$k_p$ — Cost of preferred stock

$k_{RF}$ — Rate of return on a risk-free security

$k_s$ — (1) Cost of retained earnings
(2) Required return on a stock

M — Maturity value of a bond

M/B — Market to book ratio

MCC — Marginal cost of capital

n — (1) Life of a project
(2) Number of shares outstanding

NPV — Net present value

NWC — Net working capital

P — (1) Price of a share of stock; $P_0$ = price of the stock today
(2) Sales price per unit of product sold

P/E — Price/earnings ratio

PI — Profitability index

PMT — Periodic level payment or annuity

PV — Present value

PVIF — Present value interest factor for a lump sum

PVIFA — Present value interest factor for an annuity

Q — Quantity produced or sold

r — (1) Rate of return
(2) Correlation coefficient
(3) Internal rate of return

ROA — Return on assets

ROE — Return on equity

RP — Risk premium

S — (1) Total market value of a firm's stock
(2) Sales

SML — Security market line

$S_n$ — Future value of an annuity

$\Sigma$ — Summation sign (capital sigma)

$\sigma$ — Standard deviation (lower case sigma)

$\sigma^2$ — Variance

t — Time period

T — Marginal income tax rate

TIE — Times-interest-earned ratio

V — (1) Variable cost per unit
(2) Market value of a firm

VC — Total variable costs

YTM — Yield to maturity

# FUNDAMENTALS OF FINANCIAL MANAGEMENT

**FOURTH EDITION**

# FUNDAMENTALS OF FINANCIAL MANAGEMENT

## FOURTH EDITION

# EUGENE F. BRIGHAM
*University of Florida*

**THE DRYDEN PRESS**
Chicago   New York   Philadelphia   San Francisco   Montreal
Toronto   London   Sydney   Tokyo   Mexico City   Rio de Janeiro   Madrid

**Acquisitions Editor:** Ann Heath
**Developmental Editor:** Judy Sarwark
**Project Editor:** Cate Rzasa
**Managing Editor:** Jane Perkins
**Design Director:** Alan Wendt
**Production Manager:** Mary Jarvis
**Copy Editor:** Nancy Maybloom
**Compositor:** The Clarinda Company
**Text Type:** 10/12 ITC Garamond Book

**Library of Congress Cataloging-in-Publication Data**
Brigham, Eugene F., 1930–
    Fundamentals of financial management.

    Includes bibliographical references and index.
    1. Corporations—Finance. I. Title.
    HG4026.B6693   1986        658.1′5        85–16141
    ISBN 0–03–004382–4

Printed in the United States of America
678–039–987654321

Address orders: ·
383 Madison Avenue
New York, NY   10017

Address editorial correspondence:
One Salt Creek Lane
Hinsdale, IL   60521

CBS COLLEGE PUBLISHING
The Dryden Press
Holt, Rinehart and Winston
Saunders College Publishing

**Acknowledgments**

Logos courtesy of the following companies: Delta Air Lines, AT&T, International Business Machines Corporation, Homestake Mining Company, Albertson's, Polaroid Corporation, Leaseway Transportation Corporation, MCI, Con Edison of New York, Tampa Electric Company, Transamerica Corporation, Xerox Corporation, and Chevron Corporation.

# THE DRYDEN PRESS SERIES IN FINANCE

Brigham
**Financial Management:**
**Theory and Practice,**
*Fourth Edition*

Brigham
**Fundamentals of Financial Management,**
*Fourth Edition*

Brigham and Gapenski
**Intermediate Financial Management**

Brigham and Johnson
**Issues in Managerial Finance,**
*Second Edition*

Campsey and Brigham
**Introduction to Financial Management**

Clayton and Spivey
**The Time Value of Money**

Cretien, Ball, and Brigham
**Financial Management with *Lotus 1-2-3*®**

Crum and Brigham
**Cases in Managerial Finance,**
*Sixth Edition*

Fama and Miller
**The Theory of Finance**

Gitman
**Personal Finance,**
*Third Edition*

Greer and Farrell
**Contemporary Real Estate:**
**Theory and Practice**

Greer and Farrell
**Investment Analysis for**
**Real Estate Decisions**

Harrington
**Case Studies in Financial**
**Decision Making**

Johnson and Johnson
**Commercial Bank Management**

Kidwell and Peterson
**Financial Institutions, Markets, and Money,**
*Second Edition*

Lorie and Brealey
**Modern Developments in**
**Investment Management,**
*Second Edition*

Mayo
**Investments: An Introduction**

Mayo
**Finance: An Introduction,**
*Second Edition*

Myers
**Modern Developments in**
**Financial Management**

Pettijohn
**PROFIT**

Reilly
**Investment Analysis and**
**Portfolio Management,**
*Second Edition*

Reilly
**Investments,** *Second Edition*

Tallman and Neal
**Financial Analysis and Planning Package**

Weston and Brigham
**Essentials of Managerial Finance,**
*Seventh Edition*

Weston and Copeland
**Managerial Finance,**
*Eighth Edition*

# PREFACE

*Fundamentals of Financial Management* is intended for use in the introductory finance course. It begins with a discussion of such basic concepts as security markets, interest rates, taxes, and risk/return valuation models, after which it goes on to explain how financial management can be used to help maximize the value of a firm. This organization has three important advantages:

**1.** Explaining early in the book how financial markets operate, and how security prices are determined within these markets, helps students see how financial management can affect the value of the firm. Also, early coverage of valuation models and risk analysis permits us to use and reinforce these key concepts throughout the book.

**2.** Structuring the book around markets and valuation concepts enhances continuity—students can better see how the various topics interrelate with one another.

**3.** Most students—even those who do not plan to major in finance—are generally interested in stock and bond prices and returns on investments. Since people's ability to learn a subject is a function of their interest and motivation, and since *Fundamentals* begins by showing the relationship between security markets, security values, and financial management, this organization is sound from a pedagogic standpoint.

## Changes in the Fourth Edition

The world of finance is dynamic—new developments occur frequently, and many of them simply must be incorporated into textbooks such as this one. However, it is often easier to add than to subtract, with the result that introductory texts gradually become intermediate or even advanced texts as they move through successive editions. We recognized this problem, and we attacked it as follows: (1) We developed an organization plan that set forth the background knowledge, theory, and financial management methodology students need before going into a case course, a finance position in business, or graduate school. (2) We then divided that material into the body of knowledge that all business students need versus knowledge needed primarily by finance majors. In both instances, we limited coverage to the amount of material that could realistically be covered in a one-term course, plus slightly more to provide flexibility for instructors and reference materials for students. (3) We then put into this fourth edition of *Fundamentals* what we believe should be covered in the introductory course, while other materials that are interesting and important, but too advanced or specialized for the first course, were incorporated into a new book (Eugene F. Brigham and Louis C. Gapenski, *Intermediate Financial Management*, Dryden Press, 1985).

As a result of this process, *Fundamentals* has been streamlined, and we reduced the number of chapters from 25 to 21 to make it easier to cover at least the basics of most important topics in a one-term course. Other important changes include the following:

**1.** All sections were updated to reflect current interest rates, tax laws, mergers, and the like.

**2.** Capital budgeting is now covered in two chapters rather than three. Some of the more complex subjects that are better left for advanced courses were deleted.

**3.** The old chapters on leasing and on warrants, options, and convertibles were combined with preferred stock to form one comprehensive chapter on "hybrid" types of long-term financing. This arrangement makes it feasible to actually cover these subjects in a one-term course.

**4.** The working capital section was reorganized and streamlined. It now begins with an overview of working capital policy, and credit policy was simplified by using an easy-to-understand comparative income statement approach rather than the complex set of equations used in the last edition.

**5.** The degree of leverage concept was moved from an appendix directly into the capital structure chapter.

**6.** The bankruptcy chapter was shortened and placed as an appendix to the long-term debt chapter.

**7.** The small business chapter was deleted, but discussions of small business topics were integrated into appropriate chapters.

**8.** We replaced the old end-of-book glossary with a new running glossary. The key terms in each chapter are boldfaced, and their definitions appear in the margin next to the point where they are defined. Each key term is, of course, indexed.

**9.** The number of end-of-chapter problems has been increased by approximately 50 percent, and the range of difficulty expanded. In addition, computerized problems were added to most chapters; a diskette with *Lotus 1-2-3*® models for these problems is available to instructors from The Dryden Press. The computerized problems are designed to show students the power of computers in financial analysis, and no knowledge of computers or programming is needed to use them. These problems are indicated by a diskette logo next to the problem number (for example, see Problem 2-4 on page 45).

**10.** We added an appendix to Chapter 8, "Financial Forecasting," which discusses the use of microcomputers in financial management. Here we describe in general terms applications of computers in finance and illustrate them with a *Lotus 1-2-3* model that forecasts financial requirements under a variety of conditions. Since microcomputers are now essential in real-world finance, we debated extending the discussion to other areas, such as capital budgeting, capital structure, leasing, and cash budgeting. However, we concluded that the time pressures of the course would preclude the use of this material even if it were included. We note, though, that our end-of-chapter computer problems do provide a good sampling of how computers can be used in finance, and, if time and hardware permit, they can even be used as the basis for a computer-oriented introductory course. Also, our advanced text (*Intermediate Financial Management*) provides extensive discussions of a number of applications, and The Dryden Press will publish a paperback book, *Financial Management with Lotus 1-2-3®*, that covers this key subject in even greater depth.

## Ancillary Materials

A number of additional items are available as aids to both students and instructors:

**1.** *Study Guide*. This supplement outlines the key sections of the text, provides students with self-test questions for each chapter, and provides a set of problems and solutions similar to those in the text.

**2.** *Casebook*. The revised edition of *Cases in Managerial Finance*, sixth edition (Dryden Press, 1987), by Roy L. Crum and Eugene F. Brigham, is well suited for use with this text. The cases show real-world applications of the methodologies and concepts developed in the text.

**3.** *Readings Book*. A revised readings book, *Issues in Managerial Finance*, third edition (Dryden Press, 1987), edited by Ramon E. Johnson, provides an excellent mix of theoretical and practical articles which can be used to supplement the text.

**4.** *Financial Management with Lotus 1-2-3®* by Paul D. Cretien, Susan E. Ball, and Eugene F. Brigham. As noted above, a new Dryden manual and diskette will be available to teach students how to use *Lotus 1-2-3* and to explain how many commonly encountered problems in financial management can be analyzed with electronic spreadsheets.

**5.** *Instructor's Manual*. An exceptionally complete manual is available to instructors who adopt the book. The manual contains answers to all text questions and problems, as well as a set of lecture notes (including notes on how to use the transparencies).

**6.** *Transparencies*. A comprehensive set of acetate transparencies, designed to highlight key materials in each chapter, is available to instructors who adopt the text.

**7.** *Test Bank*. A test bank with more than 600 class-tested questions and problems in objective format is available both in book form and on computer diskettes (Apple II® and IBM PC®). The new questions are more challenging than those in many test banks, and they are well suited for exams.

**8.** *Supplemental Problems*. A set of additional problems, organized according to topic and level of difficulty, is also available to instructors.

**9.** *Problem Diskette*. A diskette containing *Lotus 1-2-3®* models for selected end-of-chapter problems is also available.

**10.** *PROFIT.* This software supplement by James Pettijohn of Southwest Missouri State University contains 18 user-friendly programs that include the time value of money, forecasting, and capital budgeting. The program includes a user's manual, and it is available for the IBM PC and Apple IIe.

## Acknowledgments

This book reflects the efforts of a great many people. First, I would like to thank the following, whose reviews and comments contributed to the first three editions: Ed Altman, Bob Aubey, Peter Bacon, Tom Bankston, Bill Beranek, Bill Brueggeman, Bob Carleson, S. K. Choudhury, Phil Cooley, Roy Crum, Robert Hehre, George Hettenhouse, Craig Johnson, Ramon Johnson, Ray Jones, Don Knight, Harold Krogh, Charles Kronke, Wayne Lee, Jim Longstreet, Bob Magee, Phil Malone, Andy McCollough, Bob Moore, Tim Nantell, Bill Nelson, Tom O'Brien, Jim Pappas, Jim Pettijohn, Rich Pettit, Dick Pettway, John Pinkerton, Bill Rentz, Dilip Shome, Don Sorenson, Mel Tysseland, Paul Vanderheiden, Steve Vinson, and Don Woods. In addition, the following professors reviewed the manuscript and provided comments and suggestions for improving this fourth edition:

| | | |
|---|---|---|
| Thomas Berry | John Harris | Stephen Parrish |
| Scott Besley | Paul Hastings | Franklin Potts |
| G. Geoffrey Booth | Del Hawley | Jerry Prock |
| Joseph Brandt | Thomas Hindelang | Herbert Quigley |
| Elizabeth Brannigan | John Houston | Pietra Rivoli |
| Kate Brown | Steven Isberg | Thomas Scampini |
| Susan Chaplinsky | Manuel Jose | Alan Severn |
| Maclyn Clouse | William Kennedy | Frederic Shipley |
| Joe Copeland | Dorothy Koehl | G. Stacy Sirmans |
| David Cordell | Martin Laurence | David Speairs |
| Joel Dauten | Edward Lawrence | Alan Stephens |
| Steve Dawson | Ileen Malitz | Jerry Stevens |
| Les Dlabay | Chris Manning | Dennis Tanner |
| Dean Dudley | John Mathys | Richard Teweles |
| Charles Edwards | John McAlhany | Andrew Thompson |
| John Ellis | William McDaniel | Paul Vanderheiden |
| Michael Ferri | Barry Morris | Patrick Vincent |
| Bernie Grablowsky | Chris Muscarella | John Wachowicz |
| Gerald Hamsmith | William Nelson | Kuo Chiang Wei |
| William Hardin | Robert Niendorf | Bill Welch |

Chris Barry, Southern Methodist University, wrote the small business sections; Art Herrmann, University of Hartford, wrote the bankruptcy appendix; Roy Crum, University of Florida, wrote the multinational finance chapter; and Bob Porter, University of South Carolina, reviewed the manuscript and also worked through the end-of-chapter problems, including the computer problems, to help ensure that they are as clear, accurate, and relevant as possible. Also, several students and colleagues at the University of Florida worked through and/or discussed with me all or major parts of the book and ancillaries to help eliminate errors and confusing sections: Dana Aberwald, Barbara Bruening, Lou Gapenski, Richard Kish, and Craig Tapley. In addition, Kay Mangan had the primary responsibility for developing the computerized problem models; Terry Sicherman, Melissa Davis, and Debbie Sperlich typed and helped proof the various manuscripts; and The Dryden Press staff, especially Ann Heath, Mary Jarvis, Nancy Maybloom, Jane Perkins, Cate Rzasa, Judy Sarwark, Bill Schoof, Alan Wendt, and Liz Widdicombe, helped greatly with all phases of the revision. Last, but certainly not least, Susan Ball worked closely with me at every stage of the revision; her assistance was absolutely invaluable.

## Errors in the Text

At this point, most authors make a statement like this: "I appreciate all the help I received from the people listed above, but any remaining errors are, of course, my own responsibility." And generally there are more than enough remaining errors. As a part of my quest for clarity, I resolved to avoid this problem in *Fundamentals*, and as a result of the error detection procedures we used, I am convinced that it is virtually free of mistakes.

Some of my colleagues suggested that if I am so confident about the book's accuracy, I should offer a reward to people who find errors. With this in mind, but primarily because I want to detect any remaining errors and correct them in subsequent printings, I hereby offer a reward of $5 per error (misspelled word, arithmetic mistake, and the like) to the first person who reports it to me. (Any error that has follow-through effects is counted as two errors only.) Two accounting students have set up a foolproof audit system to make sure I pay off—accounting students tend to be skeptics! Please report any errors to me at the address below.

## Conclusion

Finance is, in a real sense, the cornerstone of the enterprise system—good financial management is vitally important to the economic health of business firms, and, hence, to the nation and the world. Because of its importance, finance should be widely and thoroughly understood, but this is easier said than done. The field is relatively complex, and it is undergoing constant change in response to shifts in economic conditions. All of this makes finance stimulating and exciting but also challenging and sometimes perplexing. I sincerely hope that *Fundamentals* will meet its own challenge by contributing to a better understanding of our financial system.

Eugene F. Brigham
*College of Business*
*University of Florida*
*Gainesville, Florida 32611*
*November 1985*

# CONTENTS

# FUNDAMENTALS OF
# FINANCIAL MANAGEMENT

**FOURTH EDITION**

# I

# FUNDAMENTAL CONCEPTS IN FINANCIAL MANAGEMENT

Each financial decision must be analyzed in terms of its effect on the value of the firm's stock. This requires a knowledge of how alternative decisions will influence stock prices. Accordingly, in Part I we develop a basic stock valuation model for use throughout the remainder of the book.

Chapter 1 presents an overview of financial management. Chapter 2 looks at the different types of business firms, the securities they issue, and the way both firms and their owners are taxed. Chapter 3 describes how capital is allocated, the institutions used to facilitate the flow of capital from savers to borrowers, and the way interest rates are established. Chapter 4 covers discounted cash flow analysis, and the concepts developed there are extended in Chapter 5 to show how stock and bond values are determined. Finally, Chapter 6 discusses the concept of risk, ways of measuring risk, and the impact risk has on stock prices and rates of return.

# 1 AN OVERVIEW OF FINANCIAL MANAGEMENT

## DIFFERENCES IN FINANCIAL POLICY: DELTA VS. EASTERN

In 1964 Eastern Airlines' stock sold for over $60 per share, while Delta's sold for $20. By the mid-1980s Eastern had dropped below $4, while Delta was up to $50. Delta's earnings and dividends had increased steadily over the years, while Eastern paid its last dividend in 1969 and has recently been suffering heavy losses. Further, Delta's employees have reasonably secure, well-paid positions, while Eastern has been laying off people and slashing the salaries of those who remain.

Although many factors combined to produce these divergent results, financial decisions exerted a major influence. Eastern has traditionally used a great deal of debt, while Delta has a policy of financing primarily with common equity. (In 1985 Delta had about 71 percent equity and 29 percent debt; Eastern had about 12 percent equity and 88 percent debt.) The dramatic increase in interest rates (for example, the prime business loan rate rose from 6 percent in the 1960s to 21 percent in the early 1980s) greatly increased Eastern's costs and lowered its profits, but it had only a minor effect on Delta. Further, when the airlines saw the need to buy new, fuel-efficient planes, because fuel prices had risen by over 1,000 percent, Delta was able to do so. Eastern, however, was not. Finally, when the airlines were deregulated in the late 1970s, Delta was strong enough to expand into developing markets and to cut prices as necessary to attract business, but Eastern was not.

Similar stories could be told about hundreds of companies in scores of industries—autos, computers, insurance, banking, or you name it. One company does well while another goes under—and a major reason for the divergent results is a difference in some basic financial policy. In this chapter we outline the major types of financial decisions that must be made. Then, in the remainder of the book, we discuss how these decisions should be made.

---

Finance consists of three interrelated subareas: (1) *money and capital markets*, or macro finance, which deals with many of the topics covered in macroeconomics; (2) *investments*, which focuses on the decisions of individuals and financial institutions as they choose securities for their investment portfolios; and (3) *financial management*, or "business finance," which involves decisions within the firm. Each of these areas interacts with the others; therefore, a corporate financial manager must have some knowledge of money and capital markets as well as the way in which individuals and institutions are likely to appraise the firm's securities.

*Financial management* has undergone significant changes over the years. When it first emerged as a separate field of study in the early 1900s, the emphasis was on the legal aspects of such matters as mergers, consolidations, the formation of new firms, and the various types of securities issued by corporations. Industrialization was sweeping the country, and the critical problem firms such as U.S. Steel and Reynolds Tobacco faced was obtaining capital for expansion. The capital markets were relatively primitive, which made transfers of funds from individual savers to businesses difficult. The earnings and asset values reported in accounting statements were unreliable, while stock trading by insiders and manipulators caused prices to fluctuate wildly. Consequently, investors were reluctant to purchase stocks and bonds. As a result of these environmental conditions, finance in the early 1900s focused on legal issues relating to the issuance of securities.

The emphasis remained on securities through the 1920s. However, radical changes occurred during the depression of the 1930s, when an unprecedented number of business failures shifted the focus to bankruptcy and reorganization, to corporate liquidity, and to governmental regulation of securities markets. Finance was still a descriptive, legalistic subject, but the emphasis shifted from expansion to survival.

During the 1940s and early 1950s, finance continued to be taught as a descriptive, institutional subject, viewed from the outside rather than from the standpoint of management. However, managerial finance techniques designed to help firms maximize their profits and stock prices were beginning to receive attention.

The evolutionary pace toward rigorous analysis quickened during the late 1950s. Also, the major emphasis began to shift from the right-hand side of the balance sheet (liabilities and capital) to asset analysis. Computers were beginning to be used, and models were being developed to help manage inventories, cash, accounts receivable, and fixed assets. Increasingly, the focus of finance shifted from the outsider's to the insider's point of view, as financial decisions within the firm were recognized as the critical issue in corporate finance. Descriptive, institutional materials on capital markets and financing instruments were still studied, but these topics were considered within the context of corporate financial decisions.

The 1960s and 1970s witnessed a renewed interest in the liabilities and capital side of the balance sheet, with a focus (1) on the optimal mix of securities and (2) on the way in which individual investors make investment decisions, or *portfolio theory*, and its implications for corporate finance. Corporate financial management is designed to help general management take actions that will maximize the value of the firm and the wealth of its stockholders; therefore, soundness of corporate financial decisions depends upon how investors are likely to react to them. *This was recognized in the 1960s and 1970s, and with this recognition came a merging of investments with corporate finance.*

Thus far in the 1980s three issues have received emphasis: (1) inflation and interest rates, (2) deregulation of financial institutions and the accompanying trend away from specialized institutions and toward broadly diversified financial service corporations, and (3) a dramatic increase in the use of computers for analyzing financial decisions. Inflation is being worked into the fabric of both financial theories and financial decision processes, and it has even led to the creation of new financial institutions and industries—for example, money market funds and interest rate futures markets. Older institutions have been forced into major structural changes, and it is getting harder and harder to tell a bank from a savings and loan, or an insurance company from a brokerage firm: Bank of America owns a stock brokerage firm; Merrill Lynch offers checking account services; and Sears, Roebuck is one of the largest U.S. financial institutions, owning such firms as Allstate Insurance and Coldwell Banker. At the same time, technological developments in the computer hardware and telecommunications areas, and the availability of software packages that make otherwise very difficult numerical analyses relatively easy, are bringing about fundamental changes in the way managers manage. Data storage, transmittal, and retrieval techniques are reducing the "judgmental" aspects of management, as financial managers can often obtain relatively precise estimates of the effects of various courses of action.

## Increasing Importance of Financial Management

These evolutionary changes have greatly increased the importance of financial management. In earlier times the marketing manager would project sales, the engineering and production staffs would determine the assets necessary to meet these demands, and the financial manager's job was simply to raise the money needed to purchase the required plant, equipment, and inventories. This mode of operation is no longer prevalent. Decisions are now made in a much more coordinated manner, with the financial manager having direct responsibility for the control process.

Public Service of Indiana (PSI) can be used to illustrate this change. A few years ago, PSI's economic forecasters would project power demand on the basis of historic trends and give these forecasts to the engineers, who would then proceed to build the new plants necessary to meet the forecasted demand. The finance department simply had the task of raising the capital the engineers told them was needed. However, inflation, environmental regulations, and other factors combined to double or even triple plant construction costs, and this caused a corresponding increase in the need for new capital. At the same time, rising fuel costs caused dramatic increases in electricity prices, which lowered demand and made some of the new construction unnecessary. Thus, PSI not only found itself building a nuclear power plant that it did not really need, but it was also unable to raise the capital necessary to pay for the plant. Eventually, a $2.5 billion investment had to be written off, and the price of the company's stock declined from about $35 in the late 1970s to a 1985 low of $6.88. As a result of this experience, PSI (and most other utilities) now places far more emphasis on the planning and control process, and this has greatly increased the importance of the finance staff.

The direction in which business is moving, as well as the increasing importance of finance, was described in *Fortune*. After pointing out that well over half of today's top executives had majored in business administration versus about 25 percent a few years earlier, *Fortune* continued:

> Career patterns have followed the educational trends. Like scientific and technical schooling, nuts-and-bolts business experience seems to have become less important. The proportion of executives with their primary experience in production, operations, engineering, design, and research and development has fallen from a third of the total to just over a quarter. And the number of top officers with legal and financial backgrounds has increased more than enough to make up the difference. Lawyers and financial men now head two out of five corporations.
>
> It is fair to assume that the changes in training, and in the paths that led these men to the top, reflect the shifting priorities and needs of their corporations. In fact, the expanding size and complexity of corporate organizations, coupled with their continued expansion overseas, have greatly increased the importance of financial planning and controls. And the growth of government regulation and of obligations companies face under the law has heightened the need for legal advice. The engineer and the production man have become, in consequence, less important in management than the finance man and the lawyer.
>
> Today's chief executive officers have obviously perceived the shift in emphasis, and many of them wish they had personally been better prepared for it. Interestingly enough, a majority of them say they would have benefited from additional formal training, mainly in business administration, accounting, finance, and law.[1]

These same trends are evident at lower levels within firms of all sizes, as well as in nonprofit and governmental organizations. Thus, it is becoming increasingly important for people in marketing, accounting, production, personnel, and other areas to understand finance in order to do a good job in their own fields. Marketing people, for instance, must understand how marketing decisions affect and are affected by funds availability, by inventory levels, by excess plant capacity, and so on. Accountants, to cite another example, must understand how accounting data are used in corporate planning and are viewed by investors: The function of accounting is to provide quantitative financial information for use in making economic decisions, while the main functions of financial management are to plan for, acquire, and utilize funds in order to maximize the efficiency and value of the enterprise.[2]

---

[1]Charles G. Burck, "A Group Profile of the Fortune 500 Chief Executive," *Fortune*, May 1976, 173.

[2]American Institute of Certified Public Accountants, *Statement of the Accounting Principles Board #4* (New York, October 1970).

*Thus, there are financial implications in virtually all business decisions, and nonfinancial executives simply must know enough finance to work these implications into their own specialized analyses.*[3] This point is amplified in the following sections.

## The Place of Finance in a Business Organization

Organization structures vary from firm to firm, but Figure 1-1 gives a fairly typical picture of the role of finance within a business. The chief financial officer—who has the title of vice-president: finance—reports to the president. Key subordinates are the treasurer and the controller. The treasurer has direct responsibility for managing the firm's cash and marketable securities, for planning the financial structure, for selling stocks and bonds to raise capital, and for overseeing the corporate pension fund. Under the treasurer (but in some firms under the controller) are the credit manager, the inventory manager, and the director of capital budgeting (who analyzes decisions relating to investments in fixed assets). The controller is responsible for the activities of the accounting and tax departments.

**Figure 1-1**
**Place of Finance in a Typical Business Organization**

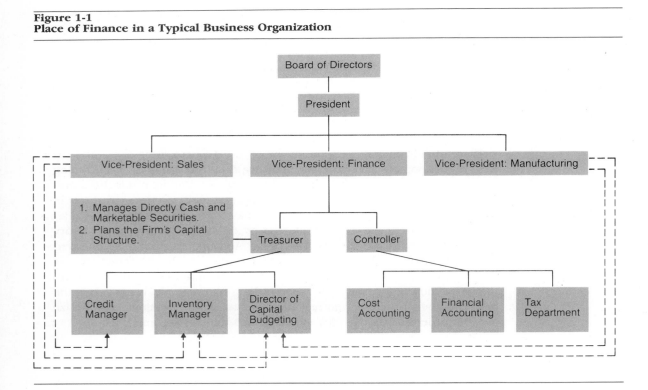

---

[3]It is an interesting fact that the course "Financial Analysis for Nonfinancial Executives" has the highest enrollment in most executive development programs.

## The Goals of the Firm

**stockholder wealth maximization**
The appropriate goal for management decisions; considers the risk and timing associated with increasing earnings per share in order to maximize the price of the firm's common stock.

Decisions are made not in a vacuum, but rather, with some objective in mind. *Throughout this book we operate on the assumption that management's primary goal is* **stockholder wealth maximization**. As we shall see, this translates into *maximizing the price of the common stock*. Firms do, of course, have other objectives—managers, who make the actual decisions, are interested in their own personal satisfaction, in employees' welfare, and in the good of the community and society at large. Still, for the reasons set forth below, *stock price maximization is the most important goal of most firms*, and it is a reasonable operating objective upon which to build decision rules in a book such as this.

### Managerial Incentives to Maximize Shareholder Wealth

Stockholders own the firm and elect the management team. Management in turn is supposed to operate in the best interests of the stockholders. We know, however, that because the stock of most large firms is widely held, the managers of such firms have a great deal of autonomy. This being the case, might not managements pursue goals other than maximization of stockholder wealth? For example, some argue that the managers of a large, well-entrenched corporation could work to keep stockholder returns at a "fair" or "reasonable" level and then devote part of their efforts and resources to public service activities, employee benefits, higher executive salaries, or golf.

Similarly, a firmly entrenched management might avoid risky ventures, even when the possible gains to stockholders are high enough to warrant taking the gamble. The theory behind this argument is that since stockholders are generally well diversified, holding portfolios of many different stocks, if one company takes a chance and loses, the stockholders lose only a small part of their wealth. Managers, on the other hand, are not diversified, so setbacks affect them more seriously. Accordingly, some maintain that corporate managers tend to "play it safe" rather than aggressively seeking to maximize the prices of their firms' stocks.

It is extremely difficult to determine whether a particular management team is trying to maximize shareholder wealth or is merely attempting to keep stockholders satisfied while pursuing other goals. For example, how can we tell whether voluntary employee or community benefit programs are in the long-run best interests of the stockholders? Are relatively high executive salaries really necessary to attract and retain excellent managers, who in turn will keep the firm ahead of its competition? When a risky venture is turned down, does this reflect management conservatism, or is it a correct judgment regarding the risks of the venture versus its potential rewards?

It is impossible to give definitive answers to these questions. However, we do know that the managers of a firm operating in a competitive market will be forced to undertake actions that are reasonably consistent with shareholder wealth maximization. If they depart from this goal, they run the risk of being removed from their jobs in a hostile takeover attempt or proxy fight.[4] Thus, while managers may have other objectives, there are reasons to view stock price maximization as the dominant goal for most firms. We shall return to this point later in the chapter.

### Social Responsibility

**social responsibility**
The concept that businesses should be actively concerned with the welfare of society at large.

**normal profits/rates of return**
Those profits and rates of return that are close to the average for all firms.

Another issue that deserves consideration is **social responsibility**: Should businesses operate strictly in the stockholders' best interest, or are firms also partly responsible for the welfare of employees, customers, the communities in which they operate, and indeed for society at large? In tackling this question, consider first those firms whose **profits** and **rates of return** on investment are close to **normal**, that is, close to the average for all firms. If some companies attempt to be social do-gooders, thereby increasing their costs over what they otherwise would have been, and if the other businesses in the industry do not follow suit, then the socially oriented firms would probably be forced by competition to abandon their efforts. Thus, any socially responsible acts that raise costs will be difficult, if not impossible, in industries subject to keen competition.

What about oligopolistic firms with profits above normal levels—can they not devote resources to social projects? Undoubtedly they can, for many large, successful firms do engage in community projects, employee benefit programs, and the like to a greater degree than would appear to be called for by pure profit or wealth maximization goals.[5] Still, publicly owned firms are constrained in such actions by capital market factors. Suppose a saver who has funds to invest is considering two alternative firms. One firm devotes a substantial part of its resources to social actions, while the other concentrates on profits and stock prices. Most investors are likely to shun the socially oriented firm, thus putting it at a disadvantage in the capital market— after all, why should the stockholders of one corporation subsidize society to a greater extent than those of other businesses? For this reason, even highly profitable firms (unless they are closely held rather than publicly owned) are generally constrained against taking unilateral cost-increasing social actions.

Does all this mean that firms should not exercise social responsibility? Not at all—it simply means that most cost-increasing actions may have to be put on a *mandatory* rather than a voluntary basis, at least initially, to insure that their burden will fall uniformly across all businesses. Thus, such social benefit

---

[4]A hostile *takeover* is the purchase by one company of the stock of another over the opposition of its management, while a *proxy fight* involves an attempt to gain control by getting stockholders to vote a new management group into office. Both actions are facilitated by low stock prices, so for the sake of self-preservation management must try to keep the stock value as high as possible. However, it is quite clear from the actions taken by some managements in resisting takeover attempts that they are far more interested in their own survival as managers than in the interests of stockholders in general. The dominant view is that takeovers would rarely present a serious threat to a well-entrenched management team if that team had succeeded in maximizing the firm's value, for people attempt to take over undervalued, bargain companies, not fully valued ones. Still, takeover experience does make it crystal clear that many, if not most, managers are more interested in their own personal positions than in maximizing shareholder wealth per se. We shall address this issue at more length later in the chapter.

[5]Even firms such as these often find it necessary to justify such projects at stockholder meetings by stating that these programs will contribute to long-run profit maximization.

programs as fair hiring practices, minority training, product safety, pollution abatement, and antitrust actions are most likely to be effective if realistic rules are established initially and then enforced by government agencies. Of course, it is critical that industry and government cooperate in establishing the rules of corporate behavior, that the costs as well as the benefits of such actions be accurately estimated and taken into account, and that firms follow the spirit as well as the letter of the law in their actions. In such a setting, the rules of the game become constraints. Throughout this book, we shall assume that managers are stock price maximizers who operate subject to a set of socially imposed constraints.

### Stock Price Maximization and Social Welfare

If firms attempt to maximize stock prices, is this good or bad for society? In general, it is good. Aside from such illegal actions as attempting to form monopolies, violating safety codes, and failing to meet pollution control requirements—all of which are constrained by the government—*the same actions that maximize stock prices also benefit society*. First, stock price maximization requires efficient, low-cost operations that produce the desired quality and quantity of output at the lowest possible cost. Second, stock price maximization requires the development of products that consumers want and need, so the profit motive leads to new technology, new products, and new jobs. Finally, stock price maximization necessitates efficient and courteous service, adequate stocks of merchandise, and well-located business establishments, because these factors are all necessary to make sales, and sales are necessary for profits. *Therefore, the types of actions that help a firm increase the price of its stock are also directly beneficial to society at large.* This is why profit-motivated, free-enterprise economies have been so much more successful than socialistic and other types of economic systems. Since financial management plays a crucial role in the operation of successful firms, and since successful firms are absolutely necessary for a healthy, productive economy, it is easy to see why finance is important from a social standpoint.[6]

## The Agency Problem

In a very important article, Michael Jensen and William Meckling defined an *agency relationship* as a contract under which one or more persons (the principals) hire another person (the agent) to perform some service on their

---

[6]People sometimes argue that firms, in their efforts to raise profits and stock prices, increase product prices and gouge the public. In a reasonably competitive economy, which we have, prices are constrained by competition and consumer resistance. If a firm raises its prices beyond reasonable levels, it will simply lose its market share. Even giant firms like General Motors lose business to the Japanese and Germans, as well as to Ford and Chrysler, if they set prices over what will cover production costs plus a "normal" profit. Of course, firms *want* to earn more, and they constantly try to cut costs, develop new products, and so on, and thereby earn above-normal profits. Yet, if they are successful and do earn above-normal profits, these very profits will attract competition and eventually drive prices down, so the main beneficiary is the consumer.

behalf and then delegate some decision-making authority to that agent.[7] Within the financial management framework, agency relationships exist (1) between stockholders and managers and (2) between bondholders (or creditors generally) and stockholders. These relationships are discussed in the following sections.

## Stockholders versus Managers

**agency problem**
A potential conflict of interest between (1) the principals (outside shareholders) and the agent (manager) or (2) stockholders and debtholders.

Jensen and Meckling contend that an **agency problem** arises whenever a manager owns less than 100 percent of the firm's common stock. If a firm is solely owned and managed by a single individual, we can assume that that person will take every possible action to increase his or her own welfare, mostly in the form of increased personal wealth but also in more leisure or perquisites.[8] If the owner-manager relinquishes a portion of his or her ownership by selling some of the firm's stock to outsiders, a potential conflict of interests will arise. For example, the owner-manager may now decide (1) to lead a more relaxed life and not work as strenuously to maximize shareholder wealth, because less of this wealth will go to him or her, or (2) to consume more perquisites, because part of those costs will now fall on the outside stockholders. This potential conflict between two parties, the principals (outside shareholders) and the agent (manager), is one type of agency problem.

**leveraged buyout**
A situation in which a firm's management, using its own line of credit, purchases the outstanding shares of the company's stock.

**tender offer**
The offer by the managers of a firm, or by another firm, to buy the stock of a firm directly from its stockholders.

Another potential conflict between management and stockholders is a **leveraged buyout**, a term used to describe the situation in which management itself (1) arranges a line of credit, (2) makes an offer, called a **tender offer**, to the stockholders to buy the stock not already owned by the management group, and (3) "takes the company private" after it buys the outstanding shares. Dozens of such buyouts of New York Stock Exchange listed companies have occurred recently, and a potential conflict clearly exists whenever one is contemplated. For example, the management of Cone Mills, the largest U.S. producer of denim, recently decided to make a leveraged buyout offer to the outside stockholders. It was in management's best interests to have the stock price minimized, not maximized, prior to the offer Aware of this, Cone's management, like most who contemplate leveraged buyouts, obtained an outside opinion as to the value of the stock so as to head off lawsuits. Also, management's offer, like most, was contested by competing offers from other parties. In spite of competing offers, Cone Mills' managers were able to purchase the stock of the company for less than its true value. Thus, leverage buyouts do constitute a type of agency problem arising between the stockholders and the managers of a firm.

---

[7]See Michael C. Jensen and William H. Meckling, "Theory of the Firm: Managerial Behavior, Agency Costs, and Ownership Structure," *Journal of Financial Economics*, October 1976, 350-360. The discussion of agency theory which follows draws heavily from their work.

[8]*Perquisites* are executive fringe benefits such as luxurious offices, use of corporate planes and yachts, personal assistants, and so on.

**agency costs**
The costs associated with monitoring management's actions to insure that these actions are consistent with contractual agreements between managers, stockholders, and debtholders.

To insure that the manager acts in the best interests of the outside shareholders, the firm must incur **agency costs**, which may take several forms: (1) expenditures to monitor managerial actions, (2) expenditures to structure the organization so that the possibility of undesirable managerial behavior will be limited, and (3) opportunity costs associated with lost profit opportunities because the organizational structure does not permit managers to take actions on as timely a basis as would be possible if the managers were also the owners.

There are two extreme positions regarding how to solve the agency problem. First, if the manager were compensated only with shares of the firm's stock, then agency costs would be low because the manager would have less incentive to take excessive leisure or perquisites. However, it would be difficult to hire managers under these terms. At the opposite extreme, owners could monitor closely every managerial activity, but this solution would be extremely costly and inefficient. The optimal solution lies somewhere between the extremes, where executive compensation is tied to performance but some monitoring is also done. Several mechanisms which tend to force managers to act in the shareholders' best interests are discussed next. These include (1) the threat of firing, (2) the threat of takeover, and (3) the proper structuring of managerial incentives.

*The Threat of Firing.* Until recently the probability of a large firm's management being ousted by its stockholders was so remote that it posed little threat. This situation existed because ownership of most firms was so widely distributed and management's control over the proxy mechanism was so strong that it was almost impossible for dissident stockholders to gain enough votes to overthrow the managers. However, stock ownership is being increasingly concentrated in the hands of large institutions rather than individuals, and the institutional money managers have the clout, if they choose to use it, to exercise considerable influence over a firm's operations.

To illustrate, consider the case of GAF Corporation, a leading producer of building materials and industrial chemicals with 1984 sales of $699 million. Its stock price was as high as $41 in 1965, after which it began a long slide; by the early 1980s it was selling below $8. At that point institutions began to buy heavily, and their ownership increased from 15 to 40 percent. Many bought shares with the expectation that GAF's chairman, Jesse Werner, would retire soon and that the company would be broken up or taken over. This expectation was fueled by the fact that Mr. Werner, who became chairman in 1964, announced that GAF would sell eight marginally profitable businesses representing about half its sales. Analysts figured that this would make the company cash-rich and a likely takeover candidate and that the price of its stock would rise—indeed, the stock price did more than double, from $7.75 in 1980 to $16.375 in 1981.

But Mr. Werner decided to keep his job. He obtained a new five-year contract and announced that the firm would reinvest internally most of the $212 million it had received from the sale of several unprofitable divisions. These actions caused GAF's stock price to drop back below $9. This in turn prompted Samuel Heyman, a Connecticut shopping center owner who held 4.2 percent of GAF's stock, to wage a proxy fight. At the 1983 annual meeting, Mr. Heyman received proxies representing about 60 percent of the shares, so he was able to oust Mr. Werner.

The victory for the dissidents was made possible because of support from large institutional holders. "We've got to outperform the market," explained one money manager. "Our clients have many money managers, and if we're performing poorly, the meter starts running. And pretty soon we'd be cut from the list." Another money manager said, "We simply can't afford to have much patience with poor management." So, whereas individual investors may be uninformed, lazy, or simply willing to "vote with their feet" by selling shares in companies whose performance is sub-par, institutional investors are more likely to work actively to oust an inefficient management. Recognizing this fact, people like Mr. Heyman are now more likely to "run against" a firmly entrenched management than would have been true some years ago.

**hostile takeover**
A takeover in which the target firm's management resists acquisition.

***The Threat of Takeover.*** **Hostile takeovers** (where management does not want the firm to be taken over) are most likely to occur when a firm's stock is undervalued relative to its potential, reflecting poor managerial decisions. In a hostile takeover, the managers of the acquired firm are generally fired, and any who are able to stay on lose the autonomy that they had prior to the acquisition. Thus, to avoid takeover, managers have an incentive to take actions which maximize share price. In the words of one company president, "If you want to keep control, don't let your company's stock sell at a bargain price."

Actions to increase the firm's stock price and keep it from being a bargain are obviously good from the standpoint of the stockholders, but other tactics that managers can take to ward off a hostile takeover may not be. Two examples of questionable tactics are (1) taking "poison pills" and (2) paying greenmail. A **poison pill** is an action that a firm can take which practically kills it and thus makes it unattractive to potential suitors. Examples include Walt Disney's decision to sell large blocks of its stock at low prices to "friendly" parties, Scott Industries' decision to make all of its debt immediately payable if its management changed, and Carleton Corporation's decision to give huge retirement bonuses, which represented a large part of the company's wealth, to its managers if the firm was taken over (such payments are called "golden parachutes"). **Greenmail**, which is like blackmail, occurs when this sequence of events takes place: (1) A potential acquirer (firm or individual) buys a block of stock in a company, (2) the target company's management becomes frightened that the acquirer will make a tender offer and gain control of the company, and (3) to head off a possible takeover, management offers to pay greenmail, buying the stock of the potential raider at a price above the existing market price without offering the same deal to other stockholders. A good example of greenmail was Texaco's 1984 buyback of 13 million shares of its stock from the Bass Brothers organization at a price of $50 at a time when the stock sold in the market at less than $40.

**poison pill**
An action taken by a firm to make it unattractive to potential buyers in an attempt to avoid a hostile takeover.

**greenmail**
A situation in which a firm, in trying to avoid a takeover, offers to buy back stock from a raider at a price above the existing market price.

As this book goes to press (summer 1985), the SEC and Congress are considering legislation to protect stockholders from poison pills, greenmail, and the like.

***Structuring Managerial Incentives.*** More and more, firms are tying managers' compensation to the company's performance, and research suggests that this motivates managers to operate in a manner consistent with stock price maximization.[9]

Performance plans have become an accepted management tool. In the 1950s and 1960s, most of these plans involved stock options on the theory that allowing managers to purchase stock at a fixed price would provide an incentive for them to take actions which would maximize the stock's price. However, this type of managerial incentive lost favor in the 1970s because the options generally did not pay off. The whole stock market was relatively flat, and stock prices did not necessarily reflect companies' earnings growth. Incentive plans ought to be based on those factors over which managers have control, and since they cannot control the general stock market, stock option plans proved to have a weakness as an incentive device. Therefore, while 61 of the 100 largest U.S. firms used stock options as their sole incentive compensation in 1970, not even one of the largest 100 companies relied exclusively on these plans in 1984.

**performance shares**
A type of incentive plan in which managers are awarded shares of stock on the basis of their performance over given intervals with respect to EPS or other measures.

The main tool now is **performance shares**, which are shares of stock given to executives on the basis of performance as measured by earnings per share, return on assets, return on equity, and so on. For example, Honeywell uses growth in earnings per share as its primary performance measure. The firm has two overlapping four-year performance periods, beginning two years apart. At the start of each period, the participating executives are allocated a certain number of performance shares, say, 10,000 shares for the president down to 1,000 shares for a lower-ranking manager. If the company achieves, say, a targeted 13 percent annual average growth in earnings per share, the managers will earn 100 percent of their shares. If the corporate performance is above the target, they can earn even more shares, up to a maximum of 130 percent, which requires a 16 percent growth rate. However, if growth is below 13 percent, they get less than 100 percent of the shares, and below a 9 percent growth rate, they get zero.

Notice that performance shares have a value even if the company's stock price does nothing because of a poor general stock market, whereas under similar conditions stock options could have no value even though managers had been successful in boosting earnings. Of course, the *value* of the shares received is dependent on market price performance, because 1,000 shares of

---

[9]See Wilbur G. Lewellen, "Management and Ownership in the Large Firm," *Journal of Finance*, May 1969, 299-322. Lewellen concluded that managers seem to make decisions that are largely oriented toward stock price maximization. Economic events since his study was published suggest that the incentives for price maximization are even stronger today than they were during the period his data covered.

Honeywell stock are a lot more valuable if the stock sells for $200 than if it sells for only $100.

All incentive compensation plans—executive stock options, performance shares, profit-based bonuses, and so forth—are supposed to accomplish two purposes. First, they offer executives incentives to act on those factors under their control in a manner that will contribute to stock price maximization. Second, the existence of such performance plans helps companies attract and retain top-level executives. Well-designed plans certainly can accomplish these goals.

## Stockholders versus Creditors

The second agency problem arises because of potential conflicts between stockholders and creditors. Creditors lend funds to the firm at rates that are based on (1) the riskiness of the firm's existing assets; (2) expectations concerning the riskiness of future asset additions; (3) the firm's existing capital structure, that is, the amount of debt financing it uses; and (4) expectations concerning future capital structure changes. These are the factors that determine the riskiness of the firm's cash flows and hence the safety of its debt issues. The creditors therefore set their required rates of return, and hence the cost of debt to the firm, on expectations regarding these factors.

Now suppose the stockholders, acting through management, cause the firm to take on new projects that have greater risks than were anticipated by the creditors. This increased risk will cause the required rate of return on the firm's debt to increase, which in turn will cause the value of the outstanding debt to fall.[10] If the riskier capital investments turn out to be successful, all of the benefits will go to the stockholders, because the creditors get only a fixed return; but if things go sour, the bondholders will share the losses. What we would have, from the stockholders' point of view, is a game of "heads I win, tails you lose," which is obviously not a good game from the creditors' standpoint. Similarly, if the firm increases its level of debt in an effort to boost profits, then the value of the old debt will decrease because the old debt's bankruptcy protection will be lessened by the issuance of the new debt. In both of these situations, stockholders would be expropriating wealth from the firm's creditors.

Should stockholders, through their managers/agents, try to expropriate wealth from the firm's creditors? In general, the answer is no. First, because such attempts have been made in the past, creditors today protect themselves against such stockholder actions through restrictions in credit agreements. Second, if creditors perceive that the firm is trying to maximize shareholder wealth at the creditors' expense, they will either refuse to deal further with the firm or else require much higher than normal rates of return to compensate for the risks of such possible exploitation. Thus, firms which try

---

[10]Basically, the higher the required rate of return on an existing debt issue, the lower its value. In Chapter 5 we will present some models which illustrate this point.

to deal unfairly with creditors either lose access to the debt markets or are saddled with higher interest rates and consequently lower returns on equity, and generally with a decrease in the long-run value of the stock.

In view of these constraints, it follows that the goal of maximizing shareholder wealth is also consistent with fair play with creditors: Stockholder wealth depends on continued access to capital markets, and access depends on fair play and abiding by both the letter and the spirit of contracts and agreements. Therefore, the managers, as agents of both the creditors and the shareholders, must act in a manner which is fairly balanced between the interests of both classes of security holders. Similarly, because of other constraints and sanctions, management actions which would expropriate wealth from the firm's employees, customers, suppliers, or community will ultimately be to the detriment of shareholders. We conclude, then, that in our society the goal of shareholder wealth maximization requires the fair treatment of other groups.

## Managerial Actions to Maximize Shareholder Wealth

**profit maximization**
The maximization of the firm's net income.

**earnings per share (EPS)**
The net income of the firm divided by the number of shares of common stock outstanding.

Assuming that a firm's management team does indeed seek to maximize the long-run value of its stock, what types of actions should it take? First, consider the question of stock prices versus profits: Will **profit maximization** also result in stock price maximization? In answering this question, we must analyze the matter of total corporate profits versus **earnings per share (EPS)**.

For example, suppose Xerox had 100 million shares outstanding and earned $400 million, or $4 per share, and you owned 100 shares of the stock, so your share of the total profits was $400. Now suppose Xerox sold another 100 million shares and invested the funds received in assets which produced $100 million of income. Total income would rise to $500 million, but earnings per share would decline from $4 to $500/200 = $2.50. Now your share of the firm's earnings would be only $250, down from $400. You (and the other original stockholders) would have suffered an earnings dilution, even though total corporate profits had risen. Therefore, other things held constant, *if management is interested in the well-being of its existing stockholders, it should concentrate on earnings per share rather than on total corporate profits.*

Will maximization of expected earnings per share always maximize stockholder welfare, or should other factors be considered? Think about the *timing of the earnings.* Suppose Xerox had one project that would cause earnings per share to rise by $0.20 per year for 5 years, or $1 in total, while another project would have no effect on earnings for 4 years but would increase earnings by $1.25 in the fifth year. Which project is better—in other words, is $0.20 per year for 5 years as good as $1.25 in Year 5? The answer depends on which project adds the most to the value of the stock, which in turn depends on the time value of money to investors. Thus, timing is an important reason to concentrate on wealth as measured by the price of the stock rather than on earnings alone.

Still another issue relates to *risk*. Suppose one project is expected to increase earnings per share by $1, while another is expected to raise earnings by $1.20 per share. The first project is not very risky; if it is undertaken, earnings will almost certainly rise by about $1 per share. The other project is quite risky, so while our best guess is that earnings will rise by $1.20 per share, we must recognize the possibility that there may be no increase whatsoever. Depending on how averse stockholders are to risk, the first project may be preferable to the second.

The riskiness inherent in projected earnings per share (EPS) also depends on *how the firm is financed*. As we shall see, many firms go bankrupt every year, and the greater the use of debt, the greater the threat of bankruptcy. *Consequently, while the use of debt financing may increase projected EPS, debt also increases the riskiness of these projected earnings.*

Still another issue is the matter of paying dividends to stockholders versus retaining earnings and reinvesting them in the firm, thereby causing the earnings stream to grow over time. Stockholders like cash dividends, but they also like the growth in EPS that results from plowing earnings back into the business. The financial manager must decide exactly how much of the current earnings should be paid out as dividends rather than retained and reinvested—this is called the **dividend policy decision**. The optimal dividend policy is the one that maximizes the firm's stock price.

**dividend policy decision**
The decision as to how much of current earnings to pay out as dividends rather than retain and reinvest in the firm.

We see, then, that the firm's stock price is dependent on the following factors:

1. Projected earnings per share
2. Timing of the earnings stream
3. Riskiness of these projected earnings
4. Manner of financing the firm
5. Dividend policy

Every significant corporate decision should be analyzed in terms of its effect on these factors and hence on the price of the firm's stock. For example, suppose Exxon's coal division is considering opening a new mine. If this is done, can it be expected to increase EPS? Is there a chance that costs will exceed estimates, that prices and output will fall below projections, and that EPS will be reduced because the new mine was opened? How long will it take for the new mine to start showing a profit? How should the capital required to open the mine be raised? If debt is used, how much will this increase Exxon's riskiness? Should Exxon reduce its current dividends and use the cash thus saved to finance the project, or should it maintain its dividends and finance the mine with external capital? Financial management is designed to help answer such questions as these, plus many more.

## The Economic Environment

Although managers can take actions which affect the values of their firms' stocks, there are additional factors which influence stock prices. Included among them are external constraints, the general level of economic activity, taxes, and conditions in the stock market. Figure 1-2 diagrams these general relationships. Working within the set of external constraints shown in the box at the extreme left, management makes a set of long-run strategic policy decisions which chart a future course for the firm. These policy decisions, along with the general level of economic activity and the level of corporate income taxes, influence the firm's expected profitability, the timing of its earnings, the eventual transfer of earnings to stockholders in the form of dividends, and the degree of uncertainty (or risk) inherent in projected earnings and dividends. Profitability, timing, and risk all affect the price of the firm's stock, but so does another factor, the state of the stock market as a whole, for all stock prices tend to move up and down together to some extent.

**Figure 1-2**
**Summary of Major Factors Affecting Stock Prices**

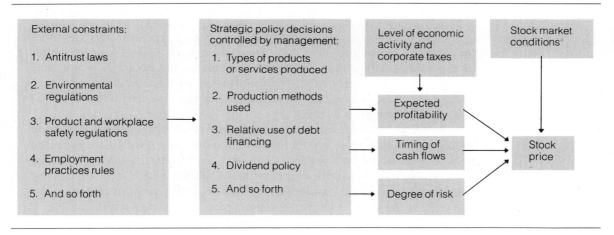

## Organization of the Book

Part I contains fundamental background materials and concepts upon which the book builds. Finance cannot be studied in a vacuum—financial decisions are profoundly influenced by the economic and social environment in which they are made. Our introduction to the economic side of this environment is continued in Chapters 2 and 3. Then, we go on to develop some financial models which can be used to help evaluate financial decisions. The specific tasks of financial managers include (1) coordinating the planning process, (2) administering the control process, (3) handling specialized finance functions such as raising capital, and (4) analyzing strategic long-term investment decisions which have a major influence on the firm's long-run future. To perform these tasks properly, it is necessary to estimate stockholders' reactions to alternative actions or events. Accordingly, our major task in Part I is to develop a set of *valuation models* which can be used to gain insights into how different actions are likely to affect the price of the firm's stock. The concepts and models developed in Part I are used extensively throughout the remainder of the book.

Part II deals with financial statements and financial forecasting. Since both long- and short-run plans are analyzed in terms of future financial statements, it is important to understand how these statements are developed and used by both managers and investors. We concentrate first on analyzing reports of past operations, then on projecting financial statements into the future under different strategic plans and operating conditions.

Beginning with Part III, we move into the execution phase of the long-range strategic planning process: In Chapters 9 and 10, we consider the vital subject of long-term investment decisions, or capital budgeting. Since major capital expenditures take years to plan and execute, and since decisions in this area are generally not reversible and hence affect operations for many years, their impact on the value of the firm is obvious.

Part IV focuses on raising long-term capital: What are the principal sources and forms of long-term capital, how much does each type cost, and how does the method of financing affect the value of the firm? This section utilizes most of the valuation concepts developed throughout the book, so it not only addresses such key issues as the optimal debt/equity mix and dividend policy, but it also serves to integrate the long-term, strategic aspects of the book and to show how the parts fit together.

In Part V we examine current, ongoing operations as opposed to long-term strategic decisions. From accounting we know that assets which are expected to be converted to cash within a year, such as inventories and accounts receivable, are called *current assets* and that liabilities which must be paid off within a year are called *current liabilities*. The management of current assets and current liabilities is known as *working capital management*, and Part V deals with this topic.

Finally, in Part VI, we consider two subjects—mergers and international financial management—that, while important, are best studied within the general framework of financial management as developed in Parts I through V.

## Summary

This chapter has provided an overview of financial management. We began with a brief review of the evolution of finance as an academic discipline, tracing developments from 1900 to the present. We next examined the place of finance in the firm, and we saw that the financial manager has been playing an increasingly important role in the organization. We also considered the goals of financial management, and we concluded that *the key goal in most publicly owned firms is stock price maximization.*

However, there does exist the potential for conflicts of interest between shareholders and managers and between shareholders and creditors; these conflicts are called *agency problems.* There are a number of incentives for motivating managers to act in the best interest of stockholders, including (1) the threat of firing, (2) the threat of takeovers, and (3) properly structured managerial compensation packages. In a competitive economy, where managers serve at the pleasure of stockholders, stock price maximization must, in general, be the dominant goal.

The book's organization reflects this primary goal. First, we discuss the economic and social environment, after which we develop valuation models that can be used to show how corporate actions affect stock prices. Then, in the remainder of the book, we examine the actions that management can take to help maximize the price of the firm's stock.

## SMALL BUSINESS

## Goals and Resources in the Small Firm

A strong set of small businesses is critical to the vitality of the U.S. economy. The Small Business Administration (SBA) reports that over 98 percent of all businesses are considered small by SBA standards, and these small businesses provide approximately 60 percent of U.S. business employment, plus almost 100 percent of *new* jobs in American industry. Also, the SBA reports that "more than half of all product and service innovations developed in the United States since World War II" have been developed by independent small business entrepreneurs.[1]

Although small business is a vital contributor to the financial health of our economy, the businesses themselves are often fragile and susceptible to failure because of their poor management, particularly their financial management. Financial management, then, is a matter of great concern to the small business.

Significant differences exist between small and big businesses: the way they are owned, the way they are managed, and the financial and managerial resources they have at their disposal. These differences affect the financial management function in small firms, and they make it necessary to modify the standard financial management principles for application in the small business area. Two especially important differences are resource shortages and goal conflicts.

### Resource Shortages

John Thompson is the owner of 75 percent of the stock in Circuit Products Corporation, a small but growing manufacturer of semiconductor components. The remainder of the stock is owned by his various friends and relatives. The company began operation with about $250,000 in cash, and it has developed a promising line of products. However, the firm has used up nearly all of its original capital.

In addition to Thompson, the company has 12 employees; 10 are engineers or technicians involved in the development and testing of new products, and the other two are clerical/secretarial personnel. Thompson uses the services of an outside accounting firm to process the company's monthly statements, which typically are completed approximately six weeks after the end of the month.

---

[1]Extracted from Small Business Administration, *Facts about Small Business and the U.S. Small Business Administration* (Washington, D.C.: U.S. Government Printing Office, 1981).

Thompson has full responsibility for the management of Circuit Products except for product development, which is run by Vice President Roland Smith. Smith is a technical whiz with no interest or background in business management, but he does have an impressive list of technical credentials. He recently left a senior engineering position at a large electronics company to join Thompson's company.

Thompson's responsibilities include making contacts with potential customers, handling all personnel decisions, giving final approval to all planned products presented by the technical staff, overseeing investor relations, handling legal issues both in the patent area and in the issuance of the firm's stock, managing the firm's relations with the bank, and managing the firm's finances. He has not taken a day off in six months, and he does not expect to do so for several more months.

Thompson is not unusual. Management in small firms is often spread very thin, and one or two key individuals end up taking on far more responsibility than they can handle properly. Thompson, for example, feels that other priorities in the business are too important to let him spend time putting together a budget or checking regularly to see how well the company is doing against such a budget. He argues, "I have a pretty good feel for how we're doing cash-wise, and I really don't have the time to go into any more detail. Making budgets doesn't make money."

Given a request by the technical staff for some new and expensive testing equipment for development purposes, Thompson would make the decision to buy or not to buy the equipment with little or no formal analysis, proceeding on the basis of his "gut feelings." He sees the analysis as being too time-consuming in view of the fact that he must this week put together a presentation for a potential customer and talk with a venture capital firm about providing Circuit Products with new capital to get its products into the market.

Not only is management often spread thin in small firms, but smaller firms have great difficulty acquiring new funds needed for business expansion, and they can often get funds only under very difficult conditions. Until Circuit Products achieves a fairly substantial size, say, $15 million or so in sales, the company cannot sell stock or bonds in public markets. Furthermore, if the company does have a public stock offering at the first opportunity, it will be very expensive by comparison to larger firms' cost of issuing stock. Thus, Circuit Products has very limited access to public capital markets.[2] Access to non-public markets is also limited. For example, its banks may also be reluctant to lend Circuit Products substantial amounts of money because of the firm's lack of a track record.

Small firms thus have constraints both on their managerial talent and on their ability to muster adequate financial resources. It is no wonder small firms often fail either because of poor (or overworked) management or because of undercapitalization.

## Goal Setting

Small businesses also differ from large firms with regard to corporate goals. We pointed out earlier that share price maximization is taken to be the goal of all firms. Thompson, however, is a good example of an owner whose life is tied up in this company. He depends on the firm for his livelihood, and he has bet his future on the success of the company. His personal wealth portfolio is not at all diversified: he has put everything he owns into the company. Given his level of commitment to the company and his lack of a fallback position, Thompson takes a very different posture toward risk-taking by his firm than would a typical investor in a public company. Most public investors hold a number of other investments, all contributing toward a well-diversified portfolio of holdings, and their employment income generally comes from a job in an altogether separate industry. On the other hand, both Thompson's salary and investment income are dependent on the success of one company, Circuit Products.

The owner-managers of small firms are interested in the value of their firms, even if this value cannot be observed in the market. Thompson and others in similar positions may have in mind "taking the firm public" or having it merged into a larger firm at some future date—at the highest possible value. But the motives of small business owners are complex, and some owners may be moti-

---

[2] The ability of small firms to acquire equity capital in public markets and the costs of doing so are explored in Hans R. Stoll, "Small Firms' Access to Public Equity Financing," forthcoming in *Financing Small Business*, eds. Paul M. Horvitz and R. Richardson Pettit.

vated primarily by such considerations as the desire to be their "own boss" even if this means not letting the firm grow at the fastest rate possible or be as profitable as it could be. In other words, there is value to being in control, and that value is not easily discernible. As a result, we often observe small businesses taking actions, such as refusing to bring in new stockholders, that do not make sense when judged on the basis of value maximization but that do make sense when seen in the light of the true objectives of the owners.

To the extent that the goals of the small firm differ from value maximization, some of the prescriptions in this text may not be entirely applicable. However, most of the tools we develop will be useful for small businesses, even though the tools may have to be modified somewhat. In any event, brief "Small Business" sections to various chapters will serve as a vehicle for exploring special issues of importance to small firms.

## Questions

**1-1**   Define each of the following terms:
   a. Stockholder wealth maximization
   b. Takeover; proxy fight; tender offer
   c. Social responsibility
   d. Normal profits; normal rate of return
   e. Agency problem; agency costs
   f. Leveraged buyout
   g. Poison pill; greenmail
   h. Performance shares
   i. Profit maximization
   j. Earnings per share
   k. Dividend policy decision

**1-2**   Would the "normal" rate of return on investment be the same in all industries? Would "normal" rates of return change over time? Explain.

**1-3**   Would the role of the financial manager be likely to increase or decrease in importance relative to other executives if the rate of inflation increased? Explain.

**1-4**   Should stockholder wealth maximization be thought of as a long-run or a short-run goal—for example, if one action would probably increase the firm's stock price from a current level of $20 to $25 in 6 months and then to $30 in 5 years but another action would probably keep the stock at $20 for several years but then increase it to $40 in 5 years, which action would be better? Can you think of some actions which might have these general tendencies?

**1-5**   Drawing on your background in accounting, can you think of any accounting procedure differences which might make it difficult to evaluate the relative performance of different firms?

**1-6**   Would the management of a firm in an oligopolistic or in a competitive industry be more likely to engage in what might be called "socially conscious" practices? Explain your reasoning.

**1-7**   What is the difference between stock price maximization and profit maximization? Under what conditions might profit maximization not lead to stock price maximization?

1-8    If you were running a large, publicly owned corporation, would you make decisions to maximize stockholders' welfare or your own personal interests? What are some actions stockholders could take to insure that your interests and theirs coincided? What are some other factors which might influence your actions?

1-9    The president of Union Manufacturing Corporation made this statement in the company's annual report: "Union's primary goal is to increase the value of the common stockholders' equity over time." Later on in the report, the following announcements were made:

a.  The company contributed $1 million to the symphony orchestra in its home office city.

b.  The company is spending $300 million to open a new plant in South America. No revenues will be produced by the plant for 3 years, so earnings will be depressed during this period versus what they would have been had the decision been made not to open the new plant.

c.  The company is increasing its relative use of debt. Whereas assets were formerly financed with 40 percent debt and 60 percent equity, henceforth the financing mix will be 50-50.

d.  The company uses a great deal of electricity in its manufacturing operations, and it generates most of this power itself. Plans are to utilize nuclear fuel rather than coal to produce electricity in the future.

Discuss how each of these factors might affect Union's stock price.

## Selected Additional References

For alternative views on firms' goals and objectives, see the following articles:

Anthony, Robert N., "The Trouble with Profit Maximization," *Harvard Business Review*, November-December 1960, 126-134.

Donaldson, Gordon, "Financial Goals and Strategic Consequences," *Harvard Business Review*, May-June 1985, 57-66.

Seitz, Neil, "Shareholder Goals, Firm Goals and Firm Financing Decisions," *Financial Management*, Autumn 1982, 20-26.

The following articles extend our discussion of the agency problem:

Barnea, Amir, Robert A. Haugen, and Lemma W. Senbet, "Market Imperfections, Agency Problems, and Capital Structure: A Review," *Financial Management*, Summer 1981, 7-22.

Hand, John H., William P. Lloyd, and Robert B. Rogow, "Agency Relationships in the Close Corporation," *Financial Management*, Spring 1982, 25-30.

For a general review of the state of the art in academic finance, together with an extensive bibliography of key research articles, see:

Beranek, William, "Research Directions in Finance," *Quarterly Review of Economics and Business*, Spring 1981, 6-24.

Cooley, Philip L., and J. Louis Heck, "Significant Contributions to Finance Literature," *Financial Management*, Tenth Anniversary Issue, 1981, 23-33.

Weston, J. Fred, "Developments in Finance Theory," *Financial Management*, Tenth Anniversary Issue, 1981, 5-22.

For more information on managerial compensation, see:

Cooley, Philip L., and Charles E. Edwards, "Ownership Effects on Managerial Salaries in Small Business," *Financial Management*, Winter 1982, 5-9.

Patton, Arch, "Those Million-Dollar-a-Year Executives," *Harvard Business Review*, January-February 1985, 56-62.

# 2

# BUSINESS ORGANIZATIONS, FINANCIAL STATEMENTS, AND TAXES

What do General Electric, Bank of America, Safeway Stores, and Armstrong Rubber all have in common? They, and virtually all other big businesses, all started out as proprietorships, later became partnerships, and eventually converted to corporations. Why does this pattern emerge? The answer is that organizational form affects risk, returns, and growth opportunities—and hence the market value—of a business. This chapter will give you some insights into why General Electric is a corporation rather than a partnership or proprietorship, and some ideas as to the form of organization you should choose if you decide to go into business for yourself.

General Electric's stock value is based on its current and projected earnings, which in turn depend on the company's assets and liabilities. Income, assets, and liabilities are all reported in GE's financial statements. Consequently, the information given in these statements is important to anyone thinking of investing in GE's stock. Its balance sheets and income statements show where GE has been, where it is now, and where it seems to be headed in the future. In a sense, GE's financial statements are like its report card; analysts can examine the statements and determine whether the company should receive an A, B, C, D, or F. The central task of GE's management is to take actions now, in 1986, that will lead to good "report cards" in future years.

Finally, it must be recognized that GE and other companies have a major "silent partner" who takes a large (but somewhat controllable) share of the profits, and this same "silent partner" takes a further share of all the interest and dividends GE pays to its investors. This silent partner is, of course, the Internal Revenue Service, which takes its share of the pie as taxes. The Tax Code is quite complicated, and, depending on how a firm is structured and the types of actions it takes, the firm can pay rates of up to 46 percent or as low as zero. GE has, in fact, managed to pay essentially no taxes in recent years, even though it is one of the most profitable U.S. corporations. GE has a tax liability, but it has kept that liability low by making huge investments that generate depreciation tax shelters and by "buying" the tax shelters of

23

less profitable companies that have no taxable income to shelter. Studying the tax issues discussed in this chapter will not assure anyone of achieving GE's success, but it will give you a good idea of how the U.S. tax system operates and of how to live with, if not beat, the system.

Financial management cannot be studied in a vacuum—if the value of a firm is to be maximized, the financial manager must understand the legal environment in which financial decisions are made. This requires a consideration of the forms of business organizations and of the types of securities firms issue. Further, value depends on the *usable income* available to investors, and this means the *after-tax income* as reported to investors. Accordingly, this chapter presents some background information on forms of business organizations, the major types of business securities, and the federal income tax system.[1]

## Alternative Forms of Business Organization

There are three major forms of business organization: the sole proprietorship, the partnership, and the corporation. In terms of numbers, about 80 percent of business firms are operated as sole proprietorships, while the remainder are divided equally between partnerships and corporations. By dollar value of sales, however, about 80 percent of business is conducted by corporations, about 13 percent by sole proprietorships, and about 7 percent by partnerships. Since most business is conducted by corporations, we shall concentrate on them in this book. However, it is important to understand the differences among the three forms, as well as their advantages and disadvantages.

### Sole Proprietorship

**proprietorship**
A business owned by one individual.

A **proprietorship** is a business owned by one individual. Going into business as a single proprietor is very simple—one merely begins business operations. However, most cities require even the smallest establishments to be licensed, and occasionally state licenses are required as well.

The proprietorship has two important advantages for small operations: (1) it is easily and inexpensively formed, since no formal charter for operations is required, and it is subject to few government regulations. (2) The business pays no corporate income taxes; however, as we shall see, this is

---

[1]This chapter contains essential information, but many business students will have been exposed to some or all of it in economics, accounting, or business law courses. Even if they have not, the material is both straightforward and descriptive. Therefore, some instructors may prefer to have students cover Chapter 2 on their own rather than to cover it in class.

not always a net advantage, as all earnings of the firm, whether they are reinvested in the business or withdrawn, are subject to personal income taxes.

The proprietorship also has three important limitations: (1) as we shall see shortly, it is difficult for a proprietorship to obtain large sums of capital; (2) the proprietor has unlimited personal liability for business debts and can lose assets beyond those invested in the company; and (3) the life of a business organized as a proprietorship is limited to the life of the individual who created it. For these three reasons, the individual proprietorship is restricted primarily to small business operations. *However, businesses are frequently started as proprietorships and then converted to corporations if and when their growth causes the disadvantages of the proprietorship form to outweigh its advantages.*

### Partnership

**partnership**
An unincorporated business owned by two or more persons.

A **partnership** exists whenever two or more persons associate to conduct a business. Partnerships may operate under different degrees of formality, ranging from informal, oral understandings to formal agreements filed with the secretary of the state in which the partnership does business. The major advantage of a partnership is its low cost and ease of formation. The disadvantages are similar to those associated with proprietorships: (1) unlimited liability, (2) limited life of the organization, (3) difficulty of transferring ownership, and (4) difficulty of raising large amounts of capital. The tax treatment of a partnership is similar to that for proprietorships, and when compared to that of a corporation, this can be either an advantage or a disadvantage, depending on the situation; this point is discussed later in the chapter.

Regarding liability, the partners must all risk their personal assets, even those assets not invested in the business, for under partnership law each partner is liable for the business's debts. This means that if any partner is unable to meet his or her pro rata claim in the event the partnership goes bankrupt, the remaining partners must take over the unsatisfied claims, drawing on their personal assets if necessary.[2]

The first three disadvantages—unlimited liability, impermanence of the organization, and difficulty of transferring ownership—combine to cause the fourth, the difficulty partnerships have in attracting substantial amounts of capital. This is no particular problem for a slow-growing business, but if a business's products really catch on and it needs to raise large amounts of capital to expand and thus capitalize on its opportunities, the difficulty in attracting large amounts of capital becomes a real drawback. Thus, companies such as Hewlett-Packard and Apple Computer generally begin life as proprietorships or partnerships, but at some point they find it necessary to convert into corporations.

---

[2]However, it is possible to limit the liabilities of some of the partners by establishing a *limited partnership*, wherein certain partners are designated *general partners* and others *limited partners*. Limited partnerships are quite common in the area of real estate investment, but they do not work well with most types of businesses.

## Corporation

A **corporation** is a legal entity, or "person," created by a state. It is separate and distinct from its owners and managers. This separateness gives the corporation three major advantages: (1) it has an *unlimited life*—it can continue after its original owners and managers are deceased; (2) it permits *easy transferability of ownership interest*, because ownership interests can be divided into shares of stock, which in turn can be transferred far more easily than can partnership interests; and (3) it permits *limited liability*. To illustrate, if you invested $10,000 in a partnership which then went bankrupt owing a considerably larger sum of money, you could be assessed for a share of these debts. Thus, an investor in a partnership is exposed to unlimited liability. On the other hand, if you invested $10,000 in the stock of a corporation, your potential loss on the investment would be $10,000—your liability would be limited to the amount of your investment in the business.[3]

While a proprietorship or a partnership can commence operations without much paperwork, setting up a corporation is a bit more involved. The incorporators must prepare a charter and a set of bylaws. The *charter* includes the following information: (1) name of the proposed corporation, (2) type of activities it will pursue, (3) amount of capital stock, (4) number of directors, and (5) names and addresses of directors. The charter is filed with the secretary of the state in which the firm will be headquartered, and when it is approved, the corporation is officially in existence.

The *bylaws* are a set of rules drawn up by the founders of the corporation to aid in governing the internal management of the company. Included are such points as (1) how directors are to be elected (all elected each year or, say, one-third each year); (2) whether the existing stockholders shall have the first right to buy any new shares the firm issues; (3) what provisions there are for management committees, such as an executive committee or a finance committee, and their duties; and (4) what procedures there are for changing the bylaws themselves, should conditions require it. Lawyers have standard form charters and bylaws in their word processors, and they can set up a corporation with very little effort. For about $500—less if you find a hungry young lawyer fresh out of law school—a business can be incorporated.

The value of any business other than a very small one will probably be maximized if it is organized as a corporation. The reasons are as follows:

**1.** Limited liability reduces risk to investors, and the lower the firm's risk, other things held constant, the higher its value.

**2.** Value is dependent on growth opportunities, which in turn are dependent on a firm's ability to attract capital. Since corporations can attract capital more easily than unincorporated businesses, they have superior growth opportunities.

---

[3]In the case of small corporations, the limited liability feature is often a fiction, since bankers and credit managers frequently require personal guarantees from the stockholders of small, weak businesses.

3. The value of an asset also depends on its *liquidity*, which means the ease of selling the asset and converting it to cash. Since an investment in the stock of a corporation is much more liquid than a similar investment in a proprietorship or partnership, this too means that the corporate form of organization can enhance the value of a business.

4. Corporations are taxed differently than proprietorships and partnerships, and under certain conditions the tax laws favor corporations. This point is discussed in detail later in the chapter.

Since most firms are managed with value maximization in mind, it is easy to see why most business is conducted by corporations.

## Securities and Financial Statements

Irrespective of its form of organization, any business must have *assets* if it is to operate, and in order to acquire assets, the firm must raise *capital*. Capital comes in two basic forms, *debt* and *equity*. There are many different types of debt—long-term and short-term, interest-bearing and non-interest-bearing, secured and unsecured, and so on. Similarly, there are different types of equity. The equity of a proprietorship is called *proprietor's interest* or *proprietor's net worth*; for a partnership, the word *partner* is inserted in lieu of *proprietor*. For a corporation, equity is represented by *preferred stock* and *common stockholders' equity*. Common equity, in turn, includes both *paid-in capital* and *retained earnings*.

Table 2-1 shows a simplified balance sheet for Teletron Electronics Company, a large electronic components manufacturer, as of December 31, 1985. Teletron began life in 1951 as a proprietorship, then became a partnership, and finally converted to a corporation in 1962. Its 1985 sales were $401 million, and the $280 million of assets shown in Table 2-1 were necessary to support these sales. Teletron and other companies obtain the bulk of the funds used to buy assets (1) by buying on credit from their suppliers (accounts payable); (2) by borrowing from banks, insurance companies, pension funds, and other institutions; (3) from the sale of preferred and common stock to investors; and (4) by "saving money" as reflected in the retained earnings account.[4] Also, since wages and taxes are not paid on a daily basis, Teletron obtains some "credit" from its labor force and from the government in the form of accrued wages and taxes.

The first claim against Teletron's income and assets is by its creditors—all those claims items listed on the balance sheet above preferred stock. However, the creditors' claims are limited to fixed amounts; for example, most of the long-term debt bears interest at a rate of 9 percent per year, so the bond-

---

[4]Corporate saving occurs whenever a company pays dividends which are less than its net income. The savings that have accumulated since the company began are reported as retained earnings on its balance sheet.

**Table 2-1**
**Teletron Electronics Company:**
**Balance Sheet as of December 31, 1985**
**(Thousands of Dollars)**

| Assets | | Claims on Assets | |
|---|---|---|---|
| Cash and marketable securities | $ 12,081 | Accounts payable | $ 23,818 |
| Accounts receivable | 50,262 | Notes payable to banks | 30,000 |
| Inventories | 91,611 | Accrued wages and taxes | 2,568 |
| Prepaid expenses and other current assets | 1,605 | Other current liabilities | 5,151 |
| Total current assets | $155,559 | Total current liabilities | $ 61,537 |
| Net fixed assets | 124,718 | Long-term bonds | 107,015 |
| | | Preferred stock (111,500 shares) | 11,150 |
| | | Common stockholders' equity: | |
| | | Common stock and paid-in capital (1,706,351 shares) | 10,375 |
| | | Retained earnings | 90,200 |
| | | Total common equity | $100,575 |
| Total assets | $280,277 | Total claims | $280,277 |

holders in total get interest of about 0.09 x $107,015,000 = $9,631,350 per year. If Teletron did extremely well and had profits of, say, $80 million, the bondholders would still get only $9.6 million. However, if Teletron lost money, the bondholders would nevertheless get their $9.6 million—assets would be sold, the cash would be used to pay the bond interest, and common equity would be reduced. Further, if the company's situation were so bad that it simply could not generate the cash needed to make the required payments to the bondholders and other creditors, then as a rule (1) it would be forced into bankruptcy, (2) the assets would be sold off (generally at less than the values stated on the balance sheet), and (3) the creditors would have first claim on the proceeds from the bankruptcy liquidation.

The preferred stockholders stand next in line, after the creditors, for the firm's income and assets. Teletron has 111,500 shares of preferred stock, each with a par value of $100. This preferred pays a dividend of $8.125 per year, or 8.125 percent on its $100 par value. The preferred dividends must be paid before any dividends can be paid on the common, and in the event of bankruptcy the preferred must be paid off in full before anything goes to the common stockholders.[5]

---

[5]The status of the different types of investors, and bankruptcy proceedings in general, are discussed in more detail in Chapters 11 and 12. As a general rule, here is the order of priority of different claimants in the event of bankruptcy: (1) secured creditors' claims on the proceeds from the sale of the specific assets securing their loans, such as a building which secures a mortgage; (2) federal and state governments for accrued taxes; (3) employees for accrued wages and unfunded pension benefits; (4) other creditors; (5) preferred stockholders; and (6), in last place, common stockholders. This priority system has a major effect on the riskiness and consequently on the rates of return on different classes of securities.

Teletron has 1,706,351 shares of common stock outstanding. Investors actually paid about $6.08 on the average for these shares ( $10,375,000/ 1,706,351 = $6.08), but the company has saved through retention of earnings $90,200,000/1,706,351 = $52.86 per share since it was incorporated in 1962. Therefore, stockholders on the average have a total investment of $6.08 + $52.86 = $58.94 per share in the company; this is the stock's *book value*.

Teletron's debt and preferred stock is held primarily by its suppliers, by five banks, and by some institutions such as life insurance companies and pension funds. The debt is rarely if ever traded, since this particular set of investors tends to hold debt until it matures. Teletron's common stock, on the other hand, is traded fairly actively. Individuals own about 65 percent of the stock, while institutions own the remaining 35 percent; these are typical percentages. In the fall of 1985, the stock traded in the general range of $60 to $70 per share, and it has ranged from a high of $75 to a low of $10 over the past 12 years. The price rises and falls depending (1) on how the company is doing at a given point in time, (2) on what is happening to other stock prices, and (3) most important, on how investors expect the company to do in the future. The *market value* (or price) does not depend directly on, and is usually different from, the book value. We will return to the question of how stock prices are determined in Chapter 5.

## The Federal Income Tax System

The value of any financial asset, such as stocks or bonds, and most real assets, such as plants or even whole firms, depends on the stream of *usable* income produced by the asset. Usable income means income *after taxes*. Proprietorship and partnership income must be reported and taxed as personal income to the owners. Most corporations must first pay taxes on their own income, and stockholders must then pay taxes on corporate after-tax income distributed to them as dividends. Therefore, both *personal* and *corporate* income taxes are important.

Federal income tax rates for individuals go up to 50 percent, and when state and city income taxes are included, the marginal tax rate on an individual's income can approach 70 percent. Business income is also taxed heavily. The income from partnerships and proprietorships is reported by the individual owners and consequently taxed at rates going up to about 70 percent, while corporate profits are subject to federal income tax rates of up to 46 percent, in addition to state income taxes. Because of the magnitude of the tax bite, taxes play an important role in many financial decisions.

Taxes are so complicated that university law schools offer master's degrees in taxation to practicing lawyers, many of whom also have CPA licenses. In a field complicated enough to warrant such detailed study, we can cover only the highlights. This is all that is really necessary, though, because business people and investors should and do rely on tax specialists rather than trust their own limited knowledge. Still, it is important to know the basic elements of the tax system as a starting point for discussions with tax experts.

## Individual Income Taxes

**progressive tax**
A tax that requires a higher percentage payment on higher incomes. The personal income tax in the United States, which goes from a rate of 11 percent on its lowest increments of income to 50 percent on the highest increments, is progressive.

**taxable income**
Gross income minus allowable deductions as set forth in the Tax Code.

**marginal tax rate**
The tax applicable to the last unit of income.

**average tax rate**
Taxes paid divided by taxable income.

Individuals pay taxes on wages and salaries, on investment income (dividends, interest, and profits from the sale of securities), and on the profits of proprietorships and partnerships. Our tax rates are **progressive**—that is, the higher the income, the larger the percentage paid in taxes. Table 2-2 gives the current tax rates for single individuals and married couples filing joint returns under the rate schedules that existed in the summer of 1985.[6] Here are the highlights of the table:

**1. Taxable income** is defined as gross income less a set of deductions which are spelled out in the instructions to the tax forms people must file (Forms 1040, 1040A, or 1040EZ).

**2.** The **marginal tax rate** is the tax on the last unit of income; marginal tax rates are zero on the first units of income, but they rise to 50 percent.

**3.** One can calculate **average tax rates** from the data in the table. For example, if Jane Vincent, a single individual, had a taxable income of $30,000 in 1985, then her tax bill would be $5,705 + 0.34($30,000 − $28,800) = $5,705 + 0.34($1,200) = $6,113. Her *average tax rate* would be $6,113/$30,000 = 0.204 = 20.4 percent versus a *marginal rate* of 34 percent. If Jane received a raise of $1,000, bringing her income to $31,000, she would have to pay $340 of it as taxes, so her net raise would be $660.

**4.** It is not shown in the table, but Congress committed itself (though it could change its mind) to *index tax rates* beyond 1984 to avoid the **bracket creep** which occurred during the 1970s and which de facto raised tax rates substantially.[7]

**bracket creep**
A situation that occurs when progressive tax rates combine with inflation to cause a greater portion of each taxpayer's real income to be paid as taxes.

***Taxes on Dividend and Interest Income.*** Dividend and interest income received by individuals from corporate securities is taxed at rates going up to 50 percent. Since corporations pay dividends out of earnings that have

---

[6]It should be noted that Congress changes the tax laws fairly often. The provisions given here are those for 1985 as they existed in the summer of that year.

[7]For example, if you were single and had a 1985 taxable income of $10,800, your tax bill would be $1,203. Now suppose inflation caused prices to double and your income, being tied to a cost of living index, rose to $21,600. Because our tax rates are progressive, your taxes (at 1985 rates) would jump to $3,621. Your after-tax income would thus increase from $9,597 to $17,979, but, since prices have doubled, your real income would *decline* from $9,597 to $8,990 (calculated as one-half of $17,979). You would be in a higher tax bracket, so you would be paying a higher percentage of your real income in taxes. If this happened to everyone, and if Congress failed to change tax rates sufficiently, then real individual incomes would decline because the federal government would be taking a larger share of the national product. This is called the federal government's "inflation dividend," and it helps explain why congressional liberals have not been too concerned about inflation, since it has given them more of the nation's real income to dispense. Bracket creep was a real problem during the 1970s, but the current (1985) law indexing rates will stop it unless Congress changes that part of the tax code.

**Table 2-2**
**Individual Tax Rates in 1985**

| Single Individuals | | | Married Couples Filing Joint Returns | | |
|---|---|---|---|---|---|
| **If Your Taxable Income Is** | **You Pay this Amount on the Base of the Bracket (Tax on Base)** | **Plus this Percentage on the Excess over the Base (Marginal Rate)** | **If Your Taxable Income Is** | **You Pay this Amount on the Base of the Bracket (Tax on Base)** | **Plus this Percentage on the Excess over the Base (Marginal Rate)** |
| Up to $2,300 | No tax | — | Up to $3,400 | No tax | — |
| $2,300 to $3,400 | $    0 | 11% | $3,400 to $5,500 | $    0 | 11% |
| $3,400 to $4,400 | 121 | 12 | $5,500 to $7,600 | 231 | 12 |
| $4,400 to $6,500 | 241 | 14 | $7,600 to $11,900 | 483 | 14 |
| $6,500 to $8,500 | 535 | 15 | $11,900 to $16,000 | 1,085 | 16 |
| $8,500 to $10,800 | 835 | 16 | $16,000 to $20,200 | 1,741 | 18 |
| $10,800 to $12,900 | 1,203 | 18 | $20,200 to $24,600 | 2,497 | 22 |
| $12,900 to $15,000 | 1,581 | 20 | $24,600 to $29,900 | 3,465 | 25 |
| $15,000 to $18,200 | 2,001 | 23 | $29,900 to $35,200 | 4,790 | 28 |
| $18,200 to $23,500 | 2,737 | 26 | $35,200 to $45,800 | 6,274 | 33 |
| $23,500 to $28,800 | 4,115 | 30 | $45,800 to $60,000 | 9,772 | 38 |
| $28,800 to $34,100 | 5,705 | 34 | $60,000 to $85,600 | 15,168 | 42 |
| $34,100 to $41,500 | 7,507 | 38 | $85,600 to $109,400 | 25,920 | 45 |
| $41,500 to $55,300 | 10,319 | 42 | $109,400 to $162,400 | 36,630 | 49 |
| $55,300 to $81,800 | 16,115 | 48 | Over $162,400 | 62,600 | 50 |
| Over $81,800 | 28,835 | 50 | | | |

already been taxed, there is *double taxation* of corporate income. However, the first $100 of dividend income for single individuals ($200 for married couples filing joint returns) is *excluded* from personal income taxes.

It should be noted that under U.S. tax laws interest on state and local government bonds, called *municipals* or *"munis,"* is not subject to federal income taxes. Thus, investors get to keep more of the interest paid on municipal bonds than on bonds issued by corporations or by the U.S. government. This means that a lower-yielding muni can provide the same after-tax return as a higher-yielding corporate bond. For example, a taxpayer in the 46 percent marginal tax bracket who could buy a muni which yielded 9 percent would have to receive a before-tax yield of 16.67 percent on a corporate or U.S. Treasury bond to have the same after-tax income:

$$\text{Equivalent pre-tax yield on taxable bond} = \frac{\text{Yield on muni}}{1 - \text{Marginal tax rate}}$$

$$= \frac{9\%}{1 - 0.46} = 16.67\%.$$

This exemption from federal taxes stems from the separation of federal and state powers, and its primary purpose is to help state and local governments borrow at lower rates than would otherwise be available to them.

***Capital Gain versus Ordinary Income.*** Assets such as stocks, bonds, and real estate are defined as *capital assets*. If you buy a capital asset and later sell it for more than your purchase price, the profit is defined as a **capital gain**; if you suffer a loss, it is called a **capital loss**.

**capital gain or loss**
The profit (loss) from the sale of a capital asset for more (less) than its purchase price.

An asset sold within 6 months of the time it was purchased produces a *short-term gain or loss*, while one held for more than 6 months produces a *long-term gain or loss.*[8] Thus, if you buy 100 shares of GE stock for $70 per share and sell it for $80, you make a capital gain of 100 × $10, or $1,000. However, if you sell the stock for $60, you will have a $1,000 capital loss. If you hold the stock for more than 6 months, the gain or loss is long-term; otherwise, it is short-term. If you sell the stock for $70, you make neither a gain nor a loss; you simply get your $7,000 back and pay no taxes on it.

Long-term capital gains are generally taxed at only 40 percent of the rate which applies to short-term gains (or other ordinary income). Under the law, 60 percent of all long-term gains are excluded from taxable income, so taxes are paid on only 40 percent of long-term gains income. Thus, if an individual had $1,000 of short-term capital gains (or dividends) and was in the 34 percent marginal tax bracket, his or her gains tax would be $340, while if the gain had been long-term, the tax would have been only 0.34($1,000 − $600) = $136. Because of this 60 percent exclusion, the effective long-term gains tax rate is only 40 percent of the ordinary tax rate.[9]

The fact that capital gains income is taxed at a lower rate than dividend or interest income has an important bearing on financial management. As we shall see, most businesses have at least some flexibility in providing returns to investors in the form of capital gains rather than as dividends. Since the tax treatment of income from an asset has a significant effect on the value of that asset, personal income taxes must be taken into account by a firm seeking to maximize the value of its stock.

## Corporate Income Taxes

The corporate tax structure, shown in Table 2-3, is relatively simple. To illustrate, if a firm had $200,000 of taxable income, its 1985 tax bill would be $71,750:

$$\text{Taxes} = 0.15(\$25,000) + 0.18(\$25,000) + 0.30(\$25,000) + 0.40(\$25,000) + 0.46(\$100,000)$$
$$= \$3,750 + \$4,500 + \$7,500 + \$10,000 + \$46,000$$
$$= \$71,750.$$

---

[8]The Deficit Reduction Act of 1984 reduced the capital gains holding period from over 1 year to over 6 months. This reduction is on a "trial basis" and is scheduled to expire on December 31, 1987, unless renewed by Congress.

[9]Some complexities in the taxation of long-term capital gains (and losses) are not discussed here. The interested reader is referred to *Federal Tax Course* (Englewood Cliffs, N.J.: Prentice-Hall, 1985).

**Table 2-3**
**Corporate Tax Rates in 1985**

| Taxable Income | Tax Rate |
|---|---|
| 1st $25,000 | 15% |
| 2nd $25,000 | 18 |
| 3rd $25,000 | 30 |
| 4th $25,000 | 40 |
| Over $100,000[a] | 46 |

[a]If a corporation's income exceeds $1,000,000, it must give up the tax savings on the first $100,000 of income. Specifically, for income over $1,000,000, the tax is increased by the lesser of either 5 percent of the excess over $1,000,000 or $20,250.

Thus, the corporate tax is very progressive up to $100,000 of income, but it is essentially constant thereafter.[10]

***Interest and Dividend Income Received by a Corporation.*** Interest income received by a corporation is taxed as ordinary income at regular corporate tax rates. However, 85 percent of the dividends received by one corporation from another is excluded from taxable income, while the remaining 15 percent is taxed at the ordinary tax rate. Thus, a corporation earning over $100,000 and paying a 46 percent marginal tax rate would pay $0.15(0.46) = 0.069 = 6.9\%$ of its dividend income as taxes. If this firm had $10,000 in pre-tax dividend income, its after-tax dividend income would be $9,310:

$$
\begin{aligned}
\text{After-tax income} &= \text{Before-tax income} - \text{Taxes} \\
&= \text{Before-tax income} - (\text{Before-tax income})(\text{Effective tax rate}) \\
&= \text{Before-tax income}(1 - \text{Effective tax rate}) \\
&= \$10,000[1 - (0.15)(0.46)] \\
&= \$10,000(1 - 0.069) \\
&= \$10,000(0.931) = \$9,310.
\end{aligned}
$$

If the corporation passes its own after-tax income on to its stockholders as dividends, the income is ultimately subjected to *triple taxation*: (1) the original corporation is first taxed, (2) the second corporation is then taxed on the dividends it received, and (3) the individuals who receive the final dividends are taxed again. This is the reason for the 85 percent exclusion on intercorporate dividends.

---

[10]As we noted at the beginning of the chapter, many large, profitable corporations pay zero income taxes. What actually happens is that (1) expenses, especially depreciation, are defined differently for purposes of calculating taxable income versus reporting earnings to stockholders, so some companies report positive profits to stockholders but losses—hence no taxes—to the Internal Revenue Service, and (2) some companies which do have tax liabilities use various tax credits, including the investment tax credit (discussed later in the chapter) to offset taxes that would otherwise be payable.

Notice that if a corporation has surplus funds which can be invested in marketable securities, the tax factor favors investment in stocks, which pay dividends, rather than in bonds, which pay interest. For example, suppose a firm had $100,000 to invest, and it could buy bonds that paid interest of $10,000 per year or stock that paid dividends of $10,000. If the firm were in the 46 percent tax bracket, its tax on the interest, if it bought bonds, would be 0.46($10,000) = $4,600 and its after-tax income would be $5,400. If it bought stock, its tax would be 0.46[(0.15)($10,000)] = $690 and its after-tax income would be $9,310. Other factors might lead the firm to invest in bonds, but the tax factor certainly favors stock investments when the investor is a corporation.[11]

***Interest and Dividends Paid by a Corporation.*** A firm's operations can be financed with either debt or equity capital. If it uses debt, it must pay interest on this debt, while if it uses equity, it will pay dividends to the equity investors (stockholders). The interest paid by a corporation is deducted from its operating income to obtain its taxable income, but dividends paid are not deductible. A firm needs $1 of pre-tax income to pay $1 of interest, but if it is in the 46 percent bracket, it needs

$$\frac{\$1}{1 - \text{Tax rate}} = \frac{\$1}{0.54} = \$1.85$$

of pre-tax income to pay $1 of dividends.

To illustrate, Table 2-4 shows the situation for a firm whose assets produced $2 million of income in 1985 before taxes. If the firm were financed entirely by bonds and it had interest payments of $2 million, then its taxable income would be zero, taxes would be zero, and investors would receive the entire $2 million. (The term *investors* includes both stockholders and bondholders.) If the firm had no debt and was therefore financed only by stock, the $2 million would be taxable income to the corporation, the tax would be $2,000,000(0.46) = $920,000, and investors would receive only $1.08 million versus $2 million under debt financing. Of course, it is generally not possible to finance exclusively with debt capital, and the risk of doing so would offset the benefits of the higher expected income. *Still, the fact that interest is a deductible expense has a profound effect on the way businesses are financed—our tax system favors debt financing over equity financing.* This point is discussed in more detail in Chapters 14 and 15.

***Corporate Capital Gains.*** Corporate long-term capital gains are taxed at rates lower than ordinary income, just as with individuals. A firm could generate capital gains by the sale of financial assets (stocks, bonds, and so on)

---

[11]Also note that corporations are restricted in their use of borrowed funds to purchase another firm's preferred or common stock. Without such restrictions firms could engage in *tax arbitrage*, whereby the interest on borrowed funds reduces taxable income on a dollar-for-dollar basis but taxable income is increased by only $0.15 per dollar of dividend income. Thus, current tax laws reduce the 85 percent dividend exclusion in proportion to the amount of borrowed funds used to purchase the stock.

**Table 2-4**
**Cash Flows to Investors under Bond and Stock Financing**

|  | Use Bonds | Use Stock |
|---|---|---|
| Before-tax income | $2,000,000 | $2,000,000 |
| Interest | 2,000,000 | 0 |
| Taxable income | $          0 | $2,000,000 |
| Taxes (46%) | 0 | 920,000 |
| After-tax income | $          0 | $1,080,000 |
| Income to investors | $2,000,000 | $1,080,000 |

which it held as part of an investment portfolio, but it could also realize capital gains on its capital assets such as land, plant, and equipment. (Remember that a capital gain occurs when an asset is sold for more than its purchase price.) As with individuals, to qualify as a long-term capital gain, the asset must be held for more than 6 months. The laws governing corporate capital gains are even more complex than those pertaining to individual capital gains. We will discuss corporate capital gains again in Chapter 10, where we analyze capital budgeting cash flows.

**tax loss carry-back
and carry-forward**
Losses that can be carried
backward or forward in
time to offset taxable
income in a given year.

*Corporate Loss Carry-Back and Carry-Forward.* Ordinary corporate operating losses can be carried back (**carry-back**) to each of the preceding 3 years and forward (**carry-forward**) for the following 15 years and used to offset taxable income in those years. For example, an operating loss in 1985 can be used to reduce taxable income in 1982, 1983, or 1984, and then any remaining losses can be carried forward and used in 1986, 1987, and so on, to the year 2000. The loss must be first applied to the earliest year, then to the next earliest year, and so on.

To illustrate, suppose Manhattan Manufacturing, Inc., had a $1 million *pre-tax* profit in 1982, 1983, and 1984 and then in 1985 it had a bad year and lost $6 million. Manhattan would use the carry-back feature to recompute taxes for 1982, using $1 million of the 1985 operating losses to reduce the 1982 pre-tax profit to zero. This would permit the company to recover the amount of taxes paid in 1982, so Manhattan would receive a refund in 1986 of 1982 taxes because of the loss experienced in 1985. Since $5 million of unrecovered losses would still be available, Manhattan would repeat this procedure for 1983 and 1984. Thus, it would pay zero taxes for 1985 and would receive in 1986 a refund of taxes paid from 1982 through 1984. The firm would still have $3 million of unrecovered losses to carry forward (subject to the 15-year limit) until the entire $6 million loss had been used to offset taxable income. The purpose of permitting this loss averaging is, of course, to avoid penalizing corporations whose incomes fluctuate significantly from year to year.

*Improper Accumulation to Avoid Payment of Dividends.* Corporations could refrain from paying dividends to permit their stockholders to avoid

**improper
accumulation**
Retention of earnings by a
business for the purpose
of enabling stockholders
to avoid personal income
taxes.

personal income taxes on dividends. To prevent this, the tax code contains
an **improper accumulation** provision which states that earnings accumulated by a corporation are subject to penalty rates *if the purpose of the accumulation is to enable stockholders to avoid the personal income tax*. A
cumulative total of $250,000 (the balance sheet item "retained earnings") is
by law exempted from the improper accumulation tax.[12] This is a benefit
primarily to small corporations.

Although there is a penalty rate on all amounts over $250,000 *shown to
be unnecessary to meet the reasonable needs of the business*, many companies do indeed have legitimate reasons for retaining earnings over $250,000
and are thus not subject to the penalty rate. Earnings during a given year may
be retained and used to pay off debt, to finance growth, or to provide the
corporation with a cushion against possible cash drains caused by losses.
How much a firm should properly accumulate for uncertain contingencies is
a matter of judgment. We shall consider this matter again in Chapter 16,
which deals with corporate dividend policy.

***Consolidated Corporate Tax Returns.*** If a corporation owns 80 percent
or more of another corporation's stock, it can aggregate income and file one
consolidated tax return; thus, losses in one company can be used to offset
profits in another. (Similarly, one division's losses can be used to offset another division's profits.) No business ever wants to incur losses (you can go
broke losing $1 to save 46¢ in taxes), but tax offsets do make it more feasible
for large, multidivisional corporations to undertake risky new ventures or
ventures that will suffer losses during a developmental period.

## Taxation of Small Businesses: S Corporations

The Internal Revenue Code provides that small businesses which meet certain restrictions as spelled out therein may be set up as corporations and thus
receive the benefits of the corporate form of organization—especially limited
liability—yet still be taxed as proprietorships or partnerships rather than as
corporations. These corporations are called **S corporations** (formerly Subchapter S corporations). There are several reasons for a small firm's electing
to be taxed as an S corporation, including the following:

**S corporation**
A small corporation which
under Subchapter S of the
Internal Revenue Code
elects to be taxed as a
proprietorship or a
partnership yet to retain
limited liability and other
benefits of the corporate
form of organization.

**1.** If an S firm is profitable, its income is reported on a pro rata basis as
taxable income to its stockholders, who may then withdraw funds without
the payment of further taxes. This avoids the double taxation that occurs
when a corporation reports income, pays taxes, and then pays dividends that
are taxable income to its stockholders. (Of course, if the owners are already
in high personal tax brackets from other income, and if they do not plan to
withdraw profits from the business, then they may elect not to use the S
option.)

**2.** If the firm has operating losses, its stockholders can claim them on a pro
rata basis as deductions against their ordinary income. This is an especially

---

[12]The limit is $150,000 for certain personal service corporations.

attractive feature for a new business that expects to incur heavy start-up costs and whose stockholders are in high marginal tax brackets because of income from other sources.

**3.** If the firm has investment tax credits, these credits can be passed along to the stockholders. (Investment tax credits are discussed later in the chapter.) Again, this is especially important for small, new firms that are making heavy capital investments yet whose income is insufficient to utilize fully the tax credits generated by these investments but whose owners have outside income that can be offset by these credits.

Many factors other than taxes bear on the question of whether or not a firm should be organized as a corporation. However, the provision for S corporation status makes it possible for most small businesses to enjoy the benefits of a corporation yet avoid double taxation problems.

## Depreciation

Suppose a firm buys a milling machine for $100,000 and uses it for 5 years, after which it is scrapped. The cost of the goods produced by the machine must include a charge for the machine, and this charge is called *depreciation*. Depreciation reduces profits as calculated by the accountants and reported to investors, but it also reduces the firm's tax bill.

Companies generally calculate depreciation one way when figuring taxes and another way when reporting income to investors: (1) they use the *straight line* method for stockholder reporting (or "book" purposes), and (2) they use the fastest rate permitted by law (Congress) for tax purposes. Under the straight line method, one simply takes the cost of the asset less its salvage value and divides this amount by the asset's economic life. For an asset with a 5-year life which costs $100,000 and has a zero salvage value, the annual depreciation charge is $100,000/5 = $20,000. For tax purposes, Congress changes the permissible tax depreciation methods from time to time. Prior to 1954 the straight line method was required for tax purposes, but in 1954 *accelerated* methods (double declining balance and sum-of-years'-digits) were permitted. Then, in 1981, the old accelerated methods were replaced by a simpler procedure known as the **Accelerated Cost Recovery System** (**ACRS**, which is pronounced "acres"). Following are the highlights of ACRS as it existed in 1985.

**Accelerated Cost Recovery System (ACRS)**
A depreciation system that allows businesses to write off the cost of an asset over a period much shorter than its operating life.

### Tax Depreciation Life

The cost of an asset is expensed gradually over its depreciable life for tax purposes. Historically, an asset's depreciable life was determined by its estimated useful economic life; it was intended that an asset would be fully depreciated at approximately the same time that it reached the end of its useful economic life. However, ACRS totally abandoned this practice and set simpler guidelines which created several classes of assets, each with a more-or-less arbitrarily prescribed life called a *recovery period* or *class life*. These ACRS class lives bear no necessary relationship to expected economic lives.

A major effect of the ACRS system has been to shorten the depreciable lives of assets, thus giving businesses larger tax deductions and increasing cash flows available for reinvestment. Table 2-5 describes what types of property fit into the different class life groups, and Table 2-6 sets forth the ACRS recovery allowances (depreciation rates) for the various classes of investment property. Consider Table 2-5 first. The first column gives the ACRS class life, while the second column describes the types of assets which fall into each category. With the straight line method, a uniform annual depreciation charge is allowed. The annual depreciation charge is equal to the cost of the asset divided by the years of the asset's class life. The ACRS recovery allowances as set by Congress always equal or exceed the straight line rates. Therefore, a firm will always obtain a faster depreciation write-off if it uses the ACRS recovery allowances than if it uses straight line.[13]

### Computing ACRS Depreciation

Under earlier depreciation methods, the rate at which the value of an asset actually declined was estimated, and this rate was then used as the basis for tax depreciation. Thus, different assets were depreciated along different paths over time. The ACRS method, however, sets forth prescribed depreciation rates, called *recovery allowance percentages*, for all assets within each class. These rates, as set forth in 1985, are shown in Table 2-6. The yearly recovery, or depreciation expense, is determined by multiplying the asset's *depreciable basis* by the applicable recovery allowance percentage. In the remainder of this section, we discuss some additional features of the ACRS system, discuss the computation of an asset's depreciable basis, and illustrate the calculation of annual depreciation expense.

---

**Table 2-5**
**Classes and Asset Lives under ACRS**

| Class | Type of Property |
|---|---|
| 3-year | Automobiles, tractor units, light-duty trucks, and certain special manufacturing tools. |
| 5-year | Personal property that is not 3-year or 10-year property. Includes most equipment, office furniture, and fixtures. |
| 10-year | Certain real property, certain public utility property, and theme park structures. Includes manufactured and mobile homes. |
| 18-year | All real property, such as buildings, other than any designated as 10-year property. |

Note: There are a few exceptions to these rules for such assets as low-income housing. Also, it is possible to use straight line depreciation, but it is not in the best interests of most profitable firms to do so.

---

[13]As a benefit to very small companies, the tax code also permits companies to *expense*, which is equivalent to depreciating over one year, up to $5,000 of equipment. Thus, if a small company bought one asset worth up to $5,000, it could write the asset off in the year it was acquired. This is called "Section 179 expensing." We shall disregard this provision throughout the book.

**Table 2-6**
**Recovery Allowances for Property**
**Placed in Service after December 31, 1980**[a]

| Ownership Year | Class of Investment | | | |
|---|---|---|---|---|
| | 3-Year | 5-Year | 10-Year | 18-Year |
| 1 | 25% | 15% | 8% | 4% |
| 2 | 38 | 22 | 14 | 8 |
| 3 | 37 | 21 | 12 | 7 |
| 4 | | 21 | 10 | 7 |
| 5 | | 21 | 10 | 6 |
| 6 | | | 10 | 6 |
| 7 | | | 9 | 6 |
| 8 | | | 9 | 6 |
| 9 | | | 9 | 5 |
| 10 | | | 9 | 5 |
| 11 | | | | 5 |
| 12 | | | | 5 |
| 13 | | | | 5 |
| 14 | | | | 5 |
| 15 | | | | 5 |
| 16 | | | | 5 |
| 17 | | | | 5 |
| 18 | | | | 5 |
| | 100% | 100% | 100% | 100% |

[a]Congress developed these recovery allowance percentages based on the 150 percent declining balance method, with a switch to straight line depreciation at some point in the asset's life. For example, consider the 10-year recovery allowances. The straight line allowance would be 10 percent per year, so the 150 percent declining balance multiplier is $1.5 \times 10\% = 15\%$. However, the half-year convention applies, so the ACRS allowance for Year 1 is 7.5 percent, rounded to 8 percent. For Year 2, there is 92 percent of the depreciable basis remaining to be depreciated, so the recovery allowance is $0.15(92\%) = 13.8\%$, rounded to 14 percent. After 3 years, straight line depreciation exceeds the declining balance depreciation, so a switch is made to straight line. This switch gives an allowance of $66\%/7 = 9.43\%$, which is rounded to 10 percent for 3 years and to 9 percent for the final 4 years to eliminate fractional percentages.

**half-year convention**
A feature of ACRS in which all assets are assumed to be put into service at mid-year and thus allowed a half-year's depreciation regardless of when they actually go into service.

*Half-Year Convention.* The ACRS recovery percentages as shown in Table 2-6 employ the **half-year convention**—that is, they assume that all assets are put into service at mid-year, and hence generate a half-year's depreciation, irrespective of when they actually go into service. The half-year convention also applies if the straight line option is used, with half of one year's depreciation being taken in the first year, a full year's depreciation in each of the remaining years of the asset's class life, and the remaining half-year's depreciation in the year following the end of the class life.

**depreciable basis**
The portion of an asset's value which can be depreciated for tax purposes. The depreciable basis is equal to the cost of the asset minus one-half the ITC.

*Depreciable Basis.* The **depreciable basis** is a critical element of ACRS, because each year's allowance (depreciation expense) depends on the asset's depreciable basis and ACRS class life. The depreciable basis under ACRS is not adjusted for *salvage value*, which is the estimated market value of the asset at the end of its useful life. However, it is affected by the investment tax credit, as discussed in the following section. The depreciable basis is the same whether ACRS or the optional straight line method is used.

investment tax credit
(ITC)
A specified percentage of
the cost of new assets
that businesses can
deduct as a credit against
their income taxes.

*Investment Tax Credit.* The **investment tax credit (ITC)** provides for a direct reduction of taxes, and it is designed to stimulate business investment.[14] The credit applies only to depreciable personal property with a life of 3 years or more, and currently it is 6 percent for assets in the 3-year class and 10 percent for assets in the 5- and 10-year classes. Nearly all new property except land and buildings qualifies for the ITC. The dollar tax deduction is determined by multiplying the capitalized cost of the asset by the applicable ITC percentage.[15]

There are four other points to bear in mind regarding the ITC: (1) the depreciable basis of an asset, that is, the amount to which the ACRS recovery allowances are applied, is reduced by one-half the amount of the ITC; (2) if an asset is sold prior to meeting the minimum qualifying life, the firm will have to repay, and the IRS will **recapture**, some of the ITC; (3) the ITC is limited to the first $25,000 of tax liability plus 85 percent of the remainder; thus, if a company's income is low in a year when it makes large capital expenditures, it may not be able to use all of its ITC; (4) if the credit during a given year exceeds the limitations noted in Point 3, the excess may be carried back to the 3 prior years and then forward for the next 15 years.[16]

recapture
The return of a portion of
the ITC to the IRS
because an asset was not
held for the minimum time
required to qualify for the
ITC.

*ACRS and ITC Illustration.* Assume that a stamping machine which falls into the 5-year class life and which costs $50,000 is placed into service on March 1, 1986. An ITC of $5,000 is taken. Salvage value is not considered, but one-half of the ITC, or $2,500, must be deducted to determine the depreciable basis, which is therefore $47,500. Each year's recovery (depreciation expense) is determined by multiplying the depreciable basis by the applicable recovery percentage. Thus, the depreciation expense for 1986 is $0.15( \$47,500 ) = \$7,125$; similarly, it is $10,450 for 1987 and $9,975 per year for 1988, 1989, and 1990. The total depreciation expense is $47,500, which is the depreciable basis of the machine.

Now assume that the stamping machine is sold after 4 years. To qualify for the full 10 percent ITC, the asset must be kept for at least 5 years. Since the asset was only in service for 4 out of 5 years, or 80 percent of the required period, 20 percent of the ITC, or $1,000, must be repaid.

---

[14]In addition to ITCs, there are also tax credits for research and development, for job training and employment programs, and for other specific expenditures. A discussion of these credits would be beyond the scope of this text.

[15]The Tax Code also provides an alternative ITC method. Rather than taking a 6 percent ITC on 3-year property along with a 3 percent reduction in depreciable basis, the firm could take a 4 percent ITC with no reduction in depreciable basis. Similarly, it can take an 8 percent ITC on property that falls into the other classes with no reduction in depreciable basis. Since the method presented above generally provides somewhat greater benefits to the firm, we will take the full ITC in our illustrations throughout the text.

[16]The carry-back and carry-forward of the ITC effectively transfers the credit from less profitable to more profitable years. Leases, which we discuss in Chapter 13, permit the transfer of the ITC from low-profit to high-profit firms. GE and IBM used leases to obtain tax credits which greatly reduced their effective tax rates.

## Summary

This chapter presented some background information on forms of business organization, business securities, and income taxes. First, we saw that firms may be organized as *proprietorships*, as *partnerships*, or as *corporations*. The first two types are easy and inexpensive to form. However, corporations have major advantages in terms of risk reduction, ability to raise capital, and investment liquidity, and these features make it possible to maximize the value of any business except very small ones by using the corporate form of organization. Accordingly, corporations are the dominant form of business.

The capital raised to acquire business assets consists of *debt* and *equity*. The debtholders, or creditors, have first claim against the earnings of the business, but these claims are limited to fixed amounts. The common equity holders are the owners of the business; thus, they have claims against all remaining earnings. The specific dollar amounts invested by both creditors and equity holders are reflected in the business's balance sheet.

The value of any asset is dependent on the effective income it produces for its owner. *Effective income* means *after-tax income*. Since corporate income is taxed at rates going up to 46 percent, and since personal income is subjected to additional federal tax rates of up to 50 percent, the tax consequences of various decisions have a most important impact on a firm's value. It is not necessary to memorize everything about taxes—indeed, this would be impossible. However, you should know the basic differences between corporate and personal taxes, that interest is a tax deduction to the payer of the interest, that capital gains and operating income are taxed differently, and so on. These matters will come up throughout the book as we examine various types of financial decisions.

Finally, we discussed the tax implications of capital investment. Our tax laws permit fixed assets to be depreciated over time, and the annual depreciation expense is a tax deduction. The current depreciation system is called the *Accelerated Cost Recovery System (ACRS)*. As we shall see in Chapter 10, where we discuss capital budgeting cash flow estimation, tax depreciation rules have a major impact on the profitability of capital investments.

# SMALL BUSINESS

## Taxes and the Small Firm

As discussed in Chapter 1, small firms face inherent disadvantages in the competition for funds. However, the federal government has made some special tax provisions to encourage the flow of equity capital into smaller firms. These are not tax "loopholes"; rather, they are measures purposefully designed to aid small business. This section considers three provisions that stimulate growth businesses: S corporation tax status, Section 1244 stock, and R&D Limited Partnerships.

### S Corporation Tax Status

Subchapter S of the Internal Revenue Code allows small businesses, known as *S corporations*, to enjoy the limited-liability benefits of the corporate form of organization yet obtain the benefits of being taxed as a partnership. To enjoy S corporation status, a corporation must qualify as a small business, must be a domestic corporation, must be owned by no more than 25 individuals, and must elect S corporation status at the beginning of the tax year. Other restrictions apply as well.[1]

Owners of S corporations are taxed as if they were partners in a partnership. This tax treatment is especially beneficial in the early stages of a firm's development, when it is making heavy investments (which produce large investment tax credits) and incurring start-up costs which lead to operating losses. Indeed, many firms anticipate having one or more unprofitable years in their early lives while they are developing new products or trying to gain footholds in new markets. If such firms were not corporations, the tax benefits of the ITCs would be passed on directly to the owners, and the businesses' losses would be used to offset the owners' other income. *S corporation status allows the corporation to pass on those benefits as if the firm were a partnership, with the shareholders receiving the benefits on a pro rata basis in accordance with their fractional ownership of the firm's equity.*

If the firm is profitable during a year in which S corporation status has been elected, the earnings are added to the individual owners' ordinary incomes and taxed at their marginal personal tax rates. This feature of Subchapter S tax treatment can be either an advantage or a disadvantage. If the corporation plans to distribute all of its earnings to shareholders, then Subchapter S allows the firm to avoid double taxation: The earnings are taxed only at the personal level, not at the corporate level and then again at the personal level. On the other hand, if the owners wish to retain all earnings in the firm to finance continued growth, S corporation status may be a disadvantage, for if the average corporate tax rate is lower than the average rates of the individual owners, then more capital will be available by allowing the income to be taxed at the corporate level.

## Section 1244 Stock

S corporation status as described above provides benefits in the treatment of the corporation's *operating income.* There are also benefits with regard to capital gains. All long-term capital gains en-joy favored treatment under the Internal Revenue Code: the maximum tax rate on long-term gains under current law is 20 percent. However, the Internal Revenue Code allows net capital losses to offset only up to $3,000 in ordinary income. Thus, if you invested $10,000 in a stock and the company went bankrupt, you could normally deduct a maximum of $3,000 in any one year. However, Section 1244 of the code contains a provision that gives favored tax treatment to capital losses incurred on the stocks of small businesses: Up to $50,000, rather than the normal $3,000, of losses per year can be deducted if the stock is that of a small business as defined in Section 1244 of the Tax Code. For an individual in a high tax bracket, this feature greatly reduces the downside risk of investment. For example, if the investor is in the 50 percent tax bracket and has made a $10,000 investment in Section 1244 stock that becomes worthless, the investor in effect gets back $5,000 in the form of reduced taxes. With Section 1244 stock, then, the investor gets the regular favored tax treatment of capital gains if the venture does well, but he or she also gets substantial benefits if the venture does badly. This treatment provides a significant enhancement to the value of an investment in a small high-risk firm, and hence it encourages investment in small businesses.

As is the case with S corporation status, the issuance of Section 1244 stock is subject to certain limitations. Since the provision was established to help small firms compete for investment capital, it is restricted to small firms, defined as those with less than $1,000,000 in invested capital. Further, it applies only to the original holders of the stock, and then only to individuals or partnerships—corporations and trusts cannot obtain Section 1244 benefits. Also, the aggregate losses that qualify for deduction against ordinary income are limited to $50,000 in any taxable year.[2]

Since S corporation status can be elected by corporations that have issued 1244 stock, investors can enjoy the benefits of favored tax treatment both on the operating income of the firm and on capital gains or losses.

[1]The full set of conditions that must be met to qualify for S corporation status is described in Ernest W. Walker and J. William Petty II, *Financial Management of the Small Firm* (Englewood Cliffs, NJ: Prentice-Hall, 1978), Chapter 2.

[2]An interesting presentation of the advantages of Section 1244 stock and the conditions for qualifying for Section 1244 treatment is given in Dick Levin, *Buy Low, Sell High, Collect Early, and Pay Late* (Englewood Cliffs, NJ: Prentice-Hall, 1983), Chapter 4.

## R&D Limited Partnerships

The past ten years have witnessed rapid growth in new high-technology businesses. Typically, such businesses undergo a start-up period during which heavy expenditures are made on research and development prior to the production and marketing of a new product. The *R&D limited partnership* is a special form of organization set up to permit the partners to treat the early losses in the project as ordinary losses and then to convert future gains from the commercial use of the product into capital gains.

The R&D limited partnership is a complex legal entity that should be established with the help of an attorney who has specialized experience in this field. The legal documents and prospectus involved can easily exceed 100 pages. However, the principles are straightforward, so the organizational structure is not difficult to describe. There is a set of general partners and a set of limited partners; the limited partners enjoy limited liability, and they typically put up the majority of the funds for the development activities; the general partners assume the liability for the partnership's debt, manage the business, and share in profits in exchange for bearing risks and managing the enterprise.

High Tech Electronic Software, Inc., (HTES) provides an illustration. Two University of Texas professors wanted to develop a new software product that runs on the IBM AT. They estimated that it would cost $1,000,000 to develop the product, and the professors did not have the required cash. They created a firm, HTES, Inc., which in turn created an R&D limited partnership in which the company acted as the general partner, and several wealthy, sophisticated investors were the limited partners and put up the full $1,000,000. The partnership then contracted with HTES to develop the product, which will remain the property of the partnership.

During the first year, the only activities were in product development. No revenues were earned, and the partnership lost $1,000,000, having spent all of the initial cash. Each of the limited partners was able to write off his or her pro rata share of the loss, and this write-off effectively reduced the cost of product development to $500,000, because the investors were all in a 50 percent marginal tax bracket. On December 31, 1985, however, the product was ready to be marketed.

The partnership agreement gave HTES an exclusive right to market the new product. In exchange for this right, HTES agreed to pay the partnership royalties from the sale of the product, and these royalties will receive capital gains treatment for the limited partners. Thus, the limited partners first received a favorable tax treatment on the losses incurred in product development, and then, if the product is successful, they will receive favorable tax treatment on the income received from marketing the product.[3]

Congress provided favorable tax treatment for R&D limited partnerships for much the same reason it established S corporations and Section 1244 stock—to help new businesses get off the ground. Large corporations are efficient producers of many goods and services, but new businesses are often more innovative, and Congress wanted to help innovation flourish.

---

[3]The R&D limited partnership can be used on relatively small development projects, such as the one just described, or on very large projects. For example, Gene Amdahl, the inventor of the famous Amdahl computer, raised $55 million in a public offering of an R&D limited partnership to start Trilogy Systems Corporation.

## Questions

2-1    Define each of the following terms:
  a. Proprietorship; partnership; corporation
  b. Progressive tax
  c. Taxable income
  d. Marginal and average tax rates
  e. Bracket creep
  f. Capital gain or loss
  g. Tax loss carry-back and carry-forward

    h. Improper accumulation

    i. ACRS depreciation; half-year convention; depreciable basis

    j. Investment tax credit (ITC); recapture

    k. S corporation

**2-2**    What are the three principal forms of business organization? What are the advantages and disadvantages of each?

**2-3**    Suppose you owned 100 shares of General Motors stock and the company just earned $6 per share. Suppose further that GM could either pay all its earnings out as dividends (in which case you would receive $600) or retain the earnings in the business, buy more assets, and cause the price of the stock to go up by $6 per share (in which case the value of your stock would rise by $600).

    a. How would the tax laws influence what you, as a typical stockholder, would want the company to do?

    b. Would your choice be influenced by how much other income you had? Why might the desires of a 45-year-old doctor differ from those of a pension fund manager or a retiree with respect to corporate dividend policy?

    c. How might the corporation's decision with regard to dividend policy influence the price of its stock?

**2-4**    What does *double taxation of corporate income* mean?

**2-5**    If you were starting a business, what tax considerations might cause you to prefer to set it up as a proprietorship or a partnership rather than as a corporation? Would the existence of S corporations have a bearing on your decision?

**2-6**    Explain how the federal income tax structure affects the choice of financing (debt versus equity) used by U.S. business firms.

**2-7**    How can the federal government influence the level of business investment by adjusting the ITC?

**2-8**    For someone planning to start a new business, is the average or the marginal tax rate more relevant?

## Problems

(Note: By the time this book is published, Congress may have changed tax rates and other provisions. Work all problems on the assumption that the information in the chapter is still current.)

Corporate tax liability    **2-1**    The Bryant Metals Company had a 1985 income of $200,000 from operations after all operating costs but before (1) interest charges of $10,000, (2) dividends paid of $20,000, and (3) income taxes. What is Bryant's income tax liability and after-tax income?

Corporate tax liability    **2-2**    The Charles River Corporation had $200,000 of taxable income from operations in 1985.

    a. What is the company's federal income tax bill for the year?

    b. Assume the firm receives an additional $20,000 of interest income from some bonds it owns. What is the tax on this interest income?

    c. Now assume that the firm does not receive the interest income but does receive an additional $20,000 as dividends on some stock it owns. What is the tax on this dividend income?

| | | |
|---|---|---|
| Loss carry-back, carry-forward | **2-3** | The Matrix Company has made $200,000 before taxes for each of the last 15 years, and it expects to make $200,000 a year before taxes in the future. However, this year (1985) Matrix incurred a loss of $1,200,000. Matrix will claim a tax credit at the time it files its 1985 income tax returns and will receive a check from the U.S. Treasury. Show how it calculates this credit, and then indicate Matrix's tax liability for each of the next 5 years. Assume a 50 percent tax rate on *all* income to ease the calculations. |
| Form of organization | **2-4** | Robert Gould has operated his small repair shop as a sole proprietorship for several years, but projected changes in his business' income have led him to consider incorporating. |

Gould is married and has two children. His family's only income, an annual salary of $40,000, is from operating the business. (The business actually earns more than $40,000, but he reinvests the additional earnings in the business.) His itemized deductions are $6,100, and with four exemptions he has total exemptions of $4 \times \$1,000 = \$4,000$, so his taxable income, given a salary of $40,000, would be $\$40,000 - \$6,100 - \$4,000 = \$29,900$. Of course, his actual taxable income, if he does not incorporate, would be higher by the amount of reinvested income. Gould estimates that his business earnings before salary and taxes for the period 1986 to 1988 will be:

| Year | Income before Salary and Taxes |
|------|-------------------------------|
| 1986 | $50,000 |
| 1987 | 70,000 |
| 1988 | 90,000 |

a. What would his total taxes (corporate plus personal) be in each year under
   1. A corporate form of organization (1986 tax = $6,290)?
   2. A proprietorship (1986 tax = $7,825)?
b. Should Gould incorporate? Discuss.
(Do Part c only if you are using the computerized problem diskette.)
c. 1. Suppose Gould decides to pay out (a) 50 percent or (b) 100 percent of the after-salary corporate income in each year as dividends. Would such dividend policy changes affect Gould's decision about whether or not to incorporate?
   2. Suppose business improves, and actual earnings before salary and taxes in each year are twice the original estimate. However, Gould will continue to receive a salary of $40,000 and to reinvest additional earnings in the business. (No dividends would be paid.) Which form of business organization would allow Gould to pay the smallest amount of total income tax over the three years?

| | | |
|---|---|---|
| Personal taxes | **2-5** | Jill Triffs has this situation for the year 1985: salary of $50,000; dividend income of $10,000; interest on IBM bonds of $5,000; interest on state of Florida municipal bonds of $8,000; proceeds of $12,500 from the sale of 100 shares of IBM stock purchased in 1981 at a cost of $6,000; and proceeds of $12,500 from the sale of 100 shares of IBM stock purchased |

in October 1985 at a cost of $12,000. Jill gets one exemption ( $1,000), and she has itemized deductions of $4,000; these amounts will be deducted from her gross income to determine her taxable income.

a. What is Jill's tax liability for 1985?

b. What are her marginal and average tax rates?

c. If she had some money to invest and was offered a choice of either Florida bonds with a yield of 7 percent or more IBM bonds with a yield of 11 percent, which should she choose, and why?

d. At what marginal tax rate would Jill be indifferent to the choice between the Florida and IBM bonds?

Depreciation        2-6        The Apex Corporation commenced operations on January 1, 1985. Here are some data on the company: Sales revenues in 1985 were $1,000,000; labor and materials costs were $700,000; on January 1, the company purchased $100,000 of equipment which had a 5-year ACRS class life; Apex received $10,000 of dividends on some stock the company owned and $10,000 of interest on some bonds it owned; also on January 1, the company issued $500,000 of long-term bonds which carried an interest rate of 12 percent. Apex also paid its shareholders a dividend of $40,000 during 1984. (Hint: Depreciation for Year 1 is $14,250.)

a. What is the depreciation expense in each year on the 5-year class life equipment?

b. What is Apex's 1985 tax liability?

c. Suppose Apex has forecasted higher costs and lower revenues for the first few years of its operations, so when you developed the income statement, you found a loss and hence no taxes. Would this mean the company would lose the tax credit? How would you recommend that it handle the situation? Assume for purposes of this question that losses were projected for 5 years, and after this start-up period substantial profits were projected.

## Selected Additional References

For a good reference guide to tax issues, see:

*Federal Tax Course* (Englewood Cliffs, N.J.: Prentice-Hall, published annually).

# 3

# FINANCIAL MARKETS, INSTITUTIONS, AND INTEREST RATES

"Money Men Are Minding the Store: The Financial Brains Have Taken Charge in Retailing." This caption appeared in a recent issue of *The New York Times*. The article went on to explain how financial executives were taking over the top spots of major U.S. retailing chains from marketing executives and the reasons behind this shift of power. The primary reason is that finance people best understand the markets wherein companies raise capital for expansion and where stock prices, which the firms seek to maximize, are established.

Another article, this one in *Business Week*, illustrates the impact that financial timing can have. Caterpillar Company executives delayed a $300 million bond issue on the grounds that the 10.5 percent interest rate the company would have had to pay was too high. Subsequently, interest rates rose sharply rather than falling as the Caterpillar executives had expected, and a year later, with rates at 15 percent, their cash needs forced them to go ahead with the issue—at an additional cost of $13.5 million per year.

Caterpillar was a victim of bad luck (or bad forecasting), but rising interest rates have been far more painful to many other companies. For example, Washington Savings and Loan Association, one of the largest companies in Miami, borrowed money on a short-term basis and then loaned it out on a long-term, fixed rate basis. This was profitable as long as short-term rates were lower than long-term rates, but when short rates rose above long rates, Washington S&L found itself with an asset portfolio that was yielding about 11 percent and liabilities which had an average cost of about 14 percent. To avoid bankruptcy, Washington S&L had to be merged into a stronger firm; many of its managers were demoted or fired.

To some extent the problems of Caterpillar, Washington S&L, and the thousands of other companies that have been hurt by high interest rates were the result of bad luck—it is hard to predict interest rates. However, some of these problems might have been avoided had these firms' financial managers had a better understanding of financial markets and institutions and of the way interest rates are established in these markets. These topics are discussed in this chapter.

## The Financial Markets

Business firms, as well as individuals and government units, often need to raise capital. For example, suppose Pacific Gas & Electric Company forecasts an increase in the demand for electricity in Northern California and decides to build a new power plant. It almost certainly will not have the $2 billion necessary to pay for the plant, so PG&E will have to raise this capital in the market. Or suppose Mr. Jones, the proprietor of a local hardware store, decides to expand into appliances. Where will he get the money to buy the initial inventory of TV sets, washers, and freezers? Similarly, if the Smith family wants to buy a home that costs $60,000, but they have only $20,000 in savings, how can they raise the additional $40,000? Or if the City of Sacramento wants to borrow $20 million to finance a new sewer plant, while the federal government needs some $180 billion to cover its 1986 deficit, they, too, need sources for raising this capital.

On the other hand, some individuals and firms have incomes which are greater than their current expenditures, so they have funds available to invest. For example, Edgar Rice has an income of $36,000, but his expenses are only $30,000, and in 1985 General Motors Corporation had accumulated about $3 billion of excess cash which it could make available for investment.

Entities wanting to borrow money are brought together with those having surplus funds in the *financial markets*. Note that "markets" is plural—there are a great many different financial markets, each one consisting of many institutions, in a developed economy. Each market deals with a somewhat different type of security, serves a different set of customers, or operates in a different part of the country. Here are some of the major types of markets:

1. *Physical asset markets* and *financial asset markets* must be distinguished. *Physical asset markets* (also called "tangible" or "real" asset markets) include those for wheat, autos, real estate, computers, machinery, and so on. *Financial markets* deal in stocks, bonds, notes, mortgages, and other *claims on real assets*.

2. *Spot markets* and *futures markets* are terms that refer to whether the assets are being bought or sold for "on the spot" delivery (literally, within a few days) or for delivery at some future date such as six months or a year in the future. The futures markets (which could include the options markets) are growing in importance, but we shall not discuss them until much later in the text.

**money markets**
The financial markets in which funds are borrowed or loaned for short periods (less than one year).

3. **Money markets** are defined as the markets for debt securities with maturities of less than one year. The New York money market is the world's largest, and it is dominated by the major U.S. banks, although branches of foreign banks are also active there. London, Tokyo, and Paris are other major money market centers.

**capital markets**
The financial markets in which funds are borrowed or loaned for long periods (one year or longer).

4. **Capital markets** are defined as the markets for long-term debt and corporate stocks. The New York Stock Exchange, which handles both the stocks and the bonds of the largest corporations, is a prime example of a capital market. The stocks and bonds of smaller corporations are handled in other segments of the capital market.

5. *Mortgage markets* deal with loans on residential, commercial, and industrial real estate and on farmland.

6. *Consumer credit markets* involve loans on autos and appliances, as well as for education, vacations, and so on.

7. *World, national, regional,* and *local markets* also exist. Thus, depending on an organization's size and scope of operations, it may be able to borrow all around the world, or it may be confined to a strictly local, even neighborhood, market.

**primary markets**
Markets in which newly issued securities are bought and sold for the first time.

8. **Primary markets** are the markets in which newly issued securities are bought and sold for the first time. If IBM were to sell a new issue of common stock to raise capital, this would be a primary market transaction.

**secondary markets**
Markets in which securities are traded after they have been issued by corporations.

9. **Secondary markets** are markets in which existing, outstanding securities are bought and sold. Thus, if Jane Vincent decided to buy 100 shares of IBM stock, the purchase would occur in the secondary market. The New York Stock Exchange is a secondary market, since it deals in "used" as opposed to newly issued stocks and bonds.

Other classifications could be made, but this breakdown is sufficient to show that there are many types of financial markets.

A healthy economy is vitally dependent on efficient transfers of funds from people who are net savers to firms and individuals who need capital—that is, the economy depends on *efficient financial markets*. Without efficient transfers the economy simply could not function: Pacific Gas & Electric could not raise capital, so San Francisco's citizens would have no electricity; the Smith family would not have adequate housing; Edgar Rice would have no place to invest his savings; and so on. Obviously, our levels of employment and productivity, and hence our standard of living, would be much lower, so it is absolutely essential that our financial markets function efficiently—not only quickly, but also at a low cost.[1]

## Financial Institutions

Transfers of capital between savers and those who need capital take place in the three different ways diagrammed in Figure 3-1:

1. *Direct transfers* of money and securities occur when a business sells its stocks or bonds directly to savers, without going through any type of intermediary.

2. Transfers may also go through an *investment banking house* such as Merrill Lynch, which serves as a middleman and facilitates the issuance of securities. A company would sell its stocks or bonds to the investment bank,

---

[1]When organizations such as the United Nations design plans to aid developing nations, just as much attention must be paid to the establishment of cost-efficient financial markets as to electrical power, transportation, communications, and other "infrastructure" systems. Economic efficiency is simply impossible without a good system for allocating capital within the economy.

**Figure 3-1**
**Diagram of the Capital Formation Process**

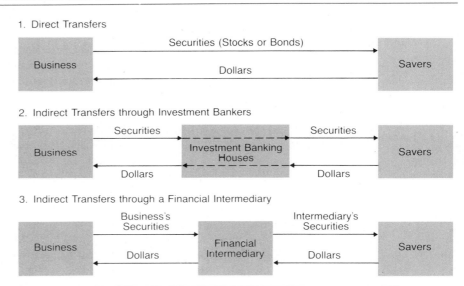

1. Direct Transfers

| Business | → Securities (Stocks or Bonds) → | Savers |

2. Indirect Transfers through Investment Bankers

| Business | → Securities → | Investment Banking Houses | → Securities → | Savers |

3. Indirect Transfers through a Financial Intermediary

| Business | → Business's Securities → | Financial Intermediary | → Intermediary's Securities → | Savers |

which in turn would sell them to ultimate savers. The businesses' securities and the savers' money merely "pass through" the investment banking house.

**3.** Transfers can also be made through a *financial intermediary*, such as a bank or mutual fund, which obtains funds from savers and then issues its own securities in exchange. Intermediaries literally transform money capital from one form to another, which increases general market efficiency. For example, a saver might give dollars to a bank and receive from it a certificate of deposit; the bank might then use the money it received to buy a General Motors bond.

For simplicity we assume that the entity which needs capital is a business, and specifically a corporation, although it is easy enough to visualize the demander of capital as a potential home purchaser, a government unit, and so on.

Direct transfers of funds from savers to businesses are possible and do occur on occasion, but it is generally more efficient for a business to obtain the services of a specialized financial institution called an **investment bank**. Merrill Lynch, Salomon Brothers, and E. F. Hutton are examples of financial institutions which offer investment banking services. Such organizations (1) help corporations design securities with the features that will be most attractive to investors, (2) buy these securities from the corporation, and (3) then resell them to savers in the primary markets. Thus, the investment bankers are *middlemen* in the process of transferring capital from savers to businesses.

**investment bank**
A financial institution that underwrites and distributes new investment securities and helps businesses obtain financing.

**financial intermediaries**
Specialized financial firms that facilitate the transfer of funds from savers to demanders of capital.

The **financial intermediaries** shown in the third section of Figure 3-1 do more than simply transfer money and securities between firms and savers—they literally create new financial products. Since the intermediaries are generally large, they gain economies of scale in analyzing the credit-worthiness of potential borrowers, in processing and collecting loans, and in pooling risks and thus helping individual savers diversify, or avoid "putting all their financial eggs in one basket." Further, a system of specialized intermediaries can enable savings to do more than just draw interest—for example, people can put money into banks and get both interest and a convenient way of making payments (checking), put money into life insurance companies and get both interest and protection for their beneficiaries, and so on.

In the United States and other developed nations, a large set of specialized, highly efficient financial intermediaries has evolved. The situation is, however, changing rapidly, and different types of institutions are performing services that were formerly reserved for others, causing institutional distinctions to become blurred. Still, there is a degree of institutional identity, and here are the major classes of intermediaries:

1. *Commercial banks*, which are the traditional "department stores" of finance, serve a wide variety of savers and those with needs for funds. Historically, the commercial banks have been the major institutions for handling checking accounts and through which the Federal Reserve System expanded or contracted the money supply. Today, however, some of the other institutions discussed below also provide checking services and significantly influence the effective money supply. Conversely, commercial banks now provide an ever widening range of services, including stock brokerage services and insurance.

2. *Savings and loan associations (S&Ls)*, which have traditionally served individual savers and residential and commercial mortgage borrowers, take the funds of many small savers and then lend this money to home buyers and other types of borrowers. The savers are provided a degree of liquidity that would be absent if they bought the mortgages or other securities directly, so perhaps the most significant economic function of the S&Ls is to "create liquidity" which would otherwise be lacking. Also, the S&Ls have more expertise in analyzing credit, setting up loans, and making collections than individual savers could possibly have, so they reduce the cost and increase the feasibility of making real estate loans. Finally, the S&Ls hold large, diversified portfolios of loans and other assets and thus spread risks in a manner that would be impossible if small savers were making direct loans. Because of these factors, savers benefit by being able to invest their savings in more liquid, better managed, and less risky accounts, while borrowers benefit by being able to obtain more capital, and at lower costs, than would otherwise be possible.

3. *Mutual savings banks*, which are similar to S&Ls, operate primarily in the northeastern states, accept savings primarily from individuals, and lend mainly on a long-term basis to home buyers and consumers.

**4. *Credit unions*** are cooperative associations whose members have a common bond, such as being employees of the same firm. Members' savings are loaned only to other members, generally for auto purchases, home improvements, and the like.

**5. *Pension funds*** are retirement plans funded by corporations or government agencies for their workers and administered primarily by the trust departments of commercial banks or by life insurance companies. Pension funds invest primarily in bonds, stocks, mortgages, and real estate.

**6. *Life insurance companies*** take savings in the form of annual premiums, then invest these funds in stocks, bonds, real estate, and mortgages, and finally make payments to the beneficiaries of the insured parties. In recent years life insurance companies have also offered a variety of tax-deferred savings plans which provide benefits to the participants when they retire.

**mutual fund**
A corporation that invests the pooled funds of savers, thus obtaining economies of scale in investing and reducing risk by diversification.

**7. Mutual funds** are corporations which accept dollars from savers and then use these dollars to buy stocks, long-term bonds, or short-term debt instruments issued by businesses or government units. These organizations pool funds and thus reduce risks by diversification. They also gain economies of scale, which lower the costs of analyzing securities, managing portfolios, and trading in the stock and bond markets. Different funds are designed to meet the objectives of different types of savers. Hence, we have bond funds for those who desire safety; stock funds for savers who are willing to accept significant risks in the hope of very high returns; and still other funds that are used as interest-bearing checking accounts (the **money market funds**). There are literally hundreds of different mutual funds with dozens of different goals and purposes.

**money market fund**
A mutual fund that invests in short-term, low-risk securities and allows investors to write checks against their accounts.

The financial institutions have historically been heavily regulated, with the major purpose of this regulation being to insure the safety of the institutions for the protection of their savers. However, these regulations—which have taken the form of prohibitions on nationwide branch banking, restrictions on the types of assets the institutions can buy, ceilings on the interest rates they can pay, and limitations on the types of services they can provide—have tended to impede the free flow of capital from surplus to deficit areas and thus have hurt the efficiency of our capital markets. Recognizing this fact, Congress has authorized some major changes, and more will be coming along.

The major result of the ongoing changes is a blurring of the distinctions among the different types of institutions. Indeed, the trend in the United States today is toward huge *financial service corporations*, which own banks, S&Ls, investment banking houses, insurance companies, pension plan operations, and mutual funds, and which have branches across the country and even around the world. Sears, Roebuck is, interestingly, one of the largest—if not *the* largest—financial service corporations. It owns Allstate Insurance, Dean Witter (a leading brokerage and investment banking firm), Coldwell

Banker (the largest real estate brokerage firm), a huge credit card business, and a host of other related businesses. Other financial service corporations, most of which started in one area and have now diversified to cover the full financial spectrum, include Transamerica, Merrill Lynch, American Express, Citicorp, and Prudential.

## The Stock Market

As has been noted, secondary markets are the markets in which outstanding, previously issued securities are traded. By far the most active market—and the most important one to financial managers—is the *stock market*. It is here that the prices of firms' stocks are established. Since the primary goal of financial management is to contribute to the maximization of a firm's stock price, a knowledge of the market in which this price is established is clearly essential for anyone involved in managing a business.

### The Stock Exchanges

There are two basic types of stock markets—the *organized exchanges*, which are typified by the New York Stock Exchange (NYSE) and the American Stock Exchange (AMEX), and the less formal *over-the-counter markets*. Since the organized exchanges have actual physical market locations and are easier to describe and understand, we shall consider them first.

**organized security exchanges**
Formal organizations having tangible, physical locations that conduct auction markets in designated ("listed") securities. The two major U.S. security exchanges are the New York Stock Exchange (NYSE) and the American Stock Exchange (AMEX).

The **organized security exchanges** are tangible, physical entities. Each of the larger ones occupies its own building, has specifically designated members, and has an elected governing body—its board of governors. Members are said to have "seats" on the exchange, although everybody stands up. These seats, which are bought and sold, represent the right to trade on the exchange. In 1968 seats on the NYSE sold at a record high of $515,000, but in 1979 they sold for as little as $40,000. They were back up to $400,000 in June of 1985.

Most of the larger investment banking houses operate *brokerage departments* which own seats on the exchanges and designate one or more of their officers as members. The exchanges are open on all normal working days, with the members meeting in a large room equipped with telephones and other electronic equipment that enable each member to communicate with its firm's offices throughout the country.

Like other markets, security exchanges facilitate communication between buyers and sellers. For example, Merrill Lynch (the largest brokerage firm) might receive an order in its Atlanta office from a customer who wants to buy 100 shares of General Motors stock. Simultaneously, E. F. Hutton's Denver office might receive an order from a customer wishing to sell 100 shares of GM. Each broker communicates by wire with the firm's representative on the NYSE. Other brokers throughout the country are also communicating with their own exchange members. The exchange members with *sell orders* offer the shares for sale, and these are bid for by the members with *buy orders*. Thus, the exchanges operate as *auction markets*.[2]

## The Over-the-Counter Market

**over-the-counter market**
A large collection of brokers and dealers, connected electronically by telephones and computers, that provides for trading in unlisted securities.

In contrast to the organized security exchanges, the **over-the-counter market** is a nebulous, intangible organization. An explanation of the term *over-the-counter* will help clarify exactly what this market is. The exchanges operate as auction markets—buy and sell orders come in more or less simultaneously, and the exchanges are used to match these orders. But if a stock is traded less frequently, perhaps because it is the stock of a new or a small firm, few buy and sell orders come in, and matching them within a reasonable length of time would be difficult. To avoid this problem, some brokerage firms maintain an inventory of such stocks; they buy when individual investors wish to sell and sell when investors want to buy. At one time the inventory of securities was kept in a safe, and the stocks, when bought and sold, were literally passed over the counter.

Today over-the-counter markets are defined as all facilities that provide for security transactions not conducted on the organized exchanges. These facilities consist (1) of the relatively few *dealers* who hold inventories of over-the-counter securities and who are said to "make a market" in these securities, (2) of the thousands of brokers who act as *agents* in bringing these dealers together with investors, and (3) of the computers, terminals, and electronic networks that facilitate communications between dealers and brokers. The dealers who make a market in a particular stock continuously post a price at which they are willing to buy the stock (the *bid price*) and a price at which they will sell shares (the *asked price*). These prices, which are

---

[2]The NYSE is actually a modified auction market, wherein people (through their brokers) bid for stocks. Originally—a hundred or so years ago—brokers would literally shout, "I have 100 shares of Union Pacific for sale; how much am I offered?" and then sell to the highest bidder. If a broker had a buy order, he or she would shout, "I want to buy 100 shares of Union Pacific; who'll sell at the best price?" The same general situation still exists, although the exchanges now have members known as *specialists* who facilitate the trading process by keeping an inventory of shares of the stocks in which they specialize. If a buy order comes in at a time when no sell order arrives, the specialist will sell off some inventory. Similarly, if a sell order comes in, the specialist will buy and add to inventory. The specialist sets a *bid price* (the price the specialist will pay for the stock) and an *asked price* (the price at which shares will be sold out of inventory). The bid and asked prices are set at levels designed to keep the inventory in balance. If many buy orders start coming in because of favorable developments, or sell orders because of unfavorable events, the specialist will raise or lower prices to keep supply and demand in balance. Bid prices are somewhat lower than asked prices, with the difference, or *spread*, representing the specialist's profit margin.

It should also be noted that special facilities are available to help institutional investors such as mutual funds or pension funds sell large blocks of stock without depressing their prices. In essence, brokerage houses which cater to institutional clients will purchase blocks (defined as 10,000 or more shares) and then resell the stock to other institutions or individuals. Also, when a firm has a major announcement which is likely to cause its stock price to change sharply, it will ask the exchanges to halt trading in its stock until the announcement has been made and digested by investors. Thus, when Texaco in 1984 announced that it planned to acquire Getty Oil, trading was halted for one day in both Texaco and Getty stock.

adjusted as supply and demand conditions change, can be read off computer screens all across the country. The spread between bid and asked prices represents the dealer's markup, or profit.

In terms of numbers of issues, the majority of stocks are traded over-the-counter. However, because the stocks of larger companies are listed on the exchanges, it is estimated that two-thirds of the dollar volume of stock trading takes place on the exchanges.

### Some Trends in Security Trading Procedures

From the NYSE's inception in the 1800s until the 1970s, the vast majority of all stock trading occurred on the Exchange and was conducted by member firms. The NYSE established a set of minimum brokerage commission rates, and no member firm could charge a commission lower than the set rate—this was a monopoly, pure and simple. However, on May 1, 1975, the Securities and Exchange Commission (SEC), with strong prodding from the Antitrust Division of the Justice Department, forced the NYSE to abandon its fixed commissions. Commission rates declined dramatically, falling in some cases as much as 80 percent from former levels. These changes were a boon to the investing public but not to the brokerage industry. A number of "full service" brokerage houses went bankrupt, and others were forced to merge with stronger firms. Many Wall Street experts predict that once the dust settles the number of brokerage houses will have declined from literally thousands in the 1960s to perhaps 20 large, strong, nationwide companies, all of which are units of diversified financial service corporations.

## The Cost of Money

Capital in a free economy is allocated through the price system. *The interest rate is the price paid to borrow capital, while in the case of equity capital, investors obtain payment in the form of dividends and capital gains.* The factors which affect the supply of and the demand for investment capital, and hence the cost of money, are discussed in this section.

**production opportunities**
The returns available within an economy from investment in productive (cash-generating) investments.

**time preferences for consumption**
The preferences of consumers for current consumption as opposed to saving for future consumption.

The two most fundamental factors affecting the cost of money are ( 1 ) **production opportunities** and ( 2 ) **time preferences for consumption**. To see how these factors operate, visualize an isolated island community where the people live on fish. They have a stock of fishing gear which permits them to survive in reasonably good shape, but they would like to have more fish. Now suppose Mr. Crusoe had a bright idea for a new type of fishnet that would enable him to double his daily catch. However, it would take him a year to perfect his design, build his net, and learn how to use it efficiently, and Mr. Crusoe would probably starve before he could put his new net into operation. Therefore, he might suggest to Ms. Robinson, Mr. Friday, and several others that if they would give him one fish each day for a year, he would return two fish a day during all of the next year. If someone accepted the offer, then the fish which Ms. Robinson or one of the others gave to Mr.

Crusoe would constitute *savings*; these savings would be *invested* in the fishnet; and the extra fish the net produced would constitute a *return on the investment*.

Obviously, the more productive Mr. Crusoe thought the new fishnet would be, the higher would be his expected return on the investment and the more he could offer to pay Ms. Robinson, Mr. Friday, or other potential investors for their savings. In this example we assume that Mr. Crusoe thought he would be able to pay, and thus he offered, a 100 percent rate of return—he offered to give back two fish for every one he received. He might have tried to attract savings for less—for example, he might have decided to offer only 1.5 fish next year for every one he received this year, which would represent a 50 percent rate of return to Ms. Robinson or the other potential savers. How attractive this offer would be to potential savers would depend in large part on their *time preferences for consumption*. For example, Ms. Robinson might be thinking of retirement, and she might be willing to trade fish today for fish in the future on a one-for-one basis. On the other hand, Mr. Friday might have a wife and several young children and need his current fish, so he might be unwilling to "lend" a fish today for anything less than three fish next year. Mr. Friday would be said to have a high time preference for consumption, and Ms. Robinson a low time preference. Note also that if the whole population were living right at the subsistence level, then time preferences for current consumption would necessarily be high, aggregate savings would be low, interest rates would be high, and capital formation would be difficult.

In a more complex society there are many businesses like Mr. Crusoe's, many products, and many savers like Ms. Robinson and Mr. Friday. Further, people use money as a medium of exchange rather than barter with fish. *Still, the interest rate paid to savers depends in a basic way on (1) the rate of return producers can expect to earn on invested capital and (2) consumers'/savers' time preferences for current versus future consumption.* Producers' expected returns on their business investments set an upper limit on how much they can pay for savings, while consumers' time preferences for consumption establish how much consumption they are willing to defer and hence how much they will save at different levels of interest offered by producers.[3]

## Interest Rate Levels

Capital is allocated among firms by interest rates: Firms with the most profitable investment opportunities can pay the most for capital, so they tend to attract it away from inefficient firms or from those whose products are not in

---

[3]The term "producers" is really too narrow. A better word might be "borrowers," which would include home purchasers, people borrowing to go to college, or even people borrowing to buy autos or to pay for vacations. Also, the wealth of the society influences people's ability to save and hence their time preferences for current versus future consumption.

demand. Of course, our economy is not completely free in the sense of being influenced only by market forces. Thus, the federal government has agencies which help individuals or groups as stipulated by Congress to obtain credit on favorable terms. Among those eligible for this kind of assistance are small businesses, certain minorities, firms willing to build plants in areas with high unemployment, and so on. Still, most capital in the U.S. economy is allocated through the price system.

Figure 3-2 shows how supply and demand interact to determine interest rates in two capital markets. Markets A and B represent two of the many capital markets in existence. The going interest rate, k, is 10 percent for the low-risk securities in Market A. Borrowers whose credit is strong enough to qualify for this market can obtain funds at a cost of 10 percent, and investors who want to put their money to work at low risk can obtain a 10 percent return. Riskier borrowers must obtain higher-cost funds in Market B. There, investors who are more willing to take risks invest with the expectation of receiving a 12 percent return but also with the realization that they might receive much less.

If the demand for funds in a market declines, as it typically does during a business recession, the demand curve will shift to the left (or down) as shown by Curve $D_2$ in Market A. The market-clearing, or equilibrium, interest rate in this example will decline to 8 percent. You can also visualize what would happen if the Federal Reserve tightened credit: The supply curve, $S_1$, would shift to the left, and this would raise interest rates and lower the current level of borrowing in the economy.

**Figure 3-2**
**Interest Rates as a Function of Supply and Demand for Funds**

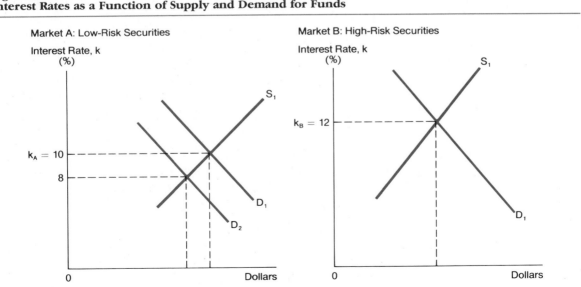

Market A: Low-Risk Securities

Market B: High-Risk Securities

Capital markets are interdependent. For example, assuming that Markets A and B were in equilibrium before the demand shift to $D_2$ in Market A, then investors were willing to accept the higher risk in Market B in exchange for a *risk premium* of 12% − 10% = 2%. After the shift to $D_2$, the risk premium would initially increase to 12% − 8% = 4%. In all likelihood, this much larger premium would induce some of the lenders in Market A to shift to Market B; this, in turn, would cause the supply curve in Market A to shift to the left (or up) and that in Market B to shift to the right. This transfer of capital between markets would raise interest rates in Market A and lower them in Market B, thus bringing the risk premium back closer to the original level (2 percent).

There are many, many capital markets in the United States. U.S. firms also invest and raise capital throughout the world, while foreigners both borrow and lend capital in the United States. There are markets in the United States for real estate loans; farm loans; business loans; federal, state, and local government loans; and consumer loans. Within each category, there are also regional markets as well as different types of submarkets. For example, in real estate there are separate markets for first and second mortgages and for loans on owner-occupied homes, apartments, office buildings, shopping centers, vacant land, and so on. Within the business sector, there are dozens of types of debt and also several sharply differentiated markets for common stocks as opposed to debt.

There are as many prices as there are types of capital, and these prices change over time as shifts occur in supply and demand conditions. Figure 3-3 shows how long- and short-term interest rates to business borrowers have varied since the 1950s. Notice that short-term interest rates are especially prone to rise during booms and then fall during recessions. (The shaded areas of the chart indicate recessions.) When the economy is expanding, firms need capital, and this demand for capital pushes rates up. Also, inflationary pressures are strongest during business booms, so at such times the Federal Reserve tends to tighten the money supply, which also exerts an upward pressure on rates. Conditions are reversed during recessions—slack business reduces the demand for credit, the Fed increases the money supply, and the result is a drop in interest rates. In addition, inflationary pressures are normally weakest during recessions, and this too helps keep interest rates down.

These tendencies do not hold exactly—the early part of the 1974-1975 recession is a case in point. The price of oil increased dramatically in 1974, exerting inflationary pressures on other prices and raising fears of serious, long-term inflation. These fears pushed interest rates to high levels. Investors "looked over the valley" of the 1974-1975 recession, forecasted a continued problem with inflation, and demanded an inflation premium that kept long-term rates high by historical standards.[4]

---

[4]Short-term rates are responsive to current economic conditions, while long-term rates primarily reflect long-run expectations for inflation. As a result, short-term rates are sometimes above and sometimes below long-term rates. The relationship between long-term and short-term rates is called the *term structure of interest rates*. This topic is discussed later in the chapter.

**Figure 3-3**
**Long- and Short-Term Interest Rates, 1953-1985**

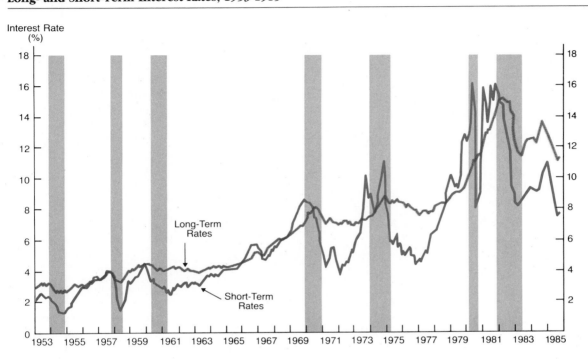

Notes:
1. The shaded areas designate business recessions.
2. Short-term rates are measured by four- to six-month loans to very large, strong corporations and long-term
rates by AAA corporate bonds.

Source: *Federal Reserve Bulletin.*

The relationship between inflation and long-term interest rates is highlighted in Figure 3-4, which plots rates of inflation along with long-term interest rates. Prior to 1965, when the average rate of inflation was about 1.0
percent, interest rates on AAA-rated bonds generally ranged from 4 to 5 percent. As the war in Vietnam accelerated in the mid-1960s, the rate of inflation
increased and interest rates began to rise. The rate of inflation dropped after
1970, and so did long-term interest rates. However, the 1973 Arab oil em-
bargo was followed by a quadrupling of oil prices in 1974, which caused a
spurt in the price level, which in turn drove interest rates to new record
highs in 1974 and 1975. Inflationary pressures eased in late 1975 and 1976
but then rose again after 1976. In 1980 inflation rates hit the highest level
on record, and fears of continued double-digit inflation pushed interest rates
up to historic highs. In 1985, as this is written, the current inflation rate has
dropped to the 4 to 5 percent level, but investors' fears of a renewal of
double-digit inflation are keeping long-term interest rates at relatively high
levels.

**Figure 3-4**
**Relationship between Annual Rates and Long-Term Interest Rates, 1953-1985**

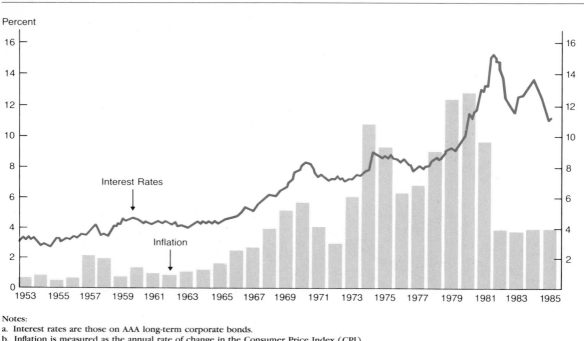

Notes:
a. Interest rates are those on AAA long-term corporate bonds.
b. Inflation is measured as the annual rate of change in the Consumer Price Index (CPI).

Source: *Federal Reserve Bulletin.*

## The Determinants of Market Interest Rates

In general, the nominal interest rate on a debt security, k, is composed of a pure rate of interest, k*, plus several premiums which reflect inflation, the riskiness of the security, and the security's marketability (or liquidity).[5] This relationship can be expressed as follows:

$$k = k* + IP + DP + LP + MP.$$

Here

k* = pure, or real, rate of interest.

---

[5]The term *nominal* as it is used here means the *stated* rate as opposed to the *real* rate, which is adjusted for inflation. If you bought a 10-year Treasury bond in February 1985, the stated, or nominal, rate would be about 11.5 percent, but if inflation averages 7 percent over the next 10 years, the real rate would be about 11.5% − 7.0% = 4.5%. In Chapter 4 we will use the term nominal in yet another way: to distinguish between stated rates and effective rates when compounding occurs more frequently than once a year.

IP = inflation premium.

DP = default risk premium.

LP = liquidity premium.

MP = maturity risk premium.

We discuss each of these components in the following sections.

### The Pure Rate of Interest

**pure rate of interest, k\***
The real, risk-free rate of interest; the rate of interest on default-free U.S. Treasury securities less the expected inflation rate.

The **pure rate of interest**, **k\***, is defined as the equilibrium interest rate on a riskless security if there were no expected inflation. Thus, the pure rate is also a "real, risk-free rate," and it may be thought of as the rate of interest on short-term U.S. Treasury securities in an inflation-free world. The pure rate is not static—it changes over time depending on economic conditions, especially (1) the rate of return borrowers can expect to earn on their real assets and (2) consumers'/savers' time preferences for current versus future consumption. Borrowers' expected returns on real asset investment set an upper limit on how much they can afford to pay for borrowed funds, while consumers' time preferences for consumption establish how much consumption they are willing to defer and hence the amount of funds they will lend at different levels of interest. It is very difficult to measure k\* precisely; many experts think that in the United States it has fluctuated in the range of 2 to 4 percent in recent years.

### Inflation Premium

Inflation has a major impact on interest rates—it can erode the purchasing power of the dollar and lower the real rate of return on investments. To illustrate its effects, suppose you saved up $1,000 and invested it in a Treasury bond which matures in 1 year and which pays 5 percent interest. At the end of the year you would receive $1,050—your original $1,000 plus $50 of interest. Now suppose the rate of inflation during the year was 10 percent, and it affected all items equally. If beer had cost $1 per bottle at the beginning of the year, it would cost $1.10 at the end. Therefore, you could have bought $1,000/$1 = 1,000 bottles at the beginning of the year but only $1,050/$1.10 = 955 bottles at the end. Thus, in *real terms*, you would be worse off—you would have received $50 of interest, but it would not have been sufficient to offset inflation. You would have been better off having bought and held 1,000 bottles of beer (or some other storable asset such as land, timber, apartment buildings, wheat, or gold) than having bought bonds.

**inflation premium (IP)**
A premium for anticipated or expected inflation that investors add to the pure rate of return.

Investors are well aware of all this, so when they lend money they add an **inflation premium** to the rate they would have been willing to accept in the absence of inflation. For a short-term, default-free U.S. Treasury bill, the actual interest rate charged, $k_{T\text{-bill}}$, would be the pure rate, k\*, plus the inflation premium (IP):

$$k_{T\text{-bill}} = k^* + IP.$$

Therefore, if the pure rate of interest were k* = 4% and if inflation were expected to be 5 percent (and hence IP = 5%) over the next year, then the rate of interest on 1-year T-bills would be 9 percent. On July 29, 1985, the expected 1-year inflation rate was about 5 percent and the yield on 1-year T-bills was 8.1 percent, which implies that the pure rate on that date was 3.1 percent.

It is important to note that the rate of inflation built into interest rates is the *rate of inflation expected in the future*, not the rate experienced in the past. Thus, the latest reported figures might show an annual inflation rate of 4 percent, but that is for a past period, and if people on the average expect a 6 percent inflation rate in the future, then 6 percent would be built into the current rate of interest. Note also that the inflation rate reflected in the interest rate on any security is the *average rate of inflation expected over the security's life*. Thus, the inflation rate built into a 1-year bond is the expected inflation rate for the next year, but the inflation rate built into a 30-year bond is the average rate of inflation expected over the next 30 years.[6]

Expectations for future inflation are closely related to, although not perfectly correlated with, rates experienced in the recent past. Therefore, if the inflation rate reported for the past few months increased, people would tend to raise their expectations for future inflation, and this change in expectations would cause an increase in interest rates as shown in Figure 3-4.

## Default Risk Premium

The risk that a borrower will *default* on a loan, which means that the borrower does not pay the interest or principal on the loan on a timely basis, also affects the market interest rate on a security: the greater the default risk, the higher the interest rate lenders charge. Treasury securities have no default risk, and hence they carry the lowest interest rates on taxable securities in the United States. For corporate bonds, the higher the bond's rating, the lower its default risk and, consequently, the lower its interest rate.[7] Here are some representative interest rates on long-term bonds during February 1985:

| | |
|---|---|
| U.S. Treasury | 11.5% |
| AAA | 12.3 |
| AA | 12.6 |
| A | 13.0 |

---

[6]To be theoretically precise, we should use a *geometric average*. Also, note that since millions of investors are active in the market, it is impossible to determine exactly the consensus expected inflation rate. However, survey data are available which give us a reasonably good idea of what investors expect over the next few years. For example, in 1980 the University of Michigan's Survey Research Center reported that people expected inflation over the next year to be 11.9 percent and the average rate of inflation expected over the next 5 to 10 years was 10.5 percent. However, the economy cooled in 1981 and 1982, and inflationary expectations dropped to 4 percent for 1983 and to the range of 6 to 7 percent for the next 5 to 10 years. As inflationary expectations dropped, so did the market rate of interest.

[7]Bond ratings, and bonds' riskiness in general, will be discussed in Chapter 12. For now, merely note that bonds rated AAA are judged to have less default risk than bonds rated AA, AA bonds are less risky than A bonds, and so on.

**default risk premium (DP)**
The difference between the interest rate on a U.S. Treasury bond and a corporate bond of equal maturity and marketability.

The difference between the interest rate on a T-bond and that on a corporate bond *with similar maturity, liquidity, and other features* is defined as the **default risk premium (DP)**. Therefore, if the bonds listed above were otherwise similar, the default risk premium would be DP = 12.3% − 11.5% = 0.8 percentage points for AAA corporate bonds, 1.1 percentage points for AA, and 1.5 percentage points for A corporate bonds. Default risk premiums vary somewhat over time, but the February 1985 figures are representative of levels in recent years.

## Liquidity Premium

**liquid asset**
An asset that can be readily converted to spendable cash.

**liquidity premium (LP)**
A premium added to the equilibrium interest rate on a security that cannot be converted to cash on short notice.

An asset which is highly **liquid** can be sold and converted to spendable cash on short notice. Active markets, which provide liquidity, exist for government bonds, for the stocks and bonds of the larger corporations, and for the securities of certain financial intermediaries. If a security is *not* liquid, investors will add a **liquidity premium (LP)** when they establish the market interest rate on the security. It is very difficult to measure liquidity premiums, but a differential of at least one and probably two percentage points exists between the least liquid and the most liquid financial assets of similar default risk and maturity.

## Maturity Risk Premium

**interest rate risk**
The risk to which investors are exposed due to changing interest rates.

**maturity risk premium (MP)**
A premium for the risk to which investors are exposed due to the length of a security's maturity.

U.S. Treasury securities are free of default risk in the sense that one can be virtually certain that the government will pay interest on its bonds and also pay them off when they mature; therefore, the default risk premium on Treasury securities is essentially zero. Further, active markets exist for Treasury securities, so their liquidity premiums are also close to zero. Thus, as a *first approximation*, the rate of interest on a Treasury bond should be equal to the pure rate, k\*, plus the inflation premium, IP. However, an adjustment is needed. The prices of long-term bonds decline sharply whenever interest rates rise, and since interest rates can and do occasionally rise, all long-term bonds, even Treasury bonds, have an element of risk called **interest rate risk.** As a general rule, the bonds of any organization, from the U.S. government to Eastern Airlines, have more interest rate risk the longer the maturity of the bond.[8] Therefore, a **maturity risk premium (MP)**, which is higher the longer the years to maturity, must be included in the required interest rate.

The effect of maturity risk premiums is to raise interest rates on long-term bonds relative to those on short-term bonds. This premium, like the others, is extremely difficult to measure, but (1) it seems to vary over time, rising when interest rates are more volatile and uncertain and falling when they are more stable, and (2) in recent years, the maturity risk premium on 30-year

---

[8]For example, if you had bought a 30-year Treasury bond for $1,000 in 1972, when the long-term interest rate was 7 3/8 percent, and held it until February 1985, when long-term rates were about 11.5 percent, the value of your bond would have declined to about $690. Had you invested in short-term bills in 1972 and subsequently reinvested your principal each time the bills matured, you would still have $1,000. This point will be discussed in detail in Chapter 5.

T-bonds appears to have generally been in the range of one to two percentage points.

We should mention that while long-term bonds have interest rate risk, short-term bonds have a **reinvestment rate risk**. When short-term bonds mature and the funds are reinvested, or "rolled over," a decline in interest rates would mean reinvestment at a lower rate and hence a decline in interest income. Thus, although the principal is preserved, the interest income provided by short-term bonds varies from year to year depending on reinvestment rates.

**reinvestment rate risk**
Risk that a decline in interest rates will lead to lower income when short-term bonds mature and funds are reinvested.

## The Term Structure of Interest Rates

A study of Figure 3-3 above reveals that at certain times such as 1985, short-term interest rates were lower than long-term rates, while at other times such as 1979 and 1980, short rates were above long rates. The relationship between long and short rates, which is known as the **term structure of interest rates**, is important to corporate treasurers who must decide whether to borrow by issuing long- or short-term debt. It is also important to investors who must decide whether to buy long- or short-term bonds. Thus, it is important to understand (1) how long- and short-term rates are related to each other and (2) what causes shifts in their relative positions.

**term structure of interest rates**
The relationship between yields and maturities of securities.

To begin, we can look up in a source such as *The Wall Street Journal* or the *Federal Reserve Bulletin* the interest rates on bonds of various maturities at a given point in time. For example, Figure 3-5 presents interest rates for Treasury issues of different maturities on two dates. The set of data for a given date, when plotted on a graph such as that in Figure 3-5, is defined as the **yield curve** for that date. The yield curve changes over time as interest rates rise and fall. In March of 1980, short-term rates were higher than long-term rates, so the yield curve on that date was *downward sloping*. However, in November of 1984, short-term rates were lower than long-term rates, so the yield curve at that time was *upward sloping*. Had we drawn the yield curve during June of 1980 it would have been essentially horizontal, for long-term and short-term bonds on that date had about the same rate of interest. (See Figure 3-3.)

**yield curve**
A graph showing the relationship between yields and maturities of securities.

Figure 3-5 shows yield curves for U.S. Treasury securities, but we could have constructed them for corporate bonds—for example, we could have developed yield curves for IBM, General Motors, Eastern Airlines, or any other company that borrows money over a range of maturities. Had we constructed such curves and plotted them on Figure 3-5, the corporate yield curves would have been above those for Treasury securities on the same date because of the addition of default risk premiums, but they would have had the same general shape as the Treasury curves. Also, the more risky the corporation, the higher its yield curve; thus, Eastern's curve would have been above that of IBM.

In a stable economy such as we had in the 1950s and early 1960s, where (1) inflation fluctuated in the 1 to 3 percent range, (2) the expected future

**Figure 3-5**
**U.S. Treasury Bond Interest Rates on Different Dates**

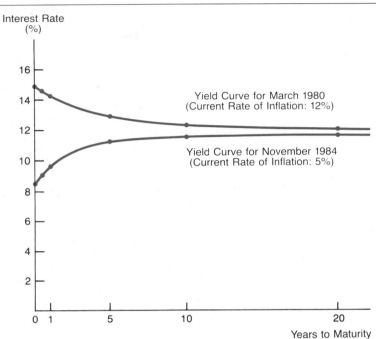

| Term to Maturity | Interest Rate | |
|---|---|---|
| | **March 1980** | **November 1984** |
| 6 months | 15.03% | 8.81% |
| 1 year | 14.03 | 9.80 |
| 5 years | 13.47 | 11.33 |
| 10 years | 12.75 | 11.57 |
| 20 years | 12.49 | 11.66 |

rate of inflation was about equal to the current rate, and (3) the Federal Reserve did not actively intervene in the markets, all interest rates were relatively low, and the yield curve generally had a slight upward slope to reflect maturity effects. People often speak of such an upward-sloping yield curve as being a **"normal" yield curve** and a yield curve which slopes downward as an **inverted,** or **"abnormal," yield curve**.

**"normal" yield curve**
An upward-sloping yield curve.

**inverted yield curve**
A downward-sloping yield curve.

## Term Structure Theories

Several theories have been used to explain the shape of the yield curve. The three major ones are (1) the *market segmentation theory*, (2) the *liquidity preference theory*, and (3) the *expectations theory*.

**market-segmentation theory**
The theory that each borrower and lender has a preferred maturity and that the slope of the yield curve depends on the supply of and demand for funds in the long-term market relative to the short-term market.

*Market Segmentation Theory.* Briefly, the **market segmentation theory** states that each lender and each borrower has a preferred maturity—for example, a person borrowing to buy a long-term asset like a house or an electric utility company borrowing to build a power plant would want a long-term loan, but a retailer borrowing in September to build its inventory for Christmas would prefer a short-term loan. Similarly, a person saving up to take a vacation next summer would want to lend in the short-term market, but someone saving for retirement 20 years hence would want to buy long-term securities. The thrust of the market segmentation theory is that the slope of the yield curve depends on supply/demand conditions in the long-term market relative to those in the short-term market. Thus, according to this theory, the yield curve could at any given time be either upward sloping or downward sloping.

**liquidity preference theory**
The theory that borrowers prefer to make short-term loans rather than long-term loans.

*Liquidity Preference Theory.* The **liquidity preference theory** states that because of risk factors borrowers would prefer to make short-term rather than long-term loans. Therefore, if long- and short-term rates were equal (that is, if the yield curve were horizontal), then people would tend to sell long-term bonds and use the proceeds to buy short-term bonds. This would drive the interest rates on long-term bonds up and those on short-term bonds down. Thus, the liquidity preference theory implies that under normal conditions the yield curve will be upward sloping.

**expectations theory**
The theory that the shape of the yield curve depends on investors' expectations about future inflation rates.

*Expectations Theory.* The **expectations theory** states that the yield curve depends on expectations about future inflation rates. Specifically, $k_t$, the nominal interest rate on a U.S. Treasury bond that matures in t years, is found as follows:

$$k_t = k^* + IP_t,$$

where $k^*$ is the real, default-free interest rate and $IP_t$ is an inflation premium which is equal to the average rate of inflation over the t-year life of the bond.

To illustrate, suppose that in late December of 1986 the real rate of interest were $k^* = 2\%$ and expected inflation rates for the next 3 years were as follows:[9]

|      | Expected Annual (1-Year) Inflation Rate | Expected Average Inflation Rate over the Indicated Period | |
|------|------|------|------|
| 1987 | 9% | 9/1 | = 9.0% |
| 1988 | 6% | (9 + 6)/2 | = 7.5% |
| 1989 | 3% | (9 + 6 + 3)/3 | = 6.0% |

---

[9]Technically we should be using geometric averages rather than arithmetic averages. However, the differences are not material in the example—for instance, a 5.97 percent geometric average versus a 6.0 percent arithmetic average in the case of the 3-year bond. For a more detailed discussion of this point, see Eugene F. Brigham and Louis C. Gapenski, *Intermediate Financial Management* (Hinsdale, Ill.: Dryden, 1985), 586-591.

Given these expectations, the following pattern of interest rates would be expected to exist:

| | Real Rate (k*) | | Inflation Premium, which is Equal to the Average Expected Inflation Rate (IP$_t$) | | Treasury Bond Rate (k$_{T\text{-}bond}$) |
|---|---|---|---|---|---|
| 1-year bond | 2% | + | 9.0% | = | 11.0% |
| 2-year bond | 2% | + | 7.5% | = | 9.5% |
| 3-year bond | 2% | + | 6.0% | = | 8.0% |

Had the pattern of expected inflation rates been reversed, with inflation expected to rise from 3 percent to 6 percent and then to 9 percent, the following situation would have existed:

| | Real Rate | | Average Inflation Rate | | Treasury Bond Rate |
|---|---|---|---|---|---|
| 1-year bond | 2% | + | 3.0% | = | 5.0% |
| 2-year bond | 2% | + | 4.5% | = | 6.5% |
| 3-year bond | 2% | + | 6.0% | = | 8.0% |

These hypothetical data are plotted in Figure 3-6. Whenever the annual rate of inflation is expected to decline, the yield curve "points down"; conversely, if inflation is expected to increase, the yield curve "points up."

**Figure 3-6**
**Hypothetical Example of the Term Structure of Interest Rates**

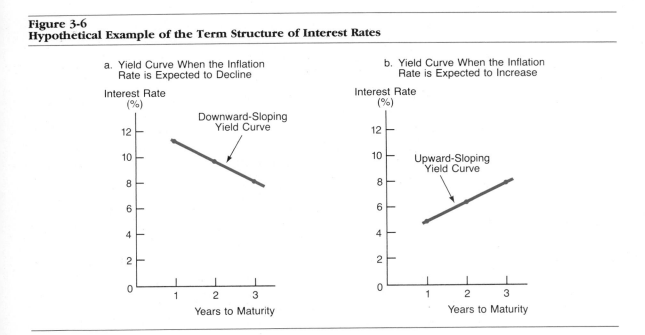

## Other Factors Influencing Interest Rate Levels

In addition to expectations for inflation and preferences for selected maturities, there are other factors which influence the general level of interest rates.

### Federal Reserve Policy

As you probably learned in your studies of economics, (1) the rate of growth in the money supply has a major effect on both the level of economic activity and the rate of inflation, and (2) in the United States the Federal Reserve System controls the money supply. If the Fed wants to stimulate the economy, it increases the money supply growth rate. The initial effect of such an action is to cause interest rates to decline, but the action may also lead to an increase in the expected rate of inflation, which in turn pushes interest rates up. The reverse holds if the Fed tightens the money supply.

To illustrate, in 1981 inflation was quite high, so the Fed tightened up the money supply. The Fed deals primarily in the short-term end of the market, so this tightening had the direct effect of pushing short-term interest rates up sharply. At the same time, the very fact that the Fed was taking strong action to reduce inflation led to a decline in expectations for long-run inflation, which led to a drop in long-term bond yields. Short-term rates decreased shortly thereafter.

During periods when the Fed is actively intervening in the markets, the yield curve will be distorted. Short-term rates will be temporarily "too high" if the Fed is tightening credit and "too low" if it is easing credit. Long-term rates are not affected as much by Fed intervention, except to the extent that such intervention affects expectations for long-term inflation.

### Business Cycles

Figure 3-3, presented earlier, can be examined to see how business conditions have influenced rates. Here are the key points revealed by the graph:

**1.** Because inflation has generally been increasing since 1953, the general tendency has been toward higher interest rates.

**2.** Until 1966, short-term rates were almost always below long-term rates. Thus, in those years the yield curve was almost always "normal" in the sense that it was upward sloping, as the liquidity preference theory suggests it should be if inflation rates are stable.

**3.** The shaded areas in the graph represent recessions, during which the demand for money falls and, at the same time, the Federal Reserve tends to increase the money supply in an effort to stimulate the economy. As a result, there is a tendency for interest rates to decline during recessions.

**4.** In recessions short-term rates experience sharper declines than long-term rates. This occurs because (1) the Fed operates mainly in the short-term sector and hence its intervention has its major effect here and (2) long-term rates reflect the average expected inflation rate over the next 20 to 30 years, and this expectation generally does not change much even when the current rate of inflation is low because of a recession.

## Interest Rate Levels and Stock Prices

Interest rates have a direct effect on corporate profits: interest is a cost, so the higher the rate of interest, the lower a firm's profits, other things held constant. Interest rates obviously affect stock prices because of their effects on profits but, even more important, they have an effect due to competition in the marketplace between stocks and bonds. If interest rates rise sharply, investors can get a higher return on their money in the bond market, which induces them to sell stocks in order to transfer funds from the stock market to the bond market. Such transfers obviously depress stock prices, but the reverse occurs if interest rates decline.

To illustrate, suppose you had $100,000 invested in Midwest Power stock and were receiving dividends of 10 percent, or $10,000, per year. Suppose further that Midwest Power's bonds returned only 7 percent, so if you switched, you would earn only $7,000 and, hence, would lose the extra $3,000 that the stock pays. (The $3,000, or 3 percent, differential reflects a risk premium.) Now suppose interest rates double, causing Midwest Power's bond prices to decline and their yields to rise to 14 percent. If the stock were still yielding 10 percent, then you could switch to bonds and increase your income from $10,000 to $14,000. You (and other stockholders) would call your broker and try to sell the stock and buy the bonds. However, the influx of sell orders would depress the price of the stock relative to that of the bond, probably before you could complete the transaction. *Thus, changes in interest rates have a major, and rapid, effect on stock prices.*

## Interest Rates and Business Decisions

The yield curve for November 1984 in Figure 3-5 shows how much the U.S. government had to pay in 1984 to borrow money for 1 year, 5 years, 10 years, and so on. A business borrower would have had to pay somewhat more, but assume for the moment that we are back in 1984 and the yield curve shown for that year also applies to your company. Now suppose you have decided (1) to build a new plant with a 20-year life which will cost $1 million and (2) to raise the $1 million by selling an issue of debt (or borrowing) rather than by selling stock. If you borrowed in 1984 on a short-term basis—say, for one year—your interest cost for that year would be only 9.8 percent, or $98,000, while if you used long-term (20-year) financing, your cost would be 11.5 percent, or $115,000. Therefore, at first glance it would seem that you should have used short-term debt.

However, this could prove to be a horrible mistake. If you use short-term debt, you will have to renew your loan every year, and the rate charged on each new loan will reflect the then-current short-term rate. Interest rates could return to their March 1980 levels, so by 1988 you could be paying 14 percent, or $140,000, per year. These high interest payments would cut into and perhaps eliminate your profits. Your reduced profitability could easily increase your firm's risk to the point where your bond rating would be lowered, causing lenders to increase the risk premium built into the interest rate they charge you, which in turn would force you to pay even higher rates. These very high interest rates would further reduce your profitability, worrying lenders even more and making them reluctant to renew your loan. If your lenders refused to renew the loan and demanded payment, as they have every right to do, you might have trouble raising the cash. If you had to make price cuts to convert physical assets to cash, you might incur heavy operating losses or even bankruptcy.

On the other hand, if you used long-term financing in 1984, your interest costs would remain constant at $116,600 per year, so an increase in interest rates in the economy would not hurt you. You might even be able to buy up some of your bankrupted competitors at bargain prices—bankruptcies increase dramatically when interest rates rise.

Does all this suggest that firms should always avoid short-term debt? Not necessarily. If the Reagan administration's economic program continues to work, inflation will remain low in the next few years, and so will interest rates. If you had borrowed on a long-term basis for 11.66 percent in November 1984, then your company would be at a major disadvantage if its debt were locked in at 11.66 percent while its competitors (who used short-term debt in 1984 and thus rode interest rates down in subsequent years) had a borrowing cost of only 8 or 9 percent. On the other hand, the administration's program might not continue to work, and large federal deficits might drive inflation and interest rates up to new record levels. In that case, you would wish you had borrowed long-term in 1984.

Financing decisions would be easy if we could predict future interest rates accurately. Unfortunately, predicting future interest rates with consistent accuracy is somewhere between difficult and impossible—people who make a living by selling interest rate forecasts say it is difficult; many others say it is impossible.

Even if it is difficult to predict future interest rate *levels*, it is easy to predict that interest rates will *fluctuate*—they always have, and they always will. This being the case, sound financial policy calls for using a mix of long- and short-term debt, as well as equity, in such a manner that the firm can survive in most interest rate environments. Further, the optimal financial policy depends in an important way on the nature of the firm's assets—the easier it is to sell off assets and thus to pay off debts, the more feasible it is to use large amounts of short-term debt. We will return to this issue later in the book.

## Summary

In this chapter we discussed the nature of financial markets, the types of institutions that operate in these markets, how interest rates are determined, and some of the ways in which interest rates affect business decisions.

The *pure interest rate, k\**, is determined (1) by the *returns on investment available to producers* and (2) by *consumers' time preferences* for current consumption as opposed to saving for future consumption. To establish the nominal interest rate for a given security, k, we must add to the pure rate an *inflation premium (IP)* which reflects expected inflation over the life of the security, a *default risk premium (DP)* which reflects the default risk inherent in the security, a *liquidity premium (LP)*, and a *maturity premium (MP)*:

$$k = k^* + IP + DP + LP + MP.$$

Interest rates fluctuate over time, with long-term rates changing primarily because of changes in the rate of expected inflation and short-term rates changing to reflect both expected inflation and Federal Reserve intervention in the markets.

The *term structure of interest rates,* or the *yield curve*, describes the relationship between long- and short-term interest rates. When inflation is expected to continue at the current rate, the yield curve tends to slope upward because of maturity effects; such a curve is called "normal." However, in recent years the yield curve has been "abnormal," or inverted, about as often as it has been normal.

Interest rate levels have a profound effect on stock prices. Higher interest rates mean (1) higher interest expenses, and thus lower corporate income, and (2) more competition from the bond market. Both of these factors tend to depress stock prices.

Finally, interest rate levels have a significant influence on financial policy. Since interest rate levels are difficult, if not impossible, to predict, sound financial policy calls for using a mix of short- and long-term debt and for positioning the firm to survive in any future interest rate environment.

## SMALL BUSINESS

## Risk Capital for Growth Businesses

The public markets for debt and common stock function well in providing capital to larger businesses. However, small businesses do not ordinarily have access to the public markets. First, an issue must be large enough to capture the attention of participants in the public markets; otherwise, it will be ignored, and its price will languish. The size of the issue also has an effect on the liquidity of the stock. Investors buying common stock in public markets want to be able to sell their stock with little delay, and without their sale driving the price down very much. A very small issue would have only a limited market and would not be actively traded, and hence it would be difficult for an investor to sell his or her stock quickly.

Second, information about the firm must be available. Because many small firms seeking funding for the first time have no track record, it is difficult for potential investors to determine a fair value for the securities. Furthermore, much of the information that management does have should remain confidential. For example, if a small firm with good prospects released information on just how favorable its prospects were, other companies might enter the market before the first firm had raised its capital and begun to exploit its opportunities. As a result, a large part of the information investors need cannot be made available to the public.

Third, while an analysis of the riskiness of an investment is always important, such analyses are especially vital when investing in a small business. The rewards for making a successful investment in a small firm can be enormous; the annals of small firms contain many stories about an investor or entrepreneur who invested a few thousand dollars that led in a few years to a payoff in the millions. High returns, however, are usually accompanied by high risks. An investment in a small firm, and especially a new small firm, is likely to be far riskier than most. Therefore, risk analysis is vital to investors in small businesses if they are to avoid making a series of investments in firms that fail. However, the general public is not equipped to make such evaluations.

For the above reasons, the public debt and equity markets are not well suited to supply risk capital to support the development of new small businesses. As a result, an industry of *venture capital firms* has been developed to fill the void and to supply both capital and managerial expertise to growth businesses. Note, though, that the venture capital industry does not supply capital to all small businesses—venture capital firms limit their investments to firms that are likely to grow rapidly and to achieve the size necessary to permit a stock flotation in the public market, or perhaps to become an attractive acquisition by a public corporation. Either action will permit the venture capital firm to get its money back, plus a profit, and to start the cycle again.

The venture capital industry consists of firms that manage a substantial amount of capital for other investors, including both individuals and larger firms, such as banks, that own the venture capital subsidiaries. Some venture capital firms are privately owned and obtain their funds from a variety of private sources, and they manage those funds for a fee. Other venture capitalists are public companies. Whether public, private, or captive (owned by another firm such as a bank), the venture capital firms are run by experienced managers who are able to evaluate risky investment propositions. Some of the venture capital firms specialize in investments in start-up companies, while others refuse to invest in any venture that has not established a record of sales and earnings. Many of the venture capital firms specialize in certain industries—for example, some invest only in energy-related companies, while others limit their investments to high-technology businesses.

The venture capital industry has grown from $2 billion in 1970 to $16 billion in 1985.[1] This ex-

traordinary growth has been associated in part with the development of the microelectronics industry, and also with promising technologies in the medical and biological fields. The needs for risk capital have increased greatly, and with them have come outstanding opportunities for high returns on the part of venture capital investors. The result has been a huge increase in the availability of venture capital to support American industry. In fact, many of the newer managers of venture capital firms have themselves been successful managers of companies funded by venture capitalists. The erstwhile start-up firm founders became wealthy when their companies went public, and they invested their profits in yet other small companies.

## A Venture Capital Company: Sevin Rosen Partners

Sevin Rosen Partners illustrates the workings of a venture capital firm. The company is a partnership formed by L. J. Sevin, the former chief executive officer of Mostek, Inc. (a semiconductor company that was acquired by United Technologies in 1980), and Ben Rosen, another well-known figure in the electronics industry. Having raised $25 million in funds from a combination of families, corporations, insurance companies, a foundation, and a university endowment, they began operations in 1981. Because of its founders' backgrounds, Sevin Rosen has tended to specialize in high-technology businesses, particularly in the electronics field, and it has emphasized investment in start-up ventures and in firms working with emerging technologies.

Sevin Rosen has been unusual among venture capital firms in that a number of its investments have proven themselves, either successfully or unsuccessfully, very quickly. For example, three of the firm's best-known investments were in Compaq Computer, Lotus Development Corporation, and Osborne Computer. Compaq was established in 1981 to manufacture portable computers that are compatible with the IBM PC. It is common for a venture capital firm to make an initial investment and later increase its investment if the firm progresses well. Accordingly, Sevin Rosen initially invested $727,000 to help get Compaq going, and then in 1982 added another $1,200,000 as a co-investor in Compaq's $8,500,000 second-round financing. Then, in the fall of 1983, when Compaq went public with an offering of $100 million in

---

[1]"The Growth of an Industry: Venture Capital, 1977-1982," *Venture Capital Journal*, October 1982, 6-11, provided estimates to 1980, and these data were extrapolated to 1985.

common stock, Sevin Rosen profited handsomely from its investment.

Sevin Rosen also invested in Lotus Development Corporation, the developers of *1-2-3*, and the result was the most fabulous success story in this young field. Sevin Rosen invested $590,000 in Lotus at the start-up stage in the spring of 1982, and followed this up with an investment of $1,500,000 in late 1982. The venture capitalist was well rewarded when Lotus went public in August 1983.

Based on the Compaq and Lotus investments, it would appear that the venture capital business is indeed attractive. But with such high returns, there is usually great risk, as is demonstrated by a third Sevin Rosen investment, this one in Osborne Computer Corporation. Osborne developed the first portable personal computer, and it grew from scratch to sales of nearly $100 million in just two years. Sevin Rosen invested $300,000 in the firm in the summer of 1982, but in the summer of 1983, Osborne filed for bankruptcy and Sevin Rosen lost all of its investment.

Like most venture capital firms, Sevin Rosen contributes more than money to the companies in its portfolio. Venture capital investors frequently put a member on the board of directors of any company in which it has made a substantial investment, and the venture firm will also assist the company in locating management personnel or scientific talent. The venture firm thus takes on the role of advisor to the small business, whose managers generally have great expertise in some areas but limited experience in others.

In order to find four or five attractive investment opportunities each year, a firm like Sevin Rosen must review literally hundreds of business plans from prospective companies. A good venture capital company has both technical and business experience, and this experience is valuable in separating attractive investments from those that are likely to fail. However, even with their careful analysis and years of experience, the venture capitalists will still make numerous investments in which all or part of their investment is lost. In fact, it has been estimated that of all venture capital investments made in the 1970s, 40 percent were partial or total losers. Venture capital is indeed risk capital.

## Questions

3-1   Define each of the following terms:
   a. Money market; capital market
   b. Primary market; secondary market
   c. Investment banker
   d. Financial intermediary
   e. Mutual fund; money market fund
   f. Organized security exchanges
   g. Over-the-counter market
   h. Production opportunities; time preferences for consumption
   i. Pure rate of interest; real, risk-free rate of interest
   j. Inflation premium (IP)
   k. Default risk premium (DP)
   l. Liquid asset; liquidity premium (LP)
   m. Interest rate risk; maturity risk premium (MP)
   n. Reinvestment rate risk
   o. Term structure of interest rates; yield curve
   p. "Normal" yield curve; inverted yield curve

3-2   Suppose interest rates on residential mortgages of equal risk were 14 percent in California and 16 percent in New York. Could this differential persist? What forces might tend to equalize rates? Would differentials in borrowing costs for businesses of equal risk located in California and New York be more or less likely than those of residential mortgage rates?

Would differentials in the cost of money for New York and California firms be more likely to exist if the firms being compared were very large or if they were very small? What are the implications of all this for the pressure now being put on Congress to permit banks to engage in nationwide branching?

3-3   What would happen to the standard of living in the United States if people lost faith in the safety of our financial institutions?

3-4   How does a cost-efficient capital market help to reduce the prices of goods and services?

3-5   Which fluctuate more, long-term or short-term interest rates? Why?

3-6   You feel that the economy is just entering a recession. Your firm must raise capital immediately, and debt will be used. Should you borrow on a long-term or a short-term basis?

3-7   Suppose the population of Area A is relatively young while that of Area B is relatively old, but everything else about the two areas is equal.
  a. Would interest rates likely be the same or different in the two areas? Explain.
  b. Would a trend toward nationwide branching by banks and S&Ls, and the development of diversified financial corporations, affect your answer to Part a?

3-8   Suppose a new type of computer-controlled industrial robot were developed which was quite expensive but which would, in time, triple the productivity of the labor force. What effect would this have on interest rates?

3-9   Suppose a new and much more liberal Congress and administration were elected, and their first order of business was to take away the independence of the Federal Reserve System and to force the Fed to greatly expand the money supply. What effect would this have
  a. On the level and slope of the yield curve immediately after the announcement?
  b. On the level and slope of the yield curve that would probably exist two or three years in the future?

3-10  The federal government (1) encouraged the development of the S&L industry; (2) forced the industry to make long-term, fixed interest rate mortgages; and (3) forced the S&Ls to obtain most of their capital as deposits that were withdrawable on demand.
  a. Would S&Ls be better off in a world with a "normal" or an inverted yield curve?
  b. If federal actions such as deficit spending and expansion of the money supply produced a sharp increase in inflation, why might a federal "bailout" of the S&L industry be necessary?

3-11  Suppose interest rates on Treasury bonds rose from 10 to 15 percent. Other things held constant, what do you think would happen to the price of an average company's common stock?

## Self-Test Problem (*Solution on Page* 76)

ST-1  Assume that it is now January 1, 1986. The rate of inflation is expected to average 5 percent throughout 1986. However, increased government deficits and renewed vigor in the economy are then expected to push inflation rates higher. Investors expect the inflation rate to be 6 percent in 1987, 7 percent in 1988, and 8 percent in 1989. The pure rate, k*, is currently 3 percent. Assume that no maturity risk premiums are required on bonds with 5 years or less to maturity. The current interest rate on 5-year T-bonds is 10 percent. Disregard maturity premiums.

a. What is the average expected inflation rate over the next 4 years?
b. What should be the prevailing interest rate on 4-year T-bonds?
c. What is the implied expected inflation rate in 1990, or Year 5?

## Problems

Yield curves        **3-1**    Suppose you and most other investors expect the rate of inflation to be 8 percent next year, to fall to 6 percent during the following year, and then to run at a rate of 4 percent thereafter. Assume that the pure rate, k*, is 2 percent and that maturity risk premiums on Treasury securities rise from zero on very short-term bonds (those that mature in a few days) by 0.2 percentage points for each year to maturity up to a limit of 1.0 percentage points on 5-year or longer-term T-bonds.

a. Calculate the interest rate on 1, 2, 3, 4, 5, 10, and 20-year Treasury securities, and plot the yield curve.
b. Now suppose IBM, an AAA company, had bonds with the same maturities as the Treasury bonds. As an approximation, plot an IBM yield curve on the same graph with the Treasury bond yield curve. (Hint: Think about the default risk premium on IBM's long-term versus its short-term bonds.)

Yield curves        **3-2**    The following yields on U.S. Treasury securities were taken from *The Wall Street Journal* of June 12, 1985:

| Term | Rate |
|------|------|
| 6 months | 7.6% |
| 1 year | 7.9 |
| 2 years | 8.8 |
| 3 years | 9.3 |
| 4 years | 9.7 |
| 5 years | 9.8 |
| 10 years | 10.1 |
| 20 years | 10.3 |
| 30 years | 10.4 |

Plot a yield curve based on these data. (Note: If you looked the data up in the *Journal*, you would find that some of the bonds—for example, the 3 percent issue which matures in February 1995—will show very low yields. These are "flower bonds," which are generally owned by older people and are associated with funerals because they can be turned in and used at par value to pay estate taxes. They always sell at close to par and have a yield which is close to the coupon yield, irrespective of the "going rate of interest." Also, the yields quoted in the *Journal* are not for the same point in time for all bonds, so random variations will appear. An interest rate series that is purged of flower bonds and random variations, and hence provides a better picture of the true yield curve, is known as the "constant maturity series" and can be obtained from the *Federal Reserve Bulletin*.)

Expected interest rates    3-3    Assume that the real rate is 3 percent and that the maturity risk premium is zero. If the nominal rate of interest on 1-year bonds is 11 percent and that on 2-year bonds 13 percent, what inflation rate is expected during Year 2? What is the 1-year interest rate that is expected for Year 2? Comment on why the average rate over the 2-year period differs from the 1-year rate expected for Year 2.

Expected interest rates    3-4    In late 1980 the U.S. Commerce Department released new figures which showed that inflation was running at an annual rate of close to 15 percent. However, many investors expected the new Reagan administration to be more effective in controlling inflation than the Carter administration had been. At the time the prime rate of interest was 21 percent, a record high. However, many observers felt that the extremely high interest rates and generally tight credit, which were brought on by the Federal Reserve System's attempts to curb the inflation rate, would shortly bring about a recession, which would in turn lead to a decline in the inflation rate and also in the rate of interest. Assume that at the beginning of 1981 the expected rate of inflation for 1981 was 12 percent; for 1982, 10 percent; for 1983, 8 percent; and for 1984 and thereafter, 6 percent.

a. What was the average expected inflation rate over the 5-year period 1981-1985? (Use the arithmetic average.)

b. What average *nominal* interest rate would, over the 5-year period, produce a 2 percent real rate of return?

c. Assuming a pure rate of 2 percent and a maturity premium which starts at 0.1 percent and increases by 0.1 percent each year, estimate the interest rate in January 1981 on bonds that mature in 1, 2, 5, 10, and 20 years, and draw a yield curve based on these data.

d. Describe the general economic conditions that could be expected to produce an upward-sloping curve.

e. If the consensus view of investors in early 1981 had been that the expected rate of inflation for every future year was 10 percent—that is, $I_t = I_{t+1} = 10\%$ for $t = 1$ to $\infty$—what do you think the yield curve would have looked like? Consider all the factors that are likely to affect the curve. Does your answer here make you question the yield curve you drew in Part c?

## Solution to Self-Test Problem

ST-1    a. Average $= (5\% + 6\% + 7\% + 8\%)/4 = 26\%/4 = 6.50\%$.

b. $k_{\text{T-bond}} = k^* + I = 0.03 + 0.0650 = 0.0950 = 9.50\%$.

c. If the 5-year T-bond rate is 10 percent, then the inflation rate is expected to average approximately $10\% - 3\% = 7\%$ over the next 5 years. Thus, the Year 5 implied inflation rate is 9.0 percent:

$$7\% = (5\% + 6\% + 7\% + 8\% + I_5)/5$$
$$35\% = 26\% + I_5$$
$$I_5 = 9\%.$$

## Selected Additional References

A number of good textbooks on interest rates and financial markets are available. Two of the most widely used are:

Kidwell, David S., and Richard L. Peterson, *Financial Institutions, Markets, and Money*, 2nd ed. (Hinsdale, Ill.: Dryden, 1984).

Van Horne, James C., *Financial Market Rates and Flows* (Englewood Cliffs, N.J.: Prentice-Hall, 1984).

For current empirical data and a forecast of monetary conditions, see the most recent edition of this annual publication:

Salomon Brothers, *Supply and Demand for Credit* (New York).

# 4 DISCOUNTED CASH FLOW ANALYSIS

## HOW THE VALUE OF MONEY CHANGES OVER TIME *or* WHAT J.C. PENNEY BONDS, YOUR COLLEGE EDUCATION, AND A GM ELECTRIC CAR HAVE IN COMMON

The managers of AT&T's pension plan were recently offered the opportunity to buy some J. C. Penney & Company bonds which cost $519.37 per bond, pay *zero* interest during their lifetime, but then will pay $1,000 when they mature 5 years later. At the same time, AT&T's fund managers were offered "regular" Penney bonds which cost $1,000, pay interest of $150 per year, and then will return the $1,000 purchase price when they mature in 5 years. Which is the better buy, the zero coupon bonds or the "regular" bonds?

A father, concerned about the rapidly rising cost of a college education, is planning a savings program to put his daughter through college. She is now 13 years old, plans to enroll at the university in 5 years, and should take 4 years to complete her education. Currently, the cost per year (for everything—food, clothing, tuition, books, transportation, and so forth) is $8,000, but a 6 percent inflation rate in these costs is forecasted. The daughter recently received $5,000 from her grandfather's estate; this money is invested in a bank account which pays 9 percent interest, compounded annually. How much will the father have to deposit each year from now to the time his daughter starts college in order to put her through school?

Suppose that in January 1986 General Motors' engineers informed top management that they had just made a breakthrough which would permit them to produce an electric auto capable of operating at an energy cost of about 3 cents per mile versus an energy cost of about 5 cents for a comparable gasoline-powered car. If GM produces the electric car, it should be able to regain the market share previously lost to the Japanese. However, the investment required to complete development of the new batteries, design the new car, and tool up for production would amount to $5 billion per year for 5 years, starting immediately. Cash flows from the $25 billion investment should amount to $3 billion per year for 15 years, starting 5 years from now, or $45 billion in total. Assuming these cost and cash flow estimates are correct (and they are obviously subject to more forecasting errors than if GM simply bought $25 billion of Treasury bonds), should management give the go-ahead for full-scale electric car production?

These are a few of the many different kinds of questions that can be answered only after an analysis based on the discounted cash flow concepts set forth in this chapter. The three questions posed above are solved in the problems at the end of the chapter.

In Chapter 1 we saw that the primary goal of management is to maximize the value of a firm's stock. We also saw that stock values depend in part on the timing of the cash flows investors expect to receive—a dollar expected soon is worth more than a dollar expected in the distant future. These concepts are extended and made more precise in this chapter, where we show how the timing of cash flows affects asset values and rates of return.

The principles of discounted cash flows as developed here also have many other applications, ranging from setting up schedules for paying off loans to making decisions about whether to acquire new equipment—*in fact, of all the techniques used in finance, none is more important than the discounted cash flow (DCF) concept.* Since this concept is used throughout the remainder of the book, it is vital to understand the material in this chapter thoroughly before going on to other topics.[1]

## Future Value

**compounding**
The arithmetic process of determining the final value of a payment or series of payments when compound interest is applied.

A dollar in hand today is worth more than a dollar to be received next year, because if you had it now you could invest it, earn interest, and end up next year with more than one dollar. To illustrate this process of **compounding,** suppose you had $100 and deposited it in a bank savings account that paid 5 percent interest compounded annually. How much would you have at the end of 1 year? Let us define terms as follows:

PV = present value of your account, or the beginning amount, $100.

k = interest rate the bank pays you = 5% per year, or, expressed as a decimal, 0.05. On financial calculators, the term i is frequently used rather than k.

---

[1]This chapter, and indeed the entire book, is written on the assumption that many students do not have financial calculators. The cost of these calculators is falling rapidly, however, so that assumption is becoming increasingly questionable. As a result, financial calculator solutions are set forth in footnotes to each of the major sections. It is important that you obtain a financial calculator and learn how to use it, for calculators—and not clumsy, rounded, and incomplete tables—are used exclusively in well-run, efficient businesses.

Even though financial calculators are efficient, they do pose a danger: People sometimes learn how to use them in a "cookbook" fashion without understanding the logical processes that underlie financial mathematics; then, when confronted with a new type of problem, they do not understand the process well enough to set it up. Therefore, you are urged not only to get a good calculator and learn how to use it but also to work through the illustrative problems "the long way" to insure that you understand the concepts involved.

$$I = \text{dollars of interest you earn during the year} = k(PV).$$

$FV_n$ = future value, or ending amount, of your account at the end of n years. Whereas PV is the value now, at the *present* time, $FV_n$ is the value n years into the future after compound interest has been earned. Note also that $FV_0$ is the future value *zero* years into the future, which is the *present*, so $FV_0 = PV$.

n = number of years or, more generally, periods, involved in the transaction.

In our example, n = 1, so $FV_n = FV_1$, calculated as follows:

$$\begin{aligned} FV_1 &= PV + I \\ &= PV + PV(k) \\ &= PV(1 + k). \end{aligned} \tag{4-1}$$

**future value, FV**
The amount to which a payment or series of payments will grow by a given future date when compounded by a given interest rate.

In words, the **future value, FV**, at the end of 1 period is the present value times 1 plus the interest rate.

We can now use Equation 4-1 to find how much your $100 will be worth at the end of 1 year at a 5 percent interest rate:

$$FV_1 = \$100(1 + 0.05) = \$100(1.05) = \$105.$$

Your account will earn $5 of interest (I = $5), so you will have $105 at the end of the year.

Now suppose you leave your funds on deposit for 5 years; how much will you have at the end of the fifth year? The answer is $127.63; this value is worked out in Table 4-1. Notice the following points: (1) You start with $100, earn $5 of interest during the first year, and end the year with $105 in your account; (2) you start the second year with $105, earn $5.25 on this now larger account, and end the second year with $110.25; your second-year earnings, $5.25, were higher because you earned interest on the first year's interest; (3) this process continues, and since in each year the beginning balance is higher, your interest income increases; (4) the total interest earned, $27.63, is reflected in the ending balance, $127.63.

Notice that the Table 4-1 value for $FV_2$, the value of the account at the end of Year 2, is equal to

$$FV_2 = FV_1(1 + k) = PV(1 + k)(1 + k) = PV(1 + k)^2.$$

**Table 4-1**
**Compound Interest Calculations**

| Year | Beginning Amount, PV | × (1 + k) = | Ending Amount, $FV_n$ | Interest Earned, PV(k) |
|------|------|------|------|------|
| 1 | $100.00 | 1.05 | $105.00 | $ 5.00 |
| 2 | 105.00 | 1.05 | 110.25 | 5.25 |
| 3 | 110.25 | 1.05 | 115.76 | 5.51 |
| 4 | 115.76 | 1.05 | 121.55 | 5.79 |
| 5 | 121.55 | 1.05 | 127.63 | 6.08 |
|  |  |  |  | $27.63 |

**Table 4-2**
**Future Value of $1 at the End of n Periods:**

$$FVIF_{k,n} = (1 + k)^n$$

| Period (n) | 1% | 2% | 3% | 4% | 5% | 6% | 7% | 8% | 9% | 10% |
|---|---|---|---|---|---|---|---|---|---|---|
| 1 | 1.0100 | 1.0200 | 1.0300 | 1.0400 | 1.0500 | 1.0600 | 1.0700 | 1.0800 | 1.0900 | 1.1000 |
| 2 | 1.0201 | 1.0404 | 1.0609 | 1.0816 | 1.1025 | 1.1236 | 1.1449 | 1.1664 | 1.1881 | 1.2100 |
| 3 | 1.0303 | 1.0612 | 1.0927 | 1.1249 | 1.1576 | 1.1910 | 1.2250 | 1.2597 | 1.2950 | 1.3310 |
| 4 | 1.0406 | 1.0824 | 1.1255 | 1.1699 | 1.2155 | 1.2625 | 1.3108 | 1.3605 | 1.4116 | 1.4641 |
| 5 | 1.0510 | 1.1041 | 1.1593 | 1.2167 | 1.2763 | 1.3382 | 1.4026 | 1.4693 | 1.5386 | 1.6105 |
| 6 | 1.0615 | 1.1262 | 1.1941 | 1.2653 | 1.3401 | 1.4185 | 1.5007 | 1.5869 | 1.6771 | 1.7716 |
| 7 | 1.0721 | 1.1487 | 1.2299 | 1.3159 | 1.4071 | 1.5036 | 1.6058 | 1.7138 | 1.8280 | 1.9487 |
| 8 | 1.0829 | 1.1717 | 1.2668 | 1.3686 | 1.4775 | 1.5938 | 1.7182 | 1.8509 | 1.9926 | 2.1436 |
| 9 | 1.0937 | 1.1951 | 1.3048 | 1.4233 | 1.5513 | 1.6895 | 1.8385 | 1.9990 | 2.1719 | 2.3579 |
| 10 | 1.1046 | 1.2190 | 1.3439 | 1.4802 | 1.6289 | 1.7908 | 1.9672 | 2.1589 | 2.3674 | 2.5937 |

Continuing, we see that $FV_3$, the balance after Year 3, is

$$FV_3 = FV_2(1 + k) = PV(1 + k)^3.$$

In general, $FV_n$, the future value at the end of n years, is found as follows:

$$FV_n = PV(1 + k)^n. \tag{4-2}$$

Applying Equation 4-2 to our 5-year, 5 percent case, we obtain

$$
\begin{aligned}
FV_5 &= \$100(1.05)^5 \\
&= \$100(1.2763) \\
&= \$127.63,
\end{aligned}
$$

which is the same as the value worked out in Table 4-1.

If an electronic calculator is handy, it is easy enough to calculate $(1 + k)^n$ directly.[2] However, tables have been constructed for values of $(1 + k)^n$ for wide ranges of k and n. Table 4-2 is illustrative; a more complete table, with more years and more interest rates, is given in Table A-3 at the end of the book. Notice that we have used the word *period* rather than *year* in Table 4-2. As we shall see later in the chapter, compounding can occur over periods of time other than one year. Thus, while compounding is often on an annual basis, it can be quarterly, semiannually, monthly, or for any other period.

---

[2]For example, to calculate $(1 + k)^n$ for k = 5% = 0.05 and n = 5 years, we multiply $(1 + k)$ = 1.05 by 1.05; multiply this product by 1.05; and so on:

$$(1 + k)^5 = (1.05)(1.05)(1.05)(1.05)(1.05) = 1.2763.$$

This same result is obtained using the exponential function of a calculator, $y^x$. Here y = 1.05; x = 5; and $(1.05)^5 = 1.2763$. If you have a financial calculator, simply punch in n = 5, k = i = 5, and PV = 1, and then punch the FV button to obtain the factor 1.2763. Alternatively, you could punch in n = 5, k = i = 5, and PV = 100 and then hit the FV button to find the final answer, $127.63. Note that some calculators will display the factor as $-1.2763$. You should ignore the negative sign.

**future value interest factor for k,n, (FVIF$_{k,n}$)**
The future value interest factor for a lump sum left in an account for n periods paying k percent per period, which is equal to $(1 + k)^n$.

We define the term **future value interest factor for k,n (FVIF$_{k,n}$)** as equal to $(1 + k)^n$. Therefore, Equation 4-2 can be written as FV$_n$ = PV(FVIF$_{k,n}$). It is necessary only to go to an appropriate interest table (4-2 or A-3) to find the proper interest factor. For example, the correct interest factor for our 5-year, 5 percent illustration can be found in Table 4-2. We look down the period column to 5 and then across this row to the 5 percent column to find the interest factor, 1.2763. Then, using this interest factor, we find the value of $100 after 5 years to be FV$_5$ = PV(FVIF$_{5\%,5 \text{ years}}$) = $100(1.2763) = $127.63, which is identical to the value obtained by the long method in Table 4-1.

### Graphic View of the Compounding Process: Growth

Figure 4-1 shows how $1 (or any other sum) grows over time at various rates of interest. The 5 and 10 percent curves are based on the values given in Table 4-2. The higher the rate of interest, the faster the rate of growth. The interest rate is, in fact, a growth rate; if a sum is deposited and earns 5 percent, then the funds on deposit grow at the rate of 5 percent per period. Note also that these formulas can be applied to anything that is growing—sales, population, earnings per share, or what have you. If you ever need to figure the growth rate of anything, the formulas in this chapter can be used.

**Figure 4-1**
**Relationship between Future Value Interest Factors, Interest Rates, and Time**

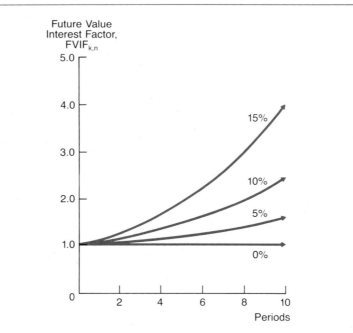

## Present Value

Suppose you are offered the alternative of receiving either $127.63 at the end of 5 years or X dollars today. There is no question that the $127.63 will be paid in full (perhaps the payer is the U.S. government). Having no current need for the money, you would deposit the X dollars in a bank account that pays 5 percent interest. (Five percent is defined to be your *opportunity cost*, or the rate of interest you could earn on alternative investments of equal risk.) What value of X would make you indifferent in your choice between X dollars today and the promise of $127.63 five years hence?

From Table 4-1 we saw that the initial amount of $100 growing at 5 percent a year is worth $127.63 at the end of 5 years. Thus, you should be indifferent to the choice between $100 today and $127.63 at the end of 5 years. The $100 is defined as the **present value**, or **PV**, of $127.63 due in 5 years when the opportunity cost is 5 percent. Therefore, if X is anything less than $100, you should prefer the promise of $127.63 in 5 years to X dollars today; if X were greater than $100, you should prefer X.

*In general, the present value of a sum due n years in the future is the amount which, if it were on hand today, would grow to equal the future sum.* Since $100 would grow to $127.63 in 5 years at a 5 percent interest rate, $100 is defined to be the present value of $127.63 due 5 years in the future when the appropriate interest rate is 5 percent.

Finding present values—or **discounting**, as it is commonly called—is simply the reverse of compounding, and Equation 4-2 can be transformed into a present value formula:

$$FV_n = PV(1 + k)^n, \tag{4-2}$$

which, when solved for PV, gives

$$PV = \frac{FV_n}{(1 + k)^n} = FV_n(1 + k)^{-n} = FV_n \left(\frac{1}{1 + k}\right)^n. \tag{4-3}$$

Tables have been constructed for the term in brackets for various values of k and n; Table 4-3 is an example. (For a more complete table, see Table A-1 in Appendix A at the end of the book.) For our illustrative case, look down the 5 percent column in Table 4-3 to the fifth row. The figure shown there, 0.7835, is the **present value interest factor (PVIF$_{k,n}$)** used to determine the present value of $127.63 payable in 5 years, discounted at 5 percent:[3]

$$PV = FV_5(PVIF_{5\%,5 \text{ years}})$$
$$= \$127.63(0.7835)$$
$$= \$100.$$

**present value, PV**
The value today of a future payment or series of payments discounted at the appropriate discount rate.

**discounting**
The process of finding the present value of a payment or a series of future cash flows; the reverse of compounding.

**present value interest factor (PVIF$_{k,n}$)**
The present value interest factor for a lump sum due n periods in the future discounted at k percent per period.

---

[3]Again, you could use a regular calculator to find PVIF and a financial calculator to find the PV of $100. With a financial calculator, just punch in n, k = i, and FV, and then hit the PV button to find the PV.

**Table 4-3**
**Present Value of $1 Due at the End of n Periods:**

$$\text{PVIF}_{k,n} = \frac{1}{(1 + k)^n} = \left(\frac{1}{1 + k}\right)^n$$

| Period (n) | 1% | 2% | 3% | 4% | 5% | 6% | 7% | 8% | 9% | 10% |
|---|---|---|---|---|---|---|---|---|---|---|
| 1 | .9901 | .9804 | .9709 | .9615 | .9524 | .9434 | .9346 | .9259 | .9174 | .9091 |
| 2 | .9803 | .9612 | .9426 | .9246 | .9070 | .8900 | .8734 | .8573 | .8417 | .8264 |
| 3 | .9706 | .9423 | .9151 | .8890 | .8638 | .8396 | .8163 | .7938 | .7722 | .7513 |
| 4 | .9610 | .9238 | .8885 | .8548 | .8227 | .7921 | .7629 | .7350 | .7084 | .6830 |
| 5 | .9515 | .9057 | .8626 | .8219 | .7835 | .7473 | .7130 | .6806 | .6499 | .6209 |
| 6 | .9420 | .8880 | .8375 | .7903 | .7462 | .7050 | .6663 | .6302 | .5963 | .5645 |
| 7 | .9327 | .8706 | .8131 | .7599 | .7107 | .6651 | .6227 | .5835 | .5470 | .5132 |
| 8 | .9235 | .8535 | .7894 | .7307 | .6768 | .6274 | .5820 | .5403 | .5019 | .4665 |
| 9 | .9143 | .8368 | .7664 | .7026 | .6446 | .5919 | .5439 | .5002 | .4604 | .4241 |
| 10 | .9053 | .8203 | .7441 | .6756 | .6139 | .5584 | .5083 | .4632 | .4224 | .3855 |

## Graphic View of the Discounting Process

Figure 4-2 shows how interest factors for discounting decrease as the discounting period increases. The curves in the figure were plotted with data taken from Table 4-3; they show that the present value of a sum to be received at some future date decreases (1) as the payment date is extended further into the future and (2) as the discount rate increases. If relatively

**Figure 4-2**
**Relationship between Present Value Interest Factors,**
**Interest Rates, and Time**

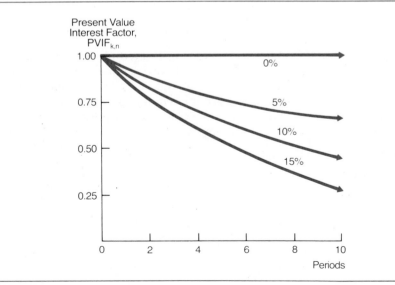

high discount rates apply, funds due in the future are worth very little today, and even at relatively low discount rates, the present values of funds due in the distant future are quite small. For example, $1 due in 10 years is worth about 61 cents today if the discount rate is 5 percent, but it is worth only 25 cents today at a 15 percent discount rate. Similarly, $1 due in 5 years at 10 percent is worth 62 cents today, but at the same discount rate $1 due in 10 years is worth only 39 cents today. At a 15 percent discount rate, $1 due in 50 years is worth only $0.0009 today.

## Future Value versus Present Value

Notice that Equation 4-2, the basic equation for compounding, was developed from the logical sequence set forth in Table 4-1; the equation merely presents in mathematical form the steps outlined in the table. The present value interest factor ($PVIF_{k,n}$) in Equation 4-3, the basic equation for discounting or finding present values, was found as the *reciprocal* of the future value interest factor ($FVIF_{k,n}$) for the same k,n combination:

$$PVIF_{k,n} = \frac{1}{FVIF_{k,n}}.$$

For example, since the *future value* interest factor for 5 percent over 5 years is seen in Table 4-2 to be 1.2763, the *present value* interest factor for 5 percent over 5 years must be the reciprocal of 1.2763:

$$PVIF_{5\%,5 \text{ years}} = \frac{1}{1.2763} = 0.7835.$$

The $PVIF_{k,n}$ found in this manner does, of course, correspond with that shown in Table 4-3.

The reciprocal nature of the relationship between present value and future value permits us to find present values in two ways—by multiplying or by dividing. Thus, the present value of $1,000 due in 5 years and discounted at 5 percent may be found as

$$PV = FV_n(PVIF_{k,n}) = FV_5 \left(\frac{1}{1+k}\right)^5 = \$1,000(0.7835) = \$783.50,$$

or as

$$PV = \frac{FV_n}{FVIF_{k,n}} = \frac{FV_5}{(1+k)^5} = \frac{\$1,000}{1.2763} = \$783.50.$$

To conclude this comparison of present and future values, compare Figures 4-1 and 4-2. Notice that the vertical intercept is at 1.0 in each case but future value interest factors rise while present value interest factors decline.[4]

---

[4]Notice that Figure 4-2 is not a mirror image of Figure 4-1. The curves in Figure 4-1 approach ∞ as n increases; in Figure 4-2 the curves approach zero, not −∞.

## Future Value of an Annuity

**annuity**
A series of payments of a fixed amount for a specified number of periods.

*An* **annuity** *is defined as a series of payments of a fixed, or constant, amount for a specified number of periods.* If payments, which are given the symbol PMT, occur at the end of each period, as they typically do, then we have an *ordinary annuity*, sometimes called a *deferred annuity*. If payments are made at the beginning of each period, then we have an *annuity due*. Since ordinary annuities are far more common in finance, when the word *annuity* is used in this book you may assume that payments are received at the end of each period unless otherwise indicated.

### Ordinary Annuities

**ordinary (deferred) annuity**
A series of payments of a fixed amount for a specified number of periods with the payments occurring at the end of the period.

A promise to pay $1,000 a year for 3 years is a 3-year annuity, and if each payment is made at the end of the year, it is an **ordinary (deferred) annuity**. If you were to receive such an annuity and were to deposit each annual payment in a savings account paying 4 percent interest, how much would you have at the end of 3 years? The answer is shown graphically as a *time line* in Figure 4-3. The first payment is made at the end of Year 1, the second at the end of Year 2, and the third at the end of Year 3. Thus, the first payment is compounded over 2 years; the second payment is compounded for 1 year; and the last payment is not compounded at all. When the future values of each of the payments are summed, their total is the future value of the annuity. In the example, this total is $3,121.60.

Expressed algebraically, with $S_n$, the sum of the annuity, defined as the future value of an annuity over n periods, PMT as the periodic payment, and **$FVIFA_{k,n}$** as the future value interest factor for an annuity, the formula is

**$FVIFA_{k,n}$**
The future value interest factor for an annuity of n periodic payments discounted at k percent.

$$S_n = PMT(1 + k)^{n-1} + PMT(1 + k)^{n-2} + \ldots + PMT(1 + k)^1 + PMT(1 + k)^0$$

$$= PMT[(1 + k)^{n-1} + (1 + k)^{n-2} + \ldots + (1 + k)^1 + (1 + k)^0]$$

$$= PMT \sum_{t=1}^{n} (1 + k)^{n-t}$$

$$= PMT(FVIFA_{k,n}) = \text{future value of an annuity.} \tag{4-4}$$

**Figure 4-3**
**Time Line for an Ordinary Annuity:**
**Future Value with k = 4%**

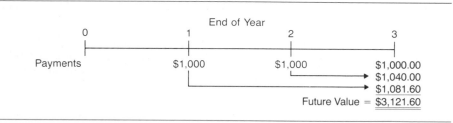

**Table 4-4**
**Sum of an Annuity of $1 per Period for n Periods:**

$$FVIFA_{k,n} = \sum_{t=1}^{n} (1 + k)^{n-t} = \frac{(1 + k)^n - 1}{k}$$

| Number of Periods (n) | 1% | 2% | 3% | 4% | 5% | 6% | 7% | 8% | 9% | 10% |
|---|---|---|---|---|---|---|---|---|---|---|
| 1 | 1.0000 | 1.0000 | 1.0000 | 1.0000 | 1.0000 | 1.0000 | 1.0000 | 1.0000 | 1.0000 | 1.0000 |
| 2 | 2.0100 | 2.0200 | 2.0300 | 2.0400 | 2.0500 | 2.0600 | 2.0700 | 2.0800 | 2.0900 | 2.1000 |
| 3 | 3.0301 | 3.0604 | 3.0909 | 3.1216 | 3.1525 | 3.1836 | 3.2149 | 3.2464 | 3.2781 | 3.3100 |
| 4 | 4.0604 | 4.1216 | 4.1836 | 4.2465 | 4.3101 | 4.3746 | 4.4399 | 4.5061 | 4.5731 | 4.6410 |
| 5 | 5.1010 | 5.2040 | 5.3091 | 5.4163 | 5.5256 | 5.6371 | 5.7507 | 5.8666 | 5.9847 | 6.1051 |
| 6 | 6.1520 | 6.3081 | 6.4684 | 6.6330 | 6.8019 | 6.9753 | 7.1533 | 7.3359 | 7.5233 | 7.7156 |
| 7 | 7.2135 | 7.4343 | 7.6625 | 7.8983 | 8.1420 | 8.3938 | 8.6540 | 8.9228 | 9.2004 | 9.4872 |
| 8 | 8.2857 | 8.5830 | 8.8923 | 9.2141 | 9.5491 | 9.8975 | 10.2598 | 10.6366 | 11.0285 | 11.4359 |
| 9 | 9.3685 | 9.7546 | 10.1591 | 10.5828 | 11.0266 | 11.4913 | 11.9780 | 12.4876 | 13.0210 | 13.5795 |
| 10 | 10.4622 | 10.9497 | 11.4639 | 12.0061 | 12.5779 | 13.1808 | 13.8164 | 14.4866 | 15.1929 | 15.9374 |

The expression in parentheses, $FVIFA_{k,n}$, has been calculated for various combinations of k and n.[5] An illustrative set of these annuity interest factors is given in Table 4-4.[6] (A full set of annuity future value factors is given in Table A-4 of Appendix A.) To find the answer to the 3-year, $1,000 annuity problem, simply refer to Table 4-4, look down the 4 percent column to the row of the third period, and multiply the factor 3.1216 by $1,000. The answer is the same as the one derived by the long method illustrated in Figure 4-3:

$$S_n = PMT(FVIFA_{k,n})$$
$$S_3 = \$1,000(FVIFA_{4\%,3 \text{ years}})$$
$$= \$1,000(3.1216) = \$3,121.60.$$

---

[5]The third step in the equation is simply a shorthand expression in which sigma ($\Sigma$) signifies "sum up," or add the values of n factors. If $t = 1$, then $(1 + k)^{n-t} = (1 + k)^{n-1}$; if $t = 2$, then $(1 + k)^{n-t} = (1 + k)^{n-2}$; and so on until $t = n$, the last year the annuity provides any returns. The symbol $\sum_{t=1}^{n}$ simply says, "Go through the following process: Let $t = 1$ and find the first factor; then let $t = 2$ and find the second factor; continue until each individual factor up to $t = n$ has been found, and then add these individual factors to find the total value of the annuity factor."

[6]The equation given with Table 4-4 recognizes that an FVIFA factor is the sum of a geometric progression. Notice that it is easy to use the equation to develop annuity factors; this is especially useful if you need the FVIFA for some interest rate not given in the tables, for example, 6.5 percent. The equation is also useful for finding factors for fractional periods—for example, 2.5 years—but one needs a calculator with an exponential function for this.

Note also that one could, with a financial calculator, find $S_n$ directly. Just punch in $n = 3$, $k = i = 4$, and PMT = 1,000, and then hit the FV button to get the answer, $S_n = \$3,121.60$. Financial calculators also handle fractional years and interest rates with no trouble. Note that on some calculators, $S_n = -\$3,121.60$. Again, ignore the negative sign.

Notice that for all positive interest rates the $\text{FVIFA}_{k,n}$ for the sum of an annuity is always equal to or greater than the number of periods the annuity runs. Also note that the entry for each period n in Table 4-4 is equal to 1.0 plus the sum of the entries in Table 4-2 up to and including Period $n - 1$, for example, the entry for Period 3 under the 4 percent column in Table 4-4 is equal to $1.000 + 1.0400 + 1.0816 = 3.1216$.

### Annuity Due

**annuity due**
A series of payments of a fixed amount for a specified number of periods with the payments occurring at the beginning of the period.

Had the three $1,000 payments in the previous example each been made at the beginning of the year, the annuity would have been an **annuity due.** In terms of Figure 4-3, each payment would have been shifted to the left, so there would have been $1,000 under Period 0 and a zero under Period 3; thus, each payment would be compounded for one extra year.

We can modify Equation 4-4 to handle annuities due as follows:

$$S_n(\text{Annuity due}) = \text{PMT}(\text{FVIFA}_{k,n})(1 + k). \qquad (4\text{-}4a)$$

Each payment is compounded for one extra year, and multiplying $\text{PMT}(\text{FVIFA}_{k,n})$ by $(1 + k)$ takes care of this extra compounding. Applying Equation 4-4a to the previous example, we obtain

$$S_n(\text{Annuity due}) = \$1,000(3.1216)(1.04) = \$3,246.46$$

versus $3,121.60 for the ordinary annuity.[7] Since its payments come in faster, the annuity due is more valuable.

## Present Value of an Annuity

Suppose you were offered the following alternatives: (1) a 3-year annuity with payments of $1,000 at the end of each year or (2) a lump sum payment today. You have no need for the money during the next 3 years, so if you accepted the annuity, you would simply deposit the payments in a savings account that pays 4 percent interest. Similarly, the lump sum payment would be deposited in an account paying 4 percent, compounded annually. How large must the lump sum payment be to make it equivalent to the annuity?

**$\text{PVIFA}_{k,n}$**
The present value interest factor for an annuity of n periodic payments discounted at k percent.

The time line shown in Figure 4-4 will help explain the problem. The present value of the first payment is $\text{PMT}[1/(1 + k)]$, the second is $\text{PMT}[1/(1 + k)]^2$, and so on. Defining the present value of an annuity of n periods as $A_n$ and **$\text{PVIFA}_{k,n}$** as the present value interest factor for an annuity, we may write the following equation in its several equivalent forms:

---

[7]Note that some financial calculators have a switch or an entry marked "Due" or "Beginning" that permits you to convert from ordinary annuities to annuities due. Be careful, though: People sometimes change the setting to work an annuity due problem, forget to switch the calculator back, and get wrong answers to subsequent ordinary annuity problems.

**Figure 4-4**
**Time Line for an Ordinary Annuity:**
**Present Value with k = 4%**

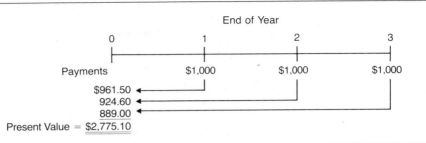

$$A_n = PMT\left(\frac{1}{1 + k}\right)^1 + PMT\left(\frac{1}{1 + k}\right)^2 + \ldots + PMT\left(\frac{1}{1 + k}\right)^n$$

$$= PMT\left(\frac{1}{(1 + k)} + \frac{1}{(1 + k)^2} + \ldots + \frac{1}{(1 + k)^n}\right)$$

$$= PMT\sum_{t=1}^{n}\left(\frac{1}{1 + k}\right)^t$$

$$= PMT(PVIFA_{k,n}). \tag{4-5}$$

Again, tables have been worked out for $PVIFA_{k,n}$. Table 4-5 is illustrative; a more complete listing is found in Table A-2 in Appendix A. From Table 4-5, the $PVIFA_{k,n}$ for a 3-year, 4 percent annuity is found to be 2.7751. Multiplying this factor by the \$1,000 annual payment gives \$2,775.10, the present value of the annuity. This value is identical to the long-method answer shown in Figure 4-4:[8]

$$A_n = PMT(PVIFA_{k,n})$$
$$A_3 = \$1,000(PVIFA_{4\%,3 \text{ years}})$$
$$= \$1,000(2.7751) = \$2,775.10.$$

Notice that the entry for each value of n in Table 4-5 is equal to the sum of the entries in Table 4-3 up to and including Period n. For example, the PVIFA for 4 percent, 3 periods, as shown in Table 4-5, could have been calculated by summing values from Table 4-3:

$$0.9615 + 0.9246 + 0.8890 = 2.7751.$$

Notice also that for all positive interest rates, $PVIFA_{k,n}$ for the *present value* of an annuity is always less than the number of periods the annuity runs, whereas $FVIFA_{k,n}$ for the *sum* of an annuity is equal to or greater than the number of periods.

---

[8]Again, the problem can be solved directly with a financial calculator. Just punch in n = 3, k = i = 4, and PMT = 1,000, and then hit the PV button to find $A_n$ = \$2,775.09. The penny difference results from rounding.

**Table 4-5**
**Present Value of an Annuity of \$1 per Period for n Periods:**

$$PVIFA_{k,n} = \sum_{t=1}^{n} \frac{1}{(1 + k)^t} = \frac{1 - \dfrac{1}{(1 + k)^n}}{k} = \frac{1}{k} - \frac{1}{k(1 + k)^n}$$

| Number of Periods (n) | 1% | 2% | 3% | 4% | 5% | 6% | 7% | 8% | 9% | 10% |
|---|---|---|---|---|---|---|---|---|---|---|
| 1 | 0.9901 | 0.9804 | 0.9709 | 0.9615 | 0.9524 | 0.9434 | 0.9346 | 0.9259 | 0.9174 | 0.9091 |
| 2 | 1.9704 | 1.9416 | 1.9135 | 1.8861 | 1.8594 | 1.8334 | 1.8080 | 1.7833 | 1.7591 | 1.7355 |
| 3 | 2.9410 | 2.8839 | 2.8286 | 2.7751 | 2.7232 | 2.6730 | 2.6243 | 2.5771 | 2.5313 | 2.4869 |
| 4 | 3.9020 | 3.8077 | 3.7171 | 3.6299 | 3.5460 | 3.4651 | 3.3872 | 3.3121 | 3.2397 | 3.1699 |
| 5 | 4.8534 | 4.7135 | 4.5797 | 4.4518 | 4.3295 | 4.2124 | 4.1002 | 3.9927 | 3.8897 | 3.7908 |
| 6 | 5.7955 | 5.6014 | 5.4172 | 5.2421 | 5.0757 | 4.9173 | 4.7665 | 4.6229 | 4.4859 | 4.3553 |
| 7 | 6.7282 | 6.4720 | 6.2303 | 6.0021 | 5.7864 | 5.5824 | 5.3893 | 5.2064 | 5.0330 | 4.8684 |
| 8 | 7.6517 | 7.3255 | 7.0197 | 6.7327 | 6.4632 | 6.2098 | 5.9713 | 5.7466 | 5.5348 | 5.3349 |
| 9 | 8.5660 | 8.1622 | 7.7861 | 7.4353 | 7.1078 | 6.8017 | 6.5152 | 6.2469 | 5.9952 | 5.7590 |
| 10 | 9.4713 | 8.9826 | 8.5302 | 8.1109 | 7.7217 | 7.3601 | 7.0236 | 6.7101 | 6.4177 | 6.1446 |

### Present Value of an Annuity Due

Had the payments in the preceding example occurred at the beginning of each year, the annuity would have been an *annuity due*. In terms of Figure 4-4, each payment would have been shifted to the left, so \$1,000 would have appeared under Period 0 and a zero would have appeared under the 3. Each payment occurs one period earlier, so it has a higher PV. To account for these shifts, we modify Equation 4-5 as follows to find the present value of an annuity due:

$$A_n(\text{Annuity due}) = PMT(PVIFA_{k,n})(1 + k). \tag{4-5a}$$

Our illustrative 4 percent, 3-year annuity, with payments made at the beginning of each year, thus has a present value of \$2,886.10 versus a value of \$2,775.10 on an ordinary annuity basis:

$$\begin{aligned} A_3 &= \$1,000(2.7751)(1.04) \\ &= \$2,775.10(1.04) \\ &= \$2,886.10. \end{aligned}$$

Since each payment comes earlier, an annuity due is worth more than an ordinary annuity.

## Perpetuities

Most annuities call for payments to be made over some definite period of time—for example, \$1,000 per year for 3 years. However, some annuities go on indefinitely; here the payments constitute an *infinite series*, and the series

**perpetuity**
A stream of equal
payments expected to
continue forever.

is defined as a **perpetuity**. The present value of a perpetuity is found by applying Equation 4-6:[9]

$$PV(\text{perpetuity}) = \frac{\text{Payment}}{\text{Discount rate}} = \frac{PMT}{k}. \qquad (4\text{-}6)$$

To illustrate, after the Napoleonic Wars in 1815, the British government sold a huge bond issue and used the proceeds to pay off many smaller issues that had been floated in prior years to pay for the wars. Since the purpose of the new bonds was to consolidate past debts, the bonds were called **consols.** Suppose each consol promised to pay $90 interest per year in perpetuity. (Actually, interest was stated in pounds.) What would each bond be worth if the going rate of interest, or the discount rate, were 8 percent? The answer is $1,125:

**consol**
A perpetual bond issued
by England to consolidate
past debts; in general, any
perpetual bond.

$$\text{Value} = \$90/0.08 = \$1,125.$$

Perpetuities are discussed further in Chapter 5, where procedures for finding the values of various types of securities (stocks and bonds) are analyzed.

## Present Value of an Uneven Series of Payments

The definition of an annuity includes the words *constant amount*—in other words, annuities involve situations in which cash flows are *identical* in every period. Although many financial decisions do involve constant cash flows, some important decisions are concerned with uneven flows of cash—for example, common stocks are typically expected to pay an increasing series of dividends over time, and capital budgeting projects do not normally provide constant cash flows. Consequently, it is necessary to expand our analysis to deal with **uneven payment streams**.

**uneven payment
stream**
A series of payments in
which the amount varies
from one period to the
next.

The PV of an uneven stream of future income is found as the sum of the PVs of the individual components of the stream. For example, suppose we are trying to find the PV of the stream of payments shown in Figure 4-5, discounted at 6 percent. As shown in the lower part of the figure, we multiply each payment by the appropriate $PVIF_{k,n}$ and then sum these products to obtain the PV of the stream, $1,413.24. The graph gives a pictorial view of the cash flow stream.[10]

The PV of the payments shown in Figure 4-5 for Years 2 through 5 can also be found by using the annuity equation. This alternative solution process involves the following steps:

---

[9]The derivation of Equation 4-6 is given in Appendix 3A of Eugene F. Brigham and Louis C. Gapenski, *Intermediate Financial Management.*

[10]This general equation may be used to find the PV of an uneven series of payments:

$$PV = \sum_{t=1}^{n} PMT_t \left( \frac{1}{1+k} \right)^t = \sum_{t=1}^{n} PMT_t(PVIF_{k,t}),$$

where $PMT_t$ is the payment in any Year t.

**Figure 4-5**
**Analysis of an Uneven Cash Flow Stream:**
**Present Value with k = 6%**

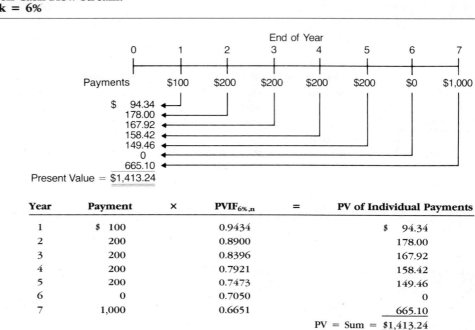

| Year | Payment | × | PVIF$_{6\%,n}$ | = | PV of Individual Payments |
|------|---------|---|--------|---|---------------------------|
| 1 | $ 100 | | 0.9434 | | $ 94.34 |
| 2 | 200 | | 0.8900 | | 178.00 |
| 3 | 200 | | 0.8396 | | 167.92 |
| 4 | 200 | | 0.7921 | | 158.42 |
| 5 | 200 | | 0.7473 | | 149.46 |
| 6 | 0 | | 0.7050 | | 0 |
| 7 | 1,000 | | 0.6651 | | 665.10 |
| | | | | PV = Sum = | $1,413.24 |

**Step 1.** Find the PV of $100 due in Year 1:

$$\$100(0.9434) = \$94.34.$$

**Step 2.** Recognize that a $200 annuity will be received during Years 2 through 5. Thus, we could determine the value of a 5-year annuity, subtract from it the value of a 1-year annuity, and have remaining the value of a 4-year annuity whose first payment is due in 2 years. This result is achieved by subtracting the PVIFA for a 1-year, 6 percent annuity from that for a 5-year annuity and then multiplying the difference by $200:

$$
\begin{aligned}
\text{PV of the annuity} &= \$200(\text{PVIFA}_{6\%,5 \text{ years}}) - \$200(\text{PVIFA}_{6\%,1 \text{ year}}) \\
&= \$200(\text{PVIFA}_{6\%,5 \text{ years}} - \text{PVIFA}_{6\%,1 \text{ year}}) \\
&= \$200(4.2124 - 0.9434) \\
&= \$200(3.2690) = \$653.80.
\end{aligned}
$$

Thus, the present value of the annuity component of the uneven stream is $653.80.[11]

---

[11]An alternative method for finding the present value of the annuity component of the cash flow stream would be (1) to find the value of the annuity at the end of Year 1 = $200(PVIFA$_{6\%,4 \text{ years}}$) = $200(3.4651) = $693.02 and (2) to discount this lump sum value for one year to the present, $693.02(PVIF$_{6\%,1 \text{ year}}$) = $693.02(0.9434) = $653.79. (Note the 1-cent rounding error.)

**Step 3.** Find the PV of the $1,000 due in Year 7:

$$\$1,000(0.6651) = \$665.10.$$

**Step 4.** Sum the components:

$$\$94.34 + \$653.80 + \$665.10 = \$1,413.24.$$

Either the Figure 4-5 method or the method utilizing the annuity formula can be used to solve problems of this type. However, the alternative annuity solution is much easier if the annuity component runs for many years. For example, the alternative solution would be clearly superior for finding the PV of a stream consisting of $100 in Year 1, $200 in Years 2 through 29, and $1,000 in Year 30.

Notice that *the present value of a stream of future cash flows can always be found by summing the present values of each individual cash flow.* However, cash flow regularities within the stream may allow the use of short-cuts such as finding the present value of several cash flows that comprise an annuity. Also, note that in some instances we may want to find the value of a stream of payments at some point other than the present (Year 0). In this situation, we proceed as before but compound and discount to some other point in time, say Year 2, rather than Year 0.[12]

## Determining Interest Rates

We can use the basic equations that were developed earlier in the chapter to determine the interest rates implicit in financial contracts.

**Example 1.** A bank offers to lend you $1,000 if you sign a note to pay $1,610.50 at the end of 5 years. What rate of interest would the bank be charging you?

**1.** Recognize that $1,000 is the PV of $1,610.50 due in 5 years:

$$PV = \$1,000 = \$1,610.50(PVIF_{k,5 \text{ years}}).$$

**2.** Solve for $PVIF_{k,5 \text{ years}}$:

$$PVIF_{k,5 \text{ years}} = \$1,000/\$1,610.50 = 0.6209.$$

---

[12]Note that problems involving unequal cash flows can be solved quite easily with a financial calculator. Some of these calculators permit the input of the separate cash flows plus the interest rate; then you hit the PV (or NPV) button to obtain the solution. However, this feature is not found on all financial calculators. Also, before closing this section, we should note that the future value of a series of uneven payments, often called the *terminal value*, is found by compounding each payment and then summing the individual future values:

$$FV_n = \sum_{t=1}^{n} PMT_t(1 + k)^{n-t}.$$

**3.** Now turn to Table 4-3 (or Table A-1). Look across the row for Period 5 until you find the value 0.6209. It is in the 10 percent column, so you would be paying a 10 percent rate of interest if you were to take out the loan.[13]

**Example 2.** A bank offers to lend you $25,000 to buy a home. You must sign a mortgage calling for payments of $2,545.16 at the end of each of the next 25 years. What interest rate is the bank offering you?

**1.** Recognize that $25,000 is the PV of a 25-year, $2,545.16 annuity:

$$PV = \$25,000 = \sum_{t=1}^{25} \$2,545.16 \frac{1}{(1 + k)^t}$$

$$= \$2,545.16(PVIFA_{k,25 \text{ years}}).$$

**2.** Solve for $PVIFA_{k,25 \text{ years}}$:

$$PVIFA_{k,25 \text{ years}} = \$25,000/\$2,545.16 = 9.8226.$$

**3.** Turn to Table A-2. Looking across the row for 25 periods, you will find 9.8226 under the column for 9 percent. Therefore, the rate of interest on this mortgage loan is 9 percent.[14]

While the tables can be used to find the interest rate implicit in single payments and annuities, it is more difficult to find the interest rate implicit in an uneven series of payments. One can use a trial-and-error procedure, a financial calculator with an IRR feature (IRRs are discussed in Chapter 9), or a graphic procedure, which is also discussed in Chapter 9. We will defer further discussion of this problem for now, but we will take it up later in our discussion of bond values and again in the capital budgeting chapters.

## Semiannual and Other Compounding Periods

In all of our examples thus far, we have assumed that returns are received once a year, or annually. Suppose, however, that you put your $1,000 in a bank which advertises that it pays 6 percent compounded *semiannually*.

---

[13]Financial calculators are especially useful for finding interest rates in problems such as this. Merely punch in PV = 1,000, n = 5, and FV = 1,610.5, and then hit the k = i button to obtain the interest rate. The calculator blinks a few times, and 10.00 percent pops up. Your calculator may require that either the PV or FV be entered as a negative. If you get an error message, try entering PV = −1,000.

[14]To solve this problem with a financial calculator, punch in PV = 25,000, n = 25, and PMT = 2,545.16, and then hit the k = i button to find the interest rate of 9 percent.

Consider also the situation in which the mortgage calls for annual payments of $2,400. Then $PVIFA_{k,n} = \$25,000/\$2,400 = 10.4167$. In Table A-2, this value lies between the $PVIFA_{k,n}$ for 8 and 9 percent, but closer to 8 percent. The approximate rate for the mortgage could be found by "linear interpolation," a topic discussed in algebra texts, but today we would use a financial calculator and find the interest rate merely by hitting the i button. The rate in this example is 8.2887 percent.

**Table 4-6**
**Future Value Calculations with Semiannual Compounding**

| Period | Beginning Amount, PV | × | (1 + k/2) | = | Ending Amount, $FV_n$ |
|--------|---------------------|---|-----------|---|----------------------|
| 1 | $1,000.00 | | (1.03) | | $1,030.00 |
| 2 | 1,030.00 | | (1.03) | | 1,060.90 |

How much will you have at the end of 1 year? Semiannual compounding means that interest is actually paid each 6 months. The procedures for semiannual compounding are illustrated in the calculations in Table 4-6. Here the annual interest rate is divided by 2, but twice as many compounding periods are used because interest is paid twice a year. Comparing the amount on hand at the end of the second 6-month period, $1,060.90, with what would have been on hand under annual compounding, $1,060, we see that semiannual compounding is better from your standpoint as a saver. This result occurs because you earn *interest on interest* more frequently.[15]

Throughout the economy, different types of investments use different compounding periods. For example, bank accounts generally pay interest monthly or daily; most bonds pay interest semiannually; stocks pay dividends quarterly; and many loans pay annual interest.[16] Thus, if we are to compare securities with different compounding periods, we need to put them on a common basis. This need has led to the development of the terms *nominal*, or *stated, interest rate* versus the *effective annual rate*, also called the *annual percentage rate (APR)*.[17] The **nominal**, or **stated**, **interest rate** is the quoted rate; thus, in our example, the nominal rate is 6 percent. The **effective annual rate**, or *annual percentage rate, is the rate that would have produced the final compound value, $1,060.90, under annual rather than semiannual compounding*. In this case, the effective annual rate is 6.09 percent, found by solving for k in the following equation:

$$\$1,000(1 + k) = \$1,060.90$$

$$k = \frac{\$1,060.90}{\$1,000} - 1 = 0.0609 = 6.09\%.$$

Thus, if one bank offered 6 percent with semiannual compounding while another offered 6.09 percent with annual compounding, they would both be paying the same effective annual rate of interest.

**nominal (stated) interest rate**
The contracted, or stated, interest rate.

**effective annual rate**
The annual rate of interest actually being earned as opposed to the stated rate; also called the *annual percentage rate (APR)*.

---

[15]Semiannual compounding is handled easily with a financial calculator. We merely set i = 3, n = 2, and PV = 1,000 and then hit the FV button to get the solution, FV = $1,060.90.

[16]Many banks and savings and loans are now paying interest compounded continuously. Continuous compounding and discounting is discussed in Appendix 4A.

[17]The term *nominal* it is used here has a different meaning from the way it was used in Chapter 3. There, nominal interest rates meant market rates as opposed to real (inflation-adjusted) rates. In this chapter, the term nominal rate means the stated rate as opposed to the effective annual rate giving consideration to compounding more frequently than once a year.

In general, we can determine the effective annual percentage rate, given the nominal rate, by solving Equation 4-7:[18]

$$\text{Effective annual rate} = \left(1 + \frac{k_{Nom}}{m}\right)^m - 1.0. \qquad (4\text{-}7)$$

Here $k_{Nom}$ is the nominal, or stated, interest rate, and m is the number of compounding periods per year. For example, to find the effective annual rate if the nominal rate is 6 percent, compounded semiannually, we make the following calculation:

$$
\begin{aligned}
\text{Effective annual rate} &= \left(1 + \frac{0.06}{2}\right)^2 - 1.0 \\
&= (1.03)^2 - 1.0 \\
&= 1.0609 - 1.0 \\
&= 0.0609 = 6.09\%.
\end{aligned}
$$

The points made about semiannual compounding can be generalized as follows. When compounding periods are more frequent than once a year, we use a modified version of Equation 4-2 to find the future value of a lump sum:

$$\text{Annual compounding: } FV_n = PV(1 + k)^n. \qquad (4\text{-}2)$$

$$\text{More frequent compounding: } FV_n = PV\left(1 + \frac{k_{Nom}}{m}\right)^{mn}. \qquad (4\text{-}2a)$$

Here m is the number of times per year compounding occurs, and n is the number of years. When banks compute daily interest, the value of m is set at 365 and Equation 4-2a is applied.[19]

The interest tables can often be used when compounding occurs more than once a year. Simply divide the nominal, or stated, interest rate by the number of times compounding occurs, and multiply the years by the number of compounding periods per year. For example, to find the amount to which $1,000 will grow after 5 years if semiannual compounding is applied to a stated 4 percent interest rate, divide 4 percent by 2 and multiply the 5 years by 2. Then look in Table A-3 under the 2 percent column and in the row for Period 10. You will find an interest factor of 1.2190. Multiplying this by the

---

[18]It should be noted that many banks define the term *APR* simply as the nominal interest rate, that is, APR = $k_{Nom}$. Although this is a widespread practice and apparently meets the minimum requirements of the "truth in lending" laws, it is somewhat deceptive because the true effective interest rate, which ought to be reported to borrowers, exceeds $k_{Nom}$ except where annual compounding is used.

[19]For example, the future value of $1 invested at 6 percent for 1 year under daily compounding is $1.0618:

$$FV_n = \$1\left(1 + \frac{0.06}{365}\right)^{365(1)}$$

$$= \$1(1.0618) = \$1.0618.$$

initial $1,000 gives a value of $1,219, the amount to which $1,000 will grow in 5 years at 4 percent, compounded semiannually. This compares with $1,216.70 for annual compounding.[20]

The same procedure is applied in all the cases covered—compounding, discounting, single payments, and annuities. To illustrate semiannual discounting in finding the present value of an annuity, consider the case described in the section "Present Value of an Annuity": $1,000 a year for 3 years, discounted at 4 percent. With annual discounting, the interest factor is 2.7751 and the present value of the annuity is $2,775.10. For semiannual discounting, look under the 2 percent column and in the Period 6 row of Table 4-5 to find an interest factor of 5.6014. This is now multiplied by half of $1,000, or the $500 received each six months, to get the present value of the annuity, $2,800.70. The payments come a little more rapidly—the first $500 is paid after only six months (similarly with other payments), so the annuity is a little more valuable if payments are received semiannually rather than annually.

By letting m approach infinity, Equation 4-2a can be modified to the special case of **continuous compounding**. Continuous compounding is useful in theoretical finance, and it also has practical applications—for example, banks and savings associations sometimes pay interest on a continuous basis. Continuous compounding is discussed in Appendix 4A.

**continuous compounding**
A situation in which interest is added continuously rather than at discrete points in time.

## Amortized Loans

One of the most important applications of compound interest involves loans that are to be paid off in installments over time. Examples include automobile loans, home mortgage loans, and most business debt other than very short-term loans. If a loan is to be repaid in equal periodic amounts (monthly, quarterly, or annually), it is said to be an **amortized loan**.[21]

**amortized loan**
One that is repaid in equal payments over the life of the loan.

To illustrate, suppose a firm borrows $1,000 to be repaid in 3 equal payments at the end of each of the next 3 years. The lender is to receive 6 percent interest on the loan balance that is outstanding at each point in time. The first task is to determine the amount the firm must repay each year, or the annual payment. To find this amount, recognize that the $1,000 represents the present value of an annuity of PMT dollars per year for 3 years, discounted at 6 percent:

---

[20]With a financial calculator, simply press in i = $k_{Nom}/m$ = 2, n = m $\times$ n = 10, and then proceed as before. It should be clear that the tables in this book are not complete enough to handle much variability of interest rates. For example, to handle 9 percent, compounded quarterly, we would need a table for 2¼ percent; 10 percent quarterly would require a table for 2½ percent; and so on. Years ago very complete tables were available, but they were replaced by financial calculators.

[21]The word *amortized* comes from the Latin *mort*, meaning "dead," so an amortized loan is one that is "killed off" over time.

$$PV \text{ of annuity} = \frac{PMT}{(1 + k)^1} + \frac{PMT}{(1 + k)^2} + \frac{PMT}{(1 + k)^3}$$

$$\$1{,}000 = \frac{PMT}{(1.06)} + \frac{PMT}{(1.06)^2} + \frac{PMT}{(1.06)^3}$$

$$= PMT(PVIFA_{6\%, \ 3 \ years}).$$

The PVIFA is 2.6730, so

$$\$1{,}000 = PMT(2.6730).$$

Solving for PMT, we obtain

$$PMT = \$1{,}000/2.6730 = \$374.11.$$

**amortization schedule**
A schedule showing precisely how a loan will be repaid, giving the required payment on each specified date and a breakdown of the payment showing how much constitutes interest and how much repayment of principal.

If the firm pays the lender $374.11 at the end of each of the next 3 years, the percentage cost to the borrower, and the rate of return to the lender, will be 6 percent.

Each payment consists partly of interest and partly of a repayment of principal. This breakdown is given in the **amortization schedule** shown in Table 4-7. The interest component is largest in the first year and declines as the outstanding balance of the loan goes down. For tax purposes, the borrower reports as a deductible cost each year the interest payments in Column 2, while the lender reports these same amounts as taxable income.

**Table 4-7**
**Loan Amortization Schedule**

| Year | Payment (1) | Interest[a] (2) | Repayment of Principal[b] (3) | Remaining Balance (4) |
|------|-------------|-----------------|-------------------------------|------------------------|
| 1 | $ 374.11 | $ 60.00 | $ 314.11 | $685.89 |
| 2 | 374.11 | 41.15 | 332.96 | 352.93 |
| 3 | 374.11 | 21.18 | 352.93 | 0 |
|   | $1,122.33 | $122.33 | $1,000.00 | |

[a]Interest is calculated by multiplying the loan balance at the beginning of the year by the interest rate. Therefore, interest in Year 1 is $1,000(0.06) = $60; in Year 2, $685.89(0.06) = $41.15; and in Year 3, $352.93(0.06) = $21.18.

[b]Repayment of principal is equal to the payment of $374.11 minus the interst charge.

## Summary

Financial decisions often involve situations in which someone pays money at one point in time and receives money at some other time. Dollars that are paid or received at two different points in time are different, and this difference must be recognized when analyzing financial decisions and transactions. All of this is called *discounted cash flow (DCF) analysis*.

Several basic equations are used in financial analysis:

Future value:
(single payment)
$$FV_n = PV(1 + k)^n = PV(FVIF_{k,n}).$$

Present value:
(single payment)
$$PV = FV_n \left[\frac{1}{1 + k}\right]^n = FV_n(1 + k)^{-n}$$
$$= FV_n(PVIF_{k,n}).$$

Future value
(annuity):
$$S_n = PMT \sum_{t=1}^{n} (1 + k)^{n-t}$$
$$= PMT \left[\frac{(1 + k)^n - 1}{k}\right]$$
$$= PMT(FVIFA_{k,n}).$$

Present value
(annuity):
$$A_n = PMT \sum_{t=1}^{n} \left(\frac{1}{1 + k}\right)^t$$
$$= PMT \left[\frac{1 - \dfrac{1}{(1 + k)^n}}{k}\right]$$
$$= PMT(PVIFA_{k,n}).$$

Present value
(perpetuity):
$$PV \text{ (perpetuity)} = \frac{PMT}{k}.$$

These equations may also be applied to find the present or future value of uneven cash flow streams and to find interest rates in situations in which the other values are given but the value of k is unknown. To find the interest rate, one simply inserts the known values into the appropriate formula, solves for the interest factor, and looks up the interest factor in the appropriate table. If fractional rates are involved, one must go through a rather tedious interpolation process or else use a financial calculator.

The chapter also covered situations in which compounding occurs more frequently than once a year, for example, semiannually or quarterly. Here the stated, or nominal, interest rate, $k_{Nom}$, is divided by m, the number of compounding periods per year; the exponent used is m × n; and the equations given above are used with these modified values. Note that the *effective annual rate* is somewhat greater than $k_{Nom}$ when compounding is more frequent than annual.

The concepts covered in this chapter will be used throughout the remainder of the book. In Chapter 5 we apply present value concepts to the process of valuing stocks and bonds; there we will see that the market prices of these securities are established by determining the present values of the cash flows they are expected to provide. Then, in Chapter 6, we examine the determinants of a stock's required rate of return (which is used to discount its expected future cash flows in order to find its present value). In later chapters, the same basic concepts are applied to corporate decisions involving both expenditures on capital assets and the types of capital that should be used to pay for assets.

# Questions

**4-1**    Define each of the following terms:

a. PV; k; I; $FV_n$; n

b. $FVIF_{k,n}$; $PVIF_{k,n}$; $FVIFA_{k,n}$; $PVIFA_{k,n}$

c. Annuity; lump sum payment; uneven payment stream

d. Ordinary (deferred) annuity; annuity due

e. Perpetuity; consol

f. Financial calculator versus "regular" calculator

g. Compounding; discounting; DCF

h. Annual, semiannual, quarterly, monthly, daily, and continuous compounding

i. Effective annual rate; nominal (stated) rate of interest

j. Amortization schedule; principal component versus interest component of a payment

**4-2**    Is it true that for all positive interest rates the following conditions hold: $FVIF_{k,n} \geq 1.0$; $PVIF_{k,n} \leq 1.0$; $FVIFA_{k,n} \geq$ number of periods the annuity lasts; and $PVIFA_{k,n} \leq$ number of periods the annuity lasts?

**4-3**    An *annuity* is defined as a series of payments of a fixed amount for a specific number of periods. Thus, $100 a year for 10 years is an annuity, but $100 in Year 1, $200 in Year 2, and $400 in Years 3 through 10 do *not* constitute an annuity. However, the second series *contains* an annuity. Is this statement true or false?

**4-4**    If a firm's earnings per share grew from $1 to $2 over a 10-year period, the *total growth* was 100 percent but the *annual growth rate* was *less than* 10 percent. Why is this so?

**4-5**    Assuming that two banks offer the same stated, or nominal, rate, would you rather have a deposit in a bank that uses annual, semiannual, or quarterly compounding? Explain.

**4-6**    To find the present value of an uneven series of payments, you can use the $PVIF_{k,n}$ tables; the $PVIFA_{k,n}$ tables can never be of use, even if some of the payments constitute an annuity (for example, $100 each for Years 3, 4, 5, and 6), because the entire series is not an annuity. Is this statement true or false?

**4-7**    The present value of a perpetuity is equal to the payment on the annuity, PMT, divided by the discount rate, k: PV = PMT/k. What is the *sum*, or future value, of a perpetuity of PMT dollars per year? (Hint: The answer is infinity, but explain why.)

# Self-Test Problems (*Solutions on Page 105*)

**ST-1**    Assume that it is now January 1, 1986. On January 1, 1987, you will deposit $1,000 into a savings account paying an 8 percent interest rate.

a. If the bank compounds interest annually, how much will you have in your account on January 1, 1990?

b. What would your January 1, 1990, balance be if the bank used quarterly compounding rather than annual compounding?

c. Suppose you deposited the $1,000 in 4 payments of $250 each on January 1 of 1987, 1988, 1989, and 1990. How much would you have

in your account on January 1, 1990, based on 8 percent annual compounding?

d. Suppose you deposited 4 equal payments in your account on January
1 of 1987, 1988, 1989, and 1990. How large would each of your
payments have to be for you to obtain the same ending balance you
calculated in Part a?

ST-2   Assume that it is now January 1, 1986, and you will need $1,000 on
January 1, 1990. Your bank compounds interest at an 8 percent rate
annually.

a. How much must you deposit on January 1, 1987, to have a balance
of $1,000 on January 1, 1990?

b. If you want to make equal payments on each January 1 from 1987
through 1990 to accumulate the $1,000, how large must each of the
4 payments be?

c. If your father were to offer either to make the payments calculated
in Part b ( $221.92) or to give you a lump sum of $750 on January 1,
1987, which would you choose?

d. If you have only $750 on January 1, 1987, what interest rate, com-
pounded annually, would you have to earn to have the necessary
$1,000 on January 1, 1990?

e. Suppose you can deposit only $186.29 each January 1 from 1987
through 1990 but you still need $1,000 on January 1, 1990. What
interest rate, with annual compounding, must you seek out to achieve
your goal?

f. To help you reach your $1,000 goal, your father offers to give you
$400 on January 1, 1987. You will get a part-time job and make 6
additional payments of equal amounts each 6 months thereafter. If all
of this money is deposited in a bank which pays 8 percent, compounded semiannually, how large must your payments be?

g. What is the effective annual rate being paid by the bank in Part f?

ST-3   Bank A pays 8 percent interest, compounded quarterly, on its money
market account. The managers of Bank B want its money market account
to equal Bank A's effective annual rate, but to be compounded on a
monthly basis. What nominal, or stated, rate must Bank B set?

## Problems

Present and future values
for different periods

4-1   Find the following values *without using tables*, and then work the problems with tables to check your answers. If you have a financial calculator,
use it also to check your answers. Disregard rounding errors.

a. An initial $200 compounded for 1 year at 7 percent.
b. An initial $200 compounded for 2 years at 7 percent.
c. The present value of $200 due in 1 year at a discount rate of 7 per-
cent.
d. The present value of $200 due in 2 years at a discount rate of 7
percent.

Present and future values
for different interest rates

4-2   Use the tables to find the following values. Check your work with a financial calculator if you have one.

a. An initial $200 compounded for 10 years at 7 percent.

b. An initial $200 compounded for 10 years at 14 percent.

c. The present value of $200 due in 10 years at a 7 percent discount rate.

d. The present value of $741.40 due in 10 years at a 14 percent discount rate.

| Time for a lump sum to double | 4-3 | To the closest year, how long will it take $200 to double if it is deposited and earns the following rates? |

a. 7 percent.

b. 9 percent.

c. 12 percent.

d. 100 percent.

**Future value of an annuity     4-4**

Find the *future value* of the following annuities. The first payment in these annuities is made at the *end* of Year 1—that is, they are *ordinary* annuities.

a. $200 per year for 10 years at 10 percent.

b. $100 per year for 5 years at 5 percent.

c. $200 per year for 5 years at 0 percent.

d. Now rework Parts a, b, and c assuming that payments are made at the *beginning* of each year, that is, they are *annuities due*.

**Present value of an       4-5**
**annuity**

Find the *present value* of the following *ordinary* annuities:

a. $200 per year for 10 years at 10 percent.

b. $100 per year for 5 years at 5 percent.

c. $200 per year for 5 years at 0 percent.

d. Now rework Parts a, b, and c assuming that payments are made at the *beginning* of each year, that is, they are *annuities due*.

**Uneven cash flow stream     4-6**

a. Find the present values of the following cash flow streams. The appropriate discount rate is 10 percent.

| Year | Cash Stream A | Cash Stream B |
|------|---------------|---------------|
| 1    | $100          | $300          |
| 2    | 400           | $400          |
| 3    | 400           | $400          |
| 4    | 400           | $400          |
| 5    | 300           | $100          |

b. What is the value of each cash flow stream at a 0 percent discount rate?

**Uneven cash flow stream     4-7**

Find the present value of the following cash flow stream, discounted at 5 percent: Year 1, $100; Year 2, $400; Years 3 through 20, $300.

**Present value comparison     4-8**

Which amount is worth more at 9 percent: $1,000 today or $2,000 after 8 years?

**Growth rates     4-9**

Spantex Corporation's 1985 sales were $4 million. Sales were $2 million 5 years earlier (in 1980).

a. To the nearest percentage point, at what rate have sales been growing?

b. Suppose someone calculated the sales growth for Spantex Corporation in Part a as follows: "Sales doubled in 5 years. This represents a growth of 100 percent in 5 years, so, dividing 100 percent by 5, we find the growth rate to be 20 percent per year." Explain what is wrong with this calculation.

Effective rate of interest · **4-10** · Find the interest rates, or rates of return, on each of the following:
a. You borrow $200 and promise to pay back $210 at the end of 1 year.
b. You lend $200 and receive a promise of $210 at the end of 1 year.
c. You borrow $20,000 and promise to pay back $32,578 at the end of 10 years.
d. You borrow $2,000 and promise to make payments of $514.18 per year for 5 years.

Expected rate of return · **4-11** · The Ossenfort Company buys a machine for $20,000 and expects a return of $4,770.42 per year for the next 10 years. What is the expected rate of return on the machine?

Expected rate of return · **4-12** · Georgia-Atlantic invests $1 million to clear a tract of land and set out some young pine trees. The trees will mature in 10 years, at which time Georgia-Atlantic plans to sell the forest at an expected price of $3 million. What is Georgia-Atlantic's expected rate of return?

Effective rate of interest · **4-13** · Your broker offers to sell you a note for $11,300 that will pay $2,000 per year for 10 years. If you buy the note, what rate of interest will you be earning?

Effective rate of interest · **4-14** · A mortgage company offers to lend you $50,000; the loan calls for payments of $5,477.36 per year for 20 years. What interest rate is the mortgage company charging you?

Required lump sum payment · **4-15** · In order to complete your last year in business school and then go through law school, you will need $8,000 per year for 4 years, starting next year (that is, you will need to withdraw $8,000 one year from today). Your rich uncle offers to put you through school and will deposit in a bank time deposit paying 8 percent interest a sum of money that is sufficient to cover all expenses. The deposit will be made today.
a. How large must the deposit be?
b. How much will be in the account immediately after you make the first withdrawal? After the last withdrawal?

Future value for various compounding periods · **4-16** · Find the amount to which $200 will grow under each of the following conditions:
a. 12 percent compounded annually for 4 years.
b. 12 percent compounded semiannually for 4 years.
c. 12 percent compounded quarterly for 4 years.
d. 12 percent compounded monthly for 1 year.

Present value for various compounding periods · **4-17** · Find the present values of $200 due in the future under each of the following conditions:
a. 12 percent nominal rate, semiannual compounding, discounted back 4 years.
b. 12 percent nominal rate, quarterly compounding, discounted back 4 years.
c. 12 percent nominal rate, monthly compounding, discounted back 1 year.

Annuity value for various   **4-18**   Find the indicated value of the following regular annuities:
compounding periods

   a. FV of $200 each 6 months for 4 years at a nominal rate of 12 percent, compounded semiannually.

   b. PV of $200 each 3 months for 4 years at a nominal rate of 12 percent, compounded quarterly.

Effective versus nominal   **4-19**   The First National Bank pays 11 percent interest, compounded annually,
interest rates   on time deposits. The Second National Bank pays 10 percent interest, compounded quarterly.

   a. In which bank would you prefer to deposit your money?

   b. Could your choice of banks be influenced by the fact that you might want to withdraw your funds during the year as opposed to the end of the year? In answering this question, assume that funds must be left on deposit during the entire compounding period in order for you to receive any interest.

Present value of a   **4-20**   What is the present value of a perpetuity of $100 per year if the appro-
perpetuity   priate discount rate is 5 percent? If interest rates in general were to double and the appropriate discount rate rose to 10 percent, what would happen to the present value of the perpetuity?

Amortization schedule   **4-21**   a. Set up an amortization schedule for a $20,000 loan to be repaid in equal installments at the end of each of the next 3 years. The interest rate is 10 percent.

   (Do Parts b through d only if you are using the computerized problem diskette.)

   b. Set up an amortization schedule for a $40,000 loan to be repaid in equal installments at the end of each of the next 3 years. The interest rate is 10 percent.

   c. Set up an amortization schedule for a $100,000 loan to be repaid in equal installments at the end of each of the next 3 years. The interest rate is 9 percent.

   d. Redo Parts b and c using a 20-year amortization schedule.

Effective rates of return   **4-22**   Look back to the introduction of this chapter, where we described the situation facing AT&T's pension fund managers. They had the choice of investing in (1) a bond which costs $519.37 today, pays nothing during its life, and then pays $1,000 after 5 years or (2) a bond which costs $1,000 today, pays $150 in interest at the end of each of the next 4 years, and pays $1,150 interest and principal at the end of Year 5.

   a. Which alternative would have provided the higher rate of return?

   b. Assume that the market interest rate dropped to 10 percent immediately after the bonds were purchased and remained at that level for the next 5 years. (1) What would be the immediate gain or loss on the two bonds? (2) If AT&T holds the bonds until they mature, what returns will it realize on the two bond alternatives over the five-year holding period.

Required annuity   **4-23**   Again refer to the introduction. How much would the father have to save
payments   each year to send his daughter to college?

Present value of an   **4-24**   Refer once more to the introduction. Should General Motors invest in
annuity   electric car production? Assume that the opportunity cost of the funds invested in the project is 10 percent.

## Solutions to Self-Test Problems

**ST-1**   a.

| 1/1/86 | 1/1/87 | 1/1/88 | 1/1/89 | 1/1/90 |
|---|---|---|---|---|

$1,000

$1,000 is being compounded for 3 years, so your balance on January 1, 1990, is $1,259.71:

$$FV = PV(1 + k)^n = \$1,000(1 + 0.08)^3 = \$1,259.71.$$

b. The effective annual rate for 8 percent, compounded quarterly, is

$$APR = \left(1 + \frac{0.08}{4}\right)^4 - 1.0$$

$$= (1.02)^4 - 1.0 = 0.0824 = 8.24\%.$$

Therefore, $FV = \$1,000(1.0824)^3 = \$1,000(1.2681) = \$1,268.10.$

Alternatively, use FVIF for 2%, $3 \times 4 = 12$ periods:

$$FV = \$1,000(FVIF_{2\%,12 \text{ periods}}) = \$1,000(1.2682) = \$1,268.20.$$

(Calculator solution = $1,268.24.)

Note that since the interest factors are carried to only four decimal places, rounding errors occur. Rounding errors also occur between calculator and tabular solutions.

c.

| 1/1/86 | 1/1/87 | 1/1/88 | 1/1/89 | 1/1/90 |
|---|---|---|---|---|
| | $250 | $250 | $250 | $250 |

As you work this problem, keep in mind that the tables assume that payments are made at the end of each period. Therefore, you may solve this problem by finding the future value of an annuity of $250 for 4 years at 8 percent:

$$PMT(FVIFA_{k,n}) = \$250(4.5061) = \$1,126.53.$$

d. $FV = \$1,259.71; k = 8\%; n = 4.$

$$PMT(FVIFA_{8\%,4 \text{ years}}) = FV$$
$$PMT(4.5061) = \$1,259.71$$
$$PMT = \$1,259.71/4.5061 = \$279.56.$$

Therefore, you would have to make 4 payments of $279.56 each to have a balance of $1,259.71 on January 1, 1990.

**ST-2**   a. Set up a time line like those above, and note that your deposit will grow for 3 years at 8 percent. The deposit on January 1, 1987, is the PV, and $1,000 = FV. Here is the solution:

$$FV = \$1,000; n = 3; k = 8\%.$$

$$FV(PVIF_{8\%,3 \text{ years}}) = PV$$

$1,000(0.7938) = \$793.80 =$ Initial deposit to accumulate $1,000.

(Calculator solution $= \$793.83$.)

b. Here we are dealing with a 4-year annuity whose first payment occurs one year from today, on 1/1/87, and whose future value must equal $1,000. Here is the solution:

$$FV = \$1,000; n = 4; k = 8\%.$$

$$PMT(FVIFA_{8\%,4 \text{ years}}) = FV$$

$$PMT = \frac{FV}{(FVIFA_{8\%,4 \text{ years}})}$$

$$= \frac{\$1,000}{4.5061}$$

$$= \$221.92$$

$$= \text{Payment necessary to accumulate } \$1,000.$$

c. This problem can be approached in several ways. Perhaps the simplest is to ask this question: "If I received $750 on 1/1/87 and deposited it to earn 8%, would I have the required $1,000 on 1/1/90?" The answer is no:

$$\$750 \ (1.08)(1.08)(1.08) = \$944.78.$$

This indicates that you should let your father make the payments rather than accept the lump sum $750.

You could also compare the $750 with the PV of the payments:

$$PMT = \$221.92; k = 8\%; n = 4.$$

$$PMT(PVIFA_{8\%,4 \text{ years}}) = PV$$

$221.92(3.3121) = \$735.02 =$ Present value of the required payments.

This is less than the $750 lump sum offer, so your initial reaction might be to accept the lump sum of $750. However, this would be a mistake. As we saw above, if you were to deposit the $750 on January 1, 1987, at an 8 percent interest rate, to be withdrawn on January 1, 1990, interest would be compounded for only 3 years, from January 1, 1987, to December 31, 1989, and the future value would be only

$$PV(FVIF_{8\%,3 \text{ years}}) = \$750(1.2597) = \$944.78.$$

The problem is that when you found the $735.02 PV of the annuity, you were finding the value of the annuity *today*, on January 1, 1986. You were comparing $735.02 today with the lump sum $750 one year from now. This is, of course, invalid. What you should have done was take the $735.02, recognize that this is the PV of an annuity as of January 1, 1986, multiply $735.02 by 1.08 to get $793.82, and compare $793.82 with the lump sum of $750. You would then take your father's offer to pay off the loan rather than the lump sum on January 1, 1987.

d.  PV = \$750; FV = \$1,000; n = 3; k = ?

$$PV(FVIF_{k,3 \text{ years}}) = FV$$

$$FVIF_{k,3 \text{ years}} = \frac{FV}{PV}$$

$$= \frac{\$1,000}{\$750} = 1.3333.$$

Use the Future Value of \$1 table (Table A-3 at the end of the book) for 3 periods to find the interest rate corresponding to an FVIF of 1.3333. Look across the Period 3 row of the table until you come to 1.3333. The closest value is 1.3310, in the 10 percent column. Therefore, you would require an interest rate of approximately 10 percent to achieve your \$1,000 goal. The exact rate required, found with a financial calculator, is 10.0642 percent.

e.  FV = \$1,000; PMT = \$186.29; n = 4; k = ?

$$PMT(FVIFA_{k,4 \text{ years}}) = FV$$

$$\$186.29(FVIFA_{k,4 \text{ years}}) = \$1,000$$

$$FVIFA_{k,4 \text{ years}} = \frac{\$1,000}{\$186.29} = 5.3680.$$

Using Table A-4 at the end of the book, we find that 5.3680 corresponds to a 20 percent interest rate. You might be able to find a borrower willing to offer you a 20 percent interest rate, but there would be some risk involved—he or she might not actually pay you your \$1,000!

(Calculator solution = 19.9997%.)

f.

| 1/1/86 | | 1/1/87 | | 1/1/88 | | 1/1/89 | | 1/1/90 |
|---|---|---|---|---|---|---|---|---|

\$400        ?        ?        ?        ?        ?        ?

Find the future value of the original \$400 deposit:

$$FV = PV(FVIF_{4\%,6}) = \$400(1.2653) = \$506.12.$$

This means that on January 1, 1990, you need an additional sum of \$493.88:

$$\$1,000.00 - 506.12 = \$493.88.$$

This will be accumulated by making 6 equal payments which earn 8% compounded semiannually, or 4% each 6 months:

$$PMT(FVIFA_{4\%,6}) = FV$$

$$PMT = \frac{FV}{(FVIFA_{4\%,6})}$$

$$= \frac{\$493.88}{6.6330} = \$74.46.$$

g.     Effective annual rate $= \left(1 + \dfrac{k_{Nom}}{m}\right)^{m} - 1.0$

$$= \left(1 + \frac{0.08}{2}\right)^{2} - 1 = (1.04)^{2} - 1$$

$$= 1.0816 - 1 = 0.0816 = 8.16\%.$$

ST-3     Bank A's effective annual rate is 8.24 percent:

$$\text{Effective annual rate} = \left(1 + \frac{0.08}{4}\right)^{4} - 1.0$$

$$= (1.02)^{4} - 1 = 1.0824 - 1$$

$$= 0.0824 = 8.24\%.$$

Now Bank B must have the same effective annual rate:

$$\left(1 + \frac{k}{12}\right)^{12} - 1.0 = 0.082432$$

$$\left(1 + \frac{k}{12}\right)^{12} = 1.082432$$

$$1 + \frac{k}{12} = (1.082432)^{1/12}$$

$$1 + \frac{k}{12} = 1.0066227$$

$$\frac{k}{12} = 0.0066227$$

$$k = 0.0794724 = 7.95\%.$$

## Selected Additional References

For a more complete discussion of the mathematics of finance, see:

Cissell, Robert, Helen Cissell, and David C. Flaspohler, *Mathematics of Finance* (Boston: Houghton Mifflin, 1978).

To learn more about using financial calculators, see the owner's handbook which came with your calculator, for example:

Hewlett-Packard, HP-12C, *Owner's Manual and Problem Solving Guide*, 1983.

## APPENDIX 4A

### Continuous Compounding and Discounting

In Chapter 4, we implicitly assumed that growth occurs at discrete intervals—annually, semiannually, and so forth. For some purposes it is better to assume instantaneous, or *continuous*, growth. In this appendix, we develop present value and future value relationships when the interest rate is compounded continuously.

### Continuous Compounding

The relationship between discrete and continuous compounding is illustrated in Figure 4A-1. Panel a shows the annual compounding case, in which interest is added once a year; in Panel b compounding occurs twice a year; and in Panel c, interest is earned continuously. As the graphs show, the more frequent the compounding period, the larger is the final compound amount, because interest is earned on interest more often.

In Chapter 4, Equation 4-2a was developed to allow for any number of compounding periods per year:

$$FV_n = PV \left( 1 + \frac{k_{Nom}}{m} \right)^{mn}. \tag{4-2a}$$

Here $k_{Nom}$ = the stated interest rate, m = the number of compounding periods per year, and n = the number of years. To illustrate, let PV = \$100, k = 10%, and n = 5. At various compounding periods per year, we obtain the following future values at the end of 5 years:

$$\text{Annual: } FV_5 = \$100 \left( 1.0 + \frac{0.10}{1} \right)^{1(5)} = \$100(1.10)^5 = \$161.05.$$

**Figure 4A-1**
**Annual, Semiannual, and Continuous Compounding:**
**Future Value with k = 25%**

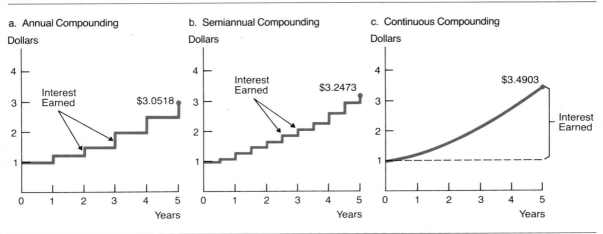

a. Annual Compounding    b. Semiannual Compounding    c. Continuous Compounding

$$\text{Semiannual: } FV_5 = \$100\left(1.0 + \frac{0.10}{2}\right)^{2(5)} = \$100(1.05)^{10} = \$162.89.$$

$$\text{Monthly: } FV_5 = \$100\left(1.0 + \frac{0.10}{12}\right)^{12(5)} = \$100(1.0083)^{60} = \$164.53.$$

$$\text{Daily: } FV_5 = \$100\left(1.0 + \frac{0.10}{365}\right)^{365(5)} = \$164.86.$$

$$\text{Hourly: } FV_5 = \$100\left(1.0 + \frac{0.10}{8,760}\right)^{365(24)(5)} = \$164.87.$$

We could keep going, compounding every minute, every second, every 1/1,000th of a second, and so on. At the limit, we could compound every instant, or *continuously*. The equation for continuous compounding is

$$FV_n = PV(e^{kn}), \qquad\qquad\qquad\qquad\qquad\text{(4A-1)}$$

where e is the value 2.7183 · · · .[1] If \$100 is invested for 5 years at 10 percent compounded continuously, then $FV_5$ is computed as follows:

$$\text{Continuous: } FV_5 = \$100[e^{0.10(5)}] = \$100(2.7183 \cdots)^{0.5}$$
$$= \$164.872.$$

## Continuous Discounting

Equation 4A-1 can be transformed into Equation 4A-2 and used to determine present values under continuous compounding:

$$PV = \frac{FV_n}{e^{kn}} = FV_n e^{-kn}. \qquad\qquad\qquad\text{(4A-2)}$$

Thus, if \$1,649 is due in 10 years, and if the appropriate *continuous* discount rate, k, is 5 percent, then the present value of this future payment is

$$PV = \$1,649\left[\frac{1}{(2.7183 \cdots)^{0.5}}\right] = \frac{\$1,649}{1.649} = \$1,000.$$

---

[1]Calculators with exponential functions can be used to evaluate Equation 4A-1.

# 5 BOND AND STOCK VALUATION MODELS

## PICKING WINNERS AND AVOIDING LOSERS IN THE STOCK AND BOND MARKETS

On August 1, 1985, some bonds Pacific Gas & Electric had issued several years ago for $1,000 were selling for only $690, while other PG&E bonds were selling for $1,155. On the same date, U.S. Treasury bonds originally sold to investors for $1,000 ranged in price from $1,250 to $732. Bank of America had some $1,000 bonds that were selling for only $442, and Baldwin United bonds sold for just $300. Ralston Purina's bonds, on the other hand, were trading at $2,700. Why do these differences exist? Why have the holders of some PG&E bonds suffered large losses while others were making gains? Why are the Ralston bonds so high, and the Baldwin United bonds so low? How could one invest in U.S. Treasury securities and lose money?

Some interesting things were also happening in the stock market. CBS, the broadcasting company which also owns the publisher of this book, fell by $1 per share, to $115, down from $125 a few weeks earlier. Even though it was down from its high, CBS stockholders have not done so bad—the stock sold for only $70 in January, and for as little as $33 two years ago. ABC, meanwhile, was doing even better than CBS—it sold for $114, up from $59 in January and from $26 two years ago. Not all stocks have been up, however. For example, Apple Computer was selling for $15, down from $31 in January and from $63 two years ago, and Storage Technology, another NYSE computer company, was down to $2 from a recent high of $40. Apple and Storage Technology both did well for awhile, but then IBM decided to move into personal computers and disk storage devices. IBM is likely to set another earnings record in 1985, and its stock price just hit a record $138, up from $99 in 1984 and $48 three years ago. Why is CBS worth $115 per share, Storage Technology $2, IBM $138, and Apple $15? More important, what actions can managers take to increase their firms' stock prices, and how can you, as an investor, decide what a stock or bond is worth and which securities are likely to rise in value rather than fall?

We will return to these questions in the last section of the chapter. Study hard, and perhaps you can pick the next big winner, or avoid the big losers.

In Chapter 4 we examined discounted cash flow concepts. Those concepts can be used to analyze the worth of any asset whose value is derived from future cash flows, including real estate, factories, machinery, oil wells, coal mines, farmland, stocks, or bonds. In this chapter we use discounted cash flow techniques to show how investors establish the values of stocks and bonds. The material covered in the chapter is obviously important to investors and potential investors and also to corporate decision makers. *All important corporate decisions should be analyzed in terms of how they will affect the price of the firm's stock, so it is clearly essential for management to know what determines stock prices.*

## Bond Values

Corporations raise capital in two primary forms—debt and common equity. Our first task in this chapter is to examine the valuation process for bonds, the primary type of long-term debt.

**bond**
A long-term debt instrument.

A **bond** is a long-term promissory note issued by a business or governmental unit. For example, on January 2, 1986, the Teletron Electronics Company borrowed $50 million by selling 50,000 individual bonds for $1,000 each. As a first step in explaining how bond values are determined, we need to define some of the terms associated with these securities.

**par value**
The nominal or face value of a stock or bond.

1. *Par value.* The **par value** is the stated face value of the bond; it is usually set as $1,000, although multiples of $1,000 are used on occasion. The par value generally represents the amount of money that the firm borrows and promises to repay at some future date.

**maturity date**
A specified date on which the par value of a bond is to be repaid.

**original maturity**
The maturity at the time a bond is issued.

2. *Maturity date.* Bonds generally have a specified **maturity date** on which the par value is to be repaid. Teletron's bonds, which were issued on January 2, 1986, will mature on January 1, 2001; thus, they had a 15-year maturity at time of issue. Most bonds have **original maturities** (the maturity at the time the bond is issued) of from 10 to 40 years, but this is not a hard and fast rule. Of course, the maturity of a bond declines each year after it has been issued. Thus, Teletron's bonds had a 15-year original maturity, but in 1987 they will have a 14-year maturity, and so on.

**call provision**
A provision in a bond contract that gives the issuer the right to redeem the bonds under specified terms prior to the normal maturity date.

3. *Call provisions.* Some bonds have a provision whereby the issuer may pay them off prior to maturity. This feature is termed a **call provision**, and it is discussed in detail in Chapter 12. If a bond is callable and interest rates in the economy decline, then the company can sell a new issue of low interest rate bonds and use the proceeds to retire the old high-interest-rate issue, just as a homeowner can refinance a home mortgage loan.

**coupon interest rate**
The stated rate of interest on a bond.

4. *Coupon interest rate.* The bond states that the issuer will pay a specified number of dollars of interest each year (or, more generally, each six months). When this *coupon payment*, as it is called, is divided by the par value, the result is the **coupon interest rate**. For example, Teletron Electronics' bonds have a $1,000 par value and pay $150 in interest each year. The bond's cou-

pon interest is $150, so its coupon interest rate is $150/$1,000 = 15 percent. The $150 is the yearly "rent" on the $1,000 loan. This payment, which is fixed at the time the bond is issued, remains in force, by contract, during the life of the bond. Incidentally, some time ago, every bond literally had a number of small (1/2-by-2-inch), dated coupons attached to it, and on the interest payment date, the owner would clip the coupon off and either cash it at his or her bank or mail it to the company's paying agent, who then mailed back an interest check. Long-term bonds had lots of coupons, while short-term bonds had only a few. However, today virtually all bonds are *registered*, and the interest checks are mailed directly to the registered owner of the bond.

**5.** *New issues versus outstanding bonds.* As we shall see, a bond's market price is determined primarily by its coupon interest payment—the higher the coupon, other things held constant, the higher the market price of the bond. At the time a bond is issued, the coupon is generally set at a level that will force the market price of the bond to equal its par value. If a lower coupon were set, investors simply would not be willing to pay $1,000 for the bond, while if a higher coupon were set, investors would clamor for the bond and bid its price up over $1,000. Investment bankers can judge quite precisely the coupon rate which will cause a bond to sell at its $1,000 par value.

A bond that has just been issued is defined as a *new issue*. (*The Wall Street Journal* classifies a new bond as a new issue for about two weeks after it has first been issued.) Once the bond has been on the market for awhile, it is classified as an *outstanding bond*, also called a *seasoned issue*. As we shall see below, although newly issued bonds do generally sell very close to par, the prices of outstanding bonds vary widely from it. Their coupon interest payments are constant; however, since economic conditions change, a bond with a $150 coupon that sells at par when it is issued can sell for more or less than $1,000 thereafter.

## The Basic Bond Valuation Model[1]

As we noted above, bonds call for the payment of a specified amount of interest for a stated number of years and for the repayment of the par value on the bond's maturity date.[2] Thus, a bond represents an annuity plus a lump sum, and its value is found as the present value of this payment stream.

---

[1]In finance the term *model* refers to an equation or set of equations designed to show how one or more variables affect some other variable. Thus, a bond valuation model shows the mathematical relationship between a bond's price and the set of variables that determine it.

[2]Actually, most bonds pay interest semiannually, not annually, which makes it necessary for us to modify our valuation equation slightly. The modification is discussed later in the chapter. Also, we should note that some bonds issued in recent years either pay no interest during their lives ("zero coupon bonds") or else pay very low coupon rates. Such bonds are sold at a discount below par, and hence they are called *original issue discount bonds*, and the "interest" earned on these bonds comes at the end, when the company pays off at par ($1,000) a bond which was purchased for, say, $321.97. The discount of $1,000 − $321.97 = $678.03 amounts to interest. Original issue discount bonds are discussed at greater length in Chapter 12.

The following equation is used to find a bond's value:

$$\text{Value} = V = \sum_{t=1}^{n} I\left(\frac{1}{1 + k_d}\right)^t + M\left(\frac{1}{1 + k_d}\right)^n \tag{5-1}$$

$$= I(\text{PVIFA}_{k_d,n}) + M(\text{PVIF}_{k_d,n}).$$

Here

I = dollars of interest paid each year = coupon interest rate × par value.

M = par value, or maturity value, which is typically $1,000.

$k_d$ = appropriate rate of interest on the bond.[3]

n = number of years until the bond matures; n declines each year after the bond is issued, so a bond which had a maturity of 30 years when it was issued (original maturity = 30 years) becomes a 29-year bond a year later, then a 28-year bond, and so on.

We can use Equation 5-1 to find the value of Teletron's bonds when they were issued. Simply substitute $150 for I, $1,000 for M, and the values of PVIFA and PVIF at 15 percent, 15 periods, as found in Tables A-2 and A-1 at the end of the book:

$$V = \$150(5.8474) + \$1,000(0.1229)$$
$$= \$877.11 + \$122.90$$
$$= \$1,000.01 \approx \$1,000 \text{ when } k_d = 15\%.$$

Figure 5-1 gives a graphic view of the bond valuation process.

If $k_d$ remained constant at 15 percent, what would the value of the bond be 1 year after it was issued? We can find this value using the same valuation formula, but now the term to maturity is only 14 years—that is, n = 14:

$$V = \$150(5.7245) + \$1,000(0.1413)$$
$$= \$999.98 \approx \$1.000.$$

The value of the bond will remain at $1,000 as long as the appropriate interest rate for it remains constant at 15 percent.[4]

---

[3]How the appropriate interest rate is determined was discussed in Chapter 3. The bond's riskiness and years to maturity, as well as supply and demand conditions in the capital markets, all have an influence.

[4]The bond prices quoted by brokers are calculated as described. However, if you bought a bond, you would have to pay this basic price plus accrued interest. Thus, if you purchased a Teletron Electronics bond 6 months after it was issued, your broker would send you an invoice stating that you must pay $1,000 as the basic price of the bond plus $75 interest, representing one-half the annual interest of $150. The seller of the bond would receive $1,075. If you bought the bond the day before its interest payment date, you would pay $1,000 + (364/365)($150) = $1,149.59. Of course, you would receive an interest payment of $150 at the end of the next day.

   Note also that if you have one of the better financial calculators, you can enter values for n, k = i, PMT, and FV = 1,000 and then press the PV button to find the value of the bond. This provides an exact solution only immediately after the interest payment date, but the same limitation applies to the Equation 5-1 solution. Expensive financial calculators have a built-in calendar which permits the calculation of exact values between interest payment dates.

**Figure 5-1**
**Time Line for Teletron Electronics Bonds**

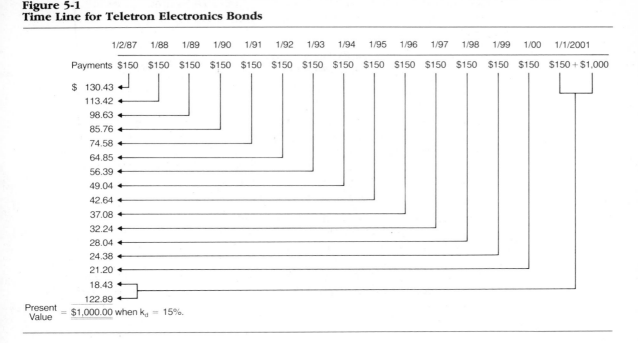

Now suppose interest rates in the economy fell after the Teletron bonds were issued, and as a result $k_d$ *decreased* from 15 to 10 percent. Both the coupon interest payments and the maturity value would remain constant, but now 10 percent values for PVIF and PVIFA would have to be used in Equation 5-1. The value of the bond at the end of the first year would be $1,368.31:

$$V = \$150(\text{PVIFA}_{10\%,14 \text{ years}}) + \$1,000(\text{PVIF}_{10\%,14 \text{ years}})$$
$$= \$150(7.3667) + \$1,000(0.2633)$$
$$= \$1,105.01 + \$263.30$$
$$= \$1,368.31.$$

Thus, the bond would sell at a *premium* over its par value.

The arithmetic of the bond price increase should be clear, but what is the logic behind it? The reason for the increase is simple. The fact that $k_d$ has fallen to 10 percent means that if you had $1,000 to invest, you could buy new bonds like Teletron's (every day some 10 to 12 companies sell new bonds), except that they would pay $100 of interest each year rather than $150. Naturally, you would prefer $150 to $100, so you would be willing to pay more than $1,000 for Teletron's bonds to obtain its higher coupons. All investors would recognize these facts, and as a result, the Teletron bonds would be bid up in price to $1,368.31, at which point they would provide the same rate of return to a potential investor as the new bonds, 10 percent.

Assuming that interest rates remain constant at 10 percent for the next 14 years, what would happen to the value of a Teletron bond? It would fall gradually from $1,368.31 at present to $1,000 at maturity, when Teletron

Electronics must redeem each bond for $1,000. This point can be illustrated by calculating the value of the bond 1 year later, when it has 13 years remaining to maturity:

$$V = \$150(PVIFA_{10\%,13\ years}) + \$1,000(PVIF_{10\%,13\ years})$$
$$= \$150(7.1034) + \$1,000(0.2897) = \$1,355.21.$$

Thus, the value of the bond will have fallen from $1,368.31 to $1,355.21, or by $13.10. If you were to calculate the value of the bond at other future dates, the price would continue to fall as the maturity date approached.

Notice also that if you purchased the bond at a price of $1,368.31 and then sold it 1 year later, with $k_d$ still at 10 percent, you would have a capital loss of $13.10, or a total return of $150.00 − $13.10 = $136.90. Your percentage rate of return would consist of an *interest yield* (also called a *current yield*) plus a *capital gains yield*, calculated as follows:

$$
\begin{aligned}
\text{Interest, or current, yield} &= \$150/\$1,368.31 &= 0.1096 &= 10.96\% \\
\text{Capital gains yield} &= -\$13.10/\$1,368.31 &= -0.0096 &= \underline{-0.96\%} \\
\text{Total rate of return, or yield} &= \$136.90/\$1,368.31 &= 0.1001 &\approx \underline{10.00\%}
\end{aligned}
$$

Had interest rates risen from 15 to 20 percent during the first year after issue rather than fallen, the value of Teletron's bonds would have declined to $769.49:

$$V = \$150(PVIFA_{20\%,14\ years}) + \$1,000(PVIF_{20\%,14\ years})$$
$$= \$150(4.6106) + \$1,000(0.0779)$$
$$= \$691.59 + \$77.90$$
$$= \$769.49.$$

In this case, the bond would sell at a *discount* below its par value. Its total expected future yield would again consist of a current yield and a capital gains yield, and the latter would be *positive*. The total yield would, of course, be 20 percent.

The discount or premium on a bond may also be calculated as follows:

$$\text{Discount or premium} = \left(\begin{array}{c}\text{Interest payment} \\ \text{on old bond}\end{array} - \begin{array}{c}\text{Interest payment} \\ \text{on new bond}\end{array}\right)\left(PVIFA_{k_d,n}\right),$$

where n = years to maturity on the old bond and $k_d$ = current rate of interest, or yield to maturity, on the new bond. For example, if interest rates had risen to 20 percent 1 year after the Teletron bonds were issued, the discount on them would have been calculated as follows:

$$\text{Discount} = (\$150 - \$200)(4.6106) = -\$230.53.$$

(The minus sign indicates discount.) This value agrees, except for rounding, with the value calculated above:

$$\text{Discount} = \text{Price} - \text{Par value} = \$769.49 - \$1,000.00 = -\$230.51.$$

From these calculations, we see that the discount is equal to the present value of the interest payment one sacrifices to buy a low-coupon old bond rather than a high-coupon new bond. The longer the bond has to run, the greater the sacrifice and hence the greater the discount.

Figure 5-2 graphs the value of the bond over time assuming that interest rates in the economy either remain constant at 15 percent, fall to 10 percent and then remain constant at that level, or rise to 20 percent and remain constant at that level. Of course, if interest rates do *not* remain constant, then the price of the bond will fluctuate. However, regardless of what interest rates do, the bond's price will approach $1,000 as it nears the maturity date (barring bankruptcy, in which case the bond's value might drop to zero).

Figure 5-2 illustrates the following key points:

**1.** Whenever the going rate of interest, $k_d$, is equal to the coupon rate, a bond will sell at its par value.

**2.** Whenever the going rate of interest is *above* the coupon rate, a bond will sell below its par value. Such a bond is called a **discount bond**.

**3.** Whenever the going rate of interest is *below* the coupon rate, a bond will sell above its par value. Such a bond is called a **premium bond**.

**4.** An increase in interest rates will cause the price of an outstanding bond to fall, while a decrease in rates will cause it to rise.

**5.** The market value of a bond will approach its par value as its maturity date approaches.

These points are very important, for they show that bondholders may suffer capital losses or make capital gains depending on whether interest rates rise or fall—and, as we saw in Chapter 3, interest rates do indeed change over time.

**discount bond**
A bond that sells below its par value; occurs when the coupon rate is lower than the going rate of interest.

**premium bond**
A bond that sells above its par value; occurs when the coupon rate is above the going rate of interest.

---

**Figure 5-2**
**Time Path of the Value of a 15% Coupon, $1,000 Par Value Bond**
**When Interest Rates Are 10%, 15%, and 20%**

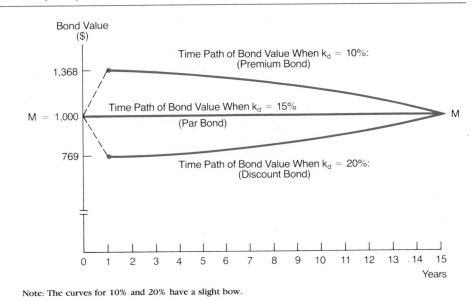

Note: The curves for 10% and 20% have a slight bow.

### Finding the Interest Rate on a Bond: Yield to Maturity

Suppose you were offered a 14-year, 15 percent coupon, $1,000 par value bond at a price of $1,368.31. What rate of interest would you earn if you bought the bond and held it to maturity? This rate is defined as the bond's **yield to maturity**, or **YTM**, and it is the interest rate discussed by bond traders when they talk about rates of return. To find the yield to maturity, you could solve the following equation for $k_d$:

**yield to maturity (YTM)**
The rate of return earned on a bond if it is held to maturity.

$$V = \$1,368.31 = \frac{\$150}{(1 + k_d)^1} + \frac{\$150}{(1 + k_d)^2} + \cdots + \frac{\$150}{(1 + k_d)^{14}} + \frac{\$1,000}{(1 + k_d)^{14}}$$

$$= \$150(\text{PVIFA}_{k_d,14}) + \$1,000(\text{PVIF}_{k_d,14}).$$

We can substitute values for PVIFA and PVIF until we find a pair that "works" and forces this equality:

$$\$1,368.31 = \$150(\text{PVIFA}_{k_d,14}) + \$1,000(\text{PVIF}_{k_d,14}).$$

What would be a good interest rate to use as a starting point? First, we know that since the bond is selling at a premium over its par value ($1,368.31 versus $1,000), the bond's yield to maturity must be *below* its 15 percent coupon rate. Therefore, we might try a rate of 12 percent. Substituting factors for 12 percent, we obtain

$$\$150(6.6282) + \$1,000(0.2046) = \$1,198.83 \neq \$1,368.31.$$

Our calculated bond value, $1,198.83, is *below* the actual market price, so the YTM is *not* 12 percent. To raise the calculated value, we must *lower* the interest rate used in the process. Inserting factors for 10 percent, we obtain

$$V = \$150(7.3667) + \$1,000(0.2633)$$
$$= \$1,105.01 + \$263.30$$
$$= \$1,368.31.$$

This calculated value is equal to the market price of the bond; thus, 10 percent is the bond's yield to maturity: $k_d = \text{YTM} = 10.0\%$.[5]

---

[5]We found the yield to maturity on this bond by trial and error. It should also be noted that some financial calculators can be used to find the YTM on a bond with very little effort. A few years ago, bond traders all had specialized tables called *bond tables* that gave yields on bonds of different maturities selling at different premiums and discounts. Because calculators are so much more efficient (and accurate), bond tables are rarely used any more.

There is also a formula that can be used to find the *approximate* YTM on a bond:

$$k_d = \text{YTM} \approx \frac{I + (M - V)/n}{(M + V)/2}.$$

In our example, I = $150, M = $1,000, V = $1,368.31, and n = 14, so

$$k_d \approx \frac{\$150 + (\$1,000 - \$1,368.31)/14}{(\$1,000 + \$1,368.31)/2} = 0.1045 = 10.45\%.$$

The exact value is 10 percent, so *this formula should be used only to obtain a starting point for the trial-and-error method.*

The yield to maturity is identical to the total rate of return as discussed in the preceding section. The YTM for a bond that sells at par consists entirely of an interest yield, but if the bond sells at a price other than its par value, the YTM consists of the interest yield plus a positive or negative capital gains yield. Note also that a bond's yield to maturity changes whenever interest rates in the economy change—and this is almost daily. One who purchases a bond and holds it until it matures will receive the YTM that existed on the purchase date, but the bond's calculated YTM will change frequently.

## Yield to Call

If you had bought a bond that was callable and the company called it, you would not have the option of holding it until it matured, so the yield to maturity would not be applicable. For example, if a firm had callable, 15 percent coupon bonds outstanding and interest rates fell from 15 percent to 10 percent, then the company could call in the 15 percent bonds, replace them with 10 percent bonds, and save \$150 − \$100 = \$50 interest per bond per year. This is beneficial to the company, but not to bondholders.

**yield to call (YTC)**
The rate of return earned on a bond if it is redeemed before its maturity date.

If current interest rates are well below an outstanding bond's coupon rate, then a callable bond is likely to be called, and investors should estimate the expected rate of return on the bond as the **yield to call (YTC)** rather than as the yield to maturity. To calculate the YTC, solve this equation for $k_d$:

$$\text{Price of bond} = \sum_{t=1}^{N} \frac{I}{(1 + k_d)^t} + \frac{\text{Call price}}{(1 + k_d)^N}.$$

Here N = years until the company can call the bond; call price is the price the company must pay in order to call the bond (it is often set equal to the par value plus one year's interest); and $k_d$ is the YTC. In the balance of the chapter, we assume that bonds are not callable unless otherwise noted.

## Bond Values with Semiannual Compounding

Although some bonds do pay interest annually, most actually pay interest semiannually. To evaluate semiannual payment bonds, we must modify the valuation model (Equation 5-1) as follows:

**1.** Divide the annual coupon interest payment by 2 to determine the amount of interest paid each 6 months.

**2.** Multiply the years to maturity, n, by 2 to determine the number of periods.

**3.** Divide the annual interest rate, $k_d$, by 2 to determine the semiannual interest rate.

By making these changes, we arrive at the following equation for finding the value of a bond that pays interest semiannually:

$$V = \sum_{t=1}^{2n} \frac{I}{2}\left(\frac{1}{1 + \dfrac{k_d}{2}}\right)^t + M\left(\frac{1}{1 + \dfrac{k_d}{2}}\right)^{2n} \tag{5-1a}$$

$$= \frac{I}{2}\left(\text{PVIFA}_{k_d/2,2n}\right) + M(\text{PVIF}_{k_d/2,2n}).$$

To illustrate, assume now that Teletron Electronics' bonds pay $75 interest each 6 months rather than $150 at the end of each year. Thus, each interest payment is only half as large, but there are twice as many of them. When the going rate of interest is 10 percent, the value of this 15-year bond is found as follows:

$$V = \$75(PVIFA_{5\%,30 \text{ periods}}) + \$1,000(PVIF_{5\%,30 \text{ periods}})$$
$$= \$75(15.3725) + \$1,000(0.2314)$$
$$= \$1,152.94 + \$231.40$$
$$= \$1,384.34.$$

The $1,384.34 value with semiannual interest payments is slightly larger than $1,380.32, the value when interest is paid annually. This higher value occurs because interest payments are received somewhat faster under semiannual compounding.

Students sometimes want to discount the maturity value at 10 percent over 15 years, rather than at 5 percent over 30 six-month periods. This is incorrect—logically, all cash flows in a given contract must be discounted on the same basis, semiannually in this instance. For consistency, bond traders *must* apply semiannual compounding to the maturity value, and they do.

### Interest Rate Risk on a Bond

As we saw in Chapter 3, interest rates go up and down over time, and as they change, the values of outstanding bonds also fluctuate. Suppose you bought some 15 percent Teletron bonds at a price of $1,000 and interest rates subsequently rose to 20 percent. As we saw above, the price of the bonds would fall to $769.49, so you would have a loss of $230.51 per bond.[6] Interest rates can and do rise, and rising rates cause a loss of value for bondholders. Thus, people or firms who invest in bonds are exposed to risk from changing interest rates, or **interest rate risk**.

**interest rate risk**
The risk to which investors are exposed due to changing interest rates.

One's exposure to interest rate risk is higher on bonds with long maturities than on those maturing in the near future. This point can be demonstrated by showing how the value of a 1-year bond with a 15 percent coupon fluctuates with changes in $k_d$ and then comparing these changes with those on a 14-year bond as calculated above. The 1-year bond's values at different interest rates are shown here:

Value at $k_d = 10\%$:

$$V = \$150(PVIFA_{10\%,1 \text{ year}}) + \$1,000(PVIF_{10\%,1 \text{ year}})$$
$$= \$150(0.9091) + \$1,000(0.9091)$$
$$= \$136.37 + \$909.10 = \$1,045.47.$$

---

[6]You would have an *accounting* (and tax) loss only if you sold the bond; if you held it to maturity, you would not have such a loss. However, even if you did not sell, you would still have suffered a *real economic loss in an opportunity cost sense*, because you would have lost the opportunity to invest at 20 percent and would be stuck with a 15 percent bond in a 20 percent market. So, in finance we regard "paper losses" as being just as bad as realized accounting losses.

Value at $k_d$ = 15%:

$$V = \$150(0.8696) + \$1,000(0.8696)$$
$$= \$130.44 + \$869.60 = \$1,000.04 \approx \$1,000.$$

Value at $k_d$ = 20%:

$$V = \$150(0.8333) + \$1,000(0.8333)$$
$$= \$125.00 + \$833.30 = \$958.30.$$

The values of the 1-year and 14-year bonds at different current market interest rates are summarized and plotted in Figure 5-3. Notice how much

**Figure 5-3**
**Value of Long- and Short-Term 15% Coupon Rate Bonds**
**at Different Market Interest Rates**

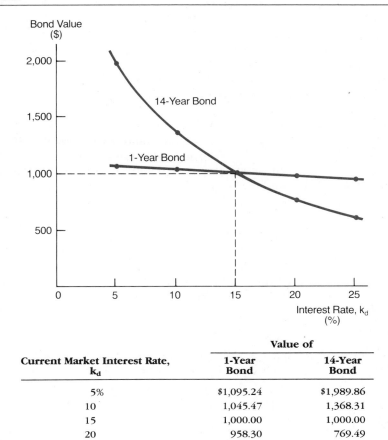

| Current Market Interest Rate, $k_d$ | Value of | |
|---|---|---|
| | 1-Year Bond | 14-Year Bond |
| 5% | $1,095.24 | $1,989.86 |
| 10 | 1,045.47 | 1,368.31 |
| 15 | 1,000.00 | 1,000.00 |
| 20 | 958.30 | 769.49 |
| 25 | 920.00 | 617.59 |

more sensitive the price of the long-term bond is to changes in interest rates. At a 15 percent interest rate, both the long- and the short-term bonds are valued at $1,000. When rates rise to 20 percent, the long-term bond falls to $769.49 while the short-term bond falls only to $958.30. A similar situation occurs when rates fall below 15 percent.

*For bonds that are selling at par, this differential sensitivity to changes in interest rates always holds true—the longer the maturity of the bond, the greater its price changes in response to a given change in interest rates.* Thus, even if the risk of default on two bonds is exactly the same, the one with the longer maturity is typically exposed to more risk from a rise in interest rates.

The logical explanation for this difference in interest rate risk is simple. Suppose you bought a 14-year bond that yielded 15 percent, or $150 a year. Now suppose interest rates on comparable-risk bonds rose to 20 percent. You would be stuck with only $150 of interest for the next 14 years. On the other hand, had you bought a 1-year bond, you would have a low return for only 1 year. At the end of the year, you would get your $1,000 back, and you could then reinvest it and receive 20 percent, or $200 per year, for the next 13 years. Thus, interest rate risk reflects the length of time one is committed to a given investment.[7]

**reinvestment rate risk**
Risk that income will decline when the funds received from maturing short-term bonds are reinvested.

However, buying a 1-year bond instead of a 14-year bond exposes the buyer to **reinvestment rate risk**. Suppose you bought a 1-year bond that yielded 15 percent and then interest rates on comparable-risk bonds fell to 10 percent. Then after 1 year, when you got your $1,000 back, you would have to invest it at only 10 percent, thus losing $150 − $100 = $50 in annual interest. Had you bought the 14-year bond, you would have continued to receive $150 in annual interest payments even if rates fell. Of course, if you intended to spend the $1,000 after 1 year, then investing in a 1-year bond would guarantee (ignoring default risk) that you would get your $1,000 back (plus interest) after 1 year. The 14-year bond investment, on the other hand, if sold after 1 year, would return less than $1,000 if interest rates had risen.

## Bond Prices in Recent Years

We know from Chapter 3 that interest rates have risen sharply in recent years, and we have just seen that the prices of outstanding bonds fall during periods when interest rates are rising. Therefore, one would expect to find that bond prices in the market have fallen in recent years. Figure 5-4 shows what has happened to the price of a typical bond, Southwestern Bell's 6⅞ percent, 40-year issue. When this bond was issued in 1971 it was worth $1,000, but by early 1985 it sold for only $570 due to the rise in interest rates. Note also that it sold as low as $450 in 1981, when interest rates hit an all-time high. The graph also shows that if interest rates remain at the

---

[7]If a 10-year bond were plotted in Figure 5-3, its curve would lie between those of the 14-year bond and the 1-year bond. The curve of a 1-month bond would be almost horizontal, indicating that its price would change very little in response to an interest rate change.

**Figure 5-4**
**Southwestern Bell 40-Year Bond: Present Value as Interest Rates Change**

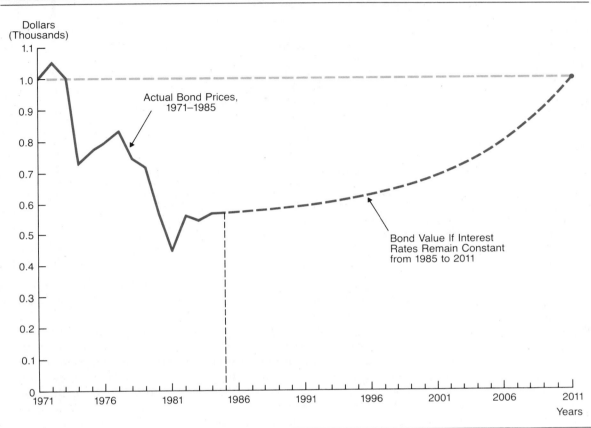

1985 level, the price of the bond will gradually rise, and the bond will be worth exactly $1,000 when it matures in 2011.

## Bond Markets

Corporate bonds are traded primarily in the over-the-counter market: Most bonds are owned by and traded among the large financial institutions (for example, life insurance companies, mutual funds, and pension funds, which deal in very large blocks of securities), and it is relatively easy for the over-the-counter bond dealers to arrange the transfer of large blocks of bonds among the relatively few holders of the bonds. It would be much more difficult to conduct similar operations in the stock market among the literally millions of large and small stockholders, so most stock trades occur on the exchanges.

Information on bond trades in the over-the-counter market is not published, but a representative group of bonds is listed and traded on the bond division of the NYSE. Figure 5-5 gives a section of the bond market page of

**Figure 5-5**
**NYSE Bond Market Transactions, February 22, 1985**

| Bonds | Cur Yld | Vol | High | Low | Close | Net Chg. |
|---|---|---|---|---|---|---|
| SwBT 8¾07 | 12. | 12 | 72⅞ | 71½ | 72½ | − ¼ |
| SwBT 6⅞11 | 12. | 63 | 58¼ | 57 | 57 | −1¼ |
| SwBT 7¾09 | 12. | 15 | 64⅝ | 64⅝ | 64⅝ | + ½ |
| SwBT 7⅜12 | 12. | 35 | 61 | 60½ | 61 | ..... |
| SwBT 7⅝13 | 12. | 10 | 63 | 63 | 63 | + ½ |
| SwBT 8¼14 | 13. | 20 | 67 | 65¾ | 65¾ | −1½ |
| SwBT 9¼15 | 13. | 35 | 74⅝ | 73¾ | 73¾ | − ¾ |
| SwBT 8½16 | 12. | 10 | 68⅝ | 68⅝ | 68⅝ | −1⅜ |
| SwBT 8¼17 | 12. | 71 | 67⅝ | 66¾ | 67 | − ½ |
| SwBT 8¾18 | 12. | 13 | 72⅛ | 70⅝ | 70⅝ | −1¾ |
| SwBT 9⅝19 | 12. | 49 | 77⅞ | 77½ | 77½ | − ⅜ |
| SwBT 11⅜20 | 13. | 164 | 90¾ | 89 | 89½ | − ⅞ |
| SwBT 14¼20 | 13. | 77 | 109⅛ | 108⅜ | 109⅛ | + ⅜ |

Notes:
1. All of the Southwestern Bell bonds traded on February 22, 1985, had 40-year maturities when they were issued except the 7¾s of 2009, which were issued in 1971 and had an original maturity of 38 years.
2. This listing contains only those Southwestern Bell bonds which were traded on the NYSE on February 22, 1985. The company has additional issues outstanding that were not traded on that date.

Source: *The Wall Street Journal,* February 25, 1985. Reprinted by permission of *The Wall Street Journal,* © Dow Jones and Company, Inc., 1985. All rights reserved.

*The Wall Street Journal* on trading for February 22, 1985. A total of 1,057 issues were traded on that date, but we show only the bonds of Southwestern Bell.

The Southwestern Bell and other bonds can have various denominations, but most have a par value of $1,000—this is how much per bond the company borrowed and how much it must someday repay. However, since other denominations are possible, for trading and reporting purposes bonds are quoted as percentages of par. Looking at the second bond listed, which is the one we analyzed in the previous section, we see that there is a 6⅞ just after the company's name; this indicates that the bond is of the series which pays 6⅞ percent interest, or 0.06875($1,000) = $68.75 of interest per year. The 6⅞ percent is the bond's *coupon rate.* The 11 which comes next indicates that this bond must be repaid in the year 2011; it is not shown in the table, but this bond was issued in 1971 and hence had a 40-year original maturity. The 12 in the fourth column is the bond's **current yield**, which is defined as the annual interest payment divided by the closing price of the bond: Current yield = $68.75/$570 = 12.1%, rounded to 12 percent. (Current yields above 9.9 percent are reported to the nearest whole percent.) The 63 in the fifth column indicates that 63 of these bonds were traded on February 22, 1985. Since the prices shown are expressed as a percentage of par, the high of 58¼ percent translates to $582.50; the low was $570; and the bond closed at $570, down 1¼ percent, or $12.50, from the previous day's close.

**current yield**
The annual interest payment on a bond divided by its closing price.

As we discussed earlier, interest rates vary over time, and companies generally set their coupon rates at levels which reflect the "going rate of interest" on the day a bond is issued. If the rates were set lower, investors simply would not buy the bonds at the $1,000 par value, so the company could not borrow the money it needed. Thus, bonds generally sell at their par value when they are issued, but their prices fluctuate whenever interest rates change. Bonds are listed in the newspaper, and hence in Figure 5-5, in the order of the dates on which they were originally issued. Thus, the fact that the coupon rates shown in the table are generally rising as we move down the list reflects the fact that interest rates have generally risen in recent years.

## Common Stock Valuation

Common stock represents the ownership of a corporation, but to the typical investor, a share of common stock is simply a piece of paper distinguished by two features:

**1.** It entitles its owner to dividends, if the company has earnings out of which dividends can be paid and if management chooses to pay dividends rather than retain earnings. Note that whereas a bond contains a *promise* to pay interest, common stock provides no such promise (in an obligatory sense) to pay dividends—if you own a stock you may *expect* a dividend, but your expectations may not in fact be met. To illustrate, Long Island Lighting Company (Lilco) had paid dividends on its common stock for over 50 years, and people expected these dividends to continue, but when the company encountered severe problems in 1984, it stopped paying dividends. However, Lilco continued paying interest on its bonds, because if it had not then it would have been declared bankrupt and the bondholders could, in effect, have taken over the company.

**2.** Stock can be sold at some future date, hopefully at a price that is greater than the purchase price. If the stock is actually sold at a price above its purchase price, the investor will receive a *capital gain*. Generally, at the time people buy common stocks, they do expect to receive capital gains; otherwise, they would not buy the stocks. However, after the fact, one can end up with capital losses rather than capital gains. Lilco's stock price dropped from $17.50 in 1983 to $3.75 in 1984, so investors' *expected* capital gains turned out to be *actual* capital losses.

In Chapter 3 we discussed the markets in which stocks are traded, and in Chapter 11 we shall discuss the rights and privileges of the common stockholders and the process by which new shares are created. Our purpose in this chapter, however, is to analyze models that help explain how stock prices are determined.

### Definitions of Terms Used in the Stock Valuation Models

Common stocks provide an expected future cash flow stream, and a stock's value is found in the same manner as the values of other financial assets, namely, as the present value of a future cash flow stream. The expected cash flows consist of two elements: (1) the dividend expected in each year and (2) the price investors expect to receive when they sell the stock. The final stock price includes the return of the original investment plus a capital gain (or minus a capital loss).

We saw in Chapter 1 that managers seek to maximize the value of their firms' stocks. Through their actions managers affect the stream of income to investors and the riskiness of this stream. Managers need to know how alternative actions will affect stock prices. Therefore, at this point we develop some models to help show how the value of a share of stock is determined under several different sets of conditions. We begin by defining the following terms:

$D_t$ = dividend the stockholder *expects* to receive at the end of Year t.[8] $D_0$ is the most recent dividend, which has already been paid; $D_1$ is the next dividend expected, which will be paid at the end of this year; $D_2$ is the dividend expected at the end of 2 years; and so forth. $D_1$ represents the first cash flow a new purchaser of the stock will receive. Note that $D_0$, the dividend which has just been paid, is known with certainty. All future dividends are expected values, so the estimate of $D_t$ may differ among investors.

**market price**
The price at which a stock sells on the security exchanges.

$P_0$ = actual **market price** of the stock today.

**intrinsic value**
The value of an asset that in the mind of the analyst is justified by the facts; may be different from the asset's current market price and/or its book value.

$\hat{P}_t$ = expected price of the stock at the end of each year t (pronounced "P hat t"). $\hat{P}_0$ is the **intrinsic**, or *expected*, **value** of the stock today as seen by the particular investor doing the analysis; $\hat{P}_1$ is the price expected at the end of 1 year; and so on. Note that $\hat{P}_0$ is the intrinsic value of the stock today based on the investor's estimate of the stock's expected dividend stream and riskiness; hence, whereas $P_0$ is fixed, $\hat{P}_0$ could differ among investors depending on how optimistic they are regarding the company. The caret, or "hat," is used to indicate that $\hat{P}_t$ is an estimated value. $\hat{P}_0$, the investor's intrinsic value, could be above or below $P_0$, the current stock price, but the investor would buy the stock only if $\hat{P}_0$ were equal to or greater than $P_0$. For the average investor, $P_0 = \hat{P}_0$; otherwise, a disequilibrium would exist, and, as we discuss in Chapter 6, buying and selling in the market would force $P_0 = \hat{P}_0$ for the average investor.

**growth rate, g**
The expected rate of growth in dividends per share.

$g$ = expected **growth rate** in dividends as predicted by the investor. (If we assume that dividends are expected to grow at a constant rate, then g is also equal to the expected rate of growth in the stock's price.) Different investors may use different g's to evaluate a firm's stock, but when we use the term g, we generally mean it as estimated by an average, or "representative," investor.

**required rate of return, $k_s$**
The minimum rate of return on common stock that stockholders consider acceptable.

$k_s$ = minimum acceptable or **required rate of return** on the stock, considering both its riskiness and the returns available on other investments. The determinants of $k_s$ will be discussed in detail in Chapter 6.

**expected rate of return, $\hat{k}_s$**
The rate of return on common stock that an individual stockholder actually expects to receive.

$\hat{k}_s$ = **expected rate of return** which the individual who buys the stock actually expects to receive. $\hat{k}_s$ (pronounced "k hat s") could be above or below $k_s$, but one would buy the stock only if $\hat{k}_s$ were equal to or greater than $k_s$.

---

[8]Stocks generally pay dividends quarterly, so theoretically we ought to evaluate them on a quarterly basis. See Appendix 5C in Eugene F. Brigham, *Financial Management*, 4th ed. (Hinsdale, Ill.: Dryden, 1985) for a discussion of quarterly models.

**actual (realized) rate of return, $\bar{k}_s$**
The rate of return on common stock actually received by stockholders. In general it will equal the expected rate of return only in the case of a short-term, riskless security.

**dividend yield**
The ratio of the expected dividend to the current price of a share of stock.

**capital gains yield**
The capital gain during any one year divided by the beginning price.

**expected total return**
The sum of the expected dividend yield and expected capital gains yield on a share of stock.

$\bar{k}_s$ = **actual,** or **realized, rate of return,** pronounced "k bar s." You may *expect* to obtain a return of $\hat{k}_s$ = 15 percent if you buy Exxon stock today, but if the market goes down you may end up with an actual, realized return that is much lower, perhaps even negative.

$D_1/P_0$ = expected **dividend yield** on the stock during the coming year. If the stock is expected to pay a dividend of $1 during the next 12 months and its current price is $10, then the expected dividend yield is $1/$10 = 0.10 = 10%.

$\dfrac{\hat{P}_1 - P_0}{P_0}$ = expected **capital gains yield** on the stock during the coming year. If the stock sells for $10 today and is expected to rise to $10.50 at the end of 1 year, then the expected capital gain is $\hat{P}_1 - P_0$ = $10.50 − $10.00 = $0.50 and the expected capital gains yield is $0.50/$10 = 0.05 = 5%.

Expected total return = expected dividend yield ($D_1/P_0$) plus expected capital gains yield $[(\hat{P}_1 - P_0)/P_0] = \hat{k}_s$ as defined above. In the above example, the **expected total return** $= \hat{k}_s$ = 10% + 5% = 15%.

## Expected Dividends as the Basis for Stock Values

In our discussion of bonds, we found the value of a bond as the present value of interest payments over the life of the bond plus the present value of the bond's maturity (or par) value:

$$V = \frac{I}{(1 + k_d)^1} + \frac{I}{(1 + k_d)^2} + \cdots + \frac{I}{(1 + k_d)^n} + \frac{M}{(1 + k_d)^n}.$$

Stock prices are likewise determined as the present value of a stream of cash flows, and the basic stock valuation equation is similar to the bond valuation equation. What are the cash flows that corporations provide to their stockholders? First, think of yourself as an investor who buys a stock with the intention of holding it (in your family) forever. In this case, all that you (and your heirs) will receive is a stream of dividends, and the value of the stock today is calculated as the present value of an infinite stream of dividends:

$$\text{Value of stock} = \hat{P}_0 = \text{PV of expected future dividends}$$

$$= \frac{D_1}{(1 + k_s)^1} + \frac{D_2}{(1 + k_s)^2} + \cdots + \frac{D_\infty}{(1 + k_s)^\infty}$$

$$= \sum_{t=1}^{\infty} \frac{D_t}{(1 + k_s)^t}. \tag{5-2}$$

What about the more typical case, where you expect to hold the stock for a finite period and then sell it—what will be the value of $\hat{P}_0$ in this case? *The value of the stock is again determined by Equation 5-2.* To see this, recognize that for any individual investor, cash flows consist of dividends plus the sale price of the stock. However, the sale price the current investor receives will be dependent upon the dividends expected by future investors. Therefore, for all present and future investors in total, expected cash flows consist only of future dividends: Unless a firm is liquidated or sold to another concern, the cash flows it provides to its stockholders consist only of a stream of dividends, so the value of a share of its stock is established as the present value of its expected stream of dividends.

The general validity of Equation 5-2 can also be seen by asking this question: Suppose I buy a stock and expect to hold it for 1 year. I will receive dividends during the year as well as the value $\hat{P}_1$ when I sell out at the end of the year. But what will determine the value of $\hat{P}_1$? It will be determined as the present value of the dividends during Year 2 plus the stock price at the end of that year, which in turn will be determined as the present value of another set of future dividends and an even more distant stock price. This process can be continued ad infinitum, and the ultimate result is Equation 5-2.[9]

Equation 5-2 is a generalized stock valuation model in the sense that the time pattern of $D_t$ can be anything: $D_t$ can be rising, falling, or constant, or it

---

[9]Assume that you and all other investors buy a stock expecting to hold it for 1 year and then sell it at price $\hat{P}_1$. $\hat{P}_0$ would be found as follows:

$$\hat{P}_0 = \frac{D_1}{1 + k_s} + \frac{\hat{P}_1}{1 + k_s}. \tag{1}$$

The value of $\hat{P}_1$ would be found as the present value of $D_2$ and $\hat{P}_2$:

$$\hat{P}_1 = \frac{D_2}{1 + k_s} + \frac{\hat{P}_2}{1 + k_s}. \tag{2}$$

We could substitute the Equation 2 value for $\hat{P}_1$ in Equation 1, obtaining Equation 3:

$$\hat{P}_0 = \frac{D_1}{1 + k_s} + \frac{\frac{D_2}{1 + k_s} + \frac{\hat{P}_2}{1 + k_s}}{1 + k_s} \tag{3}$$

$$= \frac{D_1}{(1 + k_s)^1} + \frac{D_2}{(1 + k_s)^2} + \frac{\hat{P}_2}{(1 + k_s)^2}.$$

We could continue in similar fashion, finding the values $\hat{P}_2$, $\hat{P}_3$, and so forth, and at the limit, we would have Equation 5-2:

$$\hat{P}_0 = \frac{D_1}{(1 + k_s)^1} + \frac{D_2}{(1 + k_s)^2} + \ldots + \frac{D_\infty}{(1 + k_s)^\infty}$$

$$= \sum_{t=1}^{\infty} \frac{D_t}{(1 + k_s)^t}. \tag{5-2}$$

Here we developed Equation 5-2 on the assumption that investors have a 1-year investment horizon. If they had longer horizons we would still get to Equation 5-2, but we would simply get there faster—for example, we could start with Equation 3 if investors had 2-year horizons.

We should note that investors periodically lose sight of the long-run nature of stocks as investments and forget that in order to sell a stock at a profit one must find a buyer who will pay the higher price. If you analyze a stock's value in accordance with Equation 5-2, conclude that the stock's market price exceeds a reasonable value, and then buy the stock anyway, then you are following the "bigger fool" theory of investment—you think that you may be a fool to buy the stock at its excessive price, but you also think that when you get ready to sell it you can find someone who is an even bigger fool. The bigger fool theory was widely followed in 1929, just before the Great Depression.

can even fluctuate randomly, and Equation 5-2 will still hold. Often, however, the projected stream of dividends follows a systematic pattern, in which case we can develop a simplified (that is, easier to evaluate) version of the stock valuation model expressed in Equation 5-2. In the following sections we consider the cases of zero growth, constant growth, and nonconstant growth.

## Stock Values with Zero Growth

**zero growth stock**
A common stock whose expected future dividends are equal to some constant amount.

Suppose dividends are expected not to grow at all, but to remain constant. Here we have a **zero growth stock**, for which the dividends expected in future years are equal to some constant amount—that is, $D_1 = D_2 = D_3$ and so on. Therefore, we can drop the subscripts and rewrite Equation 5-2 as follows:

$$\hat{P}_0 = \frac{D}{(1 + k_s)^1} + \frac{D}{(1 + k_s)^2} + \cdots + \frac{D}{(1 + k_s)^n} + \cdots + \frac{D}{(1 + k_s)^\infty}. \quad (5\text{-}2a)$$

**perpetuity**
A security that pays a constant amount each period forever.

As we noted in Chapter 4 in connection with the British consol bond, a security that is expected to pay a constant amount each year forever is defined as a **perpetuity**. Therefore, a zero growth stock may be thought of as a perpetuity. The stock is expected to provide a constant stream of dividends into the indefinite future, but each dividend has a smaller present value than the preceding one, and as n gets very large, the present value of the individual future dividends approaches zero. To illustrate, suppose $D = \$1.82$ and $k_s = 16\% = 0.16$. We can rewrite Equation 5-2a as follows:

$$\hat{P}_0 = \frac{\$1.82}{(1.16)^1} + \frac{\$1.82}{(1.16)^2} + \frac{\$1.82}{(1.16)^3} + \cdots + \frac{\$1.82}{(1.16)^{50}} + \cdots + \frac{\$1.82}{(1.16)^{100}} + \cdots$$

$$= \$1.57 + \$1.35 + \$1.17 + \cdots + \$0.001 + \cdots + \$0.000001 + \cdots.$$

We can also show the perpetuity in graph form, as in Figure 5-6. The horizontal line shows the constant dividend stream, $D_t = \$1.82$. The descending step function curve shows the present value of each future dividend. If we extended the analysis on out to infinity and then summed the present values of all the future dividends, the sum would be equal to the value of the stock.

As we saw in Chapter 4, the value of any perpetuity is simply the cash flow divided by the discount rate, so the value of a zero growth stock reduces to this formula:[10]

$$\hat{P}_0 = \frac{D}{k_s}. \quad (5\text{-}3)$$

Therefore, in our example the value of the stock is \$11.38:

$$\hat{P}_0 = \frac{\$1.82}{0.16} = \$11.38.$$

Thus, if you extended Figure 5-6 on out forever and then added up the present value of each individual dividend, you would end up with the intrinsic

---

[10]Equation 5-3 is derived in Appendix 4B of Eugene F. Brigham, *Financial Management*, 4th ed.

**Figure 5-6**
**Present Values of Dividends of a Zero Growth Stock (Perpetuity)**

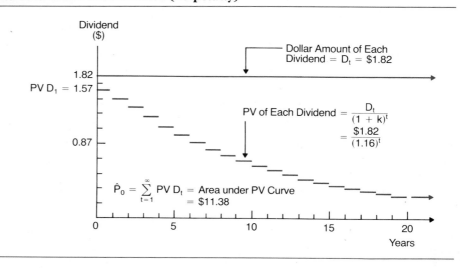

value of the stock, $11.38.[11] The actual market value of the stock, $P_0$, could be greater than, less than, or equal to $11.38, depending on other investors' perceptions of the dividend pattern and riskiness of the stock.

We could transpose the $P_0$ and the $k_s$ in Equation 5-3 and solve for $k_s$. We could then look up the price of the stock and the latest dividend, $P_0$ and D, in the newspaper, and the value $D/P_0$ would be the rate of return we could expect to earn if we bought the stock. Since we are dealing with an *expected rate of return*, we would put a "hat" on the k value to produce Equation 5-4:

$$\hat{k}_s = \frac{D}{P_0}. \qquad (5\text{-}4)$$

Thus, if we bought the stock at a price of $11.38 and expected to receive a constant dividend of $1.82, our expected rate of return would be

$$\hat{k}_s = \frac{\$1.82}{\$11.38} = 0.16 = 16\%.$$

Before leaving this section, we should note that Equations 5-3 and 5-4 are also applicable to *preferred stock*, a type of stock that (generally) pays a constant dividend in perpetuity. Preferred stock is discussed in detail in Chapter 13.

---

[11]If you think that having a stock pay dividends forever is unrealistic, then think of it as lasting only for 50 years. Here we would have an annuity of $1.82 per year for 50 years. The PV of a 50-year annuity would be $1.82(6.2463) = $11.37, which would differ by only a penny from that of the perpetuity. Thus, the dividends from Years 51 to infinity would not contribute much to the value of the stock.

## Normal, or Constant, Growth

Although the zero growth model is applicable to some companies, the earnings and dividends of most companies are expected to increase each year. While expected growth rates vary from company to company, dividend growth in general is expected to continue in the foreseeable future at about the same rate as that of the nominal gross national product (real GNP plus inflation). On this basis, it is expected that an average, or "normal," company will grow at a rate of 8 to 10 percent a year. Thus, if a **normal**, or **constant**, **growth** company's last dividend, which has already been paid, was $D_0$, its dividend in any future Year t may be forecasted as $D_t = D_0(1 + g)^t$, where g is the constant expected rate of growth. For example, if Teletron Electronics just paid a dividend of $1.82 (that is, $D_0 = \$1.82$) and investors expect a 10 percent growth rate, then the estimated dividend 1 year hence will be $D_1 = \$1.82(1.10) = \$2.00$; $D_2$ will be $2.20; and the estimated dividend 5 years hence will be

**normal (constant) growth**
Growth which is expected to continue into the foreseeable future at about the same rate as that of the economy as a whole.

$$D_t = D_0(1 + g)^t = \$1.82(1.10)^5 = \$2.93.$$

Using this method of estimating future dividends, the current value, $\hat{P}_0$, could be determined by Equation 5-2 as set forth above—in other words, we find the expected future cash flow stream (the dividends), calculate the present value of each dividend payment, and then sum these present values to find the value of the stock. Thus, the intrinsic value of the stock is equal to the present value of its expected future dividends.

However, if g is constant, then Equation 5-2 may be simplified as follows:[12]

$$\hat{P}_0 = \frac{D_0(1 + g)}{k_s - g} = \frac{D_1}{k_s - g}. \tag{5-5}$$

Inserting values into Equation 5-5, we find the value of this stock to be $33.33:

$$\hat{P}_0 = \frac{\$1.82(1.10)}{0.16 - 0.10} = \frac{\$2.00}{0.06} = \$33.33.$$

**constant growth model**
Also called the Gordon Model, it is used to find the value of a constant growth stock.

The **constant growth model** expressed in Equation 5-5 is often called the Gordon Model, after Myron J. Gordon, who did much to develop and popularize it.

Note that Equation 5-5 is sufficiently general to encompass the zero growth case described above: If growth is zero, this is simply a special case of constant growth, and Equation 5-5 is equal to Equation 5-3. Note also that a necessary condition for the derivation of Equation 5-5 is that $k_s$ be greater than g. If the equation is used where $k_s$ is not greater than g, the results will be meaningless.

The concept underlying the stock valuation process is graphed in Figure 5-7 for the case of a 10 percent constant growth rate. Dividends are growing,

---

[12]Equation 5-5 is derived in Appendix 5B of Eugene F. Brigham, *Financial Management*, 4th ed.

**Figure 5-7**
**Present Values of Dividends of a Constant Growth Stock:**
$D_0 = \$1.82, g = 10\%, k_s = 16\%$

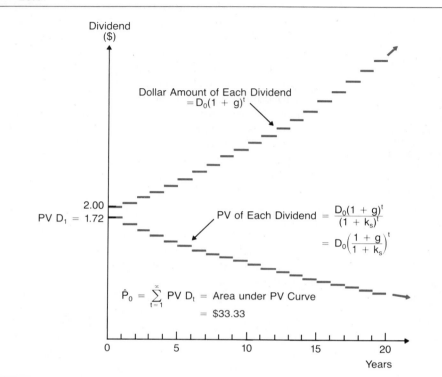

but since $k_s > g$, the present value of each future dividend is declining. For example, the dividend in Year 1 is $D_1 = D_0(1 + g)^1 = \$1.82(1.10) = \$2.00$. The present value of this dividend, discounted at 16 percent, is $PV(D_1) = \$2.00/(1.16)^1 = \$2.00/1.16 = \$1.72$. The dividend expected in Year 2 grows to $\$2.00(1.10) = \$2.20$, but the present value of this dividend falls to \$1.64. Continuing, $D_3 = \$2.42$ and $PV(D_3) = \$1.55$, and so on. Thus, the expected dividends are growing, but the present values of the successive dividends are declining.

If we added up the present values of each future dividend, this summation would be the value of the stock, $\hat{P}_0$—and, as we have seen, when g is a constant, this summation is equal to $D_1/(k_s - g)$, the value of Equation 5-5. Therefore, if we extended the lower step function curve in Figure 5-7 on out to infinity and added up the present values of each future dividend, the summation would be identical to the value given by the formula, \$33.33.

Growth in dividends occurs primarily as a result of growth in *earnings per share (EPS)*. Earnings growth, in turn, results from a number of factors, including (1) inflation and (2) the amount of earnings the company reinvests. Regarding inflation, if output (in units) is stable, and if both sales prices and input costs rise at the inflation rate, then EPS will grow. EPS will also grow as a result of the reinvestment, or plowback, of earnings. If the firm's earnings are not all paid out as dividends (that is, if some fraction of earnings is retained), then the dollars of investment behind each share will rise over time, which should lead to rising earnings and dividends.

## Expected Rate of Return on a Constant Growth Stock

We can solve Equation 5-5 for $k_s$, again using the hat to denote that we are dealing with an expected rate of return:[13]

$$\begin{array}{ccc} \text{Expected rate} \\ \text{of return} \end{array} = \begin{array}{c} \text{Expected} \\ \text{dividend} \\ \text{yield} \end{array} + \begin{array}{c} \text{Expected} \\ \text{capital} \\ \text{gains yield} \end{array}$$

$$\hat{k}_s = \frac{D_1}{P_0} + g. \qquad (5\text{-}6)$$

Thus, if you buy a stock for a price $P_0 = \$33.33$, and if you expect the stock to pay a dividend $D_1 = \$2.00$ one year from now and to grow at a constant rate $g = 10\%$ in the future, then your expected rate of return is 16 percent:

$$\hat{k}_s = \frac{\$2.00}{\$33.33} + 10\% = 6\% + 10\% = 16\%.$$

In this form, we see that $\hat{k}_s$ is the *expected total return*, and that it consists of an *expected dividend yield*, $D_1/P_0 = 6\%$, plus an *expected growth rate or capital gains yield*, $g = 10\%$.

Suppose the analysis described above had been conducted on January 1, 1986, so $P_0 = \$33.33$ was the January 1, 1986, stock price and $D_1 = \$2.00$ was the dividend expected at the end of 1986. What should the stock price be at the end of 1986 (or the beginning of 1987)? We would again apply Equation 5-5, but this time we would use the 1987 dividend, $D_2 = D_1(1 + g) = \$2.00(1.10) = \$2.20$:

$$\hat{P}_{1/1/1987} = \frac{D_{1987}}{k_s - g} = \frac{\$2.20}{0.16 - 0.10} = \$36.67.$$

---

[13]Equation 5-6 is derived from 5-5 as follows:

$$\hat{P}_0 = \frac{D_1}{k_s - g} \qquad (5\text{-}5)$$

$$k_s\hat{P}_0 - g\hat{P}_0 = D_1$$

$$k_s\hat{P}_0 = D_1 + g\hat{P}_0$$

$$\hat{k}_s = D_1/P_0 + g. \qquad (5\text{-}6)$$

The $k_s$ value of Equation 5-5 is a *required* rate of return, but when we transform to obtain Equation 5-6, we are finding an *expected* rate of return. Obviously, the transformation requires that $k_s = \hat{k}_s$. This equality holds if the stock market is in equilibrium, a condition discussed at length in Chapter 6.

Now notice that \$36.67 is 10 percent greater than $P_0$, the \$33.33 price on January 1, 1986:

$$\$36.67 \approx \$33.33(1.10).$$

Thus, we would expect to make a capital gain of $\$36.67 - \$33.33 = \$3.34$ during the year for a capital gains yield of 10 percent:

$$\text{Capital gains yield} = \frac{\$3.34}{\$33.33} = 0.10 = 10\%.$$

We could extend the analysis on out, and in each future year the expected capital gains yield would always equal g, the expected dividend growth rate.

The dividend yield in 1987 can be estimated as follows:

$$\text{Dividend yield}_{1987} = \frac{D_{1987}}{\hat{P}_{1/1/87}} = \frac{\$2.20}{\$36.67} = 0.06 = 6\%.$$

The dividend yield for 1988 could also be calculated, and again it would be 6 percent. Thus, *for a constant growth stock*, these conditions will hold:

**1.** The dividend is expected to grow at a constant rate, g.

**2.** The stock price is expected to grow at this same rate.

**3.** The expected dividend yield is a constant.

**4.** The expected capital gains yield is also a constant, and it is equal to g.

**5.** The expected total rate of return, $\hat{k}_s$, is equal to the expected dividend yield plus the expected growth rate.

## Supernormal, Or Nonconstant, Growth

Firms typically go through *life cycles*. During the early part of the cycles, their growth is much faster than that of the economy as a whole; then they match the economy's growth; and finally their growth is slower than that of the economy. Automobile manufacturers in the 1920s and computer and office equipment manufacturers in the 1980s are examples of firms in the early part of the cycle, and these firms are called **supernormal**, or **nonconstant**, **growth** firms. Figure 5-8 illustrates such nonconstant growth and compares it with normal growth, zero growth, and negative growth.[14]

The dividends of the supernormal growth firm are expected to grow at a 30 percent rate for 3 years, after which the growth rate is expected to fall to 10 percent, the assumed norm for the economy. The value of this firm, like

**supernormal (nonconstant) growth**
The part of the life cycle of a firm in which its growth is much faster than that of the economy as a whole.

---

[14]A negative growth rate indicates a declining company. A mining company whose profits are falling because of a declining ore body is an example. Someone buying such a company would expect its earnings, and consequently its dividends and stock price, to decline each year, and this would lead to capital losses rather than capital gains. Obviously, a declining company's stock price will be low, and its dividend yield must be high enough to offset the expected capital loss and still produce a competitive total return. Students sometimes argue that they would not be willing to buy a stock whose price was expected to decline. However, if the annual dividends are large enough to *more than offset* the falling stock price, the stock could be a bargain.

**Figure 5-8**
**Illustrative Dividend Growth Rates**

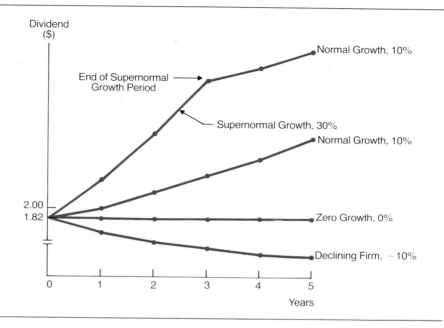

any other, is the present value of its expected future dividends as determined by Equation 5-2. In the case where $D_t$ is growing at a constant rate, we simplified Equation 5-2 to $\hat{P}_0 = D_1/(k_s - g)$. In the supernormal case, however, the expected growth rate is not a constant—it declines at the end of the period of supernormal growth. To find the value of such stock, or any nonconstant growth stock when the growth rate will eventually stabilize, we proceed in three steps:

**1.** Find the PV of the dividends during the period of nonconstant growth.

**2.** Find the price of the stock at the end of the nonconstant growth period, at which point it has become a constant growth stock, and then discount this price back to the present.

**3.** Add these two components to find the intrinsic value of the stock, $\hat{P}_0$.

To illustrate the process for valuing nonconstant growth stocks, suppose the following facts exist:

$k_s$ = stockholders' required rate of return = 16%.

N = years of supernormal growth = 3.

$g_s$ = rate of growth in both earnings and dividends during supernormal growth period = 30%.

$g_n$ = rate of growth after supernormal period = 10%.

$D_0$ = last dividend the company paid = $1.82.

The valuation process is graphed in Figure 5-9 and explained in the steps set forth below:

**Step 1.** Find the PV of dividends paid (PV $D_t$) at the end of Years 1 to 3 using this procedure:

| $D_0$ | × $FVIF_{30\%,t}$ = | $D_t$ | × $PVIF_{16\%,t}$ = | PV $D_t$ |
|---|---|---|---|---|
| $D_1$: $1.82 × | 1.3000 = | $2.366 × | 0.8621 = | $2.040 |
| $D_2$:   1.82 × | 1.6900 = | 3.076 × | 0.7432 = | 2.286 |
| $D_3$:   1.82 × | 2.1970 = | 3.999 × | 0.6407 = | 2.562 |
| | | Sum of PVs of supernormal period dividends = | | $6.888 |

**Step 2.** Find the PV of the dividends expected in Year 4 and thereafter. This requires that we (a) first find the expected value of the stock at the end of Year 3 and (b) then find the present value of the Year 3 stock price:

**a.**
$$\hat{P}_3 = \frac{D_4}{k_s - g_n} = \frac{D_0(1 + g_s)^3(1 + g_n)}{k_s - g_n} = \frac{D_3(1 + g_n)}{0.16 - 0.10}$$

$$= \frac{\$3.999(1.10)}{0.06} = \frac{\$4.399}{0.06} = \$73.32.$$

**b.**   PV $\hat{P}_3$ = $73.32($PVIF_{16\%,3\text{ years}}$) = $73.32(0.6407) = $46.98.

**Step 3.** Find $\hat{P}_0$, the value of the stock today:

$$\hat{P}_0 = \$6.89 + \$46.98 = \$53.87.$$

**Figure 5-9**
**Time Line for Finding the Value of a Supernormal Growth Stock**

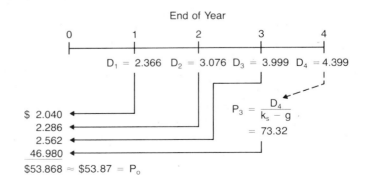

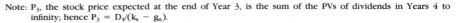

Note: $P_3$, the stock price expected at the end of Year 3, is the sum of the PVs of dividends in Years 4 to infinity; hence $P_3 = D_4/(k_s - g_n)$.

## Comparing Companies with Different Expected Growth Rates

It is useful to summarize our discussion of stock valuation models by comparing companies with the four growth situations graphed in Figure 5-8. There we have a zero growth company, one with a constant 10 percent expected growth rate, one whose earnings are expected to decline at the rate of 10 percent a year, and one whose growth rate is nonconstant.

We can use the valuation equations developed above to determine the stock prices, dividend yields, capital gains yields, total expected returns, and price/earnings (P/E) ratios for the four companies; these are shown in Table 5-1.[15] We assume that each firm had earnings per share (EPS) of $3.41 during the preceding reporting period (that is, $EPS_0 = \$3.41$) and paid out 53.3 percent of its reported earnings as dividends. Therefore, dividends per share last year, $D_0$, were $1.82 for each company, but the values of $D_1$ differ among the firms.

The value of each stock equals its market price, and the expected and required return is 16 percent on each; thus, $\hat{k}_s = k_s = 16\%$. For the declining firm, this return consists of a high current dividend yield, 26 percent, combined with a capital loss amounting to 10 percent a year. For the zero growth firm there is neither a capital gain nor a capital loss expectation, so the 16 percent return must be obtained entirely from the dividend yield. The normal growth firm provides a 6 percent current dividend yield plus a 10 percent per year capital gains expectation. Finally, the supernormal growth firm has a low current dividend yield but a high capital gains expectation.

What is expected to happen to the prices of the four illustrative firms' stocks over time? Three of the four cases are straightforward: The zero growth firm's price is expected to be constant; the declining firm is expected to have a falling stock price; and the constant growth firm's stock price is expected to grow at a constant rate, 10 percent. We do not prove it here, but we could show that the supernormal firm's stock price growth rate starts at 11.6 percent per year but declines to 10 percent as the supernormal growth period ends.

## Actual Stock Prices and Returns

Our discussion thus far has focused on *expected* stock prices and *expected* rates of return. Anyone who has ever invested in the stock market knows that there can be and generally are large differences between *expected* and *realized* prices and returns. To illustrate, on January 1, 1981, IBM's stock price

---

[15]Price/earnings ratios relate a stock's price to its earnings per share (EPS). The higher the P/E ratio, the more investors are willing to pay for a dollar of the firm's current earnings. Other things held constant, investors will pay more for a dollar of current earnings of a rapidly growing firm than for one of a slow growth company; hence, rapid growth companies generally have high P/E ratios. These ratios are discussed in more detail in Chapter 7. The relationships between the P/E ratios, shown in the last column of Table 5-1, are similar to what one would intuitively expect—the higher the expected growth rate (all other things the same), the higher the P/E ratio.

We should note too that differences in P/E ratios among firms can also arise from differences in the required rates of return, $k_s$, which investors use in capitalizing the future dividend streams. If one company has a higher P/E ratio than another, this could be caused by a higher g, a lower $k_s$, or a combination of these two factors.

**Table 5-1
Prices, Dividend Yields, and Price/Earnings Ratios
for 16 Percent Returns under Different
Growth Assumptions**

| | | Price | Current Dividend Yield ($D_1/P_0$) | Capital Gains Yield in Year 1 $[(P_1 - P_0)/P_0]$ | Total Expected Return | P/E Ratio[a] |
|---|---|---|---|---|---|---|
| Declining constant growth ($-10\%$) | $\hat{P}_0 = \dfrac{D_1}{k_s - g} = \dfrac{\$1.64}{0.16 - (-0.10)}$ = | $6.31 | 26% | $-10.0\%$ | 16% | 1.85 |
| Zero growth (0%) | $\hat{P}_0 = \dfrac{D}{k_s} = \dfrac{\$1.82}{0.16}$ = | 11.38 | 16 | 0.0 | 16 | 3.34 |
| Normal constant growth (10%) | $\hat{P}_0 = \dfrac{D_1}{k_s - g} = \dfrac{\$2.00}{0.16 - 0.10}$ = | 33.33 | 6 | 10.0 | 16 | 9.77 |
| Supernormal growth | $\hat{P}_0 =$ (See Steps 1-3 above) = | 53.87 | 4.4 | 11.6[b] | 16 | 15.79 |

[a]It was assumed at the beginning of this example that each company is earning $3.41 initially. This $3.41, divided into the various prices, gives the indicated P/E ratios.

We might also note that as the supernormal growth rate declines toward the normal rate (or as the time when this decline will occur becomes more imminent), the high P/E ratio must approach the normal P/E ratio—that is, the P/E of 15.79 will decline year by year and equal 9.77, that of the normal growth company, in the third year.

Note also that $D_1$ differs for each firm. It is calculated as follows:

$$D_1 = EPS_0(1 + g)(\text{Fraction of earnings paid out}) = \$3.41(1 + g)(0.533).$$

For the declining firm, $D_1 = \$3.41(0.90)(0.533) = \$1.64.$

[b]With k = 16% and $D_1/P_0$ = 4.4%, the capital gains yield must be 16.0% − 4.4% = 11.6%. We could calculate the expected price of the stock at the end of the year, $\hat{P}_1$, using the supernormal growth procedures to confirm that the capital gains yield in Year 1 is indeed 11.6 percent, but this is not necessary.

was $67.875 per share. Its 1980 dividend, $D_0$, had been $3.44, and the consensus view among security analysts was that IBM would experience a growth rate of about 11 percent in the future. Thus, an average investor who bought IBM at $67.875 would have expected to earn a return of about 16.6 percent:

$$\hat{k}_s = \begin{array}{c} \text{Expected} \\ \text{dividend} \\ \text{yield} \end{array} + \begin{array}{c} \text{Expected growth rate} \\ \text{or expected capital} \\ \text{gains yield} \end{array}$$

$$= \frac{D_0(1 + g)}{P_0} + g$$

$$= \frac{\$3.82}{\$67.875} + 11\%$$

$$= 5.6\% + 11.0\% = 16.6\%.$$

In fact, things did not work out as expected. The economy in 1981 was weaker than had been predicted, so IBM's earnings did not grow as expected and its dividend remained at $3.44. Further, interest rates soared during 1981, and capital was attracted out of the stock market and into the bond market to take advantage of the high interest rates. As a result of these two events, IBM's price declined, and it closed on December 31, 1981, at $46.875, down $11 for the year. Thus, on a beginning-of-the-year investment of $67.875, the actual return on IBM for 1981 was $-11.1$ percent:

$$\bar{k}_s = \begin{matrix} \text{Actual} \\ \text{dividend} \\ \text{yield} \end{matrix} + \begin{matrix} \text{Actual} \\ \text{capital gains} \\ \text{yield} \end{matrix}$$

$$= \frac{\$3.44}{\$67.875} + \frac{-\$11}{\$67.875}$$

$$= 5.1\% - 16.2\% = -11.1\%.$$

Most other stocks had experiences in 1981 that were similar to that of IBM.

However, the economy improved after 1981, and IBM's dividend and stock price improved apace. The total realized return on IBM in 1982 increased dramatically to 77 percent; in 1983 it was a strong 30 percent; it dropped to 5 percent in 1984; and thus far in 1985 it has been about 20 percent. On average, the realized return on IBM stock has been about 20 percent, which is somewhat above the rate of return investors expected. Year-to-year deviations were much greater.

Panel a of Figure 5-10 shows how the price of an average share of stock has varied in recent years, and Panel b shows how total realized returns have varied. The market has gone up in some years and down in others, and the stocks of individual companies have likewise gone up and down. We know from theory that expected returns as estimated by an average investor are always positive, but in some years, as Panel b shows, negative returns were realized. Of course, even in bad years some individual companies do well, so the "name of the game" in security analysis is to pick the winners. Also, financial managers attempt to take actions which will put their companies into the winners' column, but they do not always succeed. In subsequent chapters, we will examine the actions that managers can take to increase the odds of their firms' doing relatively well in the marketplace.

## Stock Market Reporting

Figure 5-11, taken from a daily newspaper, is a section of the stock market page which lists stocks on the NYSE. For each stock listed it provides specific data on the trading that took place on February 20, 1985, as well as other, more general information. Similar information is available on stocks listed on the other exchanges and also on stocks traded over-the-counter. Stocks are listed alphabetically, from AAR Industries to Zurn Industries; the data in Figure 5-11 were taken from the top of the listing. The two columns on the left show the highest and lowest prices at which the stocks have sold during the past year; AAR, the first company shown, has traded in the range from $23½ to $16⅛ (or from $23.50 to $16.125) during the preceding 52 weeks. The figure just to the right of the company's abbreviated name is the dividend; AAR had a current indicated annual dividend rate of 48 cents per share and a dividend yield (which is the dividend divided by the closing stock price) of 2.3 percent. Next comes the ratio of the stock's price to its annual earnings

**Figure 5-10**
**Stock Prices and Total Returns, 1953-1984**

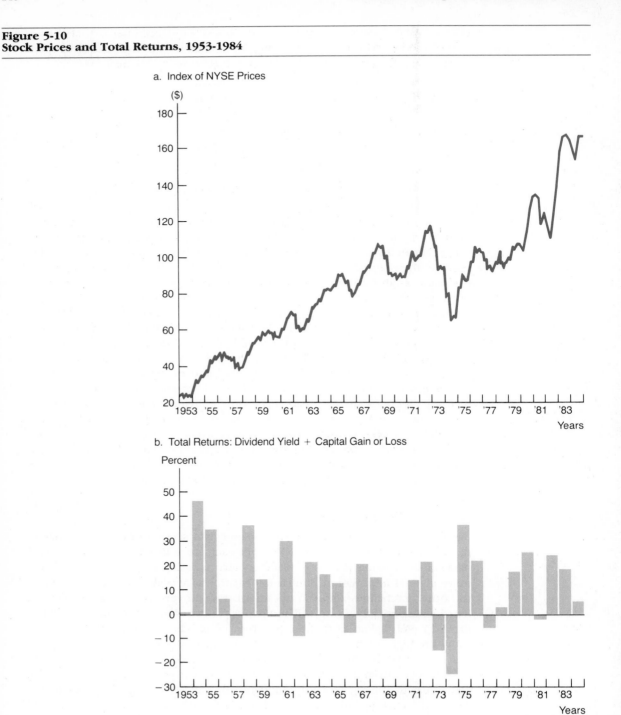

a.  Index of NYSE Prices

b.  Total Returns: Dividend Yield  +  Capital Gain or Loss

Source: *Federal Reserve Bulletins,* given years. Stock prices are based on the Standard and Poor's 500 index.

**Figure 5-11**
**Stock Market Transactions, February 20, 1985**

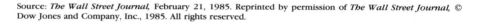

| 52 Weeks High | Low | Stock | Div. | Yld. % | P-E Ratio | Sales 100s | High | Low | Close | Net Chg. |
|---|---|---|---|---|---|---|---|---|---|---|
| | | — A – A – A — | | | | | | | | |
| $23^{1}/_2$ | $16^{1}/_8$ | AAR | .48 | 2.3 | 16 | 77 | $21^{1}/_4$ | 21 | 21 | ..... |
| $24^{1}/_8$ | $9^{3}/_8$ | AGS | .. | 12 | 50 | $15^{3}/_4$ | $15^{1}/_2$ | $15^{1}/_2$ | – $^{1}/_4$ |
| $18^{1}/_4$ | $12^{1}/_8$ | AMCA | .. | .. | 132 | $12^{3}/_8$ | d$11^{7}/_8$ | 12 | – $^{1}/_8$ |
| $17^{7}/_8$ | $13^{1}/_8$ | AMF | .50 | 3.0 | 37 | 441 | $16^{5}/_8$ | $16^{1}/_8$ | $16^{1}/_2$ + $^{1}/_4$ |
| $39^{7}/_8$ | $24^{1}/_4$ | AMR | .. | 9 | 7673 | u$40^{7}/_8$ | $38^{3}/_4$ | $40^{3}/_8$ + $^{1}/_2$ |
| $20^{1}/_4$ | $18^{1}/_4$ | AMR | pf2.18 | 11. | .. | 26 | 20 | 20 | 20 | ..... |
| $14^{1}/_4$ | $8^{1}/_2$ | APL | .. | 3 | .15 | $11^{1}/_8$ | $10^{7}/_8$ | $10^{7}/_8$ – $^{3}/_8$ |
| $69^{3}/_4$ | $44^{3}/_4$ | ASA | 2 | 4.0 | .. | 338 | $50^{3}/_8$ | 50 | $50^{1}/_8$ – $^{1}/_8$ |
| 27 | 16 | AVX | .32 | 1.3 | 15 | 303 | $25^{1}/_4$ | $24^{5}/_8$ | 25 + $^{3}/_8$ |
| $48^{3}/_4$ | $36^{3}/_4$ | AbtLab | 1.20 | 2.5 | 15 | 3881 | u49 | $48^{1}/_4$ | $48^{1}/_2$ + $^{1}/_8$ |
| $25^{7}/_8$ | $16^{1}/_2$ | AccoWd | s.44 | 1.9 | 19 | 217 | $23^{1}/_2$ | $23^{1}/_4$ | $23^{1}/_2$ ... |
| $23^{7}/_8$ | $12^{1}/_2$ | AcmeC | .40 | 2.3 | .. | 164 | 18 | $17^{1}/_2$ | $17^{3}/_4$ + $^{1}/_4$ |
| $10^{3}/_4$ | $8^{1}/_4$ | AcmeE | .32b | 3.2 | 12 | 8 | 10 | 10 | 10 + $^{1}/_8$ |
| $17^{3}/_8$ | 15 | AdaEx | 2.11e | 12. | .. | 72 | 17 | $16^{5}/_8$ | 17 + $^{1}/_4$ |
| $19^{7}/_8$ | $11^{7}/_8$ | AdmMl | .32 | 1.6 | 8 | 53 | u20 | $19^{1}/_2$ | 20 + $^{1}/_2$ |
| $19^{1}/_2$ | $8^{5}/_8$ | AdvSys | .81t | 6.8 | 19 | 167 | $11^{7}/_8$ | $11^{1}/_2$ | $11^{7}/_8$ + $^{3}/_8$ |
| $41^{1}/_8$ | $25^{1}/_8$ | AMD | .. | 14 | 3817 | $33^{7}/_8$ | $32^{5}/_8$ | $33^{3}/_4$ + $1^{1}/_8$ |
| $12^{3}/_4$ | $6^{7}/_8$ | Advest | .12 | 1.1 | .. | 88 | $11^{3}/_8$ | 11 | $11^{1}/_4$ – $^{1}/_8$ |
| $14^{5}/_8$ | $8^{3}/_4$ | Aerflex | .. | 14 | 69 | $14^{1}/_4$ | $13^{3}/_4$ | 14 | ..... |
| $42^{5}/_8$ | $27^{1}/_4$ | AetnLf | 2.64 | 6.5 | 39 | 2411 | 41 | $40^{1}/_8$ | $40^{5}/_8$ – $^{1}/_4$ |
| $58^{3}/_4$ | $52^{3}/_8$ | AetL | pf5.87e | 11. | .. | 9 | $55^{7}/_8$ | $55^{7}/_8$ | $55^{7}/_8$ + $^{1}/_4$ |
| $32^{1}/_8$ | $15^{3}/_4$ | Ahmns | 1.20 | 4.0 | 17 | 3294 | $30^{3}/_8$ | 30 | $30^{1}/_4$ ... |
| $4^{7}/_8$ | $2^{5}/_8$ | Aileen | .. | 30 | 27 | $3^{1}/_8$ | 3 | 3 | ..... |
| 51 | $36^{1}/_2$ | AirPrd | 1.20 | 2.4 | 11 | 502 | $50^{7}/_8$ | $49^{7}/_8$ | 50 – $^{5}/_8$ |
| $24^{1}/_4$ | 13 | AirbFrt | .60 | 2.5 | 13 | 59 | $23^{7}/_8$ | $23^{3}/_4$ | $23^{3}/_4$ ... |

(the P/E ratio), followed by the volume of trading for the day: 7,700 shares of AAR stock were traded on February 20, 1985. Following the volume come the high and the low prices for the day and then the closing price. On February 20, AAR traded as high as $21¼ and as low as $21, while the last trade was at $21. The last column gives the change from the closing price on the previous day. AAR had no change in price, so the previous close must have been $21.

There are two other points to note in Figure 5-11: (1) The "pf" following the stock name of the lower of the two AMR listings tells us that this is an issue of preferred rather than common stock. (Incidentally, AMR Corporation is the name of the company that owns American Airlines.) (2) The "u" preceding AbtLab's daily high indicates that the $49 price is a new 52-week high. Note that the reported yearly high and low listing in the left columns does not include the current trading day.

## Postscript

At the beginning of the chapter we discussed some recent events in the bond and stock markets, and we asked some questions about those events. We are now in a position to consider answers to the questions.

**1.** PG&E bonds, as well as U.S. Treasury bonds, sell at different prices because they were issued at different times and carry higher or lower coupons. Investors who bought when interest rates were high did well, while those who bought when rates were low have suffered losses.

**2.** The Bank of America bonds that currently sell for only $442 are zero coupon bonds—they pay no interest, but pay $1,000 when they mature in

1992. Thus, the value of these bonds is simply the PV of $1,000 discounted back from 1992 to 1985, so the bonds must sell for less than $1,000 as long as interest rates exceed zero. Investors paid less than $1,000 when the bonds were issued, so the fact that the bonds sell for only $442 does not necessarily indicate that anyone has lost on the bonds. Baldwin United's bonds, on the other hand, were issued for $1,000, and they are selling for only $300 because the company was recently forced into bankruptcy and people don't know whether or not the company will be able to pay either the interest of $100 per year or the $1,000 principal when it comes due in 2009. Because of B-U's high risk, investors assign a very high value to $k_d$—33.4% rather than the 12 percent or so that applies to stronger companies.

**3.** The stock market examples point out several interesting things. CBS and ABC were both under the influence of takeover attempts—CBS by Ted Turner and Turner Broadcasting, and ABC by Capital Cities Broadcasting. In both cases potential acquirers believed that the assets would be more profitable if they were managed differently. ABC apparently will be taken over by Capital Cities, but CBS seems to be holding off Turner. Even so, CBS has agreed to increase its use of debt, and this additional leverage may boost EPS and consequently DPS.

**4.** Apple and Storage Technology were both doing extraordinarily well until quite recently. Their sales and earnings were doubling every couple of years, and while they paid no dividends, investors were forecasting that they would begin to pay dividends soon. (Their stocks were evaluated with Equation 5-2, with the $D_t$ term set at zero for the first few years and then set at values which were based on estimated earnings.) Now, though, future profit forecasts have been revised downward, and some analysts question whether the companies can even survive as independent entities.

**5.** IBM, a primary cause of Apple's and Storage Technology's woes, epitomizes the established, stable company—its earnings are relatively predictable, as are its dividends and its stock price. "Relatively predictable" does not mean easy to predict—just easier than for firms like Apple and Storage Technology.

The most interesting questions posed in the chapter opener were these: What actions can management take to insure that its stock goes up rather than down, and how can you, as an investor, pick winners in the stock and bond markets? Most of this book is aimed at answering those questions, so at this point all we can say is: "Wait and see."

## Summary

Corporate decisions should be analyzed in terms of how alternative courses of action are likely to affect the value of a firm. It is necessary to know how bond and stock prices in general are established before attempting to measure how a given decision will affect a specific firm's value. Accordingly, this chapter showed how bond and stock values are established, as well as how investors go about estimating the rates of return they expect to receive on these securities if they purchase them at the existing market prices. In all cases, security values were found to be *the present value of the future cash flows expected from the security*. The cash flows from a bond consist of interest payments plus the bond's maturity value, while stocks provide a stream of dividends plus a sale price.

The following equation is used to find the value of an annual coupon bond:

$$V = \sum_{t=1}^{n} \frac{I}{(1 + k_d)^t} + \frac{M}{(1 + k_d)^n}$$

$$= I(PVIFA_{k_d,n}) + M(PVIF_{k_d,n}).$$

Here V is the value of the bond; I is the annual interest payment, or coupon; n is years to maturity; $k_d$ is the appropriate interest rate; and M is the bond's maturity value, generally $1,000. This equation can also be solved for $k_d$, which is called the *yield to maturity (YTM)*. If the bond pays interest semiannually, as most do, we must divide I and $k_d$ by 2 and multiply n by 2 before applying the formula.

Several different stock valuation formulas were developed, including the ones for zero and for constant growth:

$$\text{Zero growth stock: } \hat{P}_0 = \frac{D}{k_s}.$$

$$\text{Constant, or normal, growth stock: } \hat{P}_0 = \frac{D_1}{k_s - g}.$$

Here $\hat{P}_0$ is the current price of the stock; D is the expected constant dividend; $D_1$ is the dividend expected during the next year; $k_s$ is the required rate of return on the stock; and g is the expected growth rate. In the latter equation, g is a constant; if g is not a constant, then the nonconstant growth procedure must be used to find the stock's value.

We can express the equation for the *expected rate of return* on a constant growth stock as follows:

$$\hat{k}_s = \frac{D_1}{P_0} + g.$$

In this form we see that the total expected return, $\hat{k}_s$, consists of an *expected dividend yield* plus an *expected capital gains yield*. For constant growth stocks, the dividend and capital gains components of total yield are constant over time. For supernormal growth stocks, the dividend yield rises over time, while the capital gains component declines, with the total yield remaining constant.

We saw that differences can and do exist between expected and actual returns in the stock and bond markets—only for short-term, riskless assets do expected and actual (or realized) returns equal each other.

Throughout the chapter we used "appropriate" discount rates, $k_d$ for bonds and $k_s$ for stocks. In Chapter 3, we learned that $k_d$ is composed of a pure rate of interest plus premiums for inflation and risk. In Chapter 6, we shall examine the factors that determine $k_s$. Then, in the remainder of the book, we will consider the types of actions that a firm's financial manager can take to lower the discount rate and to increase the expected growth rate, both of which will increase the value of the firm's stock.

## Questions

**5-1**    Define each of the following terms:
- a. Bond
- b. Par value; maturity date; call provision
- c. Coupon interest rate
- d. Premium; discount bond
- e. Current yield (on a bond); yield to maturity (YTM); yield to call (YTC)
- f. Interest rate risk; reinvestment rate risk
- g. Intrinsic value; market price
- h. Required rate of return, $k_s$; expected rate of return, $\hat{k}_s$; actual, or realized, rate of return, $\bar{k}_s$
- i. Capital gains yield; dividend yield; expected total return
- j. Perpetuity; zero growth stock
- k. Normal, or constant, growth; supernormal, or nonconstant, growth

**5-2**    Two investors are evaluating AT&T's stock for possible purchase. They agree on the expected value of $D_1$ and also on the expected future dividend growth rate. Further, they agree on the riskiness of the stock. However, one investor normally holds stocks for 2 years, while the other holds stocks for 10 years. Based on the type of analysis done in this chapter, they should both be willing to pay the same price for AT&T's stock. True or false? Explain.

**5-3**    A bond that pays interest forever and has no maturity date is a perpetual bond. In what respect is a perpetual bond similar to a no-growth common stock and to a share of preferred stock?

**5-4**    Is it true that the following equation can be used to find the value of an n-year bond that pays interest once a year?

$$\text{Value} = \sum_{t=1}^{n} \frac{\text{Annual interest}}{(1 + k_d)^t} + \frac{\text{Par value}}{(1 + k_d)^n}.$$

**5-5**    "The values of outstanding bonds change whenever the going rate of interest changes. In general, short-term interest rates are more volatile than long-term interest rates. Therefore, short-term bond prices are more sensitive to interest rate changes than are long-term bond prices." Is this statement true or false? Explain.

**5-6**    The rate of return you would get if you bought a bond and held it to its maturity date is defined as the bond's yield to maturity. If interest rates in the economy rise after a bond has been issued, what will happen to its YTM? Does the amount of time to maturity affect its YTM?

**5-7**    If you buy a *callable* bond and interest rates decline, will the value of your bond rise as much as it would have if the bond had not been callable?

**5-8**    If you bought a share of common stock, you would typically expect to receive dividends plus capital gains. Would you expect the distribution between dividend yield and capital gains to be influenced by the firm's decision to pay more dividends rather than retain and reinvest more of its earnings?

**5-9**    The next expected dividend, $D_1$, divided by the current price of a share of stock, $P_0$, is defined as the stock's expected dividend yield. What is the relationship between the dividend yield, the total yield, and the remaining years of supernormal growth for a supernormal growth firm?

5-10   Is it true that the following expression can be used to find the value of a constant growth stock?

$$\hat{P}_0 = \frac{D_0}{k_s + g}.$$

## Self-Test Problems *(Solutions on Page 150)*

ST-1   You are considering buying the stock of two very similar companies. Both companies are expected to earn $3 per share this year. However, Company D (for "dividend") is expected to pay all of its earnings out as dividends, while Company G (for "growth") is expected to pay out only one-third of its earnings, or $1. D's stock price is $20. Which of the following is most likely to be true? G and D are equally risky.
  a. Company G will have a faster growth rate than Company D. Therefore, G's stock price should be greater than $20.
  b. Although G's growth rate should exceed D's, D's current dividend exceeds that of G, and this should cause D's price to exceed G's.
  c. An investor in Stock D will get his or her money back faster because D pays out more of its earnings as dividends. Thus, in a sense, D is like a short-term bond, and G is like a long-term bond. Therefore, if economic shifts cause $k_d$ and $k_s$ to increase, and if the expected streams of dividends from D and G remain constant, then Stocks D and G will both decline, but D's price should decline further.
  d. D's expected and required rate of return is $\hat{k}_s = k_s = 15\%$. G's expected return will be higher because of its higher expected growth rate.
  e. Based on the available information, the best estimate of G's growth rate is 10 percent.

ST-2   The Franklin Corporation issued a new series of bonds on January 1, 1966. The bonds were sold at par ($1,000), have a 12 percent coupon, and mature in 30 years, on December 31, 1996. Coupon payments are made semiannually (on June 30 and December 31).
  a. What was the YTM of the bond on January 1, 1966?
  b. What was the price of the bond on January 1, 1971, 5 years later, assuming that the level of interest rates had fallen to 10 percent?
  c. Find the current yield and capital gains yield on the bond on January 1, 1971, given the price as determined in Part b.
  d. On July 1, 1986, the bonds sold for $896.64. What was the YTM at that date?
  e. What were the current yield and capital gains yield on July 1, 1986?
  f. Now assume that you purchase an outstanding bond on March 1, 1986. The going rate of interest is 15.5 percent. How large a check must you write to complete the transaction? Hard question!

ST-3   Karp Company's current stock price is $24, and its last dividend was $1.60. In view of Karp's stong financial position and its consequent low risk, its required rate of return is only 12 percent. If dividends are expected to grow at a constant rate, g, in the future, and if $k_s$ is expected to remain at 12 percent, what is Karp's expected stock price 5 years from now?

ST-4    Miniscule Computer Chips, Inc., is experiencing a period of rapid growth. Earnings and dividends are expected to grow at a rate of 18 percent during the next 2 years, at 15 percent in the third year, and then at a constant rate of 6 percent thereafter. Miniscule's last dividend was $1.15, and the required rate of return on the stock is 12 percent.

a. Calculate the value of the stock today.

b. Calculate $\hat{P}_1$ and $\hat{P}_2$.

c. Calculate the dividend yield and capital gains yield for Years 1, 2, and 3.

## Problems

Bond valuation            5-1    The Hayes Company has two bond issues outstanding. Both bonds pay $100 annual interest plus $1,000 at maturity. Bond L has a maturity of 15 years and Bond S a maturity of 1 year.

a. What will be the value of each of these bonds when the going rate of interest is (1) 6 percent, (2) 9 percent, and (3) 12 percent? Assume that there is only one more interest payment to be made on Bond S.

b. Why does the longer-term (15-year) bond fluctuate more when interest rates change than does the shorter-term bond (1-year)?

Yield to maturity         5-2    The Coronet Company's bonds have 4 years remaining to maturity. Interest is paid annually; the bonds have a $1,000 par value; and the coupon interest rate is 8 percent.

a. What is the yield to maturity at a current market price of (1) $825 or (2) $1,107?

b. Would you pay $825 for one of these bonds if you thought that the appropriate rate of interest was 10 percent; that is, $k_d = 10\%$? Explain your answer.

Bond valuation            5-3    Suppose Exxon sold an issue of bonds with a 10-year maturity, a $1,000 par value, a 12 percent coupon rate, and semiannual interest payments.

a. Two years after the bonds were issued, the going rate of interest on bonds such as these fell to 8 percent. At what price would the bonds sell?

b. Suppose that 2 years after the issue the going interest rate had risen to 14 percent. At what price would the bonds sell?

c. Suppose the conditions in Part a existed—that is, interest rates fell to 8 percent 2 years after the issue date. Suppose further that the interest rate remained at 8 percent for the next 8 years. What would happen to the price of the Exxon bonds over time?

Perpetual bond valuation  5-4    The bonds of the Stanroy Corporation are perpetuities bearing an 11 percent coupon. Bonds of this type currently yield 10 percent, and their par value is $1,000.

a. What is the price of the Stanroy bonds?

b. Suppose interest rate levels rise to the point where such bonds now yield 14 percent? What would be the price of the Stanroy bonds?

c. Suppose interest rate levels drop to 11 percent. At what price would the Stanroy bonds sell?

d. How would your answers to Parts a, b, and c change if the bonds had a definite maturity of 20 years?

**Constant growth stock valuation**

**5-5** Your broker offers to sell you some shares of Jasper Carriage Company common stock that paid a dividend of $2 *last year*. You expect the dividend to grow at the rate of 6 percent per year for the next 3 years, and if you buy the stock you plan to hold it for 3 years and then sell it.

a. Find the expected dividend for each of the next 3 years; that is, calculate $D_1$, $D_2$, and $D_3$. Note that $D_0 = \$2$.

b. Given that the appropriate discount rate is 12 percent and that the first of these dividend payments will occur 1 year from now, find the present value of the dividend stream; that is, calculate the PV of $D_1$, $D_2$, and $D_3$, and sum these PVs.

c. You expect the price of the stock 3 years from now to be $42.08; that is, you expect $\hat{P}_3$ to equal $42.08. Discounted at a 12 percent rate, what is the present value of this expected future stock price? In other words, calculate the PV of $42.08.

d. If you plan to buy the stock, hold it for 3 years, and then sell it for $42.08, what is the most you should pay for it?

e. Use Equation 5-5 to calculate the present value of this stock. Assume that $g = 6\%$, and it is a constant.

f. Is the value of this stock dependent upon how long you plan to hold it? In other words, if your planned holding period were 2 years or 5 years rather than 3 years, would this affect the value of the stock today, $\hat{P}_0$?

**Return on common stock**

**5-6** You buy a share of stock for $35.33. You expect it to pay dividends of $1.06, $1.1236, and $1.1910 in Years 1, 2, and 3, respectively, and you expect to sell it at a price of $42.08 at the end of 3 years.

a. Calculate the growth rate in dividends.

b. Calculate the current dividend yield.

c. Assuming that the calculated growth rate is expected to continue, you can add the dividend yield to the expected growth rate to get the expected total rate of return. What is this stock's expected total rate of return?

**Constant growth stock valuation**

**5-7** Investors require a 20 percent rate of return on Company M's stock ($k_s = 20\%$).

a. What will be the stock's value if the previous dividend was $D_0 = \$2$ and investors expect dividends to grow at a constant compound annual rate of (1) $-5$ percent, (2) 0 percent, (3) 5 percent, and (4) 15 percent?

b. Using data from Part a, what is the Gordon (constant growth) model value for Company M's stock if the required rate of return is 20 percent and the expected growth rate is (1) 20 percent or (2) 25 percent? Are these reasonable results? Explain.

c. Is it reasonable to expect that a constant growth stock would have $g > k_s$?

**Stock price reporting**

**5-8** Look up the prices of IBM's stock and bonds in *The Wall Street Journal* (or some other newspaper which provides this information).

a. What was the stock's price range over the last year?

b. What is IBM's dividend? What is its dividend yield?

c. What change occurred in IBM's stock price the day the newspaper was published?

d. If IBM were to sell a new issue of $1,000 par value long-term bonds, approximately what coupon interest rate would it have to set on the bonds if it wanted to bring them out at par?

e. If you had $10,000 and wanted to invest it in IBM, what return would you expect to get if you bought the bonds, and what return if you bought IBM's stock? (Hint: Think about capital gains when you answer the latter part of this question.)

**Discount bond valuation**     **5-9**     In February 1956 the Los Angeles Airport authority issued a series of 3.4 percent, 30-year bonds. Interest rates rose substantially in the years following the issue, and as they did, the price of the bonds declined. In February 1969, 13 years later, the price of the bonds had dropped from $1,000 to $650. Assume annual interest payments.

a. Each bond originally sold at its $1,000 par value. What was the yield to maturity of these bonds at their time of issue?

b. Calculate the yield to maturity in February 1969.

c. Assume that interest rates stabilized at the 1969 level and stayed there for the remainder of the life of the bonds. What would have been their price in February 1981, when they had 5 years remaining to maturity?

d. What will the price of the bonds be the day before they mature in 1986? Disregard the last interest payment.

e. In 1969 the Los Angeles Airport bonds were called "discount bonds." What happens to the price of discount bonds as they approach maturity? Is there a "built-in capital gain" on such bonds?

f. The coupon interest divided by the market price of a bond is called the bond's *current yield*. What would have been the current yield of a Los Angeles Airport bond (1) in February 1969 and (2) in February 1981? What would have been its capital gains yields and total yields (total yield equals yield to maturity) on those same two dates?

**Declining growth stock valuation**     **5-10**     Ellis Mining Company's ore reserves are being depleted, so its sales are falling. Also, its pit is getting deeper each year, so its costs are rising. As a result, the company's earnings and dividends are declining at the constant rate of 10 percent per year. If $D_0 = \$6$ and $k_s = 15\%$, what is the value of Ellis Mining's stock?

**Supernormal growth stock valuation**     **5-11**     It is now January 1, 1986. Prosun Engineering has just developed a solar panel capable of generating 200 percent more electricity than any solar panel currently on the market. As a result, Prosun is expected to experience a 30 percent annual growth rate for the next 5 years. By the end of 5 years other firms will have developed comparable technology, and Prosun's growth rate will slow to 8 percent per year indefinitely. Stockholders require a return of 12 percent on Prosun stock. The most recent annual dividend ($D_0$), which was paid yesterday, was $1.50 per share.

a. Calculate the expected dividends for 1986, 1987, 1988, 1989, and 1990.

b. Calculate the value of the stock today, $\hat{P}_0$. Proceed by finding the present value of the dividends expected at the end of 1986, 1987, 1988, 1989, and 1990 plus the present value of the stock price which should exist at the end of 1990. The year-end 1990 stock price can be found by using the constant growth equation. Notice that to find the December 31, 1990, price you use the dividend expected in 1991, which is 8 percent greater than the 1990 dividend.

c. Calculate the current dividend yield, $D_1/P_0$, the capital gains yield expected in 1986, and the expected total return (dividend yield plus capital gains yield) for 1986. (Assume that $\hat{P}_0 = P_0$, and recognize that the capital gains yield is equal to the total return minus the dividend yield.) Also, calculate these same three yields for 1990.

d. How might an investor's tax situation affect his or her decision to purchase stocks of companies in the early stages of their lives, when they are growing rapidly, versus stocks of older, more mature firms? When does Prosun Engineering stock become "mature" in this example?

(Do Parts e and f only if you are using the computerized problem diskette.)

e. Suppose your boss tells you that she believes that Prosun's annual growth rate will be only 15 percent over the next 5 years, and that the firm's normal growth rate is only 6 percent. Calculate the expected dividends for the supernormal growth period and the value of the stock today under these assumptions.

f. Suppose your boss also tells you that she regards Prosun as being quite risky, and that she feels that the required rate of return is 15 percent, not 12 percent. Calculate the value of Prosun's stock. What is the stock's current value if you add this assumption? Do the calculations with k values of 20 percent and 25 percent to see how k affects the stock price.

**Supernormal growth stock valuation**  **5-12**  Overseas Motor Corporation (OMC) has been growing at a rate of 25 percent per year in recent years. This same growth rate is expected to last for another 2 years.

a. If $D_0 = \$2$, k = 14%, and $g_n = 6\%$, what is OMC's stock worth today? What are its current dividend yield and capital gains yield?

b. Now assume that OMC's period of supernormal growth is 5 years rather than 2 years. How does this affect its price, dividend yield, and capital gains yield? Answer in words only.

c. What will be OMC's dividend yield and capital gains yield the year after its period of supernormal growth ends? (Hint: These values will be the same regardless of whether you examine the case of 2 or 5 years of supernormal growth; the calculations are trivial.)

d.  Of what interest to investors is the changing relationship between dividend yield and capital gains yield over time?

**Yield to call**  **5-13**    It is now January 1, 1986, and you are considering the purchase of an outstanding bond that was issued on January 1, 1984. The bond has a 10.5 percent annual coupon and a 30-year original maturity (it matures in 2014). There was originally a 5-year call protection (until December 31, 1988), after which time the bond can be called at 110 (that is, at 110 percent of par, or for $1,100). Interest rates have declined since the bond was issued, and the bond is now selling at 115.174 percent, or $1,151.74. You want to determine both the yield to maturity and the yield to call for this bond. (Note: The yield to call considers the impact of a call provision on the bond's probable yield. In the calculation, we assume that the bond will be outstanding until the call date, at which time it will be called. Thus, the investor will have received interest payments for the call-protected period and then will receive the call price, in this case $1,100, on the call date.)

a. What is the yield to maturity in 1986 for this bond? What is its yield to call?

b. If you bought this bond, which return do you think you would actually earn? Explain your reasoning.

c. Suppose the bond had sold at a discount. Would the yield to maturity or the yield to call have been more relevant?

(Do Parts d and e only if you are using the computerized problem diskette.)

d. Suppose the bond's price suddenly jumps to $1,250. What is the yield to maturity now, and the yield to call?

e. Suppose the price suddenly falls to $800; now what would the YTM and YTC be?

## Solutions to Self-Test Problems

ST-1    a. This is not necessarily true. Since G plows back two-thirds of its earnings, its growth rate should exceed that of D, but D pays more dividends ($3 versus $1). We cannot say which stock should have the higher price.

b. Again, we just do not know which price would be higher.

c. This is false. The changes in $k_d$ and $k_s$ would have a greater impact on G—its price would decline more.

d. The total expected return for D is $\hat{k}_D = D_1/P_0 + g = 15\% + 0\% = 15\%$. The total expected return for G will have $D_1/P_0$ less than 15 percent and g greater than 0 percent, but $\hat{k}_G$ should be neither greater nor smaller than D's total expected return, 15 percent, because the two stocks are equally risky.

e. We have eliminated a, b, c, and d, so e should be correct. On the basis of the available information, D and G should sell at about the same price, $20; thus, $\hat{k}_s = 15\%$ for both D and G. G's current dividend yield is $1/$20 = 5\%$. Therefore, g = 15\% - 5\% = 10\%.

a. The bonds were sold at par; therefore, the original YTM equaled the coupon rate of 12%.

b.
$$V = \sum_{t=1}^{50} \frac{\$120/2}{\left(1 + \dfrac{0.10}{2}\right)^t} + \frac{\$1,000}{\left(1 + \dfrac{0.10}{2}\right)^{50}}$$

$$= \$60(PVIFA_{5\%,50}) + \$1,000(PVIF_{5\%,50})$$
$$= \$60(18.2559) + \$1,000(0.0872)$$
$$= \$1,095.35 + \$87.20 = \$1,182.55.$$

c.
$$\text{Current yield} = \text{Annual coupon payment/Price}$$
$$= \$120/\$1,182.55$$
$$= 0.1015 = 10.15\%.$$

$$\text{Capital gains yield} = \text{Total yield} - \text{Current yield}$$
$$= 10\% - 10.15\% = -0.15\%.$$

d.
$$\$896.64 = \sum_{t=1}^{19} \frac{\$60}{(1 + k_d/2)^t} + \frac{\$1,000}{(1 + k_d/2)^{19}}.$$

Use the approximate YTM formula to get a starting point:

$$\text{Approximate YTM} = \frac{I + (M - V)/n}{(M + V)/2}$$

$$= \frac{\$60 + (\$1,000 - \$896.64)/19}{(\$1,000 + \$896.64)/2}$$

$$= 6.90\%.$$

Therefore, $k_d \approx 6.9(2) = 13.8\%$.
Try $k_d = 14\%$:

$$V = I(\text{PVIFA}_{7\%,19}) + M(\text{PVIF}_{7\%,19}).$$
$$\$896.64 = \$60(10.3356) + \$1,000(0.2765)$$
$$= \$620.14 + \$276.50 = \$896.64.$$

Therefore, the YTM on July 1, 1986, was 14 percent.
e.  Current yield $= \$120/\$896.64 = 13.38\%$.

Capital gains yield $= 14\% - 13.38\% = 0.62\%$.

f.  The following time line illustrates the years to maturity of the bond:

| 1/1/86 | 7/1/86 | 1/1/87 | 7/1/87 | 1/1/88 | 12/31/95 |
|---|---|---|---|---|---|

3/1/86

Thus, there are $19\frac{2}{3}$ periods left before the bond matures. Bond traders actually use the following procedure to determine the price of the bond:
1.  Find the price of the bond on the next coupon date, July 1, 1986.

$$V_{7/1/86} = \$60(\text{PVIFA}_{7.75\%,19}) + \$1,000(\text{PVIF}_{7.75\%,19})$$
$$= \$60(9.7788) + \$1,000(0.2421)$$
$$= \$828.83.$$

Note that we could use a calculator to solve for $V_{7/1/86}$ or we could substitute $k = 7.75\%$ and $n = 19$ periods into the equations for PVIFA and PVIF:

$$\text{PVIFA} = \frac{1 - \dfrac{1}{(1 + k)^n}}{k} = \frac{1 - \dfrac{1}{(1 + 0.0775)^{19}}}{0.0775} = 9.7788.$$

$$\text{PVIF} = \frac{1}{(1 + k)^n} = \frac{1}{(1 + 0.0775)^{19}} = 0.2421.$$

2.  Add the coupon, $60, to the bond price to get the total value, TV, of the bond on the next interest payment date: TV = $828.83 + $60.00 = $888.83.

3. Discount this total value back to the purchase date:

$$\text{Value at purchase date (March 1, 1986)} = \$888.83(\text{PVIF}_{7.75\%,4/6})$$
$$= \$888.83(0.9515)$$
$$= \$845.72.$$

Here

$$\text{PVIF}_{7.75\%,2/3} = \frac{1}{(1 + 0.0775)^{2/3}} = \frac{1}{1.0510} = 0.9515.$$

4. Therefore, you would write a check for $845.72 to complete the transaction. Of this amount, $20 = (1/3)(\$60)$ would represent accrued interest and $825.72 would represent the bond's basic value. This breakdown would affect both your taxes and those of the seller.

**ST-3**  The first step is to solve for g, the unknown variable, in the constant growth equation. Since $D_1$ is unknown but $D_0$ is known, substitute $D_0(1 + g)$ as follows:

$$\hat{P}_0 = P_0 = \frac{D_1}{k_s - g} = \frac{D_0(1 + g)}{k_s - g}.$$

$$\$24 = \frac{\$1.60(1 + g)}{0.12 - g}.$$

Solving for g, we find the growth rate to be 5 percent:

$$\$2.88 - \$24\,g = \$1.60 + \$1.60g$$
$$\$25.60g = \$1.28$$
$$g = 0.05 = 5\%.$$

The next step is to use the growth rate to project the stock price 5 years hence:

$$\hat{P}_5 = \frac{D_0(1 + g)^6}{k_s - g}$$

$$= \frac{\$1.60(1.05)^6}{0.12 - 0.05}$$

$$= \$30.63.$$

(Alternatively, $\hat{P}_5 = \$24(1.05)^5 = \$30.63$.)
Therefore, Karp Company's expected stock price 5 years from now, $\hat{P}_5$, is $30.63.

**ST-4**  a. 1. Calculate the PV of the dividends paid during the supernormal growth period:

$$D_1 = \$1.1500(1.18) = \$1.3570.$$
$$D_2 = \$1.3570(1.18) = \$1.6013.$$
$$D_3 = \$1.6013(1.15) = \$1.8415.$$

$$\text{PV D} = \$1.3570(0.8929) + \$1.6013(0.7972) + \$1.8415(0.7118)$$
$$= \$1.2117 + \$1.2766 + \$1.3108$$
$$= \$3.7991 \approx \$3.80.$$

2. Find the PV of the stock's price at the end of Year 3:

$$\hat{P}_3 = \frac{D_4}{k_s - g} = \frac{D_3(1 + g)}{k_s - g}$$

$$= \frac{\$1.8415(1.06)}{0.12 - 0.06}$$

$$= \$32.53.$$

$$PV \; \hat{P}_3 = \$32.53(0.7118) = \$23.15.$$

3. Sum the two components to find the value of the stock today:

$$\hat{P}_0 = \$3.80 + \$23.15 = \$26.95.$$

b.   $\hat{P}_1 = \$1.6013(0.8929) + \$1.8415(0.7972) + \$32.53(0.7972)$
     $= \$1.4298 + \$1.4680 + \$25.9329$
     $= \$28.8307 \approx \$28.83.$

$\hat{P}_2 = \$1.8415(0.8929) + \$32.53(0.8929)$
     $= \$1.6443 + \$29.0460$
     $= \$30.6903 \approx \$30.69.$

c.

| Year | Dividend Yield + | Capital Gains Yield | = Total Return |
|------|------------------|---------------------|----------------|
| 1 | $\frac{\$1.3570}{\$26.95} = 5.04\%$ | $\frac{\$28.83 - \$26.95}{\$26.95} = 6.98\%$ | $\approx 12\%$ |
| 2 | $\frac{\$1.6013}{\$28.83} = 5.55\%$ | $\frac{\$30.69 - \$28.83}{\$28.83} = 6.45\%$ | $\approx 12\%$ |
| 3 | $\frac{\$1.8415}{\$30.69} = 6.00\%$ | $\frac{\$32.53 - \$30.69}{\$30.69} = 6.00\%$ | $\approx 12\%$ |

## Selected Additional References

Many investment textbooks cover stock and bond valuation models in depth and detail. These are some of the good recent ones:

Francis, Jack C., *Investments: Analysis and Management*, 3rd ed. (New York: McGraw-Hill, 1980).

Radcliffe, Robert C., *Investment: Concepts, Analysis, and Strategy* (Glenview, Ill.: Scott, Foresman, 1982).

Reilly, Frank K., *Investment Analysis and Portfolio Management*, 2nd ed. (Hinsdale, Ill.: Dryden, 1985).

Sharpe, William F., *Investments*, 2nd ed. (Englewood Cliffs, N.J.: Prentice-Hall, 1981).

The classic works on stock valuation models are these:

Gordon, Myron J., and Eli Shapiro, "Capital Equipment Analysis: The Required Rate of Profit," *Management Science*, October 1956, 102-110.

Williams, John B., *The Theory of Investment Value* (Cambridge, Mass.: Harvard University Press, 1938).

# 6

# RISK AND RATES OF RETURN

Common sense tells us that required rates of return on investments increase as the investments increase in risk. However, it does not tell us how to measure risk—and, indeed, the proper measurement of risk is rather subtle. To illustrate, consider these two examples:

**1.** Homestake Mining Company is a leading U.S. gold producer. Gold prices are volatile, and since Homestake's profits vary with the price of gold, its earnings also fluctuate widely from year to year. Moreover, it is one of the few New York Stock Exchange companies which has had to cut its dividend in recent years. All this suggests that Homestake is relatively risky and hence that the required rate of return on its stock, $k_s$, should be above those of most other NYSE companies. However, this is not the case; the formula $\hat{k}_s = k_s = D_1/P_0 + g$ indicates that, with any reasonable value for growth, Homestake's $k_s$ in 1985, and all other years, was quite low in relation to most other companies. This, in turn, indicates that investors regard Homestake as being a low-risk company in spite of its fluctuating profits and its unstable dividend stream.

**2.** Such large, strong, and well-diversified companies as Du Pont and General Electric (GE) have more predictable earnings and dividends than do the 1,600 or so smaller NYSE firms. This suggests that Du Pont, GE, and other giant companies should have much less risk and consequently a much lower required rate of return than smaller companies. However, this is not the case: a careful analysis indicates that Du Pont, GE, and other giant firms are not materially less risky than many smaller, more volatile companies.

The reason for these somewhat counterintuitive facts has to do with diversification and its effects on risk. It so happens that Homestake's stock price rises with inflationary expectations, whereas other stocks tend to decline as inflation heats up. Therefore, holding Homestake in a portfolio of "normal" stocks tends to stabilize returns on the entire portfolio. In the case of Du Pont and GE, it turns out that investors, by forming portfolios of the stocks of smaller companies, can and do diversify away much of the risk that would otherwise be inherent in such firms.

We also know that expectations for inflation, along with risk, have an impact on interest rates and required rates of return generally, and consequently on security prices. Inflationary expectations are worked into security prices in various ways. Sometimes the changes are slow and almost imperceptible, but sometimes they are quite rapid. For example, in the spring of 1985, Henry Kaufman, an economist and senior executive of Salomon Brothers (a major Wall Street investment banking firm) and probably the most listened-to interest rate forecaster in the United States, predicted that in 1986 interest rates would increase sharply. Kaufman's forecast caused the Dow Jones Industrial Average to drop by over 15 points within a few hours.

In this chapter we take an in-depth look at how investment risk should be measured and also at how both risk and inflation affect security prices and rates of return.

In Chapter 5 we referred frequently to the terms *appropriate interest rate on debt, $k_d$, and appropriate (or required) rate of return on a common stock, $k_s$.* These rates, which we used to help determine the values of bonds and stocks, depend primarily on the level of the riskless rate of interest, $k_{RF}$, and on the riskiness of the security in question. In this chapter we define the term *risk* as it relates to securities, examine procedures for measuring risk, and then discuss the relationship between risk, returns, and security prices.

## Defining and Measuring Risk

**risk**
The probability that actual future returns will be below expected returns.

**Risk** is defined in *Webster's* as "a hazard; a peril; exposure to loss or injury." Thus, risk refers to the chance that some unfavorable event will occur. If you engage in skydiving, you take a chance with your life—skydiving is risky. If you bet on the horses, you risk losing your money. If you invest in speculative stocks (or, really, *any* stock), you are taking a risk in the hope of making an appreciable return.

To illustrate the riskiness of financial assets, suppose an investor buys $100,000 of short-term government bonds with an interest rate of 10 percent. In this case the yield to maturity on the investment, 10 percent, can be estimated quite precisely, and the investment is defined as being risk-free. However, if the $100,000 were invested in the stock of a company just being organized to prospect for oil in the mid-Atlantic, then the investment's return could not be estimated precisely. One might analyze the situation and conclude that the *expected* rate of return, in a statistical sense, is 20 percent but recognize that the *actual* rate of return could range from, say, +1,000 percent to −100 percent and, because there is a significant danger of a return considerably less than the expected return, describe the stock as being relatively risky.

Investment risk, then, is related to the probability of returns less than the expected return—the greater the chance of low or negative returns, the riskier the investment. However, we can define risk more precisely, and it is useful to do so.

## Probability Distributions

An event's *probability* is defined as the chance that the event will occur. For example, a weather forecaster may state, "There is a 40 percent chance of rain today and a 60 percent chance that it will not rain." If all possible events, or outcomes, are listed, and if a probability is assigned to each event, then the listing is defined as a **probability distribution**. For our weather forecast, we could set up the following probability distribution:

**probability distribution**
A listing of all possible outcomes or events with a probability (chance of occurrence) assigned to each outcome.

| Outcome (1) | Probability (2) | |
|---|---|---|
| Rain | 0.4 = | 40% |
| No rain | 0.6 = | 60% |
| | 1.0 = | 100% |

The possible outcomes are listed in Column 1, while the probabilities of these outcomes, expressed both as decimals and as percentages, are given in Column 2. Notice that the probabilities must sum to 1.0, or 100 percent.

In Chapter 5 we defined the expected rate of return on a stock, $\hat{k}_s$, as the sum of the expected dividend yield plus the expected capital gain. We now examine the probability distribution concept as related to rates of return. To begin, consider the possible rates of return (dividend yield plus capital gain or loss) that you might earn next year on a $10,000 investment in the stock of either Kelly Products, Inc., or U.S. Water Company. Kelly manufactures and distributes computer terminals and equipment for the rapidly growing data transmission industry. Its sales are cyclical, so its profits rise and fall with the business cycle. Further, its market is extremely competitive, and some new company could develop better products which could literally bankrupt Kelly. U.S. Water, on the other hand, supplies an essential service, and it has city franchises which make it a monopoly, so its sales and profits are relatively stable and predictable.

The rate of return probability distributions for the two companies are shown in Table 6-1. Here we see that there is a 30 percent chance of a boom, in which case both companies will have high earnings, pay high dividends, and enjoy capital gains; a 40 percent probability of a "normal" economy and moderate returns; and a 30 percent probability of a recession, which will mean low earnings and dividends and also capital losses. Notice, however, that Kelly Products' rate of return could vary far more widely than that of U.S. Water. There is a fairly high probability that the value of the Kelly stock will drop significantly, resulting in a loss of 70 percent, while there is no chance of a loss on U.S. Water.[1]

---

[1] It is, of course, completely unrealistic to think that any stock has no chance of a loss. Only in hypothetical instances could this occur. To illustrate, the price of Commonwealth Edison's stock dropped from $27 to $21 on January 16, 1984, a decline of 22 percent in one day. Don't tell people who bought Commonwealth on the 15th that the stock had no chance of a loss!

**Table 6-1**
**Probability Distributions for Kelly Products and U.S. Water**

| State of the Economy | Probability of This State Occurring | Rate of Return on Stock under This State | |
| --- | --- | --- | --- |
| | | **Kelly Products** | **U.S. Water** |
| Boom | 0.3 | 100% | 20% |
| Normal | 0.4 | 15 | 15 |
| Recession | 0.3 | −70 | 10 |
| | 1.0 | | |

**Table 6-2**
**Calculation of Expected Rate of Return:**
**Payoff Matrix**

| State of the Economy (1) | Probability of This State Occurring (2) | Kelly Products | | U.S. Water | |
| --- | --- | --- | --- | --- | --- |
| | | Rate of Return if This State Occurs (3) | Product: (2) × (3) (4) | Rate of Return if This State Occurs (5) | Product: (2) × (5) (6) |
| Boom | 0.3 | 100% | 30% | 20% | 6% |
| Normal | 0.4 | 15 | 6 | 15 | 6 |
| Recession | 0.3 | −70 | −21 | 10 | 3 |
| | 1.0 | | $\hat{k} = $ 15% | | $\hat{k} = $ 15% |

## Expected Rate of Return

**expected rate of return, k̂**
The rate of return expected to be realized from an investment; the mean value of the probability distribution of possible results.

If we multiply each possible outcome by its probability of occurrence and then sum these products, we have a *weighted average* of outcomes. The weights are the probabilities, and the weighted average is defined as the **expected rate of return, k̂**.[2] The expected rates of return for both Kelly Products and U.S. Water are shown in Table 6-2 to be 15 percent. This type of table is known as a *payoff matrix*.

The expected rate of return calculation can also be expressed as an equation which does the same thing as the payoff matrix table:

[2]In this section we discuss only returns on stock; thus, the subscript s is unnecessary, so we use the term k̂ rather than $\hat{k}_s$. Also, keep in mind that $\hat{k} = D_1/P_0 + g$ for a constant growth stock:

$$\hat{k} = \frac{D_1}{P_0} + g = \sum_{i=1}^{n} P_i k_i.$$

Further, note that the uncertainty about k̂, the expected *total* return, reflects uncertainty about the two return components, $D_1/P_0$ and g. There is more uncertainty regarding g than there is regarding the dividend yield. Thus, companies with high growth and low current dividend yields are often regarded as being riskier than low-growth companies. This point is discussed further in Chapter 16.

$$\text{Expected rate of return} = \hat{k} = \sum_{i=1}^{n} P_i k_i. \qquad (6\text{-}1)$$

Here $k_i$ is the $i$th possible outcome, $P_i$ is the probability of the $i$th outcome, and n is the number of possible outcomes. Thus, $\hat{k}$ is a weighted average of the possible outcomes (the $k_i$ values), with each outcome's weight being equal to its probability of occurrence. Using the data for Kelly Products, we obtain its expected rate of return as follows:

$$\hat{k} = P_1(k_1) + P_2(k_2) + P_3(k_3)$$
$$= 0.3(100\%) + 0.4(15\%) + 0.3(-70\%) = 15\%.$$

U.S. Water's expected rate of return is also 15 percent:

$$\hat{k} = 0.3(20\%) + 0.4(15\%) + 0.3(10\%) = 15\%.$$

We can graph the rates of return to obtain a picture of the variability of possible outcomes; this is shown in the bar charts in Figure 6-1. The height of each bar signifies the probability that a given outcome will occur. The range of probable returns for Kelly Products is from 100 to −70 percent, with an expected return of 15 percent. The expected return for U.S. Water is also 15 percent, but its range is much narrower.

**Figure 6-1**
**Probability Distributions of Kelly Products' and**
**U.S. Water's Rates of Return**

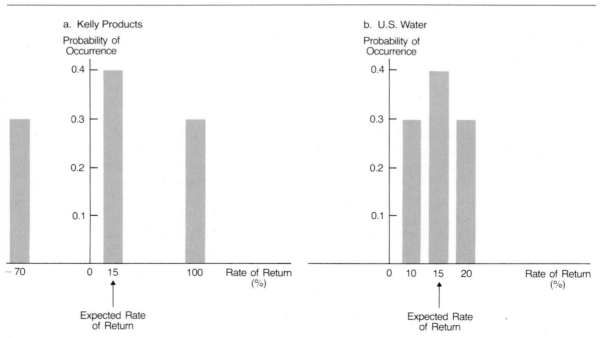

## Continuous Probability Distributions

Thus far, we have assumed that only three states of the economy can exist: recession, normal, and boom. Actually, of course, the state of the economy could range from a deep depression to a fantastic boom, and there are an unlimited number of possibilities in between. Suppose we had the time and patience to assign a probability to each possible state of the economy (with the sum of the probabilities still equaling 1.0) and to assign a rate of return to each stock for each state of the economy. We would have a table similar to Table 6-2, except that it would have many more entries in each column. This table could be used to calculate expected rates of return as shown above, and the probabilities and outcomes could be approximated by continuous curves such as those presented in Figure 6-2. Here we have changed the assumptions so that there is essentially a zero probability that the return of Kelly Products will be less than −70 percent or more than 100 percent, or that U.S. Water will return less than 10 percent or more than 20 percent, but virtually any return within these limits is possible.

**Figure 6-2**
**Continuous Probability Distributions of Kelly Products' and U.S. Water's Rates of Return**

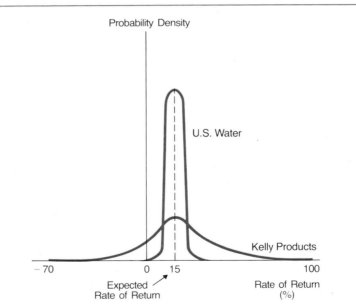

Note: The assumptions regarding the probabilities of various outcomes have been changed from those in Figure 6-1. There the probability of obtaining exactly 15 percent was 40 percent; here it is *much smaller*, because there are many possible outcomes instead of just three. With continuous distributions such as those above, it is more appropriate to ask what the probability is of obtaining at least some specified rate of return than to ask what the probability is of obtaining exactly that rate. This cumulative probability is equal to the area under the probability distribution curve to the right of the point of interest, or 1 minus the area under the curve up to that point. This topic is covered in detail in statistics courses.

The tighter, or more peaked, the probability distribution, the more likely it is that the actual outcome will be close to the expected value and consequently the less likely it is that the actual return will be far below the expected return. Thus, the tighter the probability distribution, the lower is the risk assigned to a stock. Since U.S. Water has a relatively tight probability distribution, its *actual return* is likely to be closer to its 15 percent *expected return* than is that of Kelly Products.

## Measuring Risk: The Standard Deviation

Risk is a difficult concept to grasp, and a great deal of controversy has surrounded attempts to define and measure it. However, a common definition, and one that is satisfactory for many purposes, is stated in terms of probability distributions such as those presented in Figure 6-2: *The tighter the probability distribution of expected future returns, the smaller the risk of a given investment.* According to this definition, U.S. Water is less risky than Kelly Products *because the chances of returns that are far below the expected level are smaller for U.S. Water than for Kelly Products.*

**standard deviation, σ**
A statistical measurement of the variability of a set of observations.

To be most useful, any measure of risk should have a definite value—we need a measure of the tightness of the probability distribution. One such measure is the **standard deviation**, the symbol for which is σ, pronounced "sigma." The smaller the standard deviation, the tighter the probability distribution and, accordingly, the lower the riskiness of the stock.[3] To calculate the standard deviation we proceed as shown in Table 6-3, which is explained below:

1. Calculate the expected rate of return:

$$\text{Expected rate of return} = \hat{k} = \sum_{i=1}^{n} P_i k_i. \qquad (6\text{-}1)$$

For Kelly, we previously found $\hat{k} = 15\%$.

---

[3]Since we define risk in terms of the chances of returns being less than expected, it would seem logical to measure risk in terms of the probability of returns below the expected return rather than by the entire distribution. Measures of below-expected returns, which are known as *semivariance measures*, have been developed, but they are difficult to analyze. Additionally, if the distribution is approximately symmetric, which is often the case for security returns, then the standard deviation is about as good a risk measure as the semivariance.

Note also that it is sometimes useful to calculate the *coefficient of variation*, which is the standard deviation divided by the expected value. The advantage of the coefficient of variation is that it permits better comparisons when the expected values of two alternatives are not the same.

## Table 6-3
### Calculating Kelly Products' Standard Deviation

| $k_i - \hat{k}$ (1) | $(k_i - \hat{k})^2$ (2) | $(k_i - \hat{k})^2 P_i$ (3) |
|---|---|---|
| $100 - 15 = 85$ | $7,225$ | $(7,225)(0.3) = 2,167.5$ |
| $15 - 15 = 0$ | $0$ | $(0)(0.4) = 0$ |
| $-70 - 15 = -85$ | $7,225$ | $(7,225)(0.3) = \underline{2,167.5}$ |
|  |  | Variance $= \sigma^2 = \underline{4,335.0}$ |

$$\text{Standard deviation} = \sigma = \sqrt{\sigma^2} = \sqrt{4,335} = 65.84\%.$$

2. In Column 1 of the table, subtract the expected rate of return from each possible outcome to obtain a set of deviations about $\hat{k}$:

$$\text{Deviation}_i = k_i - \hat{k}.$$

3. In Columns 2 and 3 of the table, square each deviation, multiply the result by the probability of occurrence for its related outcome, and sum these products to obtain the **variance** of the probability distribution:

**variance, $\sigma^2$**
The square of the standard deviation.

$$\text{Variance} = \sigma^2 = \sum_{i=1}^{n} (k_i - \hat{k})^2 P_i. \tag{6-2}$$

4. Now take the square root of the variance to obtain the standard deviation:

$$\text{Standard deviation} = \sigma = \sqrt{\sum_{i=1}^{n} (k_i - \hat{k})^2 P_i.} \tag{6-3}$$

Thus, the standard deviation is a probability-weighted average deviation from the expected value—it gives you an idea of how far above or below the expected value the actual value is likely to be. Kelly's standard deviation is $\sigma = 65.84\%$. Using these same procedures, we find U.S. Water's standard deviation to be 3.87 percent. Since Kelly's standard deviation is larger, it is the riskier stock according to this measure of risk.

If a probability distribution is normal, the *actual* return will be within $\pm 1$ standard deviation of the *expected* return about 68.26 percent of the time. Figure 6-3 illustrates this point and also shows the situation for $\pm 2\sigma$ and $\pm 3\sigma$. For Kelly Products, $\hat{k} = 15\%$ and $\sigma = 65.84\%$, while $\hat{k} = 15\%$ and $\sigma = 3.87\%$ for U.S. Water. Thus, there is a 68.26 percent probability that the actual return for Kelly Products will be in the range of $15 \pm 65.84$ percent, or from $-50.84$ to 80.84 percent. For U.S. Water, the 68.26 percent range is $15 \pm 3.87$ percent, or from 11.13 to 18.87 percent. With such a small $\sigma$, there is only a small probability that U.S. Water's return will be significantly

**Figure 6-3**
**Probability Ranges for a Normal Distribution**

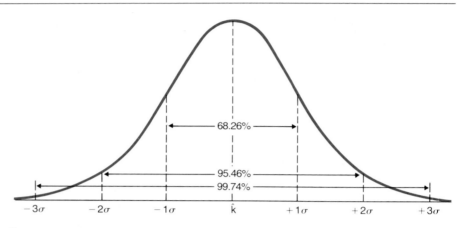

Notes:

a. The area under the normal curve equals 1.0, or 100 percent, *Thus, the areas under any pair of normal curves drawn on the same scale, whether they are peaked or flat, must be equal.*

b. Half of the area under a normal curve is to the left of the mean, indicating that there is a 50 percent probability that the actual outcome will be less than the mean and a 50 percent probability that it will be greater than the mean, or to the right of $\hat{k}$.

c. Of the area under the curve, 68.26 percent is within $\pm$ $1\sigma$ of the mean, indicating that the probability is 68.26 percent that the actual outcome will be within the range $\hat{k} - 1\sigma$ to $\hat{k} + 1\sigma$.

d. Procedures exist for finding the probability of other earnings ranges. These procedures are covered in statistics courses.

e. For a normal distribution, the larger the value of $\sigma$, the greater the probability that the actual outcome will vary widely from, and hence perhaps be far below, the expected, or most likely, outcome. *Since the probability of having the actual result turn out to be far below the expected result is our definition of risk, and since $\sigma$ measures this probability, we can use $\sigma$ as a measure of risk.* This definition may not be a good one, however, if we are dealing with an asset held in a diversified portfolio. This point is covered later in the chapter.

less than expected, so the stock is not very risky. For the average firm listed on the New York Stock Exchange, $\sigma$ has been close to 30 percent in recent years.[4]

## Risk Aversion and Required Returns

Suppose you had worked hard and saved $1 million, which you now plan to invest. You can buy a 10 percent Treasury note, and at the end of 1 year you

---

[4]In this section we have described the procedure for finding the mean and standard deviation when the data are in the form of a known probability distribution. If only sample returns data over some past period are available, then the standard deviation of returns can be estimated using this formula:

$$\text{Estimated } \sigma = S = \sqrt{\frac{\sum\limits_{t=1}^{n} (\bar{k}_t - \bar{k}_{Avg})^2}{n-1}}, \qquad \text{(6-3a)}$$

*(footnote continued)*

will have a sure $1.1 million, which is your original investment plus $100,000 in interest. Alternatively, you can buy stock in R&D Enterprises. If R&D's research programs are successful, your stock will increase in value to $2.2 million; however, if the research is a failure, the value of your stock will go to zero and you will be penniless. You regard R&D's chances of success or failure as being 50-50, so the expected value of the stock investment is $0.5(\$0) + 0.5(\$2,200,000) = \$1,100,000$. Subtracting the $1 million cost of the stock leaves an expected profit of $100,000, or an expected (but risky) 10 percent rate of return.

Thus, you have a choice between a sure $100,000 profit (a 10 percent rate of return) on the Treasury note or a risky expected $100,000 profit (also a 10 percent expected rate of return) on the R&D Enterprises stock. Which one would you choose? *If you choose the less risky investment, you are risk averse. Most investors are indeed risk averse, and certainly the average investor is risk averse, at least with regard to his or her "serious money." Since this is a well-documented fact, we shall assume* **risk aversion** *throughout the remainder of the book.*

**risk aversion**
A dislike for risk. Risk-averse investors have higher required rates of return for higher-risk securities.

What are the implications of risk aversion for security prices and rates of return? The answer is that, other things held constant, the higher a security's risk, (1) the lower its price and (2) the higher its required return. To see how this works, we can analyze the situation with U.S. Water and Kelly Products stocks. Suppose each stock sold for $100 per share and each had an expected rate of return of 15 percent. Investors are averse to risk, so there would be a general preference for U.S. Water. People with money to invest would bid for Water rather than Kelly stock, and Kelly's stockholders would start selling it and using the money to buy Water stock. The buying pressure would tend to drive up the price of Water stock, and the selling pressure would cause Kelly's price to decline.

---

where $\bar{k}_t$ ("k bar t") denotes the past realized rate of return in period t. Here is an example:

| Year | $\bar{k}_t$ |
|------|------|
| 1983 | 15% |
| 1984 | -5 |
| 1985 | 20 |

$$\bar{k}_{Avg} = \frac{(15 - 5 + 20)}{3} = 10.0\%.$$

$$\text{Estimated } \sigma \text{ (or S)} = \sqrt{\frac{(15 - 10)^2 + (-5 - 10)^2 + (20 - 10)^2}{3 - 1}}$$

$$= \sqrt{\frac{350}{2}} = 13.2\%.$$

Often the historical $\sigma$ is used as an estimate of the future $\sigma$. Much less often, and generally incorrectly, $\bar{k}_{Avg}$ for some past period is used as an estimate of $\hat{k}$, the expected future return. Past variability is likely to be repeated, but the past *level* of return (which could have been as high as $+100\%$ or as low as $-50\%$) is not necessarily expected in the future.

These price changes, in turn, would cause changes in the expected rates of return on the two securities. Suppose, for example, the price of Water stock was bid up from $100 to $150, while the price of Kelly's stock declined from $100 to $75. Further, suppose this caused Water's expected return to fall to 10 percent, while Kelly's expected return rose to 20 percent. The difference in returns, 20% − 10% = 10%, is a **risk premium**, **RP**, which represents the compensation investors require for assuming the additional risk of Kelly stock.

**risk premium, RP**
The difference between the required rate of return on a given risky asset and that on a riskless asset with the same expected life.

This example demonstrates a very important principle: *In a market dominated by risk-averse investors, riskier securities must have higher expected returns as estimated by the average investor than less risky ones, for if this situation does not hold, then actions will occur in the market to force it to occur.* We will consider the question of *how much* higher the returns on risky securities must be later in the chapter, after we examine in more depth how risk should be measured.

## Portfolio Risk and the Capital Asset Pricing Model

In the preceding section we considered the riskiness of a stock held in isolation. Now we analyze the riskiness of stocks held in portfolios.[5] As we shall see, a stock held as part of a portfolio is less risky than the same stock held in isolation. This fact has been incorporated into a generalized framework for analyzing the relationship between risk and rates of return; this framework is called the **Capital Asset Pricing Model**, or **CAPM**. The CAPM framework is, as we shall see, an extremely important analytical tool in both financial management and investment analysis. In the following sections we discuss the basic CAPM concepts and results.

**Capital Asset Pricing Model (CAPM)**
A model based on the proposition that any stock's required rate of return is equal to the riskless rate of return plus its risk premium, where risk is measured by the beta coefficient.

### Portfolio Risk and Return

Most financial assets are not held in isolation; rather, they are held as parts of portfolios. Banks, pension funds, insurance companies, mutual funds, and other financial institutions are required by law to hold diversified portfolios. Even individual investors—at least those whose security holdings constitute a significant part of their total wealth—generally hold stock portfolios, not just the stock of one firm. This being the case, from an investor's standpoint the fact that a particular stock goes up or down is not very important; *what is important is the return on his or her portfolio, and the portfolio's risk. Logically, then, the risk and return of an individual security should be analyzed in terms of how that security affects the risk and return of the portfolio in which it is held.*

---

[5]A *portfolio* is a collection of investment securities. If you owned some General Motors stock, some Exxon stock, and some IBM stock, you would be holding a three-stock portfolio. For reasons set forth in this section, the vast majority of all stocks are held as parts of portfolios.

**expected return on a portfolio, $\hat{k}_p$**
The weighted average expected return of the stocks held in the portfolio.

***Portfolio Returns.*** The **expected return on a portfolio**, $\hat{k}_p$, is simply the weighted average expected return of the individual stocks in the portfolio, with the weights being the fraction of the total portfolio invested in each stock:

$$\hat{k}_p = w_1\hat{k}_1 + w_2\hat{k}_2 + \ldots + w_n\hat{k}_n$$

$$= \sum_{i=1}^{n} w_i\hat{k}_i. \tag{6-4}$$

Here the $\hat{k}_i$'s are the expected returns on the individual stocks, the $w_i$'s are the weights, and there are n stocks in the portfolio. Note (1) that $w_i$ is the proportion of the portfolio's dollar value invested in Stock i, that is, the value of the investment in Stock i divided by the total value of the portfolio, and (2) that the $w_i$'s must sum to 1.0. To illustrate, given the following $w_i$'s and $\hat{k}_i$'s, the expected return on a hypothetical four-stock portfolio is 11.8 percent:

$$\hat{k}_p = w_1\hat{k}_1 + w_2\hat{k}_2 + w_3\hat{k}_3 + w_4\hat{k}_4$$

$$= 0.20(10\%) + 0.25(12\%) + 0.30(11\%) + 0.25(14\%)$$

$$= 2.0\% + 3.0\% + 3.3\% + 3.5\% = 11.8\%.$$

Of course, after the fact and a year later, the actual *realized* rates of return on the individual stocks—the $\bar{k}_i$ values—will probably be different from their expected values, so $\bar{k}_p$ will be somewhat different from $\hat{k}_p = 11.8\%$.

***Portfolio Risk.*** As we just saw, the expected return on a portfolio is simply a weighted average of the expected returns on the individual stocks in the portfolio, and each stock's contribution to the expected portfolio return is $w_i\hat{k}_i$. However, unlike returns, the riskiness of a portfolio, $\sigma_p$, is generally *not* a weighted average of the standard deviations of the individual securities in the portfolio, and each stock's contribution to the portfolio's risk is *not* $w_i\sigma_i$. It is theoretically possible to combine two stocks which are individually quite risky as measured by their standard deviations and to form a portfolio which is completely riskless, with $\sigma_p = 0$.

To illustrate, consider the situation in Figure 6-4. The bottom section gives data on rates of return for Stocks W and M, both individually and for a portfolio invested 50 percent in each stock. Panel a plots the data in a time series format, and Panel b shows the probability distributions of returns, assuming the future is expected to be like the past. The two stocks would be quite risky if they were held in isolation, but when they are combined to form Portfolio WM, they are not risky at all. (Note: These stocks are called W and M because their returns graphs in Figure 6-4 resemble a W and an M.)

The reason Stocks W and M can be combined to form a riskless portfolio is that their returns move countercyclically to each other—when W's returns fall, those of M rise, and vice versa. The tendency of two variables to move

**Figure 6-4**
**Rate of Return Distributions for Two Perfectly Negatively**
**Correlated Stocks (r = −1.0) and Portfolio WM**

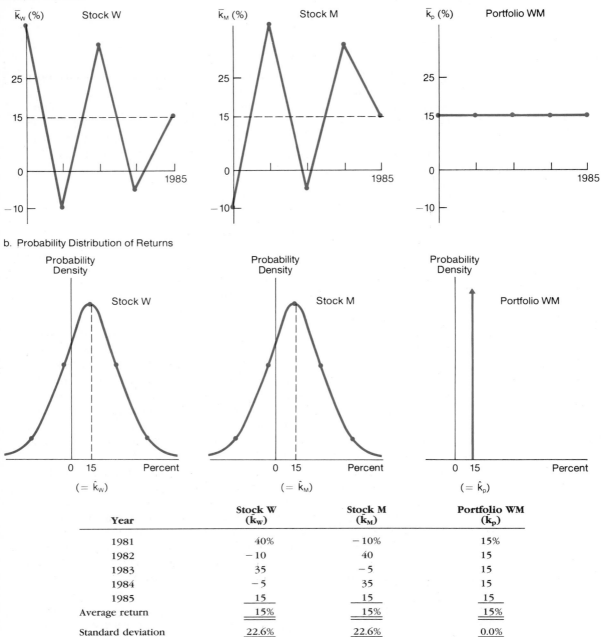

a. Rate of Return

b. Probability Distribution of Returns

| Year | Stock W ($\hat{k}_W$) | Stock M ($\hat{k}_M$) | Portfolio WM ($k_p$) |
|---|---|---|---|
| 1981 | 40% | −10% | 15% |
| 1982 | −10 | 40 | 15 |
| 1983 | 35 | −5 | 15 |
| 1984 | −5 | 35 | 15 |
| 1985 | 15 | 15 | 15 |
| Average return | 15% | 15% | 15% |
| Standard deviation | 22.6% | 22.6% | 0.0% |

**correlation
coefficient, r**
A measure of the degree
of relationship between
two variables.

together is called *correlation*, and the **correlation coefficient, r**, measures this tendency.[6] In statistical terms, we say that the returns on Stocks W and M are *perfectly negatively correlated*, with r = −1.0.

The opposite of perfect negative correlation, with r = −1.0, is *perfect positive correlation*, with r = +1.0. Returns on two perfectly positively correlated stocks would move up and down together, and a portfolio consisting of two such stocks would be just as risky as the individual stocks. This point is illustrated in Figure 6-5, where we see that the portfolio's standard deviation is equal to that of the individual stocks, indicating that diversification does nothing to reduce risk if the portfolio consists of perfectly positively correlated stocks.

Figures 6-4 and 6-5 demonstrate (1) that when stocks are perfectly negatively correlated (r = −1.0), all risk can be diversified away but (2) that when stocks are perfectly positively correlated (r = +1.0), diversification does no good whatsoever in terms of reducing risk. In reality, most stocks are positively correlated, but not perfectly so. On average, the correlation coefficient for the returns on two randomly selected stocks would be about +0.6, and for most pairs of stocks, r would lie in the range of +0.5 to +0.7. *Under such conditions, combining stocks into portfolios reduces risk but does not eliminate it completely.* Figure 6-6 illustrates this point with two stocks whose correlation coefficient is r = +0.65. The portfolio's average return is 15.0 percent, which is exactly the same as the average return for each of the two stocks, but its standard deviation is 20.6 percent, which is less than the standard deviation of either stock. Thus, the portfolio's risk is *not* an average of the risks of its individual stocks—diversification has reduced, but not eliminated, risk.

From these two-stock portfolio examples, we have seen that in one extreme case (r = −1.0) risk can be completely eliminated, while in the other extreme case (r = +1.0) diversification does no good whatever. In between these extremes, combining two stocks into a portfolio reduces, but does not eliminate, the riskiness inherent in the individual stocks.

What would happen if we included more than two stocks in the portfolio? *As a rule, the riskiness of a portfolio will be reduced as the number of stocks in the portfolio increases.* If we added enough partially correlated stocks, could we completely eliminate risk? In general, the answer is no, but the extent to which adding stocks to a portfolio reduces its risk depends on the *degree of correlation* among the stocks: The smaller the correlation coefficient, the lower the remaining risk in a large portfolio. If we could find a set of stocks whose correlation coefficients were zero or negative, all risk could be eliminated. *In the typical case, where the correlations among the individual stocks are positive but less than +1.0, some, but not all, risk can be eliminated.*

---

[6]The *correlation coefficient*, *r*, can range from +1.0, denoting that the two variables move up and down in perfect synchronization, to −1.0, denoting that the variables always move in exactly opposite directions. A correlation coefficient of zero suggests that the two variables are not related to each other—that is, changes in one variable are *independent* of changes in the other.

**Figure 6-5**
**Rate of Return Distributions for Two Perfectly Positively**
**Correlated Stocks (r = +1.0) and for Portfolio MM′**

a. Rate of Return

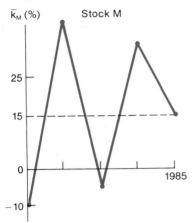

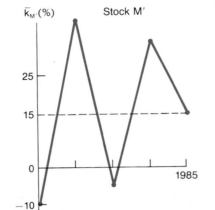

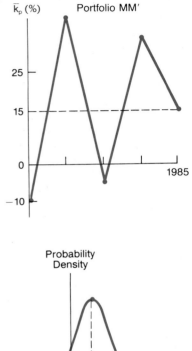

b. Probability Distribution of Returns

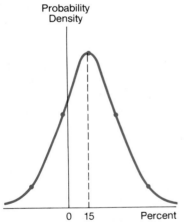

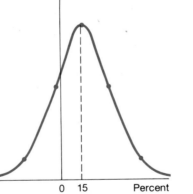

| Year | Stock M ($k_M$) | Stock M′ ($k_{M'}$) | Portfolio MM′ ($k_p$) |
|---|---|---|---|
| 1981 | −10% | −10% | −10% |
| 1982 | 40 | 40 | 40 |
| 1983 | −5 | −5 | −5 |
| 1984 | 35 | 35 | 35 |
| 1985 | 15 | 15 | 15 |
| Average return | 15% | 15% | 15% |
| Standard deviation | 22.6% | 22.6% | 22.6% |

**Figure 6-6**
**Rate of Return Distributions for Two Partially Correlated**
**Stocks (r = +0.65) and for Portfolio WY**

a. Rate of Return

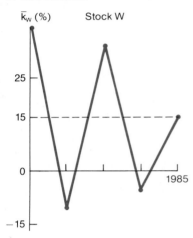
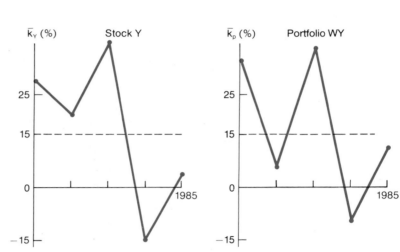

b. Probability Distribution of Returns

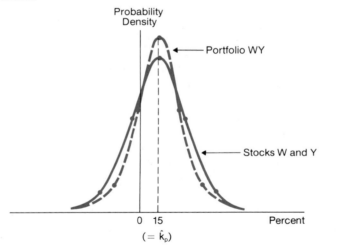

| Year | Stock W $(\bar{k}_W)$ | Stock Y $(\bar{k}_Y)$ | Portfolio WY $(\bar{k}_p)$ |
|---|---|---|---|
| 1981 | 40% | 28% | 34% |
| 1982 | −10 | 20 | 5 |
| 1983 | 35 | 41 | 38 |
| 1984 | −5 | −17 | −11 |
| 1985 | 15 | 3 | 9 |
| Average return | 15% | 15% | 15% |
| Standard deviation | 22.6% | 22.6% | 20.6% |

*Company-Specific Risk versus Market Risk.* As noted earlier, it is very difficult, if not impossible, to find stocks whose expected returns are not positively correlated—most stocks tend to do well when the national economy is strong and badly when it is weak.[7] Thus, even very large portfolios end up with a material amount of risk. For example, in Figure 5-10 in Chapter 5, we saw that actual returns varied quite a bit from year to year on a portfolio consisting of all New York Stock Exchange (NYSE) stocks. To see more precisely how portfolio size affects portfolio risk, consider Figure 6-7, which shows how portfolio risk is affected by forming larger and larger portfolios of NYSE stocks. Standard deviations are plotted for an average 1-stock portfolio, a 2-stock portfolio, and so on, up to a portfolio consisting of all 1,500-plus common stocks that were listed on the NYSE at the time the data were graphed. The graph illustrates that in general the riskiness of a portfolio consisting of average NYSE stocks tends to decline and to asymptotically approach a limit as the size of the portfolio increases. According to data accumulated in recent years, $\sigma_1$, the standard deviation of a one-stock portfolio (or an average stock), is approximately 28 percent. A portfolio consisting of all stocks, which is called "the market portfolio," would have a standard deviation of about 15.1 percent. The market portfolio's standard deviation is given the symbol $\sigma_M$, so $\sigma_M = 15.1\%$.

Thus, almost half of the riskiness inherent in an average individual stock can be eliminated if the stock is held in a reasonably well-diversified portfolio, one containing about 40 stocks. Some risk always remains, however, so it is virtually impossible to diversify away the effects of broad stock market declines that are suffered by almost all stocks.

That part of the risk of a stock which can be eliminated is called *diversifiable*, or *company-specific, risk*; that part which cannot be eliminated is called *nondiversifiable*, or *market, risk*. The name is not especially important, but the fact that part of the riskiness of any individual stock can be eliminated is vitally important.[8]

**company-specific risk**
That part of a security's risk associated with random events; can be eliminated by proper diversification.

**Company-specific risk** is caused by such things as lawsuits, strikes, successful and unsuccessful marketing programs, winning and losing major contracts, and other events that are unique to a particular firm. Since these events are essentially random, their effects on a portfolio can be eliminated by diversification—bad events in one firm will be offset by good events in another. **Market risk**, on the other hand, stems from factors which affect all firms simultaneously, such as war, inflation, recessions, and high interest rates. Since all firms are affected simultaneously by these factors, this type of risk cannot be eliminated by diversification.

**market risk**
That part of a security's risk that cannot be eliminated by diversification; measured by the beta coefficient.

We know that investors demand a premium for bearing risk—that is, the higher the riskiness of a security, the higher the expected return required to

---

[7]It is not too hard to find a few stocks that happened to rise because of a particular set of circumstances in the past while most other stocks were declining; it is much harder to find stocks that could logically be *expected* to advance in the future when other stocks are falling.

[8]Company-specific risk is also known as *unsystematic risk*, while market risk is sometimes called *systematic risk*.

**Figure 6-7**
**Effects of Portfolio Size on Portfolio Risk for Average Stocks**

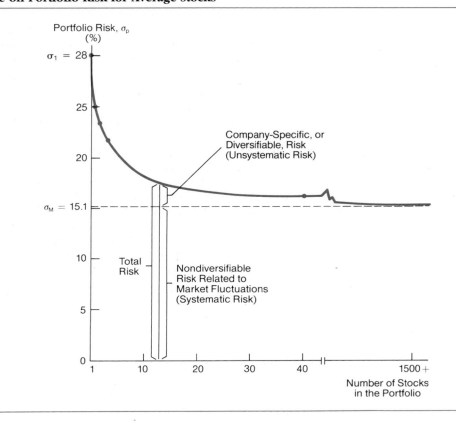

induce investors to buy (or to hold) it. But if investors are primarily concerned with *portfolio risk* rather than the risk of the individual securities in
the portfolio, how should the riskiness of an individual stock be measured?
The answer is this: *The relevant riskiness of an individual stock is its contribution to the riskiness of a well-diversified portfolio.* In other words, the
riskiness of Stock X to a doctor who has a portfolio of 40 stocks, or to a trust
officer managing a 150-stock portfolio, is the contribution that Stock X makes
to the portfolio's riskiness. The stock might be quite risky if held by itself,
but if most of its risk can be eliminated by diversification, then its **relevant
risk**, which is its *contribution to the portfolio's risk*, may be small.

A simple example will help make this point clear. Suppose you can flip a
coin once; if a head comes up you win $10,000, but you lose $8,000 if it
comes up tails. Although this may be considered a good bet—the expected
return is 0.5($10,000) + 0.5(−$8,000) = $1,000—it is a highly risky prop-
osition, because you have a 50 percent chance of losing $8,000. Alternatively,
suppose you can flip a coin 100 times and win $100 for each head but lose

**relevant risk**
The risk of a security that
cannot be diversified
away, or market risk. This
is a security's contribution
to the risk of the portfolio.

$80 for each tail. It is possible that you would flip all heads and win $10,000, and it is also possible that you would flip all tails and lose $8,000, but the chances are very high that you would actually flip about 50 heads and about 50 tails, winning a net $1,000. Although each individual flip is a risky bet, collectively you have a very low-risk proposition because you have diversified away most of the risk. This is the idea behind holding portfolios of stocks rather than just one stock, except that with stocks all of the risk cannot be eliminated by diversification—those risks related to broad changes in the stock market will remain.

Are all stocks equally risky in the sense that adding them to a well-diversified portfolio would have the same effect on the portfolio's riskiness? The answer is no—different stocks will affect the portfolio differently, so different securities have different degrees of relevant risk. How can the relevant risk of an individual stock be measured? As we have seen, all risk except that related to broad market movements can, and presumably will, be diversified away. After all, why accept risk that can easily be eliminated? *The risk that remains after diversifying is market risk, or risk that is inherent in the market, and it can be measured by the degree to which a given stock tends to move up and down with the market.*

## The Concept of Beta

**beta coefficient, b**
A measure of the extent to which the returns on a given stock move with the stock market.

The tendency of a stock to move with the market is reflected in its **beta coefficient, b**, which is a measure of the stock's volatility relative to an average stock.

An *average-risk stock* is defined as one that tends to move up and down in step with the general market as measured by some index such as the Dow Jones Industrials, the S&P 500, or the New York Stock Exchange Index. Such a stock will, by definition, have a beta, b, of 1.0, which indicates that in general, if the market moves up by 10 percent, the stock will also move up by 10 percent, while if the market falls by 10 percent, the stock will likewise fall by 10 percent. A portfolio of such b = 1.0 stocks will move up and down with the broad market averages, and it will be just as risky as the averages. If b = 0.5, the stock is only half as volatile as the market—it will rise and fall only half as much—and a portfolio of such stocks is half as risky as a portfolio of b = 1.0 stocks. On the other hand, if b = 2.0, the stock is twice as volatile as an average stock, so a portfolio of such stocks will be twice as risky as an average portfolio.

Figure 6-8 shows betas in a graphic sense. Assume that in 1983 the "market," defined as a portfolio consisting of all stocks, had a total return (dividend yield plus capital gains yield) of 10 percent, and Stocks H, A, and L also had returns of 10 percent. Now assume that in 1984 the market went up sharply and the return on the market portfolio was $\bar{k}_M = 20\%$. Returns on our three stocks also went up: H soared to 30 percent; A went up to 20 percent, the same as the market; and L went up only to 15 percent. Now suppose that the market dropped in 1985 and the market return was $\bar{k}_M = -10\%$. Our three stocks' returns also fell, H plunging to $-30$ percent, A

**Figure 6-8**
**Beta Graph**

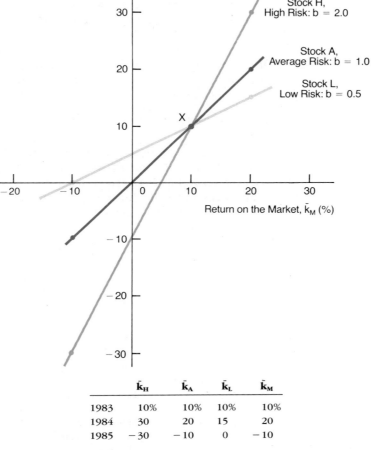

| | $\bar{k}_H$ | $\bar{k}_A$ | $\bar{k}_L$ | $\bar{k}_M$ |
|---|---|---|---|---|
| 1983 | 10% | 10% | 10% | 10% |
| 1984 | 30 | 20 | 15 | 20 |
| 1985 | −30 | −10 | 0 | −10 |

falling to −10 percent, and L going down only to $\bar{k}_L$ = 0%. Thus, our three stocks all moved in the same direction as the market, but H, the high-beta stock, was by far the most volatile. A was just as volatile as the market, and L was less volatile than average.

Betas are actually calculated by plotting lines such as those in Figure 6-8. The slopes of the lines show how each stock moves in response to a movement in the general market—*indeed, the slope coefficient of such "regression lines" is the beta coefficient.* (Procedures for actually calculating betas are described in Appendix 6A.) Betas for literally thousands of companies are calculated and published by Merrill Lynch, Value Line, and numerous other organizations. The beta coefficients of some well-known companies are shown in Table 6-4. Most stocks have betas in the range of 0.50 to 1.50; the average for all stocks is 1.0 by definition.[9]

If a higher-than-average-beta stock (one whose beta is greater than 1.0) is added to an average-risk (b = 1.0) portfolio, then the beta, and consequently the riskiness, of the portfolio will increase; conversely, if a lower-than-average-beta stock (one whose beta is less than 1.0) is added to an average-risk portfolio, the portfolio's beta and risk will decline. *Thus, since a stock's beta measures its contribution to the riskiness of a portfolio, beta is the theoretically correct measure of the stock's riskiness.*

We can summarize our analysis of the Capital Asset Pricing Model's logic to this point as follows:

**1.** A stock's risk consists of two components, market risk and company-specific risk.

**2.** Company-specific risk can be eliminated by diversification, and most investors do indeed diversify. We are left, then, with market risk, which is caused by general movements in the stock market and which reflects the fact that all stocks are affected by certain overall economic events like war, recessions, and inflation. This market risk is the only relevant risk to a rational, diversified investor.

**Table 6-4**
**Illustrative List of Beta Coefficients**

| Stock | Beta |
| --- | --- |
| E. F. Hutton | 2.00 |
| Apple Computer | 1.70 |
| Storage Technology | 1.50 |
| ABC | 1.15 |
| CBS | 1.05 |
| IBM | 1.05 |
| McDonald's | 1.00 |
| Firestone Tire | 0.95 |
| Gerber Products | 0.80 |
| Anheuser-Busch | 0.75 |
| Long Island Lighting | 0.70 |
| Pacific Gas & Electric | 0.65 |
| Boston Edison | 0.55 |

Source: *Value Line,* August 2, 1985.

---

[9]The betas we have been discussing are called *historic,* or *ex post,* betas because they are based strictly on historic, or past, data. Another type of beta, the *fundamental beta,* which is based partly on past actions and partly on expected future conditions not yet reflected in historic data, is also in wide use today. For a discussion of the various types of beta, their determination, and their use, see Eugene F. Brigham and Louis C. Gapenski, *Intermediate Financial Management,* Chapters 2 and 4. Historic betas sometimes make little sense. For example, in Table 6-4 Long Island Lighting's beta of 0.7 suggests low risks, yet LILCO is almost bankrupt and quite risky.

**3.** Investors must be compensated for bearing risk—the greater the riskiness of a stock, the higher its required return. However, compensation is required only for risk which cannot be eliminated by diversification. If risk premiums existed for diversifiable risk, well-diversified investors would buy these securities and bid up their prices, and their final expected returns would reflect only nondiversifiable market risk.

**4.** The market risk of a stock is measured by its beta coefficient, which is an index of the stock's relative volatility. Some benchmark betas follow:

b = 0.5: Stock is only half as volatile, or risky, as the average stock.

b = 1.0: Stock is of average risk.

b = 2.0: Stock is twice as risky as the average stock.

**5.** *Since a stock's beta coefficient determines how it affects the riskiness of a diversified portfolio, beta is the most relevant measure of a stock's risk.*

### Portfolio Beta Coefficients

A portfolio consisting of low-beta securities will itself have a low beta, since the beta of any set of securities is a weighted average of the individual securities' betas:

$$b_p = \sum_{i=1}^{n} w_i b_i. \tag{6-5}$$

Here $b_p$ is the beta of the portfolio, which reflects how volatile the portfolio is in relation to the market index; $w_i$ is the fraction of the portfolio invested in the $i$th stock; and $b_i$ is the beta coefficient of the $i$th stock. For example, if an investor holds a \$100,000 portfolio consisting of \$10,000 invested in each of 10 stocks, and each of the stocks has a beta of 0.8, then the portfolio will have $b_p = 0.8$. Thus, the portfolio will be less risky than the market, and it should experience relatively narrow price swings and have relatively small rate of return fluctuations.

Now suppose one of the existing stocks is sold and replaced by a stock with $b_i = 2.0$. This action will increase the riskiness of the portfolio from $b_{p1} = 0.8$ to $b_{p2} = 0.92$:

$$b_{p2} = \sum_{i=1}^{n} w_i b_i = 0.9(0.8) + 0.1(2.0) = 0.92.$$

Had a stock with $b_i = 0.2$ been added, the portfolio beta would have declined from 0.8 to 0.74. Adding a low-beta stock would, therefore, reduce the riskiness of the portfolio.

## The Relationship between Risk and Rates of Return

In the preceding section, we saw that under the CAPM framework beta is the appropriate measure of a stock's relevant risk. Now we must specify the relationship between risk and return—if beta rises by some specific amount, by how much must the stock's expected return increase to compensate for the increase in risk? To begin, let us define the following terms:

$\hat{k}_i$ = expected rate of return on the $i$th stock.

$k_i$ = required rate of return on the $i$th stock. Note that if $\hat{k}_i$ is less than $k_i$, then you would not purchase this stock, or you would sell it if you owned it.

$k_{RF}$ = risk-free rate of return, generally measured by the rate of return on U.S. Treasury securities.

$b_i$ = beta coefficient of the $i$th stock.

$k_M$ = required rate of return on a portfolio consisting of all stocks, which is the market portfolio. $k_M$ is also the required rate of return on an average ($b_A$ = 1.0) stock.

$RP_M = (k_M - k_{RF})$ = market risk premium. It is the additional return over the risk-free rate required to compensate investors for assuming an "average" amount of risk. Average means $b_A$ = 1.0.

$RP_i = b_i(k_M - k_{RF})$ = risk premium on the $i$th stock. The stock's risk premium is less than, equal to, or greater than the premium on an average stock depending on whether its beta is less than, equal to, or greater than 1.0. If $b_i = b_A = 1.0$, then $RP_i = RP_M$.

**market risk premium, $RP_M$**
The additional return over the risk-free rate needed to compensate investors for assuming an "average" amount of risk.

The **market risk premium**, **$RP_M$**, depends on the degree of aversion that investors in the aggregate have to risk.[10] Let us assume that at the current time Treasury bonds yield $k_{RF}$ = 8% and an average share of stock has a required return of $k_M$ = 12%. Therefore, the market risk premium is 4 percent:

$$RP_M = k_M - k_{RF} = 12\% - 8\% = 4\%.$$

It follows that if one stock were twice as risky as another, then its risk premium would be twice as high and, conversely, if its risk were only half as much, then its risk premium would be half as large. Further, we can measure a stock's relative riskiness by its beta coefficient. Therefore, if we know the market risk premium, $RP_M$, and the stock's risk as measured by its beta coef-

---

[10]This concept, as well as other aspects of CAPM, is discussed in more detail in Chapter 2 of Brigham and Gapenski, *Intermediate Financial Management*. It should be noted that the risk premium of an average stock, $k_M - k_{RF}$, cannot be measured with great precision because it is impossible to obtain precise values for $k_M$. However, empirical studies suggest that where long-term U.S. Treasury bonds are used to measure $k_{RF}$ and where $k_M$ is the expected return on the S&P 400 Industrial Stocks, the market risk premium varies somewhat from year to year; it has generally ranged from 3 to 6 percent during the last 20 years.

Chapter 2 of *Intermediate Financial Management* also discusses the assumptions embodied in the CAPM framework. Although some of the assumptions of the CAPM theory are unrealistic, the theory is still quite useful.

ficient, $b_i$, we can find its risk premium as the product $b_i(RP_M)$. For example, if $b_i = 0.5$ and $RP_M = 4\%$, then $RP_i$ is 2 percent:

$$\text{Risk premium for Stock i} = RP_i = b_i(RP_M) \tag{6-6}$$
$$= 0.5(4\%) = 2.0\%.$$

To summarize, given estimates of $k_{RF}$, $k_M$, and $b_i$, we can find the required rate of return on Stock i:

$$k_i = k_{RF} + b_i(k_M - k_{RF}) \tag{6-7}$$
$$= k_{RF} + b_i(RP_M) = 8\% + 0.5(12\% - 8\%)$$
$$= 8\% + 0.5(4\%) = 10\%.$$

If some other stock, j, were more risky than Stock i and had $b_j = 2.0$, then its required rate of return would be 16 percent:

$$k_j = 8\% + 2.0(4\%) = 16\%.$$

An average stock, with $b = 1.0$, would have a required return of 12 percent, the same as the market return:

$$k_{Avg} = 8\% + 1.0(4\%) = 12\% = k_M.$$

**Security Market Line (SML)**
The line that shows the relationship between risk and rate of return for individual securities. SML = Equation 6-7.

Equation 6-7 is often expressed as a graph called the **Security Market Line (SML)**; Figure 6-9 shows the SML when $k_{RF} = 8\%$ and $k_M = 12\%$. Note the following points:

**1.** Required rates of return are shown on the vertical axis, while risk as measured by beta is shown on the horizontal axis.

**2.** Riskless securities have $b_i = 0$; therefore, $k_{RF}$ appears as the vertical axis intercept.

**3.** The slope of the SML reflects the degree of risk aversion in the economy—the greater the average investor's aversion to risk, then (1) the steeper the slope of the line, (2) the greater the risk premium for any given stock, and (3) the higher the required rate of return on stocks.[11] These points are discussed further in a later section.

**4.** The values we worked out for stocks with $b_i = 0.5$, $b_i = 1.0$, and $b_i = 2.0$ agree with the values shown on the graph for $k_{Low}$, $k_{Avg}$, and $k_{High}$.

Both the Security Market Line and a company's position on it change over time as interest rates, investors' risk aversion, and individual companies' betas change. Such changes are discussed in the following sections.

---

[11]Students sometimes confuse beta with the slope of the SML. This is a mistake. The slope of the SML is actually $(k_M - k_{RF})$. As we saw earlier in connection with Figure 6-8, and as is developed further in Appendix 6A, beta does represent the slope of a line, but *not* the Security Market Line. This confusion arises partly because the SML equation is generally written, in this book and throughout the finance literature, as $k_i = k_{RF} + b_i(k_M - k_{RF})$, and in this form $b_i$ looks like the slope coefficient and $(k_M - k_{RF})$ like the variable. It would perhaps be less confusing if the second term were written $(k_M - k_{RF})b_i$. In Figure 6-9, $k_i = 8\% + 4b_i$, so a unitary increase in beta, for example from 1.0 to 2.0, would produce a 4 percent increase in $k_i$.

**Figure 6-9**
**The Security Market Line (SML)**

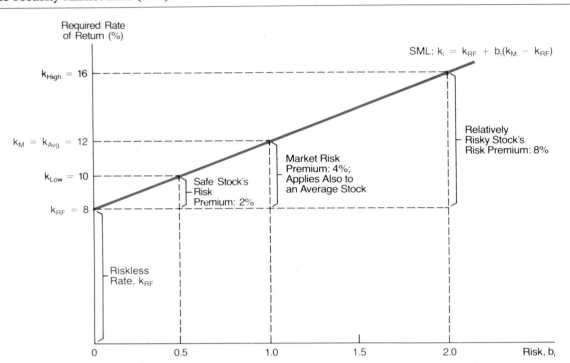

## The Impact of Inflation

As we saw in Chapter 3, interest amounts to "rent" on borrowed money, or the "price" of money; thus, $k_{RF}$ is the price of money to a riskless borrower. As we also saw, the existing market risk-free rate is called the *nominal rate*, and it consists of two elements: (1) a *real, or inflation-free, rate of return*, $k^*$, and (2) an *inflation premium, IP*, equal to the anticipated rate of inflation. Thus, $k_{RF} = k^* + IP$. The real rate on risk-free government securities has historically ranged from 2 to 4 percent, with a mean of about 3 percent. Thus, if no inflation were expected, risk-free government securities would tend to yield about 3 percent. However, as the expected rate of inflation increases, a premium must be added to the real rate of return to compensate investors for the loss of purchasing power that results from inflation. Thus, the 8 percent $k_{RF}$ shown in Figure 6-9 might be thought of as consisting of a 3 percent real rate of return plus a 5 percent inflation premium: $k_{RF} = k^* + IP = 3\% + 5\% = 8\%$.

If the expected rate of inflation rose to 7 percent, this would cause $k_{RF}$ to rise to 10 percent. Such a change is shown in Figure 6-10. Notice that under the CAPM the increase in $k_{RF}$ also causes an *equal* increase in the rate of

**Figure 6-10**
**Shift in the SML Caused by an Increase in Inflation**

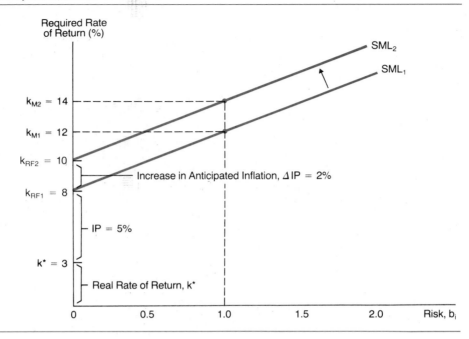

return on all risky assets, since the inflation premium is built into the required rate of return of both riskless and risky assets. For example, the rate of return on an average stock, $k_M$, increases from 12 to 14 percent. Other risky securities' returns also rise by two percentage points.

## Changes in Risk Aversion

The slope of the Security Market Line also reflects the extent to which investors are averse to risk—the steeper the slope of the line, the greater the average investor's risk aversion. If investors were indifferent to risk, and if $k_{RF}$ were 8 percent, then risky assets would also sell to provide an expected return of 8 percent—with no risk aversion there would be no risk premium, and the SML would be horizontal. As risk aversion increases, so does the risk premium and, thus, the slope of the SML.

Figure 6-11 illustrates an increase in risk aversion. The market risk premium rises from 4 to 6 percent, and $k_M$ rises from 12 to 14 percent. The returns on other risky assets also rise, with the impact of this shift in risk aversion being more pronounced on riskier securities. For example, the required return on a stock with $b_i = 0.5$ increases by only one percentage point, from 10 to 11 percent, while that on a stock with $b_i = 1.5$ increases by three percentage points, from 14 to 17 percent.

**Figure 6-11**
**Shift in the SML Caused by Increased Risk Aversion**

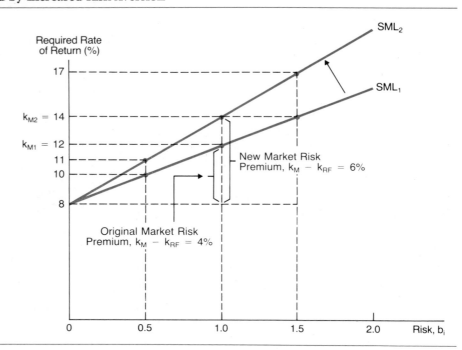

### Changes in a Stock's Beta Coefficient

As we shall see later in the book, a firm can affect its market, or beta, risk through changes in the nature and composition of its assets and also through its use of debt financing. A company's beta can also change as a result of increased competition in its industry, the expiration of basic patents, a change in management, and the like. When such changes occur, the demanded or required rate of return also changes, and this will affect the price of the firm's stock. For example, consider Teletron Electronics Corporation, a constant growth firm with $b = 1.0$, $D_1 = \$2.00$, and $g = 5\%$. Now suppose some action occurred that caused Teletron Electronics' beta to increase from 1.0 to 1.5. If the conditions depicted in Figure 6-9 held, Teletron's required rate of return would increase from

$$k_1 = k_{RF} + b_i(k_M - k_{RF}) = 8\% + 1.0(12\% - 8\%) = 12\%$$

to

$$k_2 = 8\% + 1.5(12\% - 8\%) = 14\%.$$

This change in k would cause Teletron's equilibrium stock price, assuming no change in its expected dividend and its expected growth rate, to fall from $28.57 to $22.22:[12]

$$\text{Old price} = \hat{P}_0 = \frac{D_1}{k_1 - g} = \frac{\$2.00}{0.12 - 0.05} = \$28.57.$$

$$\text{New price} = \hat{P}_0 = \frac{D_1}{k_2 - g} = \frac{\$2.00}{0.14 - 0.05} = \$22.22.$$

Notice that at its new equilibrium price of $22.22 Teletron's new expected rate of return is exactly equal to its new 14 percent required rate of return:

$$\hat{k}_2 = D_1/P_0 + g = \$2/\$22.22 + 5\% = 14.0\%.$$

$$k_2 = k_{RF} + b_i(k_M - k_{RF}) = 8\% + 1.5(12\% - 8\%) = 14.0\%.$$

Since the expected rate of return is equal to the required return, we know that $22.22 is Teletron's new equilibrium stock price.

## Security Market Equilibrium

Suppose a "typical" investor's required rate of return on Stock X, with $b_X = 2$, is 16 percent, determined as follows:

$$k_X = k_{RF} + b_X(k_M - k_{RF}) = 8\% + 2.0(12\% - 8\%) = 16\%.$$

This 16 percent required return is indicated in Figure 6-12.

Our typical investor will want to buy Stock X if the expected rate of return is more than 16 percent, will want to sell it if the expected rate of return is less than 16 percent, and will be indifferent if the expected rate of return is exactly 16 percent. Now suppose that the investor's portfolio contains X and he or she analyzes the stock's prospects and concludes that its earnings, dividends, and price can be expected to grow at a constant rate of 5 percent per year. The last dividend was $D_0 = \$2.8571$, so the next expected dividend is

$$D_1 = \$2.8571(1.05) = \$3.$$

The investor observes that the present price of the stock, $P_0$, is $30. Should he or she purchase more of Stock X, sell the present holdings, or maintain the present position?

The investor can calculate Stock X's expected rate of return as follows:

$$\hat{k}_X = \frac{D_1}{P_0} + g = \frac{\$3}{\$30} + 5\% = 15\%.$$

---

[12]Companies do sometimes deliberately increase their risk, but only if the action that will raise risk will also raise the expected earnings and the expected growth rate. Trying to determine the effects of a given action on both risk and profitability is one of the financial manager's central tasks.

**Figure 6-12**
**Expected and Required Returns on Stock X**

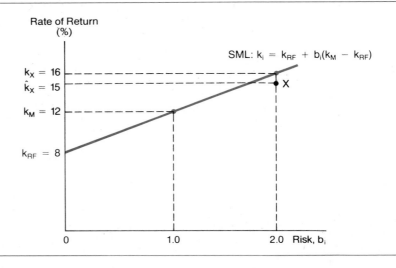

This value is plotted on Figure 6-12 as Point X, which is below the SML. Since the expected rate of return is less than the required return, this "typical" investor will want to sell the stock, as will other holders. However, few people will want to buy at the $30 price, so present owners will be able to find buyers only if they cut the price of the stock. Thus, the price will decline, and this decline will continue until the stock price reaches $27.27, at which point the market for this security will be in **equilibrium** and the expected rate of return, 16 percent, will be equal to the required rate of return:

**equilibrium**
The condition under which the expected return on a security is just equal to its required return.

$$\hat{k}_X = \frac{\$3}{\$27.27} + 5\% = 16\% = k_X.$$

Had the stock initially sold for less than $27.27, then events would have been reversed. Investors would have wanted to buy the stock, because its expected rate of return would have exceeded its required rate of return; then buy orders would have driven the stock's price up to $27.27.

To summarize, in equilibrium these two conditions must hold:

**1.** The expected rate of return as seen by the average investor must equal this investor's required rate of return, so that $\hat{k}_i = k_i$.

**2.** The market price of the stock must equal its intrinsic value as estimated by the typical investor, so that $P_0 = \hat{P}_0$.

Of course, some investors will believe that $\hat{k}_i > k$ and $\hat{P}_0 > P_0$ and hence will invest most of their funds in the stock; other investors will have an opposite view and will sell all of their shares. However, the average investor, trading at the margin, will establish the actual market price, and for this investor, $\hat{k}_i = k_i$ and $P_0 = \hat{P}_0$, for if these conditions do not exist, trading will occur until they do exist.

## Changes in Equilibrium Stock Prices

Stock market prices are not constant—they undergo violent changes at times. Let us assume that Stock X is in equilibrium, selling at a price of $27.27 per share. If all expectations were exactly met, over the next year the price would gradually rise to $28.63, or by 5 percent. However, many different events could occur to cause a change in the equilibrium price of the stock.

To illustrate, consider again the set of inputs used to develop Stock X's price of $27.27, along with a new set of assumed input variables:

|  | Variable Value | |
| --- | --- | --- |
|  | Original | New |
| Riskless rate, $k_{RF}$ | 8% | 7% |
| Market risk premium, $k_M - k_{RF}$ | 4% | 3% |
| Stock X's beta coefficient, $b_X$ | 2.0 | 1.0 |
| Stock X's expected growth rate, $g_X$ | 5% | 6% |
| Price of Stock X | $27.27 | ? |

The first three variables influence $k_X$, which declines from 16 to 10 percent as a result of the new set of variables:

$$\text{Original } k_X = 8\% + 2.0(4\%) = 16\%.$$

$$\text{New } k_X = 7\% + 1.0(3\%) = 10\%.$$

Using these values, together with the new g value, we find that $\hat{P}_0$, and presumably $P_0$, rises from $27.27 to $75.71.[13]

$$\text{Original } \hat{P}_0 = \frac{\$2.8571(1.05)}{0.16 - 0.05} = \frac{\$3}{0.11} = \$27.27.$$

$$\text{New } \hat{P}_0 = \frac{\$2.8571(1.06)}{0.10 - 0.06} = \frac{\$3.0285}{0.04} = \$75.71.$$

At the new price, the expected and required rates of return will be equal:[14]

$$\hat{k}_X = \frac{\$3.0285}{\$75.71} + 6\% = 10\% = k_X.$$

---

[13]A price change of this magnitude is by no means rare. The prices of *many* NYSE stocks double or halve during a year. For example, during 1984 Allied Products increased in value by 169 percent; on the other hand, Charter Corporation fell from 12⅞ to 1, a 92 percent loss.

[14]It should be obvious by now that actual realized rates of return are not necessarily equal to expected and required returns. Thus, an investor might have *expected* to receive a return of 15 percent if he or she had bought Charter Corporation or Allied Products stock in 1984, but after the fact, the realized return on Allied was far above 15 percent and that on Charter was far below.

Evidence suggests that stocks, and especially those of large, NYSE companies, adjust quite rapidly to disequilibrium situations. Consequently, equilibrium ordinarily exists for any given stock, and, in general, required and expected returns are equal. Stock prices certainly change, sometimes violently and rapidly, but this simply reflects changing conditions and expectations. There are, of course, times when a stock continues to react for several months to a favorable or unfavorable development, but this does not signify a long adjustment period; rather, it simply illustrates that as more new bits of information about the situation become available, the market adjusts to them. The ability of the market to adjust to new information is discussed in the next section.

### The Efficient Markets Hypothesis

**Efficient Markets Hypothesis (EMH)**
The hypothesis that securities are typically in equilibrium—that they are fairly priced in the sense that the price reflects all publicly available information on each security.

A body of theory called the **Efficient Markets Hypothesis (EMH)** holds (1) that stocks are always in equilibrium and (2) that it is impossible for an investor to consistently "beat the market." Essentially, the EMH states that there are some 100,000 or so full-time, highly trained, professional analysts and traders operating in the market and following some 3,000 major stocks. If each analyst followed only 30 stocks, there would still be 1,000 analysts following each stock. Further, these analysts work for organizations such as Merrill Lynch and Prudential Insurance, which have billions of dollars available with which to take advantage of bargains. As new information about a stock becomes available, these 1,000 analysts all receive and evaluate it at approximately the same time, so the price of the stock adjusts almost immediately to reflect the new developments.

Financial theorists generally define three forms, or levels, of market efficiency:

1. *Weak-form* efficiency implies that all information contained in past price movements is fully reflected in current market prices. Therefore, information about recent trends in a stock's price is of no use in selecting stock—the fact that a stock has risen for the past three days, for example, gives us no useful clues as to what it will do today or tomorrow. People who believe that weak-form efficiency exists also believe that "tape watchers" and "chartists" are wasting their time.[15]

2. *Semistrong-form* efficiency implies that current market prices reflect all *publicly available* information. If this is true, no abnormal returns can be gained by analyzing stocks.[16] Thus, if semistrong-form efficiency existed, it would do no good to pore over annual reports or other published data, be-

---

[15]Tape watchers are people who watch the NYSE tape, while chartists plot past patterns of stock price movements. Both believe that they can see if something is happening to the stock that will cause its price to move up or down in the near future.

[16]An abnormal return is one that exceeds the return justified by the riskiness of the investment, that is, a return that plots above the SML.

cause market prices would have adjusted to any good or bad news contained in such reports as soon as they came out. However, insiders (say, the presidents of companies) could, even under semistrong-form efficiency, still make abnormal returns on their own companies' stocks.

**3.** *Strong-form* efficiency implies that current market prices reflect all pertinent information, whether publicly available or privately held. If this form holds, then even insiders would find it impossible to earn abnormal returns in the stock market.[17]

Many empirical studies have been conducted to test for the three forms of market efficiency. Most suggest that the stock market—indeed, all well-developed capital markets—are highly efficient in the weak form and reasonably efficient in the semistrong form, at least for the larger and more widely followed stocks. However, capital markets are not strong-form efficient, so abnormal profits can be gained by those who possess insider information.

What effect does the EMH have on financial decisions? Since stock prices do reflect public information, most stocks do seem to be fairly valued. This does not mean that new information could not cause a stock's price to soar or to plummet, but it does mean that stocks, in general, are neither overvalued nor undervalued—they are fairly priced and in equilibrium. Certainly there are cases in which financial managers do have some special information not known to outsiders, but for the larger, actively traded firms, which are followed by literally hundreds of full-time security analysts backed by billions of dollars of capital, the market quickly reacts to all new developments.

If the EMH is correct, then it would be a waste of time to analyze stocks by looking for those that are undervalued—if stock prices already reflect all available information, and hence are fairly priced, one could "beat the market" only by luck, and it would be difficult if not impossible for anyone to consistently outperform the market averages. Empirical tests have shown that the EMH is, to a very large extent, valid. People such as corporate officers who have insider information can do better than the averages, and individuals and organizations that are especially good at digging out information on small, new companies also seem to do consistently well. However, the market for large firms such as those traded on the NYSE is highly efficient. Therefore, for NYSE companies, it is generally safe to assume that $\hat{k} = k$, that $\hat{P}_0 = P_0$, and that stocks plot on the SML.[18]

---

[17]In the spring of 1985, it was reported in the press that the assistant to a New York lawyer who worked on takeover deals had made $2 million in the stock market in less than a year. He went to jail, but he did help to disprove strong-form EMH.

[18]Market efficiency also has significant implications for managerial decisions, especially those pertaining to common stock issues, stock repurchases, and tender offers. Financial assets appear to be fairly valued, and decisions based on a stock's being undervalued or overvalued must be approached with caution.

## Physical Assets' Risk versus Securities' Risk

In a book on the financial management of business firms, why do we spend so much time on the riskiness of security investments? Why not begin by looking at the riskiness of such business assets as plant and equipment? *The reason is that, for a management whose goal is stock price maximization, the overriding consideration is the riskiness of the firm's stock, and the relevant risk of any physical asset must be measured in terms of its effect on the stock's risk.* For example, suppose General Motors were to go into a new operation, say, electric cars, whose sales and earnings were highly uncertain. This would seem to be a very risky investment. However, suppose the returns of this particular operation were not highly correlated with returns on GM's other operations or with returns on GM's stockholders' other investments—perhaps because electric cars could be expected to sell best if gasoline prices rose sharply, pulling down sales of both regular cars and corporate profits in general. In this case most of the new plant's risk would not be relevant, because it would be offset in a diversification sense within GM's overall operations and also within stockholders' portfolios. Thus, the riskiness of a corporate asset investment should be considered within the context of this question: What does the investment in a particular physical asset do to the riskiness of the firm as viewed by stockholders?

## A Word of Caution

A word of caution about betas and the Security Market Line is in order. Although these concepts are very logical, the entire theory is based on *ex ante*, or expected, conditions, yet we have available only *ex post*, or past, data. Thus, the betas we calculate show how volatile a stock has been in the *past*, but conditions may change and alter its *future volatility*, which is the item of real concern to investors. Additionally, the Security Market Line is but one part of the overall Capital Asset Pricing Model. Although the CAPM represents a significant step forward in security pricing theory, it does have some potentially serious deficiencies when applied in practice, so estimates of $k_i$ found through use of the SML may be subject to considerable error.[19]

---

[19]The concept of beta was discovered and developed by academicians and then seized upon and used by business practitioners. To some extent betas seem to have been oversold—the beauty of the concept has been overemphasized, and the difficulties with actually implementing the theory have not been pointed out sufficiently. In a recent article, Anise Wallace ("Is Beta Dead?" *Institutional Investor*, July 1980, 23-30) reached this conclusion: "It took nearly a decade for money managers to learn to love beta. Now it looks as if they were sold a bill of goods—and the whole MPT [Modern Portfolio Theory] house of cards could come tumbling down." This judgment is, in the minds of most observers, far too harsh. The concept of beta obviously reflects the way sophisticated investors should and do look at the risk inherent in a security. Problems arise when one attempts to measure *future* events on the basis of *past* data, but abandoning the CAPM because of these difficulties would be like throwing out the baby with the bath water!

## Summary

The primary goals of this chapter were (1) to show how risk is measured in financial analysis and (2) to explain how risk affects security prices and rates of return. We began by showing that risk is related to the variability of expected future returns. However, we soon saw that most rational investors hold *portfolios of stocks* and that such investors are more concerned with the risks of their portfolios than with the risks of individual securities.

Next, we saw that the riskiness of a given stock can be split into two components—*market risk*, which is caused by changes in the broad stock market and which cannot be eliminated by diversification, and *company-specific risk*, which can be eliminated by holding a diversified portfolio. Since investors can and do diversify and thus eliminate company risk, the most *relevant risk* inherent in stocks is their market risk, which is measured by the *beta coefficient, b.*

Betas measure the tendency of stocks to move up and down with the market— a high-beta stock is more volatile than an average stock, while a low-beta stock is less volatile than average. An average stock has b = 1.0 by definition.

The required rate of return on a stock consists of the rate of return on risk-free bonds, $k_{RF}$, plus a risk premium that depends on the stock's beta coefficient:

$$k_i = k_{RF} + b_i(k_M - k_{RF}).$$

This formula is called the *Security Market Line (SML) equation*, or, sometimes, the *Capital Asset Pricing Model (CAPM) equation*, and it is of fundamental importance in finance.

We also saw that stocks are typically in equilibrium, with their expected and required rates of return as seen by the average investor equal to each other. This is because the capital markets in the United States are, in general, *efficient*. However, even though stocks are generally in equilibrium, a number of things can happen to cause prices to change: The riskless rate can change because of changes in anticipated inflation; a stock's beta can change; or its rate of expected growth can increase or decrease. In the remainder of this book, we will examine the ways in which a firm's management can influence its stock's riskiness, its expected growth rate, and hence its price.

### Questions

6-1    Define the following terms, using graphs or equations to illustrate your answers wherever feasible:
   a. Risk; probability distribution
   b. *Expected* rate of return, $\hat{k}$
   c. Standard deviation, $\sigma$; variance, $\sigma^2$
   d. Risk aversion
   e. Risk premium, $RP_i$; market risk premium, $RP_M$
   f. Capital Asset Pricing Model (CAPM)
   g. Expected return on a portfolio, $\hat{k}_p$
   h. Correlation coefficient, r
   i. Market risk; company-specific risk; relevant risk
   j. Beta coefficient, b; average stock's beta, $b_A$
   k. Security Market Line (SML); SML equation
   l. Equilibrium
   m. Efficient Markets Hypothesis (EMH)

6-2    The probability distribution of a less risky expected return is more peaked than that of a risky return. What shape would the probability distribution have for (a) completely certain returns and (b) completely uncertain returns?

6-3    Security A has an expected return of 6 percent, a standard deviation of expected returns of 30 percent, a correlation coefficient with the market of −0.25, and a beta coefficient of −0.5. Security B has an expected return of 11 percent, a standard deviation of returns of 10 percent, a correlation with the market of 0.75, and a beta coefficient of 1.0. Which security is more risky? Why?

6-4    Suppose you owned a portfolio consisting of $500,000 worth of long-term U.S. government bonds.
       a. Would your portfolio be riskless?
       b. Now suppose you hold a portfolio consisting of $500,000 worth of 30-day Treasury bills. Every 30 days your bills mature and you reinvest the principal ($500,000) in a new batch of bills. Is your portfolio truly riskless? (Hint: Assume that you live on the investment income from your portfolio, and that you want to maintain a constant standard of living.)
       c. You should have concluded that both long-term and short-term portfolios of government securities have some element of risk. Can you think of any asset that would be completely riskless?

6-5    A life insurance policy is a financial asset. The premiums paid represent the investment's cost.
       a. How do you calculate the expected return on a life insurance policy?
       b. Suppose the owner of the life insurance policy has no other financial assets—the person's only other asset is "human capital," or lifetime earnings capacity. What is the correlation coefficient between returns on the insurance policy and returns on the policyholder's human capital?
       c. Life insurance companies have administrative costs and sales representatives' commissions; hence, the expected rate of return on insurance premiums is low or even negative. Use the portfolio concept to explain why people buy life insurance in spite of negative expected returns.

6-6    If investors' aversion to risk increased, would the risk premium on a high-beta stock increase more or less than that on a low-beta stock? Explain.

## Self-Test Problem (*Solution on Page 192*)

ST-1   Stocks A and B have the following historical dividend and price data:

| Year | Stock A | | Stock B | |
| | Dividend | Year-End Price | Dividend | Year-End Price |
| --- | --- | --- | --- | --- |
| 1980 | — | $22.50 | — | $43.75 |
| 1981 | $2.00 | 16.00 | $3.40 | 35.50 |
| 1982 | 2.20 | 17.00 | 3.65 | 38.75 |
| 1983 | 2.40 | 20.25 | 3.90 | 51.75 |
| 1984 | 2.60 | 17.25 | 4.05 | 44.50 |
| 1985 | 2.95 | 18.75 | 4.25 | 45.25 |

a. Calculate the realized rate of return (or holding period return) for each stock in each year. Then assume that someone had held a portfolio consisting of 50 percent of A and 50 percent of B. (The portfolio is rebalanced every year so as to maintain these percentages.) What would the realized rate of return on the portfolio have been in each year from 1981 through 1985? What would the average returns have been for each stock and for the portfolio?

b. Now calculate the standard deviation of returns for each stock and for the portfolio.

c. Based on the extent to which the portfolio has a lower risk than the stocks held individually, would you guess that the correlation coefficient between returns on the two stocks is closer to 0.9 or to −0.9?

d. If you added more stocks at random to the portfolio, what is the most accurate statement of what would happen to $\sigma_p$?
1. $\sigma_p$ would remain constant.
2. $\sigma_p$ would decline to somewhere in the vicinity of 15 percent.
3. $\sigma_p$ would decline to zero if enough stocks were included.

## Problems

**Expected returns**      **6-1**      Stocks A and B have the following probability distributions of expected future returns:

| Probability | A | B |
|---|---|---|
| 0.1 | −25% | −40% |
| 0.2 | 5 | 0 |
| 0.4 | 15 | 16 |
| 0.2 | 30 | 40 |
| 0.1 | 45 | 66 |

a. Calculate the expected rate of return, $\hat{k}$, for Stock B. ($\hat{k}_A = 15\%$.)

b. Calculate the standard deviation of expected returns for Stock A. (That for Stock B is 27.0 percent.) Is it possible that most investors might regard Stock B as being *less* risky than Stock A? Explain.

**Required rate of return**      **6-2**      Suppose $k_{RF} = 12\%$, $k_M = 16\%$, and $b_A = 1.4$.

a. What is $k_A$, the required rate of return on Stock A?

b. Now suppose $k_{RF}$ (1) increases to 13 percent or (2) decreases to 11 percent. The slope of the SML remains constant. How will this affect $k_M$ and $k_A$?

c. Now assume $k_{RF}$ remains at 12 percent but $k_M$ (1) increases to 17 percent or (2) falls to 14 percent. The slope of the SML does not remain constant. How will this affect $k_A$?

**Expected returns**      **6-3**      Suppose you are offered (1) $1 million or (2) a gamble where you get $2 million if a head is flipped but zero if a tail comes up.

a. What is the expected value of the gamble?

b. Would you take the sure $1 million or the gamble?

c. If you take the sure $1 million, are you a risk averter or a risk seeker?

d. Suppose you actually take the sure $1 million. You can invest it in either a U.S. Treasury bond that will return $1,075,000 at the end of a year or a common stock that has a 50-50 chance of being either worthless or worth $2,300,000 at the end of the year.

1. What is the expected profit on the stock investment? (The expected profit on the T-bond investment is $75,000.)
2. What is the expected rate of return on the stock investment? (The expected rate of return on the T-bond investment is 7.5 percent.)
3. Would you invest in the bond or the stock?
4. Just how large would the expected profit and the expected rate of return have to be on the stock investment to make *you* invest in the stock?
5. How might your decision be affected if, rather than buying one stock for $1 million, you could construct a portfolio consisting of 100 stocks with $10,000 in each? Each of these stocks has the same return characteristics as the one stock, that is, a 50-50 chance of being worth either zero or $23,000 at year-end. Would the correlation between returns on these stocks matter?

**Equilibrium stock price**    **6-4**    The risk-free rate of return, $k_{RF}$, is 12 percent; the required rate of return on the market, $k_M$, is 17 percent; and Stock X has a beta coefficient of 1.6.

a. If the dividend expected during the coming year, $D_1$, is $2.50 and g = a constant 5%, at what price should Stock X sell?

b. Now suppose the Federal Reserve Board increases the money supply, causing the riskless rate to drop to 10 percent. What would this do to the price of the stock?

c. In addition to the change in Part b, suppose investors' risk aversion declines; this fact, combined with the decline in $k_{RF}$, causes $k_M$ to fall to 14 percent. At what price would Stock X sell?

d. Now suppose Firm X has a change in management. The new group institutes policies that increase the constant growth rate to 6 percent. Also, the new management stabilizes sales and profits and thus causes the beta coefficient to decline from 1.6 to 1.3. After all these changes, what is Stock X's new equilibrium price? (Note: $D_1$ goes to $2.52.)

**Beta coefficients**    **6-5**    Suppose Kriegal Chemical Company's management conducts a study and concludes that if Kriegal expanded its consumer products division (which is less risky than its primary business, industrial chemicals), the firm's beta would decline from 1.2 to 0.9. However, consumer products have a somewhat lower profit margin, and this would cause Kriegal's constant growth rate in earnings and dividends to fall from 7 to 5 percent.

a. Should management make the change? Assume the following: $k_M$ = 12%; $k_{RF}$ = 9%; $D_0$ = $2.

b. Assume all the facts as given above except the change in the beta coefficient. What would the beta have to equal to cause the expansion to be a good one? (Hint: Set $\hat{P}_0$ under the new policy equal to $\hat{P}_0$ under the old one, and find the new beta that will produce this equality.)

**Expected rate of return**    **6-6**    The beta coefficient for Stock C is $b_C$ = 0.4, while that for Stock D is $b_D$ = −0.5. (Stock D's beta is negative, indicating that its rate of return rises whenever returns on most other stocks fall. There are very few negative beta stocks, although gold mining stocks are often cited as an example.)

a. If the risk-free rate is 9 percent and the expected rate of return on an average stock 13 percent, what are the required rates of return on Stocks C and D?

b. For Stock C, suppose the current price, $P_0$, is $25; the next expected dividend, $D_1$, is $1.50; and the stock's expected constant growth rate is 4 percent. Is the stock in equilibrium? Explain, and describe what will happen if the stock is not in equilibrium.

Security Market Line  6-7  The T. Lowe Brice Investment Fund has a total investment of $400 million in five stocks:

| Stock | Investment | Stock's Beta Coefficient |
|---|---|---|
| A | $120 million | 0.5 |
| B | 100 million | 2.0 |
| C | 60 million | 4.0 |
| D | 80 million | 1.0 |
| E | 40 million | 3.0 |

The beta coefficient for a fund such as this can be found as a weighted average of the fund's investments. The current risk-free rate is 7 percent, while expected market returns have the following estimated probability distribution for the next period:

| Probability | Market Return |
|---|---|
| 0.1 | 8% |
| 0.2 | 10 |
| 0.4 | 12 |
| 0.2 | 14 |
| 0.1 | 16 |

a. What is the estimated equation for the Security Market Line (SML)? (Hint: Determine the expected market return.)

b. Compute the Fund's required rate of return for the next period.

c. Suppose management receives a proposal for a new stock. The investment needed to take a position in the stock is $50 million; it will have an expected return of 16 percent; and its estimated beta coefficient is 2.5. Should the new stock be purchased? At what expected rate of return would management be indifferent to purchasing the stock?

Realized rates of return  6-8  Stocks A and B have the following historical dividend and price data:

| Year | Stock A Dividend | Stock A Year-End Price | Stock B Dividend | Stock B Year-End Price |
|---|---|---|---|---|
| 1979 | — | $22.50 | — | $43.75 |
| 1980 | $2.00 | 16.00 | $3.40 | 35.50 |
| 1981 | 2.20 | 17.00 | 3.65 | 38.75 |
| 1982 | 2.40 | 20.25 | 3.90 | 51.75 |
| 1983 | 2.60 | 17.25 | 4.05 | 44.50 |
| 1984 | 2.95 | 18.75 | 4.25 | 45.25 |

a. Calculate the realized rate of return (or holding period return, HPR) for each stock in each year. Then assume that someone had held a portfolio consisting of 50 percent of A and 50 percent of B (the portfolio was rebalanced at the end of each year). What would the realized rate of return on the portfolio have been in each year from 1980 through 1984? What would the average returns have been for each stock and for the portfolio?

b. Now calculate the standard deviation of returns for each stock and for the portfolio.

(Do Parts c, d, e, and f of this problem only if you are using the computerized problem diskette.)

c. Add Stock C to the portfolio; C has the following historical dividend and price data:

| Year | Dividend | Year-End Price |
|------|----------|----------------|
| 1980 | —        | $23.40         |
| 1981 | $1.85    | 23.90          |
| 1982 | 1.95     | 31.50          |
| 1983 | 2.05     | 27.20          |
| 1984 | 2.15     | 32.25          |
| 1985 | 2.25     | 26.00          |

Assume that the portfolio contains 33⅓ percent of A, 33⅓ percent of B, and 33⅓ percent of C. How does this affect the portfolio return and $\sigma_p$?

d. If you added more stocks at random to the portfolio, what is the most accurate statement of what would happen to $\sigma_p$?
1. $\sigma_p$ would remain constant.
2. $\sigma_p$ would decline to somewhere in the vicinity of 15 percent.
3. $\sigma_p$ would decline to zero if enough stocks were included.

e. Make some other changes in the portfolio percentages, making sure that the percentages sum to 100 percent. For example, put 100 percent in A; 25 percent in A, 25 percent in B, and 50 percent in C; and so forth. Explain why $k_p$ and $\sigma_p$ change.

f. Would you rather have a portfolio consisting of one-third of each stock or a portfolio with 50 percent A and 50 percent B? Explain.

## Solution to Self-Test Problem

ST-1    a. The realized return in each Period t is estimated as follows:

$$\bar{k}_t = \frac{D_t + P_t - P_{t-1}}{P_{t-1}}.$$

For example, the realized return for Stock A in 1981 was $-20.0$ percent:

$$\bar{k}_{1981} = \frac{D_{1981} + P_{1981} - P_{1980}}{P_{1980}}$$

$$= \frac{\$2.00 + \$16.00 - \$22.50}{\$22.50}$$

$$= -0.200 = -20.0\%.$$

The table that follows shows the realized returns for each stock in each year, the averages for the five years, and the same data for the portfolio:

| Year | Stock A's Return, $k_A$ | Stock B's Return, $k_B$ | Portfolio AB's Return, $k_{AB}$ |
|------|------------------------|------------------------|---------------------------------|
| 1981 | −20.0% | −11.1% | −15.6% |
| 1982 | 20.0 | 19.4 | 19.7 |
| 1983 | 33.2 | 43.6 | 38.4 |
| 1984 | −2.0 | −6.2 | −4.1 |
| 1985 | 25.8 | 11.2 | 18.5 |
| $k_{Avg}$ | 11.4% | 11.4% | 11.4% |

b. The standard deviation of returns is estimated, using Equation 6-3a, as follows (see Footnote 4, page 162):

$$\text{Estimated } \sigma = S = \sqrt{\frac{\sum_{t=1}^{n}(\bar{k}_t - \bar{k}_{Avg})^2}{n-1}}. \qquad (6\text{-}3a)$$

For Stock A, the estimated $\sigma$ is 21.9 percent:

$$\sigma_A = \sqrt{\frac{(-20.0 - 11.4)^2 + (20.0 - 11.4)^2 + \ldots + (25.8 - 11.4)^2}{5 - 1}}$$

$$= \sqrt{\frac{1,922.08}{4}} = 21.9\%.$$

The standard deviation of returns for Stock B and for the portfolio are similarly determined, and they are shown here:

|  | Stock A | Stock B | Portfolio AB |
|--|---------|---------|--------------|
| Standard deviation, $\sigma$ | 21.9 | 21.9 | 21.3 |

c. Since the risk reduction from diversification is small ($\sigma_{AB}$ falls only from 21.9 to 21.3 percent), the most likely value of the correlation coefficient is 0.9. If the correlation coefficient were −0.9, the risk reduction would be much larger. In fact, the correlation coefficient between Stocks A and B is 0.89.

d. If more randomly selected stocks were added to the portfolio, $\sigma_p$ would decline to somewhere in the vicinity of 15 percent. $\sigma_p$ would remain constant only if the correlation coefficient were +1.0, which is most unlikely. $\sigma_p$ would decline to zero only if the correlation coefficient, r, were equal to zero and a large number of stocks were added to the portfolio, or if the proper proportions were held in a two-stock portfolio with r = −1.0.

## Selected Additional References

Chapter 2 of Eugene F. Brigham and Louis C. Gapenski, *Intermediate Financial Management*, provides an extension of the basic contents of Chapter 6. Also, the investments textbooks listed in the Chapter 5 references contain both discussions of and further references to the literature on risk and the CAPM.

## APPENDIX 6A

### Calculating Beta Coefficients

The CAPM is an *ex ante* model, which means that all of the variables represent before-the-fact, *expected* values. In particular, the beta coefficient used in the SML equation should reflect the volatility of a given stock's return versus the expected return on the market during some *future* period. However, people generally calculate betas during some *past* period and then assume that the stocks' relative volatility will remain constant in the future.

To illustrate how betas are calculated, consider Figure 6A-1. The data at the bottom of the figure show the historic realized returns for Stock J and for the market over the last five years. The data points have been plotted on the scatter diagram and a regression line drawn. If all the data points fall on a straight line, as they did in Figure 6-8 in Chapter 6, it is easy to draw an accurate line. If they do not, as in Figure 6A-1, then you can fit the line either "by eye" as an approximation or by statistical procedures.

Recall what the term *regression line*, or *regression equation*, means: The equation $Y = a + bX + e$ is the standard form of a simple linear regression. It states that the dependent variable, Y, is equal to a constant, a, plus b times X, where b is the slope coefficient (or parameter) and X is the "independent" variable, plus an error term, e. Thus, the rate of return on the stock during a given time period (Y) depends on what happens to the general stock market, which is measured by $X = \bar{k}_M$.

Once the line has been drawn on graph paper, we can estimate its intercept and slope, the a and b values in $Y = a + bX$. The intercept, a, is simply the point where the line cuts the vertical axis. The slope coefficient, b, can be estimated by the "rise over run" method. This involves calculating the amount by which $\bar{k}_J$ increases for a given increase in $\bar{k}_M$. For example, we observe in Figure 6A-1 that $\bar{k}_J$ increases from $-8.9$ to $+7.1$ percent (the rise) when $\bar{k}_M$ increases from 0 to 10.0 percent (the run). Thus, b, the beta coefficient, can be measured as follows:

$$b = \text{Beta} = \frac{\text{Rise}}{\text{Run}} = \frac{\Delta Y}{\Delta X} = \frac{7.1 - (-8.9)}{10.0 - 0.0} = \frac{16.0}{10.0} = 1.6.$$

Note that rise over run is a ratio, and it would be the same if measured using any two arbitrarily selected points on the line.

The regression line equation enables us to predict a rate of return for Stock J, given a value of $\bar{k}_M$. For example, if $\bar{k}_M = 15\%$, we would predict $\bar{k}_J = -8.9\% + 1.6(15\%) = 15.1\%$. The actual return would probably differ from the predicted return: This deviation is the error term, $e_J$, for the year, and it varies randomly from year to year depending on company-specific factors.

**Figure 6A-1**
**Calculating Beta Coefficients**

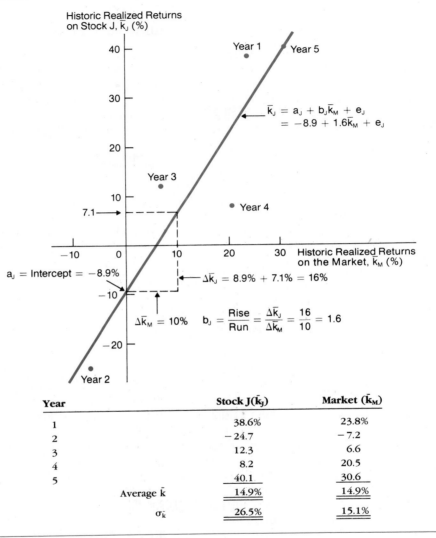

| Year | Stock J($\bar{k}_J$) | Market ($\bar{k}_M$) |
|------|----------------------|----------------------|
| 1 | 38.6% | 23.8% |
| 2 | −24.7 | −7.2 |
| 3 | 12.3 | 6.6 |
| 4 | 8.2 | 20.5 |
| 5 | 40.1 | 30.6 |
| Average $\bar{k}$ | 14.9% | 14.9% |
| $\sigma_{\bar{k}}$ | 26.5% | 15.1% |

In actual practice, monthly rather than annual returns are generally used for $\bar{k}_J$ and $\bar{k}_M$, and five years of data are employed; thus, there would be $5 \times 12 = 60$ dots on the scatter diagram. Also, in practice one would always use the *least squares method* for finding the regression coefficients a and b; this procedure minimizes the squared values of the error terms. It is discussed in statistics courses.

Note that the least squares value of beta can be obtained quite easily with a computer or even with a calculator that has statistical functions. The procedures below explain how to find the values of beta and the slope using either a Texas Instruments or a Hewlett-Packard financial calculator:

### Texas Instruments BA, BA-II, or MBA calculator

1. Press 2nd Mode until "STAT" shows in the display.
2. Enter the first X value ($\bar{k}_M$ = 23.8 in our example), press x≷y, and then enter the first Y value ($\bar{k}_J$ = 38.6) and press Σ+.
3. Repeat Step 2 until all values have been entered.
4. Press 2nd b/a to find the value of Y at X = 0, which is the value of the Y intercept (a), −8.9219, and then press x≷y to display the value of the slope (beta), 1.6031.
5. You could also press 2nd Corr to obtain the correlation coefficient, r, which is 0.9134.

Putting it all together, you should have this regression line:

$$\bar{k}_J = -8.92 + 1.60\bar{k}_M.$$

$$r = 0.9134.$$

### Hewlett-Packard 12C

1. Press f CLx to clear your memory registers.
2. Enter the first Y value ($\bar{k}_J$ = 38.6 in our example), press ENTER, and then enter the first X value ($\bar{k}_M$ = 23.8) and press Σ+.
3. Repeat Step 2 until all values have been entered.
4. Press 0 g ŷ,r to find the value of Y at X = 0, which is the value of the Y intercept (a), −8.9219.
5. Press STO 0 to store the value of the Y intercept for use in calculating the slope (beta).
6. Press 0 g x̂,r to find the value of X at Y = 0, which is the value of the X intercept, 5.5655.
7. Press RCL 0 CHS x≷y ÷ to calculate and display the value of the slope (beta), 1.6031.
8. You can also press 0 g ŷ,r x≷y to obtain the correlation coefficient, r, which is 0.9134 in this case.

Putting it all together, you should have this regression line:

$$\bar{k}_J = -8.92 + 1.60\bar{k}_M.$$

$$r = 0.9134.$$

## Problems

Beta coefficients and
rates of return

**6A-1**    You are given the following set of data:

| | Historic Rates of Return ($\bar{k}$) | |
|---|---|---|
| Year | Stock Y ($\bar{k}_Y$) | NYSE ($\bar{k}_M$) |
| 1 | 3.0% | 4.0% |
| 2 | 18.2 | 14.3 |
| 3 | 9.1 | 19.0 |
| 4 | −6.0 | −14.7 |
| 5 | −15.3 | −26.5 |
| 6 | 33.1 | 37.2 |
| 7 | 6.1 | 23.8 |
| 8 | 3.2 | −7.2 |
| 9 | 14.8 | 6.6 |
| 10 | 24.1 | 20.5 |
| 11 | 18.0 | 30.6 |
| Mean | 9.8% | 9.8% |
| $\sigma_{\bar{k}}$ | 13.8% | 19.6% |

a. Construct a "scatter diagram" graph showing the relationship between returns on Stock Y and the market as in Figure 6A-1; then draw a freehand approximation of the regression line. What is the approximate value of the beta coefficient? (If you have a calculator with statistical functions, use it to calculate beta.) Use graph paper.

b. Give a verbal interpretation of what the regression line and the beta coefficient show about Stock Y's volatility and relative riskiness as compared with other stocks.

c. Suppose the scatter of points had been more spread out, but the regression line was exactly where your present graph shows it. How would this affect (1) the firm's risk if the stock were held in a one-asset portfolio and (2) the actual risk premium on the stock if the CAPM held exactly? How would the degree of scatter (or the correlation coefficient) affect your confidence that the calculated beta will hold true in the years ahead?

d. Suppose the regression line had been downward sloping and the beta coefficient had been negative. What would this imply about (1) Stock Y's relative riskiness and (2) its probable risk premium?

e. Construct an illustrative probability distribution graph of returns (see Figure 6-6) on portfolios consisting of (1) only Stock Y, (2) 1 percent each of 100 stocks with beta coefficients similar to that of Stock Y, and (3) all stocks (that is, the distribution of returns on the market). Use as the expected rate of return the arithmetic mean as given above for both Stock Y and the market, and assume that the distributions are normal. Are the expected returns "reasonable"—that is, is it reasonable that $\hat{k}_Y = \hat{k}_M = 9.8\%$?

f. Now suppose that in the next year, Year 12, the market return was 27 percent but Stock Y increased its use of debt, which raised its perceived risk to investors. Further, this risk increase is expected to

have no effect on Firm Y's dividend stream. What would happen to
its stock price? Do you think that the return in Year 12 can be approximated by the following historic characteristic line?

$$\bar{k}_Y = 3.8\% + 0.62(\bar{k}_M) = 3.8\% + 0.62(27\%) = 20.5\%.$$

g. Now suppose $\bar{k}_Y$ in Year 12 had actually been 0 percent, with the
stock price decline exactly offsetting its dividend yield. What would
the new beta be, based on the most recent 11 years of data, that is,
Years 2 through 12? Does this beta seem reasonable—that is, is the
change in beta consistent with the other facts given in the problem?

Security Market Line        6A-2    You are given the following historic data on market returns, $\bar{k}_M$, and the
returns on Stocks A and B, $\bar{k}_A$ and $\bar{k}_B$:

| Year | $\bar{k}_M$ | $\bar{k}_A$ | $\bar{k}_B$ |
|------|------|------|------|
| 1 | 37.2% | 37.2% | 26.1% |
| 2 | 23.8 | 23.8 | 19.4 |
| 3 | −7.2 | −7.2 | 3.9 |
| 4 | 6.6 | 6.6 | 10.8 |
| 5 | 20.5 | 20.5 | 17.7 |
| 6 | 30.6 | 30.6 | 22.8 |

$k_{RF}$, the riskless rate, is 10 percent. Your probability distribution for $k_M$
for next year is as follows:

| Probability | $k_M$ |
|------|------|
| 0.1 | −15% |
| 0.2 | 0 |
| 0.4 | 15 |
| 0.2 | 30 |
| 0.1 | 45 |

a. Determine graphically the beta coefficients for Stocks A and B.
b. Graph the Security Market Line and give its equation.
c. Calculate the required rates of return on Stocks A and B.
d. Suppose a new stock, C, with $b_C = 2$, $D_1/P_0 = 8\%$, and an expected
growth rate of 8 percent becomes available. Is this stock in equilibrium? Explain. If the stock is not in equilibrium, explain how equilibrium will be restored.

# II

# FINANCIAL STATEMENTS AND FINANCIAL FORECASTING

In order to use the valuation models developed in Part I, investors need information on companies' expected earnings, dividends, and growth rates, and on the riskiness of these items. The sources of this information are described in Chapter 7. Chapter 8 then discusses how financial managers make projections of future financial statements and use these projections to help plan future operations.

# 7 ANALYSIS OF FINANCIAL STATEMENTS

## WHAT AFFECTS RETURN ON EQUITY: ALBERTSON'S, DELMARVA POWER, AND DART AND KRAFT

A firm's stock price depends to a large extent on the rate of return management is able to generate on the stockholders' equity (ROE). Consequently management seeks to raise the level of ROE, and investors are very much interested in past and prospective ROE levels.

Every year *Fortune, Business Week*, and other business magazines publish "report cards" on each of the largest firms in the United States, breaking them down into groups such as industrials (primarily manufacturing firms), retailers, utilities, and banks. A feature of these reports is the level of ROE and changes in it, along with clues as to why the changes occurred.

Data from some representative companies in the grocery chain, electric power, and manufacturing industries are given below:

|  | Profit Margin on Sales | × Turnover × | Equity Multiplier | = ROE |
|---|---|---|---|---|
|  | $\dfrac{\text{Profits}}{\text{Sales}}$ × | $\dfrac{\text{Sales}}{\text{Assets}}$ × | $\dfrac{\text{Assets}}{\text{Equity}}$ | = $\dfrac{\text{Net Income}}{\text{Common Equity}}$ |
| Albertson's | 1.70% | 7.26× | 1.46× | 18.0% |
| Delmarva Power | 13.76 | 0.56 | 2.27 | 17.5 |
| Dart and Kraft | 4.59 | 2.18 | 1.75 | 17.5 |

The three companies had about the same ROE, but they achieved it in very different ways. Albertson's, a leading food chain, made only a small profit per dollar of sales, but on average it turned over its assets 7.26 times per year, and hence it made up in volume for the small markup per item sold. Delmarva Power had a high profit per dollar of sales, but its turnover was low because it required a huge investment in assets to generate a dollar of sales revenue. Dart and Kraft, a typical manufacturing company, lies between the extremes of the utility and the grocery chain. Notice that the three companies all used debt (or "leverage") to boost their ROEs, and this was especially true for the utility.

If a company wants to increase its ROE, it must raise its profit margin on sales, boost its turnover, or increase its leverage. Of course, there are limits to raising these ratios, and hence the level of ROE, but the better management is, the better the firm's performance will be. In this chapter we look in more depth at the determinants of ROEs, see how managers can analyze operations to improve performance, and discuss how investors can analyze financial statements to anticipate future changes in profitability and hence in stock prices.

In Chapters 4, 5, and 6 we examined the discounted cash flow concept, developed bond and stock valuation models, discussed the concept of risk, and saw that risk affects the value of financial assets. Up to this point, however, we have abstracted from the actual data used in financial analysis as well as from the fundamental determinants of risk and profitability. In this chapter we first examine the basic financial data available to managers and investors, after which we look at some analytical techniques used by investors to appraise firms' relative riskiness, profit potential, and general management competence. Managers also use these same analytical techniques to measure and improve upon their own performance, judging performance in terms of maximizing the firm's stock price.

As you go through the chapter, it is important to remember that security values are established as discounted *cash flows*, yet accounting statements concentrate primarily on *reported profits*. As we shall see, there can be major differences between profits as reported by accountants and cash flows. This makes it necessary to "look behind the accounting numbers," both when appraising the performance of management and when setting a value for the firm. For the most part, accounting numbers are valid—high accounting profits generally signify high cash flows and the ability to pay high dividends, either now or in the future, but there are enough exceptions to this rule to warrant a critical examination of all accounting data. Keep this in mind as you read the chapter.

## Financial Statements and Reports

**annual report**
A report issued annually by corporations to their stockholders that contains basic financial statements as well as management's opinion of the past year's operations and the firm's future prospects.

Of the various reports corporations issue to their stockholders, the **annual report** is by far the most important. Two types of information are given in this report. First, there is a verbal section that both describes the firm's operating results during the past year and discusses new developments that will affect future operations. Second, the report presents four basic financial statements—the *income statement*, the *balance sheet*, the *statement of retained earnings*, and the *statement of changes in financial position*. Taken together, these statements give an accounting picture of the firm's operations and financial position. Detailed data are provided for the two most recent years, along with historical summaries of key operating statistics for the past five or ten years.[1]

The quantitative and verbal information are equally important. The financial statements report *what has actually happened* to earnings and dividends over the past few years, while the verbal statements attempt to explain why things turned out the way they did. For example, Texas Instruments' earnings dropped sharply in 1985. Management reported that the drop resulted from problems in the semiconductor industry, but it then went on to paint a more optimistic picture for the future. Of course, a return to profitability may not occur, and analysts should compare management's past statements with subsequent results. *In any event, the information contained in the annual report is used by investors to form expectations about future earnings and dividends, and about the riskiness of these expected values.* Therefore, the annual report is obviously of great interest to investors.

## The Income Statement

**income statement**
A statement summarizing the firm's revenues and expenses over an accounting period.

Table 7-1 gives the 1984 and 1985 **income statements** for National Metals Company, a major producer of fabricated aluminum products. Net sales are shown at the top of the statements, after which various costs, including income taxes, are subtracted to obtain the net income available to common stockholders. A report on earnings and dividends per share is given at the bottom of the statement. In financial management, earnings per share (EPS) is called "the bottom line," denoting that of all the items on the income statement, EPS is the most important.[2] National earned $2.40 per share in 1985, down from $2.60 in 1984, but it raised the dividend from $1.80 to $2.00.

## The Balance Sheet

**balance sheet**
A statement of the firm's financial position at a specific point in time.

The left-hand side of National's year-end 1984 and 1985 **balance sheet**, which is given in Table 7-2, shows the firm's assets, while the right-hand side shows claims against these assets. The assets are listed in order of their "liquidity," or the length of time it typically takes to convert them to cash. The claims are listed in the order in which they must be paid: Accounts payable must generally be paid within 30 days; notes are payable within 90 days; and so on down to the stockholders' equity accounts, which represent ownership and need never be "paid off."

---

[1]Firms also provide quarterly reports, but these are much less comprehensive than the annual reports. In addition, larger firms file even more detailed statements, giving breakdowns for each major division or subsidiary, with the Securities and Exchange Commission (SEC). These reports, called *10-K reports*, are made available to stockholders upon request to a company's secretary. Finally, many larger firms also publish *statistical supplements*, which give financial statement data and key ratios going back ten years.

[2]Dividends are important too, but the firm's ability to pay dividends is dependent on its long-run cash flows, which in turn are dependent primarily on its earnings.

**Table 7-1**
**National Metals Company:**
**Income Statements for Years**
**Ending December 31**
**(Millions of Dollars, Except for Per Share Data)**

|  | 1985 | 1984 |
|---|---|---|
| Net sales | $3,000 | $2,850 |
| Costs and expenses: |  |  |
| Labor and materials | 2,544 | 2,413 |
| Depreciation | 100 | 90 |
| Selling | 22 | 20 |
| General and administrative | 40 | 35 |
| Lease payments on buildings | 28 | 28 |
| Total costs | $2,734 | $2,586 |
| Net operating income, or earnings before interest and taxes (EBIT) | $ 266 | $ 264 |
| Less interest expense: |  |  |
| Interest on notes payable | $     8 | $     2 |
| Interest on first mortgage bonds | 40 | 42 |
| Interest on debentures | 18 | 3 |
| Total interest | $   66 | $   47 |
| Earnings before taxes | $ 200 | $ 217 |
| Taxes (at 40%) | 80 | 87 |
| Net income after taxes available to common stockholders | $ 120 | $ 130 |
| Disposition of net income: |  |  |
| Dividends to common stockholders | $ 100 | $   90 |
| Addition to retained earnings | $   20 | $   40 |
| Per share of common stock: |  |  |
| Stock price (year-end) | $28.50 | $29.00 |
| Earnings per share (EPS)[a] | $ 2.40 | $ 2.60 |
| Dividends per share (DPS)[a] | $ 2.00 | $ 1.80 |

[a]There are 50 million shares outstanding; see Table 7-2.
Calculations of EPS and DPS for 1985 are as follows:

$$\text{EPS} = \frac{\text{Net income after tax}}{\text{Shares outstanding}} = \frac{\$120,000,000}{50,000,000} = \$2.40.$$

$$\text{DPS} = \frac{\text{Dividends paid to common stockholders}}{\text{Shares outstanding}} = \frac{\$100,000,000}{50,000,000} = \$2.00.$$

Some additional points about the balance sheet are worth noting:

**1. Cash versus other assets.** Although the assets are all stated in terms of dollars, only cash represents actual money. Receivables are bills others owe National; inventories consist of raw materials, work-in-process, and finished goods available for sale; and fixed assets consist of National's plant and equipment. National can write checks at present for a total of $50 million (versus

**Table 7-2**
**National Metals Company:**
**December 31 Balance Sheets**
**(Millions of Dollars)**

| Assets | 1985 | 1984 | Claims on Assets | 1985 | 1984 |
|---|---|---|---|---|---|
| Cash | $ 50 | $ 55 | Accounts payable | $ 60 | $ 30 |
| Marketable securities | 0 | 25 | Notes payable | 100 | 60 |
| Accounts receivable | 350 | 315 | Accrued wages | 10 | 10 |
| Inventories | 300 | 215 | Accrued taxes | 130 | 120 |
| Total current assets | $ 700 | $ 610 | Total current claims | $ 300 | $ 220 |
| Gross plant and equipment | $1,800 | $1,470 | First mortgage bonds | $ 500 | $ 520 |
| Less depreciation | 500 | 400 | Debentures | 300 | 60 |
| Net plant and equipment | $1,300 | $1,070 | Total long-term debt | $ 800 | $ 580 |
| | | | Stockholders' equity: | | |
| | | | Common stock (50,000,000 shares, $1 par) | $ 50 | $ 50 |
| | | | Additional paid-in capital | 100 | 100 |
| | | | Retained earnings | 750 | 730 |
| | | | Total stockholders' equity | $ 900 | $ 880 |
| Total assets | $2,000 | $1,680 | Total claims | $2,000 | $1,680 |

Note: The first mortgage bonds have a sinking fund requirement of $20 million a year. Sinking funds are discussed in Chapter 12, but in brief, a sinking fund simply involves the repayment of long-term debt. Thus, National Metals was required to pay off $20 million from December 31, 1984, to December 31, 1985. The current portion of the long-term debt is included in notes payable here, although in a more detailed balance sheet it would be shown as a separate item under current liabilities.

current liabilities of $300 million due within a year). The noncash assets should produce cash flows eventually, but they do not represent cash-in-hand.

**2. Liabilities versus stockholders' equity.** The claims against assets are of two types—liabilities, or money the company owes, and the stockholders' ownership position.[3] The **stockholders' equity**, or **net worth**, is a residual:

$$\text{Assets} \quad - \quad \text{Liabilities} \quad = \text{Stockholders' equity.}$$
$$\$2,000,000,000 - \$1,100,000,000 = \quad \$900,000,000.$$

Suppose assets decline in value—for example, suppose some of the accounts receivable are written off as bad debts. Liabilities remain constant, so the value of the net worth must decline. Therefore, the risk of asset value fluctuations is borne by the stockholders. Note, however, that if asset values rise (perhaps because of inflation), these benefits will accrue exclusively to the stockholders.

**3. Breakdown of the stockholders' equity account.** A detailed discussion of the equity accounts is given in Chapter 11, "Common Stock and the Investment Banking Process," but a brief preview of that discussion is useful

**stockholders' equity (net worth)**
The capital supplied by stockholders—capital stock, paid-in capital, retained earnings, and occasionally certain reserves. *Common equity,* or *stockholders' equity,* is that part of the total net worth belonging to the common stockholders.

---

[3]One could divide liabilities into (1) debts owed to someone and (2) other items such as deferred taxes, reserves, and so on. We do not make this distinction, and so the terms *debt* and *liabilities* are used synonymously.

**retained earnings**
That portion of the firm's earnings that is "saved" rather than paid out as dividends.

**paid-in capital**
Funds received in excess of par value when a firm sells stock.

here. First, note that the equity section is divided into three accounts—common stock, paid-in capital, and retained earnings. The **retained earnings** account is built up over time by the firm's "saving" a part of its earnings rather than paying all earnings out as dividends. The other two accounts arise from the sale of stock by the firm to raise capital. Accountants generally assign a *par value* to common stock—National Metals' stock has a par value of $1.[4] Now suppose National were to sell 1 million additional shares at a price of $30 per share. The company would raise $30 million, and the cash accounts would go up by this amount. Of the total, $1 million would be added to common stock and $29 million to **paid-in capital**. Thus, after the sale, common stock would show $51 million, paid-in capital would show $129 million, and there would be 51 million shares outstanding.

The breakdown of the equity accounts is important for some purposes but not for others. For example, a potential stockholder would want to know if the company had actually earned the funds reported in its equity accounts or if funds had come mainly from selling stock. A potential creditor, on the other hand, would be more interested in the amount of money the owners had put up than in the form in which they put it up. In the remainder of this chapter, we generally aggregate the three equity accounts and call this sum *common equity* or *net worth*.

**4. Inventory accounting.** National uses the FIFO (first-in, first-out) method to determine the inventory value shown on its balance sheet ($300 million). It could have used the LIFO (last-in, first-out) method. During a period of rising prices FIFO causes reported inventories to show a higher value than LIFO would. At the same time, FIFO causes the cost of goods sold (materials expense as shown in the income statement in Table 7-1) to be lower than it would be if LIFO were used, and with a lower cost of goods sold, reported profits would be higher. In National's case, EPS would have been lowered by 30 cents, to $2.10, and its balance sheet figures for inventories would have been $275 million rather than $300 million, had the company elected to use LIFO. Thus, the inventory valuation method can have a significant effect on the financial statements.

**5. Depreciation methods.** Companies often use the ACRS method to calculate depreciation for tax purposes but straight line based on a longer life for stockholder reporting. However, National, IBM, and some other companies use rapid depreciation for stockholder reporting as well as for tax purposes. Had National not used ACRS for stockholder reporting, its EPS would have been raised by almost 50 cents, and the $1.3 billion shown for "net plant" on its balance sheet, and hence its retained earnings, would also have been materially higher.

**6. The time dimension.** The balance sheet may be thought of as a snapshot of the firm's financial position *at a point in time*—for example, on December 31, 1985. Thus, on December 31, 1984, National had $25 million of market-

---

[4]See Chapter 11 for a discussion of par value.

able securities, but this account was zero by the end of 1985. The income statement, on the other hand, reports on operations *over a period of time*— for example, during the calendar year 1985. National had sales of $3 billion, and its net income was $120 million. The balance sheet changes every day as inventories are increased or decreased, as fixed assets are added or retired, as bank loans are increased or decreased, and so on. Companies whose businesses are seasonal have especially large balance sheet changes. For example, most retailers have large inventories just before Christmas, but low inventories and high accounts receivable after Christmas, so their balance sheets look materially different depending on the date chosen to construct the statement.

**7. Deferred taxes.** National uses ACRS depreciation both for calculating its tax liability and for computing net income to report to its stockholders. However, most companies use ACRS for tax purposes and some other depreciation method, one that will more accurately represent the decline in assets' value, for reporting purposes. The result is that the tax liability reported on an income statement can be different from the taxes actually paid. The difference between the computed taxes and the actual tax liability is called *deferred taxes*. The balance sheet item "deferred taxes" is the cumulative taxes the firm has deferred over time. This item does not appear on National's balance sheet, but many firms do have such an entry in the liabilities section of their balance sheets.

## The Cash Flow Cycle

As a company like National Metals goes about its business, it makes sales, which lead to a reduction of inventories, to an increase in cash, and, if the sales price exceeds the cost of the item sold, to a profit. These transactions cause the balance sheet to change, and they also are reflected in the income statement. It is critically important that you understand (1) that businesses deal with *physical* units like autos, computers, or aluminum, (2) that physical transactions are translated into dollar terms through the accounting system, and (3) that financial analysis is designed to examine the accounting numbers in order to measure how efficient the firm is at making and selling physical goods and services. In other words, how good is the company at taking resources in the form of labor and materials and converting them into some product or service that people want and are willing to pay for?

Several factors make financial analysis difficult. One is accounting—different methods of inventory valuation and depreciation can lead to differences in reported profits for otherwise similar firms, and a good financial analyst must be able to adjust for these differences if he or she is to make valid comparisons among companies. Another factor involves timing—an action is taken at one point in time, but its full effects are not felt until some later period, yet we need to evaluate the effects of the action before its final results are known.

**cash flow**
The actual net cash, as opposed to accounting net income, that flows into or out of the firm during some specified period; equal to net income after taxes plus noncash expenses, including depreciation.

To understand how timing influences the financial statement, and hence financial analysis, one must understand the **cash flow** cycle within a firm as set forth in Figure 7-1. Rectangles represent balance sheet accounts—assets and claims against assets—while circles represent actions taken by the firm. Each rectangle may be thought of as a reservoir, and the wavy lines designate the amount of the asset or liability in the reservoir (account) on a balance sheet date. Various transactions cause changes in the accounts, just as adding or subtracting water changes the level in a reservoir. The diagram is by no means a complete representation of the cash flow cycle—to avoid undue complexity, it shows only the major flows.

The cash account is the focal point of the graph. Certain events, such as collecting accounts receivable or borrowing money from the bank, will cause the cash account to increase, while the payment of taxes, interest, and so on will cause it to decline. Similar comments could be made about all the balance sheet accounts—their balances rise, fall, or remain constant depending on events that occur during the period under study, which for National Metals is January 1, 1985, through December 31, 1985.

Projected sales increases may require the firm to raise cash by borrowing from its bank or selling new stock. For example, if National anticipates an increase in sales, it will (1) expend cash to buy or build fixed assets through the capital budgeting process, (2) step up purchases, thereby increasing both raw materials inventories and accounts payable, (3) increase production, which causes an increase in both accrued wages and work-in-process, and (4) eventually build up its finished goods inventory. Some cash will have been expended and hence removed from the cash account, and the firm will have obligated itself to expend still more cash to pay off its accounts payable and accrued wages within a few weeks. These events will have occurred *before* any new cash has been generated. Even when the expected sales do occur, there will still be a lag in the generation of cash until receivables are collected. For example, if National grants credit for 30 days, then it will be about 30 days after a sale is made before cash comes in. Depending on how much cash the firm had at the beginning of the buildup, on the length of its production-sales-collection cycle, and on how long it can delay payment of its own payables and accrued wages, the company may have to obtain significant amounts of additional cash by selling stock or bonds, or by borrowing from the bank.

If the firm is profitable, its sales revenues will exceed its costs, and its cash inflows will eventually exceed its cash outlays. However, even a profitable business can experience a cash shortage if it is growing rapidly. It may have to pay for plant, materials, and labor before cash from the expanded sales starts flowing in. For this reason, rapidly growing firms often require large bank loans or capital from other sources.

An unprofitable firm, such as Storage Technology in recent years, will have larger cash outlays than inflows. This, in turn, will typically cause a slowdown in the payment of accrued wages and accounts payable, and it may also lead to heavy borrowings. Thus, liabilities build up to excessive levels in unprof-

**Figure 7-1**
**Cash and Materials Flows within the Firm**

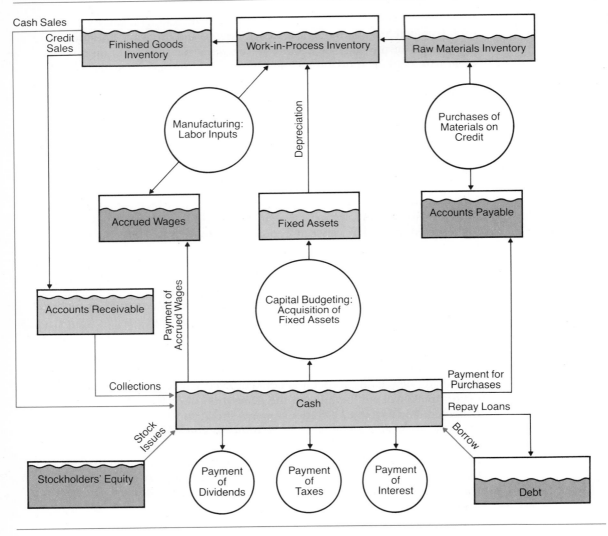

itable firms. Similarly, an overly ambitious expansion plan will be reflected in an excessive buildup of inventories and fixed assets, while a poor credit/ collection policy will result in bad debts and reduced profits that will first show up as high accounts receivable. Financial analysts are well aware of these relationships, and they use the analytical techniques discussed in the remainder of this chapter and later in the book to help discover problems before they become too serious.

**Table 7-3**
**National Metals Company:**
**Statement of Retained Earnings**
**for Year Ending December 31, 1985**
**(Millions of Dollars)**

| | |
|---|---:|
| Balance of retained earnings, December 31, 1984 | $730 |
| Add: Net income, 1985 | 120 |
| Less: Dividends to stockholders | (100)[a] |
| Balance of retained earnings, December 31, 1985 | $750 |

[a]Here, and throughout the book, parentheses are used to denote negative numbers.

## Statement of Retained Earnings

**statement of retained earnings**
A statement reporting that portion of the firm's earnings not paid out in dividends. The figure that appears on the balance sheet is the sum of retained earnings for each year of the firm's history.

Changes in the common equity accounts between balance sheet dates are reported in the **statement of retained earnings**. National's statement is shown in Table 7-3. The company earned $120 million during 1985, paid out $100 million in dividends, and plowed $20 million back into the business. Thus, the balance sheet item "Retained earnings" increased from $730 million at the end of 1984 to $750 million at the end of 1985.

Note that the balance sheet account retained earnings represents a *claim against assets*, not assets per se. Further, firms retain earnings primarily to expand the business—this means investing in plant and equipment, in inventories, and so on, *not* in a bank account. *Thus, retained earnings as reported on the balance sheet do not represent cash and are not "available" for the payment of dividends or anything else.*[5]

## Statement of Changes in Financial Position

**statement of changes in financial position**
A statement reporting the firm's sources of financing and the uses of those funds over an accounting period.

The graphic analysis set forth in Figure 7-1 is converted into numerical form and reported in annual reports as the **statement of changes in financial position**, often called the *sources and uses of funds statement*. This statement is designed to show how the company obtained funds and how they were used. It helps answer questions such as these: Was an expansion program financed by sale of debt or equity? How much of its required capital has the firm been able to generate internally? Has the firm been building up its liquid assets, or is it becoming less liquid? Is output from the new plant selling, or are inventories just building up? Are customers paying on time, or are accounts receivable building up? Information such as this is useful both for investment analysis and for corporate planning, so the statement of changes in financial position is an important part of the annual report.

---

[5]Recall from your accounting courses that the amount recorded in the retained earnings account is *not* an indication of the amount of cash the firm has. That amount (as of the balance sheet date) is found in the cash account—an asset account. A positive number in the retained earnings account indicates only that in the past, according to generally accepted accounting principles, the firm has earned an income and its dividends have been less than that reported income. Also, recall the difference between accrual and cash accounting. Even though a company reports record earnings and shows an increase in the retained earnings account, it may still be short of cash.

**depreciation**
An annual noncash charge against income that reflects a rough estimate of the dollar cost of fixed assets used in the production process.

***The Role of Depreciation.*** Before we discuss the statement of changes in financial position in detail, we should reflect for a moment on one of its most important elements—**depreciation**. First, what is depreciation? In effect, it is an annual charge against income which provides an estimate of the dollar cost of the capital equipment used in the production process. For example, suppose a machine with an ACRS class life of 5 years and a zero expected salvage value was purchased in 1984 for $100,000. This $100,000 cost is not expensed in the purchase year, but rather is charged against production over the machine's 5-year depreciable life. If the depreciation expense were not taken, then profits would be overstated and taxes would be too high. This point is illustrated in Appendix 7A. The annual depreciation allowance is deducted from sales revenues, along with such other costs as labor and raw materials, to determine income. However, depreciation is not a cash outlay; funds were expended back in 1984, so the depreciation charged against the income in Years 1985 through 1989 is not a cash outlay, as are labor or raw materials charges. *Depreciation is a noncash charge.*

This point is illustrated with data for National Metals in Table 7-4. Here Column 1 shows an abbreviated version of National's income statement, while Column 2 shows the statement on a cash flow basis. Assume for the moment (1) that all sales are for cash, (2) that all costs except depreciation were paid during 1985, and (3) that no buildups occurred in inventories or other assets. How much cash would have been generated from operations? From Column 2 we see that the answer is $220 million. The sales are all for cash, so the firm took in $3 billion of cash money. Its costs other than depreciation were $2.634 billion, and these were paid in cash, leaving $366 million. Depreciation is *not* a cash charge—the firm does not pay out the $100 million of depreciation expenses—so $366 million of cash money is still left after depreciation. Taxes and interest, however, are paid in cash, so $66 million for interest and $80 million for taxes must be deducted from the $366 million cash earnings before interest and taxes, leaving a net cash flow from operations of $220 million.[6] As shown in Column 1, this $220 million is exactly equal to profit after tax plus depreciation: $120 million plus $100 million equals $220 million. Thus, since depreciation is a noncash charge, it is added back to net income to approximate cash flows from operations, and it is included as a source of funds in the statement of changes in financial position as discussed in the next section.

Before leaving the subject of depreciation, we should sound a word of caution. Depreciation does not really *provide* funds; it is simply a noncash

---

[6]Note that if National had depreciated its assets by a depreciation method other than ACRS, its depreciation expenses would be lowered and its reported tax liability and net income would be higher. In that case, only a portion of the taxes reported would be cash expenditures and the remainder would be deferred. Therefore, the firm's cash flows would equal net income plus depreciation plus deferred taxes. We will show in Appendix 7A that a firm's *cash flows* are the same under either reporting method, but *reported earnings* are higher for the firm that uses a slower depreciation method for reporting purposes, at least initially.

**Table 7-4**
**National Metals Company:**
**Cash Flows for 1985**
**(Millions of Dollars)**

|  | Income Statement (1) | Cash Flows (2) |
|---|---|---|
| Sales | $3,000 | $3,000 |
| Costs and expenses: |  |  |
|    Costs except depreciation | 2,634 | 2,634 |
|    Depreciation (D) | 100 | — |
| Earnings before interest and taxes (EBIT) | $ 266 | $ 366 |
| Interest expense | 66 | 66 |
| Earnings before taxes | $ 200 | $ 300 |
| Taxes | 80 | 80 |
| Net income (NI) | $ 120 | n.a. |
| Cash flow: CF = NI + D = $120 + $100 = | $ 220 | $ 220 |

n.a. = Not applicable.

charge which is added back to net income to obtain an estimate of the cash flow from operations. However, if the firm made no sales, then depreciation would not provide cash flows. To see this point more clearly, consider the case of Communications Satellite Corporation (Comsat), which derives its income principally from two satellites, one positioned over the Atlantic and one over the Pacific. Comsat's cash flows are approximately equal to its net income plus its depreciation charges. Yet, if its two satellites stopped working, sales would vanish, and while accountants might still calculate depreciation, this depreciation would provide no cash flows (except possibly from some tax loss carry-backs).

***Preparing the Statement of Changes in Financial Position.*** The statement of changes in financial position is designed to answer at a glance these three questions: (1) Where did the firm get its funds during the year? (2) What did it do with its available funds? (3) Did operations during the year tend to increase or decrease the firm's liquidity as measured by the change in net working capital?[7] **Working capital** is defined as total current assets, while **net working capital** is current assets minus current liabilities. In general, the firm's financial position is stronger if net working capital increases, and weaker if it decreases.

The starting point in preparing a statement of changes in financial position is to determine the change in each balance sheet item and then to record it as either a source or a use of funds in accordance with the following rules:

**working capital**
A firm's total current assets.

**net working capital**
The difference between total current assets and total current liabilities.

---

[7]There are several different formats for presenting the statement of changes in financial position. The format we present here focuses on changes in net working capital.

*Sources*:

1. Increase in claims, that is, an increase in a liability or capital account. Borrowing from the bank is an example.

2. Decrease in an asset account. Selling some fixed assets, or reducing inventories, are examples.

*Uses*:

1. Decrease in a claim against assets. Paying off a loan is an example.

2. Increase in an asset account. Buying fixed assets, or building inventories, are examples.

Thus, sources of funds include bank loans and retained earnings, as well as money generated by selling assets, by collecting receivables, and even by drawing down the cash account. Uses include acquiring fixed assets, building up receivables or inventories, and paying off debts.

Table 7-5 shows the changes that occurred in National Metals Company's balance sheet accounts during the calendar year 1985, with each change designated as a source or a use. Sources and uses each total $470 million.[8] Note

**Table 7-5**
**National Metals Company:**
**Changes in Balance Sheet Accounts during 1985**
**(Millions of Dollars)**

|  |  |  | Change | |
|---|---|---|---|---|
|  | 12/31/85 | 12/31/84 | Source | Use |
| Cash | $    50 | $    55 | $    5 |  |
| Marketable securities | 0 | 25 | 25 |  |
| Accounts receivable | 350 | 315 |  | $  35 |
| Inventories | 300 | 215 |  | 85 |
| Gross plant and equipment | 1,800 | 1,470 |  | 330 |
| Accumulated depreciation[a] | 500 | 400 | 100 |  |
| Accounts payable | 60 | 30 | 30 |  |
| Notes payable | 100 | 60 | 40 |  |
| Accrued wages | 10 | 10 |  |  |
| Accrued taxes | 130 | 120 | 10 |  |
| Mortgage bonds | 500 | 520 |  | 20 |
| Debentures | 300 | 60 | 240 |  |
| Common stock | 50 | 50 |  |  |
| Paid-in capital | 100 | 100 |  |  |
| Retained earnings | 750 | 730 | 20 |  |
| Totals |  |  | $470 | $470 |

[a]Depreciation is a *contra-asset*, not an asset; hence, an increase in depreciation is a source of funds.

---

[8]Adjustments must be made if fixed assets were sold or retired during the year. National had no sales of assets or major retirements during 1985.

that the table does not contain any summary accounts such as total current assets or net plant and equipment. If we included summary accounts in Table 7-5 and then used these accounts to prepare the statement of changes in financial position, we would be "double counting."

The data contained in Table 7-5 are next used to prepare the formal statement of changes in financial position, or sources and uses of funds statement. The one contained in National Metals' annual report is shown in Table 7-6. Note that every item in the "change" columns of Table 7-5 is carried over to

**Table 7-6**
**National Metals Company:**
**1985 Statement of Changes in Financial Position**
**(Millions of Dollars)**

| Sources of Funds | |
|---|---|
| Net income after taxes | $120 |
| Depreciation | 100 |
|    Funds from operations | $220 |
| Proceeds from sale of debentures | 240 |
| Total sources | $460 |

| Uses of Funds | |
|---|---|
| Repayment of mortgage bonds | $ 20 |
| Increase in fixed assets | 330 |
| Dividend payments to common stockholders | 100 |
|    Total nonworking capital uses | $450 |
| Increase in net working capital[a] | 10 |
| Total uses | $460 |

| Analysis of Changes in Working Capital[a] | |
|---|---|
| Increases (decreases) in current assets: | |
|   Cash | ($ 5)[b] |
|   Marketable securities | (25) |
|   Accounts receivable | 35 |
|   Inventories | 85 |
|     Net increase in current assets | $ 90 |
| Increases (decreases) in current liabilities: | |
|   Accounts payable | $ 30 |
|   Notes payable | 40 |
|   Accrued taxes | 10 |
|     Net increase in current liabilities | $ 80 |
| Increase (decrease) in net working capital | $ 10 |

[a]If a company increases its net working capital, as National did, this is a sign of strength. If net working capital had declined, this would have represented a weakening position. If a decrease in net working capital had been calculated in the lower section, it would have been reported in the top section as a source of funds.
[b]Parentheses denote negative numbers here and throughout the book.

Table 7-6 except retained earnings: The statement of changes in financial position reports net income as a source and dividends as a use rather than netting these items out and just reporting the increase in retained earnings.

Notice that the statement provides answers to the three questions asked above: (1) The top section answers the question regarding National's major sources of long-term funds; (2) the middle section answers the question about how National used its available funds; and (3) the lower section, which deals with current assets and liabilities, shows how the company's liquidity position changed during the year. We see that National's major sources of funds were net income, depreciation, and the sale of debentures (a type of long-term debt which is described in Chapter 12). These funds were used to reduce the mortgage debt, to increase fixed assets, and to pay dividends on common stock. Also, $10 million was used to increase net working capital.

As shown in the bottom section, National decreased its cash and marketable securities but increased accounts receivable and inventories, for a net increase in current assets of $90 million. Current liabilities increased by $80 million, so there was an increase of $10 million in net working capital (current assets minus current liabilities). This net increase in working capital is reported as a use in the middle section.

National is a strong, well-managed company, and its sources and uses statement shows nothing unusual or alarming. One does, however, occasionally see situations in which huge increases in fixed assets are financed primarily by short-term debt, which must be repaid within a few months if the lender demands repayment. This would show up in the lower third of the table as a decrease in net working capital, and it is, as we shall see in detail later in the book, a dangerous situation.

## Earnings, Dividends, and Stock Prices

In addition to the four statements previously described, most annual reports today also give a summary of earnings, dividends, and stock prices over the last few years. For National, these data are analyzed in Figure 7-2. Earnings were variable, but there was a definite upward trend over the period. In 1985 a strike caused earnings to drop somewhat, but management expects the growth trend to resume in 1986.

Although dividends and dividend policy are discussed in detail in Chapter 16, we can make several comments about dividends at this point:

**1.** Dividends per share (DPS) represent the basic cash flows passed from the firm to its stockholders. As such, dividends are a key element in the stock valuation models developed in earlier chapters.

**2.** DPS in any given year can exceed EPS, but in the long run dividends are paid from earnings, so normally DPS is smaller than EPS. The percentage of earnings paid out in dividends, or the ratio of DPS to EPS, is defined as the *dividend payout ratio*. National Metals' payout ratio has varied somewhat from year to year, but it has averaged about 80 percent.

**3.** In a graph such as that in Figure 7-2, the DPS line is typically below the EPS line, while the two lines generally have about the same slope, indicating

**Figure 7-2**
**National Metals Company:**
**Earnings, Dividends, and Stock Prices, 1975-1985**

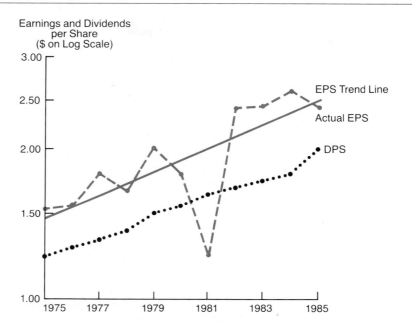

| Year | Average Stock Price | Earnings per Share | Dividends per Share |
|------|------|------|------|
| 1975 | $20 | $1.53 | $1.25 |
| 1976 | 22 | 1.55 | 1.30 |
| 1977 | 22 | 1.80 | 1.35 |
| 1978 | 23 | 1.65 | 1.40 |
| 1979 | 24 | 2.00 | 1.50 |
| 1980 | 21 | 1.80 | 1.55 |
| 1981 | 30 | 1.25 | 1.65 |
| 1982 | 31 | 2.40 | 1.70 |
| 1983 | 30 | 2.43 | 1.75 |
| 1984 | 37 | 2.60 | 1.80 |
| 1985 | 33 | 2.40 | 2.00 |

10-year growth rate:[a] EPS = 5%
                       DPS = 5%

[a]Growth rates were obtained by linear regression. The logs of EPS and DPS were regressed against years, and the slope coefficient represents the growth rate. The graphs above give plots of EPS and DPS over time and a trend line for EPS fitted by least squares regression. (The DPS growth is so smooth that a trend line is unnecessary.) By dividing the trend line figure for EPS in 1985 ($2.43) into the trend line figure for 1975 ($1.49), we obtain a PVIF for 10 years (not 11 years; 11 years of data are needed to estimate 10 years of *growth*). We can look up PVIF = $1.49/$2.43 = 0.6132 in Table A-1 in Appendix A across the row for 10 periods. The calculated interest factor is approximately equal to 0.6139, the factor for 5 percent; thus, the growth rate in EPS is approximately 5 percent.

Calculated growth rates can be highly sensitive to the beginning and ending points—for example, National's growth rate in EPS was negative from 1975 to 1981 but positive from 1975 to 1985. A *great deal* of judgment, plus qualitative information about the company, is needed when interpreting past trends and forecasting future EPS growth rates—indeed, the historic growth rate can almost never be used as more than a starting point for estimating the expected future growth rate. See Brigham and Gapenski, *Intermediate Financial Management,* Chapter 4, for a further discussion of growth rates.

that EPS and DPS are growing at about the same rate. As the data in Figure 7-2 indicate, National's earnings and dividends have both been growing at an average rate of 5 percent per year. If the type of analysis undertaken in the next section suggests that this trend will continue, then 5 percent is the value of g that will be used in the discounted cash flow valuation model to calculate National's stock price.

## Financial Statement Analysis

Financial statements report both on a firm's position at a point in time and on its operations over some past period. However, their real value lies in the fact that they can be used to help predict the firm's future earnings and dividends, as well as the riskiness of its cash flows. From an investor's standpoint, *predicting the future is what financial statement analysis is all about*, while from management's standpoint, *financial statement analysis is useful both as a way to anticipate future conditions and, more important, as a starting point for planning actions that will influence the future course of events*. In the remainder of this chapter we discuss procedures used by both investors and managers to analyze and interpret financial statements.

## Ratio Analysis[9]

Financial ratios are designed to show relationships between financial statement accounts. For example, Firm A might have debt of $5,248,760 and interest charges of $419,900, while Firm B might have debt of $52,647,980 and interest charges of $3,948,600. The true burden of these debts, and the companies' ability to repay them, can be ascertained by comparing each firm's debt to its assets, and its interest charges to the income available for payment of interest. Such comparisons are made by *ratio analysis*.

### Liquidity Ratios

One of the first concerns of most financial analysts is liquidity: Will the firm be able to meet its maturing obligations? National Metals has debts totaling $300 million that must be paid off within the coming year. Will National have trouble satisfying those obligations? A full liquidity analysis requires the use of cash budgets (described in Chapter 18), but by relating the amount of cash and other current assets to the current obligations, ratio analysis pro-

---

[9]In addition to the ratios discussed in this section, financial analysts also employ a tool known as *common size* balance sheets and income statements. To form a common size balance sheet, one simply divides each asset and liability item by total assets and expresses the result as a percentage. The resultant percentage statement can be compared with those of larger or smaller firms, or for the same firm over time. To form a common size income statement, one simply divides each item by sales.

**liquidity ratios**
Ratios that show the relationship of a firm's cash and other current assets to its current obligations.

**current ratio**
The ratio computed by dividing current assets by current liabilities; indicates the extent to which the claims of short-term creditors are covered by assets expected to be converted to cash in the near future.

vides a quick, easy-to-use measure of liquidity. Two commonly used **liquidity ratios** are discussed below.

***Current Ratio.*** The **current ratio** is computed by dividing current assets by current liabilities:

$$\text{Current ratio} = \frac{\text{Current assets}}{\text{Current liabilities}} = \frac{\$700}{\$300} = 2.3 \text{ times.}$$

$$\text{Industry average} = 2.5 \text{ times.}$$

Current assets normally include cash, marketable securities, accounts receivable, and inventories. Current liabilities consist of accounts payable, short-term notes payable, current maturities of long-term debt, accrued income taxes, and other accrued expenses (principally wages). Also, note that all dollar amounts in this section are in millions.

If a company is getting into financial difficulty, it begins paying its bills (accounts payable) more slowly, building up bank loans, and so on. If these current liabilities are rising faster than current assets, the current ratio will fall, and this could spell trouble. The current ratio provides the best single indicator of the extent to which the claims of short-term creditors are covered by assets that are expected to be converted to cash in a period roughly corresponding to the maturity of the claims. Therefore, it is the most commonly used measure of short-term solvency.

National's current ratio is slightly below the average for the industry, 2.5, but not low enough to cause concern. It appears that National is about in line with most other aluminum firms. Since current assets are scheduled to be converted to cash in the near future, it is highly probable that they could be liquidated at close to their stated value. With a current ratio of 2.3, National could liquidate current assets at only 43 percent of book value and still pay off current creditors in full.[10]

Although industry average figures are discussed later in some detail, it should be stated at this point that an industry average is not a magic number that all firms should strive to maintain—in fact, some very well-managed firms will be above it and other good firms below it. However, if a firm's ratios are far removed from the average for its industry, the analyst must be concerned about why this variance occurs. Thus, a deviation from the industry average should signal the analyst to check further.

**quick (acid test) ratio**
The ratio computed by deducting inventories from current assets and dividing the remainder by current liabilities.

***Quick, or Acid Test, Ratio.*** The **quick**, or **acid test**, **ratio** is calculated by deducting inventories from current assets and dividing the remainder by current liabilities:

$$\frac{\text{Quick, or}}{\text{acid test, ratio}} = \frac{\text{Current assets} - \text{Inventories}}{\text{Current liabilities}} = \frac{\$400}{\$300} = 1.3 \text{ times.}$$

$$\text{Industry average} = 1.0 \text{ times.}$$

---

[10] $1/2.3 = 0.43$, or 43 percent. Note that $0.43(\$700) = \$300$, the amount of current liabilities.

Inventories are typically the least liquid of a firm's current assets, and hence the assets on which losses are most likely to occur in the event of liquidation. Therefore, this measure of the firm's ability to pay off short-term obligations without relying on the sale of inventories is important.

The industry average quick ratio is 1.0, so National's 1.3 ratio compares favorably with other firms in the industry. If the accounts receivable can be collected, the company can pay off its current liabilities even without selling any inventory.

### Asset Management Ratios

**asset management ratios**
A set of ratios designed to measure how effectively a firm is managing its assets.

The second group of ratios, the **asset management ratios**, is designed to measure how effectively the firm is managing its assets. In particular, these ratios answer this question: Does the total amount of each type of asset as reported on the balance sheet seem reasonable, too high, or too low in view of current and projected operating levels? National and other companies must borrow or obtain capital from other sources in order to acquire assets. If they have too many assets, then their interest expenses will be too high and hence their profits too low. On the other hand, if assets are too low, then operations will not be as efficient as possible.

**inventory utilization ratio**
The ratio computed by dividing sales by inventories; also called the *inventory turnover ratio.*

***Inventory Utilization.*** The **inventory utilization ratio**, often called the *inventory turnover ratio*, is defined as sales divided by inventories:[11]

$$\text{Inventory utilization, or turnover, ratio} = \frac{\text{Sales}}{\text{Inventory}} = \frac{\$3,000}{\$300} = 10 \text{ times.}$$

$$\text{Industry average} = 9 \text{ times.}$$

As a rough approximation, each item of National's inventory is sold out and restocked, or "turned over," 10 times per year. Its gross profit is therefore 10 times the difference between its selling prices and the cost of its inventory.

National's turnover of 10 times compares favorably with an industry average of 9 times. This suggests that the company does not hold excessive stocks of inventory; excess stocks are, of course, unproductive and represent an investment with a low or zero rate of return. National's high inventory utilization ratio also reinforces our faith in the current ratio. If the turnover were low—say, 3 or 4 times—we might wonder whether the firm was holding damaged or obsolete materials not actually worth their stated value.

Two problems arise in calculating and analyzing the inventory utilization ratio. First, sales are stated at market prices, so if inventories are carried at cost, as they generally are, it would be more appropriate to use cost of goods

---

[11]"Turnover" is a term that originated many years ago. The old Yankee peddler would load up his wagon with goods, then go off on his route to peddle his wares. The merchandise was defined as his "working capital," because it was what he actually sold or "turned over" to produce his profits, while his "turnover" represented the number of trips he took per year.

sold in place of sales in the numerator of the formula. Established compilers of financial ratio statistics such as Dun & Bradstreet, however, use the ratio of sales to inventories carried at cost. To develop a figure that can be compared with those developed by Dun & Bradstreet, it is therefore necessary to measure inventory utilization with sales in the numerator, as we do here.

The second problem lies in the fact that sales occur over the entire year, whereas the inventory figure is for one point in time. This makes it better to use an average inventory.[12] If it were determined that the firm's business is highly seasonal, or if there has been a strong upward or downward sales trend during the year, it would become essential to make some such adjustment. To maintain comparability with industry averages, however, we did not use the average inventory figure.

**average collection period (ACP)**
The ratio computed by dividing average sales per day into accounts receivable; indicates the average length of time the firm must wait after making a sale before receiving payment.

***Average Collection Period.*** The **average collection period (ACP)**, which is used to appraise the accounts receivable, is computed by dividing average daily sales into accounts receivable to find the number of days' sales tied up in receivables. It is so called because it represents the average length of time that the firm must wait after making a sale before receiving cash. The calculations for National show an average collection period of 42 days, slightly above the 36-day industry average.[13]

$$ACP = \frac{Average}{collection\ period} = \frac{Receivables}{Average\ sales\ per\ day} = \frac{Receivables}{Annual\ sales/360}$$

$$= \frac{\$350}{\$3,000/360} = \frac{\$350}{\$8.333} = 42\ days.$$

$$Industry\ average = 36\ days.$$

The ACP can also be evaluated by comparison with the terms on which the firm sells its goods. For example, National's sales terms call for payment within 30 days, so the 42-day collection period indicates that customers, on the average, are not paying their bills on time. If the trend in the collection period over the past few years had been rising, but the credit policy had not changed, this would be even stronger evidence that steps should be taken to expedite the collection of accounts receivable.

---

[12]Preferably, the average inventory would be calculated by summing the monthly figures during the year and dividing by 12. If monthly data are not available, one can add the beginning and ending figures and divide by 2.

[13]Because information on credit sales is generally unavailable, total sales must be used. Since all firms do not have the same percentage of credit sales, there is a chance that the average collection period will be somewhat in error. Also, note that by convention the financial community generally uses 360 rather than 365 as the number of days in the year for purposes such as these. Finally, it would be better to use *average* receivables = (beginning + ending)/2 = ($315 + $350)/2 = $332.5 in the formula. Had this been done, National's ACP would have been $332.5/$8.333 = 40 days. The 40-day figure is the more accurate one, but since the industry average was based on year-end receivables, we used 42 days for the comparison. The ACP is discussed further in Chapter 19.

**fixed assets
utilization ratio**
The ratio of sales to net
fixed assets; also called
the *fixed assets turnover
ratio*.

***Fixed Assets Utilization.*** The **fixed assets utilization ratio**, often called the *fixed assets turnover ratio*, measures the utilization of plant and equipment as the ratio of sales to fixed assets:

$$\text{Fixed assets utilization, or turnover, ratio} = \frac{\text{Sales}}{\text{Net fixed assets}} = \frac{\$3,000}{\$1,300} = 2.3 \text{ times.}$$

$$\text{Industry average} = 3.0 \text{ times.}$$

National's ratio of 2.3 times compares poorly with the industry average of 3 times, indicating that the firm is not using its fixed assets to as high a percentage of capacity as are the other firms in the industry. The financial manager should bear this fact in mind when production people request funds for new capital investments.

A major potential problem exists with the use of the fixed assets utilization ratio for comparative purposes. Inflation has caused the value of many assets that were purchased in the past to be seriously understated. Therefore, if we were comparing an old firm which had acquired many of its fixed assets years ago at low prices with a new company which had acquired its fixed assets only recently, then the old firm would probably have the higher turnover. However, this would be more reflective of problems with the accounting statements than of inefficiency on the part of the new firm. The accounting profession is trying to devise ways of providing financial statements which are more reflective of current rather than historic values. If balance sheets were stated on a current basis, this would eliminate the problem of comparisons, but at the moment the problem still exists. Financial analysts typically do not have the data necessary to make adjustments, so they simply recognize that a problem exists and deal with it judgmentally. In National's case, the issue is not a serious one because all firms in the industry have been expanding at about the same rate, so the balance sheets of the comparison firms are indeed comparable.[14]

**total assets
utilization ratio**
The ratio computed by
dividing sales by total
assets; also called the
*total assets turnover ratio*.

***Total Assets Utilization.*** The final asset management ratio, the **total assets utilization ratio**, measures the utilization, or turnover, of all of the firm's assets; it is calculated by dividing sales by total assets:

$$\text{Total assets utilization, or turnover, ratio} = \frac{\text{Sales}}{\text{Total assets}} = \frac{\$3,000}{\$2,000} = 1.5 \text{ times.}$$

$$\text{Industry average} = 1.8 \text{ times.}$$

National's ratio is somewhat below the industry average, indicating that the company is not generating a sufficient volume of business for the size of its total asset investment. Sales should be increased, some assets should be disposed of, or both steps should be taken.

---

[14]See FASB #33, *Financial Reporting and Changing Prices* (September 1979), for a discussion of the effects of inflation on financial statements and what the accounting profession is trying to do to provide better and more useful balance sheets and income statements.

## Debt Management Ratios

**financial leverage**
The extent to which a firm uses debt financing.

The extent to which a firm uses debt financing, or **financial leverage**, has three important implications: (1) By raising funds through debt, the owners maintain control of the firm with a limited investment. (2) Creditors look to the equity, or owner-supplied funds, to provide a margin of safety: if the owners have provided only a small proportion of total financing, then the risks of the enterprise are borne mainly by its creditors. (3) If the firm earns more on investments financed with borrowed funds than it pays in interest, then the return on the owners' capital is magnified, or "leveraged."

The first point is obvious, but to understand better how financial leverage affects risk and return, consider Table 7-7. Here we are analyzing two companies that are identical except for the way they are financed. Firm U (for "unleveraged") has no debts, while Firm L (for "leveraged") is financed half with equity and half with debt which has an interest rate of 15 percent. Both companies have $100 of assets and $100 of sales. Their ratio of operating income to assets, or the *basic earning power ratio*, is EBIT/Total assets =

**Table 7-7**
**Effect of Financial Leverage on Stockholders' Returns**

### Firm U (Unleveraged)

| | | | |
|---|---|---|---|
| Current assets | $ 50 | Debt | $ 0 |
| Fixed assets | 50 | Common equity | 100 |
| Total assets | $100 | Total claims | $100 |

| | |
|---|---|
| Sales | $100.00 |
| Operating costs | 70.00 |
| Operating income (EBIT) | $ 30.00 |
| Interest | 0.00 |
| Taxable income | $ 30.00 |
| Taxes (50%) | 15.00 |
| Net income | $ 15.00 |
| $ROE_U = \$15/\$100 =$ | 15% |

### Firm L (Leveraged)

| | | | |
|---|---|---|---|
| Current assets | $ 50 | Debt (15%) | $ 50 |
| Fixed assets | 50 | Common equity | 50 |
| Total assets | $100 | Total claims | $100 |

| | |
|---|---|
| Sales | $100.00 |
| Operating costs | 70.00 |
| Operating income (EBIT) | $ 30.00 |
| Interest | 7.50 |
| Taxable income | $ 22.50 |
| Taxes (50%) | 11.25 |
| Net income | $ 11.25 |
| $ROE_L = \$11.25/\$50 =$ | 22.5% |

$30/\$100 = 0.30 = 30\%$. Even though both companies' assets have the same earning power, Firm L provides its stockholders with a return on equity of 22.5 percent versus only 15 percent for Firm U. This difference is caused by Firm L's use of debt.

Financial leverage raises the rate of return to stockholders for two reasons: (1) Since interest is deductible, the use of debt financing lowers the tax bill and leaves more of the firm's operating income available to its investors; (2) if the rate of return on assets (EBIT/Total assets) exceeds the interest rate on debt, as it generally does, then a company can use debt to finance assets, pay the interest on the debt, and have something left over as a "bonus" for its stockholders. For our hypothetical firms, these two effects have combined to push Firm L's rate of return on equity up to 1.5 times that of Firm U, a gain of 50 percent. Thus, debt can be used to "leverage up" the rate of return on equity.

However, financial leverage can cut both ways—if the return on assets declines, the leveraged firm's return on equity will fall further and faster. Suppose, for example, that the operating costs of Firms U and L rose to $100 because of inflation but competitive pressures during a recession kept them from increasing sales prices. Consequently, in terms of Table 7-7, operating costs would rise to $100 and EBIT would drop to zero for both firms. If we worked through the rest of the table, we would see that Firm U would be in a breakeven position, with net income = $0 and ROE = 0%, while for Firm L net income = $-\$7.5$ and ROE = $-15\%$. Firm U, because of its strong balance sheet, could ride out the recession and be ready for the next boom. Firm L, on the other hand, would be under great pressure. Because of its losses, its cash would be depleted. Therefore, it would need to raise funds. Running a loss, it would have a hard time selling stock to raise capital, and the losses would also make its debt look risky, which would cause lenders to raise the interest rate. This would amplify L's problems, and the firm just might not be around to enjoy the next boom.

We see, then, that firms with relatively low debt ratios have less risk of loss when the economy is in a recession, but they also have lower expected returns when the economy booms. Conversely, firms with high leverage ratios run the risk of large losses, but they also have a chance of earning high profits. The prospects of high returns are desirable, but investors are averse to risk. Decisions about the use of leverage, then, require us to balance higher expected returns against increased risk.

Determining the optimal amount of debt for a given firm is a complicated process, and we defer a discussion of this topic until Chapter 15, when we will be better prepared to deal with it. For now we will simply look at the two ways analysts examine the firm's use of debt in a financial statement analysis: (1) They check balance sheet ratios to determine the extent to which borrowed funds have been used to finance assets, and (2) they review income statement ratios to determine the number of times fixed charges are covered by operating profits. These two sets of ratios are complementary, and most analysts use both types.

**debt ratio**
The ratio of total debt to total assets.

***Total Debt to Total Assets.*** The ratio of total debt to total assets, generally called the **debt ratio**, measures the percentage of total funds provided by creditors:

$$\text{Debt ratio} = \frac{\text{Total debt}}{\text{Total assets}} = \frac{\$1,100}{\$2,000} = 55\%.$$

$$\text{Industry average} = 40\%.$$

Debt is defined to include both current liabilities and long-term debt. Creditors prefer low debt ratios, since the lower the ratio, the greater the cushion against creditors' losses in the event of liquidation. The owners, on the other hand, may seek high leverage either to magnify earnings or because selling new stock would mean giving up some degree of control.

National's debt ratio is 55 percent; this means that creditors have supplied more than half the firm's total financing. Since the average debt ratio for this industry—and for manufacturing generally—is about 40 percent, National would find it difficult to borrow additional funds without first raising more equity capital. Creditors would be reluctant to lend the firm more money, and management would probably be subjecting the firm to the risk of bankruptcy if it sought to increase the debt ratio still more by borrowing.[15]

**times-interest-earned (TIE) ratio**
The ratio of earnings before interest and taxes to interest charges; measures the ability of the firm to meet its annual interest payments.

***Times Interest Earned.*** The **times-interest-earned (TIE) ratio** is determined by dividing earnings before interest and taxes (EBIT in Table 7-1) by the interest charges:

$$\begin{array}{c}\text{Times-interest-earned} \\ \text{(TIE) ratio}\end{array} = \frac{\text{EBIT}}{\text{Interest charges}} = \frac{\$266}{\$66} = 4 \text{ times.}$$

$$\text{Industry average} = 6 \text{ times.}$$

The TIE ratio measures the extent to which earnings can decline before the firm is unable to meet its annual interest costs. Failure to meet this obligation can bring legal action by the creditors, possibly resulting in bankruptcy. Note that the before-tax profit figure is used in the numerator. Because income taxes are computed after interest expense is deducted, the ability to pay current interest is not affected by income taxes.

---

[15]The ratio of debt to equity is also used in financial analysis. The debt to assets (D/A) and debt to equity (D/E) ratios are simply transformations of each other:

$$D/E = \frac{D/A}{1 - D/A}, \text{ and } D/A = \frac{D/E}{1 + D/E}.$$

Both ratios increase as a firm of a given size (total assets) uses a greater proportion of debt, but D/A rises linearly and approaches a limit of 100 percent, while D/E rises exponentially and approaches infinity.

It should also be noted that for certain purposes the debt ratio should be based on the market values of the firm's assets and its debt (outstanding bonds). Market values are especially important if they differ significantly from the accounting values as shown on the balance sheet.

National's interest is covered 4 times. Since the industry average is 6 times, the company is covering its interest charges by a relatively low margin of safety. Thus, the TIE ratio reinforces our conclusion based on the debt ratio, namely, that the company might face some difficulties if it attempted to borrow additional funds.

**fixed charge coverage ratio**
A ratio that expands upon the TIE ratio to include the firm's annual long-term lease obligations.

*Fixed Charge Coverage.* The **fixed charge coverage ratio** is similar to the times-interest-earned ratio, but it is more inclusive in that it recognizes that many firms lease assets and incur long-term obligations under lease contracts.[16] Leasing has become widespread in recent years, making this ratio preferable to the times-interest-earned ratio for most financial analyses. Fixed charges are defined as interest plus annual long-term lease obligations, and the fixed charge coverage ratio is defined as follows:

$$\text{Fixed charge coverage ratio} = \frac{\overset{\text{Earnings}}{\overset{\text{before taxes}}{}} + \overset{\text{Interest}}{\overset{\text{charges}}{}} + \overset{\text{Lease}}{\overset{\text{obligations}}{}}}{\text{Interest charges} + \text{Lease obligations}}$$

$$= \frac{\$200 + \$66 + \$28}{\$66 + \$28} = \frac{\$294}{\$94} = 3.1 \text{ times.}$$

$$\text{Industry average} = 5.5 \text{ times.}$$

National's fixed charges are covered 3.1 times as opposed to an industry average of 5.5 times. Again, this indicates that the firm is somewhat weaker than creditors would prefer it to be, and it points up the difficulties National would likely encounter if it attempted to increase its debt.

**cash flow coverage ratio**
The ratio showing the margin by which the firm's operating cash flows cover its financial requirements.

*Cash Flow Coverage.* Suppose National (1) issued preferred stock which required payment of $8 million in dividends per year and (2) had to make annual repayments of principal (sinking fund payments) on its debt obligations of $20 million per year. To the numerator of the fixed charge coverage ratio we add depreciation, which is a noncash charge, and to the denominator we add preferred dividends and principal repayments, both on a before-tax basis, dividing each by $(1 - T)$ because neither is a tax-deductible expense.[17] These adjustments produce the **cash flow coverage ratio**, which shows the margin by which operating cash flows cover financial requirements:

---

[16]Generally, a long-term lease is defined as one that is at least 3 years long. Thus, rent incurred under a 1-year lease would not be included in the fixed charge coverage ratio, but rental payments under a 3-year or longer lease would be defined as fixed charges and would be included.

[17]Because preferred dividends and sinking fund payments must be made from income remaining after payment of income taxes, dividing by $(1 - T)$ "grosses up" the payments and shows the before-tax amounts necessary to produce a given after-tax amount. Also note that if National had deferred taxes, the amount of deferred taxes would be added to the numerator as a cash inflow.

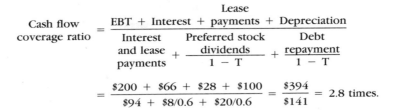

$$\text{Cash flow} \atop \text{coverage ratio} = \frac{\text{EBT} + \text{Interest} + \overset{\text{Lease}}{\text{payments}} + \text{Depreciation}}{\underset{\text{payments}}{\overset{\text{Interest}}{\text{and lease}}} + \frac{\overset{\text{Preferred stock}}{\text{dividends}}}{1 - T} + \frac{\overset{\text{Debt}}{\text{repayment}}}{1 - T}}$$

$$= \frac{\$200 + \$66 + \$28 + \$100}{\$94 + \$8/0.6 + \$20/0.6} = \frac{\$394}{\$141} = 2.8 \text{ times.}$$

While there are no generally published industry standards on this ratio, a common rule of thumb is that a cash flow coverage ratio of at least 3 times should be achieved in "normal" times. This allows for a substantial decline in cash inflows before a cash solvency problem is encountered. National does not meet this standard.

## Profitability Ratios

**profitability ratios**
A group of ratios showing the combined effects of liquidity, asset management, and debt management on operating results.

Profitability is the net result of a large number of policies and decisions. The ratios examined thus far reveal some information about the way the firm is operating, but the **profitability ratios** show the combined effects of liquidity, asset management, and debt management on operating results.

**profit margin on sales**
The ratio measuring income per dollar of sales; computed by dividing net profit after taxes by sales.

***Profit Margin on Sales.*** The **profit margin on sales**, computed by dividing net income after taxes by sales, gives the profit per dollar of sales:

$$\text{Profit margin} \atop \text{on sales} = \frac{\text{Net income after taxes}}{\text{Sales}} = \frac{\$120}{\$3,000} = 4\%.$$

$$\text{Industry average} = 5\%.$$

National's profit margin is somewhat below the industry average of 5 percent, indicating that its sales prices are relatively low, that its costs are relatively high, or both.

**basic earning power ratio**
The ratio that indicates the power of the firm's assets to generate operating income; computed by dividing earnings before interest and taxes by total assets.

***Basic Earning Power.*** The **basic earning power ratio** is calculated by dividing earnings before interest and taxes (EBIT) by total assets:

$$\text{Basic earning} \atop \text{power ratio} = \frac{\text{EBIT}}{\text{Total assets}} = \frac{\$266}{\$2,000} = 13.3\%.$$

$$\text{Industry average} = 17.2\%.$$

This ratio is useful for comparing firms in different tax situations and with different degrees of financial leverage. Because of its low turnover ratio and low profit margin on sales, National is not getting as much operating income out of its assets as is the average aluminum company.[18]

---

[18]Notice that EBIT is earned throughout the year, whereas the total assets figure is as of the end of the year. Therefore, it would be conceptually better to calculate the ratio as EBIT/Average assets = EBIT/[(Beginning assets + Ending assets)/2]. We have not made this adjustment because the published ratios used for comparative purposes do not include it. Incidentally, the same adjustment would also be appropriate for the next two ratios, ROA and ROE.

**return on total assets (ROA)**
The ratio of net income after taxes to total assets.

***Return on Total Assets.*** The ratio of net income to total assets measures the **return on total assets (ROA)** after interest and taxes:

$$\text{Return on total assets (ROA)} = \frac{\text{Net income after taxes}}{\text{Total assets}} = \frac{\$120}{\$2{,}000} = 6\%.$$

$$\text{Industry average} = 9\%.$$

National's 6 percent return is well below the 9 percent average for the industry. This low rate results from National's low basic earning power plus its above-average use of debt, which causes its interest payments to be high and its net income to be relatively low.

**return on common equity (ROE)**
The ratio of net income after taxes to common equity; measures the rate of return on stockholders' investments.

***Return on Common Equity.*** The ratio of net income after taxes to common equity measures the **return on common equity (ROE)**, or *rate of return on the stockholders' investment*:

$$\text{Return on common equity (ROE)} = \frac{\text{Net income after taxes}}{\text{Common equity}} = \frac{\$120}{\$900} = 13.3\%$$

$$\text{Industry average} = 15.0\%$$

National's 13.3 percent return is below the 15.0 percent industry average, but not as far below as the return on total assets. This results from National's greater use of debt, a point that is analyzed in detail later in the chapter.[19]

## Market Value Ratios

**market value ratios**
A set of ratios that relate the firm's stock price to its earnings and book value per share.

A final group of ratios, **market value ratios**, relates the firm's stock price to its earnings and book value per share. These ratios give management an indication of what investors think of the company's past performance and future prospects. If the firm's liquidity, asset management, debt management, and profitability ratios are all good, then its market value ratios will be high and the stock price will probably be as high as can be expected.

**price/earnings (P/E) ratio**
The ratio of price per share to earnings per share; shows the dollar amount investors will pay for $1 of current earnings.

***Price/Earnings Ratio.*** The **price/earnings (P/E) ratio**, which was discussed in Chapter 5, shows how much investors are willing to pay per dollar of reported profits. National's stock sells for $28.50, so with an EPS of $2.40 its P/E ratio is 11.9:

$$\text{Price/earnings (P/E) ratio} = \frac{\text{Price per share}}{\text{Earnings per share}} = \frac{\$28.50}{\$2.40} = 11.9 \text{ times.}$$

$$\text{Industry average} = 12.5 \text{ times.}$$

As we saw in Chapter 5, P/E ratios are higher for firms with high growth prospects but lower for riskier firms. National's P/E ratio is slightly below

---

[19]The fact that National's basic earning power and ROE are both 13.3 percent is a coincidence; normally they differ. Actually, if more decimal places had been shown, the two ratios would have been different from each other.

those of other large aluminum producers, which suggests that the company is regarded as being somewhat riskier than most, as having poorer growth prospects, or both.

***Market/Book Ratio.*** The ratio of a stock's market price to its book value gives another indication of how investors regard the company. Companies with high rates of return on equity generally sell at higher multiples of book value than those with low returns. National's book value per share is $18:

$$\text{Book value per share} = \frac{\text{Stockholders' equity}}{\text{Shares outstanding}} = \frac{\$900}{50} = \$18.$$

**market/book ratio**
The ratio of a stock's market price to its book value.

Dividing the price per share by the book value gives a **market/book ratio** of 1.6 times:

$$\text{Market/book ratio} = \frac{\text{Market price per share}}{\text{Book value per share}} = \frac{\$28.50}{\$18.00} = 1.6 \text{ times.}$$
$$\text{Industry average} = 1.8 \text{ times.}$$

Investors are willing to pay slightly less for National's book value than for that of an average aluminum company.

The typical railroad, which has a very low rate of return on assets, has a market/book value ratio of less than 0.5. On the other hand, very successful firms such as IBM achieve high rates of return on their assets, and they have market values well in excess of their book values. IBM's is 2.6 times.

## Trend Analysis

It is important to analyze trends in ratios as well as their absolute levels, for trends give clues as to whether the financial situation is improving or deteriorating. To do a **trend analysis** one simply graphs a ratio against years, as shown in Figure 7-3. This graph shows that National's rate of return on common equity has been declining since 1982, even though the industry average has been relatively stable. Other ratios could be analyzed similarly.

**trend analysis**
An analysis of a firm's financial ratios over time in order to determine the improvement or deterioration of its financial situation.

## Summary of Ratio Analysis: The Du Pont System

Table 7-8 summarizes National Metals' ratios, while Figure 7-4, which is called a **Du Pont chart** because that company's managers developed the general approach, shows the relationship between debt, asset turnover, and the profit margin. The left-hand side of the chart develops the *profit margin on sales.* The various expense items are listed and then summed to obtain National's total costs. Subtracting costs from sales yields the company's net income, which, when divided by sales, indicates that 4 percent of each sales dollar is left over for stockholders.

**Du Pont chart**
A chart designed to show the relationship between return on investment, asset turnover, and profit margin.

The right-hand side of the chart lists the various categories of assets, totals them, and then divides sales by total assets to find the number of times National "turns its assets over" each year. National's total assets turnover ratio is 1.5 times.

**Figure 7-3**
**Rate of Return on Common Equity, 1981-1985**

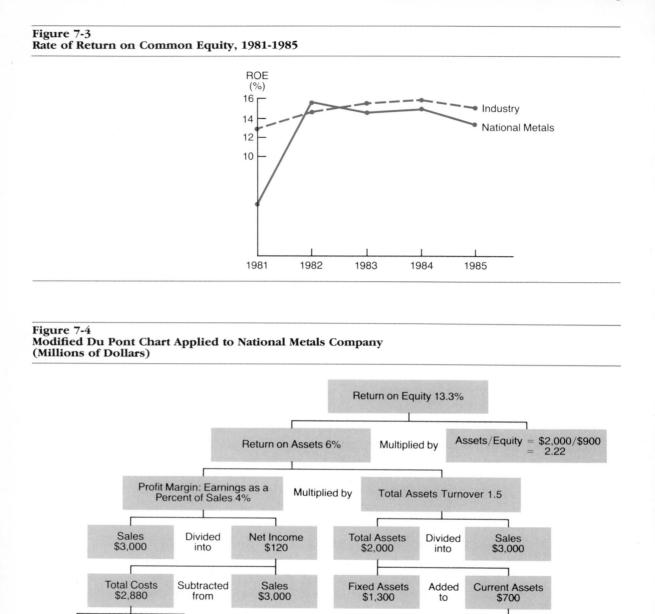

**Figure 7-4**
**Modified Du Pont Chart Applied to National Metals Company**
**(Millions of Dollars)**

**Table 7-8**
**National Metals Company:**
**Summary of Financial Ratios**
**(Millions of Dollars)**

| Ratio | Formula for Calculation | Calculation | Ratio | Industry Average | Comment |
|---|---|---|---|---|---|
| **Liquidity** | | | | | |
| Current | $\dfrac{\text{Current assets}}{\text{Current liabilities}}$ | $\dfrac{\$700}{\$300}$ | = 2.3× | 2.5× | Slightly low |
| Quick, or acid test | $\dfrac{\text{Current assets} - \text{Inventories}}{\text{Current liabilities}}$ | $\dfrac{\$400}{\$300}$ | = 1.3× | 1× | OK |
| **Asset Management** | | | | | |
| Inventory turnover | $\dfrac{\text{Sales}}{\text{Inventory}}$ | $\dfrac{\$3,000}{\$300}$ | = 10× | 9× | OK |
| Average collection period (ACP) | $\dfrac{\text{Receivables}}{\text{Sales}/360}$ | $\dfrac{\$350}{\$8.333}$ | = 42 days | 36 days | Poor |
| Fixed assets turnover | $\dfrac{\text{Sales}}{\text{Fixed assets}}$ | $\dfrac{\$3,000}{\$1,300}$ | = 2.3× | 3× | Poor |
| Total assets turnover | $\dfrac{\text{Sales}}{\text{Total assets}}$ | $\dfrac{\$3,000}{\$2,000}$ | = 1.5× | 1.8× | Poor |
| **Debt Management** | | | | | |
| Debt to total assets | $\dfrac{\text{Total debt}}{\text{Total assets}}$ | $\dfrac{\$1,100}{\$2,000}$ | = 55% | 40% | High |
| Times interest earned (TIE) | $\dfrac{\text{Earnings before interest and taxes}}{\text{Interest charges}}$ | $\dfrac{\$266}{\$66}$ | = 4× | 6× | Low |
| Fixed charge coverage | $\dfrac{\text{Earnings before taxes} + \text{Interest charges} + \text{Lease obligations}}{\text{Interest charges} + \text{Lease obligations}}$ | $\dfrac{\$294}{\$94}$ | = 3.1× | 5.5× | Poor |
| Cash flow coverage | $\dfrac{\text{Cash inflows}}{\text{Fixed charges} + \dfrac{\text{Preferred stock dividends}}{1 - T} + \dfrac{\text{Debt repayment}}{1 - T}}$ | $\dfrac{\$394}{\$141}$ | = 2.8× | n.a. | Poor |
| **Profitability** | | | | | |
| Profit margin on sales | $\dfrac{\text{Net income after taxes}}{\text{Sales}}$ | $\dfrac{\$120}{\$3,000}$ | = 4% | 5% | Low |
| Basic earning power | $\dfrac{\text{Earnings before interest and taxes}}{\text{Total assets}}$ | $\dfrac{\$266}{\$2,000}$ | = 13.3% | 17.2% | Low |
| Return on total assets (ROA) | $\dfrac{\text{Net income after taxes}}{\text{Total assets}}$ | $\dfrac{\$120}{\$2,000}$ | = 6% | 9% | Very low |
| Return on common equity (ROE) | $\dfrac{\text{Net income after taxes}}{\text{Common equity}}$ | $\dfrac{\$120}{\$900}$ | = 13.3% | 15% | Low |
| **Market Value** | | | | | |
| Price/earnings (P/E) | $\dfrac{\text{Price per share}}{\text{Earnings per share}}$ | $\dfrac{\$28.50}{\$2.40}$ | = 11.9× | 12.5× | Slightly low |
| Market/book | $\dfrac{\text{Market price per share}}{\text{Book value per share}}$ | $\dfrac{\$28.50}{\$18.00}$ | = 1.6× | 1.8× | OK |

**Du Pont equation**
A formula that gives the rate of return on assets by multiplying the profit margin by the total assets turnover.

The profit margin times the total assets turnover is called the **Du Pont equation**, and it gives the rate of return on assets (ROA):

$$\text{ROA} = \begin{matrix}\text{Rate of return}\\\text{on assets}\end{matrix} = \text{Profit margin} \times \text{Total assets turnover}$$

$$= \frac{\text{Net income}}{\text{Sales}} \times \frac{\text{Sales}}{\text{Total assets}} \qquad (7\text{-}1)$$

$$= 4\% \times 1.5 = 6\%.$$

National made 4 percent, or 4 cents, on each dollar of sales, and assets were "turned over" 1.5 times during the year, so the company earned a return of 6 percent on its assets.

If National had used only equity, the 6 percent rate of return on assets would have equalled the rate of return on equity. However, in the actual case, 55 percent of the firm's capital was supplied by creditors, and since the 6 percent return on total assets all goes to stockholders, who put up only 45 percent of the capital, the return on equity is higher than 6 percent. Specifically, the rate of return on assets (ROA) must be multiplied by the *equity multiplier*, which is the ratio of assets to common equity, to obtain the rate of return on equity (ROE):

$$\text{ROE} = \text{ROA} \times \text{Equity multiplier}$$

$$= \frac{\text{Net income}}{\text{Assets}} \times \frac{\text{Assets}}{\text{Common equity}} \qquad (7\text{-}2)$$

$$= 6\% \times \$2{,}000/\$900$$

$$= 6\% \times 2.22 = 13.3\%.$$

This 13.3 percent rate of return could, of course, be calculated directly: Net income after taxes/Common equity = \$120/\$900 = 13.3%. However, the Du Pont equation shows how the rate of return on assets and the use of debt interact to determine the return on equity.[20]

Management can use the Du Pont system to analyze ways of improving the firm's performance. On the left, or "profit margin," side of Figure 7-4, marketing people can study the effects of raising sales prices (or lowering them to increase volume), of moving into new products or markets with higher margins, and so on. Cost accountants can study the expense items and, working with engineers, purchasing agents, and other operating personnel, seek ways of holding costs down. On the "turnover" side, financial analysts, work-

---

[20]Another ratio that is frequently used is the following:

$$\text{Rate of return on investors' capital} = \frac{\text{Net income after taxes} + \text{Interest}}{\text{Debt} + \text{Equity}}.$$

The ratio is especially important in the public utility industries, where regulators are concerned about the companies' using their monopoly positions to earn excessive returns on investors' capital. In fact, regulators try to set utility prices (service rates) at levels that will force the return on investors' capital to equal a company's cost of capital as defined in Chapter 14.

ing with both production and marketing people, can investigate ways of reducing investments in various types of assets. At the same time, the treasurer can analyze the effects of alternative financing strategies, seeking to hold down interest expenses and the risks of debt while still using debt to increase the rate of return on equity. The chapter opener illustrates how the financial community uses the Du Pont equation.

## Comparative Ratios

**comparative ratio analysis**
An analysis based on a comparison of a firm's ratios with those of other firms in the same industry.

The preceding analysis of National Metals Company pointed out the usefulness of **comparative ratio analysis**. Comparative ratios are available from a number of sources. One useful set of comparative data is compiled by Dun & Bradstreet, Inc. D&B provides 14 ratios calculated for a large number of industries. Useful ratios can also be found in the *Annual Statement Studies* published by Robert Morris Associates, which is the national association of bank loan officers. The Federal Trade Commission's *Quarterly Financial Report*, which is found in most libraries, gives a set of ratios for manufacturing firms by industry group and size of firm. Trade associations and individual firms' credit departments also compile industry average financial ratios. Finally, financial statement data for thousands of publicly owned corporations are available on magnetic tapes, and since brokerage houses, banks, and other financial institutions have access to these data, security analysts can and do generate comparative ratios tailored to their individual needs.

Each of these organizations uses a somewhat different set of ratios designed for its own purposes. For example, D&B deals mainly with small firms, many of which are proprietorships, and it is concerned largely with the creditor's viewpoint. Accordingly, its ratios emphasize current assets and liabilities, and D&B is completely unconcerned with market value ratios. Therefore, when you select your comparative data source, you should be sure that your emphasis is similar to that of the agency whose ratios you use, or else recognize the limitations of those ratios for your purposes. Additionally, there are often minor definitional differences in the ratios presented by different sources. Before using any source, be sure to verify the exact definitions of the ratios.

## Uses of Ratio Analysis

As noted earlier, ratio analysis is used by three main groups: (1) *management*, to help analyze, control, and thus improve the firm's operations; (2) *credit analysts*, such as bank loan officers or credit managers for industrial companies, who analyze ratios to help ascertain a company's ability to pay its debt; and (3) *security analysts*, including stock analysts, who are interested in a company's efficiency and growth prospects, and bond analysts, who are concerned with a company's ability to pay interest on its bonds and also with the assets that would be available to bondholders in the event the company went bankrupt.

In later chapters we will look in more depth at the basic factors which underlie each ratio, after which you will have a better idea about how to interpret and use ratios.

## Limitations of Ratio Analysis

Ratio analysis can provide useful information concerning a company's operations and financial condition. However, it does have some inherent problems and limitations that necessitate care and judgment.

**1.** Many large firms operate a number of different divisions in quite different industries; in such cases it is difficult to develop a meaningful set of industry averages for comparative purposes. This tends to make ratio analysis more useful for small than for large firms.

**2.** Most firms want to be better than average (although half will be above and half below the median), so merely attaining average performance is not necessarily good. As a target for high-level performance, it is preferable to look at the industry leaders' ratios.

**3.** Inflation has badly distorted firms' balance sheets. Further, since inflation affects both depreciation charges and inventory costs, profits are also affected. Thus, a ratio analysis for one firm over time, or a comparative analysis of firms of different ages, must be interpreted with care and judgment.

**4.** Seasonal factors can also distort ratio analysis. For example, the inventory utilization ratio for a food processor will be radically different if the balance sheet figure used for inventory is the one just before versus just after the close of the canning season. This problem can be minimized by using monthly averages for the inventory figures.

**"window dressing" techniques**
Techniques employed by a firm to make its financial statements look better to credit analysts.

**5.** Firms can employ **"window dressing" techniques** to make their financial statements look better to credit analysts. To illustrate, a Chicago builder borrowed on a two-year basis on December 29, 1985, held the proceeds of the loan as cash for a few days, and then paid off the loan ahead of time on January 4, 1986. This improved his current and quick ratios and made his year-end 1985 balance sheet look good. However, the improvement was strictly temporary; a week later the balance sheet was back at the old level.

**6.** Different operating and accounting practices can distort comparisons. As noted earlier, inventory valuation and depreciation methods can affect the financial statements and thus distort interfirm comparisons. Also, if one firm leases a substantial amount of its productive equipment, then its assets may be low relative to sales because leased assets may not appear on the balance sheet; at the same time, the lease liability will not be shown as a debt. Thus, leasing can artificially improve the debt and turnover ratios. The accounting profession has recently taken steps which reduce but do not eliminate this problem; we discuss this in Chapter 13.

**7.** It is difficult to generalize about whether a particular ratio is "good" or "bad." For example, a high current ratio may show a strong liquidity position, which is good, or excessive cash, which is bad because excess cash in the bank is a nonearning asset. Similarly, a high assets utilization ratio may denote either a firm that uses assets efficiently or one that is undercapitalized and simply cannot afford to buy enough assets.

**8.** A firm may have some ratios which look "good" and others which look "bad," making it difficult to tell whether the firm is, on balance, in a strong or a weak position. However, statistical procedures can be used to analyze the *net effects* of a set of ratios. Many banks and other lending organizations use these procedures to analyze firms' financial ratios and, on the basis of their analyses, classify companies according to their probability of getting into financial distress.[21]

Ratio analysis is useful, but analysts should be aware of these problems and make adjustments as necessary. Ratio analysis conducted in a mechanical, unthinking manner is dangerous; however, used intelligently and with good judgment, it can provide useful insights into a firm's operations. Your judgment in interpreting a set of ratios is necessarily weak at this point, but it will be greatly enhanced as we go through the remainder of the book.

## Summary

The primary purposes of this chapter were (1) to describe the basic financial statements and (2) to discuss techniques used by investors and managers to analyze them. Four basic statements were covered: the *income statement,* the *balance sheet,* the *statement of retained earnings,* and the *statement of changes in financial position.*

Financial analysis is designed to determine the relative strengths and weaknesses of a company—whether the firm is financially sound and profitable relative to other firms in its industry and whether its position is improving or deteriorating over time. Investors need such information in order to estimate both future cash flows from the firm and the riskiness of these flows. Managers need to be aware of their firms' financial positions in order to detect problems and strengthen weaknesses.

Our study of financial analysis concentrated on a set of ratios designed to highlight the key aspects of a firm's operations. These ratios were broken down into five categories: (1) liquidity ratios, (2) asset management ratios, (3) debt management ratios, (4) profitability ratios, and (5) market value ratios. The ratios for a given firm are calculated and then compared with those of other firms in the same industry to judge the relative strength of the firm in question. Trends in the ratios are also analyzed, and the Du Pont system is used to pinpoint the cause of low profits. Ratio analysis has limitations, but used with care and judgment it can be most helpful.

---

[21]For a discussion of the use of discriminant analysis to predict bankruptcy, see Edward I. Altman, "Financial Ratios, Discriminant Analysis, and the Prediction of Corporate Bankruptcy," *Journal of Finance,* September 1968, 589-609, or Eugene F. Brigham and Louis C. Gapenski, *Intermediate Financial Management,* Chapter 23.

## SMALL BUSINESS

### Financial Analysis in the Small Firm

Financial ratio analysis is a useful tool for small businesses as well as for big ones. Readily available sources of key financial ratios provide comparative data by size class, with the class size varying down to some very small firms. For example, Robert Morris Associates provides comparative ratios for a number of small-firm classes, including the size range of zero to $250,000 in annual sales. Nevertheless, the financial analysis of small firms presents some unique problems that are related to the risk of the small firm and to the depth and quality of management in the particular firm. Let's examine some of those problems from the standpoint of the bank credit officer.

### The Banker Evaluates a Small Firm: Problems

One of the most common uses of financial ratios is credit analysis by commercial banks. In examining the small-business credit prospect, the banker is essentially making a prediction about the ability of the company to repay its debt if the bank extends credit. In making this prediction, the banker will be especially concerned about indicators of liquidity and about continuing prospects for profitability. The banker will elect to do business with a new customer if the banker believes that loans will be paid off on a timely basis and that the company will remain in business and therefore be a customer of the bank for some years to come. Thus, both short-run and long-run viability are of interest to the banker. On the other hand, the banker's perceptions about the business are important to the owner-manager because the bank may become a vital source of funds as the firm's needs increase in the future.

The first problem the banker is likely to encounter is that, unlike the bank's bigger customers, the small firm may not have audited financial statements. Furthermore, the statements that are available may have been produced on an irregular basis (for example, in some months or quarters but not in others). If the firm is young, it may have historical financial statements for only one year, or perhaps it may have none at all. The banker will probably require that periodic income statements and

balance sheets be produced, and by a reputable accounting firm rather than by the owner's brother-in-law.

The quality of financial data may therefore be a problem for the small business in its attempt to establish a banking relationship. If it is a serious problem, the firm may fail to get credit even though it is in reality on solid financial ground. It is in the owner's interest to make sure that the firm's financial data are credible even if it is a little more expensive to do so. Furthermore, if the banker is uncomfortable with the data, then the firm's management should also be uncomfortable. Many of the managerial decisions will depend on the numbers in the firm's accounting statements, so those numbers should be as accurate as possible.

Given a set of financial ratios, the firm may be more or less risky depending on its size. Often small firms either are single-product firms or rely heavily on a relationship with a single customer. For example, back in the 1960s a company called Yard Man, Inc. manufactured and sold lawn equipment. Most of Yard Man's sales were to Sears, Roebuck, and so most of Yard Man's revenues and profits were due to its Sears account. When Sears decided to drop Yard Man as a supplier, the company was left without its most important customer. Losing the Sears, Roebuck account was a devastating blow to Yard Man. Because large firms typically have a broad customer base, they are not as susceptible to a similar loss of a large portion of their business.

A similar danger applies to the single-product company. Just as the loss of a key customer can be disastrous for a small business, so can a shift in the tides of consumer interest in a particular fad. For example, Coleco manufactured and sold the extremely popular Cabbage Patch dolls in the Christmas season of 1983. The phenomenal popularity of the dolls was a great boom for Coleco. But the public is fickle. One can almost never predict when such a fad will suddenly die out, leaving the company with a great deal of capacity to build a product that no one will buy and with a lot of inventory (valued, incidentally, at a high dollar amount on the corporate books but in reality worth nearly nothing to the hapless banker who wins the inventory in bankruptcy).

Coleco is a sizable company that is sufficiently

diversified to withstand the loss of such a fad item. But if the Cabbage Patch doll were manufactured instead by a small company with no other products, such a shift in fads could destroy the company. No matter how good the financial ratios *look* at the moment, the creditor of a small, single-product company has to be ever-mindful of the added risks.

The extension of credit to a small company, and especially a small owner-managed company, often involves one other risk that is quite different from those discussed above. Such a company is often highly dependent on the management or leadership of a single key individual. The unexpected death of that person could cause the company to fail. Alternatively, if the company is family owned and managed, there is typically one key decision maker, but perhaps several other family members are also involved in helping to manage the company. In this case the loss of the top person does not wipe out the management, although it may create the equally serious problem of no clear management succession. The loss of a key family member is a highly emotional event, and it is not at all unusual for it to be followed by an ugly and prolonged struggle for control of the business. It is in the family's interest, and certainly of concern to prospective creditors, to see that a plan of succes-

sion of management is clearly specified before trouble arises. If all of the standard financial ratios look good, but there is a significant risk of loss of management, then an otherwise creditworthy firm may fail to get needed financing.

We have identified three concerns that must be added to standard financial analysis of the small firm. Two of them are concerns that the firm should be able to handle if it addresses them seriously. These are (1) the quality of the firm's financial data and (2) succession of management. The third concern raised is that, because of the lack of diversity of the product line or customer base, the firm may be susceptible to sudden loss of revenue. This is a risk the firm may elect not to eliminate, at least not early in its life. Entrepreneurs start businesses in hopes of earning very large returns. Very large returns ordinarily entail very large risks. Diversifying a business is a way of reducing risk, but it may also reduce returns. The entrepreneur may therefore be unwilling to use diversification as a part of his or her business strategy.

In determining the creditworthiness of a small firm, the financial analyst must look beyond the basic financial ratios and analyze the viability of the firm's product, customers, and market. It is not an easy task, but it must be done. Ratio analysis is only the starting point.

## Questions

7-1    Define each of the following terms:
   a. Annual report; income statement; balance sheet
   b. Equity, or net worth; paid-in capital; retained earnings
   c. Cash flow cycle
   d. Statement of retained earnings; statement of changes in financial position; sources and uses of funds statement
   e. Depreciation; depreciation methods
   f. Working capital; net working capital
   g. Liquidity ratio; current ratio; quick, or acid test, ratio
   h. Asset management ratio; inventory turnover ratio; average collection period (ACP); fixed assets turnover ratio; total assets turnover ratio
   i. Financial leverage; debt ratio; times-interest-earned (TIE) ratio; fixed charge coverage ratio; cash flow coverage ratio
   j. Profitability ratio; profit margin on sales; basic earning power ratio; return on total assets (ROA); return on common equity (ROE)
   k. Market value ratio; price/earnings (P/E) ratio; market/book (M/B) ratio; dividend payout ratio; book value
   l. Trend analysis; comparative analysis
   m. Du Pont chart; Du Pont equation
   n. "Window dressing"

7-2     What four statements are contained in most annual reports?

7-3     Is it true that if a "typical" firm reports $20 million of retained earnings on its balance sheet, its directors could declare a $20 million cash dividend without any qualms whatsoever?

7-4     How does inflation distort ratio analysis comparisons both for one company over time (trend analysis) and when different companies are compared? Are only balance sheet items or both balance sheet and income statement items affected?

7-5     If a firm's ROE is low and management wants to improve it, explain how using more debt might provide a solution.

7-6     Suppose a firm used debt to leverage up its ROE and in the process its EPS was also boosted. Would this necessarily lead to an increase in the price of the firm's stock? Assume the payout ratio remains constant.

7-7     How might (a) seasonal factors and (b) different growth rates over time or between companies distort a comparative ratio analysis? Give some examples. How might these problems be alleviated?

7-8     Indicate the effects of the transactions listed below on each of the following: total current assets, net working capital, current ratio, and net profit. Use ( + ) to indicate an increase, ( − ) to indicate a decrease, and (0) to indicate no effect or an indeterminate effect. Be prepared to state any necessary assumptions, and assume an initial current ratio of more than 1.0. (Note: A good accounting background is necessary to answer some of these questions; if yours is not strong, just answer the questions you can handle.)

| | Total Current Assets | Net Working Capital | Current Ratio | Effect on Net Income |
|---|---|---|---|---|
| a. Cash is acquired through issuance of additional common stock. | | | | |
| b. Merchandise is sold for cash. | | | | |
| c. Federal income tax due for the previous year is paid. | | | | |
| d. A fixed asset is sold for less than book value. | | | | |
| e. A fixed asset is sold for more than book value. | | | | |
| f. Merchandise is sold on credit. | | | | |
| g. Payment is made to trade creditors for previous purchases. | | | | |
| h. A cash dividend is declared and paid. | | | | |
| i. Cash is obtained through short-term bank loans. | | | | |
| j. Short-term notes receivable are sold at a discount. | | | | |
| k. Marketable securities are sold below cost. | | | | |
| l. Advances are made to employees. | | | | |

| | Total Current Assets | Net Working Capital | Current Ratio | Effect on Net Income |
|---|---|---|---|---|
| m. Current operating expenses are paid. | _____ | _____ | _____ | _____ |
| n. Short-term promissory notes are issued to trade creditors for past due accounts receivable. | _____ | _____ | _____ | _____ |
| o. Ten-year notes are issued to pay off accounts payable. | _____ | _____ | _____ | _____ |
| p. A fully depreciated asset is retired. | _____ | _____ | _____ | _____ |
| q. Accounts receivable are collected. | _____ | _____ | _____ | _____ |
| r. Equipment is purchased with short-term notes. | _____ | _____ | _____ | _____ |
| s. Merchandise is purchased on credit. | _____ | _____ | _____ | _____ |
| t. The estimated taxes payable are increased. | _____ | _____ | _____ | _____ |

## Self-Test Problems (*Solutions on Page 244*)

**ST-1**   A. L. Kaiser & Co. had earnings per share of $4 last year, and it paid a $2 dividend. Book value per share at year-end was $40, while total retained earnings increased by $12 million during the year. Kaiser has no preferred stock, and no new common stock was issued during the year. If Kaiser's year-end debt (which equals its total liabilities) was $120 million, what was the company's year-end debt/assets ratio?

**ST-2**   The following data apply to Cadwalader & Company (millions of dollars):

| | |
|---|---|
| Cash and marketable securities | $100.00 |
| Fixed assets | $283.50 |
| Sales | $1,000.00 |
| Net income | $50.00 |
| Quick ratio | 2.0× |
| Current ratio | 3.0× |
| ACP | 40 days |
| ROE | 12% |

Cadwalader has no preferred stock—only common equity, current liabilities, and long-term debt.

a. Find Cadwalader's (1) accounts receivable (A/R), (2) current liabilities, (3) current assets, (4) total assets, (5) ROA, (6) common equity, and (7) long-term debt.

b. In Part a you should have found Cadwalader's accounts receivable (A/R) = $111.1 million. If Cadwalader could reduce its ACP from 40 days to 30 days while holding other things constant, how much cash would it generate? If this cash were used to buy back common stock (at book value) and thus to reduce the amount of common equity, how would this affect (1) the ROE, (2) the ROA, and (3) the total debt/total assets ratio?

## Problems

Ratio analysis

**7-1**    Data for the Mainframe Company and its industry averages follow.
          a. Calculate the indicated ratios for Mainframe.
          b. Construct the Du Pont equation for both Mainframe and the industry.
          c. Outline Mainframe's strengths and weaknesses as revealed by your
             analysis.

**Mainframe Company:**
**Balance Sheet as of**
**December 31, 1985**

| Cash | $ 155,000 | Accounts payable | $ 258,000 |
|------|-----------|------------------|-----------|
| Receivables | 672,000 | Notes payable | 168,000 |
| Inventory | 483,000 | Other current liabilities | 234,000 |
| Total current assets | $1,310,000 | Total current liabilities | $660,000 |
| Net fixed assets | 585,000 | Long-term debt | 513,000 |
| | | Common equity | 722,000 |
| Total assets | $1,895,000 | Total claims | $1,895,000 |

**Mainframe Company:**
**Income Statement for Year Ended**
**December 31, 1985**

| | | |
|---|---|---|
| Sales | | $3,215,000 |
| Cost of goods sold: | | |
| Materials | $1,434,000 | |
| Labor | 906,000 | |
| Heat, light, and power | 136,000 | |
| Indirect labor | 226,000 | |
| Depreciation | 83,000 | 2,785,000 |
| Gross profit | | 430,000 |
| Selling expenses | | 230,000 |
| General and administrative expenses | | 60,000 |
| Earnings before interest and taxes | | $ 140,000 |
| Interest expense | | 49,000 |
| Net income before taxes | | 91,000 |
| Federal income taxes (40%) | | 36,400 |
| Net income | | $ 54,600 |

| Ratio | Mainframe | Industry Average |
|-------|-----------|------------------|
| Current assets/current liabilities | _____ | 2.0× |
| Average collection period | _____ | 35 days |
| Sales/inventories | _____ | 6.7× |
| Sales/total assets | _____ | 2.9× |
| Net income/sales | _____ | 1.2% |
| Net income/total assets | _____ | 3.4% |
| Net income/equity | _____ | 8.3% |
| Total debt/total assets | _____ | 60.0% |

d. Suppose Mainframe had doubled its sales and also its inventories, accounts receivable, and common equity during 1985. How would that
information affect the validity of your ratio analysis? (Hint: Think
about averages, and the effects of rapid growth on ratios if averages
are not used. No calculations are needed.)

Liquidity ratios    7-2    The Jacobs Company has $1,750,000 in current assets and $700,000 in
current liabilities. Its initial inventory level is $500,000, and it will raise
funds as additional notes payable and use them to increase inventory.
How much can its short-term debt (notes payable) increase without violating a current ratio of 2 to 1? What will the firm's quick ratio be after
the Jacobs Company has raised the maximum amount of short-term
funds?

Du Pont analysis    7-3    The Blacksburg Furniture Company, a manufacturer and wholesaler of
high-quality home furnishings, has been experiencing low profitability in
recent years. As a result, the board of directors has replaced the president of the firm with a new president, John Stockwell, who has asked
you to make an analysis of the firm's financial position using the Du Pont
system. The most recent industry average ratios and Blacksburg's financial statements are reproduced below:

### Industry Average Ratios

| | | | |
|---|---|---|---|
| Current ratio | 2× | Sales/fixed assets | 6× |
| Debt/total assets | 30% | Sales/total assets | 3× |
| Times interest earned | 7× | Net profit on sales | 3% |
| Sales/inventory | 10× | Return on total assets | 9% |
| Average collection period | 24 days | Return on common equity | 12.8% |

**Blacksburg Furniture Company:**
**Balance Sheet as of**
**December 31, 1985**
**(Millions of Dollars)**

| | | | |
|---|---|---|---|
| Cash | $ 30 | Accounts payable | $ 30 |
| Marketable securities | 22 | Notes payable | 30 |
| Net receivables | 44 | Other current liabilities | 14 |
| Inventories | 106 | Total current liabilities | $ 74 |
| Total current assets | $202 | Long-term debt | 16 |
| | | Total liabilities | $ 90 |
| Gross fixed assets | $150 | | |
| Less depreciation | 52 | Common stock | $ 76 |
| Net fixed assets | 98 | Retained earnings | 134 |
| | | Total stockholders' equity | 210 |
| Total assets | $300 | Total claims | $300 |

**Blacksburg Furniture Company:**
**Income Statement for Year Ended**
**December 31, 1985**
**(Millions of Dollars)**

| | |
|---|---:|
| Net sales | $530 |
| Cost of goods sold | 440 |
| Gross profit | $ 90 |
| Selling expenses | 49 |
| Depreciation expense | 8 |
| Interest expense | 3 |
| Total expenses | $ 60 |
| Net income before tax | $ 30 |
| Taxes (50%) | 15 |
| Net income | $ 15 |

a. Calculate those ratios that you feel would be useful in this analysis.
b. Construct a Du Pont equation for Blacksburg, and compare the company's ratios to the composite ratios for the industry as a whole.
c. Do the balance sheet accounts or the income statement figures seem to be primarily responsible for the low profits?
d. Which specific accounts seem to be most out of line in relation to other firms in the industry?
e. If Blacksburg had a pronounced seasonal sales pattern, or if it grew rapidly during the year, how might that affect the validity of your ratio analysis? How might you correct for such potential problems?

**Statement of changes in financial position**     **7-4**     The consolidated balance sheets for the Alabama-Atlantic Lumber Company at the beginning and end of 1985 follow. The company bought $150 million worth of fixed assets. The charge for depreciation in 1985 was $30 million. Earnings after taxes were $76 million, and the company paid out $20 million in dividends.

a. Fill in the amount of source or use in the appropriate column.

**Alabama-Atlantic Lumber Company:**
**Balance Sheets at**
**Beginning and End of 1985**
**(Millions of Dollars)**

| | | | Change | |
|---|---|---|---|---|
| | Jan. 1 | Dec. 31 | Source | Use |
| Cash | $ 30 | $ 14 | _____ | _____ |
| Marketable securities | 22 | 0 | _____ | _____ |
| Net receivables | 44 | 60 | _____ | _____ |
| Inventories | 106 | 150 | _____ | _____ |
| Total current assets | $202 | $224 | _____ | _____ |
| Gross fixed assets | 150 | 300 | _____ | _____ |
| Less depreciation | (52) | (82) | _____ | _____ |
| Net fixed assets | $ 98 | $218 | _____ | _____ |
| Total assets | $300 | $442 | _____ | _____ |
| Accounts payable | $ 30 | $ 36 | _____ | _____ |
| Notes payable | 30 | 6 | _____ | _____ |

(*Table continued*)

**Alabama-Atlantic Lumber Company:**
**Balance Sheets at**
**Beginning and End of 1985**
**(Millions of Dollars)**

| | Jan. 1 | Dec. 31 | Change Source | Change Use |
|---|---|---|---|---|
| Other current liabilities | 14 | 30 | | |
| Long-term debt | 16 | 52 | | |
| Common stock | 76 | 128 | | |
| Retained earnings | 134 | 190 | | |
| Total claims | $300 | $442 | | |

Note: Total sources must equal total uses.

b.  Prepare a statement of changes in financial position.

c.  Briefly summarize your findings.

Du Pont analysis     **7-5**     The Ameritronic Corporation's balance sheets for 1985 and 1984 are as follows (millions of dollars):

| | 1985 | 1984 |
|---|---|---|
| Cash | $ 21 | $ 45 |
| Marketable securities | 0 | 33 |
| Receivables | 90 | 66 |
| Inventories | 225 | 159 |
| Total current assets | $336 | $303 |
| Gross fixed assets | 450 | 225 |
| Less accumulated depreciation | (123) | (78) |
| Net fixed assets | $327 | $147 |
| Total assets | $663 | $450 |
| Accounts payable | $ 54 | $ 45 |
| Notes payable | 9 | 45 |
| Accruals | 45 | 21 |
| Total current liabilities | $108 | $111 |
| Long-term debt | 78 | 24 |
| Common stock | 192 | 114 |
| Retained earnings | 285 | 201 |
| Total long-term capital | $555 | $339 |
| Total claims | $663 | $450 |

Additionally, Ameritronic's 1985 income statement is as follows (millions of dollars):

| | |
|---|---|
| Sales | $1,365 |
| Cost of goods sold | 888 |
| General expenses | 282 |
| EBIT | $ 195 |
| Interest | 10 |
| EBT | $ 185 |
| Taxes (46%) | 85 |
| Net income | $ 100 |

a. What was Ameritronic's dividend payout ratio in 1985?
b. The following extended Du Pont equation is the industry average for 1985:

| Profit margin | × | Asset turnover | × | Equity multiplier | = | ROE |
|---|---|---|---|---|---|---|
| 6.52% | × | 1.82 | × | 1.77 | = | 21.00% |

Construct Ameritronic's 1985 extended Du Pont equation. What does the Du Pont analysis indicate about Ameritronic's expense control, asset utilization, and debt utilization? What is the industry's debt to assets ratio?
c. Construct Ameritronic's 1985 statement of changes in financial position. What does it suggest about the company's operations?

Ratio trend analysis          **7-6**    The Bangor Corporation's forecasted 1986 financial statements are given below, along with some industry average ratios.

a. Calculate Bangor's 1986 forecasted ratios, compare them with the industry average data, and comment briefly on Bangor's projected strengths and weaknesses.

**Bangor Corporation:**
**Pro Forma Balance Sheet as of December 31, 1986**

|  | 1986 |
|---|---|
| Cash | $    72,000 |
| Accounts receivable | 439,000 |
| Inventory | 894,000 |
| Total current assets | $1,405,000 |
| Land and building | 238,000 |
| Machinery | 132,000 |
| Other fixed assets | 61,000 |
| Total assets | $1,836,000 |
| Accounts and notes payable | $   432,000 |
| Accruals | 170,000 |
| Total current liabilities | $   602,000 |
| Long-term debt | 404,290 |
| Common stock | 575,000 |
| Retained earnings | 254,710 |
| Total liabilities and equity | $1,836,000 |

**Bangor Corporation:**
**Pro Forma Income Statement for 1986**

|  | 1986 |
|---|---|
| Sales | $4,290,000 |
| Cost of goods sold | 3,580,000 |
| Gross operating profit | $   710,000 |
| General administrative and selling expenses | 236,320 |
| Depreciation | 159,000 |
| Miscellaneous | 134,000 |
| Net income before taxes | $   180,680 |

(*Table continued*)

**Bangor Corporation:**
**Pro Forma Income Statement for 1986**

| | 1986 |
|---|---|
| Taxes (40%) | 72,272 |
| Net income | $ 108,408 |
| Number of shares outstanding | 23,000 |

**Per-Share Data:**

| | |
|---|---|
| EPS | $4.71 |
| Cash dividends | $0.95 |
| P/E ratio | 5× |
| Market price (average) | $23.57 |

| | Industry Financial Ratios (1986)[a] |
|---|---|
| Quick ratio | 1.0× |
| Current ratio | 2.7× |
| Inventory turnover[b] | 7× |
| Average collection period | 32 days |
| Fixed assets turnover[b] | 13.0× |
| Total assets turnover[b] | 2.6× |
| Return on total assets | 9.1% |
| Return on equity | 18.2% |
| Debt ratio | 50% |
| Profit margin on sales | 3.5% |
| P/E ratio | 6× |

[a]Industry average ratios have been constant for the past four years.
[b]Based on year-end balance sheet figures.

(Do only if you are using the computerized problem diskette.)

b. Suppose Bangor is considering installing a new computer system which would provide tighter control of inventory, accounts receivable, and accounts payable. If the new system is installed, the following data are projected rather than the data now given in certain balance sheet and income statement categories:

| | |
|---|---|
| Cash | $ 81,000 |
| AR | 400,000 |
| INV | 750,000 |
| Other fixed assets | 91,000 |
| Accounts payable | 300,000 |
| Accruals | 133,000 |
| Retained earnings | 279,710 |
| Cost of goods sold | 3,510,000 |
| Administrative and selling expense | 228,320 |
| P/E | 6 |

(1) How does this affect the projected ratios and the comparison to the industry averages?

(2) If the new computer system were either more efficient or less efficient, and caused the cost of goods sold to increase or decrease by $150,000 from the new projections, what effect would that have on the company's position?

## Solutions to Self-Test Problems

**ST-1**   Kaiser paid $2 in dividends and retained $2 per share. Since total retained earnings rose by $12 million, there must be 6 million shares outstanding. With a book value of $40 per share, total common equity must be $40(6 million) = $240 million. Since Kaiser has $120 million of debt, its debt ratio must be 33.3 percent:

$$\frac{\text{Debt}}{\text{Assets}} = \frac{\text{Debt}}{\text{Debt} + \text{Equity}} = \frac{\$120 \text{ million}}{\$120 \text{ million} + \$240 \text{ million}}$$

$$= 0.333 = 33.3\%.$$

**ST-2**   a. In answering questions such as this, always begin by writing down the relevant definitional equations, then start filling in numbers.

(1) $$\text{ACP} = \frac{\text{Accounts receivable}}{\text{Sales}/360}$$

$$40 = \frac{\text{A/R}}{\$1,000/360}$$

$$\text{A/R} = 40(\$2.778) = \$111.1 \text{ million.}$$

(2) $$\text{Quick ratio} = \frac{\text{Current assets} - \text{Inventories}}{\text{Current liabilities}} = 2.0$$

$$= \frac{\text{Cash and marketable securities} + \text{A/R}}{\text{Current liabilities}} = 2.0$$

$$2.0 = \frac{\$100 + \$111.1}{\text{Current liabilities}}$$

Current liabilities = ($100 + $111.1)/2 = $105.5 million.

(3) $$\text{Current ratio} = \frac{\text{Current assets}}{\text{Current liabilities}} = 3.0$$

$$= \frac{\text{Current assets}}{\$105.5} = 3.0.$$

Current assets = 3.0($105.5) = $316.50 million.

(4) $$\text{Total assets} = \text{Current assets} + \text{Fixed assets}$$
$$= \$316.5 + \$283.5 = \$600 \text{ million.}$$

(5) $$\text{ROA} = \text{Profit margin} \times \text{Total assets utilization}$$

$$= \frac{\text{Net income}}{\text{Sales}} \times \frac{\text{Sales}}{\text{Total assets}}$$

$$= \frac{\$50}{\$1,000} \times \frac{\$1,000}{\$600}$$

$$= 0.05 \times 1.667 = 0.833 = 8.33\%.$$

(6)

$$ROE = ROA \times \frac{Assets}{Equity}$$

$$12.0\% = 8.33\% \times \frac{\$600}{Equity}$$

$$Equity = \frac{(8.33\%)(\$600)}{12.0\%}$$

$$= \$416.50 \text{ million.}$$

(7)

$$Total\ assets = Total\ claims = \$600$$

$$Current\ liabilities + Long\text{-}term\ debt + Equity = \$600$$

$$\$105.5 + Long\text{-}term\ debt + \$416.5 = \$600$$

$$Long\text{-}term\ debt = \$600 - \$105.5 - \$416.5 = \$78 \text{ million.}$$

Note: We could have found equity as follows:

$$ROE = \frac{Net\ income}{Equity}$$

$$12.0\% = \frac{\$50}{Equity}$$

$$Equity = \$50/0.12$$

$$= \$416.67 \text{ million (rounding error difference).}$$

Then we could have gone on to find current liabilities and long-term debt.

b. Cadwalader's average sales per day were $1,000/360 = \$2.777777$ million. Its ACP was 40, so A/R $= 40(\$2,777,777) = \$111,111,080$. Its new ACP of 30 would cause A/R $= 30(\$2,777,777) = \$83,333,310$. The reduction in receivables would be $\$111,111,080 - \$83,333,310 = \$27,777,770$, which would equal the amount of cash generated.

(1)

$$New\ equity = Old\ equity - Stock\ bought\ back$$

$$= \$416,500,000 - \$27,777,777$$

$$= \$388,722,223.$$

Thus,

$$New\ ROE = \frac{Net\ income}{New\ equity}$$

$$= \frac{\$50,000,000}{\$388,722,223}$$

$$= 12.86\% \text{ (versus old ROE of 12.0\%).}$$

(2)          $$\text{New ROA} = \frac{\text{Net income}}{\text{Total assets} - \text{Reduction in A/R}}$$

$$= \frac{\$50,000,000}{\$600,000,000 - \$27,777,777}$$

$$= 8.74\% \text{ (versus old ROA of } 8.33\%).$$

(3) The old debt is the same as the new debt:

$$\text{Debt} = \text{Total claims} - \text{Equity}$$
$$= \$600 - \$416.5 = \$183.5 \text{ million.}$$

$$\text{Old total assets} = \$600 \text{ million.}$$

$$\text{New total assets} = \text{Old total assets} - \text{Reduction in A/R}$$
$$= \$600 - \$27.78$$
$$= \$572.22 \text{ million.}$$

Therefore,

$$\frac{\text{Debt}}{\text{Old total assets}} = \frac{\$183.5}{\$600} = 30.6\%,$$

while

$$\frac{\text{New debt}}{\text{New total assets}} = \frac{\$183.5}{\$572.22} = 32.1\%.$$

## Selected Additional References and Cases

The effects of alternative accounting policies on both financial statements and ratios based on these statements are discussed in many excellent texts on financial accounting. For example, see:

Kieso, Donald E., and Jeremy J. Weygandt, *Intermediate Accounting* (New York: Wiley, 1980).

Smith, Jay M., and Fred K. Skousen, *Intermediate Accounting* (Cincinnati: Southwestern, 1981).

For further information on the relative usefulness of various financial ratios, see:

Chen, Kung H., and Thomas A. Shimerda, "An Empirical Analysis of Useful Financial Ratios," *Financial Management*, Spring 1981, 51-60.

Considerable work has been done to establish the relationship between bond ratings and financial ratios. For one example, see:

Belkaoui, Ahmed, *Industrial Bonds and the Rating Process* (London: Quorum Books, 1983).

For sources of ratios and common size statements, see the following:

Dun & Bradstreet, *Key Business Ratios* (New York: Updated annually).

Financial Research Associates, *Financial Studies of the Small Business* (Arlington, Va.: Updated annually).

Robert Morris Associates, *Annual Statement Studies* (Philadelphia: Updated annually).

Troy, Leo, *Almanac of Business and Industrial Financial Ratios* (Englewood Cliffs, N. J.: Prentice-Hall, Updated annually).

The following case focuses on ratio analysis:

Case 1, "Silver River Manufacturing Company," in the Crum-Brigham casebook, which illustrates the use of ratio analysis in the evaluation of a firm's existing and potential financial positions.

APPENDIX 7A

## Effects of Depreciation Methods on Taxes, Net Income, and Cash Flows

Managers and financial analysts are concerned primarily with the stream of cash flows which accrue to a firm from its operations. As we have seen previously, net income and cash flows are rarely, if ever, the same. A firm's cash flows are approximately equal to its net income plus depreciation plus any taxes it has deferred, and all three of these quantities depend on the depreciation methods the firm uses for tax and reporting purposes.

### Tax Purposes versus Reporting Purposes

All firms are required to use either the Accelerated Cost Recovery System (ACRS) method or the optional straight line method when depreciating their assets for tax purposes. Most firms use the most rapid method, ACRS, when calculating their taxes because depreciation is a tax-deductible expense and larger depreciation write-offs allow them to decrease their current tax liability. However, larger depreciation expenses also reduce firms' net income.

Generally accepted accounting principles, which govern the accounting methods a firm uses to determine its income as reported to its stockholders, state that a firm should depreciate its assets for reporting purposes using the method which most accurately reflects the decline in the value of its assets over time. For most firms, this method is straight-line depreciation. IBM and a few other firms use ACRS for both tax and reporting purposes, but it is much more common for firms to use ACRS for calculating taxes and straight line for reporting income to investors.

***Effects on Taxes and Net Income.*** Table 7A-1 shows pre-tax income, taxes, and net income for a firm which has sales of $100 million a year, costs equal to 50 percent of sales, and a single asset which costs $100 million. This asset has a 10-year economic life, and it will have a zero salvage value at the end of the 10 years. The top section of the table shows the calculation of actual taxes owed using the ACRS method, while the bottom section shows the calculation of taxes and net income for reporting purposes using the straight line method. Notice that in the early years pre-tax income is larger—and hence taxes and net income after taxes are larger—if the straight line method is used. For example, in Year 1 the firm reports to the Internal Revenue Service $25 million in depreciation, pays $11.5 million in taxes, and has net income of $13.5 million using ACRS. However, it reports to stockholders only $10 million in depreciation, $11.5 + $6.9 = $18.4 million in taxes, and net income of $21.6 million. Clearly the firm prefers to report to its stockholders income of $21.6 million rather than of $13.5 million.

Although the firm reports taxes of $18.4 million, its tax bill is only $11.5 million. The firm does not actually pay the difference of $18.4 − $11.5 = $6.9 million in reported taxes in Year 1. The $6.9 million difference is reported on the income statement as deferred taxes—that is, the firm has deferred paying these taxes until a later date by using an accelerated depreciation method for calculating them.

Notice also that net income using ACRS depreciation fluctuates for several years, then is stable at a level above net income as reported to stockholders. Income reported to stockholders using straight line depreciation is stable over

## Table 7A-1
## Effects of Depreciation on Taxes and Profits

1. The firm has a single asset which costs $100 million, has a 10-year economic life, and has a zero salvage value. Revenues are $100 per year over the 10 years, and costs other than depreciation are $50 million per year. The firm's tax rate is 46 percent, and it has 10 million shares of stock outstanding.
2. Straight line depreciation charges are $100,000,000/10 = $10,000,000 per year. The asset has a 3-year tax life, so it can, under ACRS, be depreciated at these rates (millions of dollars):

| Year | ACRS Rate | Depreciation |
|------|-----------|--------------|
| 1 | 0.25 | $ 25.00 |
| 2 | 0.38 | 38.00 |
| 3 | 0.37 | 37.00 |
| | 1.00 | $100.00 |

3. In the following section, we show (1) how the tax liability is calculated and (2) how income is reported to investors.

| | | | Year | | |
|---|---|---|---|---|---|
| **I. Tax Calculations** | **1** | **2** | **3** | **4** . . . | **10**[a] |
| Sales | $100.00 | $100.00 | $100.00 | $100.00 | $100.00 |
| Costs | 50.00 | 50.00 | 50.00 | 50.00 | 50.00 |
| Depreciation (D) | 25.00 | 38.00 | 37.00 | 0.00 | 0.00 |
| Pre-tax income | $ 25.00 | $ 12.00 | $ 13.00 | $ 50.00 | $ 50.00 |
| Taxes paid, 46% (T) | 11.50 | 5.52 | 5.98 | 23.00 | 23.00 |
| Deferred taxes (DT) | n.a. | n.a. | n.a. | n.a. | n.a. |
| Net income after taxes (NI) | $ 13.50 | $ 6.48 | $ 7.02 | $ 27.00 | $ 27.00 |
| Earnings per share | $ 1.35 | $ 0.65 | $ 0.70 | $ 2.70 | $ 2.70 |

| | | | Year | | |
|---|---|---|---|---|---|
| **II. Calculations for Stockholder Reporting** | **1** | **2** | **3** | **4** . . . | **10**[a] |
| Sales | $100.00 | $100.00 | $100.00 | $100.00 | $100.00 |
| Costs | 50.00 | 50.00 | 50.00 | 50.00 | 50.00 |
| Depreciation (D) | 10.00 | 10.00 | 10.00 | 10.00 | 10.00 |
| Pre-tax income | $ 40.00 | $ 40.00 | $ 40.00 | $ 40.00 | $ 40.00 |
| Taxes paid, 46% (T) (from I above) | 11.50 | 5.52 | 5.98 | 23.00 | 23.00 |
| Deferred taxes (DT)[b] | 6.90 | 12.88 | 12.42 | −4.60 | −4.60 |
| Net income after taxes (NI) | $ 21.60 | $ 21.60 | $ 21.60 | $ 21.60 | $ 21.60 |
| Earnings per share | $ 2.16 | $ 2.16 | $ 2.16 | $ 2.16 | $ 2.16 |

[a]The income statements do not change for Years 4 through 10.
[b]DT = (Pre-tax income) (Tax rate) − Taxes paid from Part I = ($40)(0.46) − $11.5 = $6.9 in Year 1.

the entire period. Firms prefer stable or growing earnings to fluctuating earnings. A stable earnings stream, therefore, is another advantage of using straight line depreciation for reporting purposes.

***Effects on Cash Flows.*** The cash flows which accrue to the firm are calculated in Table 7A-2. Notice that cash flows, which are equal to net income plus depreciation plus deferred taxes, are the same regardless of the depreciation method used. This result will always occur because net income increases by $(1 − T)(\Delta Dep)$ and deferred taxes increase by $T(\Delta Dep)$, which together exactly offset

**Table 7A-2**
**Effects of Depreciation on Cash Flows**

### I. Tax Calculations

| | Year | | | | |
|---|---|---|---|---|---|
| | 1 | 2 | 3 | 4 | . . . 10[a] |
| Net income after taxes | $13.50 | $ 6.48 | $ 7.02 | $27.00 | $27.00 |
| Depreciation | 25.00 | 38.00 | 37.00 | 0 | 0 |
| Deferred taxes | 0 | 0 | 0 | 0 | 0 |
| Cash flow[b] | $38.50 | $44.48 | $44.02 | $27.00 | $27.00 |

### II. Calculations for Stockholder Reporting

| | Year | | | | |
|---|---|---|---|---|---|
| | 1 | 2 | 3 | 4 | . . . 10[a] |
| Net income after taxes | $21.60 | $21.60 | $21.60 | $21.60 | $21.60 |
| Depreciation | 10.00 | 10.00 | 10.00 | 10.00 | 10.00 |
| Deferred taxes | 6.90 | 12.88 | 12.42 | −4.60 | −4.60 |
| Cash flow[b] | $38.50 | $44.48 | $44.02 | $27.00 | $27.00 |

[a]Cash flows do not change in Years 4 through 10.
[b]Cash flows = Net income + Depreciation + Deferred taxes.

the decrease in depreciation cash flows. Thus, we can see that the depreciation method has no effect on the cash flows which accrue to a firm from its assets—provided the firm uses ACRS for tax purposes. (If it used straight line for tax purposes then taxes would be higher in early years, and cash flows lower.) The important point is that if you do not recognize depreciation and deferred taxes as cash inflows, then the firm's reported cash flows stream will be understated.

# 8  FINANCIAL FORECASTING

## POOR FINANCIAL PLANNING
## BANKRUPTS LEADING RETAILER

On August 1, 1985, the chairman of Sakowitz Inc., an 83-year-old high fashion retailing chain with 17 stores in Houston and other southwestern cities, announced to his employees that the company was bankrupt. Bankruptcies of well-established, old-line retailers are uncommon, but what makes the Sakowitz case especially interesting is the fact that its downfall can be traced so clearly to poor financial planning.

After 70 years of steady and profitable growth, Sakowitz launched an aggressive expansion program in the 1970s. Its catalogue business was increased, and new stores were opened throughout the Southwest. The company leased rather than purchased buildings, and it financed inventories with short-term bank loans that had to be renewed every 90 days. Rather than selling common stock to increase equity along with debt, the company actually bought back and retired some of its outstanding stock, thus reducing equity even while debt rose. The short-term borrowings lowered the current ratio and raised the debt ratio, and the stock buy-back increased the debt ratio still more. The lease payment commitments exacerbated potential problems by further reducing the fixed charge coverage ratio.

When oil prices fell and drilling slowed after 1983, the incomes of many people in the Texas-Oklahoma-Louisiana area also fell. In that environment, $2,000 Yves St. Laurent dresses moved slowly, and Sakowitz's sales fell dramatically. Cash flows were insufficient to cover operating costs plus interest on bank debt and lease payments. Since the bank loans were short term, they had to be either paid off or renewed every 90 days, and, while the banks had been happy to renew when the company was doing well, they became increasingly reluctant to grant extensions as profits fell. The company argued that its problems were temporary—that good times were just around the corner. The banks, though, were under pressure from their regulators to focus on cash flows rather than asset values when appraising loans.

Now Sakowitz is bankrupt. Well-financed retailers are trying to pick up its stores and merchandise at bargain prices. Good times may be just around the corner, but they won't do Sakowitz much good. Had its management practiced the financial planning techniques discussed in this chapter, perhaps the story would have ended differently.

As noted in Chapter 4, both managers and investors are vitally concerned with *future* financial statements, so they should consider how alternative courses of action will affect the projected statements. In this chapter we discuss briefly how pro forma statements are constructed, and we then show how they are used to help estimate the need for different types of capital.

## Sales Forecasts

**sales forecast**
A forecast of a firm's unit and dollar sales for some future period; generally based on recent sales trends plus forecasts of the economic prospects for the nation, region, industry, and so forth.

The **sales forecast** generally starts with a review of sales over the past five to ten years, expressed in a graph such as that in Figure 8-1. The first part of the graph shows actual sales for Telecomp Corporation, a manufacturer of computer and telecommunications equipment, from 1975 through 1985. During this 10-year period, sales grew from $150 million to $400 million, or at a compound growth rate of 10.3 percent. However, the growth rate has accelerated sharply in recent years, primarily as a result of the breakup of AT&T and the separation of its manufacturing and telephone operations, which permitted companies like Telecomp to compete for sales to telephone operating companies. Also, Telecomp's R&D program has been especially successful, so when the telecommunications market broke open, Telecomp was ready.

On the basis of the recent trend in sales, on new product introductions, and on Telecomp's economics staff's forecast that the national economy will be quite strong during the coming year, Telecomp's planning group projects a 50 percent growth rate during 1986, to a sales level of $600 million.

**Figure 8-1**
**1986 Sales Projection for Telecomp Corporation**

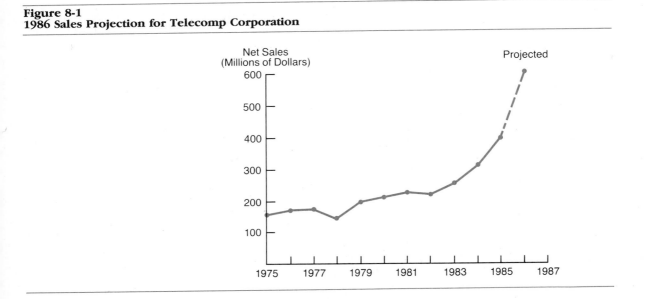

Of course, a great deal of work lies behind all good sales forecasts. Companies must project the state of the national economy, economic conditions within their own geographic areas, and conditions in the product markets they serve. Further, they must consider their own pricing strategies, credit policies, advertising programs, capacity limitations, and the like. Companies must also consider the strategies and policies of their competitors—the introduction of new products by IBM or AT&T, or more aggressive pricing by these and other companies, could seriously affect Telecomp's 1986 sales forecast.

If the sales forecast is off, the consequences can be serious. First, if the market expands *more* than Telecomp has expected and geared up for, then it will not be able to meet its customers' needs. Orders will back up, delivery times will lengthen, repair and installations will be harder to schedule, and customer unhappiness will increase. Customers will end up going elsewhere, Telecomp will lose market share, and it will have missed a major opportunity. On the other hand, if its projections are overly optimistic, Telecomp could end up with too much plant, equipment, and inventory. This would mean low turnover ratios, high costs for depreciation and storage, and, possibly, write-offs of obsolete inventory and equipment. All of this would result in a low rate of return on equity, which in turn would depress the company's stock price. If Telecomp had financed the expansion with debt, its problems would, of course, be compounded. Thus, an accurate sales forecast is critical to the well-being of the firm.[1]

## Forecasting Financial Requirements: The Percentage of Sales Method

Several methods are used to forecast financial statements. In this chapter we focus on the percentage of sales method. We also explain when this method can and cannot be used, and we discuss the growing use of computerized models for forecasting financial statements.

**percentage of sales method**
A method of forecasting financial requirements by expressing various balance sheet items as a percentage of sales and then multiplying these percentages by expected future sales to construct pro forma balance sheets.

The **percentage of sales method** is a simple but often practical method of forecasting financial statement variables. The procedure is based on two assumptions: (1) that most balance sheet accounts are tied directly to sales and (2) that the current levels of all assets are optimal for the current sales level. We illustrate the process with Telecomp Corporation, whose December 31, 1985, balance sheet and summary income statement are given in Table 8-1. Telecomp operated its fixed assets at full capacity to support its 1985 sales of $400 million, and it had no unnecessary stocks of current assets. Its profit margin on sales was 10 percent, and it distributed 60 percent

---

[1]A sales forecast is actually the *expected value of a probability distribution* of possible levels of sales. Because any sales forecast is subject to a greater or lesser degree of uncertainty, for financial planning we are often just as interested in the degree of uncertainty inherent in the sales forecast ($\sigma$ sales) as we are in the expected value of sales. See "Demand Estimation" in James L. Pappas, Eugene F. Brigham, and Mark Hirschey, *Managerial Economics* (Hinsdale, Ill.: Dryden, 1983), Chapter 5, for a detailed discussion of procedures for making demand forecasts.

**Table 8-1**
**Telecomp Corporation: 1985 Financial Statements**

### I. Balance Sheet, December 31, 1985
(Millions of Dollars)

| | | | |
|---|---|---|---|
| Cash | $ 10 | Accounts payable | $ 40 |
| Receivables | 90 | Notes payable | 10 |
| Inventories | 200 | Accrued wages and taxes | 50 |
| Total current assets | $300 | Total current liabilities | $100 |
| Net fixed assets | 300 | Mortgage bonds | 150 |
| | | Common stock | 50 |
| | | Retained earnings | 300 |
| Total assets | $600 | Total claims | $600 |

### II. Summary Income Statement

| | |
|---|---|
| 1985 Sales: | $400 million |
| 1985 Net income: | 40 million |
| 1985 Dividends paid: | 24 million |

of its net income to stockholders as dividends. If Telecomp's sales increase to $600 million in 1986, what will be the condition of its pro forma December 31, 1986, balance sheet, and how much additional financing will the company require during 1986?

The first step in the percentage of sales forecast is to isolate those balance sheet items that vary directly with sales. Since Telecomp has been operating at full capacity, each asset item must increase if the higher level of sales is to be attained. More cash will be needed for transactions; receivables will be higher; additional inventory must be stocked; and new plant must be added.[2]

If Telecomp's assets are to increase, its liabilities and net worth must likewise rise—the balance sheet must balance, so an increase in assets must be financed in some manner. **Spontaneously generated funds** come from such sources as accounts payable and accruals, which rise spontaneously with sales: As sales increase, so will purchases, and larger purchases will automatically result in higher levels of accounts payable. Thus, if sales double, accounts payable will also double. Similarly, a higher level of operations will require more labor, so accrued wages will increase and, assuming profit margins are maintained, an increase in profits will pull up accrued taxes. Retained earnings will also increase, but not in direct proportion to the increase in sales. Neither notes payable, mortgage bonds, nor common stock will rise spontaneously with sales—higher sales do not *automatically* trigger increases in these items.

We can construct a pro forma balance sheet for December 31, 1986, proceeding as outlined in the following paragraphs.

**spontaneously generated funds**
Funds that arise automatically from routine business transactions.

---

[2]Some assets, such as marketable securities, are not tied directly to operations and hence do not vary directly with sales. Also, as we shall see later in the chapter, if some assets are not being fully utilized, then sales can increase without increasing those assets.

**Step 1.** In Table 8-2, Column 1, we express those balance sheet items that vary directly with sales as a percentage of 1985 sales. An item such as notes payable that does not automatically vary with sales is designated "not applicable."

**Step 2.** We multiply these percentages (their fractions, really) by the $600 million projected 1986 sales to obtain the projected amounts as of December 31, 1986. These are shown in Column 2 of the table.

**Step 3.** We simply insert figures for notes payable, mortgage bonds, and common stock from the December 31, 1985, balance sheet. At least one of these accounts will have to be changed later in the analysis.

**Step 4.** We add the addition to retained earnings estimated for 1986 to the figure shown on the December 31, 1985, balance sheet to obtain the Decem-

**Table 8-2**
**Telecomp Corporation:**
**December 31, 1985, Balance Sheet**
**Expressed as a Percentage of Sales and**
**December 31, 1986, Pro Forma Balance Sheet**
**(Millions of Dollars)**

|  | Balance Sheet Items on 12/31/85 (as a % of the $400 1985 Sales) (1) | Pro Forma Balance Sheet on 12/31/86 (= Projected Sales of $600 Times Column 1) (2) |
|---|---|---|
| Cash | 2.5% | $ 15 |
| Receivables | 22.5 | 135 |
| Inventories | 50.0 | 300 |
| Total current assets | 75.0% | $450 |
| Net fixed assets | 75.0 | 450 |
| Total assets | 150.0% | $900 |
| Accounts payable | 10.0% | $ 60 |
| Notes payable | n.a.[a] | 10[b] |
| Accrued wages and taxes | 12.5 | 75 |
| Total current liabilities | 22.5% | $145 |
| Mortgage bonds | n.a. | 150[b] |
| Common stock | n.a. | 50[b] |
| Retained earnings | n.a. | 324[c] |
| Funds available |  | $669 |
| Additional funds needed |  | 231[d] |
| Total claims |  | $900 |

[a]n.a. = not applicable. (Item does not vary spontaneously with sales.)

[b]Initially projected at the 1985 level. Later financing decisions might change this level.

[c]December 31, 1985, balance in retained earnings plus 1986 addition to retained earnings as explained in Step 4.

[d]"Additional funds needed" is a balancing figure: $900 − $669 = $231.

ber 31, 1986, projected retained earnings. Recall that Telecomp expects to earn 10 percent on sales of $600 million, or $60 million, and to pay 60 percent of this out in dividends to stockholders; thus the **dividend payout ratio** is 60 percent. Therefore, retained earnings for the year are projected to be $60 million − 0.6($60 million) = $24 million. Adding the $24 million addition to retained earnings to the $300 million beginning balance gives the $324 million projected retained earnings shown in Column 2.

**Step 5.** We sum the asset accounts, obtaining a total projected assets figure of $900 million, and we also sum the projected liabilities and net worth items to obtain $669 million, the estimate of available funds. Since liabilities and net worth must total $900 million but only $669 million is projected, we have a shortfall of $231 million which we designate "additional funds needed"; it will presumably be raised by bank borrowing and/or by issuing securities. For simplicity, we disregard depreciation by assuming that cash flows generated by depreciation will be used to replace worn-out fixed assets.

**Step 6.** Telecomp could use short-term bank loans (notes payable), mortgage bonds, common stock, or a combination of these securities to make up the shortfall. Ordinarily, it would make this choice on the basis of the relative costs of these different types of securities. However, in Telecomp's case the company has a contractual agreement with its bondholders to keep total debt at or below 50 percent of total assets and also to keep the current ratio at a level of 3.0 or greater. These provisions restrict the financing choices as follows:[3]

1. *Restriction on additional debt*:

   Maximum debt permitted = (0.5)(Total assets)

                            = (0.5)($900 million)        = $450 million

   Less debt already projected for December 31, 1986:

      Current liabilities                   $145 million

      Mortgage bonds              150 million =  295 million

   Maximum additional debt                 = $155 million

2. *Restriction on additional current liabilities*:

   Maximum current liabilities = Projected current assets/3

                              = $450 million/3     = $150 million

   Less current liabilities already projected       145 million

   Maximum additional current liabilities      $   5 million

3. *Common equity requirements*:

   Total additional funds needed (from Table 8-2)    $231 million

   Maximum additional debt permitted           155 million

   Common equity funds required             $  76 million

---

[3]As we shall see in Chapter 12, restrictions such as these are contained in virtually all long-term debt agreements. They are designed to protect bondholders against imprudent managerial decisions that would increase the risk the bondholders face.

We see, then, that Telecomp needs a total of $231 million from external sources. Its existing debt contract limits new debt to $155 million, and only $5 million of that amount can be short-term debt. Thus, assuming that Telecomp wants to make maximum use of debt financing, it must plan to sell common stock in the amount of $76 million, in addition to its debt financing, to cover its financial requirements. Here is a summary of its planned, non-spontaneous external financings:

| | |
|---|---:|
| Short-term debt (notes payable) | $   5 million |
| Long-term debt | 150 million |
| New common stock | 76 million |
| Total | $231 million |

## Projected Financial Statements and Ratios

**pro forma financial statement**
A financial statement that shows how an actual statement will look if certain specified assumptions are realized.

Telecomp's financial manager can now construct a set of projected or **pro forma financial statements** and then analyze the ratios that are implied therein. Parts I and II of Table 8-3 give abbreviated versions of the final projected balance sheet and income statement, Part III gives the statement of changes in financial position, and Part IV gives a few key ratios. These statements can be used by the financial manager to show the other executives the implications of the planned sales increase. For example, the projected rate of return on equity is 13.3 percent. Is this a reasonable target, or can it be improved? Also, the preliminary forecast calls for the sale of $76 million of common stock—but does top management really want to sell any new stock? Suppose just over 50 percent of Telecomp's stock is owned by John Edwards, who does not want the company to sell any stock and thereby cause him to lose his majority control. How then can the needed funds be raised, or what adjustments should be made? In the remainder of the chapter, we look at approaches to answering questions such as these.

## Relationship between Growth in Sales and Capital Requirements

Although the forecast of capital requirements can be made by constructing pro forma balance sheets as has been described, it is often easier to use a simple forecasting formula. The formula can also be used to make clear the relationship between sales growth and financial requirements:

$$\begin{matrix} \text{Additional} \\ \text{funds} \\ \text{needed} \end{matrix} = \begin{pmatrix} \text{Required} \\ \text{increase} \\ \text{in assets} \end{pmatrix} - \begin{pmatrix} \text{Spontaneous} \\ \text{increase in} \\ \text{liabilities} \end{pmatrix} - \begin{pmatrix} \text{Increase in} \\ \text{retained} \\ \text{earnings} \end{pmatrix}.$$

$$\text{AFN} = (A/S)\Delta S - (L/S)\Delta S - MS_1(1 - d). \qquad \textbf{(8-1)}$$

Here

AFN = additional funds needed.

A/S = assets that increase spontaneously with sales as a percentage of sales, or required dollar increase in assets per $1 increase in sales. A/S = 150%, or 1.5, for Telecomp from Column 1 of Table 8-2.

**Table 8-3**
**Telecomp Corporation: Projected Financial Statements for 1986**
**(Millions of Dollars)**

### I. Projected Balance Sheet, December 31, 1986

| | | | |
|---|---|---|---|
| Cash | $ 15 | Accounts payable | $ 60 |
| Accounts receivable | 135 | Notes payable | 15 |
| Inventories | 300 | Accruals | 75 |
| Total current assets | $450 | Total current liabilities | $150 |
| Net fixed assets | 450 | Long-term debt | 300 |
| | | Common stock | 126 |
| | | Retained earnings | 324 |
| | | Total equity | $450 |
| Total assets | $900 | Total claims | $900 |

### II. Projected Income Statement, 1986

| | |
|---|---|
| Sales | $600 |
| Total costs | 500 |
| Net income before taxes | $100 |
| Taxes (40%) | 40 |
| Net income after taxes | $ 60 |
| Dividends (60% of income) | 36 |
| Addition to retained earnings | $ 24 |

### III. Projected Statement of Changes in Financial Position, 1986

*Sources of funds:*

| | |
|---|---|
| Net income | $ 60 |
| Funds from operations[a] | $ 60 |
| Proceeds from sale of bonds | 150 |
| Proceeds from sale of common stock | 76 |
| Total sources | $286 |

*Use of funds:*

| | |
|---|---|
| Increase in net fixed assets | $150 |
| Dividend payments | 36 |
| Increase in net working capital | 100 |
| Total uses | $286 |

*Analysis of changes in working capital:*

Increase (decrease) in current assets:

| | |
|---|---|
| Cash | $ 5 |
| Accounts receivable | 45 |
| Inventories | 100 |
| Net increase (decrease) in current assets | $150 |

Increase (decrease) in current liabilities:

| | |
|---|---|
| Accounts payable | $ 20 |
| Notes payable | 5 |
| Accruals | 25 |
| Net increase (decrease) in current liabilities | $ 50 |
| Increase (decrease) in net working capital | $100 |

### IV. Key Ratios Projected for December 31, 1986[b]

1. Current ratio     3.0 times
2. Total debt/total assets     50%
3. Rate of return on equity     13.3%

[a]The figure for funds from operations normally includes depreciation. Here we have assumed that depreciation is reinvested in fixed assets, that is, it is netted out against fixed asset additions.

[b]Other ratios could be calculated and analyzed by the Du Pont system.

L/S = liabilities that increase spontaneously with sales as a percentage of sales, or spontaneously generated financing per \$1 increase in sales. L/S = 22.5%, or 0.225, for Telecomp.

$S_1$ = total sales projected for next year. Note that $S_0$ = last year's sales. $S_1$ = \$600 million for Telecomp.

$\Delta S$ = change in sales = $S_1 - S_0$ = \$600 million − \$400 million = \$200 million for Telecomp.

M = profit margin, or rate of profits per \$1 of sales. M = 10%, or 0.10, for Telecomp.

d = percentage of earnings paid out in dividends, or the dividend payout ratio; d = 60%, or 0.60, for Telecomp. Notice that 1 − d = 1.0 − 0.6 = 0.4, or 40 percent. This is the percentage of earnings that Telecomp retains, often called the **retention rate** or *retention ratio*.

**retention rate**
The percentage of earnings retained by the firm, which is equal to 1 − the dividend payout ratio.

**additional funds needed (AFN)**
Funds that a firm must acquire through borrowing or by selling new common or preferred stock.

Inserting values for Telecomp into Equation 8-1, we find the **additional funds needed (AFN)** as follows:

$$AFN = 1.5(\Delta S) - 0.225(\Delta S) - 0.1(S_1)(1 - 0.6)$$

$$= 1.5(\$200 \text{ million}) - 0.225(\$200 \text{ million}) - 0.1(\$600 \text{ million})(0.4)$$

$$= \$300 \text{ million} - \$45 \text{ million} - \$24 \text{ million}$$

$$= \$231 \text{ million.}$$

To increase sales by \$200 million, Telecomp must increase assets by \$300 million. The \$300 million of new assets must be financed in some manner. Of the total, \$45 million will come from a spontaneous increase in liabilities, while another \$24 million will be obtained from retained earnings. The remaining \$231 million must be raised from external sources. This value agrees, of course, with the figure developed earlier in Table 8-2.

### Relationship between Growth and Funds Requirements

The faster Telecomp's growth rate in sales, the greater its need for external financing; we can use Equation 8-1, which is plotted in Figure 8-2, to indicate this relationship. The lower section shows Telecomp's external financial requirements at various growth rates, and these data are plotted in the graph. Several points that can be seen from the figure are discussed below.

*Financial Planning.* At low growth rates Telecomp needs no external financing. However, if the company grows faster than 3.239 percent, it must raise capital from outside sources—the faster the growth rate, the greater the capital requirements. If management foresees difficulties in raising this capital—perhaps because Telecomp's current stockholders do not want to sell additional stock—then management should reconsider the feasibility of the expansion plans.

*Effect of Dividend Policy on Financing Needs.* Dividend policy also affects external capital requirements, so if Telecomp foresees difficulties in raising capital, it might want to consider a reduction in the dividend payout

**Figure 8-2**
**Relationship between Growth in Sales and Financial Requirements,**
**Assuming $S_0$ = \$400 Million (Millions of Dollars)**

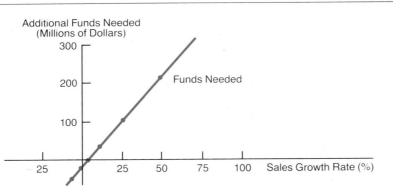

| Growth Rate in Sales (1) | Increase (Decrease) in Sales, $\Delta S$ (2) | Forecasted Sales, $S_1$ (3) | Additional Funds Needed (4) |
|:---:|:---:|:---:|:---:|
| 50% | \$200 | \$600 | \$231.0 |
| 10 | 40 | 440 | 33.4 |
| 3.239 | 12.956 | 412.956 | 0.0 |
| 0 | 0 | 400 | (16.0) |
| −10 | (40) | 360 | (65.4) |

*Explanation of Columns:*
Col. 1: Growth rate in sales, g.
Col. 2: Increase (decrease) in sales, $\Delta S = g(S_0)$.
Col. 3: Forecasted sales, $S_1 = S_0 + g(S_0) = S_0(1 + g)$.
Col. 4: Additional funds needed $= 1.5(\Delta S) - 0.225(\Delta S) - 0.04(S_1)$.

ratio. This would lower (or shift to the right) the line in Figure 8-2, indicating smaller external capital requirements at all growth rates. However, before changing its dividend policy, management should consider the effects of such a decision on stock prices. These effects are described in Chapter 16.

Notice that the line in Figure 8-2 does *not* pass through the origin; thus, at low growth rates (below 3.239%), surplus funds will be produced, because new retained earnings plus spontaneous funds will exceed the required asset increases. Only if the dividend payout ratio is 100 percent, meaning that the firm does not retain any of its earnings, will the "funds needed" line pass through the origin.

**capital intensity ratio**
The amount of assets required per dollar of sales (A/S).

*Capital Intensity.* The amount of assets required per dollar of sales, A/S in Equation 8-1, is often called the **capital intensity ratio**. This factor has a major effect on capital requirements per unit of sales growth. If the capital intensity ratio is low, then sales can grow rapidly without much outside capital. However, if the firm is capital intensive, even a small growth in output will require a great deal of outside capital.

***Profit Margin and the Need for External Funds.*** The profit margin, M, is also an important determinant of the funds-required equation—the higher the margin, the lower the funds requirements, other things held constant. Telecomp's profit margin is 10 percent. Now suppose M increased to 15 percent. This new value could be inserted into the funds-needed formula, and the effect would be to reduce the additional funds needed at all positive growth rates. In terms of the graph, an increase in the profit margin would cause the line to shift down, and its slope would also become less steep. Because of the relationship between profit margins and external capital requirements, some very rapidly growing firms do not need much external capital. For example, for many years Xerox grew at a rapid rate with very little borrowing or stock sales. However, as the company lost patent protection and as competition intensified in the copier industry, Xerox's profit margin declined, its needs for external capital rose, and it began to borrow from banks and other sources. IBM has had a similar experience.

## Forecasting Financial Requirements When the Balance Sheet Ratios Are Subject to Change

To this point we have been assuming that the balance sheet ratios of assets and liabilities to sales (A/S and L/S) will remain constant over time. For this to happen, each asset and liability item must increase at the same rate as sales. In graph form, this assumes the type of relationship indicated in Panel a of Figure 8-3, a relationship that is linear and passes through the origin. Under those conditions, if the company grows and sales expand from $200 million to $400 million, inventories will increase proportionately from $100 million to $200 million.

The assumption of constant ratios is appropriate at times, but there are times when it is incorrect. Three such conditions are described in the following sections.

### Economies of Scale

There are economies of scale in the use of many kinds of assets, and where economies occur, the ratios are likely to change over time as the size of the firm increases. For example, firms often need to maintain base stocks of different inventory items, even if sales levels are quite low. Then, as sales expand, inventories grow less rapidly than sales, so the ratio of inventory to sales (I/S) declines. This situation is depicted in Panel b of Figure 8-3. Here we see that the inventory/sales ratio is 1.5, or 150 percent, when sales are $200 million but declines to 1.0 when sales climb to $400 million.

The relationship shown for economies of scale is linear, but this is not necessarily the case. Indeed, as we shall see in Chapters 18 and 19, if the firm uses the most popular model for establishing inventory and cash levels, the EOQ model, then the levels of these items will rise with the square root of sales. This means that the graph in Figure 8-3b would tend to be a curved line whose slope decreases at higher sales levels.

**Figure 8-3**
**Three Possible Ratio Relationships (Millions of Dollars)**

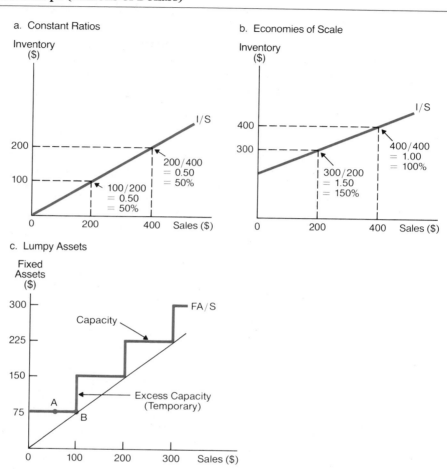

a. Constant Ratios

b. Economies of Scale

c. Lumpy Assets

## "Lumpy" Assets

**"lumpy" assets**
Assets that cannot be acquired in small increments but must be obtained in large, discrete amounts.

In many industries, technological considerations dictate that if a firm is to be competitive it must add fixed assets in large, discrete units; such assets are often referred to as **"lumpy" assets**. In the paper industry, for example, there are strong economies of scale in basic paper mill equipment, so when paper companies expand capacity they must do so in large, or lumpy, increments. This type of situation is depicted in Panel c of Figure 8-3. Here we assume that the minimum-size feasible plant has a cost of $75 million and that such a plant can produce enough output to attain a sales level of $100 million. If the firm is to be competitive, it simply must have at least $75 million of fixed assets.

This situation has a major effect on the fixed assets/sales (FA/S) ratios at different sales levels, and consequently on financial requirements. At Point A in Figure 8-3c, which represents a sales level of $50 million, the fixed assets are $75 million, so the ratio FA/S = $75/$50 = 1.5. However, sales can expand by $50 million, out to $100 million, with no required increase in fixed assets. At that point, represented by Point B, the ratio FA/S = $75/$100 = 0.75. If the firm is operating at capacity, even a small increase in sales would require a doubling of plant capacity, so a small projected sales increase would bring with it very large financial requirements.[4]

## Cyclical Changes

Panels a, b, and c of Figure 8-3 all focus on target, or projected, relationships between sales and assets. Actual sales, however, are often different from projected sales, and the actual asset/sales ratio for a given period may thus be quite different from the planned ratio. To illustrate, the firm depicted in Panel b of Figure 8-3 might, when its sales are at $200 million and its inventories at $300 million, project a sales expansion to $400 million, and then increase its inventories to $400 million in anticipation of the sales expansion. Yet suppose an unforeseen economic downturn holds sales to only $300 million. In this case, actual inventories will be $400 million, but only about $350 million will be needed to support sales of $300 million. If the firm were making its forecast for the following year, it would have to recognize that sales can expand by $100 million with no increase in inventories, but that any sales expansion beyond $100 million would require additional financing to build inventories.

## Modifying the Forecast of Additional Funds Needed

If any of the asset/sales ratios in Table 8-2 are subject to any of the conditions noted above, then the simple percentage of sales forecasting method should not be used—rather, it is necessary (1) to make separate forecasts of the requirements for each type of asset given the projected sales level, (2) to forecast spontaneously generated funds, and (3) to subtract to determine the external funds needed.

To illustrate, consider again the Telecomp example set forth in Tables 8-1 and 8-2. Now suppose a ratio analysis along the lines described in Chapter 7 suggests that the cash, receivables, and inventories ratios indicated in Table

---

[4]Several other points should be noted about Panel c of Figure 8-3. First, if the firm is operating at a sales level of $100 million or less, then any expansion that calls for a sales increase above $100 million will require a *doubling* of the firm's fixed assets. Much smaller percentage increases will be involved if the firm is large enough to be operating a number of plants. Second, firms generally go to multiple shifts and take other actions to minimize the need for new fixed asset capacity as they approach Point B. However, these efforts can go only so far, and eventually a fixed asset expansion will be required. Third, firms often make arrangements to share excess capacity with other firms in their industry. For example, consider the situation in the electric utility industry, which is very much like that depicted in Panel c. Electric companies often arrange to buy power from other utilities in order to avoid building a new plant that will be underutilized.

8-2 are appropriate, as are the liability ratios and the retained earnings calculations, but that excess capacity exists in fixed assets. Specifically, assume that fixed assets in 1985 were being utilized to only 80 percent of capacity. To use the existing fixed assets at full capacity, 1985 sales could have been as high as $500 million:

$$\begin{array}{c} \text{Full} \\ \text{capacity} \\ \text{sales} \end{array} = \frac{\text{Current sales}}{\begin{array}{c} \text{Percentage} \\ \text{at which fixed assets} \\ \text{were operated} \end{array}} = \frac{\$400 \text{ million}}{0.80} = \begin{array}{c} \$500 \text{ million sales} \\ \text{at full capacity.} \end{array}$$

This suggests that Telecomp's target fixed assets/sales ratio should be

$$\frac{\text{Fixed assets}}{\text{Full capacity sales}} = \frac{\$300 \text{ million}}{\$500 \text{ million}} = 0.6,$$

not the 0.75 that actually existed. Therefore, at the projected sales level of $600 million, Telecomp would require fixed assets of only 0.6($600 million) = $360 million, up only $60 million from the $300 million currently on hand, rather than up $150 million.[5]

We estimated earlier that Telecomp would need an additional $231 million of capital and that at least $76 million of this amount would have to be raised by selling common stock. However, those estimates were based on the assumption that $450 − $300 = $150 million of additional fixed assets would be required. If Telecomp could attain a sales level of $600 million with only $360 million of fixed assets, then the external funds needed would decline by $450 − $360 = $90 million, to $141 million.

## Computerized Financial Planning Models

Although the type of financial forecasting described in this chapter can be done with a hand calculator, most well-managed firms with sales greater than a few million dollars employ some type of computerized financial planning model. Such models can be programmed to show the effects of different sales levels, different ratios of sales to operating assets, and even different assumptions about sales prices and input costs. Plans are then made regarding how financial requirements are to be met—through bank loans, thus increasing short-term notes payable; by selling long-term bonds; or by selling new common stock. Pro forma balance sheets and income statements are generated under the different financing plans, and earnings per share are projected, along with such risk measures as the current ratio, the debt/assets ratio, and the times-interest-earned ratio.

---

[5]This $60 million of required new fixed assets could also be determined by noting (1) that sales could grow from $400 million to $500 million without any increase in fixed assets but (2) that the sales increase from $500 million to $600 million would require new fixed assets of (FA/S)(ΔS) = 0.6($100 million) = $60 million.

Depending on how these projections look, management may modify its initial plans. For example, the firm may conclude that its sales forecast must be cut because the requirements for external capital exceed the firm's ability to raise money. Or, management may decide to reduce dividends and thus generate more funds internally. Alternatively, the company may decide to investigate production processes that require fewer fixed assets, or to consider the possibility of buying rather than manufacturing certain components, thus eliminating raw materials and work-in-process inventories as well as certain manufacturing facilities.

In subsequent chapters we will look in detail at ways of analyzing policy changes such as those mentioned above. In all such considerations, the basic issue is the effect that a specific action will have on future earnings, on the riskiness of these earnings, and hence on the price of the firm's stock. Since computerized planning models help management assess these effects, they are playing an ever increasing role in corporate management. A very simple *Lotus 1-2-3* forecasting model is described in Appendix 8A, and an even simpler one is developed for Problem 8-7.[6]

## Summary

This chapter described in broad outline how firms go about projecting their financial statements and determining their overall capital requirements. In brief, management establishes a target balance sheet based on the type of ratio analysis discussed in Chapter 7. Assuming that each balance sheet ratio is at the desired level and that the optimal levels for these ratios are stable, the *percentage of sales method* can be used to forecast the external financial requirements associated with any given increase in sales. If the balance sheet ratios are subject to change, as they will be if excess capacity currently exists, if assets are lumpy, or if economies of scale exist, then each item in the projected balance sheet must be forecasted separately.

---

[6]It is becoming increasingly easy for companies to develop planning models as a result of the dramatic improvements that have been made in computer hardware and software in recent years. *Lotus 1-2-3* is one system that can be used, and a more elaborate system is *Interactive Financial Planning System* (*IFPS*). Both systems are used by literally thousands of companies, including 3M Corporation, Shell Oil, and Florida Power & Light. Increasingly, a knowledge of these or similar planning systems is becoming a requirement for getting even an entry-level job in the finance department of many corporations.

Note also that in this chapter we have concentrated on long-run, or strategic, financial planning. Within the framework of the long-run strategic plan, firms also develop short-run financial plans. For example, in Table 8-2 we saw that Telecomp Corporation expects to need $231 million by the end of 1986, and that it plans to raise this capital by using short-term debt, long-term debt, and common stock. However, we do not know when during the year the need for funds will occur or when Telecomp will obtain each of its different types of capital. To address these issues, the firm must develop a short-run financial plan, the centerpiece of which is the *cash budget*, which is a projection of cash inflows and outflows on a daily, weekly, or monthly basis during the coming year (or other budget period). Although considering the cash budget here would complete our examination of the basic types of analyses done in connection with financial planning, we shall nevertheless defer this discussion to Chapter 18, "Cash and Marketable Securities," because cash budgets can best be understood after we have discussed the firm's target cash balance.

The type of forecasting described here is important for several reasons. First, if the projected operating results are unsatisfactory, management can "go back to the drawing board" and reformulate its plans for the coming year. Second, it is possible that the funds required to meet the sales forecast simply cannot be obtained; if so, it is obviously better to know this in advance and to scale back the projected level of operations. Third, even if the required funds can be raised, it is desirable to plan for their acquisition well in advance. As we shall see in later chapters, raising capital takes time, and both time and money can be saved by careful forward planning.

## Questions

**8-1**    Define each of the following terms:
    a. Sales forecast
    b. Percentage of sales method
    c. Spontaneously generated funds
    d. Dividend payout ratio; retention ratio
    e. Pro forma financial statement
    f. Additional funds needed (AFN)
    g. Capital intensity ratio
    h. "Lumpy" assets

**8-2**    Certain liability and net worth items generally increase spontaneously with increases in sales. Put a check ($\checkmark$) by those items that typically increase spontaneously:

Accounts payable          _____

Notes payable to banks     _____

Accrued wages              _____

Accrued taxes              _____

Mortgage bonds             _____

Common stock               _____

Retained earnings          _____

Marketable securities      _____

**8-3**    The following equation can, under certain assumptions, be used to forecast financial requirements:

$$\text{Additional funds needed} = (A/S)(\Delta S) - (L/S)(\Delta S) - MS_1(1 - d).$$

Under what conditions does the equation give satisfactory predictions, and when should it not be used?

**8-4**    Assume that an average firm in the office supply business has a 6 percent after-tax profit margin, a 40 percent debt/assets ratio, a turnover of 2 times, and a dividend payout ratio of 40 percent. Is it true that if such a firm is to have *any* sales growth ($g > 0$) it will be forced to borrow or to sell common stock (that is, it will need some nonspontaneous, external capital even if g is very small)?

**8-5**    Is it true that computerized corporate planning models were a fad during the 1970s but, because of a need for flexibility in corporate planning, they have been dropped by most firms?

**8-6**    Suppose a firm makes the following policy changes. If the change means
that external, nonspontaneous financial requirements for any rate of
growth will increase, indicate this by a ( + ); indicate decreases by a
( − ); and indicate indeterminant and/or no effect by a ( 0 ). Think in
terms of the immediate, short-run effect on funds requirements.

a. The dividend payout ratio is increased.                                      _____

b. The firm contracts to buy rather than make certain com-
   ponents used in its products.                                                _____

c. The firm decides to pay all suppliers on delivery, rather
   than after a 30-day delay, in order to take advantage of discounts for rapid payment.                                                    _____

d. The firm begins to sell on credit (previously all sales had
   been on a cash basis).                                                       _____

e. The firm's profit margin is eroded by increased competi-
   tion; sales are steady.                                                      _____

f. Advertising expenditures are stepped up.                                     _____

g. A decision is made to substitute long-term mortgage bonds
   for short-term bank loans.                                                   _____

h. The firm begins to pay employees on a weekly basis (previously it had paid at the end of each month).                              _____

## Self-Test Problems (*Solutions on Page 271*)

**ST-1**    K. Billingsworth and Company has the following ratios: A/S = 1.6; L/S =
0.4; profit margin = 0.10; and dividend payout ratio = 0.45, or 45 percent. Sales last year were $100 million. Assuming that these ratios will
remain constant and that all liabilities increase spontaneously with increases in sales, what is the maximum growth rate Billingsworth can
achieve without having to employ nonspontaneous external funds?

**ST-2**    Suppose Billingsworth's financial consultants report ( 1 ) that the inventory turnover ratio is sales/inventory = 3 times versus an industry average of 4 times and ( 2 ) that Billingsworth could raise its turnover to 4
without affecting sales, the profit margin, or the other asset turnover
ratios. Under these conditions, what amount of external funds would
Billingsworth require during each of the next 2 years if sales grew at a
rate of 20 percent per year?

## Problems

Pro forma balance sheet    **8-1**    A group of investors is planning to set up a new company, The Running
Shoe, Ltd., to manufacture and distribute a novel type of running shoe.
To help determine the new operation's financial requirements, you have
been asked to construct a pro forma balance sheet for December 31,
1986, the end of the first year of operations, and to estimate Running
Shoe's external financing requirements for 1986. Sales for 1986 are projected at $10 million, and the following are industry average ratios for
athletic shoe companies:

| | |
|---|---|
| Sales to common equity | 5× |
| Current debt to equity | 50% |
| Total debt to equity | 80% |
| Current ratio | 2.2× |
| Net sales to inventory | 9× |
| Accounts receivable to sales | 10% |
| Fixed assets to equity | 70% |
| Profit margin | 3% |
| Dividend payout ratio | 30% |

a. Complete the pro forma balance sheet below, assuming that 1986 sales are $10 million and the firm maintains industry average ratios.

**The Running Shoe, Ltd.: Pro Forma Balance Sheet**
**December 31, 1986 (Millions of Dollars)**

| | | | | |
|---|---|---|---|---|
| Cash | $ | Current debt | $ | |
| Accounts receivable | | Long-term debt | _____ | |
| Inventories | _____ | Total debt | | |
| Total current assets | | Equity | _____ | |
| Fixed assets | _____ | | | |
| Total assets | $_____ | Total claims | $_____ | |

b. If the group supplies all the equity, how much capital (exclusive of retained earnings) will it be required to put up during 1986?

Long-term financing needed     **8-2**     At year-end 1985, SOS, Inc.'s total assets were $2.4 million. Sales, which were $5 million, will increase by 25 percent in 1986. The 1985 ratio of assets to sales will be maintained in 1986. Common stock amounted to $850,000 in 1985, and retained earnings were $590,000. Accounts payable will continue to be 15 percent of sales in 1986, and the company plans to sell new common stock in the amount of $150,000. Net income after taxes is expected to be 6 percent of sales; 50 percent of earnings will be paid out as dividends. (a) What was SOS's total debt in 1985, and (b) how much new, long-term debt financing will be needed in 1986? (Hint: AFN − New stock = New long-term debt.)

Pro forma statements and ratios     **8-3**     Dandy Computers makes bulk purchases of small computers, stocks them in conveniently located warehouses, and then ships them to its chain of retail stores. Dandy's balance sheet as of December 31, 1985, is shown here (millions of dollars):

| | | | |
|---|---|---|---|
| Cash | $ 3.5 | Accounts payable | $ 9.0 |
| Receivables | 26.0 | Notes payable | 17.5 |
| Inventories | 58.0 | Accruals | 9.0 |
| Total current assets | $ 87.5 | Total current liabilities | $ 35.5 |
| Net fixed assets | 35.0 | Mortgage loan | 6.0 |
| | | Common stock | 15.0 |
| | | Retained earnings | 66.0 |
| Total assets | $122.5 | Total claims | $122.5 |

Sales for 1985 were $350 million, while net income after taxes for the year was $9,930,000. Dandy paid dividends of $3,972,000 to common stockholders. The firm is operating at full capacity.

a. If sales are projected to increase by $70 million, or 20 percent, during 1986, what are Dandy's projected external capital requirements?

b. Construct Dandy's pro forma balance sheet for December 31, 1986. Assume that all external capital requirements are met by bank loans and are reflected in notes payable.

c. Now calculate the following ratios, based on your projected December 31, 1986, balance sheet. Dandy's 1985 ratios and industry average ratios are shown here for comparison:

|  | Dandy Computers | | Industry Average |
|---|---|---|---|
|  | 12/31/86 | 12/31/85 | 12/31/85 |
| Current ratio | ———— | 2.5× | 3× |
| Debt/total assets | ———— | 33.3% | 30% |
| Rate of return on equity | ———— | 12.1% | 12% |

d. Now assume that Dandy grows by the same $70 million but that the growth is spread over 5 years, that is, sales grow by $14 million each year.

1. Calculate total additional financial requirements over the 5-year period. (Hint: Use 1985 ratios, $\Delta S = 70$, but *total* sales.)

2. Construct a pro forma balance sheet as of December 31, 1990, using notes payable as the balancing item.

3. Calculate the current ratio, debt/assets ratio, and rate of return on net worth as of December 31, 1990. [Hint: Be sure to use *total sales*, which amount to $1,960 million, to calculate retained earnings but 1990 profits to calculate the rate of return on net worth—that is, (1990 profits)/(12/31/90 net worth).]

e. Do the plans outlined in Parts c and d seem feasible to you? That is, do you think Dandy could borrow the required capital, and would the company be raising the odds on its bankruptcy to an excessive level in the event of some temporary misfortune?

Additional funds needed          8-4    Tom River Textile's 1985 sales were $48 million. The percentage of sales of each balance sheet item that varies directly with sales is given below:

| Cash | 3% |
|---|---|
| Receivables | 20 |
| Inventories | 25 |
| Net fixed assets | 40 |
| Accounts payable | 15 |
| Accruals | 10 |

The dividend payout ratio is 40 percent; the profit margin is 5 percent; the December 31, 1984, balance sheet account for retained earnings was $16.4 million; and both common stock and mortgage bonds are constant and equal to the amounts shown on the balance sheet below.

a. Complete the balance sheet below as of December 31, 1985:

**Tom River Textile**
**Balance Sheet**
**December 31, 1985**
**(Thousands of Dollars)**

| Cash | $ | Accounts payable | $ |
|---|---|---|---|
| Receivables | | Notes payable | 4,400 |
| Inventories | ___ | Accruals | |
|   Total current assets | | Total current liabilities | ___ |
| Net fixed assets | ___ | Mortgage bonds | 4,000 |
| | | Common stock | 4,000 |
| | | Retained earnings | |
| Total assets | $ | Total claims | $ |

b. Now suppose 1986 sales are projected to increase by 10 percent over 1985 sales. Determine the additional funds needed. Assume that the company was operating at full capacity in 1985, that it cannot sell off any of its fixed assets, and that any required financing will be borrowed as notes payable. Use Equation 8-1 to answer this question.

c. Develop a pro forma balance sheet for December 31, 1986. Assume that any required financing is borrowed as notes payable. Note that 12/31/85 retained earnings are $17,840,000.

Excess capacity      **8-5**      Alabama Textile's 1985 sales were $72 million. The percentage of sales of each balance sheet item except notes payable, mortgage bonds, and common stock is given here:

| | |
|---|---|
| Cash | 4% |
| Receivables | 25 |
| Inventories | 30 |
| Net fixed assets | 50 |
| Accounts payable | 15 |
| Accruals | 5 |
| Profit margin (after taxes) on sales | 5 |

The dividend payout ratio is 60 percent; the December 31, 1984, balance sheet account for retained earnings was $41.8 million; and both common stock and mortgage bonds are constant and equal to the amounts shown on the following balance sheet.

a. Complete the following balance sheet.

**Alabama Textile**
**Balance Sheet**
**December 31, 1985**
**(Thousands of Dollars)**

| Cash | $ | Accounts payable | $ |
|---|---|---|---|
| Receivables | | Notes payable | 6,840 |
| Inventories | ___ | Accruals | |
|   Total current assets | | Total current liabilities | ___ |
| Net fixed assets | ___ | Mortgage bonds | 10,000 |
| | | Common stock | 4,000 |
| | | Retained earnings | |
| Total assets | $ | Total claims | $ |

b. Assume that the company was operating at full capacity in 1985 with regard to all items *except* fixed assets; had the fixed assets been used to full capacity, the fixed assets/sales ratio would have been 40 percent in 1985. By what percentage could 1986 sales increase over 1985 sales without the need for an increase in fixed assets?

c. Now suppose that 1986 sales increase by 20 percent over 1985 sales. How much additional external capital will be required? Assume that Alabama Textile cannot sell any fixed assets. (Hint: Equation 8-1 can no longer be used. You must develop a pro forma balance sheet as in Table 8-2.) Assume that any required financing is borrowed as notes payable. (Another hint: Notes payable = $10,728.)

d. Suppose that industry averages for receivables and inventories are 20 percent and 25 percent, respectively, and that Alabama Textile matches these figures in 1986 and then uses the funds released to reduce equity. (It could pay a special dividend out of retained earnings.) What would this do to the rate of return on year-end 1986 equity?

Additional funds needed     8-6     The 1985 sales of Koehlman Technologies, Inc., were $3 million. Common stock and notes payable are constant. The dividend payout ratio is 50 percent. Retained earnings as shown on the December 31, 1984, balance sheet were $105,000. The percentage of sales in each balance sheet item that varies directly with sales is expected to be as follows:

| | |
|---|---|
| Cash | 4% |
| Receivables | 10 |
| Inventories | 20 |
| Net fixed assets | 35 |
| Accounts payable | 12 |
| Accruals | 6 |
| Profit margin (after taxes) on sales | 3 |

a. Complete the balance sheet given below.

b. Suppose that in 1986 sales will increase by 10 percent over 1985 sales. How much additional capital will be required? Assume the firm operated at full capacity in 1985.

c. Construct the year-end 1986 balance sheet. Assume 50 percent of the additional capital required will be financed by selling common stock and the remainder by borrowing as notes payable.

d. If the profit margin after taxes remains at 3 percent and the dividend payout rate remains at 50 percent, at what growth rate in sales will the additional financing requirements be exactly zero?

**Koehlman Technologies, Inc.**
**Balance Sheet December 31, 1985**

| | | | |
|---|---|---|---|
| Cash | $ | Accounts payable | $ |
| Receivables | | Notes payable | 130,000 |
| Inventories | _____ | Accruals | |
| Total current assets | | Total current liabilities | |
| Fixed assets | _____ | | |
| | | Common stock | 1,250,000 |
| | | Retained earnings | _____ |
| Total assets | $_____ | Total claims | $_____ |

Forecasting

8-7

(Do only if you are using the computerized problem diskette.)
The 1985 sales of Danman Industries, Inc., were $100 million. The percentage of sales of each balance sheet item except for long-term debt and common stock (which do not vary directly with sales) is given below:

| | |
|---|---|
| Cash | 5% |
| Receivables | 15 |
| Inventories | 25 |
| Net fixed assets | 50 |
| Current liabilities | 15 |

The dividend payout ratio is 40 percent, and the profit margin is 5 percent. The long-term debt at December 31, 1985, was $20 million; common stock was $25 million, and the balance sheet amount for retained earnings was $35 million. Projected annual sales growth for the next 5 years is 20 percent.

a. Danman plans to finance its additional funds needed with 50 percent short-term debt and 50 percent long-term debt. Prepare the 1985 balance sheet, and pro forma balance sheets for 1986 through 1990, and determine (1) additional funds needed, (2) the current ratio, (3) the debt ratio, and (4) the return on equity.

b. Sales growth could be 5 percentage points above or below the projected 20 percent. Determine the impact of such variances on AFN and the key ratios.

c. Perform a sensitivity analysis on AFN and the key ratios under each of the following conditions, assuming sales grow at a constant 20 percent:

1. Profit margin (1) rises from 5 to 6 percent or (2) falls from 5 to 4 percent.

2. With the profit margin at 5 percent, the dividend payout ratio (1) is raised from 40 to 70 percent or (2) is lowered from 40 to 20 percent.

## Solutions to Self-Test Problems

ST-1    To solve this problem, we will define $\Delta S$ as the change in sales and g as the growth rate in sales, and then use the following three equations:

$$\Delta S = gS_0.$$
$$S_1 = S_0(1 + g).$$
$$AFN = (A/S_0)(\Delta S) - (L/S_0)(\Delta S) - MS_1(1 - d).$$

Set $AFN = 0$, substitute in known values for A/S, L/S, M, d, and $S_0$, and then solve for g:

$$
\begin{aligned}
0 &= 1.6(\$100g) - 0.4(\$100g) - 0.10[\$100(1 + g)](0.55) \\
&= \$160g - \$40g - 0.055(\$100 + \$100g) \\
&= \$160g - \$40g - \$5.5 - \$5.5g \\
\$114.5g &= \$5.5 \\
g &= \$5.5/\$114.5 = 0.048 = 4.8\% \\
&= \text{Maximum growth rate without external financing.}
\end{aligned}
$$

ST-2   Note that assets consist of cash, marketable securities, receivables, inventories, and fixed assets. Therefore, we can break the A/S ratio into its components—cash/sales, inventories/sales, and so forth. Then,

$$\frac{A}{S} = \frac{A - \text{Inventories}}{S} + \frac{\text{Inventories}}{S} = 1.6.$$

We know that the inventory turnover ratio is sales/inventories = 3 times, so inventories/sales = 1/3 = 0.3333. Further, if the inventory turnover ratio could be increased to 4 times, then the inventory/sales ratio would fall to 1/4 = 0.25, a difference of 0.3333 − 0.2500 = 0.0833. This in turn would cause the A/S ratio to fall from A/S = 1.6 to A/S = 1.6 − 0.0833 = 1.5167.

This change would have two effects: (1) It would change the AFN equation, and (2) it would mean that Billingsworth currently has excessive inventories, so there could be some sales growth without any additional inventories. Therefore, we could set up the revised AFN equation, estimate the funds needed next year, and then subtract out the excess inventories currently on hand:

*Present Conditions:*

$$\frac{\text{Sales}}{\text{Inventories}} = \frac{\$100}{\text{Inventories}} = 3,$$

so

Current level of inventories = $100/3 = $33.3 million.

*New Conditions:*

$$\frac{\text{Sales}}{\text{Inventories}} = \frac{\$100}{\text{Inventories}} = 4,$$

so

New level of inventories = $100/4 = $25 million.

Therefore,

Excess inventories = $33.3 − 25 = $8.3 million.

*Forecast of Funds Needed, First Year:*

$\Delta S$ in first year = 0.2($100 million) = $20 million.
AFN = 1.5167($20) − 0.4($20) − 0.1(0.55)($120) − $8.3
= $30.3 − $8 − $6.6 − $8.3
= $7.4 million.

*Forecast of Funds Needed, Second Year:*

$\Delta S$ in second year = $gS_1$ = 0.2($120 million) = $24 million.
AFN = 1.5167($24) − 0.4($24) − 0.1(0.55)($144)
= $36.4 − $9.6 − $7.9
= $18.9 million.

## Selected Additional References and Cases

The heart of successful financial planning is the sales forecast. On this key subject, see:

Pan, Judy, Donald R. Nichols, and O. Maurice Joy, "Sales Forecasting Practices of Large U.S. Industrial Firms," *Financial Management*, Fall 1977, 72-77.

Pappas, James L., Eugene F. Brigham, and Mark Hirschey, *Managerial Economics* (Hinsdale, Ill.: Dryden, 1983).

Computer modeling is becoming increasingly important. For general references, see:

Carleton, Willard T., Charles L. Dick, Jr., and David H. Downes, "Financial Policy Models: Theory and Practice," *Journal of Financial and Quantitative Analysis*, December 1973, 691-709.

Cretien, Paul, Susan E. Ball, and Eugene F. Brigham, *Financial Management with* Lotus 1-2-3 (Hinsdale, Ill.: Dryden, 1986).

Francis, Jack Clark, and Dexter R. Rowell, "A Simultaneous Equation Model of the Firm for Financial Analysis and Planning," *Financial Management*, Spring 1978, 29-44.

Grinyer, P. H., and J. Wooller, *Corporate Models Today—A New Tool for Financial Management* (London: Institute of Chartered Accountants, 1978).

Traenkle, J. W., E. B. Cox, and J. A. Bullard, *The Use of Financial Models in Business* (New York: Financial Executives' Research Foundation, 1975).

The Crum-Brigham casebook contains the following applicable case:

Case 3, "Ceramic Structures Engineering, Inc.," which focuses on the importance and mechanics of financial planning.

## APPENDIX 8A
## Microcomputers and Financial Forecasting

In Chapter 8 we presented a method for forecasting financial requirements, the percentage of sales method, which required only paper, pencil, and a calculator. While this simple procedure is useful to help gain an understanding of the basics of financial forecasting, pencil and paper computations are no longer used in the forecasting process by corporations—virtually all corporate forecasts are made with the aid of computerized forecasting models. Such models vary greatly in complexity, ranging from simple electronic spreadsheets that can be run on personal computers to complex models that require mainframe computers. In this appendix we discuss computerized forecasting models in general, and we illustrate the use of an electronic spreadsheet model which forecasts earnings and calculates key financial ratios for the Telecomp Corporation.

### Computerized Forecasting Models

The most simple computerized financial models are based on electronic spreadsheets. The user inputs historical data and formulas, which the computer uses to calculate key relationships among sales and income statement and balance sheet items, and future sales levels or sales growth rates, with which the computer performs essentially the same calculations as the forecaster would have done using a calculator. The spreadsheet has two major advantages over pencil and paper calculations: (1) It is much faster to construct a spreadsheet model than to make a "by hand" forecast if the forecast period extends beyond two or three years, and (2) the spreadsheet model automatically recomputes all forecasts if one of the input variables is changed. As we shall see, this second feature is especially valuable.

Electronic spreadsheets, which are available for most personal computers, are simply computer programs which (1) set up an electronic matrix as a series of rows and columns—that is, like a sheet of accounting paper—and then (2) do arithmetic on the rows and columns automatically. For example, Column 1 can be set up as last year's balance sheet, and then Columns 2, 3, and so forth can be the balance sheets for Years 1, 2, and so forth, with each account programmed to increase at a specified rate. A "lower section" of the spreadsheet can be designated as a corresponding series of projected income statements, and a still lower section can calculate the projected ratios for each year. Some of the more popular spreadsheets are *Lotus 1-2-3*, *Multiplan*, and *SuperCalc*.

Interactive financial forecasting models operate much like the spreadsheets, but they are more powerful. Some interactive models are available for use on large-memory personal computers; others require a mainframe computer. The most widely used interactive model is *Interactive Financial Planning System*, or *IFPS*, for which both mainframe and personal computer versions are available. Interactive models allow the forecaster to "work backwards" to find the value of a particular variable which will produce a desired outcome. For example, instead of determining the expected ROE which will result if sales grow at a specified rate, the model can determine the level of sales growth required to produce a desired ROE. This function helps financial managers plan their growth (and other variables) to maximize the value of the firm. Interactive systems can also be linked with other personal and mainframe computers within a firm, allowing many users to share data and programs.[1]

Interactive models also allow the user to specify variables as probability distributions rather than as discrete values. The model simulates real-world situations by randomly selecting a value from each probability distribution and then computing a set of outcomes associated with the values chosen. This process can be repeated several hundred times in a matter of minutes, and it results in a distribution of the possible outcomes. For example, sales growth can be specified as a random variable, and the distribution of possible net incomes and ROEs associated with the sales distribution can be generated.

Among the most complex computerized forecasting models are integrated, data-based financial planning systems. These systems link all areas of a corporation's operations in order to help it plan for the most efficient utilization of its financial and physical resources. Further, these models can use the firm's data base of historic information to form probability distributions for use in the forecasting models. Oil companies, for example, use integrated planning models to forecast regional and worldwide demands for different types of petroleum products, to plan the best way to utilize their resources to meet this demand, and finally to forecast the financial conditions that will result under different operating plans. These models analyze a number of variables, including the company's own oil production, the cost of purchased crude oil, the capacity and operating costs of its plants, the type of fuel used by each, and so on. These input-costs and

---

[1]Electronic spreadsheets and interactive models can do many different types of things, such as (1) setting up a schedule for paying off a mortgage (amortization schedule), (2) figuring taxes, (3) managing security portfolios, (4) analyzing proposed capital budgeting projects, (5) analyzing bond refunding decisions, (6) analyzing lease proposals, (7) analyzing alternative capital structures for a firm, and an almost limitless list of other applications. Because of the power of spreadsheets and interactive models like *IFPS* and the ease with which one can learn to use them, most business school programs, including MBA programs, are now having students learn how to use software packages rather than how to program in FORTRAN, BASIC, or other languages (unless the student is interested in computer science per se).

output-prices are then worked into financial statements and used to forecast the firm's future financial condition, need for outside capital, and so forth.

Even small firms, such as retail stores and auto repair shops, are finding that they simply cannot compete effectively if they do not use computers for planning and control purposes. Indeed, now that hardware and software costs have fallen so drastically, most businesses larger than shoeshine stands can use computers in a cost-effective way—and competing in business without a computer is almost like competing on a finance exam without a calculator. So, our advice is this: If you want to be a success (or even a non-failure) in the business world, learn something about computers!

## A Simplified Financial Forecasting Model

We can best demonstrate the usefulness of financial forecasting systems by discussing one such model. In Table 8A-1 we show a simplified electronic spreadsheet model, which was developed using *Lotus 1-2-3*, for making a 6-year financial forecast for the Telecomp Corporation. The model was constructed under the following assumptions: (1) Sales and assets will grow at 20 percent a year, (2) the additional funds requirement will be met by using debt, (3) fixed costs will grow at 10 percent a year, (4) variable costs, including interest, will grow at 22 percent a year (variable costs will grow at a faster rate than sales because in this particular case the firm's debt level, hence interest, will increase at a faster rate than sales), and (5) both the dividend payout ratio and the common stock

**Table 8A–1**
**Simplified Forecasting Model for the Telecomp Corporation**

|  | | (A) | (B) | (C) | (D) | (E) | (F) | (G) | (H) |
|---|---|---|---|---|---|---|---|---|---|
| | 1 | Year | | 1985 | 1986 | 1987 | 1988 | 1989 | 1990 |
| | 2 | Sales | +C2*1.2 | 400 | 480 | 576 | 691 | 829 | 995 |
| | 3 | FC | +C3*1.1 | 140 | 154 | 169 | 186 | 205 | 225 |
| | 4 | VC | +C4*1.22 | 230 | 281 | 342 | 418 | 510 | 622 |
| | 5 | EBT | +C2-C3-C4 | 30 | 45 | 64 | 87 | 115 | 148 |
| | 6 | Tax (46%) | +C5*.46 | 14 | 21 | 30 | 40 | 53 | 68 |
| | 7 | Net income | +C5-C6 | 16 | 25 | 35 | 47 | 62 | 80 |
| | 8 | Dividend payout | +C8 | .5 | .5 | .5 | .5 | .5 | .5 |
| | 9 | Dividends | +C7*C8 | 8 | 12 | 17 | 24 | 31 | 40 |
| | 10 | Additions to RE | +C7-C9 | 8 | 12 | 17 | 24 | 31 | 40 |
| | 11 | Assets | +C11*1.2 | 276 | 331 | 397 | 477 | 572 | 687 |
| | 12 | Debt | +C11-C13-C14 | 116 | 159 | 207 | 264 | 328 | 403 |
| | 13 | Common stock | +C13 | 80 | 80 | 80 | 80 | 80 | 80 |
| | 14 | RE | +C14+D10 | 80 | 92 | 110 | 133 | 164 | 204 |
| | 15 | Profit margin | +C7/C2 | 0.04 | 0.05 | 0.06 | 0.07 | 0.07 | 0.08 |
| | 16 | ROE | +C7/(C13+C14) | 0.10 | 0.14 | 0.18 | 0.22 | 0.25 | 0.28 |
| | 17 | ROI | +C7/C11 | 0.06 | 0.07 | 0.09 | 0.10 | 0.11 | 0.12 |
| | 18 | D/A | +C12/C11 | 0.42 | 0.48 | 0.52 | 0.55 | 0.57 | 0.59 |

Note: The formulas in Column B would not appear on the printout of an actual *Lotus 1-2-3* model; they are presented here to show the relationships among items in the income statements and balance sheets from one year to the next year.

account will remain constant. The model calculates net income, additions to re-tained earnings, and the forecasted level of assets, and it then solves for the level of debt needed to finance those assets. The model also computes the company's key financial ratios.

The *Lotus 1-2-3* spreadsheet designates columns as A, B, C, . . . and rows as 1, 2, 3, . . ., and each cell in the matrix has a designation such as A1, A2, B1, B2, and so forth. Thus, in Table 8A-1 the years are in Row 1; sales are in Row 2; fixed costs are in Row 3; and so forth. Column A provides labels; Column B shows the formulas used in the model; and Columns C through H give data for the different years. Thus, Cell C3 gives the 1985 value for fixed costs (FC), Cell C4 gives the 1985 value for variable costs (VC), and so on. The 1986 value for sales is the 1985 value increased by 20 percent, and the electronic spreadsheet automatically computes this using the formula D2 = C2*1.2, replicated for 1986 through 1990. Similarly, fixed costs, variable costs, and assets are increased in each year. The remainder of the income statement and balance sheet items are calculated, and then the ratios are developed.

We can see from Table 8A-1 that, as Telecomp's sales grow, its profit margin, ROE, and ROA also increase. This result occurs in part because a larger percent-age of assets is being financed by debt rather than by equity—in fact, from 1985 until 1990, the firm's debt ratio is projected to increase from 42 percent of assets to 59 percent.

The model allows us to examine the trends in the firm's profitability and debt ratios; however, it does not show us what is happening to the firm's liquidity and activity ratios. It would be easy enough to provide more detail on the income statement and balance sheet, and this might show us that Telecomp's current ratio was weak, that the firm was holding excess stocks of inventory, and so on. We could also build in constraints, such as requirements that the debt ratio not exceed 50 percent and the current ratio be maintained at 2.0 times or higher.

Note that it is extremely easy to change the assumptions built into computer models to see the results under alternative scenarios. For example, if we wanted to see what would happen at a sales growth rate of 10 percent rather than 20 percent, we would simply move the cursor to Cell B2, delete the "2" and replace it with a "1" (leaving the cell +C2*1.1), and the computer would immediately and automatically recalculate everything and produce a new Table 8A-1. Similar changes could be made with the profit margin, the tax rate, and so on. This type of analysis is called "what if" analysis—"What if the sales growth rate drops to 10 percent or the profit margin increases to 5 percent? Then what results would we get?" Being able to answer this type of question is extremely useful in all forms of financial planning.

We have illustrated computer modeling with a simple financial forecast. It should be noted that computerized models are used to analyze many of the finan-cial decisions covered in this book, including cash budgeting, capital budgeting, capital structure analysis, lease analysis, and bond refunding decisions. Illustra-tions of some of these models are provided in Cretien, Ball, and Brigham, *Finan-cial Management with* Lotus 1-2-3® (Hinsdale, Ill.: Dryden, 1986).

Finally, note that in most chapters of this book, one or more of the end-of-chapter problems is designated with a floppy disk logo; in Chapter 8, for example, Problem 8-7 is so designated. You can get a diskette from your instructor which contains *Lotus 1-2-3* models for each of the computer problems, go through them fairly rapidly, and gain a good understanding of just how useful computer models can be in dealing with the types of analyses addressed in this book.

# III

# STRATEGIC LONG-TERM INVESTMENT DECISIONS: CAPITAL BUDGETING

Capital budgeting, which involves the decision to acquire fixed assets, is an exceptionally important subject. Since "fixed assets" last for a number of years, investment decisions concerning them affect the long-run course of a business. Chapter 9 describes the fundamentals of capital budgeting, while Chapter 10 extends and refines the basic analysis, and discusses how risk is handled in capital budgeting.

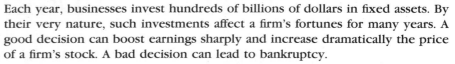

# 9

# THE BASICS OF CAPITAL BUDGETING

Each year, businesses invest hundreds of billions of dollars in fixed assets. By their very nature, such investments affect a firm's fortunes for many years. A good decision can boost earnings sharply and increase dramatically the price of a firm's stock. A bad decision can lead to bankruptcy.

A classic example of a bad capital budgeting decision which could have easily been avoided involved Lockheed's production of the L-1011 Tri-Star commercial jet. At the time Lockheed made the final decision to go forward with Tri-Star production, it estimated the breakeven volume at about 200 planes. The company had orders for about 180 planes, and it was sure of getting at least 20 more orders. Consequently, it decided to commit $1 billion and commence production.

However, Lockheed's analysis was flawed—it failed to account properly for the cost of the capital tied up in the project. Had its analysts appraised the project correctly, they would have found that the breakeven point was far above 200 planes—so far above that the Tri-Star program was almost certainly doomed to financial failure. This mistake contributed to a decline in Lockheed's stock from $73 per share to $3. Had Lockheed's managers read Chapter 9 and heeded its advice, at least some of that loss might have been avoided.

**capital budgeting**
The process of planning expenditures on assets whose returns are expected to extend beyond one year.

In previous chapters we have seen how investors value corporate securities and how investors determine required rates of return. Now we turn to **capital budgeting**, which involves investment decisions relating to fixed assets. The term *capital* refers to fixed assets used in production, while a *budget* is a plan which details projected inflows and outflows during some future period. Thus, the *capital budget* outlines the planned expenditures on fixed assets, and *capital budgeting* is the whole process of analyzing projects and deciding whether they should be included in the capital budget. This process is of fundamental importance to the success or failure of the firm, for its fixed asset investment decisions chart its course for many years into the future—indeed, these decisions *determine* its future.

Our treatment of capital budgeting is divided into two parts. First, Chapter 9 gives an overview and explains the basic techniques used in capital budgeting analysis. Then, Chapter 10 goes on to consider how cash flows are estimated and to discuss risk analysis in capital budgeting. Also, in Chapter 9 we take as given the firm's cost of capital; again, that subject is addressed in Chapter 10 and also in Chapter 14.

## Project Proposals and Classifications

The same general concepts are involved in both capital budgeting and security analysis. However, whereas a set of stocks and bonds exists in the securities market, and investors select portfolios from this set, *capital projects are created by the firm*. For example, a Hewlett-Packard sales representative recently reported that customers were asking for a particular type of oscilloscope that the company was not then producing. The sales manager discussed the idea with the marketing research group to determine the size of the market for the proposed product. It appeared likely that a significant market did exist, so cost accountants and engineers were asked to estimate production costs. The whole analysis suggested that the product could be produced and sold to yield a good profit, and the project was therefore undertaken.

The growth and development of a firm like Hewlett-Packard, even its ability to remain competitive and to survive, depend upon a constant flow of new investment ideas. Accordingly, well-managed firms like H-P go to great lengths to develop good capital budgeting proposals. For example, a senior executive recently made this statement:

> Our R&D department is constantly searching both for new products and for ways to improve existing products. In addition, our executive committee, which consists of senior executives in marketing, production, and finance, identifies the products and markets in which our company will compete, and the committee sets long-run targets for each division. These targets, which are formalized in the corporation's strategic business plan, provide a general guide to the operating executives who must meet them. These executives then seek new products, set expansion plans for existing products, and look for ways to reduce production and distribution costs. Since bonuses and promotions are based in large part on each unit's ability to meet or exceed its targets, these economic incentives encourage our operating executives to seek out profitable investment opportunities.
>
> While our senior executives are judged and rewarded on the basis of how well their units perform, people further down the line are given bonuses for specific suggestions, including ideas that lead to profitable investments. Additionally, a percentage of our corporate profit is set aside for distribution to nonexecutive employees. Our objective is to encourage lower level workers to keep on the lookout for good ideas, including those that lead to capital investments.

If a firm has capable and imaginative executives and employees, and if its incentive system is working properly, many ideas for capital investment will be advanced. Since some ideas will be good ones but others will not, procedures must be established for screening projects.

Screening capital expenditure proposals is not a costless operation—benefits can be gained from a careful analysis, but such an investigation does have a cost. For certain types of projects, a relatively detailed analysis may be warranted; for others, cost/benefit studies may suggest that a simpler procedure should be used. To aid in the screening process, firms generally classify projects into the following categories:

**1.** *Replacement: maintenance of business.* Expenditures necessary for replacing worn-out or damaged equipment used to produce profitable products are in this group.

**2.** *Replacement: cost reduction.* Expenditures to replace serviceable but obsolete equipment fall into this category. The purpose of these expenditures is to lower the cost of labor, materials, or other items such as electricity.

**3.** *Expansion of existing products or markets.* Expenditures to increase output of existing products or to expand outlets or distribution facilities in markets now being served are included here.

**4.** *Expansion into new products or markets.* These are expenditures necessary for producing a new product or expanding into a geographic area not currently being served.

**5.** *Safety and/or environmental projects.* Expenditures necessary for complying with government orders, labor agreements, or insurance policy terms are listed here. These expenditures are often called *mandatory*, or *nonrevenue-producing, investments.*

**6.** *Other.* This catchall includes office buildings, parking lots, and so on.

In general, relatively simple calculations and only a few supporting documents are required for replacement decisions, especially maintenance-type investments in profitable plants. More detailed analysis is required for cost reduction replacements, for expansion of existing product lines, and especially for investments in new products or areas. Also, within each category projects are broken down by their dollar costs: The larger the required investment, the more detailed the analysis and the higher the level of the officer who must authorize the expenditure. A plant manager may be authorized to approve maintenance expenditures up to $10,000 on the basis of a relatively unsophisticated analysis. On the other hand, the full board of directors may have to approve decisions which involve either amounts over $1 million or expansions into new products or markets, and a very detailed, refined analysis would also be required.

## Similarities between Capital Budgeting and Security Valuation

The capital budgeting process in well-managed firms such as Hewlett-Packard involves these five steps:

**1.** First, management estimates the expected cash flows from a given project, including the value of the asset at a specified terminal date. This is similar to estimating the future dividend or interest payment stream in security analysis.

**2.** Next, the riskiness of the projected cash flows must be estimated. To do this, management needs information about the probability distributions of the cash flows.

**3.** Then, given the riskiness of the projected cash flows and the general level of money costs in the economy as reflected in the riskless rate, $k_{RF}$, the firm determines the appropriate discount rate, or cost of capital, at which the project's cash flows are to be discounted. This is equivalent to finding the required rate of return on a stock or a bond as we did in Chapter 6.

**4.** Next, the expected cash flows are put on a present value basis to obtain an estimate of the asset's value to the firm. This is equivalent to finding the present value of expected future dividends.

**5.** Finally, the present value of the expected cash inflows is compared with the required outlay, or cost, of the project. If the asset's present value exceeds its cost, the project should be accepted; otherwise, it should be rejected.

If an individual investor identifies and invests in a stock or bond whose market price is less than its true value, then the value of the investor's portfolio will increase. Similarly, if a firm identifies (or creates) an investment opportunity with a present value greater than its cost, its earnings and consequently the price of its stock will rise. Thus, there is a very direct link between capital budgeting and stock values: The more effective the firm's capital budgeting procedures, the higher its growth rate and hence the higher the price of its stock.

## Capital Budgeting Decision Rules

**ranking methods**
Methods used to evaluate capital expenditure proposals.

A number of different methods are used to rank projects and to decide whether or not they should be accepted for inclusion in the capital budget. In this section we will discuss three **ranking methods** that are used by firms today: payback, net present value (NPV), and internal rate of return (IRR). Then, in the next section, we will evaluate these methods with respect to how well they help achieve our goal of value maximization.[1]

---

[1]You should also be aware of two other ranking methods that are sometimes used: (1) the *accounting rate of return*, which is found by dividing the average profits over a project's life by the firm's average investment in the project, and (2) the *profitability index*, which is found by dividing the present value of the expected cash flows by the project's cost. The accounting rate of return is dangerous and potentially misleading, because it fails to recognize that a dollar held today is worth more than a dollar to be received in the future. The profitability index is a derivative of the NPV, but is inferior to NPV in that it can lead to incorrect decisions. Both of these methods are discussed in more detail in Brigham and Gapenski, *Intermediate Financial Management*, Chapter 7.

**Table 9-1**
**Cash Flows for Projects S and L**

|  | Expected After-Tax Net Cash Flow, $CF_t$ | |
|:---:|:---:|:---:|
| Year (t) | Project S | Project L |
| 0 | ($1,000)[a] | ($1,000)[a] |
| 1 | 500 | 100 |
| 2 | 400 | 300 |
| 3 | 300 | 400 |
| 4 | 100 | 600 |

[a]Represents the net investment outlay, or initial cost. The parentheses indicate a negative number, or cash outflow.

We will use the cash flow data shown in Table 9-1 for Projects S and L to illustrate each method. (The S stands for *short* and the L for *long*: Project S is a short-term project, and L is a long-term one in the sense that S's cash inflows tend to come in sooner than L's.) We assume that the projects are equally risky. Note that the cash flows, $CF_t$, are expected values and that they are adjusted for tax, depreciation, and salvage value effects. Also, since many projects require both fixed assets plus an addition to net working capital, the investment outlays shown as $CF_0$ include any necessary changes in net working capital.[2] Finally, we assume that all cash flows occur at the end of the designated year.

### Payback Period

**payback period**
The length of time required for the net revenues of an investment to return the cost of the investment.

The **payback period**, defined as the number of years a firm expects it will take to recover its original investment from net cash flows, was the first formal method developed for use in evaluating capital budgeting projects. The easiest way to calculate the payback period is to accumulate the project's net cash flows and see when they sum to zero. For example, the *cumulative* net cash flows of Project S are listed below. We begin with $-$1,000; add $+$500 to get the Year 1 cumulative total of $-$500; then add $+$400 to get the Year 2 value of $-$100; and so on:

| | $CF_t$ for S | Cumulative CF |
|:---:|:---:|:---:|
| Year 0 | ($1,000) | ($1,000) |
| Year 1 | 500 | (500) |
| Year 2 | 400 | (100) |
| Year 3 | 300 | 200 |
| Year 4 | 100 | 300 |

[2]Perhaps the most difficult part of the capital budgeting process is the estimation of the relevant cash flows. For simplicity, the net cash flows are treated as a given in this chapter, since this will allow us to focus on our main area of concern, the capital budgeting decision rules. In Chapter 10, we will discuss cash flow estimation in detail. Also, note that *working capital* is defined as the firm's current assets while *net working capital* is current assets minus current liabilities.

This cumulative total becomes positive in Year 3, so the investment is recovered in that year. Assuming that cash flows occur evenly during the year, the recovery actually occurs one-third of the way into Year 3: $100 remains to be recovered at the end of Year 2, and since Year 3 produces $300 in net cash flow, the payback period for Project S is 2⅓ years. Using the same procedure, we find the payback of Project L to be 3⅓ years:

$$\text{Payback}_S: 2^1/_3 \text{ years.}$$

$$\text{Payback}_L: 3^1/_3 \text{ years.}$$

If the firm required a payback of three years or less, Project S would be accepted and Project L would be rejected. If the projects were *mutually exclusive*, S would be accepted over L because S has the shorter payback.[3] Thus, the payback method ranks S over L.

***Advantages of Payback Method.*** The payback method was originally used because it is easy and inexpensive to calculate and apply. This was an important consideration in the precomputer days. However, even today some very sophisticated firms still use payback to evaluate small capital expenditure decisions when the cost of using the more complex methods outweighs the possible benefits to be gained by their making "better" choices among alternatives. Also, the payback is useful in that it provides a measure of project liquidity, or the speed with which cash invested in the project will be returned. Firms that are short of cash must necessarily place a higher value on projects with a higher degree of liquidity. Finally, the payback period is often considered to be an indicator of the relative risk of projects: because firms can generally forecast near-term events better than more distant ones, projects whose returns come in relatively rapidly are, other things held constant, generally less risky than longer-term projects. In this sense, Project S is less risky than Project L because S's returns come in sooner.

***Disadvantages of Payback Method.*** One glaring weakness of the payback method is that it ignores cash flows beyond the payback period. Thus, Project L has cash flows of $500 and $600 in Years 5 and 6, respectively, but this fact does not influence either its payback or the payback ranking of Projects S and L. Ignoring returns in the distant future means that the payback method is biased against long-term projects. A second major flaw in the payback method is that it ignores the time value of money; a dollar received in Year 3 is given the same weight as a dollar received in Year 1. These two shortcomings can cause the payback method to lead to incorrect capital investment decisions; therefore, other methods should be used.

---

[3]*Mutually exclusive* means that if one project is taken on, the other must be rejected. For example, the installation of a conveyor-belt system in a warehouse and the purchase of a fleet of forklift trucks for the same warehouse would be mutually exclusive projects—accepting one would imply rejection of the other. *Independent* projects are projects whose costs and revenues are independent of one another. These terms are discussed later in the chapter.

## Net Present Value (NPV)

**discounted cash flow (DCF) techniques**
Methods of ranking investment proposals that employ time value of money concepts; two of these are the net present value and internal rate of return methods.

**net present value (NPV) method**
A method of ranking investment proposals using the NPV, which is equal to the present value of future returns, discounted at the marginal cost of capital, minus the present value of the cost of the investment.

As the flaws in the payback method were recognized, people began to search for methods that would improve the accuracy of project evaluations. This led to the development of **discounted cash flow (DCF) techniques**, which take account of the time value of money. One such DCF method is the **net present value (NPV) method**. Here is the procedure:

**1.** Find the present value of each cash flow, including the initial outflow, discounted at an appropriate percentage rate.

**2.** Add up these discounted cash flows; their sum is defined as the project's NPV.

**3.** If the NPV is positive, the project should be accepted; if negative, it should be rejected; and if two projects are mutually exclusive, the one with the higher positive NPV should be chosen.

The NPV can be expressed as follows:

$$
NPV = \frac{CF_0}{(1 + k)^0} + \frac{CF_1}{(1 + k)^1} + \ldots + \frac{CF_n}{(1 + k)^n}
$$

$$
= \sum_{t=0}^{n} \frac{CF_t}{(1 + k)^t}. \tag{9-1}
$$

Here $CF_t$ is the expected net cash flow at Period t; k is the appropriate discount rate, or the project's cost of capital; and n is the project's expected life.[4] The cost of capital, k, depends on the riskiness of the project, the level of interest rates in the economy, and several other factors. In this chapter we take k as a given, but it is discussed in detail in Chapter 14.

Cash outflows (expenditures on the project, such as the cost of buying equipment or building factories) are treated as *negative* cash flows. In evaluating Projects S and L only $CF_0$ is negative, but for many large projects, such as General Motors' Saturn project, an electric generating plant, or a new generation of computers, outflows occur for several years before operations begin and the cash flows become positive. Also, note that Equation 9-1 is quite general, so inflows and outflows could occur on any basis (say, quarterly), and t could represent quarters or months rather than years.

At a 10 percent cost of capital, the NPV of Project S is $78.82:

$$
NPV_S = \frac{-\$1,000}{(1.10)^0} + \frac{\$500}{(1.10)^1} + \frac{\$400}{(1.10)^2} + \frac{\$300}{(1.10)^3} + \frac{\$100}{(1.10)^4}
$$

$$
= -\$1,000(1.0000) + \$500(0.9091) + \$400(0.8264) + \$300(0.7513)
$$
$$
+ \$100(0.6830)
$$

$$
= -\$1,000 + \$454.55 + \$330.58 + \$225.39 + \$68.30
$$

$$
= \$78.82.
$$

---

[4]Note also that if all of the project's costs occur at t = 0, as is often true of smaller projects, then $CF_0$ = Cost and $(1 + k)^0$ = 1, so we can express the NPV equation as follows:

$$
NPV = \sum_{t=1}^{n} \frac{CF_t}{(1 + k)^t} - Cost. \tag{9-1a}
$$

Here is the same thing expressed as a time line:

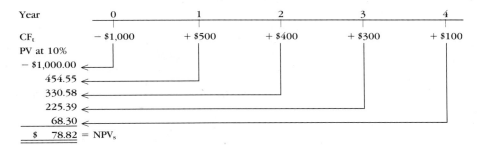

| Year | 0 | 1 | 2 | 3 | 4 |
|------|---|---|---|---|---|
| $CF_t$ | $-\$1,000$ | $+\$500$ | $+\$400$ | $+\$300$ | $+\$100$ |

PV at 10%
- $1,000.00
    454.55
    330.58
    225.39
     68.30
$  78.82 = $NPV_s$

By a similar process, we find $NPV_L = \$49.18$. Thus, based on the NPV method, both projects should be accepted if they are independent, but S should be the one chosen if they are mutually exclusive.[5] The NPVs of both projects are also calculated in Table 9-2, using the procedures developed in Chapter 4. Notice that the NPVs are the same using either procedure, except for minor rounding differences.

The rationale for the NPV method is straightforward. The value of a firm is the sum of the values of its parts. If a firm takes on a zero-NPV project, the position of the original investors is unchanged—the firm becomes larger, but the price of its stock does not change. However, if the firm takes on a project with a positive NPV, the position of the original investors is improved. In our example, the original shareholders' wealth will increase by $78.82 if the firm takes on Project S but by only $49.18 if it takes on Project L. Viewed in this way, it is easy to see why S is preferred to L, and it is also easy to see the logic of the NPV approach.[6]

### Internal Rate of Return (IRR)

**internal rate of return (IRR) method**
A method of ranking investment proposals using the rate of return on an asset investment, calculated by finding the discount rate that equates the present value of future cash flows to the investment's cost.

**discount rate, r**
The interest rate used in the discounting process. In this context, r = IRR.

In Chapter 5 we examined procedures for finding the yield to maturity, or rate of return, on a bond. Exactly the same concepts are employed in capital budgeting when the **internal rate of return (IRR) method** is used. The IRR is defined as that **discount rate, r**, which equates the present value of a project's expected costs to the present value of the expected cash inflows:

$$PV(\text{Investment costs}) = PV(\text{Inflows}),$$

or, equivalently,

$$\frac{CF_0}{(1+r)^0} + \frac{CF_1}{(1+r)^1} + \cdots + \frac{CF_n}{(1+r)^n} = 0$$

$$\sum_{t=0}^{n} \frac{CF_t}{(1+r)^t} = 0. \qquad (9\text{-}2)$$

[5]If you have one of the better financial calculators, you can input the cash flows and the cost of capital and then hit a button marked "NPV" to find a project's NPV.

[6]Of course, this description of the process is oversimplified. Both analysts and investors anticipate that firms will identify and accept positive NPV projects, and stock prices reflect these expectations. Thus, stock prices react to announcements of new capital projects only to the extent that such projects were not already expected.

**Table 9-2**
**Calculating the Net Present Value (NPV) of Projects S and L**

| Year | Project S | | | Project L | | |
|------|-----------|-----------|----------------|-----------|-----------|----------------|
| | Net Cash Flow | PVIF (10%) | PV of Cash Flow | Net Cash Flow | PVIF (10%) | PV of Cash Flow |
| 1 | $500 | 0.9091 | $ 454.55 | $100 | 0.9091 | $ 90.91 |
| 2 | 400 | 0.8264 | 330.56 | 300 | 0.8264 | 247.92 |
| 3 | 300 | 0.7513 | 225.39 | 400 | 0.7513 | 300.52 |
| 4 | 100 | 0.6830 | 68.30 | 600 | 0.6830 | 409.80 |
| PV of inflows | | | $1,078.80 | | | $1,049.15 |
| Less: Cost | | | 1,000.00 | | | 1,000.00 |
| NPV | | | $ 78.80 | | | $ 49.15 |

For our Project S, here is the set-up:

$$\frac{-\$1,000}{(1 + r)^0} + \frac{\$500}{(1 + r)^1} + \frac{\$400}{(1 + r)^2} + \frac{\$300}{(1 + r)^3} + \frac{\$100}{(1 + r)^4} = 0.$$

Here we know the value of $CF_t$ for all t, but we do not know the value of r. Thus, we have an equation with one unknown, and we can solve for the value of r. *This value of r is defined as the IRR.*

Notice that the internal rate of return formula, Equation 9-2, is simply the NPV formula, Equation 9-1, solved for the particular discount rate that causes the NPV to equal zero. Thus, the same basic equation is used for both methods, but in the NPV method the discount rate, k, is specified and the NPV is found, while in the IRR method the NPV is specified to equal zero and the value of r = IRR that forces this equality is determined.

The internal rate of return may be found by several procedures. We will discuss four here.

***Procedure 1: Trial and Error.*** In the trial and error method, we first compute the present value of cash inflows from an investment using a somewhat arbitrarily selected discount rate. Since the cost of capital for most firms is in the range of 10 to 20 percent, it is to be hoped that projects will promise a return of at least 10 percent. Therefore, 10 percent is a good starting point for most problems. We calculate the present value at a 10 percent cost of capital and see if it is positive, negative, or zero. Suppose the NPV is *negative*—what do we do then? We must *raise* the present value of the inflows; to do this we must *lower* the discount rate, say, from 10 to 8 percent, and go through the process again. Conversely, if the NPV is positive, we raise the discount rate and repeat the process. We continue until Equation 9-2 is approximately equal to zero. *The discount rate that forces this solution is defined as the internal rate of return.*

This calculation process is illustrated in Table 9-3 for the same Projects S and L that we analyzed earlier. First, the present value interest factors are

**Table 9-3**
**Finding the Internal Rates of Return for Projects S and L**

| | | Cash Flows (CF$_t$ Values) | |
|---|---|---|---|
| | Year | S | L |
| | 0 | ($1,000) | ($1,000) |
| | 1 | 500 | 100 |
| | 2 | 400 | 300 |
| | 3 | 300 | 400 |
| | 4 | 100 | 600 |

| | | NPV at 10% | | | NPV at 15% | |
|---|---|---|---|---|---|---|
| | | Present Value | | | Present Value | |
| Year | PVIF | PV$_S$ | PV$_L$ | PVIF | PV$_S$ | PV$_L$ |
| 0 | 1.0000 | ($1,000.00) | ($1,000.00) | 1.0000 | ($1,000.00) | ($1,000.00) |
| 1 | 0.9091 | 454.55 | 90.91 | 0.8696 | 434.80 | 86.96 |
| 2 | 0.8264 | 330.56 | 247.92 | 0.7561 | 302.44 | 226.83 |
| 3 | 0.7513 | 225.39 | 300.52 | 0.6575 | 197.25 | 263.00 |
| 4 | 0.6830 | 68.30 | 409.80 | 0.5718 | 57.18 | 343.08 |
| NPV | | $    78.80 | $    49.15 | | $    (8.33) | $    (80.13) |

obtained from Table A-1 in Appendix A at the end of the text; note that for t = 0, PVIF is always equal to 1.0. These factors are then multiplied by the cash flows for the corresponding years, and the present values of the annual cash flows are placed in the appropriate columns. Finally, we sum the present values of the yearly cash flows to obtain the investment's net present value. Because the net present value of both investments is positive at the 10 percent rate, we increase the rate to 15 percent and try again. At this point the net present value of S is just below zero, which indicates that its IRR is slightly less than 15 percent. L's net present value at 15 percent is well below zero, so its IRR is quite a bit less than 15 percent. These trials could be continued to obtain closer and closer approximations to the exact IRR, but the procedures described below can speed up the process.

*Procedure 2: Graphic Solution.* The graphic method for finding IRRs involves plotting curves that show the relationship between a project's NPV and the discount rate used to calculate the NPV. Such a curve is defined as the project's **net present value profile**. NPV profiles for Projects L and S are shown in Figure 9-1. To construct them, we first note that at a zero discount rate the NPV is simply the total of the undiscounted cash flows of the project; thus, at a zero discount rate, NPV$_S$ = $300 while NPV$_L$ = $400. These values are plotted as the vertical axis intercepts in Figure 9-1. Next, we calculate the projects' NPVs at three discount rates, say, 5, 10, and 15 percent, and plot these values. The data points plotted on our graph are

**net present value profile**
A curve showing the relationship between a project's NPV and the discount rate used to calculate it.

**Figure 9-1**
**Net Present Value Profiles:**
**NPVs of Projects S and L at Different Discount Rates**

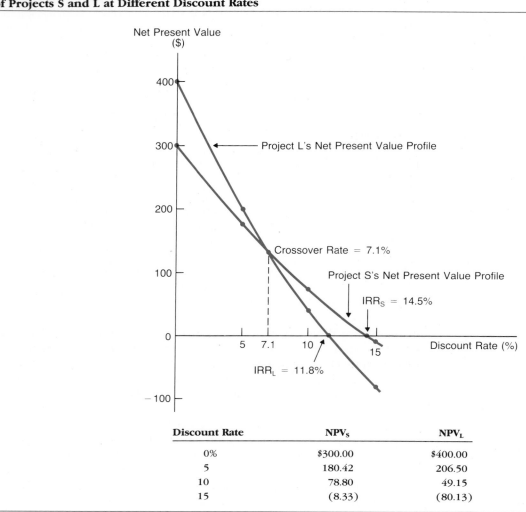

| Discount Rate | NPV$_S$ | NPV$_L$ |
|---------------|---------|---------|
| 0% | $300.00 | $400.00 |
| 5 | 180.42 | 206.50 |
| 10 | 78.80 | 49.15 |
| 15 | (8.33) | (80.13) |

shown at the bottom of the figure. When we connect these points, we have the net present value profiles.[7]

_____

[7]Notice that the present value profiles are curved—they are *not* straight lines; the degree of curvature varies from case to case, and it also depends on how the axes are scaled. Also, the NPVs approach the t = 0 cash flow (the cost of the project) as the discount rate increases without limit. The reason is that at an infinitely high discount rate the PV of the inflows would be zero and NPV = CF$_0$, which in our example is − $1,000. We should also note that under certain conditions the NPV profiles can cross the horizontal axis several times or never cross it. This point is discussed in Eugene F. Brigham and Louis C. Gapenski, *Intermediate Financial Management*, Chapter 7.

Since the IRR is defined as the discount rate at which a project's NPV equals zero, *the point at which its net present value profile crosses the horizontal axis indicates the project's internal rate of return.* Figure 9-1 shows that $IRR_S$ is 14.5 percent while $IRR_L$ is 11.8 percent. With graph paper and a sharp pencil, the graphic method yields reasonably accurate results.[8]

***Procedure 3: Financial Calculator and Computer Solutions.*** Internal rates of return can be calculated very easily by computers. Most larger firms have computerized their capital budgeting processes and automatically generate IRRs, NPVs, and paybacks for all projects. Also, many hand-held calculators have built-in functions for calculating IRRs. Thus, business firms have no difficulty whatever with the mechanical side of capital budgeting. All IRRs reported hereafter in this and the following chapters were obtained using a financial calculator. By keying in the cash flows and then pressing the IRR button, we find that Project S has $IRR_S = 14.5\%$ while $IRR_L = 11.8\%$.

***Procedure 4: IRR with Constant Cash Inflows.*** If the cash inflows from a project are constant, or equal in each year, then the project's IRR can be found by a relatively simple process. In essence, such a project is an annuity: The firm makes an outlay, C, and receives a stream of cash flow benefits, $CF_t$, for a given number of years. The IRR for the project is found by applying Equation 4-5, discussed in Chapter 4.

To illustrate, suppose a project has a cost of $10,000 and is expected to produce cash flows of $1,627.45 per year for 10 years. The cost of the project, $10,000, is the present value of an annuity of $1,627.45 per year for 10 years, so applying Equation 4-5, we obtain

$$\frac{Cost}{CF} = \frac{\$10,000}{\$1,627.45} = 6.1446 = PVIFA_{k,n}.$$

Looking up PVIFA = 6.1446 in Table A-2 in Appendix A across the row for Year 10, we find it located under the 10 percent column. Accordingly, 10 percent is the project's IRR. This procedure works only if the project has a one-time cost and constant annual inflows; if it does not, the IRR must be found by one of the methods discussed above.

### Rationale and Use of the IRR Method

What is so special about the particular discount rate that equates a project's cost with the present value of its receipts (the IRR)? To answer this question, let us first assume that our illustrative firm obtains the $1,000 needed to take on Project S by borrowing from a bank at an interest rate of 14.5 percent. Since the internal rate of return on this particular project was calculated to be 14.5 percent, the same as the cost of the bank loan, the firm can invest in the project, use the cash flows generated by the investment to pay off the

---

[8]For all practical purposes, an IRR that is accurate to within about one-half percent is sufficient, given the inaccuracy inherent in the cash flow estimates. The calculations may be carried out to several decimal places, but for most projects this is spurious accuracy.

**Table 9-4**
**Analysis of Project S's IRR as a Loan Rate**

| Year | Loan Amount at Beginning of Year (2) | Cash Flow (3) | Interest on the Loan at 14.5% 0.145 × (2) = (4) | Repayment of Principal (3) − (4) = (5) | Ending Loan Balance (2) − (5) = (6) |
|---|---|---|---|---|---|
| 1 | $1,000.00 | $500 | $145.00 | $355.00 | $645.00 |
| 2 | 645.00 | 400 | 93.53 | 306.47 | 338.53 |
| 3 | 338.53 | 300 | 49.09 | 250.91 | 87.62 |
| 4 | 87.62 | 100 | 12.70 | 87.30 | 0.32[a] |

[a]The exact value of IRR$_S$ is 14.48884. Had that value been used as the loan rate, the ending balance would have been zero.

principal and interest on the loan, and come out exactly even on the transaction. This point is demonstrated in Table 9-4, which shows that Project S provides cash flows that are just sufficient to pay 14.5 percent interest on the unpaid balance of the bank loan, retire the loan over the life of the project, and end up with a balance that differs from zero only by a rounding error of 32 cents.

If the internal rate of return exceeds the cost of the funds used to finance a project, a surplus will remain after paying for the capital. This surplus will accrue to the firm's stockholders, so taking on the project will increase the value of the firm's stock. If the internal rate of return is less than the cost of capital, taking on the project will impose a cost on existing stockholders, so accepting the project will result in a reduction of value. It is this "breakeven" characteristic that makes us interested in the internal rate of return.[9]

Continuing with our example of Projects S and L, if both projects have a cost of capital of 10 percent, the internal rate of return rule indicates that if the projects are independent, both should be accepted—they both do better than "break even." If they are mutually exclusive, S ranks higher and should be accepted, while L should be rejected. If the cost of capital is above 14.5 percent, both projects should be rejected.

## Evaluation of the Decision Rules

We have presented three possible capital budgeting rules, all of which are used to a greater or lesser extent in practice. However, the methods can lead to quite different accept/reject decisions, so we need to answer this question: Which of the methods is best? Obviously, the best method is the one that selects the set of projects which will maximize shareholder wealth. If more than one method does this, then the best method would be the one that is easiest to use in practice.

---

[9]This example illustrates the logic of the IRR method, but for technical correctness, the capital used to finance the project should be assumed to come from both debt and equity and not from debt alone.

Here are three properties that must be exhibited by a selection method if it is to lead to consistently correct capital budgeting decisions:

**1.** The method must consider all cash flows throughout the entire life of a project.

**2.** The method must consider the time value of money—that is, it must reflect the fact that dollars which come in sooner are more valuable than distant dollars.

**3.** When the method is used to select from a set of mutually exclusive projects, it must choose that project which will maximize the firm's stock value.

How do the three decision criteria stand in regard to the required properties? The payback method violates Properties 1 and 2—it does not consider all cash flows, and it ignores the time value of money. Both the NPV and IRR methods satisfy Properties 1 and 2, and both lead to identical (and correct) accept/reject decisions for independent projects. However, only the NPV method satisfies Property 3 under all conditions. As we shall see in the next section, there are certain conditions under which the IRR method fails to correctly identify that project in a set of mutually exclusive projects which will maximize the firm's stock price.

## Comparison of the NPV and IRR Methods

We noted above that the NPV method exhibits all the desired decision rule properties, and as such it is the best method for evaluating projects. Because the NPV method is theoretically superior to the IRR, we were tempted to explain only the NPV, state that it should be used for decision making, and go on to the next topic. However, the IRR method is familiar to many corporate executives, and it is widely entrenched in industry. Therefore, it is important that finance students thoroughly understand the IRR method and be prepared to explain why at times a project with a lower IRR may be preferable to one with a higher IRR. Also, for many purposes it is useful to compare alternatives in terms of their IRRs, but when such comparisons are made, it is essential that the analyst be fully aware of how the IRR is developed and know when it can be used in a rational manner.

### NPV Rankings Depend on the Discount Rate

**crossover rate**
The discount rate at which the NPV profiles of two projects cross and at which the projects' NPVs are equal.

We saw in Figure 9-1 that a project's NPV declines as the cost of capital discount rate increases. Look back at the figure and notice in the figure that Project L has the higher NPV at low discount rates while $NPV_S$ exceeds $NPV_L$ if the discount rate is above the 7.1 percent **crossover rate**. Notice also that Project L's NPV is "more sensitive" to changes in the discount rate than is $NPV_S$—that is, Project L's net present value profile has the steeper slope, indicating that a small change in k has a larger effect on $NPV_L$ than on $NPV_S$.

To see why L has the greater sensitivity, recall first that the cash flows from S are received earlier than those from L; in a payback sense, S is a short-term project while L is a long-term one. Next, recall the equation for the NPV:

$$\text{NPV} = \frac{CF_0}{(1 + k)^0} + \frac{CF_1}{(1 + k)^1} + \frac{CF_2}{(1 + k)^2} + \frac{CF_3}{(1 + k)^3} + \frac{CF_4}{(1 + k)^4}.$$

Now notice that the denominators of the terms in this equation increase as k and t increase, and that the increase is exponential—that is, the effect of a higher k is more pronounced the larger the value of t. To understand this point more clearly, consider the following data:

| | |
|---|---|
| PV of $100 due in 1 year, discounted at 5% | $95.24 |
| PV of $100 due in 1 year, discounted at 10% | 90.91 |
| Percentage decline in PV resulting from a doubling of k when t = 1 | −4.5% |
| | |
| PV of $100 due in 20 years, discounted at 5% | $37.69 |
| PV of $100 due in 20 years, discounted at 10% | 14.86 |
| Percentage decline in PV resulting from a doubling of k when t = 10 | −60.6% |

A doubling of k causes only a 4.5 percent decline in the PV of a Year 1 cash flow, but the same increase in k causes the PV of a Year 20 cash flow to fall by 61 percent. Thus, if a project has most of its cash flows coming in the early years, its NPV will not be lowered very much if the discount rate increases, but a project whose cash flows come later will be severely penalized by high discount rates. Accordingly, Project L, which has its largest cash flows in the later years, is hurt badly when the discount rate is high, while Project S, which has relatively rapid cash flows, is affected less. Thus, L's NPV profile is steeper than S's.

## Independent Projects

**independent project**
A project whose cash flows are unaffected by the decision to accept or reject some other project.

For two **independent projects**, the NPV and IRR criteria always lead to the same accept/reject decision—if NPV says accept, IRR also says accept. To see why this is so, look back at Figure 9-1 and notice (1) that the IRR criterion for acceptance requires that the project's cost of capital be less than (or to the left of) the IRR, and (2) that whenever the project's cost of capital is less than the IRR, its NPV is positive. Thus, for any cost of capital less than 11.8 percent, Project L is acceptable by both the NPV and the IRR criteria, while both methods reject the project if the cost of capital is greater than 11.8 percent. Project S—and all other independent projects under consideration—could be analyzed similarly.

## Mutually Exclusive Projects

**mutually exclusive projects**
A set of projects of which only one can be accepted.

Now assume that Projects S and L are **mutually exclusive projects**, and not independent—that is, we can choose either Project S or Project L, or we can reject both, but we cannot accept both projects. Notice in Figure 9-1 that as long as the cost of capital is *greater than* the crossover rate of 7.1 percent, $NPV_S$ is greater than $NPV_L$ and $IRR_S$ is greater than $IRR_L$. Therefore, for k greater than the crossover rate of 7.1 percent, the two methods lead to the selection of the same project. However, if the cost of capital is *less than* the crossover rate, the NPV method ranks Project L higher but the IRR method indicates that Project S is better. Thus, at any cost of capital less than the crossover rate, a conflict exists—NPV says choose mutually exclusive L, while IRR says take S. Which answer is correct? Logic leads us to conclude that the NPV method is best, since it selects the project which adds the most to shareholder wealth.

There are two basic conditions which cause NPV profiles to cross and thus lead to potential conflicts between NPV and IRR:

**1.** *Project size (or scale) differences exist.* If the cost of one project is significantly larger than that of the other, the larger project will generally have a higher vertical axis intercept than the smaller one in a graph like Figure 9-1, so it is possible for one NPV profile to cut the other.

**2.** *Timing differences exist.* If most of the cash flows from one project come in the early years while most of those from the other project come in the later years, as occurred with Projects S and L, then the long-term project will generally have a higher vertical axis intercept, so again the NPV profiles can cross each other. At low discount rates, the longer-term project will generally have the higher NPV, while at high discount rates, the shorter-term project will often have the higher NPV. This is because high discount rates impose a greater penalty on distant cash flows than on near-term cash flows. Therefore, long-term projects such as Project L have NPV profiles which decline quite steeply relative to those of projects such as S, allowing the two profiles to cross.

When either size or timing differences occur, the firm will have different amounts of funds to invest in the various years, depending on which of the two mutually exclusive projects it chooses. For example, if one project costs more than the other, then the firm will have more money at t = 0 to invest elsewhere if it selects the smaller project. Similarly, for projects of equal size, the one with the larger early cash flows will provide more funds for reinvestment in the early years. Thus, the rate of return at which differential cash flows can be invested is an important consideration.[10]

## The Reinvestment Rate Assumption

**reinvestment rate assumption**
The assumption that cash flows from a project can be reinvested (1) at the cost of capital, if using the NPV method, or (2) at the internal rate of return, if using the IRR method.

Although we do not prove it in this book, the fundamental reason behind the NPV/IRR conflict has to do with the **reinvestment rate assumptions** underlying the two methods—the NPV method assumes that the firm can reinvest cash flows at the cost of capital, while the IRR method assumes that they can be reinvested at the IRR rate itself. In most companies, cash flows are more likely to be invested at a rate close to the cost of capital than to the

---

[10]For a complete discussion of scale and timing differences, see Chapter 7 of Eugene F. Brigham and Louis C. Gapenski, *Intermediate Financial Management*.

IRR.[11] Therefore, generally speaking, the assumption upon which the NPV method is built is the better one. This fact leads us to prefer the NPV method and to recommend that if an NPV analysis suggests that one of two mutually exclusive projects is better, but an IRR analysis ranks the other one first, the firm should choose the one with the higher NPV.

## The Post-Audit

**post-audit**
A comparison of the actual and expected results for a given capital project.

An important aspect of the capital budgeting process is the **post-audit**, which involves (1) a comparison of actual results to those predicted in the request for funds and (2) an explanation for any observed differences. For example, many firms require that the operating divisions send a monthly report for the first six months after a project goes into operation and a quarterly report thereafter until the project's results are up to expectations. From then on, reports on the project are handled like those of other operations.

The post-audit can provide several benefits, including the following:

**1. Improved forecasts.** When decision makers systematically compare their projections to actual outcomes, there is a tendency for estimates to improve. Conscious or unconscious biases are observed and eliminated; new forecasting methods are sought as the need for them becomes apparent; and people simply tend to do everything better, including forecasting, if they know that their actions are being monitored.

**2. Improved operations.** Businesses are run by people, and people can perform at higher or lower levels of efficiency. When a divisional team has made a forecast about a new project, its members are, in a sense, putting their reputations on the line. If costs are above predicted levels, sales are below expectations, and so on, then executives in production, sales, and other areas will strive to improve operations and to bring results into line with forecasts.

The post-audit is not a simple process. There are a number of factors that can cause complications. First, we must recognize that since each element of

---

[11]See Eugene F. Brigham and Louis C. Gapenski, *Intermediate Financial Management*, Chapter 7, for a discussion of the NPV/IRR conflict. As noted above, the conflict has to do with the reinvestment of cash flows—the NPV method implicitly assumes reinvestment at the cost of capital, while the IRR method implicitly assumes reinvestment at the internal rate of return. For a value-maximizing firm, reinvestment at the cost of capital is the better assumption. The rationale is as follows: A value-maximizing firm will expand to the point at which it accepts all projects yielding more than the cost of capital (these projects will have NPV > 0). How these projects are financed is irrelevant—the point is that they will be financed and accepted. Now consider the question of the cash flows from a particular project: If these cash flows are reinvested, at what rate will reinvestment occur? All projects that yield more than the cost of capital have already been accepted; thus, these cash flows can be invested only in physical assets yielding *less than* the cost of capital or else be used in lieu of other capital whose cost must be the cost of capital. A rational firm will take the second alternative, so reinvested cash flows will save the firm the cost of capital. The end result of this is that cash flows are, in effect, reinvested to yield the cost of capital, the assumption implicit in the NPV method.

the cash flow forecast is subject to uncertainty, a percentage of all projects undertaken by any reasonably venturesome firm will necessarily go awry. This fact must be considered when appraising the performances of the operating executives who submit capital expenditure requests. Second, projects sometimes fail to meet expectations for reasons beyond the control of the operating executives and for reasons that no one could realistically be expected to anticipate.[12] For example, the dramatic increase in the value of the dollar in world markets in 1985 adversely affected many projects for which exports were important, and the unexpected decline in oil prices hurt others. Third, it is often difficult to separate the operating results of one investment from those of a larger system. While some projects stand alone and permit ready identification of costs and revenues, the actual cost savings that result from a replacement project may be very hard to measure. Fourth, if the post-audit process is not used with care, executives may be reluctant to suggest potentially profitable but risky projects. Fifth, the executives who were actually responsible for a given decision may have moved on by the time its results are known.

Because of these difficulties, some firms tend to play down the importance of the post-audit. However, observations of both businesses and governmental units suggest that the best-run and most successful organizations are the ones that put the greatest stress on post-audits. Accordingly, we regard the post-audit as being one of the most important elements in a good capital budgeting system.

## Other Issues in Capital Budgeting

Thus far, this chapter has outlined the basic procedures used by most firms when making decisions about investments in fixed assets. However, capital budgeting is a very complex subject, and we have by no means dealt with all the important issues. Some of the significant points that have not been covered are listed and discussed here to provide an indication of the types of questions that can arise when one actually becomes involved in the capital budgeting process.

**1.** *Conflicts between NPV and IRR may occur.* As noted earlier, conflicts may arise between NPV and IRR for mutually exclusive projects. When such conflicts are present, the NPV ranking should be used.

**2.** *Multiple IRRs may be found.* Under certain conditions, more than one value of r solves Equation 9-2, which means that the project has more than

---

[12]Because of such uncertainties, most firms require that line executives include in all "request for expenditure" packages a list of key assumptions. Top managers often have more information on national political and economic trends than do division managers, engineers, and lower-level people. Highlighting the key assumptions in a separate exhibit therefore helps to better utilize top management's unique expertise.

one IRR. This situation creates confusion for companies that rely on the IRR method, and we regard it as one more disadvantage of the IRR.[13]

**3.** *The size of the capital budget can have an effect on the cost of capital.* Throughout this chapter, we have assumed that the firm's cost of capital is a given constant. However, as is shown in Chapter 14, the size of the capital budget can influence the cost of capital and hence the acceptability of specific projects.

**4.** *Capital may be rationed.* Firms occasionally set limits on the amount of money they will spend on fixed assets; this is called *capital rationing.* Thus, it is conceivable that a firm may end up with more projects having acceptable NPVs or IRRs than it is willing to finance. This situation is discussed briefly in Chapter 10.

**5.** *Project risk must be taken into account.* Thus far we have abstracted from the riskiness of different projects. This subject is discussed in Chapter 10.

**6.** *The cost of capital is critical.* The cost of capital, which is the discount rate used in the NPV method and the cutoff rate in the IRR method, is difficult to estimate, yet it is vital to the capital budgeting process. Methods for estimating the cost of capital, and also the relationship between it and the size of the capital budget, are discussed in Chapter 14.

**7.** *Inflation must be dealt with.* The best procedure for handling inflation is to estimate inflation rates for both the product's sales price and each cost item and then to let these rates be reflected in the cash flows as shown in Table 9-1.[14]

## Summary

Capital budgeting is similar in principle to security valuation—future cash flows are estimated, risks are appraised and reflected in a project's cost of capital discount rate, all cash flows are put on a present value basis, and if a project's *net*

---

[13]Very briefly, multiple IRRs can arise if a second sign reversal occurs in the cash flows during the life of a project. In a "normal" project, the first cash flow—or perhaps the first few—are negative, after which all cash flows are positive. However, there are "nonnormal" projects in which negative cash flows occur somewhere during or at the end of the projects' lives; for example, there may be large land reclamation costs at the end of a strip mining project's life. At a low discount rate, the large negative terminal cash flow has a high present value and can cause the NPV to be negative. Then, at a higher rate, the PV of the terminal cost becomes less important, and the project's NPV becomes positive. Finally, at some still higher discount rate, PVs of the positive inflows become so small that they are swamped by the negative initial cost, and the project's NPV again becomes negative. For example, a project with $CF_0 = -\$55$, $CF_1 = +\$200$, and $CF_2 = -\$150$ has NPV $= -\$5$ at $k = 0\%$; NPV rises and hits a maximum of \$11.7 at $k = 50\%$; NPV then declines, as k increases, and becomes negative at $k = 160\%$; and, as k continues to increase, NPV $\rightarrow -\$55$. A graph of the NPV profile indicates two points where NPV $= 0$, and hence two IRRs, one at about 5.8% and one at about 158%. See Eugene F. Brigham and Louis C. Gapenski, *Intermediate Financial Management*, Chapter 7, for a further discussion of multiple IRRs.

[14]Procedures for dealing with inflation are addressed in Eugene F. Brigham and Louis C. Gapenski, *Intermediate Financial Management*, Chapter 8.

*present value (NPV)* is positive, it is accepted. Alternatively, if the project's *internal rate of return (IRR)* is greater than its cost of capital, it is accepted. Because of differing reinvestment rate assumptions, the NPV and IRR methods can lead to conflicts when evaluating *mutually exclusive* projects. When conflicts exist, they should be resolved in favor of the project with the higher NPV.

In outline form, the capital budgeting process centers around the following steps:

**1.** Ideas for projects are developed.

**2.** Projects are classified by type of investment: replacement, expansion of existing product lines, expansion into new markets, safety-related mandatory projects, and "other."

**3.** The expected future cash flows from a project are estimated. This involves estimating (a) the investment outlay required for the project and (b) the cash inflows over the project's estimated life. Cash flow estimation is the most important, yet the most difficult, step in the capital budgeting process; it will be discussed in detail in Chapter 10.

**4.** The riskiness inherent in the project is appraised; this subject is also taken up in Chapter 10.

**5.** Projects are ranked by their NPVs or IRRs; those with NPV $> 0$ or IRR $>$ the cost of capital are accepted. Conflicts between NPV and IRR rankings should be resolved in favor of the NPV. Some firms also calculate projects' *payback periods*. The payback gives an indication of a project's risk and liquidity, because it shows how long the original capital will be "at risk." However, since it does not consider all cash flows and it ignores the time value of money, firms generally use a project's NPV and/or IRR as a measure of its profitability and its payback as a risk/liquidity indicator.

**6.** A *post-audit* is conducted; this involves comparing actual to predicted results. Post-audits lead to improvements in the forecasting process and hence to better future capital budgeting decisions.

While this chapter has presented the basic elements of the capital budgeting process, there are many other aspects of this crucial topic. Some of the more important ones are discussed in Chapter 10.

## SMALL BUSINESS

## Capital Budgeting in the Small Firm

The allocation of capital in small firms is as important as it is in large ones. In fact, given their comparative lack of inexpensive access to the capital markets, it may be even more important in the small firm; a mistake in allocating capital to investment in a small firm could cost the firm its very existence. Normally, large firms with capital budgets of $100 million or more allocate capital to numerous projects. A mistake can get lost in the rounding errors associated with annual earnings per share. A small firm with relatively narrow markets, however, has less margin for errors. It follows, therefore, that capital budgeting is critical to small businesses.

In spite of the importance of capital expenditures to small business, studies of the way firms make capital budgeting decisions frequently report that small firms use very unsophisticated analysis, or perhaps even no analysis at all, in making capital budgeting decisions. For example, in a study of small manufacturing firms in Iowa 20 years ago, Robert Soldofsky[1] found that more than 50 percent of the firms relied exclusively on payback or some similar criterion, and over 40 percent of them used no formal analysis at all. More recently, Runyon[2] studied 214 firms with net worths of from $500,000 to $1,000,000. He found that almost 70 percent relied upon either payback or the accounting rate of return criteria; only 14 percent used a discounted cash flow analysis; and about 9 percent of Runyon's sample indicated that they used no formal analysis at all. Studies of larger firms typically find that well over half of the firms support their capital budgeting decisions with discounted cash flow techniques.

We are left with a puzzle. Capital budgeting decisions are clearly of great importance to small firms, yet the firms neglect to use the tools that have been developed to aid their decision making. Why does this situation exist?

One of the arguments often presented is that managers of small firms are simply not well trained; they are unsophisticated. This argument suggests that the managers would use the more sophisticated techniques if they were aware of the techniques or understood them better.

Another argument relates to the fact that managerial talent is a scarce resource in small firms. That is, even if the managers are exceptionally sophisticated, perhaps the demands on their time are such that they are unable to use elaborate techniques to analyze a problem. In other words, the managers are capable of doing a careful discounted cash flow analysis, but they cannot rationally allocate the time required for such an analysis.

The managerial time required to undertake an analysis is just one example of the cost of analysis. To some extent, the costs of doing an analysis of a capital expenditure decision are fixed; the costs are generally larger for bigger expenditures, but not necessarily. To the extent that the costs of analysis are fixed, it may not be economical to incur the costs of analysis when the project itself is relatively small. This argument suggests that small firms with projects that are comparatively small may in some cases be making the sensible decision that the cost of analysis is too great for projects when management's "gut feeling" is that the project should definitely be undertaken. Small firms may do less analysis simply because it is often not economical to perform a full-blown analysis when the dollar value of the project is small. Remember also that a major part of the capital budgeting analysis process in the large firm is for lower level analysts to marshall facts needed by higher level decision makers, and this step is less necessary in the small firm. Thus, one decision to be made is how much to spend making decisions. In many cases a reasoned appraisal might suggest that the cost of analysis is greater than the value of the expected benefits.

As Soldofsky learned in his study of manufacturing firms, small firms tend to be cash oriented. They are very concerned with basic survival, so they tend to look at expenditures from the standpoint of their effects on cash, and in the very near term. This cash and survival orientation leads the firm to look only at relatively short time horizons, and it leads to an emphasis on the payback criterion as a decision tool. The limitations of payback were discussed in this chapter, but in spite of those limitations the technique is popular in small business (and in some big business). Payback gives the firm a feel for the time required to recover the cash committed to an investment and for when cash will be available for new opportunities. Small firms that are cash oriented and have scarce managerial time resources may find the payback method an appealing compromise between the need for extensive analysis on the one hand and the high costs of analysis on the other.

Small firms often face very great uncertainty in the cash flows they might generate beyond the immediate future. Many business people are uncomfortable making forecasts beyond a short horizon. Since discounted cash flow techniques require explicit estimates of cash flows through the life of the

---

[1]Robert M. Soldofsky, "Capital Budgeting Practices in Small Manufacturing Companies," in *Studies in the Factor Markets for Small Business Firms*, ed. Dudley G. Luckett (Washington, DC: Small Business Administration, 1964).

[2]L. R. Runyon, "Capital Expenditure Decision Making in Small Firms," *Journal of Business Research*, September 1983, 389-397.

project, small business managers may feel that they cannot take seriously an analysis that hinges on "guesstimate" numbers. This argument seems to appeal to many business people, but, of course, discounting techniques contain built-in mechanisms for handling the fact that some cash flow estimates may be more uncertain than others. For example, one can increase the discount rate in accordance with the greater perceived uncertainty.

## The Value of the Firm and Capital Budgeting

The single most appealing argument for the use of net present value in capital expenditure decisions is that NPV gives an explicit measure of the effect of the investment on the value of the firm. If NPV is positive, in theory the investment will increase the value of the firm and make all owners of the firm more wealthy. In small firms, however, it is often the case that the equity of the firm is not traded in public markets, so its value cannot be easily observed. Also, for reasons of control or because their size does not permit the making of a market in their stock, many small business owners and managers may be content not to let the ownership broaden into the public markets.

It is difficult to argue for value-based techniques when the value of the firm itself is unobservable. Furthermore, in a closely held firm the objectives of the individual owner-manager may not be easily expressible in terms of the firm's value. For example, the manager may not hold a well-diversified investment portfolio but may instead have a heavy financial commitment to the firm. In that case the manager is sensitive to the total risk of the firm,

not just to its systematic or undiversifiable component. A project then might be viewed as desirable because of its contribution to risk reduction in the firm as a whole. Similarly, a project with high unsystematic risk might be unacceptable even though in a CAPM framework it would be judged acceptable.

Another problem that nonmarketability causes the firm is that the cost of equity capital is not easily determined. A cost of capital estimate is required for an NPV or IRR analysis, and such estimates are generally based on market data. The small firm in an industry of small firms may have essentially no basis for estimating its costs of capital.

### Conclusions

Small firms make less extensive use of discounted cash flow techniques than do larger firms. The decision to use relatively informal procedures may arise from conflicts between the objectives of the firms and the objectives which motivate the use of DCF, and it may result in part from a determination that the cost of analysis exceeds the benefits. However, small businesses must do all they can to compete effectively with big business. To the extent that small businesses fail to use DCF because the managers are unsophisticated or uninformed, the small firms may be putting themselves at a competitive disadvantage. Making poor capital investment decisions may cost the small firms their very existence. It follows that small firms should use every means at their disposal to insure that the projects to which they allocate scarce capital are good projects. Errors can be terribly costly.

## Questions

9-1    Define each of the following terms:
   a. Capital budgeting
   b. Payback period
   c. Discounted cash flow (DCF) techniques; net present value (NPV) method; internal rate of return (IRR) method
   d. Discount rate, r
   e. Net present value profile; crossover rate; discount rate where NPV profile crosses X-axis
   f. Independent projects; mutually exclusive projects
   g. Reinvestment rate assumption
   h. Post-audit
   i. NPV versus IRR conflict

9-2     How is a project classification scheme (for example, replacement or expansion into new markets) used in the capital budgeting process?

9-3     Explain why the NPV of a relatively long-term project— defined as one in which a high percentage of the cash flows is expected in the distant future—is more sensitive to changes in the cost of capital than is the NPV of a short-term project.

9-4     Explain why, if two mutually exclusive projects are being compared, the short-term project might have the higher ranking under the NPV criterion if the cost of capital is high but the long-term project might be deemed better if the cost of capital is low. Would changes in the cost of capital ever cause a change in the IRR ranking of two such projects?

9-5     In what sense is a reinvestment rate assumption embodied in the NPV and IRR methods? What is the implied reinvestment rate in each method?

9-6     "If a firm has no mutually exclusive projects but only independent ones, a constant cost of capital, and normal projects in the sense of having one or more outflows followed by a stream of inflows, then it will always obtain identical capital budget results from the NPV and IRR methods." Discuss this statement. What does it imply about using the IRR method in lieu of the NPV method?

9-7     A firm has $100 million available for capital expenditures. It is considering investing in one of two projects, each costing $100 million. Project A has an IRR of 20 percent and an NPV of $9 million. It will be terminated at the end of one year at a profit of $20 million, resulting in an immediate increase in earnings per share (EPS). Project B, which is not postponable, has an NPV of $50 million and an IRR of 30 percent. However, the firm's short-run EPS will be reduced if it accepts Project B, because no revenues will be generated for several years.
        a. Should the short-run effects on EPS influence the choice between the two projects?
        b. How might situations such as the one described here influence a firm's decision to use payback as a screening criterion?

9-8     Are there conditions under which a firm might be better off if it were to choose a machine with a rapid payback rather than one with a larger NPV?

## Self-Test Problem (*Solution on Page 304*)

ST-1    You are a financial analyst for Porter Electronics Company. The director of capital budgeting has asked you to analyze two proposed capital investments, Projects X and Y. Each project has a cost of $10,000 and a cost of capital of 12 percent. The projects' expected net cash flows are shown below:

|        | Net Cash Flow | |
| --- | --- | --- |
| Year   | Project X   | Project Y   |
| 0      | ($10,000)   | ($10,000)   |
| 1      | 6,500       | 3,500       |
| 2      | 3,000       | 3,500       |
| 3      | 3,000       | 3,500       |
| 4      | 1,000       | 3,500       |

a. Calculate each project's payback, net present value (NPV), and internal rate of return (IRR).
b. Which project or projects should be accepted if they are independent?
c. Which project should be accepted if they are mutually exclusive?
d. How might a change in the cost of capital produce a conflict between the NPV and IRR rankings of these two projects? At what values of k would this conflict exist?
e. Why would the conflict exist?

## Problems

**Payback, NPV, and IRR calculations**

**9-1**   Project M has a cost of $35,000, and its expected net cash inflows are $9,000 per year for 6 years.
a. What is the project's payback (to the closest year)?
b. The cost of capital is 12 percent. What is the project's NPV?
c. What is the project's IRR? (Hint: Recognize that the project is an annuity.)

**NPVs and IRRs for independent projects**

**9-2**   Dellva Engineering is considering including two pieces of equipment, a truck and an overhead pulley, in this year's capital budget. The projects are not mutually exclusive. The cash outlay for the truck is $14,399, and that for the pulley is $20,336. The firm's cost of capital is 13 percent. After-tax cash flows, including depreciation, are shown below:

| Year | Truck | Pulley |
|------|-------|--------|
| 1 | $4,200 | $6,800 |
| 2 | 4,200 | 6,800 |
| 3 | 4,200 | 6,800 |
| 4 | 4,200 | 6,800 |
| 5 | 4,200 | 6,800 |

Calculate the IRR and NPV for each project, and indicate the correct accept/reject decision for each.

**NPVs and IRRs for mutually exclusive projects**

**9-3**   Clayton Industries must choose between a gas-powered and an electric-powered forklift truck for moving materials in its factory. Since both forklifts perform the same function, the firm will choose only one. (They are mutually exclusive investments.) The electric-powered truck will cost more, but it will be less expensive to operate; it will cost $18,550, while the gas-powered truck will cost $14,950. The cost of capital that applies to both investments is 10 percent. The life for both types of truck is estimated to be 5 years, during which time the net cash flows for the electric-powered truck will be $6,200 per year and those for the gas-powered truck will be $5,000 per year. Annual net cash flows include depreciation expenses. Calculate the NPV and IRR for each type of truck, and decide which to recommend for purchase.

**Present value profiles; NPV versus IRR**

**9-4**   Two projects each involve an investment of $4,500. Expected annual net cash flows are $3,000 for 2 years for Project S and $1,200 for 6 years for Project L.
a. Compute the net present value of each project if the firm's cost of capital is 0 percent and if it is 6 percent. NPVs for S at 10 and 20 percent, respectively, are $706.50 and $83.40, while NPVs for L at 10 and 20 percent are $726.36 and − $509.40.

b. Graph the net present value profiles of the two projects, and use the graph to estimate each project's IRR.

c. Use a calculator to find the internal rate of return for each project. (If you do not have a financial calculator, note that both projects are annuities.)

d. If these projects are mutually exclusive, which one would you select, assuming a cost of capital of (1) 8 percent, (2) 10.3 percent, or (3) 12 percent? Explain.

**NPV and IRR analysis**    **9-5**    Western States Chemical Company (WSC) is considering two mutually exclusive investments. The projects' expected net cash flows are as follows:

| | Expected Net Cash Flow | |
|---|---|---|
| Year | Project A | Project B |
| 0 | ($300) | ($405) |
| 1 | (387) | 134 |
| 2 | (193) | 134 |
| 3 | (100) | 134 |
| 4 | 600 | 134 |
| 5 | 600 | 134 |
| 6 | 850 | 134 |
| 7 | (180) | 0 |

a. Construct NPV profiles for Projects A and B.

b. What is each project's IRR?

c. If you were told that each project's cost of capital is 10 percent, which project should be selected? If the cost of capital were 17 percent, what would the proper choice be?

d. What is the crossover rate, and what is its significance?

e. (Do only if you are using the computerized problem diskette.) WSC's management is confident of the projects' cash flows in Years 0 to 6 but is uncertain as to what the Year 7 cash flows will be for the two projects. Under a worst case scenario, Project A's Year 7 cash flow will be − $300 and B's will be − $150, while under a best case scenario, the cash flows will be − $70 and + $120 for Projects A and B, respectively. Answer Parts a through c using these new cash flows. Which project should be selected under each scenario?

f. Put the Year 7 cash flows back to − $180 for A and zero for B. Now change the cost of capital and observe what happens to NPV, IRR, and the crossover rate at k = 0%, 5%, 20%, and 400% (input as 4.0).

**NPV and IRR calculations**    **9-6**    Project S has a cost of $10,000 and is expected to produce benefits (cash flows) of $3,000 per year for 5 years. Project L costs $25,000 and is expected to produce cash flows of $7,400 per year for 5 years. Calculate the two projects' NPVs and IRRs, assuming a cost of capital of 12 percent. Which project would be selected, assuming they are mutually exclusive, using each ranking method? Which should actually be selected? Assume that the projects are equally risky.

NPV and IRR analysis          9-7          Each of two mutually exclusive projects involves an investment of $120,000. Net cash flows (after-tax profits plus depreciation) for the two projects have a different time pattern. Project M involves using some acreage for a mining operation. Since the expense of removing the ore is lower in the early years, when the ore will be closer to the surface, Project M will yield high returns in early years and lower returns in later years. Project O involves using the land for an orchard, and it will take a number of years for the trees to mature and be fully bearing. Thus Project O will yield low returns in the early years and higher returns in the later years. The cash flows from the two investments are as follows:

| Year | Project M | Project O |
|------|-----------|-----------|
| 1 | $70,000 | $10,000 |
| 2 | 40,000 | 20,000 |
| 3 | 30,000 | 30,000 |
| 4 | 10,000 | 50,000 |
| 5 | 10,000 | 80,000 |

a.  Calculate each project's payback.
b.  Compute the net present value of each project when the firm's cost of capital is 0 percent, 6 percent, and 20 percent. At 10 percent, the NPV for M is $12,273 and the NPV for O is $11,984.
c.  Graph the net present value profiles of the two projects. Use the graph to estimate each project's IRR. If you have a financial calculator, use it to check your graphic estimate.
d.  Which project would you select, assuming no capital rationing and a constant cost of capital of 8 percent? Of 10 percent? Of 12 percent? Explain.
e.  How might a change in the cost of capital produce a conflict between NPV and IRR? At what values of k would this conflict exist?
f.  The company's capital budgeting manual states that no project with a payback greater than 4.0 should be accepted. Please comment.

NPV and IRR analysis          9-8          The Bey Burger Company is considering two mutually exclusive investments. Project A has a cost of $20,000 and will produce after-tax net cash flows of $3,752.21 per year for 10 years. Project B also has a cost of $20,000, and it is expected to produce cash flows of $5,880.72 per year for 5 years.
a.  Assuming that Bey's average cost of capital is 12 percent and that these two projects are both of average risk, which, if either, should Bey accept?
b.  Now assume that Bey's cost of capital rises to 14 percent. What is your decision now? (Note: $NPV_B = \$189.10$.)
c.  Suppose Bey's cost of capital falls to 10 percent. How does this affect your decision? (Note: $NPV_B = \$2,292.63$.)
d.  Graph the two projects' NPV profiles. (Hint: At a zero cost of capital, $NPV_A = \$17,522.10$ and $NPV_B = \$9,403.60$.)
e.  Explain why Project A's NPV profile declines more rapidly than that of Project B. Also, explain the economic logic of why A is better at a low cost of capital while B is better at a high capital cost.

Cost minimization　　　　9-9　　Florida Power and Light must install pollution control equipment on its new St. Lucie nuclear plant. The new equipment will produce no revenues, and it will be expensive to operate, but if it is not installed and operated, then the company will have to close a $2 billion plant, so the equipment will be installed. Two alternatives are available: Project S, which involves a net investment of $10,000,000 at t = 0 plus net cash outlays of $1,000,000 per year for 30 years, and Project L, which costs $14,000,000 but can be operated at a net cash cost of $600,000 per year over its 30-year life. FP&L's cost of capital is 10 percent.

a. Which alternative should FP&L choose?

b. If the cost of capital were (1) 5% or (2) 15%, would this change the decision? Explain.

## Solution to Self-Test Problem

ST-1　　a. *Payback*:

To determine the payback, calculate the cumulative cash flows for each project:

| Year | Project X | | Project Y | |
|------|-----------|----------------|-----------|----------------|
|      | CF$_t$    | Cumulative CF  | CF$_t$    | Cumulative CF  |
| 0    | ($10,000) | ($10,000)      | ($10,000) | ($10,000)      |
| 1    | 6,500     | (3,500)        | 3,500     | (6,500)        |
| 2    | 3,000     | (500)          | 3,500     | (3,000)        |
| 3    | 3,000     | 2,500          | 3,500     | 500            |
| 4    | 1,000     | 3,500          | 3,500     | 4,000          |

At the end of Year 2, $500 still has not been recovered from X. During Year 3, $3,000 of cash flows will come in. If cash flows come in at a uniform rate during the year, daily cash flows will be $3,000/365 = $8.2192 per day. It will take $500/$8.2192 = 60.83 days to recover the $500. This is 60.83/365 = 0.1667 ≈ 0.17 of a year, so the payback is 2 + 0.17 = 2.17 years for Project X. This formula can be used:

$$\text{Payback}_X = 2 + \frac{\$500}{\$3,000} = 2.17 \text{ years.}$$

$$\text{Payback}_Y = 2 + \frac{\$3,000}{\$3,500} = 2.86 \text{ years.}$$

*Net Present Value (NPV)*:

$$NPV_X = -\$10,000 + \frac{\$6,500}{(1.12)^1} + \frac{\$3,000}{(1.12)^2} + \frac{\$3,000}{(1.12)^3} + \frac{\$1,000}{(1.12)^4}$$

$$= \$966.01.$$

$$NPV_Y = -\$10,000 + \frac{\$3,500}{(1.12)^1} + \frac{\$3,500}{(1.12)^2} + \frac{\$3,500}{(1.12)^3} + \frac{\$3,500}{(1.12)^4}$$

$$= \$630.72.$$

*Internal Rate of Return (IRR)*:

To solve for the IRR, find the discount rates which force each project's

NPV to zero. For Project Y, which is an annuity, divide $10,000 by $3,500 to obtain the interest factor 2.8571:

$$\text{PVIFA}_{r\%, \ 4 \ \text{years}} = \$10,000/\$3,500 = 2.8571.$$

Look this factor up in Appendix Table A-2 across the row for Period 4; it is in the column for 15 percent, which indicates that $\text{IRR}_Y = 15\%$. For Project X you must use trial and error, the graphic method, or a financial calculator, but $\text{IRR}_X = 18\%$.

b. The following table summarizes the project rankings by each method:

|         | Ranks Higher |
|---------|:------------:|
| Payback |      X       |
| NPV     |      X       |
| IRR     |      X       |

Note that all methods rank Project X over Project Y. Additionally, both projects are acceptable under the NPV and IRR criteria at a 12 percent cost of capital. Thus, both projects should be accepted if they are independent.

c. Choose the project with the higher NPV, which is Project X.
d. To determine the effects of changing the cost of capital, first plot the NPV profiles of each project:

**NPV Profiles for Projects X and Y**

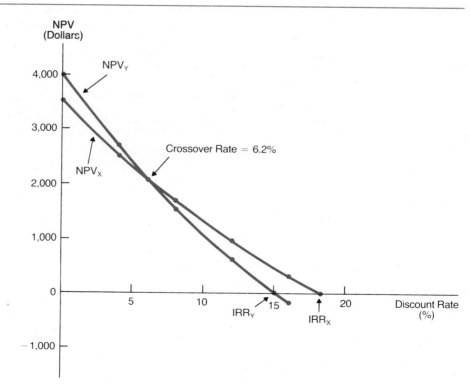

| Discount Rate | $NPV_X$ | $NPV_Y$ |
|:---:|:---:|:---:|
| 0% | $3,500 | $4,000 |
| 4 | 2,546 | 2,705 |
| 8 | 1,707 | 1,592 |
| 12 | 966 | 631 |
| 16 | 307 | (206) |
| 18 | 5 | (585) |
| 20 | (282) | (939) |

The crossover rate, where $NPV_X = NPV_Y$, is approximately 6.2 percent. Thus, if the firm's cost of capital were less than 6.2 percent, a conflict would exist, because $NPV_Y > NPV_X$ but $IRR_X > IRR_Y$.

## Selected Additional References

For an in-depth treatment of capital budgeting techniques, see:

Bierman, Harold, Jr., and Seymour Smidt, *The Capital Budgeting Decision* (New York: Macmillan, 1984).

Grant, Eugene L., William G. Ireson, and Richard S. Leavenworth, *Principles of Engineering Economy* (New York: Ronald, 1976).

Levy, Haim, and Marshall Sarnat, *Capital Investment and Financial Decisions* (Englewood Cliffs, N.J.: Prentice-Hall, 1982).

Osteryoung, Jerome, *Capital Budgeting: Long-Term Asset Selection* (Columbus, Ohio: Grid, 1974).

For a discussion of strategic considerations in capital budgeting, see:

Crum, Roy, and Frans D. J. Derkinderen, eds., *Readings in Strategies for Corporate Investments* (New York: Pitman, 1980).

Three articles related to the topics covered in Chapter 9 are:

Bacon, Peter W., "The Evaluation of Mutually Exclusive Investments," *Financial Management*, Summer 1977, 55-58.

Kim, Suk H., and Edward J. Farragher, "Current Capital Budgeting Practices," *Management Accounting*, June 1981, 26-30.

Lewellen, Wilbur G., Howard P. Lanser, and John J. McConnell, "Payback Substitutes for Discounted Cash Flow," *Financial Management*, Summer 1973, 17-23.

Additional capital budgeting references are provided in Chapter 10.

# 10

# CASH FLOW ESTIMATION, RISK, AND OTHER TOPICS IN CAPITAL BUDGETING

## A DELICATE BALANCE: PROJECTED CASH FLOWS VERSUS START-UP CAPITAL INVESTMENT COSTS

When Edwin Land invented instant photography, there was simply no question as to whether or not his Polaroid Corporation should build plants to manufacture the cameras—the projected cash flows were so large that any type of capital budgeting analysis would have given the "go" signal. However, most capital expenditure decisions are not so clear-cut. Often firms must make fairly close decisions regarding starting a new product line, replacing existing machinery versus continuing to use old equipment, and so on. Similarly, hard choices must be made between expensive, long-lived equipment and equipment that will wear out sooner but will have a lower initial cost. These "bread and butter" decisions have a major effect on the long-run success or failure of a company.

Postmortems on failed companies often reveal technical weaknesses in their capital budgeting systems. These firms did not properly analyze and compare alternative projects; they did not take account of risk in their capital budgeting analysis; and, most important, they did not estimate projects' cash flows properly. Some frequently encountered problems in capital budgeting are discussed in this chapter.

The basic principles of capital budgeting were covered in Chapter 9. Now we examine some additional issues, including (1) cash flow estimation, (2) replacement decisions, and (3) risk analysis in capital budgeting.[1]

---

[1] If time pressures do not permit coverage of the entire chapter, we suggest that cash flow estimation and replacement analysis be covered; the remainder of the chapter can be omitted without loss of continuity.

## Cash Flow Estimation

**cash flow**
The actual net cash, as opposed to accounting net income, that flows into (or out of) a firm during some specified period.

The most important, but also the most difficult, step in the analysis of a capital project is estimating its **cash flows**—the investment outlays that will be required and the annual net cash inflows the project will produce after it goes into operation. A great many variables are involved in cash flow forecasting, and many individuals and departments participate in the process. For example, the forecasts of unit sales and sales prices are normally made by the marketing department, giving consideration to price elasticity, advertising effects, the state of the economy, what competitors are doing, and trends in consumer tastes. Similarly, the capital outlays associated with a new product are generally obtained from the engineering and product development staffs, while operating costs are estimated by cost accountants, production experts, wage rate specialists, purchasing agents, and so forth.

Obtaining accurate estimates of the costs and revenues associated with a large, complex project can be exceedingly difficult, and forecast errors can be quite large. For example, when several large oil companies decided to build the Alaskan Pipeline, the original cost forecast was in the neighborhood of $700 million, but the final cost was closer to $7 billion. Similar miscalculations are common in product design cost estimates for items such as new personal computers. Further, as difficult as plant and equipment costs are to estimate, sales revenues and operating costs over the life of a project are generally even harder to forecast. For example, when AT&T developed the Picturephone, it envisaged large sales in both the residential and business markets, yet it turned out that virtually no one was willing to pay the price required to cover the project's costs. Because of its financial strength, AT&T was able to absorb losses on the project with no problem, but the Picturephone venture would surely have forced a weaker firm into bankruptcy.

The major roles of the financial staff in the forecasting process are to (1) coordinate the efforts of the other departments, such as engineering and marketing, (2) insure that everyone involved with the forecast uses a consistent set of economic assumptions, and (3) make sure that no biases are inherent in the forecasts. This last point is extremely important, because division managers often become emotionally involved with pet projects and/or develop empire-building complexes, possibly leading to cash flow forecasting biases which make bad projects look good on paper. The AT&T Picturephone project is reported to be an example of this problem.

It is not sufficient that the financial staff have unbiased point estimates of the key variables—as we shall see, data on probability distributions or other indications of the likely ranges of error are also essential. Moreover, it is useful to know the relationship between each input variable and some basic economic variable such as gross national product. If all production and sales variables are related to such a basic variable, then the financial manager will have an idea of how the project will do under different economic conditions.

It is impossible to overstate either the importance of cash flow estimates or the difficulties that are encountered in these forecasts. However, there are certain principles which, if observed, will help to minimize errors.

## Identifying the Relevant Cash Flows

One important element in cash flow estimation is the identification of the *relevant cash flows*, which are defined as those cash flows within the firm which should be considered in the decision at hand. Errors are often made here, but there are two cardinal rules which can help financial analysts avoid mistakes: (1) Capital budgeting decisions must be based on *cash flows*, not accounting income, and (2) only *incremental cash flows* are relevant to the accept/reject decision. These two rules are discussed in detail in the following sections.

### Cash Flow versus Accounting Income

In capital budgeting analysis, *annual cash flows*, *not accounting profits*, are used. Further, cash flows and accounting profits can be very different. To illustrate, consider Table 10-1, which shows how accounting profits and cash flows are related to each other. We assume that CBS Publishing is planning to start a new division at the end of 1986; that sales and all costs except depreciation are projected to be constant over time; and that the division will use accelerated depreciation, which will cause its reported depreciation charges to decline over time.

The top section of the table shows the situation in the first year of operations, 1987. Accounting profits are $12 million, but the division's net cash flow—money which is available to CBS—is $42 million. The bottom part of the table shows the situation projected for 1993. Here reported profits have

**Table 10-1**
**Accounting Profit versus Net Cash Flow (Thousands of Dollars)**

|  | Accounting Profit | Cash Flows |
|---|---|---|
| **I. 1987 Situation** |  |  |
| Sales | $100,000 | $100,000 |
| Costs except depreciation | 50,000 | 50,000 |
| Depreciation | 30,000 | 0 |
| Operating income | $ 20,000 | $ 50,000 |
| Taxes (40%) | 8,000 | 8,000 |
| Net income or net cash flow | $ 12,000 | $ 42,000 |

Net cash flow = Net income plus depreciation = $12,000 + $30,000 = $42,000.

| **II. 1993 Situation** |  |  |
|---|---|---|
| Sales | $100,000 | $100,000 |
| Costs except depreciation | 50,000 | 50,000 |
| Depreciation | 10,000 | 0 |
| Operating income | $ 40,000 | $ 50,000 |
| Taxes (40%) | 16,000 | 16,000 |
| Net income or net cash flow | $ 24,000 | $ 34,000 |

Net cash flow = $24,000 + $10,000 = $34,000.

doubled (because of the decline in depreciation), but the net cash flow is down sharply.

Accounting profits are important for some purposes, but for purposes of setting a value on a project, cash flows are more important. *Therefore, in capital budgeting, we are interested in net cash flows*, defined as

$$\text{Net cash flow} = \text{Net income after taxes} + \text{Depreciation},$$

*not in accounting profits per se.*[2]

## Incremental Cash Flows

**incremental cash flow**
The net cash flow attributable to an investment project.

In evaluating a capital project, we are concerned only with those cash flows that result directly from the project. These cash flows, called **incremental cash flows**, represent the change in the firm's total cash flows that occurs as a direct result of accepting or rejecting the project. Three special problems in determining incremental cash flows are discussed next.

**sunk cost**
A cash outlay that has already been committed for a project and is irrecoverable regardless of whether the project is accepted or rejected.

*Sunk Costs.* Sunk costs are not incremental costs, and they should not be included in the analysis.[3] A **sunk cost** refers to an outlay that has already been committed or that has already occurred and hence is not affected by the accept/reject decision under consideration. To illustrate, in 1986 Northeast BankCorp was considering the establishment of a branch office in a newly developed section of Boston. To help with its evaluation, Northeast had, back in 1985, hired a consulting firm to perform a site analysis at a cost of $100,000; this amount was expensed for tax purposes in 1985. Is this 1985 expenditure a relevant cost with respect to the 1986 capital budgeting decision? The answer is no—the $100,000 is a sunk cost, and Northeast cannot recover it regardless of whether or not the new branch is built. It often turns out that a particular project has a negative NPV when all the associated costs, including sunk costs, are considered. However, on an incremental basis the project may be a good one, because the incremental cash flows are large enough to produce a positive NPV on the incremental investment.

**opportunity cost**
The rate of return on the best *alternative* investment available; the highest return that will *not* be earned if funds are invested in a particular project.

*Opportunity Costs.* The second potential problem relates to **opportunity costs**, defined here as the cash flows that could be generated from assets the firm already owns if they are not used for the project in question. To illustrate, Northeast BankCorp already owns a piece of land that is suitable for the branch location. When evaluating the prospective branch, should the cost of the land be disregarded because no additional cash outlay would be re-

---

[2]Notice that Table 10-1 ignores interest charges, which would be present if the firm used debt. Most firms do use debt and hence finance part of their investments in capital projects with debt. Therefore, the question has been raised as to whether or not interest charges should be reflected in capital budgeting cash flow analysis. The consensus is that interest charges should *not* be dealt with explicitly in capital budgeting—rather, the effects of debt financing are reflected in the cost of capital which is used to discount the cash flows. The cost of capital is discussed in Chapter 14.

[3]For an excellent example of the improper treatment of sunk costs by a major corporation, see U. E. Reinhardt, "Break-Even Analysis for Lockheed's TriStar: An Application of Financial Theory," *Journal of Finance*, September 1973, 821-838.

quired? The answer is no, because there is an opportunity cost inherent in the use of the property. In this case, the land could be sold to yield $150,000 after taxes. Use of the site for the branch would require forgoing this inflow, so the $150,000 must be charged as an opportunity cost against the project. Note, though, that the proper land cost in this example is the $150,000 market-determined value, irrespective of whether Northeast originally paid $50,000 or $500,000 for the property. (What Northeast paid would, of course, have an effect on taxes, hence on the after-tax opportunity cost.)

***Effects on Other Parts of the Firm.*** The third potential problem involves the effects of a project on other parts of the firm. For example, some of Northeast's customers who would use the new branch are already banking with Northeast's downtown office. The loans and deposits, and hence profits, generated by these customers would not be new to the bank—rather, they would represent a transfer from the main office to the branch. Thus, the net revenues produced by these customers should not be treated as incremental income in the capital budgeting decision. On the other hand, having a suburban branch would also attract new business to the downtown office, because some potential customers could now make transactions both from home and from work. In this case, the additional revenues that would actually flow to the downtown office should be attributed to the branch. Although often difficult to quantify, "externalities" such as these must be considered.

## Changes in Net Working Capital

Normally, additional inventories are required to support a new operation, and expanded sales also produce additional accounts receivable; both of these asset increases must be financed. On the other hand, accounts payable and accruals will also increase spontaneously as a result of the expansion, and this will reduce the net cash needed to finance inventories and receivables. The difference between the increased current assets and the increase in current liabilities is defined as the **change in net working capital**. If this change is positive, as it generally is for expansion projects, this indicates that additional financing, over and above the cost of the fixed assets, is needed to fund the increase in current assets.

**change in net working capital**
The increased current assets resulting from a new project minus the increased current liabilities.

As the project approaches termination, inventories are sold off and not replaced, and receivables are also converted to cash. As these changes occur, the firm experiences an end-of-project cash flow that is equal to the net working capital requirement that occurred when the project was begun.

## Capital Budgeting Project Evaluation

Thus far the problem of measuring cash flows—the benefits used in the present value calculations in Chapter 9—has not been dealt with in any detail. In this section we discuss in depth the analysis for (1) new expansion projects and (2) replacement projects.

## Expansion Projects

expansion project
A project that is intended
to increase sales.

An **expansion project** is defined as one that calls for the firm to invest in new facilities in order to increase sales. For example, suppose Ryder Trucking Company buys a new delivery van at a cost of $10,000. The van has a 3-year ACRS life (see Chapter 2 for a review of ACRS depreciation); a 6 percent investment tax credit (ITC) is applicable; additional sales attributable to the new van will amount to $28,000 per year for three years; and Ryder expects to be able to sell the van for $500 at the end of its 3-year service life. Operating costs (fuel, labor, and so forth) will amount to $20,000 per year; Ryder's effective income tax rate is 40 percent; and its cost of capital is 10 percent. Table 10-2 works out the cash flows over the van's 3-year life.

Now we need to determine the company's initial investment, or $CF_0$. Ryder must write a check for $10,000 to pay for the van, but because of the ITC its next tax payment will drop by $0.06($10,000$) = $600$. Also, Ryder's net working capital (inventories plus accounts receivable, less accounts payable) will rise by $3,000 if it purchases the van; this net working capital will be recovered when the van is sold. Thus, the net investment in the van at (approximately) $t = 0$ is

| | |
|---|---|
| Purchase price of van | $10,000 |
| Less ITC | (600) |
| Plus investment in working capital | 3,000 |
| Net investment at $t = 0$ | $12,400 |

When the van is disposed of at the end of three years, Ryder expects to sell it for $500. Since the truck was fully depreciated, yet has a value of $500, in economic terms it was "over-depreciated." Under the tax laws, the government gets to "recapture" this depreciation by treating any salvage value in excess of the original depreciable basis as ordinary income rather than as a capital gain. Therefore, the $500 will be taxed as ordinary income at a rate of 40 percent. Thus, the after-tax proceeds from the sale will be

$$
\begin{aligned}
\text{Salvage value after tax} &= \text{Amount before tax} - \text{Tax} \\
&= \text{Amount before tax} - \text{Amount before tax(Tax rate)} \\
&= \text{Amount before tax}(1 - T) \\
&= \$500(0.6) = \$300 \text{ recovered at end of Year 3.}
\end{aligned}
$$

The annual net cash flows attributable to the investment in the van are equal to net income after taxes plus depreciation. These cash flows are developed in Table 10-2. Note that depreciation under ACRS for a 3-year class life project such as the van is calculated as follows:

**1.** The *depreciable basis* is equal to cost minus one-half the ITC, which is 6 percent of the cost, or $0.06($10,000$) = $600$:

$$\text{Depreciable basis} = \$10,000 - 0.5(\$600) = \$9,700.$$

Note that delivery, installation, and similar charges are included in the depreciable basis.

**Table 10-2**
**Analysis of an Expansion Project: Ryder Trucking Company**

|  | Year 1 | Year 2 | Year 3 |
|---|---|---|---|
| Sales attributable to the project (S) | $28,000 | $28,000 | $28,000 |
| Operating costs (OC) | 20,000 | 20,000 | 20,000 |
| Depreciation (Dep) | 2,425 | 3,686 | 3,589 |
| Income before tax | $ 5,575 | $ 4,314 | $ 4,411 |
| Taxes (40%) | 2,230 | 1,726 | 1,764 |
| Net income after taxes (NI) | $ 3,345 | $ 2,588 | $ 2,647 |
| Net cash flow (CF$_t$ = NI + Dep) | $ 5,770 | $ 6,274 | $ 6,236 |

**2.** Annual depreciation:

| Year | ACRS Percent[a] | Basis | Annual Depreciation |
|---|---|---|---|
| 1 | 0.25 | $9,700 | $2,425 |
| 2 | 0.38 | 9,700 | 3,686 |
| 3 | 0.37 | 9,700 | 3,589 |
|  | 1.00 |  | $9,700 |

[a]See Chapter 2.

Now we have all the information necessary for calculating the project's NPV at the 10 percent cost of capital:

| Year | Cash Flow | PVIF$_{10\%,t}$ | Product |
|---|---|---|---|
| 1 | $5,770 | 0.9091 | $ 5,246 |
| 2 | 6,274 | 0.8264 | 5,185 |
| 3 | 9,536[a] | 0.7513 | 7,164 |
|  |  | Total | $17,595 |
|  |  | Less: Net investment at t = 0 | 12,400 |
|  |  | Net present value (NPV) | $ 5,195 |

[a]$6,236 from operations + $3,000 recovery of net working capital + $300 after-tax salvage value.

Alternatively, we could set up the problem as follows:

$$\text{NPV} = \sum_{t=1}^{n} \frac{CF_t}{(1 + k)^t} - \text{Cost}$$

$$= \frac{\$5,770}{(1.10)^1} + \frac{\$6,274}{(1.10)^2} + \frac{\$9,536}{(1.10)^3} - \$12,400$$

$$= \$5,195.$$

Even better, we could input the cash flow data and the cost of capital into a financial calculator, press the NPV button, and obtain the NPV, $5,195.12. If the project had a fairly long life, the calculator solution would be much more efficient.

We could also solve for r in the following equation to find the van's IRR:

$$\text{NPV} = 0 = \frac{\$5,770}{(1 + r)^1} + \frac{\$6,274}{(1 + r)^2} + \frac{\$9,536}{(1 + r)^3} - \$12,400.$$

The solution value is r = IRR = 30.5%, found with a financial calculator.

Since the van has a positive NPV (and also an IRR greater than the 10 percent cost of capital), it represents a good investment, and Ryder Trucking should purchase it.

## Replacement Projects[4]

**replacement analysis**
An analysis involving the decision of whether to replace an existing asset that is still productive with a new one.

Finding the relevant cash flows in a **replacement analysis** is somewhat more involved, for here we must find a set of *incremental cash flows*. To illustrate a replacement analysis, consider Ryder Trucking's analysis of the replacement of an old, relatively inefficient packaging machine that was purchased five years ago, in 1982, at a cost of $10,000. The machine had an original expected life of 10 years and a zero estimated salvage value at the end of that period. It is being depreciated on a straight line basis and now has a book value of $5,000. The division manager reports that a new machine can be bought and installed for $12,000 which, over its 5-year life, will expand sales from $10,000 to $11,500 a year and, furthermore, will reduce labor and raw materials usage sufficiently to cut annual operating costs from $7,000 to $5,000. The new machine, which will be depreciated using the ACRS method, has an estimated salvage value of $2,000 at the end of its 5-year life. The old machine's current market value is $1,000; the firm's marginal tax rate is 40 percent; and its cost of capital is 10 percent. No investment tax credit applies. Should Ryder buy the new machine?

The decision analysis requires five steps: (1) estimate the actual cash outlay attributable to the new investment, (2) determine the incremental cash flows, (3) find the present value of the incremental cash flows, (4) add the present value of the expected salvage value to the present value of the total cash flows, and (5) see whether the NPV is positive. These steps are explained further in the following sections.

***Estimated Cash Outlay.*** The net initial cash outlay consists of these items: (1) payment to the manufacturer for the new machine, (2) proceeds from the sale of the old machine, and (3) tax effects. Ryder must make a $12,000

---

[4]In earlier editions of this book, we developed a worksheet approach to replacement analysis. That approach was useful for practical applications when calculations were performed with a calculator, but today, when most people who are actually involved in capital budgeting have access to desktop personal computers, the procedures set forth herein are most appropriate. Since the worksheet approach is no longer efficient, and since it is also harder to understand, we dropped it in this edition of the text.

payment to the manufacturer of the machine, but it will receive a cash inflow of $1,000 from the sale of the old one. Also, its current tax bill will be reduced because of the loss it will incur when it sells the old machine:

$$\text{Tax saving} = (\text{Loss})(\text{Tax rate})$$
$$= (\$4,000)(0.4) = \$1,600.$$

The tax reduction will occur because the old machine, which has a book value of $5,000, will be written down by $4,000 ($5,000 less the $1,000 salvage value) immediately upon the purchase of the new one, and this will reduce the tax bill by $1,600. No investment tax credit will be taken; but if it were, it too would reduce the net cost of the project.

The result is that the purchase of the new machine will involve an immediate net cash outlay of $9,400; this is the cost used for capital budgeting purposes:

| | |
|---|---|
| Invoice price of new machine | $12,000 |
| Less: Tax savings from loss ($4,000 × 0.4) | (1,600) |
| Salvage value of old machine | (1,000) |
| Net cash outflow (cost) | $ 9,400 |

If an investment in additional working capital were required as a result of the capital budgeting decision, as would generally be true for expansion investments (as opposed to cost-reducing replacement investments), this factor would have to be taken into account. The amount of net working capital—additional current assets required as a result of the expansion minus any spontaneous funds generated by it—would be estimated and added to the initial cash outlay. We assume that Ryder will not need any additional working capital, so that factor is not relevant in this example.

***Incremental Cash Flows.*** Ryder requires a net investment of $9,400 to buy the new machine. What will it get from this investment? Put another way, what annual cash flows can the company expect to receive from its investment? The value we seek is Ryder's *incremental net cash flow*, or the additional cash flow the company will have if it takes on the project.

Column 1 in Table 10-3 shows Ryder's estimated income from packaging for Year 1 as it would be without the new machine, while Column 2 shows how the statement would look if the new investment were made. (Cash flow estimates must be made for each year, because the depreciation expense of the new machine is not a constant annual amount.) Column 3 shows the differences between the first two columns. The $2,420 shown at the bottom of Column 3 is the *incremental net cash flow* from the project for Year 1; this is the $CF_1$ value that will be used in the NPV or IRR analysis.

We could set up a series of tables like Table 10-3, one for each year of the project's life; with computer programs such as *Lotus 1-2-3* this is a very simple process. However, if a computer is not available, we can develop a relatively simple equation to calculate the incremental cash flows. First, note

**Table 10-3**
**Comparative Income Statement Framework for Analyzing Cash Flows, Year 1**

| | Without New Investment (1) | | With New Investment (2) | | Difference: (2) − (1) (3) | |
|---|---|---|---|---|---|---|
| Sales (S) | | $10,000 | | $11,500 | | $1,500 |
| Operating costs (OC) | $7,000 | | $5,000 | | ($2,000) | |
| Depreciation (Dep)[a] | 1,000 | 8,000 | 1,800 | 6,800 | 800 | (1,200) |
| Income before taxes | | $ 2,000 | | $ 4,700 | | $2,700 |
| Taxes (40%) | | 800 | | 1,880 | | 1,080 |
| Income after taxes | | $ 1,200 | | $ 2,820 | | $1,620 |
| Net cash flows (add back depreciation) | | $ 2,200 | | $ 4,620 | | $2,420 |

[a]The old machine had a cost of $10,000 and is being depreciated by the straight line method over a 10-year life; therefore, its depreciation is $1,000 per year. The new machine is being depreciated under the ACRS allowances, so its first-year depreciation is 15 percent of its $12,000 cost, or 0.15($12,000) = $1,800. See Chapter 2 for a discussion of ACRS depreciation.

that because the project's effects on sales and operating costs were assumed to be constant in each year, the only changes in Column 3 of Table 10-3 from year to year would be those that resulted from the change in depreciation. Next, note that we could calculate the incremental net cash flow ($CF_t$) by using the following equation, which is simply an algebraic restatement of Table 10-3. The general equation is:

$$CF_t = [(S_2 - S_1) - (OC_2 - OC_1) - (Dep_2 - Dep_1)][1 - T] + (Dep_2 - Dep_1)$$
$$= (\Delta S - \Delta OC - \Delta Dep)(1 - T) + \Delta Dep$$
$$= (\Delta S - \Delta OC)(1 - T) - (\Delta Dep)(1 - T) + \Delta Dep$$
$$= (\Delta S - \Delta OC)(1 - T) - \Delta Dep + \Delta Dep(T) + \Delta Dep$$
$$= (\Delta S - \Delta OC)(1 - T) + \Delta Dep(T). \tag{10-1}$$

Applying Equation 10-1 to the data in Table 10-3, we obtain a cash flow for Year 1 of $2,420:

$$CF_1 = [(\$11,500 - \$10,000) - (\$5,000 - \$7,000)](0.6) + (\$1,800 - \$1,000)(0.4)$$
$$= [\$1,500 - (-\$2,000)](0.6) + \$800(0.4)$$
$$= (\$1,500 + \$2,000)(0.6) + \$800(0.4)$$
$$= \$2,100 + \$320$$
$$= \$2,420.$$

This value agrees with the figure shown at the bottom of Column 3 of Table 10-3.

Now notice that the only numbers in Equation 10-1 that change from year to year are the values for $\Delta Dep$, the change in depreciation that results from the purchase of the new machine. Table 10-4 shows the annual depreciation for the old and new machines, along with the change. If we insert the appro-

**Table 10-4**
**Change in Annual Depreciation Expense, Δ Dep**

| Year | Old Depreciation | New Depreciation | | Change in Depreciation, Δ Dep |
|------|------------------|------------------|------|-------------------------------|
| 1 | $1,000 | $1,800 | (15%) | $ 800 |
| 2 | 1,000 | 2,640 | (22%) | 1,640 |
| 3 | 1,000 | 2,520 | (21%) | 1,520 |
| 4 | 1,000 | 2,520 | (21%) | 1,520 |
| 5 | 1,000 | 2,520 | (21%) | 1,520 |

Note: The old machine had a cost of $10,000 and was being depreciated by the straight line method over a 10-year life, so its depreciation is $1,000 per year. The new machine will be depreciated under the ACRS system. See Chapter 2 for a discussion of ACRS; the percentages in Column 3 were taken from Chapter 2.

priate depreciation figures into Equation 10-1, we can find the yearly cash flows:

$$CF_t = (\$1,500 + \$2,000)(0.6) + \Delta Dep(0.4)$$
$$= (\$3,500)(0.6) + \Delta Dep(0.4)$$
$$= \$2,100 + \Delta Dep(0.4).$$

Thus, $CF_1$ to $CF_5$ can be found as follows:

$$CF_1 = \$2,100 + 0.4(\$800) = \$2,420.$$
$$CF_2 = \$2,100 + 0.4(\$1,640) = \$2,756.$$
$$CF_3 \text{ to } CF_5 = \$2,100 + 0.4(\$1,520) = \$2,708.$$

***PV of Benefits.*** Now that we have determined the project's incremental net cash flows, we can calculate their present value. The PV of the cash flow stream, discounted at the 10 percent cost of capital, is $10,043.

**salvage value**
The value of a capital asset at the end of a specified period. In a capital budgeting decision, it is also the current market price of an asset being considered for replacement.

***Salvage Value.*** The new machine has an estimated **salvage value** of $2,000—that is, Ryder expects to be able to sell the machine for $2,000 after 5 years of use. However, this salvage value will be taxable income; because the machine will be fully depreciated in 5 years, income from its sale will be subject to regular corporate income taxes. Thus, the after-tax cash flow from the sale of the new machine will be $1,200:

$$\text{A.T. salvage value} = \text{Salvage value (new)} - \text{Taxes}$$
$$= \text{Salvage value} - \text{Salvage value}(T)$$
$$= \text{Salvage value}(1 - T)$$
$$= \$2,000(0.6)$$
$$= \$1,200, \text{ which will occur in Year 5.}$$

Of course, when the new machine is actually retired 5 years hence, it might be sold for more or less than the expected $2,000, but $2,000 is the best present estimate of the new machine's salvage value. (Note also that if additional working capital had been required and included in the initial cash outlay, this amount would have been added to the salvage value of the machine, because the working capital would be recovered if and when the project was completed or abandoned.)

***Determining the Net Present Value.*** The replacement project's net cash flows, expressed in a time line, are shown below:

| Year | 0 | 1 | 2 | 3 | 4 | 5 |
|---|---|---|---|---|---|---|
| Cost | − $9,400 | — | — | — | — | — |
| Operating cash flow | — | $2,420 | $2,756 | $2,708 | $2,708 | $2,708 |
| A.T. salvage value | — | — | — | — | — | + $1,200 |
| Net cash flows | − $9,400 | + $2,420 | + $2,756 | + $2,708 | + $2,708 | + $3,908 |

These cash flows can now be used to determine the project's NPV based on Ryder's 10 percent cost of capital. The easiest procedure if a financial calculator is available is to simply input the values for $CF_t$ and the 10 percent cost of capital, press the NPV button, and read off the value NPV = $1,388.41. If a financial calculator is not available, then solve the following equation:

$$\text{NPV} = \sum_{t=0}^{5} \frac{CF_t}{(1 + k)^t}$$

$$= -\frac{\$9,400}{(1.10)^0} + \frac{\$2,420}{(1.10)^1} + \frac{\$2,756}{(1.10)^2} + \frac{\$2,708}{(1.10)^3} + \frac{\$2,708}{(1.10)^4} + \frac{\$3,908}{(1.10)^5}$$

$$= -\$9,400(1.0) + \$2,420(0.9091) + \$2,756(0.8264)$$

$$+ \ \$2,708(0.7513) + \$2,708(0.6830) + \$3,908(0.6209)$$

$$= -\$9,400 + \$2,200 + \$2,278 + \$2,035 + \$1,850 + \$2,426$$

$$= \$1,389 \text{ (rounding error difference from calculator solution)}.$$

Since the NPV is positive, the project should be accepted.[5] Had we set NPV = 0 and solved for the discount rate, we would have found IRR = 15.25%. Since the IRR > 10%, this method also suggests acceptance.

---

[5]A complication—the *unequal life problem*—that often arises in connection with replacement decisions should be noted. If the life of the new machine had been different from the remaining life of the old machine, a further analysis would have been necessary. Specifically, it would have been necessary to extend the analysis on out into the future to some common-denominator date, if one could be found. This refinement goes beyond the scope of an introductory text, but see Eugene F. Brigham and Louis C. Gapenski, *Intermediate Financial Management*, pp. 325-328, for a discussion.

## Risk Analysis

The cash flows associated with capital budgeting projects are not certain—they are subject to some degree of uncertainty, which varies from project to project. Thus, just as risk varies among securities such as stocks and bonds, capital budgeting projects also differ in terms of their relative risks. Further, as we saw in Chapter 6, the higher the risk associated with an investment, the higher the rate of return needed to compensate investors for assuming that risk. The same holds true for capital projects. Procedures for both measuring project risk and incorporating it into the accept/reject decision are covered in the following sections.

## Corporate Risk versus Beta Risk

**market, or beta, risk**
That part of a project's risk that cannot be eliminated by diversification; measured by the project's beta coefficient.

**total, or corporate, risk**
Risk not considering the effects of diversification; in capital budgeting, it relates to the probability that a project will incur losses that will destabilize profits.

Two separate and distinct types of risk are relevant in capital budgeting analysis: (1) **market**, or **beta**, **risk**, which is a measure of risk from the standpoint of an investor who holds the stock of the company doing the capital budgeting analysis as just one security in a highly diversified portfolio, and (2) **total**, or **corporate**, **risk**, which is the firm's risk viewed without consideration for the effects of its stockholders' personal diversification. A particular project might have highly uncertain returns, yet taking it on might not affect the firm's beta coefficient at all; hence the project's risk might be low from its stockholders' standpoint. To understand this point more clearly, recall that the beta coefficient reflects only that part of an investor's risk which cannot be eliminated by forming a large portfolio of stocks. If an investor holds a portfolio consisting of 100 stocks, and if each company is considering 100 projects, then the project in question is but one of 10,000 projects from the investor's viewpoint. Therefore, even if the project produces a return of $-100$ percent, this would not make much difference, and that loss would be completely offset if some other project had a return of $+100$ percent.

To illustrate the difference between corporate and beta risk, suppose 100 firms in the oil business each drill one wildcat well. Each company has $1 million of capital which it will invest in its one well. If a firm strikes oil, it will get a return of $2.4 million and hence earn a profit of $1.4 million, while if it hits a dry hole, it will lose its $1 million investment and go bankrupt. The probability of striking oil is 50 percent. Each firm's expected rate of return is 20 percent, calculated as follows:

$$\text{Expected rate of return} = \frac{\text{Expected profit}}{\text{Investment}}$$

$$= \frac{0.5(-\$1,000,000) + 0.5(+\$1,400,000)}{\$1,000,000}$$

$$= \frac{-\$500,000 + \$700,000}{\$1,000,000} = 20\%.$$

Note, however, that even though the expected return is 20-percent, there is a 50 percent probability of each firm being wiped out, so from the standpoint of the individual firms, this is a very risky business.

Although the riskiness of each firm is high, if a stockholder constructs a portfolio consisting of one share of each of the 100 companies' stocks, the riskiness of this portfolio will not be high at all. Some of the companies will hit oil and do well, while others will miss and go out of business, but the diversified investor's return will be very close to the expected 20 percent. Therefore, since investors can diversify away the risks inherent in each of the individual companies, these risks are *not market-related* and so do not affect the companies' beta coefficients.[6] However, the firms remain quite risky from the standpoint of their managers and employees, who bear risk similar to that borne by undiversified shareholders.

With this background, *we may define the corporate risk of a capital budgeting project as the probability that the project will incur losses which will, at a minimum, destabilize the corporation's earnings and, at the extreme, cause it to go bankrupt.* Taking on a project with a high degree of corporate risk will not necessarily affect the firm's stockholders' risk as measured by its beta coefficient to any great extent; our oil drilling example demonstrates this point. On the other hand, if a project has highly uncertain returns, and if those returns are also highly correlated with those of most other assets in the economy, then the project may have a high degree of both corporate and beta risk. For example, suppose a firm decides to undertake a major expansion to build solar-powered autos. The firm is not sure if its technology will work on a mass production basis, so there are great risks in the venture. Management also estimates that the project will have a higher probability of success if the economy is strong, for then people will have money to spend on the new autos. This means that the project will tend to do well if other companies are also doing well and to do poorly if others do poorly; hence, the project's beta coefficient will be high. A project like this would have a high degree of both corporate risk and beta risk.

Beta risk is obviously important because of beta's effect on the firm's cost of capital and the value of its stock. At the same time, corporate risk is also important for three primary reasons:

**1.** Undiversified stockholders, including the owners of small businesses, are more concerned about total risk than about beta risk.

**2.** Many financial theorists argue that investors, even those who are well diversified, consider factors other than market risk when setting required re-

---

[6]Note also that if the 100 companies were merged, the combined company would not be very risky—it would drill many wells, losing on some and hitting on others, but it would earn a relatively steady profit. This helps explain why large oil (and other) companies exhibit more stability than smaller ones, but it also explains why an investor who holds the stocks of many small companies may not have a riskier portfolio than someone who invests only in large firms. Companies often use the stabilization of income argument to explain why they engage in mergers. Some academicians argue that this is not a valid motive because investors can themselves diversify, and they can do it in the stock market more easily and less expensively than firms can through mergers. We discuss this point in more detail in Chapter 21.

turns. Empirical studies of the determinants of required rates of return generally find both beta and total risk to be important.

**3.** A firm's stability is important to its managers, workers, customers, suppliers, and creditors, and also to the community in which it operates. Firms that are in serious danger of bankruptcy, or even of suffering low profits and reduced output, have difficulty attracting and retaining good managers and workers. Also, both suppliers and customers are reluctant to depend on weak firms, and such firms have difficulty borrowing money except at high interest rates. These factors will tend to reduce risky firms' profitability, and hence the prices of their stocks.

For all of these reasons, corporate risk can be important even to well-diversified stockholders.

## Techniques for Measuring Corporate Risk

The starting point for analyzing corporate risk involves determining the uncertainty inherent in a project's cash flows. This analysis can be handled in a number of ways, ranging from informal judgments to complex economic and statistical analyses involving large-scale computer models. To illustrate what is involved here, refer back to Ryder Trucking Company's packaging machine project. Most of the elements in Table 10-3, which gave the expected Year 1 cash flows for the project, are subject to uncertainty. For example, incremental sales in each year were projected at $1,500, but incremental sales will almost certainly be somewhat higher or lower than $1,500. In effect, the sales estimates are really expected values taken from probability distributions, as are the values for the reduction in operating costs each year. The distributions could be relatively "tight," reflecting small standard deviations and low risk, or they could be "flat," denoting a great deal of uncertainty about the variable in question and hence a high degree of risk. For example, the sales estimate could have come from a distribution like A, B, or C in Figure 10-1. The more peaked the distribution, the higher the probability that actual sales will be close to the predicted level and hence the smaller the risk of the project.[7]

### Sensitivity Analysis

**sensitivity analysis**
A risk analysis technique in which key variables are changed one at a time and the resulting changes in the NPV or the rate of return are observed.

Intuitively, we know that most of the variables which determine a project's cash flows are based on some type of probability distribution rather than known with certainty. We also know that if a key input variable such as sales changes, so will the project's NPV. **Sensitivity analysis** *reveals how much NPV will change in response to a given change in an input variable, other things held constant.* Sensitivity analysis is sometimes called "what if" anal-

---

[7]For convenience, we frequently use distributions that are approximately normal. While the assumption of normality is often appropriate, at times a skewed distribution is more realistic.

**Figure 10-1**
**Probability Distributions of Incremental Sales for Ryder Trucking Company**

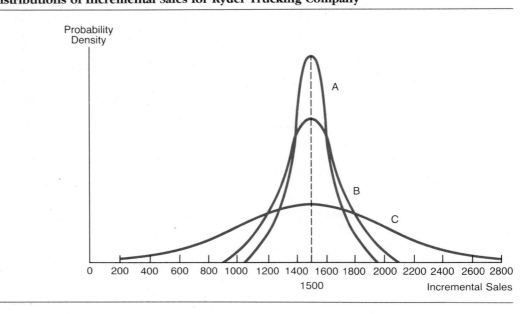

ysis, because it answers questions such as this: "What if incremental sales are only $1,000 rather than $1,500? Then what will the NPV be?"

Sensitivity analysis begins with a *base case* situation which reflects the expected value for each input variable. To illustrate the procedure, we shall consider the data that were given back in Table 10-3 and the related calculations, in which projected cash flows for Ryder's packaging machine project were developed. The values for both sales and operating costs were the *expected*, or *base case*, values, and the resulting $1,388 NPV is called the *base case NPV*. Now we ask a series of "what if" questions: "What if sales are 20 percent below the expected level?"; "What if operating costs rise?"; "What if the firm's cost of capital rises from 10 percent to 12 percent?"; "What if Congress increases the tax rate?" *Sensitivity analysis is designed to provide the decision maker with answers to questions such as these.*

In a sensitivity analysis, we change each variable by specific percentages above and below the base case value, calculate new NPVs, holding other things constant, and then plot the derived NPVs against the variable in question. Figure 10-2 shows the packaging machine project's sensitivity graphs for three of the key input variables. The table in the lower section gives the NPVs that were used to construct the graphs. The slopes of the lines show how sensitive NPV is to changes in each of the inputs: The steeper the slope, the more sensitive the NPV to a change in the particular variable. Here we see that the project's NPV is very sensitive to changes in sales volume, fairly sensitive to changes in operating costs, and relatively insensitive to changes in the cost of capital.

**Figure 10-2**
**Sensitivity Analysis for Ryder Trucking Company**

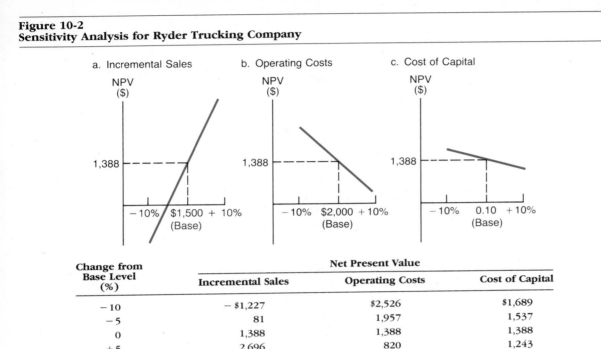

| Change from Base Level (%) | Net Present Value | | |
|---|---|---|---|
| | Incremental Sales | Operating Costs | Cost of Capital |
| −10 | − $1,227 | $2,526 | $1,689 |
| −5 | 81 | 1,957 | 1,537 |
| 0 | 1,388 | 1,388 | 1,388 |
| +5 | 2,696 | 820 | 1,243 |
| +10 | 4,004 | 251 | 1,100 |

If we were comparing two projects, then, other things held constant, the one with the steeper sensitivity lines would be regarded as riskier—relatively small errors in estimating variables such as the variable cost per unit or demand for the product would produce large errors in the project's expected NPV. Thus, sensitivity analysis provides useful insights into the relative riskiness of different projects.

## Scenario Analysis

Although sensitivity analysis is probably the most widely used method of risk analysis, it does have limitations. Consider, for example, a proposed coal mine whose NPV is highly sensitive to changes in both output and sales prices. However, if a utility company has contracted to buy most of the mine's output at a fixed price per ton plus an inflation adjustment, then the mining venture may not be very risky even if its sensitivity lines are quite steep. *In general, a project's risk depends on both (1) its sensitivity to changes in key variables and (2) the range of likely values of these variables as reflected in their probability distributions.* Because sensitivity analysis considers only the first factor, it does not provide a complete measure of a project's corporate risk.

A risk analysis technique which does consider the sensitivity of NPV both to changes in key variables and also to the range of likely variable values is

**Table 10-5**
**Scenario Analysis Results Summary**

| Scenario | Sales | NPV |
|---|---|---|
| Worst case | $10,000 | ($2,023) |
| Base case | 11,500 | 1,388 |
| Best case | 13,000 | 4,800 |

Notes:
a. NPVs were developed using *Lotus 1-2-3*.
b. Variables other than sales were set at their expected values.

**scenario analysis.** Here the operating executives pick a "bad" set of circumstances (low unit sales, low sales price, high variable cost per unit, high construction cost, and so on) and a "good" set. The NPV under the "bad" and "good" conditions is then calculated and compared to the expected, or base case, NPV.

As an example, consider again Ryder's packaging machine project. Assume that Ryder's executives are fairly confident in their estimates of all the project's cash flow variables except incremental sales. Further, assume they regard a decline in sales below the current $10,000 level or a rise above $13,000 as being extremely unlikely. Thus, incremental sales of $0 per year defines the lower bound, or the worst case scenario, while incremental sales of $3,000 defines the upper bound, or the best case scenario. Remember that the expected, or base case, value is $11,500 in annual sales, or $1,500 in incremental sales.

To carry out the scenario analysis, we use the worst case variable values to obtain the worst case NPV and the best case variable values to obtain the best case NPV.[8] We actually performed the analysis using *Lotus 1-2-3*, a popular spreadsheet program which was described in Appendix 8A, and Table 10-5 summarizes the results of our analysis. We see that the base case produces a positive NPV; the worst case produces a negative NPV; and the best case produces a large positive NPV. However, it is not easy to interpret this scenario analysis or to make a decision based on it. In our example we can say that there is a chance of losing on the project, but we cannot easily attach a specific probability to this loss. Clearly, what we need is some idea about the *probability of occurrence* of the worst case, the best case, the most likely case, and all the other cases that might arise. This leads us directly to Monte Carlo simulation, which is described in the next section.

## Monte Carlo Simulation

**Monte Carlo simulation,** so named because this type of analysis grew out of work on the mathematics of casino gambling back in the 1600s, ties together sensitivities and input variable probability distributions to quantify a

---

[8]We could have included worst and best case values for operating costs, salvage values, and so on. For illustrative purposes, however, we have limited the changes to only one variable.

**Table 10-6**
**Probability Distribution for Packaging Machine's Incremental Sales**

| Incremental Sales (1) | Probability (2) | Associated Random Numbers (3) |
|---|---|---|
| $    0 | 0.05 | 00-04 |
| 1,000 | 0.20 | 05-24 |
| 1,500 | 0.50 | 25-74 |
| 2,000 | 0.20 | 75-94 |
| 3,000 | 0.05 | 95-99 |

project's risk.[9] However, simulation requires a relatively sophisticated computer, coupled with an efficient financial planning software package, while scenario analysis can be done with a hand-held calculator.

The first step in a computer simulation is to specify a probability distribution for each of the key variables in the analysis. To illustrate, suppose we have estimated the probability distribution of Ryder's packaging machine's incremental sales as shown by Columns 1 and 2 of Table 10-6.[10] The expected incremental sales level is $1,500, but it can range from $0 to $3,000. Column 3 gives a set of random numbers associated with each price estimate. Notice that in Column 2 there is a 5 percent probability that incremental sales will be $0; therefore, 5 digits (0, 1, 2, 3, and 4) are assigned to this price. Twenty digits are assigned to incremental sales of $1,000, and so on for the other possible prices. Once the distributions and associated random numbers have been specified for each of the key variables—in other words, once a table such as 10-6 has been set up for incremental sales, operating costs, salvage value, cost of capital, and so on—the computer simulation can begin. These are the steps involved:

**1.** Computers have stored in them (or they can generate) random numbers. On Run 1, the computer will select a different random number for each uncertain variable; for example, assume that it selects 44 for incremental sales.

**2.** Depending on the random number selected, a value is determined for each variable. The 44 associated with incremental sales (in Table 10-6) indicates that the appropriate incremental sales level for use in the first run is $1,500. Values for all the other variables are set in a like manner.

**3.** Once a value has been established for each of the variables, the computer generates a set of income statements and cash flows. These cash flows are then discounted at the cost of capital (which may also be treated as a random

---

[9]The use of simulation analysis in capital budgeting was first reported by David B. Hertz, "Risk Analysis in Capital Investments," *Harvard Business Review*, January-February 1964, 95-106.

[10]Here we assume that sales is a discrete variable which can take on only five values. This simplification is purely for illustrative purposes; actual simulation models need have no such restrictions.

variable), and the result is the net present value of the project on the computer's first run.

**4.** The NPV generated on Run 1 is stored in memory, and the computer then goes on to Run 2. Here a different set of random numbers, and hence cash flows, is used. The NPV generated in Run 2 is again stored, and the model proceeds on for perhaps 500 runs. Mainframe computers can complete this operation almost instantaneously for a cost of less than $2.

**5.** The 500 stored NPVs are then printed out in the form of a frequency distribution, together with the expected NPV, the standard deviation of this NPV, and other summary statistics.

Using this procedure, we can perform a simulation analysis on Ryder's packaging machine project. As in our scenario analysis, we have simplified the illustration by specifying the distributions for only one key variable, incremental sales. For all the other variables, we merely specify their expected values.

The primary advantage of simulation is that it shows us the range of possible outcomes with attached probabilities and not just a point estimate of the NPV. The expected NPV can be used as a measure of the project's profitability, while the variability of this NPV as measured by $\sigma_{NPV}$ can be used to measure risk. However, large projects tend to have larger standard deviations of NPV than small ones, so to compare projects of different sizes, we need a statistic that standardizes for size and thus shows risk per dollar of cash flow. The **coefficient of variation (CV)** is such a statistic:

**coefficient of variation, CV**
The standard deviation divided by the mean.

$$\text{Coefficient of variation} = CV = \frac{\text{Standard deviation}}{\text{Expected value}} = \frac{\sigma_{NPV}}{\text{Expected NPV}}.$$

$$CV_{\text{Machine}} = \frac{\$1,297}{\$1,388} = 0.93.$$

The packaging machine project's expected NPV is $1,388, and the standard deviation of this NPV is $\sigma_{NPV} = \$1,297$, so its CV is 0.93. Similar calculations have been made for Ryder's other projects (and for its existing assets), and the average asset has a coefficient of variation of 0.40. Since the CV of the packaging machine project is much larger than that of Ryder's average project, the packaging project is riskier than most of its other projects.

Such risk differentials can be dealt with either subjectively or in some specific manner. Ryder employs a specific risk adjustment procedure—it adds two percentage points to the cost of capital of projects whose CVs are greater than 0.60, uses the corporate cost of capital for projects whose CVs are in the range of 0.30 to 0.59, and subtracts one percentage point from the corporate cost of capital for projects whose CVs are less than 0.30. These adjustments are arbitrary, but Ryder's management believes that this adjustment is better than no adjustment at all, which would amount to saying that all projects are equally risky.

Our analysis thus far has been based on Ryder's average cost of capital, 10 percent. Therefore, we must now reevaluate the project with a project cost of capital of 12 percent. When evaluated at this higher cost of capital, the NPV of the packaging machine project, using expected values for all variables, is $824. Thus, even at the higher risk-adjusted cost of capital, the packaging machine project still has a positive NPV; thus, it appears to be acceptable.

***Limitations of Monte Carlo Simulation Analysis.*** In spite of its obvious appeal, Monte Carlo simulation analysis has not been as widely used in industry as one might think. Five major reasons for this lack of general acceptance have been advanced.

**1.** *Cost versus benefits.* Until quite recently, developing a simulation model was a major undertaking that required a good deal of high-powered programming talent and a lot of expensive computer time. This is no longer true. Simulation software such as *IFPS*, along with the hardware necessary for operating such systems, have been developed to the point where cost is not a major consideration, at least for the larger firms. This suggests that we may see more simulation analysis in the future.

**2.** *Implementation lag.* It generally takes a while for any new managerial technology to become widely accepted, and simulation analysis may be in this position. (This point was made by several executives who reviewed this book.) Again, this suggests that the use of simulation may increase in the future.

**3.** *Difficulty of obtaining valid probability distributions.* It is difficult to obtain valid probability distributions for the key variables. Moreover, the simulation process described above assumes that the variables are independent of one another. However, it may be that such variables as unit sales and sales prices are correlated. For example, if demand is weak, sales prices may also be depressed; this suggests that if units sold is low, a low sales price should also be used.[11] Similarly, the simulation process described above assumes that the values of each variable, and hence the bottom line cash flows, are independent over time. However, in many situations it seems more reasonable to assume that high sales in the early years imply market acceptance, and hence high sales in future years, rather than that sales in one year are not correlated with sales levels in other years.

It is conceptually easy to incorporate any type of correlation among variables into a simulation analysis. However, it is extremely difficult to specify what the correlations should be—indeed, people who have tried to obtain such relationships from the operating executives who must estimate them have eloquently emphasized the difficulties involved.[12]

---

[11]This statement implies a *downward* (or *left*) *shift* in the demand curve for the product. One could also visualize *movement along the demand curve*, which would imply that low sales prices would be associated with high demand. The proper relationship must be built into the simulation by the analyst.

[12]For an excellent discussion of this problem, see K. Larry Hastie, "One Businessman's View of Capital Budgeting," *Financial Management*, Winter 1974, 36-43.

**4.** *No specific decision rule.* When a simulation analysis has been completed, no clear-cut decision rule emerges. We end up with an expected NPV and a distribution about this value, which we can use to judge the project's risk. However, the analysis has no mechanism for indicating whether the profitability as measured by the expected NPV is sufficient to compensate for the risk as indicated by $\sigma_{NPV}$ or $CV_{NPV}$. This is in sharp contrast to the beta approach discussed later in the chapter, in which a project is defined to be acceptable if its expected rate of return exceeds its beta-determined required rate of return.

**5.** *Ignores diversification.* Simulation analysis ignores the effects of diversification, both among projects within the firm and by investors in their personal investment portfolios. Thus, an individual project may have highly uncertain returns, but if those returns are not correlated with the returns on the firm's other assets, then the project may not be risky in the sense of destabilizing the firm as a whole. Indeed, if a highly variable project's returns are negatively correlated with returns on the firm's other assets, it may even stabilize earnings. Similarly, if a project's returns are not correlated with the stock market, then even a project with highly variable returns might not be regarded as risky by well-diversified stockholders, who logically should be more concerned with market risk than with total risk.

## Beta Risk

The types of corporate risk analysis discussed thus far in the chapter provide insights into projects' risks and thus help managers make better accept/reject decisions. However, as we noted above, those risk measures do not take account of portfolio risk, and they are subjective rather than objective in that they do not state specifically which projects should be accepted and which rejected. In this section, we show how the CAPM can be used to help overcome those shortcomings. Of course, the CAPM has shortcomings of its own, but it does nevertheless offer additional insights into risk analysis in capital budgeting.

To begin, recall from Chapter 6 that the Security Market Line equation expresses the risk/return relationship as follows:

$$k_s = k_{RF} + b_i(k_M - k_{RF}).$$

For example, consider the case of Erie Steel Company, an integrated steel producer operating in the Great Lakes region. Erie Steel's beta = 1.1, $k_{RF}$ = 8%, and $k_M$ = 12%; thus Erie's cost of equity is 12.4 percent:

$$k_s = 8\% + 1.1(12\% - 8\%)$$
$$= 8\% + 1.1(4\%) = 12.4\%.$$

This suggests that investors would be willing to give Erie money to invest in average-risk projects if the company could earn 12.4 percent or more on this money. Here again, by average risk we mean projects having risk similar to the firm's existing assets. *Therefore, as a first approximation, Erie should invest in capital projects if and only if these projects have an expected return of 12.4 percent or more.*[13] In other words, Erie should use 12.4 percent as its discount rate to determine the NPVs of any average-risk project which it is considering.

Suppose, however, that taking on a particular project will cause a change in Erie's beta coefficient and hence change the company's cost of equity. For example, Erie might be considering the construction of a fleet of barges to haul iron ore, and barge operations might have betas of 1.5 rather than 1.1. Since the firm itself may be regarded as a "portfolio of assets," and since the beta of any portfolio is a weighted average of the betas of the individual assets, taking on the barge project would cause the overall corporate beta to rise and to end up somewhere between the original beta of 1.1 and the barge project's beta of 1.5. The exact value would depend on the relative size of the investment in barge operations versus Erie's other assets. If 80 percent of Erie's total funds would end up in basic steel operations with a beta of 1.1 and 20 percent in barge operations with a beta of 1.5, then the new corporate beta would be 1.18:

$$\text{New } b_i = 0.8(1.1) + 0.2(1.5) = 1.18.$$

This increase in Erie's beta coefficient would cause the stock price to decline *unless the increased beta were offset by a higher expected rate of return*. Specifically, taking on the new project would cause the overall corporate cost of capital to rise to 12.72 percent:

$$k_s = 8\% + 1.18(4\%) = 12.72\%.$$

Therefore, to keep the barge investment from lowering the value of the firm, Erie's overall expected rate of return would have to rise from 12.4 to 12.72 percent.

If investments in basic steel must earn 12.4 percent, how much must the barge investment earn in order for the new overall rate of return to equal 12.72 percent? We know that if Erie undertakes the barge investment it will have 80 percent of its assets invested in basic steel earning 12.4 percent and 20 percent in barges earning X percent, and the average required rate of return will be 12.72 percent. Therefore,

$$0.8(12.4\%) + 0.2X = 12.72\%.$$

Solving for X, we find that the barge project must have an overall expected return of 14.0 percent if the corporation is to earn its new cost of capital.

In summary, if Erie takes on the barge project, its beta will rise from 1.1 to 1.18; the overall required rate of return will rise from 12.4 to 12.72 per-

---

[13]To simplify things somewhat, we assume at this point that the firm uses only equity capital. If debt is used, then the cost of capital used must be a weighted average of the costs of debt and equity. This point is discussed at length in Chapter 14.

cent; and the barge investment will have to earn 14.0 percent in order for Erie to earn its new overall cost of capital.

This line of reasoning leads to the conclusion that if the beta coefficient for each project, $b_p$, could be determined, then an individual project's cost of capital, $k_p$, could be found as follows:

$$k_p = k_{RF} + b_p(k_M - k_{RF}).$$

Thus, for basic steel projects with $b = 1.1$, Erie should use 12.4 percent as the discount rate. The barge project, with $b = 1.5$, should be evaluated at a 14 percent discount rate:

$$k_{Barge} = 8\% + 1.5(4\%) = 8\% + 6\% = 14\%.$$

On the other hand, a low-risk project, such as a new steel distribution center with a beta of only 0.5, would have a cost of capital of 10 percent:

$$k_{Center} = 8\% + 0.5(4\%) = 10\%.$$

Figure 10-3 gives a graphic summary of these concepts as applied to Erie Steel. Note the following points:

**1.** The SML is the same Security Market Line that we developed in Chapter 6. It shows how investors are willing to make trade-offs between risk as measured by beta and expected returns. The higher the beta risk, the higher the rate of return needed to compensate investors for bearing this risk, and the SML specifies the nature of this relationship.

**Figure 10-3**
**Using the Security Market Line Concept in Capital Budgeting**

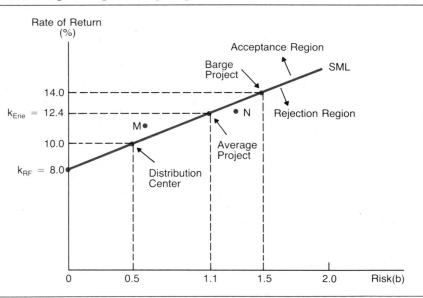

**2.** Erie Steel initially had a beta of 1.1, so its required rate of return on average-risk investments was 12.4 percent.

**3.** High-risk investments like the barge line require higher rates of return, while low-risk investments like the distribution center require lower returns. It is not shown on the graph, but if Erie makes relatively large investments in either high- or low-risk projects as opposed to average-risk ones, then the corporate beta and therefore the required rate of return on the common stock ($k_s$) will change.

**4.** If the expected rate of return on a given capital project lies *above* the SML, the expected rate of return on the project is more than enough to compensate for its risk, so it should be accepted. Conversely, if the project's rate of return lies *below* the SML, it should be rejected. Thus, Project M in Figure 10-3 is acceptable, while Project N should be rejected. N has a higher expected return than M, but the differential is not enough to offset its much higher risk.

## Techniques for Measuring Beta Risk

In Chapter 6, where we discussed the estimation of betas for stocks, we indicated that it is difficult to estimate "true future betas." The estimation of project betas is even more difficult and more fraught with uncertainty. However, there are two approaches available for the estimation of individual assets' betas: (1) the "pure play" method and (2) the accounting beta method.

### The Pure Play Method

**pure play method**
An approach used for estimating the beta of a project in which a firm locates several companies that manufacture the same product exclusively, calculates the beta for each firm, and then averages the betas to find an approximation of its own project's risk.

In the **pure play method**, the company tries to find several nonintegrated, single-product companies in the same line of business as the project being evaluated and then apply their betas to determine the cost of capital for its own project. For example, suppose Erie could find three existing single-product firms that operate barges and that Erie's management believes its barge project would be subject to the same risks as these firms. Then Erie could determine the betas of those firms by the regular regression process, average them, and use this average beta as a proxy for the barge project's beta.[14]

The pure play approach is frequently difficult to implement because it is often impossible to find pure play proxy firms. However, when IBM was considering going into personal computers, it was able to get data on Apple Computer and several other essentially pure play personal computer companies; this is often the case when firms consider major investments outside their primary fields.

---

[14]If the pure play firms employ different capital structures from that of our firm, then this fact must be dealt with by adjusting the beta coefficients. See Eugene F. Brigham and Louis C. Gapenski, *Intermediate Financial Management*, pp. 373-374.

## The Accounting Beta Method

**accounting beta method**
A method of estimating a project's beta by running a regression of the company's rate of return on assets against the average ROA for a large sample of firms.

As noted above, it is often impossible to find single-product, publicly traded firms suitable for the pure play approach. In those cases, we may be able to use the **accounting beta method**. Betas are normally found as described in Appendix 6A—by regressing the returns of a particular company's stock against returns on a stock market index. However, we could run a regression of the company's rate of return on assets (EBIT/Total assets) over time against the average return on assets for a large sample of companies such as those included in the S&P 400. Betas determined in this way—that is, by using accounting data rather than stock market data—are called *accounting betas*.

Accounting betas for projects can be calculated only after the project has been accepted and placed in operation and has begun to generate output and accounting results. However, to the extent that management thinks a given project is similar to other projects the firm has undertaken in the past, other projects' accounting betas can be used as proxies for that of the project in question. In practice, accounting betas are normally calculated for divisions or other large units, not for single projects, and divisional betas are then imputed to the project. This point is discussed later in the chapter.

## Portfolio Effects within the Firm

As we saw in Chapter 6, a security might be quite risky if held in isolation but not very risky if held as part of a well-diversified portfolio. The same thing is true of capital budgeting—the returns on an individual project might be highly uncertain, but if the project is small relative to the total firm, and if its returns are not highly correlated with the firm's other assets, then the project may not be very risky in either the corporate or the beta sense.

Many firms do make serious efforts to diversify; often this is a specific objective of the long-run strategic plan. For example, Du Pont diversified into both coal and oil to broaden its operating base, while real estate developers have diversified geographically to lessen the impact of a slowdown in one region. The major objective of many such moves is to stabilize earnings, reduce corporate risk, and thereby raise the value of the firm's stock.

The wisdom of corporate diversification designed to reduce risk has been questioned—why should a firm diversify when stockholders can so easily diversify on their own? In other words, it may be true that if the returns on Du Pont and on Conoco are not perfectly positively correlated, then merging the companies (as happened in 1982) will reduce their risks somewhat, but would it not be just as easy for investors to carry out this risk-reducing diversification directly without all the trouble and expense of a merger?

As you might suspect, the answer is not so simple. While stockholders could obtain directly some of the risk-reducing benefits from corporate diversification, other benefits can be gained only by diversification at the corporate level. A relatively stable corporation may be able to attract a better work force, and also to use more low-cost debt, than two less stable firms. And, of course, there may also be spillover effects from diversification—for example, Du Pont provided Conoco with a more stable market for its oil, while Conoco provided Du Pont with a stable supply of raw materials. Further, the two companies' research departments are reported to have gained economies of scale from combined operations.

## Project Risk Conclusions

We have discussed two types of risk in capital budgeting analyses—corporate risk and beta risk—and we have looked at ways of assessing each. However, two important questions remain: (1) Should a firm consider both corporate risk and beta risk in its capital budgeting decisions? (2) What does a firm do when its beta and corporate risk assessments lead to different conclusions?

These questions do not have easy answers. From a theoretical standpoint, well-diversified investors should be concerned primarily with beta risk and managers with stock price maximization; this leads to the conclusion that market (or beta) risk should be given the most weight in capital budgeting decisions. However, if investors are not well diversified, if market imperfections prevent the CAPM from functioning as theory says it should, or if measurement problems keep us from implementing the CAPM approach in capital budgeting, then total risk may be given more weight than theory would suggest. Moreover, the CAPM does not consider bankruptcy and other costs associated with financial weakness, even though such costs are in reality often very significant, and the probability of financial distress depends on a firm's total risk, not just on its beta risk. Therefore, one could easily conclude that even well-diversified investors should want a firm's management to give at least some consideration to total risk rather than to concentrate exclusively on beta risk.

Although it would be desirable to measure project risk on some absolute scale, the best we can do in practice is to determine project risk in a somewhat nebulous, relative sense. For example, we might be able to say with a fair degree of confidence that Project A has more total risk than the firm's average project. Then, if beta risk and corporate risk are highly correlated (as most studies suggest they are), a project with more total risk than average is also likely to have more beta risk.[15]

What does all this mean to the financial manager? He or she should make as good an assessment as possible of each project's relative total risk and beta risk. If both types of risk are higher than average for a given project, then

---

[15]For example, see M. Chapman Findlay, Arthur E. Gooding, and Wallace Q. Weaver, Jr., "On the Relevant Risk for Determining Capital Expenditure Hurdle Rates," *Financial Management*, Winter 1976, 9-16.

that project's cost of capital should be increased relative to the firm's overall cost of capital. If both types of risk are below average, then the adjustment should be reversed. Unfortunately, it is impossible to specify exactly how large the adjustments should be.

## Divisional Costs of Capital

Thus far, we have seen that capital budgeting can affect a firm's beta risk, its corporate risk, or both. We have also seen that it is exceedingly difficult to quantify either effect. In other words, it may be possible to reach the general conclusion that one project is riskier than another (in either the beta or the corporate sense), but it is difficult to develop a really good *measure* of project risk. Further, this lack of precision in measuring project risk makes it difficult to specify risk-adjusted rates of return, or project costs of capital, with which to evaluate individual projects. As we shall see in Chapter 14, it is possible to estimate a firm's overall cost of capital reasonably well. Moreover, it is generally agreed that riskier projects should be evaluated with a higher cost of capital than the overall corporate cost, while a lower cost rate should be used for lower-risk projects. Unfortunately, there is no good way of specifying exactly *how much* higher or lower these cost rates should be; given the present state of the art, risk adjustments are necessarily judgmental and somewhat arbitrary.

Debt effects must also be taken into account. For example, one division might have a lot of real estate, which is well suited as collateral for loans, whereas some other division might have most of its capital tied up in special-purpose machinery, which is not good collateral. As a result, the division with the real estate might have a higher *debt capacity* than the machinery division. In this case, the first division might calculate its cost of capital using a higher debt ratio than the second division.

**risk-adjusted discount rate**
The discount rate that applies to a particular risky (uncertain) stream of income; the riskless rate of interest plus a risk premium appropriate to the level of risk attached to the particular income stream.

Although the process is not exact, Ryder Trucking Company (and many other companies) develops **risk-adjusted discount rates** for use in capital budgeting in a two-step process: (1) Divisional costs of capital are established for each of the major operating divisions on the basis of the divisions' estimated risk and capital structures, and (2) within each division, all projects are classified into three categories—high risk, average risk, and low risk. Each of Ryder's divisions then uses its basic divisional cost of capital as the discount rate for average-risk projects, reduces the discount rate by one percentage point when evaluating low-risk projects, and raises the rate by two percentage points for high-risk projects. For example, if a division's basic cost of capital is estimated to be 10 percent, then a 12 percent discount rate would be used for high-risk projects and a 9 percent rate for low-risk ones. Average-risk projects, which constitute about 80 percent of most of its divisions' capital budgets, would be evaluated at the 10 percent divisional cost of capital. This procedure is not very elegant, but it does at least recognize that different divisions have different characteristics and hence different costs of capital, and it also acknowledges differential project riskiness within divisions. Ryder's financial staff feels that these adjustments are in the right direction and that they result in better decisions than would be obtained if no adjustments at all were made. Further discussion of the cost of capital is deferred to Chapter 14.

## Capital Rationing

Capital budgeting decisions are typically made as described in this and the preceding chapter—independent projects are accepted if their NPVs are positive, and choices among mutually exclusive projects are made by selecting the one with the highest NPV. In this analysis, it is assumed that if in a particular year the firm has an especially large number of good projects, then management will simply go into the financial markets and raise whatever funds are required to finance all of the acceptable projects. However, some firms set limits on the amount of funds they are willing to raise, and if this is done, then the capital budget also has to be limited. Such a constraint is known as **capital rationing**.

**capital rationing**
A situation in which a constraint is placed on the total size of a capital investment during a particular period.

Some elaborate and mathematically sophisticated linear programming models have been developed to help firms maximize their values subject to the capital rationing constraint. However, a firm which subjects itself to capital rationing is deliberately forgoing profitable projects and hence is not truly maximizing its value. This point is well known, so few sophisticated firms today ration capital.[16]

## Summary

This chapter has dealt with three issues in capital budgeting: cash flow estimation, replacement decisions, and risk analysis.

The most important, yet most difficult, step in capital budgeting analysis is *cash flow estimation*. The key to cash flow estimation is to consider only *incremental* after-tax cash flows. *Replacement analysis* is conceptually similar to new-project analysis except that replacement cash flow estimation requires consideration of the fact that the old asset could continue to generate additional cash flows.

Our analysis of risk focused on two issues: (1) the effect of a given project on the firm's beta coefficient (*beta risk*) and (2) the project's effect on the probability of large losses (*corporate risk*). Both types of risk are important. Although beta risk is theoretically more correct, CAPM theory itself is not completely valid, and it is more difficult to obtain the data necessary for applying the theory to projects than to stocks. Corporate risk affects the financial strength of the firm; this in turn influences its ability to use debt, to maintain smooth operations over time, and to avoid crises that might consume the energy of the firm's managers and disrupt its employees, customers, suppliers, and community.

---

[16]See Eugene F. Brigham and Louis C. Gapenski, *Intermediate Financial Management*, pp. 404-408, for a further discussion of capital rationing.

Several analytical techniques can be used to help measure a project's corporate risk; among them are (1) *sensitivity analysis*, (2) *scenario analysis*, and (3) *Monte Carlo simulation*. However, the final decision regarding a project's corporate risk remains judgmental.

The major problem with applying CAPM concepts to capital budgeting is the difficulty of estimating projects' beta coefficients. It is not really meaningful to think about the beta of a particular asset such as a truck or a machine; however, it is meaningful to think of betas for divisions that are large enough to be operated as independent firms. Therefore, in practice beta risk is usually estimated for large divisions of firms and then used to establish divisional costs of capital, which are then scaled up or down in a subjective manner to reflect a given project's own risk. Two approaches are used to measure beta risk: (1) the *pure play method* and (2) the *accounting beta method*.

## Questions

10-1    Define each of the following terms:
    a. Cash flow
    b. Incremental cash flow; sunk cost
    c. Opportunity cost
    d. Change in net working capital
    e. Expansion project; replacement analysis
    f. Salvage value
    g. Market, or beta, risk; total, or corporate, risk
    h. Sensitivity analysis; scenario analysis; Monte Carlo simulation
    i. Coefficient of variation, CV
    j. Pure play method
    k. Accounting beta method
    l. Risk-adjusted discount rate
    m. Capital rationing

10-2    The focus in Table 10-2 is on operating cash flows rather than accounting profits. What is the basis for this emphasis on cash flows as opposed to net income?

10-3    Think about Ryder Trucking Company's packaging machine project, and answer these questions:
    a. Why is the salvage value of the machine reduced for taxes?
    b. Why is depreciation on the old machine in effect deducted from the depreciation on the new machine in Table 10-3?
    c. How would the analysis be affected if the new machine permitted a *reduction* in working capital?

10-4    Why should firms not employ capital rationing?

10-5    Differentiate among (a) simulation analysis, (b) scenario analysis, and (c) sensitivity analysis. If AT&T were considering two investments, one calling for the expenditure of $100 million to develop a satellite communications system and the other involving the expenditure of $5,000 for a new truck, on which project would the company be more likely to use simulation?

10-6    Distinguish between the beta risk and the corporate risk of a project being considered for inclusion in the capital budget. Should both types of risk be given weight in the capital budgeting decisions? Explain your answer.

10-7    Suppose Lima Locomotive Company, which has a high beta and also a great deal of corporate risk, merged with Echo Bay Mines, which has a zero beta but relatively high corporate risk. What would the merger do to the cost of capital in the consolidated company's locomotive division and in its gold mining division?

## Self-Test Problems (*Solutions on Page 342*)

ST-1    You have been asked by the president of your company to evaluate the proposed acquisition of a new earthmover. The mover's basic price is $50,000, and it will cost another $10,000 to modify it for special use by your firm. The mover falls into the ACRS 3-year class and qualifies for a 6 percent investment tax credit. It will be sold after 3 years for $20,000. Use of the mover will require an increase in net working capital (spare parts inventory) of $2,000. The earthmover will have no effect on revenues, but it is expected to save the firm $20,000 per year in before-tax operating costs, mainly labor. The firm's marginal tax rate is 40 percent.
   a. What is the net cost of the earthmover? (That is, what are the Year 0 cash flows?)
   b. What are the operating cash flows in Years 1, 2, and 3?
   c. What are the additional (nonoperating) cash flows in Year 3?
   d. If the project's cost of capital is 10 percent, should the earthmover be purchased?

ST-2    The Boston Toy Corporation (BTC) currently uses an injection molding machine that was purchased 2 years ago. This machine is being depreciated on a straight line basis toward a $500 salvage value; it has 6 years of remaining life, and its current book value is $2,600. Thus, the annual depreciation expense is ($2,600 − $500)/6 = $350 per year. It can be sold for $3,000 at this time.

   BTC is offered a replacement machine which has a cost of $8,000, an estimated useful life of 6 years, and an estimated salvage value of $800. This machine falls into the ACRS 5-year class and thus qualifies for a 10 percent investment tax credit. It would permit an output expansion, so sales would rise by $1,000 per year; even so, its much greater efficiency would still cause operating expenses to decline by $1,500 per year. The new machine would require that inventories be increased by $2,000, but accounts payable would simultaneously increase by $500.

   BTC's effective tax rate is 46 percent, and its cost of capital is 15 percent. Should it replace the old machine?

## Problems

New project

10-1     You have been asked by the president of your company to evaluate the proposed acquisition of a new milling machine. The machine's basic price is $100,000, and it will cost another $20,000 to modify it for special use by your firm. The machine falls into the ACRS 3-year class, and it qualifies for a 6 percent investment tax credit. The machine will be sold after 3 years for $50,000. Use of the machine will require an increase in net working capital (inventory) of $5,000. The machine will have no effect on revenues, but it is expected to save the firm $40,000 per year in before-tax operating costs, mainly labor. The firm's marginal tax rate is 46 percent.

a. What is the net cost of the machine for capital budgeting purposes? (That is, what is the Year 0 net cash flow?)
b. What are the operating cash flows in Years 1, 2, and 3?
c. What are the additional (nonoperating) cash flows in Year 3?
d. If the project's cost of capital is 10 percent, should the machine be purchased?

(Do Parts e and f only if you are using the computerized problem diskette.)

e. Determine the NPV if the cost of capital were to (i) rise to 12 percent or (ii) fall to 8 percent.
f. There is some uncertainty about the salvage value. It could be as low as $25,000 or as high as $75,000. What would the NPV be at each of those two salvage value levels (assume k = 10 percent)? Should this increased uncertainty affect the decision to invest?

**Expansion project**

**10-2**   Vulcanized Pizza Dough, Inc. (VPD), has an opportunity to invest in a new dough machine. VPD needs more productive capacity, so the new machine will not be a replacement for any existing one. The new machine costs $120,000, has an expected useful life of 10 years, will be depreciated using the straight line method, and has an expected salvage value of $20,000 at the end of Year 10. It will require a $30,000 investment in net working capital. It will generate additional operating revenues of $140,000 per year but will increase cash operating expenses by $100,000 per year. VPD's cost of capital is 12 percent, and its marginal tax rate is 40 percent. An investment tax credit of 10 percent applies to the purchase. Depreciation per year equals $10,000. (Depreciation is calculated using straight line from a depreciable base of $100,000, which is the price minus the salvage value.) The book value at the end of Year 10 equals $20,000; therefore, no taxes will be required on the $20,000 salvage value. What is the NPV of this expansion project? Should VPD purchase the new machine?

**Cash flow estimation and replacement analysis**

**10-3**   The Hawkeye Express Company purchased a machine 5 years ago at a cost of $100,000. It had an expected life of 10 years at the time of purchase and an expected salvage value of $10,000 at the end of the 10 years. It is being depreciated using the straight line method toward a salvage value of $10,000, or by $9,000 per year.

A new machine can be purchased for $150,000, including installation costs. Over its 5-year life, it will reduce cash operating expenses by $50,000 per year. Sales are not expected to change. At the end of its useful life, the machine is estimated to be worthless. ACRS depreciation will be used, and it will be depreciated over its 3-year class life rather than its 5-year economic life.

The old machine can be sold today for $65,000. The firm's tax rate is 30 percent. Assume that an ITC equal to 10 percent of the cost of the new asset, including installation costs, is applicable. The firm's appropriate discount rate is 15 percent.

a. If the new machine is purchased, what is the amount of the initial cash flow at Year 0?
b. What incremental cash flows will occur at the end of Years 1-4 as a result of replacing the old machine?
c. What incremental cash flow will occur at the end of Year 5 if the new machine is purchased?

d. What is the NPV of this project? Should Hawkeye replace the old machine?

Replacement project  **10-4**  Bates Bottling Company is contemplating the replacement of one of its bottling machines with a newer and more efficient one. The old machine has a book value of $500,000 and a remaining useful life of 5 years. The firm does not expect to realize any return from scrapping the old machine in 5 years, but it can sell it now to another firm in the industry for $200,000. The old machine is being depreciated toward a zero salvage value, or by $100,000 per year, using the straight line method.

The new machine has a purchase price of $1.4 million, an estimated useful life and ACRS class life of 5 years, and an estimated salvage value of $150,000. It is expected to economize on electric power usage, labor, and repair costs, and also to reduce the number of defective bottles. In total, an annual saving of $225,000 will be realized if it is installed. The new machine qualifies for a 10 percent investment tax credit. The company is in the 40 percent tax bracket, and it has a 10 percent cost of capital.

a. What is the initial cash outlay required for the new machine?
b. Calculate the annual depreciation allowances for both machines, and compute the change in the annual depreciation expense if the replacement is made.
c. What are the cash flows in Years 1 to 5?
d. What is the cash flow from the salvage value in Year 5?
e. Should Bates purchase the new machine? Support your answer.
f. In general, how would each of the following factors affect the investment decision, and how should each be treated?
   1. The expected life of the existing machine decreases.
   2. The cost of capital is not constant but is increasing.

(Do Parts g, h, and i only if you are using the computerized problem diskette.)
g. Bates Bottling may be able to purchase an alternative new bottling machine from another supplier. Its purchase price would be $1,200,000, and its salvage value would be $250,000. This machine has a lower annual operating savings of $210,000. Should Bates purchase this machine?
h. If the salvage value on the alternative new machine were $225,000 rather than $250,000, how would this affect the decision?
i. With everything as in Part h, assume that the cost of capital declined from 10 percent to 9.5 percent. How would this affect the decision?

Replacement project  **10-5**  Granger Shipyards is considering the replacement of an 8-year-old riveting machine with a new one that will increase the earnings before depreciation from $30,000 to $58,000 per year. The new machine will cost $60,000 and have an estimated life of 8 years with no salvage value. The machine will be depreciated over its 3-year ACRS recovery period. The applicable corporate tax rate is 40 percent, and the firm's cost of capital is 12 percent. The old machine has been fully depreciated and has no salvage value. Calculate the net present value for the project. Should the old riveting machine be replaced by the new one? Granger will not take an ITC on this project.

Replacement project  **10-6**  Assume that Granger Shipyards (in Problem 10-5) will be able to take an investment tax credit of 10 percent on the purchase of the new machine and that this machine will have a salvage value of $8,000 at the end of 8 years. Assume further that the old machine has a book value of

$24,000 and a remaining life of 8 years. The old machine was purchased in 1978, and it is being depreciated using the straight line method toward a zero salvage value, or by $3,000 per year. If replaced, it can be sold now for $15,000. Should the replacement be made?

**Replacement project    10-7**   Twinkle Toy Company is considering the purchase of a new machine tool to replace an obsolete one. The machine being used for the operation has both a tax book value and a market value of zero; however, it is in good working order and will last physically for at least an additional 15 years. The proposed machine will perform the operation so much more efficiently that Twinkle engineers estimate that labor, material, and other direct costs will be reduced $4,500 a year if it is installed. The proposed machine costs $24,000 delivered and installed, and its economic life is estimated to be 15 years with zero salvage value. The firm's cost of capital is 12 percent, and its tax rate is 40 percent. For simplicity, assume the firm will depreciate the asset over its economic life using the straight line method. The annual depreciation is $1,600, which disregards the ½ year convention in Year 1. No ITC will be taken on the machine.

a. Should Twinkle Toy buy the new machine?
b. Assume that the tax book value of the old machine is $6,000 and the annual depreciation charge is $400. The old machine still has a market value of zero. How do these assumptions affect your answer?

**CAPM approach to risk     10-8
adjustments**   Goodtread Rubber Company has two divisions: (1) the tire division, which manufactures tires for new autos, and (2) the recap division, which manufactures recapping materials that are sold to independent tire recapping shops throughout the United States. Since auto manufacturing moves up and down with the general economy, the tire division's earnings contribution to Goodtread's stock price is highly correlated with returns on most other stocks. If the tire division were operated as a separate company, its beta coefficient would be about 1.60. The sales and profits of the recap division, on the other hand, tend to be counter-cyclical—recap sales boom when people cannot afford to buy new tires, so that division's beta is estimated to be 0.40. Approximately 75 percent of Goodtread's corporate assets are invested in the tire division and 25 percent in the recap division.

Currently, the rate of interest on Treasury securities is 10 percent, and the expected rate of return on an average share of stock is 15 percent. Goodtread uses only common equity capital; it has no debt outstanding.

a. What is the required rate of return on Goodtread's stock?
b. What discount rate should be used to evaluate capital budgeting projects? Explain your answer fully, and illustrate it with two projects, one in each division, which cost $100,000, have 10-year lives, and provide expected after-tax net cash flows of $20,000 per year.

**Risk adjustment     10-9**   The risk-free rate of return is 5 percent, and the market risk premium is 6 percent. The beta of the project under analysis is 1.6, with expected net cash flows after taxes estimated at $750 per year for 5 years. The required investment outlay on the project is $2,100.

a. What is the required risk-adjusted return on the project?
b. Should the project be accepted?

**Risky cash flows     10-10**   The Rowan Company is faced with two mutually exclusive investment projects. Each project costs $4,500 and has an expected life of 3 years.

Annual net cash flows from each project begin 1 year after the initial investment is made and have the following probability distributions:

| Project A | | Project B | |
|---|---|---|---|
| Probability | Cash Flow | Probability | Cash Flow |
| 0.2 | $4,000 | 0.2 | $ 0 |
| 0.6 | 4,500 | 0.6 | 4,500 |
| 0.2 | 5,000 | 0.2 | 12,000 |

Rowan has decided to evaluate the riskier project at a 12 percent rate and the less risky project at a 10 percent rate.

a. What is the expected value of the annual net cash flows from each project? The coefficient of variation (CV)?

b. What is the risk-adjusted NPV of each project? What is the coefficient of variation (CV)?

c. If it were known that Project B was negatively correlated with other cash flows of the firm while Project A was positively correlated, how should this knowledge affect the decision? If Project B's cash flows were negatively correlated with gross national product (GNP), would that influence your assessment of its risk?

Sensitivity analysis **10-11** Your firm is considering the purchase of a tractor which will have a net cost of $30,000, will increase pre-tax operating cash flows exclusive of depreciation effects by $10,000 per year, and will be depreciated on a straight line basis to zero over 5 years at the rate of $6,000 per year, beginning the first year. (Annual cash flows will be $10,000, reduced by taxes, plus the tax savings that result from $6,000 of depreciation.) The board of directors, however, is having a heated debate as to whether the tractor will actually last 5 years. Specifically, Wayne Brown insists that he knows of some that have lasted only 4 years. Tom Miller agrees with Brown, but he argues that most tractors do give 5 years of service. Laura Evans, on the other hand, says she has seen some last as long as 8 years.

a. Given this discussion, the board asks you to prepare a sensitivity analysis to ascertain the importance of the uncertainty about the tractor's life. Assume a 40 percent tax rate on both income and capital losses, a zero salvage value, and a cost of capital of 10 percent. (Hint: Here straight line depreciation is based on the expected life of the tractor and is not affected by the actual life. Also, ignore the ½ year convention for this problem.)

(Do Parts b and c only if you are using the computerized problem diskette.)

b. The board would also like to know how sensitive the analysis is to the cost of capital. Assume that the machine's life is 5 years, and analyze the effects of a change in the cost of capital to 8 percent or to 12 percent. Is the project very sensitive to changes in the cost of capital?

c. Finally, the board would like to determine the sensitivity of the project to changes in the increase in pretax operating revenues. The directors believe that the increase would be no less than $7,000 per year and no more than $15,000 per year. Analyze the project at these levels of operating revenue, assuming a 5-year project life and a 10 percent cost of capital.

## Solutions to Self-Test Problems

**ST-1**      a. *Estimated Investment Requirements:*

| | |
|---|---:|
| Price | ($50,000) |
| Modification | (10,000) |
| Investment tax credit* | 3,600 |
| Net working capital | (2,000) |
| Total investment | ($58,400) |

*ITC = 6% of capitalized cost
    = 0.06 ($50,000 + $10,000) = $3,600.

b. *Operating Cash Flows:*

| | Year 1 | Year 2 | Year 3 |
|---|---:|---:|---:|
| 1. After-tax cost savings* | $12,000 | $12,000 | $12,000 |
| 2. Depreciation** | 14,550 | 22,116 | 21,534 |
| 3. Depreciation tax savings*** | 5,820 | 8,846 | 8,614 |
| Net cash flow (1 + 3) | $17,820 | $20,846 | $20,614 |

*Before-tax savings (1 − Tax rate) = $20,000 (0.6) = $12,000.

**Depreciable basis = $60,000 − 0.5($3,600) = $58,200; allowances = 0.25, 0.38, and 0.37; depreciation in Year 1 = 0.25($58,200) = $14,550; and so on.

***T(Depreciation) = Tax savings.

c. *End-of-Project Cash Flows:*

| | |
|---|---:|
| Salvage value | $20,000 |
| Tax on salvage value* | (8,000) |
| Net working capital recovery | 2,000 |
| | $14,000 |

| | |
|---|---:|
| *Salvage value | $20,000 |
| Less book value | 0 |
| Taxable income | $20,000 |
| Tax at 40% | 8,000 |

d. Yes, the project has a positive NPV.

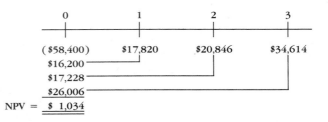

|  | 0 | 1 | 2 | 3 |
|---|---|---|---|---|
| | ($58,400) | $17,820 | $20,846 | $34,614 |
| | $16,200 | | | |
| | $17,228 | | | |
| | $26,006 | | | |

NPV = $ 1,034

ST-2   First determine the net cash outflow at t = 0:

| | |
|---|---:|
| Purchase price | $8,000 |
| Investment tax credit | (800) |
| Sale of old machine | (3,000) |
| Tax on sale of old machine | 184* |
| Net working capital | 1,500** |
| Total investment | $5,884 |

*The market value is $3,000 − $2,600 = $400 above the book value. Thus there is a $400 recapture of depreciation, and BTC would have to pay 0.46($400) = $184 in taxes.
**The change in net working capital is a $2,000 increase in current assets less a $500 increase in current liabilities, or $1,500.

Now examine the annual operating cash inflows:

| | |
|---|---:|
| Sales increase | $1,000 |
| Cost decrease | 1,500 |
| Pre-tax operating revenue increase | $2,500 |

After-tax operating revenue increase = $2,500(1 − T) = $2,500(0.54) = $1,350.

Depreciation:

| | 1 | 2 | 3 | 4 | 5 | 6 |
|---|---:|---:|---:|---:|---:|---:|
| New* | $1,140 | $1,672 | $1,596 | $1,596 | $1,596 | $ 0 |
| Old | 350 | 350 | 350 | 350 | 350 | 350 |
| ΔDepreciation | $ 790 | $1,322 | $1,246 | $1,246 | $1,246 | ($350) |
| Depreciation tax savings** | $ 363 | $ 608 | $ 573 | $ 573 | $ 573 | ($161) |

*Depreciable basis = Cost − 0.5(ITC) = $8,000 − $400 = $7,600. Depreciation expense each year equals depreciable basis times the ACRS factor of 0.15 for Year 1, 0.22 for Year 2, and 0.21 for Years 3-5.
**Depreciation tax savings = Depreciation(T).

Now recognize that at the end of Year 6 BTC will recover its working capital investment of $1,500, and it will also receive $800 from the sale of the replacement machine. However, the firm must pay 0.46($800) = $368 in taxes on the sale of the machine. Note also that by undertaking the replacement now, the firm foregoes the right to sell the old machine for $500 in Year 6; thus, this $500 in Year 6 must be considered as an opportunity cost in that year. There is no tax effect on that sale, since the $500 salvage value would equal the old machine's Year 6 book value.
    Finally, place all the cash flows on a time line:

| | 0 | 1 | 2 | 3 | 4 | 5 | 6 |
|---|---:|---:|---:|---:|---:|---:|---:|
| Net cost | ($5,884) | | | | | | |
| After-tax revenue increase | | $1,350 | $1,350 | $1,350 | $1,350 | $1,350 | $1,350 |
| Depreciation tax savings | | 363 | 608 | 573 | 573 | 573 | (161) |
| Working capital recovery | | | | | | | 1,500 |
| Salvage value on new machine | | | | | | | 800 |
| Tax on salvage value | | | | | | | (368) |
| Opportunity cost of old machine | | | | | | | (500) |
| Net cash flow | ($5,884) | $1,713 | $1,958 | $1,923 | $1,923 | $1,923 | $2,621 |

The net present value of this incremental cash flow stream, when discounted at 15 percent, is $1,539. Thus, the replacement should be made.

## Selected Additional References and Cases

Several articles have been written regarding the capital budgeting implications of the Accelerated Cost Recovery System (ACRS). Among them are the following:

Angell, Robert J., and Tony R. Wingler, "A Note on Expensing versus Depreciating under the Accelerated Cost Recovery System," *Financial Management*, Winter 1982, 34-35.

McCarty, Daniel E., and William R. McDaniel, "A Note on Expensing versus Depreciating under the Accelerated Cost Recovery System: Comment," *Financial Management*, Summer 1983, 37-39.

For further information on both replacement analysis and risk analysis, see the texts by Bierman and Smidt, by Grant, Ireson, and Leavenworth, and by Levy and Sarnat as referenced in Chapter 9.

The Crum-Brigham casebook, *Cases in Managerial Finance*, 6th ed. (Hinsdale, Ill.: Dryden, 1987), contains the following cases which focus on topics covered in Chapters 9 and 10:

Case 13, "Granville Pump Company," which focuses on the replacement decision.

Case 15, "Narwhal Sports Industries, Inc," which emphasizes the determination of relevant costs.

Case 17, "Lotis Electronics, Inc.," which provides an overview of the problem of determining relevant costs and comparing mutually exclusive projects.

The Harrington casebook contains the following relevant case:

"Federal Reserve Bank of Richmond," which analyzes the choice among three mutually exclusive methods of automating savings bond operations.

# IV

# STRATEGIC LONG-TERM FINANCING DECISIONS

A decision to increase assets brings with it the requirement to raise new capital. In Part IV we examine the primary types of long-term capital, and the analysis firms employ when deciding which of these securities to use. Chapters 11 and 12 examine the characteristics of common stock, bonds, and preferred stock. Chapter 13 discusses hybrid forms of long-term financing. Chapter 14 goes on to show how the costs of different types of capital are combined to form a weighted average cost of capital, and Chapter 15 considers the optimal mix of securities, or the capital structure decision. Finally, Chapter 16 shows how the firm's investment opportunities and cost of capital interact to determine its dividend policy.

# 11

# COMMON STOCK AND THE INVESTMENT BANKING PROCESS

In the early 1980s, after several years of strong growth, Apple Computer realized that it had some excellent investment opportunities, but it lacked the capital necessary to take advantage of them. It could have borrowed the funds, but a debt ratio constraint limited its use of debt without additional equity. To take advantage of its growth opportunities, the company needed to sell about $90 million of stock.

At the time, Apple's stock was not publicly traded—it had 50 million shares outstanding, but they were all owned by its founders and several venture capital firms. Since the stock was not traded, it had no established price. This presented a problem. To raise the required $90 million, Apple would have to create and then sell new shares. It could create 1 million shares and try to sell them for $90 each, 10 million shares for $9 each, 90 million shares for $1 each, or any other combination that would produce $90 million. If it sold a few shares at a high price, the current owners would benefit, since they would end up owning a higher percentage of the company. On the other hand, potential buyers would want to obtain shares at a lower price, so if the offering price were set too high, the issue would fail and Apple would not raise the $90 million. However, if the offering price were set too low, then the original owners would be giving away a larger share of the company than was necessary.

To help resolve the price question, and also to help market the stock, Apple brought in a group of investment bankers, including Morgan Stanley & Company. Based on a careful analysis of Apple's sales, earnings, and assets, as well as of how investors were valuing similarly situated but publicly traded firms at the time, Morgan concluded that Apple should sell 4.4 million shares at a price of $22, for a total of $96.8 million. Morgan Stanley and the other investment bankers were paid about $6 million for their services, and Apple netted just over $90 million.

Immediately after the sale, the stock moved up from the $22 offering price to the $28 to $29 range. The new stockholders were happy—they had made a quick gain of about 30 percent. The old stockholders were also happy, because (1) the public sale indicated a minimum value of 50,000,000($28) = $1.4 billion for the 50 million shares they owned and (2) with a market price established, the old stockholders' liquidity was greatly enhanced. Finally, the investment bankers were happy—they not only had made $6 million, but they also had satisfied their clients on both sides of the deal, which meant more business in the future.

Stock offerings do not always work out so well. For example, shortly after the Apple issue, Abt Computer Graphics, a Boston company, tried to sell an issue at $14 per share to raise $5 million. The issue failed to sell, so the company cut the price to $7. That did not work either, and Abt was forced to withdraw the offering entirely and to cut back its future growth plans.

Success or failure in the new equity market is a function of many things. Obviously, the fundamental position of the company is critical, but two similar firms can have very different experiences, depending on the timing of their issues, how the securities are packaged, and the sales approach taken by the investment bankers. These topics are discussed in this chapter.

In Part III we examined the analysis firms employ when making decisions regarding the investment in long-term (or fixed) assets. Any decision to acquire new assets necessitates the raising of new capital—and, generally, long-term assets are financed with long-term capital. In this chapter, we consider in some detail decisions regarding common stock financings. As a part of this analysis, we also examine in detail the procedures used by firms to raise new long-term capital, or the investment banking process.

## Balance Sheet Accounts and Definitions

**common equity**
A firm's common stock, paid-in capital, and retained earnings, which equal the amount of assets belonging to the common stockholders.

**par value**
The nominal or face value of a stock or bond.

Legal and accounting terminology is vital to both investors and financial managers if they are to avoid misinterpretations and possibly costly mistakes. Therefore, we begin our analysis of common stock with a discussion of accounting and legal issues. Consider first Table 11-1, which shows the **common equity** section of National Metals Company's balance sheet. National's owners, its stockholders, have authorized management to issue a total of 60 million shares, and management has thus far actually issued (or sold) 50 million shares. Each share has a **par value** of $1; this is the minimum amount for which new shares can be issued.[1]

---

[1] A stock's par value is an arbitrary figure that indicates the minimum amount of money stockholders have put up, or must put up in the event of bankruptcy. Actually, the firm could legally sell new shares at below par, but any purchaser would be liable for the difference between the issue price and the par value in the event the company went bankrupt. Thus, if National sold an investor 10,000 shares at 40 cents per share, for $4,000, the investor would have to put up an additional $6,000 if the company later went bankrupt. This contingent liability effectively precludes the sale of new common stock at prices below par.

Also, we should point out that firms are not required to establish a par value for their stock. Thus, National could have elected to use "no par" stock, in which case the common stock and additional paid-in capital accounts could have been consolidated under one account called *common stock*, which would show a balance of $150 million.

**Table 11-1**
**National Metals Company:**
**Stockholders' Equity Accounts as of December 31, 1985**

| | |
|---|---|
| Common stock (60 million shares authorized, 50 million shares outstanding, $1 par) | $ 50,000,000 |
| Additional paid-in capital | 100,000,000 |
| Retained earnings | 750,000,000 |
| Total common stockholders' equity (or common net worth) | $900,000,000 |

$$\text{Book value per share} = \frac{\text{Total common stockholders' equity}}{\text{Shares outstanding}} = \frac{\$900,000,000}{50,000,000} = \$18.$$

**retained earnings**
The balance sheet account which indicates the total amount of earnings the firm has not paid out as dividends throughout its history; these earnings have been reinvested in the firm.

**paid-in capital**
Funds received in excess of par value when a firm sells stock.

**book value per share**
The accounting value of a share of common stock; equal to the common equity (common stock plus paid-in capital plus retained earnings) of the firm divided by the number of shares outstanding.

National Metals is an old company—it was established back in 1873. Its initial equity capital consisted of 5,000 shares sold at the $1 par value, so on its first balance sheet the total stockholders' equity was $5,000. The initial paid-in capital and retained earnings accounts showed zero balances. Over the years National retained some of its earnings, and the firm issued new stock to raise capital from time to time. During 1985 National earned $120 million, paid $100 million in dividends, and retained $20 million. The $20 million was added to the $730 million accumulated **retained earnings** shown on the year-end 1984 balance sheet to produce the $750 million retained earnings at year-end 1985. Thus, since its inception in 1873, National has retained, or plowed back, a total of $750 million. This is money that belongs to the stockholders and that they could have received in the form of dividends. Instead, the stockholders chose to let management reinvest the $750 million in the business.

Now consider the $100 million additional **paid-in capital**. This account shows the difference between the stock's par value and what new stockholders paid when they bought newly issued shares. As has been noted, National was formed in 1873 with 5,000 shares issued at the $1 par value; thus, the first balance sheet showed a zero balance for additional paid-in capital. By 1888 the company had demonstrated its profitability and was earning 50 cents per share. Further, it had built up the retained earnings account to a total of $10,000, so the total stockholders' equity was $5,000 of par value plus $10,000 of retained earnings = $15,000, and the **book value per share** was $15,000/5,000 shares = $3. National had also borrowed heavily, and, in spite of its retained earnings, the company's debt ratio had risen to an unacceptable level, precluding further use of debt without an infusion of equity.

The company had profitable investment opportunities, so in order to take advantage of them, management decided to issue another 2,000 shares of stock. The market price at the time was $4 per share, which was eight times the 50 cents earnings per share (the price/earnings ratio was 8x). This $4 market value per share was well in excess of the $1 par value and also higher than the $3 book value per share, demonstrating that par value, book value, and market value are not necessarily equal. Had the company lost money since its inception, it would have had negative retained earnings, the book value would have been below par, and the market price might well have

**Table 11-2**
**Effects of Stock Sale on National Metals' Equity Accounts**

| Before Sale of Stock | |
| --- | --: |
| Common stock (5,000 shares outstanding, $1 par) | $ 5,000 |
| Additional paid-in capital | 0 |
| Retained earnings | 10,000 |
| Total stockholders' equity | $15,000 |
| Book value per share = $15,000/5,000 = | $3.00 |

| After Sale of Stock | |
| --- | --: |
| Common stock (7,000 shares outstanding, $1 par) | $ 7,000 |
| Additional paid-in capital ($4 − $1) × 2,000 shares | 6,000 |
| Retained earnings | 10,000 |
| Total stockholders' equity | $23,000 |
| Book value per share = $23,000/7,000 = | $3.29 |

been below book. After the 2,000 new shares had been sold to investors back in 1888 at the market price of $4 per share, National's partial balance sheet changed as shown in Table 11-2. Each share brought in $4, of which $1 represented the par value and $3 represented the excess of the sale price above par. Since 2,000 shares were involved, a total of $2,000 was added to common stock while $6,000 was entered in additional paid-in capital. Notice also that book value per share rose from $3 to $3.29; whenever stock is sold at a price above book, the book value increases, and vice versa if stock is sold below book.[2]

Similar transactions have taken place down through the years to produce the current situation, as shown on National's latest balance sheet in Table 11-1.[3]

## Legal Rights and Privileges of Common Stockholders

The common stockholders are the owners of a corporation, and as such they have certain rights and privileges. The most important of these rights are discussed in this section.

---

[2]The effects of stock sales on book value are not important for industrial firms, but they are *very* important for utility companies, whose allowable earnings per share are in effect determined by regulators as a percentage of book value. Thus, if a utility's stock is selling below book and the company sells stock to raise new equity, this will dilute the book value per share of its existing stockholders and drive down their allowable earnings per share, which in turn will drive down the market price. Most U.S. electric utilities' stocks sold below book value during the late 1970s and early 1980s. The firms needed to raise large amounts of capital, including equity, since they had to keep their capital structures in balance. This meant selling stock at prices below book, which tended to depress the market value of the stock still further.

[3]Stock dividends, stock splits, and stock repurchases (the reverse of stock issues) also affect the capital accounts. However, we shall defer a discussion of these topics until Chapter 16.

## Control of the Firm

The stockholders have the right to elect the firm's directors, who in turn select the officers who will manage the business. In a small firm, the major stockholder typically assumes the positions of president and chairman of the board of directors. In a large, publicly owned firm, the managers typically have some stock, but their personal holdings are insufficient to exercise voting control. Thus, the management of a publicly owned firm can be removed by the stockholders if they decide it is not effective.

Various state and federal laws stipulate how stockholder control is to be exercised. First, corporations must hold an election of directors periodically, usually once a year, with the vote taken at the annual meeting. Frequently, one-third of the directors are elected each year for a three-year term. Each share of stock has 1 vote; thus, the owner of 1,000 shares has 1,000 votes. Stockholders can appear at the annual meeting and vote in person, or they can transfer their right to vote to a second party by means of an instrument known as a **proxy**. Management always solicits stockholders' proxies and usually gets them. However, if earnings are poor and stockholders are dissatisfied, an outside group may solicit the proxies in an effort to overthrow management and take over control of the business. This is known as a **proxy fight**.

The question of control has become a central issue in finance in recent years. The frequency of proxy fights has increased, as have attempts by one corporation to take over another by purchasing a majority of the outstanding stock. This latter action, which is called a *takeover*, is discussed in detail in Chapter 21. Some well-known examples of recent takeover battles include Du Pont's acquisition of Conoco, and Chevron's acquisition of Gulf Oil. Managers who do not have majority control (over 50 percent) of their firms' stocks are very much concerned about takeovers, and many of them are attempting to get stockholder approval for changes in their corporate charters that would make takeovers more difficult. For example, a number of companies tried in 1985 to get their stockholders to agree (1) to elect only one-third of the directors each year (rather than electing all directors each year) and (2) to require 75 percent of the stockholders (rather than 50 percent) to approve a merger. Managements seeking such changes generally cite a fear that the firm will be picked up at a bargain price—but some stockholders wonder if management's concern over their own jobs might not be an even more important consideration.

## The Preemptive Right

Common stockholders often have the right, called the **preemptive right**, to purchase any additional shares sold by the firm. In some states the preemptive right is automatically included in every corporate charter; in others it is necessary to specifically insert it into the charter.

The purpose of the preemptive right is twofold. First, it protects the power of control of present stockholders. If it were not for this safeguard, the management of a corporation under criticism from stockholders could prevent

---

**proxy**
A document giving one person the authority to act for another, typically the power to vote shares of common stock.

**proxy fight**
An attempt by a person, group, or company to gain control of a firm by getting the stockholders to grant them the authority to vote their shares of stock in order to vote a new management into office.

**preemptive right**
A provision in the corporate charter or bylaws that gives common stockholders the right to purchase on a pro rata basis new issues of common stock (or convertible securities).

stockholders from removing it from office by issuing a large number of additional shares and purchasing these shares itself. Management would thereby secure control of the corporation to frustrate the will of the current stockholders.

The second, and by far the more important reason for the preemptive right is that it protects stockholders against a dilution of value. For example, assume that 1,000 shares of common stock, each with a price of $100, are outstanding, making the total market value of the firm $100,000. An additional 1,000 shares are sold at $50 a share, or for $50,000, thus raising the total market value of the firm to $150,000. When the total market value is divided by the new total shares outstanding, a value of $75 a share is obtained. Thus, selling common stock at below-market value would dilute its price and would transfer wealth from the present stockholders to those who purchase the new shares. The preemptive right prevents such occurrences.[4]

## Types of Common Stock

**classified stock**
Common stock that is given special designations, such as Class A, Class B, and so forth, in order to meet special needs of the company.

Although most firms have only one type of common stock, in some instances special classifications of stock are created to meet the special needs of the company. Generally, when **classified stock** is used, one type is designated *Class A*, another *Class B*, and so on. Small, new companies seeking to obtain funds from outside sources frequently use different types of common stock. For example, when Genetic Concepts, Inc., went public in 1985, its Class A stock was sold to the public, paid a dividend, and had no voting rights for five years. Its Class B stock was retained by the organizers of the company and had full voting rights for five years; the legal terms stated that dividends would not be paid on it until the company had established its earning power by building up retained earnings to a designated level. Because of the use of classified stock, the public was able to take a position in a conservatively financed growth company without sacrificing income, while the founders retained absolute control during the crucial early stages of the firm's development. At the same time, other investors were protected against excessive withdrawals of funds by the original owners. As is often the case in such situations, the Class B stock was also called **founders' shares**.

**founders' shares**
Classified stock owned by the firm's founders that has sole voting rights and restricted dividends for a specified number of years.

Note that "Class A," "Class B," and so on, have no standard meanings. Most firms have no classified shares, but one that does could designate its Class B shares as founders' shares and its Class A shares as those sold to the public, while another could reverse these designations. Still other firms could use the A and B designations for entirely different purposes.

General Motors recently introduced yet another type of common stock. When GM acquired Electronic Data Systems for $2 billion in 1984, it paid in part with a new Class E common, GME, which had limited voting rights and

---

[4]For a discussion of the procedures for issuing stock to existing stockholders, see Eugene F. Brigham and Louis C. Gapenski, *Intermediate Financial Management*, Chapter 11.

whose dividends were tied in part to the performance of EDS as it operated as a GM subsidiary. The reasons for the new stock are reported to be these: (1) GM wanted to limit voting privileges on the new stock because of management's concern about a possible takeover and (2) EDS employees and stockholders wanted to participate more directly in EDS's own performance than would have been possible through regular GM stock. GM also signaled that it planned to use this new type of stock in future acquisitions, and it did in 1985, when it announced plans to acquire Hughes Aircraft for $5 billion of newly created Class H stock, GMH.

GM's deals posed a problem for the New York Stock Exchange (NYSE), which had a rule against listing a company's common stock if the company had any nonvoting common outstanding. GM made it clear that it was willing to delist if the Exchange did not change its rules. The NYSE concluded that such arrangements as GM had made were logical and were likely to be made by other companies in the future, so it changed its rules to accommodate GM.

## Evaluation of Common Stock as a Source of Funds

Thus far this chapter has covered the main characteristics of common stock. Now we will appraise stock financing both from the viewpoint of the corporation and from a social perspective.

### From the Corporation's Viewpoint

***Advantages.*** There are several advantages to the corporation associated with common stock financing:

**1.** Common stock does not obligate the firm to make fixed payments to stockholders. If the company generates earnings and has no pressing internal needs for them, it can pay common stock dividends. Had it used debt, it would have incurred a legal obligation to pay interest on it, regardless of its operating conditions, its cash flows, and so on.

**2.** Common stock carries no fixed maturity date—it never has to be "repaid" as would a debt issue.

**3.** Since common stock provides a cushion against losses from the creditors' viewpoint, the sale of common stock increases the creditworthiness of the firm. This, in turn, raises its bond rating, lowers its cost of debt, and increases its future ability to use debt.

**4.** If a company's prospects look bright, then common stock can often be sold on better terms than debt. Stock appeals to certain groups of investors because (a) it typically carries a higher expected total return (dividends plus capital gains) than does preferred stock and debt and (b) since stock represents the ownership of the firm, it provides the investor with a better hedge against unanticipated inflation than does preferred stock or bonds. Ordinarily, common stock increases in value when real asset values rise during inflationary periods.[5]

**5.** Returns on common stock in the form of capital gains are subject to the lower personal capital gains tax rates. Hence, the effective personal income tax rate on returns from common stock may be lower than the effective tax rate on the interest received on debt.

**6.** When a company is having operating problems, it often needs new funds to overcome its problems. However, investors are reluctant to supply capital to a troubled company, and if they do, they generally require some type of security. From a practical standpoint, this means that a firm which is experiencing problems can often obtain new capital only by issuing debt. Corporate treasurers are well aware of this, so they often opt to finance with common stock so as to maintain a **reserve borrowing capacity**—indeed, surveys have indicated that maintenance of an adequate reserve of borrowing capacity is the primary consideration in most financing decisions.

**reserve borrowing capacity**
Unused debt capacity which permits borrowing if a firm needs capital in troubled times.

*Disadvantages.* Disadvantages to a company which issues common stock include the following:

**1.** The sale of common stock extends voting rights, or perhaps even control, to new stock owners. For this reason, additional equity financing is often avoided by managers who are concerned about maintaining control. The use of founders' shares and shares such as those GM issued can, however, mitigate this problem.

**2.** Common stock gives new owners the right to share in the income of the firm—if profits soar, the new stockholders get to share in this bonanza, while if debt had been used, new investors would have received only a fixed return, no matter how profitable the company.[6]

**3.** As we shall see, the costs of underwriting and distributing common stock are usually higher than those for underwriting and distributing preferred stock or debt. Flotation costs for selling common stock are characteristically higher because (a) the costs of investigating an equity security investment

---

[5]During the inflation of the last decade, the lags of product price increases behind increases in input costs depressed corporate earnings and increased the uncertainty of earnings growth, causing price/earnings multiples to fall. Thus, stocks were not a good hedge against inflation during the late 1960s and the 1970s. However, many analysts think that this period was unique and that in the future stocks will be a better inflation hedge than bonds. Indeed, the latter situation has prevailed during the 1980s—stocks have outperformed bonds and better offset the effects of inflation.

[6]This point has given rise to this interesting new theory: "If a firm sells a large issue of bonds, this is a signal that management expects the company to earn high profits on investments financed by the new capital, and it does not wish to share these profits with new stockholders. On the other hand, if the firm issues stock, this is a signal that its prospects are not so bright." There is no question but that there is some truth in the theory, but future prospects are only one element in the financing/capital structure decision. The theory is, incidentally, one aspect of the "asymmetric information problem," which is the name given to the situations in which managers have different information about the firm's prospects than public investors.

are higher than those for a comparable debt security and (b) stocks are riskier than debt, meaning investors must diversify their equity holdings, which in turn means that a given dollar amount of new stock must be sold to a greater number of purchasers than the same amount of debt.

**4.** As we shall see in Chapter 14, if the firm has more equity than is called for in its optimum capital structure, the average cost of capital will be higher than necessary. Therefore, a firm would not want to sell stock to the point where its equity ratio exceeded the optimal level.

**5.** Under current tax laws, common stock dividends are not deductible as an expense for calculating the corporation's income subject to the federal income tax, but bond interest is deductible. As we shall see in Chapter 14, the impact of this factor is reflected in the relative cost of equity capital vis-à-vis debt capital.[7]

### From a Social Viewpoint

From a social viewpoint, common stock is a desirable form of financing because it renders business firms less vulnerable to the consequences of declines in sales and earnings. Common stock financing involves no fixed charges, the payment of which might force a faltering firm into reorganization or bankruptcy. From the standpoint of the economy as a whole, if too many firms used too much debt, business fluctuations would be amplified and minor recessions could turn into major ones. During 1985, when many mergers and buyouts financed heavily with debt were occurring and raising the aggregate debt ratio (the average debt ratio of all firms), Federal Reserve Chairman Volcker and other authorities voiced concern over the situation, and congressional leaders debated the wisdom of social controls over corporations' use of debt. Like most important issues, this one is debatable, and the debate centers around who can better determine "appropriate" capital structures, corporations' managers or people in Washington.

## The Market for Common Stock

Some companies are so small that their common stocks are not actively traded—they are owned by only a few people, usually the companies' managers. Such firms are said to be *privately owned*, or **closely held**, **corporations**, and their stock is said to be *closely held stock*. On the other hand, the stocks of most larger companies are owned by a fairly large number of investors, most of whom are not active in management. Such companies are said to be

**closely held corporation**
A corporation that is not publicly owned but owned by a few individuals who are typically associated with the firm's management.

---

[7]However, as we saw in Chapter 2, the fact that capital gains are taxed at a lower personal rate than interest income provides an incentive to investors in high tax brackets to buy stock rather than bonds. This lowers the cost of equity relative to the cost of debt. In a famous article, Merton Miller ("Debt and Taxes," *Journal of Finance*, May 1977) argued that the effective costs of debt and equity to a firm are equal. Subsequent work suggests that Miller's basic arguments have merit, but that he overstated the case.

**publicly held corporation**
A corporation that is owned by a relatively large number of individuals who are not actively involved in its management.

**over-the-counter (OTC) market**
A facility that provides for trading in unlisted securities.

**organized security exchange**
A formal organization, having a tangible, physical location, that conducts auction markets in designated ("listed") securities. The two major U.S. security exchanges are the New York Stock Exchange (NYSE) and the American Stock Exchange (AMEX).

**secondary market**
The market in which securities are traded after they have been issued by corporations.

**primary market**
The market in which newly issued securities are bought and sold for the first time.

**going public**
The act of selling stock to the public at large by a closely held corporation or its principal stockholders.

**publicly owned corporations**, and their stock is said to be *publicly held stock.*

As we saw in Chapter 3, the stocks of smaller publicly owned firms are not listed on an exchange; they trade in the **over-the-counter (OTC) market**, and the companies and their stocks are said to be *unlisted*. However, larger publicly owned companies generally apply for listing on an **organized security exchange**, and they and their stocks are said to be *listed*. As a general rule, companies are first listed on a regional exchange, such as the Pacific Coast or Midwest, then move up to the American (AMEX), and finally, if they grow large enough, to the "Big Board," the New York Stock Exchange (NYSE). About 7,000 stocks are traded in the OTC market, but in terms of market value of both outstanding shares and daily transactions, the NYSE dominates with about 60 percent of the business.

Institutional investors such as pension trusts, insurance companies, and mutual funds own about 35 percent of all common stocks. However, the institutions buy and sell relatively actively, so they account for about 80 percent of all transactions. Thus, the institutional investors have a heavy influence on the price of individual stocks—in a real sense, they determine the prices of individual stocks and hence set the tone of the market.

## Types of Stock Market Transactions

We can classify stock market transactions into three distinct categories:

**1.** *Trading in the outstanding shares of established, publicly owned companies: the secondary market.* National Metals Company has 50 million shares of stock outstanding. If the owner of 100 shares sells his or her stock, the trade is said to have occurred in the **secondary market**. Thus, the market for outstanding shares, or *used shares*, is defined as the secondary market. The company receives no new money when sales occur in this market.

**2.** *Additional shares sold by established, publicly owned companies: the primary market.* If National Metals decides to sell (or issue) an additional 1 million shares to raise new equity capital, this transaction is said to occur in the **primary market**.[8]

**3.** *New public offerings by privately held firms: the primary market.* In 1975 the Coors Brewing Company, which was owned by the Coors family at the time, decided to sell some stock to raise capital needed for a major expansion program.[9] This type of transaction is defined as **going public**—

---

[8]Recall that National has 60 million shares authorized but only 50 million outstanding; thus, it has 10 million authorized but unissued shares. If it had no authorized but unissued shares, management could increase the authorized shares by obtaining stockholders' approval, which would generally be granted without any arguments.

[9]The stock Coors offered to the public was designated Class B, and it was nonvoting. The Coors family retained the founders' shares, called Class A stock, which carried full voting privileges. The company was large enough to obtain a NYSE listing, but that exchange had a requirement that listed common stock have full voting rights, which precluded Coors from obtaining a NYSE listing. Now that GM has forced the Exchange to change its rules, Coors could presumably list its stock.

**new issue market**
The market consisting of
stocks of companies that
have just gone public.

whenever stock in a closely held corporation is offered to the public for the first time, the company is said to be going public. The market for stock that has recently gone public is often called the **new issue market**.

Firms can go public without raising any additional capital. For example, in its early days, the Ford Motor Company was owned exclusively by the Ford family. When Henry Ford died, he left a substantial part of his stock to the Ford Foundation. When the Foundation later sold some of this stock to the general public, the Ford Motor Company went public, even though the company raised no capital in the transaction.

## The Decision to Go Public

As noted in Chapter 2, most businesses begin life as proprietorships or partnerships; the more successful ones, as they grow, then find it desirable at some point to convert into corporations. Initially these new corporations' stocks are owned by the firms' officers, key employees, and/or a very few investors who are not actively involved in management. However, if growth continues, the companies may decide at some point to go public. The advantages and disadvantages of public ownership are discussed next.

## Advantages of Going Public

**1.** *Facilitates stockholder diversification.* As a company grows and becomes more valuable, its founders often have most of their wealth tied up in the company. By selling some of their stock in a public offering, the founders can diversify their holdings and thereby reduce somewhat the riskiness of their personal portfolios.

**2.** *Increases liquidity.* The stock of a closely held firm is illiquid: No ready market exists for it. If one of the holders wants to sell some shares to raise cash, it is hard to find potential buyers, and even if a buyer is located, there is no established price at which to complete the transaction. These problems do not exist with publicly owned firms.

**3.** *Makes it easier to raise new corporate cash.* If a privately held company wants to raise cash by a sale of new stock, it must either go to its existing owners, who may neither have any money nor want to put any more eggs in this particular basket, or shop around for wealthy investors who are willing to make an investment in the company. However, it is usually difficult to get outsiders to put money into a closely held company, because if they do not have voting control (over 50 percent) of the stock, then the inside stockholders-managers can run roughshod over them. The insiders can pay or not pay dividends, pay themselves exorbitant salaries, have private deals with the company, and so on. For example, the president might buy a warehouse and lease it to the company or get the use of a Rolls Royce and all-the-frills travel to conventions. The insiders can even keep the outsiders from knowing the company's actual earnings, or its real worth. There are not many positions more vulnerable than that of an outside stockholder in a closely held company, and for this reason it is hard for closely held companies to raise new equity capital. Going public, which brings with it disclosure and regulation by the Securities and Exchange Commission (SEC), greatly reduces these problems and thus makes people more willing to invest in the company.

4. *Establishes a value for the firm.* For a number of reasons, it is often useful to establish a firm's value in the marketplace. For one thing, when the owner of a privately owned business dies, state and federal inheritance tax appraisers must set a value on the company for estate tax purposes. Often, these appraisers set too high a value, which creates all sorts of problems. However, a company that is publicly owned has its value established, with little room for argument. Similarly, if a company wants to give incentive stock options to key employees, it is useful to know the exact value of these options; employees much prefer to own stock, or options on stock, that is publicly traded, because public trading increases liquidity.

## Disadvantages of Going Public

1. *Cost of reporting.* A publicly owned company must file quarterly and annual reports with the SEC and/or various state officials. These reports can be costly, especially for very small firms.

2. *Disclosure.* Management may not like the idea of reporting operating data, because such data will then be available to competitors. Similarly, the owners of the company may not want people to know their net worth: Since publicly owned companies must disclose the number of shares owned by officers, directors, and major stockholders, it is easy enough for anyone to multiply shares held by price per share to estimate the net worth of insiders.

3. *Self-dealings.* The owners-managers of closely held companies have many opportunities for various types of questionable but legal self-dealings, including the payment of high salaries, nepotism, personal transactions with the business (such as a leasing arrangement), excellent retirement programs, and not-truly-necessary fringe benefits. Such self-dealings are much harder to arrange if a company is publicly owned—it must be disclosed, and the managers are also subject to stockholder suits.

4. *Inactive market/low price.* If the firm is very small and if its shares are not traded with much frequency, its stock will not really be liquid, and the market price may not be representative of the stock's true value. Security analysts and stockbrokers simply will not follow the stock, because there just will not be sufficient trading activity to generate enough sales commissions to cover the analysts' or brokers' costs of doing so.

5. *Control.* Because of the dramatic increase in tender offers and proxy fights in the 1980s, the managers of publicly owned firms who do not have at least 50 percent of the stock must be concerned about maintaining control. Further, there is pressure on such managers to produce annual earnings gains, even when it would be in the shareholders' best long-term interests to adopt a strategy that might penalize short-run earnings but lead to higher earnings in future years. These factors have led a number of public companies to "go private" in "leveraged buyout" deals in which the managers borrow the money to buy out the nonmanagement stockholders.

## Conclusions on Going Public

It should be obvious from this discussion that there are no hard and fast rules regarding whether or when a company should go public. This is an individual decision that should be made on the basis of the company's and its stockholders' own unique circumstances.

If a company does decide to go public, either by the sale of newly issued stock to raise new capital for the corporation or by the sale of stock by the current owners, one key issue is that of setting the price at which shares will be offered to the public. The company and its current owners want to set the price as high as possible—the higher the offering price, the smaller the fraction of the company the current owners will have to give up to obtain any specified amount of money. On the other hand, potential buyers will want the price set as low as possible. We will return to the establishment of the offering price later in the chapter, after we have described some other aspects of common stock financing.

## The Decision to List the Stock

The decision to go public, as discussed above, is a truly significant milestone in a company's life—it marks a major transition in the relationship between the firm and its owners. The decision to *list*, on the other hand, is not a major event. The company will have to file a few new reports with an exchange; it will have to abide by the rules of the exchange; and the stock's price will be quoted in the newspaper under a stock exchange rather than in the over-the-counter section. These are not very significant differences.

In order to have its stock listed, a company must apply to an exchange, pay a relatively small fee, and meet the exchange's minimum requirements. These requirements relate to the size of the company's net income as well as to the number of shares outstanding and in the hands of outsiders (as opposed to the number held by insiders, who generally do not trade their stock very actively). Also, the company must agree to disclose certain information to the exchange; this information is designed to help the exchange track trading patterns and thus try to prevent manipulation of the price of the stock.[10] The size qualifications increase as one moves from the regional exchanges to the AMEX and on to the NYSE.

Assuming a company qualifies, many people believe that listing is beneficial both to it and to its stockholders. Listed companies receive a certain amount of free advertising and publicity, and their status as a listed company en-

---

[10]It is illegal for anyone to attempt to manipulate the price of a stock. Prior to the creation of the SEC in the 1930s, syndicates would buy and sell stock back and forth at rigged prices for the purpose of deceiving the public into thinking that a particular stock was worth more or less than its true value. The exchanges, with the encouragement and support of the SEC, utilize sophisticated computer programs to help spot any irregularities that suggest manipulation. They can identify the exact day and time of each trade and the broker who executed it, and they can require the broker to disclose the name of the person for whom the trade was made. Such a system can obviously help identify manipulators. This same system also helps to identify illegal insider trading, as discussed in the next section.

hances their prestige and reputation. This may have a beneficial effect on the sales of the firm's products, and it is probably advantageous in terms of lowering the required rate of return on its common stock. Investors respond favorably to increased information, increased liquidity, and confidence that the quoted price is not being manipulated. By providing investors with these benefits in the form of listing their companies' stock, financial managers may lower their firms' costs of capital and increase the value of their stocks.

## Regulation of Securities Markets

**Securities and Exchange Commission (SEC)**
The U.S. government agency that regulates the issuance and trading of stocks and bonds.

Sales of new securities, and also operations in the secondary markets, are regulated by the **Securities and Exchange Commission (SEC)** and, to a lesser extent, by each of the 50 states. Here are the primary elements of SEC regulations:

**1.** The SEC has jurisdiction over all interstate offerings of new securities to the public in amounts of $1.5 million or more.

**registration statement**
A statement of facts filed with the SEC about a company planning to issue securities.

**prospectus**
A document describing a new security issue and the issuing company.

**2.** Newly issued securities must be registered with the SEC at least 20 days before they are publicly offered. The **registration statement** provides financial, legal, and technical information about the company. A **prospectus** summarizes this information for use in selling the securities. SEC lawyers and accountants analyze both the registration statement and the prospectus; if the information is inadequate or misleading, the SEC will delay or stop the public offering.

**"red herring" prospectus**
A preliminary prospectus distributed to potential buyers of a new security issue prior to approval of the registration statement by the SEC.

**3.** After the registration has become effective, new securities may be offered, but any sales solicitation must be accompanied by the prospectus. Preliminary, or "**red herring**," **prospectuses** may be distributed to potential buyers during the 20-day waiting period, but no sales may be finalized during this time. The "red herring" prospectus contains all the key information that will appear in the final prospectus except the price.

**4.** If the registration statement or prospectus contains misrepresentations or omissions of material facts, any purchaser who suffers a loss may sue for damages. Severe penalties may be imposed on the issuer or its officers, directors, accountants, engineers, appraisers, underwriters, and all others who participated in the preparation of the registration statement or prospectus.

**5.** The SEC also regulates all national securities exchanges, and companies whose securities are listed on an exchange must file annual reports similar to the registration statement with both the SEC and the exchange.

**insiders**
Officers, directors, major stockholders, or others who may have inside information on a company's operations.

**6.** The SEC has control over corporate **insiders**. Officers, directors, and major stockholders must file monthly reports of changes in their holdings of the stock of the corporation. Any short-term profits from such transactions are payable to the corporation.

**7.** The SEC has the power to prohibit manipulation by such devices as pools (aggregations of funds used to affect prices artificially) or wash sales (sales between members of the same group to record artificial transaction prices).

**8.** The SEC has control over the form of the proxy and the way the company uses it to solicit votes.

**margin requirements**
Maximum percentage of
debt that can be used to
purchase a security.

**margin call**
Call from a broker asking
for more money to support
a stock purchase loan.

Control over the flow of credit into security transactions is exercised by
the Board of Governors of the Federal Reserve System. The Fed exercises this
control through **margin requirements**, which stipulate the maximum percentage of the purchase price of a security that can be borrowed. If a great
deal of margin borrowing has been going on, then a decline in stock prices
can result in inadequate coverages; this forces the stockbrokers to issue **margin calls**, which in turn require investors either to put up more money or
to have their margined stock sold to pay off their loans. Such forced sales
further depress the stock market and can set off a downward spiral. The
margin requirement has been 50 percent since 1974.

States also have some control over the issuance of new securities within
their boundaries. This control is usually exercised by a "corporation commis-
sioner" or someone with a similar title. State laws relating to security sales
are called **blue sky laws**, because they were put into effect to keep unscru-
pulous promoters from selling securities that offered the "blue sky" but actually had little or no asset backing.

**blue sky laws**
State laws that prevent
the sale of securities
having little or no asset
backing.

The security industry itself realizes the importance of stable markets,
sound brokerage firms, and the absence of stock manipulation. Therefore, the
various exchanges work closely with the SEC to police transactions on the
exchanges and to maintain the integrity and credibility of the system. Similarly, the **National Association of Securities Dealers (NASD)** cooperates
with the SEC to police trading in the OTC market. These industry groups also
cooperate with regulatory authorities to set net worth and other standards
for securities firms, to develop insurance programs to protect the customers
of brokerage houses, and the like.

**National Association
of Securities Dealers
(NASD)**
An organization of
securities dealers that
works with the SEC to
regulate operations in the
over-the-counter market.

In general, government regulation of securities trading, and also industry
self-regulation, is designed to insure that investors receive information that is
as accurate as possible, that no one artificially manipulates the market price
of a given stock, and that corporate insiders do not take advantage of their
position to profit in their companies' stocks at the expense of other stockholders. Neither the SEC, the state regulators, nor the industry itself can prevent investors from making foolish decisions or from having "bad luck," but
they can and do help investors obtain the best data possible for making sound
investment decisions.

## The Investment Banking Process

The role of investment bankers was discussed in general terms in Chapter 3.
There we saw (1) that the major investment banking houses are often divisions of large financial service corporations engaged in a wide range of activities and (2) that these bankers help firms issue new securities in the primary
markets and also operate as brokers in the secondary markets. Sears, Roebuck
is one of the largest financial services corporations; in addition to its insurance and credit card operations, it owns a large brokerage house and a major
investment banking house. Similarly, Merrill Lynch has a brokerage department which operates thousands of offices and an investment banking depart-

ment which helps companies issue securities. Of course, Merrill Lynch's and Sears' brokers sell securities that have just been issued through their investment banking departments. In this section we describe in some detail how securities are issued, and the role of investment bankers in this process.

## Stage I Decisions

The firm itself makes some initial, preliminary decisions on its own, including these:

1. *Dollars to be raised.* How much new capital is needed?

2. *Type of securities used.* Should stock, bonds, or a combination be used? Further, if stock is to be issued, should it be offered to existing stockholders or sold directly to the general public? (See Chapter 12 for a discussion of the many different types of bonds.)

3. *Competitive bid versus a negotiated deal.* Should the company simply offer a block of its securities for sale to the highest bidder, or should it sit down with an investment banker and negotiate a deal? These two procedures are called *competitive bids* and *negotiated deals*. Only the 100 or so largest firms on the NYSE, whose issues would be very lucrative for the investment bankers, typically use the competitive bid process—the investment banks have to do a large amount of work in order to bid on an issue, and the costs are generally too high to make it worthwhile unless the bankers are sure of getting the deal. Therefore, most offerings of stock or bonds are made on a negotiated basis.

4. *Selection of an investment banker.* Assuming the issue is to be negotiated, which investment banker should the firm use? Older firms that have "been to market" before will have already established a relationship with an investment banker, although it is easy enough to change bankers if the firm is dissatisfied. However, a firm that is just going public will have to choose an investment bank, and different investment banking houses are better suited for different companies. The older, larger "establishment houses" like Morgan Stanley deal mainly with companies like AT&T, IBM, and Exxon. Other bankers handle more speculative issues. There are some houses that specialize in new issues and others that are not well suited to handle new issues because their brokerage clients are relatively conservative. (The investment banking firms sell the issues largely to their own regular investment customers, so the nature of these customers has a major effect on the ability of the house to do a good job for a corporate security issuer.) Table 11-3 lists in ranked order the ten largest investment bankers for 1984.

## Stage II Decisions

Stage II decisions, which are made jointly by the firm and its selected investment banker, include the following:

1. *Reevaluating the initial decisions.* The firm and its banker will reevaluate the initial decisions regarding the size and the type of securities to use. For example, the firm may have initially decided to raise $50 million by selling

**Table 11-3**
**Ten Largest Investment Bankers, 1984**

1. Salomon Brothers
2. Drexel Burnham Lambert
3. First Boston
4. Merrill Lynch Capital Markets
5. Goldman Sachs
6. Shearson Lehman/American Express
7. Morgan Stanley
8. Kidder Peabody
9. Prudential-Bache
10. Blyth Eastman Paine Webber

Note: Rankings are based on the dollar volume of domestic underwritings managed in 1984.

Source: *The Wall Street Journal*, January 2, 1985.

---

common stock, but the investment banker may convince management that it would be better off, in view of current market conditions, to limit the stock issue to $25 million and to raise the other $25 million as debt.

**2.** *Best efforts or underwritten issues.* The firm and its investment banker must decide whether the banker will work on a *best efforts* basis or *underwrite* the issue. In a **best efforts issue**, the banker does not guarantee that the securities will be sold or that the company will get the cash it needs. On an **underwritten issue**, the company does get a guarantee, so the banker bears significant risks in such an offering. For example, the very day IBM signed an agreement to sell $1 billion of bonds in 1979, interest rates rose sharply and the value of bond prices fell. IBM's investment bankers lost somewhere between $10 million and $20 million. Had the offering been on a best efforts basis, IBM would have been the loser.

**3.** *Issuance costs.* The investment banker's fee must be negotiated, and also the firm must estimate the other expenses it will incur in connection with the issue—lawyers' fees, accountants' costs, printing and engraving, and so on. Usually, the banker will buy the issue from the company at a discount below the price at which the securities are to be offered to the public, with this **spread** being set to cover the banker's costs and to provide a profit.

Table 11-4 gives an indication of the **flotation costs** associated with public issues of bonds, preferred stock, and common stock. As the table shows, costs as a percentage of the proceeds are higher for stocks than for bonds, and costs are higher for small than for large issues. The relationship between size of issue and flotation costs is due primarily to the existence of fixed costs—certain costs must be incurred regardless of the size of the issue, so the percentage of flotation costs is quite high for small issues.

Also, it should be noted that when relatively small companies go public to raise new capital, the investment bankers frequently take part of their compensation in the form of options to buy stock in the firm. For example, when Data Technologies, Inc., went public with a $10 million issue in 1985 by

---

**best efforts issue**
An issue of securities for which the investment bank handling the transaction gives no guarantee that the securities will be sold.

**underwritten issue**
An issue of securities for which the investment bank guarantees the sale of the securities, thus agreeing to bear any risks involved in the transaction.

**spread**
The difference between the price a security dealer offers to pay for securities (the "bid" price) and the price at which the dealer offers to sell them (the "asked" price).

**flotation costs**
The costs of issuing new stocks or bonds.

**Table 11-4**
**Costs of Flotation for Underwritten, Nonrights Offerings**
**(Expressed as a Percentage of Gross Proceeds)**

| Size of Issue (Millions of Dollars) | Bonds | | | Preferred Stock | | | Common Stock | | |
|---|---|---|---|---|---|---|---|---|---|
| | Underwriting Commission | Other Expenses | Total Costs | Underwriting Commission | Other Expenses | Total Costs | Underwriting Commission | Other Expenses | Total Costs |
| Under 1.0 | 10.0% | 4.0% | 14.0% | — | — | — | 13.0% | 9.0% | 22.0% |
| 1.0–1.9 | 8.0 | 3.0 | 11.0 | — | — | — | 11.0 | 5.9 | 16.9 |
| 2.0–4.9 | 4.0 | 2.2 | 6.2 | — | — | — | 8.6 | 3.8 | 12.4 |
| 5.0–9.9 | 2.4 | 0.8 | 3.2 | 1.9% | 0.7% | 2.6% | 6.3 | 1.9 | 8.1 |
| 10.0–19.9 | 1.2 | 0.7 | 1.9 | 1.4 | 0.4 | 1.8 | 5.1 | 0.9 | 6.0 |
| 20.0–49.9 | 1.0 | 0.4 | 1.4 | 1.4 | 0.3 | 1.7 | 4.1 | 0.5 | 4.6 |
| 50.0 and over | 0.9 | 0.2 | 1.1 | 1.4 | 0.2 | 1.6 | 3.3 | 0.2 | 3.5 |

Notes:

a. Small issues of preferred are rare, so no data on preferred issues below $5 million are given.

b. Flotation costs tend to rise somewhat when interest rates are cyclically high; because money is in relatively tight supply, the investment bankers will have a relatively hard time placing issues with permanent investors. Thus the figures shown above represent averages, and actual flotation costs vary somewhat over time.

Sources: Securities and Exchange Commission, *Cost of Flotation of Registered Equity Issues* (Washington, D.C.: U.S. Government Printing Office, December 1974); Richard H. Pettway, "A Note on the Flotation Costs of New Equity Capital Issues of Electric Companies," *Public Utilities Fortnightly*, March 18, 1982; and informal surveys of common stock, preferred stock, and bond issues conducted by the author.

selling 1 million shares at a price of $10, its investment bankers (1) bought the stock from the company at a price of $9.75, so the direct underwriting fee was only 1,000,000($10.00 − $9.75) = $250,000, or 2.5 percent, and (2) received a 5-year option to buy 200,000 shares at a price of $10. If the stock should go up to $15, which the bankers expect it to do, then they would make a $1 million profit on top of the regular underwriting fee.

**4. Setting the offering price.** If the company is already publicly owned, the **offering price** will be based on the existing market price of the stock or the yield on the bonds. For common stock, the most typical arrangement calls for the investment banker to buy the securities at a prescribed number of points below the closing price on the last day of registration. For example, on October 15, 1985, the stock of National Metals Company had a current price of $28.50, and it had traded between $25 and $30 a share during the previous three months. National and its underwriter agreed that the investment banker would buy 10 million new shares at $1 below the closing price on the last day of registration, which was expected to be in early 1986. The stock actually closed at $28 on the day the SEC released the issue, so National received $27 a share. As is typical, National's agreement had an escape clause that provided for the contract to be voided if the price of the stock had fallen below a predetermined figure. In the illustrative case, this "upset" price was set at $23 a share. Thus, if the closing price of the shares on the last day of registration had been $22.50, National would have had the option of withdrawing from the agreement.

**offering price**
The price at which common stock is sold to the public.

**Figure 11-1**
**Estimated Demand Curve for National Metals Company's Common Stock**

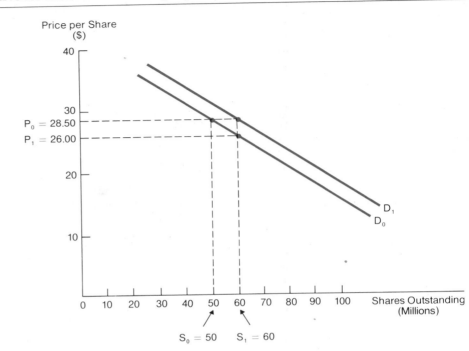

Investment bankers have an easier job if an issue is priced relatively low, but the issuer of the securities naturally wants as high a price as possible. Therefore, some conflict of interest on price arises between the investment banker and the issuer. If the issuer is financially sophisticated and makes comparisons with similar security issues, the investment banker will be forced to price close to the market.

The offering price typically has to be set at a price below the preoffering market price. Consider Figure 11-1, in which $D_0$ is the estimated market demand curve for National Metals' stock and $S_0$ is the number of shares outstanding. Initially there are 50 million shares outstanding, and the equilibrium price of the stock is $28.50. As we saw in Chapter 5, the equilibrium price of a constant-growth stock is found in accordance with this equation:

$$P_0 = \hat{P}_0 = \frac{D_1}{k_s - g} = \frac{\$2.00}{0.12 - 0.05} = \$28.57 \approx \$28.50.$$

The values shown for $D_1$, $k_s$, and g are the *estimates of the marginal stockholder*. Some stockholders doubtlessly regard National as being less risky than others and hence assign it a lower value for $k_s$. Similarly, some stockholders will estimate the company's growth rate higher than others, and so use g > 5 percent when calculating the stock's intrinsic value. Thus, there are some investors who think National's stock is worth more than $28.50 and others who think it is worth less, but the marginal investor thinks the stock is worth $28.50. Accordingly, this is its current price.

If National is to sell another 10 million shares of stock, it will either have to attract some investors who are apparently not willing to own the stock at the $28.50 price or have to induce present stockholders to buy additional shares. There are two ways this can be accomplished: (1) by reducing the price of the stock or (2) by "promoting" or "advertising" the company and thus shifting the demand curve to the right.[11] If the demand curve does not shift at all, we see from Figure 11-1 that the only way the 10 million additional shares could be sold would be by setting the offering price at $26 per share. However, if the investment bankers can promote the stock sufficiently to shift the demand curve out to $D_1$, then the offering price can be set equal to the current market price, $28.50.[12]

The extent to which the demand curve can be shifted depends primarily on two factors: (1) what investors think the company can do with the money brought in by the stock sale and (2) how effectively the brokers promote the issue. If investors can be convinced that the new money will be invested in highly profitable projects that will substantially raise earnings and the earnings growth rate, then the shift will occur and the stock price may even go above $28.50. Even if investors do not radically change their expectations about the company's fundamental factors, the fact that thousands of stockbrokers telephone their clients with suggestions that they consider purchasing National's stock may shift the demand curve. The extent to which this promotion campaign is successful in shifting the demand curve depends, of course, on the effectiveness of the investment banking firm. Therefore, National's financial manager's perceptions about the effectiveness of different investment bankers will be an important factor in its choice of an underwriter.

One final point is that *if pressure from the new shares drives down the price of the stock, all shares outstanding, and not just the new shares, will be affected*. Thus, if National's stock had fallen from $28.50 to $26 as a result of the financing, and if the price had remained at that new level, then the company would have incurred a loss of $2.50 on each of the 50 million

---

[11]It should be noted that investors can buy newly issued stock without paying normal brokerage commissions, and brokers are careful to point this out to potential purchasers. Thus, if an investor were to buy National's stock at $28.50 in the regular market, the commission would be about 1 percent, or 28 cents per share. If the stock were purchased in an underwriting, this commission would be avoided.

It should also be noted that some academicians have argued that the demand curve for a firm's stock is either horizontal or has only a slight downward slope. Most corporate treasurers, on the other hand, believe that there is a decided downward slope to the curve, especially if the sale occurs at a time when the stock is "out of favor" with the investing public. Recent empirical studies indicate that the demand curve does have a decided downward slope. See the Pettway-Radcliffe article in the references at the end of this chapter.

[12]The supply curve is a vertical line, first at 50 million shares and then, after the new issue, at 60 million.

shares previously outstanding, or a total market value loss of $125 million. In a very real sense, that loss would have been a *flotation cost*, since it would have been a cost associated with the new issue. However, empirical evidence suggests that even though pressure does drive stock prices down immediately after a new issue is announced, demand curves do shift over time, so National would not be likely to suffer a permanent loss anywhere close to $125 million on an issue such as this one.

If the company is going public, there will be no established price, so the bankers will have to estimate the *equilibrium price* at which the stock will sell after issue. Problem 11-4 at the end of this chapter illustrates in some detail the process involved. Note that if the offering price is set below the true equilibrium price, the stock will rise sharply after issue and the company and its original stockholders will have given away too much stock to raise the required capital. If the offering price is set above the true equilibrium price, either the issue will fail or investment clients, if the bankers succeed in selling them the stock, will be unhappy when the stock subsequently falls to its equilibrium level. Therefore, it is important that the equilibrium price be approximated as closely as possible.

### Selling Procedures

Once the company and its investment bankers have decided how much money to raise, the type of securities to issue, and the basis for pricing the issue, they will prepare and file an SEC registration statement and a prospectus as described earlier in the chapter. It generally takes about 20 days for the issue to be approved by the SEC. The final price of the stock (or the interest rate on a bond issue) is set at the close of business the day the issue clears the SEC, and the securities are offered to the public the following day.

Investors are not required to pay for the stock until ten days after they place their buy orders, but the investment bankers must pay the issuing firm within four days of the time the offering officially begins. Typically, the bankers sell the stock within a day or two after the offering begins, but on occasion they miscalculate, set the offering price too high, and are unable to move the issue. At still other times, the market declines during the offering period, forcing the bankers to reduce the price of the stock. In either instance, on an underwritten offering the firm receives the price that was agreed upon, and the bankers must absorb any losses that are incurred.

Because they are exposed to large potential losses, investment bankers typically do not handle the purchase and distribution of an issue singlehandedly unless it is a very small one. If the amount of money involved is large and the risk of price fluctuations substantial, investment bankers form **underwriting syndicates** in an effort to minimize the amount of risk each one carries. The banking house which sets up the deal is called the **lead**, or **managing, underwriter**.

In addition to the underwriting syndicate, on larger offerings still more investment bankers are included in a **selling group**, which handles the distribution of securities to individual investors. The selling group includes all

**underwriting syndicate**
A syndicate of investment firms formed to spread the risk associated with the purchase and distribution of a new issue of securities.

**lead, or managing, underwriter**
The member of an underwriting syndicate that actually arranges a new security issue.

**selling group**
A group of stock brokerage firms formed for the purpose of distributing a new issue of securities.

members of the underwriting syndicate plus additional dealers who take relatively small participations, or shares of the total issue, from the syndicate members. Thus, the underwriters act as *wholesalers*, while members of the selling group act as *retailers*. The number of houses in a selling group depends partly upon the the size of the issue; for example, the one set up when Communications Satellite Corporation (Comsat) went public consisted of 385 members.

### Shelf Registrations

**shelf registration**
A procedure under which a large, well-established firm can sell new securities on very short notice.

The selling procedures described above, including the 20-day minimum waiting period between registration with the SEC and sale of the issue, apply to most security sales. However, it should be noted that large, well-known public companies which issue securities frequently may file a *master registration statement* with the SEC and then update it with a *short-form statement* just prior to each individual offering. This procedure is known as **shelf registration**, because in effect the company puts its new securities "on the shelf" and then sells them to investors when it feels the market is "right."

### Maintenance of the Secondary Market

In the case of a large, established firm such as National Metals, the investment banking firm's job is finished once it has disposed of the stock and turned the net proceeds over to the company. However, in the case of a company going public for the first time, the investment banker is under an obligation to maintain a market in the shares after the issue has been completed. Such stocks are typically traded in the over-the-counter market, and the lead underwriter generally agrees to "make a market" in the stock so as to keep it reasonably liquid. The company wants a good market to exist for its stock, as do the stockholders. Therefore, if the banking house wants to do business with the company in the future, to keep its own brokerage customers happy, and to have future referral business, it will hold an inventory and help to maintain an active secondary market in the stock.

### IBM's Initial Debt Offering

IBM's first public debt offering, in 1979, provides an informative case study of the nature of investment banking.[13] The offering, still the largest in U.S. corporate history, represented a combination of $500 million in 7-year notes and $500 million in 25-year debentures (unsecured long-term debt) for a total of $1 billion. IBM's customary investment banker had been Morgan Stanley & Co. However, IBM requested separate proposals from Morgan Stanley and from Salomon Brothers, another major investment banking house. IBM's

---

[13]This summary is based on contemporary accounts in the financial press and in the article by Walter Guzzardi, Jr., "The Bomb IBM Dropped on Wall Street," *Fortune*, November 19, 1979, 52-56.

financial management was of the opinion that two managers would provide better execution of the sale and back it up with a larger amount of capital. John H. Gutfreund, Salomon Brothers' managing partner, is quoted as stating, "A major corporation is best served by two sets of eyes and ears." Robert H. B. Baldwin, president of Morgan Stanley, is said to have responded, "You need only one brain surgeon." Morgan Stanley dropped out, refusing to participate if it could not be sole manager, and Salomon Brothers and Merrill Lynch became co-managers, with an underwriting group totaling 227 members.

The Salomon and Morgan Stanley proposals were presented to IBM early in September 1979. During the next few weeks, while discussions were taking place, the prime rate was increased five times, reaching a level of 13.5 percent on September 28. A "pricing meeting" took place on Wednesday, October 3, 1979; at the time, rapidly rising yields were being experienced in the money markets. Discussions at the pricing meeting centered around prices based on a yield of 7 basis points above Treasury notes for the IBM notes and 12 basis points above Treasury bonds for the IBM debentures.[14] The result was that IBM would have to pay 9.62 percent for the 7-year notes and 9.41 percent for the 25-year debentures. The underwriting spread, or commission, was ⅝ of 1 percent, or $6.25, per note and ⅞ of 1 percent, or $8.75, per debenture.

Only hours after the pricing meeting had ended and the issue's yield and price had been fixed, the market yield for Treasury bonds moved up by 5 basis points. The IBM offering began the next day, Thursday, October 4. On that same day, the Treasury auctioned $2.5 billion of 4-year notes yielding 9.79 percent, which was higher than the 9.62 percent on the IBM 7-year notes. Naturally, the IBM securities did not sell at all well.

On Saturday, October 6, the Federal Reserve System announced an increase in its discount rate from 11 percent to 12 percent to combat the high rate of inflation that was developing. At the same time, a number of other credit-tightening policies, which Wall Street experts called "draconian" in their severity, were implemented. As a result of the Fed's actions, on Tuesday, October 9, an additional full percentage point increase in the prime rate, to 14.5 percent, was announced. The next morning, the underwriting syndicate was disbanded. The prices of both the notes and the debentures fell by about $50 each, with yields rising to 10.65 percent on the notes and to 10.09 percent on the debentures.

When the syndicate was disbanded, it was estimated that only $650 million of the $1 billion issue had been sold. The underwriting fee to syndicate members was about $5 million. When the market quotations dropped after the syndicate was disbanded, the losses on the $350 million unsold portion of the issue were estimated at between $10 and $20 million, so the underwriters "took a bath."

---

[14]One basis point is equal to one one-hundredth of 1 percent. Therefore, IBM's notes were priced to yield 0.07 percent more than Treasury notes.

A controversy arose over whether the IBM issue was priced "too tight." During the month preceding the actual offering, the prime rate and the discount rate had both been increasing. The financial markets during the week of October 3, when the pricing decision was made, were hectic, if not chaotic. Undoubtedly, the severe measures taken by the Federal Reserve System on Saturday, October 6, 1979, were being anticipated during the week. Whether the underwriters should have given themselves more cushion to avoid a subsequent price decline is a matter of judgment. From one standpoint, the price decline of $50 after the disbanding of the underwriting syndicate was relatively modest, given the sharply rising interest rates during the period and the Fed announcement on October 6. Differences in judgment on this matter are natural—and such differences are what make markets.

The IBM offering illustrates a number of basic characteristics of investment banking. First, the risks are real. Second, competition among investment bankers continues to be vigorous and tough. Third, a corporate issue of a well-managed, prestigious firm which is taking on debt for the first time, and in moderate quantity in relation to its total assets, will be rated high and priced close to Treasury issues. Fourth, turbulence in the financial markets during the period immediately preceding the offering makes the task of the underwriters and the company an extremely difficult one; it demonstrates the great risk-taking and judgment that are required in making decisions in the face of an extremely volatile financial environment. Fifth, the episode illustrates the high drama, the considerable financial sophistication, and the continued great challenges that exist in the field of financial decision making.[15]

## Emerging Trends

Important new developments are taking place in the financial markets, including commercial banking and investment banking. Some of these developments have resulted from legislative changes and others from fundamental shifts in the nature of economic and financial relationships.

Important changes in the banking environment were brought about by the Depository Institutions Deregulation and Monetary Control Act of 1980. The law directed the Federal Reserve to lower reserve requirements and to phase out deposit interest rate ceilings. It permitted depository institutions to offer interest-bearing checking accounts, savings and loan associations were given expanded lending and investing powers, and commercial banks were allowed to offer money market funds and some brokerage services.

Competition has increased dramatically among the different types of financial institutions, as "financial service corporations," which encompass invest-

---

[15]To close out the story, (1) at least some of the underwriters claim to have hedged their IBM positions in the futures market, and (2) Salomon Brothers, the lead underwriter, was at the time aggressively (and successfully) seeking to expand its operations—and that requires taking some chances. Salomon's overall strategy has certainly worked well even if this one issue did not, for in 1983 Salomon surpassed Morgan Stanley as the world's leading underwriter.

ment banking, brokerage operations, insurance, and commercial banking, are dominating the scene. Investment banking firms often earn more income in the form of interest than in commissions, and additional new sources of income for them include credit cards, money market funds, and counseling on corporate merger activity.

When the SEC ordered the end of fixed commission schedules on May 1, 1975, investment bankers were placed under severe financial pressure. To avoid financial disaster, numerous "mergers of necessity" have taken place, as is evident in the compound names of some of the surviving firms: Merrill Lynch White Weld Capital Markets Group, Blyth Eastman Paine Webber, and Dean Witter Reynolds, Inc. In addition to mergers within the investment banking and brokerage business, mergers between different types of financial institutions have taken place. Bache and Co., once the eighth largest investment banking firm, was taken over by Prudential Insurance; American Express acquired Shearson Loeb Rhoades, the second largest investment banking firm; and Sears, Roebuck bought out Dean Witter. There is a very clear trend toward *financial services conglomerates*. At the same time, institutional investors, especially pension funds, are continuing to replace individuals on the buying side—about 80 percent of all stock transactions are among institutions, and competition for institutional business has changed the way both brokerage and investment banking houses (or divisions) operate. These trends, in turn, have changed and are continuing to change the types of securities nonfinancial corporations offer to raise capital. We shall discuss some of these changes in the following chapters.

## Summary

This chapter has focused on these items: (1) the balance sheet treatment of common stock; (2) the legal rights of individual stockholders, especially their control of the firm; (3) the types of common stock that are in use (for example, founders' shares); (4) the markets in which common stocks are traded; (5) the steps a firm must go through when issuing new shares; (6) the government's regulation of security markets; (7) the decisions related to a company's going public; (8) the decisions related to having a company's stock listed on an exchange; and (9) recent changes in security markets. The chapter is more descriptive than analytical, but a knowledge of the issues discussed here is essential to an understanding of finance.

## SMALL BUSINESS

### Raising Equity Capital for the Small Firm

Small firms are generally disadvantaged in competing for funds in public equity markets. Nevertheless, the public markets are accessible, and the Securities and Exchange Commission also makes available some special facilities to help small firms raise equity funds without incurring the expense of a public offering. *Venture Capital Journal* reports that in the year 1983, 477 small firms made public offerings of common stock, raising a stunning total of $3.67 billion, an average of $7.7 million per firm. These statistics are for firms whose pre-offering net worths were all under $5 million. So, while it is true that smaller firms are at a disadvantage, the public equity markets are by no means the exclusive domain of giant companies.

Biotechnology General provides a good example of a firm with a new public offering in 1983. For the full year 1982, Biotechnology General (BTG) had total sales of $150,000. It lost $2.3 million, not unusual for a young firm in a heavily research-oriented industry. Yet, on September 29, 1983, when BTG went public at an offering price of $13 per share, it quickly raised a total of over $10 million.

How could a firm with essentially no revenues go public and obtain $10 million? How could the public decide on a value for the shares? The answers to these questions can prove problematic. BTG illustrates several features of a public offering that can have a major effect on its success for a young, small firm. The features we highlight below are market timing, the public's interest in this type of business, and the company's success in developing a new product. Another point BTG's case illustrates is the great difficulty of valuing shares by traditional means under such circumstances.

Market timing is thought by many investment underwriters to be a critical element in the success of a new public offering. The year 1983 was phenomenally successful for the stock market. The Dow Jones Industrial Average reached an all-time historical high, and many investors told stories of great success with their equity investments. Pension funds and other large institutional investors shifted huge sums into the equity markets. As public interest in the equity markets grew, public participation in new equity offerings increased concurrently, and 1983 was by far the most successful year in history for new public offerings. New offerings are especially interesting to investors during bull market periods because new-issue prices tend to be highly volatile. Volatility is attractive to investors who are optimistic—it means a higher probability of unusually high returns.

Of course, investors have to keep in mind that price volatility also means a higher probability of unusually large losses, and, indeed, the bull market of 1983 soured quickly, turning into a bear market in 1984. As investor concerns about general economic conditions worsened, prices tumbled rapidly. Companies that had delayed their offerings during the bull market period suddenly found that the markets had reduced the values of new issues. Many firms planning to go public found either that they had to sell their issues at disappointingly low prices or that, as often occurred, they were advised to postpone their offerings indefinitely.

BTG made its offering in September 1983, just as the market was beginning to turn. At that time the market was still receptive to new issues, though subsequent events indicate how volatile the initial market reception can be. BTG was able to sell its shares at the desired price, and despite substantial problems with the offering, the firm was able to successfully raise $10 million. Had BTG waited and come to market three or four months later, however, the shares would not have sold at all.

The second factor is the firm's line of business. The market is very sensitive to this point since there tend to be general expectations about particular industries. For example, earlier in 1983 Osborne Computer Corporation had filed for bankruptcy. The market was at that time especially careful in evaluating new computer hardware firms. BTG, however, was a member of the exciting new breed of genetic engineering firms. Spurred on by the incredible success of Genentech, the market had a very strong interest in new issues of biological and genetic engineering companies.

The third factor is the existence of a product, and BTG had completed the development of its first product, a promising new biological wonder that demonstrated the firm's expertise in biological engineering. The firm needed funds for continued product development, and it had already demonstrated its ability to deliver.

We are still left with the question of how BTG's underwriters came up with a market value for the stock. The answer is unclear. Although the firm was three years old at the time, it had never produced positive earnings, and it had certainly never paid a dividend. In fact, there could be no reasonable expectation of dividends for the foreseeable future, so clearly one could not apply the valuation models discussed in Chapter 5. One could not even apply a price/earnings multiple to current earnings since there were no current earnings. In essence, the underwriters had to do the best they could to set a price at which the issue would be appealing to the public in spite of the huge uncertainty about the future financial performance of the firm. As it was, the issue price was dropped from

$15-$17 to $13 per share even before the offering was ever made public. Had the firm not been in biogenetics, it is doubtful the issue would have been offered at all. BTG's decision to sell stock illustrates the value of being in the right place at the right time: it was in a hot industry, with a promising new product, and in a fairly receptive market.

We can see that there can be a market for the stock of very promising small and young firms. A number of factors figure in the success of a public offering of a small firm's equity, and not all of the factors are under the firm's control. But small firms do have some access to public markets if they have at least some promise of growing into more substantial enterprises. Managing those growth opportunities is something that *is* under the control of the firm and its managers.

## Questions

**11-1**   Define each of the following terms:
   a.  Common equity; paid-in capital; retained earnings
   b.  Par value; book value per share; market value per share
   c.  Proxy; proxy fight
   d.  Preemptive right
   e.  Classified stock; founders' shares
   f.  Closely held corporation; publicly held corporation
   g.  Over-the-counter (OTC) market; organized security exchange
   h.  Primary market; secondary market
   i.  Going public; new issue market
   j.  Securities and Exchange Commission (SEC); registration statement; shelf registration; blue sky laws; margin; insiders
   k.  Prospectus; "red herring" prospectus
   l.  National Association of Securities Dealers (NASD)
   m.  Best efforts issue; underwritten issue
   n.  Spread; flotation costs; offering price
   o.  Underwriting syndicate; lead, or managing, underwriter; selling group

**11-2**   Examine Table 11-1. Suppose National sold 2 million shares, with the company netting $25 per share. Construct a pro forma statement of the equity accounts to reflect this sale.

**11-3**   Is it true that the "flatter," or more nearly horizontal, the demand curve for a particular firm's stock, the more important the role of investment bankers when the company sells a new issue of stock?

**11-4**   The SEC attempts to protect investors who are purchasing newly issued securities by making sure that the information put out by a company and its investment bankers is correct and is not misleading. However, the SEC does not provide an opinion about the real value of the securities; hence, an investor might pay too much for some new stock and consequently lose heavily. Do you think the SEC should, as a part of every new stock or bond offering, render an opinion to investors on the proper value of the securities being offered? Explain.

**11-5**   How do you think each of the following items would affect a company's ability to attract new capital and the flotation costs involved in doing so?
   a.  A decision to list a company's over-the-counter stock.
   b.  A decision of a privately held company to go public.
   c.  The increasing institutionalization of the "buy side" of the stock and bond markets.

   d. The trend toward "financial conglomerates" as opposed to stand-alone investment banking houses.
   e. Elimination of the preemptive right.
   f. The introduction of "shelf registrations" in 1981.

**11-6**    Before entering a formal agreement, investment bankers carefully investigate the companies whose securities they underwrite; this is especially true of the issues of firms going public for the first time. Since the bankers do not themselves plan to hold the securities but intend to sell them to others as soon as possible, why are they so concerned about making careful investigations?

**11-7**    It is frequently stated that the primary purpose of the preemptive right is to allow individuals to maintain their proportionate share of the ownership and control of a corporation.
   a. How important do you suppose this consideration is for the average stockholder of a firm whose shares are traded on the New York or American Stock Exchanges?
   b. Is the preemptive right likely to be of more importance to stockholders of publicly owned or closely held firms? Explain.

**11-8**    a. Is a firm likely to get a wider distribution of shares if it sells new stock through a preemptive rights offering to existing stockholders or directly to underwriters?
   b. Why would management be interested in getting a wider distribution of its shares?

## Problems

Book value per share    **11-1**    The Harmonic Recording Company had the following balance sheet at the end of 1985:

**Harmonic Recording Company:**
**Balance Sheet**
**December 31, 1985**

|  |  |  |  |
|---|---|---|---|
|  |  | Accounts payable | $ 32,000 |
|  |  | Notes payable | 36,000 |
|  |  | Long-term debt | 72,000 |
|  |  | Common stock (30,000 shares authorized, 20,000 shares outstanding) | 180,000 |
|  |  | Retained earnings | 150,000 |
| Total assets | $470,000 | Total claims | $470,000 |

   a. What is the book value per share of Harmonic's common stock?
   b. Suppose the firm sold the remaining authorized shares and netted $13.50 per share from the sale. What would the new book value per share be?

Profit (loss) on new stock    **11-2**    Security Brokers, Inc., specializes in underwriting new issues by small
issue    firms. On a recent offering of Med-Tek, the terms were as follows:

| | |
|---|---|
| Price to public | $10 per share |
| Number of shares | 1 million |
| Proceeds to Med-Tek | $9,500,000 |

The out-of-pocket expenses incurred by Security Brokers in the design and distribution of the issue were $200,000. What profit or loss would Security Brokers incur if the issue were sold to the public at an average price of:

a. $10 per share?
b. $11 per share?
c. $9 per share?

**Underwriting and flotation expenses**    **11-3**    The Jet Company, whose stock price is now $30, needs to raise $15 million in common stock. Underwriters have informed Jet's management that they must price the new issue to the public at $28 per share because of a downward-sloping demand curve. The underwriters' compensation will be 5 percent of the issue price, so Jet will net $26.60 per share. It will also incur expenses in the amount of $150,000.

How many shares must Jet sell to net $15 million after underwriting and flotation expenses?

**New stock issue**    **11-4**    The Callaway Company, a small jewelry manufacturer, has been successful and has enjoyed a good growth trend. Now Callaway is planning to go public with an issue of common stock, and it faces the problem of setting an appropriate price on the stock. The company and its investment bankers feel that the proper procedure is to select several similar firms with publicly traded common stock and to make relevant comparisons.

Several jewelry manufacturers are reasonably similar to Callaway with respect to product mix, size, asset composition, and debt/equity proportions. Of these companies, Sonnet and Mailers are most similar. When analyzing the following data, assume that 1980 and 1985 were reasonably "normal" years for all three companies—that is, these years were neither especially good nor especially bad in terms of sales, earnings, and dividends. At the time of the analysis, $k_{RF}$ was 10 percent and $k_M$ was 15 percent. Sonnet is listed on the AMEX and Mailers on the NYSE, while Callaway will be traded in the OTC market.

|  | Sonnet | Mailers | Callaway (Totals) |
|---|---|---|---|
| **Earnings per share** | | | |
| 1985 | $ 4.50 | $ 7.50 | $1,200,000 |
| 1980 | 3.00 | 5.50 | 816,000 |
| **Price per share** | | | |
| 1985 | $36.00 | $65.00 | — |
| **Dividends per share** | | | |
| 1985 | $ 2.25 | $ 3.75 | $ 600,000 |
| 1980 | 1.50 | 2.75 | 420,000 |
| Book value per share, 1985 | $30.00 | $55.00 | $9,000,000 |
| Market/book ratio, 1985 | 120% | 118% | — |
| | | | |
| Total assets, 1985 | $28 million | $ 82 million | $20 million |
| Total debt, 1985 | $12 million | $ 30 million | $11 million |
| Sales, 1985 | $41 million | $140 million | $37 million |

a. Assume that Callaway has 100 shares of stock outstanding. Use this information to calculate earnings per share (EPS), dividends per share

(DPS), and book value per share for Callaway. (Hint: Callaway's 1985 EPS = $12,000.)

b. Calculate earnings and dividend growth rates for the three companies. (Hint: Callaway's EPS g is 8%.)

c. Based on your answer to Part a, do you think Callaway's stock would sell at a price in the same "ballpark" as that of Sonnet and Mailers, that is, in the range of $25 to $100 per share?

d. Assuming that Callaway's management can split the stock so that the 100 shares could be changed to 1,000 shares, 100,000 shares, or any other number, would such an action make sense in this case? Why?

e. Now assume that Callaway did split its stock and has 400,000 shares. Calculate new values for EPS, DPS, and book value per share. (Hint: Callaway's new 1985 EPS is $3.00.)

f. Return on equity (ROE) can be measured as EPS/book value per share or as total earnings/total equity. Calculate ROEs for the three companies. (Hint: Callaway's 1985 ROE = 13.3%.)

g. Calculate dividend payout ratios for the three companies. (Hint: Callaway's 1985 payout ratio is 50%.)

h. Calculate debt/total assets ratios for the three companies. (Hint: Callaway's 1985 debt ratio is 55%.)

i. Calculate the P/E ratios for Sonnet and Mailers. Are these P/Es reasonable in view of relative growth, payout, and ROE data? If not, what other factors might explain them? (Hint: Sonnet's P/E = $8\times$.)

j. Now determine a range of values for Callaway's stock price, with 400,000 shares outstanding, by applying Sonnet's and Mailers' P/E ratios, price/dividends ratios, and price/book value ratios to your data for Callaway. For example, one possible price for Callaway's stock is (P/E Sonnet) (EPS Callaway) = 8($3) = $24 per share. Similar calculations would produce a range of prices based on both Sonnet and Mailers data. (Hint: Our range was $24 to $27.)

k. Using the equation $k = D_1/P_0 + g$, find approximate k values for Sonnet and Mailers. Then use these values in the constant growth stock price model to find a price for Callaway's stock. (Hint: We averaged the EPS and DPS g's for Callaway.)

l. At what price do you think Callaway's shares should be offered to the public? You will want to select a price that will be low enough to induce investors to buy the stock but not so low that it will rise sharply immediately after it was issued. Think about relative growth rates, ROEs, dividend yields, and total returns ($k = D/P + g$).

## Selected Additional References and Cases

For a wealth of facts and figures on a major segment of the stock market, see:

New York Stock Exchange, *Fact Book* (New York, published annually).

For both a description of the stock market and some further facts and figures, see:

Frances, Jack C., *Investments: Analysis and Management* (New York: McGraw-Hill, 1980).

Radcliffe, Robert C., *Investment Concepts, Analysis, and Strategy* (Glenview, Ill.: Scott, Foresman, 1982).

Reilly, Frank K., *Investment Analysis and Portfolio Management*, (Hinsdale, Ill.: Dryden, 1985).

Sharpe, William F., *Investments* (Englewood Cliffs, N.J.: Prentice-Hall, 1981).

Other good references on specific aspects of equity financing include the following:

Block, Stanley, and Marjorie Stanley, "The Financial Characteristics and Price Movement Patterns of Companies Approaching the Unseasoned Securities Market in the Late 1970s," *Financial Management*, Winter 1980, 30-36.

Fabozzi, Frank J., "Does Listing on the AMEX Increase the Value of Equity?" *Financial Management*, Spring 1981, 43-50.

Hansen, Robert S., and John M. Pinkerton, "Direct Equity Financing: A Resolution to a Paradox," *Journal of Finance*, June 1982, 651-665.

Logue, Dennis E., and Robert A. Jarrow, "Negotiation versus Competitive Bidding in the Sale of Securities by Public Utilities," *Financial Management*, Autumn 1978, 31-39.

Pettway, Richard H., and Robert C. Radcliffe, "Impacts of New Equity Sales upon Electric Utility Share Prices," *Financial Management*, Spring 1985, 16-25.

The Harrington casebook contains the following applicable case:

"Hop-In Food Stores, Incorporated," which focuses on a firm's decision to go public.

# 12  LONG-TERM DEBT

**Leaseway Transportation**

On any given day, corporations go to the market for vast amounts of new debt capital, and they issue many forms of securities. For example, in a recent issue of *The Wall Street Journal* it was announced that Houston Lighting and Power had just sold $125 million of 13⅛ percent, 10-year, first mortgage bonds; that a Carolina Power & Light subsidiary was raising $60 million in Europe on 7-year notes guaranteed by the parent company; that Leaseway Transportation Corp. was raising $75 million using collateral trust notes; that Moran Energy had obtained a $75 million revolving line of credit from a group of banks, with interest to vary over time and to be set at a rate based on the lower of the First National Bank of Houston's prime rate or the London Inter-Bank Offered Rate (LIBOR); that Occidental Petroleum was selling $100 million of long-term debt and using the money to reduce its short-term debt; and that Southwestern Bell was selling 40-year, Aaa debenture bonds at a rate of 14⅛ percent. Another story in the same issue of the *Journal* reported that the bond rating of Fedders Corporation, an air conditioning manufacturer, was being lowered, with the result that the company would have to pay more for debt in the future.

Why are there so many different types of debt having so many different maturities, ratings, and so on? Does it cost more to raise debt capital by selling 40-year bonds or 7-year notes? What are the pros and cons of paying a fixed rate of interest on a bond versus letting the coupon rate float up and down as rates in the economy fluctuate? How can a company keep its bond rating up, or get it back up if it is lowered? These are some of the issues discussed in this chapter.

---

Different groups of investors favor different types of securities, and investors' tastes change over time. Thus, astute financial managers offer a variety of securities, "packaging" their new security offerings at each point in time so as to attract the greatest possible number of potential investors, and thereby holding their costs of capital to a minimum. In this chapter, we consider various types of long-term debt.

**funded debt**
Long-term debt; "funding" means replacing short-term debt with securities of longer maturity.

Long-term debt is often called **funded debt**. When a firm is said to be planning to "fund" its short-term debt, it is in essence planning to replace short-term debt with securities of longer maturity. Funding does not imply placing money with a trustee or other repository; it is simply part of the jargon of finance and means "replacing short-term debt with permanent capital." Tampa Electric Company provides a good example of funding. This company has a continuous construction program and typically uses short-term debt to finance construction expenditures. However, once short-term debt has built up to about $100 million, the company sells a stock or bond issue, uses the proceeds to pay off (or fund) its bank loans, and starts the cycle again. There is a fixed cost involved in selling stocks or bonds which makes it quite expensive to issue small amounts of these securities. Therefore, the process used by Tampa Electric and other companies is very logical.

## Traditional Debt Instruments

There are many types of long-term debt instruments: term loans, bonds, secured and unsecured notes, marketable and nonmarketable notes, and so on. In this section, we discuss briefly the traditional long-term debt instruments. In the next major section, we discuss some important features of debt contracts, after which we discuss recent innovations in long-term debt financing.

### Term Loans

**term loan**
A loan, generally obtained from a bank or insurance company, with a maturity period greater than one year.

A **term loan** is a contract under which a borrower agrees to make a series of interest and principal payments on specific dates to a lender.[1] Term loans are usually negotiated directly between the borrowing firm and a financial institution—generally a bank, an insurance company, or a pension fund. Although the maturities of term loans vary from 2 to 30 years, most are for periods in the 3-year to 15-year range.

Term loans have three major advantages over public offerings—*speed, flexibility*, and *low issuance costs*. Also, because they are negotiated directly between the lender and the borrower, formal documentation is minimized. The key provisions of term loans can be worked out much more quickly and with more flexibility than can those for a public issue, and it is not necessary for the loans to go through the Securities and Exchange Commission registration process. A further advantage of term loans has to do with future flexibility: If a bond issue is held by many different bondholders, it is virtually impossible to obtain permission to alter the terms of the agreement, even though new economic conditions may make such changes desirable. With a term loan, the borrower can generally negotiate with the lender to work out modifications to the contract.

---

[1] Most term loans are *amortized*, which means paid off in equal installments over the life of the loan. Amortization protects the lender against the possibility that the borrower will not make adequate provisions for the loan's retirement during the life of the loan. See Chapter 4 for a review of amortization. Also, if the interest and maturity payments required under a term loan agreement are not met on schedule, the borrowing firm is said to have *defaulted*, and it can then be forced into bankruptcy. See Appendix 12A for a discussion of bankruptcy.

The interest rate on a term loan can be either fixed for the life of the loan or variable. If a fixed rate is used, it will be close to the rate on bonds of equivalent maturity for companies of comparable risk. If the rate is variable, it will usually be set at a certain number of percentage points over the prime rate, the commercial paper rate, the T-bill rate, or the London Inter-Bank Offered Rate (LIBOR). Thus, when the index rate goes up or down, so does the rate on the outstanding balance of the term loan. (Often, rates are adjusted annually, but the contract can state that they are to be adjusted monthly, quarterly, or semiannually.) In 1984 about 50 percent of the dollar amount of term loans made by banks had floating rates, up from virtually zero in 1970. Banks obtain most of the funds they themselves lend to corporations by selling certificates of deposit, and since the CD rate rises along with other market rates, banks need to raise the rate they charge in order to meet their own interest costs. With the increased volatility of interest rates in recent years, banks and other lenders have become increasingly reluctant to make long-term, fixed rate loans.

## Bonds

**bond**
A long-term debt instrument.

A **bond** is a long-term contract under which a borrower agrees to make payments of interest and principal on specific dates to the holder of the bond. While bonds have traditionally been issued with maturities of between 20 and 30 years, in the 1980s shorter maturities, such as 7 to 10 years, have been used to an increasing extent. Although bonds are similar to term loans, a bond issue is generally advertised, offered to the public, and actually sold to many different investors—indeed, thousands of individual and institutional investors may purchase bonds when a firm sells a bond issue, while there is generally only one lender in the case of a term loan.[2] With bonds the interest rate is generally fixed, although in recent years there has been an increase in the use of various types of floating rate bonds. There are a number of different types of bonds, the more important of which are discussed next.

**mortgage bond**
A bond backed by fixed assets. *First mortgage bonds* are senior in priority to claims of *second mortgage bonds*.

*Mortgage Bonds.* Under a **mortgage bond**, the corporation pledges certain assets as security for the bond. To illustrate, in 1985 Ryder Trucking needed $10 million to purchase land and to build a major distribution center. Bonds in the amount of $4 million, secured by a mortgage on the property, were issued. (The remaining $6 million was financed with equity funds.) If Ryder defaults on the bonds, the bondholders can foreclose on the property and sell it to satisfy their claims.

If Ryder chose to, it could issue *second mortgage bonds* secured by the same $10 million plant. In the event of liquidation, the holders of these second mortgage bonds would have a claim against the property only after the

---

[2]However, for very large term loans, 20 or more financial institutions may form a syndicate to grant the credit. Also, it should be noted that a bond issue can be sold to one lender (or to just a few); in this case, the issue is said to be "privately placed." Companies that place bonds privately do so for the same reasons that they use term loans—speed, flexibility, and low issuance costs.

first mortgage bondholders had been paid off in full. Thus, second mortgages are sometimes called *junior mortgages* because they are junior in priority to claims of *senior mortgages*, or *first mortgage bonds*.

The first mortgage indentures of most major corporations were written 20, 30, 40, or more years ago.[3] These indentures are generally "open ended," meaning that new bonds may be issued from time to time under the existing indenture. However, the amount of new bonds that can be issued is virtually always limited to a specified percentage of the firm's total "bondable property," which generally includes all plant and equipment. For example, Savannah Electric Company can issue first mortgage bonds totaling up to 60 percent of its fixed assets. If its fixed assets totaled $1 billion and it had $500 million of first mortgage bonds outstanding, then it could, by the property test, issue another $100 million of bonds (60% of $1 billion = $600 million).

In recent years, Savannah Electric has at times been unable to issue any new first mortgage bonds because of another indenture provision: Its times-interest-earned (TIE) ratio was below 2.5, the minimum coverage that it must maintain in order to sell new bonds. Thus, Savannah Electric passed the property test but failed the coverage test; hence, it could not issue first mortgage bonds, and it had to finance with junior securities. Since first mortgage bonds carry lower rates of interest than junior long-term debt, this restriction was a costly one.

Savannah Electric's neighbor, Georgia Power Company, has more flexibility under its indenture—its interest coverage requirement is only 2.0. In hearings before the Georgia Public Service Commission, it was suggested that Savannah Electric change its indenture coverage to 2.0 so that it could issue more first mortgage bonds. However, this is simply not possible—the holders of the outstanding bonds would have to approve the change, and it is inconceivable that they would vote for a change that would seriously weaken their position.

**debenture**
A long-term debt instrument that is not secured by a mortgage on specific property.

***Debentures.*** A **debenture** is an unsecured bond, and as such it provides no lien against specific property as security for the obligation. Debenture holders are therefore general creditors whose claims are protected by property not otherwise pledged. In practice, the use of debentures depends both on the nature of the firm's assets and on its general credit strength. An extremely strong company such as IBM will tend to use debentures—it simply does not need to put up property as security for its debt issues. Debentures are also issued by companies in industries where it would not be practical to provide security through a mortgage on fixed assets. Examples of such industries are the large mail-order houses and commercial banks, which characteristically hold most of their assets in the form of inventory or loans, neither of which is satisfactory security for a mortgage bond.

---

[3]Bond indentures, which are the actual debt contracts, will be discussed in detail in the next section of this chapter.

**subordinated debenture**
A bond having a claim on assets only after the senior debt has been paid off in the event of liquidation.

*Subordinated Debentures.* The term *subordinate* means "below," or "inferior," and in the event of bankruptcy subordinated debt has claims on assets only after senior debt has been paid off. Debentures may be subordinated either to designated notes payable—usually bank loans—or to all other debt. In the event of liquidation or reorganization, holders of subordinated debentures cannot be paid until all senior debt, as named in the debentures' indenture, has been paid. Precisely how subordination works, and how it strengthens the position of senior debtholders, is explained in Appendix 12A.

**convertible bond**
A bond that is exchangeable at the option of the holder for common stock of the issuing firm.

**warrant**
A long-term option to buy a stated number of shares of common stock at a specified price.

*Other Types of Bonds.* Several other types of bonds are used sufficiently often to warrant mention. First, **convertible bonds** are securities that are convertible into shares of common stock, at a fixed price, at the option of the bondholder. Basically, convertibles provide investors with a chance for capital gains in exchange for a lower coupon rate, while the issuing firm gets the advantage of that lower rate. Bonds issued with **warrants** are similar to convertibles. Warrants are options which permit the holder to buy stock for a stated price, thereby providing a capital gain if the price of the stock rises. Bonds that are issued with warrants, like convertibles, carry lower coupon rates than straight bonds. Warrants and convertibles are discussed in detail in Chapter 13.

**income bond**
A bond that pays interest to the holder only if the interest is earned.

**Income bonds** pay interest only when the interest is earned. Thus, these securities cannot bankrupt a company, but from an investor's standpoint they are riskier than "regular" bonds.

**indexed (purchasing power) bond**
A bond that has interest payments based on an inflation index so as to protect the holder from inflation.

Yet another type of bond that has been discussed in the United States but not yet used here to any extent is the **indexed**, or **purchasing power**, **bond**, which is popular in Brazil, Israel, and a few other countries long plagued by high rates of inflation. The interest rate paid on these bonds is based on an inflation index such as the consumer price index and rises when the inflation rate rises, thus protecting the bondholders against inflation. In a similar vein, Mexico has used bonds whose interest rate is pegged to the price of oil to finance the development of its huge petroleum reserves; since oil prices and inflation are correlated, these bonds also protect investors against inflation. At the same time, Mexico's ability to pay interest depends on the price of oil, so it too is protected by this indexing scheme. The British government has issued an indexed bond whose interest rate is set equal to the British inflation rate plus 3 percent. Thus, these bonds provide a "real rate" of 3 percent.

## Specific Debt Contract Features

A firm's managers are vitally concerned about (1) the effective cost of debt and (2) any restrictions or provisions which might limit the firm's future alternatives. In this section, we discuss features which could affect either the cost of the firm's debt or its future flexibility.

## Bond Indentures

**indenture**
A formal agreement between the issuer of a bond and the bondholders.

An **indenture** is a legal document that spells out the rights of both the bondholders and the issuing corporation; a **trustee** is an official (usually a bank officer) who represents the bondholders and makes sure that the terms of the indenture are carried out. The indenture may be several hundred pages in length, and it will include **restrictive covenants** that cover such points as the conditions under which the issuer can pay off the bonds prior to maturity, the level at which the issuer's times-interest-earned ratio must be maintained if the company is to sell additional bonds, and restrictions against the payment of dividends when earnings do not meet certain specifications. Overall, these covenants relate to the agency problem discussed in Chapter 1, and they are designed to insure, insofar as possible, that the firm does nothing to cause the quality of its bonds to deteriorate after they are issued.

**trustee**
An official who ensures that the bondholders' interests are protected and that the terms of the indenture are carried out.

**restrictive covenant**
A provision in debt contracts that constrains the actions of the borrower.

The trustee is responsible for making sure the covenants are not violated and for taking appropriate action if they are. What constitutes "appropriate action" varies with the circumstances. It might be that to insist on immediate compliance would result in bankruptcy, which in turn might lead to large losses on the bonds. In such a case, the trustee might decide that the bondholders would be better served by giving the company a chance to work out its problems rather than forcing it into bankruptcy.

The Securities and Exchange Commission (1) approves indentures and (2) makes sure that all indenture provisions are met before allowing a company to sell new securities to the public. Also, it should be noted that the indentures of most larger corporations were actually written back in the 1930s or 1940s and that many issues of new bonds, all covered by the same indenture, have been sold down through the years. The interest rates on the bonds, and perhaps also the maturities, will change from issue to issue, but bondholders' protection as spelled out in the indenture will be the same for all bonds of a given type.[4]

## Call Provisions

**call provision**
A provision in a bond contract that gives the issuer the right to redeem the bonds under specified terms prior to the normal maturity date.

Most bonds contain a **call provision** which gives the issuing corporation the right to call the bonds for redemption. The call provision generally states that the company must pay the bondholder an amount greater than the par value for the bond when the bond is called. The additional sum, which is defined as a *call premium*, is typically set equal to one year's interest if the bond is called during the first year; the premium declines at a constant rate of $I/n$ each year thereafter, where $I$ = Annual interest and $n$ = Original maturity in years. For example, the call premium on a $1,000 par value, 10-year, 10 percent bond would generally be $100 if it were called during the first year, $90 during the second year (calculated by reducing the $100, or 10 percent, premium by one-tenth), and so on.

Suppose a company sold bonds or preferred stock when interest rates were relatively high. Provided the issue is callable, the company could sell a new

---

[4]A firm will have different indentures for each of the major types of bonds it issues, including its first mortgage bonds, its debentures, and so on.

issue of low-yielding securities if and when interest rates drop. It could then use the proceeds to retire the high-rate issue and thus reduce its interest or preferred dividend expenses. This is called a *refunding operation*. Refunding operations are discussed in detail in Appendix 12B.

The call privilege is valuable to the firm but potentially detrimental to the investor, especially if the bond is issued in a period when interest rates are cyclically high. Accordingly, the interest rate on a new issue of callable bonds will exceed that on a new issue of noncallable bonds. For example, on February 1, 1985, Great Falls Timber Company sold a bond issue yielding 13.375 percent; these bonds were callable immediately. On the same day, Midwest Milling Company sold an issue of similar risk and maturity which yielded 13.0 percent; its bonds were noncallable for 10 years. (This is known as a *deferred call*.) Investors were apparently willing to accept a 0.375 percent lower interest rate on Midwest's bonds for the assurance that the relatively high (by historic standards) rate of interest would be earned for at least 10 years. Great Falls, on the other hand, had to incur a 0.375 percent higher annual interest rate to obtain the option of calling the bonds in the event of a subsequent decline in interest rates.

## Sinking Funds

**sinking fund**
A required annual payment designed to amortize a bond or preferred stock issue.

A **sinking fund** is a provision that facilitates the orderly retirement of a bond issue (or, in some cases, an issue of preferred stock). Typically, the sinking fund provision requires the firm to retire a portion of the bond issue each year. On rare occasions the firm may be required to deposit money with a trustee, who invests the funds and then uses the accumulated sum to retire the bonds when they mature. A failure to meet the sinking fund requirement causes the bond issue to be thrown into default, which may force the company into bankruptcy. Obviously, then, a sinking fund can constitute a dangerous cash drain on the firm.

In most cases, the firm is given the right to handle the sinking fund in either of two ways:

**1.** It may call in for redemption (at par value) a certain percentage of the bonds each year—for example, it might be able to call 2 percent of the total original amount of the issue at a price of $1,000 per bond. The bonds are numbered serially, and those called for redemption are determined by a lottery.

**2.** It may buy the required amount of bonds on the open market. Since the firm will choose the least-cost method, if interest rates have risen, causing bond prices to fall, it will elect to use the option of buying bonds in the open market at a discount; otherwise, it will call them. Note that a call for sinking fund purposes is quite different from a refunding call as discussed above. A sinking fund call requires no call premium; however, only a small percentage of the issue is normally callable in any one year.

Although sinking funds are designed to protect bondholders by insuring that an issue is retired in an orderly fashion, it must be recognized that they will at times work to the detriment of bondholders. For example, if the bond carries a 15 percent interest rate and if yields on similar bonds have fallen to

10 percent, then the bond will sell above par. A sinking fund call at par would thus greatly disadvantage those bondholders whose bonds were called. On balance, however, securities that provide for a sinking fund and continuing redemption are regarded as being safer than those without such provisions, so at the time they are issued they have lower coupon rates than otherwise similar bonds without sinking funds.

## Recent Innovations

### Zero (or Very Low) Coupon Bonds

**zero coupon bond**
A bond that pays no annual interest but sells at a discount below par, therefore providing compensation to investors in the form of capital appreciation.

Some bonds pay no interest but are offered at a substantial discount below their par values and hence provide capital appreciation rather than interest income. These securities are called **zero coupon bonds** ("*zeros*"), or *original issue discount bonds*. Zeros were first used in a major way in 1981. In recent years IBM, Alcoa, J. C. Penney, ITT, Cities Service, GMAC, Martin-Marietta, and many other companies have used them to raise billions of dollars. Moreover, investment bankers have in effect created zero coupon Treasury bonds. To understand what zeros are, consider Penney's $200 million par value issue of bonds which have no coupons and which pay no annual interest. These zero coupon bonds were sold in 1981 and mature after 8 years, in 1989, at which time holders will be paid $1,000. The bonds were sold at a discount below par, for $332.41 per $1,000 bond. The compound interest rate which causes $332.41 to grow to $1,000 over 8 years is 14.76 percent. Penney received $66.482 million less underwriting expenses for the issue, but it will have to pay back $200 million in 1989.

The advantages of the zeros to Penney include the following: (1) no cash outlays are required for either interest or principal until the bonds mature; (2) the bonds have a relatively low yield to maturity (Penney would have had to pay over 15.25 percent versus 14.76 percent had it issued regular coupon bonds at par); and (3) Penney receives an annual tax deduction equal to the yearly amortization of the discount, which means that the bonds provide a positive cash flow in the form of tax savings over their life. There are also two disadvantages to Penney: (1) the bonds are simply not callable, because they would have to be called at their $1,000 par value, and, since it is better to pay the $1,000 in 1989 than at some earlier date, in effect, Penney cannot refund the issue if interest rates should fall; and (2) Penney will have a very large nondeductible cash outlay coming up in 1989.

There are two principal advantages to investors in zero coupon bonds: (1) they have no danger whatever of a call, and (2) they are guaranteed a "true" yield (14.76 percent in the Penney case) irrespective of what happens to interest rates—the holders of Penney's bonds do not have to worry about having to reinvest coupon payments at low rates if interest rates should fall, which would result in a "true" yield to maturity of less than 14.76 percent. This second feature is extremely important to pension funds, life insurance companies, and other institutions which make actuarial contracts based on assumed reinvestment rates. For such investors, the risk of declining interest rates, and hence an inability to reinvest cash inflows at the assumed rate, is greater than the risk of an increase in rates and the accompanying fall in bond values. To illustrate, suppose an insurance company or pension plan signed a contract to pay $100,000 in 8 years in exchange for a lump sum premium of $33,241 today. The premium was based on the assumption that the company could invest the $33,241 at a return of 14.76 percent. If the $33,241 were invested in regular coupon bonds paying a 14.76 percent annual coupon rate, then the accumulated value 8 years hence would be equal to the required $100,000 only if all coupon payments could be reinvested at 14.76 percent over the next 8 years. If interest rates were to fall, then the accumulated amount would fall short of the required $100,000. Note, however, that if the $33,241 were invested in a zero coupon bond with a 14.76 percent yield, the insurance company would end up with the required $100,000 irrespective of what happened to interest rates in the future. Thus, the insurance company (or pension fund) would have been "immunized" against a decline in interest rates.

To analyze a zero coupon bond and compare it with a regular coupon bond, a corporate treasurer (or pension fund administrator) must employ the valuation models developed in Chapter 5. Consider again Penney's bonds. Penney will receive $332.41 per bond at t = 0. Also, it will have a tax deduction each year equal to the $83.45 amortization of the discount: ($1,000 − $332.41)/8 = $83.45.[5] This deduction will save taxes each year in the amount of T(Deduction) = 0.46($83.45) = $38.39 per bond. Penney will have to make a payment of $1,000 at t = 8. Thus, the after-tax cash flow time line is as follows:

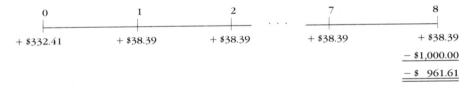

The discount rate which solves the equation below is Penney's after-tax cost of debt capital from the zero coupon bond, $k_d$:

$$\sum_{t=0}^{n} \frac{C_t}{(1 + k_d)^t} = 0$$

$$\frac{C_0}{(1 + k_d)^0} + \frac{C_1}{(1 + k_d)^1} + \cdots + \frac{C_n}{(1 + k_d)^n} = 0$$

$$\frac{\$332.41}{(1 + k_d)^0} + \frac{\$38.39}{(1 + k_d)^1} + \cdots + \frac{\$38.39}{(1 + k_d)^7} - \frac{\$961.61}{(1 + k_d)^8} = 0.$$

---

[5]Although we use straight line amortization in our example, the Tax Code requires the use of an amortization procedure which produces lower early-year deductions and hence a slightly higher effective cost to the company. Also, since most bonds pay interest on a semiannual basis, people often analyze zeros on a semiannual compounding basis to make the calculated yields comparable to those on regular coupon bonds. We did the analysis on an annual basis for simplicity.

The solution value for $k_d$ is 7.6 percent; this is Penney's after-tax cost of zero coupon debt.[6]

If Penney had sold an annual payment coupon bond, it would have had to pay about 15.25 percent. Its after-tax interest payments would have been (Coupon)$(1 - T)$ = ($152.50)(0.54) = $82.35, and its after-tax cost of debt would have been $k_d$ in this equation:

$$\frac{\$1,000}{(1 + k_d)^0} - \frac{\$82.35}{(1 + k_d)^1} - \cdots - \frac{\$82.35}{(1 + k_d)^7} - \frac{\$1,082.35}{(1 + k_d)^8} = 0.$$

The solution value is $k_d$ = 8.235 percent, so on an after-tax basis, the zero coupon bond will have had a lower cost to Penney than a regular coupon bond—7.6 percent versus 8.235 percent. For a purchaser, of course, the reverse is true: A tax-exempt bond buyer would receive the yield to maturity, which is 14.76 percent for the zero coupon bond and 15.25 percent for the regular coupon bond. Purchasers apparently believed that call protection plus interest rate immunization were worth the 0.49 percentage point cost.

Shortly after corporations began to issue zeros, investment bankers figured out a way to create zeros out of U.S. Treasury bonds, which are issued only in coupon form. In 1982 Salomon Brothers bought $1 billion of 12 percent, 30-year Treasuries. Each bond had 60 coupons worth $60 each, which represented the interest payments due every 6 months. Salomon then in effect clipped the coupons and placed them in 60 piles; the last pile also contained the now "stripped" bond itself, which represented a promise of $1,000 in the year 2012. These 60 piles of U.S. Treasury promises were then placed with the trust department of a bank and used as collateral for "zero coupon U.S. Treasury Trust Certificates," which are in essence zero coupon Treasury bonds. A pension fund that expected to need money in 1993 could buy 11-year certificates backed by the interest the Treasury will pay in 1993. Treasury zeros are, of course, safer than corporate zeros, so they are very popular with pension fund managers.

## Floating Rate Debt

In the early 1980s, inflation pushed interest rates up to unprecedented levels, causing sharp declines in the prices of long-term bonds. Even some supposedly "risk-free" U.S. Treasury bonds lost fully half their value, and a similar situation occurred with corporate bonds, mortgages, and other fixed rate, long-term securities. The lenders who held the fixed rate debt were of course hurt very badly. Bankruptcies (or forced mergers to avoid bankruptcy) were commonplace in the banking and especially the savings and loan industries. Insurance company reserves also plummeted, causing those companies severe problems, including the bankruptcy of Baldwin-United, a $9 billion diversified insurance firm. As a result, many lenders became reluctant to lend

---

[6]Since interest is a deductible expense, the government in effect pays a portion of the interest on a bond. This point is discussed in detail in Chapter 14, where we will see that the after-tax cost of debt is equal to the pre-tax cost times $(1 - \text{Tax rate})$.

money at fixed rates on a long-term basis, and they would do so only at high rates.

There is normally a *maturity risk premium* embodied in long-term interest rates—this is a risk premium designed to offset the risk of declining bond prices if interest rates rise. Prior to the 1970s, this maturity risk premium on 30-year bonds was about one percentage point, meaning that under "normal" conditions a firm might expect to pay about one percentage point more to borrow on a long-term than on a short-term basis. However, in the early 1980s, the maturity risk premium is estimated to have jumped to about three percentage points, which made long-term debt very expensive relative to short-term debt. Lenders were able and willing to lend on a short-term basis, but corporations were rightly reluctant to borrow short-term to finance long-term assets—such action is, as we shall see in Chapter 17, extremely dangerous. Therefore, we had a situation in which lenders did not want to lend on a long-term basis but corporations needed long-term money. The problem was solved by the introduction of *long-term, floating rate debt*.

**floating rate bond**
A bond whose interest rate fluctuates with shifts in the general level of interest rates.

A typical **floating rate bond** works as follows. The coupon rate is set for, say, the initial six-month period, after which it is adjusted every six months based on some market rate. For example, Gulf Oil sold a floating rate bond that was pegged at 35 basis points above the going rate on 30-year Treasury bonds. Other companies' issues have been tied to short-term rates. Many additional provisions have been included in floating rate issues; for example, some are convertible to fixed rate debt, while others have a stated minimum coupon rate and also a cap on how high the rate can go.

Floating rate debt is advantageous to lenders because the interest rate moves up if market rates rise, which ( 1 ) causes the market value of the debt to be stabilized and ( 2 ) provides lenders such as banks with more income to meet their own obligations (for example, a bank which owns floating rate bonds can use the interest it earns to pay interest on its own deposits ). Moreover, floating rate debt is advantageous to corporations because by using it they can obtain debt with a long maturity without committing themselves to paying an historically high rate of interest for the entire term of the loan. Of course, if interest rates increase after a floating rate note has been signed, then the borrower would have been better off issuing conventional, fixed rate debt.[7]

## "Junk Bond"

**junk bond**
A high-risk, high-yield bond used to finance mergers, leveraged buyouts, and troubled companies.

Another new type of bond is the **junk bond**, a high-risk, high-yield bond either issued to finance a leveraged buyout or a merger, or issued by a troubled company. For example, when Ted Turner attempted to buy CBS, he planned to finance the acquisition by issuing junk bonds to CBS's stockholders in exchange for their shares. Similarly, Merrill Lynch has helped Public

---

[7]For a general discussion of floating rate debt, see Kenneth R. Marks and Warren A. Law, "Hedging against Inflation with Floating-Rate Notes," *Harvard Business Review*, March-April 1980, 106-112.

Service of New Hampshire finance construction of its troubled Seabrook nuclear plant with junk bonds. In all junk bond deals, the debt ratio is extremely high, so the bondholders must bear as much risk as stockholders normally would. The bonds' yields reflect this fact—Ted Turner's bonds would have carried a coupon rate of about 16 percent, and Merrill Lynch has reported that it will have to set a coupon rate in the 25 to 30 percent range to sell the Public Service of New Hampshire bonds.

The emergence of junk bonds as an important type of debt is another example of how the investment banking industry adjusts to—and facilitates—new developments in capital markets. In the 1980s, mergers and takeovers increased dramatically. People like T. Boone Pickens and Ted Turner thought that certain old-line, established companies were run inefficiently and financed too conservatively, and they wanted to take these companies over and restructure them. To help finance these takeovers, the investment banking firm of Drexel Burnham Lambert began an active campaign to persuade certain institutions to purchase high-yield bonds. Drexel developed expertise in putting together deals that would be attractive to the institutions yet feasible in the sense that cash flows were sufficient to meet the required interest payments. The fact that interest on the bonds is tax deductible, combined with the much higher debt ratios of the restructured firms, also increased after-tax cash flows and helped make the whole deal feasible.

The development of junk bond financing has done as much as any single factor to reshape the U.S. financial scene. It has led directly to the loss of Gulf Oil and hundreds of other companies as independent entities, and it has led to major shake-ups in such companies as CBS. It also caused Drexel Burnham Lambert to leap from essentially nowhere in the 1970s to become the number two investment banking firm in 1985.

## Bond Ratings

Since the early 1900s, bonds have been assigned quality ratings that reflect their probability of going into default. The two major rating agencies are Moody's Investors Service (Moody's) and Standard & Poor's Corporation (S&P). These agencies' rating designations are shown in Table 12-1.[8] The triple and double A bonds are extremely safe. Single A and triple B bonds are strong enough to be called *investment grade*, and they are the lowest-rated bonds that many banks and other institutional investors are permitted by law to hold. Double B and lower bonds are speculations; they have a significant probability of going into default, and many financial institutions are prohibited from buying them.

---

[8]In the discussion to follow, reference to the S&P code is intended to imply the Moody code as well. Thus, for example, triple B bonds mean both BBB and Baa bonds; double B bonds, both BB and Ba bonds; and so on.

**Table 12-1**
**Comparison of Bond Ratings**

| | High Quality | | Investment Grade | | Substandard | | Speculative | |
|---|---|---|---|---|---|---|---|---|
| Moody's | Aaa | Aa | A | Baa | Ba | B | Caa | C |
| S&P | AAA | AA | A | BBB | BB | B | CCC | D |

Note: Both Moody's and S&P use "modifiers" for bonds rated below triple A. S&P uses a plus and minus system; thus, A+ designates the strongest A-rated bonds and A− the weakest. Moody's uses a 1, 2, or 3 designation, with 1 denoting the strongest and 3 the weakest; thus, within the double A category, Aa1 is the best, Aa2 is average, and Aa3 is the weakest.

## Bond Rating Criteria

Although the rating assignments are judgmental, they are based on both qualitative and quantitative factors, some of which are listed below:

1. Debt ratio.

2. Times-interest-earned ratio.

3. Fixed charge coverage ratio.

4. Current ratio.

5. Mortgage provisions: Is the bond secured by a mortgage? If it is, and if the property has a high value in relation to the amount of bonded debt, the bond's rating is enhanced.

6. Subordination provisions: Is the bond subordinated to other debt? If so, it will be rated at least one notch below the rating it would have if it were not subordinated. Conversely, a bond with other debt subordinated to it will have a somewhat higher rating.

7. Guarantee provisions: Some bonds are guaranteed by other firms. If a weak company's debt is guaranteed by a strong company (usually the weak company's parent), then the bond will be given the strong company's rating.

8. Sinking fund: Does the bond have a sinking fund to insure systematic repayment? This feature is a plus factor to the rating agencies.

9. Maturity: Other things the same, a bond with a shorter maturity will be judged less risky than a longer-term bond, and this will be reflected in the ratings.

10. Stability: Are the issuer's sales and earnings stable?

11. Regulation: Is the issuer regulated, and could an adverse regulatory climate cause the company's economic position to decline? Regulation is especially important for utilities, railroads, and telephone companies.

12. Antitrust: Are any antitrust actions pending against the firm that could erode its position?

13. Overseas operations: What percentage of the firm's sales, assets, and profits are from overseas operations, and what is the political climate in the host countries?

**14.** Environmental factors: Is the firm likely to face heavy expenditures for pollution control equipment?

**15.** Pension liabilities: Does the firm have unfunded pension liabilities that could pose a future problem?

**16.** Labor unrest: Are there potential labor problems on the horizon that could weaken the firm's position? As this is written, the entire airline industry faces this problem, and it has caused ratings to be lowered.

**17.** Resource availability: Is the firm likely to face supply shortages that could force it to curtail operations?

**18.** Accounting policies: If a firm uses relatively conservative accounting policies, then its reported earnings will be of "higher quality" than if it uses less conservative procedures. Thus, conservative accounting policies are a plus factor in bond ratings.

Representatives of the rating agencies have consistently stated that no precise formula is used to set a firm's rating—all the factors listed, plus others, are taken into account, but not in a mathematically precise manner. Statistical studies have borne out this contention. Researchers who have tried to predict bond ratings on the basis of quantitative data have had only limited success, indicating that the agencies do indeed use a good deal of subjective judgment when establishing a firm's rating.[9]

### Importance of Bond Ratings

Bond ratings are important both to firms and to investors. First, a bond's rating is an indicator of its default risk; hence, the rating has a direct, measurable influence on the bond's interest rate and the firm's cost of debt capital. Second, most bonds are purchased by institutional investors rather than individuals, and many institutions are restricted to investment-grade securities. Thus, if a firm's bonds fall below BBB, it will have a difficult time trying to sell new bonds, since many of the potential purchasers will not be allowed to buy them.

Ratings also have an effect on the availability of debt capital. If an institutional investor buys BBB bonds and these bonds are subsequently downgraded to BB or lower, then (1) the institution's regulators will reprimand or perhaps impose restrictions on it if it continues to hold the bonds, but (2) since many other institutional investors will not be able to purchase them, the institution that owns them will probably not be able to sell them except at a sizable loss. Because of this fear of downgrading, many institutions restrict their bond portfolios to at least A, or even AA, and some even confine purchases to AAA bonds. Thus, the lower a firm's rating, the smaller the group of available purchasers for its new issues.

As a result of their higher risk and more restricted market, lower-grade bonds have higher required rates of return, $k_d$, than high-grade bonds. Figure 12-1 illustrates this point. In each of the years shown on the graph, U.S. gov-

---

[9]See Ahmed Belkaoui, *Industrial Bonds and the Rating Process* (London: Quorum Books, 1983).

**Figure 12-1**
**Yields on U.S. Government Bonds,**
**AAA Corporates, and BBB Corporates, 1953-1984**

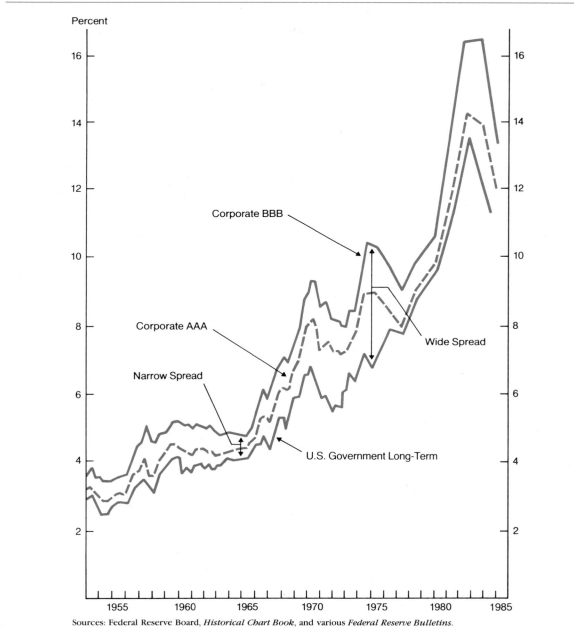

Sources: Federal Reserve Board, *Historical Chart Book*, and various *Federal Reserve Bulletins*.

**Figure 12-2**
**Relationship between Bond Ratings and Bond Yields, 1963, 1975, and 1985**

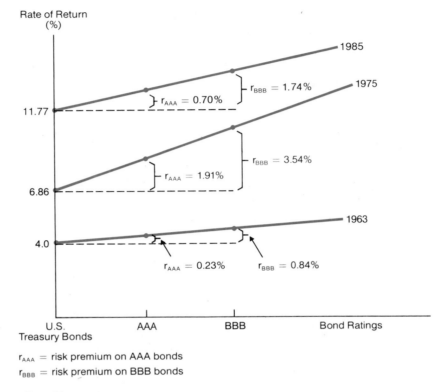

$r_{AAA}$ = risk premium on AAA bonds
$r_{BBB}$ = risk premium on BBB bonds

| | Long-Term Government Bonds (Default-Free) (1) | AAA Corporate Bonds (2) | BBB Corporate Bonds (3) | Risk Premiums | |
|---|---|---|---|---|---|
| | | | | AAA (4) = (2) − (1) | BBB (5) = (3) − (1) |
| June 1963 | 4.00% | 4.23% | 4.84% | 0.23% | 0.84% |
| June 1975 | 6.86 | 8.77 | 10.40 | 1.91 | 3.54 |
| March 1985 | 11.77 | 12.47 | 13.51 | 0.70 | 1.74 |

Sources: *Federal Reserve Bulletin*, December 1963, December 1975, and May 1985.

ernment bonds have had the lowest yields, AAAs have been next, and BBB bonds have had the highest yields of the three types. The figure also shows that the gaps between yields on the three types of bonds vary over time; in other words, the cost differentials, or risk premiums, fluctuate from year to year. This point is highlighted in Figure 12-2, which gives the yields on the three types of bonds and the risk premiums for AAA and BBB bonds in June

1963, June 1975, and March 1985.[10] Note first that the riskless rate, or vertical axis intercept, rose over 7 percentage points from 1963 to 1985, reflecting the increase in realized and anticipated inflation. Second, the slope of the line also has increased since 1963, indicating an increase in investors' risk aversion; this increase was quite pronounced from 1963 to 1975 but fell somewhat between 1975 and 1985. Thus, the penalty for having a low credit rating varies over time. Occasionally, as in 1963, it is quite small, but at other times, as in 1975, it is very large. These differences reflect investors' risk aversion—in 1975 we were emerging from a severe recession caused by a quadrupling of oil prices in 1973-1974, and investors were afraid the economy would slip back into a slump. At such times people seek safety in bonds, Treasuries are in great demand, and the premium on low-quality over high-quality bonds increases.

### Changes in Ratings

A change in a firm's bond rating will have a significant effect on its ability to borrow long-term capital and on the cost of that capital. Rating agencies review outstanding bonds on a periodic basis, occasionally upgrading or downgrading a bond as a result of its issuer's changed circumstances. For example, in the spring of 1985, when Mobil Oil announced that it was planning to spin off its Montgomery Ward unit (Mobil had acquired Montgomery Ward in a diversification move back in the early 1970s), S&P immediately placed Ward on its *CreditWatch* list. (*CreditWatch* is a weekly publication that discusses developing situations that may lead to upgradings or downgradings.) The statement made in *CreditWatch* was that without Mobil's backing, Montgomery Ward's credit position might deteriorate to the point where its first mortgage bonds would have to be lowered from BBB − to BB and its debentures from BB + to some lower rating. The final outcome will depend on Ward's condition when Mobil does spin it off. Similarly, when it was announced that Chevron would buy Gulf in 1984, borrowing much of the money for the purchase, Chevron was immediately placed on the *CreditWatch* list with negative implications, and its bonds were downgraded when it became clear that the deal was going through.

---

[10]The term *risk premium* ought to reflect only the difference in expected (and required) returns between two securities that results from differences in their risk. However, the differences between *yields to maturity* on different types of bonds consist of (1) a true risk premium; (2) a liquidity premium, which reflects the fact that U.S. Treasury bonds are more readily marketable than most corporate bonds; (3) a call premium, because most Treasury bonds are not callable while corporate bonds are; and (4) an expected loss differential, which reflects the probability of loss on the corporate bonds. As an example of the last point, suppose the yield to maturity on a BBB bond was 10 percent versus 7 percent on government bonds, but there was a 5 percent probability of total default loss on the corporate bond. In this case, the expected return on the BBB bond would be 0.95(10%) + 0.05(0%) = 9.5%, and the risk premium would be 2.5 percent and not the full 3.0 percentage point difference in "promised" yields to maturity. Therefore, the risk premiums given in Figure 12-2 overstate somewhat the true (but unmeasurable) risk premiums.

If a company announces a large new bond issue, a rating agency review will generally be triggered. If the firm's situation has recently deteriorated but its bonds have not been reviewed and downgraded, then it may choose to use a term loan or short-term debt rather than finance through a public bond issue. This will perhaps postpone a rating agency review until the situation has improved. For example, Midwest Utilities delayed a bond issue in 1984, financing with short-term debt until a rate increase could be obtained to raise interest coverage ratios to acceptable levels. After the rate increase was in effect and coverages improved, the company sold bonds and used the proceeds to retire the short-term debt.

## Rationale for Using Different Types of Securities

Why are there so many different types of long-term securities? At least a partial answer to this question may be seen from Figure 12-3, which depicts the now familiar risk/return trade-off function drawn to show the risk and the expected after-personal-tax returns for the various securities of the Montpelier Company.[11] First, U.S. Treasury bills, representing the risk-free rate, are shown for reference. The lowest-risk long-term securities offered by Montpelier are its floating rate notes; these securities are free of interest rate risk, but they are exposed to some risk of default. The first mortgage bonds are somewhat riskier than the notes, and they sell at a somewhat higher required and expected after-tax return. The second mortgage bonds are even riskier, and they have a still higher expected return. Subordinated debentures, income bonds, and preferred stocks are all increasingly risky, and their expected returns increase accordingly. The firm's convertible preferred is riskier than its straight preferred but less risky than its common stock. Montpelier's warrants, the riskiest security it issues, have the highest required return of any of its offerings. (Preferred stock, warrants, and convertibles are all discussed in Chapter 13.)

Why does Montpelier issue so many different classes of securities? Why does it not offer just one type of bond plus common stock? The answer lies in the fact that different investors have different risk/return trade-off preferences, so to appeal to the broadest possible market, Montpelier must offer securities that attract as many different types of investors as possible. Also, different securities are in demand at different points in time, so firms tend to sell whatever is popular at the time they need money. Used wisely, a policy of selling differentiated securities to take advantage of market conditions can lower a firm's overall cost of capital below what it would be if the firm issued only one class of debt plus common stock.

---

[11]The yields in Figure 12-3 are after taxes to the recipient. If yields were on a before-personal-tax basis, those on preferred stocks would lie below those on bonds because of the tax treatment of preferreds. In essence, 85 percent of preferred dividends are tax exempt to corporations owning preferred shares, so a preferred stock with a 10 percent pre-tax yield will have a higher after-tax return to a corporation in the 46 percent tax bracket than will a bond with a 12 percent yield. This point is discussed in Chapter 13.

**Figure 12-3**
**Montpelier Company: Risk and Expected Returns**
**on Different Classes of Securities**

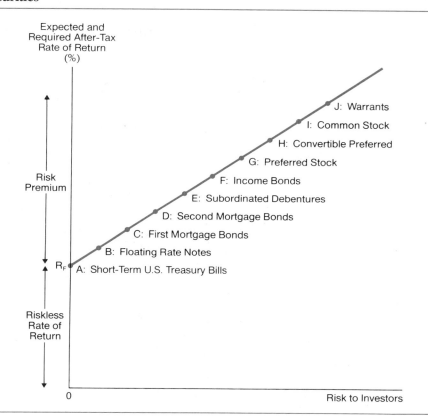

## Factors Influencing Long-Term Financing Decisions

As we show in this section, many factors influence a firm's long-term financing decisions. The factors' relative importance varies among firms at any point in time and for any given firm over time, but any company planning to raise new long-term capital should consider each of these points.

### Target Capital Structure

As we shall see in Chapter 15, firms typically establish target capital structures, or target debt/equity mixes. One of the most important considerations in any financing decision is how the firm's actual capital structure compares to its target structure. Of course, few firms in any one year finance exactly in accordance with their target capital structures, primarily because of flotation costs: Since smaller issues of new securities have proportionally larger flotation costs, firms tend to use debt one year and stock the next.

For example, Consolidated Tools, Inc., a Cincinnati machine tool manufacturer, requires $10 million of new external capital in each of the next two years. Its target capital structure calls for 40 percent debt, so if Consolidated were to raise debt each year, it would issue $4 million of new bonds each year. The flotation costs, based on data back in Table 11-4, would be 6.2 percent of each $4 million issue. To net $4 million, Consolidated would have to sell $4,000,000/0.938 = $4,264,392 each year and pay $264,392 in flotation costs on each issue for a total of $528,784 in flotation costs over the two years.

Alternatively, Consolidated could elect to raise the total $8 million of debt in one year. The flotation cost for an $8 million issue would be about 3.2 percent, so the firm would float an issue for $8,000,000/0.968 = $8,264,463 and pay $264,463 in total flotation costs. By issuing debt only once, Consolidated could cut its debt flotation costs almost in half. The same relationship would apply to sales of preferred stock and new common equity issues. Note that making fewer but larger security offerings would cause Consolidated's capital structure to fluctuate about its optimal level rather than stay right on target. However, as we shall see in Chapter 15, small fluctuations about the optimal capital structure have little effect either on a firm's required returns on debt and equity or on its overall cost of capital. Also, investors would recognize that its actions were prudent and that the firm would save substantial amounts of flotation costs by financing in this manner. Therefore, while firms such as Consolidated do tend to finance over the long haul in accordance with their target capital structures, flotation costs plus the other factors discussed in the following sections have a definite influence on the specific financing decisions in any given year.

## Maturity Matching

Assume that Consolidated decides to float a single $8 million nonconvertible bond issue with a sinking fund. It must next choose a maturity for the issue, taking into consideration the shape of the yield curve, management's own expectations about future interest rates, and the maturity of the assets being financed. In the case at hand, Consolidated's capital projects over the next two years consist primarily of new, automated milling and stamping machinery for its Cincinnati plant. This machinery has an expected economic life of 10 years (even though it falls into the ACRS 5-year class life). Should Consolidated finance the debt portion of this equipment with 5-year, 10-year, 20-year, or 30-year debt, or debt of some other maturity? *The typical approach is to match the maturity of the liabilities with the maturity of the assets being financed.*

Note that some of the new capital for the machinery will come from common stock, which is generally considered to be a perpetual security with an infinite maturity. Of course, common stock can always be repurchased on the open market or by a tender offer, so its effective maturity can be reduced significantly.

On the other hand, debt maturities are specified at the time of issue. If Consolidated financed its capital budgets over the next two years with 10-

year sinking fund bonds, it would be matching asset and liability maturities. Since the cash flows resulting from the new machinery could be used to make the interest and sinking fund payments on the issue, the bonds would be retired as the machinery wore out. If Consolidated had used 1-year debt, it would have to pay off the loan with cash flows derived from assets other than the machinery in question. Of course, it could probably roll over the 1-year debt. However, if it did so and interest rates rose, it would then have to pay a higher rate. If Consolidated subsequently experienced difficulties, lenders would be hesitant to extend the loan, and the company might be unable to obtain new short-term debt at any reasonable rate. Conversely, if it used 20-year or 30-year debt, Consolidated would still be servicing the debt long after the assets that were purchased with it had been scrapped and had ceased providing cash flows; this would worry the lenders.

For all these reasons, the best financing strategy, in general, is to match debt maturities with asset maturities. In recognition of this fact, firms do consider maturity relationships, and this factor often determines the debt portion of the financing decision.

## Interest Rate Levels

Financial managers also consider interest rate levels, both absolute and relative, when making financing decisions. For example, long-term interest rates were high by historic standards in 1981 and 1982, so many managers were reluctant to issue long-term debt and thus lock in those costs for long periods. We already know that one solution to this problem is to use long-term debt with a call provision. Callability permits refunding of the issue should interest rates drop, but there is a cost, because firms must pay more for callable debt. Alternatively, firms may finance with short-term debt whenever long-term rates are historically high and then, assuming that interest rates subsequently fall, sell a long-term issue to replace the short-term debt. Of course, this strategy has its risks. If interest rates move even higher, firms will be forced to renew the debt at higher and higher short-term rates or to replace the short-term debt with a long-term bond which will now cost even more than it would have when the original decision was made.

## Interest Rate Forecasts

In early September of 1983, the interest rate on AAA corporate bonds was about 12.5 percent, up from 11.5 percent in April. Exxon's investment bankers advised the company to tap the Eurodollar bond market for relatively cheap fixed rate financing.[12] At the time, Exxon could have issued its bonds in London at 0.4 percentage points *below* comparable-maturity Treasury bonds. However, one of Exxon's officers was quoted as saying, "I say so what. The absolute level of rates is too high. Our people would rather wait." The managers of Exxon, as well as those of many other companies, were betting

---

[12]A *Eurodollar bond* is a bond sold outside of the United States but denominated in U.S. dollars. See Chapter 20 for a further discussion.

that the next move in interest rates would be down. This belief was also openly expressed by executives of ITT, Ontario Hydro, and RCA, among others.

The above example confirms that many firms base their financing decisions on expectations about future interest rates. In Exxon's case, the financial staff was correct. However, the success of such a strategy requires that interest rate forecasts be right more often than they are wrong—and it is very difficult to find someone with a long-term forecasting track record better than 50-50.

### The Firm's Current and Forecasted Condition

Earlier in the chapter, we discussed bond ratings and the effects of changes in ratings on the cost and availability of capital. If a firm's current financial condition is poor, its managers may be reluctant to issue new long-term debt because ( 1 ) a new bond issue would probably trigger a review by the rating agencies, and ( 2 ) long-term debt issued when a firm is in poor financial condition would probably cost more and have more severe restrictive covenants than debt issued from strength. Thus, a firm that is in a weakened condition but is forecasting a better time in the future would be inclined to delay permanent financing of any type until things improved. Conversely, a firm that is strong now but whose forecasts indicate a potentially bad time in the period just ahead would be motivated to finance long-term now rather than to wait. These scenarios imply that the capital markets are inefficient in the sense that investors do not have as much information about the firm's future as does its financial manager. This situation is undoubtedly true at times.

The firm's earnings outlook, and the extent to which forecasted higher earnings per share are reflected in stock prices, also has an effect on the choice of securities. If a successful R&D program has just been concluded and management forecasts higher earnings than do most investors, then the firm would not want to issue common stock. It would use debt and then, once earnings have risen and pushed up the stock price, sell common stock to restore the capital structure to its target level.[13]

### Restrictions in Existing Debt Contracts

Earlier we discussed the fact that Savannah Electric has at times been restricted from issuing new first mortgage bonds by its indenture coverage requirements. This is just one example of how indenture covenants can influence a firm's financing decision. Restrictions on the current ratio, the debt/equity ratio, and so on, could also restrict a firm's ability to use different types of financing at a given time.

---

[13]Many of the factors discussed in this section imply an ability on the part of managers to forecast capital market conditions. While managers can probably forecast their own firms' internal conditions better than outside investors, no one can consistently forecast interest rates and the general level of stock prices. A manager can minimize the adverse effects of changes in capital costs through transactions in the *futures market*. For a discussion of the futures market, see Eugene F. Brigham and Louis C. Gapenski, *Intermediate Financial Management*, Chapter 15.

## Availability of Collateral

Generally, secured debt will be less costly than unsecured debt. Thus, firms with large amounts of unencumbered fixed assets having a ready resale value are likely to use a relatively large amount of debt, especially mortgage bonds. Additionally, each year's financing decision would be influenced by the amount of new qualified assets that are available as security for new bonds.

## Summary

This chapter has described the characteristics, advantages, and disadvantages of the major types of long-term debt securities. The key difference between *bonds* and *term loans* is the fact that term loans are sold directly by a corporate borrower to between 1 and 20 lenders while bonds are generally sold to many public investors through investment bankers.

It is impossible to state as a generalization that long-term debt is the "best" method of financing at a particular time. Each type of security has advantages and disadvantages vis-à-vis the others, and the relative advantages of long-term debt vary over time and from company to company. There are many factors that influence a firm's long-term financing decisions, including (1) its target capital structure, (2) maturity matching, (3) current interest rate levels, (4) forecasts of future interest rates, (5) the firm's current and forecasted condition, (6) restrictive covenants, and (7) the availability of collateral.

Two related issues are discussed in Appendices 12A and 12B: bankruptcy and bond refundings. Bankruptcy is an important consideration both to companies that issue debt and to investors, for the sequence of events which occur if a firm is unable to meet scheduled interest and maturity payments on debt has a profound effect on all parties. Refunding, or paying off high interest rate debt with new, lower rate debt, is also an important consideration, especially today (1985), for many firms that previously issued long-term debt at rates of 18 percent or more have an opportunity to refund this debt at a cost of 12 percent or less.

## Questions

12-1    Define each of the following terms:
   a. Funded debt
   b. Term loan; bond
   c. Mortgage bond
   d. Debenture; subordinated debenture
   e. Convertible bond; warrant; income bond; indexed, or purchasing power, bond
   f. Indenture; restrictive covenant
   g. Trustee
   h. Call provision; sinking fund
   i. Zero coupon bond
   j. Floating rate bond
   k. "Junk bond"
   l. Bond rating; rating agency
   m. Maturity matching

12-2    What effect would each of the following items have on the interest rate a firm must pay on a new issue of long-term debt? Indicate whether each factor would tend to raise, lower, or have an indeterminate effect on the interest rate, and then explain *why*.

a. The firm uses bonds rather than a term loan.

b. The firm uses nonsubordinated debentures rather than first mortgage bonds.

c. The firm makes its bonds convertible into common stock.

d. The firm makes its debentures subordinate to its bank debt. What will the effect be

    1. On the cost of the debentures?

    2. On the cost of the bank debt?

    3. On the average cost of total debt?

e. The firm sells income bonds rather than debentures.

f. The firm must raise $100 million, all of which will be used to construct a new plant, and is debating the sale of first mortgage bonds or debentures. If it decides to issue $50 million of each type, as opposed to $75 million of first mortgage bonds and $25 million of debentures, how will this affect

    1. The cost of debentures?

    2. The cost of mortgage bonds?

    3. The average cost of the $100 million?

g. The firm puts a call provision on its new issue of bonds.

h. The firm includes a sinking fund on its new issue of bonds.

i. The firm's bonds are downgraded from A to BBB.

12-3    Rank the following securities from lowest (1) to highest (9) in terms of their riskiness for an investor. All securities (except the government bond) are for a given firm. If you think two or more securities are equally risky, indicate so.

a. Income bond _____

b. Subordinated debentures—noncallable _____

c. First mortgage bond—no sinking fund _____

d. Common stock _____

e. U.S. Treasury bond _____

f. First mortgage bond—with sinking fund _____

g. Subordinated debentures—callable _____

h. Amortized term loan _____

i. Nonamortized term loan _____

12-4    A sinking fund can be set up in one of two ways:

1. The corporation makes annual payments to the trustee, who invests the proceeds in securities (frequently government bonds) and uses the accumulated total to retire the bond issue at maturity.

2. The trustee uses the annual payments to retire a portion of the issue each year, either calling a given percentage of the issue by a lottery and paying a specified price per bond or buying bonds on the open market, whichever is cheaper.

Discuss the advantages and disadvantages of each procedure from the viewpoint of both the firm and the bondholders.

12-5    Draw an SML graph. Put dots on the graph to show (approximately) where you think a particular company's (a) common stock and (b) bonds would lie. Now put on dots to represent a riskier company's stock and bonds.

## Self-Test Problem (*Solution on Page 403*)

**ST-1**   The Montreal Development Company has just issued a $100 million, 10-year, 8 percent bond. A sinking fund will retire the issue over its life. Sinking fund payments are of equal amounts and will be made *semiannually*, and the proceeds will be used to retire bonds as the payments are made. Bonds can be called at par for sinking fund purposes, or the funds paid into the sinking fund can be used to buy bonds in the open market.

a. How large must each semiannual sinking fund payment be?

b. What will happen, under the conditions of the problem thus far, to the company's debt service requirements per year for this issue over time?

c. Now suppose Montreal Development had set its sinking fund so that *equal annual amounts*, payable at the end of each year, were paid into a sinking fund trust held by a bank, with the proceeds being used to buy government bonds that pay 6 percent interest. The payments, plus accumulated interest, must total $100 million at the end of 10 years, and the proceeds will be used to retire the bonds at that time. How large must the annual sinking fund payment now be?

d. What are the annual cash requirements for covering bond service costs under the trusteeship arrangement described in Part c? (Note: Interest must be paid on Montreal's outstanding bonds but not on bonds that have been retired.)

e. What would have to happen to interest rates to cause the company to buy bonds on the open market rather than call them under the original sinking fund plan?

## Problems

Loan amortization

**12-1**   Suppose a firm is setting up an amortized term loan. What are the annual payments for a $2 million loan under the following terms:

a. 8 percent, 5 years?

b. 8 percent, 10 years?

c. 10 percent, 5 years?

d. 10 percent, 10 years?

Amortization schedule

**12-2**   Set up an amortization schedule for a $1 million, 3-year, 9-percent loan.

Yield to call

**12-3**   Three years ago a firm issued some 18-year bonds with a 13 percent coupon rate and a 10 percent call premium. Today the firm called the bonds. The bonds originally were sold at their face value of $1,000. Compute the realized rate of return for investors who purchased the bonds when they were issued and will surrender them today in exchange for the call price.

Perpetual bond analysis

**12-4**   In 1936 the Canadian government raised $55 million by issuing bonds at a 3 percent annual rate of interest. Unlike most bonds issued today, which have a specific maturity date, these bonds can remain outstanding forever; they are, in fact, perpetuities.

At the time of issue, the Canadian government stated in the bond indenture that cash redemption was *possible* at face value ($100) on or after September 1966; in other words, the bonds were callable at par after September 1966. Believing that the bonds would in fact be called, many investors purchased these bonds in 1965 with expectations of receiving $100 in 1966 for each perpetual they had. In 1965 the bonds sold for $55, but a rush of buyers drove the price to just below the $100 par value by 1966. Prices fell dramatically, however, when the Canadian government announced that these perpetual bonds were indeed perpetual and would not be paid off. A new, 30-year supply of coupons was sent to each bondholder.

The bonds' market price declined to $42 in December 1965. Because of their severe losses, hundreds of Canadian bondholders formed the Perpetual Bond Association to lobby for face value redemption of the bonds, claiming that the government had reneged on an implied promise to redeem the bonds. Government officials in Ottawa insisted that claims for face value payment were nonsense, for the bonds were and always had been clearly identified as perpetuals. One Ottawa official stated, "Our job is to protect the taxpayer. Why should we pay $55 million for less than $25 million worth of bonds?"

The issue heats up again every few years, and it recently resurfaced once more. Here are some questions relating to the Canadian issue that will test your understanding of bonds in general:

a. Would it make sense for a business firm to issue bonds such as the Canadian bonds described above? Would it matter whether the firm were a proprietorship or a corporation?

b. Suppose the U.S. government today sold $100 million each of these four types of bonds: 5-year bonds, 50-year bonds, "regular" perpetuities, and Canadian-type perpetuities. What do you think the relative order of interest rates would be? In other words, rank the bonds from the one with the lowest to the one with the highest rate of interest. Explain your answer.

c. 1. Suppose that because of pressure by the Perpetual Bond Association you believe that the Canadian government will redeem this particular perpetual bond issue in 5 years. Which course of action would be more advantageous to you if you owned the bonds—(a) to sell your bonds today at $42 or (b) to wait 5 years and have them redeemed? Assume that similar-risk bonds earn 8 percent today and that interest rates are expected to remain at this level for the next 5 years.

  2. If you had the opportunity to invest your money in bonds of similar risk, at what rate of return would you be indifferent to the choice of selling your perpetuals today or having them redeemed in 5 years—that is, what is the expected yield to maturity on the Canadian bonds?

d. Show mathematically the perpetuities' value if they yield 7.15 percent, pay $3 interest annually, and are considered "regular" perpetuities. Show what would happen to the price of bonds if the going interest rate fell to 2 percent.

e. Are the Canadian bonds more likely to be valued as "regular" perpetuities if the going rate of interest is above or below 3 percent? Why?

f. Do you think the Canadian government would have taken the same action with regard to retiring the bonds if the interest rate had fallen rather than risen after they were issued?

g. Do you think the Canadian government was "fair" or "unfair" in its actions? Give the pros and cons, and justify your reason for thinking that one outweighs the other. Would it matter if the bonds had been sold to "sophisticated" as opposed to "naive" purchasers?

Zero coupon bond    **12-5**    Suppose Midland Insurance Company needed to raise $400 million and its investment bankers indicated that 10-year zero coupon bonds could be sold at a YTM of 15 percent while a 16 percent yield would be required on *annual* payment coupon bonds sold at par. Midland's tax rate is 46 percent. (Assume that the discount can be amortized by the issuer using the straight line method. Although this cannot be done under current tax laws, assume it anyway.)

a. How many $1,000 par value bonds would Midland have to sell under each plan?

b. What would be the after-tax YTM on each type of bond (1) to a holder who is tax exempt and (2) to a taxpayer in the 50 percent bracket?

c. What would be the after-tax cost of each type of bond to Midland?

d. Why would investors be willing to buy the zero coupon bonds?

e. Why might Midland turn down the offer to issue zero coupon bonds?

(Do only if you are using the computerized problem diskette.)

f. Redo Parts a, b, and c assuming that the YTM on zero coupon bonds falls to 12 percent and that on annual coupon bonds falls to 13 percent. As in the previous analysis, the after-tax yield to investors on the annual coupon bond exceeds that of the zero coupon bond. Has the differential between the annual and zero coupon bond yields changed? Would investors be more willing to purchase the zero coupon bond under the original assumptions or under the new assumptions? If the before-tax YTM were 12 percent on each type of bond, what would the after-tax YTMs be to zero and to 50 percent taxpayers, what would the after-tax cost be to the company, and what type of investors would be likely to hold the zeros and what type the regular coupon bonds?

## Solution to Self-Test Problem

**ST-1**   a. $100,000,000/10 = $10,000,000 per year, or $5 million each 6 months. Since the $5 million will be used to retire bonds immediately, no interest will be earned on it.

b. The debt service requirements will decline. As the amount of bonds outstanding declines, so will the interest requirements:

| Semiannual Payment Period (1) | Sinking Fund Payment (2) | Outstanding Bonds on Which Interest Is Paid (3) | Interest Payment[a] (4) | Total Bond Service (2) + (4) = (5) |
|---|---|---|---|---|
| 1 | $5 | $100 | $4.0 | $9.0 |
| 2 | 5 | 95 | 3.8 | 8.8 |
| 3 | 5 | 90 | 3.6 | 8.6 |
| . | . | . | . | . |
| . | . | . | . | . |
| . | . | . | . | . |
| 20 | 5 | 5 | 0.2 | 5.2 |

[a]Interest is calculated as (0.5)(0.08)(Column 3); for example, interest in Period 2 = (0.5)(0.08)($95) = $3.8.

The company's total cash bond service requirement will be $9.0 + $8.8 = $17.8 million per year for the first year. The requirement will decline by $0.8 million, or 0.08 ($10,000,000), per year for the remaining years.

c. Here we have a 10-year, 6 percent annuity whose compound value is $100 million, and we are seeking the annual payment, PMT, in this equation:

$$\$100 \text{ million} = \sum_{t=1}^{10} PMT(1 + k)^t$$

$$= PMT(FVIFA_{6\%,10})$$

$$= PMT(13.1808)$$

$$PMT = \$7,586,793 = \text{Sinking fund payment.}$$

The solution could also be obtained with a financial calculator: Input FV = 100, n = 10, and i = 6, and press the PMT key to obtain 7.586796 = $7,586,796. The $3 difference is due to rounding the FVIFA to 4 decimal places.

d. Annual debt service costs will be $100,000,000(0.08) + $7,586,793 = $15,586,793.

e. If interest rates rose, causing the bond's prices to fall, the company would use open market purchases. This would reduce its debt service requirements.

## Selected Additional References and Cases

The chapters on fixed-income securities in the investment textbooks listed in the Chapter 11 references provide useful information on bonds and the markets in which they are traded. In addition, the following articles offer useful insights, and more references are cited in Chapter 12 of Eugene F. Brigham and Louis C. Gapenski, *Intermediate Financial Management.*

Backer, Morton, and Martin L. Gosman, "The Use of Financial Ratios in Credit Downgrade Decisions," *Financial Management*, Spring 1980, 53-56.

Clark, John J., with Brenton W. Harries, "Some Recent Trends in Municipal and Corporate Securities Markets: An Interview with Brenton W. Harries, President of Standard & Poor's Corporation," *Financial Management*, Spring 1976, 9-17.

Ferri, Michael G., "An Empirical Examination of the Determinants of Bond Yield Spreads," *Financial Management*, Autumn 1978, 40-46.

Kalotay, Andrew J., "Innovations in Corporation Finance: Deep Discount Private Placements," *Financial Management*, Spring 1982, 55-57.

Zwick, Burton, "Yields on Privately Placed Corporate Bonds," *Journal of Finance*, March 1980, 23-29.

The following cases focus on the topics covered in this chapter:

Case 20, "Seminole Gas and Electric," in the Crum-Brigham casebook, illustrates the bond refunding decision.

The Harrington case "Exxon Corporation" describes three early 1980 Exxon debt/equity swaps.

## APPENDIX 12A

## Bankruptcy and Reorganization

Debtholders have a prior claim to a firm's income, and to its assets in the event of bankruptcy, over common and preferred stockholders. Also, different classes of debtholders are accorded different treatments in the event of bankruptcy, so it is important that one know who gets what if a firm fails. These topics are discussed in this appendix.[1]

### Federal Bankruptcy Laws

Bankruptcy actually begins when a debtor is unable to meet scheduled payments to creditors or when the firm's cash flow projections indicate that it will soon be unable to do so. As the bankruptcy proceedings go forward, these central issues arise:

**1.** Is the firm's inability to meet scheduled debt payments a temporary cash flow problem, or is it a permanent problem caused by asset values having fallen below debt obligations?

**2.** If the problem is a temporary one, then an extension which gives the firm time to recover and to satisfy everyone will be worked out. However, if basic long-run asset values have truly declined, economic losses will have occurred. In this event, who should bear the losses?

**3.** Is the company "worth more dead than alive"—that is, would the business be more valuable if it were maintained and continued in operation or if it were liquidated and sold off in pieces?

**4.** Who should control the firm while it is being liquidated or rehabilitated? Should the existing management be left in control, or should a *trustee* be placed in charge of operations? These are the primary issues that are addressed in the federal bankruptcy statutes.

Our bankruptcy laws were first enacted in 1898, modified substantially in 1938, changed again in 1978, and further fine-tuned in 1984. The 1978 act was a major revision designed to streamline and expedite proceedings, and it consists of eight odd-numbered chapters, the even-numbered chapters of the earlier act having been deleted. Chapters 1, 3, and 5 of the 1978 act contain general provisions applicable to the other chapters; Chapter 7 details the procedures to be followed when liquidating a firm; Chapter 9 deals with financially distressed municipalities; Chapter 11 is the business reorganization chapter; Chapter 13 covers the adjustment of debts for "individuals with regular income"; and Chapter 15 sets up a system of trustees who help administer proceedings under the new act.

When you read in the paper that Manville Corporation or some other company has "filed for Chapter 11," this means that the company is bankrupt and is trying

---

This appendix was coauthored by Arthur L. Herrmann of the University of Hartford.

[1]Much of the current work in this area is based on writings by Edward I. Altman. For a summary of his work, and that of others, see Edward I. Altman, "Bankruptcy and Reorganization," in *Financial Handbook*, Edward I. Altman, ed. (New York: Wiley, 1981), Chapter 35. Also, Chapter 23 of Eugene F. Brigham and Louis C. Gapenski, *Intermediate Financial Management*, provides additional discussion of bankruptcy issues.

to reorganize under Chapter 11 of the Act. If a reorganization plan cannot be worked out, then the company will be liquidated as prescribed in Chapter 7 of the Act.

The 1978 act is quite flexible and provides much scope for informal negotiations between a company and its creditors and stockholders. Under this act, a case is opened by the filing of a petition with a federal district bankruptcy court. The petition may be either voluntary or involuntary—that is, it may be filed by either the firm's management or its creditors. A committee of unsecured creditors is then appointed by the court to negotiate with management for a reorganization, which may include the restructuring of debt and other claims against the firm. A trustee may be appointed by the court if that is deemed to be in the best interests of the creditors and stockholders; otherwise, the existing management will retain control. Under the new Chapter 11, if no fair and feasible reorganization can be worked out, the firm will be liquidated under the procedures spelled out in Chapter 7.

## Financial Decisions in Bankruptcy

When a business becomes insolvent, a decision must be made whether to dissolve the firm through *liquidation* or to keep it alive through *reorganization*. Fundamentally, this decision depends on a determination of the value of the firm if it is rehabilitated versus the value of its assets if they are sold off individually. The procedure that promises higher returns to the creditors and owners will be adopted. If the decision is made to reorganize the firm, the courts, and possibly the SEC, will be called upon to determine the *fairness* and the *feasibility* of the proposed reorganization plan.

***Standard of Fairness.*** The basic doctrine of *fairness* states that claims must be recognized in the order of their legal and contractual priority. Carrying out this concept of fairness in a reorganization (as opposed to a liquidation) involves the following steps:

**1.** Future sales must be estimated.

**2.** Operating conditions must be analyzed so that the future earnings and cash flows can be predicted.

**3.** A capitalization (or discount) rate to be applied to these future cash flows must be determined.

**4.** This capitalization rate must then be applied to the estimated cash flows to obtain a present value figure, which is the indicated value for the reorganized company.

**5.** Provision for distributions to the claimants must be made.

***Standard of Feasibility.*** The primary test of *feasibility* in a reorganization is whether the fixed charges after reorganization will be sufficiently covered by cash flows. Adequate coverage generally requires an improvement in operating earnings, a reduction of fixed charges, or both. Among the actions that must generally be taken are the following:

**1.** Debt maturities are usually lengthened, and some debt is usually converted into equity.

**2.** When the quality of management has been substandard, a new team must be given control of the company.

**3.** If inventories have become obsolete or depleted, they must be replaced.

**4.** Sometimes the plant and equipment must be modernized before the firm can operate and compete successfully on a cost basis.

## Liquidation Procedures

If a company is too far gone to be reorganized, it must be liquidated. Liquidation should occur if a business is worth more dead than alive or if the possibility of restoring it to financial health is so remote that the creditors would face a high risk of even greater losses if operations were continued.

Chapter 7 of the 1978 Bankruptcy Act is designed to do these three things: (1) provide safeguards against the withdrawal of assets by the owners of the bankrupt firm; (2) provide for an equitable distribution of the assets among the creditors; and (3) allow insolvent debtors to discharge all their obligations and start over unhampered by a burden of prior debt.

The distribution of assets in a liquidation under Chapter 7 of the Bankruptcy Act is governed by the following priority of claims:

**1.** *Secured creditors, who are entitled to the proceeds of the sale of specific property pledged for a lien or a mortgage.* If the proceeds do not fully satisfy the secured creditors' claims, the remaining balance is treated as a general creditor claim. (See Item 9.)

**2.** *Trustee's costs to administer and operate the bankrupt firm.*

**3.** *Expenses incurred after an involuntary case has begun but before a trustee is appointed.*

**4.** *Wages due workers if earned within three months prior to the filing of the petition in bankruptcy.* The amount of wages is limited to $2,000 per person.

**5.** *Claims for unpaid contributions to employee benefit plans that were to be paid within six months prior to filing.* However, these claims, plus wages in Item 4, are not to exceed the $2,000 per wage earner limit.

**6.** *Unsecured claims for customer deposits, not to exceed a maximum of $900 per individual.*

**7.** *Taxes due to federal, state, county, and any other government agency.*

**8.** *Unfunded pension plan liabilities.* Unfunded pension plan liabilities have a claim above that of the general creditors for an amount up to 30 percent of the common and preferred equity; any remaining unfunded pension claims rank with the general creditors.

**9.** *General, or unsecured, creditors.* Holders of trade credit, unsecured loans, the unsatisfied portion of secured loans, and debenture bonds are classified as *general creditors.* Holders of subordinated debt also fall into this category, but they must turn over required amounts to the holders of senior debt, as discussed later in this section.

**10.** *Preferred stockholders, who can receive an amount up to the par value of the issue.*

**11.** *Common stockholders, who receive any remaining funds.*

**Table 12A-1**
**Whitman, Inc.: Balance Sheet at Liquidation**
**(Thousands of Dollars)**

| | | | | |
|---|---|---|---|---|
| Current assets | $80,000 | | Accounts payable | $20,000 |
| Net fixed assets | 10,000 | | Notes payable (to bank) | 10,000 |
| | | | Accrued wages, 1,400 @ $500 | 700 |
| | | | U.S. taxes | 1,000 |
| | | | State and local taxes | 300 |
| | | | Current liabilities | $32,000 |
| | | | First mortgage | $ 6,000 |
| | | | Second mortgage | 1,000 |
| | | | Subordinated debentures[a] | 8,000 |
| | | | Total long-term debt | $15,000 |
| | | | Preferred stock | $ 2,000 |
| | | | Common stock | 26,000 |
| | | | Paid-in capital | 4,000 |
| | | | Retained earnings | 11,000 |
| | | | Total equity | $43,000 |
| Total assets | $90,000 | | Total claims | $90,000 |

[a]Subordinated to $10 million in notes payable to the bank.

To illustrate how this priority system works, consider the balance sheet of Whitman, Inc., shown in Table 12A-1. The assets have a book value of $90 million. The claims are indicated on the right-hand side of the balance sheet. Note that the debentures are subordinate to the notes payable to banks. Whitman has filed for bankruptcy under Chapter 11, and since no fair and feasible reorganization could be arranged, the trustee is liquidating the firm under Chapter 7.

The assets as reported in the balance sheet in Table 12A-1 are greatly overstated; they are, in fact, worth less than half of the $90 million at which they are carried. The following amounts are realized on liquidation:

| | |
|---|---|
| From sale of current assets | $28,000,000 |
| From sale of fixed assets | 5,000,000 |
| Total receipts | $33,000,000 |

The order of priority of the claims is shown in Table 12A-2. The first mortgage holders receive the $5 million in net proceeds from the sale of fixed assets, leaving $28 million available to the remaining creditors. Note that a $1 million unsatisfied claim of the first mortgage holders remains; this claim is added to that of the other general creditors. Next come the fees and expenses of administration, which are typically about 20 percent of gross proceeds; in this example, they are assumed to be $6 million. Next in priority are wages due workers, which total $700,000, and taxes due, which amount to $1.3 million. Thus far, the total of claims paid from the $33 million is $13 million, leaving $20 million for the general creditors. In this example, we assume that there are no claims for unpaid benefit plans or unfunded pension liabilities; if there were, they would have priority over the general creditors.

**Table 12A-2**
**Whitman, Inc.: Order of Priority of Claims**

### Distribution of Proceeds on Liquidation

| | |
|---|---|
| 1. Proceeds from sale of assets | $33,000,000 |
| 2. First mortgage, paid from sale of fixed assets | 5,000,000 |
| 3. Fees and expenses of administration of bankruptcy | 6,000,000 |
| 4. Wages due workers earned within three months prior to filing of bankruptcy petition | 700,000 |
| 5. Taxes | 1,300,000 |
| 6. Available to general creditors | $20,000,000 |

### Distribution to General Creditors

| Claims of General Creditors | Claim[a] (1) | Application of 50 Percent[b] (2) | After Subordination Adjustment[c] (3) | Percentage of Original Claims Received[d] (4) |
|---|---|---|---|---|
| Unsatisfied portion of first mortgage | $ 1,000,000 | $ 500,000 | $ 500,000 | 92% |
| Unsatisfied portion of second mortgage | 1,000,000 | 500,000 | 500,000 | 50 |
| Notes payable | 10,000,000 | 5,000,000 | 9,000,000 | 90 |
| Accounts payable | 20,000,000 | 10,000,000 | 10,000,000 | 50 |
| Subordinated debentures | 8,000,000 | 4,000,000 | 0 | 0 |
| | $40,000,000 | $20,000,000 | $20,000,000 | |

[a]Column 1 is the claim of each class of general creditor. Total claims equal $40 million.

[b]From Line 6 in the upper section of the table, we see that $20 million is available for general creditors. This sum, divided by the $40 million of claims, indicates that general creditors will initially receive 50 percent of their claims; this is shown in Column 2.

[c]The debentures are subordinated to the notes payable, so $4 million is reallocated from debentures to notes payable in Column 3.

[d]Column 4 shows the results of dividing the amount in Column 3 by the original claim amount given in Column 1, except for the first mortgage, where the $5 million received from the sale of fixed assets is included.

The claims of the general creditors total $40 million. Since $20 million is available, claimants would initially be allocated 50 percent of their claims, as shown in Column 2, before the subordination adjustment. This adjustment requires that the subordinated debentures turn over to the notes payable all amounts received until the notes are satisfied. In this situation, the claim of the notes payable is $10 million, but only $5 million is available; the deficiency is therefore $5 million. After transfer of $4 million from the subordinated debentures, there remains a deficiency of $1 million on the notes; this amount will remain unsatisfied.

Note that 90 percent of the bank claim is satisfied, whereas a maximum of 50 percent of other unsecured claims will be satisfied. These figures illustrate the usefulness of the subordination provision to the security to which the subordination is made. Since no other funds remain, the claims of the holders of preferred and common stock are completely wiped out. Studies of bankruptcy liquidations reveal that unsecured creditors receive on the average about 15 cents on the dollar while common stockholders generally receive nothing.

## Problems

**12A-1**    The Florida Tile Company has the following balance sheet:

| | | | | |
|---|---|---|---|---|
| Current assets | $2,800 | Accounts payable | | $ 600 |
| Fixed assets | 1,500 | Notes payable (to bank) | | 300 |
| | | Accrued taxes | | 100 |
| | | Accrued wages | | 100 |
| | | Total current liabilities | | $1,100 |
| | | First mortgage bonds | | $ 500 |
| | | Second mortgage bonds | | 500 |
| | | Total mortgage bonds | | $1,000 |
| | | Subordinated debentures | | 600 |
| | | Total debt | | $2,700 |
| | | Preferred stock | | 200 |
| | | Common stock | | 1,400 |
| Total assets | $4,300 | Total claims | | $4,300 |

The debentures are subordinated only to the notes payable. Suppose Florida Tile goes bankrupt and is liquidated, with $700 being received from the sale of the fixed assets, which were pledged as security for the first and second mortgage bonds, and $1,300 from the sale of current assets.

a.  How much will each class of investors receive?

(Do only if you are using the computerized problem diskette.)

b.  How much would each class of investors receive if

1.  $500 were received from the sale of fixed assets and $1,000 from the sale of current assets?

2.  $1,000 were received from the sale of fixed assets and $2,000 from the sale of current assets?

**12A-2**    A firm has the following balance sheet:

| | | | |
|---|---|---|---|
| Current assets | $1,500,000 | Bank debt | $ 300,000 |
| Fixed assets | 1,500,000 | Trade credit | 600,000 |
| | | Subordinated debentures | 600,000 |
| | | Total debt | $1,500,000 |
| | | Common equity | 1,500,000 |
| Total assets | $3,000,000 | Total claims | $3,000,000 |

If the debentures are subordinated only to the bank debt and the firm goes bankrupt, how much will each class of investors receive under each of the following conditions?

a.  A total of $2 million is received from sale of assets.

b.  A total of $1.5 million is received from sale of assets.

(Do Parts c and d only if you are using the computerized problem diskette.)

c.  A total of $1 million is received from sale of assets.

d.  A total of $500,000 is received from sale of assets.

e.  What is the significance of these findings for the banks, the trade creditors, the debenture holders, and the common stockholders?

## APPENDIX 12B
## Refunding Operations

A great deal of long-term debt was sold during the period 1979-1982 at interest rates going up to 18 percent or more even for double A companies. Since the period of call protection on this debt is, or soon will be, ending, many companies are analyzing the pros and cons of bond refundings. Refunding decisions actually involve two separate questions: (1) Is it profitable to call an outstanding issue in the current period and replace it with a new issue, and (2) even if refunding is currently profitable, would the expected value of the firm be increased even more if the refunding were postponed to a later date? We consider both questions in this appendix.[1]

First, note that the decision to refund a security is analyzed in much the same way as a capital budgeting expenditure. The costs of refunding—the investment outlays—are (1) the call premium paid for the privilege of calling the old issue and (2) the flotation costs incurred in selling the new issue. The annual benefits, in a capital budgeting sense, are the interest payments that are saved each year. For example, if the interest expense on the old issue is $1,000,000 while that on the new issue is $700,000, the $300,000 savings constitutes an annual benefit.

The net present value method is used to analyze the advantages of refunding—discount the future interest savings back to the present, and then compare this discounted value with the cash outlays associated with the refunding. The firm should refund the bond if the present value of the savings exceeds the cost, that is, if the NPV of the refunding operation is positive.

*In the discounting process, the after-tax cost of the new debt, $k_d$, should be used as the discount rate.* The reason is that there is relatively little risk to the savings—cash flows in a refunding are known with relative certainty, which is quite unlike the situation with cash flows in most capital budgeting decisions.

The easiest way to examine the refunding decision is through an example. Microchip Computer Company has outstanding a $60 million bond issue which has a 15 percent coupon interest rate and 20 years remaining to maturity. This issue, which was sold 5 years ago, had flotation costs of $3 million, which the firm has been amortizing on a straight line basis over the 25-year original life of the issue. The bond has a call provision which makes it possible for the company to retire the issue at this time by calling the bonds in at a 10 percent call premium. Investment bankers have assured the company that it could sell an additional $60 million to $70 million worth of new 20-year bonds at an interest rate of 12 percent. To insure that the funds required to pay off the old debt will be available, the new bonds would be sold one month before the old issue is called, so for one month, interest would have to be paid on two issues. Current short-term interest rates are 11 percent. Predictions are that long-term interest rates

---

[1]During the early 1980s, there was a flurry of work on the pros and cons of refunding bond issues that had fallen to deep discounts as a result of rising interest rates. At such times a company could go into the market, buy its debt at a low price, and retire it. The difference between the bonds' par value and the price the company paid would be reported as income, and taxes would have to be paid on it. The results of the research on the refunding of discount issues suggest that in general bonds should not be refunded after a rise in rates. See Andrew J. Kalotay, "On the Structure and Valuation of Debt Refundings," *Financial Management*, Spring 1982, 41-42; and Robert S. Harris, "The Refunding of Discounted Debt: An Adjusted Present Value Analysis," *Financial Management*, Winter 1980, 7-12.

are unlikely to fall below 12 percent.[2] Flotation costs on a new refunding issue would amount to $2,650,000. Microchip's marginal tax rate is 40 percent. Should the company refund the $60 million of 15 percent bonds?

The following steps outline the decision process; they are summarized in worksheet form in Table 12B-1.

**Step 1.** Determine the investment outlay required to refund the issue.

**a.** *Call premium*:

$$\text{Before tax: } 0.10(\$60,000,000) = \$6,000,000.$$
$$\text{After tax: } \$6,000,000(1 - T) = \$6,000,000(0.6)$$
$$= \$3,600,000.$$

Although Microchip must expend $6 million on the call premium, this is a deductible expense in the year the call is made. Since the company is in the 40 percent tax bracket, it saves $2.4 million in taxes; therefore, the after-tax cost of the call is only $3.6 million. This amount is shown on Line 1 of Table 12B-1.

**b.** *Flotation costs on the new issue*:
Flotation costs on the new issue will be $2,650,000. For tax purposes, flotation costs must be amortized over the life of the new bond, or 20 years. Therefore, the annual tax deduction is

$$\frac{\$2,650,000}{20} = \$132,500.$$

Since Microchip is in the 40 percent tax bracket, it has a tax savings of $132,500(0.4) = $53,000 a year for 20 years. This is an annuity of $53,000 for 20 years. In a refunding analysis, all cash flows should be discounted at the after-tax cost of new debt, in this case, 12%(1 - T) = 12%(0.6) = 7.2%. The present value of the tax savings, discounted at 7.2 percent, is $552,859.[3] Thus, the net after-tax cost of flotation for the new issue is

| | |
|---|---|
| Gross flotation costs on new issue | $2,650,000 |
| PV of associated tax savings | (552,859) |
| Net after-tax flotation cost on new issue | $2,097,141 |

The gross costs and tax savings are reflected on Lines 2 and 3 of Table 12B-1.

**c.** *Flotation costs on old issue*:
The old issue has an unamortized flotation cost of (20/25)($3,000,000)

---

[2]The firm's management has estimated that interest rates will probably remain at their present level of 12 percent or else rise; there is only a 25 percent probability that they will fall further.

[3]The PVIFA for 7.2 percent over 20 years is 10.4313, found with a financial calculator.

**Table 12B-1**
**Worksheet for the Bond Refunding Decision**

| | Amount before Tax | Amount after Tax | Time Event Occurs | PV Factor at 7.2% | PV |
|---|---|---|---|---|---|
| **Cost of Refunding at t = 0** | | | | | |
| 1. Call premium on old bond | $6,000,000 | $3,600,000 | 0 | 1.0000 | $ 3,600,000 |
| 2. Flotation costs on new issue | 2,650,000 | 2,650,000 | 0 | 1.0000 | 2,650,000 |
| 3. Tax savings on new issue flotation cost amortization | (132,500) | (53,000) | 1–20 | 10.4313 | (552,859) |
| 4. Immediate tax savings on old flotation cost expense | (2,400,000) | (960,000) | 0 | 1.0000 | (960,000) |
| 5. Periodic tax benefits no longer received on old flotation costs | 120,000 | 48,000 | 1–20 | 10.4313 | 500,702 |
| 6. Extra interest on old issue | 750,000 | 450,000 | 0 | 1.0000 | 450,000 |
| 7. Interest on short-term investment | (550,000) | (330,000) | 0 | 1.0000 | (330,000) |
| 8. Total after-tax investment (PV of investment) | | | | | $ 5,357,843 |
| **Savings over the Life of the New Issue: t = 1 to 20** | | | | | |
| 9. Interest on old bond | $9,000,000 | $5,400,000 | | | |
| 10. Interest on new bond | (7,200,000) | (4,320,000) | | | |
| 11. Net savings of interest | $1,800,000 | $1,080,000 | 1–20 | 10.4313 | $11,265,804 |

**Refunding NPV**

12. NPV = PV of interest savings − PV of investment
    = $11,265,804 − $5,357,843
    = $5,907,961.

= $2,400,000 at this time. If the issue is retired, the unamortized flotation cost may be recognized immediately as an expense, thus creating an after-tax savings of $2,400,000(T) = $960,000. The firm will, however, no longer receive a tax deduction of $120,000 a year for 20 years, which is equivalent to an after-tax benefit of $48,000 a year. The present value of this tax savings, discounted over 20 years at 7.2 percent, is $500,702. Thus, the net after-tax effect of the old flotation costs is − $459,298:

| | |
|---|---|
| Tax savings from immediate write-off of old flotation costs | ($960,000) |
| PV of tax savings on old flotation costs had refunding not occurred | 500,702 |
| Net after-tax savings on old flotation costs | ($459,298) |

These figures are reflected on Lines 4 and 5 of Table 12B-1.

Note that, because of the refunding, the flotation costs provide an immediate tax saving rather than annual savings over the next 20 years. Thus, the $459,298 net savings simply reflects the difference between the present value of benefits received in the future without the refunding versus an immediate benefit if the refunding occurs.

**d.** *Additional interest*:

One month's "extra" interest on the old issue, after taxes, costs $450,000:

$$\text{(Dollar amount)}\left(\frac{1}{12}\text{ of }15\%\right)(1 - T) = \text{Interest cost}$$
$$(\$60,000,000)(0.0125)(0.6) = \$450,000.$$

However, the proceeds from the new issue can be invested in short-term securities for one month. Thus, $60 million invested at a rate of 11 percent will return $330,000 in after-tax interest:

$$(\$60,000,000)\left(\frac{1}{12}\text{ of }11\%\right)(1 - T) = \text{Interest earned}$$
$$(\$60,000,000)(0.009167)(0.6) = \$330,000.$$

The net after-tax additional interest cost is thus $120,000:

| | |
|---|---:|
| Interest paid on old issue | $450,000 |
| Interest earned on short-term securities | (330,000) |
| Net additional interest | $120,000 |

These figures are reflected on Lines 6 and 7 of Table 12B-1.

**e.** *Total after-tax investment*:

The total investment outlay required to refund the bond issue, which will be financed by debt, is thus $5,357,843.[4]

| | |
|---|---:|
| Call premium | $3,600,000 |
| Flotation costs, new, net of tax savings | 2,097,141 |
| Flotation costs, old, net savings | (459,298) |
| Net additional interest | 120,000 |
| Total investment | $5,357,843 |

This total is shown on Line 8 of Table 12B-1.

---

[4]The investment outlay (in this case, $5,357,843) is usually obtained by increasing the amount of the new bond issue. In the example given, the new issue would be $65,357,843. However, the interest on the additional debt *should not* be deducted at Step 2, because the $5,357,843 itself will be deducted at Step 3. If additional interest on the $5,357,843 were deducted at Step 2, then interest would in effect be deducted twice. The situation here is exactly like that in regular capital budgeting decisions. Even though some debt may be used to finance a project, interest on that debt is not subtracted when developing the annual cash flows—rather, the annual cash flows are *discounted* by the project's cost of capital.

***Step 2.*** Calculate the PV of the annual interest savings.

**a.** *Interest on old bond, after tax*:
The annual after-tax interest on the old issue is $5.4 million:

$$( \$60,000,000)(0.15)(0.6) = \$5,400,000.$$

This is shown on Line 9 of Table 12B-1.

**b.** *Interest on new bond, after tax*:
The new issue has an annual after-tax cost of $4,320,000:

$$( \$60,000,000)(0.12)(0.6) = \$4,320,000.$$

This is shown on Line 10 as a negative saving.

**c.** *Net Annual savings*:
Thus, the net annual after-tax savings is $1,080,000:

| | |
|---|---:|
| Interest on old bonds, after tax | $5,400,000 |
| Interest on new bonds, after tax | (4,320,000) |
| Annual net savings | $1,080,000 |

This is shown on Line 11.

**d.** *PV of annual savings*:
The PV of $1,080,000 a year for 20 years is $11,265,804:

$$PV = \$1,080,000(PVIFA_{7.2\%,20})$$
$$= \$1,080,000(10.4313) = \$11,265,804.$$

This is also shown on Line 11.

***Step 3.*** Determine the NPV of the refunding.

| | |
|---|---:|
| PV of annual savings | $11,265,804 |
| Net investment | (5,357,843) |
| NPV from refunding | $ 5,907,961 |

Since the net present value of the refunding is positive, it would be profitable to refund the old bond issue.

Several other points should be noted. First, since the cash flows are based on differences between contractual obligations, their risk is the same as that of the underlying obligations. Therefore, the present values of the cash flows should be found by discounting at the firm's least risky rate—its after-tax cost of marginal debt. Second, since the refunding operation is advantageous to the firm, it must be disadvantageous to bondholders; they must give up their 15 percent bonds and reinvest in new ones yielding 12 percent. This points out the danger of the call provision to bondholders, and it also explains why bonds without a call feature command higher prices than callable bonds. Third, although it is not emphasized in the example, we assumed that the firm raises the investment required to undertake the refunding operation (the $5,357,843 shown on Line 8 of Table

12B-1) as debt. This should be feasible, since the refunding operation will improve the interest coverage ratio even though a larger amount of debt is outstanding.[5] Fourth, we set up our example in such a way that the new issue had
the same maturity as the remaining life of the old one. Often the old bond has
only a relatively short time to maturity (say, 5 to 10 years), while the new bond
would have a much longer maturity (say, 25 to 30 years). In this situation, the
analysis should include only cash flows up to the maturity of the old issue.[6] Fifth,
refunding decisions are well suited for analysis with a computer spreadsheet such
as *Lotus 1-2-3* or *IFPS*. The spreadsheet is simple to set up, and once it is, it is
easy to vary the assumptions, especially that about the interest rate on the refunding issue, and see how such changes affect the NPV.

One final point should be addressed: Although our analysis shows that the refunding would increase the value of the firm, would refunding *at this time* truly
maximize the firm's expected value? Note that if interest rates continue to fall,
then the company might be better off waiting, for this could increase the NPV of
the refunding operation even more. The mechanics of calculating the NPV of a
refunding are easy, but the decision of *when* to refund is not a simple one at all,
because it requires a forecast of future interest rates. Thus, the final decision on
refunding now versus waiting for a possibly more favorable time is a judgmental
decision.

## Problem

**12B-1**   Cannon Container Corporation (CCC) is considering whether to refund
a $50 million, 14 percent coupon, 30-year bond issue that was sold 5
years ago. It is amortizing $3 million of flotation costs on the 14 percent
bonds over the issue's 30-year life. CCC's investment bankers have indicated that the company could sell a new, 25-year issue at an interest rate
of 12 percent in today's market. Neither they nor CCC's management
sees much chance that interest rates will fall below 12 percent any time
soon, but there is a chance that rates will increase.

A call premium of 14 percent would be required to retire the old
bonds, and flotation costs on the new issue would amount to $3 million.
CCC's marginal federal plus state tax rate is 50 percent. The new bonds
would be issued one month before the old bonds were called, with the
proceeds being invested in short-term government securities returning
9 percent annually during the interim period.

---

[5]See Ahron R. Ofer and Robert A. Taggart, Jr., "Bond Refunding: A Clarifying Analysis," *Journal
of Finance*, March 1977, 21-30, for a discussion of how the method of financing the refunding
affects the analysis. Ofer and Taggart prove that (1) if the refunding investment outlay is to be
raised as debt, then the after-tax cost of debt is the proper discount rate, while (2) if these funds
are to be raised as common equity, then the before-tax cost of debt is the proper rate. Since a
profitable refunding will virtually always raise the firm's debt-carrying capacity (because total
interest charges after the refunding will be lower than before it), it is more logical to use debt
than either equity or a combination of debt and equity to finance the operation. Therefore, firms
generally do use additional debt to finance refunding operations, and we therefore assume debt
financing for the costs of refunding and discount at the after-tax cost of debt.

[6]It should also be noted that to be exactly precise the old bond in our example should have had
a maturity of 20 years plus one month at the time the analysis was undertaken so that it would
have a 20-year remaining maturity when it is actually refunded. This is a detail that should not
concern you.

a. Perform a complete bond refunding analysis. What is the bond refunding's NPV?
b. What factors would influence CCC's decision to refund now rather than later?

(Do only if you are using the computerized problem diskette.)

c. Determine the interest rate on new bonds at which CCC would be indifferent to refunding, that is, the interest rate at which the NPV of the refunding decision would be approximately zero. (Hint: You will need to perform the analysis using different rates of interest on new bonds until you find the one which causes NPV to be zero.)

# 13

# HYBRID FINANCING: PREFERRED STOCK, LEASING, AND OPTION SECURITIES

**MCI**

U.S. Steel recently decided to build a $690 million plant to manufacture seamless pipe. This capital expansion could have been financed conventionally, using both debt and equity. However, the steel industry was in the midst of a severe recession, and U.S. Steel had a depressed stock price, a high marginal cost of debt, and virtually no projected retained earnings. Thus, conventional financing would have required U.S. Steel to go to the capital markets at the worst possible time. To avoid this problem, U.S. Steel considered leasing the plant from General Electric Credit Corporation (GECC), one of the largest providers of commercial and industrial financing. GECC arranged for 17 banks in 6 countries to put up most of the required funds, with it supplying some equity and owning the plant. U.S. Steel would then lease the plant for 10 years, after which it would have an option to buy the plant. Its effective financing cost was estimated to be 40 percent less under the lease arrangement than under conventional financing.

The lease arrangement looked attractive because of the differential value of tax benefits to U.S. Steel and GECC. U.S. Steel, with past losses and a slow recovery in sight, could not immediately use the plant's investment tax credit and depreciation deductions. GECC, on the other hand, consolidates its income with its parent, General Electric, and the tax benefits of the plant could be used immediately to offset General Electric's own high current income. In effect, U.S. Steel would be transferring tax benefits that it could not use because of its low earnings situation to General Electric, to whom tax credits were valuable, and General Electric would pay for these credits by charging U.S. Steel a relatively low lease rate.

At that time, the bond market was in shambles. Interest rates were near all-time highs, and even AAA-rated corporations could only issue regular long-term bonds by offering yields close to 18 percent. Even so, MCI Communications Corporation, the biggest and fastest growing of the new competitors in long-distance telephone service, sold a B-rated $100 million issue of 20-year subordinated debentures which carried a coupon of only 10.25 percent.

The issue sold out in an hour, and within a month each bond was selling at a premium of $70 over its $1,000 par value.

How was MCI able to sell this low-coupon issue so easily? The key was convertibility—bondholders could swap their bonds for 40 shares of stock, so if the price of the stock rose, the value of the convertible bond would also rise. Thus, the purchaser of an MCI convertible bond was buying a fixed-income security with a yield of 10¼ percent plus a chance for capital gains if MCI's stock price rose. MCI's convertibles appealed to investors because they offered steady income plus potential capital gains, and they were attractive to the company because they saved it interest expense and, when converted, would result in the replacement of debt with equity and thus strengthen the balance sheet.

When we discussed long-term financing in Chapters 11 and 12, we concentrated on common stock and various types of debt. In this chapter, we examine other types of long-term financing which firms such as U.S. Steel and MCI use to lower their costs of capital. We first discuss preferred stock, which is a hybrid security that represents a cross between debt and equity. Then we look at leasing, which is an alternative to borrowing to purchase assets. Finally, we examine the use of option features, particularly warrants and convertibles, which allow debtholders to acquire common stock at bargain prices and thus to share in the capital gains if a company is especially successful in its business operations.

Even though all three of the topics covered in this chapter are important, time pressures may preclude detailed coverage of all of them. Accordingly, the chapter is written in modular form, so instructors may choose to cover one, two, or all three topics. When we are under time pressure in the basic course at Florida, we require students to read the entire chapter, but to know for exam purposes only how to answer the end-of-chapter questions, not how to work the problems.

## Preferred Stock

Preferred stock is a *hybrid*—it is similar to bonds in some respects and to common stock in others. The hybrid nature of preferred stock becomes apparent when we try to classify it in relation to bonds and common stock. Like bonds, preferred stock has a par value. Preferred dividends are also similar to interest payments on bonds in that they are fixed in amount and generally must be paid before common stock dividends can be paid. However, if the preferred dividend is not earned, the directors can omit (or "pass") it without throwing the company into bankruptcy. So, while preferred stock has a fixed payment like bonds, a failure to make this payment will not lead to bankruptcy.

Preferred stock is sometimes treated as debt and sometimes as equity, depending on the type of analysis being made. If the analysis is being made by a common stockholder considering the fixed charge which must be paid ahead of common stock dividends, then the preferred stock will be viewed much like debt. Suppose, however, that the analysis is being made by a bondholder studying the firm's vulnerability to failure due to a future decline in sales and income. Since the dividends on preferred stock are not a fixed charge in the sense that failure to pay them represents a default on an obligation, preferred stock provides an additional equity base. We see, then, that common stockholders view preferred stock much like debt, while creditors view it as equity.[1]

## Major Provisions of Preferred Stock Issues

Preferred stock has a number of features, the most important of which are covered in the following sections.

***Priority in Assets and Earnings.*** Preferred stockholders have priority over common stockholders with regard to earnings and assets. Thus, dividends must be paid on preferred stock before they can be paid on the common stock, and in the event of bankruptcy, the claims of the preferred shareholders must be satisfied before the common stockholders receive anything. To reinforce these features, most preferred stock certificates have coverage requirements similar to those on bonds which limit the amount of preferred stock a company can use; they also require that a minimum level of retained earnings be maintained before common dividends are permitted.

***Par Value.*** Unlike common stock, preferred stock always has a par value (or its equivalent under some other name), and this value is a meaningful quantity. First, the par value establishes the amount due the preferred stockholders in the event of liquidation. Second, the preferred dividend is frequently stated as a percentage of the par value. For example, J. I. Case's preferred stock has a par value of $100 and a stated dividend of 7 percent of par. It would, of course, be just as appropriate for the Case preferred stock to simply call for an annual dividend of $7.

**cumulative dividends**
A protective feature on preferred stock that requires all past preferred dividends to be paid before any common dividends.

**arrearage**
An omitted dividend on preferred stock.

***Cumulative Dividends.*** Most preferred stock provides for **cumulative dividends**—that is, all preferred dividends **arrearages** must be paid before common dividends can be paid. The cumulative feature is a protective device, for if the preferred stock dividends were not cumulative, a firm could do the following: (1) avoid paying preferred and common stock dividends

---

[1] Accountants generally include preferred stock in the equity portion of the capital structure, calling it "preferred equity" as opposed to "common equity." Still, from an economic standpoint, preferred is as much like debt as common equity.

for, say, 10 years and thus "save" a large amount of earnings and then (2) pay a large common stock dividend, but pay only the stipulated annual amount to the preferred stockholders. Obviously, such an action could be used to effectively void the preferred position that the preferred stockholders have tried to obtain, but the cumulative feature prevents such abuses.[2]

***Convertibility.*** Approximately 40 percent of the preferred stock that has been issued in recent years is convertible into common stock. For example, each share of InterNorth's $10.50 Class J preferred stock can be converted into 3.413 shares of its common stock at the option of the preferred shareholders. (Convertibility is discussed in more detail later in this chapter.)

***Some Infrequent Provisions.*** Some other provisions one occasionally encounters in preferred stocks include the following:

**1.** *Voting rights.* Sometimes preferred stockholders are given the right to vote for directors if the company has not paid the preferred dividend for a specified period, say, four, eight, or ten quarters. This feature certainly motivates management to make every effort to pay preferred dividends.

**2.** *Participating.* A rare type of preferred stock is one that participates with the common stock in sharing the firm's earnings. The following sequence generally relates to participating preferred stocks: (a) the stated preferred dividend is paid, for example, $5 a share; (b) income is allocated to common stock dividends up to an amount equal to the preferred dividend—in this case, $5; and (c) any remaining income is shared equally between the common and preferred stockholders.

**3.** *Sinking fund.* Some preferred issues have a sinking fund requirement, which ordinarily calls for the purchase and retirement of a given percentage of the preferred stock each year. For example, 2 percent, which is a common amount, gives the relevant preferred issue an average life of 25 years and a maximum life of 50 years.

**4.** *Maturity.* Preferred stocks almost never have maturity dates on which they must be retired. However, if the issue has a sinking fund, this effectively creates a maturity date.

**5.** *Call provision.* A call provision gives the issuing corporation the right to call in the preferred stock for redemption, as in the case for bonds. Call provisions generally state that the company must pay an amount greater than the par value of the preferred stock, the additional sum being defined as a **call premium**. For example, IBES Corporation's 12 percent, $100 par value preferred stock, issued in 1984, is noncallable for 10 years, but it may be called at a price of $112 after 1995.

**call premium**
The amount in excess of par value that a company must pay when it calls a security.

---

[2]Note, however, that compounding is absent in most cumulative plans—in other words, the arrearages themselves earn no return. Also, many preferred issues have a limited cumulative feature—for example, arrearages might accumulate for only three years.

## Evaluation of Preferred Stock

There are both advantages and disadvantages to financing with preferred stock. These are discussed in the following sections.

***Issuer's Viewpoint.*** By using preferred stock, a firm can fix its financial costs and thus keep more of the potential future profits for its existing set of common stockholders, as with bonds, yet avoid the danger of bankruptcy if earnings are too low to meet these fixed charges. Also, since preferred stock typically has no maturity and often no sinking fund, this too reduces cash flow problems vis-à-vis bonds. Finally, by selling preferred rather than common stock, the firm avoids sharing either control or earnings with the new investors.

However, preferred does have a major disadvantage from the issuer's standpoint: It has a higher after-tax cost of capital than debt. There are two reasons for this high cost. First, preferred stock often carries a higher coupon yield than bonds.[3] Second, preferred dividends are not deductible as a tax expense, which makes the component cost of preferred stock much greater than that of bonds: The after-tax cost of debt is approximately half the stated coupon rate for profitable firms, while the cost of preferred stock is the full percentage amount of the preferred dividend. Of course, the deductibility differential is most important for issuers that are in relatively high tax brackets—if a company pays little or no taxes because it is unprofitable or because it has a great deal of accelerated depreciation or investment tax credits, then the deductibility of interest does not make much difference. Thus, the higher a company's tax bracket, the less likely it is to use preferred stock financing.

***Investor's Viewpoint.*** In designing securities, the financial manager must also consider the investor's point of view. Frequently it is asserted that preferred stock has so many disadvantages to both the issuer and the investor that it should never be issued. Nevertheless, preferred stock is issued in substantial amounts. It provides investors with reasonably steady and assured income plus a preference over common stockholders in the event of liquidation. In addition, 85 percent of the preferred dividends received by corporations are not taxable. For this reason, a large percentage of outstanding preferred stock is owned by corporations.

The principal disadvantage of preferred stock from an investor's standpoint is that although preferred stockholders bear a substantial portion of owner-

---

[3]One would think that a given firm's preferred stock would always carry a higher coupon rate than its bonds because of the preferred's greater risk from the holder's viewpoint. However, the fact that 85 percent of preferred dividends received by corporate owners are exempt from income taxes has made preferred stock very attractive to corporate investors. Therefore, a lot of preferred stock is owned by corporations, and in recent years, high-grade preferreds on average have sold on a lower-yield basis than high-grade bonds. As an example, Alabama Power recently sold a preferred issue yielding 11 percent to investors. On the day the preferred was issued, Alabama Power's bonds yielded 13 percent, or two percentage points more than the preferred. The tax treatment accounted for this differential; the *after-tax* yield to a corporate investor was greater on the preferred stock than on the bonds.

ship risk, their returns are limited. Other disadvantages are that (1) preferred stockholders have no legally enforceable right to dividends, even if a company earns a profit, and (2) for individual as opposed to corporate investors, bond yields are frequently higher than those of even riskier preferred stock.[4]

## Recent Trends

Since preferred dividends are not tax deductible, many companies have retired their preferred stocks and replaced them with debentures or subordinated debentures. However, as the following examples illustrate, preferred is still used to raise long-term capital when conditions are such that neither common stock nor long-term debt can be issued on reasonable terms and a hybrid like preferred is useful.

**1.** The Chrysler Corporation's issue of preferred stock and warrants in the late 1970s proved a successful attempt at raising capital in the face of adverse circumstances. Due to first-quarter losses, Chrysler's stock price was depressed and very much out of favor—investors were simply too worried about the company's ability to survive to make additional commitments without receiving some sort of senior position—so common stock was ruled out. Various incentives were offered to the brokers who handled the issue, and a relatively high yield was set on the preferred stock, making the issue so successful that its size was raised from $150 to $200 million. Chrysler got the money it needed, and that money helped the company regain profitability.

**2.** Utility companies often use preferred stock to bolster the equity component of their capital structure. These companies are capital intensive and make heavy use of debt financing, but lenders and rating agencies require minimum equity ratios as a condition for further sales of bonds. Also, the utilities have made very heavy investments, and thus have had large tax credits and high depreciation, which has held down their effective tax rates and therefore has lowered the tax disadvantage of preferred stock for them.

**3.** In recent years there has also been a pronounced movement toward convertible preferred, which is used primarily in connection with mergers. For example, in 1983, when Belco Petroleum was negotiating its acquisition by InterNorth, it was pointed out that if the buyout were for cash, Belco's stockholders would be required to pay immediately substantial amounts of capital gains taxes. However, under the tax laws, if preferred stock were exchanged, this would constitute a tax-free exchange of securities. Thus, Belco's stockholders could obtain a fixed-income security and at the same time postpone the payment of capital gains taxes.

InterNorth actually offered a choice of straight or convertible preferred to Belco's stockholders. Those stockholders who were interested primarily in

---

[4]Another disadvantage of owning preferred stock is the fact that companies often manage to avoid paying off all accumulated dividends when they emerge from a troubled, low-income period. Such companies frequently go through reorganization under the Bankruptcy Act, and preferred stockholders often do not fare well in these proceedings.

income could take the straight preferred, while those interested in capital gains could take the convertible preferred. (After the exchange, both preferred issues traded on the NYSE; the straight preferred had a yield of 11 percent and the convertible preferred 7.5 percent, but the latter had a chance of gains—indeed, by 1985 the InterNorth convertible preferred had risen from $100 to $150 per share due to an increase in the price of the common into which it could be converted, while the nonconvertible preferred had declined from $100 to $97 because of an increase in interest rates.)

**floating rate preferred stock**
Preferred stock whose interest rate fluctuates with changes in the general level of interest rates.

**4.** In 1984 Alabama Power sold a new type of security, **floating rate preferred stock**. Since this stock has a floating rate, its price stays relatively constant, making it suitable for liquidity portfolios (marketable securities held by corporations to provide funds either for planned expenditures or to meet emergencies, as discussed in Chapter 18). The combination of a floating rate, and hence a stable price, plus the 85 percent tax exemption for corporations makes these preferreds quite attractive, and thus they enable Alabama Power and other firms to obtain capital at a relatively low cost.

## Leasing

Firms generally own fixed assets and report them on their balance sheets, but it is the *use* of buildings and equipment that is important, not their ownership per se. One way of obtaining the use of facilities and equipment is to buy them, but an alternative is to lease them. Prior to the 1950s, leasing was generally associated with real estate—land and buildings. Today, however, it is possible to lease virtually any kind of fixed asset, and in 1985 about 20 percent of all new capital equipment acquired by businesses was financed through lease arrangements.

### Types of Leases

Leasing takes several different forms, the three most important of which are (1) *sale-and-leaseback* arrangements, (2) *operating leases*, and (3) straight *financial*, or *capital, leases*.

**sale and leaseback**
An operation whereby a firm sells land, buildings, or equipment to a financial institution and simultaneously leases the property back for a specified period under specific terms.

**lessee**
The party leasing a property.

**lessor**
The owner of property that is leased.

*Sale and Leaseback.* Under a **sale-and-leaseback**, a firm that owns land, buildings, or equipment sells the property to another party and simultaneously executes an agreement to lease the property back for a specified period under specific terms. The purchaser of the property could be an insurance company, a commercial bank, a specialized leasing company, or even an individual investor. The sale-and-leaseback plan is an alternative to a mortgage.

Note that the firm which is selling the property, or the **lessee**, immediately receives the purchase price put up by the buyer, or the **lessor**.[5] At the same

---

[5]The term *lessee* is pronounced "less-ee," not "lease-ee," and *lessor* is pronounced "less-or."

time, the seller-lessee retains the use of the property just as if it had borrowed and used the property to secure the loan. This parallel to borrowing is carried over to the lease payment schedule. Under a mortgage loan arrangement, the financial institution would normally receive a series of equal payments just sufficient to amortize the loan while providing a specified rate of return to the lender on the outstanding balance. Under a sale-and-leaseback arrangement, the lease payments are set up in exactly the same manner—the payments are set so as to return the full purchase price to the investor-lessor and to provide a specified rate of return on the lessor's outstanding investment.

**operating lease**
A lease under which the lessor maintains and finances the property; also called a *service lease*.

*Operating Leases.* **Operating leases**, sometimes called *service leases*, provide for both *financing* and *maintenance*. IBM is one of the pioneers of the operating lease contract, and computers and office copying machines, together with automobiles and trucks, are the primary types of equipment involved. Ordinarily, these leases call for the lessor to maintain and service the leased equipment, and the cost of the maintenance is built into the lease payments.

Another important characteristic of operating leases is the fact that they are frequently *not fully amortized*—in other words, the payments required under the lease contract are not sufficient to recover the full cost of the equipment. However, the lease contract is written for a period considerably shorter than the expected economic life of the leased equipment, and the lessor expects to recover all investment costs either through subsequent renewal payments, through subsequent leases to other lessees, or by sale of the leased equipment.

A final feature of operating leases is that they frequently contain a *cancellation clause* which gives the lessee the right to cancel the lease before the expiration of the basic agreement. This is an important consideration to the lessee, for it means that the equipment can be returned if it is rendered obsolete by technological developments or is no longer needed because of a decline in the lessee's business.

**financial lease**
A lease that does not provide for maintenance services, is not cancelable, and is fully amortized over its life; also called a *capital lease*.

*Financial, or Capital, Leases.* **Financial leases**, sometimes called *capital leases*, are differentiated from operating leases in three respects: (1) they do *not* provide for maintenance service, (2) they are *not* cancelable, and (3) they *are* fully amortized (that is, the lessor receives rental payments equal to the full price of the leased equipment plus a return on investment). In a typical leasing arrangement, the firm that will use the equipment (the lessee) selects the specific items it requires and then negotiates the price and delivery terms with the manufacturer. The user firm then negotiates terms with a leasing company and, once the lease terms are set, arranges to have the lessor buy the equipment from the manufacturer or the distributor. When the equipment is purchased, the user firm simultaneously executes the lease agreement.

Financial leases are quite similar to sale-and-leaseback arrangements, the major difference being that the leased equipment is new and the lessor buys

**Table 13-1**
**Balance Sheet Effects of Leasing**

| Before Asset Increase | | | | After Asset Increase | | | | | | | |
|---|---|---|---|---|---|---|---|---|---|---|---|
| Firms P and L | | | | Firm P, Which Borrows and Purchases | | | | Firm L, Which Leases | | | |
| Current assets | $ 50 | Debt | $ 50 | Current assets | $ 50 | Debt | $150 | Current assets | $ 50 | Debt | $ 50 |
| Fixed assets | 50 | Equity | 50 | Fixed assets | 150 | Equity | 50 | Fixed assets | 50 | Equity | 50 |
| Total | $100 | | $100 | Total | $200 | | $200 | Total | $100 | | $100 |
| | | Debt ratio: | 50% | | | Debt ratio: | 75% | | | Debt ratio: | 50% |

it from a manufacturer or a distributor instead of from the user-lessee. A sale and leaseback may thus be thought of as a special type of financial lease, and both sale-and-leasebacks and financial leases are analyzed in the same manner.[6]

### Financial Statement Effects

**off balance sheet financing**
Financing in which the assets and liabilities under the contract do not appear on the firm's balance sheet.

Lease payments are shown as operating expenses on a firm's income statement, but under certain conditions, neither the leased assets nor the liabilities under the lease contract appear on the firm's balance sheet. For this reason, leasing is often called **off balance sheet financing**. This point is illustrated in Table 13-1 by the balance sheets of two hypothetical firms, P (for Purchase) and L (for Lease). Initially, the balance sheets of both firms are identical, and both have debt ratios of 50 percent. Next, each firm decides to acquire fixed assets costing $100. Firm P borrows $100 to make the purchase, so both an asset and a liability go on its balance sheet, and its debt ratio is increased to 75 percent. Firm L leases the equipment. The lease may call for fixed charges as high as or even higher than those on the loan, and the obligations assumed under the lease may be equally or more dangerous from the standpoint of financial safety, but the firm's debt ratio remains at 50 percent.

**FASB #13**
The statement of the Financial Accounting Standards Board that details the conditions and procedures for capitalizing leases.

To correct this problem, the Financial Accounting Standards Board has issued **FASB #13**, which requires that for an unqualified audit report, firms that enter into financial (or capital) leases must restate their balance sheets to report leased assets as fixed assets and the present value of future lease payments as a debt.[7] This process is called *capitalizing the lease*, and its net effect is to cause Firms P and L to have similar balance sheets—both of which will in essence resemble the one shown for Firm P.

The logic behind FASB #13 is as follows. If a firm signs a lease contract, its obligation to make lease payments is just as binding as if it had signed a loan agreement—the failure to make lease payments can bankrupt a firm just

---

[6]In order for a lease transaction to qualify as a lease for tax purposes, and thus for the lessee to be able to deduct the lease payments, the life of the lease must approximate the life of the asset, and the lessee cannot be permitted to buy the asset at a nominal value. It is important to consult lawyers and accountants to insure that a lease is valid under current IRS regulations.

[7]FASB #13, "Accounting for Leases," November 1976, spells out in detail the conditions under which the lease must be capitalized and the procedures for doing so.

as surely as can the failure to make principal and interest payments on a loan. Therefore, for all intents and purposes, a financial lease is identical to a loan.[8] This being the case, if a firm signs a lease agreement, this has the effect of raising its "true" debt ratio and thereby changing its "true" capital structure. Therefore, if the firm had previously established a target capital structure, and if there is no reason to think that the optimal capital structure has changed, then using lease financing requires additional equity backing in exactly the same manner as does debt financing.

If a disclosure of the lease in our Table 13-1 example were not made, then Firm L's investors could be deceived into thinking that its financial position is stronger than it really is. Even if the lease were disclosed, investors might not fully recognize its impact and in effect might not see that Firms P and L are in essentially the same financial position. If this were the case, then a firm could increase its true amount of debt through a lease arrangement, which would have a smaller effect on its cost of conventional debt, $k_d$, on its cost of equity, $k_s$, and consequently on its average cost of capital, $k_a$, than if it had borrowed directly. These benefits of leasing would accrue to existing investors at the expense of new investors, who were in effect being deceived by the fact that the firm's balance sheet did not fully reflect its true liability situation. This is why FASB #13 was issued.

A lease is classified as a capital lease, and hence is capitalized and shown directly on the balance sheet, if any one of the following conditions exists:

**1.** Under the terms of the lease, ownership of the property is effectively transferred from the lessor to the lessee.

**2.** The lessee can purchase the property or renew the lease at less than true market value when the lease expires.

**3.** The lease runs for a period equal to or greater than 75 percent of the asset's life. Thus, if an asset has a 10-year life and the lease is written for more than 7.5 years, the lease must be capitalized.

**4.** The present value of the lease payments is equal to or greater than 90 percent of the initial value of the asset, less any tax credit taken by the lessor.[9]

---

[8]There are, however, certain legal differences between loans and leases. In a bankruptcy liquidation, the lessor is entitled to take possession of the leased asset. If the value of the asset is less than the required payments under the lease, the lessor can enter a claim (as a general creditor) for one year's lease payments; in a bankruptcy reorganization, the lessor receives the asset plus three years' lease payments if needed to bring the value of the asset up to the remaining investment in the lease. Under a secured loan arrangement, on the other hand, the lender has a security interest in the asset, meaning that if it is sold, the lender will be given the proceeds, and the full unsatisfied portion of the lender's claim will be treated as a general creditor obligation (see Appendix 12A). It is not possible to state as a general rule whether a supplier of capital is in a stronger position as a secured creditor or as a lessor. Since one position is usually regarded as being about as good as the other at the time the financial arrangements are being made, a lease is about as risky as a secured term loan from both the lender's and the lessee-borrower's viewpoints.

[9]The discount rate used to calculate the present value of the lease payments must be the lower of (1) the rate used by the lessor to establish the lease payments or (2) the rate of interest which the lessee would have paid for new debt with a maturity equal to that of the lease.

These rules, together with strong footnote disclosure rules for operating leases, are sufficient to insure that no one will be fooled by lease financing. Thus, leases are recognized to be essentially the same as debt; they will have the same effects as debt on $k_d$, $k_s$, and the firm's overall cost of capital as discussed in Chapter 14. Therefore, leasing will not generally permit a firm to use more financial leverage than could be obtained with conventional debt.

## Evaluation by the Lessee

Any prospective leases must be evaluated by both the lessee and the lessor. The lessee must determine whether leasing an asset will be less costly than buying it; the lessor must decide whether or not the lease will provide a reasonable rate of return. Since our focus in this book is primarily on corporations, we restrict our analysis to that conducted by the lessee.[10]

In the typical case, the events leading to a lease arrangement follow the sequence described below. We should note that a great deal of uncertainty exists regarding the theoretically correct way to evaluate lease versus purchase decisions—some very complex decision models have been developed to aid in the analysis. However, the analysis given here leads to the correct decision in every case we have ever encountered.

**1.** The firm decides to acquire a particular building or piece of equipment; this decision is based on regular capital budgeting procedures and is not an issue in the typical lease analysis. In a lease analysis, we are concerned simply with whether to obtain the use of the machine by lease or by purchase. However, if the effective cost of the lease is substantially lower than that of debt—and this could occur for several reasons, including the situation in which the lessor is able to utilize the investment tax credit but the lessee is not—then the cost of capital used in capital budgeting would have to be recalculated, and projects formerly deemed unacceptable might become acceptable.

**2.** Once the firm has decided to acquire the asset, the next question is how to finance it. Well-run businesses do not have excess cash lying around, so new assets must be financed in some manner.

**3.** Funds to purchase the asset could be obtained by borrowing, by retaining earnings, or by selling new equity. Alternatively, the asset could be leased. Because of the FASB #13 capitalization/disclosure provision for leases, we assume that a lease would have the same capital structure effect as a loan.

As indicated earlier, a lease is comparable to a loan in the sense that the firm is required to make a specified series of payments, and a failure to meet these payments will result in bankruptcy. Thus, it is most appropriate to com-

---

[10]The lessee is typically offered lease terms by the lessor, which is generally a bank, a finance company such as GECC, or some other institutional lender, and it can accept the lease terms or shop around for a better deal. In this chapter, we take the lease terms as given for purposes of our analysis. Chapter 14 of Eugene F. Brigham and Louis C. Gapenski, *Intermediate Financial Management*, considers lease analysis from the lessor's standpoint and discusses how a potential lessee can use such an analysis in bargaining for better terms.

pare the cost of lease financing versus that of debt financing.[11] The lease versus borrow-and-purchase analysis is illustrated with data on the Porter Electronics Company. The following conditions are assumed:

**1.** Porter plans to acquire equipment with a cost of $11,111,111, delivered and installed. An investment tax credit of $1,111,111, which is 10 percent, applies. Thus, the net financing required if Porter borrows and buys is $10 million.

**2.** Porter can borrow the required $10 million with a 10 percent loan to be amortized over 5 years. Therefore, the loan will call for payments of $2,637,965.60 per year, calculated as follows:

$$\text{Payment} = \frac{\$10,000,000}{\text{PVIFA}_{10\%,5}} = \frac{\$10,000,000}{3.7908} = \$2,637,965.60.$$

**3.** Alternatively, Porter can lease the equipment for 5 years at a rental charge of $2,791,670 per year, but the lessor will own it upon the expiration of the lease. (The lease payment schedule is established by the potential lessor, and Porter can accept it, reject it, or negotiate.)

**4.** The equipment will definitely be used for 5 years, at which time its estimated net salvage value will be $715,000. Porter plans to continue using the equipment, so (1) if it purchases the equipment, Porter will keep it, and (2) if it leases the equipment, we assume Porter will have the option to buy it at its estimated salvage value, $715,000.

**5.** The lease contract stipulates that the lessor will maintain the equipment. However, if Porter borrows and buys, it will have to bear the cost of maintenance, which will be performed by the equipment manufacturer at a fixed contract rate of $500,000 per year, payable at year-end.

**6.** The equipment falls in the ACRS 5-year class life, and for this analysis we assume that Porter's effective tax rate is 40 percent. Also, note that the depreciable basis is the original cost less one-half of the ITC, or $11,111,111 − $555,556 = $10,555,555.

***NPV Analysis.***[12] Table 13-2 shows the outflows that would be incurred each year under the two financing plans. The table is set up to form a time line of cash flows:

---

[11]The analysis should compare the cost of leasing to the cost of debt financing *regardless* of how the asset is actually financed. The asset may actually be purchased with available cash if it is not leased, but since in the long run leasing is a substitute for debt financing, the comparison between the two would still be the most appropriate.

[12]This section is relatively technical, so some instructors may choose to omit it if time pressures do not permit coverage. Also, the format of the lease analysis is somewhat different in this edition of the text than the worksheet presented in the last one. People are increasingly using computer spreadsheets such as *Lotus 1-2-3* to analyze leases, and such analysis is easier if it is set up to resemble a time line, which is the format used here. Also, we have broken the analysis into several steps to make it easier for students to understand what is being done.

**Table 13-2**
**Porter Electronics Company: NPV Lease Analysis**
**(Thousands of Dollars)**

| I. Borrow and Purchase Analysis | Year | | | | |
|---|---|---|---|---|---|
| | 1 | 2 | 3 | 4 | 5 |
| a. Amortization schedule | | | | | |
| (1) Loan payment | $ 2,638 | $ 2,638 | $ 2,638 | $ 2,638 | $ 2,638 |
| (2) Interest | 1,000 | 836 | 656 | 458 | 240 |
| (3) Principal payment | 1,638 | 1,802 | 1,982 | 2,180 | 2,398 |
| (4) Remaining balance | 8,362 | 6,560 | 4,578 | 2,398 | 0 |
| b. Depreciation schedule | | | | | |
| (5) Depreciable basis | 10,556 | 10,556 | 10,556 | 10,556 | 10,556 |
| (6) Allowance | .15 | .22 | .21 | .21 | .21 |
| (7) Depreciation | 1,583 | 2,322 | 2,217 | 2,217 | 2,217 |
| c. Cash outflows | | | | | |
| (8) Loan payment | $ 2,638 | $ 2,638 | $ 2,638 | $ 2,638 | $ 2,638 |
| (9) Interest tax savings | (400) | (334) | (262) | (183) | (96) |
| (10) Depreciation tax savings | (633) | (929) | (887) | (887) | (887) |
| (11) Maintenance (AT) | 300 | 300 | 300 | 300 | 300 |
| (12) Net cash outflows (buy) | $ 1,905 | $ 1,675 | $ 1,789 | $ 1,868 | $ 1,955 |
| (13) PVIF | 0.9434 | 0.8900 | 0.8396 | 0.7921 | 0.7473 |
| (14) PV of owning | $ 1,797 | $ 1,491 | $ 1,502 | $ 1,480 | $ 1,461 |
| (15) Total PV cost of owning | | | Sum of Line 14 = PV cost of owning: | | $ 7,731 |
| **II. Lease Analysis** | | | | | |
| (16) Lease cost after taxes | $ 1,675 | $ 1,675 | $ 1,675 | $ 1,675 | $ 1,675 |
| (17) Purchase option price | | | | | 715 |
| (18) Net cash outflows (lease) | $ 1,675 | $ 1,675 | $ 1,675 | $ 1,675 | $ 2,390 |
| (19) PVIF | 0.9434 | 0.8900 | 0.8396 | 0.7921 | 0.7473 |
| (20) PV of leasing | $ 1,580 | $ 1,491 | $ 1,406 | $ 1,327 | $ 1,786 |
| (21) Total PV cost of leasing | | | Sum of Line 20 = PV cost of leasing: | | $ 7,590 |

**III. Cost Comparison**

Advantage to leasing: Total PV cost of owning − Total PV cost of leasing = $7,731 − $7,590
$$= \$141.$$

All cash flows occur at the end of the year, and the $CF_t$ values are shown on Lines 12 and 18 for buying and for leasing, respectively.

The top section of the table is devoted to the costs of borrowing and buying, and Line 12 shows net cash flows. The loan amortization schedule is given first, followed by the depreciation schedule. Then the annual net cash

**Explanation of lines:**

(1) Payments under the loan were determined in the text.

(2) Interest is calculated at 10 percent of the remaining balance from the prior year. Initially, the remaining balance is $10 million, so the first year's interest is 0.1 ($10,000) = $1,000.

(3) The principal payment is equal to the payment minus the interest component, $2,638 − $1,000 = $1,638 in Year 1.

(4) The remaining balance is calculated as the remaining balance from the prior year minus the principal repayment, $10,000 − $1,638 = $8,362 in Year 1.

(5) Depreciable basis is equal to the purchase price minus one-half of the ITC: $11,111,111 − (0.5)($1,111,111) = $10,555,555.

(6 and 7) Depreciation is calculated by ACRS, using rates of 0.15, 0.22, 0.21, 0.21, and 0.21. Refer back to Chapter 2 for a discussion of the ACRS depreciation system.

(8) Loan payment, which is taken from Line 1.

(9) The interest tax savings is calculated as Interest(Tax rate) = Interest(0.40). This amount is shown as a negative because it reduces outflows.

(10) The depreciation tax savings is equal to Depreciation(Tax rate) = Depreciation(0.40). It is shown as a negative number because it also reduces outflows.

(11) Maintenance costs are $500 per year on a pre-tax basis, or $300 on an after-tax basis: $500(1 − T) = $500(0.6) = $300.

(12) Net cash outflows if Porter borrows and buys are calculated as follows: Line 12 = Line 8 + Line 9 + Line 10 + Line 11.

(13) PVIFs are based on the 6 percent after-tax cost of debt and are taken from Appendix Table A-1. Why 6 percent is used is discussed later in the chapter.

(14) The PV of the cost of owning for each year is the product of Line 12 times Line 13.

(15) The total PV cost of owning is the sum of the entries on Line 14.

(16) The lease payment is given in the text as $2,791,670 before taxes and $1,675,002 after taxes. This payment includes all maintenance costs.

(17) Porter may purchase the machinery for $715,000 at the end of 5 years. Since it plans to continue the operation, it must incur this expense in Year 5. No taxes are involved.

(18) Net cash outflows if Porter elects to lease consist of the after-tax amount of the lease payment plus the Year 5 purchase option cost.

(19) PVIFs are the same as those shown on Line 13.

(20) PV costs of leasing are Line 18 times Line 19.

(21) The total PV cost of leasing is the sum of the entries on Line 20.

outflows—loan payment, interest tax savings, depreciation tax savings, and after-tax maintenance expense—that Porter will incur if it borrows and buys the equipment are summed, and the present values of these cash flows are found by multiplying each cash flow by the appropriate present value interest factor. Note that the interest and depreciation tax savings are shown as negative outflows, since they are actually cash inflows resulting from the deductibility of interest and depreciation expenses. The present value of these cash flows is shown on Line 15 in the Year 5 column.

The next section of the table calculates the present value cost of leasing. The lease payments are $2,791,670 per year; this rate, which includes maintenance, was established by the prospective lessor and offered to Porter Electronics. If Porter accepts the lease, the full $2,791,670 will be a deductible expense, so the after-tax cost of the lease is calculated as follows:

$$
\begin{aligned}
\text{After-tax cost} &= \text{Lease payment} - \text{Tax savings} \\
&= \text{Lease payment} - (\text{Tax rate})(\text{Lease payment}) \\
&= \text{Lease payment} (1 - \text{Tax rate}) \\
&= \$2,791,670(1 - 0.4) \\
&= \$1,675,002.
\end{aligned}
$$

This amount is shown on Line 16.

Line 17 in the lease section shows the $715,000 expected Year 5 purchase price. We include this amount as a cost of leasing because Porter will almost certainly want to continue the operation and thus will be forced to purchase the equipment from the lessor. If we had assumed that the operation would not be continued, then no entry would appear on this line. However, in that case, we would have included the $715,000, less taxes, as a Year 5 inflow (with parens around it) in the purchase analysis because if the asset were purchased originally, it would be sold after 5 years. It would be subtracted because it would then be an inflow, whereas all other cash flows are outflows. Line 20 calculates the present value of the cost of leasing for each year, and Line 21 sums these costs and shows the total PV cost of leasing in the Year 5 column.

The rate used to discount the cash flows is a critically important issue. In Chapter 6, we saw that the riskier the cash flow, the higher will be the discount rate used to find present values. This same principle was observed in our discussion of capital budgeting, and it also applies in lease analysis. Just how risky are the cash flows under consideration here? Most of them are relatively certain, at least when compared with the types of cash flow estimates that were developed in capital budgeting. For example, the loan payment schedule is set by contract, as is the lease payment schedule. The depreciation expenses are also established by law and are not subject to change, and the $500,000 annual maintenance cost is fixed by contract as well. The tax savings are somewhat uncertain, but they will be as projected so long as Porter's effective tax rate remains at 40 percent. The residual value is the least certain of the cash flows, but even here Porter's management is fairly confident that it will want to acquire the property and also that the estimated salvage value will be close to $715,000.

Since the cash flows under the lease and borrow-and-purchase alternatives are both reasonably certain, they should be discounted at a relatively low rate. Most analysts recommend that the company's cost of debt be used, and this rate seems reasonable in our example. Further, since all the cash flows are on an after-tax basis, *the after-tax cost of debt, which is 6 percent, should be used*. Accordingly, in Table 13-2 we multiplied the cash outflows by the 6 percent PVIFs shown below each set of cash flows, and we summed these discounted cash flows to obtain the present values of the costs of owning and leasing. The financing method that produces the smaller present value of costs is the one that should be selected. The example shown in Table 13-2 indicates that leasing has a net advantage over buying: the present value of the costs of leasing is $141,000 less than that of buying. In this instance, it is to Porter's advantage to lease.[13]

***Estimated Residual Value.*** It is important to note that the lessor will own the property upon the expiration of the lease. The value of the property at that time is called its **residual value**. Superficially, it would appear that if residual values are expected to be large, owning would have an advantage over leasing. However, this apparent advantage of owning is subject to substantial qualification: if expected residual values are large—as they may be under inflation for certain types of equipment and also if real property is involved—competition among leasing companies will force leasing rates down to the point where potential residual values will be fully recognized in the lease contract rates. Thus, the existence of large residual values on equipment is not likely to result in materially lower costs of owning.

***Increased Credit Availability.*** As noted earlier, leasing is sometimes said to have an advantage for firms that are seeking the maximum degree of financial leverage. First, it is sometimes argued that firms can obtain more money for longer terms under a lease arrangement than under a loan secured by a specific piece of equipment. Second, since some leases do not appear on the balance sheet, lease financing has been said to give the firm a stronger appearance in a *superficial* credit analysis and thus permit it to use more leverage than it could if it did not lease. There may be some truth to these claims for smaller firms. However, now that large firms are required to capitalize major leases and to report them on their balance sheets, this point is of questionable validity.

***Investment Tax Credit and Depreciation.*** The investment tax credit, discussed in Chapter 2, can be taken only if the firm's profits and taxes exceed prescribed levels. If a firm is unprofitable or is expanding so rapidly and generating such large tax credits that it cannot use all available tax shelters, then it may be worthwhile for it to enter a lease arrangement. Here the lessor (generally a bank or a leasing subsidiary of a profitable company such as IBM or GE) will take the credit and give the lessee a corresponding reduction in

**residual value**
The value of leased property at the end of the lease term.

---

[13]The more complicated methods that exist for analyzing leasing generally focus on the issue of which discount rate should be used to discount the cash flows. See Brigham and Gapenski, *Intermediate Financial Management*, Chapter 14, for a discussion.

lease charges. Railroads and airlines have been large users of leasing in recent years, as have industrial companies such as U.S. Steel whose profits have been eroded by international competition.

Depreciation has the same type of effect as the investment tax credit: a firm that is suffering losses cannot benefit from the tax deductibility of depreciation as much as a lessor who is in a high marginal tax bracket. Tax considerations—the investment tax credit and accelerated depreciation—are without a doubt the dominant force behind most financial leases written today.

## Options

**option**
A contract giving the option holder the right to buy or sell an asset at some predetermined price within a specified period of time.

An **option** is a contract that gives its holder the right to buy (or sell) an asset at some predetermined price within a specified period of time. "Pure options" are instruments that are created by outsiders (generally investment banking firms) rather than the firm itself; they are bought and sold primarily by investors (or speculators). However, financial managers should understand the nature of options, because this will help them structure warrant and convertible financings.

### Option Types and Markets

There are many types of options and option markets.[14] To understand how options work, suppose you owned 100 shares of IBM stock which on April 11, 1985, sold for $126.875 per share. You could give (or sell) someone else the right to buy your 100 shares at any time during the next 6 months at a price of, say, $130 per share. The $130 is called the **striking**, or **exercise**, **price**. Such options exist, and they are traded on a number of stock exchanges, with the Chicago Board Options Exchange (CBOE) being the oldest and largest. This type of option is defined as a **call option**, as the purchaser has a "call" on 100 shares of stock. The seller of a call option is defined as an *option writer*. An investor who writes a call option against stock held in his or her portfolio is said to be selling *covered options*; options sold without the stock to back them up are called *naked options*.

**striking (exercise) price**
The price that must be paid for a share of common stock when it is bought by exercising an option.

**call option**
An option to buy, or "call," a share of stock at a certain price within a specified period.

On April 11, 1985, IBM's 6-month, $130 call options sold on the CBOE for $5.50 each. Thus, for ($5.50)(100) = $550 you could buy an option contract that would give you the right to purchase 100 shares of IBM at a price of $130 per share at any time during the next 6 months. If the stock price stayed below $130 during that period, you would lose your $550, but if it rose to $150, then your $550 investment would be worth ($150 − $130)(100) = $2,000. That translates into a very healthy rate of return. Incidentally, if the stock price did go up, you would probably not actually exercise your

---

[14]For more on options, see Brigham and Gapenski, *Intermediate Financial Management*, Chapter 13. For a really in-depth treatment, see one of the investment texts listed in the references to Chapter 5.

option and buy the stock—you would sell the option, which would then have a price of at least $20 versus the $5.50 you paid, to another option buyer.

You can also buy an option which gives you the right to *sell* a stock at a specified price at some time in the future—this is called a **put option**. For example, suppose you expect IBM's stock price to decline from its current level sometime during the next 6 months. For $237.50 you could buy a 6-month put option giving you the right to sell 100 shares (which you would not necessarily own) at a price of $120 per share ($120 is the striking price). If you bought a 100-share put contract for $237.50 and IBM's stock price actually fell to $100, you would make ($120 − $100)(100) = $2,000, less the $237.50 you paid for the put option, for a net profit (before taxes and commissions) of $1,762.50.

**put option**
An option to sell a share of stock at a certain price within a specified period.

Options trading is one of the "hottest" financial activities in the United States today. The leverage involved makes it possible for speculators with just a few dollars to make a fortune almost overnight. Also, investors with sizable portfolios can sell options against their stocks and earn the value of the options (less brokerage commissions) even if the stocks' prices remain constant. Still, perhaps those who have profited most from the development of options trading are security brokers, who earn very healthy commissions on such trades.

The corporations on whose stocks options are written, such as IBM, have nothing to do with the options market. They neither raise money in that market nor have any direct transactions in it, and option holders do not vote for corporate directors (unless they exercise their options to purchase the stock, which few actually do). There have been studies by the SEC and others as to whether options trading stabilizes or destabilizes the stock market and whether it helps or hinders corporations seeking to raise new capital. The studies have not been conclusive, but options trading is here to stay, and many regard it as the most exciting game in town.

### Formula Value versus Option Price

**formula value**
The value of an option security on its expiration date, calculated as the stock price minus the striking, or exercise, price.

How is the actual price of an option determined in the market? To begin, we define an option's **formula value** as follows:

$$\text{Formula value} = \text{Current price of the stock} - \text{Striking price.}$$

For example, if a stock sells for $50 and its options have a striking price of $20, then the formula value of the option is $30. The formula value can be thought of as the value of the option on its expiration date.

Now consider Figure 13-1, which presents some data on Space Technology, Inc. (STI), a company which recently went public and whose stock has fluctuated widely during its short history. Column 1 in the lower section shows the trading range of the stock; Column 2 shows the striking price of the option; Column 3 shows the formula values for STI's options when the stock was selling at different prices; Column 4 gives the actual market prices of the option; and Column 5 shows the premium, or excess of the actual

**Figure 13-1**
**Space Technology, Inc.: Option Price and Formula Value**

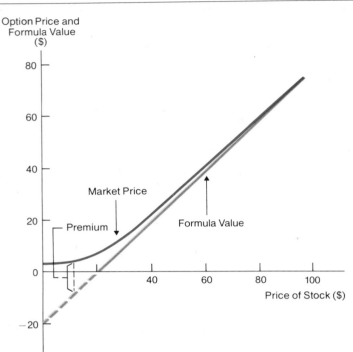

| Price of Stock (1) | Striking Price (2) | Formula Value of Option (1) − (2) = (3) | Market Price of Option (4) | Premium (4) − (3) = (5) |
|---|---|---|---|---|
| $12.00 | $20.00 | − $ 8.00 | $ 5.00 | $13.00 |
| 20.00 | 20.00 | 0.00 | 9.00 | 9.00 |
| 21.00 | 20.00 | 1.00 | 9.75 | 8.75 |
| 22.00 | 20.00 | 2.00 | 10.50 | 8.50 |
| 35.00 | 20.00 | 15.00 | 21.00 | 6.00 |
| 42.00 | 20.00 | 22.00 | 26.00 | 4.00 |
| 50.00 | 20.00 | 30.00 | 32.00 | 2.00 |
| 73.00 | 20.00 | 53.00 | 54.00 | 1.00 |
| 98.00 | 20.00 | 78.00 | 78.50 | 0.50 |

option price over its formula value. These data are plotted in the graph. At any stock price below $20, the formula value is negative; beyond $20, each $1 increase in the price of the stock brings with it a $1 increase in the option's formula value. Note, however, that the actual market price of the option lies above the formula value at each price of the common stock but the premium declines as the price of the stock increases. For example, when the common stock sold for $20 and the option had a zero formula value, its actual price, and the premium, was $9. Then, as the price of the stock rose, the *formula value* matched the increase dollar for dollar, but the *market price* of the option climbed less rapidly, and the premium declined. Thus, the premium was $9 when the stock sold for $20 a share, but it had declined to $1 by the time the stock price reached $73 a share, and beyond this point the premium virtually disappeared.

Why does this pattern exist? Why should the option ever sell for more than its formula value, and why does the premium decline as the price of the stock increases? The answer lies in the speculative appeal of options—they provide an investor with a high degree of leverage when buying securities. To illustrate, suppose STI's stock were selling for $21 and its options for exactly their formula value, $1. Now suppose you were thinking of investing in the company. If you bought a share of stock and the price rose to $42, you would make a 100 percent capital gain. However, if you bought the option at its $1 formula value, your capital gain would be $21 on a $1 investment, or 2,000 percent! At the same time, your total loss potential with the option would be only $1, while the potential loss if you purchased the stock would be $21. The huge capital gains potential, combined with the loss limitation, is clearly worth something—the exact amount it is worth to investors is the amount of the premium.

But why does the premium decline as the price of the stock rises? Part of the answer is that both the leverage effect and the loss protection feature decline at high stock prices. For example, if you were thinking of buying the stock when its price was $73 a share, the formula value of the option would be $53. If the stock price doubled to $146, the formula value of STI's option would go from $53 to $126, an increase of 138 percent versus the previous 2,000 percent gain when the stock price doubled. Notice also that the potential loss on the option is much greater when the option is selling at high prices. These two factors, the declining leverage impact and the increasing danger of losses, help explain why the premium diminishes as the price of the common stock rises.

In addition to the stock price and the striking price, the value of an option depends on the option's time to maturity and the variability of the underlying stock's price:

1. The longer an option has to run, the greater its value and the larger its premium. If an option expires at 4 p.m. today, there is not much chance that the stock price will go way up. Therefore, the option will sell at close to its formula value, and its premium will be small. On the other hand, if it has a year to go, the stock price could rise sharply, pulling the option's value up with it.

2. An option on an extremely volatile stock will be worth more than one on a very stable stock. For example, an option on a stock whose price rarely moves would not provide much chance of a large gain. On the other hand, an option on a stock that is highly volatile could provide a large gain, so such an option is more valuable. Note also that losses on options are limited, so large declines in a stock's price do not have a corresponding bad effect on

option holders. Therefore, stock price volatility can only enhance the value of an option.

**3.** If everything else were held constant, then in a graph such as Figure 13-1, the longer an option's life, the higher its market price line will be above the formula value line, and the more volatile the price of the underlying stock, the higher is the market price line.

## Warrants

**warrant**
A long-term option to buy a stated number of shares of common stock at a specified price.

A **warrant** is an option issued by a company which gives the holder the right to buy a stated number of shares of the company's stock at a specified price. Generally, warrants are distributed along with debt, and they are used to induce investors to buy a firm's long-term debt at a lower interest rate than would otherwise be required. For example, when Pan Pacific Airlines (PPA) wanted to sell $50 million of 20-year bonds in 1985, the company's investment bankers informed the financial vice-president that straight bonds would be difficult to sell and that an interest rate of 14 percent would be required. However, the bankers suggested as an alternative that investors would be willing to buy bonds with a coupon rate as low as 10⅜ percent if the company would offer 30 warrants with each $1,000 bond, each warrant entitling the holder to buy one share of common stock at a price of $22 per share. The stock was selling for $20 per share at the time. The warrants would expire in 1995 if they had not been exercised previously.

Why would investors have been willing to buy Pan Pacific's bonds at a yield of only 10⅜ percent in a 14 percent market just because warrants were offered as part of the package? Warrants, since they are long-term options, have a value for the reasons set forth in the previous section. In the PPA case, this value offset the low interest rate on the bonds and made the entire package of below-market-yield-bonds plus warrants attractive to investors.

### Initial Market Price of Bond with Warrants

If the PPA bonds had been issued as straight debt, they would have carried a 14 percent interest rate. However, with warrants attached, the bonds were sold to yield 10⅜ percent. Someone buying one of the bonds at its $1,000 initial offering price would thus have been receiving a package consisting of a 10⅜ percent, 20-year bond plus 30 warrants. Since the going interest rate on bonds as risky as those of PPA was 14 percent, we can find the straight-debt value of the bonds, assuming an annual coupon, as follows:

$$\text{Value} = \sum_{t=1}^{20} \frac{\$103.75}{(1.14)^t} + \frac{\$1,000}{(1.14)^{20}}$$

$$= \$103.75(\text{PVIFA}_{14\%,20}) + \$1,000(\text{PVIF}_{14\%,20})$$

$$= \$687.15 + \$72.80$$

$$= \$759.95 \approx \$760.$$

Thus, a person buying the bonds in the initial underwriting would pay $1,000 and receive in exchange a straight bond worth about $760 plus warrants presumably worth about $1,000 − $760 = $240:

$$\begin{array}{ccc}
\text{Price paid for} \\
\text{bond with warrants}
\end{array} = \begin{array}{c}
\text{Straight-debt} \\
\text{value of bond}
\end{array} + \begin{array}{c}
\text{Value of} \\
\text{warrants}
\end{array}$$

$$\$1,000 \quad = \quad \$760 \quad + \quad \$240$$

Since investors receive 30 warrants with each bond, each warrant has an implied value of $240/30 = $8.

The key issue in setting the terms of a bond-with-warrants offering is that of valuing the warrants. The straight-debt value of the bond can be estimated quite accurately. However, it is much more difficult to estimate the value of the warrants. If in setting the terms the value of the warrants is overestimated relative to their true market value, then it will be difficult to sell the issue at its par value. Conversely, if the warrants' value is underestimated, then investors in the issue will receive a windfall profit, because they can sell the warrants in the market for more than they implicitly paid for them. This windfall profit would come out of the pockets of PPA's stockholders.

## Use of Warrants in Financing

In the past, warrants have generally been used by small, rapidly growing firms as "sweeteners" when they were selling either debt or preferred stock. Such firms are frequently regarded as being highly risky, and their bonds could be sold only if the firms were willing to pay extremely high rates of interest and to accept very restrictive indenture provisions. To avoid this, firms such as Pan Pacific often offered warrants along with their bonds. In the 1970s, however, AT&T raised $1.57 billion by selling bonds with warrants. This was the largest financing of any type ever undertaken by a business firm, and it marked the first use ever of warrants by a large, strong corporation. Following AT&T, other sound companies began to use warrants.

Getting warrants along with bonds enables investors to share in a company's growth if that firm does in fact grow and prosper; therefore, investors are willing to accept a lower bond interest rate and less restrictive indenture provisions. A bond with warrants has some characteristics of debt and some of equity—it is a hybrid security that provides the financial manager with an opportunity to expand the firm's mix of securities and appeal to a broader group of investors, thus possibly lowering the firm's cost of capital.

**detachable warrant**
A warrant that can be detached from a bond issue and traded independently of it.

Virtually all warrants today are **detachable warrants**. Thus, after a bond with attached warrants has been sold, the warrants can be detached and traded separately from the bond. Further, when these warrants are exercised, the bond issue (with its low coupon rate) remains outstanding; the warrants thus bring in additional funds to the firm while leaving its interest costs relatively low.

The warrants' exercise price is generally set at from 10 to 30 percent above the market price of the stock on the date the bond is issued. If the firm does grow and prosper, and if its stock price rises above the exercise price at which shares may be purchased, warrant holders will turn in their warrants, along with cash equal to the stated exercise price, in exchange for the stock. However, without some incentive, many warrants would never be exercised prior to maturity—their value in the market would be greater than their formula, or exercise, value, and hence holders would sell warrants rather than exercise them.

There are three conditions which encourage holders to exercise their warrants: (1) Warrant holders will *surely* exercise warrants and buy stock if the warrants are about to expire with the market price of the stock above the exercise price. (2) Warrant holders will tend to exercise *voluntarily* and buy stock if the company raises the dividend on the common stock by a sufficient amount. Since no dividend is paid on the warrant, it provides no current income. However, if the common stock pays a high dividend, it provides an attractive dividend yield; the higher the stock's dividend, the greater the opportunity cost of holding the warrant rather than exercising it. (3) Warrants sometimes have **stepped-up exercise prices**, which prod owners into exercising them. For example, the Williamson Scientific Company has warrants outstanding with an exercise price of $25 until December 31, 1988, at which time that price will rise to $30. If the price of the common stock is over $25 just before December 31, 1988, many warrant holders will exercise their options before the stepped-up price takes effect.

**stepped-up exercise price**
An exercise price that is specified to be higher if a warrant is exercised after a designated date.

Another useful feature of warrants is that they generally bring in funds only if such funds are needed. If the company grows, it will probably need new equity capital. At the same time, this growth will cause the price of the stock to rise and the warrants to be exercised, thereby allowing the firm to obtain additional cash. If the company is not successful and cannot profitably employ additional money, the price of its stock will probably not rise sufficiently to induce exercise of the options.

## Convertibles

**convertible security**
A security, usually a bond or preferred stock, that is exchangeable at the option of the holder for the common stock of the issuing firm.

**Convertible securities** are bonds or preferred stocks that can be exchanged for common stock at the option of the holder. Unlike the exercise of warrants, which provides the firm with additional funds, conversion does not bring in additional capital—debt (or preferred stock) is simply replaced by common stock. Of course, this reduction of debt or preferred stock will strengthen the firm's balance sheet and thus make it easier to obtain additional capital, but this is a separate action.

**conversion ratio, R**
The number of shares of common stock that may be obtained by converting a convertible bond or share of convertible preferred stock.

### Conversion Ratio and Conversion Price

One of the most important provisions of a convertible security is the **conversion ratio**, **R**, defined as the number of shares of stock the convertible holder receives upon conversion. Related to the conversion ratio is the **conversion price**, $P_c$, which is the effective price the company receives for its common stock when conversion occurs. The relationship between the con-

**conversion price, $P_c$**
The effective price paid for common stock obtained by converting a convertible security.

version ratio and the conversion price can be illustrated by the Mountain States Oil (MSO) convertible debentures, issued at their $1,000 par value in 1985. At any time prior to maturity on July 1, 2005, a debenture holder can exchange a bond for 20 shares of common stock; therefore, R = 20. The bond has a par value of $1,000, so the holder would be relinquishing this amount upon conversion. Dividing the $1,000 par value by the 20 shares received gives a conversion price of $P_c$ = $50 a share:

$$\text{Conversion price} = P_c = \frac{\text{Par value of bond}}{\text{Shares received}}$$

$$= \frac{\$1,000}{R} = \frac{\$1,000}{20} = \$50.$$

Similarly, if we know the conversion price, we can find R:

$$R = \frac{\$1,000}{P_c} = \frac{\$1,000}{\$50} = 20 \text{ shares.}$$

Once R is set, the value of $P_c$ is established, and vice versa.

Like a warrant's exercise price, the conversion price is characteristically set at from 10 to 30 percent above the prevailing market price of the common stock at the time the convertible issue is sold. Generally, the conversion price and ratio are fixed for the life of the bond, although sometimes a stepped-up conversion price is used. Litton Industries' convertible debentures, for example, were convertible into 12.5 shares until 1972; into 11.76 shares from 1972 until 1982; and into 11.11 shares from 1982 until maturity in 1987. The conversion price thus started at $80, rose to $85 in 1972, and then went to $90 in 1982. Litton's convertibles, like most, became callable at the option of the company after a 10-year call protection period.

Another factor that may cause a change in the conversion price and ratio is a standard feature of almost all convertibles—the clause protecting the convertible against dilution from stock splits, stock dividends, and the sale of common stock at prices below the conversion price. The typical provision states that if common stock is sold at a price below the conversion price, then the conversion price must be lowered (and the conversion ratio raised) to the price at which the new stock was issued. Also, if the stock is split (or if a stock dividend is declared), the conversion price must be lowered by the percentage amount of the stock dividend or split. For example, if MSO were to have a two-for-one stock split, the conversion ratio would automatically be adjusted from 20 to 40 and the conversion price lowered from $50 to $25. If this protection were not contained in the contract, a company could completely thwart conversion by the use of stock splits. Warrants are similarly protected against such dilution.

The standard protection against dilution from selling new stock at prices below the conversion price can, however, get a company into trouble. For example, Litton Industries' stock was selling for only $62 in 1985. Thus, Litton would have to give the bondholders a tremendous advantage by lowering the conversion price from $90 to $62 if it wanted to sell new common stock.

Problems such as this must be kept in mind by firms considering the use of convertibles or bonds with warrants.

## Convertible Bond Model

In 1985 Mountain States Oil was thinking of issuing 20-year convertible bonds at a price of $1,000 each. Each bond would pay a 10 percent annual coupon interest rate, or $100 per year, and could be converted into 20 shares of stock; the conversion price therefore would be $1,000/20 = $50. If the bonds were not convertible, the required rate of return would be 13 percent and the bonds would initially sell at a price of $789:

$$B_0 = \sum_{t=1}^{20} \frac{\$100}{(1.13)^t} + \frac{\$1,000}{(1.13)^{20}} = \$789.$$

The firm's stock is expected to pay a dividend of $2.80 in the coming year; it sells at $35 per share; and this price is expected to grow at a constant rate of 8 percent per year.

The convertible bonds would not be callable for 10 years, after which they could be called at a price of $1,000. If after 10 years the conversion value exceeds the call price by at least 20 percent, management has indicated that it will probably call the bonds.

Figure 13-2 shows the expectations of both an average investor and the company:[15]

**1.** The horizontal line at M = $1,000 represents the par (and maturity) value. Also, $1,000 is the price at which the bond is initially offered to the public.

**2.** The "straight-bond" value of the convertible is initially $789, but it rises to $1,000 over the 20-year life of the bond. The bond's straight-debt value is shown by the line $B_t$ in Figure 13-2.

**conversion value, $C_t$**
The value of common stock obtained by converting a convertible security.

**3.** The bond's initial **conversion value**, $C_t$, or the value of the stock the investor would receive if the bond were converted at t = 0, is $700: Conversion value = $P_0(R)$ = $35(20 shares) = $700. The stock's price is expected to grow at an 8 percent rate, so $P_t$ = $35(1.08)^t$. If the price of the stock rises over time, then so will the conversion value of the bond—for example, in Year 5 the conversion value should be $C_t$ = $P_5(R)$ = $35(1.08)^5(20)$ = $1,029. The expected conversion value over time is given by the line $C_t$ in Figure 13-2.

**4.** The actual market price of the bond must always be equal to or greater than the higher of its straight-debt value or its conversion value. Therefore, the higher of the bond value or conversion value curves in Figure 13-2 represents a "floor price" for the bond; this is represented by the heavy line $B_0XC_t$.

---

[15]For a more complete discussion of how the terms are set on a convertible offering, see M. Wayne Marr and G. Rodney Thompson, "The Pricing of New Convertible Bond Issues," *Financial Management*, Summer 1984, 31-37.

**Figure 13-2**
**Model of a Convertible Bond**

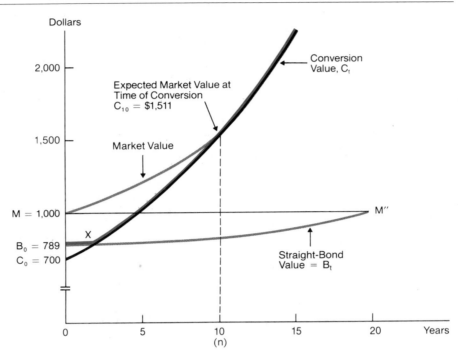

**5.** Initially, however, the convertible bond will sell for $1,000, which is substantially more than either its straight-bond value or its conversion value. Investors are willing to pay a premium over the straight-bond value (which establishes the initial floor) because of the possibility of earning large capital gains if the stock price shoots up. After about Year 2, when the conversion value exceeds the straight-bond value and thus establishes the floor, the market price will still exceed the floor. This is because the convertible is safer than the stock, for even if profits decline and the stock price drops, the bond's value will never fall below its straight-debt value.[16]

**6.** The gap between the market price of the convertible and the floor, or the premium investors are willing to pay, declines over time and is zero in Year 10. This decline occurs for two reasons. First, the dividends received on the stock are presumably growing at 8 percent a year, while the interest on the bond is fixed at $100 annually. At some point, the dividends which would be received from 20 shares of stock ( $2.80 \times 20 = $56$ initially) will exceed

---

[16]Note, however, that the bond value line $B_0M''$ would fall if interest rates rose in the economy or if the company's credit risk deteriorated and its $k_d$ consequently rose.

the $100 of interest paid by the bond; beyond that point the opportunity cost of holding the bond rather than converting it will become increasingly heavy. Second, after 10 years the bond will become callable at a price of $1,000. If MSO calls the issue, the bondholder can either convert the bond to common stock worth $C_t = \$1,511$ or receive $1,000 in cash. The holder will, of course, choose the $1,511 of stock. Note, however, that if the convertible were selling at a price greater than $C_t = \$1,511$ when the call occurred, the holder would suffer an immediate loss equal to the difference between the bond's price and $1,511. Therefore, due to the call provision, the market value of the bond will equal the conversion price in Year 10.

## Use of Convertibles in Financing

Convertibles offer two important advantages from the issuer's standpoint: ( 1 ) Convertibles, like bonds with warrants, permit a company to sell debt with lower interest rates and less restrictive covenants than straight bonds, and ( 2 ) they provide a way of selling common stock at prices higher than those currently prevailing. Many companies actually want to sell common stock and not debt, but they believe that the price of their stock is temporarily depressed. Management may know, for example, that earnings are depressed because of start-up costs associated with a new project but expect earnings to rise sharply during the next year or so, pulling the price of the stock along. Management thinks that if it sold stock now it would be giving up too many shares to raise a given amount of money. However, if it set the conversion price at 20 to 30 percent above the present market price of the stock, then 20 to 30 percent fewer shares would be given up when the bonds were converted. Notice, however, that management is counting on the stock price's rising sufficiently above the conversion price to make the bonds attractive in conversion. If earnings do not rise and pull the stock price up, and hence conversion does not occur, then the company could be saddled with debt in the face of low earnings, which could be disastrous.

How can the company be sure that conversion will occur if the price of the stock rises above the conversion price? Typically, convertibles contain a call provision that enables the issuing firm to force bondholders to convert. Suppose the conversion price is $50, the conversion ratio is 20, the market price of the common stock has risen to $60, and the call price on the convertible bond is $1,050. If the company calls the bond, bondholders can either convert into common stock with a market value of $1,200 or allow the company to redeem the bond for $1,050. Naturally, bondholders prefer $1,200 to $1,050, so conversion will occur. The call provision therefore gives the company a means of forcing conversion, provided the market price of the stock is greater than the conversion price.

Convertibles may be useful, but they do have three important disadvantages. ( 1 ) Although the use of a convertible security does in effect give the issuer the opportunity to sell common stock at a price higher than it could otherwise, if the common stock increases greatly in price, the issuer would probably have been better off if it had used straight debt in spite of its higher cost and then later sold common stock and refunded the debt. (2) If the company truly wants to raise equity capital, and if the price of the stock does not rise sufficiently after the bond is issued, then the firm will be stuck with debt. (3) Convertibles typically have a low coupon interest rate, an advantage that will be lost when conversion occurs. Warrant financings, on the other hand, permit the company to continue to use the low-coupon debt for a longer period.

## Reporting Earnings When Warrants or Convertibles Are Outstanding

If warrants or convertibles are outstanding, a firm could theoretically report earnings per share in one of three ways:

**1.** *Simple EPS.* The earnings available to common stockholders are divided by the average number of shares actually outstanding during the period.

**2.** *Primary EPS.* The earnings available are divided by the average number of shares that would have been outstanding if warrants and convertibles likely to be converted in the near future had actually been exercised or converted.

**3.** *Fully diluted EPS.* This is similar to primary EPS except that *all* warrants and convertibles are assumed to be exercised or converted regardless of the likelihood of either occurring.

Simple EPS is virtually never reported by firms which have warrants or convertibles likely to be exercised or converted—the SEC prohibits use of this figure, and it requires that primary and fully diluted earnings be shown on the income statement.

## Summary

This chapter discussed three hybrid forms of long-term financing: (1) preferred stock, (2) leasing, and (3) option securities. Preferred stock has characteristics similar to both debt and equity. It has priority over common stock with respect to claims on earnings and assets, and yet it has a fixed dividend, but nonpayment of the dividend cannot bankrupt the company. Preferred stocks are usually cumulative; they have no maturity but are sometimes callable, and they may have a sinking fund. Preferred dividends are not deductible to the issuer, but 85 percent of preferred dividends are excludable from taxable income to corporate owners.

There are three major types of leases: (1) *operating leases*, (2) *sale-and-lease-back arrangements*, and (3) *financial leases for new assets*. Operating leases generally provide for both the financing of an asset and its maintenance; sale-and-leaseback plans and regular financial leases usually provide only financing, and they are alternatives to debt financing. Lease plans are evaluated by a cash flow analysis. We start with the assumption that an asset will be acquired and that the acquisition will be financed either by debt or through a lease arrangement. Next, we develop the annual net cash outflows associated with each financing plan in a table similar to a time line. Then we discount the two sets of outflows at the company's after-tax cost of debt. Finally, we compare the alternatives and choose the one with the lower present value of costs.

*Warrants* and *convertibles* are forms of options used to finance business firms. Both are used as "sweeteners"—the option privileges they grant may make it possible for small companies to sell debt or preferred stock that otherwise could not be sold; for large companies, they result in lower costs of the securities sold.

The conversion of bonds or preferred stock by their holders does not provide additional funds to the company, but it does result in a lower debt ratio. The exercise of warrants provides additional funds, which strengthens the firm's equity position, but it still leaves the debt or preferred stock on the balance sheet. Note, however, that low interest rate debt remains outstanding when warrants are exercised, but the firm loses this advantage when convertibles are converted.

## Questions

13-1    Define each of the following terms:
        a. Cumulative dividends; arrearages; floating rate preferred stock
        b. Call premium
        c. Lessee; lessor
        d. Sale and leaseback; operating lease; financial lease
        e. Off balance sheet financing
        f. FASB #13
        g. Residual value
        h. Option; striking, or exercise, price; call option; put option
        i. Formula value; warrant; detachable warrant; stepped-up exercise price
        j. Convertible security; conversion ratio, R; conversion price, $P_c$; conversion value, $C_t$; straight bond value, $B_t$
        k. Simple EPS; primary EPS; fully diluted EPS

13-2    You are told that one corporation just issued $100 million of preferred stock and another purchased $100 million of preferred stock as an investment. You are also told that one firm has an effective tax rate of 20 percent while the other is in the 46 percent bracket. Which firm is more likely to have bought the preferred? Explain.

13-3    One often finds that a company's bonds have a higher yield than its preferred stock, even though the bonds are considered to be less risky than the preferred to an investor. What causes this yield differential?

13-4    Why would a company choose to issue floating rate as opposed to fixed rate preferred stock?

13-5    Distinguish between operating leases and financial leases. Would a firm be more likely to finance a fleet of trucks or a manufacturing plant with an operating lease?

13-6    One alleged advantage of leasing voiced in the past was that it kept liabilities off the balance sheet, thus making it possible for a firm to obtain more leverage than it otherwise could have. This raised the question of whether or not both the lease obligation and the asset involved should be capitalized and shown on the balance sheet. Discuss the pros and cons of capitalizing leases and related assets.

13-7      Suppose there were no IRS restrictions on what constitutes a valid lease. Explain in a manner that a legislator might understand why some restrictions should be imposed.

13-8      Suppose Congress changed the tax laws in a way that (1) permitted equipment to be depreciated over a shorter period, (2) lowered corporate tax rates, and (3) increased the investment tax credit. Discuss how each of these changes would affect the relative use of leasing versus conventional debt in the U.S. economy.

13-9      Why do options typically sell at prices higher than their formula values?

13-10     What effect does the trend in stock prices (subsequent to issue) have on a firm's ability to raise additional funds through (a) convertibles and (b) warrants?

13-11     How would a firm's decision to pay out a higher percentage of its earnings as dividends affect each of the following?
          a. The value of its long-term warrants.
          b. The likelihood that its convertible bonds will be converted.
          c. The likelihood that its warrants will be exercised.

13-12     Evaluate the following statement: "Issuing convertible securities represents a means by which a firm can sell common stock at a price above the existing market price."

13-13     Suppose a company simultaneously issues $50 million of convertible bonds with a coupon rate of 10 percent and $50 million of straight bonds with a coupon rate of 14 percent. Both bonds have the same maturity. Does the fact that the convertible issue has the lower coupon rate suggest that it is less risky than the straight bond? Is the cost of capital lower on the convertible than on the straight bond? Explain.

## Self-Test Problem (*Solution on Page 452*)

ST-1      The Olson Company has decided to acquire a new truck. One alternative is to lease the truck on a 4-year contract for a lease payment of $10,000 per year, with payments to be made at the *beginning* of each year. The lease would include maintenance. Alternatively, Olson could purchase the truck outright for $40,000, financing with a bank loan for the net purchase price and amortizing the loan over a 4-year period at an interest rate of 10 percent per year. Under the borrow-to-purchase arrangement, Olson would have to maintain the truck at a cost of $1,000 per year, payable at year-end. The truck qualifies for a 6 percent investment tax credit; it falls into the ACRS 3-year class; and it has a salvage value of $10,000, which is the expected market value after 4 years, at which time Olson plans to replace the truck irrespective of whether it leases or buys. Olson has a tax rate of 40 percent.
          a. What is Olson's PV cost of leasing?
          b. What is Olson's PV cost of owning? Should the truck be leased or purchased?
          c. The appropriate discount rate for use in Olson's analysis is the firm's after-tax cost of debt. Why?
          d. The salvage value is the least certain cash flow in the analysis. How might Olson incorporate the higher riskiness of this cash flow into the analysis?

## Problems

Balance sheet effects
of leasing

**13-1**  Two electronics companies, Minicorp and Microcorp, began operations with identical balance sheets. A year later, both required additional manufacturing capacity at a cost of $50,000. Minicorp obtained a 5-year, $50,000 loan at an 8 percent interest rate from its bank. Microcorp, on the other hand, decided to lease the required $50,000 capacity from Leasecorp for 5 years; an 8 percent return was built into the lease. The balance sheet for each company, before the asset increases, is as follows:

|              |           | Debt         | $ 50,000  |
|--------------|-----------|--------------|-----------|
|              |           | Equity       | 100,000   |
| Total assets | $150,000  | Total claims | $150,000  |

a. Show the balance sheet of each firm after the asset increase, and calculate each firm's new debt ratio.

b. Show how Microcorp's balance sheet would look immediately after the financing if it had capitalized the lease.

c. Would the rate of return (1) on assets and (2) on equity be affected by the choice of financing? How?

Lease versus buy

**13-2**  Silverton Mining Company must install $1 million of new machinery in its Colorado mine. It can obtain a bank loan for 100 percent of the required amount net of the ITC. Alternatively, a Denver investment banking firm which represents a group of investors believes that it can arrange for a lease financing plan. *Assume* that these facts apply:

1. The equipment falls in the ACRS 3-year class.
2. An ITC of 6 percent is allowed.
3. Estimated maintenance expenses are $50,000 per year.
4. Silverton's tax rate is 20 percent.
5. If the money is borrowed, the bank loan will be at a rate of 14 percent, amortized in 3 equal installments at the end of each year.
6. The tentative lease terms call for payments of $320,000 per year for 3 years.
7. Under the proposed lease terms, the lessee must pay for insurance, property taxes, and maintenance.
8. Silverton must use the equipment if it is to continue in business, so it will almost certainly want to acquire the property at the end of the lease. If it does, then under the lease terms it can purchase the machinery at its fair market value at that time. The best estimate of this market value is the $200,000 salvage value, but it could be much higher or lower under certain circumstances.

To assist management in making the proper lease-versus-buy decision, you are asked to answer the following questions:

a. Assuming that the lease can be arranged, should Silverton lease or borrow and buy the equipment? Explain. (Hints: PV cost of owning = $784,585 versus $768,897 for leasing; use these as check figures. Also, we used a discount rate of 11.2%. Loan payment = $404,888.)

b. Consider the $200,000 estimated salvage value. Is it appropriate to discount it at the same rate as the other cash flows? What about the other cash flows— are they all equally risky? (Hint: Riskier cash flows are normally discounted at higher rates, but when the cash flows are *costs* rather that *inflows*, the normal procedure must be reversed.)

(Do only if you are using the computerized problem diskette.)

c. Determine the lease payment at which Silverton would be indifferent to buying or leasing, that is, the lease payment which equates the NPV of leasing to that of buying. (Hint: Use trial and error.)

d. Using the $320,000 lease payment, what would be the effect if Silverton's tax rate rose to 46 percent? What generalization does this suggest?

Lease analysis               **13-3**      As part of its overall plant modernization and cost reduction program, Confederate Mills' management has decided to install a new automated weaving loom. In the capital budgeting analysis of this equipment, the IRR of the project was found to be 29 percent versus a project required return of 14 percent.

The loom has an invoice price of $100,000, including delivery and installation charges. The net financing requirement, if Confederate Mills borrows the funds, would be the purchase price less the applicable investment tax credit of 10 percent. The funds needed could be borrowed from the bank through a 4-year amortized loan at a 15 percent interest rate, with payments to be made at the end of each year. In the event that the loom is purchased, the manufacturer will contract to maintain and service it for a fee of $8,000 per year paid at the end of each year. The loom falls in the ACRS 5-year class, and Confederate's marginal tax rate is 40 percent.

Brooks Automation, Inc., maker of the loom, has offered to lease the loom to Confederate for $27,100 upon delivery and installation (at t = 0) plus 4 additional annual lease payments of $27,100 to be made at the end of Years 1 to 4. (Note that there are 5 lease payments in total.) The lease agreement includes maintenance and servicing. Actually, the loom has an expected life of 8 years, at which time its expected salvage value is zero; however, after 4 years, its market value is expected to equal its book value. Confederate plans to build an entirely new plant in 4 years, so it has no interest in either leasing or owning the proposed loom for more than that period.

a. Should the loom be leased or purchased?

(Do the remainder of the problem only if you are using the computerized problem diskette.)

b. Confederate's managers disagree on the appropriate discount rate to be used in the analysis. What effect would a discount rate change have on the lease-versus-purchase decision?

c. The salvage value is clearly the most uncertain cash flow in the analysis. What effect would a salvage value risk adjustment have on the analysis? (Assume that the appropriate salvage value pre-tax discount rate is 18 percent.)

d. The original analysis assumed that Confederate would not need the loom after 4 years. Now assume that the firm will continue to use it after the lease expires. Thus, if it leased, Confederate would have to buy the asset after 4 years at the then existing market value, which is assumed to equal the book value. What effect would this requirement have on the basic analysis? (No numerical analysis is required; just verbalize.)

e. Under the original lease terms, it was to Confederate's advantage to purchase the loom. However, if you had analyzed the lease from the lessor's viewpoint, you would have found that it was more profitable for Brooks Automation to lease the machine than to sell it—in fact, the manager of Brooks has found that the company can lower the lease payment to $26,400 and still make $816 more by leasing the machine than by selling it. With an annual lease payment of $26,400, should the loom be leased or bought?

f. Perform the lease analysis assuming that Confederate's marginal tax rate is (1) 0 percent and (2) 46 percent. Assume a lease payment of $27,100 and a 15 percent pre-tax discount rate. What effect, if any, would the lessee's tax rate have on the lease-buy decision?

**Warrants**          **13-4**    Weatherford Industries, Inc., has warrants outstanding that permit their holders to purchase one share of stock per warrant at a price of $25.

a. Calculate the formula value of Weatherford's warrants if the common sells at each of the following prices: $20, $25, $30, and $100.

b. At what approximate price do you think the warrants would actually sell under each condition indicated above? What premium is implied in your price? Your answer is a guess, but your prices and premiums should bear reasonable relationships to each other.

c. How would each of the following factors affect your estimates of the warrants' prices and premiums in Part b?
   1. The life of the warrant is lengthened.
   2. The expected variability ($\sigma_p$) in the stock's price decreases.
   3. The expected growth rate in the stock's EPS increases.
   4. The company announces a change in dividend policy: whereas it formerly paid no dividends, henceforth it will pay out *all* earnings as dividends.

d. Assume Weatherford's stock now sells for $20 per share. The company wants to sell some 20-year, annual interest, $1,000 par value bonds. Each bond will have attached 50 warrants, each exercisable into one share of stock at an exercise price of $25. Weatherford's straight bonds yield 12 percent. Regardless of your answer to Part b above, assume that the warrants will have a market value of $3 when the stock sells at $20. What coupon interest rate and dollar coupon must the company set on the bonds with warrants if they are to clear the market? Round to the nearest dollar or percentage point.

**Convertibles**      **13-5**    The Boca Grande Company was planning to finance an expansion in the summer of 1985. The principal executives of the company agreed that an industrial company such as theirs should finance growth by means of common stock rather than by debt. However, they felt that the price of the company's common stock did not reflect its true worth, so they decided to sell a convertible security. They considered a convertible debenture but feared the burden of fixed interest charges if the common stock did not rise in price to make conversion attractive. They decided on an issue of convertible preferred stock, which would pay a dividend of $2.10 per share.

The common stock was selling for $42 a share at the time. Management projected earnings for 1985 at $3 a share and expected a future growth rate of 10 percent a year in 1986 and beyond. It was agreed by the investment bankers and management that the common stock would sell at 14 times earnings, the current price/earnings ratio.

a. What conversion price should be set by the issuer? The conversion ratio will be 1.0—that is, each share of convertible preferred can be converted into one share of common. Therefore, the convertible's par value (and also the issue price) will be equal to the conversion price, which in turn will be determined as a percentage over the current market price of the common. Your answer will be a guess, but make it a reasonable one.

b. Should the preferred stock include a call provision? Why or why not?

Financing alternatives     **13-6**     The Drake Computer Company has grown rapidly during the past 5 years. Recently its commercial bank urged the company to consider increasing its permanent financing. Its bank loan under a line of credit has risen to $250,000, carrying an 8 percent interest rate, and Drake has been 30 to 60 days late in paying trade creditors.

Discussions with an investment banker have resulted in the decision to raise $500,000 at this time. Investment bankers have assured Drake that the following alternatives are feasible (flotation costs will be ignored):

*Alternative 1*: Sell common stock at $8.

*Alternative 2*: Sell convertible bonds at an 8 percent coupon, convertible into 100 shares of common stock for each $1,000 bond (that is, the conversion price is $10 per share).

*Alternative 3*: Sell debentures at an 8 percent coupon, each $1,000 bond carrying 100 warrants to buy one share of common stock at $10.

Melissa Davis, the president, owns 80 percent of the common stock of Drake and wishes to maintain control of the company; 100,000 shares are outstanding. The following are extracts of Drake's latest financial statements:

**Balance Sheet**

|  |  |  |  |
|---|---|---|---|
|  |  | Current liabilities | $400,000 |
|  |  | Common stock, $1 par | 100,000 |
|  |  | Retained earnings | 50,000 |
| Total assets | $550,000 | Total claims | $550,000 |

**Income Statement**

|  |  |
|---|---|
| Sales | $1,100,000 |
| All costs except interest | 990,000 |
| EBIT | 110,000 |
| Interest | 20,000 |
| EBT | 90,000 |
| Taxes at 50% | 45,000 |
| Net income | $   45,000 |
| Shares outstanding | 100,000 |
| Earnings per share | $0.45 |
| Price/earnings ratio | 19× |
| Market price of stock | $8.55 |

a. Show the new balance sheet under each alternative. For Alternatives 2 and 3, show the balance sheet after conversion of the debentures or exercise of the warrants. Assume that one-half of the funds raised will be used to pay off the bank loan and one-half to increase total assets.

b. Show Davis' control position under each alternative, assuming that she does not purchase additional shares.

c. What is the effect on earnings per share of each alternative if it is assumed that profits before interest and taxes will be 20 percent of total assets?

d. What will be the debt ratio under each alternative?

e. Which of the three alternatives would you recommend to Davis, and why?

**Convertibles**    **13-7**    Disk Drives, Inc. (DDI), needs to raise $25 million to begin producing a new disk drive. DDI's straight, nonconvertible debentures currently yield 14 percent. Its stock sells for $30 per share; the last dividend was $2; and the expected growth rate is a constant 9 percent. Investment bankers have tentatively proposed that DDI raise the $25 million by issuing convertible debentures. These convertibles would have a $1,000 par value, carry a coupon rate of 10 percent, have a 20-year maturity, and be convertible into 20 shares of stock. The bonds would be noncallable for 5 years, after which they would be callable at a price of $1,075; this call price would decline by $5 per year in Year 6 and each year thereafter. Management has called convertibles in the past (and presumably will call them again in the future), once they were eligible for call, when their conversion value was about 20 percent above their par value (not their call price).

a. Draw an accurate graph similar to Figure 13-2 representing the expectations set forth above.

b. Suppose the projects outlined above work out on schedule for 2 years, but then DDI begins to experience extremely strong competition from Japanese firms. As a result, DDI's expected growth rate drops from 9 percent to zero. Assume that the dividend at the time of the drop is $2.38. The company's credit strength is not impaired, and its value of $k_s$ is also unchanged. What would happen (1) to stock price and (2) to the convertible bond's price? Be as precise as you can.

## Solution to Self-Test Problem

**ST-1**    a. *Cost of leasing*:

|  | Year | | | |
| --- | --- | --- | --- | --- |
|  | **0** | **1** | **2** | **3** |
| Lease payment (AT)[a] | $ 6,000 | $6,000 | $6,000 | $6,000 |
| PVIFs (6%) | 1.000 | 0.9434 | 0.8900 | 0.8396 |
| PV of leasing | $ 6,000 | $5,660 | $5,340 | $5,038 |
| Total PV cost of leasing | = | $22,038 | | |

[a]After-tax payment = $10,000 (1 − T) = $10,000(0.6) = $6,000.

b. *Cost of owning*:

ITC 0.06( $40,000 ) = $2,400.
Net purchase price = $40,000 − $2,400 = $37,600.

Loan payment = $37,600/(PVIFA$_{10\%,4}$)

= $37,600/3.1699

= $11,862.

Depreciable basis = $40,000 − 0.5( $2,400 ) = $38,800.

Here are the cash flows under the borrow-and-buy alternative.

|  | Year | | | |
|---|---|---|---|---|
|  | **1** | **2** | **3** | **4** |
| 1. Amortization schedule | | | | |
| (a) Loan payment | $11,862 | $11,862 | $11,862 | $11,862 |
| (b) Interest | 3,760 | 2,950 | 2,059 | 1,078 |
| (c) Principal payment | 8,102 | 8,912 | 9,803 | 10,784 |
| (d) Remaining balance | 29,498 | 20,586 | 10,783 | 0 |
| 2. Depreciation schedule | | | | |
| (e) Depreciation basis | $38,800 | $38,800 | $38,800 | $38,800 |
| (f) Allowance | .25 | .38 | .37 | 0 |
| (g) Depreciation | 9,700 | 14,744 | 14,356 | 0 |
| 3. Cash outflows | | | | |
| (h) Loan payment | $11,862 | $11,862 | $11,862 | $11,862 |
| (i) Interest tax savings | (1,504) | (1,180) | (824) | (431) |
| (j) Depreciation tax savings | (3,880) | (5,898) | (5,742) | — |
| (k) Maintenance (AT) | 600 | 600 | 600 | 600 |
| (l) Salvage value (AT) | | | | (6,000) |
| (m) Total cash outflows | $ 7,078 | $ 5,384 | $ 5,896 | $ 6,031 |
| PVIFs | 0.9434 | 0.8900 | 0.8396 | 0.7921 |
| PV of owning | $ 6,677 | $ 4,792 | $ 4,950 | $ 4,777 |

Total PV cost of owning = $21,196

Since the present value of the cost of owning is less than that of leasing, the truck should be purchased: $22,038 − $21,196 = $842.

c. Use the cost of debt, because most cash flows are fixed by contract and consequently are relatively certain; thus, lease cash flows have about the same risk as the firm's debt. Also, leasing is considered as a substitute for debt. Use an after-tax cost rate, because the cash flows are stated net of taxes.

d. Olson could increase the discount rate on the salvage value cash flow.

## Selected Additional References and Cases

For a more detailed discussion of all the materials in this chapter, see:

Brigham, Eugene F., and Louis C. Gapenski, *Intermediate Financial Management*, Chapters 12, 13, and 14.

For a description of lease analysis in practice, as well as a comprehensive bibliography of the leasing literature, see:

O'Brien, Thomas J., and Bennie H. Nunnally, Jr., "A 1982 Survey of Corporate Leasing Analysis," *Financial Management*, Summer 1983, 30-36.

The investments texts listed in Chapter 6 provide extended discussions of options, warrants, and convertibles. For more insights into convertible pricing and use, see:

Alexander, Gordon J., Roger D. Stover, and D. B. Kuhnau, "Market Timing Strategies in Convertible Debt Financing," *Journal of Finance*, March 1979, 143-155.

The Crum-Brigham casebook contains several cases which deal with the issues discussed in this chapter:

Case 26, "Biotech Services, Inc.," which illustrates the standard lease-versus-purchase decision.

Case 27, "Sure Strike Tackle Company," which focuses on the analysis of sale and leaseback versus conventional mortgage financing.

Case 29, "Biolog Development Corporation," which illustrates convertible bond valuation.

"FLX, Incorporated," in the Harrington casebook, focuses on the retirement of convertible subordinated debentures which are selling below par.

# 14 THE COST OF CAPITAL

## RECOVERING COST OF CAPITAL:
## SHELL OIL TANKERS RUN AGROUND

In 1984, Shell Oil Company and the Newport News Shipbuilding and Dry-dock division of Tenneco, Inc., were involved in a lawsuit regarding two large tankers which Newport News had built for Shell at a cost of $100 million. Shell paid in advance for the ships and was to take delivery on a specified date. The contract stated that if the ships were not completed on time, Shell could sue for damages based on the cost of the capital which it had invested. Newport News did fail to complete the ships on time, so Shell sued.

The theory behind the contract clause, and hence the lawsuit, was (1) that Shell was investing money, (2) that this money had a cost, (3) that Shell expected to earn a return on the ships that would cover the cost of the money invested, (4) that if Shell did not get the ships, then it could not earn the cost of the capital it had invested in them, and (5) that it should be entitled to recover its capital costs from Newport News. The principal issue in the suit was this: What was the cost of the approximately $100 million which Shell had invested in the tankers? That determination required an assessment of how Shell had actually raised the $100 million (it had been raised partly as debt and partly as equity) and how much the funds from each source cost. The techniques discussed in this chapter were used to help ascertain the proper amount of the damages. Exactly the same procedures are (or should be) used by Shell and other companies for many other purposes.

The cost of capital is a critically important topic for three main reasons: (1) to maximize its value, a firm must minimize the costs of all inputs, including capital, and to minimize the cost of capital, the firm must be able to estimate it; (2) proper capital budgeting decisions require an estimate of the cost of capital; and (3) many other types of decisions, including those related to leasing, to bond refunding, and to working capital policy, require estimates of the cost of capital.[1]

---

[1]The cost of capital is also vitally important in regulated industries, including electric, gas, telephone, and water companies. In essence, regulatory commissions seek to measure a utility's cost of capital and then set prices so that the company will just earn this rate of return. If the estimate of the cost of capital is too low, then the company will not be able to attract sufficient capital to meet long-run demands for service, and the public will suffer. If the estimate is too high, customers will pay too much for service.

Our first topic in this chapter is the logic of the weighted average cost of capital. Next, we will consider the costs of the major types of capital. Then, we will see how the costs of the individual components of the capital structure are brought together to form a weighted average cost of capital. Finally, we will examine the relationship between capital budgeting and the cost of capital.

## The Logic of the Weighted Average Cost of Capital

When we discussed capital budgeting, we assumed the firms under consideration were financed entirely with equity funds. In those cases, the cost of capital used to analyze capital budgeting decisions was the firm's required return on equity. However, most firms finance a substantial portion of their capital budget with long-term debt, and many also use preferred stock as a source of capital. In these cases, a firm's cost of capital must reflect the average cost of the various sources of long-term funds it uses and not just its cost of equity.

Suppose a particular firm's cost of debt is estimated to be 13 percent, its cost of equity is 18 percent, and the decision has been made to finance next year's projects by selling debt. The argument is sometimes made that the cost of capital for these projects is 13 percent because only debt will be used to finance them. However, this position is incorrect. If it finances a particular set of projects with debt, the firm will be using up some of its potential for obtaining new debt in the future. As expansion occurs in subsequent years, the firm will at some point find it necessary to use additional equity financing to prevent the debt ratio from becoming too large.

To illustrate, suppose the firm borrows heavily at 13 percent during 1985, using up its debt capacity in the process, to finance projects yielding 15 percent. In 1986 it has new projects available that yield 17 percent, well above the return on 1985 projects, but it cannot accept them because they would have to be financed with 18 percent equity money. To avoid this problem the firm should be viewed as an ongoing concern, and the cost of capital used in capital budgeting should be calculated as a weighted average, or composite, of the various types of funds it generally uses regardless of the specific financing used to fund a particular project.

## Basic Definitions

**capital component**
One of the types of capital used by firms to raise money.

The items on the right-hand side of a firm's balance sheet—various types of debt, preferred stock, and common equity—are defined as its **capital components**. Any net increase in assets must be financed by an increase in one or more capital components.

*Capital* is a necessary factor of production, and like any other factor it has a cost. The cost of each component is defined as the *component cost* of that particular type of capital—for example, if a firm can borrow money at 13 percent, its component cost of debt is defined to be 13 percent.[2] Throughout this chapter we concentrate on debt, preferred stock, retained earnings, and new issues of common stock, which are the major capital structure components; their component costs are identified by the following symbols:

$k_d$ = interest rate on the firm's new debt = before-tax component cost of debt.

$k_d(1 - T)$ = after-tax component cost of debt, where T is the firm's marginal tax rate. $k_d(1 - T)$ is the debt cost used to calculate the weighted average cost of capital.

$k_p$ = component cost of preferred stock.

$k_s$ = component cost of retained earnings (or internal equity). It is identical to the $k_s$ developed in Chapter 6 and defined there as the required rate of return on common stock.

$k_e$ = component cost of external capital obtained by issuing new common stock, or external equity as opposed to internal equity. As we shall see, it is necessary to distinguish between equity raised by retaining earnings and that raised by selling new stock. This is why we distinguish between $k_s$ and $k_e$.

$k_a$ = the average, or composite, cost of capital. It is also called the weighted average cost of capital, WACC, so $k_a$ = WACC. If a firm raises new capital to finance asset expansion, and if it is to keep its capital structure in balance (that is, if it is to keep the same percentage of debt, preferred stock, and common equity funds), then it will raise part of its new funds as debt, part as preferred stock, and part as common equity (with equity coming either from retained earnings or from the issuance of new common stock).[3] Also, $k_a$ is a *marginal cost of capital (MCC)*; it reflects the cost of each additional dollar of capital used to finance an investment program.

These definitions and concepts are explained in detail in the remainder of the chapter, where we seek to accomplish two goals: (1) to develop a marginal cost of capital schedule ($k_a$ = MCC) that can be used in capital budgeting and (2) to determine the mix of types of capital that will minimize the MCC schedule. If the firm finances so as to minimize its MCC schedule, uses this MCC to calculate NPVs, and makes capital budgeting decisions on the basis of the NPV method, then the value of its stock will be maximized.

---

[2]We will see shortly that there is a before-tax and an after-tax cost of debt; for now it is sufficient to know that 13 percent is the before-tax component cost of debt.

[3]Firms try to keep their debt, preferred stock, and common equity in optimal proportions; we will see how they establish these proportions in Chapter 15. However, firms do not try to maintain any proportional relationship between the common stock and retained earnings accounts as shown on the balance sheet—common equity is common equity, whether it is represented by common stock or by retained earnings.

## Cost of Debt, $k_d$

**after-tax cost of debt,**
**$k_d(1 - T)$**
The relevant cost of new
debt financing, taking into
account the tax
deductibility of interest.

The **after-tax cost of debt, $k_d(1 - T)$**, used to calculate the weighted average cost of capital is the interest rate on debt, $k_d$, multiplied by $(1 - T)$, where T is the firm's tax rate:[4]

$$\text{Component cost of debt} = k_d(1 - T). \qquad (14\text{-}1)$$

For example, if a firm can borrow at an interest rate of 10 percent and it has a tax rate of 40 percent, then its after-tax cost of debt is 6 percent:

$$k_d(1 - T) = 10\%(1.0 - 0.4) = 10\%(0.6) = 6.0\%.$$

The reason for making the tax adjustment is as follows. The value of the firm's stock, which we want to maximize, depends on *after-tax* cash flows. Since interest is a deductible expense, it produces tax savings which reduce the net cost of debt, so the after-tax cost of debt is less than the before-tax cost. We are concerned with after-tax cash flows, and since cash flows and rates of return should be on a comparable basis, we adjust the interest rate downward to take account of the preferential tax treatment of debt.[5]

Note that the cost of debt is the interest rate on *new* debt, not that on any previously outstanding debt; in other words, we are interested in the cost of new debt, or the *marginal* cost of debt. Our primary concern with the cost of capital is to use it in a decision-making process—for example, the decision of whether to obtain the capital needed to buy a new machine tool. The rate at which the firm has borrowed in the past is irrelevant for this purpose.

## Cost of Preferred Stock, $k_p$

**cost of preferred**
**stock, $k_p$**
The preferred dividend,
$D_p$, divided by the net
issuing price, $P_n$.

The component **cost of preferred stock, $k_p$**, used to calculate the weighted cost of capital is the preferred dividend, $D_p$, divided by the net issuing price, $P_n$, or the price the firm receives after deducting flotation costs:

$$\text{Component cost of preferred stock} = k_p = \frac{D_p}{P_n}. \qquad (14\text{-}2)$$

For example, suppose a firm has preferred stock that pays a $11.70 dividend per share and sells for $100 per share in the market. If it issues new shares of preferred, it will incur an underwriting (or flotation) cost of 2.5 percent,

---

[4]Note that the cost of debt is considered in isolation. The impact of debt on the cost of equity, as well as on future increments of debt, is treated when the weighted cost of a combination of debt and equity is derived. Also, *flotation costs*, or the costs of selling the debt, are ignored. Flotation costs for debt issues are generally quite low—in fact, most debt is placed directly with banks, insurance companies, pension funds, and the like, and involves only administrative costs.

[5]It should also be noted that the tax rate is *zero* for a firm with losses. Therefore, for a company that does not pay taxes, the cost of debt is not reduced—that is, in Equation 14-1 the tax rate equals zero, so the after-tax cost of debt is equal to the interest rate.

or $2.50 per share, so it will net $97.50 per share. Therefore, the cost of preferred stock would be 12 percent:

$$k_p = \$11.70/\$97.50 = 12\%.$$

Note that no tax adjustments are made when calculating $k_p$ because preferred dividends, unlike interest expense on debt, are *not* deductible.

## Cost of Retained Earnings, $k_s$

**cost of retained earnings, $k_s$**
The rate of return required by stockholders on a firm's common stock.

The costs of debt and preferred stock are based on the returns investors require on these securities. Similarly, the **cost of retained earnings**, $k_s$, is the rate of return stockholders require on the firm's common stock.[6]

The reason why we must assign a cost of capital to retained earnings involves the *opportunity cost principle*. The firm's after-tax earnings literally belong to the stockholders. Bondholders are compensated by interest payments and preferred stockholders by preferred dividends, while the earnings remaining after interest and preferred dividends belong to the common stockholders and compensate them for the use of their capital. Management may either pay out earnings in the form of dividends or retain earnings and reinvest them in the business. If management decides to retain earnings, there is an opportunity cost involved—stockholders could have received the earnings as dividends and invested this money in other stocks, in bonds, in real estate, or in anything else. Thus, the firm should earn on its retained earnings at least as much as the stockholders themselves could earn in alternative investments of comparable risk.

What rate of return can stockholders expect to earn on equivalent-risk investments? The answer is $k_s$. *Therefore, if the firm cannot invest retained earnings and earn at least $k_s$, then it should pay these funds to its stockholders and let them invest directly in other assets that do provide this return.*[7]

Whereas debt and preferred stock are contractual obligations that have easily determined costs, it is not at all easy to measure $k_s$. However, we can employ the principles developed in Chapters 5 and 6 to produce reasonably good cost of equity estimates. To begin, recall that for stocks in equilibrium (which is the typical situation) the required rate of return, $k_s$, is also equal to the expected rate of return, $\hat{k}_s$. Further, the required return is equal to a riskless rate, $k_{RF}$, plus a risk premium, RP, while the expected return on a

---

[6]The term *retained earnings* can be interpreted to mean either the balance sheet item "retained earnings," consisting of all the earnings retained in the business throughout its history, or the income statement item "additions to retained earnings." The latter definition is used in this chapter—for our purpose, *retained earnings* refers to that part of current earnings not paid out in dividends and hence available for reinvestment in the business this year.

[7]One complexity in estimating the cost of retained earnings is the fact that dividends and capital gains are taxed differently. Retaining earnings rather than paying them out as dividends can convert ordinary income to capital gains. This point is discussed in detail in Chapter 16.

constant growth stock is equal to a dividend yield, $D_1/P_0$, plus an expected growth rate, g:

$$\text{Required rate of return} = \text{Expected return}$$

$$k_s = k_{RF} + RP = D_1/P_0 + g = \hat{k}_s. \qquad (14\text{-}3)$$

Therefore, we can estimate $k_s$ either directly as $k_s = k_{RF} + RP$ or indirectly as $k_s = \hat{k}_s = D_1/P_0 + g$. Actually, we can use three methods for finding the cost of retained earnings: (1) the CAPM approach, (2) the bond yield plus risk premium approach, and (3) the discounted cash flow (DCF) approach, each of which is discussed below.

## The CAPM Approach

One method of estimating the cost of equity is to use the Capital Asset Pricing Model (CAPM) as developed in Chapter 6. Here we proceed as follows:

**Step 1.** Estimate the riskless rate, $k_{RF}$, generally taken to be either the U.S. Treasury bond rate or the short-term (30-day) Treasury bill rate.

**Step 2.** Estimate the stock's beta coefficient, b, and use this as an index of the stock's market risk.

**Step 3.** Estimate the rate of return on the "market," or on an "average" stock, $k_M$.

**Step 4.** Use the above values to estimate the required rate of return on the stock in question as follows:

$$k_s = k_{RF} + b(k_M - k_{RF}). \qquad (14\text{-}4)$$

Thus, the CAPM estimate of $k_s$ begins with the risk-free rate, $k_{RF}$, and then adds a risk premium which is equal to the premium on an average stock, $k_M - k_{RF}$, scaled up or down to reflect the stock's relative risk by multiplying by its beta coefficient.

To illustrate the CAPM approach, assume that $k_{RF} = 10\%$, $k_M = 16\%$, and $b_i = 0.7$ for a given stock. The stock's $k_s$ is calculated as follows:

$$\begin{aligned} k_s &= 10\% + 0.7(16\% - 10\%) \\ &= 10\% + 0.7(6\%) \\ &= 10\% + 4.2\% \\ &= 14.2\%. \end{aligned}$$

Had $b_i$ been 1.8, indicating that the stock was riskier than average, $k_s$ would have been

$$k_s = 10\% + 1.8(6\%) = 10\% + 10.8\% = 20.8\%.$$

For an average stock,

$$k_s = k_M = 10\% + 1.0(6\%) = 16\%.$$

It should be noted that while the CAPM approach appears to yield accurate, precise estimates of $k_s$, there are actually several problems with it. First, as we saw in Chapter 6, if a firm's stockholders are not well diversified, they may be concerned with *total risk* rather than market risk only; in this case the firm's true investment risk will not be measured by beta, and the CAPM procedure will understate the correct value of $k_s$. Further, even if the CAPM method is valid, it is hard to obtain correct estimates of the inputs required to make it operational: there is uncertainty over whether to use long-term or short-term Treasury bonds for $k_{RF}$; it is hard to estimate the beta that investors expect the company to have in the future; and it is difficult to estimate the market risk premium. This latter problem has been especially vexing in the 1980s, because the riskiness of stocks versus bonds has been changing, making the market risk premium unstable.

## Bond Yield plus Risk Premium Approach

Although it is essentially an ad hoc, subjective procedure, analysts often estimate a firm's cost of common equity by adding a risk premium of some two to four percentage points to the interest rate on the firm's own long-term debt. It is logical to think that firms with risky, low-rated, and consequently high interest rate debt will also have risky, high-cost equity, and the procedure of basing the cost of equity on a readily observable debt cost utilizes this precept. For example, if an Aaa-rated firm's bonds yield 11 percent, then its cost of equity might be estimated as follows:

$$k_s = \text{Bond rate} + \text{Risk premium} = 11\% + 3\% = 14\%.$$

A Baa firm's debt might carry a yield of 13 percent, making its estimated cost of equity 16 percent:

$$k_s = 13\% + 3\% = 16\%.$$

Note that the 3 percent risk premium is a judgmental estimate, so the estimated value of $k_s$ is also judgmental. Empirical work in recent years suggests that the over-own-debt risk premium has ranged from about 1.0 to about 4.5 percentage points, so this method is not likely to produce a very accurate cost of equity—about all it can do is "get us into the right ballpark." The low premium occurs when interest rates are quite high and people are reluctant to invest in long-term bonds because they fear runaway inflation, further increases in interest rates, and losses on investments in bonds.

## Dividend Yield plus Growth Rate, or Discounted Cash Flow (DCF), Approach

In Chapter 5 we saw that both its price and the expected rate of return on a share of common stock depend ultimately on the dividends paid on the stock:

$$P_0 = \frac{D_1}{(1 + k_s)^1} + \frac{D_2}{(1 + k_s)^2} + \dots \tag{14-5}$$

Here $P_0$ is the current price of the stock; $D_t$ is the dividend expected to be paid at the end of Year t; and $k_s$ is the required rate of return. If dividends are expected to grow at a constant rate, then, as we saw in Chapter 5, Equation 14-5 reduces to the following expression:

$$P_0 = \frac{D_1}{k_s - g}. \tag{14-6}$$

We can solve for $k_s$ to obtain the required rate of return on common equity, which in equilibrium is also equal to the expected rate of return:[8]

$$k_s = \hat{k}_s = \frac{D_1}{P_0} + \text{Expected g}. \tag{14-7}$$

Thus, investors expect to receive a dividend yield, $D_1/P_0$, plus a capital gain, g, for a total expected return of $\hat{k}_s$, and in equilibrium this expected return is also equal to the required return. This method of estimating the cost of equity is called the *discounted cash flow, or DCF, method.* Henceforth in this chapter, we will assume that equilibrium exists and thus use the terms $k_s$ and $\hat{k}_s$ interchangeably.

It is relatively easy to determine the dividend yield, but it is difficult to establish the proper growth rate. If past growth rates in earnings and dividends have been relatively stable, and if investors appear to be projecting a continuation of past trends, then g may be based on the firm's historic growth rate. *However, if the company's growth has been abnormally high or low, either because of its own unique situation or because of general economic conditions, then investors will not project the past growth rate into the future.* In this case, g must be estimated in some other manner. Security analysts regularly make earnings and dividends growth forecasts, looking at such factors as projected sales, profit margins, and competitive factors. Some-one making a cost of capital estimate can obtain such analysts' forecasts and use them as a proxy for the growth expectations of investors in general, then combine g with the current dividend yield, and estimate $\hat{k}_s$ as follows:

$$\hat{k}_s = \frac{D_1}{P_0} + \text{Growth rate as projected by security analysts}.$$

Again, note that this estimate of $\hat{k}_s$ is based on the assumption that g is expected to remain constant in the future. If this assumption is not correct,

---

[8]Note also that dividends are actually paid quarterly, and $D_1$ is generally taken to be the dividends expected to be paid during the next four quarters. The model could be worked out on a quarterly basis; for a discussion of a quarterly payment model, see Appendix 5C of Eugene F. Brigham, *Financial Management: Theory and Practice,* 4th ed., 1985.

then it will be necessary to solve for $\hat{k}_s$ in the nonconstant growth model developed in Chapter 5.[9]

To illustrate the DCF approach, suppose a firm's stock sells for $18.82; its next expected dividend is $1.43; and its expected growth rate is 6.6 percent. The firm's expected and required rate of return, and hence its cost of retained earnings, is 14.2 percent:

$$\hat{k}_s = k_s = \frac{\$1.43}{\$18.82} + 6.6\% = 7.6\% + 6.6\% = 14.2\%.$$

This 14.2 percent is the minimum rate of return that management must expect to earn to justify retaining earnings and plowing them back into the business rather than paying them out to stockholders as dividends.

In practice, it is generally easiest to obtain reliable inputs for the DCF model; therefore, financial analysts tend to rely most heavily upon that approach. Although they do consider the other methods, they normally give estimates obtained with them less weight than DCF estimates. People experienced in estimating equity capital costs recognize that both careful analysis and some very fine judgments are required. It would be nice to pretend that these judgments are unnecessary and to specify an easy, precise way of determining the exact cost of equity capital. Unfortunately, this is not possible—finance is in large part a matter of judgment, and we simply must face that fact.

## Cost of Newly Issued Common Stock, or External Equity, $k_e$

**cost of new common equity, $k_e$**
The cost of external equity based on the cost of retained earnings, adjusted for flotation costs.

The **cost of new common equity, $k_e$**, or external equity capital, is higher than the cost of retained earnings, $k_s$, because of flotation costs involved in selling new common stock. What rate of return must be earned on funds raised by selling stock in order to make issuing new stock worthwhile? To put it another way, what is the cost of new common stock?

---

[9]When using the DCF method, we are implicitly assuming that the stock's price is in equilibrium, with $\hat{k}_s = D_1/P_0 + g = k_{RF} + RP = k_s$. Thus, the DCF and the CAPM methods will, if all inputs are estimated correctly, produce similar cost of capital estimates. Also, as we have just indicated, growth rates may be estimated (1) by projecting past trends if there is reason to think they will continue or (2) by asking security analysts what growth rates they are projecting (or, alternatively, looking up projected growth rates in such publications as *Value Line*, a financial service subscribed to by many investors). A third procedure for estimating g involves first projecting the firm's dividend payout ratio and its complement, the *retention rate*, and then multiplying the retention rate by the company's projected rate of return on equity (ROE):

$$g = (\text{Retention rate})(\text{ROE}) = (1.0 - \text{Payout rate})(\text{ROE}).$$

This last method is correct only if the retention rate and ROE are expected to remain constant in the future.

*For a firm with a constant growth rate, the answer is found by applying the following formula:*

$$k_e = \frac{D_1}{P_0(1 - F)} + g. \tag{14-8}$$

**flotation cost, F**
The percentage cost of issuing new common stock.

Here F is the percentage **flotation cost** incurred in selling the new stock issue, so $P_0(1 - F)$ is the net price per share received by the company when it sells a new stock issue.[10]

Assuming that the illustrative firm has a flotation cost of 10 percent, its cost of new outside equity is computed as follows:

$$k_e = \frac{\$1.43}{\$18.82(1 - 0.10)} + 6.6\% = \frac{\$1.43}{\$16.94} + 6.6\%$$

$$= 8.4\% + 6.6\% = 15.0\%.$$

Investors require a return of $k_s = 14.2\%$ on the stock. However, because of flotation costs the company must earn *more* than 14.2 percent on funds obtained by selling stock in order to provide this return. Specifically, if the firm earns 15 percent on funds obtained from new common stock issues, then earnings per share will not fall below previously expected earnings; its expected dividend can be maintained; and as a result of all this, the price per share will not decline. If the firm earns less than 15 percent, then earnings, dividends, and growth will fall below expectations, causing the price of the stock to decline; if it earns more, the price of the stock will rise.[11]

---

[10]Equation 14-8 is derived as follows:

*Step 1.* The old stockholders expect the firm to pay a stream of dividends, $D_t$, which will be derived from existing assets. New investors will likewise expect to receive the same stream of dividends. For them to do so *without impairing the $D_t$ stream of the old investors*, the new funds obtained from the sale of stock must be invested at a return high enough to provide a dividend stream whose present value will be equal to the price the firm will receive:

$$P_0(1 - F) = P_n = \sum_{t=1}^{\infty} \frac{D_t}{(1 + k_e)^t}. \tag{14-9}$$

Here $D_t$ is the dividend stream to new stockholders and $k_e$ is the cost of new outside equity.

*Step 2.* When growth is a constant, Equation 14-9 reduces to

$$P_n = P_0(1 - F) = \frac{D_1}{k_e - g}. \tag{14-9a}$$

*Step 3.* Equation 14-9a may be solved for $k_e$ to produce Equation 14-8:

$$k_e = \frac{D_1}{P_0(1 - F)} + g. \tag{14-8}$$

[11]On occasion it is useful to use another equation to calculate the cost of external equity:

$$k_e = \frac{\text{Dividend yield}}{(1 - F)} + g = \frac{D_1/P_0}{(1 - F)} + g. \tag{14-8a}$$

Equation 14-8a is derived algebraically from 14-8, and it is useful when information on dividend yields, but not on dollar dividends and stock prices, is available.

## Weighted Average, or Composite, Cost of Capital, WACC = $k_a$

**target capital structure**
The optimal capital structure; the percentage of debt, preferred stock, and common equity that will maximize the price of the firm's stock.

**weighted average cost of capital, WACC = $k_a$**
A weighted average of the component costs of debt, preferred stock, and common equity.

As we shall see in Chapter 15, each firm has an optimal capital structure, which is that mix of debt, preferred, and common equity that causes its stock price to be maximized. Therefore, a rational, value-maximizing firm will establish its **target capital structure** and then raise new capital in a manner that will keep the actual capital structure on target over time. In this chapter we assume that the firm has identified its optimal capital structure, that it uses this optimum as the target, and that it finances so as to remain constantly on target. How the target is established will be examined in Chapter 15.

The target proportions of debt, preferred, and common equity, along with the component costs of capital, are used to calculate the firm's **weighted average cost of capital, WACC = $k_a$**. To illustrate, suppose Universal Machine Company has a target capital structure calling for 30 percent debt, 10 percent preferred stock, and 60 percent common equity. Its before-tax cost of debt, $k_d$, is 10 percent; its cost of preferred stock, $k_p$, is 12 percent; its cost of common equity from retained earnings, $k_s$, is 15 percent; and its marginal tax rate is 40 percent. First, note that Universal's after-tax, or component, cost of debt = $k_d(1 - T) = 10\%(0.6) = 6.0\%$. Now we can calculate Universal's weighted average cost of capital, $k_a$, as follows:

$$\text{WACC} = k_a = w_d k_d(1 - T) + w_p k_p + w_s k_s \qquad (14\text{-}10)$$

$$= 0.3(10\%)(0.6) + 0.1(12\%) + 0.6(15\%) = 12\%.$$

Here $w_d$, $w_p$, and $w_s$ are the weights used for debt, preferred, and common equity, respectively.

Every dollar of new capital that Universal Machine obtains consists of 30 cents of debt with an after-tax cost of 6 percent, 10 cents of preferred with a cost of 12 percent, and 60 cents of common equity with a cost of 15 percent. The average cost of each whole dollar, $k_a$, is 12 percent.

The weights could be based either on the accounting values shown on the firm's balance sheet (book values) or on the market values of the different securities. Theoretically, the weights should be based on market values, but if a firm's book value weights are reasonably close to its market value weights, book value weights can be used as a proxy for market value weights. This point is discussed further in Chapter 15, but in the remainder of this chapter we shall assume that the firm's market values are approximately equal to its book values and then use book value capital structure weights.

## The Marginal Cost of Capital

The *marginal cost* of any item is the cost of another unit of that item; for example, the marginal cost of labor is defined as the cost of adding one additional worker. The marginal cost of labor might be $25 per person if 10 workers are added but $35 per person if the firm tries to hire 100 new workers, because it would be harder to find that many people willing and able to do the work. The same concept applies to capital. As the firm tries to attract more new dollars, the cost of each dollar will at some point rise. *Thus, the **marginal cost of capital**, MCC, is defined as the cost of obtaining another dollar of new capital, and the marginal cost rises as more and more capital is raised during a given period.*

**marginal cost of capital, MCC**
The cost of obtaining another dollar of new capital; the weighted average cost of the last dollar of capital raised.

We can use Universal Machine to illustrate the marginal cost of capital concept. The company's target capital structure and other data follow:[12]

| | | |
|---|---|---|
| Debt | $ 3,000,000 | 30% |
| Preferred | 1,000,000 | 10 |
| Common equity | 6,000,000 | 60 |
| Total capital | $10,000,000 | 100% |

$P_0 = \$20$.

$D_0 = \$1.495 = $ dividends per share in the *last* period. $D_0$ has already been paid, so someone purchasing this stock today would *not* receive $D_0$—rather, he or she would receive $D_1$, the *next* dividend.

$g = 7\%$, expected to remain constant.

$k_s = D_1/P_0 + g = [D_0(1 + g)]/P_0 + g = [\$1.495(1.07)]/\$20.00 + 0.07$
$= (\$1.60/\$20.00) + 0.07 = 0.08 + 0.07 = 0.15 = 15\%$.

$k_d = 10\%$.

$k_p = 12\%$.

$T = 40\%$.

Based on these data, the weighted average cost of capital, WACC $= k_a$, is 12 percent:

$$k_a = \left(\begin{matrix}\text{Fraction of}\\ \text{debt}\end{matrix}\right)\left(\begin{matrix}\text{Interest}\\ \text{rate}\end{matrix}\right)(1 - T) + \left(\begin{matrix}\text{Fraction of}\\ \text{preferred}\end{matrix}\right)\left(\begin{matrix}\text{Cost of}\\ \text{preferred}\end{matrix}\right)$$
$$+ \left(\begin{matrix}\text{Fraction of}\\ \text{common equity}\end{matrix}\right)\left(\begin{matrix}\text{Cost of}\\ \text{equity}\end{matrix}\right)$$
$$= 0.3(10\%)(0.6) + 0.1(12\%) + 0.6(15\%)$$
$$= 1.8\% + 1.2\% + 9.0\% = 12\%.$$

As long as Universal keeps its capital structure on target, and as long as its debt has an after-tax cost of 6 percent, its preferred a cost of 12 percent, and its common equity a cost of 15 percent, then its weighted average cost of capital will be 12 percent. Each dollar that it raises will consist of some debt,

---

[12]We assume that Universal has only a negligible amount of payables and accruals, which have no explicit cost, so these items are ignored. For a discussion of how "free credit" is handled, see Eugene F. Brigham and Louis C. Gapenski, *Intermediate Financial Management*, Chapter 4.

**Figure 14-1**
**Marginal Cost of Capital (MCC) Schedule for Universal Machine Company**

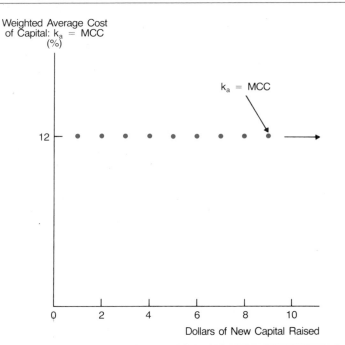

some preferred stock, and some common equity, and the cost of the dollar will be 12 percent.

The graph shown in Figure 14-1 is defined as Universal's **marginal cost of capital schedule**. Here the dots represent dollars raised. Since each dollar of new capital has a cost of 12 percent, the marginal cost of capital (MCC) for Universal is constant at 12 percent under the assumptions we have used thus far.[13]

**marginal cost of capital schedule**
A graph or table that relates the firm's weighted average cost of each dollar of capital to the total amount of new capital raised.

### Breaks in the MCC Schedule

Could Universal raise an unlimited amount of new capital at the 12 percent cost? The answer is no. As a practical matter, as a company raises larger and larger sums during a given time period, the costs of debt, preferred, and common equity begin to rise, and as this occurs, the weighted average cost of each new dollar also rises. Thus, just as corporations cannot hire unlimited

---

[13]Universal's MCC schedule in Figure 14-1 would be different (higher) if the company used any capital structure other than 30 percent debt, 10 percent preferred, and 60 percent equity. This point will be developed in Chapter 15; however, as a general rule, a different MCC schedule would exist for every possible capital structure, and the optimal structure is the one that produces the lowest MCC schedule.

numbers of workers at a constant wage, they cannot raise unlimited amounts of capital at a constant cost—at some point, the cost of each new dollar will increase.

Where will this point occur for Universal? As a first step to determining the point where the MCC begins to rise, recognize that although the company's balance sheet shows total long-term capital of $10 million, all of this capital was raised in the past, and it has been invested in assets which are being used in operations. New (or marginal) capital will presumably be raised so as to maintain the 30/10/60 debt/preferred/common relationship. Therefore, if Universal wants to raise $1 million in new capital, it should obtain $300,000 of debt, $100,000 of preferred stock, and $600,000 of common equity. The new common equity could come from two sources: (1) retained earnings, defined as that part of this year's profits which management decides to retain in the business rather than use for dividends (but not from earnings retained in the past, for these have already been invested in plant, equipment, inventories, and so on) or (2) proceeds from the sale of new common stock.

The debt will have an interest rate of 10 percent, or an after-tax cost of 6 percent, while the preferred stock will have a cost of 12 percent. The cost of common equity will be $k_s$ so long as the equity is obtained as retained earnings, but it will become $k_e$ once the company uses up all of its retained earnings and is thus forced to sell new common stock.

Consider first the case in which all the new equity comes from retained earnings. Universal's stock now sells for $20 per share; its last dividend ($D_0$) was $1.495; its expected growth rate is 7 percent; and its next expected dividend is $1.60. Thus, we estimate the expected and required rate of return on its common equity, $k_s$, to be 15 percent:

$$k_s = \frac{D_1}{P_0} + g = \frac{\$1.60}{\$20} + 7\% = 8\% + 7\% = 15\%.$$

Now suppose the company expands so rapidly that its retained earnings for the year are not sufficient to meet its needs for new equity, forcing it to sell new common stock. Since the flotation cost on new stock is $F = 10$ percent, Universal's cost of equity after it exhausts its retained earnings will rise from 15 to 15.9 percent:

$$k_e = \frac{D_1}{P_0(1 - F)} + g = \frac{\$1.60}{\$20(0.9)} + 7\% = \frac{\$1.60}{\$18} + 7\% = 15.9\%.$$

The company will net $18 when it sells new stock, and it must earn 15.9 percent on these net proceeds in order to provide investors with a 15.0 percent return on the $20 that investors actually put up.

Universal's weighted average cost of capital, using first new retained earnings (earnings retained this year, not in the past) and then new common stock, is shown in Table 14-1. We see that the weighted average cost of each dollar, or the marginal cost of capital, is 12 percent so long as retained earn-

**Table 14-1**
**Universal's Marginal Cost of Capital Using New**
**Retained Earnings and New Common Stock**

**I. MCC When Equity Is from New Retained Earnings**

| Component | Weight | Component Cost | Product |
|---|---|---|---|
| Debt | 0.3 | 6.0% | 1.8% |
| Preferred | 0.1 | 12.0 | 1.2 |
| Common equity (R.E.) | 0.6 | 15.0 | 9.0 |
| | 1.0 | MCC = WACC = $k_a$ = | 12.0% |

**II. MCC When Equity Is from Sale of New Common Stock**

| Component | Weight | Component Cost | Product |
|---|---|---|---|
| Debt | 0.3 | 6.0% | 1.8% |
| Preferred | 0.1 | 12.0 | 1.2 |
| Common equity (New C.S.) | 0.6 | 15.9 | 9.5 |
| | 1.0 | MCC = WACC = $k_a$ = | 12.5% |

ings are used but it jumps to 12.5 percent as soon as the firm exhausts its retained earnings and is forced to sell new common stock.[14]

How much new capital can Universal raise before it exhausts its retained earnings and is forced to sell new common stock—that is, where will the break point in the MCC occur? We find this point as follows:

**1.** The company expects to have total earnings of $840,000 for the year, and it has a policy of paying out half of its earnings as dividends. Thus, the addition to retained earnings will be $420,000 during the year.

**2.** We now want to know how much *total financing*—debt, preferred, and retained earnings—can be done before the $420,000 of retained earnings is exhausted and Universal is forced to sell new common stock. In effect, we are seeking some amount of capital, X, which is defined as a **break point** and which represents the total financing that can be done before Universal is forced to sell new common stock.

**break point**
The dollar value of new capital that can be raised before an increase in the firm's weighted average cost of capital occurs.

**3.** We know that 60 percent, or 0.6, of X, the total capital raised, will be retained earnings while 40 percent will be debt plus preferred. We also know that retained earnings will amount to $420,000. Therefore,

$$0.6X = \text{Retained earnings} = \$420,000.$$

[14]At relatively low growth rates expansion could be financed by spontaneously generated debt and retained earnings, but at higher growth rates external capital is needed. If Universal needed no external equity, its marginal cost of capital would be MCC = 12%. However, if its growth rate were rapid enough to require it to sell new common stock, its marginal cost of capital would rise to MCC = 12.5%.

**4.** Solving for X, which is the *retained earnings break point*, we obtain $BP_{RE}$ = \$700,000:

$$X = BP_{RE} = \frac{\text{Retained earnings}}{\text{Equity fraction}} = \frac{\$420,000}{0.6} = \$700,000.$$

**5.** Thus, Universal can raise a total of \$700,000, consisting of 0.6(\$700,000) = \$420,000 of retained earnings plus 0.10(\$700,000) = \$70,000 of preferred stock and 0.30(\$700,000) = \$210,000 of new debt supported by these new retained earnings, without altering its capital structure:

| | | |
|---|---:|---:|
| New debt supported by retained earnings | \$210,000 | 30% |
| Preferred stock supported by retained earnings | 70,000 | 10 |
| Retained earnings | 420,000 | 60 |
| Total expansion supported by retained earnings, or break point for retained earnings | \$700,000 | 100% |

**6.** The value of X, or $BP_{RE}$ = \$700,000, is defined as the *retained earnings break point*, or the amount of total capital at which a break, or jump, occurs in the MCC schedule.

Figure 14-2 graphs Universal's marginal cost of capital schedule. Each dollar has a weighted average cost of 12 percent until the company has raised a

**Figure 14-2**
**Marginal Cost of Capital Schedule for Universal Machine Company**
**Using Both Retained Earnings and New Common Equity**

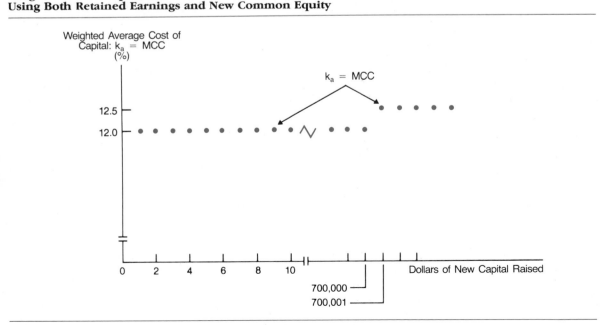

total of $700,000. This $700,000 will consist of $210,000 of new debt with an after-tax cost of 6 percent, $70,000 of preferred stock with a cost of 12 percent, and $420,000 of retained earnings with a cost of 15 percent. However, if Universal raises $700,001, the last dollar will contain 60 cents of equity *obtained by selling new common equity at a cost of 15.9 percent*; therefore, MCC = WACC = $k_a$ rises from 12 percent to 12.5 percent, as calculated in Table 14-1.

## Other Breaks in the MCC Schedule

There is a jump, or break, in Universal's MCC schedule at $700,000 of new capital. Could there be other breaks in the schedule? Yes, there could. For example, suppose Universal could obtain only $300,000 of debt at a 10 percent interest rate, with additional debt costing 12 percent. This would result in a second break point in the MCC schedule at the point where the $300,000 of 10 percent debt is exhausted. At what amount of *total financing* would the 10 percent debt be used up? If we let $BP_{Debt}$ represent the total financing at this second break point, then we know that 30 percent, or 0.3, of $BP_{Debt}$ will be debt, so

$$0.3(BP_{Debt}) = \$300,000,$$

and, solving for $BP_{Debt}$, we obtain

$$BP_{Debt} = \frac{\text{Amount of 10\% debt}}{\text{Debt fraction}} = \frac{\$300,000}{0.3} = \$1,000,000.$$

Thus, there will be another break in the MCC schedule after Universal has raised a total of $1 million.

As we have seen, from $0 to $700,000 of new capital the MCC is 12 percent, while just beyond $700,000 the MCC rises to 12.5 percent. Then, as a result of the increase in $k_d$ from 10 percent to 12 percent, the MCC rises again, at $1,000,001, to 12.9 percent:

**MCC above $1 Million**

| Component | Weight | | Component Cost | | Product |
|---|---|---|---|---|---|
| Debt | 0.3 | × | 7.2[a] | = | 2.2% |
| Preferred | 0.1 | × | 12.0 | = | 1.2 |
| Common equity | 0.6 | × | 15.9 | = | 9.5 |
| | | | | MCC = WACC = $k_a$ = | 12.9% |

[a]12%(1 − T) = 12%(0.6) = 7.2%, up from 6%.

In other words, the next dollar beyond $1 million will consist of 30 cents of 12 percent debt (7.2 percent after taxes), 10 cents of 12 percent preferred, and 60 cents of new common stock (retained earnings were used up much earlier), and this marginal dollar will have an average cost of 12.9 percent.

The effect of this new MCC increase is shown in Figure 14-3. We now have two break points, one caused by using up all the retained earnings and the other by using up all the 10 percent debt. With the two breaks, we have three different MCCs: $MCC_1$ = 12% for the first $700,000 of new capital;

**Figure 14-3**
**Marginal Cost of Capital Schedule for Universal Machine Company**
**Using Retained Earnings, New Common Stock, and Higher-Cost Debt**

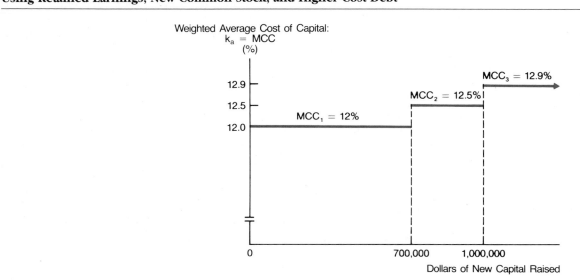

$MCC_2$ = 12.5% in the interval between $700,001 and $1 million; and $MCC_3$ = 12.9% for all new capital beyond $1 million.[15]

There could, of course, be still more break points which would occur if the interest rate continued to rise, if the cost of preferred stock rose,[16] or if the cost of common stock rose. *In general, a break point will occur whenever the cost of one of the capital components rises, and the break point can be determined by Equation 14-11:*

---

[15]When we use the term *weighted average cost of capital*, we are referring to $k_a$, which is the cost of $1 raised partly as debt, partly as preferred, and partly as equity. We could also calculate the average cost of all the capital the firm raises during a given year. For example, if Universal raised $2 million, then the first $700,000 would have a cost of 12 percent, the next $300,000 a cost of 12.5 percent, and the last $1 million a cost of 12.9 percent. The entire $2 million would have an average cost of

$$(0.7/2)(12\%) + (0.3/2)(12.5\%) + (1/2)(12.9\%) = 12.53\%.$$

*This particular cost of capital should not be used for financial decisions—it has no relevance in finance.*

[16]The first break point is not necessarily the point at which retained earnings are used up—it is possible that low-cost debt could be exhausted *before* retained earnings have been used up. For example, if Universal had available only $150,000 of 10 percent debt, then $BP_{Debt}$ would occur at $500,000:

$$BP_{Debt} = \frac{\$150,000}{0.3} = \$500,000.$$

This is well before the break point for retained earnings, which occurs at $700,000.

**Figure 14-4**
**Smoothed, or Continuous, Marginal Cost of Capital Schedule**

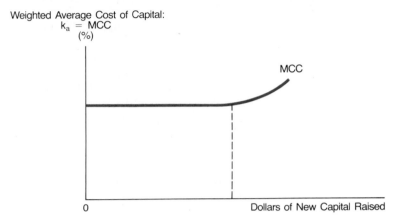

Weighted Average Cost of Capital:
$k_a = MCC$
(%)

MCC

0                                                Dollars of New Capital Raised

$$\text{Break point} = \frac{\text{Total amount of lower-cost}}{\text{Fraction of this type of capital}} \qquad (14\text{-}11)$$

We see, then, that numerous break points can occur. At the limit, we can even think of an MCC with so many break points that it rises almost continuously beyond some given level of new financing. Such an MCC schedule is shown in Figure 14-4.

The easiest sequence for calculating MCC schedules is as follows:

**1.** Identify the points at which breaks occur. A break will occur any time the cost of one of the capital components rises. (However, it is possible that two capital components could both increase at the same point.) Use Equation 14-11 to determine the exact break points, and make a list of them.

**2.** Determine the cost of capital for each component in the intervals between breaks.

**3.** Calculate the weighted averages of these component costs to obtain the MCCs in each interval. The MCC is constant within each interval, but it rises at each break point.

Notice that if there are n separate breaks, there will be n + 1 different MCCs—for example, in Figure 14-3 we see two breaks and three different MCCs.

Before closing this section, we should note again that a different MCC schedule would result if a different capital structure were used. As we will show in Chapter 15, the optimal capital structure produces the lowest MCC schedule.

## Combining the MCC and Investment Opportunity Schedules

Now that we have calculated the MCC schedule, we can use it to determine a discount rate for use in the capital budgeting process—*that is, we can use the MCC schedule to find the cost of capital for use in determining projects' net present values (NPVs) as discussed in Chapter 9.*

To understand how the MCC schedule is used in capital budgeting, assume that Universal has three financial executives: financial vice-president, treasurer, and director of capital budgeting (DCB). The financial VP asks the treasurer to develop the firm's MCC schedule, and the treasurer produces the schedule shown earlier in Figure 14-3. At the same time, the financial VP asks the DCB to determine the dollar amounts of all projects that are potentially acceptable, using the IRR method. The DCB then prepares the listing of all of the firm's potential projects, including each one's cost and projected annual net cash inflows, as shown in Table 14-2. For example, Project A has a cost of $200,000, is expected to produce inflows of $55,757 per year for 5 years, and therefore has an IRR of 12.2 percent, while Project B has a cost of $150,000, is expected to produce inflows of $33,917 per year for 7 years, and thus has an IRR of 13 percent. For simplicity, we assume now that all projects are independent, that they are equally risky, and that their risk is equal to that of the firm's average existing asset.

**investment opportunity schedule (IOS)**
A listing or graph of the firm's investment opportunities ranked in order of the projects' rates of return.

The DCB then plots the IRR data given in Table 14-2 as the **investment opportunity schedule (IOS)** shown in Figure 14-5. The IOS schedule shows how much money Universal could invest at different rates of return. Figure 14-5 also shows Universal's MCC schedule as it was developed by the treasurer and plotted in Figure 14-3. Consider first Project D: its IRR is 14 percent and it can be financed with capital that costs only 12 percent; consequently it should be accepted. Also, recall from Chapter 9 that if a project's IRR exceeds the cost of capital, its NPV will also be positive, so Project D is also acceptable by the NPV criterion. Projects F, B, and E can be analyzed similarly; they are all acceptable because IRR > MCC and NPV > 0. Projects A and C, on the other hand, should be rejected because IRR < MCC and NPV < 0.

Notice also that if the cost of capital had started at a point above 14 percent, none of the available projects would have positive NPVs; hence, none

**Table 14-2**
**Potential Capital Budgeting Projects Available to Universal Machine Company**

| Project | Cost | Annual Inflows | Project Life (Years) | IRR, or Discount Rate at Which NPV = 0 |
|---|---|---|---|---|
| A | $200,000 | $ 55,757 | 5 | 12.2% |
| B | 150,000 | 33,917 | 7 | 13.0 |
| C | 250,000 | 43,344 | 10 | 11.5 |
| D | 350,000 | 90,005 | 6 | 14.0 |
| E | 200,000 | 41,250 | 8 | 12.7 |
| F | 250,000 | 106,781 | 3 | 13.5 |

**Figure 14-5**
**Combining Universal Machine Company's MCC and IOS Curves to**
**Determine Its Optimal Capital Budget**

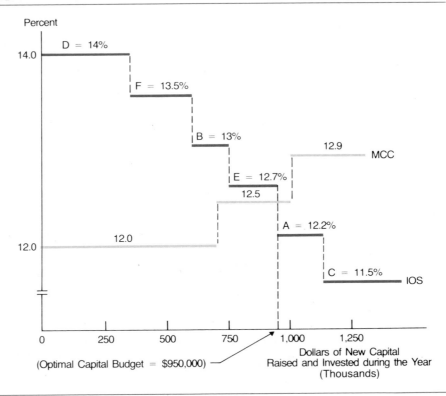

of them should be accepted. In that case, Universal simply should not expand. However, in the actual situation, where the MCC starts at 12 percent and then rises, Universal should accept the four projects (D, F, B, and E) which have rates of return in excess of the cost of the capital that would be used to finance them, ending up with a capital budget of $950,000.[17]

---

[17]People sometimes ask this question: "If we took Project A first, it would be acceptable, because its 12.2 percent return would exceed the 12 percent cost of money used to finance it. Why couldn't we do this?" The answer is that we are seeking in effect to maximize the *excess of returns over costs*, or the area that is above the MCC but below the IOS. We accomplish this by graphing (and accepting) the most profitable projects first.

   Another question that sometimes arises is this: "What would happen if the MCC cut through one of the projects? For example, suppose the second break point in the MCC schedule has occurred at $900,000 rather than at $1 million so that the MCC cut through Project E. Should we then accept Project E?" If Project E could be accepted in part, then we would take on only part of it. Otherwise, the answer would be determined by (1) finding the average cost of the funds needed to finance Project E (some of the money would cost 12.5 percent and some 12.9 percent) and (2) comparing the average cost of this money to the 12.7 percent return on the project. We should accept Project E if its return exceeds the average cost of the $200,000 needed to finance it.

The above analysis as summarized in Figure 14-5 reveals a very important point: *The cost of capital used in the capital budgeting process as discussed in Chapter 9 is actually determined at the intersection of the IOS and MCC schedules. If this intersection rate is used, then the firm will make correct accept/reject decisions, and its level of financing and investment will be optimal. If it uses any other rate, its capital budget will not be optimal.*

If Universal had fewer good investment opportunities, its IOS schedule would be shifted to the left, causing the intersection to occur at a lower level on the MCC curve. Conversely, if the firm had more and better investment opportunities, the IOS would be shifted to the right, and the intersection would occur at a higher MCC. Thus, we see that the discount rate used in capital budgeting is influenced both by the shape of the MCC curve and by the set of available projects.

We have, of course, abstracted from differential project riskiness in this chapter—implicitly, we have assumed that all projects are equally risky. As noted in Chapter 10, the cost of capital used to evaluate riskier projects should be adjusted upward, while a lower rate should be used for projects with below-average risk. The MCC as determined in Figure 14-5 should be used to find the NPVs of new projects that are about as risky as the firm's existing assets, but it should be adjusted up or down to find NPVs for projects with higher or lower risk than the average project.[18]

### Some Problem Areas in Cost of Capital

A number of difficult issues relating to the cost of capital either have not been mentioned or have been glossed over lightly thus far in the chapter. These topics are covered in advanced finance courses, but they deserve some mention now so that the reader may be alerted to potential dangers, as well as provided with a preview of some of the matters dealt with in advanced courses.

***The Effects of Personal Income Taxes.*** Our discussion of the cost of capital has dealt with *corporate* income taxes, but we abstracted from *personal* income taxes. When we use the equation $k_s = D_1/P_0 + g$, we often assume that investors are indifferent between dividend yield and capital gains. However, dividends are taxed at higher rates than capital gains, so investors may prefer capital gains (g) to dividend yield ($D_1/P_0$). This, in turn, might cause the differential between the cost of retained earnings ($k_s$) and new common stock ($k_c$) to be greater than can be accounted for by flotation costs alone.

***Depreciation-Generated Funds.*** The largest single source of capital for many firms is depreciation, yet we have not discussed the cost of funds from this source. In brief, depreciation cash flows can be either reinvested or returned to investors (stockholders *and* creditors). The cost of depreciation-generated funds is approximately equal to the weighted average cost of capital in the interval in which capital comes from retained earnings and low-

---

[18]For a discussion of cost of capital risk adjustments, see Brigham and Gapenski, *Intermediate Financial Management*, Chapter 10.

cost debt. See Eugene F. Brigham and Louis C. Gapenski, *Intermediate Financial Management*, Chapter 4, for a discussion.

***Deferred Taxes.*** Many companies show, as a liability, an item called "deferred taxes." Deferred taxes arise principally from accelerated tax depreciation and delays in payments of regular taxes, and these deferrals can constitute an important source of funds. Since deferred taxes are, in effect, an interest-free loan from the federal government, they have a zero cost. Again, see Brigham and Gapenski, Chapter 4, for a discussion of how deferred taxes are handled in cost of capital calculations.

***Privately Owned Firms.*** Our whole discussion of the cost of equity has been related to publicly owned corporations, and we have concentrated on the rate of return required by stockholders at large. However, there is a serious question as to how one should measure the cost of equity for a firm whose stock is not traded. Tax issues also become especially important in these cases. As a general rule, the same principles of cost of capital estimation apply to both privately held and publicly owned firms, but the problems of obtaining input data are somewhat different for each.

***Small Businesses.*** Small businesses are generally privately owned, making it difficult to estimate their cost of equity, and they also often obtain debt from government sources, such as the Small Business Administration. However, the same theoretical principles apply to both large and small firms.

***Measurement Problems.*** One cannot overemphasize the practical difficulties encountered in actually estimating the cost of equity. It is very difficult to obtain good input data for the CAPM, for g in the formula $k_s = D_1/P_0 + g$, and for the risk premium in the formula $k_s =$ Bond yield + Risk premium.

***Costs of Capital for Projects of Differing Riskiness.*** As noted in Chapter 10, care must be taken to assign different risk-adjusted discount rates to capital budgeting projects of differing degrees of riskiness.

***Capital Structure Weights.*** In this chapter we have simply taken as given the target capital structure and used this target to obtain the weights used to calculate k. As we shall see in Chapter 15, establishing the target capital structure is a major task in itself.

***Dynamic Considerations.*** Capital budgeting and cost of capital estimates are a part of the *planning process*—they deal with ex ante, or estimated, data rather than ex post, or historical, data. Hence, we can be wrong about the location of the IOS and the MCC—for example, we can underestimate the MCC and hence accept projects that with 20-20 foresight we would have rejected. In a dynamic, changing world this is a real problem. Interest rates and money costs could be low at the time plans are being laid and contracts to build plants are being let, but six or eight months later these figures could have risen substantially. Thus, a project that formerly looked good could turn out to be a bad one because we improperly forecasted our MCC schedule.

Although this listing of problem areas may appear formidable, the state of the art in cost of capital estimation is really not in bad shape. The procedures outlined in this chapter can be used to obtain cost of capital estimates that are sufficiently accurate for practical purposes, and the problems listed here merely indicate the desirability of certain refinements. The refinements are not unimportant, but the problems identified certainly do not invalidate the usefulness of the procedures outlined in the chapter.

## Summary

This chapter showed how the MCC schedule is developed and used in the capital budgeting process. We began by discussing the process of estimating the cost of each capital structure component. The *cost of debt* is simply $k_d(1 - T)$. The first increment of *common equity* is raised as *retained earnings*, whose cost, $k_s$, may be estimated in one of three ways: (1) by the CAPM equation, $k_s = k_{RF} + b(k_M - k_{RF})$; (2) by the dividend growth model, $k_s = D_1/P_0 + g$; or (3) by adding a risk premium of 2 to 4 percent to the firm's cost of long-term debt. Once retained earnings have been exhausted, the firm must sell new common stock, or *external equity*, whose cost is $k_e = D_1/[P_0(1 - F)] + g$ in the case of a constant growth stock.

Our next task is to combine the component costs to form a *weighted average cost of capital*, WACC $= k_a$. The weights used to develop the WACC should be based on the firm's target capital structure. If these weights are used, the stock price will be maximized and the cost of capital simultaneously minimized.

Capital typically has a higher cost if the firm expands beyond certain limits. This means that the MCC curve turns upward beyond some point. We used the *break point concept* to develop a step function MCC schedule, which we then combined with the IOS schedule to determine both the optimal capital budget and the cost of capital that should be used in capital budgeting.

The concepts developed here are extended in Chapter 15, in which we consider the effect of the capital structure on the cost of capital.

## SMALL BUSINESS

### Cost of Equity Capital for Small Firms

The three methods for estimating the cost of equity capital that were discussed in this chapter have serious limitations when applied to small firms, increasing the need for the small-business manager to use judgment. Consider first the constant growth model, $k_s = D_1/P_0 + g$. Imagine a small, rapidly growing firm, such as Biotechnology General (BTG), which does not now and will not in the foreseeable future pay dividends. For firms such as this, the constant growth model is simply not applicable—in fact, it is difficult to imagine any dividend model that would be of practical benefit in such a case due to the difficulty of estimating growth rates.

The second method is to use the yield on the firm's bonds plus a risk premium of, say, 4 percent. A small firm is unlikely to have a public debt issue outstanding. BTG, for example, has no such debt issue outstanding; therefore, we could not use the bond yield plus risk premium approach for BTG.

The third approach suggested is the CAPM. If the firm's equity is not publicly traded, then we cannot calculate the firm's beta and hence cannot use this approach. However, even if the firm has no publicly traded equity, it can still use the so-called "pure play" CAPM technique. This involves finding a firm in the same line of business that does have public equity, estimating its beta, and then using this beta as a proxy for that of the small business in question in the CAPM model.

To illustrate the pure play approach, again consider BTG. The firm went public quite recently, so not enough data are available to estimate its beta. However, the data available for more established firms, such as Genentech and Genetic Industries, could be used to provide an estimate of the beta for the biological and genetic engineering industry. Of course, these firms' betas would have to be subjectively modified in order to reflect their relatively established records and the differences in the nature of their products versus those of BTG. Still, as long as there are public companies in similar lines of business available for comparison, the estimates of their betas can be used in estimating the cost of capital of a firm whose equity is not publicly traded. Note, however, that a "liquidity premium" as discussed in Chapter 3 would have to be added to reflect the illiquidity of the stock of a small, nonpublic firm.

## Flotation Costs for Small Issues

When external equity capital is raised, flotation costs increase the cost of equity capital beyond what it would be for internal funds. These external flotation costs are especially significant for smaller issues and can substantially affect capital budgeting decisions involving external equity funds. To illustrate this point, consider a firm that is expected to pay constant dividends forever. In this case, if F is the percentage flotation cost, then the cost of equity capital is $D_1/[P_0(1 - F)]$. The higher the flotation cost, the higher the cost of external equity.

How big is F? According to the latest Securities and Exchange Commission data, the average flotation cost of large common stock offerings (over $50 million) is only about 4 percent. For a firm that is expected to provide a 15 percent dividend yield—that is, $D_1/P_0 = 15\%$—the cost of equity is $15\%/(1 - 0.04)$, or 15.6 percent.

The SEC's data on small stock offerings (less than $1 million) show that flotation costs for such issues average about 21 percent. Thus, the cost of equity capital in the above example would be $15\%/(1 - 0.21)$, or about 19 percent. Compared to the 15.6 percent for large offerings, it is clear that a small firm will have to earn considerably more on the same project than would a large firm. Small firms are therefore at a substantial disadvantage because of the effects of flotation costs.

## The Small-Firm Effect

A number of researchers have observed that portfolios of small-firm stocks have earned consistently higher average returns than those of large-firm stocks; this is called the "small-firm effect." On the surface, it would seem to be beneficial for small firms to produce average returns that are higher than those of large firms. In reality, it is bad news for them: what the small-firm effect means is that the capital market demands higher returns for stocks of small firms than for otherwise similar stocks of large firms. In short, the cost of equity capital is higher for small firms, even ignoring the flotation costs at the time of issuance.

It might be argued that the stocks of small firms are more risky than those of large ones, and that this accounts for the differences in returns. It is true that research usually finds that betas are higher on average for small firms than for large ones. However, the larger returns for small firms remain larger even after adjusting for the effects of their higher risks, at least the higher risks in observed beta values.

The small-firm effect is an anomaly; that is, it is not consistent with presently available theory. In other words, we do not understand why small firms have higher returns—we just know that they do. Until a satisfactory explanation is developed for the small-firm effect, we can say only that the required returns (and cost of equity capital) are greater for small firms than they would be for otherwise similar large firms, and the manager of a small firm should take this factor into account in estimating his or her cost of equity capital. In general, the cost of equity capital appears to be about four percentage points higher for small firms (those with market values of less than $20 million) than for large firms with similar risk characteristics.

## Questions

**14-1**  Define each of the following terms:
  a. After-tax cost of debt, $k_d(1 - T)$; component cost
  b. Cost of preferred stock, $k_p$
  c. Cost of retained earnings, $k_s$
  d. Cost of new common equity, $k_e$
  e. Flotation cost, F
  f. Target capital structure; capital structure components
  g. Weighted average cost of capital, WACC $= k_a$
  h. Marginal cost of capital, MCC
  i. Marginal cost of capital schedule; break point
  j. Investment opportunity schedule (IOS)

**14-2**  In what sense is the marginal cost of capital an average cost?

**14-3**  How would each of the following affect a firm's cost of debt, $k_d(1 - T)$; its cost of equity, $k_s$; and its weighted average cost of capital, $k_a$? Indicate by a plus ( + ), a minus ( − ), or a zero ( 0 ) if the factor would raise, lower, or have an indeterminate effect on the item in question. Assume other things are held constant. Be prepared to justify your answer, but recognize that several of the parts probably have no single correct answer; these questions are designed to stimulate thought and discussion.

|  | Effect on | | |
| --- | --- | --- | --- |
|  | $k_d(1 - T)$ | $k_s$ | $k_a$ = WACC |
| a. The corporate tax rate is lowered. | | | |
| b. The Federal Reserve tightens credit. | | | |
| c. The firm uses more debt—that is, it increases the debt/assets ratio. | | | |
| d. The dividend payout ratio is increased. | | | |
| e. The firm doubles the amount of capital it raises during the year. | | | |
| f. The firm expands into a risky new area. | | | |
| g. The firm merges with another firm whose earnings are countercyclical to those of the first firm and to the stock market. | | | |

|  | Effect on | | |
|---|---|---|---|
|  | $k_d(1 - T)$ | $k_s$ | $k_a = WACC$ |
| h. The stock market falls drastically, and our firm's stock falls along with the rest. | _____ | _____ | _____ |
| i. Investors become more risk averse. | _____ | _____ | _____ |
| j. The firm is an electric utility with a large investment in nuclear plants. Several states propose a ban on nuclear power generation. | _____ | _____ | _____ |

14-4    Suppose a firm estimates its MCC and IOS schedules for the coming year and finds that they intersect at the point 10%, $10 million. What cost of capital should be used to evaluate average projects, high-risk projects, and low-risk projects?

14-5    What effects would you expect the introduction of "shelf registrations" as discussed in Chapter 11 to have on the MCC schedule of an average firm?

14-6    Suppose a firm decided to issue zero coupon bonds as discussed in Chapter 12. How would you determine the component cost of these bonds?

## Self-Test Problem (*Solution on Page 486*)

ST-1    Lancaster Engineering, Inc. (LEI), has the following capital structure, which it considers to be optimal:

| Debt | 25% |
|---|---|
| Preferred stock | 15 |
| Common equity | 60 |
|  | 100% |

LEI's expected net income this year is $34,285.72; its established dividend payout ratio is 30 percent; its tax rate is 40 percent; and investors expect earnings and dividends to grow at a constant rate of 9 percent in the future. LEI paid a dividend of $3.60 per share last year, and its stock currently sells at a price of $60 per share. (Note: All dollars except per share figures are in thousands.)

LEI can obtain new capital in the following ways:

*Common*: New common stock would have a flotation cost of 10 percent for up to $12,000 of new stock and 20 percent for all common over $12,000.

*Preferred*: New preferred can be sold to the public at a price of $100 per share, with a dividend of $11. However, flotation costs of $5 per share will be incurred for up to $7,500 of preferred, rising to $10, or 10 percent, on all preferred over $7,500.

*Debt*: Up to $5,000 of debt can be sold at an interest rate of 12 percent; debt in the range of $5,001 to $10,000 must carry an interest rate of 14 percent; and all debt over $10,000 will have an interest rate of 16 percent.

LEI has the following investment opportunities:

| Project | Cost at t = 0 | Annual Net Cash Flow | Project Life | IRR |
|---------|---------------|----------------------|--------------|-----|
| A | $10,000 | $2,191.20 | 7 years | 12.0% |
| B | 10,000 | 3,154.42 | 5 | 17.4 |
| C | 10,000 | 2,170.18 | 8 | 14.2 |
| D | 20,000 | 3,789.48 | 10 | 13.7 |
| E | 20,000 | 5,427.84 | 6 | |

a. Find the break points in the MCC schedule.
b. Determine the component costs of capital for each capital structure component.
c. Calculate the weighted average cost of capital (or the MCC) in the interval between each break in the MCC schedule.
d. Calculate the IRR for Project E.
e. Construct a graph showing the MCC and IOS schedules.
f. Which projects should LEI accept?

## Problems

After-tax cost of debt    **14-1**    Calculate the after-tax cost of debt under each of the following conditions:
a. Interest rate, 10 percent; tax rate, 0 percent.
b. Interest rate, 10 percent; tax rate, 40 percent.
c. Interest rate, 10 percent; tax rate, 60 percent.

After-tax cost of debt    **14-2**    The Graham Company's financing plans for next year include the sale of long-term bonds with a 12 percent coupon. The company believes it can sell the bonds at a price that will provide a yield to maturity of 14 percent. If the tax rate is 40 percent, what is Graham's after-tax cost of debt?

Cost of preferred stock    **14-3**    Infinity Industries plans to issue some $100 par preferred stock with a 10 percent dividend. The stock is selling on the market for $96.17, and Infinity must pay flotation costs of 6 percent of the market price. What is the cost of the preferred stock for Infinity?

Cost of retained earnings    **14-4**    The earnings, dividends, and stock price of the Abbott Company are expected to grow at 9 percent per year after this year. Abbott's common stock sells for $30 per share, its last dividend was $2.18, and the company will pay a dividend of $2.40 at the end of the current year. What is its cost of retained earnings?

Cost of retained earnings    **14-5**    The Iversen Company's EPS was $5 in 1985 and $3.40 in 1980. The company pays out 40 percent of its earnings as dividends, and the stock sells for $40.

a. Calculate the past growth rate in earnings. (Hint: This is a 5-year growth period.)

b. Calculate the *next* expected dividend per share, $D_1$. ($D_0 = 0.4(\$5) = \$2$.) Assume the past growth rate will continue.

c. What is the cost of retained earnings, $k_s$, for the Iversen Company?

**Break point calculations**   **14-6**   The Iversen Company expects earnings of $25 million next year. Its dividend payout ratio is 40 percent and its debt/assets ratio 50 percent. Iversen uses no preferred stock.

a. What amount of retained earnings does Iversen expect next year?

b. At what amount of financing will there be a break point in the MCC schedule?

c. If Iversen can borrow $10 million at an interest rate of 8 percent, another $10 million at a rate of 9 percent, and any additional debt at a rate of 10 percent, at what points will rising debt costs cause breaks in the MCC schedule?

**Cost of new common stock**   **14-7**   The Iversen Company's next expected dividend, $D_1$, is $2.16; its growth rate is 8 percent; and the stock now sells for $40. New stock can be sold at a price of $34.

a. What is Iversen's percentage flotation cost, F?

b. What is Iversen's cost of new common stock, $k_e$?

**Weighted average cost of capital**   **14-8**   The Renoir Company's cost of equity is 15 percent. Its before-tax cost of debt is 10 percent, and its tax rate is 40 percent. The stock sells at book value. Using the following balance sheet, calculate Renoir's after-tax weighted average cost of capital:

| Assets | | Liabilities | |
|---|---|---|---|
| Cash | $ 100 | | |
| Accounts receivable | 200 | | |
| Inventories | 300 | Long-term debt | 800 |
| Plant and equipment, net | 1,800 | Equity | 1,600 |
| Total assets | $2,400 | Total liabilities | $2,400 |

**Return on common stock**   **14-9**   Parnelli Products' stock is currently selling for $50 a share. The firm is expected to earn $5 per share and to pay a year-end dividend of $2.

a. If investors require a 10 percent return, what rate of growth must be expected for Parnelli?

b. If Parnelli reinvests retained earnings in projects whose average return is equal to the stock's expected rate of return, what will be next year's EPS? (Hint: $g = b(ROE)$, where $b$ = fraction of earnings retained.)

**Optimal capital budget**   **14-10**   On January 1, 1986, the total assets of the Rossiter Company were $90 million. During the year, the company plans to raise and invest $45 million. The firm's present capital structure, shown below, is considered to be optimal. Assume there is no short-term debt.

| | |
|---|---|
| Long-term debt | $45,000,000 |
| Common equity | 45,000,000 |
| Total liabilities and capital | $90,000,000 |

New bonds will have a 10 percent coupon rate and will be sold at par. Common stock, currently selling at $30 a share, can be sold to net the company $27 a share. Stockholders' required rate of return is estimated to be 12 percent, consisting of a dividend yield of 4 percent and an expected growth of 8 percent. (The next expected dividend is $1.20, so $1.20/$30 = 4%.) Retained earnings are estimated to be $4.5 million. The marginal corporate tax rate is 40 percent. Assuming all asset expansion (gross expenditures for fixed assets plus related working capital) is included in the capital budget, the dollar amount of the capital budget ignoring depreciation is $45 million.

a. To maintain the present capital structure, how much of the capital budget must be financed by equity?
b. How much of the new equity funds needed must be generated internally? Externally?
c. Calculate the cost of each of the equity components.
d. At what level of capital expenditure will there be a break in the MCC schedule?
e. Calculate the MCC (1) below and (2) above the break in the schedule.
f. Plot the MCC schedule. Also, draw in an IOS schedule that is consistent with the MCC schedule and the projected capital budget. (Any IOS schedule that is consistent will do.)

Marginal cost of capital          14-11    The following tabulation gives earnings per share figures for the Riley Company during the preceding 10 years. The firm's common stock, 4 million shares outstanding, is now (1/1/86) selling for $50 per share, and the expected dividend at the end of the current year (1986) is 50 percent of the 1985 EPS. Since investors expect past trends to continue, g may be based on the earnings growth rate. (Note that 9 years of growth are reflected in the data.)

| Year | EPS | Year | EPS |
|------|------|------|------|
| 1976 | $3.00 | 1981 | $4.41 |
| 1977 | 3.24 | 1982 | 4.76 |
| 1978 | 3.50 | 1983 | 5.14 |
| 1979 | 3.78 | 1984 | 5.55 |
| 1980 | 4.08 | 1985 | 6.00 |

The current interest rate on new debt is 8 percent. The firm's marginal tax rate is 40 percent. Its capital structure, considered to be optimal, is as follows:

| | |
|---|---|
| Debt | $ 80,000,000 |
| Common equity | 120,000,000 |
| Total liabilities and capital | $200,000,000 |

a. Calculate the after-tax cost of new debt and of common equity, assuming new equity comes only from retained earnings. Calculate the cost of equity as $k_s = D_1/P_0 + g$.
b. Find the marginal cost of capital, again assuming that no new common stock is sold and that all debt costs 8 percent.

c. How much can be spent on capital investments before external equity must be sold? (Assume that retained earnings available for 1986 are 50 percent of 1985 earnings. Obtain 1985 earnings by multiplying 1985 EPS by the shares outstanding.)

d. What is the marginal cost of capital (cost of funds raised in excess of the amount calculated in Part c) if new common stock can be sold to the public at $50 a share to net the firm $45 a share? The cost of debt is constant.

Optimal capital budget    14-12        Austen Enterprises has the following capital structure, which it considers to be optimal under present and forecasted conditions:

| | |
|---|---|
| Debt (long-term only) | 40% |
| Common equity | 60 |
| Total liabilities and capital | 100% |

For the coming year, management expects after-tax earnings of $1 million. The past dividend policy of paying out 60 percent of earnings will continue. Present commitments from its banker will allow Austen to borrow according to the following schedule:

| Loan Amount | Interest Rate |
|---|---|
| $0 to $300,000 | 10% on this increment of debt |
| $300,001 to $600,000 | 12% on this increment of debt |
| $600,001 and above | 14% on this increment of debt |

The company's tax rate is 40 percent, the current market price of its stock is $20 per share, its *last* dividend was $1.10 per share, and the expected growth rate is 9 percent. External equity (new common) can be sold at a flotation cost of 15 percent.

The firm has the following investment opportunities for the next year:

| Project | Cost | Annual Cash Flows | Project Life | IRR |
|---|---|---|---|---|
| 1 | $450,000 | $ 93,105 | 10 years | |
| 2 | 600,000 | 158,452 | 6 | 15.0% |
| 3 | 250,000 | 151,822 | 2 | |
| 4 | 375,000 | 123,463 | 4 | 12.0 |
| 5 | 500,000 | 97,161 | 8 | 11.0 |

Management asks you to help determine which projects (if any) should be undertaken. You proceed with this analysis by answering the following questions as posed in a logical sequence:

a. How many breaks are there in the MCC schedule?
b. At what dollar amounts do the breaks occur, and what causes them?
c. What is the weighted average cost of capital, $k_a$, in each of the intervals between the breaks?
d. What are the IRR values for Projects 1 and 3?
e. Graph the IOS and MCC schedules.
f. Which projects should Austen's management accept?

g. What assumptions about project risk are implicit in this problem? If you learned that Projects 1, 2, and 3 were of above-average risk, yet Austen chose the projects which you indicated in Part f, how would this affect the situation?

h. The problem stated that Austen pays out 60 percent of its earnings as dividends. In words, how would the analysis change if the payout ratio were changed to zero, to 100 percent, or somewhere in between? If you are using the computerized problem diskette, re-analyze the firm's capital budgeting decision using dividend payout ratios of zero, 100 percent, and 40 percent.

(Do the remaining parts if you are using the computerized problem diskette.)

i. Suppose the tax rate fell to zero, with other variables remaining constant. How would that affect the MCC schedule and the capital budget?

j. Return the tax rate to 40 percent. Now assume the debt ratio is increased to 65 percent. That causes all interest rates to rise by 1 percentage point, to 11 percent, 13 percent, and 15 percent, and g to increase from 9 percent to 10 percent. What happens to the MCC schedule and the capital budget?

k. New information becomes available. Change the Part j scenario to assume earnings of only $500,000, but a growth rate of 12 percent. How does that affect the capital budget?

l. Would it be reasonable to use the model to analyze the effects of a change in the payout ratio without changing other variables?

## Solution to Self-Test Problem

ST-1   a. A break point will occur each time a low-cost type of capital is used up. We establish the break points as follows, after first noting that LEI has $24,000 of retained earnings:

$$\text{Retained earnings} = (\text{Total earnings})(1.0 - \text{Payout})$$
$$= \$34,285.72(0.7)$$
$$= \$24,000.$$

$$\text{Break point} = \frac{\text{Total amount of low-cost capital of a given type}}{\text{Fraction of this type of capital in the capital structure}}$$

| Capital Used Up | Break Point Calculation | | Break Number |
|---|---|---|---|
| Retained earnings | $BP_{RE} = \dfrac{\$24,000}{0.60}$ | $= \$40,000$ | 2 |
| 10% flotation common | $BP_{10\% \ E} = \dfrac{\$24,000 + \$12,000}{0.60}$ | $= \$60,000$ | 4 |
| 5% flotation preferred | $BP_{5\% \ P} = \dfrac{\$7,500}{0.15}$ | $= \$50,000$ | 3 |
| 12% debt | $BP_{12\% \ D} = \dfrac{\$5,000}{0.25}$ | $= \$20,000$ | 1 |
| 14% debt | $BP_{14\% \ D} = \dfrac{\$5,000 + \$5,000}{0.25}$ | $= \$40,000$ | 2 |

### Summary of Break Points

1. There are three common equity costs (and hence two changes and two equity-induced breaks) in the MCC. There are two preferred costs and hence one preferred break. There are three debt costs and hence two debt breaks.
2. The numbers in the third column of the table designate the sequential order of the breaks, determined after the break points had been calculated. Note that the second debt break and the break for retained earnings both occur at $40,000.
3. The first break point occurs at $20,000, when the 12 percent debt is used up. The second break point, $40,000, results from using up both retained earnings and the 14 percent debt. The MCC curve also rises at $50,000 and $60,000 as preferred stock with a 5 percent flotation cost and common stock with a 10 percent flotation cost, respectively, are used up.

b. Component costs within indicated total capital intervals are shown below:

Retained earnings (used in interval $0 to $40,000):

$$k_s = \frac{D_1}{P_0} + g = \frac{D_0(1 + g)}{P_0} + g$$

$$= \frac{\$3.60(1.09)}{\$60} + 0.09$$

$$= 0.0654 + 0.09 \qquad\qquad = 15.54\%.$$

Common with F = 10% ($40,001 to $60,000):

$$k_e = \frac{D_1}{P_0(1.0 - F)} + g = \frac{\$3.924}{\$60(0.9)} + 9\% \qquad = 16.27\%.$$

Common with F = 20% (over $60,000):

$$k_e = \frac{\$3.924}{\$60(0.8)} + 9\% \qquad\qquad = 17.18\%.$$

Preferred with F = 5% ($0 to $50,000):

$$k_p = \frac{\text{Preferred dividend}}{P_n} = \frac{\$11}{\$100(0.95)} \qquad = 11.58\%.$$

Preferred with F = 10% (over $50,000):

$$k_p = \frac{\$11}{\$100(0.9)} \qquad\qquad = 12.22\%.$$

Debt at $k_d$ = 12% ($0 to $20,000):

$$k_d(1 - T) = 12\%(0.6) \qquad\qquad = 7.20\%.$$

Debt at $k_d$ = 14% ($20,001 to $40,000):

$$k_d(1 - T) = 14\%(0.6) \qquad\qquad = 8.40\%.$$

Debt at $k_d = 16\%$ (over \$40,000):

$$k_d(1 - T) = 16\%(0.6) \qquad\qquad = 9.60\%.$$

c. MCC calculations within indicated total capital intervals:

1. \$0 to \$20,000 (Debt = 7.2%, Preferred = 11.58%, and RE = 15.54%):

$$MCC = k_a = w_d k_d(1 - T) + w_p k_p + w_s k_s$$
$$= 0.25(7.2\%) + 0.15(11.58\%) + 0.60(15.54\%) \quad = 12.86\%.$$

2. \$20,001 to \$40,000 (Debt = 8.4%, Preferred = 11.58%, and RE = 15.54%):

$$MCC = k_a = 0.25(8.4\%) + 0.15(11.58\%) + 0.60(15.54\%) = 13.16\%.$$

3. \$40,001 to \$50,000 (Debt = 9.6%, Preferred = 11.58%, and Equity = 16.27%):

$$MCC = k_a = 0.25(9.6\%) + 0.15(11.58\%) + 0.60(16.27\%) = 13.90\%.$$

4. \$50,001 to \$60,000 (Debt = 9.6%, Preferred = 12.22%, and Equity = 16.27%):

$$MCC = k_a = 0.25(9.6\%) + 0.15(12.22\%) + 0.60(16.27\%) = 14.00\%.$$

5. Over \$60,000 (Debt = 9.6%, Preferred = 12.22%, and Equity = 17.18%):

$$MCC = k_a = 0.25(9.6\%) + 0.15(12.22\%) + 0.60(17.18\%) = 14.54\%.$$

d. IRR calculation for Project E:

$$PVIFA_{k,6} = \frac{\$20,000}{\$5,427.84} = 3.6847.$$

This is the factor for 16 percent, so $IRR_E = 16\%$.

e. See the graph of the MCC and IOS schedules for LEI on page 489.

f. LEI clearly should accept Projects B, E, and C. It should reject Projects A and D, because their IRRs do not exceed the marginal costs of funds needed to finance them. The firm's capital budget would total \$40,000.

**MCC and IOS Schedule for LEI**

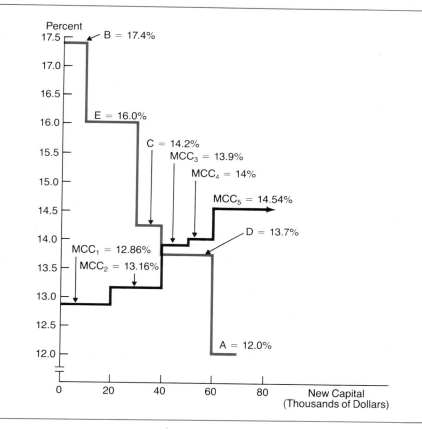

## Selected Additional References and Cases

The following articles provide some valuable insights into the CAPM approach to estimating the cost of equity:

Beaver, William H., Paul Kettler, and Myron Scholes, "The Association between Market Determined and Accounting Determined Risk Measures," *Accounting Review*, October 1970, 654-682.

Bowman, Robert G., "The Theoretical Relationship between Systematic Risk and Financial (Accounting) Variables," *Journal of Finance*, June 1979, 617-630.

Chen, Carl R., "Time-Series Analysis of Beta Stationarity and Its Determinants: A Case of Public Utilities," *Financial Management*, Autumn 1982, 64-70.

Cooley, Philip L., "A Review of the Use of Beta in Regulatory Proceedings," *Financial Management*, Winter 1981, 75-81.

The weighted average cost of capital as described in this chapter is widely used in both industry and academic circles. It has been criticized on several counts, but to date it has withstood the challenges. See the following articles:

Arditti, Fred D., and Haim Levy, "The Weighted Average Cost of Capital as a Cutoff Rate: A Critical Examination of the Classical Textbook Weighted Average," *Financial Management*, Fall 1977, 24-34.

Beranek, William, "The Weighted Average Cost of Capital and Shareholder Wealth Maximization," *Journal of Financial and Quantitative Analysis*, March 1977, 17-32.

Boudreaux, Kenneth J., and Hugh W. Long; John R. Ezzell and R. Burr Porter; Moshe Ben Horim; and Alan C. Shapiro, "The Weighted Average Cost of Capital: A Discussion," *Financial Management*, Summer 1979, 7-23.

Reilly, Raymond R., and William E. Wacker, "On the Weighted Average Cost of Capital," *Journal of Financial and Quantitative Analysis*, January 1973, 123-126.

Some other works that are relevant include the following:

Alberts, W. W., and Stephen H. Archer, "Some Evidence on the Effect of Company Size on the Cost of Equity Capital," *Journal of Financial and Quantitative Analysis*, March 1973, 229-242.

Chen, Andrew, "Recent Developments in the Cost of Debt Capital," *Journal of Finance*, June 1978, 863-883.

Myers, Stewart C., "Interactions of Corporate Financing and Investments Decisions—Implications for Capital Budgeting," *Journal of Finance*, March 1974, 1-25.

Nantell, Timothy J., and C. Robert Carlson, "The Cost of Capital as a Weighted Average," *Journal of Finance*, December 1975, 1343-1355.

For some insights into the cost of capital techniques used by major firms, see

Gitman, Lawrence J., and Vincent A. Mercurio, "Cost of Capital Techniques Used by Major U.S. Firms: Survey and Analysis of Fortune's 1000," *Financial Management*, Winter 1982, 21-29.

The following cases focus on the estimation of a firm's cost of capital:

"American Telephone & Telegraph," which illustrates the estimation of AT&T's cost of capital in the summer of 1983. Harrington, *Case Studies in Financial Decision Making* (Hinsdale, Ill.: Dryden, 1985).

"Communications Satellite Corporation," which examines the problems in estimating equity costs when new technology is involved. Available from HBS Case Services, Cambridge, Mass.

# 15 CAPITAL STRUCTURE AND LEVERAGE

In the summer of 1985, the New York Public Service Commission was involved in an important series of hearings. Consolidated Edison, the utility that provides electric and gas service to New York City and the surrounding area, had a capital structure with only 32 percent debt versus 47 percent for the average utility. The NYPSC staff argued that Con Ed's debt ratio was too low, and they recommended that the commission force the company to issue bonds, use the proceeds to buy back its stock on the open market, and thus raise the debt ratio. According to the staff, the company's weighted average cost of capital, which is built into customers' bills, would be reduced if it raised the debt ratio.

Con Ed's management disagreed. According to them, the utility industry had undergone and was continuing to undergo fundamental changes in operating conditions, which were giving rise to the need for a stronger balance sheet, one with less debt and more equity. The company supported its argument by pointing out that it very nearly went bankrupt in the 1970s, when its bonds were downgraded from AAA to BB, its stock fell from $25 to $3 per share, and it was forced to sell off fixed assets to get the cash it needed to pay interest on its bonds. Con Ed also pointed out that most other utilities were reducing their debt ratios as fast as they could, and that the federal government had recently required New York Telephone and the other telephone companies created by the breakup of AT&T to operate with the equity level Con Ed wanted to use.

Most capital structure decisions are made behind closed doors—although companies sell debt or equity and hence have a given capital structure, the analysis underlying the decision is not revealed. In this case, however, Con Ed was required to defend its capital structure, and its financial experts were subjected to intense cross-examination. In theory, choosing the optimal capital structure is easy—one simply finds that mix of debt, preferred, and common equity that minimizes the weighted average cost of capital. In practice, however, the task is much tougher, because we just do not have the inputs necessary for implementing the theory. Good judgment is required when choosing a capital structure, but the types of analysis set forth in this chapter provide a necessary underpinning for the exercise of that judgment.

In Chapter 14, when we calculated the weighted average cost of capital for use in capital budgeting, we took the capital structure weights as given. However, if the weights were changed, the calculated cost of capital and consequently the set of acceptable projects would change. Also, changing the capital structure would affect the riskiness inherent in the firm's common stock and thus affect $k_s$ and consequently $P_0$. Therefore, the choice of a capital structure, or the mix of securities the firm uses to finance its assets, is a potentially important decision.

**target capital structure**
The optimal capital structure; the capital structure that will maximize the price of the firm's stock and hence the value of the firm.

As we shall see, the firm first analyzes a number of factors and then establishes a **target capital structure**. This target may change over time as conditions vary; however, at any given moment the firm's management has a specific capital structure in mind, and individual financing decisions should be consistent with this target. If the actual debt ratio is below the target level, expansion capital will probably be raised by issuing debt, while stock will probably be sold if the debt ratio is above the target.

Capital structure policy involves a trade-off between risk and return. Using more debt raises the riskiness of the firm's earnings stream, but it also generally means a higher expected rate of return. Higher risk tends to lower the stock's price, but a higher expected rate of return raises it. *The optimal capital structure strikes that balance between risk and return which maximizes the price of the stock and simultaneously minimizes the firm's overall cost of capital.* Since stock price maximization and capital cost minimization occur simultaneously, one can approach the problem of finding the optimal capital structure as one of value maximization or cost minimization.

Several factors influence capital structure decisions. The first is the firm's *business risk*, or the riskiness inherent in its type of business: The greater its business risk, the lower the optimal debt ratio. A second key factor is the firm's *tax position*. A major reason for using debt is the fact that interest is deductible, which lowers the effective cost of debt. However, if much of a firm's income is already sheltered from taxes by accelerated depreciation, investment tax credits, or tax loss carry-forwards, then its tax rate will be low and debt will not be as advantageous as it would to a firm with a higher effective tax rate. A third important consideration is *financial flexibility*, or the ability to raise capital on reasonable terms under adverse conditions. Corporate treasurers know that a steady supply of capital is necessary for stable operations, which in turn are vital for long-run success. They also know that when money is tight in the economy, or when a firm is experiencing operating difficulties, suppliers of capital are much more willing to advance funds to companies with strong balance sheets. Therefore, potential future needs for funds, and the consequences of a funds shortage, have a major influence on the target capital structure. We shall show how these three factors, along with others, combine to determine the optimal capital structure for a given firm.

## Business and Financial Risk

In Chapter 6, when we examined risk from the viewpoint of the individual investor, we distinguished between *market risk*, which is measured by the firm's beta coefficient, and *total risk*, which includes both beta risk and an element of risk which can be eliminated by diversification. Then, in Chapter 10, we examined risk from the viewpoint of the corporation and considered how capital budgeting decisions affect the riskiness of the firm. There again we distinguished between beta risk (the effect of a project on the firm's beta) and corporate risk (the effect of the project on the firm's total risk).

Now we introduce two new dimensions of risk: (1) *business risk*, or the riskiness of the firm's operations if it used no debt, and (2) *financial risk*, which is the additional risk placed on the common stockholders as a result of the firm's decision to use debt.[1] Conceptually, the firm has a certain amount of risk inherent in its operations—this is its business risk. When it uses debt, it partitions this risk and concentrates most of it on one class of investors—the common stockholders. However, the common stockholders must be compensated for this extra risk by a higher expected return.

### Business Risk

**business risk**
The risk associated with a firm's projections of its future operating income.

**Business risk**, which is defined as the uncertainty inherent in projections of future *operating income*, or *earnings before interest and taxes (EBIT)*, is the single most important determinant of a firm's capital structure. Figure 15-1 gives some clues about Porter Electronics Company's business risk. The top graph shows the trend in EBIT over the past 11 years; this gives both security analysts and Porter's management an idea of the degree to which EBIT has varied in the past and might vary in the future. The bottom graph shows a subjectively estimated probability distribution of Porter's EBIT for 1985. The estimate was made at the beginning of 1985, and the expected value of $275 million was read from the trend line in the top section of the figure. As the graphs indicate, actual EBIT in 1985 fell below the expected value.

Porter's past fluctuations in EBIT were caused by many factors—booms and recessions in the national economy, successful new products introduced both by Porter and by its competitors, labor strikes, price controls, fires in Porter's major plants, and so on. Similar events will doubtless occur in the future, and when they do EBIT will rise or fall. Further, there is always the possibility that a long-term disaster might strike, permanently depressing the company's earning power—for example, a competitor could introduce a new product that permanently lowered Porter's earnings.[2] This element of uncer-

---

[1]Using preferred stock also adds to financial risk. To simplify matters somewhat, in this chapter we shall consider only debt and common equity.

[2]Two examples of "safe" industries that turned out to be risky are the railroads just before automobiles, airplanes, and trucks took away most of their business and the telegraph business just before telephones came on the scene. Numerous individual companies have been hurt, if not destroyed, by antitrust actions, fraud, or just plain bad management.

**Figure 15-1**
**Porter Electronics Company: Trend in EBIT, 1975-1985, and**
**Subjective Probability Distribution of EBIT, 1985**

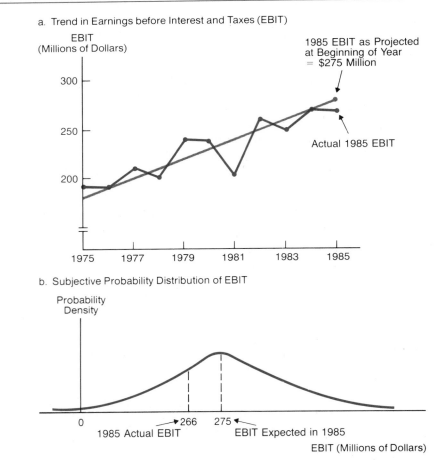

a. Trend in Earnings before Interest and Taxes (EBIT)

b. Subjective Probability Distribution of EBIT

tainty regarding Porter's future operating income is defined as the company's *basic business risk*.

Business risk varies not only from one industry to another but also among firms in a given industry. Further, business risk can change over time. For example, the electric utilities were regarded for years as having little business risk, but a combination of events in the 1970s and 1980s altered their situation, producing huge losses for some companies and greatly increasing the industry's business risk. Today food processors and grocery retailers are frequently given as examples of industries with low business risks, while cyclical manufacturing industries such as steel are regarded as having especially high business risks. Smaller companies, as well as single-product firms, also have a relatively high degree of business risk.[3]

Business risk depends on a number of factors, the more important of which include the following:

**1.** *Demand variability.* The more stable the demand for a firm's products, other things held constant, the lower its business risk.

**2.** *Sales price variability.* Firms whose products are sold in highly volatile markets are exposed to more business risk than similar firms whose output prices are relatively stable.

**3.** *Input price variability.* Firms whose input prices are highly uncertain are exposed to a high degree of business risk.

**4.** *Ability to adjust output prices for changes in input prices.* Some firms are better able to raise their own output prices when input costs rise than are others, and the greater the ability to adjust output prices, the lower the degree of business risk, other things held constant. This factor is especially important during periods of high inflation.

**5.** *The extent to which costs are fixed: operating leverage.* If a high percentage of a firm's costs are fixed and hence do not decline when demand falls off, then the company is exposed to a relatively high degree of business risk. This factor is called *operating leverage*, and it is discussed at length in the next section.

Each of these factors is determined partly by the firm's industry characteristics, but each is also controllable to some extent by management. For example, most firms can, through their marketing policies, take actions to stabilize both unit sales and sales prices; however, this stabilization may require large expenditures on advertising and/or price concessions in order to get customers to commit to purchasing fixed quantities at fixed prices in the future. Similarly, firms such as Porter Electronics can reduce the volatility of future input costs by negotiating long-term labor and materials supply contracts, but they may have to agree to pay prices above the current spot price level in order to obtain these contracts.[4]

## Operating Leverage

As noted above, business risk depends in part on the extent to which a firm's costs are fixed—if fixed costs are high, even a small decline in sales can lead to a large decline in EBIT. Therefore, other things held constant, the higher

---

[3]We have avoided any discussion of market versus company-specific risk in this section. We note now (1) that any action which increases business risk will generally increase a firm's beta coefficient but (2) that a part of business risk as we define it will generally be company specific and hence subject to elimination by diversification by the firm's stockholders. This point is discussed at some length later in the chapter.

[4]For example, in 1985 utilities could buy coal in the spot market for about $30 per ton, but under a 5-year contract, coal cost about $50 per ton. Clearly, the price for reducing uncertainty was high!

a firm's fixed costs, the greater its business risk. Higher fixed costs are generally associated with more highly automated, capital-intensive firms and industries; electric utilities, telephone companies, and airlines are three examples. Also, businesses that employ highly skilled workers who must be retained and paid even during recessions have relatively high fixed costs.

**operating leverage**
The extent to which fixed costs are used in a firm's operations.

*If a high percentage of a firm's total costs are fixed, then the firm is said to have a high degree of* **operating leverage**. In physics, leverage implies the use of a lever to raise a heavy object with a small force. In politics, people who have leverage can accomplish a lot with their smallest word or action. *In business terminology, a high degree of operating leverage, other things held constant, implies that a relatively small change in sales will result in a large change in operating income.*

Figure 15-2 illustrates the concept of operating leverage by comparing the results that a new firm can expect if it uses different degrees of operating

**Figure 15-2**
**Illustration of Operating Leverage**

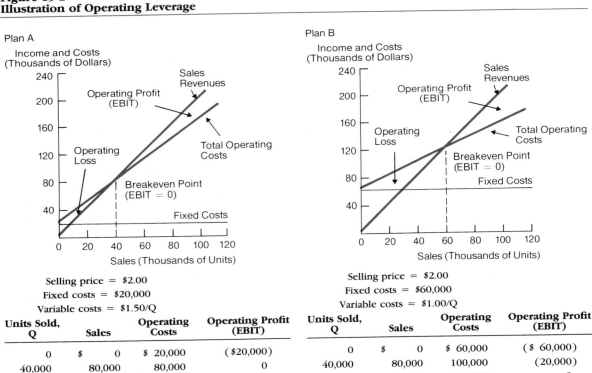

Plan A

Selling price = $2.00
Fixed costs = $20,000
Variable costs = $1.50/Q

| Units Sold, Q | Sales | Operating Costs | Operating Profit (EBIT) |
|---|---|---|---|
| 0 | $ 0 | $ 20,000 | ($20,000) |
| 40,000 | 80,000 | 80,000 | 0 |
| 60,000 | 120,000 | 110,000 | 10,000 |
| 110,000 | 220,000 | 185,000 | 35,000 |
| 160,000 | 320,000 | 260,000 | 60,000 |
| 180,000 | 360,000 | 290,000 | 70,000 |
| 220,000 | 440,000 | 350,000 | 90,000 |

Plan B

Selling price = $2.00
Fixed costs = $60,000
Variable costs = $1.00/Q

| Units Sold, Q | Sales | Operating Costs | Operating Profit (EBIT) |
|---|---|---|---|
| 0 | $ 0 | $ 60,000 | ($ 60,000) |
| 40,000 | 80,000 | 100,000 | (20,000) |
| 60,000 | 120,000 | 120,000 | 0 |
| 110,000 | 220,000 | 170,000 | 50,000 |
| 160,000 | 320,000 | 220,000 | 100,000 |
| 180,000 | 360,000 | 240,000 | 120,000 |
| 220,000 | 440,000 | 280,000 | 160,000 |

leverage. Plan A calls for a relatively small amount of fixed charges—here the firm would not have much automated equipment, so its depreciation, maintenance, property taxes, and so on would be low. Note, however, that under Plan A the total cost line has a relatively steep slope, indicating that variable costs per unit are higher than they would be if the firm used more leverage. Plan B calls for a higher level of fixed costs. Here the firm uses automated equipment (with which one operator can turn out a few or many units at the same labor cost) to a much larger extent. The **breakeven point** is higher under Plan B: Breakeven occurs at 40,000 units under Plan A versus 60,000 units under Plan B.

**breakeven point**
The volume of sales at which total costs equal total revenues, and profits equal zero.

We can develop a formula to find the breakeven quantity by recognizing that breakeven occurs when operating income (EBIT) is equal to zero, which implies that sales revenues are equal to costs:

$$\text{Sales} = \text{Costs}$$
$$PQ = VQ + F$$
$$PQ - VQ - F = 0. \tag{15-1}$$

Here P is average sales price per unit of output, Q is units of output, V is variable cost per unit, and F is fixed operating costs. We can solve Equation 15-1 for the breakeven quantity, $Q_{BE}$:

$$Q_{BE} = \frac{F}{P - V}. \tag{15-1a}$$

Thus for Plan A,

$$Q_{BE} = \frac{\$20,000}{\$2.00 - \$1.50} = 40,000 \text{ units,}$$

and for Plan B,

$$Q_{BE} = \frac{\$60,000}{\$2.00 - \$1.00} = 60,000 \text{ units.}$$

How does operating leverage affect business risk? *Other things held constant, the higher a firm's operating leverage, the higher its business risk.* This point is demonstrated in Figure 15-3, where we show how probability distributions for EBIT under Plans A and B are developed.

The top section of Figure 15-3 gives the probability distribution of sales. This distribution depends on how demand for the product varies and not on whether the product is manufactured by Plan A or by Plan B. Therefore, the same sales probability distribution applies to both production plans: expected sales are $220,000, but with a range of from zero to about $500,000, under either plan.

If we had actually specified the sales probability distribution, then we could have used this information, together with the operating profit (EBIT) at each sales level as shown in the lower part of Figure 15-2, to develop probability distributions for EBIT under Plans A and B. Typical EBIT distributions are shown in the lower section of Figure 15-3. Plan B has a higher

**Figure 15-3**
**Analysis of Business Risk**

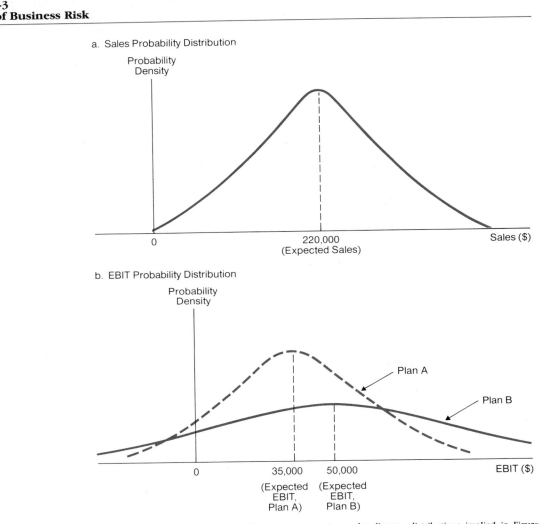

a. Sales Probability Distribution

b. EBIT Probability Distribution

Note: We are using continuous distributions to approximate the discrete distributions implied in Figure 15-2.

expected level of EBIT, but it also entails a much higher probability of large losses. Therefore, Plan B, the one with more fixed costs and a higher degree of operating leverage, is riskier. *In general, holding other things constant, the higher the degree of operating leverage, the greater the degree of business risk as measured by variability of EBIT.*

To what extent can firms control their operating leverage? To a large degree, operating leverage is determined by technology. Electric utilities, telephone companies, airlines, steel mills, and chemical companies simply *must* make heavy investments in fixed assets, resulting in high fixed costs and operating leverage. Grocery stores, on the other hand, have significantly lower fixed costs and hence lower operating leverage. Still, all firms have some control over their operating leverage. For example, an electric utility can expand its generating capacity by building either a nuclear reactor or a coal-fired plant. The nuclear generator would require a larger investment, and hence higher fixed costs, but its variable operating costs would be relatively low. The coal plant, on the other hand, would require a smaller investment and have lower fixed costs, but its variable costs (for coal) would be high. Thus, by its capital budgeting decisions the utility (or any other company) can influence its operating leverage and hence its basic business risk.

The concept of operating leverage was in fact originally developed for use in making capital budgeting decisions. Alternative methods for producing a given product often have different degrees of operating leverage and hence different breakeven points and different degrees of risk. Porter Electronics and other companies regularly undertake a type of breakeven analysis (the sensitivity analysis discussed in Chapter 10) as a part of their capital budgeting processes. Still, once a corporation's operating leverage has been established, the degree of this leverage influences the firm's capital structure decisions.

### Financial Risk

**financial leverage**
The extent to which fixed-income securities (debt and preferred stock) are used in a firm's capital structure.

**financial risk**
The portion of stockholders' risk over and above basic business risk resulting from financial leverage.

**Financial leverage** refers to the use of fixed-income securities—debt and preferred stock—and **financial risk** is the additional risk placed on the common stockholders as a result of financial leverage. Conceptually, the firm has a certain amount of risk inherent in its operations—this is its business risk, which is defined as the uncertainty inherent in projections of future EBIT. By using debt and preferred stock (financial leverage), the firm concentrates its business risk on the common stockholders. To illustrate, suppose 10 people decide to form a corporation to manufacture steel roof trusses. There is a certain amount of business risk in the operation. If the firm is capitalized only with common equity, and if each person buys 10 percent of the stock, then the investors will all share the business risk equally. However, suppose the firm is capitalized with 50 percent debt and 50 percent equity, with 5 of the investors putting up their capital as debt and the other 5 putting up their money as equity. In this case, the investors who put up the equity will have to bear essentially all of the business risk, so the common stock will be twice as risky as it would have been had the firm been financed only with equity. Thus, the use of debt concentrates the firm's business risk on its stockholders.

In the next section, we will see how financial leverage affects a firm's expected earnings per share, the riskiness of those earnings, and consequently the price of the firm's stock. As we shall see, the value of a firm that has no debt first rises as it substitutes debt for equity, then hits a peak, and finally declines as the use of debt becomes excessive. The objective of our analysis is to determine the point at which value is maximized; this point is then used as the *target capital structure*.[5]

## Determining the Optimal Capital Structure

We can illustrate the effects of financial leverage with the data for an illustrative company which we shall call Firm B. As shown in the top section of Table 15-1, the company has no debt. Should it continue the policy of using no debt, or should it start using financial leverage? If it does decide to substitute debt for equity, how far should it go? As in all such decisions, *the correct answer is that it should choose the capital structure that will maximize the price of its stock.*

**Table 15-1**
**Data on Firm B**

**I. Balance Sheet on 12/31/85**

| | | | | |
|---|---|---|---|---|
| Current assets | $100,000 | Debt | $ | 0 |
| Net fixed assets | 100,000 | Common equity (10,000 shares) | | 200,000 |
| Total assets | $200,000 | Total claims | | $200,000 |

**II. Income Statement for 1985**

| | | |
|---|---|---|
| Sales | | $200,000 |
| Fixed operating costs | $ 40,000 | |
| Variable operating costs | 120,000 | 160,000 |
| Earnings before interest and taxes (EBIT) | | $ 40,000 |
| Interest | | 0 |
| Taxable income | | $ 40,000 |
| Taxes (40%) | | 16,000 |
| Net income after taxes | | $ 24,000 |

**III. Other Data**

1. Earnings per share = EPS = $24,000/10,000 shares = $2.40.
2. Dividends per share = DPS = $24,000/10,000 shares = $2.40. (Thus, Firm B pays all of its earnings out as dividends.)
3. Book value per share = $200,000/10,000 shares = $20.
4. Market price per share = $P_0$ = $20. (Thus, the stock sells at its book value.)
5. Price/earnings ratio = P/E = $20/$2.40 = 8.33 times.

---

[5] In this chapter we examine capital structures on a *book value* (or *balance sheet*) *basis*. An alternative approach is to calculate the market values of debt, preferred stock, and common equity and then reconstruct the balance sheet on a *market value basis*. Although the market value approach is more consistent with financial theory, bond rating agencies and most financial executives focus their attention on book values. Moreover, the conversion from book to market values is a complicated process, and market value capital structures are thought by many to be too unstable to serve as operationally useful targets. Finally, exactly the same insights are gained from the book value and market value analyses. For all these reasons, the market value analysis of capital structure is better suited for advanced than for introductory finance courses. For a market value analysis, see Eugene F. Brigham and Louis C. Gapenski, *Intermediate Financial Management*, Chapters 5 and 6.

**Table 15-2**
**Interest Rates for Firm B**
**with Different Debt/Assets Ratios**

| Amount Borrowed | Debt/Assets Ratio[a] | Interest Rate, $k_d$, on All Debt |
|---|---|---|
| $ 20,000 | 10% | 8.0% |
| 40,000 | 20 | 8.3 |
| 60,000 | 30 | 9.0 |
| 80,000 | 40 | 10.0 |
| 100,000 | 50 | 12.0 |
| 120,000 | 60 | 15.0 |

[a]We assume that the firm must borrow in increments of $20,000. Also, we assume that Firm B is unable to borrow more than $120,000, or 60 percent of assets, because of restrictions in its corporate charter.

### EBIT/EPS Analysis of the Effects of Financial Leverage

Changes in the use of debt will cause changes in earnings per share (EPS) and consequently in the stock price. To understand the relationship between financial leverage and EPS, consider first Table 15-2, which shows how Firm B's cost of debt would vary if it used different percentages of debt in its capital structure. Naturally, the higher the percentage of debt, the riskier the debt, and hence the higher the interest rate lenders will charge.

Table 15-3 shows how expected EPS varies with changes in financial leverage. The top third of the table gives operating income data. It begins with a probability distribution of sales; we assume for simplicity that sales can take on only three values, $100,000, $200,000, or $300,000. Next, the table calculates EBIT at each of the three sales levels. Note that EBIT is independent of financial leverage—that is, for any given level of sales, say, $200,000, EBIT is constant regardless of the amount of debt the firm uses.[6]

The middle third of Table 15-3 calculates Firm B's earnings per share under each sales level assuming that the company continues to use no debt. Net income after taxes is divided by the 10,000 shares outstanding to obtain

---

[6]In the real world, capital structure *does* at times affect EBIT. First, if debt levels are excessive, the firm will probably not be able to finance at all if its earnings are low at a time when interest rates are high. This could lead to stop-start construction and R&D programs and also to the necessity of passing up good investment opportunities. Second, a weak financial condition (too much debt) could cause a firm to lose contracts. For example, companies such as General Motors examine closely the financial strength of their parts suppliers; if a supplier is thought to be so weak that it might not be able to deliver materials as called for in the contract, then GM will stop using it. Third, financially strong companies are able to bargain hard with unions as well as with their suppliers, while weaker ones may have to give in simply because they do not have the financial resources to carry on the fight. Finally, a company with so much debt that bankruptcy is a serious threat will have difficulty attracting and retaining managers and employees, or it will have to pay premium salaries; people value job security, and financially weak companies simply cannot provide such protection. For these four reasons, it is not totally correct to say that a firm's financial policy has no effect on its operating income.

Note also that EBIT is dependent on operating (but not financial) leverage. If we were analyzing a firm with either more or less operating leverage, the top section of Table 15-3 would be quite different. The range of EBIT over the different sales levels would be narrower if the company used a lower degree of operating leverage but wider if it used more operating leverage.

**Table 15-3**
**Firm B: EPS with Different Amounts of Financial Leverage**
**(Thousands of Dollars, except Per Share Figures)**

| Probability of Indicated Sales | 0.2 | 0.6 | 0.2 |
|---|---|---|---|
| Sales | $100.0 | $200.0 | $300.0 |
| Fixed costs | 40.0 | 40.0 | 40.0 |
| Variable costs (60% of sales) | 60.0 | 120.0 | 180.0 |
| Total costs (except interest) | $100.0 | $160.0 | $220.0 |
| Earnings before interest and taxes (EBIT) | $ 0.0 | $ 40.0 | $ 80.0 |
| **Debt/Assets (D/A) = 0%** | | | |
| Less: Interest | 0.0 | 0.0 | 0.0 |
| Earnings before taxes | $ 0.0 | $ 40.0 | $ 80.0 |
| Taxes (40%) | 0.0 | (16.0) | (32.0) |
| Net income after taxes | $ 0.0 | $ 24.0 | $ 48.0 |
| Earnings per share on 10,000 shares (EPS)[b] | $ 0.0 | $ 2.40 | $ 4.80 |
| Expected EPS | | $ 2.40 | |
| Standard deviation of EPS | | $ 1.52 | |
| **Debt/Assets (D/A) = 50%** | | | |
| Less: Interest (0.12 × $100,000) | $ 12.0 | $ 12.0 | $ 12.0 |
| Earnings before taxes | ($ 12.0) | $ 28.0 | $ 68.0 |
| Taxes (40%)[a] | 4.8 | (11.2) | (27.2) |
| Net income after taxes | ($ 7.2) | $ 16.8 | $ 40.8 |
| Earnings per share on 5,000 shares (EPS)[b] | ($ 1.44) | $ 3.36 | $ 8.16 |
| Expected EPS | | $ 3.36 | |
| Standard deviation of EPS | | $ 3.04 | |

[a]Assumes tax credit on losses.

[b]The EPS figures can also be obtained using the following formula, where the numerator amounts to an income statement at a given sales level laid out horizontally:

$$\text{EPS} = \frac{(\text{Sales} - \text{Fixed costs} - \text{Variable costs} - \text{Interest})(1 - \text{Tax rate})}{\text{Shares outstanding}}$$
$$= \frac{(\text{EBIT} - I)(1 - T)}{\text{Shares outstanding}}.$$

For example, at Sales (S) = $200,000,

$$\text{EPS}_{D/A=0} = \frac{(\$200,000 - \$40,000 - \$120,000 - 0)(0.6)}{10,000}$$
$$= \$2.40.$$
$$\text{EPS}_{D/A=0.5} = \frac{(\$200,000 - \$40,000 - \$120,000 - \$12,000)(0.6)}{5,000}$$
$$= \$3.36.$$

Since the equation is linear, the indifference level of sales, $S_I$, can be found by setting $\text{EPS}_{D/A=0}$ equal to $\text{EPS}_{D/A=0.5}$ and solving for $S_I$:

$$\text{EPS}_{D/A=0} = \frac{(S_I - \$40,000 - 0.6S_I - 0)(0.6)}{10,000}$$
$$= \frac{(S_I - \$40,000 - 0.6S_I - \$12,000)(0.6)}{5,000} = \text{EPS}_{D/A=0.5}.$$
$$S_I = \$160,000.$$

By substituting this value of sales into either equation, we can find $\text{EPS}_I$, the earnings per share at this indifference point, as $\text{EPS}_I = \$1.44$.

EPS. If sales are as low as $100,000, EPS will be zero, but it will rise to $4.80 at sales of $300,000. The EPS at each sales level is then multiplied by the probability of that sales level to calculate the expected EPS, which is $2.40 if Firm B uses no debt. We also show the standard deviation of EPS to provide an idea of the firm's risk at a zero debt ratio: $\sigma_{EPS} = \$1.52$.[7]

The bottom third of the table shows the financial results that would occur if Firm B were financed with a debt/assets ratio of 50 percent. In this situation, $100,000 of the $200,000 total capital would be debt. The interest rate on the debt, 12 percent, is taken from Table 15-2. With $100,000 of 12 percent debt outstanding, the company's interest expense in Table 15-3 would be $12,000 per year. This is a fixed cost, and it is deducted from EBIT as calculated in the top section. Next, taxes are taken out to derive net income. Then we calculate EPS as net income after taxes divided by shares outstanding. With debt = 0, there were 10,000 shares outstanding. However, if half of the equity were replaced by debt (debt = $100,000), then there would be only 5,000 shares outstanding, and we use this fact to determine the EPS figures that would result at each of the three possible sales levels.[8] With a debt/assets ratio of 50 percent, EPS would be − $1.44 if sales were as low as $100,000; it would rise to $3.36 if sales were $200,000; and it would soar to $8.16 if sales were as high as $300,000.

The EPS distributions under the two financial structures are graphed in Figure 15-4, where we use continuous distributions to approximate the discrete distributions contained in Table 15-3. Although expected EPS would be much higher if financial leverage were employed, the graph makes it clear that the risk of low or even negative EPS would also be higher if debt were used.

These relationships among expected EPS, risk, and financial leverage are extended in Figure 15-5. The tabular data in the lower section were calculated in the manner set forth in Table 15-3, and the graphs plot this data. Here we see that expected EPS rises for a while as the use of debt increases—interest charges rise, but the declining number of shares outstanding as debt is substituted for equity still causes EPS to increase. However, EPS peaks at a

---

[7]See Chapter 5 for a review of procedures for calculating standard deviations. Also, it should be noted that it is sometimes useful to go one step further in this analysis and calculate the *coefficient of variation*, which, as defined in Chapter 5, is the standard deviation divided by the expected value:

$$\text{Coefficient of variation}_{EPS} = (\sigma_{EPS})/(\text{Expected EPS})$$

$$= \$1.52/\$2.40 = 0.63.$$

The advantage of the coefficient of variation is that it permits better comparisons when the mean values of EPS vary, as they do here in the 50 percent and zero debt situations. Still, for illustrative purposes we shall use the standard deviation rather than the coefficient of variation.

[8]We assume in this example that the firm could repurchase common stock at its book value of $100,000/5,000 shares = $20 per share. However, the firm may actually have to pay a higher price to repurchase its stock on the open market. If Firm B had to pay $22 per share, then it could repurchase only $100,000/$22 = 4,545 shares and expected EPS would be only $16,800/(10,000 − 4,545) = $16,800/5,455 = $3.08. A model in which the stock repurchase price is a variable is discussed in advanced texts.

**Figure 15-4**
**Firm B: Probability Distribution of EPS with**
**Different Amounts of Financial Leverage**

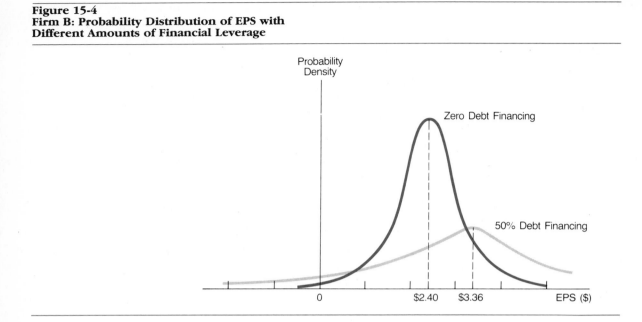

debt ratio of 50 percent. Beyond this amount, interest rates rise so rapidly that EPS is depressed in spite of the falling number of shares outstanding. Risk, as measured by the standard deviation of EPS, rises continuously and at an increasing rate as debt is substituted for equity.

We see, then, that using leverage involves a risk/return trade-off: Higher leverage increases expected earnings per share (at least for a while), but it also increases the firm's risk. Exactly how this trade-off should be resolved is discussed in the next section.

### EPS Indifference Analysis

**EPS indifference point**
The level of sales at which EPS will be unaffected whether the firm uses debt or common stock financing.

Another way of presenting the data on Firm B's two financing methods is shown in Figure 15-6, which depicts the **EPS indifference point**, that is, the point of indifference with regard to EPS between the use of debt and common stock. At a low level of sales, EPS is much higher if stock rather than debt is used. The debt line has a steeper slope and rises faster, however, showing that earnings per share will go up faster with increases in sales if debt is used. The two lines cross at sales of $160,000. Below that level, the firm would be better off using more common stock; above it, debt financing would produce higher earnings per share.

If the managers of Firm B knew with certainty that sales would never again fall below $160,000, bonds would be the preferred method of financing the asset increase. But they cannot know this for certain—in fact, they know that in a number of previous years sales have fallen below this critical level, and that if any of several detrimental events occur in the future then sales could

**Figure 15-5**
**Firm B: Relationships among Expected EPS, Risk, and Financial Leverage**

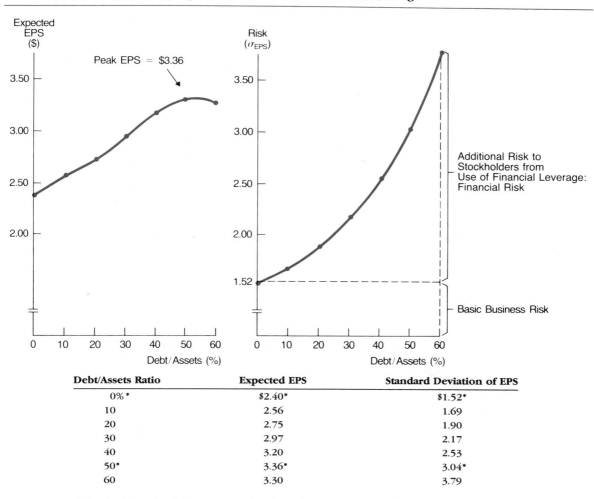

| Debt/Assets Ratio | Expected EPS | Standard Deviation of EPS |
|---|---|---|
| 0%* | $2.40* | $1.52* |
| 10 | 2.56 | 1.69 |
| 20 | 2.75 | 1.90 |
| 30 | 2.97 | 2.17 |
| 40 | 3.20 | 2.53 |
| 50* | 3.36* | 3.04* |
| 60 | 3.30 | 3.79 |

*Values for D/A = 0 and 50 percent are taken from Table 15-3. Values at other D/A ratios were calculated similarly.

again fall well below $160,000. On the other hand, if sales continued to expand, higher earnings per share would result from the use of bonds, an advantage that no officer or director would want to forgo.

### The Effect of Capital Structure on Stock Prices and the Cost of Capital

As we saw in Figure 15-5, Firm B's expected EPS is maximized at a debt/assets ratio of 50 percent. Does this mean that Firm B's optimal capital structure calls for 50 percent debt? The answer is no—*the optimal capital struc-*

**Figure 15-6**
**Earnings per Share for Stock and Debt Financing**

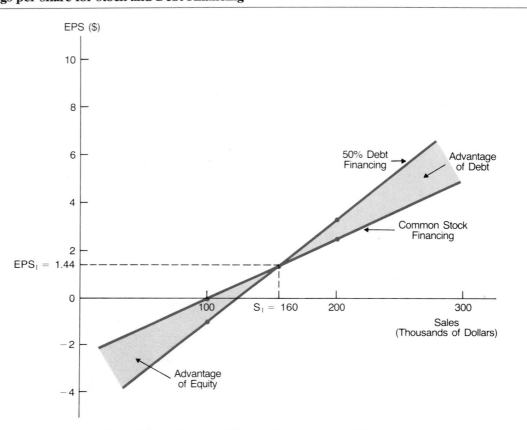

Note that these values of the indifference level of sales, $S_I$ and $EPS_I$, are the same as those obtained algebraically in Table 15-3.

*ture is the one that maximizes the price of the firm's stock, and this almost always calls for a debt ratio which is lower than the one that maximizes expected EPS.*

This statement is demonstrated in Table 15-4, which develops Firm B's estimated stock price and weighted average cost of capital at different debt/ assets ratios. The data in Columns 1, 2, and 3 were taken from Table 15-2 and Figure 15-5. The beta coefficients shown in Column 4 were estimated. Recall from Chapter 6 that a stock's beta measures its relative volatility as compared with an average stock. It has been demonstrated both theoretically and empirically that a firm's beta increases with its degree of financial leverage. The exact nature of this relationship for a given firm is difficult to estimate, but the values given in Column 4 do show the approximate nature of the relationship for Firm B.

## Table 15-4
## Stock Price and Cost of Capital Estimates for Firm B
## with Different Debt/Assets Ratios

| Debt/ Assets (1) | $k_d$ (2) | Expected EPS (and DPS)[a] (3) | Estimated Beta (4) | $k_s =$ $[k_{RF} + b(k_M - k_{RF})]$[b] (5) | Estimated Price[c] (6) | Resulting P/E Ratio (7) | Weighted Average Cost of Capital,[d] WACC = $k_a$ (8) |
|---|---|---|---|---|---|---|---|
| 0% | — | $2.40 | 1.50 | 12.0% | $20.00 | 8.33 | 12.00% |
| 10 | 8.0% | 2.56 | 1.55 | 12.2 | 20.98 | 8.20 | 11.46 |
| 20 | 8.3 | 2.75 | 1.65 | 12.6 | 21.83 | 7.94 | 11.08 |
| 30 | 9.0 | 2.97 | 1.80 | 13.2 | 22.50 | 7.58 | 10.86 |
| 40 | 10.0 | 3.20 | 2.00 | 14.0 | 22.86 | 7.14 | 10.80 |
| 50 | 12.0 | 3.36 | 2.30 | 15.2 | 22.11 | 6.58 | 11.20 |
| 60 | 15.0 | 3.30 | 2.70 | 16.8 | 19.64 | 5.95 | 12.12 |

[a]Firm B pays all of its earnings out as dividends, so EPS = DPS.

[b]We assume that $k_{RF}$ = 6% and $k_M$ = 10%. Therefore, at debt/assets equal to zero, $k_s$ = 6% + 1.5(10% − 6%) = 6% + 6% = 12%. Other values of $k_s$ are calculated similarly.

[c]Since all earnings are paid out as dividends, no retained earnings will be plowed back into the business, and growth in EPS and DPS will be zero. Hence, the zero growth stock price model developed in Chapter 5 can be used to estimate the price of Firm B's stock. For example, at debt/assets = 0,

$$P_0 = \frac{DPS}{k_s} = \frac{\$2.40}{0.12} = \$20.$$

Other prices were calculated similarly.

[d]Column 8 is found by use of the weighted average cost of capital (WACC) equation developed in Chapter 14:

$$WACC = k_a = w_d k_d(1 - T) + w_s k_s$$
$$= (D/A)(k_d)(1 - T) + (1 - D/A)k_s.$$

For example, at D/A = 40%,

$$k_a = 0.4(10\%)(0.6) + 0.6(14.0\%) = 10.80\%.$$

Assuming that the riskless rate of return, $k_{RF}$, is 6 percent and that the required return on an average stock, $k_M$, is 10 percent, we use the CAPM equation to develop estimates of the required rates of return, $k_s$, for Firm B as shown in Column 5. Here we see that $k_s$ is 12 percent if no financial leverage is used but rises to 16.8 percent if the company finances with 60 percent debt, the maximum permitted by its charter.

The zero growth stock valuation model developed in Chapter 6 is used, along with the Column 3 values of DPS and the Column 5 values of $k_s$, to develop the estimated stock prices shown in Column 6. Here we see that the expected stock price first rises with financial leverage, hits a peak of $22.86 at a debt/assets ratio of 40 percent, and then begins to decline. *Thus, Firm B's optimal capital structure calls for 40 percent debt.*

The price/earnings ratios shown in Column 7 were calculated by dividing the price in Column 6 by the expected earnings given in Column 3. We use the pattern of P/E ratios as a check on the "reasonableness" of the other data.

Other things held constant, P/E ratios decline as the riskiness of a firm increases. Also, at the time Firm B's data were being analyzed, the P/Es shown here were generally consistent with those of zero growth companies with varying amounts of financial leverage. Thus, the data in Column 7 reinforce our confidence that the estimated prices shown in Column 6 are reasonable.

Finally, Column 8 shows Firm B's weighted average cost of capital, WACC $= k_a$, calculated as described in Chapter 14, at the different capital structures. If the company uses zero debt, its capital is all equity; hence, WACC $= k_a = k_s = 12\%$. As the firm begins to use lower-cost debt, its weighted average cost of capital declines. However, as the debt ratio increases, the costs of both debt and equity rise, and the increasing costs of the two components begin to offset the fact that larger amounts of the lower-cost component are being used. At 40 percent debt, WACC $= k_a$ hits a minimum, and it rises after that as the debt ratio is increased.

The EPS, cost of capital, and stock price data shown in Table 15-4 are plotted in Figure 15-7. As the graph shows, the debt/assets ratio that maximizes Firm B's expected EPS is 50 percent. However, the expected stock price is maximized, and the cost of capital minimized, at a 40 percent debt ratio. *Thus, the optimal capital structure calls for 40 percent debt and 60 percent equity.* Management should set its target capital structure at these ratios and, if the present ratios are off target, it should move toward the target when new security offerings are made.

## Degree of Leverage

In our discussion of operating leverage earlier in the chapter, we made no mention of financial leverage, and when we discussed financial leverage, operating leverage was assumed to be given. Actually, the two types of leverage are interrelated. For example, if Firm B *reduced* its operating leverage, this would probably lead to an *increase* in the optimal amount of financial leverage. On the other hand, if it decided to *increase* its operating leverage, then its optimal capital structure would probably call for *less* debt. Thus, there is a trade-off between operating risk and financial risk.

The theory of finance has not been developed to the point where we can actually specify simultaneously the optimal levels of operating and financial leverage. However, we can gain a better understanding of how operating and financial leverage interact through an analysis of the *degree of leverage concept.*

### Degree of Operating Leverage (DOL)

**degree of operating leverage (DOL)**
The ratio of the percentage change in operating income to the percentage change in sales.

The **degree of operating leverage (DOL)** is defined as the percentage change in operating income (or EBIT) associated with a given percentage change in sales volume, or

$$DOL = \frac{\text{Percentage change in EBIT}}{\text{Percentage change in sales}} = \frac{\dfrac{\Delta EBIT}{EBIT}}{\dfrac{\Delta Q}{Q}}. \tag{15-2}$$

**Figure 15-7**
**Relationship between Firm B's Capital Structure and**
**Its EPS, Cost of Capital, and Stock Price**

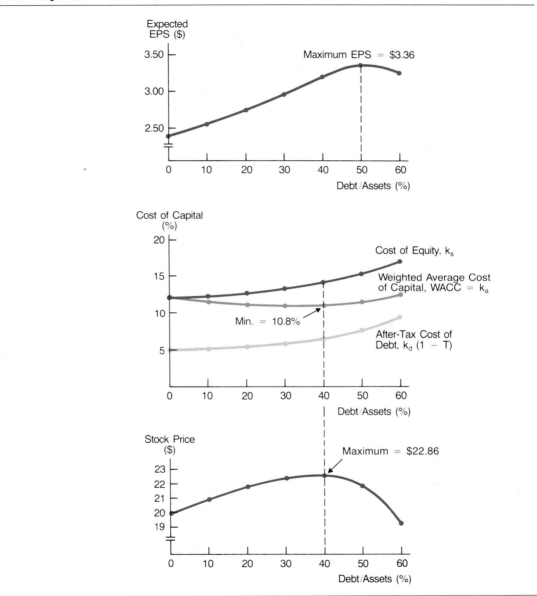

DOL can be calculated by using Equation 15-3, which is derived from Equation 15-2:[9]

$$DOL_Q = \text{Degree of operating leverage at Point Q} = \frac{Q(P - V)}{Q(P - V) - F}, \quad (15\text{-}3)$$

or, based on dollar sales rather than units,

$$DOL_S = \frac{S - VC}{S - VC - F}. \quad (15\text{-}3a)$$

Here Q is units of output, P is the average sales price per unit of output, V is the variable cost per unit, F is fixed operating costs, S is sales in dollars, and VC is total variable costs. Equation 15-3 is normally used to analyze a single product, such as IBM's PC, while Equation 15-3a is used to evaluate an entire firm with many types of products and hence where "quantity in units" and "sales price" are not meaningful.

Applying Equation 15-3 to data for Firm B at a sales level of $200,000 as shown in Table 15-3, we find its degree of operating leverage to be 2.0; thus, an X percent increase in sales will produce a 2X percent increase in EBIT:

$$DOL_{\$200,000} = \frac{\$200,000 - \$120,000}{\$200,000 - \$120,000 - \$40,000}$$

$$= \frac{\$80,000}{\$40,000} = 2.0.$$

Therefore, a 50 percent increase in sales, starting from sales of $200,000, would result in a 50%(2.0) = 100% increase in EBIT. This situation is confirmed by examining the top section of Table 15-3, where we see that a 50 percent increase in sales, from $200,000 to $300,000, causes EBIT to double. Notice also that the DOL is specific to the beginning sales level; thus, if we evaluated it from a sales base of $300,000, there would be a different DOL:

$$DOL_{\$300,000} = \frac{\$300,000 - \$180,000}{\$300,000 - \$180,000 - \$40,000}$$

$$= \frac{\$120,000}{\$80,000} = 1.5.$$

In general, if a firm is operating at close to its breakeven level, the degree of operating leverage will be high, and DOL declines the higher the base level

---

[9]Equation 15-3 is developed from 15-2 as follows. The change in units of output is defined as $\Delta Q$. Since both price and fixed costs are constant, the change in EBIT is $\Delta Q(P - V)$, where P is the price per unit and V is the variable cost per unit. The initial EBIT is $Q(P - V) - F$, so the percentage change in EBIT is

$$\% \Delta EBIT = \frac{\Delta Q(P - V)}{Q(P - V) - F}.$$

The percentage change in output is $\Delta Q/Q$, so the ratio of the percentage change in EBIT to the percentage change in output is:

$$DOL = \frac{\dfrac{\Delta Q(P - V)}{Q(P - V) - F}}{\dfrac{\Delta Q}{Q}} = \left(\frac{\Delta Q(P - V)}{Q(P - V) - F}\right)\left(\frac{Q}{\Delta Q}\right) = \frac{Q(P - V)}{Q(P - V) - F}. \quad (15\text{-}3)$$

of sales is above breakeven sales. Looking back at the top section of Table 15-3, we see that the company's breakeven point (before consideration of financial leverage) is at sales of $100,000. At that level, DOL is infinite:

$$DOL_{\$100,000} = \frac{\$100,000 - \$60,000}{\$100,000 - \$60,000 - \$40,000}$$

$$= \frac{\$40,000}{0} = \text{undefined but} \approx \text{infinity.}$$

When evaluated at higher and higher sales levels, DOL progressively declines.

### Degree of Financial Leverage (DFL)

Operating leverage affects earnings before interest and taxes (EBIT), while financial leverage affects earnings after interest and taxes, or the earnings available to common stockholders. In terms of Table 15-3, operating leverage affects the top section, while financial leverage affects the lower sections. Thus, if Firm B had more operating leverage, its fixed costs would be higher than $40,000, its variable cost ratio would be lower than 60 percent of sales, and EBIT would vary with sales to a greater extent. Financial leverage takes over where operating leverage leaves off, further magnifying the effects on earnings per share of changes in the level of sales. For this reason, operating leverage is sometimes referred to as *first-stage leverage* and financial leverage as *second-stage leverage*.

**degree of financial leverage (DFL)**
The percentage change in earnings available to common stockholders that is associated with a given percentage change in earnings before interest and taxes.

The **degree of financial leverage (DFL)** is defined as the percentage change in earnings per share (EPS) that is associated with a given percentage change in earnings before interest and taxes (EBIT), and it may be calculated as follows:[10]

$$DFL = \frac{\%\,\Delta EPS}{\%\,\Delta EBIT}$$

$$= \frac{EBIT}{EBIT - I}. \qquad (15\text{-}4)$$

---

[10]Equation 15-4 is developed as follows:

1. Notice that EBIT = Q(P − V) − F.

2. Earnings per share are found as EPS = [(EBIT − I)(1 − T)]/N, where I is interest paid, T is the corporate tax rate, and N is the number of shares outstanding.

3. I is a constant, so $\Delta I = 0$; hence, $\Delta EPS$, the change in EPS, is

$$\Delta EPS = \frac{(\Delta EBIT - \Delta I)(1 - T)}{N} = \frac{\Delta EBIT(1 - T)}{N}.$$

4. The percentage change in EPS is the change in EPS divided by the original EPS:

$$\frac{\dfrac{\Delta EBIT(1 - T)}{N}}{\dfrac{(EBIT - I)(1 - T)}{N}} = \left[\frac{\Delta EBIT(1 - T)}{N}\right]\left[\frac{N}{(EBIT - I)(1 - T)}\right] = \frac{\Delta EBIT}{EBIT - I}.$$

5. The degree of financial leverage is the percentage change in EPS over the percentage change in EBIT:

$$DFL = \frac{\dfrac{\Delta EBIT}{EBIT - I}}{\dfrac{\Delta EBIT}{EBIT}} = \left(\frac{\Delta EBIT}{EBIT - I}\right)\left(\frac{EBIT}{\Delta EBIT}\right) = \frac{EBIT}{EBIT - I}. \qquad (15\text{-}4)$$

6. This equation must be modified if the firm has preferred stock outstanding.

For Firm B at sales of \$200,000 and an EBIT of \$40,000, the degree of financial leverage with a 50 percent debt ratio is

$$\text{DFL}_{S = \$200,000,\ D = 50\%} = \frac{\$40,000}{\$40,000 - \$12,000}$$

$$= 1.43.$$

Therefore, a 100 percent increase in EBIT would result in a $100(1.43) =$ 143% increase in earnings per share. This may be confirmed by referring to the lower section of Table 15-3, where we see that a 100 percent increase in EBIT, from \$40,000 to \$80,000, produces a 143 percent increase in EPS:

$$\% \Delta \text{EPS} = \frac{\Delta \text{EPS}}{\text{EPS}_0} = \frac{\$8.16 - \$3.36}{\$3.36} = \frac{\$4.80}{\$3.36} = 1.43 = 143\%.$$

If no debt were used, the degree of financial leverage by definition would be 1.0, so a 100 percent increase in EBIT would produce exactly a 100 percent increase in EPS. This can be confirmed by the data in the center section of Table 15-3.

### Combining Operating and Financial Leverage (DTL)

We have seen that operating leverage causes a change in sales volume to have a magnified effect on EBIT, and that if financial leverage is superimposed on operating leverage, changes in EBIT will have a magnified effect on earnings per share. Therefore, if a firm uses a considerable amount of both operating and financial leverage, then even small changes in sales will produce wide fluctuations in EPS.

**degree of total leverage (DTL)**
The percentage change in EPS brought about by a given percentage change in sales; the product of the degree of operating leverage and the degree of financial leverage.

Equation 15-3 for the degree of operating leverage can be combined with Equation 15-4 for the degree of financial leverage to produce the **degree of total leverage (DTL)**, which shows how a given change in sales will affect earnings per share. Here are three equivalent equations for DTL:[11]

---

[11]Equation 15-5 is true by definition. Equations 15-5a and 15-5b are developed as follows:

1. Recognize that EBIT $= Q(P - V) - F$; then rewrite Equation 15-4 as follows:

$$\text{DFL} = \frac{\text{EBIT}}{\text{EBIT} - I} = \frac{Q(P - V) - F}{Q(P - V) - F - I} = \frac{S - VC - F}{S - VC - F - I}. \qquad \textbf{(15-4a)}$$

2. The degree of total leverage is equal to the degree of operating leverage times the degree of financial leverage, or Equation 15-3 times Equation 15-4a:

$$\text{DTL} = (\text{DOL})(\text{DFL}) \qquad \textbf{(15-5)}$$

$$= (\text{Equation 15-3})(\text{Equation 15-4a})$$

$$= \left[ \frac{Q(P - V)}{Q(P - V) - F} \right] \left[ \frac{Q(P - V) - F}{Q(P - V) - F - I} \right]$$

$$= \frac{Q(P - V)}{Q(P - V) - F - I} \qquad \textbf{(15-5a)}$$

$$= \frac{S - VC}{S - VC - F - I} \qquad \textbf{(15-5b)}$$

$$DTL = (DOL)(DFL). \tag{15-5}$$

$$DTL = \frac{Q(P - V)}{Q(P - V) - F - I}. \tag{15-5a}$$

$$DTL = \frac{S - VC}{S - VC - F - I}. \tag{15-5b}$$

For Firm B at sales of \$200,000, the degree of total leverage using 50 percent debt is

$$DTL_{\$200,000, \ 50\%} = \frac{\$200,000 - \$120,000}{\$200,000 - \$120,000 - \$40,000 - \$12,000}$$

$$= \frac{\$80,000}{\$28,000} = 2.86,$$

or

$$DFL = (2.00)(1.43) = 2.86.$$

We can use the degree of total leverage (DTL) to find the new earnings per share ($EPS_1$) for a given percentage increase in sales (% $\Delta$ Sales) as follows:

$$EPS_1 = EPS_0 + EPS_0[(DTL)(\% \Delta \ Sales)]$$

$$= EPS_0[1.0 + (DTL)(\% \Delta \ Sales)].$$

For example, a 50 percent (or 0.5) increase in sales, from \$200,000 to \$300,000, would cause $EPS_0$ ( \$3.36 as shown in the bottom section of Table 15-3) to increase to \$8.16:

$$EPS_1 = \$3.36[1.0 + (2.86)(0.5)]$$

$$= \$3.36(2.43)$$

$$= \$8.16.$$

This figure agrees with the one for EPS shown in Table 15-3.

The degree of leverage concept is useful for two reasons: (1) it enables us to estimate the effect of a change in sales volume on earnings per share, and (2) it permits us to show the interrelationship between operating and financial leverage. The concept can be used to show the management of a business, for example, that a decision to automate a plant and to finance the new equipment with debt would result in a situation wherein a 10 percent decline in sales would produce a 50 percent decline in earnings, whereas a different operating and financial leverage package would be such that a 10 percent sales decline would cause earnings to decline by only 20 percent. Having the alternatives stated in this manner gives decision makers a better idea of the ramifications of the possible actions.[12]

---

[12]The concept is also useful for investors. If firms in an industry are classified as to their degrees of total leverage, an investor who is optimistic about prospects for the industry might favor those firms with high leverage, and vice versa if industry sales are expected to decline. The major difficulty is in separating fixed from variable costs: Accounting statements simply do not make this breakdown, so the analyst must make the separation. Note too that costs are really fixed, variable, and "semivariable," for if times get tough enough, firms will sell off depreciable assets and thus reduce depreciation charges (a fixed cost), lay off "permanent" employees, reduce salaries of remaining personnel, and so on. For this reason, the degree of leverage concept is generally more useful in explaining the general nature of the relationship than in developing precise numbers, and any numbers developed should be thought of as approximate rather than exact.

## Liquidity and Cash Flow Analysis

There are some practical difficulties with the types of analyses described thus far in the chapter, including the following:

**1.** It is virtually impossible to determine exactly how either P/E ratios or equity capitalization rates ($k_s$ values) are affected by different degrees of financial leverage—the best we can do is make educated guesses as to these relationships. Therefore, management rarely if ever has sufficient confidence in the type of analysis set forth in Table 15-3 and Figure 15-7 to use it as the sole determinant of the target capital structure.

**2.** The managers may be more or less "conservative" than the average stockholder and hence may set a somewhat different target capital structure than the one that would maximize the stock price. The managers of a publicly owned firm would never admit this, for unless they owned voting control, they would quickly be removed from office. However, in view of the uncertainties about what constitutes the value-maximizing structure, management could always say that the target capital structure employed is, in its judgment, the value-maximizing structure, and it would be difficult to prove otherwise. Still, if management is far off target, especially on the low side, then chances are very high that some other firm or management group will take over the company, increase its leverage, and thereby raise its value. This point is discussed in more detail later in the chapter.

**3.** Managers of large firms, especially those providing vital services such as electricity or telephones, have a responsibility to provide *continuous* service, so they must refrain from using leverage to the point where the firms' long-run viability is endangered. Long-run viability may conflict with short-run stock price maximization and capital cost minimization.[13]

For all of these reasons, managers are concerned with the effects of financial leverage on the risk of bankruptcy, and an analysis of this factor is therefore an important input in the capital structure decision. Accordingly, managements give considerable weight to financial strength indicators such as the **times-interest-earned (TIE) ratio**. The lower this ratio, the higher the probability that a firm will default on its debt and be forced into bankruptcy.

Table 15-5 shows how Firm B's expected TIE ratio would decline if its debt/assets ratio were increased. If the debt/assets ratio were only 10 percent, the expected TIE would be a high 25 times, but the interest coverage

**times-interest-earned (TIE) ratio**
A ratio that measures the firm's ability to meet its annual interest obligations, calculated by dividing earnings before interest and taxes by interest charges.

---

[13]Recognizing this fact, most public service commissions require utilities to obtain their approval before issuing long-term securities, and Congress has empowered the SEC to supervise the capital structures of public utility holding companies. However, in addition to concern over the firms' safety, which suggests low debt ratios, both managers and regulators recognize a need to keep all costs as low as possible, including the cost of capital. Since a firm's capital structure affects its cost of capital, regulatory commissions and utility managers try to select capital structures that will minimize the cost of capital, subject to the constraint that the firm's solvency not be endangered.

**Table 15-5**
**Firm B: Expected Times-Interest-Earned Ratio**
**at Different Debt/Assets Ratios**

| Debt/Assets | Expected TIE[a] |
|---|---|
| 0% | Undefined |
| 10 | 25.0 |
| 20 | 12.1 |
| 30 | 7.4 |
| 40 | 5.0 |
| 50 | 3.3 |
| 60 | 2.2 |

[a]$TIE = \dfrac{EBIT}{Interest}$. For example, when debt/assets = 50%, TIE = \$40,000/\$12,000 = 3.3. Data are from Tables 15-2 and 15-3.

ratio would decline rapidly if the debt ratio were increased. Note, however, that these coverages are expected values at different debt ratios—the actual TIE for any non-zero debt capital structure will be higher if sales exceed the expected \$200,000 level but lower if sales fall below \$200,000.

The variability of the TIE ratio is highlighted in Figure 15-8, which shows the probability distributions of the TIEs at debt/assets ratios of 40 percent and 60 percent. The expected TIE is much higher if only 40 percent debt is used. Even more important, with less debt there is a much lower probability

**Figure 15-8**
**Firm B: Probability Distributions of Times-Interest-Earned Ratios with**
**Different Capital Structures**

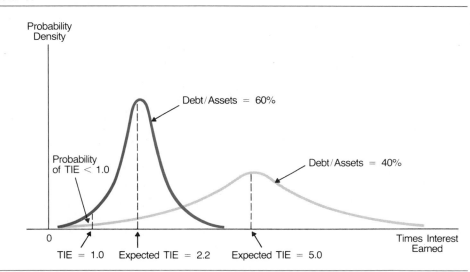

of a TIE of less than 1.0, the level at which the firm is not earning enough to meet its required interest payment and is thus seriously exposed to the threat of bankruptcy.[14]

## Capital Structure Theory

Capital structure theory really began in 1958, when Professors Franco Modigliani and Merton Miller (hereafter MM) published what has been called the most influential finance article ever written.[15] MM proved, under a very restrictive set of assumptions, that due to the tax deductibility of interest on debt, a firm's value rises continuously as it uses more debt, and hence value will be maximized by financing almost entirely with debt. MM's assumptions included the following: (1) there are no brokerage costs, (2) there are no personal taxes, (3) investors can borrow at the same rate as corporations, (4) all debt is riskless, and (5) EBIT is not affected by the use of debt. Since several of these assumptions are obviously unrealistic, MM's position was only a beginning.

Subsequent researchers, and MM themselves, extended the basic theory by relaxing the assumptions. Other researchers attempted to test the various theoretical models with empirical data to see exactly how stock prices and capital costs are affected by capital structure. Both the theoretical and the empirical results have been revealing, but neither set of studies has produced results that can be used to precisely identify a firm's optimal capital structure. A summary of the theoretical and empirical research to date is expressed graphically in Figure 15-9. Here are the key points in the figure:

**1.** Debt provides tax shelter benefits; under the assumptions of the original Modigliani-Miller paper, the line labeled "Pure MM Result" would express the relationship between stock prices and debt.

**2.** The MM assumptions do not hold in the real world. Debt costs rise as the debt ratio rises; EBIT declines at extreme leverage; expected tax rates fall and reduce the value of the debt tax shelter; and the probability of lawyers' fees and other costs associated with bankruptcy increases.

**3.** There is some threshold level of debt ($D_1$) below which the effects noted in Point 2 are immaterial. Beyond $D_1$, the bankruptcy-related costs become increasingly important in reducing the benefits of the debt tax shelter. Be-

---

[14]It should be noted that cash flows, which include depreciation, can be sufficient to cover required interest payments even though the TIE is less than 1.0. Thus, at least for a while, a firm may be able to avoid bankruptcy even though its operating income is less than its interest charges. Note also, however, that most firms' debt contracts stipulate that they must maintain the TIE ratio above some minimum level, say, 2.0 or 2.5, or else they cannot borrow any additional funds, which can severely constrain operations. Such potential constraints, as much as the threat of actual bankruptcy, limit the use of debt.

[15]Franco Modigliani and Merton H. Miller, "The Cost of Capital, Corporation Finance, and the Theory of Investment," *American Economic Review*, June 1958.

**Figure 15-9**
**Effect of Leverage on the Value of Firm B's Stock**

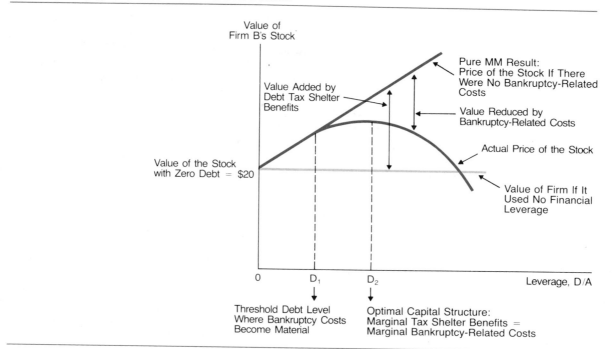

In summary, although capital structure theory provides a useful framework for considering capital structure decisions, such decisions in real life must be made on the basis of judgment rather than pure theoretical analysis.[16]

yond $D_2$, bankruptcy-related costs exceed the tax shelter benefits. Therefore, $D_2$ denotes the optimal capital structure.

**4.** Both theory and empirical evidence support the discussion above. However, statistical problems prevent researchers from identifying Points $D_1$ and $D_2$ for firms in general or for any given firm.

**5.** The theoretical and empirical work also supports the general shape of the curves in Figures 15-7 and 15-9—but again, these graphs must be taken as approximations and not as precisely defined functions. The numbers in Figure 15-7 are shown out to two decimal places, but that is merely for illustrative purposes—the figures are not nearly that accurate in view of the fact that the data on which the graph is based are judgmental estimates.

In summary, although capital structure theory provides a useful framework for considering capital structure decisions, such decisions in real life must be made on the basis of judgment rather than pure theoretical analysis.[16]

---

[16]For a more detailed discussion of capital structure theories, see Chapter 5 of Eugene F. Brigham and Louis C. Gapenski, *Intermediate Financial Management*.

## Capital Structure and Mergers

One of the most exciting developments in the financial world during the 1980s has been the high level of merger activity, especially takeovers. A *takeover* occurs when one firm buys out another over the opposition of the acquired firm's management. The target firm's stock is considered to be undervalued, so the acquiring firm will pay a premium of perhaps 50 percent to gain control. Mergers are discussed at length in Chapter 21, but it is useful to make these points now: (1) very often the acquiring firm issues debt and uses it to buy the target firm's stock; (2) this action effectively changes the enterprise's capital structure; and (3) the value enhancement resulting from the use of debt is apparently sufficient to cover the premium offered for the stock and still leave a profit for the acquiring company.

Recognizing the validity of the types of analysis described in this chapter has literally led to the creation of companies whose major function is to acquire other companies through takeovers. The managers of these acquiring companies (often called "conglomerates") have frequently made huge personal fortunes. Shrewd individual investors, even including a few professors, have selected stock portfolios heavily weighted with prime acquisition targets and then done well in the market. Of course, the managements of firms with low leverage ratios who do not want to be taken over can be expected to react by attempting to find their optimal debt levels and then issuing debt and repurchasing stock, thus bringing their actual debt ratios up to the level that maximizes the prices of their stock, which will make their companies less attractive acquisition targets. CBS, for example, did this in 1985 when fighting off an acquisition attempt by Ted Turner.

The game is far from over—indeed, it can never end, because economic shifts lead to continuing changes in optimal capital structures. This makes it especially important that the lessons to be learned from this chapter be thoroughly understood by everyone actively involved in financial management.

## Checklist for Capital Structure Decisions

In addition to the types of analysis discussed above, a firm must also consider the following factors, which have an important, though hard to measure, bearing on the choice of a target capital structure:

1. *Sales stability.* A firm whose sales are relatively stable can safely take on more debt and incur higher fixed charges than a company with unstable sales. Utility companies, because of their stable demand, have historically been able to use more financial leverage than industrial firms.

2. *Asset structure.* Firms whose assets are suitable as security for loans tend to use debt rather heavily. Thus, real estate companies are usually highly leveraged, while companies involved in technological research employ less debt.

**3.** *Operating leverage.* Other things the same, a firm with less operating leverage is better able to employ financial leverage because, as we saw, the interaction of operating and financial leverage determines the overall impact of a decline in sales on operating income and net cash flows.

**4.** *Growth rate.* Other things the same, faster-growing firms must rely more heavily on external capital (see Chapter 8). Further, the flotation costs involved in selling common stock exceed those incurred when selling debt. Thus, rapidly growing firms tend to use somewhat more debt than slower-growth companies.

**5.** *Profitability.* One often observes that firms with very high rates of return on investment use relatively little debt. Although there is no theoretical justification for this fact, the practical reason seems to be that very profitable firms such as IBM, 3M, and Kodak simply do not need to do much debt financing—their high rates of return enable them to do most of their financing with retained earnings.

**6.** *Taxes.* Interest is a deductible expense, while dividends are not. Hence, the higher a firm's corporate tax rate, the greater the advantage of using debt.

**7.** *Control.* The effect that debt or stock might have on a management's control position may influence its capital structure decision. If management has voting control (over 50 percent of the stock) but is not in a position to buy any more stock, it may choose debt for new financings. On the other hand, a management group that is not concerned about voting control may decide to use equity rather than debt if the firm's financial situation is so weak that the use of debt might subject the firm to serious risk of default—if the firm goes into default, the managers will almost surely lose their jobs. However, if too little debt is used, management runs the risk of a takeover. In general, control considerations do not necessarily suggest the use of debt or equity; however, if management is at all insecure, it will certainly take the effects of capital structure on control into account.

**8.** *Management attitudes.* In the absence of proof that one capital structure will lead to higher stock prices than another, management can exercise its own judgment about a proper choice. Some managements tend to be more conservative than others and thus use less debt than the average firm in their industry, while for other managements the reverse is true.

**9.** *Lender and rating agency attitudes.* Regardless of managers' own analyses of the proper leverage factors for their firms, there is no question but that lenders' and rating agencies' attitudes are frequently important determinants of financial structures. In the majority of cases, the corporation discusses its financial structure with lenders and rating agencies and gives much weight to their advice. But when management is so confident of the future that it seeks to use leverage beyond the norms for its industry, lenders may be unwilling to accept such debt increases or may do so only at a high price.

**10.** *Market conditions.* Conditions in the stock and bond markets undergo both long- and short-run changes which can have an important bearing on a firm's optimal capital structure. For example, during the credit crunch in the winter of 1982, there was simply no market at any "reasonable" interest rate for new long-term bonds rated below A. Low-rated companies that needed capital were forced to go to the stock market or to the short-term debt market. Actions such as this could represent either permanent changes in target capital structures or temporary departures from stable targets; the important point, however, is that stock and bond market conditions do influence the type of securities used for a given financing.

**11.** *The firm's internal condition.* A firm's own internal condition can also have a bearing on its target capital structure. For example, suppose a firm has just successfully completed an R&D program, and it projects higher earnings in the immediate future. However, the new earnings are not yet anticipated by investors and hence are not reflected in the price of the stock. This company would not want to issue stock—it would prefer to finance with debt until the higher earnings materialize and are reflected in the stock price, at which time it might want to sell an issue of common stock, retire the debt, and return to its target capital structure.

**12.** *Financial flexibility.* It has been noted that firms can earn a lot more money from good capital budgeting and operating decisions than they can from good financing decisions—indeed, we really are not sure how (or even if) financing decisions affect stock prices, but we do know that having to turn down a large order because funds are not available for buying the raw materials or equipment needed to fill it will lower profits. For this reason, many treasurers have as their primary goal to always be in a position to raise the capital needed to support operations. We also know that when times are good, firms can raise capital with either stock or bonds, but when times are bad, suppliers of capital are much more willing to make funds available if they are given a secured position, and this means bonds.

Putting these two thoughts together gives rise to the goal of *maintaining financial flexibility*, which from an operational viewpoint means *maintaining adequate reserve borrowing capacity*. What constitutes "adequate" reserve borrowing capacity is judgmental, but it clearly depends on the factors mentioned previously in the chapter, including the firm's forecasted need for funds, predicted capital market conditions, management's confidence in these forecasts, and the consequences of a capital shortage.

## Variations in Capital Structures among Firms

As might be expected, wide variations in the use of financial leverage occur both among industries and among the individual firms in each industry. Table 15-6 illustrates differences for selected industries; the ranks are in descending order of equity ratios as shown in Column 1.[17]

---

[17]Information on capital structures and financial strength is available from a multitude of sources. We used the *Compustat* data tapes to develop Table 15-6, but other published sources include *The Value Line Investment Survey, Robert Morris Association Annual Studies, and Dun & Bradstreet Key Business Ratios.*

**Table 15-6**
**Capital Structure Percentages, 1985:**
**Selected Industries Ranked by Common Equity Ratios**

| Industry | Common Equity (1) | Preferred Stock (2) | Total Debt (3) | Long-Term Debt (4) | Short-Term Debt (5) | Times-Interest-Earned Ratio (6) |
|---|---|---|---|---|---|---|
| Drugs | 78.4% | 0.1% | 21.5% | 12.5% | 9.0% | 9.1× |
| Electrical/electronics | 75.3 | 1.5 | 23.2 | 15.4 | 7.8 | 6.9 |
| Automotive | 74.0 | 2.0 | 24.0 | 19.0 | 5.0 | 7.6 |
| Retailing | 51.8 | 1.4 | 46.8 | 32.1 | 14.7 | 3.1 |
| Utilities (electric, gas, and telephone) | 44.8 | 6.8 | 48.4 | 45.9 | 2.5 | 3.2 |
| Steel | 44.0 | 3.0 | 53.0 | 48.5 | 4.5 | 0.9 |
| Composite (average of all industries, not just those listed above) | 47.2% | 2.7% | 50.1% | 31.8% | 18.3% | 2.3× |

Note: These ratios are based on accounting (or book) values. Stated on a market value basis, the results would be somewhat different. Most important, the equity percentage would rise, because most stocks sell at prices that are much higher than their book values.

Source: *Industrial Compustat* data tape, 1985.

The drug and electronics companies do not use much debt; these companies have generally been quite profitable and hence able to finance through retained earnings. Also, the uncertainties inherent in industries that are oriented toward research and/or subject to huge product liability suits render the heavy use of leverage unwise. Retailers, steel, and utility companies, on the other hand, use debt relatively heavily, but for different reasons. Retailers use short-term debt to finance inventories and long-term debt secured by mortgages on their stores. The steel companies have been losing money in recent years, and these losses have reduced their equity positions and also made it difficult for them to sell new common stock, hence requiring them to use debt financing. The utilities have traditionally used large amounts of debt—their fixed assets make good security for mortgage bonds, and their relatively stable sales and profits enable them to carry more debt than would be possible for firms in less stable industries.

Particular attention should be given to the times-interest-earned ratio. This ratio is a function of (1) financial leverage and (2) profitability. Generally, the least-leveraged industries, such as the drug companies, have the highest coverage ratios, while industries such as the steel industry, which had profit problems in 1984, have low ratios.

Wide variations in capital structures among firms within given industries also exist—for example, while the average common equity ratio in 1984 for the drug industry was 78.4 percent, Upjohn's equity ratio was only 66.4 percent but Bristol-Myers was near 90 percent. Thus, factors unique to individual firms, including management attitudes, still play an important role in setting target capital structures.

## Summary

In this chapter we examined the effects of financial leverage on stock prices, earnings per share, and the cost of capital. The analysis suggests that some *optimal capital structure* exists which simultaneously maximizes the firm's stock price and minimizes its average cost of capital. However, although it is theoretically possible to determine the optimal capital structure, as a practical matter we cannot estimate this structure with precision. Accordingly, financial executives generally treat the optimal capital structure as a range—for example, 40 to 50 percent debt—rather than as a precise point such as 45 percent. Also, they analyze the effects of different capital structures on expected earnings per share and interest coverage ratios rather than concentrating exclusively on imprecisely estimated stock prices. Firms also tend to analyze such factors as sales stability, asset structure, effects on control, and so on, and the final target capital structure is more judgmentally than quantitatively determined.

The primary advantage of debt is the tax shelter it provides—corporate income distributed to investors as interest payments on debt is not subject to corporate income taxes. The primary disadvantages of debt are associated with costs that arise as a result of actual or potential bankruptcy. The optimal capital structure involves a trade-off between these tax advantages and bankruptcy-related costs.

# SMALL BUSINESS

## Capital Structure in the Small Firm

Small businesses rely heavily on banks and other suppliers of debt funds for a large portion of their capital—in fact, as indicated in earlier chapters, small firms have relatively limited access to the public equity markets, which means that they must turn either to private equity or to debt. As a result, debt financing is very important to small businesses.

In spite of the importance of debt to small firms, there are a number of factors which may limit the extent to which the owner-manager of a small business may wish to use the debt markets. These factors include the risks inherent in debt financing, the increased likelihood of bankruptcy, and the effect of taxes.

Earlier in the chapter, we noted that, as financial leverage increases, EPS becomes more sensitive to changes in sales or operating profits. This variability in earnings may be even more important for small firms than for large ones whose securities are widely traded in the capital markets. In fact, some financial theorists argue that in firms with widely traded stock, additional debt increases expected returns by just enough to offset the added risk that debt entails. Under these hypothesized circumstances, there is no optimal capital structure because the value of the firm is unaffected by debt. However, the theory does not hold if a firm's shares are unmarketable or if the owner-managers want to retain their shares of stock in order to maintain control of the firm. In these cases, the increased variability in earnings per share caused by additional debt is a risk that cannot be transferred to others through the sale of the owner-managers' shares in the capital markets. Therefore, owner-managers may be especially sensitive to the level of debt employed.

While debt increases the variability in EPS for any firm, other factors may cause a more pronounced earnings variability in small firms. For example, small businesses typically have narrower product lines and smaller customer bases than do larger firms. Since their sales do not represent well-diversified sources of income, there is likely to be greater uncertainty in their earnings, which tends to keep the debt level relatively low.

Of course, a small customer base can be an advantage for a firm. If a small firm's key customer is willing to make a long-term commitment to take its output, that will be viewed as a definite plus by a financial institution considering a loan to the firm, assuming the customer has reasonable financial strength. Under normal circumstances, however, a small customer base is a disadvantage because of the increased risk of sudden loss of income.

Bankruptcy costs are thought by many researchers to be a significant factor in limiting the debt used by a firm. Two factors which influence capital structure decisions are (1) the actual costs of bankruptcy if it occurs and (2) the probability that bankruptcy will occur. As we have already seen, the probability of earnings fluctuation is greater in small firms, and greater earnings variability means higher risk of failure. The probability of bankruptcy would therefore normally be higher in a small firm, other things being equal.

In addition to a higher probability of bankruptcy in the small firm, there is the problem of some of the costs of bankruptcy being fixed. Although the actual costs of bankruptcy are normally higher for large firms than small ones, the costs do not rise proportionately with the size of the firm; as a result, bankruptcy costs tend to be relatively higher in the small firm. Therefore, these concerns probably reduce the amount of debt financing that managers of small firms would consider optimal.

One of the obvious benefits of debt financing is that the interest payments on debt are tax deductible, making the after-tax cost of debt lower. However, firms with earnings under $100,000 pay taxes at a lower marginal rate than do those with earnings over $100,000. For example, a firm earning $250,000 pays taxes at a 46 percent marginal tax rate, while one with earnings of only $45,000 has a marginal tax rate of only 18 percent. The after-tax cost of, say, an 18 percent loan, would be only

9.7 percent to the firm with the higher profits, but it would be 14.8 percent to the less profitable firm.

The purpose of this example is not to suggest that higher taxes are beneficial but rather to indicate that the tax deductibility of interest has a greater advantage to firms with higher marginal tax rates. If most of the debt available in the financial markets is demanded by firms in high tax brackets, that debt may carry interest rates that are relatively unattractive to less profitable smaller firms. As a result, the relative desirability of debt may be much less in a small firm when the cost of that debt is correctly measured on an after-tax basis.

Of course, there are certain factors that may make debt more attractive to small firms. That small businesses have limited access to equity markets has already been mentioned. In addition, a number of programs exist that make it easier for small firms to borrow money. Perhaps the best known are those of the Small Business Administration (SBA). Although the SBA makes direct loans to small businesses, it also guarantees small-business loans made by commercial banks and small-business investment companies. These loans are generally made on more attractive terms than conventional loans, and they are made to businesses that would otherwise have difficulty qualifying for loans.

A small business faces an interesting dilemma. Because access to other sources of funds is relatively difficult, the small firm is motivated to make heavy use of debt financing in its capital structure. On the other hand, factors that influence the target level of debt financing generally bias the small firm toward a lower use of debt than would otherwise be indicated. The owner-manager's dilemma is to balance these conflicting pressures in selecting a method of financing the firm. In achieving such a balance, the use of small-business debt sources that are unavailable to larger firms may be a help.

## Questions

15-1   Define each of the following terms:
     a. Target capital structure
     b. Business risk; financial risk
     c. Operating leverage; financial leverage
     d. Breakeven point; EPS indifference point
     e. Degree of operating leverage (DOL)

     f. Degree of financial leverage (DFL)
     g. Degree of total leverage (DTL)
     h. Times-interest-earned (TIE) ratio
     i. Modigliani-Miller (MM) theory
     j. Financial flexibility

**15-2** "One type of leverage affects both EBIT and EPS. The other type affects only EPS." Explain what this statement means.

**15-3** Explain why the following statement is true: "Other things being the same, firms with relatively stable sales are able to carry relatively high debt ratios."

**15-4** Why do public utility companies usually pursue a different financial policy than that of retail firms?

**15-5** Why is EBIT generally considered to be independent of financial leverage? Why might EBIT actually be influenced by financial leverage at high debt levels?

**15-6** If a firm went from zero debt to successively higher levels of debt, why would you expect its stock price to first rise, then hit a peak, and then begin to decline?

**15-7** Why is the debt level that maximizes a firm's expected EPS generally higher than the one that maximizes its stock price?

**15-8** In 1984 the Bell System was broken up, with the old AT&T being split into a new AT&T plus seven regional telephone companies. The reason for the breakup was to increase competition in the telephone industry. In the court order which laid out the terms of the breakup, the capital structures of the surviving companies were specified, and much attention was given to the increased competition telephone companies could expect in the future. Do you think the optimal capital structure would call for less debt in a more competitive environment, or would competition force companies to use more debt in order to reduce taxes? Explain your position.

**15-9** Assume that you are advising the management of a firm that is about to double its assets to serve its rapidly growing market. It must choose between a highly automated production process and a less automated one, and it must also choose a capital structure for financing the expansion. Should the asset investment and financing decisions be jointly determined? How would they affect each other? How could the degree of leverage concept be used to help management analyze the situation?

**15-10** Your firm's R&D department has been working on a new process which, if it works, can convert coal to oil at a cost of about $20 per barrel versus a current market price of $28 per barrel. The company needs $10 million of external funds at this time to complete the research. The results of the research will be known in about a year, and there is about a 50-50 chance of success. If the research is successful, then your company will need to raise a substantial amount of new money to put the idea into production. Your economists forecast that the economy will be depressed next year but that interest rates will be high because of international monetary problems. You must recommend how the currently needed $10 million should be raised—as debt or as equity. How would the factors discussed above influence your decision?

## Self-Test Problems (*Solutions on Page 529*)

**ST-1**   Simmons Electronics, Inc., produces stereo components which sell for P = $100 per unit. Simmons' fixed costs are $200,000; 5,000 units are produced and sold each year; profits total $50,000; and Simmons' assets (all equity financed) are $500,000. Simmons estimates that it can change its production process, adding $400,000 to investment and $50,000 to fixed operating costs. This change will (1) reduce variable costs per unit by $10 and (2) increase output by 2,000 units, but (3) the sales price on all units will have to be lowered to $95 to permit sales of the additional output. Simmons has tax loss carry-forwards that cause its tax rate to be zero. It uses no debt, and its average cost of capital is 10 percent.

a. Should Simmons make the change?

b. Would Simmons' operating leverage as measured by DOL increase or decrease if it made the change? What about its breakeven point?

c. Suppose the investment totaled $800,000, and Simmons had to borrow $400,000 at an interest rate of 10 percent. Find the ROE on the $400,000 incremental equity investment. Should Simmons make the change if debt financing must be used?

**ST-2**   Gentry Motors, Inc., a producer of turbine generators, is in this situation: (1) EBIT = $4 million; (2) tax rate = T = 35%; (3) debt outstanding = D = $2 million; (4) $k_d$ = 10%; (5) $k_s$ = 15%; (6) shares of stock outstanding = $N_0$ = 600,000; and book value per share = $10. Since Gentry's product market is stable and the company expects no growth, all earnings are paid out as dividends. The debt consists of perpetual bonds.

a. What are Gentry's earnings per share (EPS) and its price per share ($P_0$)?

b. What is Gentry's weighted average cost of capital ($k_a$)?

c. Gentry can increase its debt by $8 million, to a total of $10 million, using the new debt to buy back and retire some of its shares at the current price. Its interest rate on debt will be 12 percent (it will have to call and refund the old debt), and its cost of equity will rise from 15 percent to 17 percent. EBIT will remain constant. Should Gentry change its capital structure?

d. If Gentry did not have to refund the $2 million of old debt, how would this affect things? Assume the new and the still outstanding debt are equally risky, with $k_d$ = 12%, but the coupon rate on the old debt is 10 percent.

e. What is Gentry's TIE coverage ratio under the original situation and under the conditions in Part c?

## Problems

Risk analysis

**15-1**   a. Given the following information, calculate the expected value for Firm C's EPS: $EPS_A$ = $3.40, and $\sigma_A$ = $2.41; $EPS_B$ = $2.80, and $\sigma_B$ = $1.97; and $\sigma_C$ = $2.74.

| | Probability | | | | |
|---|---|---|---|---|---|
| | 0.1 | 0.2 | 0.4 | 0.2 | 0.1 |
| Firm A: $EPS_A$ | ($1.00) | $1.20 | $3.40 | $5.60 | $7.80 |
| Firm B: $EPS_B$ | ( 0.80) | 1.00 | 2.80 | 4.60 | 6.40 |
| Firm C: $EPS_C$ | ( 1.60) | 0.90 | 3.40 | 5.90 | 8.40 |

b. Discuss the relative riskiness of the three firms' earnings.

Degree of leverage                15-2    a. Refer back to Figure 15-2. Calculate the degree of operating leverage for Plans A and B at sales of $120,000 and $160,000. At sales of $80,000, $DOL_A$ = undefined (or $\infty$) and $DOL_B$ = $-2.0$, while at sales of $240,000, $DOL_A$ = 1.50 and $DOL_B$ = 2.0.

b. Is it true that the DOL is approximately equal to infinity just above the breakeven point, implying that a very small change in sales will produce a huge percentage increase in EBIT, but that DOL will decline when calculated at higher levels of sales?

c. Is it true that, for all sales levels at which DOL > 0 for both plans, $DOL_B$ < $DOL_A$? Explain.

d. Assume that Plans A and B can be financed in either of the following ways: (1) no debt or (2) $90,000 of debt at 10 percent. Calculate the DFL for Plan A at sales of $120,000 and $160,000. The DFLs for Plan B at these sales levels with debt are 0 and 1.82, respectively.

e. Calculate the degree of total leverage (DTL) under Plan A with debt at sales of $120,000 and $160,000. The DTLs under Plan B at these sales levels are $-6.67$ and 7.27, respectively.

f. Several of the degree of leverage figures were negative—for example, $DTL_B$ at S = $120,000 in Part e was $-6.67$. Does a negative degree of leverage imply that an increase in sales will *lower* profits?

Operating leverage effects        15-3    Varifixed Corporation will begin operations next year to produce a single product at a price of $12 per unit. Varifixed has a choice of two methods of production: Method A, with variable costs of $4 per unit and fixed operating costs of $650,000, and Method B, with variable costs of $7 per unit and fixed operating costs of $326,000. To support operations under either production method, the firm requires $1,500,000 in assets, and it has established a debt ratio of 30 percent. The cost of debt is $k_d$ = 10 percent. The tax rate is irrelevant for the problem, and fixed *operating* costs do not include interest.

a. Calculate the breakeven point for each method, and then find the level of sales in units at which the firm should be indifferent between the two methods with respect to expected operating income (that is, EBIT). (Hint: Let $EBIT_A$ = $EBIT_B$, and solve for the value of Q which produces the equality.)

b. The sales forecast for the coming years is 150,000 units. Under which method would EBIT be most adversely affected if sales did not reach expected levels? (Hint: Compare DOLs under the two production methods.)

c. Given the present debt of the firm, which method would produce the greatest percentage increase in earnings per share for a given increase in EBIT? (Hint: Compare DFLs under the two methods.)

d. Calculate DTL under each method, and then evaluate the firm's total risk under each method.

e. Is there some debt ratio, under Method A, which would produce the same $DTL_A$ as the $DTL_B$ which you calculated in Part d? (Hint: Let $DTL_A$ = $DTL_B$ as calculated in Part d, then solve for I, and then determine the amount of debt that is consistent with this level of I. Conceivably, debt could be *negative*, which implies holding liquid assets rather than borrowing. Also, you should have found $DTL_B$ = 1.98 in Part d.)

**15-4**   Astrocom Corporation supplies headphones to airplanes for use with movie and stereo programs. The headphones sell for $200 per set, and this year's sales are expected to be 35,000 units. Variable production costs for the expected sales under present production methods are estimated at $5,400,000, and fixed production (operating) costs at present are $840,000. Astrocom has $2,000,000 of debt outstanding at an interest rate of 8 percent. There are 200,000 shares of common stock outstanding, and there is no preferred stock. The dividend payout ratio is 80 percent, and Astrocom is in the 40 percent tax bracket.

The company is considering investing $6,000,000 in new equipment. Sales would not increase, but variable costs per unit would decline by 20 percent, while fixed operating costs would increase from $840,000 to $1,000,000. Astrocom could raise the required capital by borrowing $6,000,000 at 11 percent or by selling 200,000 additional shares at $30 per share.

a. What would Astrocom's EPS be (i) under the old production process, and under the new process if it uses (ii) debt or (iii) common stock?

b. Calculate DOL, DFL, and DTL under the existing setup and under the new setup with each type of financing. Assume that the expected sales level is 35,000 units, or $7,000,000.

c. Calculate the operating breakeven point (which does not consider interest expenses) under each setup. Explain how the breakeven volume could decline even though fixed costs increase. (Hint: Units sold = Sales revenues/Sales price.)

d. At what unit sales level would Astrocom have the same EPS, assuming it undertakes the investment and finances it with debt or with stock? (Hint: $V$ = variable cost/unit = $4,320,000/35,000, and EPS = $[(PQ - VQ - FC - I)(1 - T)]/N$. Set $EPS_{Stock} = EPS_{Debt}$ and solve for $Q$.)

e. At what unit sales level would EPS = 0 under the three production/ financing setups, that is, under the old plan, the new plan with debt financing, and the new plan with stock financing? (Hint: Note that $V_{Old} = $5,400,000/35,000$, and use the hints for Part d, setting the EPS equation equal to zero.)

f. On the basis of the analysis in Parts a through e, which plan is the most risky, which has the highest expected EPS, and which would you recommend? Assume here that there is a fairly high probability of sales falling as low as 10,000 units, and determine $EPS_{Debt}$ and $EPS_{Stock}$ at that sales level to help assess the riskiness of the two financing plans.

**15-5**   The Crothers Company and the Hollister Company are identical except for their leverage ratios and interest rates on debt. Each has $25 million in assets, earned $5 million before interest and taxes in 1985, and has a 40 percent corporate tax rate. Crothers, however, has a leverage ratio (D/TA) of 30 percent and pays 12 percent interest on its debt, while Hollister has a 50 percent leverage ratio and pays 14 percent interest on debt.

a. Calculate the rate of return on equity (net income/equity) for each firm.

b. Observing that Hollister has a higher return on equity, Crothers' treasurer decides to raise the leverage ratio from 30 to 60 percent, which will increase Crothers' interest rate on all debt to 17 percent. Calculate the new rate of return on equity for Crothers.

Effects of financial leverage on ROE    **15-6**    The Tanner Company wishes to calculate next year's return on equity under different leverage ratios. Tanner's total assets are $10 million, and its tax rate is 40 percent. The company is able to estimate next year's earnings before interest and taxes for three possible states of the world: $3 million with a 0.2 probability, $2 million with a 0.5 probability, and $500,000 with a 0.3 probability. Calculate Tanner's expected return on equity, standard deviation, and coefficient of variation for each of the following leverage ratios, and analyze the results:

| Leverage (Debt/Total Assets) | Interest Rate |
|---|---|
| 0% | — |
| 10 | 10% |
| 50 | 12 |
| 60 | 15 |

Financing alternatives    **15-7**    The Nordlund Company plans to raise a net amount of $180 million to finance new equipment and working capital in early 1986. Two alternatives are being considered: Common stock may be sold to net $40 per share, or debentures yielding 10 percent may be issued. The balance sheet and income statement of the Nordlund Company prior to financing are given below:

**The Nordlund Company:**
**Balance Sheet as of December 31, 1985**
**(Millions of Dollars)**

| | | | | |
|---|---|---|---|---|
| Current assets | $ 600 | Accounts payable | $ 115 |
| Net fixed assets | 300 | Notes payable to bank | 185 |
| | | Other current liabilities | 150 |
| | | Total current liabilities | $ 450 |
| | | Long-term debt | 185 |
| | | Common stock, $2 par | 40 |
| | | Retained earnings | 225 |
| Total assets | $ 900 | Total claims | $ 900 |

**The Nordlund Company:**
**Income Statement for Year Ended December 31, 1985**
**(Millions of Dollars)**

| | |
|---|---|
| Sales | $1,650 |
| Operating costs | 1,485 |
| Earnings before interest and taxes (10%) | $ 165 |
| Interest on debt | 30 |
| Earnings before taxes | $ 135 |
| Tax (40%) | 54 |
| Net income after tax | $ 81 |

The probability distribution for annual sales is as follows:

| Annual Sales (Millions of Dollars) | Probability |
|---|---|
| $1,500 | 0.30 |
| 1,800 | 0.40 |
| 2,100 | 0.30 |

a. Assuming that EBIT is equal to 10 percent of sales, calculate earnings per share under both the debt financing and the stock financing alternatives at each possible level of sales, and then calculate expected earnings per share and $\sigma_{EPS}$ under both debt and stock financing. Also, calculate the debt ratio and the times-interest-earned (TIE) ratio at the expected sales level under each alternative. The old debt will remain outstanding. Which financing method would you recommend? (Do only if you are using the computerized problem diskette.)

b. Suppose each of the following happens, with other values held at the base case (Part a) levels:

(1) The interest rate on new debt falls to 5 percent.
(2) The interest rate on new debt rises to 20 percent.
(3) The stock price falls to $20. (Return $k_d$ to 0.10 = 10%.)
(4) The stock price rises to $70.
(5) With $P_0$ = $40 and $k_d$ = 0.10 = 10%, now change the sales probability distribution to the following:

| | Sales | Probability | | Sales | Probability |
|---|---|---|---|---|---|
| (a) | $1,500 | 0 | (b) | $  0 | 0.3 |
| | 1,800 | 1.0 | | 1,800 | 0.4 |
| | 2,100 | 0 | | 5,000 | 0.3 |

What are the implications of these changes?

## Solutions to Self-Test Problems

ST-1    a.  1. Determine the variable cost per unit at present, using the following definitions and equations:

P = average sales price per unit of output = $100.

F = fixed operating costs = $200,000.

Q = units of output (sales) = 5,000.

V = variable costs per unit, found as follows:

$$\text{Profit} = P(Q) - F - V(Q)$$
$$\$50,000 = \$100(5,000) - \$200,000 - V(5,000)$$
$$5,000V = \$250,000$$
$$V = \$50.$$

2. Determine the new profit level if the change is made:

$$\text{New profit} = P_2(Q_2) - F_2 - V_2(Q_2)$$
$$= \$95(7,000) - \$250,000 - \$40(7,000)$$
$$= \$135,000.$$

3. Determine the incremental profit:

$$\Delta\text{Profit} = \$135,000 - \$50,000 = \$85,000.$$

4. Estimate the approximate rate of return on the new investment:

$$\text{ROI} = \frac{\Delta\text{Profit}}{\text{Investment}} = \frac{\$85,000}{\$400,000} = 21.25\%.$$

Since the ROI exceeds Simmons' average cost of capital, this analysis suggests that Simmons should go ahead and make the investment.

b.
$$\text{DOL} = \frac{Q(P - V)}{Q(P - V) - F}.$$

$$\text{DOL}_{\text{Old}} = \frac{5,000(\$100 - \$50)}{5,000(\$100 - \$50) - \$200,000} = 5.00.$$

$$\text{DOL}_{\text{New}} = \frac{7,000(\$95 - \$40)}{7,000(\$95 - \$40) - \$250,000} = 2.85.$$

This indicates that operating income will be less sensitive to changes in sales if the production process is changed. That suggests that the change would reduce risks. However, the change would increase the breakeven point. Still, with a lower sales price, it might be easier to achieve the higher new breakeven volume:

$$\textit{Old}: \ Q_{\text{BE}} = \frac{F}{P - V} = \frac{\$200,000}{\$100 - \$50} = 4,000 \text{ units.}$$

$$\textit{New}: \ Q_{\text{BE}} = \frac{F_2}{P_2 - V_2} = \frac{\$250,000}{\$95 - \$40} = 4,545 \text{ units.}$$

c. The incremental ROE is:

$$\text{ROE} = \frac{\Delta\text{Profit}}{\Delta\text{Equity}}.$$

Using debt financing, the incremental profit associated with the equity investment is equal to that found in Part a minus the interest expense incurred as a result of the investment:

$$\Delta\text{Profit} = \text{New profit} - \text{Old profit} - \text{Interest}$$
$$= \$135,000 - \$50,000 - 0.10(\$400,000)$$
$$= \$45,000.$$
$$\text{ROE} = \frac{\$45,000}{\$400,000}$$
$$= 11.25\%.$$

The return on the new equity investment still exceeds the average cost of capital, so Simmons should make the investment.

ST-2   a.

| | |
|---|---|
| EBIT | $4,000,000 |
| Interest ( $2,000,000 × 0.10) | 200,000 |
| Net income before taxes | $3,800,000 |
| Taxes (35%) | 1,330,000 |
| Net income after taxes | $2,470,000 |

$$\text{EPS} = \$2,470,000/600,000 = \$4.116667.$$
$$P_0 = \$4.116667/0.15 = \$27.44.$$

b.

$$\text{Equity} = 600,000 \times (\$10) = \$6,000,000$$
$$\text{Debt} = \$2,000,000$$
$$\text{Total capital} = \$8,000,000$$
$$k_a = w_d k_d (1 - T) + w_s k_s$$
$$= (2/8)(10\%)(1 - 0.35) + (6/8)(15\%)$$
$$= 1.63\% + 11.25\%$$
$$= 12.88\%.$$

c.

| | |
|---|---|
| EBIT | $4,000,000 |
| Interest ( $10,000,000 × 0.12) | 1,200,000 |
| Net income before taxes | $2,800,000 |
| Taxes (35%) | 980,000 |
| Net income after taxes | $1,820,000 |

Shares bought and retired:

$$\Delta N = \Delta \text{Debt}/P_0 = \$8,000,000/\$27.44 = 291,545.$$

New outstanding shares:

$$N_1 = N_0 - \Delta N = 600,000 - 291,545 = 308,455.$$

New EPS:

$$\text{EPS} = \$1,820,000/308,455 = \$5.90.$$

New price per share:

$$P_0 = \$5.90/0.17 = \$34.71 \text{ versus } \$27.44.$$

Therefore, Gentry should change its capital structure.

d. In this case, the company's net income after taxes would be higher by $(0.12 - 0.10)(\$2,000,000)(1 - 0.35) = \$26,000$, because its interest charges would be lower. The new price would be

$$P_0 = \frac{(\$1,820,000 + \$26,000)/308,455}{0.17} = \$35.20.$$

In the first case, where the debt had to be refunded, the bondholders were compensated for the increased risk of the higher debt position.

In the second case, the old bondholders were not compensated; their 10 percent coupon perpetual bonds would now be worth

$$\$100/0.12 \; = \; \$833.33,$$

or $1,666,667 in total, down from the old $2 million, or a loss of $333,333. The stockholders would have a gain of

$$(\$35.20 \; - \; \$34.71)(308,455) \; = \; \$151,143.$$

This gain would, of course, be at the expense of the old bondholders. (There is no reason to think that bondholders' losses would exactly offset stockholders' gains.)

e.
$$\text{TIE} \; = \; \frac{\text{EBIT}}{\text{I}}.$$

$$\text{Original TIE} \; = \; \frac{\$4,000,000}{\$200,000} \; = \; 20 \text{ times.}$$

$$\text{New TIE} \; = \; \frac{\$4,000,000}{\$1,200,000} \; = \; 3.33 \text{ times.}$$

## Selected Additional References and Cases

The references provided here are oriented more toward capital structure policy applications than theory.

Donaldson's work on the setting of debt targets is old but still relevant:

Donaldson, Gordon, "New Framework for Corporate Debt Capacity," *Harvard Business Review*, March-April 1962, 117-131, and "Strategy for Financial Emergencies," *Harvard Business Review*, November-December 1969, 67-79.

To learn more about the link between market risk and the degrees of operating and financial leverage, see:

Gahlon, James M., and James A. Gentry, "On the Relationship between Systematic Risk and the Degrees of Operating and Financial Leverage," *Financial Management*, Summer 1982, 15-23.

See the following two articles for additional insight into the relationship between industry characteristics and financial leverage:

Bowen, Robert M., Lane A. Daley, and Charles C. Huber, Jr., "Evidence on the Existence and Determinants of Inter-Industry Differences in Leverage," *Financial Management*, Winter 1982, 10-20.

Scott, David F., Jr., and John D. Martin, "Industry Influence on Financial Structure," *Financial Management*, Spring 1975, 67-73.

The following Crum-Brigham cases contain many of the concepts we present in Chapter 15:

Case 30, "Floral Fancy Plant Company," which shows the effect of financial leverage on EPS and stock price.

Case 31, "Elektra Aerospace Corporation," which consists of two parts that illustrate how operating and financial leverage interact to affect firm value.

Case 32, "Sanitary Solutions, Inc.," which concentrates on the effect of financial leverage on firm value and the weighted average cost of capital.

# 16 DIVIDEND POLICY

TAMPA ELECTRIC
A TECO ENERGY COMPANY

Several years ago Jim Taggart, financial vice-president for Tampa Electric Company (TECO), and George Schreiber, vice-president of Kidder Peabody & Company, a major investment banking house, met with a group of students at the University of Florida to discuss corporate dividend policy. Taggart led off the discussion. He presented information on TECO's forecasted capital requirements, its cost of money from various sources, the earnings and dividend growth rates that TECO could achieve if it plowed back a higher percentage of its earnings, and the tax advantages that would accrue to stockholders from receiving returns as capital gains rather than as dividends. His conclusion, which the students seemed to second, was that a low-dividend, high-plowback policy was best for TECO's stockholders.

Schreiber then took the floor. He explained that he and the Kidder Peabody sales representatives were in constant contact with investors and that in their judgment, the higher the payout, the higher the price of a given utility's stock. He went on to say that Kidder Peabody's surveys showed that most utility stocks were owned by investors in low tax brackets (for example, retirees and tax-exempt pension plans), so dividends were just as good as capital gains. Further, he pointed out that utility stockholders often live on their dividend income and that it was much more convenient to cash a dividend check to obtain cash income than to sell some stock (and incur brokerage costs). Finally, he gave an example of a "typical" investor with $10,000. The person could (1) buy bonds and get an income of $1,200 per year, (2) purchase a low-dividend utility stock and get $800 cash and perhaps some capital gains, or (3) choose a high-dividend stock and get $1,100 cash plus smaller expected capital gains. Schreiber's strong opinion was that utility investors give little weight to growth; his conclusion, therefore, was that the higher the dividend, the more people will pay for a given stock.

After listening to both presentations, the students were thoroughly confused. First, the utility executive had convinced them that maximizing stock prices called for holding down dividend payout ratios; then the investment banker made a convincing argument for higher payout ratios. The professor was uncharacteristically quiet. After reading Chapter 16, see if you can decide who was right.

Dividend policy involves the decision whether to pay out earnings or to retain them for reinvestment in the firm. Our basic constant growth stock price model, $P_0 = D_1/(k_s - g)$, shows that a policy of paying out more cash dividends will raise $D_1$, which will tend to increase the price of the stock. However, if cash dividends are raised and consequently less money is available for reinvestment, the expected future growth rate will be lowered, which in turn will depress the price of the stock. Thus, dividend policy has two opposing effects, and *an* **optimal dividend policy** *strikes exactly the balance that investors in the aggregate prefer between current dividends and future growth and thus maximizes the price of the firm's stock.*

**optimal dividend policy**
The dividend policy that strikes a balance between current dividends and future growth and thereby maximizes the firm's stock price.

A firm that pays out some of its earnings as dividends has less retained earnings, which limits the asset expansion it can finance with relatively cheap internal equity. Further expansion is possible, of course, but it will have to be supported by the sale of more expensive new common stock to keep the capital structure in balance. Thus, for any given rate of asset expansion, decisions on dividend policy also imply decisions on new stock sales.

In this chapter, we examine factors which affect the optimal dividend policy for the firm. In Appendix 16A, we take up stock repurchases as an alternative to dividends.

## Dividend Policy Theories

A number of factors influence dividend policy, including the differential tax rates on dividends and capital gains, the investment opportunities available to the firm, alternative sources of capital, and stockholders' preferences for current versus future income. Our major goal in this chapter is to show how these and other factors interact to determine a firm's optimal dividend policy. We begin by examining three theories of dividend policy: (1) the dividend irrelevance theory, (2) the "bird-in-the-hand" theory, and (3) the tax differential theory.

### Dividend Irrelevance Theory

It has been asserted that dividend policy has no effect on either the price of a firm's stock or its cost of capital—that is, dividend policy is *irrelevant*. The principal proponents of this **dividend irrelevance theory** are Merton Miller and Franco Modigliani (MM).[1] MM argue that the value of the firm is determined by its basic earnings power and its business risk; thus, the value of the firm depends on asset investment policy only and not on how the firm's earnings are split between dividends and retained earnings.

**dividend irrelevance theory**
The theory that a firm's dividend policy has no effect on either the firm's value or its cost of capital.

MM base their proposition on theoretical arguments. However, as in all theoretical work, they must make some assumptions with which to develop a manageable theory. In their dividend analysis, they assume that (1) there are

---

[1]Merton H. Miller and Franco Modigliani, "Dividend Policy, Growth, and the Valuation of Shares," *Journal of Business*, October 1961, 411-433.

no personal or corporate income taxes, (2) there are no stock flotation or transactions costs, (3) financial leverage has only a very limited effect, if any, on the cost of capital, (4) dividend policy has no effect on the firm's cost of equity, and (5) a firm's asset investment policy is independent of its dividend policy. Obviously these assumptions do not hold precisely—firms and investors do pay income taxes; firms do incur flotation costs; investors do incur transactions costs; and both taxes and transactions costs may cause $k_s$ to be affected by dividend policy. MM argue (correctly) that all economic theories are based on simplifying assumptions and that the validity of a theory must be judged on its ability to predict behavior, not on the realism of its assumptions. Still, the MM conclusions on dividend irrelevance may not be valid under real-world conditions, so a conclusion can be reached only through empirical testing.

### "Bird-in-the-Hand" Theory

The most critical assumption of MM's dividend irrelevance theory is that dividend policy does not affect investors' required rate of return on equity, $k_s$, a view that has been hotly debated in academic circles. Myron Gordon and John Lintner, on the one hand, argue that $k_s$ increases as the dividend payout is reduced because investors are less certain of receiving income from the capital gains which should result from retained earnings than they are of receiving dividend payments.[2] They say, in effect, that investors value a dollar of expected dividends more highly than a dollar of expected capital gains because the dividend yield component, $D_1/P_0$, is less risky than the g component in the total expected return equation, $\hat{k}_s = D_1/P_0 + g$.

On the other hand, MM argue that $k_s$ is independent of dividend policy, which implies, if we ignore tax effects, that investors are indifferent between $D_1/P_0$ and g, and, hence, between dividends and capital gains. They call the Gordon-Lintner argument the "**bird-in-the-hand**" fallacy because, in MM's view, many if not most investors are going to reinvest their dividends in the same or similar firms anyway, and, in any event, the riskiness of the firm's cash flows to investors in the long run is determined only by the riskiness of its operating cash flows and not by its dividend payout policy.

**"bird-in-the-hand"**
MM's name for the theory that a firm's value will be maximized by a high dividend payout ratio because investors regard dividends as being less risky than capital gains.

Figure 16-1 presents two graphs which highlight the MM versus Gordon-Lintner arguments. Panel a shows the Miller-Modigliani position. Here the company has $\hat{k}_s = D_1/P_0 + g = k_s = k_{RF} + RP = $ a constant 13.3% for any dividend policy. Thus, the equilibrium total return, $k_s$, is assumed to be a constant 13.3 percent whether it comes entirely as a dividend yield, entirely as expected capital gains, or in any combination of the two. For example, an average investor would be indifferent between a dividend yield of 13.3 percent with zero expected capital gains, a 10 percent yield plus a 3.3 percent expected capital gains yield, a 3.3 percent dividend yield and 10 percent

---

[2]Myron J. Gordon, "Optimal Investment and Financing Policy," *Journal of Finance*, May 1963, 264-272, and John Lintner, "Dividends, Earnings, Leverage, Stock Prices, and the Supply of Capital to Corporations," *Review of Economics and Statistics*, August 1962, 243-269.

**Figure 16-1**
**The Miller-Modigliani and Gordon-Lintner Dividend Hypotheses**

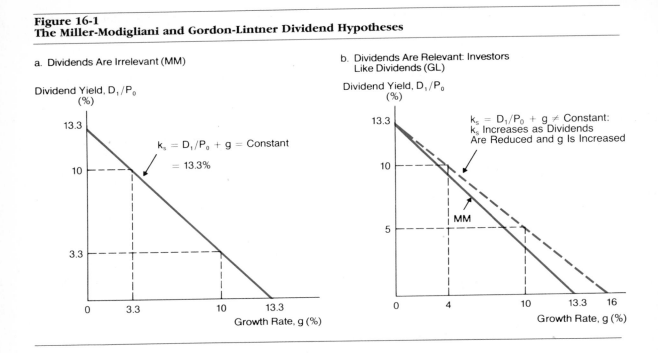

a. Dividends Are Irrelevant (MM)

b. Dividends Are Relevant: Investors Like Dividends (GL)

expected capital gains, and a zero dividend yield with a 13.3 percent expected capital gains return.

The graph in Panel b repeats the MM relationship and adds the Gordon-Lintner view. Gordon-Lintner argue that a possible capital gain in the bush is riskier than a dividend in the hand, so investors require a larger total return, $k_s$, if that return has a larger capital gains yield component, g, than dividend yield, $D_1/P_0$. In other words, Gordon-Lintner argue that *more than 1 percent* of additional g is required to offset a 1 percent reduction of dividend yield. Thus, the required rate of return, or cost of equity, would be 13.3 percent if the firm paid all of its earnings out in dividends, but as it lowered the payout and hence the dividend portion of the total return, the cost of equity would increase, up to 16 percent at a zero payout, where the dividend yield was zero.

## Tax Differential Theory

In Chapter 2, where we discussed the federal tax system, we pointed out that in the United States only 40 percent of long-term capital gains are taxed. Thus, an investor in the 48 percent marginal tax bracket would pay 48 percent in taxes on his or her dividend income but only $(0.4)(0.48) = 19.2\%$ on long-term capital gains. As a result, investors might prefer companies to pay less of their earnings out as dividends and be willing to accept a lower total return if more of it came in the form of expected capital gains. Accord-

**tax differential theory**
The theory that a firm's value will be maximized by a low dividend payout ratio because dividends are taxed at higher rates than capital gains.

ing to the **tax differential theory**, an average investor might be indifferent between a 13.3 percent return that came as dividends and a 10 percent return expected in the form of capital gains. Note that for a taxpayer in the 48 percent bracket, the after-tax return on the 13.3 percent dividend yield would be pre-tax return − tax = 13.3% − 13.3%(0.48) = 13.3%(1 − 0.48) = 6.9%, while the after-tax return on a 10 percent capital gain would be 10% − 10%(0.4)(0.48) = 10%(1 − 0.192) = 8.1%, so even though the pre-tax capital gains yield is lower than the pre-tax dividend yield, the after-tax capital gains yield is larger. Thus, even if capital gains are regarded as being riskier than dividend income, tax differentials could still cause investors to prefer low payout stocks.

At this point, we are not prepared to say which of these three theories is most correct. Before reaching such a conclusion, we must examine the empirical evidence.

## Tests of Dividend Theories

In the preceding section, we presented the following three dividend theories:

**1.** MM argue that dividend policy is irrelevant; that is, it does not affect a firm's value or its cost of capital. Thus, according to MM, there is no optimal dividend policy—one dividend policy is as good as any other.

**2.** Gordon and Lintner disagree with MM, arguing that dividends are less risky than capital gains, so a firm should set a high dividend payout ratio and offer a high dividend yield in order to minimize its cost of capital. MM call this the "bird-in-the-hand" fallacy.

**3.** The third position is the reverse of the Gordon-Lintner position, namely, that since dividends are taxed at higher rates than capital gains, investors require higher rates of return on high dividend yield stocks. Thus, according to this theory, in order to minimize its cost of capital and thereby maximize its value, a firm should establish a low dividend payout ratio.

These three theories offer contradictory advice to corporate managers. Which one should we believe? The most logical way to proceed is to test the theories empirically. Actually, many empirical tests have been used in attempts to determine the true relationship between dividend yield and required return. The earliest type of test was designed along the lines set forth in Figure 16-1.[3] In theory, we could take a sample of companies which have

---

[3]The earliest such test was that described in Eugene F. Brigham and Myron J. Gordon, "Leverage, Dividend Policy, and the Cost of Capital," *Journal of Finance*, March 1968, 85-104. In work done in conjunction with writing this chapter, we reexamined the issue and reached the conclusions reported in this section.

different dividend policies, and hence different dividend yield and growth rate components, and plot them on graphs such as those shown in Figure 16-1. If the points all fell on the line labeled MM in Panel b, so that the slope of the resulting regression line was approximately $-1.0$, this would support the MM irrelevance hypothesis. If the points all fell on the dashed line, so that the slope was less negative (less steep) than $-1.0$ (say, $-0.8$), this would support the Gordon-Lintner hypothesis. If the slope were more negative (steeper) than $-1.0$ (say, $-1.2$), this would support the tax differential position.

When such tests have been conducted, the results have been unclear—with one set of data the slope might be low, say, $-0.5$; the second data set might show a high slope, for example, $-1.5$; and the third data set might show a slope close to $-1.0$. In all cases, the standard deviation has been too large to permit much confidence in the slope coefficient. For example, one test we conducted showed a slope coefficient of $-1.2$ but a standard deviation of 0.5, which meant that we could say only that the true slope was probably within the range of $-0.7$ and $-1.7$—which in turn meant that any of the theories could be correct. There are two reasons for this situation: (1) for a valid statistical test, things other than dividend policy must be held constant—that is, the sample companies must differ only in their dividend policies, and (2) we must be able to measure with a high degree of accuracy the expected growth rates for the sample firms. Neither of these two conditions actually holds: we can neither find a set of publicly owned firms that differ only in their dividend policies nor get precise estimates of investors' expected growth rates. Therefore, we cannot determine with much precision what effect, if any, dividend policy has on the cost of equity. Hence, this particular type of test has been unable to solve the dividend policy puzzle.

Academic researchers have also studied the dividend yield effect from a CAPM perspective. These studies hypothesize that required returns are a function of both market risk, as measured by beta, and dividend yield. As with the earlier studies, the results of this line of research have been mixed. Litzenberger and Ramaswamy showed, using NYSE data from 1936 through 1977, that stocks with high dividend yields did have greater total yields than did stocks with low dividend yields, after adjusting for market risk.[4] Their study indicated that required total returns increased by about 0.24 of a percentage point for every percentage point increase in dividend yield; thus, a company might have had a 10 percent cost of equity if it retained all of its earnings but a 12.4 percent cost if it paid out all of its earnings as dividends. However, other studies have reached the opposite conclusion.[5] The major problem with the CAPM studies is that they have used historic earned rates of return as proxies for required returns, and with such a poor proxy, the

---

[4]Robert H. Litzenberger and Krishna Ramaswamy, "The Effect of Personal Taxes and Dividends on Capital Asset Prices," *Journal of Financial Economics*, June 1979, 163-196.

[5]For example, see Fischer Black and Myron Scholes, "The Effects of Dividend Yield and Dividend Policy on Common Stock Prices and Returns," *Journal of Financial Economics*, May 1974, 1-22.

tests are almost bound to have mixed results. Thus, the CAPM-based empirical tests, like the purely DCF-based ones, have not led to definitive conclusions as to which dividend theory is most correct. Unfortunately, the issue is still unresolved—academicians at this time cannot tell corporate decision makers how dividend policy affects stock prices and capital costs.

## Other Dividend Policy Issues

Before we discuss dividend policy in practice, we need to examine two other theoretical issues that could affect our views toward the three theories presented earlier. These issues are (1) the *information content*, or *signaling, hypothesis* and (2) the *clientele effect*.

### Information Content, or Signaling, Hypothesis

It has been observed that an increase in the dividend—for example, an increase in the annual dividend per share from $2 to $2.50—is often accompanied by an increase in the price of the stock, while a dividend cut generally leads to a stock price decline. This suggests to some that investors in the aggregate prefer dividends to capital gains. However, MM argued differently. They noted the well-established fact that corporations are always reluctant to cut dividends and hence do not raise dividends unless they anticipate higher, or at least stable, earnings in the future. Thus, MM argue that a dividend increase is a "signal" to investors that the firm's management forecasts improved future earnings, while a dividend reduction signals a poor earnings forecast. Thus, MM claim that investor reactions to changes in dividend payments do not necessarily show that investors prefer dividends to retained earnings—rather, in their view the fact that stock price changes follow dividend actions simply indicates that there is important information inherent in dividend announcements. This theory is referred to as the **information content**, or **signaling, hypothesis**.

**information content (signaling) hypothesis**
The theory that investors regard dividend changes as signals of management's earnings forecasts.

Like most other aspects of dividend policy, empirical studies on this topic have been inconclusive. Although there clearly is some information content in dividend announcements, it is not necessarily the complete explanation for the stock price changes that follow increases or decreases in dividends, especially if these dividend changes include a change in the percentage payout ratio as well as in the dollars of dividends paid.

### Clientele Effect

**clientele effect**
The tendency of a firm to attract the type of investor who likes its dividend policy.

MM also suggest that a **clientele effect** might exist—that is, the firm sets a particular dividend payout policy, which then tends to attract a "clientele" consisting of those investors who like its particular dividend policy. For example, some stockholders, such as university endowment funds and retired individuals, prefer current income and thus would want the firm to pay out a higher percentage of its earnings. Other stockholders have no need for current investment income and therefore would simply reinvest any dividend income received, after first paying income taxes on it.

If the firm retains and reinvests income rather than paying dividends, those stockholders who need current income will be disadvantaged. They will presumably receive capital gains, but they will also have to go to the trouble and expense of selling some of their shares in order to obtain cash. Also, some institutional investors (or trustees for individuals) are precluded from selling stock and then "spending capital." On the other hand, if the firm pays out most of its income, those stockholders who are saving rather than spending dividends will have to pay taxes and then go to the trouble and expense of reinvesting their dividends. We conclude from all this that investors who desire current investment income should own shares in high dividend payout firms, while those with no such need for current investment income should own shares in low payout firms.

To the extent that stockholders can shift their investments among firms, a firm can establish the specific policy that seems most appropriate to its management and then have stockholders who do not like it sell their shares to other investors who do. However, switching may be inefficient because of (1) brokerage costs, (2) the likelihood that selling stockholders will have to pay capital gains taxes, and (3) a possible shortage of investors in the aggregate who like the firm's newly stated dividend policy.

Evidence from several studies suggests that there is in fact a clientele effect.[6] However, MM and others argue that one clientele is as good as another. If this is so, the existence of a clientele effect does not imply that one dividend policy is better than any other. Still, MM offer no proof that the aggregate makeup of investors permits firms to disregard clientele effects. Thus, the importance of the clientele effect, like most other issues in the dividend arena, is still up in the air.

## Dividend Policy in Practice

In the preceding sections, we noted that there are three conflicting theories as to what dividend policy firms *should* follow. We also noted that empirical tests do not answer the question of which theory is most correct. In this section, we present four alternative dividend payment policies that firms actually *do* follow. As a part of this discussion, we discuss a multitude of factors which are not generally discussed by the theorists but which do influence dividend policy in practice.

### Residual Dividend Policy

In practice, dividend policy is very much influenced by investment opportunities and by the availability of funds with which to finance them. This fact

---

[6]For example, see R. Richardson Pettit, "Taxes, Transactions Costs, and the Clientele Effect of Dividends," *Journal of Financial Economics*, December 1977, 419-436.

**residual dividend policy**
A policy in which dividends paid equals actual earnings minus the amount of retained earnings necessary to finance the firm's optimal capital budget.

has led to the development of a **residual dividend policy**, which states that a firm should follow these four steps when deciding its payout ratio: (1) determine the optimal capital budget; (2) determine the amount of capital needed to finance that budget; (3) use retained earnings to supply the equity component as far as possible; and (4) pay dividends only if more earnings are available than are needed to support the optimal capital budget. The word *residual* implies "left over," and the residual policy implies that dividends should be paid only out of "leftover" earnings.

The basis of the residual policy is the belief that *most investors prefer to have the firm retain and reinvest earnings rather than pay them out in dividends if the rate of return the firm can earn on reinvested earnings exceeds the rate investors themselves could obtain on other investments of comparable risk.* For example, if the corporation could reinvest retained earnings at a 14 percent rate of return while the best rate stockholders could obtain if the earnings were passed on in the form of dividends was 12 percent, then stockholders would prefer to have the firm retain the profits.

To continue, we saw in Chapter 14 that the cost of retained earnings is an *opportunity cost* which reflects rates of return available to equity investors. If a firm's stockholders could buy other stocks of equal risk and obtain a 12 percent dividend-plus-capital-gains yield, then 12 percent would be the firm's cost of retained earnings. The cost of new outside equity raised by selling common stock would be higher than 12 percent because of the costs of floating the issue.

Note also that most firms have a target capital structure that calls for at least some debt, so new financing is done partly with debt and partly with equity. As long as the firm finances with the optimal mix of debt and equity, and provided it uses only internally generated equity (retained earnings), its marginal cost of each new dollar of capital will be minimized. Internally generated equity is available for financing a certain amount of new investment, but beyond that amount the firm must turn to more expensive new common stock. At the point where new stock must be sold, the cost of equity, and consequently the marginal cost of capital, rises.

These concepts, which were developed in Chapter 14, are illustrated in Figure 16-2 with data from the Texas and Western (T&W) Transport Company. T&W has a marginal cost of capital of 10 percent as long as retained earnings are available, but its MCC begins to rise at the point where new stock must be sold. T&W has $60 million of net income and a 40 percent optimal debt ratio. Provided it does not pay cash dividends, T&W can make net investments (investments in addition to asset replacements financed from depreciation) of $100 million, consisting of $60 million from retained earnings plus $40 million of new debt supported by the retained earnings, at a 10 percent marginal cost of capital. Therefore, its MCC is constant at 10 percent up to $100 million of capital, beyond which it rises as the firm begins to use more expensive new common stock.

Of course, if T&W does not retain all of its earnings, its MCC will begin to rise before $100 million. For example, if T&W retained only $30 million,

**Figure 16-2**
**T&W Transport Company: Marginal Cost of Capital**

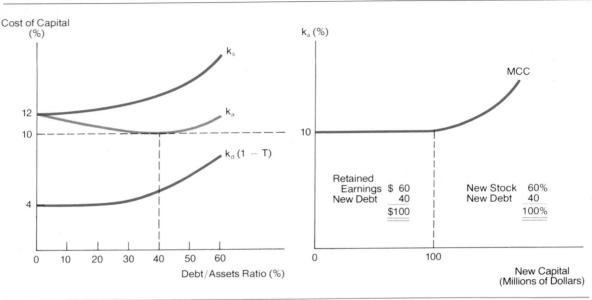

then its MCC would begin to rise at $30 million retained earnings + $20 million debt = $50 million.

Now suppose T&W's director of capital budgeting constructs several investment opportunity schedules and plots them on a graph. The investment opportunity schedules for three different years—a good year ($IOS_G$), a normal year ($IOS_N$), and a bad year ($IOS_B$)—are shown in Figure 16-3. T&W can invest the most money and earn the highest rates of return when the investment opportunities are given as $IOS_G$.

In Figure 16-4, we combine these investment opportunity schedules with the cost of capital schedule based on retaining all earnings. The point where the relevant IOS curve cuts the MCC curve defines the proper level of new investment: when investment opportunities are relatively bad ($IOS_B$) the optimal level of investment is $40 million, when opportunities are normal ($IOS_N$) $70 million should be invested, and when opportunities are relatively good ($IOS_G$) T&W should make new investments in the amount of $150 million.

Consider the situation in which $IOS_G$ is the appropriate schedule. T&W should raise and invest $150 million. It has $60 million in earnings and a 40 percent target debt ratio. Thus, it can finance $100 million, consisting of $60 million of retained earnings plus $40 million of new debt, at an average cost of 10 percent if it retains all of its earnings. The remaining $50 million will include external equity and thus have a higher cost. If T&W paid out part of its earnings in dividends, it would have to begin to use more costly new

**Figure 16-3**
**T&W Transport Company: Investment Opportunity (or IRR) Schedules**

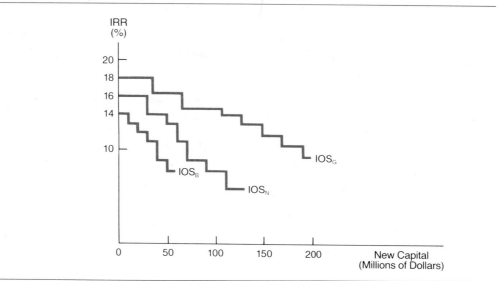

**Figure 16-4**
**T&W Transport Company: Interrelationships between**
**Cost of Capital, Investment Opportunities, and New Investment**

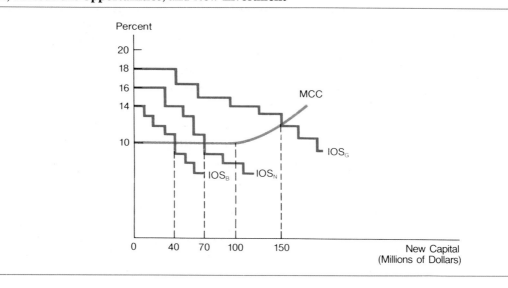

common stock earlier than need be, so its MCC curve would rise earlier than it otherwise would. *This suggests that, under the conditions of IOS$_G$, T&W should retain all of its earnings. According to the residual policy, its payout ratio should be zero if IOS$_G$ applies.*

Under the conditions of IOS$_N$, however, T&W should invest only $70 million. How should this investment be financed? First, notice that if T&W retained all of its earnings, $60 million, it would need to sell only $10 million of new debt. However, if T&W retained $60 million and sold only $10 million of new debt, it would move away from its target capital structure. To stay on target, T&W must finance 60 percent of the required $70 million with equity—retained earnings—and 40 percent with debt; this means that it must retain $42 million and sell $28 million of new debt. Since T&W retains only $42 million of its $60 million total earnings, it must distribute the residual, $18 million, to its stockholders. Thus, its optimal payout ratio is $18/$60 = 30%.

Under the conditions of IOS$_B$, T&W should invest only $40 million. Because it has $60 million in earnings, it could finance the entire $40 million out of retained earnings and still have $20 million available for dividends. Should this be done? Under our assumptions this would not be a good decision, because T&W would move away from its optimal capital structure. To stay at the 40 percent target debt/assets ratio, T&W must retain $24 million of earnings and sell $16 million of debt. When the $24 million of retained earnings is subtracted from the $60 million total earnings, T&W will be left with a residual of $36 million, the amount that should be paid out in dividends. Thus, the payout ratio, as prescribed by the residual policy, is 60 percent.

If either the IOS schedule or the earnings level varies from year to year, strict adherence to the residual dividend policy will result in dividend variability—one year the firm might declare zero dividends because investment opportunities were good but the next year it might pay a large dividend because investment opportunities were poor. Similarly, fluctuating earnings will lead to variable dividends even if investment opportunities are stable over time. Thus, a residual dividend policy can be optimal only if investors do not object to fluctuating dividends; if they do object, then k$_s$ will be higher for a firm that follows the residual theory in a strict sense than for an otherwise similar firm which attempts to stabilize its dividends over time.

## Constant, or Steadily Increasing, Dividends

In the past, many firms set a specific annual dollar dividend per share and then maintained it, increasing the annual dividend only if it seemed clear that future earnings would be sufficient to allow the new dividend to be maintained. A corollary of that policy was this rule: *Never reduce the annual dividend.*

More recently, inflation has tended to push up earnings; therefore, most firms that would otherwise have followed the stable dividend payment policy have switched over to what is called the "stable growth rate" policy. Here the firm sets a target growth rate for dividends—say, 6 percent per year— and strives to increase dividends by this amount each year. Obviously, earnings must be growing at about the same rate in order for this to be feasible.

Both a stable payment policy and a stable growth rate policy are illustrated in Figure 16-5 using data for the Morris Equipment Company over a 35-year period. Initially, earnings were $2 a share and dividends $1 a share, so the payout ratio was 50 percent. During most of the 1950s earnings fluctuated, but no clear trend was evident, so the dividend was kept at the $1 level. However, by the early 1960s earnings were substantially above earlier levels, causing the payout ratio to drop below 50 percent; further, management believed the new earnings would be sustained. Therefore, the company raised the dividend in three steps to $1.50 to reestablish the 50 percent payout.

During 1964 and 1965, a strike caused earnings to fall below the regular dividend. Expecting this decline to be temporary, management maintained the $1.50 dividend.

Earnings fluctuated on a fairly high plateau from 1966 through 1973, during which time dividends remained constant. However, due in large part to

**Figure 16-5**
**Morris Equipment Company: Dividends and Earnings over Time**

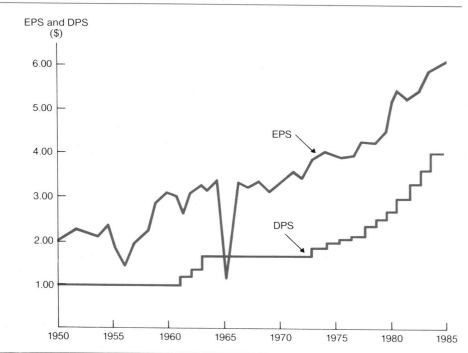

inflation, earnings grew rather steadily during the 1970s and early 1980s, and investors came to expect most successful companies to increase dividends at a rate that, they hoped, would offset inflation. Therefore, after 1973 Morris' management adopted the policy of increasing the dividend annually.

There are several logical reasons for following a stable, predictable dividend policy. First, given the existence of the information content, or signaling, idea, a fluctuating payment policy might lead to greater uncertainty and hence a higher $k_s$ and a lower stock price than would exist under a stable policy. Second, since stockholders who use dividends for current consumption want to be able to count on receiving dividends on a regular basis, irregular dividends might lower demand for the stock and cause its price to decline. Third, even though the optimal dividend as prescribed by the residual policy might vary somewhat from year to year, actions such as delaying some investment projects, departing from the target capital structure during a particular year, or even selling common stock might all be preferable to cutting the dividend or reducing its growth rate. Finally, setting a steady dividend growth rate will confirm investors' estimates of g as used in the stock valuation model, reduce risk perceptions, and thus enhance the price of the stock.

### Constant Payout Ratio

A very few firms follow a policy of paying out a constant percentage of earnings. Since earnings will surely fluctuate, following this policy necessarily means that the dollar amount of dividends will vary. For reasons discussed in the preceding section, this policy is not likely to maximize a firm's stock price. However, before its bankruptcy, Penn Central Railroad did follow the policy of paying out one-half its earnings—"A dollar for the stockholders and a dollar for the company," as one director put it. Logic like this could drive any company to bankruptcy!

### Low Regular Dividend plus Extras

A policy of paying a low regular dividend plus a year-end extra in good years is a compromise between the previous two policies. It gives the firm flexibility, yet investors can count on receiving at least a minimum dividend. Therefore, if a firm's earnings and cash flows are quite volatile, this policy may well be its best choice. The directors can set a relatively low regular dividend— low enough so that it can be maintained even in low-profit years or in years when a considerable amount of retained earnings is needed—and then supplement it with an **extra dividend** in years when excess funds are available. General Motors, whose earnings fluctuate widely from year to year, has long followed such a policy.

**extra dividend**
A supplementary dividend paid in years when excess funds are available.

### Payment Procedures

Dividends are normally paid quarterly. For example, General Electric paid dividends of $2.00, 50 cents each quarter, during 1984. In common financial language, we say that GE's *regular quarterly dividend* was 50 cents, or its *regular annual dividend* was $2.00, in 1984. GE raised its dividend for 1985 by 10 percent, to 55 cents per quarter or $2.20 per year.

The actual payment procedure is as follows:

**declaration date**
The date on which a firm's directors issue a statement declaring a dividend.

**1. Declaration date**. On the declaration date—say, on November 15—the directors meet and declare the regular dividend, issuing a statement similar to the following: "On November 15, 1985, the directors of the XYZ Company met and declared the regular quarterly dividend of 50 cents per share, plus an extra dividend of 25 cents per share, payable to holders of record on December 15, payment to be made on January 2, 1986."

**holder-of-record date**
If the company lists the stockholder as an owner on this date, then the stockholder receives the dividend.

**2. Holder-of-record date**. At the close of business on the holder-of-record date, December 15, the company closes its stock transfer books and makes up a list of the shareholders as of that date. If XYZ Company is notified of the sale and transfer of some stock before 5 P.M. on December 15, the new owner receives the dividend. However, if notification is received on or after December 16, the previous owner of the stock gets the dividend check.

**ex-dividend date**
The date on which the right to the current dividend no longer accompanies a stock; for a listed stock, it is usually four working days prior to the holder-of-record date.

**3. Ex-dividend date**. Suppose Jean Buyer buys 100 shares of stock from John Seller on December 13. Will the company be notified of the transfer in time to list Buyer as the new owner and thus pay the dividend to her? To avoid conflict, the securities industry has set up a convention of declaring that the right to the dividend remains with the stock until four business days prior to the holder-of-record date; on the fourth day before that date, the right to the dividend no longer goes with the shares. The date when the right to the dividend leaves the stock is called the *ex-dividend date*. In this case, the ex-dividend date is four days prior to December 15, or December 11:

|                        |             |
|------------------------|-------------|
|                        | December 10 |
| Ex-dividend date:      | December 11 |
|                        | December 12 |
|                        | December 13 |
|                        | December 14 |
| Holder-of-record date: | December 15 |

Therefore, if Buyer is to receive the dividend, she must buy the stock on or before December 10. If she buys it on December 11 or later, Seller will receive the dividend because he will be the holder of record.

The XYZ dividend, regular plus extra, amounts to 75 cents, so the ex-dividend date is important. Barring fluctuations in the stock market, we would normally expect the price of a stock to drop by approximately the amount of the dividend on the ex-dividend date. Thus, if XYZ closed at $30¾ on December 10, it would probably open at about $30 on December 11.[7]

**4. Payment date.** The company actually mails the checks to the holders of record on January 2, the payment date.

### Dividend Reinvestment Plans

During the 1970s most of the larger companies instituted **dividend reinvestment plans (DRPs)**, whereby stockholders can automatically reinvest dividends received in the stock of the paying corporation.[8] *There are two types of DRPs: (1) plans which involve only "old" stock that is already outstanding and (2) plans which involve newly issued stock.* In either case, the stockholder must pay income taxes on the amount of the dividends even though he or she receives stock rather than cash.

Under the "old-stock" type of plan, the stockholder elects either to receive dividend checks or to have the company use the dividends to buy more stock in the corporation. If the stockholder elects reinvestment, a bank, acting as trustee, takes the total funds available for reinvestment (less a fee), purchases the corporation's stock on the open market, and allocates the shares purchased to the participating stockholders' accounts on a pro rata basis. The transactions costs of buying shares (brokerage costs) are low because of volume purchases, so these plans benefit small stockholders who do not need cash dividends for current consumption.

The "new-stock" type of DRP provides for dividends to be invested in newly issued stock; hence, these plans raise new capital for the firm. AT&T, Florida Power & Light, Union Carbide, and many other companies have had

---

**payment date**
The date on which a firm actually mails dividend checks.

**dividend reinvestment plan (DRP)**
A plan that enables a stockholder to automatically reinvest dividends received back into the stock of the paying firm.

---

[7]Tax effects cause the price decline on average to be less than the full amount of the dividend. Suppose you were an investor in the 50 percent tax bracket. If you bought XYZ's stock on December 10, you would receive the dividend but almost immediately pay half of it out in taxes. Thus, you would want to wait until December 11 to buy the stock if you thought you could get it for 75 cents per share less. Your reaction, and that of others, would influence stock prices around dividend payment dates. Here is what would happen:

1. Other things held constant, a stock's price should rise during the quarter, with the daily price increase (for XYZ) equal to $0.75/90 = $0.0083. Therefore, if it started at $30 just after its last ex-dividend date, it would rise to $30.75 on December 10.

2. In the absence of taxes, the stock's price would fall to $30 on December 11 and then start up as the next dividend accrual period began. Thus, over time, if everything else were held constant, the stock's price would follow a sawtooth pattern if it were plotted on a graph.

3. Because of taxes, the stock's price will neither rise by the full amount of the dividend nor fall by the full dividend amount when it goes ex-dividend.

4. The amount of the rise and subsequent fall depends on the average investor's marginal tax rate and the differential between taxes on dividends and capital gains.

See Edwin J. Elton and Martin J. Gruber, "Marginal Stockholder Tax Rates and the Clientele Effect," *Review of Economics and Statistics*, February 1970, 68-74, for an interesting discussion of all this.

[8]See Richard H. Pettway and R. Phil Malone, "Automatic Dividend Reinvestment Plans," *Financial Management*, Winter 1973, 11-18, for an excellent discussion of this topic.

such plans in effect in recent years, using them to raise substantial amounts of new equity capital. No fees are charged to stockholders, and many companies offer stock at a discount of 5 percent below the actual market price. The companies absorb these costs as a trade-off against flotation costs that would have been incurred had they sold stock through investment bankers rather than through the dividend reinvestment plans.[9]

## Summary of Factors Influencing Dividend Policy

In earlier sections, we described the major theories dealing with the effects of dividend policy on the value of a firm, and we discussed four alternative payment policies. Firms choose a particular policy based on managements' beliefs concerning the dividend theories plus a host of other factors. All of the factors which are taken into account may be grouped into four broad categories: (1) constraints on dividend payments, (2) investment opportunities, (3) availability and cost of alternative sources of capital, and (4) effects of dividend policy on $k_s$. Each of these categories has several subparts, discussed in the following paragraphs.

### Constraints

1. *Bond indentures.* Debt contracts generally constrain dividend payments to earnings generated after the loan was granted. Also, they often stipulate that no dividends can be paid unless the current ratio, times-interest-earned ratio, and other safety ratios exceed stated minimums.

2. *Impairment of capital rule.* Dividend payments cannot exceed the balance sheet item retained earnings. This legal restriction, known as the *impairment of capital rule*, is designed to protect creditors. (*Liquidating dividends* can be paid out of capital, but they must be indicated as such and must not reduce capital below the limits stated in debt contracts.)

3. *Availability of cash.* Cash dividends can be paid only with cash. Thus, a shortage of cash in the bank can restrict dividend payments. However, unused borrowing capacity can offset this factor.

4. *Penalty tax on improperly accumulated earnings.* To prevent wealthy individuals from using corporations to avoid personal taxes, the Tax Code provides for a special surtax on improperly accumulated income. Thus, if the

---

[9]One interesting aspect of DRPs is that they are forcing corporations to reexamine their basic dividend policies. A high participation rate in a DRP suggests that stockholders might be better off if the firm simply reduced cash dividends, as this would save stockholders some personal income taxes. Quite a few firms are surveying their stockholders to learn more about their preferences and to find out how they would react to a change in dividend policy. A more rational approach to basic dividend policy decisions may emerge from this research.

   Also, it should be noted that companies either use or stop using new-stock DRPs depending on their need for equity capital. Thus, Florida Power & Light recently stopped offering a new-stock DRP with a 5 percent discount because its need for equity capital declined.

IRS can demonstrate that a firm's dividend payout ratio is being deliberately held down to help its stockholders avoid personal taxes, the firm is subject to heavy penalties. To date, this factor has been applied only to privately owned firms.

### Investment Opportunities

**1.** *Location of the IOS schedule.* If the relevant IOS schedule in Figure 16-4 is far to the right, this will tend to produce a low payout ratio, and vice versa if the IOS is far to the left. Also, the steeper the slope of the IOS, the more costly a failure to use the payout prescribed by a residual analysis.

**2.** *Possibility of accelerating or delaying projects.* The ability to accelerate or postpone projects will permit more flexibility in a firm's dividend policy.

### Alternative Sources of Capital

**1.** *Cost of selling new stock.* If a firm needs to finance a given level of investment, it can obtain equity by retaining earnings or by selling new common stock. If flotation costs are high, $k_e$ will be well above $k_s$, making it much better to finance through retention than through sale of new common stock. On the other hand, if flotation costs are low, dividend policy will be less important. Flotation costs differ among firms—for example, they are generally higher for small firms. Hence, the importance of these costs, and consequently the degree of flexibility in setting a dividend policy, varies among firms.

**2.** *Ability to substitute debt for equity.* A firm can finance a given level of investment with either debt or equity. As we have seen, if stock flotation costs are low, a more flexible dividend policy may be followed because equity can be raised by retaining earnings or by selling new stock. A similar situation holds for debt policy: if the firm is willing to adjust its debt ratio, it can maintain a constant dollar dividend by using a variable debt ratio. The shape of the average cost of capital curve (in the left-hand panel of Figure 16-2) determines the practical extent to which the debt ratio can be varied. If the average cost of capital curve is relatively flat over a wide range, then dividend policy is less critical than it would be if the curve had a distinct minimum.

**3.** *Control.* If management is concerned about maintaining control, it may be reluctant to sell new stock and hence may retain more earnings than it otherwise would. This factor is especially important for small firms whose managers own a relatively high percentage of the outstanding stock.

### Effects of Dividend Policy on $k_s$

The effects of dividend policy on $k_s$ may be considered in terms of these four factors: (1) differential tax rates, (2) stockholders' desire for current versus future income, (3) perceived riskiness of dividends versus capital gains, and (4) the information content of dividends (signaling). Since we discussed each of these factors in detail earlier, we need only note here that the importance of each factor in terms of its effect on $k_s$ varies from firm to firm depending on the makeup of its stockholders. Management certainly ought to take its own stockholders into account when it sets its dividend policy.

It should be apparent from our discussion thus far in the chapter that dividend policy decisions are truly exercises in informed judgment and not decisions that can be quantified precisely. Even so, in order to make rational dividend decisions, financial managers need to take account of all the points we have raised in the preceding sections.

## Stock Dividends and Stock Splits

Stock dividends and stock splits are related to the firm's cash dividend policy. The rationale for stock dividends and splits can best be explained through an example. We will use the Porter Electronics Company, a $700 million electronic components manufacturer, for this purpose. Since its inception, Porter's markets have been expanding, and the company has enjoyed growth in sales and earnings. Some of the earnings were paid out in dividends, but some were also retained each year; therefore, earnings per share and market price per share have also grown. The company began its life with only a few thousand shares outstanding. After some years of growth, each share had a very high EPS and DPS. When a "normal" P/E ratio was applied, the derived market price was so high that few people could afford to buy a "round lot" of 100 shares. This limited demand for the stock and thus kept the total market value of the firm below what it would have been if more shares, at a lower price, were outstanding. To correct this situation, Porter "split its stock" as described below.

### Stock Splits

Although there is little empirical evidence to support the contention, there is nevertheless a widespread belief in financial circles that an *optimal price range* exists for stocks. "Optimal" means that if the price is within this range, the price/earnings ratio, and hence the value of the firm, will be maximized. Many observers, including Porter's management, believe that the best range for most stocks is from $20 to $80 per share. Accordingly, if the price of Porter's stock rose to $80, management would probably declare a two-for-one **stock split**, thus doubling the number of shares outstanding, halving the earnings and dividends per share, and thereby lowering the price of the stock. Each stockholder would have more shares, but each share would be worth less. If the post-split price were $40, Porter's stockholders would be exactly as well off as they were before the split. However, if the price of the stock were to stabilize above $40, stockholders would be better off. Stock splits can be of any size—for example, the stock could be split two-for-one, three-for-one, 1.5-for-one, or in any other way.[10]

**stock split**
An action taken by a firm to increase the number of shares outstanding, such as doubling the number of shares outstanding by giving each stockholder two new shares for each one formerly held.

---

[10]*Reverse splits*, which reduce the shares outstanding, can even be used—for example, a company whose stock sells for $5 might employ a one-for-five reverse split, exchanging 1 new share for 5 old ones and raising the value of the shares to about $25, which is within the "acceptable" range. LTV Corporation did this after several years of losses drove its stock price down below the "optimal" range.

## Stock Dividends

**stock dividend**
A dividend paid in the form of additional shares of stock rather than of cash.

**Stock dividends** are similar to stock splits in that they divide the "pie" into smaller slices without affecting the fundamental position of the current stockholders. On a 5 percent stock dividend, the holder of 100 shares would receive an additional 5 shares (without cost); on a 20 percent stock dividend, the same holder would receive 20 new shares; and so on. Again, the total number of shares is increased, so earnings, dividends, and price per share all decline.

If a firm wants to reduce the price of its stock, should it use a stock split or a stock dividend? Stock splits are generally used after a sharp price run-up to produce a large price reduction. Stock dividends are frequently used on a regular annual basis to keep the stock price more or less constrained. For example, if a firm's earnings and dividends were growing at about 10 percent per year, the price would tend to go up at about that same rate, and it would soon be outside the desired trading range. A 10 percent annual stock dividend would maintain the stock price within the optimal trading range.

### Balance Sheet Effects

Although the economic effects of stock splits and stock dividends are virtually identical, accountants treat them somewhat differently. On a two-for-one split, the shares outstanding are doubled and the stock's par value is halved. This treatment is shown in the middle section of Table 16-1 for Porter Electronics, using a pro forma 1986 balance sheet.

With a stock dividend the par value is not reduced, but an accounting entry is made transferring capital from the retained earnings account to the common stock and paid-in capital accounts. The transfer from retained earnings is calculated as follows:

$$\begin{pmatrix} \text{Dollars} \\ \text{transferred from} \\ \text{retained earnings} \end{pmatrix} = \begin{pmatrix} \text{Number} \\ \text{of shares} \\ \text{outstanding} \end{pmatrix} \begin{pmatrix} \text{Percentage} \\ \text{of the} \\ \text{stock dividend} \end{pmatrix} \begin{pmatrix} \text{Market} \\ \text{price of} \\ \text{the stock} \end{pmatrix}.$$

For example, if Porter Electronics, with 5 million shares outstanding selling at $80 each, declared a 20 percent stock dividend, the transfer would be

$$\text{Dollars transferred} = (5,000,000)(0.2)(\$80) = \$80,000,000.$$

As shown in the bottom section of Table 16-1, of this $80 million transfer, $1 million is added to the common stock account and $79 million to the additional paid-in capital account. The retained earnings account is reduced to $75 million.[11]

---

[11]Note that Porter could not pay a stock dividend that exceeded 38.75 percent; a stock dividend of that percentage would exhaust the retained earnings. Thus, a firm's ability to declare stock dividends is constrained by the amount of its retained earnings. Of course, if Porter had wanted to pay a 50 percent stock dividend, it could just switch to a 1.5-for-one stock split and accomplish the same thing.

**Table 16-1**
**Porter Electronics Company:**
**Stockholders' Equity Accounts, Pro Forma, December 31, 1986**

### Before a Stock Split or Stock Dividend

| | |
|---|---:|
| Common stock (6 million shares authorized, 5 million outstanding, $1 par) | $   5,000,000 |
| Additional paid-in capital | 10,000,000 |
| Retained earnings | 155,000,000 |
| Total common stockholders' equity | $170,000,000 |

### After a Two-for-One Stock Split

| | |
|---|---:|
| Common stock (12 million shares authorized, 10 million shares outstanding, $0.50 par) | $   5,000,000 |
| Additional paid-in capital | 10,000,000 |
| Retained earnings | 155,000,000 |
| Total common stockholders' equity | $170,000,000 |

### After a 20 Percent Stock Dividend

| | |
|---|---:|
| Common stock (6 million shares authorized, 6 million outstanding, $1 par)[a] | $   6,000,000 |
| Additional paid-in capital[b] | 89,000,000 |
| Retained earnings[b] | 75,000,000 |
| Total common stockholders' equity | $170,000,000 |

[a]Shares outstanding are increased by 20 percent, from 5 million to 6 million.

[b]A transfer equal to the market value of the new shares is made from the retained earnings account to the additional paid-in capital and common stock accounts:

$$\text{Transfer} = (5,000,000 \text{ shares})(0.2)(\$80) = \$80,000,000.$$

Of this $80 million, ($1 par)(1,000,000 shares) = $1,000,000 goes to common stock and $79 million to paid-in capital.

## Price Effects

Several empirical studies have examined the effects of stock splits and stock dividends on stock prices.[12] The findings of the Barker study are presented in Table 16-2. When stock dividends were associated with a cash dividend increase, the value of the company's stock six months after the ex-dividend date had risen by 8 percent. On the other hand, when stock dividends were not accompanied by cash dividend increases, stock values fell by 12 percent, which approximated the percentage of the average stock dividend.

These data seem to suggest that stock dividends are seen for what they are—simply additional pieces of paper—and that they do not represent true income. When stock dividends are accompanied by higher earnings and cash

---

[12]See C. A. Barker, "Evaluation of Stock Dividends," *Harvard Business Review*, July-August 1958, 99-114. Barker's study has been replicated several times in recent years, and his results are still valid—they have withstood the test of time. Another excellent study, using an entirely different methodology yet reaching similar conclusions, is that of Eugene F. Fama, Lawrence Fisher, Michael C. Jensen, and Richard Roll, "The Adjustment of Stock Prices to New Information," *International Economic Review*, February 1969, 1-21.

**Table 16-2**
**Price Effects of Stock Dividends**

|  | Price at Selected Dates (Percent) | | |
|---|---|---|---|
|  | 6 Months before Ex-Dividend Date | At Ex-Dividend Date | 6 Months after Ex-Dividend Date |
| Cash dividend increase after stock dividend | 100 | 109 | 108 |
| No cash dividend increase after stock dividend | 100 | 99 | 88 |

dividends, investors bid up the value of the stock. However, when they are not accompanied by increases in earnings and cash dividends, the dilution of earnings and dividends per share causes the price of the stock to drop by about the same percentage as the stock dividend. The fundamental determinants of price are the underlying earnings and cash dividends per share.

## Establishing a Dividend Policy: Some Illustrations

As we have seen, many factors interact to determine a firm's optimal dividend policy. Moreover, since the interactions are too complex to permit the development of a rigorous model for use as a guide to dividend policy, firms are forced to consider their policies in a relatively subjective manner. Some illustrations of how dividend policies are actually set are given in the following sections.

### Dayton Publishing Company

Dayton analyzed its situation in terms of the residual theory as shown in Figure 16-4. The residual theory suggested a dividend of $1.80 per share during 1986, or a 30 percent payout ratio. Dayton's stock is publicly owned, and a number of tax-exempt institutions are important stockholders. A questionnaire to its stockholders revealed no strong preferences for dividends versus capital gains. Dayton's long-range planning group projected a cost of capital and a set of investment opportunities during the next three to five years that are similar to those estimated for this year.

On the basis of this information, Dayton's treasurer recommended to the board of directors that it establish a dividend of $1.80 for 1986, payable 45 cents quarterly. The 1985 dividend was $1.70, so the $1.80 represents an increase of about 6 percent. The treasurer also reported to the board that in the event of an unforeseen earnings downturn the company could obtain additional debt to meet its capital expenditure requirements. The board accepted the treasurer's recommendation, and on December 18, 1985, it declared a quarterly dividend of 45 cents per share, payable January 15, 1986. The board also announced its intention to maintain this dividend for all of 1986.

## Watkins Electronics

Watkins Electronics has a residual theory position resembling $IOS_G$ in Figure 16-4, which suggests that no dividend be paid. Watkins has, in fact, paid no dividend since its inception in 1975, even though it has been continuously profitable and its earnings have recently been growing at a 25 percent rate. Informal conversations with the firm's major stockholders, all of whom are in high tax brackets, suggest that they neither expect nor want dividends—they would prefer to have the firm retain earnings, generate a high earnings growth rate, and provide capital gains, which are taxed at relatively low rates. The stock now sells for $106 per share. Watkins' treasurer recommended a three-for-one split, no cash dividend, and a future policy of declaring an annual stock dividend geared to earnings for the year. The board of directors concurred.

## Southwest Electric Company

Southwest Electric has an acute need for new equity capital. The company has a major expansion program underway and absolutely must come up with the money to meet construction payments. The debt ratio is high, and if the times-interest-earned ratio falls any lower, then (1) the company's bonds will be downgraded, and (2) it will be barred by bond indenture provisions from further debt issues. These facts suggest a cut in dividends from the $2.50 per share paid last year. However, the treasurer knows that many of the stockholders rely on dividends for current living expenses; thus, if dividends are cut, these stockholders may be forced to sell, hence driving down the price of the stock. This would be especially bad in view of the treasurer's forecast that there will be a need to sell new common stock during the coming year. (New outside equity would be needed even if the company totally eliminated the dividend.) The treasurer is aware that many other utilities face a similar problem. Some have cut their dividends, which has invariably led to stock price declines of from 30 to 70 percent.

Southwest's earnings are forecasted to increase from $3.33 to $3.60. The treasurer has recommended that the dividend be raised from $2.50 to $2.70, with the increase being announced a few weeks before the company floats a new common stock issue. The hope is that this action will cause the price of the stock to increase, after which the company can sell the new issue at a better price.

## North American Oil (NAO)

NAO's 1985 dividend was $2.45 per share, up from $2.30 in 1984. Both dividend figures represented about 50 percent of earnings, and this payout was consistent with a residual theory analysis. The company's growth rate in EPS and DPS had been in the 5 to 10 percent range during the previous few years, and management was projecting a continuation of this trend. The financial vice-president foresaw a cash flow problem in 1986—earnings were projected to increase in line with the historical average, but an especially large number of good investment opportunities (along with some unprofitable but required pollution control expenditures) were expected. A preliminary analysis using the residual theory suggested that the dividend in 1986 be cut back sharply, if not eliminated.

The financial vice-president quickly rejected this cutback, recommending instead a 6 percent *increase* in the dividend, to $2.60. He noted that the company could easily borrow funds during the coming year to meet its capital requirements. The debt ratio would rise somewhat above the target, but the firm's average cost of capital curve was relatively flat, and cash flows from the 1986 investments would likely permit a reduction in the debt ratio over the next few years. The vice-president believed that it was more important to maintain the steady growth in dividends than to adhere strictly to the target debt ratio.

## Summary

*Dividend policy* involves the decision of whether to pay out earnings or to retain them for reinvestment in the firm. Any change in dividend policy has both favorable and unfavorable effects on the price of the firm's stock. Higher dividends mean higher cash flows to investors, which is good, but lower future growth, which is bad. The optimal dividend policy balances these opposing forces and maximizes the price of the stock.

We first identified three dividend theories: (1) *dividend irrelevance*, (2) *"bird-in-the-hand"*, and (3) *tax differential*. Then we described four dividend payment policies that are used by firms. Most companies analyze the *residual dividend approach* when they establish their long-run target payout ratio, but they then tend to use one of these three payment policies: (1) a *stable or continuously increasing dollar dividend per share*; (2) a *low regular dividend plus extras* that depend on annual earnings; or (3) a *constant payout ratio*, which will cause the dollar dividend to fluctuate. Most firms follow the first policy, a few use the second, and almost none use the third. Also, we noted that many firms today are using *dividend reinvestment plans (DRPs)* to help stockholders reinvest dividends at minimal brokerage costs. In Appendix 16A, we also show that some firms use stock repurchase plans in lieu of more cash dividends.

There are a number of factors that bear on dividend policy, including the following: *legal constraints*, such as bond indenture provisions, *investment opportunities*, the *availability and cost of funds from other sources* (new stock and debt), *tax rates, stockholders' desire for current income*, and the *information content* of dividend changes. Because of the large number of factors that bear on dividend policy, and also because the relative importance of these factors changes over time and across companies, it is impossible to develop a precise, generalized model for use in establishing dividend policy.

*Stock splits* and *stock dividends* were also discussed. Our conclusion was that these actions may be beneficial if the firm's stock price is quite high but otherwise they have little effect on the value of the firm.

## Questions

16-1    Define each of the following terms:
        a. Optimal dividend policy
        b. Dividend irrelevance theory; "bird-in-the-hand" theory; tax differential theory

c. Information content, or signaling, hypothesis; clientele effect

d. Residual dividend policy

e. Extra dividend

f. Declaration date; holder-of-record date; ex-dividend date; payment date

g. Dividend reinvestment plan (DRP)

h. Stock split; stock dividend

16-2    As an investor, would you rather invest in a firm that has a policy of maintaining (a) a constant payout ratio, (b) a constant dollar dividend per share, (c) a target dividend growth rate, or (d) a constant regular quarterly dividend plus a year-end extra when earnings are sufficiently high or corporate investment needs sufficiently low? Explain your answer, stating how these policies would affect your $k_s$.

16-3    How would each of the following changes tend to affect aggregate (that is, the average for all corporations) payout ratios, other things held constant? Explain your answers.

a. An increase in the personal income tax rate, but with the 60 percent long-term capital gains exclusion remaining in effect.

b. A liberalization of depreciation for federal income tax purposes, that is, faster tax write-offs.

c. A rise in interest rates.

d. An increase in corporate profits.

e. A decline in investment opportunities.

f. Permission for corporations to deduct dividends as they now do interest charges.

16-4    Discuss the pros and cons of having the directors formally announce what a firm's dividend policy will be in the future.

16-5    Most firms would like to have their stock selling at a high P/E ratio, and they would also like to have an extensive public ownership (many different shareholders). Explain how stock dividends or stock splits may help achieve these goals.

16-6    What is the difference between a stock dividend and a stock split? As a stockholder, would you prefer to see your company declare a 100 percent stock dividend or a two-for-one split? Assume that either action is feasible.

16-7    "The cost of retained earnings is less than the cost of new outside equity capital. Consequently, it is totally irrational for a firm to sell a new issue of stock and to pay dividends during the same year." Discuss this statement.

16-8    Would it ever be rational for a firm to borrow money in order to pay dividends? Explain.

16-9    "Executive salaries have been shown to be more closely correlated to the size of the firm than to its profitability. If a firm's board of directors is controlled by management instead of by outside directors, this might result in the firm's retaining more earnings than can be justified from the stockholders' point of view." Discuss the statement, being sure (a) to use Figure 16-4 in your answer and (b) to explain the implied relationship between dividend policy and stock prices.

16-10   Modigliani and Miller (MM) on the one hand and Gordon and Lintner (GL) on the other have expressed strong views regarding the effect of dividend policy on a firm's cost of capital and value.

a. In essence, what are the MM and GL views regarding the effect of dividend policy on cost of capital and stock prices?

b. How does the tax differential theory differ from the views of MM and GL?

c. According to the text, which of these three theories, if any, has received statistical confirmation from empirical tests?

d. How could MM use the *information content*, or *signaling*, *hypothesis* to counter their opponents' arguments? If you were debating MM, how would you counter them?

e. How could MM use the *clientele effect* concept to counter their opponents' arguments? If you were debating MM, how would you counter them?

16-11   More NYSE companies had stock dividends and stock splits during the first 9 months of 1983 than during the whole 12 months of the previous record year, 1971. Would you guess that the stock market was strong or weak in 1983? Explain the rationale that a financial vice-president might give his or her board of directors to support a stock split/dividend recommendation.

## Self-Test Problem (*Solution on Page 562*)

ST-1   Components Manufacturing Corporation (CMC) has an all-equity capital structure which includes no preferred stock. It has 200,000 shares of $2 par value common stock outstanding.

When CMC's founder, who was also its research director and most successful inventor, died unexpectedly in late 1985, CMC was left suddenly and permanently with materially lower growth expectations and relatively few attractive new investment opportunities. Unfortunately, there was no way to replace the founder's contributions to the firm. Previously, CMC has found it necessary to plow back most of its earnings to finance growth, which has been averaging 12 percent per year. Future growth at a 5 percent rate is considered realistic, but that level would call for an increase in the dividend payout. Further, it now appears that new investment projects with at least the 14 percent rate of return required by CMC's stockholders ($k_s = 14\%$) would amount to only $800,000 for 1986 in comparison to a projected $2,000,000 of net income after taxes. If the existing 20 percent dividend payout were continued, retained earnings would be $1.6 million in 1986, but, as noted, investments which yield the 14 percent cost of capital amount to only $800,000.

The one encouraging thing is that the high earnings from existing assets are expected to continue and net income of $2 million is still expected for 1986. Given the dramatically changed circumstances, CMC's management is reviewing the firm's dividend policy.

a. Assuming that the acceptable 1986 investment projects would be financed entirely by earnings retained during the year, calculate DPS in 1986 assuming CMC uses the residual payment policy.

b. What payout ratio does this imply for 1986?

c. If the increased payout ratio is maintained for the foreseeable future, what should be the present market price of the common stock? How does this compare with the market price that should have prevailed under the assumptions existing just prior to the news about the death of the founder? If the two values of $P_0$ are different, comment on why.

d. What are the implications of continuing the 20 percent payout? Assume that if this payout is maintained then the average rate of return on the retained earnings will be 7.5 percent and the new growth rate will be

$$g = (1.0 - \text{Payout ratio})(\text{ROE})$$
$$= (1.0 - 0.2)(7.5\%)$$
$$= (0.8)(7.5\%) = 6.0\%.$$

## Problems

**Residual policy**

**16-1**  One position expressed in the financial literature is that firms set their dividends as a residual after using income to support new investment.

a. Explain what a residual dividend policy implies, illustrating your answer with a graph showing how different conditions could lead to different dividend payout ratios.

b. Could the residual dividend policy be consistent with (1) a constant growth rate policy, (2) a constant payout policy, and/or (3) a low-regular-plus-extras policy? Answer in terms of both short-run, year-to-year consistency and longer-run consistency.

c. Think back to Chapter 15, where we considered the relationship between capital structure and the cost of capital. If the $k_a$ versus debt ratio plot were shaped like a sharp V, would this have a different implication for the importance of setting dividends according to the residual policy than if the plot were shaped like a shallow bowl (or a flattened U)?

d. Assume that Companies A and B both have IOS schedules that intersect their MCC schedules at a point which, under the residual policy, calls for a 20 percent payout. In both cases, a 20 percent payout would require a cut in the annual dividend from $2 to $1. One company cut its dividend, while the other did not. One company had a relatively steep IOS curve, while the other had a relatively flat one. Explain which company probably had the steeper curve.

**External equity financing**

**16-2**  Arizona Heating and Cooling, Inc., has a six-month backlog of orders for its patented solar heating system. Management plans to expand production capacity by 30 percent, with a $6 million investment in plant machinery, to meet this demand. The firm wants to maintain a 45 percent debt to total assets ratio in its capital structure; it also wants to maintain its past dividend policy of distributing 20 percent of last year's after-tax earnings. In 1985 after-tax earnings were $2.6 million. How much external equity must the firm seek at the beginning of 1986 in order to expand capacity as desired?

**Dividend payout**

**16-3**  Warner Company expects next year's after-tax income to be $8 million. The firm's debt ratio is currently 50 percent. Warner has $7 million of profitable investment opportunities, and it wishes to maintain its existing debt ratio. According to the residual dividend policy, how large should the firm's dividend payout ratio be next year?

**Stock split**  16-4  After a three-for-one stock split, Omaha Company paid a dividend of $2 per new share, which represents a 9 percent increase over last year's pre-split dividend. What was last year's dividend per share?

**Stock dividend**  16-5  Cartwright Corporation declared a 4 percent stock dividend, plus a cash dividend of 40 cents per share. The cash dividend was paid on both the old shares and the new shares received from the stock dividend. Construct a pro forma balance sheet showing the effect of these actions; use one new balance sheet that incorporates both actions. The stock was selling for $25 per share, and a condensed version of Cartwright's balance sheet as of December 31, 1985, before the dividends, follows (millions of dollars):

| | | | |
|---|---|---|---|
| Cash | $   50 | Debt | $1,000 |
| Other assets | 1,950 | Common stock (60 million shares authorized, 50 million shares outstanding, $1 par) | 50 |
| | | Paid-in capital | 200 |
| | | Retained earnings | 750 |
| Total assets | $2,000 | Total claims | $2,000 |

**Alternative dividend policies**  16-6  In 1985 the Vawter Company paid dividends totaling $2,250,000 on after-tax income of $7.5 million. 1985 was a "normal" year, and for the past 10 years, earnings have grown at a constant rate of 10 percent. However, in 1986, earnings are expected to jump to $12 million, and the firm expects to have profitable investment opportunities of $9 million. It is predicted that Vawter will not be able to maintain the 1986 level of earnings growth—an exceptionally profitable new product line was introduced that year—and will return to its previous 10 percent growth rate. The company's target debt ratio is 30 percent. Calculate its total dividends for 1986 if Vawter follows each of the following policies:

a. Its 1986 dividend payment is set to force dividends to grow at the long-run growth rate in earnings.

b. It continues the 1985 dividend payout ratio.

c. It uses a pure residual dividend policy (30 percent of the $9 million investment is financed with debt).

d. It employs a regular-dividend-plus-extras policy, with the regular dividend being based on the long-run growth rate and the extra dividend being set according to the residual policy.

e. Which of the above policies would you recommend? Restrict your choices to the ones listed, but justify your answer.

f. Assume that investors expect Vawter to pay total dividends of $2,500,000 in 1986 and to have the dividend grow at 10% after 1986. The total market value of the stock is $50 million. What is its cost of equity?

g. What is Vawter's long-run average return on equity? (Hint: $g = b(ROE)$.)

h. Does a 1986 dividend of $2,500,000 seem reasonable in view of your answers to Parts f and g? If not, should the dividend be higher or lower?

**Dividend policy and capital structure**   **16-7**

Tampa Tobacco Company has for many years enjoyed a moderate but stable growth in sales and earnings. However, cigar consumption and consequently Tampa's sales have been falling recently, primarily because of an increasing awareness of the dangers of smoking to health. Anticipating further declines in tobacco sales for the future, Tampa's management hopes eventually to move almost entirely out of the tobacco business and into a newly developed, diversified product line in growth-oriented industries. The company is especially interested in the prospects for pollution-control devices, because its research department has already done much work on the problems of filtering smoke. Right now the company estimates that an investment of $24 million is necessary to purchase new facilities and to begin operations on these products, but the investment could be earning a return of about 18 percent within a short time. The only other available investment opportunity totals $9.6 million, is expected to return about 10.2 percent, and is indivisible, that is, it must be accepted in its entirety or else be rejected.

The company is expected to pay a $2.40 dividend on its 6 million outstanding shares, the same as its dividend last year. The directors might, however, change the dividend if there are good reasons for doing so. Total earnings for the year are expected to be $22.8 million; the common stock is currently selling for $45; the firm's target debt ratio (debt/assets ratio) is 45 percent; and its tax rate is 50 percent. The costs of various forms of financing are listed below:

New bonds, $k_d = 11\%$. This is a before-tax rate.

New common stock sold at $45 per share will net the firm $41.

Required rate of return on retained earnings, $k_s = 14\%$.

a. Calculate Tampa's expected payout ratio, the break point where MCC rises, and its marginal cost of capital above and below the point of exhaustion of retained earnings at the current payout. (Hint: $k_s$ is given, and $D_1/P_0$ can be found. Then, knowing $k_s$ and $D_1/P_0$, g can be determined.)

b. How large should Tampa's capital budget be for the year?

c. What is an appropriate dividend policy for Tampa? How should the capital budget be financed?

d. How might risk factors influence Tampa's cost of capital, capital structure, and dividend policy?

e. What assumptions, if any, do your answers to the above make about investors' preferences for dividends versus capital gains, that is, their preferences regarding the $D_1/P_0$ and g components of $k_s$?

(Do only if you are using the computerized problem diskette.)

f. Assume that Tampa's management is considering a change in its capital structure to include more debt, and thus it would like to analyze the effects of an increase in the debt ratio to 60 percent. However, the treasurer believes that such a move would cause lenders to increase the required rate of return on new bonds to 12 percent and $k_s$ would rise to 14.5 percent. How would this change affect the optimal capital budget? If $k_s$ rose to 16 percent, would the low-return project be acceptable? Would the project selection be affected if the dividend were reduced to $1.50 from $2.40, still assuming $k_s = 16$ percent?

## Solution to Self-Test Problem

ST-1  a.

| | |
|---|---:|
| Projected net income | $2,000,000 |
| Less: Projected capital investments | 800,000 |
| Available residual | $1,200,000 |
| Shares outstanding | 200,000 |

$$DPS = \$1,200,000/200,000 \text{ shares} = \$6 = D_1.$$

b. EPS $= \$2,000,000/200,000$ shares $= \$10$.
Payout ratio $=$ DPS/EPS $= \$6/\$10 = 60\%$, or
Total dividends/NI $= \$1,200,000/\$2,000,000 = 60\%$.

c. $P_0 = \dfrac{D_1}{k_s - g} = \dfrac{\$6}{0.14 - 0.05} = \dfrac{\$6}{0.09} = \$66.67.$

Under the former circumstances, $D_1$ would be equal to the 20 percent payout on $10 EPS, or $2. With $k_s = 14\%$ and $g = 12\%$, we solve for $P_0$:

$$P_0 = \frac{D_1}{k_s - g} = \frac{\$2}{0.14 - 0.12} = \frac{\$2}{0.02} = \$100.$$

Although CMC has suffered a severe setback, its existing assets will continue to provide a good income stream. More of these earnings should now be passed on to the shareholders, as the slowed internal growth has reduced the need for funds. However, the net result is a decrease in the value of the shares of 33.3 percent.

d. If the payout ratio were held at 20 percent even after internal investment opportunities had declined, the price of the stock would drop to $2/(0.14 - 0.06) = $25 rather than to $66.67. Thus, the increase in dividend payout is consistent with maximizing shareholder wealth.

Due to the downward-sloping IOS curve (see Figure 16-4), the greater the firm's level of investment, the lower the average ROE. Thus, if CMC retains and invests more money, its average ROE will decline further. We can determine the average ROE under different conditions as follows:

*Old Situation (with Founder Alive and a 20 Percent Payout):*

$$g = (1.0 - \text{Payout ratio})\text{Average ROE}$$
$$12\% = (1.0 - 0.2)\text{Average ROE}$$
$$\text{Average ROE} = 12\%/0.8 = 15\% > k_s = 14\%.$$

Note that the *average* ROE is 15 percent while the *marginal* ROE is presumably equal to 14 percent.

*New Situation (with Founder Dead and a 60 Percent Payout):*

$$g = 6\% = (1.0 - 0.6)\text{ROE}$$
$$\text{ROE} = 6\%/0.4 = 15\% > k_s = 14\%.$$

This suggests that the new payout is appropriate and that the firm is taking on investments down to the point where marginal returns are equal to the cost of capital. Note, however, that if the 20 percent payout were maintained, the *average* ROE would be only 7.5 percent, which would imply that the marginal ROE was far below the 14 percent cost of capital.

## Selected Additional References and Cases

Dividend policy has been studied extensively by academicians. The first major academic work, and still a highly recommended classic, is Lintner's analysis of how corporations actually set their dividend payment policies:

Lintner, John, "Distribution of Incomes of Corporations among Dividends, Retained Earnings, and Taxes," *American Economic Review*, May 1956, 97-113.

The effects of dividend policy on stock prices and capital costs have been examined by many researchers. The classic theoretical argument that dividend policy is important and that stock-holders like dividends was set forth by Gordon, while Miller and Modigliani (MM) developed the notion that dividend policy is not important. Many researchers have extended both Gordon's and MM's theoretical arguments and have attempted to test the effects of dividend policy in a variety of ways. Although statistical problems have precluded definitive conclusions, the following articles, among others, have helped to clarify the issues:

Baker, H. Kent, Gail E. Farrelly, and Richard B. Edelman, "A Survey of Management Views on Dividend Policy," *Financial Management*, Autumn 1985, 78-84.

Hayes, Linda S., "Fresh Evidence That Dividends Don't Matter," *Fortune*, May 4, 1981, 351-354.

Lewellen, Wilbur G., Kenneth L. Stanley, Ronald C. Lease, and Gary G. Schlarbaum, "Some Direct Evidence on the Dividend Clientele Phenomenon," *Journal of Finance*, December 1978, 1385-1399.

Mukherjee, Tarun J., and Larry M. Austin, "An Empirical Investigation of Small Bank Stock Valuation and Dividend Policy," *Financial Management*, Spring 1980, 27-31.

On stock dividends and stock splits, see:

Baker, H. Kent, Gail E. Farrelly, and Richard B. Edelman, "A Survey of Management Views on Dividend Policy," *Financial Management*, Autumn 1985, 78-84.

Copeland, Thomas E., "Liquidity Changes Following Stock Splits," *Journal of Finance*, March 1979, 115-141.

The following cases from the Crum-Brigham casebook focus on the issues contained in this chapter:

Case 35, "Hansen Mineral Resources, Inc.," which emphasizes the effect of dividend policy on stock price.

Case 36, "Warner Body Works," which deals with virtually all aspects of dividend policy.

The following Harrington case is also appropriate for this chapter:

"New Hampshire Savings Bank Corporation," which illustrates the traditional issues that are discussed when a board of directors attempts to establish a company's dividend policy.

## APPENDIX 16A

# Stock Repurchases

The April 29, 1985, issue of *Fortune* contained an article entitled "Beating the Market by Buying Back Stock." It went on to discuss the fact that during 1984 over 600 major companies had repurchased significant amounts of their own stock. It also gave illustrations of some specific companies' repurchase programs and their effects. The article's conclusion was that "buybacks have made a mint for shareholders who stuck with the companies carrying them out." This appendix explains what repurchases are, how they are carried out, and how the financial manager should analyze a possible repurchase program.

There are really two principal types of repurchases: (1) situations in which the firm has cash available for distribution to its stockholders, and it distributes this cash by repurchasing shares rather than by paying cash dividends, and (2) situations in which the firm concludes that its capital structure is too heavily weighted with equity, and therefore it sells debt and uses the proceeds to buy back its stock.

Stock that has been repurchased by a firm is called *treasury stock*. If some of the outstanding stock is repurchased, fewer shares will remain outstanding. Assuming the repurchase does not adversely affect the firm's earnings, the earnings per share on the remaining shares will increase, resulting in a higher market price per share. Capital gains, then, will have been substituted for dividends.

## The Effects of Stock Repurchases

Many companies have been repurchasing their stock in recent years. Until recently, most repurchases amounted to a few million dollars, but in 1984 Standard Oil of Indiana announced plans for the largest repurchase on record—30 million of its shares at a price of about $60 per share, or about $1.8 billion in total. Almost simultaneously, Teledyne announced plans to buy back another 8.7 million of its shares at a price of $200 per share for a total of $1.7 billion. Other large repurchases have been made by Texaco, IBM, CBS, and Coca Cola.

The effects of a repurchase can be illustrated with data on American Development Corporation (ADC). The company earned $4.4 million in 1985, and 50 percent of this amount, or $2.2 million, had been allocated for distribution to common shareholders. There were 1.1 million shares outstanding, and the market price was $20 a share. ADC felt that it could either use the $2.2 million to repurchase 100,000 of its shares through a tender offer for $22 a share or it could pay a cash dividend of $2 a share.[1]

The effect of the repurchase on the EPS and market price per share of the remaining stock can be determined in the following way:

---

[1] Stock repurchases are commonly made in one of three ways. First, a publicly owned firm can simply buy its own stock through a broker on the open market. Second, it can issue a *tender offer* under which it would permit stockholders to send in (that is, "tender") their shares to the firm in exchange for a specified price per share. When a firm makes a tender offer, it generally indicates that it will buy up a specified number of shares within a particular time period (usually about two weeks); if more shares are tendered than the company wishes to purchase, then purchases are made on a pro rata basis. Finally, the firm can purchase a block of shares from one large holder on a negotiated basis. If a negotiated purchase is employed, care must be taken to

1. Current EPS $= \dfrac{\text{Total earnings}}{\text{Number of shares}} = \dfrac{\$4.4 \text{ million}}{1.1 \text{ million}} = \$4$ per share.

2. P/E ratio $= \dfrac{\$20}{\$4} = 5\times$.

3. EPS after repurchase of 100,000 shares $= \dfrac{\$4.4 \text{ million}}{1 \text{ million}} = \$4.40$ per share.

4. Expected market price after repurchase $= (P/E)(EPS) = (5)(\$4.40)$
$$= \$22 \text{ per share.}$$

   It should be noted from this example that investors would receive benefits of $2 per share in any case, in the form of either a $2 cash dividend or a $2 increase in the stock price. This result would occur because we assumed that (1) shares could be repurchased at exactly $22 a share and (2) the P/E ratio would remain constant. If shares could be bought for less than $22, the operation would be even better for *remaining* stockholders, but the reverse would hold if ADC paid more than $22 a share. Furthermore, the P/E ratio might change as a result of the repurchase operation, rising if investors viewed it favorably and falling if they viewed it unfavorably. Some factors that might affect P/E ratios are considered next.

## Advantages of Repurchases from the Stockholder's Viewpoint

From the stockholder's viewpoint, advantages of repurchases are as follows:

1. Profits earned on repurchases are typically taxed at the capital gains rate, whereas a dividend distribution is taxed at the personal tax rate. This is significant. For example, it has been estimated that on average individual stockholders pay a tax of about 45 percent on marginal income. Since the capital gains tax rate is only 40 percent of the personal tax rate, the typical shareholder clearly benefits, other things the same, if the distribution is in the form of a stock repurchase rather than a dividend. Teledyne, a $3 billion conglomerate, earns about $400 million per year, yet has not paid a cash dividend in 20 years and is not expected to do so in the foreseeable future. Profits are, however, used to repurchase stock and thus stimulate growth in earnings per share. Teledyne's stock rose from $4 in 1975 to over $300 in 1985, so the company is clearly doing something right!

2. The stockholder has a choice—to sell or not to sell. On the other hand, one must accept a dividend payment and pay the tax. Thus, those Teledyne stockholders who need cash can sell some of their shares, while those who do not can simply retain their stock. From a tax standpoint, both types of stockholders come out ahead.

---

insure that this one stockholder will not receive preferential treatment over other stockholders, or that any preference given can be justified by "sound business reasons." In 1984, Texaco's management was being sued by stockholders who were unhappy over the company's repurchase of about $600 million of stock from the Bass Brothers' interests at a substantial premium over the market price. The suit charges that Texaco's management, afraid the Bass Brothers would attempt a takeover, used the buyback to get them off its back. Such payments have been dubbed "greenmail."

**3.** A qualitative advantage advanced by market practitioners is that a repurchase can often remove a large block of stock which is overhanging the market and keeping the price per share down.

## Advantages of Repurchases from Management's Viewpoint

From management's viewpoint, the major advantages of repurchases are these:

**1.** As noted in Chapter 16, dividends are "sticky" in the short run because managements are reluctant to raise them if the new dividend cannot be maintained in the future—managements dislike cutting cash dividends. Hence, if the excess cash flow is thought to be only temporary, management may prefer to make the distribution in the form of a share repurchase rather than to declare a cash dividend that cannot be maintained.

**2.** Repurchased stock can be used for acquisitions or to provide shares when stock options are exercised, when convertibles are converted, or when warrants are exercised. Discussions with financial managers indicate that they often like to use repurchased stock rather than newly issued stock for these purposes in order to avoid dilution in earnings per share.

**3.** If directors have large holdings themselves, they may have especially strong preferences for repurchases rather than dividend payments because of the tax factor.

**4.** Repurchases can be used to effect large-scale changes in capital structures. For example, in 1985 Consolidated Edison decided to repurchase up to $400 million of its common stock in order to reduce its equity ratio. The repurchase was necessary because even if the company financed its capital budget only with debt, it would have taken years to get the debt ratio up to the new target level. Con Ed decided to sell long-term debt and to use the proceeds to repurchase its common stock, thus producing an instantaneous change in its capital structure.

**5.** Repurchases have also been used in two ways to help ward off hostile takeovers. For example, Seagram Company made an offer of $45 per share for St. Joe Minerals' common stock. St. Joe's management then borrowed heavily and used the funds to make a repurchase offer for 7 million of its shares at $60 per share; thus, it held off Seagram. Another type of takeover-related repurchase is represented by Disney's repurchase of its stock from Saul Steinberg and Mobil's repurchase from T. Boone Pickens. These "raiders" had acquired stock in Disney and Mobil and had announced plans to take the companies over. Management bought them out, paying a premium price which is often called "greenmail."

## Disadvantages of Repurchases from the Stockholder's Viewpoint

From the stockholder's viewpoint, disadvantages of repurchases include the following:

**1.** Stockholders may not be indifferent between the choices of dividends and capital gains, and the price of the stock might benefit more from cash dividends than from repurchases. Cash dividends are generally thought to be relatively dependable, but repurchases are not. Further, if a firm announces a regular, dependable repurchase program, the improper accumulation tax would probably become more of a threat. Although Teledyne has apparently had no problems in this regard, its repurchases are irregular, which may make a difference.

**2.** The *selling* stockholders either may not be fully aware of all the implications of a repurchase or they may not have all pertinent information about the corporation's present and future activities. Therefore, firms generally announce a repurchase program before embarking on it to avoid potential stockholder suits.

**3.** The corporation may pay too high a price for the repurchased stock, to the disadvantage of remaining stockholders. If the shares are inactively traded, and if the firm seeks to acquire a relatively large amount of its own stock, the price may be bid above a maintainable price and then fall after the firm ceases its repurchase operations.

## Disadvantages of Repurchases from Management's Viewpoint

From management's viewpoint, disadvantages of repurchases are as follows:

**1.** Some people have argued that firms which repurchase substantial amounts of stock often have poorer growth rates and fewer good investment opportunities than firms which do not engage in repurchases. Thus, to some extent, announcing a repurchase program is like announcing that management cannot locate good investment projects. One could argue that instituting a repurchase program should be regarded in the same manner as announcing a higher dividend payout; however, if it is true that repurchases are regarded as indicating especially unfavorable growth opportunities, then they could have an adverse impact on the firm's image and therefore on the price of its stock. In our view, there is little empirical support for this position—indeed, the available evidence is very much to the contrary.

**2.** Repurchases might involve some risk from a legal standpoint. If the Internal Revenue Service established that the primary purpose of the repurchases was to avoid paying taxes on dividends, then penalties could be imposed on the firm under the improper accumulation of earnings provision of the Tax Code. Congress would also probably act if tax avoidance implications were blatant. IRS suits have been brought against privately held companies, but no actions have been instituted against publicly owned firms, even though some have retired over one-half of their outstanding stock.

**3.** The SEC could raise questions if it appears that the firm may be manipulating the price of its shares. This factor in particular keeps firms from doing much repurchasing if they plan offerings of other types of securities in the near future or if they contemplate merger negotiations in which their stock would be exchanged for that of the acquired company.

## Conclusions on Stock Repurchases

When all the pros and cons on stock repurchases have been totaled, where do we stand? Our conclusions may be summarized as follows:

**1.** Repurchases on a regular, systematic, dependable basis may not be feasible because of uncertainties about their tax treatment and such things as the market price of the shares, how many shares would be tendered, and so forth.

**2.** However, repurchases do offer investors some significant tax advantages over dividends and therefore should be given careful consideration on the basis of the firm's unique situation.

**3.** Repurchases can be especially valuable to a firm that wants to make a significant shift in its capital structure within a short period of time.

On balance, companies probably ought to be doing more repurchasing than they are, and distributing less cash as dividends. Increases in the size and frequency of repurchases in recent years suggest that companies are increasingly sharing this conclusion.

# V

# WORKING CAPITAL MANAGEMENT

In prior chapters we dealt primarily with long-run, strategic financial decisions. Now we turn to short-run, operating decisions, or *working capital management*. Chapter 17 discusses working capital policies and the various types of short-term credit that can be used to finance current assets, Chapter 18 analyzes the management of cash and marketable securities, and Chapter 19 considers accounts receivables and inventory management.

# 17

# WORKING CAPITAL POLICY AND SHORT-TERM CREDIT

## AFTER RIDING THE WAVE OF SHORT-TERM INTEREST RATES, TRANSAMERICA'S DEBT EXPENSES TAKE A REFRESHING PLUNGE ·

**Transamerica**

In the early 1970s, Transamerica Corporation, a major financial services company, was financing a significant portion of its total assets with short-term, variable-rate debt. Up until that time short-term rates had generally been lower than long-term rates, and thus Transamerica had reduced its interest expense by following this financing policy. However, in the mid-1970s short-term interest rates soared to unprecedented levels, and Transamerica's interest costs rose equally sharply, contributing to a severe drop in profits. Transamerica's chairman later described the situation as follows:

> In the past two years we have reduced our variable-rate [short-term] debt by about $450 million. We aren't going to go through the enormous increase in debt expense again. The company's earnings fell sharply when money rates rose to record levels because we were almost entirely in variable-rate debt. Now, out of total debt of slightly more than $1 billion, about 65 percent is fixed rate and 35 percent variable. We've come a long way, and we'll keep plugging away at it.

Transamerica's earnings and stock price were hurt by the rise in interest rates, but other companies were even less fortunate—they simply could not pay the rising interest charges, and this forced them into bankruptcy.

Working capital policy involves decisions relating to current assets, including decisions about financing them. Since about 40 percent of the typical firm's capital is invested in current assets, efficient working capital management is vitally important to the firm's profitability.

## Working Capital Terminology

It is useful to begin our discussion of working capital by defining some basic terms and concepts:

**Table 17-1**
**Drexel Card Company:**
**Balance Sheet as of January 1 and June 30, 1986**
**(Thousands of Dollars)**

|  | January 1 | June 30 |  | January 1 | June 30 |
|---|---|---|---|---|---|
| Cash and marketable securities | $ 20 | $ 20 | Accounts payable | $ 30[a] | $ 50[a] |
| Accounts receivable | 80 | 20 | Accrued wages | 15 | 10 |
| Inventories | 100 | 200 | Accrued taxes | 15 | 10 |
|  |  |  | Notes payable | 50 | 80 |
|  |  |  | Current maturities of long-term debt | 40 | 40 |
| Current assets | $200 | $240 | Current liabilities | $150 | $190 |
| Fixed assets | 500 | 500 | Long-term debt | 150 | 140 |
|  |  |  | Stockholders' equity | 400 | 410 |
| Total assets | $700 | $740 | Total claims | $700 | $740 |

[a]DCC takes discounts, so this is "free" trade credit. This point is discussed in detail later in the chapter, but it should be noted here that accounts payable are free to a firm which takes discounts because the firm gets credit but pays no interest on it.

**working capital**
A firm's investment in short-term assets—cash, marketable securities, inventory, and accounts receivable.

**net working capital**
Current assets minus current liabilities.

**1. Working capital**, sometimes called *gross working capital*, simply refers to current assets.[1]

**2. Net working capital** is defined as current assets minus current liabilities.

**3.** One key working capital ratio is the ***current ratio***, which was defined in Chapter 7 as current assets divided by current liabilities. This ratio measures a firm's liquidity, that is, its ability to meet current obligations.

**4.** The ***quick ratio***, or ***acid test***, is current assets less inventories divided by current liabilities. The quick ratio, which also measures liquidity, removes inventories from current assets since they are the least liquid of those assets. It thus provides an "acid test" of a company's ability to meet its current obligations.

**working capital policy**
Basic policy decisions regarding target levels and financing for each category of current assets.

**5. Working capital policy** refers to the firm's basic policies regarding (1) target levels for each category of current assets and (2) how current assets will be financed.

**6.** ***Working capital management*** involves the administration, within policy guidelines, of current assets and current liabilities.

We must also be careful to distinguish between (1) those current liabilities which are specifically used to finance current assets and (2) those current liabilities which represent either current maturities of long-term debt or financing associated with a construction program which will, after the project is completed, be funded with the proceeds of a long-term security issue.

Table 17-1 contains the balance sheets of Drexel Card Company (DCC), a manufacturer of greeting cards, as of January 1 and June 30 of 1986. Note

---

[1]The term *working capital* originated with the old Yankee peddler, who would load up his wagon with goods and then go off on his route to peddle his wares. The merchandise was defined as his "working capital" because it was what he actually sold, or "turned over," to produce his profits; the wagon and horse were his "fixed assets."

that according to the definitions above, DCC's working capital on January 1 is $200,000 while its net working capital is $200,000 − $150,000 = $50,000. Also, DCC's initial current ratio is 1.33, and its initial quick ratio is 0.67. However, the total current liabilities of $150,000 include the current portion of long-term debt, which is $40,000. This account is unaffected by changes in working capital policy, since it is a function of the firm's long-term financing decisions. Thus, even though we define the long-term debt coming due in the next accounting period as a current liability, it is not a working capital decision variable. Similarly, if DCC were building a new factory and financing it with short-term loans that were to be converted to a mortgage bond when the building was completed, the construction loans would be separated from the current liabilities associated with working capital management.

## Requirement for External Working Capital Financing

The manufacture of greeting cards is a seasonal business. In June of each year, DCC begins producing Christmas and New Year cards for sale in the July-November period, and by the end of the year it has sold most of them; thus, its inventories are relatively low at year-end. However, most of its buyers purchase on credit, so the year-end receivables are at a seasonal high. Now look again at Table 17-1, this time at DCC's projected balance sheet for June 30, 1986. Here we see that inventories will be relatively high ($200,000 versus $100,000), as will accounts payable ($50,000 versus $30,000), but receivables are projected to be relatively low ($20,000 versus $80,000).

Now consider what happens to DCC's current assets and current liabilities over the period from January 1 to June 1986. Current assets increase from $200,000 to $240,000, so the firm must finance this $40,000 projected increase. However, at the same time, payables and accruals will spontaneously increase by $10,000—from $30,000 + $15,000 + $15,000 = $60,000 to $50,000 + $10,000 + $10,000 = $70,000—which will leave a $30,000 projected working capital financing requirement. This requirement could be obtained from various sources, but typically such seasonal needs are met by bank financing; thus, we assume the $30,000 will be obtained from the bank. Therefore, on June 30, 1986, we show notes payable of $80,000, up from $50,000 on January 1.

The fluctuations in DCC's working capital position shown in Table 17-1 resulted from seasonal variations. Similar fluctuations in working capital requirements, and hence in financing needs, also occur over business cycles—such needs typically contract during recessions and expand during booms. In the following sections we look in more detail at working capital variations, at alternative strategies for establishing the target level of current assets, and at strategies for financing current assets.

## The Working Capital Cash Flow Cycle

The concept of the *working capital cash flow cycle* is important in working capital management. This cycle can be described for a typical manufacturing firm as follows. (1) The firm orders and then receives the raw materials which it needs to produce the goods it expects to sell; since firms usually purchase their raw materials on credit, this transaction creates an account payable. (2) Labor is used to convert the raw materials into finished goods; to the extent that wages are not fully paid at the time the work is done, accrued wages build up. (3) The finished goods are sold, usually on credit, which creates receivables; no cash has been received yet. (4) At some point during the cycle, accounts payable and accruals must be paid, usually before the receivables have been collected, so a net cash drain occurs and must be financed. (5) The working capital cash flow cycle is completed when the firm's receivables have been collected; at this point, the firm is ready to repeat the cycle and/or pay off the loans that were used to finance the cycle.

Verlyn Richards and Eugene Laughlin developed a useful approach to analyzing the working capital cash cycle.[2] Their approach centers on the conversion of operating events to cash flows, and it is thus called the **cash conversion cycle** model. Here are some terms used in the model:

**cash conversion cycle** The length of time between the purchase of raw materials and the collection of accounts receivable generated in the sale of the final product.

1. *Inventory conversion period*, which is the average length of time required to convert raw materials into finished goods, and then to sell these goods.

2. *Receivables conversion period*, which is the average length of time required to convert the firm's receivables into cash, that is, to collect cash following a sale.

3. *Payables deferral period*, which is the length of time between the purchase of raw materials and the cash payment for them.

4. *Cash conversion cycle*, which is the length of time between actual cash expenditures on productive resources (raw materials and labor) and actual cash receipts from the sale of products, that is, from the day labor and/or suppliers are paid to the day receivables are collected.

Now we can use these definitions to analyze the cash conversion cycle. First, the concept is diagrammed in Figure 17-1. Each component is given a number, and the cash conversion cycle can be expressed by this equation:

$$
\underset{(1)}{\substack{\text{Inventory} \\ \text{conversion} \\ \text{period}}} + \underset{(2)}{\substack{\text{Receivables} \\ \text{conversion} \\ \text{period}}} - \underset{(3)}{\substack{\text{Payables} \\ \text{deferral} \\ \text{period}}} = \underset{(4)}{\substack{\text{Cash} \\ \text{conversion} \\ \text{cycle.}}}
$$

---

[2]See Verlyn D. Richards and Eugene J. Laughlin, "A Cash Conversion Cycle Approach to Liquidity Analysis," *Financial Management*, Spring 1980, 32-38. A similar approach was set forth earlier by Lawrence J. Gitman, "Estimating Corporate Liquidity Requirements: A Simplified Approach," *The Financial Review*, 1974, 79-88.

**Figure 17-1**
**The Cash Conversion Cycle**

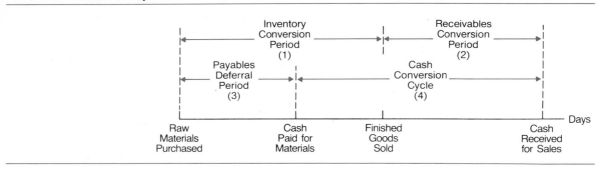

To illustrate, suppose it takes an average of 50 days to convert raw materials to inventory and to sell the goods, and 40 days to collect on receivables, while 30 days normally lapse between purchase of materials and payment of the associated account payable. In this case, the cash conversion cycle is 60 days:

$$50 \text{ days} + 40 \text{ days} - 30 \text{ days} = 60 \text{ days.}$$

Given these data, the firm knows when it receives an order that it will have to finance the costs of processing the order for a 60-day period. The firm's goal should be to shorten the cash conversion cycle as much as possible without hurting operations. This would improve profits, because the longer the cash conversion cycle, the greater the need for external financing—and such financing has a cost.

The cash conversion cycle can be shortened (1) by reducing the inventory conversion period, that is, by processing and selling goods more quickly, (2) by reducing the receivables conversion period, that is, by speeding up collections, or (3) by lengthening the payables deferral period, that is, by slowing down its own payments. To the extent that these actions can be taken *without increasing costs or depressing sales*, they should be carried out. You should keep the cash conversion cycle in mind as we go through the remainder of this chapter and the other working capital chapters.

## Working Capital Investment and Financing Policies

Working capital policy involves two basic questions: (1) What is the appropriate level of current assets, both in total and by specific accounts? (2) How should the required level of current assets be financed? In this section we examine alternative policies regarding (1) the level of investment in current assets and (2) the maturities of the liabilities used to finance those assets.

## Alternative Current Asset Investment Policies

Figure 17-2 depicts three alternative policies regarding the level of current assets. Essentially, these policies differ in that different amounts of working capital are carried to support any given level of sales. The line with the steepest slope in Figure 17-2 represents a relatively "loose" working capital policy. The word "loose" as used here has no negative connotation; we mean merely that relatively large amounts of cash, marketable securities, and inventories are carried, and that sales are stimulated by the use of a credit policy which provides liberal financing to customers and a corresponding high level of receivables. Conversely, under the "tight" policy the holdings of cash, securities, inventories, and receivables are minimized. The moderate policy is between the two extremes.

Under conditions of certainty—when sales, costs, order lead times, collection periods, and so on are known for sure—all firms would hold the same

**Figure 17-2**
**Alternative Current Asset Investment Policies**
**(Millions of Dollars)**

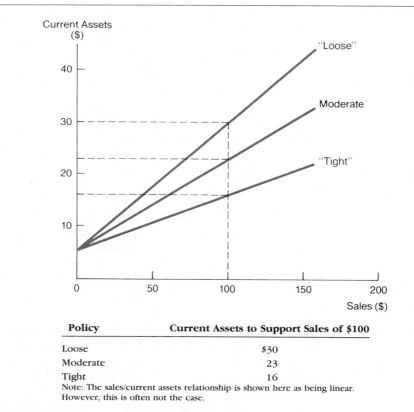

| Policy | Current Assets to Support Sales of $100 |
|---|---|
| Loose | $30 |
| Moderate | 23 |
| Tight | 16 |

Note: The sales/current assets relationship is shown here as being linear. However, this is often not the case.

level of current assets. Any larger amounts would increase the need for external funding without a corresponding increase in profits, while any smaller holdings would involve late payments to suppliers, lost sales, and production inefficiencies because of inventory shortages.

However, the picture changes when uncertainty is introduced. Here the firm requires some minimum amount of cash and inventories based on expected payments, sales, order lead times, and so on, plus additional amounts, or *safety stocks*, to account for variances from expected values. Similarly, accounts receivable are based on credit terms, and the tougher those terms, the lower the receivables for any given level of sales. With a tight working capital policy, the firm would hold minimal levels of safety stocks for cash and inventories, and it would have a tight credit policy even though this meant running the risk of a decline in sales. Generally, a tight policy provides the highest expected return on investment, but also the greatest risk, while the reverse is true under a loose policy. The moderate policy falls in between the two extremes in terms of expected risk and return.

The policy with regard to the level of current assets is never set in a vacuum—it is always established in conjunction with the firm's working capital financing policy. This is the topic we consider next.

## Alternative Financing Policies

Most businesses experience seasonal and/or cyclical fluctuations. For example, construction firms have peaks in the spring and summer, retail sales often peak around Christmas, and manufacturers who supply either construction companies or retailers follow patterns similar to those of their customers. Similarly, virtually all businesses must build up working capital when the economy is strong, but their inventories and receivables fall when the economy slacks off. However, even when business is seasonally or cyclically low, current assets do not drop to zero; this realization has led to the development of the idea of **permanent current assets**, diagrammed in Figure 17-3. Applying this idea to DCC, Table 17-1 suggests that DCC's total assets fluctuate between $700,000 and $740,000. Thus, DCC has $700,000 in permanent assets, composed of $500,000 of fixed assets plus a minimum of $200,000 in current assets—defined as the *permanent level of current assets*—plus additional seasonal, or **temporary**, **current assets** which fluctuate from zero to a maximum of $40,000. The manner in which the permanent and temporary current assets are financed constitutes the firm's *working capital financing policy*.

**permanent current assets**
Current assets that are still on hand at the trough of a firm's cycles.

**temporary current assets**
Current assets that fluctuate with seasonal or cyclical variations in a firm's business.

***Maturity Matching.*** One commonly used financing policy is that of matching asset and liability maturities as shown in Panel a of Figure 17-3. This strategy reduces the risk that the firm will be unable to pay off its maturing obligations. To illustrate, suppose a firm borrows $1 million at 10 percent on a 1-year basis and uses the funds obtained to build and equip a plant. It expects to earn 15 percent after taxes on its investment and will depreciate the building by the straight line method over 20 years. Thus, expected cash

**Figure 17-3**
**Alternative Current Asset Financing Policies**

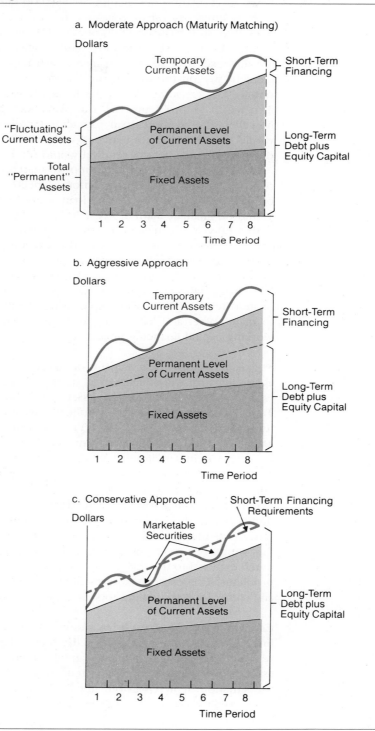

flows are $150,000 net income + $50,000 depreciation = $200,000. However, it must pay off or refinance the $1 million loan plus pay interest of $100,000, so it has cash flows of $200,000 versus a cash requirement of $1.1 million. In this case, as in most similar situations in which long-term assets are financed with short-term loans, cash flows from the plant are not sufficient to pay off the loan at the end of only one year, so the loan must be renewed. If for some reason the lender refuses to renew the loan, then the firm will have problems. Had the plant been financed with long-term debt, however, the required loan payments (interest plus part of the principal) would have been better matched with cash flows from profits and depreciation, and the problem of renewal would not have arisen.

At the limit, a firm could attempt to match exactly the maturity structure of its assets and liabilities. Inventory expected to be sold in 30 days would be financed with a 30-day bank loan; a machine expected to last for 5 years would be financed with a 5-year loan; a 20-year building would be financed with a 20-year mortgage bond; and so forth. Actually, of course, uncertainty about the lives of assets prevents this exact maturity matching in an ex post sense. For example, a firm may finance inventories with a 30-day loan, expecting to sell the inventories and to use the cash generated to retire the loan. But if sales are slow, the cash will be not be forthcoming, and the use of short-term credit may end up causing a problem. Still, if the firm attempted to match asset and liability maturities, we would define this as a moderate working capital financing policy.

***Aggressive Approach.*** Panel b of Figure 17-3 illustrates the situation for an aggressive firm which finances all of its fixed assets with long-term capital but part of its permanent current assets with short-term credit. A look back at Table 17-1 will show that DCC follows this strategy. Even at the low point in its operations, DCC has $200,000 of current assets plus $500,000 of fixed assets, or $700,000 of permanent assets. At the same time, its equity plus long-term debt (including the current portion of long-term debt) is only about $590,000, so about $110,000 of short-term credit is being used to finance permanent assets.

Returning to Figure 17-3, the dashed line in Panel b could have been drawn *below* the line designating fixed assets, indicating that all of the current assets plus part of the fixed assets were financed with short-term credit; this would be a risky, nonconservative position, and the firm would be very much exposed to the danger of rising interest rates as well as to loan renewal problems. However, short-term debt is often cheaper than long-term debt, and some firms are willing to sacrifice safety for the chance of higher profits.

***Conservative Approach.*** As shown in Panel c of Figure 17-3, the dashed line could also be drawn *above* the line designating permanent current assets, indicating that permanent capital is being used to finance all permanent asset requirements and also to meet some or all of the seasonal demands. In the situation depicted in our graph, the firm uses a small amount of short-term credit to meet its peak requirements, but it also meets a part of its seasonal needs by "storing liquidity" in the form of marketable securities during the off-season. The humps above the dashed line represent short-term financing; the troughs below it represent short-term security holdings. Panel c represents a very safe, conservative working capital financing policy.

## Advantages and Disadvantages of Short-Term Credit

The distinction among the three possible financing policies described above was the relative amount of short-term debt financing used under each. The aggressive policy called for the greatest amount of short-term debt, the conservative policy required the least, and maturity matching fell in between. Although using short-term credit is generally riskier than using long-term credit, short-term credit does have some significant advantages. The advantages and disadvantages of short-term credit are considered in this section.

### Speed

A short-term loan can be obtained much more quickly than a long-term loan. Lenders will insist on a more thorough financial examination before granting long-term credit, and the loan agreement will have to be spelled out in considerably more detail because a lot can happen during the life of a 10- to 20-year loan. Therefore, if funds are needed in a hurry, the firm should look to the short-term markets.

### Flexibility

If its needs for funds are seasonal or cyclical, a firm may not want to commit itself to long-term debt for the following reasons. (1) Flotation costs are generally much higher for long-term debt. (2) While long-term debt can be repaid early provided the loan agreement includes a prepayment provision, prepayment penalties can be expensive; accordingly, if a firm thinks its need for funds will diminish in the near future, it should choose short-term debt for the flexibility it provides. (3) Long-term loan agreements always contain provisions, or covenants, which constrain the firm's future actions, but short-term credit agreements are generally less restrictive.

### Cost of Long-Term versus Short-Term Debt

In Chapter 3, we saw that the yield curve is normally upward sloping, indicating that interest rates are generally lower on short-term than on long-term debt. Thus, under normal conditions, interest expense at the time the funds are obtained will be lower if the firm borrows on a short-term rather than a long-term basis.

### Risk to the Borrower

Even though short-term debt is often less expensive than long-term debt, financing with short-term debt subjects the borrowing firm to greater risk than does financing with long-term debt. This added risk occurs for two reasons. (1) If a firm borrows on a long-term basis, its interest costs will be fixed and therefore stable over time, but if it uses short-term credit, its interest expense will fluctuate widely, at times going quite high. The Transamerica example cited at the beginning of the chapter illustrated that risk. (2) If a firm borrows heavily on a short-term basis, it may find itself unable to repay this debt, and it may be in such a weak financial position that the lender will not extend the loan; this could force the firm into bankruptcy. Braniff Airlines, which failed during a recent credit crunch, is an example.

Statements about the flexibility, cost, and riskiness of short-term versus long-term credit depend to a large extent on the nature of the short-term credit that is actually used. To make these distinctions clear, the major types of short-term credit are discussed in the following sections.

## Accruals

**accruals**
Continually recurring short-term liabilities.

Since firms generally pay employees on a weekly, biweekly, or monthly basis, a balance sheet will typically show some accrued wages. Similarly, the firm's own estimated income taxes, plus social security and income taxes withheld from employee payrolls, and sales taxes collected, are generally paid on a weekly, monthly, or quarterly basis, so the balance sheet will typically show some accrued taxes along with its accrued wages. These **accruals** increase automatically as a firm's operations expand. Further, this type of debt is "free" in the sense that no explicit interest is paid on funds raised through it. However, a firm cannot ordinarily control its accruals: Payrolls and the timing of wage payments are set by economic forces and industry custom, while tax payment dates are established by law. Thus, firms use all the accruals they can, but they have little control over the level of these accounts.

## Accounts Payable, or Trade Credit

**trade credit**
Interfirm debt arising through credit sales and recorded as an account receivable by the seller and as an account payable by the buyer.

Firms generally make purchases from other firms on credit, recording the debt as an *account payable*. Accounts payable, or **trade credit**, as it is commonly called, is the largest single category of short-term debt, representing about 40 percent of the current liabilities of the average nonfinancial corporation. This percentage is somewhat larger for smaller firms—because small companies often do not qualify for financing from other sources, they rely especially heavily on trade credit.[3]

---

[3] In a credit sale, the seller records the transaction as a receivable and the buyer does so as a payable. We will examine accounts receivable as an asset investment in Chapter 19. Our focus in this chapter is on accounts payable, a liability item. We might also note that if a firm's accounts payable exceed its receivables, it is said to be *receiving net trade credit*, while if its receivables exceed its payables, it is *extending net trade credit*. Smaller firms frequently receive net credit, while larger firms extend it.

Trade credit is a spontaneous source of financing in the sense that it arises from ordinary business transactions. For example, suppose a firm makes average purchases of $2,000 a day on terms of "net 30," meaning that it must pay for goods 30 days after the invoice date. On average it will owe 30 times $2,000, or $60,000, to its suppliers. If its sales, and consequently its purchases, were to double, then its accounts payable would also double, to $120,000. Simply by growing, the firm would have spontaneously generated an additional $60,000 of financing. Similarly, if the terms under which it bought goods were extended from 30 to 40 days, its accounts payable would expand from $60,000 to $80,000, so lengthening the credit period, as well as expanding sales and purchases, generates additional financing.

## The Cost of Trade Credit

Firms that sell on credit have a *credit policy* that includes certain *terms of credit*. For example, Porter Electronics sells on terms of "2/10, net 30," meaning that a 2 percent discount is given if payment is made within 10 days of the invoice date, and the full invoice amount is due and payable within 30 days if the discount is not taken.

Suppose Pineapple Computers, Inc., buys an average of $12 million of electronic components from Porter each year, less a 2 percent discount, for net purchases of $11,760,000/360 = $32,666.67 per day. For simplicity, suppose Porter is Pineapple's only supplier. If Pineapple takes the discount, paying at the end of the tenth day, its payables will average (10)($32,666.67) = $326,667; it will on average be receiving $326,667 of credit from its only supplier, Porter Electronics Company.

Now suppose Pineapple decides *not* to take the discount—what will happen? First, Pineapple will begin paying invoices after 30 days, so its accounts payable will increase to (30)($32,666.67) = $980,000.[4] Porter Electronics will now be supplying Pineapple with an *additional* $653,333 of credit. Pineapple could use this additional credit to pay off bank loans, to expand inventories, to increase fixed assets, to build up its cash account, or even to increase its own accounts receivable.

Pineapple's new credit from Porter Electronics has a cost—since Pineapple is forgoing a 2 percent discount on its $12 million of purchases, its costs will rise by $240,000 per year. Dividing this $240,000 by the additional credit, we find the implicit cost of the added trade credit as follows:

$$\text{Approximate percentage cost} = \frac{\$240,000}{\$653,333} = 36.7\%.$$

---

[4]A question arises here: Should accounts payable reflect gross purchases or purchases net of discounts if a company does not plan to take discounts? Although generally accepted accounting practices permit either treatment, most accountants prefer recording both inventories and payables net of discounts and then reporting the higher payments that result from not taking discounts as an additional expense, called "discounts lost." *Thus, we show accounts payable net of discounts even when the company does not expect to take the discount.*

Assuming that Pineapple can borrow from its bank (or from other sources) at an interest rate of less than 36.7 percent, it should not expand its payables by forgoing discounts.

The following equation may be used to calculate the approximate percentage cost, on an annual basis, of not taking discounts:

$$\begin{array}{l} \text{Approximate} \\ \text{percentage} \\ \text{cost} \end{array} = \frac{\text{Discount percent}}{100 - \text{Discount percent}} \times \frac{360}{\begin{array}{c} \text{Days credit is} \\ \text{outstanding} - \text{Discount} \\ \text{period} \end{array}}. \quad \textbf{(17-1)}$$

The numerator of the first term, discount percent, is the cost per dollar of credit, while the denominator (100 − discount percent) represents the funds made available by not taking the discount. The second term shows how many times each year this cost is incurred. To illustrate the equation, the approximate cost of not taking a discount when the terms are 2/10, net 30, is computed as follows:[5]

$$\text{Approximate percentage cost} = \frac{2}{98} \times \frac{360}{20} = 0.0204(18)$$

$$= 0.367 = 36.7\%.$$

Notice, however, that the cost of trade credit can be reduced by paying late. Thus, if Pineapple can get away with paying in 60 days rather than in the specified 30, then the effective credit period becomes 60 − 10 = 50 days, and the approximate cost drops from 36.7 percent to (2/98)(360/50) = 14.7%. In periods of excess capacity, firms may be able to get away with late payments, but they may also suffer a variety of problems associated with **"stretching" accounts payable** and being branded a "slow payer" account. These problems are discussed later in the chapter.

**stretching payables**
The practice of deliberately paying accounts payable late.

The cost of the additional trade credit obtained by not taking discounts can be worked out for other purchase terms. Some illustrative costs are shown below:

| Credit Terms | Approximate Cost |
|---|---|
| 1/10, net 20 | 36% |
| 1/10, net 30 | 18 |
| 2/10, net 20 | 73 |
| 3/15, net 45 | 37 |

---

[5]In effective annual interest terms, the rate is even higher. In the case of trade discounts, the discount amounts to interest, and with terms of 2/10, net 30, the firm gains use of the funds for 30 − 10 = 20 days, so there are 360/20 = 18 "interest periods" per year. The first term in our equation is (Discount percent)/(100 − Discount percent) = 0.02/0.98 = 0.0204. This "interest rate" is the periodic rate which is "paid" 18 times each year, so the effective annual rate cost of trade credit is

$$\text{Effective rate} = (1.0204)^{18} - 1.0 = 1.438 - 1.0 = 43.8\%.$$

Thus, it could be argued that the 36.7 percent cost calculated by the approximation formula, Equation 17-1, understates the true cost of trade credit. Equation 17-1 would be correct if the cost of the discounts was incurred at the end of the year, but in actuality these costs are incurred all during the year.

As these figures show, the cost of not taking discounts can be substantial. Incidentally, throughout the chapter we assume that payments are made either on the *last day* for taking discounts or on the *last day* of the credit period unless otherwise noted. It would be foolish to pay, say, on the fifth day or on the twentieth day if the credit terms were 2/10, net 30.

## Effects of Trade Credit on the Financial Statements

A firm's policy with regard to taking or not taking discounts can have a significant effect on its financial statements. To illustrate, let us assume that Pineapple is just beginning its operations. On the first day, it makes net purchases of $32,666.67; this amount is recorded on its balance sheet under accounts payable.[6] The second day it buys another $32,666.67. The first day's purchases are not yet paid for, so at the end of the second day accounts payable total $65,333.34. Accounts payable increase by another $32,666.67 on the third day, for a total of $98,000, and after 10 days they are up to $326,667.

If Pineapple takes discounts, then on the eleventh day it will have to pay for the $32,666.67 of purchases made on the first day, which will reduce accounts payable. However, it will buy another $32,666.67, which will increase payables. Thus, after the tenth day of operations, Pineapple's balance sheet will level off, showing a balance of $326,667 in accounts payable, assuming that the company pays on the tenth day in order to take discounts.

Now suppose Pineapple decides not to take discounts. In this case, on the eleventh day it will add another $32,666.67 to payables, but it will not pay for the purchases made on the first day. Thus, the balance sheet figure for accounts payable will rise to $(11)($32,666.67) = $359,333.37$. This buildup will continue through the thirtieth day, at which point payables will total $(30)($32,666.67) = $980,000$. On the thirty-first day, Pineapple will buy another $32,667 of goods, thus increasing accounts payable, but it will also pay for the purchases made the first day, which will reduce payables. Thus, the balance sheet item accounts payable will stabilize at $980,000 after 30 days, assuming Pineapple does not take discounts.

Part I of Table 17-2 shows Pineapple's balance sheet, after it reaches a steady state, under the two trade credit policies. Total assets are unchanged by this policy decision, and we also assume that the accruals and common equity accounts are unchanged. The differences show up in accounts payable and notes payable; when Pineapple elects to take discounts and thus gives up some of the trade credit it otherwise could have obtained, it will have to raise $653,333 from some other source. It could have sold more common stock or used long-term bonds, but it chose to use bank credit, which has a 10 percent cost and is reflected in the notes payable account.

Part II of Table 17-2 shows Pineapple's income statement under the two policies. If the company does not take discounts, then its interest expense will be zero but it will have a $240,000 expense for discounts lost. On the other hand, if it does take discounts, it will incur an interest expense of

---

[6]Inventories also increase by $32,666.67, but we are not now concerned with this account.

**Table 17-2**
**Pineapple Computers' Financial Statements**
**with Different Trade Credit Policies**

|  | Does Not Take Discounts; Uses Maximum Trade Credit | Takes Discounts; Borrows from Bank | Difference |
|---|---|---|---|
| **I. Balance Sheets** | | | |
| Cash | $     500,000 | $     500,000 | $            0 |
| Receivables | 1,000,000 | 1,000,000 | 0 |
| Inventories | 2,000,000 | 2,000,000 | 0 |
| Fixed assets | 2,980,000 | 2,980,000 | 0 |
| Total assets | $  6,480,000 | $  6,480,000 | $            0 |
| Accounts payable | $     980,000 | $     326,667 | $ + 653,333 |
| Notes payable | 0 | 653,333 | − 653,333 |
| Accruals | 500,000 | 500,000 | 0 |
| Common equity | 5,000,000 | 5,000,000 | 0 |
| Total claims | $  6,480,000 | $  6,480,000 | $            0 |
| **II. Income Statements** | | | |
| Sales | $15,000,000 | $15,000,000 | $            0 |
| Less:   Purchases | 11,760,000 | 11,760,000 | 0 |
|           Labor | 2,000,000 | 2,000,000 | 0 |
| Interest | 0 | 65,333 | − 65,333 |
| Discounts lost | 240,000 | 0 | + 240,000 |
| Net income before tax | $  1,000,000 | $  1,174,667 | $ + 174,667 |
| Tax (40%) | 400,000 | 469,867 | + 69,867 |
| Net income | $     600,000 | $     704,800 | $ + 104,800 |

$65,333, but it will avoid the cost of discounts lost. Since discounts lost will exceed the interest expense, the take-discounts policy will result in the higher net income and thus in a higher stock price.

## Components of Trade Credit: Free versus Costly

Based on the preceding discussion, trade credit can be divided into two components: (1) **free trade credit**, which involves credit received during the discount period and which for Pineapple amounts to 10 days' net purchases, or $326,667, and (2) **costly trade credit**, which involves credit in excess of the free credit and whose cost is an implicit one based on the forgone discounts.[7] Pineapple could obtain $653,333, or 20 days' net purchases, of nonfree trade credit at a cost of approximately 37 percent. *Financial managers should always use the free component, but they should use the costly com-*

---

[7]There is some question as to whether any credit is really "free," because the supplier will have a cost of carrying receivables which must be passed on to the customer in the form of higher prices. Still, where suppliers sell on standard terms such as 2/10, net 30, and where the base price cannot be negotiated downward for early payment, for all intents and purposes the 10 days of trade credit is indeed "free."

*ponent only after analyzing its cost to make sure that it is less than the cost of funds that could be obtained from other sources.* Under the terms of trade found in most industries, the costly component involves a relatively high percentage cost; therefore, firms with access to bank credit should use only the free component of trade credit.

We noted earlier that firms sometimes can and do deviate from the stated credit terms, thus altering the percentage cost figures cited above. For example, a California manufacturing company that buys on terms of 2/10, net 30, makes a practice of paying in 15 days (rather than 10), but it still takes discounts—its treasurer simply waits until 15 days after receipt of the goods and still writes a check for the invoiced amount less the 2 percent discount. Since the company's suppliers want its business, they tolerate this practice. Similarly, a Wisconsin firm that also buys on terms of 2/10, net 30, does not take discounts, but it pays in 60 rather than 30 days, thus "stretching" its trade credit. As we saw earlier, both practices reduce the cost of trade credit. Although neither of these firms is "loved" by its suppliers, and neither could continue these practices in times when suppliers were operating at full capacity and had order backlogs, these practices can and do reduce the costs of trade credit during periods when suppliers have excess capacity.

## Short-Term Bank Loans

Commercial banks, whose loans generally appear on firms' balance sheets under the notes payable account, are second in importance to trade credit as a source of short-term financing.[8] Their influence is actually greater than appears from the dollar amounts they lend because banks provide *nonspontaneous* funds. As a firm's financing needs increase, it requests its bank to provide the additional funds. If the request is denied, the firm may be forced to abandon attractive growth opportunities.

### Bank Loan Features

Some features of bank loans are discussed in the following paragraphs.

*Maturity.* Although banks do make longer-term loans, *the bulk of their lending is on a short-term basis*—about two-thirds of all bank loans mature in a year or less. Bank loans to businesses are frequently written as 90-day notes, so the loans must be repaid or renewed at the end of 90 days. Of course, if a borrower's financial position has deteriorated, the bank may well refuse to renew the loan. This can mean serious trouble for the borrower.

---

[8]Although commercial banks remain the primary source of short-term loans, other sources are available. For example, in 1985 General Electric Credit Corporation (GECC) had several billion dollars of commercial loans outstanding. Firms such as GECC, which was initially established to finance consumers' purchases of GE's durable goods, often find business loans to be more profitable than consumer loans.

**promissory note**
A document specifying the terms and conditions of a loan, such as the amount, interest rate, and repayment schedule.

*Promissory Note.* When a bank loan is approved, the agreement is executed by signing a **promissory note**. The note specifies (1) the amount borrowed; (2) the percentage interest rate; (3) the repayment schedule, which can involve either a lump sum or a series of installments; (4) any collateral that might be put up as security for the loan; and (5) any other terms and conditions to which the bank and the borrower have agreed. When the note is signed, the bank credits the borrower's demand deposit (checking account) with the amount of the loan. On the borrower's balance sheet, both the cash and notes payable accounts increase.

**compensating balance (CB)**
A minimum checking account balance that a firm must maintain with a commercial bank, generally equal to 15 to 20 percent of the amount of loans outstanding.

*Compensating Balances.* Banks typically require that a regular borrower maintain an average demand deposit balance equal to a specified percentage of the face amount of the loan; generally, the required balance is set at from 10 to 20 percent. This is called a **compensating balance (CB)**, and it raises the effective interest rate on the loan. For example, if a firm needs $80,000 to pay off outstanding obligations but must maintain a 20 percent compensating balance, then it must borrow $100,000 to obtain a usable $80,000. If the stated interest rate is 8 percent, the effective cost is actually 10 percent: $8,000 interest divided by $80,000 of usable funds equals 10 percent.[9] The effective cost of a loan with a compensating balance will be discussed in more detail in the next section.

**line of credit**
An arrangement in which a financial institution commits itself to lend up to a specified maximum amount of funds during a designated period.

*Line of Credit.* A **line of credit** is a formal or informal understanding between the bank and the borrower indicating the maximum credit the bank will extend to the borrower. For example, on December 31 a bank loan officer may indicate to a corporate treasurer that the bank regards the firm as being "good" for up to $80,000 for the forthcoming year. On January 10 the treasurer signs a promissory note for $15,000 for 90 days; this is called "taking down" $15,000 of the total line of credit. This amount is credited to the firm's checking account at the bank. Before repayment of the $15,000, the firm may borrow additional amounts up to a total outstanding at any one time of $80,000.

**revolving credit agreement**
A formal line of credit extended to a firm by a bank or other lending institution.

*Revolving Credit Agreement.* A **revolving credit agreement** is a formal line of credit often used by large firms. To illustrate, Porter Electronics negotiated a revolving credit agreement for $100 million with a group of banks. The banks were formally committed for 4 years to lend Porter up to $100 million if the funds were needed. Porter in turn paid a commitment fee of one-quarter of 1 percent on the unused balance of the committed funds to compensate the banks for making the commitment. Thus, if Porter did not take down any of the $100 million commitment during a given year, it would still be required to pay a $250,000 fee. If it borrowed $50 million, the un-

---

[9]Note, however, that the compensating balance may be set as a minimum monthly *average*; if the firm maintains this average anyway, the compensating balance requirement will not raise the effective interest rate.

used portion of the line of credit would fall to $50 million and the fee would fall to $125,000. Of course, interest also had to be paid on the amount of money Porter actually borrowed. As a general rule, the rate of interest on "revolvers" is pegged to the prime rate, so the cost of the loan "floats" over time as interest rates vary. Porter's rate was set at prime plus 0.5 percentage points.

Note that a revolving credit agreement is very similar to a line of credit. However, there is an important distinguishing feature: The bank has a legal obligation to honor a revolving credit agreement, and it charges a fee for this commitment. No legal obligation exists under the less formal line of credit.

## The Cost of Bank Loans

**prime rate**
A published rate of interest charged by commercial banks to very large, strong corporations.

The cost of bank loans varies for different types of borrowers at a given point in time and for all borrowers over time. Interest rates are higher for riskier borrowers, and they are also higher on smaller loans because of the fixed costs involved in making and servicing loans. If a firm can qualify as a "prime risk" because of its size and financial strength, it can borrow at the **prime rate**, which has traditionally been the lowest rate banks charge. Rates on other loans tend to be scaled up from the prime rate.[10]

Bank lending rates vary widely over time depending on economic conditions and Federal Reserve policy. When the economy is weak, loan demand is usually slack, and the Fed also makes plenty of money available to the system. As a result, interest rates on all types of loans decline. Conversely, when the economy is booming, loan demand is typically strong, and the Fed restricts the money supply; the result is an increase in interest rates. As an indication of the kinds of fluctuations that can occur, in just five months (August to December of 1980) the prime rate rose from 11 percent to 21 percent. Interest rates on other bank loans also vary, but generally they are kept in phase with the prime rate.

Interest rates on bank loans are quoted in three ways: as *simple interest*, as *discount interest*, and as *add-on interest*. These three methods are explained next.

---

[10]Each bank sets its own prime rate, but because of competitive forces, most banks' prime rates are identical. Further, most banks follow the rate set by the large New York City banks, which in turn often follow the rate set by Citibank, New York's (and the world's) largest. Citibank at one time had a policy of setting the prime rate each week at 1¼ to 1½ percentage points above the average rate on large certificates of deposit (CDs) during the three weeks immediately preceding. CD rates represent the "price" of money in the open market; since they rise and fall with the supply and demand of money, CD rates are "market-clearing" rates. By tying the prime rate to CD rates, the banking system has insured that the prime rate will also be a market-clearing rate.

However, in recent years the prime rate has been held relatively constant even while open market rates have fluctuated sharply. Also, in recent years many banks have been lending to the very strongest companies at rates well below the prime rate. As we note later in this chapter, larger firms have ready access to the commercial paper market, and if banks want to do a significant volume of business with them, they must match or at least come close to the commercial paper rate. As competition in financial markets increases, as it has been doing as a direct result of the deregulation of banks and other financial institutions, "administered" rates such as the prime rate are giving way to flexible, negotiated rates based on market forces.

**simple interest**
Interest that is charged on the basis of the amount borrowed; it is paid when the loan ends rather than when it begins.

***Regular, or Simple, Interest.*** Simple interest is charged on many bank loans, and it also provides a basis for comparison of all other loan rates. In a **simple interest** loan, the borrower receives the face value of the loan and then repays the principal and interest at maturity. For example, on a simple interest loan of $10,000 at 12 percent for 1 year, the borrower receives the $10,000 upon approval of the loan and pays back the $10,000 principal plus $10,000(0.12) = $1,200 of interest at maturity (1 year later). The 12 percent is the stated, or nominal, rate. The effective annual rate is also 12 percent:

$$\text{Effective rate}_{\text{Simple}} = \frac{\text{Interest}}{\text{Amount received}} = \frac{\$1,200}{\$10,000} = 12\%.$$

On a simple interest loan of 1 year or more, the nominal rate equals the effective rate. However, if the loan has a term of less than 1 year—say, 90 days—then the effective rate will be higher. To see why, suppose someone borrowed $10,000 at a 12 percent simple interest rate for 90 days. Here the interest charge would be $(0.12/360)(90)(\$10,000) = \$300$. If this loan were "rolled over" three times, the total interest for the year would be $(4)(\$300) = \$1,200$, the same as the interest paid on the 1-year, 12 percent loan. However, with the 90-day loan, the $300 of interest would have to be paid every 90 days rather than at the end of the year. Because of compounding effects, the 90-day, 12 percent loan has a higher effective rate, calculated as follows:

$$\begin{aligned}\text{Effective rate}_{\text{Simple}} &= \left(1 + \frac{k_{\text{Nom}}}{m}\right)^m - 1.0 \\ &= (1 + 0.12/4)^4 - 1.0 \\ &= 12.55\%.\end{aligned}$$

Here $k_{\text{Nom}}$ is the nominal, or stated, rate and m is the number of loan periods per year, or $360/90 = 4$. The bank gets the interest sooner than under a 1-year loan, which makes the effective rate higher.

**discount interest**
Interest calculated on the face amount of a loan but deducted in advance.

***Discount Interest.*** In a **discount interest** loan, the bank deducts the interest in advance; this is called *discounting*. Thus, the borrower receives less than the face value of the loan. On a 1-year, $10,000 loan with a 12 percent (nominal) rate, discount basis, the interest (discount) is $10,000(0.12) = $1,200, so the borrower obtains the use of only $10,000 − $1,200 = $8,800. The effective rate is 13.64 percent versus 12 percent on a 1-year, simple interest loan:[11]

---

[11]Note that if the borrowing firm actually requires $10,000, it must borrow $11,363.64:

$$\begin{aligned}\text{Face value} &= \frac{\text{Funds required}}{1.0 - \text{Nominal rate (fraction)}} \\ &= \frac{\$10,000}{1.0 - 0.12} = \frac{\$10,000}{0.88} \\ &= \$11,363.64.\end{aligned}$$

The borrower will sign a note for $11,363.64 but receive only $11,363.64 − 0.12($11,363.64) = $10,000. Increasing the face value of the loan does not change the effective rate of 13.64 percent on the $10,000 of usable funds.

$$\text{Effective rate}_{\text{Discount}} = \frac{\text{Interest}}{\text{Amount received}}$$

$$= \frac{\text{Interest}}{\text{Face value} - \text{Interest}}$$

$$= \frac{\$1,200}{\$10,000 - \$1,200} = 13.64\%.$$

An alternative procedure for finding the effective annual rate on a discount interest loan is

$$\text{Effective rate}_{\text{Discount}} = \frac{\text{Nominal rate (\%)}}{1.0 - \text{Nominal rate (fraction)}}$$

$$= \frac{12\%}{1.0 - 0.12} = \frac{12\%}{0.88} = 13.64\%.$$

If the discount loan were for a period of less than 1 year, its effective annual rate would be found as follows:

$$\text{Effective rate}_{\text{Discount}} = \left(1.0 + \frac{\text{Interest}}{\text{Face value} - \text{Interest}}\right)^m - 1.0.$$

For example, if we borrowed $10,000 face value at a nominal rate of 12 percent, discount interest, for 3 months, then m = 12/3 = 4, the interest payment would be (0.12/4)( $10,000) = $300, and the effective rate would be 12.96 percent:

$$\text{Effective rate}_{\text{Discount}} = \left(1.0 + \frac{\$300}{\$10,000 - \$300}\right)^4 - 1.0$$

$$= 0.1296 = 12.96\%.$$

Thus, discount interest imposes less of a penalty on shorter-term than on longer-term loans because the interest is paid closer to the average date of use of the funds (half the life of the loan).

**add-on interest**
Interest calculated and added to funds received to determine the face amount of an installment loan.

***Installment Loans: Add-on Interest.*** Lenders typically charge **add-on interest** on automobile, appliance, and other types of small installment loans. The term "add-on" means that the interest is calculated based on the nominal rate and then added to the amount received to obtain the loan's face value. To illustrate, suppose someone borrows $10,000 on an add-on basis at a nominal rate of 12 percent, with the loan to be repaid in 12 monthly installments. At a 12 percent nominal rate, the borrower pays a total interest charge of $1,200; thus, the face amount of the note is $10,000 + $1,200 = $11,200. However, since the loan is paid off in monthly installments, (1) the borrower has the use of the full $10,000 for only the first month, (2) the amount of usable funds declines by $10,000/12 = $833.33 per month, and (3) the average amount of usable funds during the year is $10,000 − ($833.33 × 6) = $10,000 − $5,000 = $5,000. Thus, the lender receives $1,200 for the use of only about half the amount of funds borrowed. Therefore, we can approximate the effective rate as follows:

$$\text{Approximate effective rate}_{\text{Add-on}} = \frac{\text{Interest}}{(\text{Amount received})/2}$$

$$= \frac{\$1,200}{\$10,000/2} = 24\%.$$

The main point to note here is that interest is paid on the *original* amount of funds received, not the amount actually outstanding, which causes the effective rate to be almost double the stated rate.[12]

**Simple Interest with Compensating Balances.** Compensating balances tend to raise the effective rate on a loan. To illustrate this, suppose a firm needs $10,000 to pay for some equipment that it recently purchased. A bank offers to lend the company money for one year at a 12 percent simple rate, but the firm must maintain a compensating balance (CB) equal to 20 percent of the loan amount. If the firm did not take the loan, it would keep no deposits with the bank. What is the effective annual rate on the loan?

First, note that if the firm requires $10,000 it must, assuming it does not have spare cash to use as the compensating balance, borrow $12,500:

$$\text{Face value} = \frac{\text{Funds required}}{1.0 - \text{CB (fraction)}}$$

$$= \frac{\$10,000}{1.0 - 0.20} = \$12,500.$$

---

[12]This is only an approximation of the true rate of interest. To determine the precise effective rate under add-on, we proceed as follows:
1. The total loan to be repaid is $10,000 of principal plus $1,200 of interest, or $11,200.
2. The monthly payment is $11,200/12 = $933.33.
3. The bank is in effect buying a 12-period annuity of $933.33 for $10,000, so $10,000 is the PV of the annuity. Expressed in equation form,

$$PV = \$10,000 = \sum_{t=1}^{12} \$933.33 \left(\frac{1}{1 + k_d}\right)^t$$

4. This equation can be solved for $k_d$, which is the rate per month, using a financial calculator. Here $k_d = 1.788\% = 0.01788$.
5. The precise effective rate is found as follows:

$$\text{Effective rate}_{\text{Add-on}} = (1 + k_d)^{12} - 1.0$$

$$= (1.01788)^{12} - 1.0$$

$$= 1.2370 - 1.0 = 23.7\%.$$

6. Under the truth-in-lending laws, banks, department stores, and other installment lenders are required to report the *annual percentage rate (APR)* in boldface type on the first page of all installment loan contracts to prevent lenders from calling a loan with an effective rate of 23.7 percent a 12 percent loan. Note, however, that existing laws do not in all cases define the effective rate the same way we do— for example, many institutions would report our sample add-on loan as having an APR of $12 \times 1.788 = 21.46\%$ versus the 23.7 percent we calculated.
7. Note that if an installment loan is paid off ahead of schedule, additional complications will arise. For a discussion of this point see Dick Bonker, "The Rule of 78," *Journal of Finance*, June 1976, 877-888.

The interest paid at the end of the year will be $12,500(0.12) = $1,500, but the firm will only get the use of the $10,000. Therefore, the effective annual rate is 15 percent:

$$\text{Effective rate}_{\text{Simple/CB}} = \frac{\text{Interest}}{\text{Amount received}}$$

$$= \frac{\$1,500}{\$10,000} = 15\%.$$

An alternative formulation is

$$\text{Effective rate}_{\text{Simple/CB}} = \frac{\text{Nominal rate (\%)}}{1.0 - \text{CB (fraction)}}$$

$$= \frac{12\%}{1.0 - 0.2} = 15\%.$$

***Discount Interest with Compensating Balances.*** The above analysis can be extended to the case where compensating balances are required and the loan is also on a discount basis. In this situation, if a firm required $10,000 for 1 year and a 20 percent compensating balance (CB) is required on a 12 percent discount loan, it would have to borrow $14,705.88:

$$\text{Amount borrowed} = \frac{\text{Funds required}}{1.0 - \text{Nominal rate (fraction)} - \text{CB (fraction)}}$$

$$= \frac{\$10,000}{1.0 - 0.12 - 0.2}$$

$$= \$10,000/0.68 = \$14,705.88.$$

The firm would record this $14,705.88 under current liabilities as a note payable, which would be offset by these asset accounts:

| | |
|---|---|
| To cash account; subsequently write check | $10,000.00 |
| Prepaid interest (12% of $14,705.88) | 1,764.71 |
| Compensating balance (20% of $14,705.88) | 2,941.18 |
| | $14,705.89 |

The effective annual rate on this loan would be 17.65 percent:

$$\text{Effective rate}_{\text{Discount/CB}} = \frac{\text{Nominal rate}}{1.0 - \text{Nominal rate (fraction)} - \text{CB (fraction)}}$$

$$= \frac{12\%}{1.0 - 0.12 - 0.2}$$

$$= 12\%/0.68 = 17.65\%.$$

In this example, compensating balances and discount interest combined to push the effective rate of interest up from 12 to 17.65 percent. Note, how-

ever, that in our analysis we assumed that the compensating balance requirements forced the firm to increase its bank deposits. Had the company had
transactions balances which could have been used to supply all or part of the
compensating balances, the effective annual rate would have been less than
17.65 percent. Also, if the firm earned interest on its bank deposits, including
the compensating balance, then the effective annual rate would be decreased.

### Choosing a Bank

Individuals whose only contact with their bank is through the use of its
checking services generally choose a bank for the convenience of its location
and the competitive cost of its services. However, a business that borrows
from banks must look at other criteria, for important differences exist among
banks. Some of these differences are considered below.

***Willingness to Assume Risks.*** Banks have different basic policies toward
risk. Some follow relatively conservative lending practices, while others engage in what are properly termed "creative banking practices." These policies
reflect both the personalities of officers of the bank and the characteristics of
the bank's deposit liabilities. Thus, a bank with fluctuating deposit liabilities
in a static community will tend to be a conservative lender, while a bank
whose deposits are growing with little interruption may follow "liberal"
credit policies. A large bank with broad diversification over geographic regions and across industries served can obtain the benefit of combining and
averaging risks. Thus, marginal credit risks that might be unacceptable to a
small, specialized bank can be pooled by a branch banking system to reduce
the overall risk of a group of marginal accounts.

***Advice and Counsel.*** Some bank loan officers are active in providing counsel and in making developmental loans to firms in their early and formative
years. Certain banks have specialized departments which make loans to firms
that are expected to grow and thus become more important customers. The
personnel of these departments can provide valuable counseling to customers: Their experience with other firms in growth situations may enable them
to spot, and then warn their customers about, developing problems.

***Loyalty to Customers.*** Banks differ in the extent to which they will support
the activities of their borrowers in bad times. This characteristic is referred
to as the bank's degree of *loyalty*. Some banks may put great pressure on a
business to liquidate its loans when the firm's outlook becomes clouded,
whereas others will stand by the firm and work diligently to help it get back
on its feet. An especially dramatic illustration of this point was Bank of America's recent bailout of Memorex Corporation. The bank could have forced
Memorex into bankruptcy, but instead it loaned the company additional capital and helped it survive a bad period. Since Memorex's stock price subsequently rose on the New York Stock Exchange from $1.50 to $68, Bank of
America's help was indeed substantial.

*Specialization.* Banks differ greatly in their degree of loan specialization. Larger banks have separate departments that specialize in different kinds of loans, for example, real estate, farm, and commercial loans. Within these broad categories there may be a further specialization by line of business, such as steel, machinery, cattle, or textiles. The strengths of banks are also likely to reflect the nature of the business and the economic environment in which they operate—for example, Texas banks have become specialists in lending to oil companies, while many midwestern banks are agricultural specialists. A sound firm can obtain more creative cooperation and more active support by going to the bank that has the greatest experience and familiarity with its particular type of business, and financial managers should take this factor into account. A bank that is excellent for one firm may be unsatisfactory for another.

*Maximum Loan Size.* The size of a bank can be an important factor. Since the maximum loan a bank can make to any one customer is limited to 10 percent of the bank's capital accounts (capital stock plus retained earnings), it is generally not appropriate for large firms to develop borrowing relationships with small banks.

*Other Services.* Banks also provide lockbox systems (see Chapter 18), assist with electronic funds transfers, help firms obtain foreign currencies, and the like, and such services should be taken into account when selecting a bank. Also, if the firm is a small business whose manager owns most of its stock, the bank's willingness and ability to provide trust and estate services should also be considered.

## Commercial Paper

**commercial paper**
Unsecured, short-term promissory notes of large firms, usually issued in denominations of $100,000 or more and having an interest rate somewhat below the prime rate.

**Commercial paper** is the name given to the unsecured promissory notes of large, strong firms; it is sold primarily to other business firms, to insurance companies, to pension funds, to money market mutual funds, and to banks. Commercial paper is traded in the secondary markets, and a firm which holds the commercial paper of another firm can sell it to raise cash in a matter of hours—it is highly liquid. Although the amount of commercial paper outstanding is smaller than bank loans outstanding, this form of financing has grown rapidly in recent years. At the end of 1985, there was approximately $250 billion of commercial paper outstanding versus about $500 billion of bank loans to businesses.

### Maturity and Cost

Maturities of commercial paper generally vary from two to six months, with an average of about five months.[13] The rates on commercial paper fluctuate

---

[13]The maximum maturity without SEC registration is 270 days. Also, commercial paper can be sold only to "sophisticated" investors; otherwise, SEC registration would be required even for maturities of 270 days or less.

with supply and demand conditions—they are determined in the market-place, varying daily as conditions change. Recently, commercial paper rates have generally ranged from one to two percentage points below the stated prime rate and about one-quarter of a percentage point above the T-bill rate. For example, in October 1985 the average rate on 3-month commercial paper was 7.8 percent, while the stated prime rate was 9.50 percent and the T-bill rate was 7.55 percent. Also, since compensating balances are not required for commercial paper, the *effective* cost differential is still wider.[14]

### Use of Commercial Paper

The use of commercial paper is restricted to a comparatively small number of concerns that are exceptionally good credit risks. Purchasers of commercial paper hold it in their temporary marketable securities portfolios, or as liquidity reserves, as discussed in Chapter 18, and for these purposes safety is a paramount concern. Dealers prefer to handle the paper of firms whose net worth is $50 million or more and whose annual borrowing exceeds $10 million.

One potential problem with commercial paper is that a debtor who is in temporary financial difficulty may receive little help because commercial paper dealings are generally less personal than bank relationships. Thus, banks are usually more able and willing to help a good customer weather a temporary storm than is the commercial paper market. On the other hand, using commercial paper permits a corporation to tap a wide range of credit sources, including both financial institutions outside its own area and industrial corporations across the country, and this can reduce interest costs.

## Use of Security in Short-Term Financing

**secured loan**
A loan backed by collateral, often inventories or receivables.

Thus far we have not addressed the question of whether or not loans should be secured. Commercial paper is never secured by specific collateral, but all the other types of loans can be secured if this is deemed necessary or desirable. Given a choice, it is ordinarily better to borrow on an unsecured basis, since the bookkeeping costs of **secured loans** are often high. However, weak firms may find that they can borrow only if they put up some type of security to protect the lender or that by using security they can borrow at a much lower rate.

Several different kinds of collateral can be employed, including marketable stocks or bonds, land or buildings, equipment, inventory, and accounts receivable. Marketable securities make excellent collateral, but few firms hold

---

[14]However, this factor is offset to some extent by the fact that firms issuing commercial paper are required by commercial paper dealers to have unused revolving credit agreements to back up their outstanding commercial paper, and fees must be paid on these lines. In other words, to sell $1 million of commercial paper, a firm must have revolving credit available to pay off the paper when it matures, and commitment fees on this unused credit line (about 0.5 percent) increase the paper's effective cost.

portfolios of stocks and bonds. Similarly, real property (land and buildings) and equipment are good forms of collateral, but they are generally used as security for long-term loans rather than for working capital loans. Therefore, most secured short-term business borrowing involves the use of accounts receivable and inventories as collateral.

To understand the use of security, consider the case of a Chicago hardware dealer who wanted to modernize and expand his store. He requested a $200,000 bank loan. After examining his business's financial statements, the bank indicated (1) that it would lend him a maximum of $100,000 and (2) that the interest rate would be 15 percent, discount interest, for an effective rate of 17.6 percent. The owner had a substantial personal portfolio of stocks, and he offered to put up $300,000 of high-quality stocks to support the $200,000 loan. The bank then granted the full $200,000 loan, and at a rate of only 13 percent, simple interest. The store owner might also have used his inventories or receivables as security for the loan, but processing costs would have been high.

**Uniform Commercial Code**
A system of standards that simplifies and standardizes the procedure for establishing loan security.

In the past, state laws varied greatly with regard to the use of security in financing. Today, however, all states except Louisiana operate under the **Uniform Commercial Code**, which standardizes and simplifies the procedure for establishing loan security. The heart of the Uniform Commercial Code is the *Security Agreement*, a standardized document on which the specific pledged assets are stated. The assets can be items of equipment, accounts receivable, or inventories. Procedures under the Uniform Commercial Code for using accounts receivable and inventories as security for short-term credit are described in Appendix 17A.

## Summary

This chapter began with a discussion of the *working capital cash flow cycle* and alternative *working capital policies*. Working capital policy involves (1) target levels for current assets and (2) the manner in which current assets are to be financed. We saw that because short-term credit offers the advantages of speed, flexibility, and generally lower costs, most firms use at least some current debt to finance current assets in spite of the fact that such debt increases their risk.

The chapter also examined the four major types of short-term credit available to a firm: (1) *accruals*, (2) *accounts payable* (or *trade credit*), (3) *bank loans*, and (4) *commercial paper*. Companies use accruals on a regular basis, but this usage is not subject to discretionary actions; the other three types of credit are controllable, at least within limits.

Accounts payable may be divided into two components, *free trade credit* and *costly trade credit*. The cost of the latter is based on discounts lost, and it can be quite high. The financial manager should use all the free trade credit that is available, but costly trade credit should be used only if other credit is not available on better terms.

Bank loans may either be negotiated on an individual basis as the need arises or obtained on a regular basis under a *line of credit*. There are three types of interest rates that may be quoted on bank loans: (1) *simple interest*, (2) *discount interest*, and (3) *add-on interest* for installment loans. Banks often require borrowers to maintain *compensating balances*. If the required balance exceeds the balance the firm would otherwise maintain, a compensating balance will raise the effective cost of the loan.

*Commercial paper* is an important source of short-term credit, but it is available only to large, financially strong firms. Interest rates on commercial paper are generally below the prime bank rate, and the relative cost of paper is even lower when compensating balances on bank loans are considered. However, commercial paper does have disadvantages—if a firm that depends heavily on this type of credit experiences problems, its source of funds will immediately dry up. Commercial bankers are much more likely to help their customers ride out bad times.

Although we mentioned it only briefly in the chapter, short-term credit is often secured by inventories and accounts receivable. Techniques for using security to obtain short-term credit are discussed in Appendix 17A.

## SMALL BUSINESS

### Growth and Working Capital Needs

Working capital is one of the requirements of a new firm most often underestimated by the entrepreneur seeking funds to start the business. The entrepreneur makes provisions for research and development and for plant and equipment required to produce the firm's products. But working capital is frequently a surprise to the entrepreneur—he or she expects to come up with a product that the market will immediately accept and for which it will pay a very substantial premium; this premium price will lead to very high profit margins, which will in turn "finance" all of the firm's other needs. As naive as this point of view appears to be, it is nevertheless common among less experienced founders of new businesses.

Mike was one of the founders of a new microcomputer software company that began seeking venture capital to support its products in the latter part of 1980. In speaking with a venture capitalist who was concerned about the low level of funding being sought, Mike explained that the company's products would have such a high profit margin that the firm would be essentially self-financing after marketing was under way—in fact, there would even be funds available from internal sources to support continued new product development. The venture capitalist—we'll call him John—was a little disconcerted. He asked which firm was currently most successful in the microcomputer software business in which Mike would be competing.

Mike instantly responded, "Personal Software" (the company is now known as Visicorp). John asked, "Why, then, do you suppose that Personal Software has just completed raising an additional $2,500,000 in new venture capital? Isn't it as profitable as you expect it to be?" Mike fumbled around for a while with no answer; to his credit, he got the point.

Rapid growth consumes cash rather than generates it. Rapid growth does generate profits, but profits do not pay the bills—cash does. Consider what a firm must do to sustain a very high growth rate. If it is a manufacturing firm, the components of its assets include raw materials inventory, work-in-process inventory, finished goods inventory, and accounts receivable, as well as fixed assets. With the exception of fixed assets, these items are all components of gross working capital. When the firm produces a product, it must make an investment in each of these working capital items before any cash is received from collection of receivables, assuming all sales are credit sales.

Now imagine a small firm that has limited access to external financing or that chooses to finance itself internally from its retained earnings. It secures enough funding to acquire its fixed assets and to get started producing its product. When receivables are collected, the company will have a little more money than it used to create the products that generated the collections. Excluding any noncash expenses, suppose that for each dollar of sales the company spends about 95 cents. That leaves a nickel in profit. Of course, the firm's silent partner (Uncle Sam) takes a cut, and perhaps the firm pays out a little to its stockholders. The bottom line is that the firm has 3 cents left in cash from each dollar of sales. Since the firm puts in 97 cents for each dollar that it has left at the end of a single "manufacture and sales cycle," it now has about 3 percent more to put into manufacturing and selling the next round of production. In other words, after one sales cycle, the firm can afford another sales cycle with about a 3 percent increase in sales without external financing.

Now recall the financial analysis in Chapter 7. Suppose the firm has an average of 120 days of sales in inventory and an average of 60 days of sales tied up in accounts receivable. If the firm pays cash for all of its materials and labor, then it essentially "turns" cash about twice a year (360/180). In other words, from the time new investment is made in inventory and receivables, it is 180 days on average before the invested cash is returned. The firm then has two complete cash cycles per year, in each of which it ends up with a 3 percent growth in available funds. Therefore, the firm can grow at about a 6 percent annual rate from its internal sources. If the firm is actually growing at, say, 20 percent, then it is experiencing a constant need for new funds. These must come from new equity or new debt; retained earnings will not be adequate.

The analysis above is only a crude approximation of the firm's internally fundable annual growth rate, but it does give a clear indication of how working capital requirements constrain growth. The small firm planning for supernormal growth must therefore also make provisions for capital to support its growth. The manager has some alternatives, and each of them should be considered. For example, the firm can vary its working capital policy in such a way as to limit or control growth. Tightening its credit policies, for instance, may cost the firm some sales but will reduce the average collection period, thereby increasing the number of cash cycles per year. Reducing inventory investment will probably cost the firm some lost sales in the event of stock-outs, but it will again reduce the cash cycle and increase the number of cycles per year. Both of these measures will tend to reduce sales growth and to increase the rate at which sales growth can be financed internally. For the firm with constraints on available financing, these discretionary policies may help it to bring its rate of growth into balance with its ability to finance that growth.

## Questions

17-1   Define each of the following terms:
   a. Working capital; net working capital; working capital policy
   b. Permanent current assets; temporary current assets
   c. Cash conversion cycle
   d. Accruals
   e. Trade credit; free trade credit; stretching payables
   f. Promissory note; line of credit; revolving credit agreement
   g. Prime rate
   h. Simple interest; discount interest; add-on interest
   i. Compensating balance (CB)
   j. Commercial paper
   k. Secured loan
   l. Uniform Commercial Code

17-2   "Firms can control their accruals within fairly wide limits; depending on the cost of accruals, financing from this source will be increased or decreased." Discuss.

17-3   Is it true that both trade credit and accruals represent a spontaneous source of capital for financing growth? Explain.

17-4    Is it true that most firms are able to obtain some "free" trade credit and that additional trade credit is often available, but at a cost? Explain.

17-5    What kinds of firms use commercial paper? Could Mama and Papa Gus's Corner Grocery borrow using this form of credit?

17-6    From the standpoint of the borrower, is long-term or short-term credit riskier? Explain. Would it ever make sense to borrow on a short-term basis if short-term rates were above long-term rates?

17-7    If long-term credit exposes a borrower to less risk, why would people or firms ever borrow on a short-term basis?

17-8    Suppose a firm can obtain funds by borrowing at the prime rate or selling commercial paper.
   a. If the prime rate is 12 percent, what is a reasonable estimate for the cost of commercial paper?
   b. If a substantial cost differential exists, why might a firm such as this one actually borrow some of its funds from both markets?

## Self-Test Problems *(Solutions on Page 603)*

ST-1    Nelson Press, Inc., and the Craig Publishing Company have the following balance sheets as of December 31, 1985 (thousands of dollars):

|                      | Nelson Press | Craig Publishing |
|----------------------|-------------:|-----------------:|
| Current assets       | $100,000     | $100,000         |
| Fixed assets (net)   | 100,000      | 100,000          |
| Total assets         | $200,000     | $200,000         |
|                      |              |                  |
| Current liabilities  | $ 20,000     | $ 80,000         |
| Long-term debt       | 80,000       | 20,000           |
| Common stock         | 50,000       | 50,000           |
| Retained earnings    | 50,000       | 50,000           |
| Total claims         | $200,000     | $200,000         |

Earnings before interest and taxes for both firms are $30 million, and the average tax rate is 40 percent.
   a. What is the return on equity for each firm if the interest rate on current liabilities is 10 percent and the rate on long-term debt is 13 percent?
   b. Assume the short-term rate rises to 20 percent while the rate on the long-term debt remains unchanged. What would be the return on equity for Nelson Press and Craig Publishing under these conditions?
   c. Which company is in a riskier position? Why?

ST-2    The Calgary Company is attempting to establish a current assets policy. Fixed assets are $600,000, and the firm plans to maintain a 50 percent debt to assets ratio. The interest rate is 10 percent on all debt. Three alternative current asset policies are under consideration: 40, 50, and 60 percent of projected sales. The company expects to earn 15 percent before interest and taxes on sales of $3 million. Calgary's average tax rate is 40 percent. What is the expected return on equity under each alternative?

## Problems

Cash conversion cycle

**17-1**  For the Evergreen Bell Company, the average age of accounts receivable is 53 days, the average age of accounts payable is 42 days, and the average age of inventory is 70 days.
a.  What is the length of the firm's cash conversion cycle?
b.  If Evergreen's annual sales are $1,323,000, what is the firm's investment in accounts receivable?

Working capital policy

**17-2**  The Jansen Siding Corporation is attempting to determine the optimal level of current assets for the coming year. Management expects sales to increase to approximately $1.2 million as a result of an asset expansion presently being undertaken. Fixed assets total $500,000, and the firm wishes to maintain a 60 percent debt ratio. Jansen's interest cost is currently 10 percent on both short-term and longer-term debt (which the firm uses in its permanent structure). Three alternatives regarding the projected current asset level are available to the firm: (1) an aggressive policy requiring current assets of only 45 percent of projected sales; (2) an average policy of 50 percent of sales in current assets; and (3) a conservative policy requiring current assets of 60 percent of sales. The firm expects to generate earnings before interest and taxes at a rate of 12 percent on total sales.
a.  What is the expected return on equity under each current asset level? (Assume a 40 percent average tax rate.)
b.  In this problem we have assumed that the level of expected sales is independent of current asset policy. Is this a valid assumption?
c.  How would the overall riskiness of the firm vary under each policy? (Do only if you are using the computerized problem diskette.)
d.  What would the return on equity be under each current asset level if actual sales for the year were $1.6 million? $800,000? If sales were $1.2 million under the average policy, but $1.6 million under the conservative policy and $0.8 million under the aggressive policy? Which current asset level is the least risky over the range of probable sales from $800,000 to $1.6 million? Which current asset level do you recommend that Jansen maintain? Why?

Alternative working capital financing policies

**17-3**  (Do only if you are using the computerized problem diskette.)
Three companies—Aggressive, Between, and Conservative— have different working capital management policies as implied by their names—for example, Aggressive employs only minimal current assets, and it finances almost entirely with current liabilities plus equity. This "tight-ship" approach has a dual effect. It keeps total assets low, which tends to increase return on assets; but because of stock-outs and credit rejections, total sales are reduced, and since inventory is ordered more frequently and in smaller quantities, variable costs are increased. Condensed balance sheets for the three companies are presented on page 600.

|                                      | Aggressive | Between   | Conservative |
|--------------------------------------|-----------|-----------|--------------|
| Current assets                       | $150,000  | $200,000  | $300,000     |
| Fixed assets                         | 200,000   | 200,000   | 200,000      |
| Total assets                         | $350,000  | $400,000  | $500,000     |
|                                      |           |           |              |
| Current liabilities (cost = 12%)     | $200,000  | $100,000  | $ 50,000     |
| Long-term debt (cost = 10%)          | 0         | 100,000   | 200,000      |
| Total debt                           | $200,000  | $200,000  | $250,000     |
| Equity                               | 150,000   | 200,000   | 250,000      |
| Total claims on assets               | $350,000  | $400,000  | $500,000     |
|                                      |           |           |              |
| Current ratio                        | 0.75:1    | 2:1       | 6:1          |

The cost of goods sold functions for the three firms are as follows:

$$\text{Cost of goods sold} = \text{Fixed costs} + \text{Variable costs.}$$

*Aggressive*: Cost of goods sold = $200,000 + 0.70(Sales).

*Between*: Cost of goods sold = $270,000 + 0.65(Sales).

*Conservative*: Cost of goods sold = $385,000 + 0.60(Sales).

Because of the working capital differences, sales for the three firms under different economic conditions are expected to vary as indicated below:

|                  | Aggressive  | Between     | Conservative |
|------------------|-------------|-------------|--------------|
| Strong economy   | $1,200,000  | $1,250,000  | $1,300,000   |
| Average economy  | 900,000     | 1,000,000   | 1,150,000    |
| Weak economy     | 700,000     | 800,000     | 1,050,000    |

a. Construct income statements for each company for strong, average, and weak economies using the following format:

> Sales
> Less cost of goods sold
> Earnings before interest and taxes (EBIT)
> Less interest expense
> Taxable income
> Less taxes (at 40%)
> Net income

b. Compare the basic earning power (EBIT/assets) and return on equity for the companies. Which company is best in a strong economy? In an average economy? In a weak economy?

c. Suppose, with sales at the normal-economy level, short-term interest rates rose to 25 percent. How would this affect the three firms?

d. Suppose that because of production slowdowns caused by inventory shortages, the aggressive company's variable cost ratio rose to 80 percent. What would happen to its ROE?

e. What considerations for management of working capital are indicated by this problem?

| | | |
|---|---|---|
| Cost of trade credit | 17-4 | Calculate the implicit cost of nonfree trade credit under each of the following terms. Assume payment is made either on the due date or on the discount date. |

a. 1/15, net 20
b. 2/10, net 60
c. 3/10, net 30
d. 2/10, net 45
e. 1/10, net 40

| | | |
|---|---|---|
| Cost of credit | 17-5 | a. If a firm buys under terms of 2/10, net 40, but actually pays on the 20th day and *still takes the discount*, what is the cost of its nonfree trade credit? |

b. Does it receive more or less credit than it would if it paid within 10 days?

| | | |
|---|---|---|
| Cash discounts | 17-6 | Suppose a firm makes purchases of $2.4 million per year under terms of 2/10, net 30, and takes discounts. |

a. What is the average amount of accounts payable net of discounts? (Assume that the $2.4 million of purchases is net of discounts—that is, gross purchases are $2,448,980, discounts are $48,980, and net purchases are $2.4 million. Also, use 360 days in a year.)
b. Is there a cost of the trade credit it uses?
c. If it did not take discounts, what would be its average payables and the cost of this nonfree trade credit?
d. What would its cost of not taking discounts be if it could "stretch" its payments to 40 days?

| | | |
|---|---|---|
| Cost of bank loans | 17-7 | Green Thumb Garden Shop is negotiating with Millstone Bank for a $12,000, 1-year loan. Millstone has offered Green Thumb the following alternatives. Which alternative has the lowest effective interest rate? |

1. A 16 percent annual rate on a simple interest loan, with no compensating balance required and interest due at the end of the year.
2. A 12 percent annual rate on a simple interest loan, with a 15 percent compensating balance required and interest again due at the end of the year.
3. An 11 percent annual rate on a discounted loan with a 10 percent compensating balance.
4. Interest is figured as 12 percent of the $12,000 amount, payable at the end of the year, but the $12,000 is repayable in monthly installments during the year.

| | | |
|---|---|---|
| Trade credit versus bank credit | 17-8 | Selfridge Corporation projects an increase in sales from $2 million to $3 million, but it needs an additional $600,000 of current assets to support this expansion. The money can be obtained from the bank at an interest rate of 14 percent, discount interest; no compensating balance is required. Alternatively, Selfridge can finance the expansion by no longer taking discounts, thus increasing accounts payable. Selfridge purchases under terms of 2/10, net 30, but it can delay payment for an additional 30 days—paying in 60 days and thus becoming 30 days past due—without a penalty because of its suppliers' current excess capacity problems. |

a. Based strictly on an interest rate comparison, how should Selfridge finance its expansion?
b. What additional qualitative factors should Selfridge consider before reaching a decision?

**Bank financing**             **17-9**   The Kriebel Corporation had sales of $3.5 million last year, and it earned a 5 percent return, after taxes, on sales. Recently the company has fallen behind in its accounts payable. Although its terms of purchase are net 30 days, its accounts payable represent 60 days' purchases. The company's treasurer is seeking to increase bank borrowings in order to become current (that is, to have 30 days' payables outstanding) in meeting its trade obligations. The company's balance sheet is shown below (thousands of dollars):

| | | | |
|---|---|---|---|
| Cash | $  100 | Accounts payable | $  600 |
| Accounts receivable | 300 | Bank loans | 700 |
| Inventory | 1,400 | Accruals | 200 |
| Current assets | $1,800 | Current liabilities | $1,500 |
| Land and buildings | 600 | Mortgage on real estate | 700 |
| Equipment | 600 | Common stock, $0.10 par | 300 |
| | | Retained earnings | 500 |
| Total assets | $3,000 | Total claims | $3,000 |

a. How much bank financing is needed to eliminate the past-due accounts payable?

b. Would you as a bank loan officer make the loan? Why?

**Cost of trade credit**       **17-10**   C. Charles Smith & Sons sells on terms of 2/10, net 40. Gross sales last year were $6 million, and accounts receivable averaged $583,333. Half of Smith's customers paid on the tenth day and took discounts. What is the cost of trade credit to Smith's nondiscount customers? (Hint: Calculate sales/day based on a 360-day year; then get average receivables of discount customers; then find the ACP for the nondiscount customers.)

**Short-term financing**       **17-11**   Granulated Grain, Inc., buys on terms of 1/10, net 30, but it has not been
**analysis**                              taking discounts and has actually been paying in 60 rather than 30 days. Granulated's balance sheet follows (thousands of dollars):

| | | | |
|---|---|---|---|
| Cash | $   50 | Accounts payable[a] | $  500 |
| Accounts receivable | 450 | Notes payable | 50 |
| Inventories | 750 | Accruals | 50 |
| Current assets | $1,250 | Current liabilities | $  600 |
| | | Long-term debt | 150 |
| Fixed assets | 750 | Common equity | 1,250 |
| Total assets | $2,000 | Total claims | $2,000 |

[a]Stated net of discounts.

Now Granulated's suppliers are threatening to stop shipments unless the company begins making prompt payments (that is, paying in 30 days or less). The firm can borrow on a 1-year note (call this a current liability) from its bank at a rate of 15 percent, discount interest, with a 20 percent compensating balance required. (Granulated's $50,000 of cash is needed for transactions; it cannot be used as part of the compensating balance.)

a. Determine what action Granulated should take by calculating (1) the costs of nonfree trade credit and (2) the cost of the bank loan.

b. Assume that Granulated foregoes discounts and then borrows the amount needed to become current on its payables from the bank. How large will the bank loan be?

c. Based on your conclusion in Part b, construct a pro forma balance sheet. (Hint: You will need to include an account entitled "prepaid interest" under current assets.)

**Alternative financing arrangements**   **17-12**   Sunlight Sailboats estimates that due to the seasonal nature of its business, it will require an additional $350,000 of cash for the month of July. Sunlight has the following four options available for raising the needed funds:

1. Establish a one-year line of credit for $350,000 with a commercial bank. The commitment fee will be 0.5 percent per year on the unused portion, and the interest charge on the used funds will be 12 percent per annum. Assume that the funds are needed only in July, and that there are 30 days in July and 360 days in the year.

2. Forego the trade discount of 3/10, net 40, on $350,000 of purchases during July.

3. Issue $350,000 of 30-day commercial paper at an 11.4 percent per annum interest rate. The total transactions fee, including the cost of a backup credit line, on using commercial paper is 0.5 percent of the amount of the issue.

4. Issue $350,000 of 60-day commercial paper at an 11.0 percent per annum interest rate, plus a transactions fee of 0.5 percent. Since the funds are required for only 30 days, the excess funds ($350,000) can be invested in 10.8 percent per annum marketable securities for the month of August. The total transactions cost of purchasing and selling the marketable securities is 0.4 percent of the amount of the issue.

a. What is the cost of each financing arrangement?

b. Is the source with the lowest expected cost necessarily the one to select? Why or why not?

## Solutions to Self-Test Problems

**ST-1**   a. and b.

**Income Statements For Year Ended December 31, 1985 (Thousands of Dollars)**

|  | Nelson Press | | Craig Publishing | |
|---|---|---|---|---|
|  | a | b | a | b |
| EBIT | $ 30,000 | $ 30,000 | $ 30,000 | $ 30,000 |
| Interest | 12,400 | 14,400 | 10,600 | 18,600 |
| Taxable income | $ 17,600 | $ 15,600 | $ 19,400 | $ 11,400 |
| Taxes (40%) | 7,040 | 6,240 | 7,760 | 4,560 |
| Net income | $ 10,560 | $ 9,360 | $ 11,640 | $ 6,840 |
| Equity | $100,000 | $100,000 | $100,000 | $100,000 |
| Return on equity | 10.56% | 9.36% | 11.64% | 6.84% |

The Nelson Press has a higher ROE when short-term interest rates are high, while Craig Publishing does better when rates are lower.

c. Craig's position is riskier. First, note that its profits and return on equity are much more volatile than Nelson's. Second, Craig must renew its large short-term loan every year; if the renewal comes up at a time when money is very tight, its business is depressed, or both, then it could be denied credit, which could put it out of business.

ST-2

### The Calgary Company: Alternative Balance Sheets

|  | "Tight" (40%) | Middle-Ground (50%) | "Loose" (60%) |
|---|---|---|---|
| Current assets | $1,200,000 | $1,500,000 | $1,800,000 |
| Fixed assets | 600,000 | 600,000 | 600,000 |
| Total assets | $1,800,000 | $2,100,000 | $2,400,000 |
| Debt | $ 900,000 | $1,050,000 | $1,200,000 |
| Equity | 900,000 | 1,050,000 | 1,200,000 |
| Total claims | $1,800,000 | $2,100,000 | $2,400,000 |

### The Calgary Company: Alternative Income Statements

|  | "Tight" | Middle-Ground | "Loose" |
|---|---|---|---|
| Sales | $3,000,000 | $3,000,000 | $3,000,000 |
| EBIT | 450,000 | 450,000 | 450,000 |
| Interest (10%) | 90,000 | 105,000 | 120,000 |
| Earnings before taxes | $ 360,000 | $ 345,000 | $ 330,000 |
| Taxes (40%) | 144,000 | 138,000 | 132,000 |
| Net income | $ 216,000 | $ 207,000 | $ 198,000 |
| ROE | 24.0% | 19.7% | 16.5% |

## Selected Additional References and Case

The following articles provide more information on overall working capital policy and management:

Lambrix, R. J., and S. S. Singhvi, "Managing the Working Capital Cycle," *Financial Executive*, June 1979, 32-41.

Maier, Steven F., and James H. Vander Weide, "A Practical Approach to Short-Run Financial Planning," *Financial Management*, Winter 1978, 10-16.

Merville, Larry J., and Lee A. Tavis, "Optimal Working Capital Policies: A Chance-Constrained Programming Approach," *Journal of Financial and Quantitative Analysis*, January 1973, 47-60.

Smith, Keith V., "State of the Art of Working Capital Management," *Financial Management*, Autumn 1973, 50-55.

For more on trade credit, see:

Brosky, John J., *The Implicit Cost of Trade Credit and Theory of Optimal Terms of Sale*, Credit Research Foundation, New York, 1969.

Schwartz, Robert A., "An Economic Analysis of Trade," *Journal of Financial and Quantitative Analysis*, September 1974, 643-658.

For more on bank lending and commercial credit in general, see:

Stone, Bernell K., "Allocating Credit Lines, Planned Borrowing, and Tangible Services over a Company's Banking System," *Financial Management*, Summer 1975, 65-78.

For a discussion of effective yields, see:

Finnerty, John D., "Bank Discount, Coupon Equivalent, and Compound Yields: Comment," *Financial Management*, Summer 1983, 40-44.

Glasgo, Philip W., William J. Landes, and A. Frank Thompson, "Bank Discount, Coupon Equivalent, and Compound Yields," *Financial Management*, Autumn 1982, 80-84.

The following case from the Crum-Brigham casebook is appropriate for use with this chapter:

Case 10, "Conover Container Corporation," which illustrates how changes in working capital policy affect expected profitability and risk.

## APPENDIX 17A
## Secured Short-Term Financing

This appendix discusses procedures for using accounts receivable and inventories as security for short-term loans. As noted in Chapter 17, secured loans involve quite a bit of paperwork and other administrative costs, which makes them relatively expensive. However, this is often the only type of financing available to weaker firms.

### Accounts Receivable Financing

**pledging receivables**
Putting accounts receivables up as security for a loan.

**factoring**
Outright sale of accounts receivable.

**recourse**
The lender can seek payment from the selling firm if an account receivable is uncollectable.

Accounts receivable financing involves either the pledging of receivables or the selling of receivables (factoring). The **pledging of accounts receivable** is characterized by the fact that the lender not only has a claim against the receivables but also has recourse to the borrower: If the person or firm that bought the goods does not pay, the selling firm must take the loss. Therefore, the risk of default on the accounts receivable pledged remains with the borrower. Also, the buyer of the goods is not ordinarily notified about the pledging of the receivables, and the financial institution that lends on the security of accounts receivable is generally either a commercial bank or one of the large industrial finance companies.

**Factoring**, or *selling accounts receivable*, involves the purchase of accounts receivable by the lender, generally without **recourse** to the borrower, which means that if the purchaser of the goods does not pay for them, the lender rather than the seller of the goods takes the loss. Under factoring, the buyer of the goods is typically notified of the transfer and is asked to make payment directly to the financial institution. Since the factoring firm assumes the risk of default on bad accounts, it must make the credit check. Accordingly, factors provide not only money but also a credit department for the borrower. Incidentally, the same financial institutions that make loans against pledged receivables also serve as factors. Thus, depending on the circumstances and the wishes of the borrower, a financial institution will provide either form of receivables financing.

***Procedure for Pledging Accounts Receivable.*** The financing of accounts receivable is initiated by a legally binding agreement between the seller of the goods and the financing institution. The agreement sets forth in detail the procedures to be followed and the legal obligations of both parties. Once the working relationship has been established, the seller periodically takes a batch of invoices to the financing institution. The lender reviews the invoices and makes credit appraisals of the buyers. Invoices of companies that do not meet the lender's credit standards are not accepted for pledging.

The financial institution seeks to protect itself at every phase of the operation. First, selection of sound invoices is one way the lender safeguards itself. Second, if the buyer of the goods does not pay the invoice, the lender still has recourse against the seller. Third, additional protection is afforded the lender in that the loan will generally be for less than 100 percent of the pledged receivables—for example, the lender may advance the selling firm only 75 percent of the amount of the pledged invoices.

***Procedure for Factoring Accounts Receivable.*** The procedures used in factoring are somewhat different from those for pledging. Again, an agreement between the seller and the factor specifies legal obligations and procedural arrangements. When the seller receives an order from a buyer, a credit approval slip is written and immediately sent to the factoring company for a credit check. If the factor approves the credit, shipment is made and the invoice is stamped to notify the buyer to make payment directly to the factoring company. If the factor does not approve the sale, the seller generally refuses to fill the order; if the sale is made anyway, the factor will not buy the account.

The factor normally performs three functions: (1) credit checking, (2) lending, and (3) risk bearing. However, the seller can select various combinations of these functions by changing provisions in the factoring agreement. For example, a small- or medium-sized firm may have the factor perform the risk-bearing function and thus avoid having to establish a credit department. The factor's service might well be less costly than a credit department that would have excess capacity for the firm's credit volume. At the same time, if the selling firm uses someone who is not really qualified for the job to perform credit checking, then that person's lack of education, training, and experience could result in excessive losses.

The seller may have the factor perform the credit-checking and risk-taking functions without performing the lending function. The following procedure illustrates the handling of a $10,000 order under this arrangement. The factor checks and approves the invoices. The goods are shipped on terms of net 30. Payment is made to the factor, who remits to the seller. But if the buyer defaults, the $10,000 must still be remitted to the seller, and if the $10,000 is never paid, the factor sustains a $10,000 loss. Note, however, that in this situation the factor does not remit funds to the seller until either they are received from the buyer of the goods or the credit period has expired. Thus, the factor does not supply any credit.

Now consider the more typical situation in which the factor performs the lending, risk-bearing, and credit-checking functions. The goods are shipped, and even though payment is not due for 30 days, the factor immediately makes funds available to the seller. Suppose $10,000 worth of goods are shipped. Further, assume that the factoring commission for credit checking and risk bearing is 2.5 percent of the invoice price, or $250, and that the interest expense is computed at a 9 percent annual rate on the invoice balance, or $75.[1] The selling firm's accounting entry is as follows:

---

[1]Since the interest is only for 1 month, we multiply 1/12 of the stated rate (9 percent) by the $10,000 invoice price:

$$(1/12)(0.09)(\$10,000) = \$75.$$

Note that the effective rate of interest is really above 9 percent because (1) the term is for less than 1 year and (2) a discounting procedure is used and the borrower does not get the full $10,000. In many instances, however, the factoring contract calls for interest to be computed on the invoice price *less* the factoring commission and the reserve account.

| Cash | $9,175 | |
| Interest expense | 75 | |
| Factoring commission | 250 | |
| Reserve due from factor on collection of account | 500 | |
| Accounts receivable | | $10,000 |

The $500 due from the factor upon collection on the account is a reserve established by the factor to cover disputes between the seller and buyers over damaged goods, goods returned by the buyers to the seller, and the failure to make an outright sale of goods. The reserve is paid to the selling firm when the factor collects on the account.

Factoring is normally a continuous process instead of the single cycle just described. The firm that sells the goods receives an order; it transmits this order to the factor for approval; upon approval, the firm ships the goods; the factor advances the invoice amount less withholdings to the seller; the buyer pays the factor when payment is due; and the factor periodically remits any excess in the reserve to the seller of the goods. Once a routine has been established, a continuous circular flow of goods and funds takes place between the seller, the buyers of the goods, and the factor. Thus, once the factoring agreement is in force, funds from this source are *spontaneous* in the sense that an increase in sales will automatically generate additional credit.

### Cost of Receivables Financing.

Both accounts receivable pledging and factoring are convenient and advantageous, but they can be costly. The credit-checking and risk-bearing fee is 1 to 3 percent of the amount of invoices accepted by the factor, and even more if the buyers are poor credit risks. The cost of money is reflected in the interest rate (usually 2 to 3 percentage points over the prime rate) charged on the unpaid balance of the funds advanced by the factor.

### Evaluation of Receivables Financing.

It cannot be said categorically that accounts receivable financing is always either a good or a poor method of raising funds for an individual business. Among the advantages is, first, the flexibility of this source of financing: As the firm's sales expand, causing more financing to be needed, a larger volume of invoices, and hence receivables financing, is generated automatically. Second, receivables can be used as security for a loan that a firm might otherwise not be able to obtain. Third, factoring can provide the services of a credit department that might otherwise be available to the firm only under much more expensive conditions.

Accounts receivable financing also has disadvantages. First, when invoices are numerous and relatively small in dollar amount, the administrative costs involved may be excessive. Second, since the firm is using its most liquid noncash assets as security, some trade creditors may refuse to sell on credit to firms that are factoring or pledging their receivables on the grounds that this practice weakens the position of other creditors.

### Future Use of Receivables Financing.

We might make a prediction at this point: In the future, accounts receivable financing will increase in relative importance. Computer technology is rapidly advancing toward the point where credit records of individuals and firms can be kept on disks and magnetic tapes. For example, one device used by retailers consists of a box which, when an individual's magnetic credit card is inserted, gives a signal that the credit is "good" and that a bank is willing to "buy" the receivable created as soon as the store completes the sale. The cost of handling invoices will be greatly reduced over present-day costs because the new systems will be so highly automated. This will make it possible to use accounts receivable financing for very small sales, and it will reduce the cost of all receivables financing. The net result will be a marked expansion of accounts receivable financing. In fact, when consumers use credit cards such as MasterCard or Visa, the seller is in effect factoring receivables. The seller receives the amount of the purchase, less a percentage fee, the next working day. The buyer receives 30 days' (or so) credit, at which time he or she remits payment directly to the credit card company or sponsoring bank.

## Inventory Financing

A substantial amount of credit is secured by business inventories. If a firm is a relatively good credit risk, the mere existence of the inventory may be a sufficient basis for receiving an unsecured loan. However, if the firm is a relatively poor risk, the lending institution may insist upon security in the form of a *lien* against the inventory. Methods for using inventories as security are discussed in this section.

**Blanket Liens.** The *inventory blanket lien* gives the lending institution a lien against all of the borrower's inventories. However, the borrower is free to sell inventories, and thus the value of the collateral can be reduced below the level that existed when the loan was granted.

**Trust Receipts.** Because of the inherent weakness of the blanket lien, another procedure for inventory financing has been developed—the *trust receipt*, which is an instrument acknowledging that the goods are held in trust for the lender. In this method the borrowing firm, as a condition for receiving funds from the lender, signs and delivers a trust receipt for the goods. The goods can be stored in a public warehouse or held on the premises of the borrower. The trust receipt states that the goods are held in trust for the lender or are segregated on the borrower's premises on the lender's behalf and that any proceeds from the sale of the goods must be transmitted to the lender at the end of each day. Automobile dealer financing is one of the best examples of trust receipt financing.

One defect of trust receipt financing is the requirement that a trust receipt be issued for specific goods. For example, if the security is autos in a dealer's inventory, the trust receipts must indicate the cars by registration number. In order to validate its trust receipts, the lending institution must send someone to the borrower's premises periodically to see that the auto numbers are correctly listed, because auto dealers who are in financial difficulty have been known to sell cars backing trust receipts and then use the funds obtained for other operations rather than to repay the bank. Problems are compounded if borrowers have geographically diversified operations or if they are separated geographically from the lender. To offset these inconveniences, *warehousing* has come into wide use as a method of securing loans with inventory.

**Warehouse Receipts.** Like trust receipts, warehouse receipt financing uses inventory as security. A *public warehouse* is an independent third-party operation engaged in the business of storing goods. Items which must age, such as tobacco and liquor, are often financed and stored in public warehouses. Sometimes a public warehouse is not practical because of the bulkiness of goods and the expense of transporting them to and from the borrower's premises. In such cases, a *field warehouse* may be established on the borrower's grounds. To provide inventory supervision, the lending institution employs a third party in the arrangement, the field warehousing company, which acts as its agent.

Field warehousing can be illustrated by a simple example. Suppose a firm which has iron stacked in an open yard on its premises needs a loan. A field warehouse can be established by the field warehousing concern merely placing a temporary fence around the iron, erecting a sign stating "This is a field warehouse supervised and conducted by the Smith Field Warehousing Corporation," and assigning an employee to supervise and control the inventory.

This example illustrates the three essential elements for the establishment of a field warehouse: (1) public notification, (2) physical control of the inventory, and (3) supervision by a custodian of the field warehousing concern. When the field warehousing operation is relatively small, the third condition is sometimes violated by hiring an employee of the borrower to supervise the inventory. This practice is viewed as undesirable by most lenders, because there is no control over the collateral by a person independent of the borrowing firm.[2]

The field warehouse financing operation is best described by an actual case. A California tomato cannery was interested in financing its operations by bank borrowing. It had sufficient funds to finance 15 to 20 percent of its operations during the canning season. These funds were adequate to purchase and process an initial batch of tomatoes. As the cans were put into boxes and rolled into the storerooms, the cannery needed additional funds for both raw materials and labor. Because of the cannery's poor credit rating, the bank decided that a field warehousing operation was necessary in order to secure its loans.

The field warehouse was established, and the custodian notified the bank of the description, by number, of the boxes of canned tomatoes in storage and under warehouse control. With this inventory as collateral, the lending institution established for the cannery a deposit on which it could draw. From this point on, the bank financed the operations. The cannery needed only enough cash to initiate the cycle. The farmers brought in more tomatoes; the cannery processed them; the cans were boxed; the boxes were put into the field warehouse; field warehouse receipts were drawn up and sent to the bank; the bank established further deposits for the cannery on the basis of the additional collateral, and the cannery could draw on the deposits to continue the cycle.

Of course, the cannery's ultimate objective was to sell the canned tomatoes. As it received purchase orders, it transmitted them to the bank, and the bank directed the custodian to release the inventories. It was agreed that as remittances were received by the cannery they would be turned over to the bank. These remittances thus paid off the loans.

Note that a seasonal pattern existed. At the beginning of the tomato harvesting and canning season, the cannery's cash needs and loan requirements began to

---

[2]This absence of independent control was the main cause of the breakdown that resulted in over $200 million of losses on loans to the Allied Crude Vegetable Oil Company by Bank of America and other banks. American Express Field Warehousing Company was handling the operation, but it hired men from Allied's own staff as custodians. Their dishonesty was not discovered because of another breakdown—the fact that the American Express touring inspector did not actually take a physical inventory of the warehouses. As a consequence, the swindle was not discovered until losses running into the hundreds of millions of dollars had been suffered.

rise, and they reached a peak just as the season ended. It was hoped that well before the new canning season began, the cannery would have sold a sufficient volume to pay off the loan. If the cannery had had a bad year, the bank might have carried the loan over for another year to enable the company to work off its inventory.

***Acceptable Products.*** In addition to canned foods, which account for about 17 percent of all field warehouse loans, many other types of products provide a basis for field warehouse financing. Some of these are miscellaneous groceries, which represent about 13 percent; lumber products, about 10 percent; and coal and coke, about 6 percent. These products are relatively nonperishable and are sold in well-developed, organized markets. Nonperishability protects the lender if it should have to take over the security. For this reason, a bank would not make a field warehousing loan on perishables such as fresh fish; however, frozen fish, which can be stored for a long time, can be field warehoused.

***Cost of Financing.*** The fixed costs of a field warehousing arrangement are relatively high; such financing is therefore not suitable for a very small firm. If a field warehousing company sets up a field warehouse, it will typically set a minimum charge of about $5,000 per year, plus about 1 to 2 percent of the amount of credit extended to the borrower. Furthermore, the financing institution will charge an interest rate of two to three percentage points over the prime rate. An efficient field warehousing operation requires a minimum inventory of at least $1 million.

***Evaluation of Inventory Financing.*** The use of inventory financing, especially field warehouse financing, as a source of funds for business firms has many advantages. First, the amount of funds available is flexible because the financing is tied to the growth of inventories, which in turn is related directly to financing needs. Second, the field warehousing arrangement increases the acceptability of inventories as loan collateral; some inventories simply would not be accepted by a bank as security without such an arrangement. Third, the necessity for inventory control and safekeeping as well as the use of specialists in warehousing often results in improved warehouse practices, which in turn save handling costs, insurance charges, theft losses, and so on. Thus, field warehousing companies have often saved money for firms in spite of the costs of financing that we have discussed. The major disadvantages of a field warehousing operation are the paperwork, physical separation requirements, and, for small firms, the fixed-cost element.

## Problem

Receivables financing

**17A-1**   The Funtime Company manufactures plastic toys. It buys raw materials, manufactures the toys in the spring and summer, and ships them to department stores and toy stores by late summer or early fall. Funtime factors its receivables; if it did not, its October 1985 balance sheet would appear as shown on page 611 (thousands of dollars):

| Cash | $    40 | Accounts payable | $1,200 |
| Receivables | 1,200 | Notes payable | 800 |
| Inventory | 800 | Accruals | 80 |
| Current assets | $2,040 | Current liabilities | $2,080 |
| | | Mortgages | 200 |
| | | Common stock | 400 |
| Fixed assets | 800 | Retained earnings | 160 |
| Total assets | $2,840 | Total claims | $2,840 |

Funtime provides extended credit to its customers, so its receivables are not due for payment until January 31, 1986. Also, Funtime would have been overdue on some $800,000 of its accounts payable if the above situation had actually existed.

Funtime has an agreement with a finance company to factor the receivables for the period October 31 through January 31 of each selling season. The factoring company charges a flat commission of 2 percent, plus 6 percent per year interest on the outstanding balance; it deducts a reserve of 8 percent for returned and damaged materials. Interest and commissions are paid in advance. No interest is charged on the reserved funds or on the commission.

a. Show Funtime's balance sheet on October 31, 1985, including the purchase of all the receivables by the factoring company and the use of the funds to pay accounts payable.

b. If the $1.2 million is the average level of outstanding receivables, and if they turn over four times a year (hence the commission is paid four times a year), what are the total dollar costs of receivables financing (factoring) and the effective annual interest rate?

# 18

# CASH AND MARKETABLE SECURITIES

## DON'T LISTEN TO E.F. HUTTON WHEN MANAGING YOUR CASH

Cash is the oil that lubricates the wheels of business. Without adequate oil, machines grind to a halt, and businesses with inadequate cash do likewise. On the other hand, carrying cash is expensive—since it is a nonearning asset, any cash beyond a bare minimum lowers a firm's potential earnings.

As a result, cash management is developing into a very professional, highly refined system. The following excerpt from a United California Bank (UCB) advertisement illustrates what is involved:

> Using any lock box will accelerate cash flow. But a UCB Lock Box System does it with maximum efficiency. One difference is our unique city-wide zip code system for California lock box customers. It speeds the receipt of your lock box mail by several hours.
>
> Another difference: We work around the clock, seven days a week. So you can be sure your funds will be deposited, regardless of absenteeism or seasonal work loads.
>
> A third difference: We're the only west coast bank using helicopters to speed collections of checks, thus reducing float.
>
> Also, using our computerized optimization models, we can determine how many lock boxes you should use, where they should be located, and how much money you'll save with them.
>
> The cost is surprisingly reasonable. Call us, and let us show you how UCB can make your cash work harder.

These ideas make good sense, but E.F. Hutton, the big brokerage house, pushed its cash management system too far. Hutton had accounts with hundreds of banks all across the country. Every day, balances in excess of the amounts needed as compensating balances were sent electronically to *money center concentration banks*, where the funds were immediately invested in interest-bearing securities. Hutton's profits on these investments were large, and some people in the company soon learned how to make them larger yet: (1) they began to use *estimated* deposits rather than actual deposits for purposes of sending the wire transfers to the concentration banks, (2) they deliberately overestimated deposits, and (3) as a result they ended up transferring money out of the local accounts that was not actually on deposit. Thus, they were chronically overdrawn at the local banks, so most of the money they were investing at the concentration bank level actually belonged to the local banks, not to Hutton! Since the errors were deliberate, Hutton's actions were deemed to be defrauding the banking system, and hence they were illegal. When a local bank in upstate New York finally blew the whistle, Hutton was forced to compensate the defrauded banks and to pay a large fine. A number of employees were fired, the chairman resigned, and Hutton lost an incalculable amount of business to people who thought, "If you can't trust your broker, who can you trust?" As you read this chapter, keep in mind that good cash management—indeed, good financial management of all types—requires a knowledge of both what *can* be done and what *should* be done, and that the consequences of unethical behavior can be severe.

Approximately 1.5 percent of the average industrial firm's assets are held in the form of cash, which is defined as the total of bank demand deposits plus currency. In addition, sizable holdings of near-cash marketable securities such as U.S. Treasury bills (T-bills) or bank certificates of deposit (CDs) are often reported on corporations' financial statements. However, cash balances vary widely both among industries and among the firms within a given industry, depending on the individual firms' specific conditions and on their owners' and managers' aversion to risk. In this chapter, we analyze the factors that determine firms' cash and marketable securities balances. These same factors, incidentally, apply to the cash holdings of individuals and nonprofit organizations, including government agencies.

## Cash Management

Cash is generally called a "nonearning" asset—while it is needed to pay for labor and raw materials, to buy fixed assets, to pay taxes, to service debt, to pay dividends, and so on, cash itself (and most commercial checking accounts) earns no interest. Thus, the goal of cash management is to reduce the amount of cash held to the minimum necessary to conduct business. We begin our analysis with a discussion of reasons for holding cash.

### Rationale for Holding Cash

Firms hold cash for two primary reasons:

**1.** *Transactions.* Cash balances are necessary in business operations. Payments must be made in cash, and receipts are deposited in the cash account.

**transactions balance**
A cash balance associated with payments and collections; the balance necessary for a firm to conduct day-to-day business.

**compensating balance**
A minimum checking account balance that a firm must maintain with a commercial bank.

**precautionary balance**
A cash balance held in reserve for random, unforeseen fluctuations in cash inflows and outflows.

**speculative balance**
A cash balance that is held to enable the firm to take advantage of any bargain purchases that might arise.

Those cash balances associated with routine payments and/or collections are known as **transactions balances**.

*2. Compensation to banks for providing loans and services.* A bank makes money by lending out funds which have been deposited with it; thus, depositing money in a bank helps improve the bank's profit position. If a bank is providing services to a customer, it generally requires the customer to leave a minimum balance on deposit to help offset the costs of doing so. This type of balance, defined as a **compensating balance**, is discussed in detail later in this chapter.

Two other reasons for holding cash have been noted in the finance and economics literature: (1) for precaution and (2) for speculation. Cash inflows and outflows are somewhat unpredictable, with the degree of predictability varying among firms and industries. Therefore, firms need to hold some cash in reserve for random, unforeseen fluctuations in inflows and outflows. These "safety stocks" are defined as **precautionary balances**, and the less predictable the firm's cash flows, the larger such balances should be. However, if the firm has easy access to borrowed funds—that is, if it can borrow on short notice—its need to hold cash for precautionary purposes is reduced. Also, as we note later in this chapter, firms that would otherwise need large precautionary balances tend to hold highly liquid marketable securities rather than cash per se; such holdings accomplish the same purposes as cash balances, but they provide greater interest income than bank deposits.

Some cash balances may be held to enable the firm to take advantage of any bargain purchases that might arise; these funds are defined as **speculative balances**. However, as with precautionary balances, firms today are more likely to rely on reserve borrowing power and on marketable securities portfolios than on cash per se for speculative purposes.

Although the cash accounts of most firms can be thought of as consisting of transactions, compensating, precautionary, and speculative balances, we cannot calculate the amount needed for each purpose, sum them, and produce a total desired cash balance, because the same money often serves more than one purpose—for instance, precautionary and speculative balances can also be used to satisfy compensating balance requirements. Firms do, however, consider these four factors when establishing their target cash positions.

## The Cash Budget

The firm estimates its needs for cash as a part of its general budgeting, or forecasting, process. First, it forecasts sales. Next, it forecasts the fixed assets and inventories that will be required to meet the forecasted sales levels. Asset purchases and the actual payments for them are then put on a time scale, along with the actual timing of the sales and the timing of collections for sales. For example, the typical firm makes a 5-year sales forecast, which is then used to help plan fixed asset acquisitions (capital budgeting). Next, the firm develops an annual forecast, in which sales and inventory purchases are projected on a monthly basis, along with the times when payments for both fixed assets and inventory purchases must be made. These forecasts are combined with projections about the timing of the collection of accounts receivable, the schedule for payment of taxes, the dates when dividend and interest payments will be made, and so on. Finally, all of this information is summarized in the **cash budget**, which shows the firm's projected cash inflows and outflows over some specified period of time.

**cash budget**
A schedule showing cash flows (receipts, disbursements, and net cash) for a firm over a specified period.

Cash budgets can be constructed on a monthly, a weekly, or even a daily basis. Generally, firms use a monthly cash budget forecasted over the next 6 to 12 months, plus a more detailed daily or weekly cash budget for the coming month. The longer-term budget is used for planning purposes, and the shorter one for actual cash control.

## Constructing the Cash Budget

We shall illustrate the process with a monthly cash budget covering the last six months of 1986 for the Drexel Card Company, a leading producer of greeting cards. Drexel's birthday and get-well cards are sold year round, but the bulk of sales occurs during September, when retailers are stocking up for Christmas. All sales are made on terms that allow a cash discount for payments made within 10 days, but if the discount is not taken, the full amount must be paid in 40 days. However, Drexel, like most other companies, finds that some of its customers delay payment up to 70 days—indeed, its experience shows that on 20 percent of the sales, payment is made during the month in which the sale is made; on 70 percent of the sales, payment is made during the first month after the month of the sale; and on 10 percent of the sales, payment is made during the second month after the month of the sale. Drexel offers a 2 percent discount for payments received within 10 days of sales. Typically, payments received in the month of sale are discount sales.

Rather than produce at a uniform rate throughout the year, Drexel prints cards immediately before they are required for delivery. Paper, ink, and other materials amount to 70 percent of sales and are bought the month before the company expects to sell the finished product. Its own purchase terms permit Drexel to delay payment on its purchases for 1 month. Accordingly, if July sales are forecasted at $10 million, then purchases during June will amount to $7 million, and this amount will actually be paid in July.

**target cash balance**
The minimum cash balance that a firm must maintain in order to conduct business.

Such other cash expenditures as wages and rent are also built into the cash budget. Further, Drexel must make tax payments of $2 million on September 15 and December 15, and a payment for a new plant in October. Assuming that it needs to keep a **target cash balance** of $2.5 million at all times and that it will have $3 million on July 1, what are Drexel's financial requirements for the period July through December?[1]

---

[1] Setting the target cash balance is an important part of cash management. We will discuss this topic later in the chapter.

The monthly cash requirements are worked out in Table 18-1. The top half of the table provides a worksheet for calculating collections on sales and payments on purchases. The first line in the worksheet gives the sales forecast for the period May through December; May and June sales are necessary to determine collections for July and August. Next, cash collections are given. The first line of this section shows that 20 percent of the sales during any given month are collected that month. However, customers who pay in the first month typically take the discount; therefore, the cash collected in the month of a sale is reduced by 2 percent—for example, collections during May for the $5,000 of sales in that month will be $(0.2)($5,000)(0.98) =$ $980. The second line shows the collections on the prior month's sales, or 70 percent of sales in the preceding month—for example, in June 70 percent of the $5,000 May sales, or $3,500, will be collected. The third line gives collections from sales two months earlier, or 10 percent of sales in that month—for example, the July collections for May sales are $(0.10)($5,000)$ $= $500. The collections are summed to find the total cash receipts from sales during each month covered by the cash budget; thus, the July collections represent 20 percent of July sales (less the discount) plus 70 percent of June sales plus 10 percent of May sales.

With the worksheet completed, the cash budget itself can be constructed. Cash from collections is given on Line 1. Lines 2 through 9 summarize payments during each month. The difference between cash receipts and cash payments (Line 1 minus Line 9) is the net cash gain or loss during the month; for July there is a net cash loss of $2,140,000.

Next, the initial cash on hand at the beginning of the month is added to the net cash gain or loss during the month to obtain the cumulative cash that would be on hand if no financing were done; at the end of July, Drexel would have cumulative cash of $860,000.

The target cash balance, $2.5 million, is then subtracted from the cumulative cash to determine the firm's borrowing requirements or surplus cash. In July, Drexel expects to have cumulative cash, as shown on Line 12, of $860,000. Thus, to maintain the target cash balance it must borrow $1,640,000 by the end of July. Assuming that this amount is indeed borrowed, loans outstanding will total $1,640,000 at the end of July.

This same procedure is used in the following months. Sales will expand seasonally in August, accompanied by increased payments for purchases, wages, and other items. Receipts from sales will also go up, but the firm will still be left with a $1,460,000 cash outflow during the month. The total financial requirements at the end of August will be $3.1 million, the cumulative cash plus the target cash balance. This amount is also equal to the $1,640,000 needed at the end of July plus the $1,460,000 cash deficit for August. Thus, loans outstanding will total $3.1 million at the end of August.

Sales peak in September, and the cash deficit during this month will hit a high of $2,280,000. The total borrowing requirements through September will increase to $5,380,000. Sales, purchases, and payments for past purchases will fall sharply in October, but collections will be the highest of any month because they will reflect the high September sales. As a result, Drexel

**Table 18-1**
**Drexel Card Company:**
**Worksheet and Cash Budget**
**(Thousands of Dollars)**

| | May | June | July | Aug. | Sept. | Oct. | Nov. | Dec. |
|---|---|---|---|---|---|---|---|---|
| **I. Worksheet** | | | | | | | | |
| Sales (gross)[a] | $5,000 | $5,000 | $10,000 | $15,000 | $20,000 | $10,000 | $10,000 | $5,000 |
| Collections: | | | | | | | | |
| During month of sale (20% less 2% discount) | 980 | 980 | 1,960 | 2,940 | 3,920 | 1,960 | 1,960 | 980 |
| During first month after sale month (70%) | | 3,500 | 3,500 | 7,000 | 10,500 | 14,000 | 7,000 | 7,000 |
| During second month after sale month (10%) | | | 500 | 500 | 1,000 | 1,500 | 2,000 | 1,000 |
| Total collections | $ 980 | $4,480 | $ 5,960 | $10,440 | $15,420 | $17,460 | $10,960 | $8,980 |
| | | | | | | | | |
| Purchases (70% of next month's gross sales) | $3,500 | $7,000 | $10,500 | $14,000 | $ 7,000 | $ 7,000 | $ 3,500 | |
| Payments (1-month lag) | | $3,500 | $ 7,000 | $10,500 | $14,000 | $ 7,000 | $ 7,000 | $3,500 |
| **II. Cash Budget** | | | | | | | | |
| (1) Collections (from worksheet) | | | $ 5,960 | $10,440 | $15,420 | $17,460 | $10,960 | $8,980 |
| (2) Payments: | | | | | | | | |
| (3)   Purchases (from worksheet) | | | $ 7,000 | $10,500 | $14,000 | $ 7,000 | $ 7,000 | $3,500 |
| (4)   Wages and salaries | | | 750 | 1,000 | 1,250 | 750 | 750 | 500 |
| (5)   Rent | | | 250 | 250 | 250 | 250 | 250 | 250 |
| (6)   Other expenses | | | 100 | 150 | 200 | 100 | 100 | 50 |
| (7)   Taxes | | | | | 2,000 | | | 2,000 |
| (8)   Payment for plant construction | | | | | | 5,000 | | |
| (9)   Total payments | | | $ 8,100 | $11,900 | $17,700 | $13,100 | $ 8,100 | $6,300 |
| (10) Net cash gain (loss) during month (Line 1 − Line 9) | | | ($ 2,140) | ($ 1,460) | ($ 2,280) | $ 4,360 | $ 2,860 | $2,680 |
| (11) Cash at start of month if no borrowing is done (start July with $3,000; calculated thereafter)[b] | | | 3,000 | 860 | (600) | (2,880) | 1,480 | 4,340 |
| (12) Cumulative cash (= cash at start + gains or − losses = Line 10 + Line 11) | | | $ 860 | ($ 600) | ($ 2,880) | $ 1,480 | $ 4,340 | $7,020 |
| (13) Deduct: Target cash balance | | | 2,500 | 2,500 | 2,500 | 2,500 | 2,500 | 2,500 |
| (14) Total loans outstanding required to maintain $2,500 target cash balance if Line 13 exceeds Line 12[c] | | | $ 1,640 | $ 3,100 | $ 5,380 | $ 1,020 | — | — |
| (15) Surplus cash if Line 12 exceeds Line 13[c] | | | — | — | — | — | $ 1,840 | $4,520 |

Notes:

[a]Although the budget period is July through December, sales and purchases data for May and June are needed to determine collections and payouts during July and August.

[b]The amount shown on Line 11 for the first budget period month, the $3,000 balance on July 1, is assumed to be on hand initially. The values shown for each of the following months on Line 11 represent the cumulative cash as shown on Line 12 for the preceding month; for example, the $860 shown on Line 11 for August is taken from Line 12 in the July column.

[c]When the target cash balance of $2,500 (Line 13) is deducted from the cumulative cash balance (Line 12), a resulting negative figure is shown on Line 14 as a required loan while a positive figure is shown on Line 15 as surplus cash.

will enjoy a healthy $4,360,000 cash surplus during October. This surplus can be used to pay off borrowings, so loans outstanding will decline by $4,360,000, to $1,020,000.

Drexel will have another cash surplus in November, which will permit it to pay off all of its loans—in fact, the company is expected to have $1,840,000 in surplus cash by the month's end, and another cash surplus in December will swell the extra cash to $4,520,000. With such a large amount of unneeded funds, Drexel's treasurer will doubtless want to invest in interest-bearing securities or to put the funds to use in some other way.

Before concluding our discussion of the cash budget, we should make some additional points:

**1.** Our cash budget does not reflect interest on loans or income from the investment of surplus cash. This refinement could be added easily.

**2.** More important, if cash inflows and outflows are not uniform during the month, we could be seriously understating or overstating our financing requirements. The data in Table 18-1 show the situation expected on the last day of each month, but on any given day during the month it could be quite different. For example, if all payments had to be made on the fifth of each month but collections came in uniformly throughout the month, then we would need to borrow much larger amounts than those shown in Table 18-1. In this case we would need to prepare a cash budget centered on the fifth of the month, which would identify the peak borrowing requirements or, better yet, prepare a cash budget identifying requirements on a daily basis.

**3.** Since depreciation is a noncash charge, it does not appear on the cash budget other than through its effect on taxes paid.

**4.** Since the cash budget represents a forecast, all the values in the table are *expected* values. If actual sales, purchases, and so on are different from the forecasted levels, then the projected cash deficits and surpluses will also be incorrect.

**5.** Computerized spreadsheet programs such as *Lotus 1-2-3* are particularly well suited for constructing and analyzing the cash budget, especially with respect to the sensitivity of cash flows to changes in sales levels, collection periods, and the like. These models can be used to answer instantly such questions as "What if collections slow down—then what will our cash needs be?" Problem 18-3 at the end of the chapter is an example.

**6.** Finally, we should note that the target cash balance would probably be adjusted over time, rising and falling with seasonal patterns and with long-term changes in the scale of the firm's operations. Thus, Drexel would probably need more cash during August and September than at other times, and as the company grows, so will its required cash balance. Factors that influence the target cash balance are discussed in the following sections.

## Other Factors Influencing the Target Cash Balance

Any firm's target cash balance is normally set as the larger of (1) its transactions balances plus precautionary (safety stock) balances or (2) its required compensating balances as determined by its agreements with its banks. Both the transactions balances and the precautionary balances depend on the firm's volume of business, the degree of uncertainty inherent in its forecasts of cash inflows and outflows, and its ability to borrow on short notice to meet cash shortfalls. Consider again the cash budget for the Drexel Card Company. The target cash balance (or desired cash balance) is shown on Line 13 of Table 18-1. Other things held constant, the target cash balance would increase if Drexel expanded but decrease if it contracted. Similarly, Drexel could afford to operate with a smaller target balance if it could forecast better and thus be more certain that inflows would come in as scheduled and that no unanticipated outflows, such as might result from uninsured fire losses, lawsuits, and the like, would occur. The higher the cash balance, the smaller the probability that reduced inflows or unexpected outflows would cause the firm to actually run out of cash.

Statistics are not available on whether transactions balances or compensating balances actually control most firms' target cash balances, but compensating balance requirements do often dominate, especially during periods of high interest rates and tight money.[2] Also, while our discussion of the target cash balance in this section has been more intuitive than rigorous, formal models designed to optimize cash holdings have been developed. One of these models is discussed later in the chapter.

## Increasing the Efficiency of Cash Management

While a carefully prepared cash budget is a necessary starting point, there are other elements of a good cash management program, some of which we describe in this section.

### Cash Flow Synchronization

If you as an individual were to receive income once a year, you would probably put it in the bank, draw down your account periodically, and have an average balance during the year of about half your annual income. If you received income monthly, or even daily, instead of once a year, you would operate with a lower average checking account balance—indeed, if you could arrange to receive income daily and to pay rent, tuition, and other charges on a daily basis, and if you were quite confident of your forecasted inflows and outflows, this would enable you to hold a very small average cash

---

[2]This point is underscored by an incident that occurred at a professional finance meeting. A professor presented a scholarly paper that used operations research techniques to determine "optimal cash balances" for a sample of firms. He then reported that the firms' actual cash balances greatly exceeded their "optimal" balances, suggesting inefficiency and the need for more refined techniques. The discussant of the paper made her comments short and sweet. She reported that she had written each of the sample firms and asked them why they had so much cash; they had uniformly replied that their cash holdings were set by compensating balance requirements. The model was useful to determine the optimal cash balance in the absence of compensating balance requirements, but it was precisely those requirements that determined actual balances. Since the model did not include compensating balances as a determinant of cash balances, its usefulness was questionable.

balance. Exactly the same situation holds for business firms—by improving their forecasts and arranging things so that their cash receipts coincide with the timing of their cash outflows, firms can hold their transactions balances to a minimum. Recognizing this point, utility companies, oil companies, and others arrange to bill customers and to pay their own bills on regular "billing cycles" throughout the month. In our cash budgeting example, if the Drexel Card Company could arrange more **synchronized cash flows** and increase the certainty of its forecasts, it could reduce its minimum cash balance and therefore its required bank loans.

**synchronized cash flows**
A situation in which inflows coincide with outflows, thereby permitting a firm to hold transactions balances to a minimum.

**float**
The amount of funds tied up in checks that have been written but are still in process and have not yet been collected.

### Using Float

**Float** is defined as the difference between the balance shown in a firm's (or individual's) checkbook and the balance on the bank's books. Suppose a firm writes, on the average, checks in the amount of $5,000 each day, and it takes about six days for these checks to clear and to be deducted from the firm's bank account. Thus, the firm's own checking records show a balance $30,000 smaller than the bank's records. If the firm receives checks in the amount of $5,000 daily but loses four days while they are being deposited and cleared, its own books will have a balance that is, because of this factor, $20,000 larger than the bank's balance. Thus, the firm's *net float*—the difference between the $30,000 positive float and the $20,000 negative float—will be $10,000.

If the firm's own collection and clearing process is more efficient than that of the recipients of its checks—which is generally true of larger, more efficient firms—then the firm could show a *negative* balance on its own records but a *positive* balance on the books of its bank. Some firms indicate that they *never* have positive book cash balances. One large manufacturer of construction equipment has stated that while its account, according to its bank's records, shows an average cash balance of about $20 million, its *book* cash balance is *minus* $20 million—it has $40 million of net float. Obviously the firm must be able to forecast its positive and negative clearings accurately in order to make such heavy use of float.[3]

Basically, a firm's net float is a function of its ability to speed up collections on checks received and to slow down collections on checks written. Efficient firms go to great lengths to speed up the processing of incoming checks, thus putting the funds to work faster, and they try to stretch their own payments out as long as possible.

---

[3]E.F. Hutton, in the example cited at the beginning of the chapter, told its banks that checks were coming when in fact it knew they were not coming. It is quite proper to forecast what your bank will have recorded as your balance, even if that balance is different from the balance your own books show. It is not proper to forecast an overdrawn situation but then to tell the bank that you forecast a positive balance.

A question raised during the Hutton investigation was this: "Why didn't the banks recognize that Hutton was generally overdrawn and call the company to task?" The answer is that some banks, with tight controls, did exactly that and refused to let Hutton get away with the practice. Other banks were lax. Still other banks apparently let Hutton get away with being chronically overdrawn out of fear of losing its business. In many people's opinion, the banks were as much at fault as Hutton. Still, in business dealings honesty is presumed, and Hutton was dishonest in its dealings with the banks.

**check clearing**
The process of converting a check that has been written and mailed into cash in the payee's account.

When a customer writes and mails a check, this does *not* mean that the funds are immediately available to the receiving firm. Most of us have deposited a check in our account and then been told that we cannot write our own checks against this deposit until the **check-clearing** process has been completed. Our bank must (1) make sure that the check we deposited is good and (2) receive funds itself from the customer's bank before releasing funds for us to spend.

As shown on the left side of Figure 18-1, quite a bit of time may be required for a firm to process incoming checks and obtain the use of the money. A check must first be delivered through the mail and then cleared

**Figure 18-1**
**Diagram of the Check-Clearing Process**

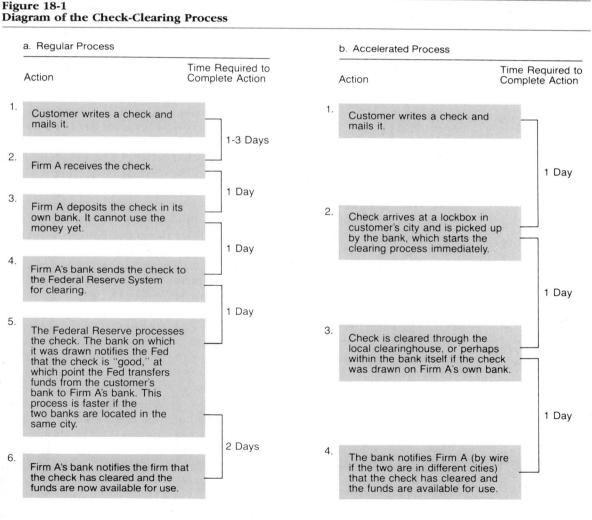

a. Regular Process

| Action | Time Required to Complete Action |
|---|---|

1. Customer writes a check and mails it.

   1-3 Days

2. Firm A receives the check.

   1 Day

3. Firm A deposits the check in its own bank. It cannot use the money yet.

   1 Day

4. Firm A's bank sends the check to the Federal Reserve System for clearing.

   1 Day

5. The Federal Reserve processes the check. The bank on which it was drawn notifies the Fed that the check is "good," at which point the Fed transfers funds from the customer's bank to Firm A's bank. This process is faster if the two banks are located in the same city.

   2 Days

6. Firm A's bank notifies the firm that the check has cleared and the funds are now available for use.

6-8 Working Days

b. Accelerated Process

| Action | Time Required to Complete Action |
|---|---|

1. Customer writes a check and mails it.

   1 Day

2. Check arrives at a lockbox in customer's city and is picked up by the bank, which starts the clearing process immediately.

   1 Day

3. Check is cleared through the local clearinghouse, or perhaps within the bank itself if the check was drawn on Firm A's own bank.

   1 Day

4. The bank notifies Firm A (by wire if the two are in different cities) that the check has cleared and the funds are available for use.

3 Working Days

through the banking system before the money can be put to use. Checks received from customers in distant cities are especially subject to delays because of mail time and also because more parties are involved. For example, assume that we receive a check and deposit it in our bank. Our bank must send the check to the bank on which it was drawn. Only when this latter bank transfers funds to our bank are they available for us to use. Checks are generally cleared through the Federal Reserve System or through a clearinghouse set up by the banks in a particular city. Of course, if the check is deposited in the same bank on which it was drawn, that bank merely transfers funds by bookkeeping entries from one of its depositors to another. The length of time required for other checks to clear is thus a function of the distance between the payer's and the payee's banks; in the case of private clearinghouses, it can range from one to three days. The maximum time required for checks to clear through the Federal Reserve System is two days, but mail delays can slow down things on each end of the Fed's involvement in the process.

The right side of Figure 18-1 shows how the process can be speeded up. First, to reduce mail and clearing delays, a **lockbox plan** can be used. Suppose a New York firm makes sales to customers all across the country. It can arrange to have its customers send payments to post office boxes (lockboxes) in their own local areas. A local bank will pick up the checks, have them cleared in the local area, and then transfer the funds by wire to the company's New York bank. In this way, collection time can be reduced by one to five days. Examples of freeing funds in the amount of $5 million or more by this method are not uncommon.

Just as expediting the collection process conserves cash, slowing down disbursements accomplishes the same thing by keeping cash on hand for longer periods. One obviously could simply delay payments, but this would involve equally obvious difficulties. Firms have in the past devised rather ingenious methods for "legitimately" lengthening the collection period on their own checks, primarily by writing checks on banks in out-of-the-way places. Since such practices are usually recognized for what they are, there are severe limits to their use.

Another widely used procedure for delaying payouts is the use of *drafts*. While a check is payable on demand, a draft must be transmitted to the issuer, who approves it and deposits funds to cover it, after which it can be collected. Insurance companies often use drafts. In handling claims, for instance, Aetna can pay a claim by draft on Friday. The recipient deposits the draft at a local bank, which must then send it to Aetna's Hartford bank. It may be Wednesday or Thursday before the draft arrives. The bank then sends it to the company's accounting department, which has until 3 P.M. that day to inspect and approve it. Not until then does Aetna have to deposit funds in its bank to pay the draft.

## Cash Management in the Multidivisional Firm

The concepts, techniques, and procedures described thus far in the chapter must be extended when applied to large, national firms. Such corporations have plants and sales offices all across the nation (or the world), and they

**lockbox plan**
A procedure used to speed up collections and reduce float through the use of post office boxes in payers' local areas.

deal with banks in all of their operating territories. These companies must maintain compensating balances in each of their banks, and they must be sure that no bank account becomes overdrawn. Cash inflows and outflows are subject to random fluctuations, so in the absence of close control and coordination, there would be a tendency for some accounts to have shortages while others had excess balances. Thus, a sound cash management program for such a multibank corporation necessarily includes provisions for keeping strict control over the level of funds in each account and for shifting funds among accounts so as to minimize the total corporate cash balance. Mathematical models and electronic connections between a central computer and each branch location have been developed to help with such situations, but a discussion of these topics would go beyond the scope of this book.

## Bank Relationships

Banks provide a great many services to firms—they clear checks, operate lockbox plans, supply credit information, and the like. Since these services cost the bank money, the bank must be compensated for rendering them.

### Compensating Balances

Banks earn most of their income by lending money at interest, and most of the funds they lend are obtained in the form of deposits. If a firm maintains a deposit account with an average balance of $100,000, and the bank can lend these funds at a net return of $8,000, then the account is, in a sense, worth $8,000 to the bank. Thus, it is to the bank's advantage to provide services worth up to $8,000 to attract and hold the account.

Banks first determine the costs of the services rendered to their larger customers and then estimate the average account balances necessary to provide enough income to compensate for these costs. Firms could make direct payments for these services, but they often find it cheaper to maintain compensating balances in order to avoid paying cash service charges to the bank.[4]

Compensating balances are also required by some banks under loan agreements. During periods when the supply of credit is restricted and interest rates are high, banks frequently insist that borrowers maintain accounts averaging a specified percentage of the loan amount as a condition for granting a loan; 15 percent is a typical figure. If the balance is larger than the firm would otherwise maintain, then the effective cost of the loan is increased; the excess balance presumably "compensates" the bank for making a loan at a rate below what it could earn on the funds if they were invested elsewhere.[5]

Compensating balances can be established (1) as an *absolute minimum*—say, $100,000—below which the actual balance must never fall or (2) as a

---

[4]Compensating balance arrangements apply to individuals as well as to business firms. Thus, you might get "free" checking services if you maintain a minimum balance of $200 but be charged 10 cents per check if your balance falls below that amount during the month.

[5]The interest rate effect of compensating balances was discussed in Chapter 17.

*minimum average* balance—perhaps $100,000—over some period, generally a month. The absolute minimum is a much more restrictive requirement, because the total amount of cash held during the month must be above $100,000 by the amount of the firm's transactions balances. The $100,000 in this case is "dead money" from the firm's standpoint. With a minimum average balance, however, the account could fall to zero on one day provided it was $200,000 on some other day, with the average working out to $100,000. Thus, the $100,000 in this case is available for transactions.

Statistics on compensating balance requirements are not available, but average balances are typical and absolute minimums rare for business accounts. Discussions with bankers, however, indicate that absolute balance requirements are less rare during times of extremely tight money.

### Overdraft Systems

**overdraft system**
A system whereby depositors may write checks in excess of their balances with the banks automatically extending loans to cover the shortages.

Most countries outside the United States use **overdraft systems**. In such systems depositors write checks in excess of their actual balances, and their banks automatically extend loans to cover the shortages. The maximum amount of such loans must, of course, be established beforehand. Although statistics are not available on the usage of overdrafts in the United States, a number of firms have worked out informal, and in some cases formal, overdraft arrangements. Also, both banks and credit card companies regularly establish "cash reserve" systems for individuals. In general, the use of overdrafts has been increasing in recent years, and as this trend continues it will lead to a reduction of cash balances.

## Matching the Costs and Benefits of Cash Management

Although a number of procedures may be used to hold down cash balance requirements, implementing these methods is not a costless operation. How far should a firm go in making its cash operations more efficient? As a general rule, the firm should incur these expenses so long as marginal returns exceed marginal expenses.

For example, suppose that by establishing a lockbox system and increasing the accuracy of cash inflow and outflow forecasts, a firm can reduce its investment in cash by $1 million without increasing the risk of running short of cash. Further, suppose the firm borrows at a cost of 12 percent. The steps taken have released $1 million, which can be used to reduce bank loans and thus save $120,000 per year. If the costs of the procedures necessary to release the $1 million are less than $120,000, the move is a good one; if they exceed $120,000, the greater efficiency is not worth the cost. It is clear that larger firms, which have larger cash balances, can better afford to hire the personnel necessary to maintain tight control over their cash positions. Cash management is thus one element of business operations in which economies of scale are present.

Very clearly, the value of careful cash management depends on the costs of funds invested in cash, which in turn depend on the current rate of interest. In the 1980s, when interest rates have often been near the historic highs, firms have been devoting a great deal of care to cash management.

## Marketable Securities

**marketable securities**
Securities that can be sold on short notice for close to their quoted market prices.

Sizable holdings of such short-term **marketable securities** as U.S. Treasury bills (T-bills) or bank certificates of deposit (CDs) are often reported on corporations' financial statements. The reasons for such holdings, as well as the factors that influence the choice of securities held, are discussed in this section.

### Reasons for Holding Marketable Securities

Marketable securities typically provide much lower yields than operating assets—for example, International Business Machines (IBM) recently held a multibillion-dollar portfolio of marketable securities that yielded about 9 percent, while its operating assets provided a return of about 18 percent. Why would a company such as IBM have such large holdings of low-yielding assets? There are two basic reasons for these holdings: (1) they serve as a substitute for cash balances, and (2) they are used as a temporary investment. These points are considered next.

***Marketable Securities as a Substitute for Cash.*** Some firms hold portfolios of marketable securities in lieu of larger cash balances, then sell some securities from the portfolios to increase the cash account when cash outflows exceed inflows. In such situations the marketable securities are a substitute for transactions balances, for precautionary balances, and for speculative balances. However, in most cases the securities are held primarily for precautionary purposes—most firms prefer to rely on bank credit to make temporary transactions or to meet speculative needs, but they still want some liquid assets to guard against a possible shortage of bank credit.

During the late 1970s, IBM had approximately $6 billion in marketable securities. This large liquid balance had been built up as a reserve for possible damage payments resulting from pending antitrust suits. When it became clear that IBM would win most of the suits, the liquidity need declined, and the company spent some of the funds on other assets, including repurchases of its own stock and the acquisition of other firms (mergers). This is a prime example of a firm's building up its precautionary balances to handle possible emergencies.

***Marketable Securities as a Temporary Investment.*** Temporary investments in marketable securities generally occur in one of the following three situations:

**1.** *When the firm must finance seasonal or cyclical operations.* Firms engaged in seasonal operations frequently have surplus cash flows during one part of the year and deficit cash flows during the other. Such firms may purchase marketable securities during their surplus periods and then liquidate them when cash deficits occur. Other firms, however, choose to use bank financings to cover such shortages.

**2.** *When the firm must meet some known financial requirements.* If a major plant construction program is planned for the near future, or if a bond issue is about to mature, a firm may build up its marketable securities portfolio to provide the required funds. Furthermore, marketable securities holdings are frequently built up immediately preceding quarterly corporate tax payment dates.

**3.** *When the firm has just sold long-term securities.* Expanding firms generally have to sell long-term securities (stocks or bonds) periodically. The proceeds from such sales are often invested in marketable securities, which are then sold off to provide cash as it is needed to pay for operating assets.

### Marketable Securities versus Borrowing

Actually, each of the needs listed above can be met either by taking short-term loans or by holding marketable securities. Consider a firm such as the Drexel Card Company, whose cash budget we discussed earlier. Drexel's sales are growing over time, but they fluctuate on a seasonal basis; as we saw from Drexel's cash budget (Table 18-1), the firm plans to borrow to meet seasonal needs. As an alternative financial policy, Drexel could hold a portfolio of marketable securities and then liquidate these securities to meet its peak cash needs.

A firm's marketable securities policy is an integral part of its overall working capital policy. If the firm has a conservative working capital financing policy, then its long-term capital will exceed its permanent assets, and it will hold marketable securities when inventories and receivables are low. With an aggressive policy, it will never carry any securities and will borrow heavily to meet peak needs. With a moderate policy, under which maturities are matched, the firm will match permanent assets with long-term financing and it will meet most seasonal increases in inventories and receivables with short-term loans, but it will also carry marketable securities at certain times.

Figure 18-2 illustrates three alternative policies for a firm such as Drexel. Under Plan A, which represents an aggressive financing policy, Drexel would hold no marketable securities, relying completely on bank loans to meet seasonal peaks. Under the conservative Plan B, Drexel would stockpile marketable securities during slack periods and then sell them to raise funds for peak needs. Plan C is a compromise: Under this alternative, the company would hold some securities but not enough to meet all of its peak needs. Drexel actually follows Plan C.

There are advantages and disadvantages to each of these strategies. Plan A is clearly the most risky—the firm's current ratio is always lower than under the other plans, indicating that it might encounter difficulties either in borrowing the funds needed or in repaying the loan. On the other hand, Plan A requires no holdings of low-yielding marketable securities, and this will prob-

**Figure 18-2**
**Alternative Strategies for Meeting Seasonal Cash Needs**

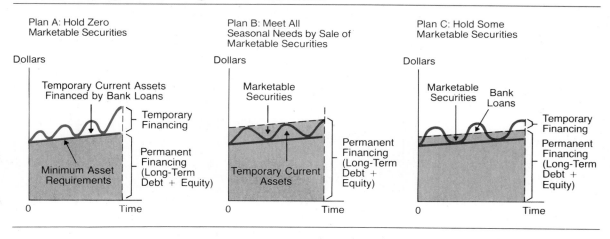

ably lead to a relatively high expected rate of return on both total assets and equity.

Exactly the same types of choices are involved with regard to meeting known financial needs such as plant construction as well as deciding whether to issue long-term securities before or after the actual need for the funds arises. Commonwealth Edison, the electric utility serving Chicago, can be used to illustrate the issues involved in timing the sale of long-term securities. Commonwealth has a permanent, ongoing construction program, generating a continuous need for new outside capital. As we saw in Chapters 11 and 12, there are substantial fixed costs involved in stock or bond flotations, so these securities are issued infrequently and in large amounts. During the 1960s, Commonwealth followed the practice of selling bonds and stocks *before* the capital was needed, investing the proceeds in marketable securities, and then liquidating these assets to finance plant construction. Plan A in Figure 18-3 illustrates this procedure. However, during the 1970s and 1980s Commonwealth encountered financial stress. It was forced to use up its liquid assets and to switch to its present policy of financing plant construction with short-term bank loans and then selling long-term securities to retire these loans when they have built up to some target level. This policy is illustrated by Plan B of Figure 18-3.

Plan A is the more conservative, less risky one. First, the company is minimizing its liquidity problems because it has no short-term debt hanging over its head. Second, it is sure of having the funds available to meet construction payments as they come due. On the other hand, when firms borrow they generally have to pay interest rates that are higher than the return they receive on marketable securities; following the less risky strategy therefore does have a cost. Again, firms are faced with a risk/return trade-off.

It is difficult to "prove" that one strategy is better than another. In principle, the practice of holding marketable securities reduces the firm's expected

**Figure 18-3**
**Alternative Methods of Financing a Continuous Construction Program**

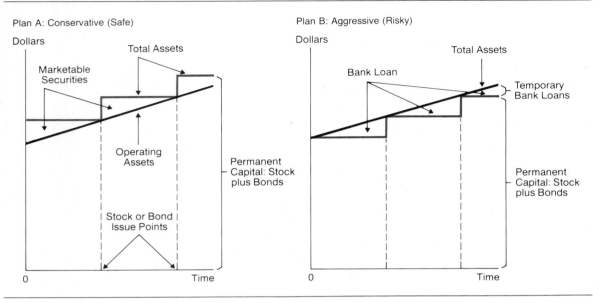

rate of return, but it also reduces $k_s$, the required rate of return on its stock. Although we can quantify the cost of following a more conservative policy—it is the average percentage differential between the return received on marketable securities and the interest rate paid on the long-term debt—it is almost impossible to quantify the benefits in terms of how much such a policy reduces risk and how this risk reduction affects $k_s$. Further, it is impossible to measure the higher sales and profits, if any, that a liquid asset portfolio might make possible should a credit crunch occur. Accordingly, the basic policies with regard to securities holdings are generally set either on the basis of judgment or, as in the case of Commonwealth Edison, by circumstances beyond the company's control.

### Criteria for Selecting Marketable Securities

A wide variety of securities, differing in terms of default risk, interest rate risk, liquidity risk, and expected rate of return, are available to firms that do choose to hold marketable securities. In this section we first consider the characteristics of different securities and then show how the financial manager selects the specific instruments to be held in the portfolio.

**default risk**
The risk that a borrower will not pay the interest or principal on a loan.

***Default Risk.*** The risk that a borrower will be unable to make interest payments or to repay the principal amount on schedule is known as **default risk**. If the issuer is the U.S. Treasury, default risk is negligible, so Treasury securities are regarded as being free of such risk. Corporate securities and bonds issued by state and local governments are subject to some degree of default risk and are rated with regard to their chances of going into default.[6]

***Interest Rate Risk.*** We saw in Chapter 5 that bond prices vary with changes in interest rates and that the prices of long-term bonds are much more sensitive to changes in interest rates than are prices of short-term securities—long-term bonds have more **interest rate risk**. Therefore, even Treasury bonds are not completely free of risk—they are subject to risk due to interest rate fluctuations. Thus, if Drexel's treasurer purchased at par $1 million of 25-year U.S. government bonds paying 9 percent interest and if interest rates rose to 14.5 percent, the market value of the bonds would fall from $1 million to approximately $638,000—a loss of almost 40 percent. (This actually happened from 1980 to 1982.) Had 90-day Treasury bills been held, the capital loss resulting from the change in interest rates would have been negligible.

**interest rate risk**
The risk to which investors are exposed due to changing interest rates.

***Purchasing Power Risk.*** Another type of risk is **purchasing power risk**, or the risk that inflation will reduce the purchasing power of a given sum of money. Purchasing power risk, which is important both to firms and to individual investors during times of inflation, is generally regarded as being lower on assets whose returns can be expected to rise during inflation than on assets whose returns are fixed. Thus, real estate, short-term debt, and common stocks are often thought of as being better "hedges against inflation" than are bonds and other long-term fixed-income securities.

**purchasing power risk**
The risk that inflation will reduce the purchasing power of a given sum of money.

***Liquidity, or Marketability, Risk.*** An asset that can be sold on short notice for close to its quoted market price is defined as being highly liquid. If Drexel purchased $1 million of infrequently traded bonds of a relatively obscure company such as Gainesville Pork Products, it would probably have to accept a price reduction in order to sell the bonds on short notice. On the other hand, if Drexel invested in U.S. Treasury bonds or bonds issued by AT&T, General Motors, or Exxon, it would be able to dispose of them almost instantaneously at close to the quoted market price. These latter bonds are therefore said to have very little **liquidity, or marketability, risk**.[7]

**liquidity (marketability) risk**
The risk that securities cannot be sold at a reasonable price on short notice.

***Returns on Securities.*** As we know from earlier chapters, the higher a security's risk, the higher its expected and required return. Thus, corporate treasurers, like other investors, must make a trade-off between risk and return when choosing investments for their marketable securities portfolios. Since

---

[6]Bond ratings were discussed in detail in Chapter 12.

[7]Some people define "liquidity" to encompass an absence of default risk, interest rate risk, and marketability risk, and also "market risk" such as any stock would have. By this definition, short-term Treasury bills, CDs, and the like, are the only "liquid assets," and IBM stock is not liquid. These definitions are not really important, but the characteristics of different securities are important.

the liquidity portfolio is generally held for a specific known need or else for use in emergencies, the firm might be financially embarrassed should the portfolio decline in value. Further, most nonfinancial corporations do not have investment departments specializing in appraising securities and determining the probability of their going into default. Accordingly, the marketable securities portfolio is generally confined to safe, highly liquid, short-term securities issued by either the U.S. government or the very strongest corporations. Given the purpose of the securities portfolio, treasurers are unwilling to sacrifice safety for higher rates of return.

### Types of Marketable Securities

Table 18-2 provides a listing of the major types of securities available for investment, with yields as of June 10, 1977, February 10, 1982, and June 3, 1985. Depending on how long they will be held, the financial manager decides upon a suitable maturity pattern for the firm's holdings. Because the securities' characteristics change with shifts in financial market conditions, it would be misleading to attempt to give detailed descriptions of them here.

It should be noted that large corporations which have larger amounts of surplus cash tend to make direct purchases of Treasury bills, commercial paper, and CDs as well as the Euromarket securities which will be described in Chapter 20. Smaller firms, on the other hand, are more likely to use money market mutual funds as **near-cash reserves** because their volume of investment simply does not warrant their hiring investment specialists to manage the portfolios and to make sure that the securities held mature (or can be sold) at the same time cash is required. Such firms can use money funds and then literally write checks on them to meet cash needs as they arise. Interest rates on money funds are somewhat lower than those on direct investments of equivalent risk, but net returns, which have the expenses of managing the portfolio already deducted, are often higher on money funds for smaller companies.

**near-cash reserves**
Reserves that can be quickly and easily converted to cash.

## The Baumol Model for Balancing Cash and Marketable Securities

Earlier in the chapter, when we discussed the Drexel Card Company's cash budget, we took as a given the $2.5 million target cash balance. Subsequently we discussed how the use of lockboxes, the synchronization of cash inflows and outflows, and so on, can be used to reduce the size of the required cash balance. Now we shall consider a formal model for establishing a target cash balance.

William Baumol first noted that cash balances are in many respects similar to inventories and that the EOQ inventory model, which will be developed in Chapter 19, can be used to establish a target cash balance.[8] Baumol's

---

[8]William J. Baumol, "The Transactions Demand for Cash: An Inventory Theoretic Approach," *Quarterly Journal of Economics,* November 1952, 545-556.

**Table 18-2**
**Securities Available for Investment of Surplus Cash**

| Security | Typical Maturity at Time of Issue | Approximate Yields as of: | | |
|---|---|---|---|---|
| | | 6/10/77 | 2/10/82 | 6/3/85 |
| **Suitable to Hold as Near-Cash Reserve** | | | | |
| U.S. Treasury bills | 91 days to 1 year | 4.8% | 15.1% | 7.2% |
| Commercial paper | Up to 270 days | 5.5 | 15.3 | 7.5 |
| Negotiable certificates of deposit (CDs) of U.S. banks | Up to 1 year | 6.0 | 15.5 | 7.7 |
| Money market mutual funds | Instant liquidity | 5.1 | 14.0 | 8.9 |
| Floating rate preferred stock mutual funds[a] | Instant liquidity | n.a. | n.a. | 7.9 |
| Eurodollar market time deposits | Up to 1 year | 6.1 | 16.2 | 8.0 |
| **Not Suitable to Hold as Near-Cash Reserve** | | | | |
| U.S. Treasury notes | 3 to 5 years | 6.8 | 14.8 | 9.3 |
| U.S. Treasury bonds | Up to 30 years | 7.6 | 14.6 | 10.6 |
| Corporate bonds (AAA)[b] | Up to 40 years | 8.2 | 16.0 | 11.3 |
| State and local government bonds (AAA)[b,c] | Up to 30 years | 5.7 | 12.8 | 9.0 |
| Preferred stocks (AAA)[b,c] | 30 years to perpetual | 7.5 | 14.0 | 9.3 |
| Common stocks of other corporations | Unlimited | Variable | Variable | Variable |
| Common stock of the firm in question | Unlimited | Variable | Variable | Variable |

[a]Floating rate preferred stock is a recent innovation in near-cash securities, first marketed in 1983. It is held by corporations (often through money funds designed for this purpose) because of the 85 percent dividend tax exclusion.

[b]Rates shown for corporate and state/local government bonds and preferred stock are for longer maturities rated AAA. Lower-rated securities have higher yields. The slope of the yield curve determines whether shorter- or longer-term securities of a given rating would have higher yields.

[c]Rates are lower on state and municipal government bonds because the interest they pay is exempt from federal income taxes and on preferred stocks because 85 percent of the dividends paid on them is exempt from federal taxes for corporate owners, who own most preferred stocks.

model assumes (1) that the firm uses cash at a steady, predictable rate—say, $1 million per week—and (2) that the firm's cash inflows from operations also occur at a steady, predictable rate—say, $900,000 per week—so (3) that the firm's net cash outflows, or net need for cash, also occur at a steady rate—in this case, $100,000 per week.[9] Under these steady-state assumptions, the firm's cash position will resemble the situation shown in Figure 18-4.

If our illustrative firm started at Time 0 with a cash balance of C = $300,000, and if its outflows exceeded its inflows by $100,000 per week, then (1) its cash balance would drop to zero at the end of Week 3 and (2) its average cash balance would be C/2 = $300,000/2 = $150,000. Therefore,

---

[9]Our hypothetical firm is experiencing a $100,000 weekly cash shortfall, but this does not necessarily imply that it is headed for bankruptcy. The firm could, for example, be highly profitable and be enjoying high earnings but be expanding so rapidly that it is experiencing chronic cash shortages that must be made up by borrowing or by selling common stock. (See Chapter 8 for examples.) Or, the firm could be in the construction business and therefore receive major cash inflows at wide intervals but have net cash outflows of $100,000 per week between major inflows.

**Figure 18-4**
**Cash Balances under the Baumol Model's Assumptions**

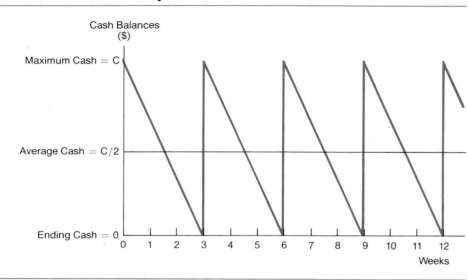

at the end of Week 3 the firm would have to replenish its cash balance, either by selling marketable securities, if it has any, or by borrowing.

If C were set at a higher level, say, $600,000, then the cash supply would last longer (6 weeks) and the firm would have to sell securities (or borrow) less frequently, but its average cash balance would rise from $150,000 to $300,000. Brokerage or some other type of transaction cost must be incurred in order to sell securities (or to borrow), so establishing larger cash balances will lower the "transactions costs" associated with obtaining cash. On the other hand, cash provides no income, so the larger the average cash balance, the higher the "opportunity cost," which is the return that could have been earned on securities or other assets held in lieu of cash. Thus, we have the situation that is graphed in Figure 18-5. The optimal cash balance is found by using the following variables and equations:

C = amount of cash raised by selling marketable securities or by borrowing. C/2 = average cash balance.

C* = optimal amount of cash to be raised by selling marketable securities or by borrowing. C*/2 = optimal average cash balance.

F = fixed costs of making a securities trade or of obtaining a loan.

T = total amount of net new cash needed for transactions over the entire period (usually a year).

k = opportunity cost of holding cash (equals the rate of return forgone on marketable securities or the cost of borrowing to hold cash).

**Figure 18-5**
**Determination of the Target Cash Balance**

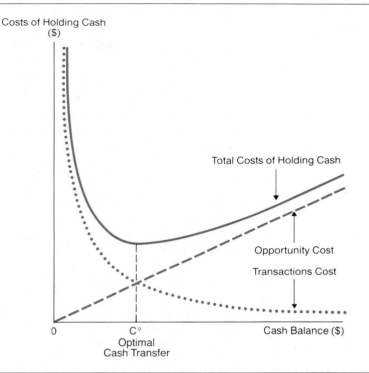

The total costs of cash balances consist of a holding, or opportunity, cost plus a transactions cost:[10]

$$\text{Total costs} = \text{Holding cost} + \text{Transactions cost}$$

$$= \left(\begin{array}{c}\text{Average cash}\\\text{balance}\end{array}\right)\left(\begin{array}{c}\text{Opportunity}\\\text{cost}\end{array}\right) + \left(\begin{array}{c}\text{Number of}\\\text{transactions}\end{array}\right)\left(\begin{array}{c}\text{Cost per}\\\text{transaction}\end{array}\right)$$

$$= \frac{C}{2}(k) + \frac{T}{C}(F). \qquad\qquad\qquad\qquad\qquad (18\text{-}1)$$

The minimum total costs are achieved when C is set equal to C*, the optimal cash transfer. C* is found as:[11]

$$C^* = \sqrt{\frac{2(F)(T)}{k}}. \qquad\qquad\qquad\qquad\qquad (18\text{-}2)$$

---

[10]Total costs can be expressed on both a before-tax and an after-tax basis. Both methods generally lead to the same conclusions regarding target cash balances and comparative costs. For simplicity, we present the model here on a before-tax basis.

[11]Equation 18-1 is differentiated with respect to C; the derivative is set equal to zero; and we then solve for C = C* to derive Equation 18-2. This model, applied to inventories and called the "EOQ Model," is discussed further in Chapter 19.

**Baumol model**
An economic model that determines the optimal cash balance by using economic ordering quantity (EOQ) concepts.

Equation 18-2 is the **Baumol model** for determining optimal cash balances. To illustrate its use, suppose F = $150; T = 52 weeks × $100,000/week = $5,200,000; and k = 15% = 0.15. Then

$$C^* = \sqrt{\frac{2(\$150)(\$5,200,000)}{0.15}} = \$101,980.$$

Therefore, the firm should sell securities in the amount of $101,980 when its cash balance approaches zero, thus building its cash balance back up to $101,980. If we divide T by C*, we have the number of transactions per year: $5,200,000/$101,980 = 50.99 ≈ 51, or about once a week. The firm's average cash balance would be $101,980/2 = $50,990 ≈ $51,000.

Notice that the optimal cash balance increases less than proportionately with increases in the amount of cash needed for transactions. For example, if the firm's size and consequently its net new cash needs doubled from $5,200,000 to $10,400,000 per year, average cash balances would increase by only 41 percent, from $51,000 to $72,000. This suggests that there are economies of scale in holding cash balances, and this in turn gives larger firms an edge over smaller ones.[12]

Of course, the firm would probably want to hold a "safety stock" of cash designed to reduce the probability of a cash shortage to some specified level. However, if the firm is able to sell securities or to borrow on short notice—and most larger firms can do so in a matter of just a couple of hours simply by making a telephone call—then the safety stock of cash can be quite low.

The Baumol model is obviously simplistic in many respects. Most important, it assumes relatively stable, predictable cash inflows and outflows, and it does not take account of any seasonal or cyclical trends. Other models as described in the end-of-chapter references have been developed to deal both with uncertainty in the cash flows and with trends. Any of these models—including the Baumol model—can provide a useful starting point for establishing a target cash balance, but all of them have limitations and must be applied with a great deal of judgment.

## Summary

The first topic covered in this chapter was *cash management*. We saw that the key element in any cash management system is the *cash budget*, which is a forecast of cash inflows and outflows during a given planning period. The cash budget shows whether the firm can expect a cash deficit, in which case plans must be made to obtain external capital, or a cash surplus, in which case plans should be made to invest the available funds. We also discussed ways of speeding up cash

---

[12]This edge may, of course, be more than offset by other factors—after all, cash management is only one aspect of running a business.

flows by the use of *lockboxes*, what *float* is and how it can be used to hold down bank loans, and *compensating balances*.

Our study of marketable securities began with a discussion of why securities are held—primarily they are held (1) as a reserve for future contingencies, (2) to meet seasonal needs, with holdings being built up during the slack season and then liquidated when cash requirements are high, (3) to meet known future cash requirements, such as construction progress payments or taxes, and (4) immediately after the sale of long-term securities. Given their motives for holding marketable securities, treasurers generally do not want to gamble by holding high-yield, risky securities—safety is the watchword, and rarely will a treasurer sacrifice it for the higher yields offered on risky securities.

The final section of the chapter dealt with the Baumol model, one of several models designed to determine the optimal cash balance. These models are generally based on the standard EOQ inventory model as described in Chapter 19, and they balance the opportunity cost of holding cash against the transactions costs associated with replenishing the cash account either by selling off marketable securities or by raising cash through the issuance of debt or equity securities.

## Questions

**18-1**   Define each of the following terms:
a. Transactions balance; compensating balance; precautionary balance; speculative balance
b. Cash budget; target cash balance
c. Synchronized cash flows
d. Float; check clearing; net float
e. Lockbox plan
f. Overdraft system
g. Marketable securities; near-cash reserves
h. Default risk; interest rate risk; purchasing power risk; liquidity (marketability) risk
i. Baumol model

**18-2**   What are the two principal reasons for holding cash? Can a firm estimate its target cash balance by summing the cash held to satisfy each of the two?

**18-3**   Explain how each of the following factors would probably affect a firm's target cash balance if all other factors were held constant.
a. The firm institutes a new billing procedure which better synchronizes its cash inflows and outflows.
b. The firm develops a new sales forecasting technique which improves its forecasts.
c. The firm reduces its portfolio of U.S. Treasury bills.
d. The firm arranges to use an overdraft system for its checking account.
e. The firm borrows a large amount of money from its bank and also begins to write far more checks than it did in the past.
f. Interest rates on Treasury bills rise from 5 percent to 10 percent.

**18-4**   In the cash budget shown in Table 18-1, is the projected maximum funds requirement of $5,380,000 in September known with certainty, or should it be regarded as the expected value of a probability distribution?

Consider how this peak would probably be affected by each of the following:

a. A lengthening of the average collection period.

b. An unanticipated decline in sales that occurred in a month when sales were supposed to peak.

c. A sharp drop in sales prices required to meet competition.

d. A sharp increase in interest rates for a firm with a large amount of short-term debt outstanding.

**18-5**   Would a lockbox plan make more sense for a firm that makes sales all over the United States or for a firm with the same volume of business but concentrated in its home city?

**18-6**   Would a corporate treasurer be more tempted to invest the firm's liquidity portfolio in long-term as opposed to short-term securities when the yield curve was upward sloping or downward sloping?

**18-7**   What does the term *liquidity* mean? Which would be more important to a firm that held a portfolio of marketable securities as precautionary balances against the possibility of losing a major lawsuit—liquidity or rate of return? Explain.

**18-8**   Firm A's management is very conservative, while Firm B's is more aggressive. Is it true that, other things the same, Firm B would probably have larger holdings of short-term marketable securities? Explain.

**18-9**   Is it true that interest rate risk refers to the risk that a firm will be unable to pay the interest on its bonds? Explain.

**18-10**  When selecting securities for portfolio investments, corporate treasurers must make a trade-off between risk and returns. Is it true that most treasurers are willing to assume a fairly high exposure to risk to gain higher expected returns?

## Self-Test Problem (*Solution on Page 640*)

**ST-1**   Olinde, Inc., has grown from a small Boston firm with customers concentrated in New England to a large, national firm serving customers throughout the United States. It has, however, maintained its central billing system in Boston. On average, 5 days elapse from the time customers mail payments until Olinde is able to receive, process, and deposit them. To shorten the collection period, Olinde is considering the installation of a lockbox system consisting of 30 local depository banks, or lockbox operators, and 8 regional concentration banks. The fixed costs of operating the system are estimated to be $14,000 per month. Under this system, customers' checks should be received by the lockbox operator 1 day after they are mailed, and daily collections should average $30,000 at each location. The collections will be transferred daily to the regional concentration banks. One transfer mechanism involves having the local depository banks use "mail depository transfer checks," or DTCs, to move the funds to the concentration banks; the alternative is to use electronic ("wire") transfers. A DTC would cost only 75 cents, but it would take 2 days before funds were in the concentration bank and thus available to Olinde. Therefore, float time under the DTC system would be 1 day for mail plus 2 days for transfer, or 3 days total, down from 5 days.

A wire transfer would cost $11, but funds would be available immediately, so float time would be only 1 day. If Olinde's opportunity cost is 11 percent, should it initiate the lockbox system? If so, which transfer method should be used? (Assume that there are 52 × 5 = 260 working days in a year.)

## Problems

Net float

**18-1**   The McShane-Blarney Company is setting up a new checking account with the First National Bank. McShane-Blarney plans to issue checks in the amount of $1 million each day and to deduct them from its own records at the close of business on the day they are written. On average, the bank will receive and clear (that is, deduct from the firm's bank balance) the checks at 5 P.M. the fourth day after they are written—for example, a check written on Monday will be cleared on Friday afternoon. The firm's agreement with the bank requires it to maintain a $750,000 average compensating balance; this is $250,000 greater than the cash balance the firm would otherwise have on deposit. It makes a $750,000 deposit at the time it opens the account.

a. Assuming that the firm makes deposits at 4 P.M. each day (and the bank includes them in that day's transactions), how much must it deposit daily in order to maintain a sufficient balance once it reaches a steady state? Indicate the required deposit on Day 1, Day 2, Day 3, Day 4, if any, and each day thereafter, assuming that the company will write checks for $1 million on Day 1 and each day thereafter.

b. How many days of float does McShane-Blarney carry?

c. What ending daily balance should the firm try to maintain (1) on the bank's records and (2) on its own records?

d. Explain how net float can help increase the value of the firm's common stock.

Cash budgeting

**18-2**   Rick and Marlo Petteway recently leased space in the Southside Mall and opened a new business, Petteway's Coin Shop. Business has been good, but the Petteways have frequently run out of cash. This has necessitated late payment on certain orders, which in turn is beginning to cause a problem with suppliers. The Petteways plan to borrow from the bank to have cash ready as needed, but first they need a forecast of just how much they must borrow. Accordingly, they have asked you to prepare a cash budget for the critical period around Christmas, when needs will be especially high.

Sales are made on a cash basis only. Petteway's purchases must be paid for the following month. The Petteways pay themselves a salary of $4,800 per month, and the rent is $2,000 per month. In addition, they must make a tax payment of $12,000 in December. The current cash on hand (on December 1) is $400, but the Petteways have agreed to maintain an average bank balance of $6,000—this is their target cash balance. (Disregard till cash, which is insignificant because the Petteways keep only a small amount on hand in order to lessen the chances of robbery.)

The estimated sales and purchases for December, January, and February are shown below. Purchases during November amounted to $140,000.

|           | Sales     | Purchases |
|-----------|-----------|-----------|
| December  | $160,000  | $40,000   |
| January   | 40,000    | 40,000    |
| February  | 60,000    | 40,000    |

a. Prepare a cash budget for December, January, and February.

b. Now suppose the Petteways were to start selling on a credit basis on December 1, giving customers 30 days to pay. All customers accept these terms, and all other facts in the problem are unchanged. What would the company's loan requirements be at the end of December in this case? (Hint: The calculations required to answer this question are minimal.)

Cash budgeting        **18-3**    The Torrence Company is planning to request a line of credit from its

bank. The following sales forecasts have been made for 1985 and 1986:

| May 1985       | $150,000 |
|----------------|----------|
| June           | 150,000  |
| July           | 300,000  |
| August         | 450,000  |
| September      | 600,000  |
| October        | 300,000  |
| November       | 300,000  |
| December       | 75,000   |
| January, 1986  | 150,000  |

Collection estimates were obtained from the credit and collection department as follows: collected within the month of sale, 5 percent; collected the month following the month of sale, 80 percent; and collected the second month following the month of sale, 15 percent. Payments for labor and raw materials are typically made during the month following the month in which these costs are incurred. Total labor and raw materials costs are estimated for each month as follows (payments are made the following month):

| May 1985   | $ 75,000 |
|------------|----------|
| June       | 75,000   |
| July       | 105,000  |
| August     | 735,000  |
| September  | 255,000  |
| October    | 195,000  |
| November   | 135,000  |
| December   | 75,000   |

General and administrative salaries will amount to approximately $22,500 a month; lease payments under long-term lease contracts will be $7,500 a month; depreciation charges will be $30,000 a month; miscellaneous expenses will be $2,250 a month; income tax payments of $52,500 will be due in both September and December; and a progress payment of $150,000 on a new research laboratory must be paid in October. Cash on hand on July 1 will amount to $110,000, and a minimum cash balance of $75,000 should be maintained throughout the cash budget period.

a. Prepare a monthly cash budget for the last six months of 1985. How much money will Torrence need to borrow (or how much will it have available to invest) each month?

b. Suppose receipts from sales come in uniformly during the month— that is, cash payments come in 1/30 each day—but all outflows are paid on the fifth of the month. Would this have an effect on the cash budget— in other words, would the cash budget you have prepared be valid under these assumptions? If not, what could be done to make a valid estimation of financing requirements? No calculations are required, although calculations can be used to illustrate the effects.

c. Torrence produces on a seasonal basis, just ahead of sales. Without making any calculations, discuss how the company's current ratio and debt ratio would vary during the year assuming all financial requirements were met by short-term bank loans. Could changes in these ratios affect the firm's ability to obtain bank credit?

d. If you prepared the cash budget in Part a correctly, you show a surplus of $85,250 at the end of July. Suggest some alternative investments for this money. Be sure to consider the pros and cons of long-term versus short-term debt instruments, and the appropriateness of investing in common stock.

e. Would your choice of securities in Part e be affected if the cash budget showed continuous cash surpluses versus alternating surpluses and deficits?

(Do only if you are using the computerized problem diskette.)

f. (1) By offering a 2 percent cash discount for paying within the month of sale, the credit manager has revised the collection percentages to 50 percent, 35 percent, and 15 percent, respectively. How will this affect the loan requirements?

(2) Return the payment percentages to their base case values and the discount to zero. Now suppose sales fall to only 70 percent of the forecasted level. Production is maintained, so cash outflows are unchanged. How does this affect Torrence's financial requirements?

(3) Return sales to the forecasted level (100%), and suppose collections slow down to 3%, 10%, and 87% for the three months, respectively. How does this affect financial requirements? If Torrence went to a cash-only sales policy, how would that affect requirements, other things held constant?

**Lockbox system**          **18-4**          Arlan, Inc., currently has a centralized billing system located in Los Angeles. However, over the years its customers gradually have become less concentrated on the West Coast and now cover the entire United States. On average, it requires 5 days from the time customers mail payments until Arlan is able to receive, process, and deposit them. To shorten this period, Arlan is considering the installation of a lockbox collection system. It estimates that the system will reduce the time lag from customer mailing to deposit by 3½ days, to 1½ days. Arlan has a daily average collection of $850,000.

a. How many days of float now exist (Arlan's customers' float, really), and what would it be under the lockbox system? What reduction in cash balances could Arlan achieve by initiating the lockbox system?

b. If Arlan has an opportunity cost of 11 percent, how much is the lockbox system worth on an annual basis?

c. What is the maximum monthly charge Arlan should pay for the lockbox system?

Optimal cash transfer       **18-5**       United Industries projects that cash outlays of $3,750,000 will occur uniformly throughout the coming year. United plans to meet its cash requirements by periodically selling marketable securities from its portfolio. The firm's marketable securities are invested to earn 12 percent, and the cost per transaction of converting securities to cash is $40.

a. Use the Baumol model to determine the optimal transaction size for transfers from marketable securities to cash.

b. What will be United's average cash balance?

c. How many transfers per year will be required?

d. What will be the total annual cost to United of maintaining cash balances? What would the total cost be if the company maintained an average cash balance of $100,000 or of $0 (it put in funds daily to meet cash requirements)?

## Solution to Self-Test Problem

**ST-1**       First, determine the annual benefit to Olinde from the reduction in cash balances under each plan:

$$\text{Average daily collections} = (30)(\$30,000)$$
$$= \$900,000.$$

*DTC*:

| | | |
|---|---|---|
| Current float: | $900,000 per day × 5 days = | $4,500,000 |
| New float: | $900,000 per day × 3 days = | 2,700,000 |
| Float reduction: | | $1,800,000 |

Olinde can reduce its cash balances by $1,800,000 by using DTCs, and it can earn 11 percent, which will provide $198,000:

$$\text{Annual benefit} = (\$1,800,000)(0.11)$$
$$= \$198,000.$$

*Wire Transfer*:

| | | |
|---|---|---|
| Current float: | $900,000 per day × 5 days = | $4,500,000 |
| New float: | $900,000 per day × 1 day = | 900,000 |
| Float reduction: | | $3,600,000 |

Olinde can reduce its cash balances by $3,600,000 by using wire transfers, which will earn $396,000:

$$\text{Annual benefit} = (\$3,600,000)(0.11)$$
$$= \$396,000.$$

Next, compute the annual cost of each transfer method:

$$\text{Number of transfers} = 30 \times 260 = 7,800 \text{ per year.}$$
$$\text{Fixed costs} = \$14,000 \times 12 = \$168,000 \text{ per year.}$$

*DTC*:

$$(7,800)(\$0.75) + \$168,000 = \$173,850.$$

*Wire Transfer*:

$$(7,800)(\$11) + \$168,000 = \$253,800.$$

Finally, calculate the net annual benefit resulting from each transfer method:

*DTC*:

$$\$198,000 - \$173,850 = \$24,150.$$

*Wire Transfer*:

$$\$396,000 - \$253,800 = \$142,200.$$

Therefore, Olinde should adopt the lockbox system and transfer funds from the lockbox operators to the regional concentration banks using wire transfers.

## Selected Additional References and Cases

*Perhaps the best way to get a good feel for the current state of the art is to look through recent issues of the* Journal of Cash Management, *a publication aimed at professionals in the field.*

Some key references on cash balance models include the following:

Daellenbach, Hans G., "Are Cash Management Optimization Models Worthwhile?" *Journal of Financial and Quantitative Analysis*, September 1974, 607-626.

Miller, Merton H., and Daniel Orr, "The Demand for Money by Firms: Extension of Analytic Results," *Journal of Finance*, December 1968, 735-759.

Mullins, David Wiley, Jr., and Richard B. Homonoff, "Applications of Inventory Cash Management Models," in *Modern Developments in Financial Management*, Stewart C. Myers, ed. (New York: Praeger, 1976).

For more information on float management, see:

Batlin, C. A., and Susan Hinko, "Lockbox Management and Value Maximization," *Financial Management*, Winter 1981, 39-44.

Gitman, Lawrence J., D. Keith Forrester, and John R. Forrester, Jr., "Maximizing Cash Disbursement Float," *Financial Management*, Summer 1976, 32-41.

Nauss, Robert M., and Robert E. Markland, "Solving Lockbox Location Problems," *Financial Management*, Spring 1979, 21-31.

The following articles provide more information on cash concentration systems:

Stone, Bernell K., and Ned C. Hill, "Cash Transfer Scheduling for Efficient Cash Concentration," *Financial Management*, Autumn 1980, 35-43.

———, "The Design of a Cash Concentration System," *Journal of Financial and Quantitative Analysis*, September 1981, 301-322.

For greater insights into compensating balance requirements, see:

Campbell, Tim S., and Leland Brendsel, "The Impact of Compensating Balance Requirements on the Cash Balances of Manufacturing Corporations," *Journal of Finance*, March 1977, 31-40.

Frost, Peter A., "Banking Services, Minimum Cash Balances and the Firm's Demand for Money," *Journal of Finance*, December 1970, 1029-1039.

For more information on marketable securities, see any of the investment textbooks referenced in Chapter 5, or see:

Stigum, Marcia, *The Money Market: Myth, Reality, and Practice* (Homewood, Ill.: Dow Jones-Irwin, 1978).

Van Horne, James C., *Financial Market Rates and Flows* (Englewood Cliffs, N.J.: Prentice-Hall, 1984).

The following cases focus on cash management:

Case 7, "Bollinger Corporation," in the Crum-Brigham casebook, which illustrates the mechanics of the cash budget and the rationale behind its use.

"Austin, Ltd.," in the Harrington casebook, which examines changes in a firm's cash disbursement system.

# 19 RECEIVABLES AND INVENTORY MANAGEMENT

XEROX®

Most security analysts were forecasting Xerox's sales and earnings to fall during the recent recession. But it did not happen—earnings rose 10 percent on a 23 percent sales gain. The secret, analysts learned, was that Xerox had instituted a major change in its credit policy—it had built up a pool of cash which it then loaned to its customers at bargain rates in order to increase sales of its products. Profits on the added sales more than offset the cost to Xerox of the low-rate loans, boosting the company's net income at a time when its competitors' profits were falling.

Although Xerox had good success with its liberal credit policy, other companies under other circumstances have increased their profits by reducing or even eliminating credit. For example, Atlantic Richfield Company (Arco) recently announced plans to eliminate the use of credit cards at all of its service stations. Its management believed (1) that customers were very sensitive to gasoline prices; (2) that the cost of extending credit to customers amounted to about 4 cents per gallon; (3) that if it eliminated credit sales it could cut gas prices at the pump by 3 cents a gallon, which would boost profit per gallon by 1 cent and at the same time double its number of customers; and (4) that consequently it would enjoy a substantial increase in net profits. Thus far the plan has worked beautifully, and its credit policy has contributed to Arco's success.

Besides their credit policies, companies are also very much concerned about their inventory policies. The cost of money used to buy and carry inventories is about 15 percent for most firms, and storage, insurance, pilferage, and obsolescence amount to another 10 to 15 percent. Thus, holding $100 of inventory for a year has a cost in the range of $25 to $30. With these high costs, holding excessive inventories can literally ruin a company. On the other hand, inventory shortages lead to lost sales, to production interruptions, and to customer ill will, so shortages can be just as harmful as excesses.

Many firms today are using computerized inventory controls to match stocks on hand with forecasted sales levels, and they are coordinating closely with suppliers to reduce average inventory levels. For example, Huffy Corporation, the largest U.S. bicycle manufacturer, was able to reduce its peak spring inventory from $69 million to $36 million over a 2-year period through better inventory control procedures. Huffy is saving millions of dollars in interest and storage costs by keeping a pared-down inventory, with no adverse effect on sales. However, such a policy is not without dangers—if bicycle sales surge, Huffy's inventories might not be sufficient to meet demand, causing the company to lose sales to its rivals, who are continuing to carry higher inventories. Note, however, that if sales fall, Huffy will be in a better position than its rivals, and if consumers begin to demand bicycles of different styles, Huffy will be able to adapt more easily than its competitors, who will be stuck with obsolete bicycles.

Our goal in this chapter is to examine the factors that companies like Xerox, Arco, and Huffy—or much smaller firms—must consider when they establish credit and inventory policies. From the standpoint of profitability, no decisions have a greater effect.

Since the typical firm has about 20 percent of its assets in receivables and another 20 percent in inventories, its effectiveness in managing these two accounts is obviously important to its profitability and risk—and thus to its stock price.

## Receivables Management

**account receivable**
A balance due from a customer.

In general, firms would rather sell for cash than on credit, but competitive pressures force most companies to offer credit. When goods are shipped, inventories are reduced, and an **account receivable** is created.[1] Eventually the customer will pay the account, at which time receivables will decline and cash will increase. Managing receivables has both direct and indirect costs, but granting credit normally increases sales. The optimal credit policy is the one which maximizes the value of the firm.

Receivables management begins with the decision of whether or not to grant credit. In this section, we discuss the manner in which receivables build up, and we present a method for monitoring them. A good receivables control system is important, because without it receivables will build up to excessive levels, cash flows will decline, and bad debts will rise to unacceptable levels.

---

[1]Whenever goods are sold on credit, two accounts actually are created—an asset item entitled "*accounts receivable*" appears on the books of the selling firm, and a liability item called "*accounts payable*" appears on the books of the purchaser. At this point we are analyzing the transaction from the viewpoint of the seller, so we are concentrating on the variables under its control, in this case, the receivables. We examined the transaction from the viewpoint of the purchaser in Chapter 17, where we discussed accounts payable as a source of funds and considered their cost relative to the cost of funds obtained from other sources.

## The Accumulation of Receivables

The total amount of accounts receivable outstanding at any given time is determined by two factors: (1) the volume of credit sales and (2) the average length of time between sales and collections. For example, suppose someone opens a store on January 1 and, starting the first day, makes sales of $100 each day. Customers are given 10 days in which to pay. At the end of the first day, accounts receivable will be $100; they will rise to $200 by the end of the second day; and by January 10 they will have risen to 10 × $100 = $1,000. On January 11 another $100 will be added to receivables, but payments for sales made on January 1 will reduce receivables by $100; total accounts receivable will therefore remain constant at $1,000. In general, once the firm's operations are stable,

$$\frac{\text{Accounts}}{\text{receivable}} = \frac{\text{Credit sales}}{\text{per day}} \times \frac{\text{Length of}}{\text{collection period}}$$

$$= \$100 \times 10 \text{ days} = \$1,000.$$

However, any changes in either sales or the collection period will cause accounts receivable to change.

Notice that the $1,000 investment in receivables must be financed. To illustrate, suppose that when our firm started on January 1 the owner had put up $100 as common stock and used this money to buy the goods sold the first day. Thus, the initial balance sheet would be as follows:

| | | | |
|---|---|---|---|
| Inventories | $100 | Common equity | $100 |
| Total assets | $100 | Total claims | $100 |

At the end of the day, the balance sheet would look like this:[2]

| | | | |
|---|---|---|---|
| Accounts receivable | $100 | | |
| Inventories | 0 | Common equity | $100 |
| Total assets | $100 | Total claims | $100 |

In order to remain in business, the owner must replenish inventories. To do so requires that $100 of goods be purchased, and this requires $100. Assuming the owner borrows the $100 from the bank, the balance sheet at the start of the second day will be as follows:

| | | | |
|---|---|---|---|
| Accounts receivable | $100 | Notes payable to bank | $100 |
| Inventories | 100 | Common equity | 100 |
| Total assets | $200 | Total claims | $200 |

---

[2]Of course, a profit might have been earned on the sales, but for a retail business it would amount to only about 2 percent, or $2. Also, the firm would need other assets, such as cash, fixed assets, and a permanent stock of inventory. We abstract from these details so that we may focus on receivables.

At the end of the day, the inventories will have been converted to receivables, and the firm will have to borrow another $100 to restock for the third day.

This process will continue, provided the bank is willing to lend the necessary funds, until the eleventh day, when the balance sheet will read as follows:

| | | | |
|---|---|---|---|
| Accounts receivable | $1,000 | Notes payable to bank | $1,000 |
| Inventories | 100 | Common equity | 100 |
| Total assets | $1,100 | Total claims | $1,100 |

This balance sheet is in a "steady-state" condition—from now on, $100 of receivables will be collected every day, and the money will be used to finance the sales made that day. Thus, the balance sheet will remain stable until the situation changes.

Now suppose sales doubled to $200 per day. After a brief transition period (10 days), the balance sheet would be as follows:

| | | | |
|---|---|---|---|
| Accounts receivables | $2,000 | Notes payable to bank | $2,100 |
| Inventories | 200 | Common equity | 100 |
| Total assets | $2,200 | Total claims | $2,200 |

These examples should make it clear (1) that accounts receivable depend jointly on the level of sales and the collection period and (2) that any increase in receivables must be financed in some manner. We assumed bank financing, but other possibilities include having the firm itself buy on credit (in which case the financing would be done by accounts payable rather than notes payable), selling bonds, or selling more common stock.[3] Methods of financing accounts receivable (and other current assets) were considered in Chapter 17.

## Monitoring the Receivables Position

The optimal credit policy, and hence the optimal level of accounts receivable, depends on the firm's own unique operating conditions. Thus, a firm with excess capacity and low variable production costs should extend credit more liberally and thus carry a higher level of accounts receivable than a firm operating at full capacity or having a slim profit margin. However, even though optimal credit policies vary among firms, or even for a single firm over time, it is still useful to analyze the effectiveness of the firm's credit policy in an aggregate sense.

As we saw in connection with the Du Pont analysis in Chapter 7, an excessive investment in any asset account will lead to a low rate of return on

---

[3]In time, profits will presumably be earned and reinvested in the business, but with normal profit margins, external funds will always be needed to support rapid growth. This point was discussed in Chapter 8 in connection with the Telecomp Corporation.

equity. For comparative purposes, we can focus on the average collection period (ACP) as discussed in Chapter 7. There we saw that National Metals Company's average collection period was 42 days compared to an industry average of 36 days. If National lowered its ACP by 6 days, to 36 days, this would mean a reduction of $(6)(\$8,333,333) = \$50,000,000$ in the amount of capital tied up in receivables. If the cost of the funds tied up in receivables were 10 percent, this would mean a savings of $5 million per year, other things held constant.

The ACP can also be compared with National's credit terms. National typically sells on terms of 1/10, net 30. Since the 42-day average collection period is greater than the 30-day maximum credit period, its customers, on average, are not paying their bills on time. Note also that if some of the customers are paying within 10 days to take advantage of the discount, then others are taking much longer than 42 days to pay—the accounts may, in fact, be so old as to suggest that they really represent bad debts. One way to get a better view of the situation is to construct an **aging schedule**, which breaks down accounts receivable according to how long they have been outstanding. National Metals' aging schedule is shown in Table 19-1. Most of the accounts pay on schedule or after only a slight delay, but a significant number are over 1 month past due. This indicates that even though the average collection period is close to the 30-day credit period, National has quite a bit of capital tied up in slow-paying accounts, some of which may eventually result in losses.

**aging schedule**
A report showing how long accounts receivable have been outstanding; gives the percentage of receivables currently past due and the percentage past due by a specified period.

Management should constantly monitor the firm's average collection period and aging schedule to detect trends, to see how the firm's collection experience compares with its credit terms, and to see how effectively the credit department is operating in comparison with other firms in the industry. If the ACP starts to lengthen, or if the aging schedule begins to show an increasing percentage of past-due accounts, then the firm's credit policy may have to be tightened. In any event, the average collection period and the aging schedule are useful tools for reviewing the credit department's performance.

Investors—both stockholders and bank loan officers—should pay close attention to accounts receivable management; otherwise, they could be misled by the firm's financial statements and later suffer serious losses on their in-

**Table 19-1**
**National's Aging Schedule**
**as of December 31, 1985**

| Age of Account (Days) | Percentage of Total Value of Accounts Receivable |
|---|---|
| 0-10 | 52% |
| 11-30 | 20 |
| 31-45 | 13 |
| 46-60 | 4 |
| Over 60 | 11 |
| | Total 100% |

vestments. When a sale is made, the following events occur: (1) Inventories are reduced by the cost of goods sold, (2) accounts receivable are increased by the sales price, and (3) the difference is recorded as a profit. If the sale is for cash, the profit is definitely earned, but if the sale is on credit, the profit is not actually earned unless and until the account is collected. Firms have been known to use credit policy to encourage "sales" to very weak customers in order to inflate reported profits. This could boost the stock price, at least until credit losses begin to show up and to lower earnings, at which time the stock price will fall. An analysis along the lines suggested above would detect any such questionable practice as well as any unconscious deterioration in the quality of accounts receivable. Such early detection could help both investors and bankers avoid losses.[4]

## Credit Policy

**credit policy**
A set of decisions that include a firm's credit period, credit standards, collection procedures, and discounts offered.

The success or failure of a business depends primarily on demand for its products—as a rule, the higher its sales, the greater its profits and the healthier the firm. Sales, in turn, depend on a number of factors, some exogenous but others controllable by the firm. The major controllable variables that affect sales are sales prices, product quality, advertising, and the firm's credit policy. **Credit policy**, in turn, consists of these four elements:

**1.** The *credit period*, which is the length of time buyers have before they must pay for their purchases.

**2.** *Credit standards*, which refers to the minimum financial strength of acceptable credit customers.

**3.** The *collection policy*, which reflects the firm's toughness or laxity in following up on slow-paying accounts.

**4.** *Discounts* given for early payment.

The credit manager has the responsibility for administering the firm's credit policy. However, because of the pervasive importance of credit, the credit policy itself is established by the executive committee, which usually consists of the president and the vice-presidents in charge of finance, marketing, and production.

### Credit Period

**credit period**
The length of time for which credit is granted.

The **credit period** is the length of time a company gives its customers to pay—for example, credit might be extended for 30, 60, or 90 days. Generally there is a relationship between the normal inventory holding period of the

---

[4]Accountants are increasingly interested in these matters. Investors have sued several of the Big Eight accounting firms for substantial damages in cases where (1) profits were overstated and (2) it could be shown that the auditors should have conducted an analysis along the lines described here and then reported the results to stockholders on the audited financial statements.

customer and the credit period. Thus, fresh fruits and vegetables are normally sold on very short credit terms, while jewelry may involve a 90-day credit period.

## Credit Standards

**credit standards**
Standards that stipulate the minimum financial strength that an applicant must demonstrate in order to be granted credit.

**Credit standards** refer to the strength and "creditworthiness" a customer must exhibit in order to qualify for credit. If a customer does not qualify for the regular credit terms, it can still purchase from the firm, but on more restrictive terms. For example, a firm's "regular" credit terms might call for payment after 30 days, and these terms might be extended to all "acceptable" customers. Its credit standards would be applied to determine which customers qualified for the regular credit terms and how much credit each customer should receive. The major factors to consider when setting credit standards relate to the likelihood that a given customer will pay slowly or perhaps even end up as a bad debt loss.

Setting credit standards implicitly requires a measurement of *credit quality*, which is defined in terms of the probability of a customer's default. The probability estimate for a given customer is for the most part a subjective judgment; nevertheless, credit evaluation is a well-established practice, and a good credit manager can make reasonably accurate judgments of the probability of default by different classes of customers. In this section we discuss some of the methods used by firms to measure credit quality.

*The Five Cs System.* The traditional method of measuring credit quality is to investigate potential credit customers with respect to five factors called the **five Cs of credit**:

**five Cs of credit**
The factors used to evaluate credit risk: character, capacity, capital, collateral, and conditions.

**1.** *Character*, which refers to the probability that customers will *try* to honor their obligations. This factor is of considerable importance, because every credit transaction implies a *promise* to pay. Will debtors make an honest effort to pay their debts, or are they likely to try to get away with something? Experienced credit managers frequently insist that the moral factor is the most important issue in a credit evaluation. Thus, credit reports provide background information on people's and firms' performances. Often credit analysts will seek this type of information from a firm's bankers, its other suppliers, its customers, and even its competitors.

**2.** *Capacity*, which is a subjective judgment of customers' ability to pay. It is gauged in part by their past records and business methods, and it may be supplemented by physical observation of customers' plants or stores. Again, credit analysts will obtain judgmental information on this factor from a variety of sources.

**3.** *Capital*, which is measured by the general financial condition of a firm as indicated by an analysis of its financial statements. Special emphasis is given to the risk ratios—the debt/assets ratio, the current ratio, and the times-interest-earned ratio.

**4.** *Collateral*, which is represented by assets that customers may offer as security in order to obtain credit.

**5.** *Conditions*, which refers both to general economic trends and to special developments in certain geographic regions or sectors of the economy that might affect a customer's ability to meet its obligations.

Information on these five factors comes from the firm's previous experience with its customers, and it is supplemented by a well-developed system of external information gatherers. Of course, once the information on the five Cs is developed, the credit manager must still make a final decision on the potential customer's overall credit quality. This decision is normally judgmental in nature, and credit managers must rely on their background knowledge and instincts.

***Sources of Credit Information.*** Two major sources of external information are available. The first is the work of the *credit associations*, which are local groups that meet frequently and correspond with one another to exchange information on credit customers. These local groups have also banded together to create Credit Interchange, a system developed by the National Association of Credit Management for assembling and distributing information about customers' past payment performances. The interchange reports show the paying records of different debtors, the industries from which they are buying, and the geographic areas in which they are making purchases. The second source of external information is the work of the *credit-reporting agencies*, which collect credit information and sell it for a fee. The best known of these agencies are Dun & Bradstreet (D&B) and TRW, Inc. D&B, TRW, and other agencies supply factual data that can be used in credit analysis; they also provide ratings similar to those available on corporate bonds.[5]

Managing a credit department requires fast, accurate, up-to-date information; to help make it available, the National Association of Credit Management (a group with 43,000 member firms) persuaded TRW, Inc., to develop a computer-based telecommunications network for the collection, storage, retrieval, and distribution of credit information. The TRW system transmits credit reports electronically, so they are available within seconds to its thousands of subscribers. Dun & Bradstreet has a similar system plus a service which provides more detailed reports through the U.S. mail.

A typical credit report would include the following pieces of information:

**1.** A summary balance sheet and income statement.

**2.** A number of key ratios, with trend information.

**3.** Information obtained from the firm's banks and suppliers about whether it has been paying promptly or slowly, and whether it has recently failed to make a payment.

---

[5]For additional information see Christie and Bracuti, *Credit Management*, a publication of the National Association of Credit Management. Also, see Peter Nulty, "An Upstart Takes on Dun & Bradstreet," *Fortune*, April 9, 1979, 98-100.

**4.** A verbal description of the physical condition of the firm's operations.

**5.** A verbal description of the backgrounds of the firm's owners, including any previous bankruptcies, lawsuits, fraud, and the like.

**6.** A summary rating, ranging from A+ for the best credit risks down to F for those who are most likely to default.

Although a great deal of credit information is available, it must still be processed in a judgmental manner. Computerized information systems can assist in making better credit decisions, but in the final analysis these determinations are really exercises in informed judgment.

***Management by Exception.*** Modern credit managers practice *management by exception.* Under such a system, (1) statistical procedures are used to classify customers into five or six categories according to degree of risk, and (2) the credit manager then concentrates time and attention on the customers that are most likely to cause problems. For example, the following classes might be established:

| Risk Class | Percentage of Uncollectable Credit Sales | Percentage of Customers in This Class |
|------------|------------------------------------------|---------------------------------------|
| 1 | 0-½% | 60% |
| 2 | ½-2 | 20 |
| 3 | 2-5 | 10 |
| 4 | 5-10 | 5 |
| 5 | Over 10 | 5 |

Firms in Class 1 might be extended credit automatically, and their credit status reviewed only once a year. Those in Class 2 might also receive credit (up to specified limits) automatically, but a ratio analysis of their financial condition would be conducted more frequently (perhaps every quarter), and they would be moved down to Class 3 if their position deteriorated. Specific approvals might be required for credit sales to Classes 3 and 4, while sales to Class 5 might be on a COD (cash-on-delivery) basis only.

## Collection Policy

**collection policy**
The procedures that a firm follows to collect accounts receivable.

**Collection policy** refers to the procedures the firm follows to collect receivables. For example, a letter might be sent to any account holder that is 10 days past due; a more severe letter, followed by a telephone call, might be used if payment is not received within 30 days; and the account might be turned over to a collection agency after 90 days. The collection process can be expensive in terms of both out-of-pocket expenditures and lost goodwill, but at least some firmness is needed to prevent an undue lengthening of the collection period and to minimize outright losses. A balance must be struck between the costs and benefits of different collection policies.

Changes in collection policy influence sales, the collection period, the bad debt loss percentage, and the percentage of customers who take discounts. The effects of a change in collection policy, along with changes in the other credit policy variables, will be analyzed later in the chapter.

## Cash Discounts

**cash discount**
A reduction in the price of goods given for early payment.

The last element in the credit policy decision, the use of **cash discounts** for early payment, is analyzed by balancing the costs and benefits of different discount terms. For example, Stylish Fashions might decide to change its credit terms from "net 30," which means that customers must pay within 30 days, to "2/10, net 30," which means that it will allow a 2 percent discount if payment is received within 10 days, while the full invoice price must otherwise be paid within 30 days. This change should produce two benefits: (1) it would attract new customers who consider discounts a type of price reduction and (2) it would cause a reduction in the average collection period, since some old customers will pay more promptly in order to take advantage of the discount. Offsetting these benefits is the dollar cost of the discounts taken. The optimal discount is established at the point where the costs and benefits are exactly offsetting. The methodology for analyzing changes in the discount is developed later in the chapter.

**seasonal dating**
A procedure for inducing customers to buy early by dating the invoice during the purchaser's selling season regardless of when the merchandise is shipped.

If sales are seasonal, a firm may use **seasonal dating** on discounts. For example, Slimwear, Inc., a swimsuit manufacturer, sells on terms of 2/10, net 30, May 1 dating. This means that the effective invoice date is May 1 even if the sale was made back in January. If the discount is not taken by May 10, the full amount must be paid on May 30. Slimwear produces throughout the year, but retail sales of bathing suits are concentrated in the spring and early summer. By offering seasonal datings, the company induces some customers to stock up early, saving itself storage costs and also "nailing down" sales.

## Other Factors Influencing Credit Policy

In addition to the factors discussed above, several other conditions also influence a firm's overall credit policy.

***Profit Potential.*** Thus far we have emphasized the costs of granting credit. *However, if it is possible to sell on credit and also assess a carrying charge on the receivables that are outstanding, then credit sales can actually be more profitable than cash sales.* This is especially true for consumer durables (autos, appliances, clothing, and so on), but it is also true for certain types of industrial equipment. Thus, the General Motors Acceptance Corporation (GMAC) unit, which finances automobiles, is highly profitable, as is Sears, Roebuck's credit subsidiary.[6] Some encyclopedia companies even lose

---

[6]Companies that do a large volume of sales financing typically set up subsidiary companies called *captive finance companies* to do the actual financing. Thus, General Motors, Chrysler, and Ford all have captive finance companies, as do Sears and Montgomery Ward. The reason for this is that consumer finance companies, because their assets are highly liquid, tend to use far more debt—especially short-term debt—than manufacturers or retailers. Thus, if GM did not use a captive finance company, its balance sheet would show an exceptionally high debt ratio and a low current ratio. By having General Motors Acceptance Corporation (GMAC) as a separate but wholly owned corporation, GM avoids distorting its own balance sheet, which presumably helps it raise capital on more favorable terms.

money on cash sales but more than make up these losses from the carrying charges on their credit sales; obviously, such firms would rather sell on credit than for cash!

The carrying charges on outstanding credit are generally about 18 percent on an annual interest rate basis (1.5 percent per month, so 1.5% × 12 = 18%). Except in the early 1980s, when short-term interest rates rose to unprecedented levels, having receivables outstanding that earn over 18 percent has been highly profitable.

*Legal Considerations in Granting Credit.* Under the Robinson-Patman Act, it is illegal for a firm to offer more favorable credit terms to one customer or class of customers than to another unless the differences are cost justified.

**open account**
A credit instrument consisting simply of an invoice that is signed by the buyer upon receipt of goods, after which both the buyer and the seller record the purchase on their books.

**promissory note**
A document specifying the amount, percentage interest rate, repayment schedule, and other terms and conditions of a loan.

**commercial draft**
A post-dated draft drawn up by and made out to the seller that must be signed by the buyer before taking possession of goods.

**sight draft**
A draft that is payable upon acceptance by the buyer.

**time draft (trade acceptance)**
A draft that is payable on a specified future date.

*Credit Instruments.* Most credit is offered on **open account**, which means that the only formal evidence of the credit is an invoice which accompanies the shipment and which the buyer signs to indicate that goods have been received. Then, the buyer and the seller each record the purchase on their books. Under certain circumstances, the selling firm may require the buyer to sign a **promissory note** evidencing the credit obligation. Promissory notes are useful (1) if the order is very large, (2) if the seller anticipates the possibility of having trouble collecting, because a note is a stronger legal claim than a simple invoice, and (3) if the buyer wants a longer than usual time period in which to pay for the order for, in that case, interest charges can be built into a promissory note.

Another instrument used in trade credit, especially in international trade, is the **commercial draft**. Here the seller draws up a draft—which looks like a check made out to the seller and to be signed by the buyer, but dated at some future date. This draft is then sent to the buyer's bank, along with the shipping invoices necessary for taking possession of the goods. The bank forwards the draft to the buyer, who signs it and returns it to the bank. The bank then delivers the shipping documents to the customer, who at this point can claim the goods. If the draft is a **sight draft**, then upon delivery of the shipping documents and acceptance of the draft by the buyer, the bank actually withdraws money from the buyer's account and forwards it to the selling firm. If the draft is a **time draft**, or **trade acceptance**, payable on a specified future date, then the bank returns it to the selling firm, which can hold it for future payment, use it as collateral for a loan, or sell it on the open market to raise immediate cash. In each of these situations, the bank has served as an intermediary, making sure that the buyer does not receive title to the goods until the note (or draft) has been executed for the benefit of the seller.

A seller who lacks confidence in the ability or willingness of the buyer to pay off a time draft may refuse to ship without a guarantee of payment by the buyer's bank. Presumably the bank knows its customer and, for a fee, will

**banker's acceptance**
A time draft that has been guaranteed by a bank. A promissory note by a business debtor arising out of a business transaction; a bank, by endorsing it, assumes the obligation of payment at the due date, while the debtor maintains a deposit at the bank that will be charged for the amount plus interest.

**conditional sales contract**
A method of financing in which the seller retains title to the goods until the buyer has completed payment.

guarantee payment of the draft. In this instance, the draft is called a **banker's acceptance**. Such instruments are widely used, especially in foreign trade. They have a low degree of risk if guaranteed by a strong bank, and there is a ready market for them, making it easy for the seller of the goods to sell the acceptances to raise immediate cash. (Banker's acceptances as well as trade acceptances are sold at a discount below face value and then paid off at face value when they mature, so the discount amounts to interest on the acceptance. The effective interest rate on a strong banker's acceptance is a little above the Treasury bill rate of interest.)

A final type of credit instrument that should be mentioned is the **conditional sales contract**. Here the seller retains legal ownership of the goods until the buyer has completed payment. Conditional sales contracts are used primarily for sales of such items as machinery, dental equipment, and the like, which are often paid for on an installment basis over a period of two or three years. The significant advantage of a conditional sales contract is that it is easier for the seller to repossess the equipment in the event of default since title to it remains with the seller until payment has been completed. This feature makes possible some credit sales that otherwise would not be feasible. Conditional sales contracts generally carry an interest rate that is equivalent to what the buyer would have to pay on a bank loan.

## Analyzing Changes in the Credit Policy Variables

If the firm's credit policy is *eased* by such actions as lengthening the credit period, relaxing credit standards, following a less tough collection policy, or offering cash discounts, then sales should increase: *Easing the credit policy normally stimulates sales.* However, if credit policy is eased and sales do rise, then costs will also rise (1) because more labor, more materials, and so on will be required to produce more goods, (2) because receivables outstanding will increase, which will raise carrying costs, and (3) because bad debt and/or discount expenses will also rise. Thus, the key question when deciding on a credit policy change is this: Will sales revenues rise more than costs, causing net income to increase, or will the increase in sales revenues be more than offset by higher costs?

Table 19-2 illustrates the general idea behind credit policy analysis. Column 1 shows the projected 1986 income statement for Monroe Manufacturing under the assumption that the firm's current credit policy is maintained throughout the year. Column 2 shows the expected effects of easing the credit policy by extending the credit period, offering larger discounts, relaxing credit standards, and easing collection efforts. Specifically, Monroe is analyzing the effects of changing its credit terms from 1/10, net 30, to 2/10, net 40, relaxing its credit standards, and putting less pressure on slow-paying customers. Column 3 shows the projected 1986 income statement incorporating the expected effects of an easing in credit policy. The generally looser policy is expected to increase sales and lower collection costs, but discounts and several other types of costs would rise. The overall, bottom line effect is

**Table 19-2**
**Monroe Manufacturing Company:**
**Analysis of Changing Credit Policy**
**(Millions of dollars)**

| | Projected 1986 Income Statement under Current Credit Policy (1) | Effect of Credit Policy Change (2) | Projected 1986 Income Statement under New Credit Policy (3) |
|---|---|---|---|
| Gross sales | $400 | + $130 | $530 |
| Less discounts | 2 | + 4 | 6 |
| Net sales | $398 | + $126 | $524 |
| Production costs, including overhead | 280 | + 91 | 371 |
| Gross profit before credit costs | $118 | + $ 35 | $153 |
| Credit-related costs: | | | |
|    Cost of carrying receivables | 3 | + 2 | 5 |
|    Credit analysis and collection expenses | 5 | − 3 | 2 |
|    Bad debt losses | 10 | + 22 | 32 |
| Gross profit | $100 | + $ 14 | $114 |
| Taxes (50%) | 50 | + 7 | 57 |
| Net income | $ 50 | + $ 7 | $ 57 |

a $7 million increase in projected profits. In the following paragraphs, we explain how the numbers in the table were calculated.

Monroe's annual sales are $400 million. Under its current credit policy, 50 percent of those customers who pay do so on Day 10 and take the discount, 40 percent pay on the thirtieth day, and 10 percent pay late, on Day 40. Thus, Monroe's average collection period is $(.50)(10) + (.40)(30) + (.10)(40) = 21$ days, and discounts total $(0.01)(\$400,000,000)(0.5) = \$2,000,000$. The cost of carrying receivables is equal to the average receivables balance times the variable cost percentage times the cost of money used to carry receivables. The firm's variable cost ratio is 70 percent, and its cost of funds invested in receivables is 20 percent. Its cost of carrying receivables is therefore $3 million:

$$(ACP)\begin{pmatrix} \text{Sales} \\ \text{per} \\ \text{day} \end{pmatrix}\begin{pmatrix} \text{Variable} \\ \text{cost} \\ \text{ratio} \end{pmatrix}\begin{pmatrix} \text{Cost} \\ \text{of} \\ \text{funds} \end{pmatrix} = \text{Cost of carrying receivables}$$

$$(21)(\$400,000,000/360)(0.70)(0.20) = \$3,266,667 \approx \$3 \text{ million.}$$

Only variable costs enter this calculation because this is the only cost element that must be financed as a result of a change in the credit policy. We are seeking the cost of carrying receivables, and variable costs represent the firm's investment in the cost of goods sold.

Even though Monroe spends $5 million annually to analyze accounts and to collect bad debts, 2.5 percent of sales will never be collected. Bad debt losses therefore amount to $(0.025)(\$400,000,000) = \$10,000,000$.

Monroe's new credit policy calls for a larger discount, a longer payment period, a relaxed collection effort, and lower credit standards. The company believes that these changes will lead to an increase in sales to $530 million per year. Under the new terms, management believes that 60 percent of the customers who pay will take the 2 percent discount, so discounts will increase to $(0.02)($530,000,000)(0.60) = $6,360,000 \approx $6$ million. Half of the remaining customers will pay on the fortieth day, and the remainder on Day 50. The new ACP is thus estimated to be 24 days:

$$(.6)(10) + (.2)(40) + (.2)(50) = 24 \text{ days.}$$

Also, the cost of carrying receivables will increase to $5 million:

$$(24)($530,000,000/360)(0.70)(0.20) = $4,946,667 \approx $5 \text{ million.}[7]$$

The company plans to reduce its annual credit analysis and collection expenditures to $2 million. The reduced credit standards and the relaxed collection effort are expected to raise bad debt losses to about 6 percent of sales, or to $(0.06)($530,000,000) = $31,800,000 \approx $32,000,000$.

The combined effect of all the changes in credit policy is a projected $7 million increase in net income. There would, of course, be corresponding changes on the projected balance sheet—the higher sales would necessitate somewhat larger cash balances, inventories, and perhaps (depending on the existence of excess capacity) more fixed assets. Accounts receivable would also increase. Since these asset increases would have to be financed, certain liabilities and/or equity would have to be increased.

The $7 million expected increase in net income is, of course, an estimate, and the actual effects of the change could be quite different. In the first place, there is uncertainty—perhaps quite a lot—about the projected $130 million increase in sales. Conceivably, if the firm's competitors matched its changes, sales would not rise at all. Similar uncertainties must be attached to the number of customers who would take discounts, to production costs at higher or lower sales levels, to the costs of carrying additional receivables, and to bad debt losses. In view of all the uncertainties, management would perhaps deem the projected $7 million increase in net income insufficient to justify the change. In the final analysis, the decision to make the change will be

---

[7]Since the credit policy change will result in a longer ACP, the firm will have to wait longer to receive its profit on the goods it sells. Therefore, the firm will incur an opportunity cost due to not having the cash from these profits available for investment. The dollar amount of this opportunity cost is equal to the old sales per day times the change in ACP times the contribution margin times the firm's required return on receivables, or

$$\begin{aligned} \text{Opportunity cost} &= (\text{Old sales}/360)(\Delta\text{ACP})(1 - v)(k). \\ &= ($400/360)(3)(0.3)(0.20) \\ &= $0.2 = $200,000. \end{aligned}$$

For simplicity, we have ignored this cost in our analysis. For a more complete discussion of the analysis of changes in credit policy, see Eugene F. Brigham and Louis C. Gapenski, *Intermediate Financial Management*, Chapter 19.

based on judgment, but the type of quantitative analysis set forth above is essential to a good judgmental decision.

The preceding paragraphs give an overview of the way changes in credit policy are analyzed. As noted, the most important considerations have to do with changes in sales and production costs. Specific estimations of these effects are handled by the marketing and production departments within the framework set forth above. The financial manager has the responsibility for the overall analysis plus a primary role in estimating several specific factors, including discounts taken, the cost of carrying accounts receivable, and bad debt losses. To evaluate a proposed change in credit policy, one could compare projected income statements, such as Column 1 versus Column 3 in Table 19-2. Alternatively, one could simply analyze Column 2, which shows the incremental effect, or the effect holding other things constant, of the proposed change. Of course, the two approaches are based on exactly the same data, so they must produce identical results. However, it is often preferable to focus on the incremental approach—because firms usually change their credit policies in specific divisions or on particular products and not across the board, an analysis of complete income statements could be swamped by other factors.

## Inventory Management

Inventories may be grouped into three classifications: (1) *raw materials*, (2) *work-in-process*, and (3) *finished goods*; each is an essential part of most business operations. As is true of accounts receivable, inventory levels depend heavily upon sales. However, whereas receivables build up *after* sales have been made, inventories must be acquired *ahead* of sales. This is a critical difference, and the necessity of forecasting sales before establishing target inventory levels makes inventory management a difficult task. Also, since errors in establishing inventory levels can lead either to lost sales and profits or to excessive costs and hence profit problems, inventory management is as important as it is difficult.

Inventory management focuses on three basic questions. (1) How many units of each inventory item should the firm hold in stock? (2) How many units should be ordered (or produced) at a given time? (3) At what point should inventory be ordered (or produced)? The remainder of this chapter is devoted to answering these questions.

### Typical Inventory Decisions

Two examples will make clear the types of issues involved in inventory management, as well as the problems poor inventory control can cause.

*Retail Clothing Store.* Glamour Galore Boutique must order bathing suits in January for sales the following summer, and it must take delivery by April to be sure of having enough suits to meet the heavy May-June demand. Bathing suits come in many styles, colors, and sizes. If the buyer stocks incorrectly, either in total or in terms of the style-color-size distribution, then the store will have trouble—it will lose potential sales if it stocks too few suits, and it will be forced to mark them down and take losses if it stocks too many or the wrong types.

The effects of inventory changes on the balance sheet are important. For simplicity, assume that Glamour Galore has a $100 base stock of inventories, financed by common stock. Its initial balance sheet is as follows:

| | | | |
|---|---|---|---|
| Inventories (base stock) | $100 | Common stock | $100 |
| Total assets | $100 | Total claims | $100 |

Now it anticipates a seasonal increase in sales of $300 and takes on additional inventories in that amount, financing them with a bank loan:

| | | | |
|---|---|---|---|
| Inventories | $400 | Notes payable to bank | $300 |
| | | Common stock | 100 |
| Total assets | $400 | Total claims | $400 |

If everything works out as planned, sales will be made, inventories will be converted to cash, the bank loan will be retired, and the company will earn a profit. The balance sheet after a successful season might look like this:

| | | | |
|---|---|---|---|
| Cash and marketable securities | $ 50 | Notes payable to bank | $ 0 |
| Inventories (base stock) | 100 | Common stock | 100 |
| | | Retained earnings | 50 |
| Total assets | $150 | Total claims | $150 |

The company is now in a highly liquid position and is ready to begin a new season.

But what if the season had not gone well? Suppose sales were slow and as fall approached the balance sheet looked like this:

| | | | |
|---|---|---|---|
| Inventories | $300 | Notes payable to bank | $200 |
| | | Common stock | 100 |
| Total assets | $300 | Total claims | $300 |

Now suppose the bank insists on repayment of its loan, and it wants cash, not bathing suits. But if the bathing suits did not sell well in the summer, how will out-of-style suits sell in the fall? Assume that Glamour Galore is forced to mark the suits down to half price in order to sell them to raise cash to repay the bank loan. The result will be:

| | | | |
|---|---|---|---|
| Cash | $150 | Notes payable to bank | $200 |
| | | Common equity | (50) |
| Total assets | $150 | Total claims | $150 |

At this point, Glamour Galore goes bankrupt. The bank gets the $150 of cash and takes a $50 loss on its loan. The stockholders are wiped out, and the company goes out of business.

***Appliance Manufacturer.*** Now consider a different type of situation, that of Whirlwind Corporation, a well-established appliance manufacturer, whose inventory position follows (millions of dollars):

| | |
|---|---:|
| Raw materials | $  200 |
| Work-in-process | 200 |
| Finished goods | 600 |
| | $1,000 |

Suppose Whirlwind anticipates that the economy is about to get much stronger and that the demand for appliances is likely to rise sharply. If it is to share in the expected boom, Whirlwind will have to increase production. This means it will have to increase inventories and, since that increase will precede sales, additional financing will be required. The details are not shown here, but some liability account, perhaps notes payable, would have to be increased in order to support the inventory buildup.

Proper inventory management requires close coordination among the sales, purchasing, production, and finance departments. The sales/marketing department is generally the first to spot changes in demand. These changes must be worked into the company's purchasing and manufacturing schedules, and the financial manager must arrange any financing that will be needed to support the inventory buildup. Either improper coordination among departments or poor sales forecasts can lead to disaster. For example, Varner Corporation, a manufacturer of home computers, was recently forced into bankruptcy because of a poor system of internal controls. The company set its production schedules for 1986 on the basis of 1985 sales. However, the introduction of new, improved computers by competitors caused sales to drop sharply during the first half of 1986. Production schedules were not adjusted downward, so both inventories and bank debt built up. By the time the situation had been properly assessed, inventories of now obsolete components had risen to over $10 million. The situation was like this (millions of dollars):

| | | | | |
|---|---:|---|---:|---|
| Cash | $  1 | Accounts payable | $  3 | |
| Receivables | 8 | Notes payable to bank | 15 | |
| Inventories:  Good | 6 | Total current liabilities | $18 | |
| Bad | 10 | Long-term debt | 10 | |
| Total current assets | $25 | Common equity | 7 | |
| Fixed assets | 10 | | | |
| Total assets | $35 | Total claims | $35 | |

The bank insisted upon payment of the note. Varner simply could not generate the necessary cash, and it was thus forced into bankruptcy.[8] The company had some good products on the drawing board, but it did not survive to bring them to fruition.

## Inventory Costs

The goal of inventory management is to provide the inventories required to sustain operations at the minimum cost. The first step is to identify all the costs involved in purchasing and maintaining inventories. Table 19-3 gives a listing of the typical costs associated with inventories, broken down into three categories: costs associated with carrying inventories, costs associated with ordering and receiving inventories, and costs associated with running short of inventory.

Although they may well be the most important element, we shall at this point disregard the third category of costs—the costs of running short; these are dealt with by adding safety stocks, as we will discuss later. The costs that remain for consideration at this stage, then, are carrying costs and ordering, shipping, and receiving costs.

**carrying costs**
The costs associated with carrying inventories, including storage, capital, and depreciation costs; generally increase in proportion to the average amount of inventory held.

***Carrying Costs.*** **Carrying costs** generally rise in direct proportion to the average amount of inventory carried, which in turn depends on the frequency with which orders are placed. To illustrate, if a firm sells S units per year and places equal-sized orders N times per year, then, assuming no safety stocks are carried, the average inventory, A, is:

$$A = \frac{S/N}{2}. \tag{19-1}$$

For example, if the firm sells S = 120,000 units in a year and orders inventory N = 4 times a year, then its average inventory will be A = 15,000 units:

$$A = \frac{S/N}{2} = \frac{120,000/4}{2} = \frac{30,000}{2} = 15,000 \text{ units.}$$

Now assume that the firm purchases its inventory at a price P = $2 per unit. The average inventory value is thus (P)(A) = ($2)(15,000) = $30,000.

If the firm has a cost of capital of 10 percent, it incurs $3,000 in capital costs to carry the inventory. Further, assume that each year the firm incurs $2,000 of storage costs (space, utilities, security, taxes, and so forth), $500 of inventory insurance costs, and $1,000 of depreciation and obsolescence costs. The firm's total costs of carrying the $30,000 average inventory is $3,000 + $2,000 + $500 + $1,000 = $6,500; thus, its percentage cost of carrying inventory is $6,500/$30,000 = 0.217 = 21.7%. Defining the per-

---

[8]As we saw in Chapter 17, bank loans are generally written as 90-day notes. Thus, the loan must be repaid or renewed every 90 days. If the bank thinks the firm's situation has deteriorated, as Varner's had, it will refuse to renew. Then, if the firm cannot raise cash to repay the loan, it will be bankrupt.

**Table 19-3**
**Costs Associated with Inventories**

|  | Approximate Annual Percentage Cost |
|---|---|
| **Carrying Costs** | |
| Cost of capital tied up | 15.0% |
| Storage and handling costs | 0.5 |
| Insurance | 0.5 |
| Property taxes | 1.0 |
| Depreciation and obsolescence | 12.0 |
| Total | 29.0% |
| **Ordering, Shipping, and Receiving Costs** | |
| Cost of placing orders, including production and set-up costs | varies |
| Shipping and handling costs | 2.5% |
| **Costs of Running Short** | |
| Loss of sales | varies |
| Loss of customer goodwill | varies |
| Disruption of production schedules | varies |

Note: These costs vary from firm to firm, from item to item, and also over time. The figures shown are U.S. Department of Commerce estimates for an average manufacturing firm. Where costs vary so widely that no meaningful numbers can be assigned, we simply report "varies."

centage cost as C, we can in general find the annual total carrying costs, TCC, as the percentage carrying cost, C, times the purchase price per unit, P, times the average number of units, A:

$$\text{Total carrying costs} = \text{TCC} = (C)(P)(A). \tag{19-2}$$

In our example,

$$\text{TCC} = (0.217)(\$2)(15,000)$$
$$\approx \$6,500.$$

*Ordering Costs.* Although carrying costs are entirely variable and rise in direct proportion to the average size of inventories, **ordering costs** are fixed.[9] For example, the costs of placing and receiving an order—interoffice memos, long-distance telephone calls, setting up a production run, taking delivery, and executive time—are essentially a fixed amount for each order, so this part of inventory cost is simply the fixed cost of placing and receiving

**ordering costs**
The costs of placing and receiving orders; this cost is fixed regardless of the average size of inventories.

---

[9]For certain purposes it is useful to add another term to the inventory cost model: *shipping and receiving costs.* This term should be added if there are economies of scale in shipping such that the cost of shipping a unit is smaller if shipments are larger. However, in most situations shipping costs are not sensitive to order size, so total shipping costs are simply the shipping cost per unit times the units ordered (and sold) during the year. Under this condition, shipping costs are not influenced by inventory policy and hence may be disregarded for purposes of determining the optimal inventory level and order size.

orders times the number of orders placed. We define the fixed costs associated with ordering inventories as F, and if we place N orders per year, the annual total ordering costs, TOC, are:

$$\text{Total ordering costs} = \text{TOC} = (F)(N). \tag{19-3}$$

Equation 19-1 may be solved for N to produce $N = S/2A$, which may then be substituted for N in Equation 19-3:

$$\text{TOC} = \text{Total ordering costs} = F\left(\frac{S}{2A}\right). \tag{19-4}$$

To evaluate Equation 19-4, suppose $F = \$100$, $S = 120,000$ units, and $A = 15,000$ units; then TOC, the total annual ordering costs, are

$$\text{TOC} = (F)(S/2A) = \$100\left(\frac{120,000}{30,000}\right) = \$100(4) = \$400.$$

***Total Inventory Costs.*** Total carrying costs, TCC, as defined in Equation 19-2, and total ordering costs, TOC, as defined in Equation 19-4, may be combined to find total inventory costs, TIC, as follows:

$$\begin{aligned} \text{TIC} &= \text{Total inventory costs} \\ &= \text{TCC} + \text{TOC} \\ &= (C)(P)(A) + F\left(\frac{S}{2A}\right). \end{aligned} \tag{19-5}$$

Recognizing that the average inventory carried is $A = Q/2$, or one-half the size of each order quantity, Q, Equation 19-5 may be rewritten as follows:

$$\text{TIC} = (C)(P)\left(\frac{Q}{2}\right) + \frac{(F)(S)}{Q}. \tag{19-6}$$

This equation can be used to find the minimum total inventory cost, which is the goal of inventory management.

## The Optimal Ordering Quantity

Inventories are obviously necessary, but it is equally obvious that a firm will suffer if it has too much or too little inventory. How can we determine the *optimal* inventory level? One commonly used approach utilizes the *economic ordering quantity (EOQ) model*, which is described in this section.

Figure 19-1 illustrates the basic premise on which inventory theory is built, namely, that some costs rise with larger inventories while other costs decline, and there is an optimal order size which minimizes the total costs associated with inventories, TIC. First, as noted earlier, the average investment in inventories depends on how frequently orders are placed—if we place a small order every day, average inventories will be much smaller than if we place one large order per year. Further, as Figure 19-1 shows, some of

**Figure 19-1**
**Determination of the Optimal Order Quantity**

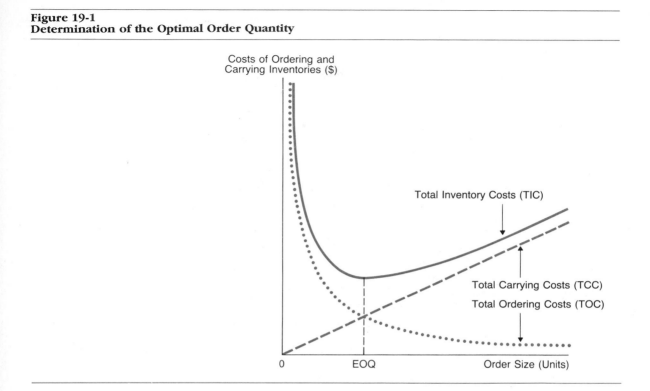

Costs of Ordering and
Carrying Inventories ($)

Total Inventory Costs (TIC)

Total Carrying Costs (TCC)

Total Ordering Costs (TOC)

0          EOQ                        Order Size (Units)

the firm's costs rise with larger orders: Larger orders mean larger average inventories, so warehousing costs, interest on funds tied up in inventory, insurance, and obsolescence will all increase. At the same time, ordering costs decline with larger orders and inventories, because the costs of placing orders, setting up production runs, and handling shipments will all decline if we order infrequently and consequently hold larger quantities.

When the carrying and ordering cost curves in Figure 19-1 are added together, the sum represents the total cost of ordering and carrying inventories, TIC. The point where the total cost curve is minimized represents the **economic ordering quantity (EOQ)**, and this in turn determines the optimal average inventory level.

It can be shown that under certain reasonable assumptions the order quantity that minimizes the total cost curve in Figure 19-1, or the EOQ, can be found by using the following formula:[10]

**economic ordering quantity (EOQ)**
The optimal, or least-cost, quantity of inventory that should be ordered.

---

[10]The EOQ model is derived in Chapter 17 of Eugene F. Brigham and Louis C. Gapenski, *Intermediate Financial Management*. The total cost function is differentiated with respect to Q, and the first derivative is set equal to zero to locate the minimum point on the total cost curve in Figure 19-1. Equation 19-7 results from this operation.

$$EOQ = \sqrt{\frac{2(F)(S)}{(C)(P)}}.$$  (19-7)

Here

EOQ = the economic ordering quantity, or the optimum quantity to be ordered each time an order is placed.

F = fixed costs of placing and receiving an order.

S = annual sales in units.

C = carrying cost expressed as a percentage of inventory value.

P = purchase price the firm must pay per unit of inventory.

**EOQ model**
A formula for determining the order quantity that will minimize total inventory cost: $EOQ = \sqrt{2FS/CP}$.

The assumptions of the **EOQ model**, which will be relaxed shortly, include the following: (1) Sales can be forecasted perfectly, (2) sales are evenly distributed throughout the year, and (3) orders are received with no delays whatever.

To illustrate the EOQ model, consider the following data supplied by Romantic Books, Inc., publisher of the classic novel *Madame Boudoir*:

S = sales = 26,000 copies per year.

C = carrying cost = 20 percent of inventory value.

P = purchase price per book to Romantic Books from a printing company = $6.1538 per copy. (The sales price Romantic Books charges is $9, but this is irrelevant for our purposes.)

F = fixed cost per order = $1,000. The bulk of this cost is the labor cost of setting the page plates on the presses as well as of setting up the binding equipment for the production run. The printer bills this cost separately from the $6.1538 cost per copy.

Substituting these data into Equation 19-7, we obtain

$$EOQ = \sqrt{\frac{2(F)(S)}{(C)(P)}}$$

$$= \sqrt{\frac{(2)(\$1,000)(26,000)}{(0.2)(\$6.1538)}}$$

$$= \sqrt{42,250,317}$$

$$= 6,500 \text{ copies.}$$

Average inventory holdings depend directly on the EOQ; this relationship is illustrated graphically in Figure 19-2. Immediately after an order is re-

**Figure 19-2**
**Inventory Position without Safety Stock**

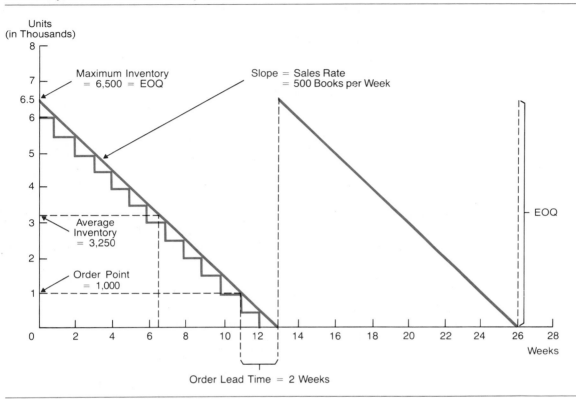

ceived, 6,500 copies are in stock. The usage rate, or sales rate, is 500 copies per week (26,000/52 weeks), so inventories are drawn down by this amount each week. Thus, the actual number of units held in inventory will vary from 6,500 books just after an order is received to zero just before the next order arrives. On average, the number of units held will be 6,500/2 = 3,250 books. At a cost of $6.1538 per book, the average investment in inventories will be (3,250)($6.1538) = $19,999.85 ≈ $20,000. If inventories are financed by a bank loan, the loan will vary from a high of $40,000 to a low of $0, but the average amount outstanding over the course of a year will be $20,000.

Notice that the EOQ, and hence average inventory holdings, rises with the square root of sales. Therefore, a given increase in sales will result in a less than proportionate increase in inventories, and the inventory/sales ratio will thus decline as sales grow. For example, Romantic Books' EOQ is 6,500 copies at an annual sales level of 26,000, and the average inventory is 3,250 copies, or $20,000. However, if sales increase by 100 percent, to 52,000 copies per year, the EOQ will rise to only 9,192 copies, or by 41 percent, and the average inventory will rise by this same percentage. This suggests that there are economies of scale in the holding of inventories.[11]

## Setting the Reorder Point

**reorder point**
The point at which stock on hand must be replenished.

If a 2-week lead time is required for production and shipping, what is Romantic Books' **reorder point**, or inventory level at which an order should be placed? If we use a 52-week year, Romantic Books sells 26,000/52 = 500 books per week. Thus, if a 2-week lag occurs between ordering and receipt, Romantic Books must place the order when there are 2(500) = 1,000 books on hand. At the end of the 2-week production and shipping period, the inventory balance will be down to zero—but just at that time the order of new books will arrive.

## Safety Stocks

**safety stocks**
Additional inventories carried to guard against changes in sales rates or production/shipping delays.

If Romantic Books knew for certain that both the sales rate and the order lead time would never vary, it could operate exactly as shown in Figure 19-2. However, since sales do change and production and shipping delays are frequently encountered, the firm will carry additional inventories, or **safety stocks**.

The concept of a safety stock is illustrated in Figure 19-3. First, note that the slope of the sales line measures the expected rate of sales. The company *expects* sales of 500 copies per week, but let us assume that the maximum possible sales rate is twice that amount, or 1,000 copies each week. Further, assume that Romantic Books sets the safety stock at 1,000 books. Thus, it initially orders 7,500, which is the EOQ of 6,500 copies plus the safety stock. Subsequently, it reorders the EOQ whenever the inventory level falls to 2,000 copies, which is the safety stock of 1,000 copies plus the 1,000 copies expected to be used while awaiting delivery of the order. Notice that the company could, over the 2-week delivery period, sell 1,000 copies a week, or double its normal expected sales; this maximum rate of sales is shown by the steep, dashed line in Figure 19-3. The condition that makes it possible to achieve this higher sales rate is the introduction of a safety stock of 1,000 copies—without it, the firm would run out of stock if the sales rate rose from 500 to 1,000 per week.

The safety stock is also useful to guard against delays in receiving orders. The expected delivery time is 2 weeks, but with a 1,000-copy safety stock the company could maintain sales at the expected rate of 500 copies per week for an additional 2 weeks if shipping delays held up an order.

Safety stocks are obviously useful, but they do have a cost. For Romantic Books, the average inventory is now EOQ/2 plus a safety stock of 1,000, or

---

[11]Note, however, that these scale economies relate to the particular item, not to the entire firm. Thus, a large publishing company with $500 million of sales may have a higher inventory/sales ratio than a much smaller company if the latter has only a few high-volume books while the former publishes a great many low-volume books.

**Figure 19-3**
**Inventory Position with Safety Stock Included**

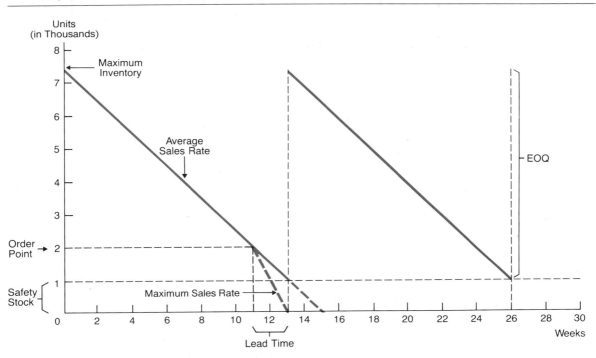

6,500/2 + 1,000 = 3,250 + 1,000 = 4,250 books, and the average inventory value is (4,250)($6.1538) = $26,154. The increase in average inventory resulting from the safety stock causes an increase in inventory carrying costs.

The optimum safety stock varies from one situation to another, but in general it *increases* (1) with the uncertainty of sales forecasts, (2) with the costs (in terms of lost sales and lost goodwill) that would result from an inventory shortage, and (3) with the probability of delays in receiving shipments. The optimum safety stock *decreases* as the cost of carrying it increases.[12]

---

[12]For a more detailed discussion of safety stocks, see Dileep R. Mehta, *Working Capital Management* (Englewood Cliffs, N.J.: Prentice-Hall), 1974. If we knew (1) the probability distribution of usage rates and (2) the probability distribution of order lead times, we could determine joint probabilities of stock-outs with various safety stock levels. With a safety stock of 1,000 copies, for example, the probability of a stock-out for *Madame Boudoir* might be 5 percent. If the safety stock were reduced to 500 copies, the stock-out probability might rise to 15 percent, while it might be reduced to 1 percent with a safety stock of 2,000 copies. If we had additional information on the precise cost of a stock-out, we could compare it with the cost of carrying larger safety stocks. The optimum safety stock is determined at the point where the marginal stock-out cost is equal to the marginal inventory carrying cost.

## Inventory Control Systems

The EOQ model, along with an analysis of safety stocks, can be used to establish the proper inventory level, but inventory management also involves the *inventory ordering and control system*. One simple control procedure is the **red-line method**—here inventory items are stocked in a bin, a red line is drawn around the inside of the bin at the level of the order point, and the inventory clerk places an order when the red line shows. The **two-bin method** has inventory items stocked in two bins; when the working bin is empty, an order is placed and inventory is drawn from the second bin. These procedures work well for such items as bolts in a manufacturing process, and for many items in retail businesses.

Companies are increasingly employing **computerized inventory control systems**. A computer starts with an inventory count in memory. Withdrawals are recorded by the computer as they are made, and the inventory balance is constantly revised. When the order point is reached, the computer automatically places an order; when this new order is received, the recorded balance is increased. Retail stores have carried this system quite far—each item has a magnetic code, and, as an item is checked out, it passes over an electronic reader, which then adjusts the computer's inventory balance at the same time the price is fed to the cash register tape. When the balance drops to the order point, an order is placed.

A good inventory control system is dynamic. Companies such as IBM and General Motors stock hundreds of thousands of different items, and the sales (or use) of these items can rise or fall quite separately from fluctuating overall corporate sales. As the usage rate for an individual item begins to fall, the inventory manager must adjust its balance to avoid ending up with obsolete items—either finished goods or parts and materials for use in producing them.

The EOQ model is useful for establishing order sizes and average inventory levels *given a correctly forecasted sales or usage rate*. However, usage rates change over time, and a good inventory management system must respond promptly to any change in sales. One system that is used to monitor inventory usage rates and in turn to modify EOQs and inventory item levels is the **ABC system**. Here the firm analyzes each inventory item on the basis of its cost, frequency of usage, seriousness of a stock-out, order lead time, and other criteria. Items that are expensive, are frequently used, and have long order lead times are put in the A category; less important items are put in the B category; and the least important items are designated C. Management reviews the A items' recent usage rates, stock positions, and delivery time situations quite frequently—say, monthly—and adjusts the EOQ as necessary. Category B items are reviewed and adjusted less frequently—say, every quarter—and C items are reviewed perhaps annually. Thus, the inventory control group's resources are concentrated where they will do the most good.

Efficient inventory management will result in a relatively high inventory turnover ratio, in low write-offs of obsolete or deteriorated inventories, and

---

**red-line method**
An inventory control procedure in which a red line is drawn around the inside of an inventory-stocked bin to indicate the order point level.

**two-bin method**
An inventory control procedure in which the order point is reached when one of two inventory-stocked bins is empty.

**computerized inventory control system**
A system of inventory control in which computers are used to determine order points and to adjust inventory balances.

**ABC system**
A system used to categorize inventory items to insure that the most important ones are reviewed most often.

in few instances of work stoppages or lost sales due to stock-outs. All this, in turn, will contribute to a high profit margin, a high total assets turnover, a high rate of return on investment, and a strong stock price.

## Effects of Inflation on Inventory Management

Moderate inflation—say, 3 percent per year—can largely be ignored for purposes of inventory management, but at higher rates of inflation it becomes important to consider this factor. If the rate of inflation in the types of goods the firm stocks tends to be relatively constant, it can be dealt with easily—one simply deducts the expected annual rate of inflation from the carrying cost percentage, C, in Equation 19-7 and uses this modified version of the EOQ model to establish the working stock. The reason for making this deduction is that inflation causes the value of the inventory to rise, thus offsetting somewhat the effects of depreciation and other carrying cost factors. Since C will now be smaller, the calculated EOQ, and hence the average inventory, will increase. However, the higher the rate of inflation, the higher interest rates will be, and this will cause C to increase and thus lower the EOQ and average inventories.

On balance, there is no evidence that inflation either raises or lowers the optimal inventories of firms in the aggregate. It should still be thoroughly considered, however, for it will raise the individual firm's optimal holdings if the rate of inflation for its own inventories is above average (and is greater than the effects of inflation on interest rates), and vice versa.

## Other Inventory Issues

Two other inventory-related issues should be mentioned. The first is the *just-in-time* system, where a manufacturer coordinates production with suppliers so that raw materials or components arrive from suppliers just as they are needed in the production process. For example, beer companies frequently arrange to have a can maker set up a manufacturing plant adjacent to a brewery, and then the can company and the brewery coordinate their production schedules. The Japanese have carried the just-in-time system to great lengths, and U.S. companies are increasingly adopting this in our manufacturing plants. Of course, a just-in-time system reduces the need for the purchaser to carry inventories by passing the problem back to its suppliers. Still, coordination between suppliers and users can lessen total inventory requirements.

Another important development related to inventories is *out-sourcing*, which is the practice of purchasing components rather than making them in-house. Thus, if General Motors arranges to buy radiators from a supplier rather than making them itself, then it has increased its use of out-sourcing. Out-sourcing is often combined with just-in-time systems to reduce inventory levels. However, perhaps the major reason for out-sourcing has nothing to do with inventory policy—a heavily unionized company like GM can often buy parts from a non-unionized supplier at a lower cost because of wage rate differentials.

A final point relating to inventory levels is *the relationship between production scheduling and inventory levels*. A company like Drexel Card Company, whose cash budget was discussed in Chapter 18, has sales which are highly seasonal. Drexel could produce on a steady, year-round basis, or it could let production rise and fall with sales. If it followed a level production schedule, its inventories would rise sharply during periods when sales were low and would decline during peak sales periods, and the average would be substantially higher than if production were geared to rise and fall with sales.

Just-in-time, out-sourcing, and our discussion of production scheduling all point out the necessity of coordinating inventory policy with manufacturing/procurement policies. Companies try to minimize *total costs*, and inventory costs are just one part of total costs. Still, they are an important cost, and financial managers should be aware of the determinants of inventory costs and how they can be minimized.

## Summary

Since the typical manufacturing firm has about 42 percent of its assets invested in inventories and receivables, the management of these assets is obviously important. The investment in receivables is dependent on the firm's *credit policy*, which consists of four variables: (1) the *credit standards*, or the financial strength customers must exhibit in order to be granted credit; (2) the *credit period*, or the length of time for which credit is extended; (3) *cash discounts*, which are designed to encourage rapid payment; and (4) the *collection policy*, which helps determine how long accounts remain outstanding. Credit policy has an important impact on the volume of sales, and the optimal policy involves a trade-off between the costs inherent in various credit policies and the profits generated by higher sales. From a practical standpoint, it is impossible to determine the optimal credit policy in a mathematical sense—good credit management involves a blending of quantitative analysis and business judgment.

*Inventory management* centers around the balancing of a set of costs that increase with larger inventory holdings (storage costs, cost of capital, and physical deterioration) and a set of costs that decline with larger holdings (ordering costs, lost sales, and disruption of production schedules). Inventory management has been quantified to a greater extent than most aspects of business, with the EOQ model being one important part of most inventory systems. This model can be used to determine the optimal order quantity, which, when combined with a specified safety stock, determines the average inventory level. Inventory control systems are used to keep track of actual inventory levels and to insure that inventory levels are adjusted to changing sales levels.

## Questions

19-1    Define each of the following terms:
     a. Account receivable
     b. Aging schedule
     c. Credit policy; credit period; credit standards; five Cs of credit; collection policy
     d. Cash discounts

    e. Seasonal dating

    f. Open account; promissory note; commercial draft; sight draft; time draft, or trade acceptance; banker's acceptance; conditional sales contract

    g. Carrying costs; ordering costs; total inventory costs

    h. Economic ordering quantity (EOQ); EOQ model

    i. Reorder point; safety stock

    j. Red-line method; two-bin method; computerized inventory control system; ABC system

    k. Average collection period (ACP)

    l. Just-in-time; out-sourcing

**19-2** Is it true that when one firm sells to another on credit the seller records the transaction as an account receivable while the buyer records it as an account payable and that, disregarding discounts, the receivable typically exceeds the payable by the amount of profit on the sale?

**19-3** What are the four elements in a firm's credit policy? To what extent can firms set their own credit policies as opposed to having to accept policies that are dictated by "the competition"?

**19-4** Suppose a firm makes a purchase and receives the shipment on February 1. The terms of trade as stated on the invoice read "2/10, net 40, May 1 dating." What is the latest date on which payment can be made and the discount still be taken? What is the date on which payment must be made if the discount is not taken?

**19-5** a. What is the average collection period (ACP) for a firm whose sales are $2,880,000 per year and whose accounts receivable are $312,000? (Use 360 days per year.)

    b. Is it true that if this firm sells on terms of 3/10, net 40, its customers probably all pay on time?

**19-6** Is it true that if a firm calculates its average collection period, it has no need for an aging schedule?

**19-7** Firm A had no credit losses last year, but 1 percent of Firm B's accounts receivable proved to be uncollectible and resulted in losses. Should Firm B fire its credit manager and hire A's?

**19-8** Indicate by a ( + ), ( − ), or ( 0 ) whether each of the following events would probably cause accounts receivable (A/R), sales, and profits to increase, decrease, or be affected in an indeterminant manner:

|  | A/R | Sales | Profits |
|---|---|---|---|
| a. The firm tightens its credit standards. | _____ | _____ | _____ |
| b. The terms of trade are changed from 2/10, net 30, to 3/10, net 30. | _____ | _____ | _____ |
| c. The terms are changed from 2/10, net 30, to 3/10, net 40. | _____ | _____ | _____ |
| d. The credit manager gets tough with past-due accounts. | _____ | _____ | _____ |

**19-9**      If a firm calculates its optimal inventory of widgets to be 1,000 units when the general rate of inflation is 2 percent, is it true that the optimal inventory (in units) will almost certainly rise if the general rate of inflation climbs to 10 percent?

**19-10**     Indicate by a $(+)$, $(-)$, or $(0)$ whether each of the following events would probably cause average annual inventories (the sum of the inventories held at the end of each month of the year divided by 12) to rise, fall, or be affected in an indeterminant manner:

a.  Our suppliers switch from delivering by train to
    air freight.                                                   _____
b.  We change from producing just in time to meet
    seasonal sales to steady, year-round production.
    (Sales peak at Christmas.)                                      _____
c.  Competition in the markets in which we sell increases.    _____
d.  The rate of general inflation increases.                       _____
e.  Interest rates rise; other things are constant.               _____


## Self-Test Problems (*Solutions on Page 675*)

**ST-1**      The Mallory Company expects to have sales of $10 million this year under its current operating policies. Its variable costs as a percentage of sales is 80 percent, and its cost of capital is 16 percent. Currently Mallory's credit policy is net 25 (no discount for early payment). However, its ACP is 30 days, and its bad debt loss percentage is 2 percent. Mallory spends $50,000 per year to collect bad debts, and its effective tax rate is 50 percent.

The credit manager is considering two alternative proposals, given below, for changing Mallory's credit policy. Find the expected change in net income, taking into consideration anticipated changes in carrying costs for accounts receivable, the probable bad debt losses, and the discounts likely to be taken, for each proposal. Should a change in credit policy be made?

*Proposal 1*: Lengthen the credit period by going from net 25 to net 30. The bad debt collection expenditures will remain constant. Under this proposal, sales are expected to increase by $1 million annually, and the bad debt loss percentage on *new* sales is expected to rise to 4 percent (the loss percentage on old sales should not change). In addition, the ACP is expected to increase from 30 to 45 days on all sales.

*Proposal 2*: Shorten the credit period by going from net 25 to net 20. Again, collection expenses will remain constant. The anticipated effects of this change are (1) a decrease in sales of $1 million per year, (2) a decline in the ACP from 30 to 22 days, and (3) a decline in the bad debt loss percentage to 1 percent on all sales.

**ST-2**      The Best Breads Company buys and then sells (as bread) 2.6 million bushels of wheat annually. The wheat must be purchased in multiples of 2,000 bushels. Ordering costs, which include grain elevator removal charges of $3,500, are $5,000 per order. Annual carrying costs are 2 percent of the purchase price per bushel of $5. The company maintains a safety stock of 200,000 bushels. The delivery time is 6 weeks.

a.  What is the EOQ?

b. At what inventory level should a reorder be placed to prevent having to draw on the safety stock?

c. What are the total inventory costs?

d. The wheat processor agrees to pay the elevator removal charges if Best Breads will purchase wheat in quantities of 650,000 bushels. Would it be to Best Breads' advantage to order under this alternative?

## Problems

**Receivables investment**   **19-1**   Provencial, Inc., sells on terms of 2/10, net 30. Total sales for the year are $600,000. Forty percent of the customers pay on the tenth day and take discounts; the other 60 percent pay, on average, 40 days after their purchases.

a. What is the average collection period?

b. What is the average amount of receivables?

c. What would happen to the average investment in receivables if Provencial toughened up on its collection policy with the result that all nondiscount customers paid on the thirtieth day?

**Easing credit terms**   **19-2**   Milburn Auto Parts is considering changing its credit terms from 2/15, net 30, to 3/10, net 30, in order to speed collections. At present, 60 percent of Milburn's customers take the 2 percent discount. Under the new terms, discount customers are expected to rise to 70 percent. Regardless of the credit terms, half of the customers who do not take the discount are expected to pay on time, while the remainder will pay 10 days late. The change does not involve a relaxation of credit standards; therefore, bad debt losses are not expected to rise above their present 2 percent level. However, the more generous cash discount terms are expected to increase sales from $1 million to $1.2 million per year. Milburn's variable cost ratio is 75 percent, the interest rate on funds invested in accounts receivable is 12 percent, and its tax rate is 50 percent.

a. What is the average collection period before and after the change?

b. Calculate the discount costs before and after the change.

c. Calculate the dollar cost of carrying receivables before and after the change.

d. Calculate the bad debt losses before and after the change.

e. What is the incremental profit from the change in credit terms? Should Milburn change its credit terms?

(Do only if you are using the computerized problem diskette.)

f. 1. Suppose the sales forecast is lowered to $1,100,000. Should Milburn change its credit policy? What if the sales forecast dropped to $1,037,265?

   2. Suppose the payment pattern of customers remains unchanged with the new credit plan; that is, 60 percent still take the discount, 20 percent pay on time, and 20 percent pay late. Also, the variable cost ratio rises to 78 percent. How does all this affect the decision, assuming the sales forecast remains at $1,200,000?

**Credit analysis**   **19-3**   Valley Distributors makes all sales on a credit basis, selling on terms of 2/10, net 30. Once a year it evaluates the creditworthiness of all its customers. The evaluation procedure ranks customers from 1 to 5, with 1 indicating the "best" customers. Results of the ranking are as follows:

| Customer Category | Percentage of Bad Debts | Average Collection Period (Days) | Credit Decision | Annual Sales Lost Due to Credit Restrictions |
|---|---|---|---|---|
| 1 | None | 10 | Unlimited credit | None |
| 2 | 1.0 | 12 | Unlimited credit | None |
| 3 | 3.0 | 20 | Limited credit | $365,000 |
| 4 | 9.0 | 60 | Limited credit | $182,500 |
| 5 | 16.0 | 90 | Limited credit | $230,000 |

The variable cost ratio is 75 percent. The cost of capital invested in receivables is 15 percent. What would be the effect on the profitability of extending unlimited credit to each of the Categories 3, 4, and 5? (Hint: Determine the effect of changing each policy separately on the income statement. In other words, find the change in sales, change in production costs, change in receivables and cost of carrying receivables, change in bad debt costs, and so forth, down to the change in gross profits.)

Tightening credit terms  **19-4**  Daniel Richards, the new credit manager of the Haskell Corporation, was alarmed to find that Haskell sells on credit terms of net 90 days while industrywide credit terms have recently been lowered to net 30 days. On annual credit sales of $2.5 million, Haskell currently averages 95 days' sales in accounts receivable. Richards estimates that tightening the credit terms to 30 days would reduce annual sales to $2,375,000, but accounts receivable would drop to 35 days of sales and the savings on investment in them should more than overcome any loss in profit.

Haskell's variable cost ratio is 85 percent, and taxes are 50 percent. If the interest rate on funds invested in receivables is 18 percent, should the change in credit terms be made?

Relaxing collection efforts  **19-5**  The Lehigh Corporation has annual credit sales of $1.6 million. Current expenses for the collection department are $35,000, bad debt losses are 1.5 percent, and the average collection period is 30 days. Lehigh is considering easing its collection efforts such that collection expenses will be reduced to $22,000 per year. The change is expected to increase bad debt losses to 2.5 percent and to increase the average collection period to 45 days. In addition, sales are expected to increase to $1,625,000 per year.

Should Lehigh relax collection efforts if the opportunity cost of funds is 16 percent, the variable cost ratio is 75 percent, and taxes are 50 percent?

Economic ordering quantity  **19-6**  The Rosecrans Garden Center sells 90,000 bags of lawn fertilizer annually. The optimal safety stock (which is on hand initially) is 1,000 bags. Each bag costs Rosecrans $1.50, inventory carrying costs are 20 percent, and the cost of placing an order with its supplier is $15.

a. What is the economic ordering quantity?
b. What is the maximum inventory of fertilizer?
c. What will Rosecrans' average inventory be?
d. How often must the company order?

EOQ and total ordering costs  **19-7**  The following inventory data have been established for the Sealfast Corporation:
1. Orders must be placed in multiples of 100 units.
2. Annual sales are 338,000 units.

3. The purchase price per unit is $3.
4. Carrying cost is 20 percent of the purchase price of goods.
5. Cost per order placed is $24.
6. Desired safety stock is 14,000 units; this amount is on hand initially.
7. Two weeks are required for delivery.

a. What is the EOQ?
b. How many orders should Sealfast place each year?
c. At what inventory level should a reorder be made? (Hint: Reorder point = Safety stock + Weeks to deliver × Weekly usage − Goods in transit.)
d. Calculate the total cost of ordering and carrying inventories if the order quantity is (1) 4,000 units, (2) 4,800 units, or (3) 6,000 units. What are the total costs if the order quantity is the EOQ?
e. (Do only if you are using the computerized problem diskette.)

What are the EOQ and total inventory cost if

1. Sales increase to 500,000 units?
2. Fixed order costs increase to $30? Sales remain at 338,000 units.
3. Purchase price increases to $4? Leave sales and fixed costs at original values.

## Solutions to Self-Test Problems

ST-1   Under the current credit policy, the Mallory Company has no discounts, collection expenses of $50,000, bad debt losses of $(0.02)($10,000,000) = $200,000$, and average accounts receivable of (ACP)(Average sales per day) = $(30)($10,000,000/360) = $833,333$. The firm's cost of carrying these receivables is (Variable cost ratio)(A/R)(Cost of capital) = $(0.80)($833,333)(0.16) = $106,667$. It is necessary to multiply by the variable cost ratio because the actual *investment* in receivables is less than the dollar amount of the receivables.

*Proposal 1*: Lengthen the credit period such that
1. Sales increase by $1 million.
2. Discounts = $0.
3. Bad debt losses = $(0.02)($10,000,000) + (0.04)($1,000,000)$

$$= $200,000 + $40,000$$

$$= $240,000.$$

4. ACP = 45 days on all sales.
5. New average receivables = $(45)($11,000,000/360)$

$$= $1,375,000.$$

6. Cost of carrying receivables = (v)(k)(Average accounts receivable)

$$= (0.80)(0.16)($1,375,000)$$

$$= $176,000.$$

7. Change in cost of carrying receivables = $176,000 − $106,667

$$= $69,333.$$

8. Collection expenses = $50,000.

Analysis of proposed change:

|  | Income Statement under Current Policy | Effect of Change | Income Statement under New Policy |
|---|---|---|---|
| Gross sales | $10,000,000 | + $1,000,000 | $11,000,000 |
| Less discounts | 0 | + 0 | 0 |
| Net sales | $10,000,000 | + $1,000,000 | $11,000,000 |
| Production costs (80%) | 8,000,000 | + 800,000 | 8,800,000 |
| Gross profits before credit costs | $ 2,000,000 | + $ 200,000 | $ 2,200,000 |
| Credit-related costs: |  |  |  |
| Cost of carrying receivables | 106,667 | + 69,333 | 176,000 |
| Collection expenses | 50,000 | + 0 | 50,000 |
| Bad debt losses | 200,000 | + 40,000 | 240,000 |
| Gross profit | $ 1,643,333 | + $ 90,667 | $ 1,734,000 |
| Taxes (50%) | 821,666 | + 45,333 | 867,000 |
| Net income | $ 821,667 | + 45,334 | $ 867,000 |

The proposed change appears to be a good one, assuming the assumptions are correct.

*Proposal 2*: Shorten the credit period to net 20 such that
1. Sales decrease by $1 million.
2. Discount = $0.
3. Bad debt losses = $(0.01)($9,000,000)$
   = $90,000.
4. ACP = 22 days.
5. New average receivables = $(22)($9,000,000/360)$
   = $550,000.
6. Cost of carrying receivables = $(v)(k)$(Average accounts receivable)
   = $(0.80)(0.16)($550,000)$
   = $70,400.
7. Collection expenses = $50,000.

Analysis of proposed change:

|  | Income Statement under Current Policy | Effect of Change | Income Statement under New Policy |
|---|---|---|---|
| Gross sales | $10,000,000 | − $1,000,000 | $9,000,000 |
| Less discounts | 0 | 0 | 0 |
| Net sales | $10,000,000 | − $1,000,000 | $9,000,000 |
| Production costs (80%) | 8,000,000 | − 800,000 | 7,200,000 |
| Gross profits before credit costs | $ 2,000,000 | − $ 200,000 | $1,800,000 |
| Credit-related costs: |  |  |  |
| Cost of carrying receivables | 106,667 | − 36,267 | 70,400 |
| Collection expenses | 50,000 | 0 | 50,000 |
| Bad debt losses | 200,000 | − 110,000 | 90,000 |
| Gross profit | $ 1,643,333 | − $ 53,733 | $1,589,600 |
| Taxes (50%) | 821,666 | − 26,866 | 794,800 |
| Net income | $ 821,667 | − $ 26,867 | $ 794,800 |

This change reduces net income, so it should be rejected. Mallory will increase profits by accepting Proposal 1 to lengthen the credit period from 25 days to 30 days, assuming all assumptions are correct. This may or may not be the *optimal*, or profit-maximizing, credit policy, but it does appear to be a movement in the right direction.

ST-2

a. $EOQ = \sqrt{\dfrac{2(F)(S)}{(C)(P)}}$

$= \sqrt{\dfrac{(2)(\$5,000)(2,600,000)}{(0.02)(\$5.00)}}$

$= 509,902$ bushels.

Since the firm must order in multiples of 2,000 bushels, it should order in quantities of 510,000 bushels.

b. Average weekly sales $= 2,600,000/52$

$= 50,000$ bushels.

Reorder point $= 6$ weeks' sales $+$ Safety stock

$= 6(50,000) + 200,000$

$= 300,000 + 200,000$

$= 500,000$ bushels.

c. Total inventory costs:

$$TIC = CP\left(\frac{Q}{2}\right) + F\left(\frac{S}{Q}\right) + CP(\text{Safety stock})$$

$$= (0.02)(\$5)\left(\frac{510,000}{2}\right) + (\$5,000)\left(\frac{2,600,000}{510,000}\right)$$

$+ (0.02)(\$5)(200,000)$

$= \$25,500 + \$25,490.20 + \$20,000$

$= \$70,990.20.$

d. Ordering costs would be reduced to $1,500. By ordering 650,000 bushels at a time, total inventory costs would be:

$$TIC = (0.02)(\$5)\left(\frac{650,000}{2}\right) + (\$1,500)\left(\frac{2,600,000}{650,000}\right)$$

$+ (0.02)(\$5)(200,000)$

$= \$32,500 + \$6,000 + \$20,000$

$= \$58,500.$

Since the firm can reduce its total inventory costs by ordering 650,000 bushels at a time, it should accept the offer and place larger orders. (Incidentally, this same type of analysis is used to consider any quantity discount offer.)

## Selected Additional References and Cases

Some articles which address credit policy and receivables management include the following:

Atkins, Joseph C., and Yong H. Kim, "Comment and Correction: Opportunity Cost in the Evaluation of Investment in Accounts Receivable," *Financial Management*, Winter 1977, 71-74.

Ben-Horim, Moshe, and Haim Levy, "Management of Accounts Receivable under Inflation," *Financial Management*, Spring 1983, 42-48.

Dyl, Edward A., "Another Look at the Evaluation of Interest in Accounts Receivable," *Financial Management*, Winter 1977, 67-70.

Hill, Ned C., and Kenneth D. Riener, "Determining the Cash Discount in the Firm's Credit Policy," *Financial Management*, Spring 1979, 68-73.

Kim, Yong H., and Joseph C. Atkins, "Evaluating Investments in Accounts Receivable: A Wealth Maximizing Framework," *Journal of Finance*, May 1978, 403-412.

Oh, John S., "Opportunity Cost in the Evaluation of Investment in Accounts Receivable," *Financial Management*, Summer 1976, 32-36.

Roberts, Gordon S., and Jeremy A. Viscione, "Captive Finance Subsidiaries: The Manager's View," *Financial Management*, Spring 1981, 36-42.

Sachdeva, Kanwal S., and Lawrence J. Gitman, "Accounts Receivable Decisions in a Capital Budgeting Framework," *Financial Management*, Winter 1981, 45-49.

Walia, Tinlochan S., "Explicit and Implicit Cost of Changes in the Level of Accounts Receivable and the Credit Policy Decision of the Firm," *Financial Management*, Winter 1977, 75-78.

Weston, J. Fred, and Pham D. Tuan, "Comment on Analysis of Credit Policy Changes," *Financial Management*, Winter 1980, 59-63.

The following articles provide additional insights into the problems of inventory management:

Bierman, H., Jr., C. P. Bonini, and W. H. Hausman, *Quantitative Analysis for Business Decisions* (Homewood, Ill.: Irwin, 1977).

Brooks, L. D., "Risk-Return Criteria and Optimal Inventory Stocks," *Engineering Economist*, Summer 1980, 275-299.

Magee, John F., "Guides to Inventory Policy, I," *Harvard Business Review*, January-February 1956, 49-60.

———, "Guides to Inventory Policy, II," *Harvard Business Review*, March-April 1956, 103-116.

———, "Guides to Inventory Policy, III," *Harvard Business Review*, May-June 1956, 57-70.

Mehta, Dileep R., *Working Capital Management* (Englewood Cliffs, N.J.: Prentice-Hall, 1974).

Shapiro, A., "Optimal Inventory and Credit Granting Strategies under Inflation and Devaluation," *Journal of Financial and Quantitative Analysis*, January 1973, 37-46.

Smith, Keith V., *Guide to Working Capital Management* (New York: McGraw-Hill, 1979).

The following cases focus on the credit policy decision:

"Zukowski Meats, Incorporated," in the Harrington casebook, which stresses forecasting the effect of a credit policy change on the working capital accounts.

Case 8, "Englehardt Kitchens, Inc.," in the Crum-Brigham casebook, which demonstrates how the various credit policy variables interact to determine (1) the firm's level of accounts receivable and (2) its risk and rate of return.

The Crum-Brigham casebook also has a useful case on inventory management:

Case 9, "Good Connection, Inc.," which focuses on the EOQ model and safety stocks.

# VI

# SPECIAL TOPICS IN FINANCIAL MANAGEMENT

Parts I through V developed the basic framework of financial management. However, we have deferred two important topics that can best be analyzed on an integrated basis using the tools developed in Chapters 1 through 19. Chapter 20 covers international finance, and Chapter 21 deals with mergers, divestitures, and holding companies.

# 20 INTERNATIONAL FINANCE

## THE SCALES TIP:
## FOREIGN INVESTMENT IN THE UNITED STATES NOW OUTWEIGHS AMERICAN INVESTMENT ABROAD

In 1984 roughly 25 percent of the assets of U.S.-based manufacturing corporations were located outside the United States, and an even larger percentage of their total income was generated by overseas operations. Moreover, the rate of growth of international investment now exceeds the growth rate of aggregate U.S. domestic investment. The rapid expansion of foreign investment by U.S. companies has been caused in large part by lower overseas labor costs resulting in generally higher rates of return on foreign investments, especially in developing nations, as compared with equivalent-risk domestic projects. Thus, it is not surprising that General Electric has television assembly plants in Mexico, South Korea, and Singapore; that IBM has computer hardware manufacturing and servicing subsidiaries in many parts of Europe and the Far East; that Caterpillar produces tractors and farm equipment in the Middle East, Europe, the Far East, and Africa; and so on.

The past decade has also seen an increasing amount of investment in the United States by foreign corporations. This "reverse" investment, which is of growing concern to U.S. government officials, has actually been occurring at a higher rate in the past few years than has U.S. investment abroad. By the end of 1984, the level of foreign investment in the United States was about 46 percent of U.S. international investment and was concentrated in manufacturing operations, trading companies, and the petroleum industry. The fastest growth has been by Japanese firms in the manufacturing and trade sectors.

These trends are significant because of their implications for eroding the traditional doctrine of independence and self-reliance that has always been a hallmark of U.S. policy. Just as American corporations with extensive overseas operations are said to use their enormous economic power to exert substantial economic and political influence over host governments in many parts of the world, it is feared that foreign corporations could gain similar sway over U.S. policy. Taken together, these developments suggest an increasing degree of mutual influence and interdependence among business enterprises and nations from which even the United States is not immune.

This chapter was coauthored by Roy L. Crum of the University of Florida.

We should state at the outset that international finance is, in a sense, like taxes—it is too important for you to know nothing about, but too complicated to be covered adequately in one chapter. However, even a quick reading of this chapter will give you a good idea of what is involved in the financial management of a multinational firm, get you ready to talk with people actually involved in multinational operations, or prepare you for a course in international business.

## The Multinational Corporation

**multinational corporation**
A firm that operates in two or more countries.

The term **multinational corporation** is used to describe a firm that operates in two or more nations. However, such a simple characterization obscures some essential attributes of the modern corporation. In the period since World War II, a new and fundamentally different format for international commercial activity has been developed, and it has greatly increased the degree of worldwide economic and political interdependence. The distinguishing characteristic between the new form of commercial transaction and earlier activities is that firms, rather than merely buying resources from foreign concerns, now make direct investments in fully integrated operations, with worldwide entities controlling all phases of the production process—from extraction of raw materials, through the manufacturing process, to distribution to consumers throughout the world. Today, multinational corporate networks control a large and growing share of the world's technological, marketing, and productive resources.

For the most part, these supranational corporations are relatively unconstrained in how they allocate resources among the various nations in which they operate. Thus, goods and services can often be transferred among the different elements of the corporate system at "prices" that do not reflect arm's-length transactions or market values. Rather, transfer prices can be set to enable the organization to locate production and marketing where these activities can be done most efficiently, yet cause taxable income to be "earned" in countries that have low tax rates, thus breaking the link between the country in which economic value is created and the country in which it is recognized. Not surprisingly, such activities lead to friction between multinational corporations and the nations in which they operate. One serious challenge to multinational corporations today comes from developing (formerly called "underdeveloped") countries, which charge that the fair value of their national resources has been—and continues to be—siphoned off and transferred to the owners of the firms, who reside in the developed world, particularly the United States, Japan, and Europe. At the same time, developed nations, which generally have relatively high wage rates, are challenging the tendency of multinational firms to move manufacturing plants—and hence jobs—to locations in developing nations with lower wage rates.

## Multinational versus Traditional Financial Management

In theory, the models and analytical procedures developed in Chapters 1 through 19 for traditional financial management remain valid even when the operating environment is expanded to include operations in more than one country. However, problems unique to multinational operations increase the complexity of the management task and make it necessary to alter the way alternative courses of action are evaluated and compared. The complexity arises because it becomes necessary to consider explicitly, as an integral part of the analyses, various issues that are unimportant in traditional financial decision making. The five major factors that distinguish the financial management of firms operating entirely in a single country from that of firms with operations spanning several countries are these:

**1.** Cash flows in various parts of the corporate system are denominated in different currencies. Hence, exchange rates and the impact of changing currency values must be included in multinational financial analysis.

**2.** Each country in which the firm operates has its own unique political and economic institutions, a fact that can cause significant problems when the corporation tries to coordinate and control the worldwide operations of its subsidiaries. For instance, differences in tax laws among countries can cause a given economic transaction to have strikingly dissimilar after-tax consequences depending on where it occurs. Similarly, differences in legal systems of host nations, such as the Common Law of Great Britain versus the French Civil Law, complicate matters ranging from negotiating the terms of a contract to the role of the judiciary in resolving conflicts.

**3.** Even within geographic regions that have long been considered relatively homogeneous, different countries have their own unique cultural heritages which shape their values and define the role of business in the society. Multinational corporations find that such matters as the appropriate goals of the firm and attitudes toward risk-taking can vary dramatically from one country to the next—for instance, capital structure norms, and even the concept of equity capital, are perceived differently in Japan than in the United States.[1]

**4.** Most traditional financial models assume the existence of a competitive marketplace, in which the terms of competition are determined through the actions of participants with only slight involvement by the government. Thus, the market provides both the primary barometer of success and the indicator of actions that need to be taken in order to remain competitive. However, in many countries the terms of competition, actions that must be taken or avoided, and the terms of trade for various transactions are largely defined

---

[1]In Japan, banks can take both debt and equity positions in a firm, whereas in the U.S. banks are precluded from owning stocks of nonfinancial corporations. Further, Japanese firms often operate with very high debt ratios. Thus, it is not unusual for a firm to have a debt ratio of 90 to 95 percent, with all of the debt and part of the equity supplied by large banks. This causes Japanese banks to have an influence over corporate affairs that extends well beyond that of a typical U.S. bank.

by direct negotiation between the host government and the multinational corporation. This is as much a political process as an economic one, and it must be treated as such. Thus, traditional financial models have to be recast to include political and other noneconomic factors.

**5.** The characteristic of a nation-state that distinguishes it from a multinational corporation is that the nation-state exercises sovereignty over people and property in its territory. Hence, a nation-state is free to place constraints on corporate resource transfers and even to expropriate the assets of the firm without compensation. This "political risk" tends to be largely a given risk rather than one that can be changed by negotiation. It varies from country to country, and it must be addressed explicitly in financial analyses.

These five major differences complicate the financial management process and clearly increase the business risk of the firms involved. However, the higher profitability mentioned earlier often makes it well worthwhile for firms to accept these risks and to learn how to minimize or at least live with them.

## Exchange Rates and the International Monetary System

In this section we examine exchange rates, showing how to convert among rates expressed in different currencies, and we discuss the world monetary system and its impact on exchange rates.

### Exchange Rates

**exchange rate**
The number of units of a given currency that can be purchased for one unit of another currency.

An **exchange rate** designates the number of units of a given currency that can be purchased with one unit of another currency. Hence, an exchange rate is the price of one currency stated in terms of another. Exchange rates for the leading trading partners of the United States appear each day in *The Wall Street Journal*; selected rates on April 30, 1985, are given in Table 20-1. The value shown in Column 1 of Table 20-1 is the number of U.S. dollars required to purchase one unit of foreign currency; this is called a *direct quotation*. Thus, the direct U.S. dollar quotation for the West German mark is $0.3227, as one German mark can be bought for $0.3227. The exchange rates given in Column 2 represent the number of units of foreign currency that can be purchased for one U.S. dollar; these are *indirect quotations*. The indirect quotation for the mark is DM3.0985. (The "DM" stands for "deutsche mark"; it is equivalent to the symbol "$".) Normal practice in the United States is to use indirect quotations (Column 2) for all currencies other than British pounds, for which direct quotations are given. Thus, we speak of the pound as "selling at $1.24" but of the mark as "being at 3.10."

It is a universal convention on the world's foreign currency exchanges to state all exchange rates except British pounds on a "dollar basis"—the foreign currency price of one U.S. dollar as reported in Column 2 of Table 20-1. Thus, in all currency trading centers, whether New York, Frankfurt, Lon-

**Table 20-1**
**Selected Exchange Rates, April 30, 1985**

|  | Direct Quotations: U.S. Dollars Required to Buy One Unit of Foreign Currency (1) | Indirect Quotations: Number of Units of Foreign Currency per U.S. Dollar[a] (2) |
|---|---|---|
| Austria (schilling) | 0.0462 | 21.65 |
| Britain (pound) | 1.2440 | 0.8039 |
| Canada (dollar) | 0.7320 | 1.3662 |
| Denmark (krone) | 0.0895 | 11.17 |
| France (franc) | 0.1063 | 9.410 |
| Greece (drachma) | 0.007369 | 135.70 |
| Hong Kong (dollar) | 0.1286 | 7.7785 |
| India (rupee) | 0.0806 | 12.41 |
| Italy (lira) | 0.0005048 | 1981.00 |
| Japan (yen) | 0.003976 | 251.50 |
| Netherlands (guilder) | 0.2861 | 3.4950 |
| Norway (krone) | 0.1124 | 8.9000 |
| Saudi Arabia (riyal) | 0.2770 | 3.0609 |
| South Africa (rand) | 0.5140 | 1.9455 |
| Spain (peseta) | 0.0057889 | 172.75 |
| Sweden (krona) | 0.1114 | 8.98 |
| Switzerland (franc) | 0.3854 | 2.5950 |
| Taiwan (dollar) | 0.02509 | 39.86 |
| Venezuela (bolivar) | 0.07943 | 12.59 |
| West Germany (mark) | 0.3227 | 3.0985 |

[a]Column 2 = 1.0/Column 1.

Source: *The Wall Street Journal*, May 1, 1985.

don, Tokyo, or anywhere else, the exchange rate for the German mark on April 30, 1985, would be displayed as DM3.0985.[2] This convention eliminates confusion when comparing quotations from one trading center with those from another.

Let us use the rates in Table 20-1 to show how one figures exchange rates. Suppose a U.S. tourist on holiday flies from New York to London, then to Paris, then on to Munich, and finally back to New York. When she arrives at London's Heathrow airport, she goes to the bank to check the foreign exchange listing. The rate she observes for U.S. dollars is $1.2440; this means that 1 pound will cost her $1.2440. Assume that she exchanges $2,000 for

---

[2]Actually, two rates would be given. The first rate is the *bid rate*, or the exchange rate at which the dealer is willing to buy U.S. dollars. This is the rate to use if you have U.S. dollars and wish to exchange them for German marks. The second rate is the *asked*, or *offer, rate*, or the exchange rate at which the dealer is willing to sell U.S. dollars. If a tourist is returning to the United States and wants to exchange unspent marks for U.S. dollars, the asked rate is the correct one to use. Convention dictates that the first rate given is always the bid rate. The difference between the bid rate and the asked rate is the *spread*, or dealer's profit. Since the spread tends to be fairly small for most major currencies, only a single rate will be used in the examples discussed in this chapter.

$2,000/$1.2440 = £1,607.72 and enjoys a week's vacation in London, spending £607.72 while there.

At the end of the week she travels to Dover to catch the Hovercraft to Calais on the coast of France and realizes that she needs to exchange her 1,000 remaining British pounds for French francs. However, what she sees on the board is the direct quotation between pounds and dollars ($1.2440) and the indirect quotation between francs and dollars (FF9.410). The exchange rate between pounds and francs is called a *cross rate*, and it is computed as follows:

$$\text{Cross rate} = \frac{\text{Dollars}}{\text{Pound}} \times \frac{\text{Francs}}{\text{Dollar}} = \frac{\text{Francs}}{\text{Pound}}$$

$$= \frac{1.2440 \text{ dollars}}{\text{per pound}} \times \frac{9.410 \text{ francs}}{\text{per dollar}} = \frac{11.7060 \text{ francs}}{\text{per pound}}.$$

Therefore, for every British pound she would receive 11.7060 French francs.[3] Thus, she would receive 11.7060 × 1,000 = 11,706 francs.

When she finishes her touring in France and arrives in Germany, she again needs to determine a cross exchange rate, this time between French francs and West German marks. The dollar-basis quotes she sees are FF9.410 per dollar and DM3.0985 per dollar. To find the cross rate, she must divide the two dollar-basis rates:

$$\text{Cross rate, francs to marks} = \frac{\text{DM3.0985/\$}}{\text{FF9.410/\$}} = \text{DM0.3293/FF}.$$

Thus, if she had FF5,000 remaining, she could exchange them for 0.3293 × 5,000 = DM1,646.5, or 1,646.5 marks.

Finally, when her vacation ends and she returns to New York, the quotation she will see is DM3.0985, which tells her she can buy 3.0985 marks for a dollar. However, she now holds marks (150 of them) and not dollars, and thus she wants to know how many U.S. dollars she will receive for her marks. First, she must find the reciprocal of the quoted rate:

$$\frac{1}{\text{DM3.0985}} = \$0.3227/\text{DM}.$$

Then she will end up with

$$0.3227 \times 150 = \$48.41.$$

In this example, we have made one very strong and probably incorrect assumption: that exchange rates remain constant over time. Actually, exchange rates vary every day—often dramatically. For instance, in 1984 the pound was selling for about $1.50, but in the spring of 1985 it was down to $1.10, a 27 percent decline. Thus, it took fewer dollars to purchase a given amount

---

[3]At the retail level, the larger stores and hotels would also display the franc-pound cross rate, so no computations would actually be required. This would also hold true for other commonly used cross rates, such as the franc-mark and franc-yen rates. Obviously, however, it would be almost impossible to display all conceivable cross rates, so travelers often use hand-held calculators to compute them as well as to convert foreign prices to their domestic currency prices.

of pounds in 1985 than in 1984, and this strengthening of the dollar (or cheapening of the pound) would be of sufficient magnitude to introduce serious errors into financial decisions if it were not anticipated. For example, if a U.S. firm had invested $1 million in Britain in 1984, its pound investment would have been $1,000,000/1.5 = £666,667. If its pound investment rose by a healthy 15 percent, the pound value of the investment would be 1.15(£666,667) = £766,667. However, those pounds would now be worth only $1.10(766,667) = $843,333, down from the original $1,000,000. Thus, although the U.S. firm's British investment was superficially profitable, the exchange rate differential turned its 15 percent profit into a substantial loss.

We see, then, that exchange rate fluctuations can have a substantial impact on the profitability of foreign investments. To understand what causes exchange rates to change over time, and thus to be able to predict exchange rates, it is necessary to look at the factors which affect currencies and the world monetary system.

## Recent History of the World Monetary System

**fixed exchange rate system**
The world monetary system in existence prior to 1971 under which the value of the U.S. dollar was tied to gold and the values of other currencies were pegged to the U.S. dollar.

From the end of World War II until August 1971, the world was on a **fixed exchange rate system** administered by the *International Monetary Fund (IMF)*. Under that system, the U.S. dollar was linked to gold at $35 per ounce and other currencies were then tied to the dollar. Exchange rates between other currencies and the dollar were controlled within narrow limits. For example, in 1964 the British pound was fixed at $2.80 for 1 pound, and it was allowed to fluctuate within only 1 percent of this rate:

|  | Value of the Pound (Exchange Rate in Dollars per Pound) |
| --- | --- |
| Upper limit ( +1% ) | 2.828 |
| Official rate | 2.800 |
| Lower limit ( −1% ) | 2.772 |

Fluctuations occurred because of changes in the supply of and demand for pounds. The demand for pounds tended to increase whenever Britain's exports exceeded its imports, because then people in other nations had to buy more pounds to pay for British goods than they received in payment for their shipments to Britain. This increased demand for pounds, in turn, tended to drive up their price relative to other currencies—for example, more dollars had to be paid for each pound. Under the fixed exchange rate system, this increase in value was, of course, subject to the 1 percent upper limit.[4]

---

[4]For example, the dollar value of the pound might move up from $2.800 to $2.828. Thus, a box of candy costing 1 pound in England would rise in price in the United States from $2.80 to $2.828. Conversely, U.S. goods would be cheaper in England: the British would now be able to buy goods worth $2.828 for 1 pound, whereas before the exchange rate change, 1 pound would buy merchandise worth only $2.80. These price changes would, of course, tend to *reduce* British exports and to *increase* imports, which in turn would lower the exchange rate because people in other nations would need fewer pounds to pay for British goods. However, the 1 percent limit severely constrained the market's ability to reach an equilibrium.

The demand for different currencies, and hence their exchange rates, also depended on capital movements. For example, suppose interest rates in Britain were higher than those in the United States. Americans would buy pounds with dollars and then use those pounds to purchase high-yielding British securities. These purchases of pounds would tend to drive up their price.[5]

Finally, current rates were (and still are) affected by international speculators (including the Arab and Swiss money managers, as well as the treasurers of major U.S. corporations) who buy a currency whenever they expect its value to rise relative to others.

Prior to 1972, the effects of supply/demand fluctuations were kept within the narrow 1 percent limit by regular market intervention by the British and U.S. governments. Whenever the value of the pound was falling and threatening to go below the 1 percent limit, the Bank of England would step in and buy pounds, offering gold or foreign currencies in exchange. These government purchases would hold up the pound rate. Conversely, whenever the pound rate was rising, the Bank of England would sell pounds. The central banks of other countries operated similarly, and the U.S. central bank (the Federal Reserve System) and the Treasury bought and sold gold to maintain its price at $35 per ounce.

**devaluation**
The process of officially reducing the value of a country's currency relative to other currencies.

If the Bank of England (or some other central bank) was running short on gold and foreign currencies and hence was unable to hold to the 1 percent limit, then (1) it could borrow from the International Monetary Fund (IMF) or (2) it could **devalue** its currency, with the approval of the IMF, if it was experiencing persistent difficulty over a long period in preventing its exchange rate from falling below the lower limit. For just these reasons, the British pound was devalued from $2.80 to $2.50 in 1967. This lowered the price of British goods in the United States and elsewhere and raised the prices of foreign goods in Britain, thus reversing the British export deficit that had been putting pressure on the pound in the first place. Conversely, a nation with an export surplus and a strong currency could, under the old system, **revalue** its currency upward, as West Germany did twice in the 1960s.

**revaluation**
The process of officially increasing the value of a country's currency relative to other currencies.

If the U.S. was exporting more than it was importing, there would be net purchases of dollars, which would tend to raise the price of the dollar. Conversely, if the U.S. was importing more than it was exporting, the value of the dollar would decline. In fact, in the late 1960s the U.S. was importing more than it was exporting, the dollar was declining, and foreigners were building up holdings of dollars. They then began turning those dollars in to the U.S.

---

[5]Such capital inflows also tended to drive down British interest rates—more foreign capital in Britain meant more money to lend and hence lower interest rates. If rates were high in the first place because of efforts by the British monetary authorities to curb inflation, then international currency flows would tend to thwart that effort. A good example of the effects of capital flows occurred during 1985. In an effort to control inflation, the Federal Reserve was attempting to keep U.S. interest rates at high levels. This in turn caused an outflow of capital from European nations to the United States. The Europeans were suffering from a severe recession and wanted to get their interest rates down in order to stimulate investment, but the U.S. policy made the European governments' job difficult.

Treasury and asking for gold at $35 per ounce. Gold was thus flowing out of the United States, and by 1970 it was becoming clear that a fundamental imbalance existed.

## Today's Floating Exchange Rate System

Devaluations and revaluations occurred only rarely before 1971. They were usually accompanied by severe international financial repercussions, partly because nations tended to postpone these needed measures until economic pressures had built up to explosive proportions. For this and other reasons, the old international monetary system came to a dramatic close in the early 1970s, when the U.S. dollar, the foundation upon which all other currencies were anchored, was cut loose from gold and, in effect, allowed to "float."

**floating exchange rates**
Exchange rates not fixed by government policy but allowed to float up or down in accordance with supply and demand.

Under a system of **floating exchange rates**, currency prices are allowed to seek their own levels without much government intervention. The present world monetary system is known as a **managed floating system**: Major world currency rates move (float) with market forces unrestricted by any internationally agreed-upon limits, such as the old 1 percent limit on pound fluctuations. However, the central bank of each country does intervene to some extent in the foreign exchange market, buying and selling its currency to smooth out random fluctuations in its exchange rate. Each central bank also tries to keep its average exchange rate at a level deemed desirable by its government's exchange policy. This is important, because exchange rates can have a profound effect on the levels of imports and exports, which in turn can influence the level of domestic employment. For example, if a country were having a problem with high unemployment, its central bank might encourage a decline in the value of its currency, which would cause its goods to be cheaper in world markets and thus stimulate exports, production, and domestic employment. Conversely, the central bank of a country whose industry is operating at full capacity and that is experiencing inflation might try to raise the value of its currency in order to reduce exports and increase imports. However, under the current floating rate system, such intervention can affect the situation only temporarily—market forces will prevail in the long run.

**managed floating system**
A system in which major currency rates move with market forces unrestricted by any internationally agreed-upon limits, but each country's central bank does try to smooth out random fluctuations.

Figure 20-1 shows how German marks, Japanese yen, and British pounds moved in comparison to the dollar from 1960 to 1985. Until 1971, when the fixed rate system was terminated, rates were stable except for an occasional revaluation or devaluation. The pound's fluctuations against the dollar were too small to even show up on the graph prior to 1967, when a devaluation occurred. The mark was revaluated upward in 1961 and again in 1969. The yen was stable until 1971, when the dollar was allowed to float. After 1971, economic forces became the major factor in setting relative currency values, and Figure 20-1 illustrates the volatility that has occurred since then. (Note that Figure 20-1 plots *cumulative* changes in relative value.) The pound has drifted down, while the yen has risen. The mark rose sharply against the dollar until 1979, but it has fallen rapidly since then.

The volatility of exchange rates that is inherent under a floating system increases the uncertainty of the cash flows of a multinational corporation.

**Figure 20-1**
**Changes in the Values of Marks, Yen, and Pounds**
**Relative to the Value of the U.S. Dollar, 1960-1985**

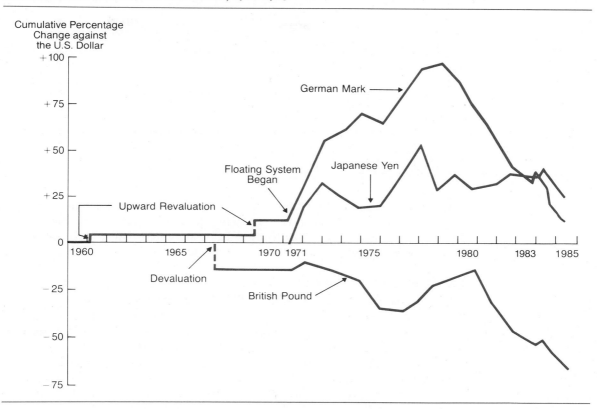

Because these cash flows are generated in many parts of the world, they are denominated in numerous currency units. But since exchange rates change, the dollar-equivalent value of the consolidated cash flows is uncertain. This is known as *exchange rate risk*, and it is a major factor differentiating the multinational corporation from a purely domestic one. However, there are numerous ways for a multinational corporation to manage and limit its exchange rate risk, several of which are discussed in later sections.

## Trading in the Foreign Exchange Market

Importers, exporters, and tourists, as well as governments, buy and sell currencies in the foreign exchange market. For example, when a U.S. trader imports automobiles from West Germany, payment will probably be made in German marks. The importer buys marks (through its bank) in the foreign exchange market, much as one buys common stocks on the New York Stock Exchange or pork bellies on the Chicago Mercantile Exchange. However,

**Table 20-2**
**Selected Spot and Forward Exchange Rates, April 30, 1985**
**(Number of Units of Foreign Currency per U.S. Dollar)**

|  | | Forward Rates | | | Spot Rate at a Premium or Discount |
|---|---|---|---|---|---|
|  | Spot Rate | 30 days | 90 days | 180 days |  |
| Britain (pound) | 0.8039 | 0.8067 | 0.8112 | 0.8163 | Discount |
| France (franc) | 9.410 | 9.425 | 9.450 | 9.4875 | Discount |
| Japan (yen) | 251.50 | 250.98 | 249.98 | 248.02 | Premium |
| Switzerland (franc) | 2.5950 | 2.5872 | 2.5715 | 2.5450 | Premium |
| West Germany (mark) | 3.0985 | 3.0913 | 3.0758 | 3.0505 | Premium |

Note: These are representative quotes as provided by a sample of New York banks. Forward rates for other currencies and for other lengths of time can often be negotiated.

Source: *The Wall Street Journal*, May 1, 1985.

while the stock and commodity exchanges have organized trading floors, the foreign exchange market consists of a network of brokers and banks based in New York, London, Tokyo, and other financial centers. Most buy and sell orders are conducted by cablegram and telephone.[6]

## Spot Rates and Forward Rates

**spot rate**
The effective exchange rate for a foreign currency for delivery on (approximately) the current day.

**forward exchange rate**
An agreed-upon price at which two currencies are to be exchanged at some future date.

The exchange rates shown in Table 20-1 are known as **spot rates**, which means the rates paid for delivery of the currencies "on the spot" or, in reality, two days after the day of the trade. It is also possible to buy (or sell) most of the world's major currencies for delivery at some agreed-upon future date, usually 30, 90, or 180 days after the transaction is negotiated. This rate is known as a **forward exchange rate**. For example, if a U.S. firm must make payment to a Swiss firm in 90 days, the U.S. firm's treasurer can buy Swiss francs today for delivery in 90 days, paying the 90-day forward rate. The contract is signed today, and the dollar cost of the Swiss francs is then known with certainty. Purchase of a forward contract is one technique for eliminating the volatility of future cash flows caused by fluctuations in exchange rates.

Forward rates for 30-, 90-, and 180-day delivery, along with the spot rates, for April 30, 1985, are given in Table 20-2. If one can obtain *more* of the foreign currency for a dollar in the forward than in the spot market, then the forward currency is less valuable than the spot currency, and the forward currency is said to be selling at a **discount**. Thus, 1 dollar could buy 0.8039 British pounds in the spot market but 0.8163 pounds in the 180-day forward market, so forward pounds sell at a discount vis-à-vis spot pounds. Conversely, if a dollar will buy *fewer* units of a currency in the forward than in the spot market, then the forward currency is worth more dollars than the spot currency and the forward currency is said to be selling at a **premium**. Thus, we see in Table 20-2 that on April 30, 1985, the pound and the French

**discount on forward rate**
Situation when the spot rate is less than the forward rate.

**premium on forward rate**
Situation when the spot rate is greater than the forward rate.

[6]For a more detailed explanation of exchange rate determination and operations of the foreign exchange market, see Steven Bell and Bryan Kettell, *Foreign Exchange Handbook* (Westport, Conn.: Quorum Books, 1983).

franc were selling at a discount but the forward yen, Swiss franc, and mark were all selling at premiums.

## Hedging in the Exchange Markets

**hedging exchange rate exposure**
The process whereby a firm protects itself against loss due to future exchange rate fluctuations.

Individuals and corporations buy or sell forward currencies as a means of **hedging exchange rate exposure**. For example, suppose that on April 30, 1985, a U.S. jewelry chain buys 5,000 watches from a Swiss manufacturer for 1 million Swiss francs. Payment is to be made in Swiss francs in 180 days, so the Swiss firm is extending trade credit for that period. The Swiss franc has been strong recently, and the U.S. company is apprehensive that the dollar will weaken because of large trade deficits. If the Swiss franc appreciates (dollar depreciates), each dollar will buy fewer francs; therefore, more dollars will be required to buy the 1 million francs, and the profits expected on the watches could be lost. Still, the U.S. firm does not want to forego 180 days of free trade credit by paying cash. It can take the trade credit and protect itself by purchasing 1 million Swiss francs for delivery in 180 days. The 180-day rate is SF2.5450, so the dollar cost is SF1,000,000/SF2.5450 = $392,927. When payment comes due in 180 days the U.S. company will have the needed 1 million Swiss francs at a cost of $392,927, regardless of the spot rate on that day. It will have *covered* its trade payable by a *forward market hedge*.

The forward market gives multinational corporation managers a device for passing exchange rate risk, for a price, on to a professional risk taker. Forward contracts can be written for any amount, for any length of time, and between any two currencies as long as the parties involved are in agreement. Some forward contracts are entered into by individuals or firms without going through an intermediary. Usually, however, forward contracts are negotiated between banks and their clients and are tailored to the specific needs of the latter—for example, Citibank might contract with the watch importer to supply the SF1,000,000 in 180 days for $392,927.

## Inflation, Interest Rates, and Exchange Rates

The currencies of countries with inflation rates higher than that of the United States tend to depreciate against the dollar. Some countries where this is the case are France, Italy, Mexico, and all the South American nations. On the other hand, the currencies of countries such as West Germany, Switzerland, and Japan, which have had less inflation than the United States, have on average tended to appreciate relative to the dollar—*in fact, a foreign currency will, over the long run, typically depreciate against the dollar at a percentage rate approximately equal to the amount by which that country's inflation rate exceeds our own.*

Relative inflation rates are also reflected in interest rates. The interest rate in any country is largely determined by its inflation rate; this point was made back in Chapter 3. Therefore, countries which are experiencing higher rates of inflation than the United States tend to have higher interest rates, while the reverse is true for countries with lower inflation rates.

It might be tempting for the treasurer of a multinational corporation to borrow heavily in countries with relatively low interest rates. However, this is not necessarily the best strategy. For example, suppose interest rates in West Germany were lower than those in the United States because of Germany's lower inflation rate. A U.S. multinational firm could save interest by borrowing in Germany. However, the mark could be expected to appreciate in the future, causing annual interest and principal payments on this debt to cost an increasing number of dollars over time. Thus, the lower interest rate could be more than offset by losses from currency appreciation. Similarly, one should not expect multinational corporations to avoid borrowing in a country like Brazil, where interest rates are very high, because future depreciation of the Brazilian cruzeiro might make such borrowing relatively inexpensive.

## International Money and Capital Markets

Direct foreign investment by U.S. multinational corporations is one way for Americans to invest in world markets. Another way is for U.S. citizens to purchase stocks, bonds, or various money market instruments issued by corporations and governments in foreign countries. Americans actually do invest substantial amounts in the stocks and bonds of large corporations headquartered in Europe and, to a lesser extent, in those operating out of the Far East and South Africa. They also buy securities issued by foreign governments. Such investments in foreign capital markets are known as *portfolio investments*, as distinguished from *direct investments* by U.S. corporations in physical assets.

### Eurocurrency Market

**Eurodollar**
A U.S. dollar on deposit in a foreign bank, generally a European bank.

A **Eurodollar** is a U.S. dollar deposited in a bank outside the United States. The bank in which the deposit is made may be a host country institution, such as Barclay's Bank in London, the foreign branch of a U.S. bank such as Citibank's Paris branch, or even a foreign branch of a third-country bank such as Barclay's Munich branch. Most Eurodollar deposits are for $500,000 or more, and they have maturities ranging from call money (or overnight funds) up to 5 years. Approximately 85 percent of all Eurodollars are held as withdrawable, interest-bearing deposits; the remaining 15 percent take the form of negotiable certificates of deposit (CDs).[7]

---

[7]It should be noted that today U.S. dollar deposits in any part of the world outside the United States, and not just in Europe, are called Eurodollars. It is also interesting to note that Eurodollars were first created by the Russians in Paris in the late 1940s. The Russians wanted to use dollars to conduct trade with parties who did not want to be paid in Russian currency. At the same time, they did not want to leave dollar balances in U.S. banks for fear that these balances would be taken over and used to pay off defaulted Czarist bonds. Thus, they decided to purchase dollars, leave them on deposit in a Paris bank, and use them to conduct trade. The idea of Eurodollars expanded rapidly thereafter. The dollar was a strong and stable currency, which made it ideal for international trade. Gold had been used earlier to settle international balances, but it is much simpler to make electronic transfers of bank accounts than to ship gold bullion.

The major difference between regular U.S. time deposits and Eurodollar deposits is their geographic locations. The deposits do not involve different currencies—in both cases, dollars are on deposit—so exchange rate considerations do not arise. However, Eurodollars are outside the direct control of the U.S. monetary authorities; therefore, such requirements as fractional reserves, interest rate ceilings, and FDIC insurance premiums do not apply. Absence of these costs means that the interest rate paid on Eurodollar deposits tends to be higher than domestic U.S. rates on equivalent instruments.[8] Hence, Eurodollar deposits serve as a favorite short-term investment for banks, governments, and multinational corporations with temporary excess dollar-denominated liquidity.

Note also that while the dollar is the leading international currency, German marks, Swiss francs, and so on, are also deposited outside their home countries; these *Eurocurrencies* are handled in exactly the same way as Eurodollars.

### International Bond Markets

The Eurocurrency market is essentially a short-term money market—most deposits and loans are for less than one year. However, since corporations, governments, and similar entities also need long-term debt capital, international bond markets have also been developed. Two types of international bonds exist.

**foreign bond**
A bond sold by a foreign borrower but denominated in the currency of the country in which it is sold.

*Foreign Bonds.* When a borrower raises long-term debt capital in the domestic capital market of a foreign country, it is said to be selling a **foreign bond**. For instance, Bell Canada may need U.S. dollars to finance the operations of its subsidiaries in the United States. If it decides to raise the needed capital in the domestic U.S. bond market, the bond will be underwritten by a syndicate of U.S. investment bankers, denominated in U.S. dollars, and sold to U.S. investors in accordance with SEC and applicable state regulations. Except for the foreign origin of the borrower—Canada—this bond will be indistinguishable from those issued by equivalent U.S. corporations. Since Bell Canada is a foreign corporation, however, this bond will be called a foreign bond

**Eurobond**
A bond that is sold in a country other than the one in whose currency it is denominated.

*Eurobonds.* The second type of international bond is the **Eurobond**, which is denominated in a currency other than that of the country in which it is sold. For example, if Exxon sold bonds in England that were denominated in marks, these would be Eurobonds. The institutional arrangements by which Eurobonds are marketed are different from those for most other bond issues, with the most important distinction being a far lower level of required

---

[8]Interest rates on Eurodollar deposits (and loans) are tied to a standard rate known by the acronym *LIBOR*, which stands for *London Inter-Bank Offer Rate*. LIBOR is the rate of interest offered on deposits of other large banks by the largest London banks of the highest credit standing. In April 1985, LIBOR rates were approximately five-eighths of a percentage point above domestic U.S. bank rates on time deposits of the same maturity: $7\frac{1}{2}$ percent for 3-month CDs versus $8\frac{1}{8}$ percent for LIBOR CDs.

disclosure than would usually be found for bonds issued in domestic markets, particularly in the United States. Governments tend not to apply as strict regulations on securities denominated in foreign currencies as they would on home-currency securities because of the nature of the bonds' probable purchasers. This often leads to lower total transaction costs on Eurobonds.

## Financial Management in the Multinational Firm

In Chapter 1, we stated that the primary objective of the firm is to maximize shareholder wealth. Although this remains a valid statement when international activities are added, several new facets complicate the task of identifying the actions that will maximize the stock price. We have already seen how multinational corporations have access to broader capital markets than do purely domestic ones. These additional sources of capital could lower the marginal cost of capital curve of a multinational company, giving it an advantage over domestic firms in that it might be able to invest profitably in projects that domestic companies would have to reject. However, when operating in many different currencies, multinational corporations open themselves to exchange rate and other risks that could offset capital market advantages. The hedging techniques described earlier can offset, or at least partially mitigate, the exchange rate risk associated with future foreign currency cash flows. Even so, exposure to currency fluctuations is still a far greater problem for multinational companies than one might gather from the previous discussion, and it deserves further exploration.

### Foreign Exchange Exposure

Because of the high volume of commercial transactions among countries and their ramifications for all sectors of the economy, no one other than a hermit is immune from the effects of changes in exchange rates. Just after the recent devaluation of the Mexican peso, a U.S. tourist who visited Mexico City would have quickly associated the change in currency value with the vastly increased purchasing power of the dollars in his or her purse. At the same time, the U.S. consumer who purchased a pineapple at the local supermarket may or may not have been aware that it was grown in Mexico, but he or she would probably have noticed that its price had fallen recently. While the linkage is not quite as obvious, the same economic event that led to bargains in Mexico City—the devaluation of the peso—caused the price of the pineapple to fall. Domestic companies also experience similar changes in the prices they must pay for goods and services as a result of exchange rate fluctuations.

**foreign exchange exposure**
Exposure to losses due to fluctuating exchange rates.

Even though individuals and domestic companies feel some effects of exchange rate changes, multinational corporations are most affected. The term used to describe how much a firm will be affected by currency fluctuations is **foreign exchange exposure**, which is divided into three types: economic exposure, transaction exposure, and translation exposure.

*Economic exposure* refers to the impact of exchange rate fluctuations on cash flows at the operating level. For example, if the dollar depreciated against the franc, this would increase the competitiveness of U.S. products in France, which in turn would increase the sales and cash flows of U.S. firms.

*Transaction exposure* refers to the situation in which a firm makes an agreement with terms that are (1) fixed at the time of signing, (2) stated in a foreign currency, but (3) will not be consummated or settled until some future date. Such a firm stands to gain or lose if the exchange rate changes. Our earlier example of the importer of Swiss watches involved this type of risk. Covering the transaction by contracting to buy at a fixed price the exact amount of the required foreign currency, to be delivered at the time needed to complete the transaction, serves to hedge the exposure.

*Translation exposure* refers to the danger that a subsidiary will have high profits in the currency of the country in which it operates but the value of that currency will depreciate vis-à-vis the parent company's home country currency, so that when the subsidiary's profits are "translated" into dollars, they will be relatively small. When balance sheet, as opposed to income statement, figures are translated, the impacts become even greater. For example, suppose Du Pont had a Canadian mining subsidiary with assets valued at $100 million stated in Canadian dollars that was financed only with equity supplied by Du Pont. Now assume that the Canadian dollar depreciated against the U.S. dollar, halving from $0.75 U.S. per Canadian dollar to $0.375 U.S. per Canadian dollar. The Du Pont subsidiary's assets, stated in Canadian dollars, would remain unchanged; however, since Canadian dollars would now be worth half as many U.S. dollars, its value in U.S. dollars would now be $50 million, and one could argue that Du Pont had lost $50 million as a result of this exchange rate change. (Du Pont would now have to spend only $50 million U.S. dollars to acquire the same physical assets, assuming the accounting statements correctly reflected true values.) Such losses are defined as **translation losses**, and exposure to them is called *translation exposure*. If foreign currencies fluctuate randomly, however, then gains in one period will offset losses in another, and over time the cumulative effect of translation losses will be small.

**translation gain or loss**
The gain or loss resulting from translating financial statements from a foreign subsidiary's currency to the parent company's currency.

## Reporting Requirements

Translation exposure arises from financial reporting, which requires the periodic preparation of consolidated financial statements. In a multinational corporation with subsidiary operations in numerous foreign countries, the job of consolidation is rendered especially difficult by the fact that host nations require the local subsidiaries to keep their financial records in terms of the local currency. Therefore, when such a firm prepares consolidated financial statements, it must translate all local currency accounts of its subsidiaries into the currency used for reporting purposes (usually the currency of the parent company's home country). If the exchange rate between the parent country's currency and the currency of any subsidiary changes during the accounting period, this can lead to accounting gains or losses. Two issues arise in the accounting area: (1) how to determine the appropriate exchange rate to use in translating each balance sheet account and (2) how to handle unrealized accounting gains and losses in the consolidated financial statements.

**FASB #52**
The publication of the Financial Accounting Standards Board that tells how translation gains or losses are to be reported.

Translations are done under rules prescribed in **FASB #52**, "Foreign Currency Translation," which was issued in December 1981. The whole question of translations, and how they ought to be reflected on a multinational corporation's books and in its reported profits, is a complex and controversial one. While it is certainly important, it goes beyond the scope of this book and is best left for accounting courses.

## Cash Flow Repatriation

**repatriation of earnings**
The process of sending cash flows from a foreign subsidiary to its parent company.

When a corporation makes an investment in a foreign country, resources in the form of an equity investment flow from the parent to the subsidiary. In order for the undertaking to be profitable, future value must flow back to the parent as compensation for undertaking the investment. Foreign governments, however, often place restrictions on such **repatriation of earnings**. For example, some governments place a ceiling on the amount of cash dividends that may be sent back, or *repatriated*, to the parent company. Restrictions may also be placed on the firm's ability to transfer depreciation cash flows back to the parent, or to other countries, until the subsidiary is sold or liquidated—and perhaps not even then. Such restrictions are normally intended to force multinational corporations to reinvest earnings in the host country, although they are also imposed to prevent large currency outflows that might destabilize the exchange rate.

**blocked currency**
Funds in a foreign country that cannot be repatriated.

Capital that cannot be sent out of the country is said to be **blocked** and thus unavailable to the parent for paying cash dividends to its shareholders or for other purposes. There are several means available for reducing the amount of blocked funds, including (1) transfer pricing, (2) royalties, and (3) management fees.

**transfer pricing**
The setting of prices by a corporation on sales among its subsidiaries; can in theory be used to increase repatriated earnings or shift profits to lower-tax areas.

*Transfer Pricing.* **Transfer pricing** refers to the prices set by the company on sales between two elements of the corporate system. Assume that the government of the island of Caribia places severe restrictions on a subsidiary's ability to repatriate capital and profits back to its parent. The Caribia subsidiary buys most of the subassemblies used in its production process from its parent in the United States and ships all of its finished products to the parent's marketing subsidiary in Puerto Rico for worldwide distribution. The cost of goods sold for the subassemblies in the United States is $100, the normal markup is 25 percent, and the arm's-length price of the finished goods is $250; however, the firm desires to set transfer prices between the United States and Caribia and between Caribia and Puerto Rico to minimize the profits realized in Caribia.

By setting the price of the subassemblies at $150 instead of $125, the firm can realize an extra profit of $25 in the United States. Assume that the Caribia subsidiary adds $50 to the value of the finished goods. Then an artificially low transfer price of $205, instead of the arm's-length price of $250, is used. This reduces the subsidiary's profit to only $205 − $150 − $50 = $5 instead of $75. This low transfer price allows the Puerto Rico marketing subsidiary to earn a higher profit. The firm's total profit is the same regardless of the transfer prices, but these manipulations have allowed the firm to repatriate $70 of profits that otherwise would have been blocked in Caribia.

Transfer pricing manipulation can also be used to shift profits to lower-tax areas. Thus, on an after-tax basis a company can increase its cash flow, and hence its value, by manipulating transfer prices. This is an important aspect of tax planning by the multinational firm.

However, host governments also understand how transfer prices can be manipulated to the benefit of the multinational corporation, and they are concerned with the lost tax revenue and the reduction of capital for local reinvestment that could be caused by companies' actions. Because transfer pricing strategies can be used as devices for removing value from a subsidiary in violation of local regulations, they are watched very carefully by local authorities. If abuses are detected, heavy fines or even nationalization may result.

**royalty**
A payment made by a subsidiary to another element of the corporation for the use of patents, processes, and the like.

*Royalties.* **Royalties** are payments made by a subsidiary to another element of the firm for use of patents, processes, or other technical assistance. Host country governments realize that royalties can represent legitimate payments for value received, but they must monitor royalty payments carefully to insure that they are not excessive. Often the amount of the royalty is set in direct negotiations between the company and the host government. If the host country perceives that contrary to its policy the corporation is attempting to use royalties to illegally channel profits out of the country, it is likely to impose fines and severe restrictions.

**management fees**
Payments made by a subsidiary to its parent for centralized management functions.

*Management Fees.* Payments for services rendered, such as the subsidiary's share of centralized management functions, are included in **management fees**. Thus, fees are in a sense similar to royalties, but host government officials, particularly in developing countries, tend to be less willing to approve them. When using this device to remove funds from a subsidiary, the company needs to be particularly careful to justify the charges; otherwise the payments may be regarded as disguised dividends and disallowed.

## Procedures for Analyzing Foreign Investments

Although the same basic principles of investment analysis apply to both foreign and domestic operations, there are several crucial differences: (1) estimating cash flows is generally more complex for overseas investments; (2) cash flows are not denominated in dollars, so exchange rate risk is an issue; and (3) the possibility of deliberate government acts to truncate or divert cash flows must be considered.

If the Dutch subsidiary of a U.S. multinational corporation is evaluating a capital investment, what cash flows are relevant to the decision? Is it the projected cash flows of the subsidiary, or is it the incremental cash flow that could be sent back to the U.S. parent? As long as there are no restrictions on the repatriation of dividends and depreciation cash flows, there is no major difference between the two cash flow streams. However, if there are local withholding taxes on dividends, restrictions on return of capital, or other blockages of international cash flows, both the timing and the magnitude of the cash flows back to the parent will be different from the operating cash flows of the project. The parent corporation cannot use cash flows blocked in a foreign country to pay current dividends to its shareholders, nor does it have the flexibility to reinvest cash flows elsewhere in the world, where expected returns may be higher. Hence, from the perspective of the parent organization, *the relevant cash flows for analysis of an international investment are the financial cash flows that the subsidiary can legally send back to the parent*. The present value of these cash flows is found by applying an appropriate discount rate; this present value is then compared to the parent's investment in the project to determine the project's NPV.

Exchange rate effects can be included in the project analysis by adding an **exchange risk** premium to the cost of capital used to discount the cash flows. Alternatively, if it is possible to hedge exchange rate risks, then the cost of the hedge is subtracted from the cash flows and no adjustment is required in the discount rate. The second method for handling exchange rate risks is superior to the first, but it is not generally possible to hedge cash flows expected in the distant future.

The final characteristic that differentiates international investment decisions from domestic capital budgeting is the existence of **sovereignty risk**. *Sovereignty* refers to the supreme and independent political authority of a nation-state to do as it pleases within its own borders. Since foreign subsidiaries are physically located within the jurisdiction of the host country, they are subject to rules and regulations established by local government authorities, no matter how arbitrary and unfair such requirements may be. Sovereignty risk includes both the possibility of expropriation or nationalization without adequate compensation and unanticipated restrictions of cash flows to the parent company, such as tighter controls on repatriation of dividends or higher taxes. The risk of expropriation of U.S. assets abroad is small in traditionally friendly and stable countries such as the United Kingdom or Switzerland. However, in Eastern Bloc countries and in most parts of the developing world of Latin America, Africa, and the Far East, the risk may be substantial. Past expropriations include those of ITT and Anaconda Copper in Chile, Gulf Oil in Bolivia, Occidental Petroleum in Libya, International Petroleum in Peru, and many companies in both Cuba and Iran.

The combined impact of exchange and sovereignty risks, as well as such "regular" risk factors as the stability and predictability of product markets, labor supplies, and government regulations, can be summarized as the *investment climate* of a foreign country. A number of organizations provide advice for a fee to multinational companies regarding investment climates. An illustrative list is shown in Table 20-3. The countries are rated in descend-

**exchange risk**
The risk that the basic cash flows of a foreign project will be worth less in the home currency of the parent company.

**sovereignty risk**
The risk of expropriation of a foreign subsidiary's assets by the host country and of unanticipated restrictions on cash flows to the parent company.

**Table 20-3**
**Risks of Foreign Investment in Various Countries**

| Country | Risk Rating | Country | Risk Rating |
|---|---|---|---|
| United States | AAA | South Africa | BBB |
| West Germany | AAA | Portugal | BBB |
| Canada | AA | Brazil | BBB |
| France | AA | Mexico | BBB |
| Australia | AA | Malaysia | BBB |
| Sweden | AA | Indonesia | BBB |
| Netherlands | AA | Philippines | BBB |
| Japan | AA | Argentina | BB |
| Saudi Arabia | AA | Chile | BB |
| Belgium | A | Kenya | BB |
| Spain | A | Pakistan | BB |
| Great Britain | A | South Korea | BB |
| New Zealand | A | Peru | BB |
| Singapore | A | Thailand | BB |
| Italy | A | Egypt | BB |
| | | India | B |

ing order from AAA to B, in much the same way that Moody's rates corporate bonds for risk of default. These ratings, or other criteria as established by an individual multinational corporation, may be used as a basis for estimating the cost of capital for capital budgeting purposes in each country in which the firm operates.

Generally, premiums are not added to the cost of capital to adjust for sovereignty risk. If corporate management has a serious concern that a given country might expropriate foreign assets, no significant investment will be made. Expropriation is viewed as a catastrophic event, and managers are generally extraordinarily risk averse in the presence of ruinous loss possibilities. However, as we will discuss next, companies can take steps to reduce the potential loss from expropriation by financing the subsidiary with local sources of capital or by structuring operations so that the subsidiary has value only as a part of the integrated corporate system. Also, to eliminate substantially or completely economic losses from expropriation, insurance can sometimes be obtained from such sources as the Overseas Private Investment Corporation (OPIC). If so, insurance premiums must be added to the project's cost to cover sovereignty risk.

## Sources of Funds for Foreign Investments

Foreign subsidiaries generally obtain a major part of their capital as common equity supplied by their parent companies. Several other sources of funds exist, including (1) sale of common stock to local residents, (2) borrowing from local residents, and (3) borrowing in world financial markets.

Selling common stock to residents of foreign countries has both advantages and disadvantages. One disadvantage is the possible loss of control of the subsidiary if the parent company owns fewer than 50 percent of the shares. Note too that some countries require majority ownership by local residents, allowing them to have some control over major decisions made by corporations operating within their boundaries and to retain a majority of the companies' profits. Local ownership requirements have limited IBM's operations in Mexico and have led IBM and a number of other large companies to virtually withdraw from manufacturing in India. However, local ownership is not necessarily bad from the point of view of the multinational corporation—it may even be a desirable feature in countries with less stable governments, since it provides an incentive for the local residents to exert pressure against the threat of expropriation or other interference. Similar protection is obtained by borrowing funds in the subsidiary's country: If the subsidiary is highly leveraged with debt from local sources, expropriation will result in only minimal losses to the parent.

Aside from protecting against expropriation, borrowing locally may be advantageous if local sources of funds offer attractive interest rates. In comparing foreign and domestic interest rates, however, one must be careful to take into account expected future changes in the exchange rate. As was pointed out earlier, a country with interest rates lower than those in the United States also has a currency that is likely to appreciate, causing the number of dollars required to meet interest and principal payments to increase over time and thus offset its lower interest rate.

The decision of whether to use local or parent country financing necessarily depends in part on projections of future trends in foreign exchange rates. Because such projections are not always accurate, using foreign debt may be riskier than using domestic debt. With the growth of multinational corporations and the uncertainties of world inflation and floating rates, corporate treasurers are making increasing use of expertise offered by commercial bankers, who make such projections and advise firms on the best way to meet their foreign currency requirements. It should come as no surprise to learn that the international divisions have been among the fastest-growing departments of the larger banks in recent years.

## Summary

As the world economy becomes more integrated, the role of *multinational firms* is ever increasing, and new companies are joining the ranks of the multinationals every day. Although the same basic principles of financial management apply to multinational corporations as to domestic ones, the financial manager of a multinational firm faces a more complex task. The primary problem from a financial standpoint is the fact that cash flows must cross national boundaries. These flows may be constrained in various ways and, equally important, their value in dollars may rise or fall depending on exchange rate fluctuations. Thus, the multinational manager must be constantly aware of the many complex interactions among national economies and their effects on multinational operations.

Efficient markets for foreign currencies and securities tie together the various national money markets, and the *forward* and *spot currency markets* can be used to smooth out the effects of exchange rate fluctuations over time. Because of the central role the U.S. dollar plays in international commerce, large markets have developed for U.S. dollar deposits (*Eurodollars*) and dollar-denominated bonds (*Eurobonds*) in Europe and Asia. These markets have also expanded to include many other currencies held in Euro-form. The *Euromarkets* are popular with multinational corporations and banks as well as with governments, because they offer safe yet relatively high-return havens for those with cash to invest and very competitive rates for those needing working capital loans.

The ability to redeploy worldwide resources quickly in response to environmental signals gives multinational corporations a distinct advantage over domestic firms. However, many complex issues must be taken into consideration in order to make good decisions, thus making multinational financial management both important and challenging. The risks inherent in international operations are high, but so are the potential rewards. In a world economy that grows more interdependent each year, the multinational manager can look forward to an ever expanding role in the corporate boardroom.

## Questions

20-1    Define each of the following terms:
    a. Multinational corporation
    b. Exchange rate
    c. Fixed exchange rate system; floating exchange rates; devaluation; revaluation; managed floating system
    d. Spot rate; forward exchange rate; discount or premium on forward rates
    e. Hedging exchange rate exposure
    f. Eurodollar; foreign bond; Eurobond
    g. Foreign exchange exposure; translation gain or loss; FASB #52
    h. Repatriation of earnings; transfer pricing; royalty; management fees
    i. Exchange risk; sovereignty risk; blocked currency

20-2    Under the old fixed exchange rate system, what was the currency against which all other currency values were defined? How did gold enter the picture?

20-3    Exchange rates fluctuate under both the old fixed exchange rate and floating exchange rate systems. What, then, is the difference between the two systems?

20-4    If the French franc *depreciates* against the U.S. dollar, can a dollar then buy more or fewer French francs?

20-5    If the United States imports more goods from abroad than it exports, foreigners will tend to accumulate a surplus of U.S. dollars. What will this do to the value of the dollar vis-à-vis foreign currencies? What will be the corresponding effect on foreign investments in the United States?

20-6    Why do U.S. corporations build manufacturing plants abroad when they could build them at home?

20-7    Most firms require higher rates of return on foreign projects than on identical investments at home. Why?

**20-8**  What is a Eurodollar? If a French citizen deposits $10,000 in Chase Manhattan Bank in New York, have Eurodollars been created? What if the deposit is made in Barclay's Bank in London? In Chase Manhattan's Paris branch?

## Problems

Exchange rate

**20-1**  If British pounds sold for $1.50 per pound, what should dollars sell for in pounds per dollar?

Currency appreciation

**20-2**  Suppose one French franc could be purchased in the foreign exchange market for 20 cents today. If the franc appreciated 10 percent tomorrow against the dollar, how many francs would a dollar buy? How many dollars would a franc buy?

Foreign investment analysis

**20-3**  After all foreign and U.S. taxes, a U.S. corporation expects to receive 2 pounds of dividends per share from a British subsidiary this year. The exchange rate at the end of the year is expected to be $1.40 per pound, and the pound is expected to depreciate 5 percent against the dollar each year for an indefinite period. The dividend (in pounds) is expected to grow at 10 percent a year indefinitely. The parent corporation owns 10 million shares of the subsidiary. What is the present value of its equity ownership in the subsidiary? Assume a cost of equity capital of 12 percent for the subsidiary.

Translation gains and losses

**20-4**  You are the financial vice-president of International Widgets, Inc., headquartered in Miami, Florida. All shareholders of International Widgets live in the United States. Earlier this month, you obtained a loan of 10 million Canadian dollars from a bank in Toronto to finance the construction of a new plant in Montreal. At the time you received the loan, the exchange rate was 78 U.S. cents to the Canadian dollar, but by the end of the month, it has unexpectedly dropped to 74 cents. Has your company made a gain or a loss as a result? How large is the gain or loss?

## Selected Additional References and Cases

Useful texts and other books that describe international financial management in some detail include the following:

Aggarwal, Raj Kumar, *The Management of Foreign Exchange: Optimal Policies of a Multinational Company* (New York: Arno, 1980).

Aliber, Robert C., *Exchange Risk and Corporate International Finance* (New York: Wiley, 1978).

Eiteman, David K., and Arthur I. Stonehill, *Multinational Business Finance* (Reading, Mass.: Addison-Wesley, 1982).

Levi, M., *International Finance: Financial Management and the International Economy* (New York: McGraw-Hill, 1983).

Rodriguez, Rita M., and E. Eugene Carter, *International Financial Management* (Englewood Cliffs, N.J.: Prentice-Hall, 1984).

For more on capital budgeting by multinational firms, see:

Oblak, David J., and Roy J. Helm, Jr., "Survey and Analysis of Capital Budgeting Methods Used by Multinationals," *Financial Management*, Winter 1980, 37-41.

Shapiro, Alan C., "Capital Budgeting for the Multinational Corporation," *Financial Management*, Spring 1978, 7-16.

Regarding decisions to use financing outside the parent company's home country, see:

Eaker, Mark R., "Denomination Decision for Multinational Transactions," *Financial Management*, Autumn 1980, 23-29.

Folks, William R., Jr., and Ramesh Advani, "Raising Funds with Foreign Currency," *Financial Executive*, February 1980, 44-49.

Severn, Alan K., and David R. Meinster, "The Use of Multicurrency Financing by the Financial Manager," *Financial Management*, Winter 1978, 45-53.

The Crum-Brigham casebook contains two cases which deal with multinational financial decisions:

Case 41, "Nysa Resources," which focuses on the overall riskiness of international capital investment.

Case 42, "Paisano Vineyards," which illustrates the complexities of international capital budgeting cash flow estimation.

The Harrington casebook contains the following applicable case:

"Philip Morris Incorporated: Swiss Franc Financing," which focuses on the choice between foreign and U.S. debt financing.

# 21 MERGERS, DIVESTITURES, AND HOLDING COMPANIES

In 1984 the Federal Trade Commission granted approval for the Chevron Corporation to buy Gulf Oil for a record $13.3 billion. Chevron offered $80 per share for Gulf, which had been selling for approximately $65 shortly before the tender offer was announced. Chevron's primary motive for the offer was Gulf's 1.8 billion barrels of worldwide oil reserves. Chevron had in recent years been significantly affected by the wide swings in crude oil prices—for example, earnings hit $2.4 billion in 1980 but dropped to $1.6 billion in 1983. With the merger, Chevron increased its supply of light, easier-to-refine crude oil.

The price Chevron paid was high, and it ended up borrowing about $10 billion to finance the purchase. This caused both Moody's and S&P to downgrade Chevron's debt issues. However, the new ratings were still AA, due largely to Chevron's plans to reduce its new debt by selling off part of Gulf's assets.

Who are the winners in this biggest-of-all-time merger? The Gulf shareholders who saw their stock almost double in price in six months are certainly winners, as are the investment bankers who helped orchestrate the deal. Salomon Brothers and Merrill Lynch split a $46.5 million fee for advising Gulf, and Morgan Stanley got $16.5 million for helping Chevron fashion its bid. But are there any losers? Right now it's hard to say. If Gulf's assets were truly undervalued at $65 per share, or if Chevron can assimilate and use these assets significantly more efficiently than Gulf could on its own, then the Chevron shareholders will also benefit from the merger. Only time will tell.

**merger**
The combination of two firms to form a single firm.

Most corporate growth occurs through *internal expansion*, which takes place when a firm's existing divisions grow through normal capital budgeting activities. However, the most dramatic examples of growth, and often the largest increases in firms' stock prices, are the result of **mergers**, which is

**divestiture**
A company's selling one of its divisions to another company.

one subject of this chapter.[1] On the other hand, the conditions of corporate life do change over time, and as a result firms occasionally find it desirable to *divest*, or sell off, major divisions to other firms that can better utilize them; therefore, **divestitures** are also discussed in the chapter. Finally, this chapter discusses the *holding company* form of organization, wherein one corporation owns the stock of one or more other companies.

## Rationale for Mergers

Many reasons have been proposed by both financial managers and theorists to account for the high level of U.S. merger activity. In this section we present some of the motives behind corporate mergers.

### Synergy

**synergy**
The condition wherein the whole is greater than the sum of its parts; in a synergistic merger, the postmerger value exceeds the sum of the separate companies' premerger values.

The primary motivation for most mergers is to increase the value of the combined enterprise. If Companies A and B merge to form Company C, and if C's value exceeds that of A and B taken separately, then **synergy** is said to exist. Such a merger should be beneficial to both A's and B's stockholders.[2] Synergistic effects can arise from four sources: (1) *operating economies of scale* in management, production, or distribution; (2) *financial economies*, which could include a higher price/earnings ratio, a lower cost of debt, and/or a greater debt capacity; (3) *differential management efficiency*, which implies that the management of one firm is inefficient and its effectiveness can be improved by merger; and (4) *increased market power* due to reduced competition. Operating and financial economies are socially desirable, as are mergers that increase managerial efficiency, but mergers that reduce competition are both undesirable and illegal.[3]

### Tax Considerations

Tax considerations have stimulated a number of mergers. For example, a firm which is highly profitable and in the highest corporate tax bracket could acquire a company with large accumulated tax losses; these losses could then

---

[1]As we use the term, *merger* means any combination that forms one firm from two or more existing firms. For legal purposes, there are distinctions among the various ways these combinations can occur, but our emphasis is on the fundamental business and financial aspects of mergers.

[2]If synergy exists, then the whole is greater than the sum of the parts. Synergy is also called the "2 plus 2 equals 5 effect." The distribution of the synergistic gain between A's and B's stockholders is determined by negotiation, a point discussed later in the chapter.

[3]In the 1880s and 1890s, many mergers occurred in the United States, and some of them were rather obviously directed toward gaining market power rather than increasing operating efficiency. As a result, Congress passed a series of acts designed to insure that mergers are not used as a method of reducing competition. The principal acts include the Sherman Act (1890), the Clayton Act (1914), and the Celler Act (1950). These acts make it illegal for firms to combine in any manner if the combination will tend to lessen competition. They are administered by the antitrust division of the Justice Department and by the Federal Trade Commission.

be used to shelter the income of the acquiring firm.[4] Similarly, a company with large losses can acquire profitable firms. Also, tax considerations may cause mergers to represent a desirable use for excess cash. For example, if a firm has a shortage of internal investment opportunities compared to its cash flow, it could (1) pay an extra dividend, (2) invest in marketable securities, (3) repurchase its own stock, or (4) purchase another firm. If the firm pays an extra dividend, the stockholders will have to pay ordinary taxes on the distribution. Marketable securities such as Treasury bonds provide a good temporary parking place for money, but the rate of return on such securities is less than that required by stockholders. A stock repurchase might result in a capital gain for the remaining stockholders, but it could be disadvantageous if the company paid too high a price for the stock and, if it had been designed solely to avoid dividend payment, a repurchase might be challenged by the IRS. However, using surplus cash to acquire another firm has no immediate tax consequences for the acquiring firm or its stockholders, and this fact has motivated a number of mergers.

## Purchase of Assets below Their Replacement Cost

Sometimes a firm will be touted as a possible acquisition candidate because the replacement value of its assets is considerably higher than their market value. For example, in the early 1980s oil companies could acquire reserves more cheaply by buying out other oil companies than by exploratory drilling. This factor was a motive in Chevron's acquisition of Gulf Oil. Similarly, steel companies find it less costly to buy an existing steel firm than to construct a new mill; for this reason LTV (the fourth largest steel company) acquired Republic Steel (the sixth largest) for $700 million in 1984, resulting in the second largest firm in the industry.

At the time the LTV-Republic merger was announced, Republic was selling for less than one-third of its book value. Even though LTV bought Republic's capacity at a lower cost than would have been required to build new plants, the purchase will not benefit its stockholders unless LTV can do something with Republic's assets beyond what was previously being done. LTV's management has argued that sufficient economies of scale exist to make the merger synergistic. The least efficient plants of both companies are being closed; plants that make similar products (say, sheet steel for autos or oil drilling pipe) are being consolidated; and distribution systems are being integrated. If these moves do result in sizable cost savings, the merger will be successful. Otherwise, the fact that LTV could buy Republic's assets at below their replacement value will be immaterial, and the consolidated company will have trouble.

---

[4]Mergers undertaken only to use accumulated tax losses would probably be challenged by the IRS. However, because many factors are present in any given merger, it is hard to prove that a merger was motivated only, or even primarily, by tax considerations.

### Diversification

Managers often claim that diversification helps to stabilize the firm's earnings stream and thus benefits its owners; therefore, diversification is often given as a reason for mergers. Stabilization of earnings is certainly beneficial to the firm's employees, suppliers, and customers, but what is its value to the firm's stockholders and debtholders? If an investor is worried about the variability of a firm's earnings, he or she could probably diversify more easily than could the firm. Why should Firms A and B merge to stabilize earnings when a stockholder in Firm A could sell half of his or her stock in A and use the proceeds to purchase stock in Firm B more easily than the firms could merge?

Of course, if you were the owner-manager of a closely held firm, it might be virtually impossible for you to sell part of your stock to diversify, because this would dilute your ownership and also generate a large capital gains tax liability. In this case, a diversification merger might well be the best way to effect personal diversification. However, for publicly held firms, diversification alone is a questionable motive for any merger.

### Control

As we discuss in the following section, in recent years many hostile mergers and takeovers by individual raiders have occurred. The managers of the target companies generally lose their jobs or at least their autonomy. Therefore, managers who own less than 51 percent of the stock in their firms look to devices that will lessen the chances of their firms' being taken over. Mergers can serve as such a device. For example, when InterNorth was under attack, it arranged to buy Houston Natural Gas Company, paying for Houston primarily with debt. That merger made InterNorth much larger and hence harder for any potential acquirer to "digest." Also, the much higher debt level resulting from the merger would make it hard for any acquiring company to use debt to buy InterNorth. Such **defensive mergers** are hard to defend on economic grounds. The managers involved invariably argue that synergy, not a desire to protect their own jobs, motivated the acquisition, but there can be no question that many mergers today are indeed designed more to benefit managers than stockholders.

**defensive merger**
A merger designed to make a company less vulnerable to a takeover.

## Types of Mergers

Economists classify mergers into four groups: (1) horizontal, (2) vertical, (3) congeneric, and (4) conglomerate. A **horizontal merger** occurs when one firm combines with another in its same line of business—for example, when one widget manufacturer acquires another, or one retail food chain merges with a second. An example of a **vertical merger** is a steel producer's acquisition of one of its own suppliers, such as an iron or coal mining firm, or an oil producer's acquisition of a company which uses its products, such as a petrochemical firm. *Congeneric* means "allied in nature or action"; hence, a

**horizontal merger**
The combination of firms that produce the same type of good or service.

**vertical merger**
A merger between a firm and one or more of its suppliers or customers.

**congeneric merger**
A merger of firms in the same general industry wherein no customer or supplier relationship exists.
**conglomerate merger**
A merger of companies in different industries.

**congeneric merger** involves related enterprises but not producers of the same product (horizontal) or firms in a producer-supplier relationship (vertical). Examples of congeneric mergers would be American Express's 1981 takeover of Shearson Hammill, a stock brokerage firm, or Prudential's acquisition of Bache & Company, another brokerage house. A **conglomerate merger** occurs when unrelated enterprises combine, as illustrated by Mobil Oil's acquisition of Montgomery Ward.

Operating economies (and also anticompetitive effects) are at least partially dependent on the type of merger involved. Vertical and horizontal mergers generally provide the greatest synergistic operating benefits, but they are also the ones most likely to be attacked by the U.S. Department of Justice. In any event, it is useful to think of these economic classifications when analyzing the feasibility of a prospective merger.

## Level of Merger Activity

Four major "merger waves" have occurred in the United States. The first was in the late 1800s, when consolidations occurred in the oil, steel, tobacco, and other basic industries. The second was in the 1920s, when the stock market boom helped financial promoters consolidate firms in a number of industries, including utilities, communications, and autos. The third was in the 1960s, when conglomerate mergers were the rage. The fourth began in the early 1980s, and it is still going strong.

The "merger mania" of the 1980s has been sparked by five factors: (1) the relatively depressed condition of the stock market (for example, the Dow Jones Industrial Index in early 1982 was below its 1968 level); (2) the unprecedented level of inflation that existed during the 1970s and early 1980s, which increased the replacement value of firms' assets even while a weak stock market reduced their market values; (3) the Reagan administration's stated view that "bigness is not necessarily badness," which resulted in a more tolerant attitude toward large mergers; (4) the general belief among the major natural resource companies that it is cheaper to "buy reserves on Wall Street" through mergers than to explore and find them in the field; and (5) attempts to ward off raiders by use of defensive mergers. Financial historians have not yet compiled the statistics and done the analysis necessary to compare the 1980s merger wave with the earlier ones, but it is virtually certain that the current wave will rank among the largest. As illustrated in Table 21-1, the top five mergers of all time in terms of dollar value have occurred in the 1980s—and, even as this is written, R. J. Reynolds is working out the details of a merger with Nabisco, General Motors with Hughes Aircraft, Texas Airways with TWA, and so on, indefinitely.

Brief descriptions of some different types of recent mergers will help explain how the deals are worked out:

**1.** Getty Oil, the fourteenth largest U.S. oil company, was acquired by Texaco, the fourth largest, in February 1984 at a cost of $10.1 billion. Prior to

**Table 21-1**
**The Five Biggest Mergers**
**(Billions of Dollars)**

| Companies | Year | Value | Price Paid for Stock ÷ Book Value | Type of Transaction |
|---|---|---|---|---|
| Chevron-Gulf | 1984 | $13.3 | 136% | Acquisition for cash |
| Texaco-Getty | 1984 | 10.1 | 191 | Acquisition for cash and notes |
| Du Pont-Conoco | 1981 | 7.2 | 156 | Acquisition for cash and common stock |
| U.S. Steel-Marathon | 1982 | 6.0 | 289 | Acquisition for cash and notes |
| ELF Aquitaine-Texas Gulf | 1981 | 4.3 | 212 | Acquisition for cash |

the merger activity, Getty's shares were selling at around $65, and the descendants of J. Paul Getty, the founder, were complaining of inefficient management. At that point, the controlling trustees of the Sarah C. Getty Trust, together with Pennzoil Company, announced plans to take the firm private by buying the shares which they did not already control at a price of $112.50 per share. Texaco then jumped in with an offer of $125 per share.

The merger doubled Texaco's domestic oil and gas reserves and, with Getty's retail outlets, gave Texaco a larger share of the gasoline market. Some analysts claim that Texaco, with its sprawling network of refineries and rapidly dwindling reserves, made the correct decision by acquiring Getty, with its large reserves and minimal refining operations. Other analysts contend that Texaco paid too much for Getty. Whether Texaco will get its money's worth remains to be seen. Acquiring Getty's reserves may have been cheaper for Texaco than finding new oil, but the value of these reserves depends on the price of oil, which by 1985 was down by more than 20 percent.

A side issue which arose at the end of the Getty merger concerned the Bass Brothers of Texas, an immensely wealthy family that had acquired over $1 billion of Texaco stock during all the action. Texaco's management was afraid the Basses would try to take over Texaco, so they bought out the Bass interests at a premium of about 20 percent over the market value. Some of Texaco's stockholders argued that the payment amounted to "greenmail," or a payoff made with stockholders' money just to insure that Texaco's managers could keep their jobs. This situation, along with several similar ones, has led to the introduction of bills in Congress to limit the actions that a management group can take in its efforts to avoid being taken over. However, Congress has not actually taken any action to date.

**2.** Conoco, which had book value assets of $11 billion and which was, based on sales, the fourteenth largest company in the United States, was recently the target of three other giants: Mobil (the second largest U.S. corporation), Du Pont (the fifteenth largest U.S. corporation), and Seagram (a large Canadian company). This 1981 merger alone almost surpassed in dollar amount the previous record for all mergers in a single year (book value assets of $12 billion in 1968). Conoco's stock sold for about $50 just before the bidding for it started; the bid price got up to over $100 per share before it was over, because Conoco's oil and coal reserves, plus its plant and equipment, were thought to be worth far more than their stock market values.

If Mobil had won, it would have been a horizontal merger. If Seagram had won, it would have been a conglomerate merger. Yet Du Pont won, and it was classified as a vertical merger because Du Pont uses petroleum in its production processes. The Justice Department would have fought a merger with Mobil, but it indicated that it would not do so in the case of Seagram or Du Pont. For this reason, even though Mobil made the highest bid ($115 per share), Du Pont ended up the winner with a bid of $98; stockholders chose the Du Pont bid over that of Mobil because they were afraid a Mobil merger would be blocked, causing Conoco's stock to fall below the level of the Du Pont bid price.

This was a *hostile merger*—Conoco's management would rather have had the company remain an independent entity. Obviously, though, this was not to be, and Conoco's top managers found themselves working for someone else (or out of a job). This is a good illustration of a point made in Chapter 1, namely, that managers have a very strong motivation to operate in a manner that will maximize the value of their firms' stock—otherwise, they could find themselves in the same boat as Conoco's managers.

**3.** Marathon Oil, a company only slightly smaller than Conoco, was the object of an attempted acquisition by Mobil after that company lost its bid for Conoco. Marathon's management resisted strongly, and again other bidders entered the picture. In March of 1982, U.S. Steel picked up Marathon for about $6 billion, making this the fourth largest merger of all time. (In this and the Conoco merger, the prices we quote refer to the price paid for the equity of the acquired firms. The acquired firms also had debt, which remained outstanding after the mergers, so the assets involved were larger than the amounts quoted.) U.S. Steel's bid for Marathon was unusual in that the firm offered to purchase only 51 percent of the stock and to exchange bonds for the remainder, with cash going to those stockholders who agreed to the merger the earliest. This is called a **two-tier offer**, and it prompted many stockholders to tender their stock to U.S. Steel out of fear of having to accept bonds if they waited to see if the bid might go higher.

**two-tier offer**
A merger offer which provides different (better) terms to those who tender their stock earliest.

**4.** Bendix, after one of the most dramatic merger fights of all time, was acquired by Allied Corporation. A four-way takeover battle began when Bendix made an unfriendly takeover offer for Martin Marietta. However, Martin Marietta responded with a "shark-eats-shark" bid to buy Bendix; in addition, it enlisted the aid of United Technologies, which then made a separate bid for Bendix. While this three-way struggle was going on, it looked as though Bendix would own 70 percent of Martin Marietta, which in turn would own over 50 percent of Bendix. Who controlled whom would then depend on who could vote the other's shares first in the annual election of directors.

At this point, Allied Corporation entered the fray with an even higher bid for Bendix. The final agreement found Allied acquiring Bendix for over $1.8 billion and Bendix and Martin Marietta swapping the shares each held of the other on the basis of their market values. This left Allied with 8.8 million shares of Martin Marietta, which it got when it completed the purchase of Bendix. Martin Marietta was then afraid Allied would gobble it up too, so it worked out a deal to buy its stock back from Allied. Martin Marietta retained its independence, but at a heavy price: the company had taken on $892 million of new debt to buy its Bendix stock, and it then had to issue even more to buy back Allied's shares. Wall Street analysts predict that it will take Martin Marietta about 10 years to get its debt ratio back to the target level.

**5.** Schlitz, once the largest U.S. brewer, had been losing both money and market share. By the early 1980s it had become only the fourth largest brewer, with a market share of 8.5 percent, and it seemed to be on a collision course with bankruptcy. Schlitz's troubles arose from its poor marketing strategy, a problem that it was unable to conquer. G. Heileman, the sixth largest brewer, with a market share of 7.5 percent, had been better managed, and its sales had been growing rapidly. (Heileman's ROE was 27.3 percent; Schlitz's was negative.) Because of its successful marketing programs, Heileman needed more brewing capacity, while, because of its poor sales performance, Schlitz had 50 percent excess capacity. Heileman offered to buy Schlitz's common stock for $494 million. If the takeover attempt had been successful, Heileman would have acquired capacity at an effective cost of $19 per barrel versus a construction cost of about $50 per barrel. The merger would also have made Heileman the third largest brewer in the nation. Although the Justice Department under the Reagan administration had previously taken the position that "bigness is not necessarily badness," it opposed this merger because in its judgment the resulting concentration would substantially reduce competition in the brewing industry. Therefore, Heileman abandoned the merger effort. However, Schlitz was still in trouble, and it was later acquired by Stroh Brewery (another good marketer).

**6.** In the summer of 1984, General Motors announced that it planned to buy Electronics Data Systems (EDS), the world's largest data processing company, for $2.2 billion. GM had excess cash, and it wanted to diversify outside the auto industry in order to stabilize earnings. Also, its management felt that EDS could help GM set up better internal management control systems. Ross Perot, the founder and a 50 percent owner of EDS, was offered over $1 billion plus a seat on the GM board for his stock, as well as a chance to continue to run EDS.

**7.** In the spring of 1985, GM announced that it would acquire Hughes Aircraft, a privately held company that was started by the late Howard Hughes in the 1930s, for about $6 billion. Hughes is one of the largest defense contractors and is highly profitable, but what GM really wants is its high-tech expertise in electronic controls. GM must utilize such technology in its design and manufacturing of autos if it is to compete effectively with the Japanese. Investment analysts believe that there are tremendous potential synergistic benefits to GM from both the Hughes and the EDS mergers, but at this point one can only wait and see if this $8 billion of investments will really pay off.

As we write this, the merger wave of the 1980s is still alive and well, and no end is in sight.

## Procedures for Combining Firms

In the vast majority of merger situations, one firm (generally the larger of the two) simply decides to buy another company, negotiates a price, and then acquires the target company. Occasionally the acquired firm will initiate the action, but it is much more common for a firm to seek acquisitions than to seek to be acquired.[5] Following convention, we shall call a company that seeks to acquire another the *acquiring company* and the one which it seeks to acquire the *target company*.

Once an acquiring company has identified a possible target, it must establish a suitable price, or range of prices, that it is willing to pay. With this in mind, its managers must decide how to approach the target company's managers. If the acquiring firm has reason to believe that the target company's management will approve the merger, then it will simply propose a merger and try to work out some suitable terms. If an agreement can be reached, then the two management groups will issue statements to their stockholders recommending that they approve the merger. Assuming that the stockholders do approve, the acquiring firm will simply buy the target company's shares from its stockholders, paying for them either with its own shares (in which case the target company's stockholders become stockholders of the acquiring company), with cash, or with bonds. This is a **friendly merger**.

**friendly merger**
A merger whose terms are approved by the managements of both companies.

Under other circumstances, the target company's management may resist the merger. Perhaps the managers feel that the price offered for the stock is too low, or perhaps they simply want to keep their jobs. In either case, the target firm's management is said to be *hostile* rather than friendly, and the acquiring firm must make a direct appeal to the target firm's stockholders. In **hostile mergers**, the acquiring company generally makes a **tender offer**, in which it asks the stockholders of the firm it is seeking to control to submit, or "tender," their shares in exchange for a specified price. The price is generally stated as so many dollars per share of the stock to be acquired, although it can be stated in terms of shares of stock of the acquiring firm. Since the tender offer is a direct appeal to stockholders, it need not be approved by the target firm's management. Tender offers are not new, but their frequency of use has increased greatly in recent years.[6]

**hostile merger**
A merger in which the target firm's management resists acquisition.

**tender offer**
The offer of one firm to buy the stock of another by going directly to the stockholders, frequently over the opposition of the target company's management.

---

[5]However, if a firm is in financial difficulty, if its managers are elderly and do not feel that suitable replacements are on hand, or if it needs the support (often the capital) of a larger company, then it may seek to be acquired. Thus, when a number of Ohio and Maryland savings and loans were in trouble in 1985, they lobbied to get the state legislatures to pass laws that would make it easier for them to be acquired. Out-of-state banks did move in to help salvage the situation and minimize depositor losses.

[6]Tender offers can be friendly, with the target firm's management recommending that stockholders go ahead and tender their stock.

## Merger Analysis

In theory, merger analysis is quite simple. The acquiring firm simply performs a capital budgeting analysis to determine whether the present value of the cash flows expected to result from the merger exceeds the price that must be paid for the target company. The target company's stockholders, on the other hand, should accept the proposal if the price offered exceeds the present value of the expected future cash flows that would result if it continued to operate independently. Theory aside, however, some difficult issues are involved: (1) The acquiring company must estimate the cash flows that will result from the acquisition; (2) it must also determine what effect, if any, the merger will have on its own required rate of return on equity; (3) it must decide how to pay for the merger—with cash, its own stock, or some other type or package of securities; and (4) having estimated the benefits of the merger, the acquiring and target firms' managers and stockholders must bargain—or fight—over how to share these benefits. The Conoco and Marathon cases discussed above illustrate just how complex this analysis can be.

### Operating Mergers versus Financial Mergers

From the standpoint of financial analysis, there are two basic types of mergers, operating mergers and financial mergers.

**operating merger**
A merger in which operations of the firms involved are integrated with the expectation of achieving synergistic benefits.

**1.** An **operating merger** is one in which the operations of two companies are integrated with the expectation of obtaining synergistic effects. The GM mergers provide good examples of operating mergers.

**financial merger**
A merger in which the firms involved will not be operated as a single unit and from which no operating economies are expected.

**2.** A **financial merger** is one in which the merged companies will not be operated as a single unit and from which no operating economies are expected. Coca-Cola's acquisition of Columbia Pictures with $748 million of surplus cash is an example of a financial merger.

Of course, mergers may actually combine these two features. Thus, if Mobil had acquired Conoco or Marathon, the merger would have been primarily an operating one. However, with Du Pont and U.S. Steel emerging as the victors, the mergers were more financial than operating in nature.

### Estimating Future Operating Income

In a pure financial merger, the postmerger cash flows are simply the sum of the expected cash flows of the two companies if they were to continue to operate independently. However, if the two firms' operations are to be integrated, or if the acquiring firm plans to change the target firm's management in order to get better results, then accurate projected cash flow statements, which are absolutely essential to sound merger decisions, will be difficult to construct.

*The basic rationale for any operating merger is synergy.* Del Monte Corporation provides a good example of a series of well-thought-out, favorable operating mergers. Del Monte successfully merged and integrated numerous small canning companies into a very efficient, highly profitable organization. It used standardized production techniques to increase the efficiency of all of its plants, a national brand name and national advertising to develop customer brand loyalty, a consolidated distribution system, and a centralized purchasing office to obtain substantial discounts from volume purchases. Because of these economies, Del Monte became the most efficient and profitable U.S. canning company, and its merger activities helped make possible the size that produced these economies. Consumers also benefited, because Del Monte's efficiency enabled the company to sell high-quality products at relatively low prices.

An example of poor pro forma analysis that resulted in a disastrous merger was the consolidation of the Pennsylvania and New York Central railroads. The premerger analysis suggested large cost savings, but it was grossly misleading because it failed to observe that certain key elements in the two rail systems were incompatible and hence could not be meshed together. Thus, rather than gaining synergistic benefits, the combined system actually incurred additional overhead costs that helped lead to its bankruptcy. *In planning operating mergers, the development of accurate pro forma statements is the single most important aspect of the analysis.*[7]

## Merger Terms

The terms of a merger include two important elements: (1) Who will control the combined enterprise? (2) How much will the acquiring firm pay for the acquired company? These points are discussed next.

***Postmerger Control.*** The employment/control situation is often of vital interest. First, consider the situation in which a small, owner-managed firm sells out to a larger concern. The owner-manager may be anxious to retain a high-status position; he or she may also have developed a camaraderie with the employees and thus be concerned about keeping operating control of the organization after the merger. Thus, these points are likely to be stressed during the merger negotiations.[8] When a publicly owned firm not controlled by its managers is merged into another company, the acquired firm's manage-

---

[7]It should be noted that firms heavily engaged in mergers have "acquisition departments" whose functions include (1) seeking suitable merger candidates and (2) taking over and integrating acquired firms into the parent corporation. The first step involves the development of both pro forma statements and a plan for making the projections materialize. The second step involves (1) streamlining the operations of the acquired firm, if necessary, and (2) instituting a system of controls that will permit the parent to effectively manage the new division and to coordinate its operations with those of other units.

[8]The acquiring firm may also be concerned about this point, especially if the acquired firm's management is quite good. A condition of the merger may be that the management team agree to stay on for a period, such as five years, after the merger. Also, the price paid may be contingent on the acquired firm's performance subsequent to the merger. For example, when International Holdings acquired Walker Products, the price paid was 100,000 shares of International Holdings stock (which sold for $63 per share) at the time the deal was closed plus an additional 30,000 shares each year for the next three years provided Walker Products earned at least $1 million during each of these years. Since Walker's managers owned the stock and would receive the bonus, they had incentive to stay on and to help the firm meet its targets.

*(footnote continued)*

ment also is worried about its postmerger position. If the acquiring firm agrees to retain the old management, then management may be willing to support the merger and to recommend its acceptance to the stockholders. If the old management is to be removed, then it will probably resist the merger.[9]

***The Price Paid.*** The second key element in a merger is the price to be paid for the target company—the cash or securities to be given to the target firm's stockholders. The analysis is similar to a regular capital budgeting analysis: The incremental earnings are estimated; a discount rate is applied to find the present value of those earnings; and if the present value of the future incremental earnings exceeds the price to be paid for the target firm, then the merger is approved. Thus, only if the target firm is worth more to the acquiring firm than its market value as a separate entity will the merger be feasible. Obviously, the acquiring firm tries to buy at as low a price as possible, while the target firm tries to sell out at the highest possible price. The final price is determined by negotiations, with the party that negotiates better capturing most of the incremental value. *The larger the synergistic benefits, the more room for bargaining and the higher the probability that the merger will actually be consummated.*[10]

## Valuing the Target Firm

To determine the value of the target firm, two key items are needed: (1) a set of pro forma financial statements which develop the expected cash flows and (2) a discount rate, or cost of capital, to apply to the projected cash flows.

### Pro Forma Income Statements

Table 21-2 contains the projected income statements for Microchip Corporation, which is being considered for acquisition by Allied Technologies, a large conglomerate. The projected data are postmerger, so all synergistic ef-

---

Also, if the managers of the target company are highly competent but do not wish to remain on after the merger, the acquiring firm may build into the merger contract a noncompetitive agreement with the old management. Typically, the acquired firm's principal officers must agree not to affiliate with a new business which is competitive with the one they sold for a specified period, say, five years. Such agreements are especially important with service-oriented businesses.

[9]Managements of firms that are thought to be attractive merger candidates occasionally arrange "golden parachutes" for themselves. Golden parachutes are extremely lucrative retirement plans which take effect if a merger is consummated. Thus, when Bendix was acquired by Allied, Bill Agee, Bendix's chairman, "pulled the ripcord of his golden parachute" and walked away with $4 million. Congress is currently considering controls on golden parachutes as a part of its "greenmail" legislative proposals.

[10]It has been estimated that of all merger negotiations seriously begun, fewer than one-third actually result in merger. Also, note that in contested merger situations the company that offers the most will usually make the acquisition, and the company that will gain the greatest synergistic benefits should bid the most.

**Table 21-2**
**Microchip Corporation: Projected Postmerger Income Statements**
**as of December 31**
**(Millions of Dollars)**

|                                        | 1986  | 1987  | 1988  | 1989  | 1990  |
|----------------------------------------|-------|-------|-------|-------|-------|
| Net sales                              | $105  | $126  | $151  | $174  | $191  |
| Cost of goods sold                     | 80    | 94    | 111   | 127   | 137   |
| Selling and administrative expenses    | 10    | 12    | 13    | 15    | 16    |
| EBIT                                   | $ 15  | $ 20  | $ 27  | $ 32  | $ 38  |
| Interest[a]                            | 3     | 4     | 5     | 6     | 6     |
| EBT                                    | $ 12  | $ 16  | $ 22  | $ 26  | $ 32  |
| Taxes[b]                               | 6     | 7     | 10    | 12    | 15    |
| Net income                             | $ 6   | $ 9   | $ 12  | $ 14  | $ 17  |
| Retentions for growth[c]               | 2     | 2     | 4     | 6     | 8     |
| Cash available to Allied               | $ 4   | $ 7   | $ 8   | $ 8   | $ 9   |
| Terminal value[d]                      |       |       |       |       | 121   |
| Net cash flow[e]                       | $ 4   | $ 7   | $ 8   | $ 8   | $130  |

[a]Interest payment estimates are based on Microchip's existing debt plus additional debt to increase the debt ratio to 50 percent, plus additional debt after the merger to finance asset expansion but subject to the 50 percent target capital structure.

[b]Allied will file a consolidated tax return after the merger. Thus, the taxes shown here are the full corporate taxes attributable to Microchip's operations, and there will be no additional taxes on the cash flowing from Microchip to Allied.

[c]Some of the net income generated by Microchip after the merger will be retained to finance asset growth, while some will be transferred to Allied to pay dividends on its stock or for redeployment within the corporation. It is assumed that depreciation-generated funds are used to replace worn-out and obsolete plant and equipment.

[d]Microchip's available cash flows are expected to grow at a constant 10 percent after 1990. The value of all post-1990 cash flows to Allied, as of December 31, 1990, is estimated by use of the constant growth model to be $121 million: $V_{1990} = \$9(1.10)/(0.1815 - 0.10) = \$121$ million. In the next section, we discuss the estimation of the 18.15 percent cost of equity.

[e]These are the net cash flows which are available to Allied by virtue of the acquisition of Microchip. They may be used for dividend payments to Allied's stockholders or to finance asset expansion in Allied's other divisions and subsidiaries.

fects are included. Microchip currently uses 30 percent debt, but if it were acquired, Allied would increase Microchip's debt ratio to 50 percent. Both Allied and Microchip have 46 percent marginal tax rates.

The net cash flows shown in Table 21-2 are the flows that would be available to Allied's stockholders, and these are the basis of the valuation.[11] Of course, the postmerger cash flows attributable to the target firm are extremely difficult to estimate. In a complete merger valuation, just as in a complete capital budgeting analysis, the component cash flow probability distributions should be specified, and sensitivity, scenario, and simulation analyses should be conducted. Indeed, in a friendly merger, the acquiring firm would send a team consisting of literally dozens of accountants, engineers,

---

[11]We purposely kept the cash flows relatively simple to help focus in on the key issues of the valuation process. In an actual merger valuation, the cash flows would be much more complex, normally including such items as additional capital furnished by the acquiring firm, tax loss carryforwards, and tax effects of plant and equipment valuation adjustments.

and so forth, to the target firm's headquarters to go over its books, to estimate required maintenance expenditures, to set values on assets such as petroleum reserves, and the like.

### Estimating the Discount Rate

The bottom line net cash flows shown in Table 21-2 are equity flows, so they should be discounted at the cost of equity rather than at the overall cost of capital. Further, the cost of equity used must reflect the riskiness of the net cash flows in the table; thus, the appropriate discount rate is Microchip's cost of equity and not that of Allied or the consolidated postmerger firm. Microchip's market-determined premerger beta was 1.30; however, this reflects its premerger 30 percent debt ratio, while its postmerger debt ratio will increase to 50 percent. Allied's investment bankers estimate that Microchip's beta would rise to 1.63 if its debt ratio were increased to 50 percent.

We can use the Security Market Line to determine Microchip's approximate cost of equity. If the risk-free rate is 10 percent and the market risk premium is 5 percent, then Microchip's cost of equity, $k_s$, after the merger with Allied would be 18.15 percent:[12]

$$k_s = k_{RF} + b(RP_M)$$
$$= 10\% + 1.63(5\%) = 18.15\%.$$

### Valuing the Cash Flows

The value of Microchip to Allied in 1985 is the present value of the cash flows expected to accrue to Allied, discounted at 18.15 percent (in millions of dollars):

$$V_{1985} = \frac{\$4}{(1.1815)^1} + \frac{\$7}{(1.1815)^2} + \frac{\$8}{(1.1815)^3} + \frac{\$8}{(1.1815)^4} + \frac{\$130}{(1.1815)^5} = \$74.$$

Thus, if Allied could acquire Microchip for $74 million or less, the merger would appear to be acceptable from Allied's standpoint.

## The Role of Investment Bankers

The investment banking community is involved with mergers in a number of ways: (1) helping to arrange mergers, (2) aiding target companies in resisting mergers, and (3) helping to value target companies. These merger-related

---

[12]In actual merger situations, the companies often hire investment banking firms to help develop valuation estimates. For example, when General Electric acquired Utah International in the largest merger up to that time, it hired Morgan Stanley to determine Utah's value. We discussed the valuation process with the Morgan Stanley analyst in charge of the appraisal. Morgan Stanley considered using the CAPM but chose instead to base the discount rate on DCF methodology. However, other analysts, and Morgan Stanley people in other situations, have used CAPM analysis as we describe it here. Merger analysis, like the analysis of any other complex issue, requires judgment, and people's judgments differ as to which method is most appropriate for any given situation.

activities have been quite profitable. For example, the investment bankers who arranged RCA's recent acquisition of C.I.T. Financial earned fees of $5.8 million. Du Pont's investment banker in the Conoco contest, First Boston, earned fees of over $15 million, while Morgan Stanley, Conoco's investment banker, had an arrangement under which it would earn fees of about $15 million regardless of who won. No wonder investment banking houses are able to make top offers to finance graduates!

### Arranging Mergers

The major investment banking firms have merger and acquisition groups which operate within their corporate finance departments. (Corporate finance departments offer advice, as opposed to underwriting or brokerage services, to business firms.) Members of these groups strive to identify firms with excess cash that might want to buy other firms, companies that might be willing to be bought, and firms that might for a number of reasons be attractive to others. Also, if an oil company, for instance, decided to expand into coal mining, then it might enlist the aid of an investment banker to help it locate and then negotiate with a target coal company. Similarly, dissident stockholders of firms with poor track records may work with investment bankers to oust management by helping to arrange a merger. Drexel Burnham Lambert, the investment banking house that developed "junk bond financing," has offered packages of financing to corporate raiders, where the package includes both designing the securities to be used in the tender offer and getting people and firms to buy the target firm's stock now and then tender it once the final offer is made.

### Fighting Off Mergers

Target firms that do not want to be acquired generally enlist the help of an investment banking firm, along with a law firm that specializes in helping to block mergers. Defenses include such tactics as (1) changing the by-laws so that only one-third of the directors are elected each year and/or a 75 percent approval versus a simple majority is required to approve a merger, (2) trying to convince the target firm's stockholders that the price being offered is too low, (3) raising antitrust issues in the hope that the Justice Department will intervene, (4) repurchasing stock in the open market in an effort to push the price above that being offered by the potential acquirer, (5) getting a **white knight** that is more acceptable to the target firm's management to compete with the potential acquirer, and (6) taking a "poison pill" as described below.

Some examples of **poison pills**—which really do amount to virtually committing suicide to avoid a takeover—are such tactics as borrowing on terms that require immediate repayment of all loans if the firm is acquired, selling off at bargain prices the assets that originally made the firm a desirable target, granting such lucrative **golden parachutes** to their executives that the cash drain from these payments would render the merger infeasible, and defensive mergers which would leave the firm with new assets of questionable value and a huge amount of debt to service. The blatant use of poison pills is

**white knight**
A company that is more acceptable to a company subject to a hostile tender offer.

**poison pill**
An action which will seriously hurt a company if it is acquired by another.

**golden parachutes**
Large payments made to managers of a firm which is acquired.

constrained by directors' awareness that it would trigger personal suits by stockholders against directors who voted for it and, perhaps in the near future, by laws that would limit management's use of this tactic. Still, investment bankers are busy thinking up new poison pill formulas, and others are just as actively trying to come up with antidotes.[13]

### Establishing a Price

If a friendly merger is being worked out between two firms' managements, it is important to be able to document that the agreed-upon price is a fair one; otherwise the stockholders of either company may sue to block the merger. Therefore, in many large mergers, each side will engage an investment banking firm to evaluate the target company and to help establish the fair price. For example, General Electric employed Morgan Stanley to determine a fair price for Utah International, as did Royal Dutch to help establish the price it paid for Shell Oil in 1985. Even if the merger is not friendly, investment bankers may still be asked to help establish a price. If a surprise tender offer is to be made, the acquiring firm will want to know the lowest price at which it might be able to acquire the stock, while the target firm may seek help in "proving" that the price being offered is too low.[14]

## Joint Ventures

**joint venture**
An undertaking in which two or more independent companies combine their resources to achieve specified, limited objectives.

A merger is not the only way in which the resources of two firms can be combined. In contrast to mergers, in which all resources are combined under a single management, **joint ventures** involve the joining together of parts of companies to accomplish specific, limited objectives.[15] Joint ventures are controlled by the combined management of the two (or more) parent companies.

---

[13]In large part because of shareholder suits arising out of poison pills, greenmail, or other attempts to block mergers that would be profitable to stockholders, it is becoming both harder and more expensive for companies to buy insurance which protects directors from stockholder suits. This in turn is forcing directors to be more careful about approving management's proposals, and the whole situation is making it harder for companies to get good people to serve as directors. The final result, however, will probably be less rubber stamping by directors and more concern for stockholder as opposed to management interests.

[14]Such investigations must obviously be done in secret, for if someone knew that Company A was thinking of offering, say, $50 per share for Company T, which was currently selling at $35 per share, then huge profits could be made. The biggest scandal to hit Wall Street thus far in the 1980s was the disclosure that a member of Morgan Stanley's merger analysis group was himself buying the stock of target companies that Morgan Stanley was analyzing for others. His purchases, of course, raised the prices of the stocks and thus forced his clients to pay more than they otherwise would have had to pay. Incidentally, he went to jail for improper use of inside information.

[15]Cross-licensing, consortia, joint bidding, and franchising are still other ways for firms to combine resources. For more information on joint ventures, see Sanford V. Berg, Jerome Duncan, and Phillip Friedman, *Joint Venture Strategies and Corporate Innovation* (Cambridge, Mass.: Oelgeschlager, Gunn, and Hain, 1982).

In one widely publicized joint venture, General Motors and Toyota, the first and third largest automakers in the world, set up an operation to produce 200,000 cars annually at an idle GM plant in Fremont, California. Toyota contributed an estimated $150 million to the venture, while GM put up $20 million in cash in addition to the California plant. Although both firms appointed an equal number of directors, Toyota got to name the chief executive. GM is reported to have sought the venture in order to gain better insights into how the Japanese can produce higher-quality cars at a substantially lower cost than U.S. automakers, while Toyota wanted to increase its production in the United States because of import quota limitations.

## Divestitures

Although corporations do more buying than selling of productive facilities, a good bit of selling does occur. In this section we briefly discuss the major types of divestitures, and then we present some recent examples and rationales for divestitures.

### Types of Divestitures

There are four primary types of divestitures: (1) sale of an operating unit to another firm, (2) sale to the managers of the unit being divested, (3) setting up the business to be divested as a separate corporation and then giving (or "spinning off") its stock on a pro rata basis to the divesting firm's stockholders, and (4) outright liquidation of assets.

*Sale to another firm* generally involves the sale of an entire division or unit, usually for cash but sometimes for stock of the acquiring firm. In a *managerial buyout*, the managers of the division purchase the division themselves, usually for cash plus notes; then, as owners/managers, they reorganize it as a closely held firm. In a **spin-off**, the firm's existing stockholders are given new stock representing separate ownership rights in the company that was divested. The new company establishes its own board of directors and officers and operates as a separate company. The stockholders end up owning shares of two firms instead of one, but no cash has been transferred. Finally, in a *liquidation*, the assets of a division are sold off piecemeal rather than as a single entity. We present some recent examples of the different types of divestitures in the next section.

**spin-off**
A divestiture in which the divested asset or division is given to the parent company's stockholders.

### Divestiture Illustrations

**1.** Esmark, Inc., a holding company which owns such consumer products companies as Swift meats and Playtex, has been aggressively selling off non-consumer-oriented divisions. For example, it recently sold its petroleum properties for $1.1 billion to Mobil, Petro-Lewis, and Total North American. Investors generally thought of Esmark as a meat packing and consumer products company, and its stock price reflected this image rather than that of a company with huge holdings of valuable oil reserves. Thus, Esmark's stock was undervalued, according to its managers, and the company was in danger of a Conoco-type takeover bid. Selling the oil properties helped Esmark raise its market value from $19 in 1980 to $45 in 1982. The Esmark divestiture is an example of a firm's selling assets to another company.

**2.** ITT, in a move to streamline and rationalize its holdings, recently divested itself of 27 separate companies with a value of $1.2 billion. Some of these units were suffering losses and were holding down the parent company's earnings, while others simply no longer fitted into ITT's corporate strategy. Also, ITT had a debt ratio that many regarded as excessive, and it has used the proceeds from its asset sales to reduce debt.

**3.** International Paper (IP) recently sold its Canadian subsidiary to Canadian Pacific for $1.1 billion. IP plans to spend $4 billion during the next five years to modernize its facilities, and the sale of the Canadian unit will help finance these expenditures.

**4.** IU International, a multimillion-dollar conglomerate listed on the NYSE, recently spun off three major subsidiaries—Gotaas-Larson, an ocean shipping company involved in petroleum transportation; Canadian Utilities, an electric utility; and Echo Bay Mining, a gold mining company. IU also owned (and retained) some major trucking companies (Ryder and PIE), several manufacturing businesses, and some large agribusiness operations. IU's management originally acquired and combined several highly cyclical businesses such as ocean shipping and gold mining with stable ones such as utilities in order to gain overall corporate stability through diversification. The strategy worked reasonably well from an operating standpoint, but it failed in the financial markets. According to its management, IU's very diversity kept it from being assigned to any particular industrial classification, so security analysts tended not to follow the company and therefore did not understand it or recommend it to investors. (Analysts tend to concentrate on an industry, and they do not like to recommend—and investors do not like to invest in—a company they do not understand.) As a result, IU had a low P/E ratio and a low market price. After the spin-offs, IU's stock price rose from $10 to $25.

**5.** U.S. Steel recently sold certain coal operations to Standard Oil of Ohio for $600 million. Sohio wanted the properties to diversify its energy base, and U.S. Steel apparently wanted to start building its "war chest" for the Marathon Oil acquisition.

**6.** Occidental Petroleum (Oxy), facing over $800 million in annual debt service requirements due mostly to its acquisition of Cities Service, has been scrambling to sell assets to help reduce its debt burden. In the last few years, Oxy has sold Cities Service Gas Company for $530 million; a copper division for $75 million; a half interest in its Columbia oil fields to Shell for $1 billion; and all of Cities Service's refining and marketing operations to the Southland Corporation, operator and franchiser of over 7,000 7-Eleven stores.

**7.** In 1984 AT&T was broken up to settle a Justice Department antitrust suit against it. For almost 100 years AT&T had operated as a holding company which owned Western Electric (its manufacturing subsidiary), Bell Labs (its research arm), a huge long-distance network system which was operated as a division of the parent company, and 22 Bell operating companies, such as Pacific Telephone, New York Telephone, Southern Bell, and Southwestern Bell. AT&T was reorganized into eight separate companies—a slimmed-down AT&T which kept Western Electric, Bell Labs, and all interstate long-distance operations plus seven new regional telephone holding companies which were created from the 22 old operating telephone companies. The stock of the seven new telephone companies was then spun off to the old AT&T's stockholders. Thus, a person who held 100 shares of AT&T stock owned after the divestiture 100 shares of the "new" AT&T plus 10 shares of each of the seven new operating companies. The 170 shares were backed by the same assets that had previously backed 100 shares of AT&T common.

The AT&T divestiture occurred as a result of a suit by the Justice Department, which wanted to break up the Bell System into a regulated monopoly segment (the seven regional telephone companies) and a manufacturing/long-distance segment which would be subjected to competition. The breakup was designed to strengthen competition in those parts of the telecommunications industry which are not natural monopolies.

**8.** Woolworth recently liquidated every one of its 336 Woolco discount stores in the United States. This reduced the company, which had had sales of $7.2 billion before the liquidation, by 30 percent. Woolco had posted operating losses of $19 million in the year before the liquidation, and its losses in the six months preceding it had climbed to an alarming $21 million. Woolworth's CEO, Edward F. Gibbons, was quoted as saying: "How many losses can you take?" Woolco's demise necessitated an after-tax write-off of $325 million, but management believed that it was better to go ahead and "bite the bullet" than to let the losing stores bleed the company indefinitely.

**9.** RCA sold Gibson Greeting Cards to a group which included Gibson's managers and some financiers for $81 million. The purchasing group put up $1 million in cash and raised the remaining $80 million through bank loans. A year later Gibson went public, and the equity held by the financiers had a market value of $140 million, which is not a bad return on a $1 million investment. This is one example of a hot new divestiture technique called a **leveraged buyout**, in which managers (often with some help from financiers) buy a company by borrowing heavily against its assets.

**leveraged buyout**
Situation in which a firm's own managers buy a firm from outside stockholders, borrowing most of the required funds.

**10.** In 1984 Continental Illinois, one of the largest U.S. bank holding companies, was struggling to avoid bankruptcy as a result of its imprudent loans to oil companies and to developing nations. Continental sold off several profitable divisions, such as its leasing and credit card operations, in an effort to raise the funds it needed to cover its bad-loan losses and deposit withdrawals. Thus, Continental's asset sales were part of an effort to stay alive. Ultimately, Continental was bailed out by the Federal Deposit Insurance Corporation and the Federal Reserve, which (1) arranged a $7.5 billion rescue package and (2) provided a blanket guarantee for Continental's entire $40 billion of liabilities.

The above examples illustrate the varied reasons for divestitures. Sometimes the market does not appear to properly recognize the value of a firm's assets when they are held as part of a conglomerate; the Esmark oil properties case is an example. Similarly, if IU International's management is correct, there are cases in which a company has become so complex and diverse that analysts and investors just do not understand it and consequently ignore it. Other companies need cash either to finance expansion in its primary business lines or to reduce a large debt burden, and divestitures can be used to raise this cash; the International Paper and Occidental Petroleum examples illustrate this point. The ITT example illustrates the fact that running a business is a dynamic process—conditions change, corporate strategies must change in response, and, as a result, firms must alter their asset portfolios by acquisitions and/or divestitures. Some divestitures, such as Woolworth's liquidation of its Woolco stores, occur in order to unload losing assets that would otherwise drag the company down, while the AT&T example is one of the many instances in which a divestiture is the result of an antitrust settlement. Finally, Continental Illinois' actions represent a desperate effort to get the cash needed to stay alive.

## Holding Companies

**holding company**
A corporation that owns sufficient common stock of other firms to achieve working control of them.

**operating company**
A subsidiary of a holding company; a separate legal entity.

Strictly defined, any company that owns stock in another could be called a holding company. However, as the term is generally used, a **holding company** is a firm that holds large blocks of stock in other companies and exercises control over those firms. The holding company is often called the *parent company*, and the controlled companies are known as *subsidiaries* or **operating companies**. The parent can own 100 percent of the subsidiaries' stock, but often control is exercised with less than this amount.

Many of the advantages and disadvantages of holding companies are identical to those of large-scale operations already discussed in connection with mergers and consolidations. Whether a company is organized on a divisional basis or with the divisions kept as separate corporations does not affect the basic reasons for conducting a large-scale, multiproduct, multiplant operation. However, as we show next, the holding company form of large-scale operation has some distinct advantages and disadvantages over those of completely integrated, divisionalized operations.

### Advantages of Holding Companies

Holding companies have three potential advantages: (1) control with fractional ownership, (2) isolation of risks, and (3) legal and accounting separation where regulations make such separation desirable.

**1. Control with fractional ownership.** Through a holding company operation a firm may buy 5, 10, or 50 percent of the stock of another corporation. Such fractional ownership may be sufficient to give the acquiring company effective working control over the operations of the firm in which it has acquired stock ownership. Working control is often considered to require more than 25 percent of the common stock, but it can be as low as 10 percent if the stock is widely distributed. One financier recently stated that the attitude of management is more important than the number of shares owned: "If they think you can control the company, then you do."

**2. Isolation of risks.** Because the various operating companies in a holding company system are separate legal entities, the obligations of any one unit are separate from those of the others. Therefore, catastrophic losses incurred by one unit of the holding company system may not be transmitted as claims on the assets of the other units. However, while this is a customary generalization, it is not always valid. First, the parent company may feel obligated to make good on the subsidiary's debts, even though it may not be legally bound to do so, in order to keep its good name and thus retain customers. Examples of this would include American Express' payment of over $100 million in connection with a swindle that was the responsibility of one of its subsidiaries, and United California Bank's coverage of a multimillion-dollar fraud loss incurred by its Swiss affiliate. Second, a parent company may feel obligated to supply capital to an affiliate in order to protect its initial investment; General Public Utilities' continued support of its subsidiaries' Three Mile Island nuclear plant is an example. Third, when lending to one of the units of a holding company system, an astute loan officer may require a guarantee by the parent holding company. To some degree, therefore, the assets in the various elements of a holding company are joined. Finally, an accident such as the one at Union Carbide's Bhopal, India, plant may be deemed the responsibility of the parent company, voiding the limited liability rules that would otherwise apply. Still, holding companies can be used to prevent purely financial losses in one unit from bringing down other units in the system.

**3. Legal separation.** Certain regulated companies such as utilities and financial institutions find it easier to operate as holding companies than as divisional corporations. For example, an electric utility such as Southern Company, which operates in several states and is regulated by each one, finds it more practical to set up a holding company (Southern) which in turn owns a set of subsidiaries (Georgia Power, Alabama Power, Mississippi Power, and Gulf Power). Even utilities which operate only within a single state are finding it beneficial to operate within a holding company format in order to separate those assets under the control of regulators from those not subject to utility commission regulation. Thus, Florida Power & Light reorganized in 1985 and changed its corporate name to FPL Group, which owns a utility (Florida Power & Light) plus subsidiaries engaged in real estate development, orange groves, insurance, and the like.

Banks, insurance companies, and other financial service corporations have also found it convenient to be organized as holding companies. Thus, Citicorp is a holding company which owns Citibank of New York, a leasing company, a mortgage service company, and so on. Transamerica is a holding company which owns insurance companies, small loan companies, title companies, auto rental companies, and so on.

## Disadvantages of Holding Companies

Holding companies have two major disadvantages: (1) partial multiple taxation and (2) ease of enforced dissolution.

**1. Partial multiple taxation.** Provided the holding company owns at least 80 percent of a subsidiary's voting stock, the Tax Code permits the filing of consolidated returns, in which case dividends received by the parent are not taxed. However, if less than 80 percent of the stock is owned, then returns cannot be consolidated and 15 percent of the dividends received by the holding company represents taxable income. With a tax rate of 46 percent, this means that the effective tax rate on intercorporate dividends is 0.15 $\times$ 46% = 6.9%. This partial double taxation somewhat offsets the benefits of holding company control with limited ownership, but whether the penalty of 6.9 percent of dividends received is sufficient to offset other possible advantages is a matter that must be decided in individual situations.

**2. Ease of enforced dissolution.** It is relatively easy for the Justice Department to require dissolution by disposal of stock ownership of a holding company operation that it finds unacceptable. For instance, Du Pont was required to dispose of its 23 percent stock interest in General Motors Corporation, an interest that had been acquired back in the early 1920s. Because there was no fusion between the two corporations, there were no difficulties, from an operating standpoint, in requiring their separation. However, if complete amalgamation had taken place, it would have been much more difficult to break up the company after so many years, and the likelihood of forced divestiture would have been reduced.

## Holding Companies as a Leveraging Device

The holding company vehicle has been used to obtain huge degrees of financial leverage. In the 1920s, several tiers of holding companies were established in the electric utility and other industries. In those days, an operating company at the bottom of the pyramid might have had $100 million of assets, financed by $50 million of debt and $50 million of equity. A first-tier holding company might have owned the stock of the operating firm as its only asset and have been financed with $25 million of debt and $25 million of equity. A second-tier holding company, which owned the $25 million of stock of the first-tier company as its only asset, might have been financed with $12.5 million of debt and $12.5 million of equity. Such systems were extended to four or more levels, but with only two holding companies, we see that $100 million of operating assets could have been controlled at the top by $12.5 million of second-tier equity, and $100 million of operating assets would have had to provide enough cash income to support $87.5 million of debt. *Such a holding company system was highly leveraged, even though the individual components had only 50 percent debt/assets ratios.* Because of this *consolidated leverage*, even a small decline in profits at the operating company level could have brought the whole system down like a house of cards.[16]

## Summary

A *merger* involves the consolidation of two or more firms. Mergers can provide economic benefits through economies of scale or through the concentration of assets in the hands of more efficient managers. However, they also have the potential for reducing competition, and for this reason they are carefully regulated by governmental agencies.

In most mergers, one company (the acquiring firm) initiates action to take over another (the target firm). The acquiring company must analyze the situation and determine the value of the target company. Often there will be operating economies, or synergistic benefits, which will raise the earnings of the combined enterprise over the sum of the earnings of the two separate companies. In this circumstance, the merger is potentially beneficial to both sets of stockholders, but the two firms' managers and stockholders must agree on how the net benefits will be shared.

Although the acquisition of assets through merger is more common, firms also on occasion get rid of assets—this is called *divestiture*. Sometimes divestitures involve a firm's selling one of its division's assets to some other firm; at other times they involve setting up a separate corporation and then *spinning off* the stock of the new company to the stockholders of the old one. The reasons for divestitures vary from antitrust to cleaning up a company's image to raising capital needed to strengthen the corporation's core business.

In a merger, one firm disappears. However, an acquiring firm may wish to buy all or a majority of the common stock of another and to run the acquired firm as an operating subsidiary. When this occurs, the acquiring firm is said to be a *holding company*. Holding company operations have both advantages and disadvantages. The major advantages are (1) that control can often be obtained for a smaller cash outlay and (2) that regulated companies can separate regulated from unregulated assets. The disadvantages include tax penalties and the fact that incomplete ownership, if it exists, can lead to control problems.

## Questions

21-1    Define each of the following terms:
        a. Synergy
        b. Horizontal merger; vertical merger; congeneric merger; conglomerate merger

---

[16]Excessive leverage through holding companies caused problems for the electric utilities during the 1930s. Accordingly, Congress passed the Holding Company Act, which specifically forbids electric utility holding companies from issuing debt for the purpose of buying the stock of operating electric utilities. The same situation does not exist in the telephone industry. Therefore, telephone holding companies can and do sell bonds and use the proceeds to buy stock in operating companies, with the purpose being to obtain capital at the lowest overall cost.

    c. Friendly merger; hostile merger; defensive merger; tender offer; two-tier tender offer

    d. Operating merger; financial merger

    e. Joint venture

    f. Divestiture; spin-off

    g. Holding company; operating company

    h. White knight; poison pill; golden parachute

**21-2**    Four economic classifications of mergers are (1) horizontal, (2) vertical, (3) conglomerate, and (4) congeneric. Explain the significance of these terms in merger analysis with regard to (a) the likelihood of governmental intervention and (b) possibilities for operating synergy.

**21-3**    Firm A wants to acquire Firm B. Firm B's management agrees that the merger is a good idea. Might a tender offer be used?

**21-4**    Distinguish between operating mergers and pure financial mergers.

**21-5**    In the spring of 1984, Disney Productions' stock was selling for about $50 per share. Then Saul Steinberg, a New York financier, began acquiring it, and after he had 12 percent he announced a tender offer for another 37 percent of the stock—which would bring his holdings up to 49 percent—at a price of $67.50 per share. Disney's management then announced plans to buy Gibson Greeting Cards and Arvida properties, paying for them with stock. It also lined up bank credit and (according to Steinberg) was prepared to borrow up to $2 billion and use the funds to repurchase shares at a higher price than Steinberg was offering. All of these efforts were designed to keep Steinberg from taking control. In June Disney's management agreed to pay Steinberg $77.45 per share, which gave him a gain of about $60 million on a two-month investment of about $26.5 million.

    When Disney's buyback of Steinberg's shares was announced, the stock price fell almost instantly from $68 to $46. Many Disney stockholders were irate, and they sued to block the buyout. Also, the Disney affair added fuel to the fire in a Congressional committee that was holding hearings on proposed legislation that would (1) prohibit someone from acquiring more than 10 percent of a firm's stock without making a tender offer for all the remaining shares, (2) prohibit "poison pill" tactics such as those Disney's management had used to fight off Steinberg, (3) prohibit buybacks such as the deal eventually offered to Steinberg ("greenmail") unless there was an approving vote by stockholders, and (4) prohibit (or significantly curtail) the use of "golden parachutes" (the one thing Disney's management did not try).

    Set forth the arguments for and against the type of legislation discussed above. What provisions, if any, should it contain? Also, look up Disney's current stock price to see how its stockholders have actually fared.

**21-6**    Two large, publicly owned firms are contemplating a merger. No operating synergy is expected; however, since returns on the two firms are not perfectly positively correlated, the standard deviation of earnings would be reduced for the combined corporation. One group of consultants argues that this risk reduction is sufficient grounds for the merger. Another group thinks this type of risk reduction is irrelevant because stockholders could themselves hold the stock of both companies and thus gain the risk reduction benefits without all the hassles and expenses of the merger. Whose position is correct?

## Problems

Capital budgeting analysis    **21-1**    Lorraine's Dress Shop wishes to acquire Cathi's Casuals for $175,000. Lorraine expects the merger to provide incremental earnings of about $30,000 a year for 10 years. She has also calculated her marginal cost of capital for this investment to be 10 percent. Conduct a capital budgeting analysis for Lorraine to determine whether or not she should purchase Cathi's shop.

Merger analysis    **21-2**    Giant, Inc., a large conglomerate, is evaluating the possible acquisition of the Tiny Company, a small aluminum window manufacturer. Giant's
 analysts project the following postmerger data for Tiny (in thousands of dollars):

|                                      | 1986  | 1987  | 1988  | 1989  |
| ------------------------------------ | ----- | ----- | ----- | ----- |
| Net sales                            | $200  | $230  | $250  | $270  |
| Selling and administrative expense   | 20    | 25    | 30    | 32    |
| Interest                             | 10    | 12    | 13    | 14    |

Tax rate after merger: 40%
Cost of goods sold as a percent of sales: 65%
Beta after merger: 1.63
Risk-free rate: 10%
Market risk premium: 6%
Terminal growth rate of cash flow available to Giant: 10%

Note: Data do not add exactly because of rounding errors.

If the acquisition is made, it will occur on January 1, 1986. All cash flows shown in the income statements are assumed to occur at end-of-year. Tiny currently has a market value capital structure of 40 percent debt, but Giant would increase that to 50 percent if the acquisition were made. Tiny, if independent, would pay taxes at 30 percent, but its income would be taxed at 40 percent if it were consolidated. Tiny's current market-determined beta is 1.50, and its investment bankers think that its beta would rise to 1.63 if the debt ratio were increased to 50 percent. The cost of goods sold is expected to be 65 percent of sales, but it could vary somewhat.

Depreciation-generated funds would be used to replace worn-out equipment, so they would not be available to Giant's shareholders. The risk-free rate is 10 percent, and the market risk premium is 6 percent.

a. What is the appropriate discount rate for valuing the acquisition?
b. What is the terminal value? What is the value of the Tiny Company to Giant?

(Do only if you are using the computerized problem diskette.)

c. 1. If sales in each year were $100 higher than the base case amounts, and if the cost of goods sold/sales ratio were 60 percent, what would Tiny be worth to Giant?

2. With sales and the cost of goods sold ratio at the Part c-1 levels, what would Tiny's value be if its beta were 1.8, $k_{RF}$ rose to 12 percent, and $RP_M$ rose to 7 percent?

3. Leaving all values at the Part c-2 levels, what would the value of the acquisition be if the terminal growth rate rose to 20 percent or dropped to 3 percent?

Merger analysis   **21-3**   Jensen Electric Corporation is considering a merger with the Shady Lamp Company. Shady is a publicly traded company, and its current beta is 1.40. Shady has barely been profitable, so it has paid only 20 percent in taxes over the last several years. Additionally, it uses little debt, having a market value debt ratio of just 25 percent.

If the acquisition is made, Jensen plans to operate Shady as a separate, wholly owned subsidiary. Jensen would pay taxes on a consolidated basis, and thus the federal-plus-state tax rate would increase to 50 percent. Additionally, Jensen would increase the debt capitalization in the Shady subsidiary on a market value basis to 40 percent of assets, which would increase beta to 1.48. Jensen's acquisition department estimates that Shady, if acquired, would produce the following net cash flows to Jensen's shareholders (in millions of dollars):

| Year | Net Cash Flow |
|------|---------------|
| 1 | $1.20 |
| 2 | 1.40 |
| 3 | 1.65 |
| 4 | 1.80 |
| 5 and beyond | Constant growth at 5% |

These cash flows include all acquisition effects. Jensen's cost of equity is 16 percent, its beta is 1.0, and its cost of debt is 12 percent. The risk-free rate is 10 percent.

a. What discount rate should be used to discount the estimated cash flows? (Hint: Use Jensen's $k_s$ to determine the market risk premium.)

b. What is the dollar value of Shady to Jensen?

c. Shady has 1.2 million common shares outstanding. What is the maximum price per share that Jensen should offer for Shady? If the tender offer were accepted at this price, what would happen to Jensen's stock price?

## Selected Additional References and Cases

Chapter 22 of *Intermediate Financial Management* goes somewhat more deeply into merger analysis, including accounting issues and their effects on merger valuations. Also, considerable empirical work has been done to determine whether stockholders of acquiring or acquired companies benefit more from corporate mergers. One of the most recent works is:

Wansley, James W., William R. Lane, and Ho C. Yang, "Abnormal Returns to Acquired Firms by Type of Acquisition and Method of Payment," *Financial Management*, Autumn 1983, 16-22.

For a comprehensive review of the empirical literature on mergers, see:

Elgers, Pieter T., and John J. Clark, "Merger Types and Shareholder Returns: Additional Evidence," *Financial Management*, Summer 1980, 66-72.

Mueller, Dennis C., "The Effects of Conglomerate Mergers," *Journal of Banking and Finance*, December 1977, 315-347.

The following case in the Crum-Brigham casebook illustrates merger analysis:

Case 37, "Dustain Industries, Inc.," which examines the effects of different types of mergers on EPS, P/E ratios, and stock prices.

The following cases in the Harrington casebook focus on the material in this chapter:

"Philip Morris, Incorporated: Seven-Up Acquisition (A)," which describes the firm's acquisition goals and value analysis as it contemplated acquiring the Seven-Up Company.

"Kennecott Corporation," which illustrates how management's attempt to maintain its position can conflict with shareholder interests.

"Piedmont Transmission Co.," which illustrates divestiture analysis.

# A    MATHEMATICAL TABLES

**Table A-1**
**Present Value of $1 Due at the End of n Periods:**

$$PVIF_{k,n} = \frac{1}{(1 + k)^n}$$

| Period | 1% | 2% | 3% | 4% | 5% | 6% | 7% | 8% | 9% | 10% |
|---|---|---|---|---|---|---|---|---|---|---|
| 1 | .9901 | .9804 | .9709 | .9615 | .9524 | .9434 | .9346 | .9259 | .9174 | .9091 |
| 2 | .9803 | .9612 | .9426 | .9246 | .9070 | .8900 | .8734 | .8573 | .8417 | .8264 |
| 3 | .9706 | .9423 | .9151 | .8890 | .8638 | .8396 | .8163 | .7938 | .7722 | .7513 |
| 4 | .9610 | .9238 | .8885 | .8548 | .8227 | .7921 | .7629 | .7350 | .7084 | .6830 |
| 5 | .9515 | .9057 | .8626 | .8219 | .7835 | .7473 | .7130 | .6806 | .6499 | .6209 |
| 6 | .9420 | .8880 | .8375 | .7903 | .7462 | .7050 | .6663 | .6302 | .5963 | .5645 |
| 7 | .9327 | .8706 | .8131 | .7599 | .7107 | .6651 | .6227 | .5835 | .5470 | .5132 |
| 8 | .9235 | .8535 | .7894 | .7307 | .6768 | .6274 | .5820 | .5403 | .5019 | .4665 |
| 9 | .9143 | .8368 | .7664 | .7026 | .6446 | .5919 | .5439 | .5002 | .4604 | .4241 |
| 10 | .9053 | .8203 | .7441 | .6756 | .6139 | .5584 | .5083 | .4632 | .4224 | .3855 |
| 11 | .8963 | .8043 | .7224 | .6496 | .5847 | .5268 | .4751 | .4289 | .3875 | .3505 |
| 12 | .8874 | .7885 | .7014 | .6246 | .5568 | .4970 | .4440 | .3971 | .3555 | .3186 |
| 13 | .8787 | .7730 | .6810 | .6006 | .5303 | .4688 | .4150 | .3677 | .3262 | .2897 |
| 14 | .8700 | .7579 | .6611 | .5775 | .5051 | .4423 | .3878 | .3405 | .2992 | .2633 |
| 15 | .8613 | .7430 | .6419 | .5553 | .4810 | .4173 | .3624 | .3152 | .2745 | .2394 |
| 16 | .8528 | .7284 | .6232 | .5339 | .4581 | .3936 | .3387 | .2919 | .2519 | .2176 |
| 17 | .8444 | .7142 | .6050 | .5134 | .4363 | .3714 | .3166 | .2703 | .2311 | .1978 |
| 18 | .8360 | .7002 | .5874 | .4936 | .4155 | .3503 | .2959 | .2502 | .2120 | .1799 |
| 19 | .8277 | .6864 | .5703 | .4746 | .3957 | .3305 | .2765 | .2317 | .1945 | .1635 |
| 20 | .8195 | .6730 | .5537 | .4564 | .3769 | .3118 | .2584 | .2145 | .1784 | .1486 |
| 21 | .8114 | .6598 | .5375 | .4388 | .3589 | .2942 | .2415 | .1987 | .1637 | .1351 |
| 22 | .8034 | .6468 | .5219 | .4220 | .3418 | .2775 | .2257 | .1839 | .1502 | .1228 |
| 23 | .7954 | .6342 | .5067 | .4057 | .3256 | .2618 | .2109 | .1703 | .1378 | .1117 |
| 24 | .7876 | .6217 | .4919 | .3901 | .3101 | .2470 | .1971 | .1577 | .1264 | .1015 |
| 25 | .7798 | .6095 | .4776 | .3751 | .2953 | .2330 | .1842 | .1460 | .1160 | .0923 |
| 26 | .7720 | .5976 | .4637 | .3604 | .2812 | .2198 | .1722 | .1352 | .1064 | .0839 |
| 27 | .7644 | .5859 | .4502 | .3468 | .2678 | .2074 | .1609 | .1252 | .0976 | .0763 |
| 28 | .7568 | .5744 | .4371 | .3335 | .2551 | .1956 | .1504 | .1159 | .0895 | .0693 |
| 29 | .7493 | .5631 | .4243 | .3207 | .2429 | .1846 | .1406 | .1073 | .0822 | .0630 |
| 30 | .7419 | .5521 | .4120 | .3083 | .2314 | .1741 | .1314 | .0994 | .0754 | .0573 |
| 35 | .7059 | .5000 | .3554 | .2534 | .1813 | .1301 | .0937 | .0676 | .0490 | .0356 |
| 40 | .6717 | .4529 | .3066 | .2083 | .1420 | .0972 | .0668 | .0460 | .0318 | .0221 |
| 45 | .6391 | .4102 | .2644 | .1712 | .1113 | .0727 | .0476 | .0313 | .0207 | .0137 |
| 50 | .6080 | .3715 | .2281 | .1407 | .0872 | .0543 | .0339 | .0213 | .0134 | .0085 |
| 55 | .5785 | .3365 | .1968 | .1157 | .0683 | .0406 | .0242 | .0145 | .0087 | .0053 |

## Table A-1
## (continued)

| Period | 12% | 14% | 15% | 16% | 18% | 20% | 24% | 28% | 32% | 36% |
|--------|------|------|------|------|------|------|------|------|------|------|
| 1 | .8929 | .8772 | .8696 | .8621 | .8475 | .8333 | .8065 | .7813 | .7576 | .7353 |
| 2 | .7972 | .7695 | .7561 | .7432 | .7182 | .6944 | .6504 | .6104 | .5739 | .5407 |
| 3 | .7118 | .6750 | .6575 | .6407 | .6086 | .5787 | .5245 | .4768 | .4348 | .3975 |
| 4 | .6355 | .5921 | .5718 | .5523 | .5158 | .4823 | .4230 | .3725 | .3294 | .2923 |
| 5 | .5674 | .5194 | .4972 | .4761 | .4371 | .4019 | .3411 | .2910 | .2495 | .2149 |
| 6 | .5066 | .4556 | .4323 | .4104 | .3704 | .3349 | .2751 | .2274 | .1890 | .1580 |
| 7 | .4523 | .3996 | .3759 | .3538 | .3139 | .2791 | .2218 | .1776 | .1432 | .1162 |
| 8 | .4039 | .3506 | .3269 | .3050 | .2660 | .2326 | .1789 | .1388 | .1085 | .0854 |
| 9 | .3606 | .3075 | .2843 | .2630 | .2255 | .1938 | .1443 | .1084 | .0822 | .0628 |
| 10 | .3220 | .2697 | .2472 | .2267 | .1911 | .1615 | .1164 | .0847 | .0623 | .0462 |
| 11 | .2875 | .2366 | .2149 | .1954 | .1619 | .1346 | .0938 | .0662 | .0472 | .0340 |
| 12 | .2567 | .2076 | .1869 | .1685 | .1372 | .1122 | .0757 | .0517 | .0357 | .0250 |
| 13 | .2292 | .1821 | .1625 | .1452 | .1163 | .0935 | .0610 | .0404 | .0271 | .0184 |
| 14 | .2046 | .1597 | .1413 | .1252 | .0985 | .0779 | .0492 | .0316 | .0205 | .0135 |
| 15 | .1827 | .1401 | .1229 | .1079 | .0835 | .0649 | .0397 | .0247 | .0155 | .0099 |
| 16 | .1631 | .1229 | .1069 | .0980 | .0708 | .0541 | .0320 | .0193 | .0118 | .0073 |
| 17 | .1456 | .1078 | .0929 | .0802 | .0600 | .0451 | .0258 | .0150 | .0089 | .0054 |
| 18 | .1300 | .0946 | .0808 | .0691 | .0508 | .0376 | .0208 | .0118 | .0068 | .0039 |
| 19 | .1161 | .0829 | .0703 | .0596 | .0431 | .0313 | .0168 | .0092 | .0051 | .0029 |
| 20 | .1037 | .0728 | .0611 | .0514 | .0365 | .0261 | .0135 | .0072 | .0039 | .0021 |
| 21 | .0926 | .0638 | .0531 | .0443 | .0309 | .0217 | .0109 | .0056 | .0029 | .0016 |
| 22 | .0826 | .0560 | .0462 | .0382 | .0262 | .0181 | .0088 | .0044 | .0022 | .0012 |
| 23 | .0738 | .0491 | .0402 | .0329 | .0222 | .0151 | .0071 | .0034 | .0017 | .0008 |
| 24 | .0659 | .0431 | .0349 | .0284 | .0188 | .0126 | .0057 | .0027 | .0013 | .0006 |
| 25 | .0588 | .0378 | .0304 | .0245 | .0160 | .0105 | .0046 | .0021 | .0010 | .0005 |
| 26 | .0525 | .0331 | .0264 | .0211 | .0135 | .0087 | .0037 | .0016 | .0007 | .0003 |
| 27 | .0469 | .0291 | .0230 | .0182 | .0115 | .0073 | .0030 | .0013 | .0006 | .0002 |
| 28 | .0419 | .0255 | .0200 | .0157 | .0097 | .0061 | .0024 | .0010 | .0004 | .0002 |
| 29 | .0374 | .0224 | .0174 | .0135 | .0082 | .0051 | .0020 | .0008 | .0003 | .0001 |
| 30 | .0334 | .0196 | .0151 | .0116 | .0070 | .0042 | .0016 | .0006 | .0002 | .0001 |
| 35 | .0189 | .0102 | .0075 | .0055 | .0030 | .0017 | .0005 | .0002 | .0001 | * |
| 40 | .0107 | 0053 | .0037 | .0026 | .0013 | .0007 | .0002 | .0001 | * | * |
| 45 | .0061 | .0027 | .0019 | .0013 | .0006 | .0003 | .0001 | * | * | * |
| 50 | .0035 | .0014 | .0009 | .0006 | .0003 | .0001 | * | * | * | * |
| 55 | .0020 | .0007 | .0005 | .0003 | .0001 | * | * | * | * | * |

*The factor is zero to four decimal places.

**Table A-2**
**Present Value of an Annuity of $1 per Period for n Periods:**

$$\text{PVIFA}_{k,n} = \sum_{t=1}^{n} \frac{1}{(1 + k)^t} = \frac{1 - \dfrac{1}{(1 + k)^n}}{k} = \frac{1}{k} - \frac{1}{k(1 + k)^n}$$

| Number of Periods | 1% | 2% | 3% | 4% | 5% | 6% | 7% | 8% | 9% |
|---|---|---|---|---|---|---|---|---|---|
| 1 | 0.9901 | 0.9804 | 0.9709 | 0.9615 | 0.9524 | 0.9434 | 0.9346 | 0.9259 | 0.9174 |
| 2 | 1.9704 | 1.9416 | 1.9135 | 1.8861 | 1.8594 | 1.8334 | 1.8080 | 1.7833 | 1.7591 |
| 3 | 2.9410 | 2.8839 | 2.8286 | 2.7751 | 2.7232 | 2.6730 | 2.6243 | 2.5771 | 2.5313 |
| 4 | 3.9020 | 3.8077 | 3.7171 | 3.6299 | 3.5460 | 3.4651 | 3.3872 | 3.3121 | 3.2397 |
| 5 | 4.8534 | 4.7135 | 4.5797 | 4.4518 | 4.3295 | 4.2124 | 4.1002 | 3.9927 | 3.8897 |
| 6 | 5.7955 | 5.6014 | 5.4172 | 5.2421 | 5.0757 | 4.9173 | 4.7665 | 4.6229 | 4.4859 |
| 7 | 6.7282 | 6.4720 | 6.2303 | 6.0021 | 5.7864 | 5.5824 | 5.3893 | 5.2064 | 5.0330 |
| 8 | 7.6517 | 7.3255 | 7.0197 | 6.7327 | 6.4632 | 6.2098 | 5.9713 | 5.7466 | 5.5348 |
| 9 | 8.5660 | 8.1622 | 7.7861 | 7.4353 | 7.1078 | 6.8017 | 6.5152 | 6.2469 | 5.9952 |
| 10 | 9.4713 | 8.9826 | 8.5302 | 8.1109 | 7.7217 | 7.3601 | 7.0236 | 6.7101 | 6.4177 |
| 11 | 10.3676 | 9.7868 | 9.2526 | 8.7605 | 8.3064 | 7.8869 | 7.4987 | 7.1390 | 6.8052 |
| 12 | 11.2551 | 10.5753 | 9.9540 | 9.3851 | 8.8633 | 8.3838 | 7.9427 | 7.5361 | 7.1607 |
| 13 | 12.1337 | 11.3484 | 10.6350 | 9.9856 | 9.3936 | 8.8527 | 8.3577 | 7.9038 | 7.4869 |
| 14 | 13.0037 | 12.1062 | 11.2961 | 10.5631 | 9.8986 | 9.2950 | 8.7455 | 8.2442 | 7.7862 |
| 15 | 13.8651 | 12.8493 | 11.9379 | 11.1184 | 10.3797 | 9.7122 | 9.1079 | 8.5595 | 8.0607 |
| 16 | 14.7179 | 13.5777 | 12.5611 | 11.6523 | 10.8378 | 10.1059 | 9.4466 | 8.8514 | 8.3126 |
| 17 | 15.5623 | 14.2919 | 13.1661 | 12.1657 | 11.2741 | 10.4773 | 9.7632 | 9.1216 | 8.5436 |
| 18 | 16.3983 | 14.9920 | 13.7535 | 12.6593 | 11.6896 | 10.8276 | 10.0591 | 9.3719 | 8.7556 |
| 19 | 17.2260 | 15.6785 | 14.3238 | 13.1339 | 12.0853 | 11.1581 | 10.3356 | 9.6036 | 8.9501 |
| 20 | 18.0456 | 16.3514 | 14.8775 | 13.5903 | 12.4622 | 11.4699 | 10.5940 | 9.8181 | 9.1285 |
| 21 | 18.8570 | 17.0112 | 15.4150 | 14.0292 | 12.8212 | 11.7641 | 10.8355 | 10.0168 | 9.2922 |
| 22 | 19.6604 | 17.6580 | 15.9369 | 14.4511 | 13.1630 | 12.0416 | 11.0612 | 10.2007 | 9.4424 |
| 23 | 20.4558 | 18.2922 | 16.4436 | 14.8568 | 13.4886 | 12.3034 | 11.2722 | 10.3711 | 9.5802 |
| 24 | 21.2434 | 18.9139 | 16.9355 | 15.2470 | 13.7986 | 12.5504 | 11.4693 | 10.5288 | 9.7066 |
| 25 | 22.0232 | 19.5235 | 17.4131 | 15.6221 | 14.0939 | 12.7834 | 11.6536 | 10.6748 | 9.8226 |
| 26 | 22.7952 | 20.1210 | 17.8768 | 15.9828 | 14.3752 | 13.0032 | 11.8258 | 10.8100 | 9.9290 |
| 27 | 23.5596 | 20.7069 | 18.3270 | 16.3296 | 14.6430 | 13.2105 | 11.9867 | 10.9352 | 10.0266 |
| 28 | 24.3164 | 21.2813 | 18.7641 | 16.6631 | 14.8981 | 13.4062 | 12.1371 | 11.0511 | 10.1161 |
| 29 | 25.0658 | 21.8444 | 19.1885 | 16.9837 | 15.1411 | 13.5907 | 12.2777 | 11.1584 | 10.1983 |
| 30 | 25.8077 | 22.3965 | 19.6004 | 17.2920 | 15.3725 | 13.7648 | 12.4090 | 11.2578 | 10.2737 |
| 35 | 29.4086 | 24.9986 | 21.4872 | 18.6646 | 16.3742 | 14.4982 | 12.9477 | 11.6546 | 10.5668 |
| 40 | 32.8347 | 27.3555 | 23.1148 | 19.7928 | 17.1591 | 15.0463 | 13.3317 | 11.9246 | 10.7574 |
| 45 | 36.0945 | 29.4902 | 24.5187 | 20.7200 | 17.7741 | 15.4558 | 13.6055 | 12.1084 | 10.8812 |
| 50 | 39.1961 | 31.4236 | 25.7298 | 21.4822 | 18.2559 | 15.7619 | 13.8007 | 12.2335 | 10.9617 |
| 55 | 42.1472 | 33.1748 | 26.7744 | 22.1086 | 18.6335 | 15.9905 | 13.9399 | 12.3186 | 11.0140 |

**Table A-2**
**(continued)**

| Number of Periods | 10% | 12% | 14% | 15% | 16% | 18% | 20% | 24% | 28% | 32% |
|---|---|---|---|---|---|---|---|---|---|---|
| 1 | 0.9091 | 0.8929 | 0.8772 | 0.8696 | 0.8621 | 0.8475 | 0.8333 | 0.8065 | 0.7813 | 0.7576 |
| 2 | 1.7355 | 1.6901 | 1.6467 | 1.6257 | 1.6052 | 1.5656 | 1.5278 | 1.4568 | 1.3916 | 1.3315 |
| 3 | 2.4869 | 2.4018 | 2.3216 | 2.2832 | 2.2459 | 2.1743 | 2.1065 | 1.9813 | 1.8684 | 1.7663 |
| 4 | 3.1699 | 3.0373 | 2.9137 | 2.8550 | 2.7982 | 2.6901 | 2.5887 | 2.4043 | 2.2410 | 2.0957 |
| 5 | 3.7908 | 3.6048 | 3.4331 | 3.3522 | 3.2743 | 3.1272 | 2.9906 | 2.7454 | 2.5320 | 2.3452 |
| 6 | 4.3553 | 4.1114 | 3.8887 | 3.7845 | 3.6847 | 3.4976 | 3.3255 | 3.0205 | 2.7594 | 2.5342 |
| 7 | 4.8684 | 4.5638 | 4.2883 | 4.1604 | 4.0386 | 3.8115 | 3.6046 | 3.2423 | 2.9370 | 2.6775 |
| 8 | 5.3349 | 4.9676 | 4.6389 | 4.4873 | 4.3436 | 4.0776 | 3.8372 | 3.4212 | 3.0758 | 2.7860 |
| 9 | 5.7590 | 5.3282 | 4.9464 | 4.7716 | 4.6065 | 4.3030 | 4.0310 | 3.5655 | 3.1842 | 2.8681 |
| 10 | 6.1446 | 5.6502 | 5.2161 | 5.0188 | 4.8332 | 4.4941 | 4.1925 | 3.6819 | 3.2689 | 2.9304 |
| 11 | 6.4951 | 5.9377 | 5.4527 | 5.2337 | 5.0286 | 4.6560 | 4.3271 | 3.7757 | 3.3351 | 2.9776 |
| 12 | 6.8137 | 6.1944 | 5.6603 | 5.4206 | 5.1971 | 4.7932 | 4.4392 | 3.8514 | 3.3868 | 3.0133 |
| 13 | 7.1034 | 6.4235 | 5.8424 | 5.5831 | 5.3423 | 4.9095 | 4.5327 | 3.9124 | 3.4272 | 3.0404 |
| 14 | 7.3667 | 6.6282 | 6.0021 | 5.7245 | 5.4675 | 5.0081 | 4.6106 | 3.9616 | 3.4587 | 3.0609 |
| 15 | 7.6061 | 6.8109 | 6.1422 | 5.8474 | 5.5755 | 5.0916 | 4.6755 | 4.0013 | 3.4834 | 3.0764 |
| 16 | 7.8237 | 6.9740 | 6.2651 | 5.9542 | 5.6685 | 5.1624 | 4.7296 | 4.0333 | 3.5026 | 3.0882 |
| 17 | 8.0216 | 7.1196 | 6.3729 | 6.0472 | 5.7487 | 5.2223 | 4.7746 | 4.0591 | 3.5177 | 3.0971 |
| 18 | 8.2014 | 7.2497 | 6.4674 | 6.1280 | 5.8178 | 5.2732 | 4.8122 | 4.0799 | 3.5294 | 3.1039 |
| 19 | 8.3649 | 7.3658 | 6.5504 | 6.1982 | 5.8775 | 5.3162 | 4.8435 | 4.0967 | 3.5386 | 3.1090 |
| 20 | 8.5136 | 7.4694 | 6.6231 | 6.2593 | 5.9288 | 5.3527 | 4.8696 | 4.1103 | 3.5458 | 3.1129 |
| 21 | 8.6487 | 7.5620 | 6.6870 | 6.3125 | 5.9731 | 5.3837 | 4.8913 | 4.1212 | 3.5514 | 3.1158 |
| 22 | 8.7715 | 7.6446 | 6.7429 | 6.3587 | 6.0113 | 5.4099 | 4.9094 | 4.1300 | 3.5558 | 3.1180 |
| 23 | 8.8832 | 7.7184 | 6.7921 | 6.3988 | 6.0442 | 5.4321 | 4.9245 | 4.1371 | 3.5592 | 3.1197 |
| 24 | 8.9847 | 7.7843 | 6.8351 | 6.4338 | 6.0726 | 5.4509 | 4.9371 | 4.1428 | 3.5619 | 3.1210 |
| 25 | 9.0770 | 7.8431 | 6.8729 | 6.4641 | 6.0971 | 5.4669 | 4.9476 | 4.1474 | 3.5640 | 3.1220 |
| 26 | 9.1609 | 7.8957 | 6.9061 | 6.4906 | 6.1182 | 5.4804 | 4.9563 | 4.1511 | 3.5656 | 3.1227 |
| 27 | 9.2372 | 7.9426 | 6.9352 | 6.5135 | 6.1364 | 5.4919 | 4.9636 | 4.1542 | 3.5669 | 3.1233 |
| 28 | 9.3066 | 7.9844 | 6.9607 | 6.5335 | 6.1520 | 5.5016 | 4.9697 | 4.1566 | 3.5679 | 3.1237 |
| 29 | 9.3696 | 8.0218 | 6.9830 | 6.5509 | 6.1656 | 5.5098 | 4.9747 | 4.1585 | 3.5687 | 3.1240 |
| 30 | 9.4269 | 8.0552 | 7.0027 | 6.5660 | 6.1772 | 5.5168 | 4.9789 | 4.1601 | 3.5693 | 3.1242 |
| 35 | 9.6442 | 8.1755 | 7.0700 | 6.6166 | 6.2153 | 5.5386 | 4.9915 | 4.1644 | 3.5708 | 3.1248 |
| 40 | 9.7791 | 8.2438 | 7.1050 | 6.6418 | 6.2335 | 5.5482 | 4.9966 | 4.1659 | 3.5712 | 3.1250 |
| 45 | 9.8628 | 8.2825 | 7.1232 | 6.6543 | 6.2421 | 5.5523 | 4.9986 | 4.1664 | 3.5714 | 3.1250 |
| 50 | 9.9148 | 8.3045 | 7.1327 | 6.6605 | 6.2463 | 5.5541 | 4.9995 | 4.1666 | 3.5714 | 3.1250 |
| 55 | 9.9471 | 8.3170 | 7.1376 | 6.6636 | 6.2482 | 5.5549 | 4.9998 | 4.1666 | 3.5714 | 3.1250 |

**Table A-3**
**Future Value of $1 at the End of n Periods:**

$$FVIF_{k,n} = (1 + k)^n$$

| Period | 1% | 2% | 3% | 4% | 5% | 6% | 7% | 8% | 9% | 10% |
|--------|------|------|------|------|------|------|------|------|------|------|
| 1 | 1.0100 | 1.0200 | 1.0300 | 1.0400 | 1.0500 | 1.0600 | 1.0700 | 1.0800 | 1.0900 | 1.1000 |
| 2 | 1.0201 | 1.0404 | 1.0609 | 1.0816 | 1.1025 | 1.1236 | 1.1449 | 1.1664 | 1.1881 | 1.2100 |
| 3 | 1.0303 | 1.0612 | 1.0927 | 1.1249 | 1.1576 | 1.1910 | 1.2250 | 1.2597 | 1.2950 | 1.3310 |
| 4 | 1.0406 | 1.0824 | 1.1255 | 1.1699 | 1.2155 | 1.2625 | 1.3108 | 1.3605 | 1.4116 | 1.4641 |
| 5 | 1.0510 | 1.1041 | 1.1593 | 1.2167 | 1.2763 | 1.3382 | 1.4026 | 1.4693 | 1.5386 | 1.6105 |
| 6 | 1.0615 | 1.1262 | 1.1941 | 1.2653 | 1.3401 | 1.4185 | 1.5007 | 1.5869 | 1.6771 | 1.7716 |
| 7 | 1.0721 | 1.1487 | 1.2299 | 1.3159 | 1.4071 | 1.5036 | 1.6058 | 1.7138 | 1.8280 | 1.9487 |
| 8 | 1.0829 | 1.1717 | 1.2668 | 1.3686 | 1.4775 | 1.5938 | 1.7182 | 1.8509 | 1.9926 | 2.1436 |
| 9 | 1.0937 | 1.1951 | 1.3048 | 1.4233 | 1.5513 | 1.6895 | 1.8385 | 1.9990 | 2.1719 | 2.3579 |
| 10 | 1.1046 | 1.2190 | 1.3439 | 1.4802 | 1.6289 | 1.7908 | 1.9672 | 2.1589 | 2.3674 | 2.5937 |
| 11 | 1.1157 | 1.2434 | 1.3842 | 1.5395 | 1.7103 | 1.8983 | 2.1049 | 2.3316 | 2.5804 | 2.8531 |
| 12 | 1.1268 | 1.2682 | 1.4258 | 1.6010 | 1.7959 | 2.0122 | 2.2522 | 2.5182 | 2.8127 | 3.1384 |
| 13 | 1.1381 | 1.2936 | 1.4685 | 1.6651 | 1.8856 | 2.1329 | 2.4098 | 2.7196 | 3.0658 | 3.4523 |
| 14 | 1.1495 | 1.3195 | 1.5126 | 1.7317 | 1.9799 | 2.2609 | 2.5785 | 2.9372 | 3.3417 | 3.7975 |
| 15 | 1.1610 | 1.3459 | 1.5580 | 1.8009 | 2.0789 | 2.3966 | 2.7590 | 3.1722 | 3.6425 | 4.1772 |
| 16 | 1.1726 | 1.3728 | 1.6047 | 1.8730 | 2.1829 | 2.5404 | 2.9522 | 3.4259 | 3.9703 | 4.5950 |
| 17 | 1.1843 | 1.4002 | 1.6528 | 1.9479 | 2.2920 | 2.6928 | 3.1588 | 3.7000 | 4.3276 | 5.0545 |
| 18 | 1.1961 | 1.4282 | 1.7024 | 2.0258 | 2.4066 | 2.8543 | 3.3799 | 3.9960 | 4.7171 | 5.5599 |
| 19 | 1.2081 | 1.4568 | 1.7535 | 2.1068 | 2.5270 | 3.0256 | 3.6165 | 4.3157 | 5.1417 | 6.1159 |
| 20 | 1.2202 | 1.4859 | 1.8061 | 2.1911 | 2.6533 | 3.2071 | 3.8697 | 4.6610 | 5.6044 | 6.7275 |
| 21 | 1.2324 | 1.5157 | 1.8603 | 2.2788 | 2.7860 | 3.3996 | 4.1406 | 5.0338 | 6.1088 | 7.4002 |
| 22 | 1.2447 | 1.5460 | 1.9161 | 2.3699 | 2.9253 | 3.6035 | 4.4304 | 5.4365 | 6.6586 | 8.1403 |
| 23 | 1.2572 | 1.5769 | 1.9736 | 2.4647 | 3.0715 | 3.8197 | 4.7405 | 5.8715 | 7.2579 | 8.9543 |
| 24 | 1.2697 | 1.6084 | 2.0328 | 2.5633 | 3.2251 | 4.0489 | 5.0724 | 6.3412 | 7.9111 | 9.8497 |
| 25 | 1.2824 | 1.6406 | 2.0938 | 2.6658 | 3.3864 | 4.2919 | 5.4274 | 6.8485 | 8.6231 | 10.835 |
| 26 | 1.2953 | 1.6734 | 2.1566 | 2.7725 | 3.5557 | 4.5494 | 5.8074 | 7.3964 | 9.3992 | 11.918 |
| 27 | 1.3082 | 1.7069 | 2.2213 | 2.8834 | 3.7335 | 4.8223 | 6.2139 | 7.9881 | 10.245 | 13.110 |
| 28 | 1.3213 | 1.7410 | 2.2879 | 2.9987 | 3.9201 | 5.1117 | 6.6488 | 8.6271 | 11.167 | 14.421 |
| 29 | 1.3345 | 1.7758 | 2.3566 | 3.1187 | 4.1161 | 5.4184 | 7.1143 | 9.3173 | 12.172 | 15.863 |
| 30 | 1.3478 | 1.8114 | 2.4273 | 3.2434 | 4.3219 | 5.7435 | 7.6123 | 10.063 | 13.268 | 17.449 |
| 40 | 1.4889 | 2.2080 | 3.2620 | 4.8010 | 7.0400 | 10.286 | 14.974 | 21.725 | 31.409 | 45.259 |
| 50 | 1.6446 | 2.6916 | 4.3839 | 7.1067 | 11.467 | 18.420 | 29.457 | 46.902 | 74.358 | 117.39 |
| 60 | 1.8167 | 3.2810 | 5.8916 | 10.520 | 18.679 | 32.988 | 57.946 | 101.26 | 176.03 | 304.48 |

**Table A-3**
**(continued)**

| Period | 12% | 14% | 15% | 16% | 18% | 20% | 24% | 28% | 32% | 36% |
|---|---|---|---|---|---|---|---|---|---|---|
| 1 | 1.1200 | 1.1400 | 1.1500 | 1.1600 | 1.1800 | 1.2000 | 1.2400 | 1.2800 | 1.3200 | 1.3600 |
| 2 | 1.2544 | 1.2996 | 1.3225 | 1.3456 | 1.3924 | 1.4400 | 1.5376 | 1.6384 | 1.7424 | 1.8496 |
| 3 | 1.4049 | 1.4815 | 1.5209 | 1.5609 | 1.6430 | 1.7280 | 1.9066 | 2.0972 | 2.3000 | 2.5155 |
| 4 | 1.5735 | 1.6890 | 1.7490 | 1.8106 | 1.9388 | 2.0736 | 2.3642 | 2.6844 | 3.0360 | 3.4210 |
| 5 | 1.7623 | 1.9254 | 2.0114 | 2.1003 | 2.2878 | 2.4883 | 2.9316 | 3.4360 | 4.0075 | 4.6526 |
| 6 | 1.9738 | 2.1950 | 2.3131 | 2.4364 | 2.6996 | 2.9860 | 3.6352 | 4.3980 | 5.2899 | 6.3275 |
| 7 | 2.2107 | 2.5023 | 2.6600 | 2.8262 | 3.1855 | 3.5832 | 4.5077 | 5.6295 | 6.9826 | 8.6054 |
| 8 | 2.4760 | 2.8526 | 3.0590 | 3.2784 | 3.7589 | 4.2998 | 5.5895 | 7.2058 | 9.2170 | 11.703 |
| 9 | 2.7731 | 3.2519 | 3.5179 | 3.8030 | 4.4355 | 5.1598 | 6.9310 | 9.2234 | 12.166 | 15.917 |
| 10 | 3.1058 | 3.7072 | 4.0456 | 4.4114 | 5.2338 | 6.1917 | 8.5944 | 11.806 | 16.060 | 21.647 |
| 11 | 3.4785 | 4.2262 | 4.6524 | 5.1173 | 6.1759 | 7.4301 | 10.657 | 15.112 | 21.199 | 29.439 |
| 12 | 3.8960 | 4.8179 | 5.3503 | 5.9360 | 7.2876 | 8.9161 | 13.215 | 19.343 | 27.983 | 40.037 |
| 13 | 4.3635 | 5.4924 | 6.1528 | 6.8858 | 8.5994 | 10.699 | 16.386 | 24.759 | 36.937 | 54.451 |
| 14 | 4.8871 | 6.2613 | 7.0757 | 7.9875 | 10.147 | 12.839 | 20.319 | 31.691 | 48.757 | 74.053 |
| 15 | 5.4736 | 7.1379 | 8.1371 | 9.2655 | 11.974 | 15.407 | 25.196 | 40.565 | 64.359 | 100.71 |
| 16 | 6.1304 | 8.1372 | 9.3576 | 10.748 | 14.129 | 18.488 | 31.243 | 51.923 | 84.954 | 136.97 |
| 17 | 6.8660 | 9.2765 | 10.761 | 12.468 | 16.672 | 22.186 | 38.741 | 66.461 | 112.14 | 186.28 |
| 18 | 7.6900 | 10.575 | 12.375 | 14.463 | 19.673 | 26.623 | 48.039 | 85.071 | 148.02 | 253.34 |
| 19 | 8.6128 | 12.056 | 14.232 | 16.777 | 23.214 | 31.948 | 59.568 | 108.89 | 195.39 | 344.54 |
| 20 | 9.6463 | 13.743 | 16.367 | 19.461 | 27.393 | 38.338 | 73.864 | 139.38 | 257.92 | 468.57 |
| 21 | 10.804 | 15.668 | 18.822 | 22.574 | 32.324 | 46.005 | 91.592 | 178.41 | 340.45 | 637.26 |
| 22 | 12.100 | 17.861 | 21.645 | 26.186 | 38.142 | 55.206 | 113.57 | 228.36 | 449.39 | 866.67 |
| 23 | 13.552 | 20.362 | 24.891 | 30.376 | 45.008 | 66.247 | 140.83 | 292.30 | 593.20 | 1178.7 |
| 24 | 15.179 | 23.212 | 28.625 | 35.236 | 53.109 | 79.497 | 174.63 | 374.14 | 783.02 | 1603.0 |
| 25 | 17.000 | 26.462 | 32.919 | 40.874 | 62.669 | 95.396 | 216.54 | 478.90 | 1033.6 | 2180.1 |
| 26 | 19.040 | 30.167 | 37.857 | 47.414 | 73.949 | 114.48 | 268.51 | 613.00 | 1364.3 | 2964.9 |
| 27 | 21.325 | 34.390 | 43.535 | 55.000 | 87.260 | 137.37 | 332.95 | 784.64 | 1800.9 | 4032.3 |
| 28 | 23.884 | 39.204 | 50.066 | 63.800 | 102.97 | 164.84 | 412.86 | 1004.3 | 2377.2 | 5483.9 |
| 29 | 26.750 | 44.693 | 57.575 | 74.009 | 121.50 | 197.81 | 511.95 | 1285.6 | 3137.9 | 7458.1 |
| 30 | 29.960 | 50.950 | 66.212 | 85.850 | 143.37 | 237.38 | 634.82 | 1645.5 | 4142.1 | 10143. |
| 40 | 93.051 | 188.88 | 267.86 | 378.72 | 750.38 | 1469.8 | 5455.9 | 19427. | 66521. | * |
| 50 | 289.00 | 700.23 | 1083.7 | 1670.7 | 3927.4 | 9100.4 | 46890. | * | * | * |
| 60 | 897.60 | 2595.9 | 4384.0 | 7370.2 | 20555. | 56348. | * | * | * | * |

*FVIF > 99,999.

**Table A-4**
**Sum of an Annuity of $1 per Period for n Periods:**

$$FVIFA_{k,n} = \sum_{t=1}^{n} (1 + k)^{n-t} = \frac{(1 + k)^n - 1}{k}$$

| Number of Periods | 1% | 2% | 3% | 4% | 5% | 6% | 7% | 8% | 9% | 10% |
|---|---|---|---|---|---|---|---|---|---|---|
| 1 | 1.0000 | 1.0000 | 1.0000 | 1.0000 | 1.0000 | 1.0000 | 1.0000 | 1.0000 | 1.0000 | 1.0000 |
| 2 | 2.0100 | 2.0200 | 2.0300 | 2.0400 | 2.0500 | 2.0600 | 2.0700 | 2.0800 | 2.0900 | 2.1000 |
| 3 | 3.0301 | 3.0604 | 3.0909 | 3.1216 | 3.1525 | 3.1836 | 3.2149 | 3.2464 | 3.2781 | 3.3100 |
| 4 | 4.0604 | 4.1216 | 4.1836 | 4.2465 | 4.3101 | 4.3746 | 4.4399 | 4.5061 | 4.5731 | 4.6410 |
| 5 | 5.1010 | 5.2040 | 5.3091 | 5.4163 | 5.5256 | 5.6371 | 5.7507 | 5.8666 | 5.9847 | 6.1051 |
| 6 | 6.1520 | 6.3081 | 6.4684 | 6.6330 | 6.8019 | 6.9753 | 7.1533 | 7.3359 | 7.5233 | 7.7156 |
| 7 | 7.2135 | 7.4343 | 7.6625 | 7.8983 | 8.1420 | 8.3938 | 8.6540 | 8.9228 | 9.2004 | 9.4872 |
| 8 | 8.2857 | 8.5830 | 8.8923 | 9.2142 | 9.5491 | 9.8975 | 10.260 | 10.637 | 11.028 | 11.436 |
| 9 | 9.3685 | 9.7546 | 10.159 | 10.583 | 11.027 | 11.491 | 11.978 | 12.488 | 13.021 | 13.579 |
| 10 | 10.462 | 10.950 | 11.464 | 12.006 | 12.578 | 13.181 | 13.816 | 14.487 | 15.193 | 15.937 |
| 11 | 11.567 | 12.169 | 12.808 | 13.486 | 14.207 | 14.972 | 15.784 | 16.645 | 17.560 | 18.531 |
| 12 | 12.683 | 13.412 | 14.192 | 15.026 | 15.917 | 16.870 | 17.888 | 18.977 | 20.141 | 21.384 |
| 13 | 13.809 | 14.680 | 15.618 | 16.627 | 17.713 | 18.882 | 20.141 | 21.495 | 22.953 | 24.523 |
| 14 | 14.947 | 15.974 | 17.086 | 18.292 | 19.599 | 21.015 | 22.550 | 24.215 | 26.019 | 27.975 |
| 15 | 16.097 | 17.293 | 18.599 | 20.024 | 21.579 | 23.276 | 25.129 | 27.152 | 29.361 | 31.772 |
| 16 | 17.258 | 18.639 | 20.157 | 21.825 | 23.657 | 25.673 | 27.888 | 30.324 | 33.003 | 35.950 |
| 17 | 18.430 | 20.012 | 21.762 | 23.698 | 25.840 | 28.213 | 30.840 | 33.750 | 36.974 | 40.545 |
| 18 | 19.615 | 21.412 | 23.414 | 25.645 | 28.132 | 30.906 | 33.999 | 37.450 | 41.301 | 45.599 |
| 19 | 20.811 | 22.841 | 25.117 | 27.671 | 30.539 | 33.760 | 37.379 | 41.446 | 46.018 | 51.159 |
| 20 | 22.019 | 24.297 | 26.870 | 29.778 | 33.066 | 36.786 | 40.995 | 45.762 | 51.160 | 57.275 |
| 21 | 23.239 | 25.783 | 28.676 | 31.969 | 35.719 | 39.993 | 44.865 | 50.423 | 56.765 | 64.002 |
| 22 | 24.472 | 27.299 | 30.537 | 34.248 | 38.505 | 43.392 | 49.006 | 55.457 | 62.873 | 71.403 |
| 23 | 25.716 | 28.845 | 32.453 | 36.618 | 41.430 | 46.996 | 53.436 | 60.893 | 69.532 | 79.543 |
| 24 | 26.973 | 30.422 | 34.426 | 39.083 | 44.502 | 50.816 | 58.177 | 66.765 | 76.790 | 88.497 |
| 25 | 28.243 | 32.030 | 36.459 | 41.646 | 47.727 | 54.865 | 63.249 | 73.106 | 84.701 | 98.347 |
| 26 | 29.526 | 33.671 | 38.553 | 44.312 | 51.113 | 59.156 | 68.676 | 79.954 | 93.324 | 109.18 |
| 27 | 30.821 | 35.344 | 40.710 | 47.084 | 54.669 | 63.706 | 74.484 | 87.351 | 102.72 | 121.10 |
| 28 | 32.129 | 37.051 | 42.931 | 49.968 | 58.403 | 68.528 | 80.698 | 95.339 | 112.97 | 134.21 |
| 29 | 33.450 | 38.792 | 45.219 | 52.966 | 62.323 | 73.640 | 87.347 | 103.97 | 124.14 | 148.63 |
| 30 | 34.785 | 40.568 | 47.575 | 56.085 | 66.439 | 79.058 | 94.461 | 113.28 | 136.31 | 164.49 |
| 40 | 48.886 | 60.402 | 75.401 | 95.026 | 120.80 | 154.76 | 199.64 | 259.06 | 337.88 | 442.59 |
| 50 | 64.463 | 84.579 | 112.80 | 152.67 | 209.35 | 290.34 | 406.53 | 573.77 | 815.08 | 1163.9 |
| 60 | 81.670 | 114.05 | 163.05 | 237.99 | 353.58 | 533.13 | 813.52 | 1253.2 | 1944.8 | 3034.8 |

**Table A-4**
**(continued)**

| Number of Periods | 12% | 14% | 15% | 16% | 18% | 20% | 24% | 28% | 32% | 36% |
|---|---|---|---|---|---|---|---|---|---|---|
| 1 | 1.0000 | 1.0000 | 1.0000 | 1.0000 | 1.0000 | 1.0000 | 1.0000 | 1.0000 | 1.0000 | 1.0000 |
| 2 | 2.1200 | 2.1400 | 2.1500 | 2.1600 | 2.1800 | 2.2000 | 2.2400 | 2.2800 | 2.3200 | 2.3600 |
| 3 | 3.3744 | 3.4396 | 3.4725 | 3.5056 | 3.5724 | 3.6400 | 3.7776 | 3.9184 | 4.0624 | 4.2096 |
| 4 | 4.7793 | 4.9211 | 4.9934 | 5.0665 | 5.2154 | 5.3680 | 5.6842 | 6.0156 | 6.3624 | 6.7251 |
| 5 | 6.3528 | 6.6101 | 6.7424 | 6.8771 | 7.1542 | 7.4416 | 8.0484 | 8.6999 | 9.3983 | 10.146 |
| 6 | 8.1152 | 8.5355 | 8.7537 | 8.9775 | 9.4420 | 9.9299 | 10.980 | 12.136 | 13.406 | 14.799 |
| 7 | 10.089 | 10.730 | 11.067 | 11.414 | 12.142 | 12.916 | 14.615 | 16.534 | 18.696 | 21.126 |
| 8 | 12.300 | 13.233 | 13.727 | 14.240 | 15.327 | 16.499 | 19.123 | 22.163 | 25.678 | 29.732 |
| 9 | 14.776 | 16.085 | 16.786 | 17.519 | 19.086 | 20.799 | 24.712 | 29.369 | 34.895 | 41.435 |
| 10 | 17.549 | 19.337 | 20.304 | 21.321 | 23.521 | 25.959 | 31.643 | 38.593 | 47.062 | 57.352 |
| 11 | 20.655 | 23.045 | 24.349 | 25.733 | 28.755 | 32.150 | 40.238 | 50.398 | 63.122 | 78.998 |
| 12 | 24.133 | 27.271 | 29.002 | 30.850 | 34.931 | 39.581 | 50.895 | 65.510 | 84.320 | 108.44 |
| 13 | 28.029 | 32.089 | 34.352 | 36.786 | 42.219 | 48.497 | 64.110 | 84.853 | 112.30 | 148.47 |
| 14 | 32.393 | 37.581 | 40.505 | 43.672 | 50.818 | 59.196 | 80.496 | 109.61 | 149.24 | 202.93 |
| 15 | 37.280 | 43.842 | 47.580 | 51.660 | 60.965 | 72.035 | 100.82 | 141.30 | 198.00 | 276.98 |
| 16 | 42.753 | 50.980 | 55.717 | 60.925 | 72.939 | 87.442 | 126.01 | 181.87 | 262.36 | 377.69 |
| 17 | 48.884 | 59.118 | 65.075 | 71.673 | 87.068 | 105.93 | 157.25 | 233.79 | 347.31 | 514.66 |
| 18 | 55.750 | 68.394 | 75.836 | 84.141 | 103.74 | 128.12 | 195.99 | 300.25 | 459.45 | 700.94 |
| 19 | 63.440 | 78.969 | 88.212 | 98.603 | 123.41 | 154.74 | 244.03 | 385.32 | 607.47 | 954.28 |
| 20 | 72.052 | 91.025 | 102.44 | 115.38 | 146.63 | 186.69 | 303.60 | 494.21 | 802.86 | 1298.8 |
| 21 | 81.699 | 104.77 | 118.81 | 134.84 | 174.02 | 225.03 | 377.46 | 633.59 | 1060.8 | 1767.4 |
| 22 | 92.503 | 120.44 | 137.63 | 157.41 | 206.34 | 271.03 | 469.06 | 812.00 | 1401.2 | 2404.7 |
| 23 | 104.60 | 138.30 | 159.28 | 183.60 | 244.49 | 326.24 | 582.63 | 1040.4 | 1850.6 | 3271.3 |
| 24 | 118.16 | 158.66 | 184.17 | 213.98 | 289.49 | 392.48 | 723.46 | 1332.7 | 2443.8 | 4450.0 |
| 25 | 133.33 | 181.87 | 212.79 | 249.21 | 342.60 | 471.98 | 898.09 | 1706.8 | 3226.8 | 6053.0 |
| 26 | 150.33 | 208.33 | 245.71 | 290.09 | 405.27 | 567.38 | 1114.6 | 2185.7 | 4260.4 | 8233.1 |
| 27 | 169.37 | 238.50 | 283.57 | 337.50 | 479.22 | 681.85 | 1383.1 | 2798.7 | 5624.8 | 11198.0 |
| 28 | 190.70 | 272.89 | 327.10 | 392.50 | 566.48 | 819.22 | 1716.1 | 3583.3 | 7425.7 | 15230.3 |
| 29 | 214.58 | 312.09 | 377.17 | 456.30 | 669.45 | 984.07 | 2129.0 | 4587.7 | 9802.9 | 20714.2 |
| 30 | 241.33 | 356.79 | 434.75 | 530.31 | 790.95 | 1181.9 | 2640.9 | 5873.2 | 12941. | 28172.3 |
| 40 | 767.09 | 1342.0 | 1779.1 | 2360.8 | 4163.2 | 7343.9 | 22729. | 69377. | * | * |
| 50 | 2400.0 | 4994.5 | 7217.7 | 10436. | 21813. | 45497. | * | * | * | * |
| 60 | 7471.6 | 18535. | 29220. | 46058. | * | * | * | * | * | * |

*FVIFA > 99,999.

# B ANSWERS TO SELECTED END-OF-CHAPTER PROBLEMS

We present here some intermediate steps and final answers to selected end-of-chapter problems. Please note that your answer may differ slightly from ours due to rounding errors. Also, though we hope not, some of the problems may have more than one correct solution, depending upon what assumptions are made in working the problem. Finally, many of the problems involve some verbal discussion as well as numerical calculations; this verbal material is not presented here.

**2-1** Tax = $67,150.

**2-2** a. Tax = $71,750.
  b. $9,200.
  c. $1,380.

**2-4** a. 1986 = $1,535;
  1987 = $5,690;
  1988 = $10,486.

**2-5** a. $19,859.
  c. IBM yield = 5.72%.
  d. 36.4%.

**2-6** a. $14,250; $20,900;
  $19,950; $19,950;
  $19,950.

**3-1** a. $k_1$ = 10.20%;
  $k_5$ = 8.20%.

**3-3** Year 2 inflation = 12%;
  k = 15%.

**3-4** a. 8.40%.
  b. 10.40%.
  c. $k_5$ = 10.9%.

**4-1** a. $214.
  d. $174.69.

**4-2** a. $393.44.
  b. $741.44.
  c. $101.66.
  d. $199.97.

**4-3** a. 10 years.

**4-4** a. $3,187.48.
  d. $1,000.

**4-5** a. $1,228.92.
  c. $1,000.
  d(a). $1,351.81.

**4-6** a. Stream A: $1,181.46.

**4-7** $3,638.78.

**4-9** a. 15% (or 14.87%).

**4-10** b. 5%.
  c. 5%.
  d. 9%.

**4-12** 11.61%.

**4-13** 12%.

**4-15** a. $26,496.80.
  b. $20,616.54 and $0.

**4-16** a. $314.70.
  b. $318.76.
  c. $320.94.
  d. $225.36.

**4-17** a. $125.48.
  b. $124.63.
  c. $177.48.

**4-19** a. 1st National = 11%;
  2nd National = 10.38%.

**4-20** $PV_{5\%}$ = $2,000;
  $PV_{10\%}$ = $1,000.

**4-21** a. PMT = $8,042.29.

**4-23** PMT = $4,439.

**4-24** PV Benefits = $15.59
  billion vs. PV
  Costs = $20.85 billion.

**5-1** a. $V_L$ at 6 percent =
  $1,388.52;
  $V_L$ at 9 percent =
  $1,080.57;
  $V_L$ at 12 percent =
  $863.79.

**5-2** a. YTM at $825 = 14%.

**5-3** a. $1,233.04.
  b. $905.50.

**5-4** a. $1,100.
  b. $785.71.
  c. At 10%, V =
  $1,085.10.

**5-5** b. PV = $5.38.
  d. $35.33.

**5-7** a-1. $7.60. a-2. $10.00.
  b-1. Undefined.

**5-9** a. YTM = 3.4%.
  b. YTM = 7%.
  c. $852.

**5-10** $21.60.

**5-11** a. Div. 1988 = $3.30.
  b. $P_0$ = $97.32.
  c. Div. yield 1986 =
  2%, 1990 = 4%.

**5-12** a. $P_0$ = $36.46.

**5-13** a. YTM = 9%;
  YTC = 7.73%.
  d. YTM = 8.20%;
  YTC = 4.58%.

**6-1** a. 17%.
  b. 17.75%.
**6-2** a. 17.6%.
  b-1. $k_M = 17\%$;
  $k_A = 18.6\%$.
  c-1. $k_M = 17\%$;
  $k_A = 19.0\%$.
**6-4** a. $P_0 = \$16.67$.
  b. $P_0 = \$19.23$.
  d. $P_0 = \$27.39$.
**6-5** a. New price = $31.34.
  b. beta = 0.49865.
**6-6** a. $k_C = 10.6\%$;
  $k_D = 7\%$.
**6-7** a. $k_i = 7\% + b_i(5\%)$.
  b. 15.75%.
**6-8** a. $\bar{k}_A = 11.4\%$;
  b. $\sigma_A = 21.9\%$.
**6A-1** a. b = 0.62.
**6A-2** a. $b_A = 1.0$; $b_B = 0.5$.
  c. $k_A = 15\%$.

**7-1** a. Current ratio = $1.98\times$;
  ACP = 75 days; Total assets turnover = $1.70\times$;
  Debt ratio = 61.9%.
**7-2** $350,000; 1.19.
**7-5** a. 16%.
  b. Profit margin = 7.33%;
  Equity multiplier = 1.39;
  Industry D/A = 44%.
**7-6** a. Quick ratio = $0.8\times$;
  ACP = 37 days;
  ROE = 13.1%;
  Debt ratio = 54.8%.

**8-1** a. Total assets = $3.6 million.
  b. $1,790,000.
**8-2** a. $960,000.
  b. $75,000.
**8-3** a. $13.75 million.

b. Notes payable = $31.25 million.
  c. Current ratio = $1.99\times$;
  ROE = 13.5%.
  d. (1) − $12.46 million.
  d. (2) Total assets = $147 million; Notes payable = $5.04 million.
  d. (3) Current ratio = $3.94\times$;
  ROE = 10.4%.
**8-4** a. Total assets = $42,240.
  b. $1,440.
  c. Notes payable = $5,840.
**8-5** a. Total assets = $78,480.
  b. 25%.
  c. Additional external capital = $3,888.
  d. ROE = 10.7%.

**9-1** a. 4 years.
  b. NPV = $2,002.60.
  c. IRR = 14%.
**9-2** IRR (Truck) = 14%;
  NPV (Truck) = $373.
**9-3** Electric-powered NPV = $4,953,
  IRR = 20%;
  Gas-powered NPV = $4,004,
  IRR = 20%.
**9-5** b. $IRR_A = 18.1\%$;
  $IRR_B = 24.0\%$.
  d. Crossover rate = 14.53%.
  e. Worst case (k = 10%)
  $NPV_A = \$221.76$,
  $IRR_A = 16.67\%$;
  $NPV_B = \$101.63$,
  $IRR_B = 19.86\%$; Best case (k = 10%)
  $NPV_A = \$339.79$,
  $IRR_A = 19.30\%$;

$NPV_B = \$240.18$,
  $IRR_B = 26.54\%$.
**9-6** $NPV_S = \$814.40$,
  $IRR_S = 15.24\%$.
**9-7** a. $Payback_M = 2.33$.
  b. $NPV_M$ at 6% = $22,220.
  c. $IRR_M = 15.78\%$.
**9-8** a. $NPV_A = \$1,201$;
  $NPV_B = \$1,199$.
  b. $NPV_A = -\$428$;
  $NPV_B = \$189$.
  c. $NPV_A = \$3,056$;
  $NPV_B = \$2,293$.

**10-1** a. Net cost = $117,800.
  b. Year 1 = $34,986;
  Year 2 = $41,947;
  Year 3 = $41,411.
  c. $32,000.
  d. NPV = $3,827.
**10-3** a. − $73,000.
  b. Year 1 = $42,988;
  Year 2 = $48,545;
  Year 3 = $48,118;
  Year 4 = $32,300.
  c. $32,300.
  d. NPV = $67,253.
**10-4** a. $940,000.
  b. $\Delta$Dep Year 1 = $99,500.
  c. $CF_1 = \$174,800$.
  d. $90,000.
  e. NPV = − $125,107.
**10-5** NPV = $42,405.
**10-6** NPV = $62,035.
**10-7** a. NPV = − $1,252.
  b. NPV = $59.
**10-8** a. $k_s = 16.5\%$.
**10-9** a. $k_s = 14.6\%$.
  b. NPV = $438.
**10-10** a. $CF_A = \$4,500$;
  $CV_A = 0.0703$.
  b. $NPV_A = \$6,691$.
**10-11** a. NPV with 5-year actual life = $1,843.
  b. NPV if k = 8%: $3,539.

**11-1** a. $16.50/share.
　　b. $15.50/share.

**11-2** a. $300,000.

**11-3** 569,549 shares.

**11-4** b. Sonnet $g_{EPS}$ = 8.4%,
　　$g_{DPS}$ = 8.4%;
　　Mailers $g_{EPS}$ = 6.4%,
　　$g_{DPS}$ = 6.4%;
　　Callaway $g_{EPS}$ = 8.0%,
　　$g_{DPS}$ = 7.4%.
　　f. Sonnet$_{ROE}$ = 15.00%,
　　Mailers$_{ROE}$ = 13.64%,
　　Callaway$_{ROE}$ = 13.33%.
　　k. $k_{Sonnet}$ = 15.2%,
　　$k_{Mailers}$ = 12.54%,
　　Callaway$_{Sonnet}$ = $21.54,
　　Callaway$_{Mailers}$ = $33.38.

**12-1** a. PMT = $500,914.17.
　　b. PMT = $298,058.15.

**12-2** PMT = $395,053.92

**12-3** k = 15.9%.

**12-4** c-1. $80.04 = value
　　in 5 years.
　　c-2. 24%.
　　d. $41.96, $150.

**12-5** a. 1,618,123 or
　　400,000 bonds.
　　b. YTM, Tax exempt =
　　15%, 50% taxpayer =
　　6.91%.
　　c. Zero coupon bond =
　　7.51%, annual coupon
　　bond = 8.64%.

**12A-1** a. Accounts payable =
　　61.17%, 2nd mortgage =
　　76.6%, subordinated
　　debentures = 41.67%.

**12B-1** a. Investment cost =
　　$5,226,334,
　　NPV = $1,165,344.

**13-2** c. PMT = $328,055.

**13-3** a. Disadvantage to
　　leasing = $1,602.

**13-4** a. $P_s$ = $20:
　　FV = −$5;
　　$P_s$ = $25: FV = $0.
　　d. Coupon rate =
　　10%, I = $100.

**13-6** b. Percent ownership,
　　Original = 80%,
　　Plan 1 = 49%,
　　Plan 2 = 53%,
　　Plan 3 = 53%.
　　c. EPS, Original =
　　$0.45, Plan 1 =
　　$0.49, Plan 2 =
　　$0.53, Plan 3 =
　　$0.73.
　　d. Debt ratio, Original =
　　73%, Plan 1 = 19%,
　　Plan 2 = 19%,
　　Plan 3 = 50%.

**13-7** a. PV of bond at t = 0:
　　$735; $CV_0$ = $600;
　　$CV_8$ = $1,196.
　　b. Percent change in
　　stock price = −59%.

**14-1** a. $k_d$ = 10%.
　　b. $k_d$ = 6%.

**14-2** $k_d$ = 8.4%.

**14-3** $k_{ps}$ = 11.06%.

**14-4** $k_s$ = 17%.

**14-5** a. g = 8%.
　　b. $D_1$ = $2.16.
　　c. $k_s$ = 13.4%.

**14-6** a. $15 million.
　　b. $30 million.
　　c. $20 million and
　　$40 million.

**14-7** a. F = 15%.
　　b. $k_e$ = 14.35%.

**14-8** $k_a$ = 12%.

**14-9** a. g = 6%.
　　b. EPS = $5.30.

**14-10** a. $22,500,000.
　　b. External equity =
　　$18 million.
　　c. $k_s$ = 12%,
　　$k_e$ = 12.4%.

**　　** d. Break at $9,000,000.
　　e. MCC = 9% and 9.2%.

**14-12** a. 3.
　　b. $666,667, $750,000,
　　$1,500,000.
　　c. 11.4%, 12.0%,
　　12.5%, and 13.0%.
　　d. $IRR_1$ = 16%,
　　$IRR_3$ = 14%.

**15-1** a. $EPS_C$ = $3.40.

**15-2** a. $DOL_{A(\$160,000)}$ =
　　2.0; $DOL_{B(\$160,000)}$ = 4.0.
　　d. $DFL_{A,zero\ debt}$ =
　　1.0; $DFL_{A,D=\$90,000}$ =
　　10 and 1.82.
　　e. $DTL_{A,D=\$90,000}$ =
　　30 and 3.64.

**15-3** a. Method A =
　　81,250 units,
　　Method B =
　　65,200 units,
　　108,000 units.
　　b. $DOL_A$ = 2.18,
　　$DOL_B$ = 1.77.
　　c. $DFL_A$ = 1.09,
　　$DFL_B$ = 1.12.
　　d. $DTL_A$ = 2.38,
　　$DTL_B$ = 1.98.
　　e. −$560,610.

**15-4** a. EPS = $1.80, $2.58,
　　and $2.28.
　　b. $DOL_{Old}$ = 2.11,
　　$DFL_{Old}$ = 1.27,
　　$DTL_{Old}$ = 2.67.
　　c. $Q_{BE(Old)}$ =
　　18,375 units.
　　d. 32,389 units.
　　e. $EPS_{Old}$ = 0
　　at 21,877 units.

**15-5** a. $ROE_{Crothers}$ = 14.1%,
　　$ROE_{Hollister}$ = 15.6%.
　　b. ROE = 14.7%.

**15-7** a. Debt: EPS = $3.05,
　　$3.95, and $4.85;
　　Expected EPS = $3.95;
　　Std. dev. = $0.70.

**16-2** $1,220,000.

**16-3** 56 percent.

**16-4** $5.50.

**16-5** T.A. = $1,979.2; R.E. = $679.2; Cash = $29.2.

**16-6** a. $2,475,000.
   b. $3,600,000.
   c. $5,700,000.
   d. Regular = $2,475,000, extra = $3,225,000.
   f. 15%.
   g. ROE = 14.3%.

**16-7** a. Payout = 63.16%, B.P. = $15.27 million or $41.45 million, MCC = 10.18% and 10.46%.
   b. $24 million.

**17-1** a. 81.
   b. $194,775.

**17-2** a. ROE = 11.8%, 10.6%, or 8.7%.

**17-4** b. 14.69%.
   d. 20.99%.
   e. 12.12%.

**17-5** a. 36.74%.

**17-6** a. $66,667.
   c. 36.73%.
   d. 24.48%.

**17-8** a. 16.28% versus 14.69% (approximate cost) or 15.66% (exact cost).

**17-9** a. $300,000.

**17-10** 14.69% (approximate rate) or 15.67% (exact rate).

**17-11** a. 18.18% (approximate cost) or 19.83% (exact cost) versus 23.08%.
   b. $384,615.

**18-1** a. $1,000,000.
   b. 4 days.
   c. $750,000 and −$3,250,000.

**18-2** a. December loans = $4,400, February surplus cash = $2,000.

**18-3** a. July surplus cash = $85,250, October loans = $26,500.

**18-4** a. 5 vs. 1½ days, $2,975,000.
   b. $327,250.
   c. $27,271.

**18-5** a. $50,000.
   b. $25,000.

   c. 75.
   d. $6,000.

**19-1** a. 28 days.
   b. $46,666.67.

**19-2** a. 23 days and 17.5 days.
   b. $25,200 and $12,000.
   c. $5,750 and $5,250.
   d. $20,000 and $24,000.
   e. $16,650.

**19-4** Net income = + $23,430.

**19-6** a. 3,000.
   b. 4,000.
   c. 2,500.
   d. Every 12 days.

**19-7** a. 5,200.
   b. 65.
   c. 16,600.
   d. $11,628, $11,530, $11,552, $11,520.

**20-2** 4.546 francs.

**20-3** $400 million.

**21-2** a. 19.8%.
   b. $326, $227.

**21-3** a. 18.9%.
   b. $13.60.

# C SELECTED EQUATIONS

**Chapter 2**

| | ACRS Class | |
| Year | 3-Year | 5-Year |
| --- | --- | --- |
| 1 | 25% | 15% |
| 2 | 38 | 22 |
| 3 | 37 | 21 |
| 4 | | 21 |
| 5 | | 21 |
| ITC | 6% | 10% |

**Chapter 3**

$$k = k^* + IP + DP + LP + MP.$$

**Chapter 4**

$$FV_n = PV(1 + k)^n = PV(FVIF_{k,n}).$$

$$PV = FV_n\left(\frac{1}{1 + k}\right)^n = FV_n(1 + k)^{-n} = FV_n(PVIF_{k,n}).$$

$$PVIF_{k,n} = \frac{1}{FVIF_{k,n}}.$$

$$FVIFA_{k,n} = [(1 + k)^n - 1]/k.$$

$$PVIFA_{k,n} = [1 - (1/(1 + k)^n)]/k.$$

$$\frac{\text{Present value}}{\text{of a perpetuity}} = \frac{\text{Payment}}{\text{Discount rate}} = \frac{\text{PMT}}{k}.$$

$$S_n = PMT(FVIFA_{k,n}).$$

$$S_n \text{ (Annuity due)} = PMT(FVIFA_{k,n})(1 + k).$$

$$A_n = PMT(PVIFA_{k,n}).$$

$$A_n \text{ (Annuity due)} = PMT(PVIFA_{k,n})(1 + k).$$

$$FV_n = PV\left(1 + \frac{k_{Nom}}{m}\right)^{mn}.$$

$$\text{Effective annual}_{\text{rate}} = \left(1 + \frac{k_{Nom}}{m}\right)^{m} - 1.0.$$

$$FV_n = PVe^{kn}.$$

$$PV = FV_n e^{-kn}.$$

$$\text{Effective annual}_{\text{rate}} = e^{k} - 1.0.$$

## Chapter 5

$$V = \sum_{t=1}^{n} I\left(\frac{1}{1 + k_d}\right)^{t} + M\left(\frac{1}{1 + k_d}\right)^{n}$$

$$= I(PVIFA_{k_d,n}) + M(PVIF_{k_d,n}).$$

$$V = \sum_{t=1}^{2n} \frac{I}{2}\left(\frac{1}{1 + \frac{k_d}{2}}\right)^{t} + M\left(\frac{1}{1 + \frac{k_d}{2}}\right)^{2n}$$

$$= \frac{I}{2}(PVIFA_{k_d/2,2n}) + M(PVIF_{k_d/2,2n}).$$

$$P_0 = \frac{D}{k_p}.$$

$$\hat{k}_p = \frac{D}{P_0}.$$

$$\hat{P}_0 = \frac{D_0(1 + g)}{k_s - g} = \frac{D_1}{k_s - g}.$$

$$\hat{k}_s = \frac{D_1}{P_0} + g.$$

## Chapter 6

$$\text{Expected rate of return} = \hat{k} = \sum_{i=1}^{n} k_i P_i.$$

$$\text{Variance} = \sigma^2 = \sum_{i=1}^{n} (k_i - \hat{k})^2 P_i.$$

$$\text{Standard deviation} = \sigma = \sqrt{\sum_{i=1}^{n} (k_i - \hat{k})^2 P_i}.$$

$$CV = \frac{\sigma}{\hat{k}}.$$

$$\hat{k}_p = \sum_{i=1}^{n} w_i \hat{k}_i.$$

$$\sigma_p = \sqrt{\sum_{j=1}^{n} (k_{pj} - \hat{k}_p)^2 P_j}.$$

Security Market Line (SML): $k_i = k_{RF} + b_i(k_M - k_{RF})$.

$$b_p = \sum_{i=1}^{n} w_i b_i.$$

## Chapter 7

$$ROE = \left(\begin{array}{c}\text{Profit}\\\text{margin}\end{array}\right)\left(\begin{array}{c}\text{Total asset}\\\text{turnover}\end{array}\right)\left(\begin{array}{c}\text{Equity}\\\text{multiplier}\end{array}\right)$$

$$= \left(\frac{\text{Net income}}{\text{Sales}}\right)\left(\frac{\text{Sales}}{\text{Total assets}}\right)\left(\frac{\text{Total assets}}{\text{Common equity}}\right)$$

$$= \frac{\text{Net income}}{\text{Common equity}}.$$

$$\text{Current ratio} = \frac{\text{Current assets}}{\text{Current liabilities}}.$$

$$\text{Quick, or acid test, ratio} = \frac{\text{Current assets} - \text{Inventories}}{\text{Current liabilities}}.$$

$$\text{Inventory utilization,}\atop\text{or turnover, ratio} = \frac{\text{Sales}}{\text{Inventory}}.$$

$$\text{ACP} = {\text{Average}\atop \text{collection}\atop \text{period}} = \frac{\text{Receivables}}{\text{Average sales per day}} = \frac{\text{Receivables}}{\text{Annual sales}/360}.$$

$$\text{Fixed assets utilization,}\atop\text{or turnover, ratio} = \frac{\text{Sales}}{\text{Net fixed assets}}.$$

$$\text{Total assets utilization,}\atop\text{or turnover, ratio} = \frac{\text{Sales}}{\text{Total assets}}.$$

$$\text{Debt ratio} = \frac{\text{Total debt}}{\text{Total assets}}.$$

$$\text{D/E} = \frac{\text{D/A}}{1 - \text{D/A}}, \text{ and D/A} = \frac{\text{D/E}}{1 + \text{D/E}}.$$

$$\text{Times-interest-earned}\atop\text{(TIE) ratio} = \frac{\text{EBIT}}{\text{Interest charges}}.$$

$$\text{Fixed charge}\atop\text{coverage ratio} = \frac{\text{EBIT + Lease payments}}{\text{Interest}\atop\text{charges} + \text{Lease}\atop\text{payments} + \frac{\text{Sinking fund payments}}{1 - \text{T}}}.$$

$$\text{Profit margin} = \frac{\text{Net income}}{\text{Sales}}.$$

$$\text{Basic earning power ratio} = \frac{\text{EBIT}}{\text{Total assets}}.$$

$$\text{Return on total assets}\atop\text{(ROA)} = \frac{\text{Net income}}{\text{Total assets}}.$$

$$\text{Return on}\atop\text{equity (ROE)} = \frac{\text{Net income available to}\atop\text{common stockholders}}{\text{Common equity}}.$$

$$\text{Price/earnings}\atop\text{(P/E) ratio} = \frac{\text{Price per share}}{\text{Earnings per share}}.$$

$$\text{Book value per share} = \frac{\text{Common equity}}{\text{Shares outstanding}}.$$

$$\text{Market/book ratio} = \frac{\text{Price per share}}{\text{Book value per share}}.$$

## Chapter 9

$$NPV = \sum_{t=0}^{n} \frac{CF_t}{(1 + k)^t}.$$

$$IRR: \sum_{t=0}^{n} \frac{CF_t}{(1 + r)^t} = 0.$$

## Chapter 10

$$CV = \frac{\sigma_{NPV}}{\text{Expected NPV}}.$$

## Chapter 13

$$\text{Formula value} = \frac{\text{Current price}}{\text{of the stock}} - \frac{\text{Striking}}{\text{price}}.$$

$$\frac{\text{Price paid for}}{\text{bond with warrants}} = \frac{\text{Straight debt}}{\text{value of bond}} + \frac{\text{Value of}}{\text{warrants}}.$$

$$\text{Conversion price} = P_c = \frac{\text{Par value of bond}}{\text{Shares received}}.$$

$$\frac{\text{Price paid for}}{\text{convertible bond}} = \sum_{t=1}^{n} \frac{I}{(1 + k_c)^t} + \frac{\text{Expected market value at}\ \text{time of conversion}}{(1 + k_c)^n}.$$

## Chapter 14

$$\text{Component cost of debt} = k_d(1 - T).$$

$$\frac{\text{Component cost}}{\text{of preferred stock}} = k_p = \frac{D_p}{P_n}.$$

$$k_s = \hat{k}_s = \frac{D_1}{P_0} + g.$$

$$k_s = k_{RF} + b_i(k_M - k_{RF}).$$

$$k_s = \text{Bond yield} + \text{Risk premium}.$$

$$k_e = \hat{k}_e = \frac{D_1}{P_0(1 - F)} + g.$$

$$WACC = k_a = w_d k_d(1 - T) + w_p k_p + w_s(k_s \text{ or } k_e).$$

## Chapter 15

$$Q_{BE} = \frac{F}{P - V}.$$

$$DOL = \frac{Q(P - V)}{Q(P - V) - F}.$$

$$DFL = \frac{EBIT}{EBIT - I}.$$

$$DTL = \frac{Q(P - V)}{Q(P - V) - F - I} = (DOL)(DFL).$$

## Chapter 17

$$\begin{matrix} \text{Percentage} \\ \text{cost} \end{matrix} = \frac{\text{Discount percent}}{100 - \begin{matrix} \text{Discount} \\ \text{percent} \end{matrix}} \times \frac{360}{\begin{matrix} \text{Days credit is} \\ \text{outstanding} \end{matrix} - \begin{matrix} \text{Discount} \\ \text{period} \end{matrix}}.$$

$$\text{Effective rate}_{\text{Simple}} = \frac{\text{Interest}}{\text{Amount borrowed}}.$$

$$\text{Effective rate}_{\text{Discount}} = \frac{\text{Nominal rate (\%)}}{1.0 - \text{Nominal rate (fraction)}}.$$

$$\text{Effective rate}_{\text{Simple/CB}} = \frac{\text{Nominal rate (\%)}}{1.0 - \text{CB (fraction)}}.$$

$$\text{Approximate effective rate}_{\text{Installment}} = \frac{\text{Average annual interest}}{\text{Loan amount/2}}.$$

## Chapter 18

$$\text{Total costs} = \text{Holding cost} + \text{Transaction cost} = \frac{C}{2}(k) + \frac{T}{C}(F).$$

$$C^* = \sqrt{\frac{2(F)(T)}{k}}.$$

## Chapter 19

$$TIC = TCC + TOC$$

$$= (C)\,(P)\left(\frac{Q}{2}\right) + \frac{F(S)}{Q}.$$

$$EOQ = \sqrt{\frac{2(F)\,(S)}{(C)\,(P)}}.$$

$$Receivables = (ADS)\,(ACP).$$

# INDEX

---

Running glossary items are set in bold face type. They are indexed either under their main
subject heading or as individual items, or in both those ways.